HENRIK IBSEN

THE COMPLETE
MAJOR PROSE PLAYS

TRANSLATED AND INTRODUCED BY

Rolf Fjelde

Farrar   Straus   Giroux

NEW YORK

To Michele, Eric, Christopher,
and the theater of their time
in the spirit of truth and freedom

321978-X

Copyright © 1965, 1970, 1978 by Rolf Fjelde

All rights reserved

Printed in the United States of America

Published simultaneously in Canada by

McGraw-Hill Ryerson Ltd., Toronto

First edition, 1978

DURHAM, NORTH CAROLINA

Library of Congress Cataloging in Publication Data

Ibsen, Henrik, 1828-1906. The complete major prose plays.

Bibliography: p.

CONTENTS: Pillars of society.—A doll house.—

Ghosts.—An enemy of the people. [etc.]

I. Fjelde, Rolf. II. Title.

PT8854.F5   1978   839.8'2'26   77-28349

ACKNOWLEDGMENTS

The appended stage history of American productions of the major Ibsen prose plays was compiled with assistance from a variety of sources, including the artistic directors and public-relations personnel of a number of the regional repertory theaters cited; but I would particularly like to express my appreciation to Louis A. Rachow, custodian of the Walter Hampden–Edwin Booth Collection and Library of the Players Club, and the respective staffs of the Library of the International Theater Institute of the United States, the Theater Collection of the Performing Arts Research Center at Lincoln Center, and the Information and Research Program of the Theater Communications Group.

For my growing awareness of both the audacity and the intricacy of Ibsen's thought and art I am indebted to many studies and biographies, especially those published over approximately the last quarter-century. The introductions following have been framed in a context of insights from the most perennially valuable of those works; and their presence in the bibliography included herewith, designed for those whose readings in and about Ibsen are confined to English, will I hope serve as a further advertisement of their merits.

My awareness of another Ibsen, the master of practical stagecraft, has grown through warmly remembered associations with those directors and actors throughout the country whom I have joined, at one stage or another, in the engrossing process of bringing these translations into performance. By their insistence on questioning a word here, a phrase there, they have often forced me back to refine what exhaustion had declared could no longer be improved upon. Paul Valéry has said that no translation is ever finished, it is abandoned. If so, I can only be thankful to my friends in the theater, without whom I might have ended this unendable endeavor too soon.

Phases of this project have been substantially forwarded by a travel grant to the University of Oslo from the American-Scandinavian Foundation, and a Ford Foundation Fellowship from the National Translation Center. It has been aided as well by the sympathetic interest of three chairmen of the Pratt Institute Department of English and Humanities: the late Edwin C. Knowles, and Professors Sherwood Weber and Carl Craycraft. The early encouragement of Eric Bentley, Einar Haugen, John Houseman, and Maurice Valency meant more than they could have known at the time. Finally, to my wife Christel, who has shared these plays in many towns, theaters, discussions, drafts, revisions, and now in print complete, I owe a gratitude that I am still learning daily how to translate.

CONTENTS

INTRODUCTION

On March 20, 1828, Henrik Johan Ibsen was born in the tiny coastal town of Skien, in the province of Telemark, near the mouth of what now is the Oslofjord, the eldest surviving child of Knut and Marichen Altenburg Ibsen. Three years later the growing family, prospering from a boom in the shipping trade, moved from the writer's birthplace, the Stockmann house on the town square, to the more attractive, spacious Altenburg villa, better suited for entertaining; and in 1833, Ibsen's gregarious father acquired country property, a farm at Venstøp several miles outside town. When Ibsen was seven, this lavishly outgoing life ceased. Overextended in his speculations, the merchant and importer Knut Ibsen was ruined financially; and the family of seven—Ibsen had three brothers and a sister, Hedvig—was forced to move out to the isolated farm. Here the sensitive boy turned inward, read intensively, painted and drew, staged puppet shows, and, increasingly over the next eight years, felt himself an onlooker, an outsider, unable to compete in the narrowly provincial and snobbish local society that earlier had feasted at his father's table.

In 1843, following his confirmation at age fifteen, after the custom of the time, Ibsen left home to seek his fortune or, more prosaically, to become an apothecary's apprentice in the still smaller village of Grimstad, farther down the coast. In his scant free hours, aided by an iron physique that required little rest, Ibsen began to write and, in time, published poetry and to prepare himself to study medicine at the university. In another bitter formative experience, at eighteen he fathered an illegitimate child by one of his employer's servants, Else Sophie Jensdatter, a woman of good family that like his had succumbed to adversity. Though apparently sympathetic to Ibsen's literary ambitions, she was ten years his senior; there was no question of

marriage, and for the next fourteen years of his most difficult struggles, Ibsen had to contribute support for the boy.
The Grimstad period was deeply stamped also by repercussions of the year of revolutions, 1848, which fired the
young poet to write his first play, a blank-verse tragedy
about the Roman conspirator and rebel Catiline. In April
1850, he left for the capital, Christiania (present-day
Oslo), where his failing entrance-exam grades in Greek
and mathematics deprived the world of a doctor and gave
it one of its handful of supremely great playwrights.

From this point on, Ibsen's life is inextricably bound,
and increasingly subordinated, to his art. If the first two
decades call for more detailed summary, it is because they
contain the seeds of so many of the themes and motifs that
found their way into that series of masterpieces composed
between Ibsen's forty-seventh and seventy-first years. The
devastating, lasting effects of financial ruin, the hypocrisy
of the so-called best people in society, the bittersweet
compensations of a withdrawn life, the humiliations of
being déclassé, the virtual mystique (shared with Emerson,
Carlyle and other authors of the century) of self-reliance,
the rankling in one's past of a guilty secret, compounding
remorse with strangled affections: all this disorder and
early sorrow can be traced in such indelible characterizations as Hjalmar and Hedvig Ekdal, John Gabriel Borkman, Hedda Gabler, Karsten Bernick, Thomas Stockmann,
Rebecca West, Helene Alving. Innumerable others, of
course, have undergone the same, or comparable experiences; and any cross-check of Beethoven's notebooks
against his scores will verify that, not the theme, but its
development, is the test and revelation of genius. The
events of the raw life can only be peripheral to the au-
tonomous world that comes filtered and modified through
the imagination.

For more than another decade, Ibsen's imagination and
his livelihood were in close, if restless, conjunction. On the
strength of *Catiline* and a second play, *The Warrior's
Barrow*, he was appointed "theater-poet"—that is, playwright in residence—at the newly formed Bergen Theater,
a post he held, along with that of stage manager, for six
years, followed by a second, more responsible term of five
years as artistic director of the impoverished Norwegian

Theater in Christiania. During this, the harsh course of his true apprenticeship, he campaigned tenaciously, through repeated discouragements, to create a national theater with its own repertory, contributing seven dramas of his own, mainly in verse or poetic prose and on Norwegian historical subjects, toward this goal. The weight of the odds against him can be gauged by noting that drama internationally had rarely been at a lower ebb of quality than in the 1850s, and that the fledgling playwright-director was compelled to serve this thin diet of, most typically, Scribean melodrama and knockabout French farce to audiences of provincially unformed tastes through the medium of badly trained actors, in a cultural situation where inordinately admired Danish theater personnel held the dominant positions of artistic influence and decision. "What destroys a writer is indifference and rejection," Ibsen later wrote. "That is what I encountered." Indeed, his sheer survival is a wonder, and his steady artistic maturation little short of miraculous, a tribute in good part to an indomitable will.

Fortunately, Ibsen had chosen well in his wife, Suzannah Thoresen, spirited and independent, whom he married in 1858. The couple's only son, Sigurd, was born a year later; and his upbringing and schooling was made as serious and strategic an ongoing project by his largely self-educated father as the conduct of his own vocation as a dramatist. That education had to be entirely pursued abroad, for in 1864, in exasperation and despair, Ibsen abandoned the Norwegian theatrical scene and, partly on the prospects of a contract from the Copenhagen publishing house of Gyldendal, commenced what became twenty-seven years of voluntary exile, the crucial period that transformed him from an obscure Scandinavian author to a master builder of world drama, a creator and a diagnostician of the mind of modern Western man.

The bulk of the dozen plays that compose this volume were written in the latter half of that odyssey of wanderings, when the place names of Ibsen's residences—Rome, Ariccia, Frascati, Ischia, Sorrento, Amalfi; Berchtesgarden, Kitzbühel, Dresden, Gossensass, Munich—were like a cross-stitch weaving together the old, antiquity-steeped Mediterranean culture of the south with the new, future-oriented Germanic culture of the north. Interrelated by theme, locale, format and, in one instance, even a character shared between two plays, the twelve segments of Ibsen's final span of productivity, for which all the rest of his life and writings were preparation, are preceded by three oversized dramas crucial to their comprehension. These are *Brand*, the stark tragedy of a promethean country pastor whose faith is steeled by uncompromising will; *Peer Gynt*, the picaresque comedy of an amiable rogue whose amours, abortive careers and shifty escapades are prompted by ungovernable wish; and *Emperor and Galilean*, an epic and prophetic account of Julian the Apostate that ranges freely over the fourth-century Roman Empire, depicting the ideological combat between paganism and Christianity for determination of the future of Western civilization. Prototypal characters and conflicts from these massive dramas, the products of the first half of Ibsen's exile, recur in the major prose plays that grew out of them. Ibsen would want them assimilated in their sequence of composition, after the procedure Ibsen urged for his work in its totality:

> Only by grasping and comprehending my entire production as a continuous and coherent whole will the reader be able to receive the precise impression I sought to convey in the individual parts of it.
>
> I therefore appeal to the reader that he not put any play aside, and not skip anything, but that he absorb the plays—by reading himself into them and by experiencing them intimately—in the order in which I wrote them.

It is in obedience to this injunction to see at least the major prose plays as a subtly and significantly interconnected dramatic cycle that the present collection has been designed. The plays, which have often, perhaps necessarily under certain circumstances, been issued piecemeal and in a broken sequence, have been gathered here in a single volume, arranged in the chronological order of their completion, their first publication and their premieres in the theaters of Scandinavia and Germany—in short, the order of their original impact on readers and playgoers. Each of the plays has been provided with a brief introduction, aimed at defining its particular tone and atmosphere, for as similar as the twelve dramas may initially appear in style, none can be adequately understood unless sensed out in its uniqueness, as a distinctive microcosm of its own.

Not merely sensed out, but thought out as well. "It may be questioned," James Joyce once wrote of Ibsen, "whether any man has held so firm an empire over the thinking world in modern times." Thinking, not at the expense of feeling, but collateral with it, has such a hold on both Ibsen and the companions in his quests because jointly they recognize that they share a new and unprecedented age where every position—intellectual, moral, political and religious—must be thought out afresh. For the fact is that through a dual revolution in politics and technology a gulf had been opened up in and around the mid-nineteenth century, dividing the period Joyce calls "modern times" from all that had gone before. The historian W. H. McNeil has termed that radical break with the past "a mutation in the economic and social life of mankind comparable in magnitude with the Neolithic transition from predation to animal husbandry"—in other words, the most tumultuous upheaval in patterns of living in some eleven thousand years. In this climate of unpredictable and accelerating change, no personal solution, whether of antiquity or the future, can be adopted without the most searching examination. Thus even the introductions that follow would be a betrayal of Ibsen's purpose if they failed to rise above documentation and received opinion and participate in that vital thinking process through interpretation, however brief, of the idea content of the plays. Though no analysis can be presumed definitive, strong lines of inquiry may at least obviate certain past approaches that have deadened or demeaned the incisive complexity of Ibsen's art. If these introductions act to stimulate such strongly conceived rethinking and discussion of the plays, they will have fulfilled their intent.

The other phase of interpretation, at the opposite end of the playwright's creative shuttle between ideas and imaginary characters, is the fully realized theatrical performance. It was Ibsen's tireless effort to find vivid theatrical equivalents for his sense of having crossed over into new territory—an unmapped wilderness of potentialities for human existence—that gained him the title of the father of modern drama. His driving fervor to explore the frontiers of consciousness struck a responsive chord almost from the start in the American theater, which like the nation itself is the maturing product of a frontier situation and mentality. As a native-born American whose Norwegian ancestry is three generations removed, I have sought to translate my pursuit, over some years, of the immediate experience of Ibsen in our theater—something that can never be captured between the covers of a book—into something that can: a distillate of the record. The appendix covering principal professional productions in the United States of the cycle from *Pillars of Society* to *When We Dead Awaken* is the result. I hope it will prove useful as an American counterpart to the listing of principal British Ibsen productions, organized along somewhat different lines, appended to Volumes V–VIII of *The Oxford Ibsen*.

The record is restricted to English-language performances and therefore begins the year after the world premiere of *Ghosts*, presented in Norwegian in 1882 at the Aurora Turner Hall in Chicago. Limitation of space also prevents the inclusion of selected amateur productions, which have sometimes had historic importance, high artistic merit, or simply curiosity value. There is thus, perhaps luckily, no occasion to list the first Ibsen play in English ever staged here, by a Milwaukee amateur group in 1882. The victim was *A Doll House*, renamed *A Child Wife*, reset in England, recast with a jovial Irish widow for comic relief and rehabilitated with a happy ending. As Einar Haugen has documented it, in Act Two, one of Nora's children sang a song to such charming effect that the applause of the audience compelled her to repeat it. Lack of the amateur record, nevertheless, is a loss. In my own experience, one of the most sensitive Eilert Løvborgs I have yet seen was the avant-garde playwright Robert Wilson in a student production at Pratt Institute.

The approximate century of professionally performed Ibsen drama in the United States raises an important question: if one can speak, with no prejudice of typecasting, of a born Shakespearian or Shavian actor, is there a histrionic sensibility particularly right for Ibsen? Probably so. What traits, then, would the born Ibsenian actor or actress possess? First, a relish for detail. Role interpretation of Ibsen's people demands to be built after the model of the characterizations themselves, stroke by stroke, with a savoring of the quirks and mannerisms which individualize behavior (contra the more generalized Brechtian actor). Second, the emotional stamina for a sustained, if rarely overt, passion. Perhaps the most unwisely violated of all Ibsen's prescriptions for playing his work is his statement to the French director Lugné-Poë: "People have not fully appreciated that a passionate writer needs to be acted with passion, and not otherwise." Thirdly, a related appreciation of the texts, not as prose, but poetry. Here Stark Young can hardly be improved upon, in writing that "dramatic poetry is not the dramatic situation poetically expressed; it is the dramatic expression of the poetic that lies in a situation." Ibsen's major prose plays, with their compression of experience, their metaphoric resonances, their unsettling juxtapositions of the commonplace and the extraordinary, their formal patterning, are of the very essence of poetry.

Overriding all these properties, though, must be an instinctive gravitation to what Henry James called Ibsen's "peculiar blessedness to actors." After paying tribute to the playwright's "independence, his perversity, his intensity, his vividness, the hard compulsion of his strangely inscrutable art," James observes on behalf of actors that "no dramatist of our time has had more the secret, and kept it better, of making their work interesting to them. The subtlety with which he puts them into relation to it eludes analysis, but operates none the less strongly as an incitement. Does it reside mainly in the way he takes hold of their imagination, or in some special affinity with their technical sense; in what he gives them or in what he leaves it to them to give; in the touches by which the moral nature of the character opens out a vista for them; or in the simple fact of connection with such a vivified whole. . . ? What is incontestable is the excitement, the amusement, the inspiration of dealing with material so solid and so fresh. The very difficulty of it makes a common cause, as the growing ripeness of preparation makes a common enthusiasm."

So solid and so fresh—those two adjectives, which the conventional mind might set in opposition, are for James the consummate summary of Ibsen's appeal. The solidity derives from the diversity of perspectives infolded into each play in the long compositional process of meditating, embodying and refining its basic idea. As a result, whenever the dramatic material appears to be most symbolic, most archetypal, most fully explicable by transpersonal agencies and forces, one finds its realism of social and psychological causation reasserting an inescapable claim for attention. Conversely, any attempt to psychologize the plays down to a purely naturalistic dissection of character and motive soon demonstrates its inadequacy, for their larger cohering structures grow out of the perspectives of history, of religion, of folktale, ritual and myth. The truth is that there is psychology behind Ibsen's metaphysics, and metaphysics behind his psychology; they interpenetrate as close and distant views of the same reality.

Not merely as the focus of mutually commutable perspectives, but also as a comprehensive image expressed in dramatic poetry, the reality that the cycle presents in its cumulative progression is ultimately a cosmos. Like any of the supreme dramatic poets, Ibsen is the creator of his own inimitable universe. One knows in Ibsen the rooms and the landscapes, the light and the weather, as one knows their less specified counterparts in Shakespeare, with the haunting immediacy of the country of one's childhood. The plays of the cycle and their possibilities in performance have, finally, the same inexhaustibility as that larger cosmos they reflect, preserving the paradox of their enduring freshness. To interpret these plays is to rediscover life.

ROLF FJELDE

PILLARS OF SOCIETY

Pillars of Society (1877)—fifteenth of Ibsen's dramas, yet only the second to be neither wholly nor partly written in verse, nor set in the historical past—ranks in complexity and power well above its exuberantly farcical, satirically exaggerated predecessor in prose of eight years before, *The League of Youth*. As a transitional learning piece that functions as a prototype to initiate the entire final twelve-play group, it cost its author a great deal of time and effort. References to, and notes for, a comedy on a contemporary theme exist from as early as 1869–70. The project was almost totally eclipsed during the composition of the enormous ten-act "world-historical" *Emperor and Galilean* (1873); then the hard struggle toward mastering a dramatic form and technique that could sensitively register the outer shocks and inner strains of modern life resumed over, for Ibsen, the unusually extended period of February 1875 to June 1877.

The result that was published and premiered near the end of that year proved an immediate success, playing the following February, for example, in as many as five theaters in Berlin simultaneously. The lesser, but hardly negligible, reason for its swift acceptance, and the starting point for its interpretation in both text and performance, lies in the fact that *Pillars of Society* is exactly what William Archer declared it to be, the perfect model of the French well-made play. Scorned by serious critics, relished by all but the most sophisticated playgoers of the time, the elements of Scribean stagecraft, as adapted by Ibsen, were here given a new ironic subtlety and an often, if not always, more substantial psychological content. First, we encounter the familiar device of the crucially withheld secret, twofold in this instance: Karsten Bernick's affair with the actress Madame Dorf, the suppression of which permits, and later protects, his marriage, revealing in the process the hollowness of his private, emotional life; and the coverup of mismanagement in the family firm through an alleged embezzlement by the same convenient scapegoat for the affair, his emigrant brother-in-law, Johan, disclosing the manipulations of his public, business career. Supplementing this is the orderly unfolding of the well-made exposition, whereby the audience is brought to see, through the various transparent misconceptions the characters have about him, the full scope of Bernick's past opportunism. Later one finds the Scribean telltale letters, used unconventionally at a critical moment, not to expose Bernick, but through their destruction to shame him instead out of his habitual lies and deceptions. Finally, the play climaxes in an obligatory scene wherein the suffering hero rescued, and the fraudulent opponent defeated, by the disclosure of the secret turn out to be the two halves of Bernick's own personality.

As this last ironic twist begins to suggest, the power of the play to affect audiences then, and still today, has a larger cause than such well-oiled, refurbished machinery of the *pièce bien faite*. Its theatricalism supports a burning concern for the betterment of society through the regeneration of the individual. In its main plot and subplot, the dual action lines out two ways to save oneself from a community whose dim awareness of its own deficiencies is symbolized by its glass-walled, curtained single set, initially a half-lit room that resembles Plato's cave of shadowy illusions. Dina Dorf takes the easier course, flight to an idealized America of wider skies and more spacious prospects. The other, dominant, more difficult option, which Bernick finally adopts, is to stand one's native ground, freely confess one's involvement in corruption and, with those whom such honesty can reach, work to reconstitute society from within.

The catalyst inciting both action lines is Lona Hessel, who has been aptly compared to a clear-eyed goddess Athena hovering over the crowded scene. Returning from the American frontier, she understands a vital mercantile economy as the way the world works, and Bernick as its inevitable product. Likewise, she respects his substantial accomplishments, the civic contributions that have made him an ostensible pillar of society. But the base on which that society rests has its analogy in the coffin ships held together by patchwork, the businessman's improvisations from one profit statement to the next. Without seeing the details, but perceiving the result—that, as Ibsen expressed it elsewhere, civilization is sailing with a corpse in the cargo, namely its own expired integrity of being—Lona determines to confront Bernick with the reality of his life and induce a fundamental change of heart.

How are we meant to regard his conversion? Probably with ambivalence. On the one hand, it is truly felt, and the conclusion of the play is legitimately moving, because it draws on Ibsen's most profound convictions about the transforming power of truth and freedom—those very convictions that the ensuing plays in the cycle will test and question, modify and transmute. On the other hand, Bernick is that most dangerous type of public man, the born opportunist who, with the agility of a dropped cat, can turn even contrition to his own advantage. Undoubtedly, he must continue to be closely watched. The last message of one of the resistance martyrs of World War II concludes with the words, "Mankind . . . be vigilant." *Pillars of Society*, seen in its affirmative, yet ironic totality, would appear to close on much the same note.

THE CHARACTERS

KARSTEN BERNICK
BETTY BERNICK, his wife
OLAF, their son, aged thirteen
MARTHA BERNICK, Karsten's sister
JOHAN TØNNESEN, Betty's younger brother
LONA HESSEL, her elder half-sister
HILMAR TØNNESEN, Betty's cousin
RØRLUND, a schoolmaster
RUMMEL, a wholesale merchant
VIGELAND, a tradesman
SANDSTAD, a tradesman
DINA DORF, a young girl living with the Bernicks
KRAP, Bernick's head clerk
AUNE, foreman in Bernick's shipyard
MRS. RUMMEL
MRS. HOLT, the postmaster's wife
MRS. LYNGE, the doctor's wife
MISS HILDA RUMMEL
MISS NETTA HOLT

Townspeople and other residents, sailors from abroad, steamship passengers, etc.

The action takes place in Karsten Bernick's house in a small Norwegian seaport.

⌒ ACT ONE ⌒

A spacious garden room in CONSUL BERNICK's *house.*
Downstage left, a door opening into BERNICK's *study; far-*
ther back in the same wall, a similar door. Centered in the
opposite wall, a large entrance door. The rear wall is glass
almost entirely, with a door in it standing open on a broad
flight of steps decked by an awning. A portion of the
garden below the steps can be seen, bounded by a fence
with a small entry gate. Just beyond and parallel to the
fence is a street, lined on the far side with small, colorfully
painted wooden houses. It is summer; the sunlight is warm.
From time to time people pass by on the street; some stop
and converse, others patronize a little corner shop, etc.
   In the garden room a group of ladies are seated around a
table. MRS. BERNICK *is sitting at the middle of the table. On*
her left sit MRS. HOLT *and her* DAUGHTER, *with* MRS.
RUMMEL *and* MISS RUMMEL *next to them. On* MRS. BER-
NICK's *right sit* MRS. LYNGE, MISS BERNICK *and* DINA DORF.
All the ladies are busy sewing. Linen, cut into patterns and
half finished, lies piled up on the table, along with other
articles of clothing. Farther back, at a little table on which
stand two potted plants in bloom and a glass of sugar
water, RØRLUND *sits reading aloud from a book with gilt*
edges, though only a few words can now and then be heard
by the audience. Out in the garden OLAF BERNICK *is run-*
ning about, target-shooting with a bow and arrow.
   After a moment AUNE, *foreman of the shipyard, slips in*

15

the door to the right. The reading is briefly interrupted, as
MRS. BERNICK *nods to him and points toward the door to*
the left. AUNE *goes quietly across and knocks softly on*
BERNICK's *door, waits, then knocks again.* KRAP, BERNICK's
assistant, with hat in hand and papers under his arm,
comes out of the room.

KRAP. Oh, was that you knocking?

AUNE. Mr. Bernick sent for me.

KRAP. That's right. But he can't see you. He's authorized
me to—

AUNE. You? I'd really prefer—

KRAP. —authorized me to tell you this: You've got to
stop these Saturday speeches of yours to the workmen.

AUNE. Oh? I'd thought I could use my own free time—

KRAP. You can't use your free time to make other people
useless on the job. Last Saturday you talked about the
dangers to the men from our new machines and the new
working methods at the yard. Why did you do that?

AUNE. I did it for the betterment of society.

KRAP. That's funny! Mr. Bernick says it'll be the ruin of
society.

AUNE. My society isn't Consul Bernick's society, Mr.
Krap. As head of the Workmen's Federation, let me—

KRAP. Above all else, you're foreman in Mr. Bernick's
shipyard. And, above all else, you have your duties to that
society called Bernick and Company, because *that's* what
supports every one of us. All right—now you know what
Mr. Bernick had to say to you.

AUNE. But *he* wouldn't have said it that way, Mr. Krap!
Anyhow, I know who I have to thank for this. It's that
damned American hulk in for repair. Those people want
the work to go like they do it over there, and that's—

KRAP. Yes, yes, yes, I can't get into these complications.
You have Mr. Bernick's message now—so that's it! You'd
better go back to the yard; no doubt you're needed. I'll be
down myself shortly. Beg pardon, ladies!

(*He bows and goes out through the garden and along the street.* AUNE *departs quietly, to the right.* RØRLUND, *who has continued to read throughout the foregoing subdued conversation, finishes the book soon after and claps it shut.*)

RØRLUND. And with that, dear ladies, the tale is told.

MRS. RUMMEL. Ah, what an uplifting story!

MRS. HOLT. And—so moral!

MRS. BERNICK. A book like that really does make you think.

RØRLUND. Oh, yes; it's a refreshing contrast to what, unhappily, we're fed every day in our newspapers and magazines. Those gilded, glittering facades that the great societies hold up—what do they actually hide? Emptiness and corruption—if you ask me. No moral foundation underfoot. In a word, they're whited sepulchers, these great modern societies.

MRS. HOLT. Yes, that's a fact.

MRS. RUMMEL. Why, look at the crew on that American ship in port here.

RØRLUND. Such scum of the earth I wouldn't even waste my breath on. But even in higher circles—what do you find *there?* Doubt and distraction on every side; troubled minds and unstable relationships. How family life's been undermined out there! How arrogantly they delight in perverting the most sacred truths!

DINA (*without looking up*). But haven't great things been done out there as well?

MRS. HOLT (*dumfounded*). Good gracious, Dina—!

MRS. RUMMEL (*simultaneously*). Dina, how could you—?

RØRLUND. I don't think it would be good for us if such things gained entree here. No, we ought to thank God, here in this town, that we live as we do. No denying, of course, that weeds grow among our good grain as well, but we strive in good faith to root them out the best we can. What matters, ladies, is to keep our community pure. We have to stand firm against all this experimentation that a restless age would like to foist on us.

MRS. HOLT. And there's more than enough of that, I'm afraid.

MRS. RUMMEL. Yes, last year we came within a hair of having a railroad built into town.

MRS. BERNICK. Well, Karsten put a stop to that.

RØRLUND. Providence, Mrs. Bernick. You can rest assured your husband was the instrument of a higher power in refusing to go along with that scheme.

MRS. BERNICK. And still he had to take such vile abuse from the newspapers. But we're completely forgetting to thank you, Mr. Rørlund. You've really been more than kind to give up so much time for us.

RØRLUND. Oh, come; now that school's out—

MRS. BERNICK. Yes, all right; but it's a sacrifice nevertheless, Mr. Rørlund.

RØRLUND (*moving his chair closer*). My dear woman, don't mention it. Aren't you all sacrificing in a good cause? And doing it willingly and gladly? These moral cripples that we're working to reclaim can be looked at as wounded soldiers on a field of battle. And you, dear ladies, are the nursing order, the sisters of mercy, winding the bandages for these unfortunate victims, binding their wounds with gentle fingers, tending and healing them—

MRS. BERNICK. It must be a great comfort to be able to see everything in such a lovely light.

RØRLUND. To a large degree it's an inborn gift, but it can also be acquired. It's really a matter of having a serious calling in life, and seeing things accordingly. What do you say, Miss Bernick? Don't you find you've gained a surer footing in life since you've been devoting yourself to your school work?

MARTHA BERNICK. Oh, I don't know what to say. Often, when I'm down there in the schoolroom, I wish I were far, far out on the wild sea.

RØRLUND. The sirens of temptation, my dear Miss Bernick. You have to bar the door to such unruly guests. The wild sea—of course you don't mean that literally. You mean the vast, surging tide of human society in which so many go down. And do you really place such value on the

life you hear rushing and roaring by outside? Look down
there in the street. There goes sunstruck humanity, sweating and haggling over its petty affairs. No, the truth of it is,
we're better off sitting here, in the cool of this room, and
turning our backs on the source of all that distraction.

MARTHA BERNICK. Yes, I'm sure you're perfectly right—

RØRLUND. And in a house like this—a fine, decent home,
where family life shows itself in its highest form—where
peace and harmony rule—(*To* MRS. BERNICK.) Do you
hear something, Mrs. Bernick?

MRS. BERNICK (*having turned toward the door of*
BERNICK's *room*). They're talking so loud in there.

RØRLUND. Is it anything special?

MRS. BERNICK. I don't know. I hear someone in there
with my husband.

(HILMAR TØNNESEN, *a cigar in his mouth, enters through
the door, right, but stops short at the sight of all the
ladies.*)

HILMAR. Oh, excuse me— (*Turns to go out.*)

MRS. BERNICK. No, do come in, Hilmar. You're not disturbing us. Was there something you wanted?

HILMAR. No, just looking in. Good morning, ladies. (*To*
MRS. BERNICK.) Well, what's the verdict?

MRS. BERNICK. On what?

HILMAR. You knew Bernick called a meeting.

MRS. BERNICK. Really? But why?

HILMAR. Oh, it's this crazy railroad thing again.

MRS. RUMMEL. No, it can't be!

MRS. BERNICK. Poor Karsten, is he in for more trouble—?

RØRLUND. But there's no rhyme or reason to this, Mr.
Tønnesen. Last year Mr. Bernick made it plain as day he'd
have nothing to do with a railroad.

HILMAR. Yes, that's what I thought, too. But I just met
Mr. Krap, and he tells me that the whole railroad issue's

been reopened, and that Bernick's in conference with three of our local tycoons.

MRS. RUMMEL. I knew I heard my husband's voice.

HILMAR. Oh, yes, Mr. Rummel's in there, of course, and Sandstad who has the store on the hill, and Michael Vigeland—or, as he's sometimes called, "Saint Michael."

RØRLUND. Hm—!

HILMAR. My apologies, Doctor.

MRS. BERNICK. And it was all so nice and peaceful here.

HILMAR. Well, for my part, I wouldn't mind it if they started bickering again. At least it would be a diversion.

RØRLUND. That kind of diversion I think we can do without.

HILMAR. That all depends on your disposition. Certain natures need a good rousing scrap now and then. But small-town life doesn't have much to offer along that line, and it isn't everyone who can— (*Leafing through* RØRLUND'*s book.*) *Woman as the Servant of Society.* What kind of hogwash is this?

MRS. BERNICK. Mercy, Hilmar, don't say that! I'm sure you haven't read it.

HILMAR. No, and I don't plan to, either.

MRS. BERNICK. You're really not quite yourself today.

HILMAR. No, I'm not.

MRS. BERNICK. Didn't you sleep well last night?

HILMAR. No, I slept miserably. I took a walk last evening for my constitution and wound up at the club, reading an account about an expedition to the North Pole. There's something exhilarating about human beings battling the elements.

MRS. RUMMEL. But it obviously didn't agree with you, Mr. Tønnesen.

HILMAR. No, it upset me. I lay tossing and turning all night, half asleep, dreaming I was chased by a hideous walrus.

OLAF (*who has come up the steps from the garden*). Have you been chased by a walrus, Uncle?

HILMAR. I dreamed it, you lunkhead! Are you still playing with that ridiculous bow and arrow? Why don't you get yourself a real rifle?

OLAF. Oh, that's what I want, but—

HILMAR. An honest-to-God rifle—there's some sense to that. It tones up the entire nervous system to shoot it off.

OLAF. And then I could shoot bears, Uncle. But Father won't let me.

MRS. BERNICK. Really, Hilmar, you mustn't put ideas like that in his head.

HILMAR. Hm! What a generation we're raising these days! Everywhere you hear talk about sports, sports—but, so help me, it's all just play. There's no serious effort toward toughening oneself by staring danger straight in the eye, like a man. Don't stand there and point that thing at me, you numskull; it might go off.

OLAF. But Uncle, there's no arrow.

HILMAR. How do you know? It could still be dangerous. Take it away, will you! Why the devil don't you run off to America on one of your father's ships? You could see them hunt buffalos there, or fight the Indians.

MRS. BERNICK. No, Hilmar—

OLAF. Oh, I'd like that, Uncle! Then maybe I'd meet Uncle Johan and Aunt Lona.

HILMAR. Hm—that's stuff and nonsense.

MRS. BERNICK. Go back down in the garden, Olaf.

OLAF. Can I go out in the street, too, Mother?

MRS. BERNICK. Yes, but not too far now.

(OLAF *runs out through the garden gate.*)

RØRLUND. That's not the kind of notion to put in a boy's head, Mr. Tønnesen.

HILMAR. No, obviously he ought to stay here and be a stick-in-the-mud, like nearly everyone else.

RØRLUND. Then why don't you go over yourself?

HILMAR. I? With my bad health? Well, as usual, no one in this town shows any regard for that. And, after all, one does have some obligations toward the society one lives in. *Someone* here has to keep the banner of the ideal flying high. Uff, now he's yelling again.

THE WOMEN. Who's yelling?

HILMAR. Oh, I don't know. When they raise their voices in there, it gets on my nerves.

MRS. RUMMEL. That's probably my husband, Mr. Tønnesen. You see, he's so accustomed to public speaking—

RØRLUND. Seems to me, the others aren't exactly soft-spoken.

HILMAR. Lord no! Not when they're defending their bankbooks— Everything here revolves around petty, material gains. Uff!

MRS. BERNICK. At least that's better than the old days, when everything revolved around pleasure.

MRS. LYNGE. Was it really so bad here in the old days?

MRS. BERNICK. Oh, I don't have to tell you, Mrs. Lynge. Just thank your lucky stars you weren't around here then.

MRS. HOLT. Yes, there have been some changes, haven't there! When I think back to when I was a girl—

MRS. RUMMEL. Or even back fourteen—fifteen years. Dear God, the life in this town! We had a dance club then, and a musical society, both—

MARTHA BERNICK. And the drama group. I remember that so well.

MRS. RUMMEL. Yes, it was *there* your play was put on, Mr. Tønnesen.

HILMAR (*moving upstage*). Oh, honestly—!

RØRLUND. A play? By Mr. Tønnesen?

MRS. RUMMEL. Yes, that was long before *you* came here, Mr. Rørlund. Anyway, it lasted only one night.

MRS. LYNGE. Isn't that the piece you told me about, Mrs. Rummel, where you played one of the young lovers?

MRS. RUMMEL (*glancing at* RØRLUND). I? I really don't remember, Mrs. Lynge. But I remember all the loud partying that went on in some people's homes.

MRS. HOLT. Yes, I could name the houses where they gave two big dinner parties a week.

MRS. LYNGE. And then I hear there was a theater company that used to come here.

MRS. RUMMEL. Oh, they were impossible—!

MRS. HOLT (*uneasily*). Hm, hm—

MRS. RUMMEL. Really—actors? No, I don't remember that.

MRS. LYNGE. Oh yes, I heard they played all sorts of practical jokes. How much truth is there in those stories?

MRS. RUMMEL. Not a single word, Mrs. Lynge.

MRS. HOLT. Dina, sweet, would you hand me that linen there?

MRS. BERNICK (*simultaneously*). Dina, dear, would you go ask Katrine to bring in the coffee?

MARTHA BERNICK. I'll come with you, Dina.

(DINA *and* MARTHA BERNICK *leave by the upstage door to the left.*)

MRS. BERNICK (*getting up*). If you'll just excuse me a moment, ladies. I think we'll have our coffee outside.

(*She goes out on the terrace and sets a table, as* RØRLUND *stands in the doorway, talking with her.* HILMAR *sits outside, smoking.*)

MRS. RUMMEL (*in an undertone*). Oh, Mrs. Lynge, what a fright you gave me!

MRS. LYNGE. *I* did?

MRS. HOLT. Yes, but really, Mrs. Rummel, you started it.

MRS. RUMMEL. I? No, how can you say that, Mrs. Holt? I never breathed a word.

MRS. LYNGE. What *is* all this?

MRS. RUMMEL. How could you start talking about—! Of all things—right in front of Dina—?

MRS. LYNGE. Dina? Good gracious, is anything wrong with—?

MRS. HOLT. And *here*, in this house! Don't you realize it was Mrs. Bernick's brother—?

MRS. LYNGE. What about him? I don't realize anything. I'm new around here—

MRS. RUMMEL. You never heard that—? Hm— (*To her daughter.*) Hilda, dear, you should spend a little time in the garden.

MRS. HOLT. You go too, Netta. And be very sweet to poor Dina when she comes back.

(MISS RUMMEL *and* MISS HOLT *go out into the garden.*)

MRS. LYNGE. Well, what happened with Mrs. Bernick's brother?

MRS. RUMMEL. You don't know about his wicked past?

MRS. LYNGE. *That* Mr. Tønnesen has a wicked past?

MRS. RUMMEL. Good Lord, no—he's her cousin, Mrs. Lynge. I'm talking about the brother—

MRS. HOLT. The worthless Tønnesen—

MRS. RUMMEL. His name was Johan. He ran off to America.

MRS. HOLT. Let's say, he *had* to run off.

MRS. LYNGE. So *he* had the wicked past.

MRS. RUMMEL. Yes, it was something—how can I put this? It involved Dina's mother. Oh, I remember it as if it were yesterday. Johan Tønnesen was in old Mrs. Bernick's office then. Karsten Bernick had only just come back from Paris—this was before he got engaged—

MRS. LYNGE. Well, so, what happened?

MRS. RUMMEL. Yes, you see—that winter the theater company was here in town—

MRS. HOLT. —and Dorf and his wife were acting with them. All the young men were wild about her.

MRS. RUMMEL. Yes, God only knows what they could see in *her*. Anyway, one night Dorf, her husband, came home late—

MRS. HOLT. Quite unexpectedly—

MRS. RUMMEL. And he found her—no, there's simply no way to say this.

MRS. HOLT. But, Mrs. Rummel, he didn't find anything, because the door was locked from the inside.

MRS. RUMMEL. Yes, that's what I was just saying: he found the door locked. And can you imagine—the man who was inside had to jump out the window.

MRS. HOLT. All the way from the top floor!

MRS. LYNGE. And that was Mrs. Bernick's brother?

MRS. RUMMEL. Exactly.

MRS. LYNGE. And that's why he ran off to America?

MRS. HOLT. Yes. You can well imagine, he had to.

MRS. RUMMEL. Because afterward something else came to light almost as bad: he'd embezzled some money from the company—

MRS. HOLT. But we don't know that for a fact, Mrs. Rummel. It was only hearsay.

MRS. RUMMEL. Well, of all things—! Didn't everyone in town know about it? And didn't old Mrs. Bernick nearly go bankrupt because of it? My husband told me so himself. I'm not going to say one more blessed word!

MRS. HOLT. Well, at least none of the money went to Mrs. Dorf, because she—

MRS. LYNGE. Yes, what became of Dina's parents?

MRS. RUMMEL. Dorf left the two of them, wife and child. But Madame had the nerve to stay on here for an entire year. Of course, she didn't dare parade herself anymore in the theater, but she took in sewing and washing and managed to get by—

MRS. HOLT. And she tried starting a school of dance.

MRS. RUMMEL. Naturally, it failed. What parents would trust their children to a woman like that? Besides, she wasn't around very long. She was too fine a lady to do real work. It affected her lungs, and she died.

MRS. LYNGE. Uff, really! What a nasty business!

MRS. RUMMEL. Yes, you can imagine what a strain that

was for the Bernicks. It's been the one dark spot in their sunlit happiness, as my husband once put it. So don't ever speak of these things in this house, Mrs. Lynge.

MRS. HOLT. Or of the half-sister, either, for heaven's sake!

MRS. LYNGE. Yes, Mrs. Bernick does have a half-sister, doesn't she?

MRS. RUMMEL. *Did* have—fortunately. Because now they've broken off completely. Oh, *she* was a character! Would you believe it, she cut her hair short and walked around in the rain in men's boots.

MRS. HOLT. And when that half-brother—the worthless creature—had run off, and the whole town was properly incensed about him—you know what she did? She went off after him—over there!

MRS. RUMMEL. Yes, but the scandal she made before she left, Mrs. Holt!

MRS. HOLT. Shh! Don't talk about it.

MRS. LYNGE. Mercy, she made a scandal, too?

MRS. RUMMEL. Oh yes. It was this way, Mrs. Lynge. Bernick had just got engaged to Betty Tønnesen; and he was bringing her in on his arm to see her aunt and break the news—

MRS. HOLT. You understand, the Tønnesens had lost their parents—

MRS. RUMMEL. —when Lona Hessel got up out of her chair and gave that suave, debonair Karsten Bernick a box on the ear to make his head swim.

MRS. LYNGE. Well, I never—!

MRS. HOLT. Yes, it's the honest truth.

MRS. RUMMEL. And then she packed her bags and went to America.

MRS. LYNGE. So she must have been eying him for herself.

MRS. RUMMEL. Yes, you can bet she was. She went around here deluding herself that they'd make a match of it when he returned from Paris.

MRS. HOLT. Yes, imagine her with ideas like that! Bernick —a polished young man of the world—a perfect gentleman—the darling of all the girls—

MRS. RUMMEL. And nevertheless, so upright, Mrs. Holt. So moral.

MRS. LYNGE. But what became of Miss Hessel in America?

MRS. RUMMEL. Well, as my husband once put it, there's a veil drawn over that which better not be lifted.

MRS. LYNGE. What do you mean?

MRS. RUMMEL. She's no part of the family anymore, as you can imagine. But one thing the whole town knows is that she's sung for money in saloons over there—

MRS. HOLT. And she's been lecturing in public—

MRS. RUMMEL. And she's brought out an idiotic book—

MRS. LYNGE. Really!

MRS. RUMMEL. Oh, yes, Lona Hessel's been another dark spot on the Bernick's happiness. So, now you know the story, Mrs. Lynge. Of course, I'm only telling you this so you'll watch your step.

MRS. LYNGE. Oh, don't worry, I will. But that poor Dina Dorf! I really feel sorry for her.

MRS. RUMMEL. Actually, for her it was a rare piece of luck. Can you imagine, if she'd remained in her parent's care! We all took an interest in her, of course, and tried to guide her the best we could. Finally Miss Bernick arranged for her to live in this house.

MRS. HOLT. But she's always been a difficult child. You can imagine—with all those bad examples. Her kind isn't like one of ours, Mrs. Lynge. She has to be handled delicately.

MRS. RUMMEL. Shh—she's coming. (*Raising her voice.*) Yes, that Dina, she's really a clever girl. Oh, is that you, Dina? We're just about finished here.

MRS. HOLT. Oh, but your coffee smells simply lovely, Dina dear. There's nothing like midmorning coffee—

MRS. BERNICK (*from the garden steps*). If you will, ladies.

(MARTHA BERNICK *and* DINA *have, in the meantime, been helping the* MAID *with the coffee things. All the* LADIES *go out and are seated; they talk with conspicuous concern to* DINA. *After a moment she comes into the room and looks for her sewing.*)

MRS. BERNICK (*from the coffee table*). Dina, don't you want—?

DINA. No, thanks; I won't have any.

(*She sits down and begins sewing.* MRS. BERNICK *and* RØRLUND *exchange some words; a moment later he reenters the room.*)

RØRLUND (*moves on a pretext to the table and speaks softly*). Dina.

DINA. Yes.

RØRLUND. Why are you staying in here?

DINA. When I came in with the coffee, I could see by that new woman's face that they'd been talking about me.

RØRLUND. But then didn't you also see how friendly she was to you out there?

DINA. But I can't stand that!

RØRLUND. You have a stubborn spirit, Dina.

DINA. Yes.

RØRLUND. Why?

DINA. It's the way I am.

RØRLUND. Couldn't you try to change?

DINA. No.

RØRLUND. Why not?

DINA (*looks at him*). Because I'm one of the moral cripples.

RØRLUND. Dina!

DINA. And Mother was, too.

RØRLUND. Who's been telling you these things?

DINA. No one. They never speak out. Why don't they? They all treat me so delicately, as if I'd go to pieces if— Oh, how I hate all this kindness!

RØRLUND. My dear Dina, I understand so well that you feel trapped here, but—

DINA. Yes, if I could only go far away somewhere. I could get along all right, if only I didn't have to live with people who were so—so—

RØRLUND. What?

DINA. So moral and proper.

RØRLUND. But, Dina, you don't mean that.

DINA. Oh, you know just what I mean. Every day Hilda and Netta come here to set me an example. I could never be as well behaved as they are. I don't *want* to be! Oh, if I were far away, I could be good, too.

RØRLUND. But, Dina dear, you *are* good.

DINA. Who cares, around here?

RØRLUND. About going—are you serious about that?

DINA. I wouldn't stay here a day longer if it weren't for *you*.

RØRLUND. Tell me, Dina—just why are you so fond of being with me?

DINA. Because you teach me so much that's beautiful.

RØRLUND. Beautiful? You call what I can teach you beautiful?

DINA. Yes. Or actually—you don't teach me anything; but when I listen to you talk, I begin to see so much that's beautiful.

RØRLUND. What do you understand, really, by a beautiful thing?

DINA. I've never thought about that.

RØRLUND. Then think about it now. What do you understand by a beautiful thing?

DINA. A beautiful thing is something great—and far away.

RØRLUND. Hm. Dina dear, I have such a deep concern for you.

DINA. Is *that* all?

RØRLUND. You know perfectly well how dear beyond words you are to me.

DINA. If I were Hilda or Netta, you wouldn't be afraid to let the world see.

RØRLUND. Oh, Dina, you haven't the least idea how many considerations I have to— When a man's called forth to be, morally, a pillar of the society he lives in, then—he can't be careful enough. If I could only be sure that people wouldn't misjudge my motives— Well, never mind about that. You *must* and you *will* be helped. Dina, is it understood that, when I come—when circumstances permit me to come—and say to you: "Here's my hand"— that you'll accept it and be my wife? You'll promise me that, Dina?

DINA. Yes.

RØRLUND. Thank you, thank you! Because for me, too— Oh, Dina, I'm so fond of you— Shh, someone's coming. Dina, for my sake—go out to the others.

(*She goes to the coffee table. At the same moment* RUMMEL, SANDSTAD *and* VIGELAND *come in from the room downstage left, followed by* BERNICK, *carrying a sheaf of papers in his hand.*)

BERNICK. So, it's all settled, then.

VIGELAND. Yes, in God's name, let's hope so.

RUMMEL. It's settled, Bernick! A Norseman's word stands firm as a rock, you know that!

BERNICK. And no wavering, no turning back—no matter what opposition we meet.

RUMMEL. We stand or fall together, Bernick!

HILMAR (*coming in by the garden door*). Fall? Excuse me, but it's not the railroad that's fallen through?

BERNICK. No, on the contrary; it's going ahead—

RUMMEL. Full steam, Mr. Tønnesen.

HILMAR (*approaching them*). Really?

RØRLUND. What?

MRS. BERNICK (*in the garden doorway*). But, Karsten dear, what's going on—?

BERNICK. Betty dear, you can't be interested in this? (*To the three men.*) But we'd better draw up the lists now, as soon as possible. Obviously, we four ought to be the first signers. With our positions in the community, we're duty-bound to extend ourselves as much as we can.

SANDSTAD. That's right, Mr. Bernick.

RUMMEL. It's *got* to go, Bernick. We've committed ourselves.

BERNICK. Oh yes, I'm not worried at all about the outcome. We'll have to use our influence in our own special circles; once we can demonstrate an active interest in every sector of the community, then the municipality will have to put in its share.

MRS. BERNICK. Karsten, you really must come out and tell us—

BERNICK. My dear Betty, this is nothing for ladies.

HILMAR. So you're actually going to back this railroad scheme?

BERNICK. Why, of course.

RØRLUND. But last year, Mr. Bernick—

BERNICK. Last year was a very different story. Then there was talk of a coast line—

VIGELAND. Which would have been completely superfluous, Mr. Rørlund. We have steamers, you know—

SANDSTAD. And it would have been an extravagant expense—

RUMMEL. Yes, and it plainly would have damaged vital interests here in town.

BERNICK. The fact of the matter was that it simply wouldn't have benefited the community as a whole. That's why I came out against it. So the interior route was chosen.

HILMAR. Yes, but then it's hardly going to affect the towns around here.

BERNICK. It's going to affect *our* town, my dear Hilmar. Because now we'll have a branch line brought in.

HILMAR. Aha! That's a new idea.

RUMMEL. Yes, isn't that a terrific idea? Uh!

RØRLUND. Hm—

VIGELAND. There's no denying that it's almost as if Divine Providence had made that terrain for a branch line.

RØRLUND. You really think so, Mr. Vigeland?

BERNICK. Yes, I must say I also find it providential that I traveled inland on business last spring and happened to go down a valley where I'd never been before. Like a bolt out of the blue, it struck me that here, exactly, was the right-of-way for a branch line into our town. I've had an engineer survey the area; I have his preliminary calculations and estimates right here. There's nothing to hold us back.

MRS. BERNICK (*still in the garden doorway with the other ladies*). But Karsten dear, why have you kept all this such a secret?

BERNICK. Betty, my dear, you really couldn't be expected to grasp the complexities. In any case, I haven't mentioned this to a living soul before today. But now the decisive moment's at hand. From now on we proceed openly, with all our strength. Yes, even if I have to stake my whole existence on this thing, I'm going to push it through.

RUMMEL. We're with you, Bernick; you can bank on that.

RØRLUND. You really expect so much from this venture, gentlemen?

BERNICK. Well, I should hope so! Think what a lift this will give the whole community! Just think of the vast tracts of forest that'll be opened up! The rich lodes of ore to mine! And the river, with one waterfall after another! The possibilities of industrial development are limitless!

RØRLUND. And you're not afraid that more contact with the corrupt world out there—?

BERNICK. No, set your mind at ease, Mr. Rørlund. Our hard-working little town rests now, thank God, on a solid moral foundation. We've all had a hand in draining it, so to speak—and we'll go on doing so, each in his own way. You, Mr. Rørlund, will keep up your inspired work in the schools and homes. We practical businessmen will sustain the community by expanding its prosperity to the widest sphere possible. And our women—yes, come closer, ladies; I want you to hear this—our women—yes, I tell you, our wives and daughters—yes, you go on undisturbed in your charitable activities, ladies, and also go on being an aid and comfort to your nearest and dearest, as my dear Betty and Martha are to me and Olaf— (*Looking about.*) Yes, where is Olaf today?

MRS. BERNICK. Oh, now with vacation, it's impossible to keep him home.

BERNICK. So that means he's down by the water again! You'll see, he won't stop till he has an accident.

HILMAR. Pah! A little brush with the powers of nature—

MRS. RUMMEL. How lovely of you to have so much family feeling, Mr. Bernick.

BERNICK. Well, let's remember, the family is the core of society. A good home, some true and honored friends, a little close-knit circle where no disturbing elements can cast a shadow—

(KRAP *enters from the right, carrying letters and news-papers.*)

KRAP. The foreign mail, Mr. Bernick—and a telegram from New York.

BERNICK (*taking it*). Ah, from the owners of the *Indian Girl*.

RUMMEL. So the mail's here? Well, then, if you'll excuse me—

VIGELAND. Yes, me too.

SANDSTAD. Good day, Mr. Bernick.

BERNICK. Good day, good day, gentlemen. And don't forget, we meet this afternoon at five.

THE THREE MEN. Yes. Oh, yes. Of course.

(*They go out right.*)

BERNICK (*who has read the telegram*). Well, how typically American! Absolutely disgusting!

MRS. BERNICK. Goodness, Karsten, what is it?

BERNICK. Look at that, Mr. Krap. Read it!

KRAP (*reading*). "Do least possible repairs. Send *Indian Girl* over soon as seaworthy. Profitable season. Cargo will float her in emergency." Well, I must say—

BERNICK. "Cargo will float her"! Those men know very well, with that cargo she'd go down like a stone if anything happened.

RØRLUND. Yes, there we see what goes on in these celebrated great societies.

BERNICK. You're right. No concern for human life the moment there's profit involved. (*To* KRAP.) Can the *Indian Girl* put to sea in four, five days?

KRAP. Yes, if Mr. Vigeland will let us stop work on the *Palm Tree* till then.

BERNICK. Hm, he won't do that. Go through the mail, would you? Incidentally, you didn't see Olaf down by the pier?

KRAP. No, Mr. Bernick.

(*He goes downstage left into* BERNICK's *study*.)

BERNICK (*glancing again at the telegram*). Those gentlemen don't hesitate a moment to risk eighteen human lives—

HILMAR. Well, it's a seaman's job to brave the elements; there must be something spine-tingling in having just a thin plank between you and the abyss—

BERNICK. I'd like to see the shipowner among us who could stoop to anything like this! Not *one*, not a single *one*— (*Catching sight of* OLAF.) Ah, thank heaven, there he is.

(OLAF, *with a fishline in his hand, comes running up the street and in through the garden door*.)

OLAF (*still in the garden*). Uncle Hilmar, I was down to see the steamer.

BERNICK. Have you been out on the pier again?

OLAF. No, I was only out in a boat. But guess what, Uncle Hilmar! A whole circus came ashore, with horses and animals. And there were so many passengers.

MRS. RUMMEL. No, are we really going to have a circus!

RØRLUND. We? I seriously doubt it.

MRS. RUMMEL. Naturally, not *us*, I mean—

DINA. I'd like to see the circus.

OLAF. Yes, me too.

HILMAR. You lunkhead, is *that* anything to see? Just a fancy horse show. No, it's something else to see the gaucho galloping over the pampas on his fiery mustang. Ah, but there's your small-town mentality—

OLAF (*tugging on* MARTHA BERNICK's *dress*). Aunt Martha, look, look—there they come!

MRS. HOLT. My gracious, yes, it's them.

MRS. LYNGE. Uff! What awful people!

(*Numbers of* PASSENGERS *and a crowd of* TOWNSPEOPLE *can be seen coming up the street.*)

MRS. RUMMEL. Yes, they're a pack of rowdies, all right. Will you look at her in the gray dress, Mrs. Holt; she's carrying a carpetbag on her shoulder.

MRS. HOLT. Yes, imagine that; she's slung it on the handle of her parasol. That would be the ringmaster's wife, no doubt.

MRS. RUMMEL. And there we have the ringmaster himself —the man with the beard. My, he really does look like a pirate. Don't look at him, Hilda!

MRS. HOLT. Nor you, Netta!

OLAF. Mother, the ringmaster's waving to us.

BERNICK. What?

MRS. BERNICK. What did you say, child?

MRS. RUMMEL. 'God of mercy, that female—she's waving, too!

BERNICK. Well, if *that* isn't nerve!

MARTHA BERNICK (*involuntarily cries out*). Ah—!

MRS. BERNICK. What is it, Martha?

MARTHA BERNICK. Oh, nothing. Just that I thought—

OLAF (*with a whoop of delight*). Look, look! There come the rest of them, with horses and animals! And the Americans, too! All the sailors from the *Indian Girl*—

(*The strains of "Yankee Doodle" are heard, accompanied by a clarinet and drum.*)

HILMAR (*claps his hands over his ears*). Uff, uff, uff!

RØRLUND. I think we should retire for a while, ladies. This is nothing for us. Let's go back to our work.

MRS. BERNICK. Maybe we ought to draw the curtains?

RØRLUND. Yes, just what I was thinking.

(*The ladies take their places at the table.* RØRLUND *closes the garden door and draws the curtains over it and the windows. The room is in semi-darkness.*)

OLAF (*peeking out*). Mother, now the ringmaster's wife is standing by the fountain, washing her face.

MRS. BERNICK. What? In the public square!

MRS. RUMMEL. In broad daylight!

HILMAR. Look, if I was crossing a desert and stumbled upon a well, I don't think I'd stand on ceremony either— Uff, that insufferable clarinet!

RØRLUND. There's really every reason for the police to step in.

BERNICK. Oh, now—you can't be so strict with foreigners. Those people don't have the deep-rooted sense of decorum that governs *our* ways. Let them run wild. What's that to us? All this riotousness that makes a mockery of custom and breeding happily has no hold in our community, if I may say so— What on earth!

(*The* STRANGE WOMAN *comes in briskly through the door, right.*)

THE LADIES (*in frightened whispers*). The circus woman! The ringmaster's wife!

MRS. BERNICK. Mercy! What's going on?

MARTHA BERNICK (*springs to her feet*). Ah—!

THE WOMAN. Hello, Betty dear! Hello, Martha! Hello, brother-in-law!

MRS. BERNICK (*in an outcry*). Lona—!

BERNICK (*reels back a step*). Well, I'll be—!

MRS. HOLT. God preserve us—!

MRS. RUMMEL. It's not possible—!

HILMAR. No! Uff!

MRS. BERNICK. Lona—! Is it really—?

LONA. Me, you mean? Well, it better be! If you want, give me a hug and find out.

HILMAR. Uff! Uff!

MRS. BERNICK. And you're coming back as—?

BERNICK. You actually perform—

LONA. Perform? In what way, perform?

BERNICK. You know—in the circus—

LONA (*in a gale of laughter*). Karsten, are you crazy? You think I belong to the circus? No! I've pulled some tricks in my time and made a fool of myself in lots of ways—

MRS. RUMMEL. Hm—

LONA. But I've never done tricks on a horse's back.

BERNICK. Then it isn't true—

MRS. BERNICK. Oh, thank God!

LONA. No, we came just like any other honest people—in second class, naturally. But we're used to that.

MRS. BERNICK. You say, *we?*

LONA. I and the child, of course.

THE LADIES (*crying out*). The child!

HILMAR. What!

RØRLUND. Well, I must say—!

MRS. BERNICK. Lona, what do you mean?

LONA. I mean John, of course. I don't know any other child I have beside John—or Johan, as you used to call him.

MRS. BERNICK. Johan—!

MRS. RUMMEL (*quietly to* MRS. LYNGE). The worthless brother!

BERNICK (*falteringly*). Is Johan with you?

LONA. Of course, of course. I wouldn't travel without him. But you all look so lugubrious. And here you sit in the shadows, sewing these white things. There hasn't been a death in the family, has there?

RØRLUND. My good woman, these are members of the Society for the Morally Disabled—

LONA (*her voice hushed*). Honestly? You mean all these nice, genteel ladies are—

MRS. RUMMEL. Now, really—!

LONA. Oh, foolish me! I understand! But what the deuce, it's Mrs. Rummel! And Mrs. Holt, too! Well, we three haven't grown any younger since we last met. But listen now, let the morally disabled take a day off; they won't be the worse for it. A joyous occasion like this—

RØRLUND. A homecoming isn't always a joyous occasion.

LONA. Really? Is that the text in your Bible, Reverend?

RØRLUND. I am not a Reverend.

LONA. Well, then you will be soon. Ecch, but all this moral linen reeks of decay—like a bundle of shrouds, I swear. I prefer the air off the prairie, I can tell you.

BERNICK (*mopping his brow*). Yes, it is quite stuffy in here.

LONA. Wait, wait, we'll make it out of the tomb yet. (*Drawing the curtains aside.*) Broad daylight's in order when the boy comes. Yes, then you'll see what a well-scrubbed look he has—

HILMAR. Uff!

LONA (*opening the door and windows to the garden*). —I should say, if he gets to wash himself up at the hotel—because on that ship he grew filthy as a pig.

HILMAR. Uff! Uff!

LONA. Uff? Well, so help me, if it isn't— (*Points at* HILMAR *and asks the others.*) Does *he* still come maundering around here, barking out "Uff"?

HILMAR. I'm not maundering; I've been taking a stroll for my health.

RØRLUND. Hm—ladies, I don't believe—

LONA (*having caught sight of* OLAF). Is that *yours*, Betty? Give me your paw, boy! Or maybe you're afraid of your grim old aunt?

RØRLUND (*tucking his book under his arm*). Ladies, I don't believe we have the proper atmosphere to continue our work today. But tomorrow we'll meet once again?

LONA (*as the* LADIES *rise to take their leave*). Yes, let's. I'll be here on the dot.

RØRLUND. *You?* Excuse me, Miss Hessel, but what can *you* do for *our* society?

LONA. I can air it out—Reverend.

⌐◄ ACT TWO ►¬

The garden room in BERNICK'S *house.* MRS. BERNICK *sits alone at the work table with her sewing. After a moment* BERNICK *enters, right, wearing a hat and gloves and carrying a stick.*

MRS. BERNICK. You're home already, Karsten?

BERNICK. Yes. There's someone I'm meeting here.

MRS. BERNICK (*sighs*). Oh yes, I suppose Johan will be coming by again.

BERNICK. No, in fact, it's one of the men. (*Taking off his hat.*) Where are all the ladies today?

MRS. BERNICK. Mrs. Rummel and Hilda haven't the time.

BERNICK. Oh? They backed out?

MRS. BERNICK. Yes, they had too much to do at home.

BERNICK. It figures. And, naturally, the others can't make it either.

MRS. BERNICK. No, they also had engagements.

BERNICK. I could have predicted it. Where's Olaf?

MRS. BERNICK. I let him go for a walk with Dina.

BERNICK. Hm, Dina. Giddy little flirt! Yesterday, to throw herself at Johan that way—!

MRS. BERNICK. But, Karsten dear, Dina doesn't know anything about—

BERNICK. Well, then Johan ought to have had the tact not to give her any attention. I could see how Vigeland was eying them.

MRS. BERNICK (*lowers her sewing to her lap*). Karsten, can you fathom what it is they want here?

BERNICK. Well, you know he has that farm over there that doesn't seem to be exactly flourishing. And of course *she* made clear yesterday that they'd had to sail second class—

MRS. BERNICK. Yes, I'm afraid it's got to be something like that. But for *her* to come, too! Her! After the outrageous way she insulted you—!

BERNICK. Oh, forget those old stories.

MRS. BERNICK. As things are, how can I possibly forget them? After all, he *is* my brother—but it isn't on his account; it's all the unpleasantness it'll make for *you*. Karsten, I'm so terribly afraid—

BERNICK. Afraid of what?

MRS. BERNICK. Won't there be some move to arrest him for the money taken from your mother?

BERNICK. Oh, that's absurd! Who can prove any money was taken?

MRS. BERNICK. But, my Lord, the whole town knows. And you said yourself—

BERNICK. I said nothing. The town hasn't the faintest clue about this; it's all just idle gossip.

MRS. BERNICK. Oh, Karsten, how good-hearted you are!

BERNICK. Enough of these memories! You don't know how it pains me, to have all this raked up again. (*He paces back and forth, then hurls down his stick.*) And they had to come home just now—now, when I need an ironclad reputation, both in town and in the press. There'll be stories sent out to every paper in the district. Whether I take them in or turn them away, it'll all be picked over and discussed. They'll go probing into the past—just the way *you* do. In a community like ours— (*Throws his gloves on the table.*) And I haven't one single person here I can talk to, or count on for support.

MRS. BERNICK. No one at all, Karsten?

BERNICK. Well, *who*, for instance—? Oh, at this moment, to have *them* on my neck! There's no question that they'll make a scandal, one way or another. She, in particular. What a curse it is, to have people like that in your family!

MRS. BERNICK. Well, *I* can't help it if—

BERNICK. If—what? If they're your relatives? No, that's perfectly true.

MRS. BERNICK. And I didn't ask them here, either.

BERNICK. Ah, now, here it comes. "I didn't ask them here; I didn't write them to come; I didn't drag them home by the hair." Oh, I can reel that whole speech off by heart.

MRS. BERNICK (*bursts out crying*). You're being so unkind—

BERNICK. Yes, that's right. Have a good cry, so the town can talk about *that*, too. Stop this foolishness, Betty. Go sit outside; anyone could come in here. You want them to see you with red eyes? A pretty business that would be if it got around that— Shh, somebody's in the hall. (*A knock at the door.*) Come in!

(MRS. BERNICK *goes out on the terrace with her sewing.* AUNE *enters, right.*)

AUNE. Good morning, Consul.

BERNICK. Good morning. Well, you probably can guess why I want to see you.

AUNE. Mr. Krap said yesterday that you weren't satisfied with—

BERNICK. I'm not satisfied in *any* respect with the way the yard's being run, Aune. You've gotten nowhere with the repair work. The *Palm Tree* should have sailed days ago. Mr. Vigeland's been here every day, plaguing me about it. He's a hard man to have as a partner.

AUNE. The *Palm Tree* will be seaworthy the day after tomorrow.

BERNICK. Well, at last. But the American ship, the *Indian Girl*. She's been laid up here five weeks, and—

AUNE. The American? I understood it that our first order of business was to concentrate on your own ship.

BERNICK. I've never given you any cause to think that. There should have been all possible progress on the American, too. But nothing's been done.

AUNE. The hull's rotted out, Mr. Bernick. The more we patch it, the worse it gets.

BERNICK. That's not the problem. Mr. Krap's told me the truth of it. You don't know how to work with the new machines I had installed—or, better, you *won't* work with them.

AUNE. Mr. Bernick, I'm near sixty, and up from a boy I've been used to the old ways—

BERNICK. They're out of date now. Don't think this is just a matter of profit, Aune. Happily, I don't have to consider that. But I do have a concern for the community I live in and the business I run. Progress has to come from me, or it won't come at all.

AUNE. I also want progress, Mr. Bernick.

BERNICK. Yes, for your own narrow faction, for the working class. Oh, I know you agitators: you make speeches, you stir people up—but as soon as there's some real progress at hand, like this with our machines, then you won't go along with it. You get scared.

AUNE. Yes, I'm scared all right, Mr. Bernick. What scares me is all those people who'll have their bread taken away from them by those machines. You're always talking about caring for society, Mr. Bernick, but I think society has a few obligations of its own. What right do technology and capitalism have to introduce all these new inventions before society's trained a generation in how to use them?

BERNICK. You read and think too much, Aune. It isn't good for you. It only makes you dissatisfied with your position.

AUNE. That isn't it, Mr. Bernick. I can't stand seeing one good workman after another turned out to go hungry, all on account of these machines.

BERNICK. Hm. When printing was invented, a lot of scribes went hungry.

AUNE. How'd you like it, Mr. Bernick, if you'd been a scribe at the time?

BERNICK. I didn't send for you to stage a debate. I called you here to tell you that the *Indian Girl* must be ready to sail the day after tomorrow.

AUNE. But, Mr. Bernick—

BERNICK. Day after tomorrow, understood? At the same time as our own ship, not an hour later. I have my own good grounds for pushing this. Did you read the paper this morning? Well, then you know that the Americans have been making trouble again. That pack of animals are turning the whole town upside down. There isn't a night goes by now without a brawl in the taverns or on the streets—along with other abominations I don't even want to talk about.

AUNE. No question they're a bad bunch.

BERNICK. And who gets the blame for all this turmoil? I do! Yes, I'm the one who suffers. All these newspaper stories with their vile innuendoes that we're putting our whole work force on the *Palm Tree*. I, who's expected to set a strong example for our fellow citizens, have to have that flung up in my face. I won't stand for it. I don't want that kind of dirt on my name.

AUNE. Oh, a name as fine as yours can take that, and more.

BERNICK. At the moment, no. Just now I need all the respect and good will my fellow citizens can give me. I have a big project underway, as no doubt you've heard. But if low-minded people manage to shake the absolute trust that's vested in me, I could find myself in fearsome difficulties. That's why, at any price, I want to put a stop to these vicious smears in the papers. And that's why I've set the deadline for the day after tomorrow.

AUNE. Mr. Bernick, you might as well set it for this afternoon.

BERNICK. You mean I'm asking the impossible?

AUNE. Yes, with the work force we have now—

BERNICK. All right—then we'll have to try another approach—

AUNE. You're not going to lay off still more old-timers?

BERNICK. No, I wasn't thinking of that.

AUNE. Because I'm sure that would sit bad both in town and with the papers, if you did that.

BERNICK. Most likely. So we won't try it. But if the *Indian Girl* isn't cleared to sail by the day after tomorrow, I'm firing you.

AUNE (*with a start*). Me! (*He laughs.*) You're joking, Mr. Bernick.

BERNICK. Don't bank on it.

AUNE. You could fire *me?* Me, whose father and grandfather worked all their lives in this yard, as I have, too—

BERNICK. Who's forcing me to?

AUNE. It's impossible, what you ask, Mr. Bernick.

BERNICK. Oh, a little willpower can work miracles. Yes or no? Give me a straight answer—or you're out, as of now.

AUNE (*coming a step closer*). Mr. Bernick, do you really understand what it means to let out an old workman? You think he can look around for something else? Oh, yes, he can look—but you suppose that's the end of it. Sometime you ought to be there, in the house of a workman who's been let out, when he comes home and puts his toolbox back of the door.

BERNICK. You think it's easy for me to fire you? As an employer, haven't I always been fair?

AUNE. All the worse for me, Mr. Bernick. That's exactly why no one at home is going to blame you. They won't say anything to me, because they wouldn't dare. But they'll look at me behind my back, and think: he probably deserved it. You understand, I—I couldn't take that. As poor a man as I am, I've always been accounted the head of my family. My simple home is a little community, too, Mr. Bernick. I've been able to support it and carry the load because my wife's believed in me and because my children have believed in me. And now it all goes down the drain.

BERNICK. Well, if there's no other course, then the lesser has to give way to the greater. God knows, the individual *has* to be sacrificed for the common good. I can't give you any other answer; that's the way the world is. But you're a stubborn man, Aune! You're blocking me, not because you've no other choice, but because you won't concede the superiority of machines over manual labor.

AUNE. And you're so hard and fast on this, Mr. Bernick, because you know throwing me out will show the news-papers you only wanted the best.

BERNICK. And suppose that's true? I've told you what this means to me—I either get all the papers down on my neck, or else line them up behind me, right at a time when I'm working on a big project in the public interest. So? What else can I do? I'd say the question, in essence, is this: either to support *your* home, as you put it, or maybe to cancel out hundreds of new homes—hundreds of homes that'll never be started, never know a warm hearth, if I don't succeed in what I'm working on. It's why I'm leaving the choice to you.

AUNE. Well, if that's it, then I've no more to say.

BERNICK. Hm—my dear Aune, I'm truly sorry that we have to part.

AUNE. We're not parting, Mr. Bernick.

BERNICK. How so?

AUNE. A plain, ordinary workman has his pride, too.

BERNICK. Why, yes, of course. Then you think you could promise—?

AUNE. The *Indian Girl* will be cleared for sailing by the day after tomorrow.

(*He bows and goes out, right.*)

BERNICK. Ah, so I got the old ramrod to bend. That's a good sign—

(HILMAR TØNNESEN, *with a cigar in his mouth, appears at the garden door.*)

HILMAR (*on the steps to the garden*). Good morning, Betty! Good morning, Bernick!

MRS. BERNICK. Good morning.

HILMAR. I see you've been crying. Then you must know.

MRS. BERNICK. Know what?

HILMAR. That the scandal's in full career. Uff!

BERNICK. What does that mean?

HILMAR (*coming in*). Those two Americans are promenading the town in Dina Dorf's company.

MRS. BERNICK (*following him*). Hilmar, that's impossible—

HILMAR. I'm afraid it's the absolute truth. Lona was even tactless enough to call after me, but of course I pretended not to hear.

BERNICK. And I suppose this hasn't gone unnoticed.

HILMAR. No, you can bet on that. People stopped in their tracks and stared at them. It seemed to get around the town like wildfire—like one of those prairie fires out West. In every house there were people at the windows, waiting for the parade to pass; heads together behind the curtains —uff! You have to excuse me, Betty; I keep saying "Uff" because this makes me nervous. If it goes on, I'll have to think of taking a nice long trip.

MRS. BERNICK. But you should have spoken to him and made clear that—

HILMAR. Right there, on the street? No, if you don't mind! Imagine that man having the nerve even to show himself in this town! We'll see if the newspapers can't put a damper on him. Pardon me, Betty, but—

BERNICK. You say, the newspapers? Have you heard rumors to that effect?

HILMAR. Oh, no doubt about it. When I left you all last evening, I took a little stroll over to the club—for my constitution, you know. It was easy to tell by the sudden silence that they'd been going on about the two Americans. And then that insolent editor, Hammer, breezes in and congratulates me in a big, booming voice on my rich cousin's homecoming.

BERNICK. Rich—?

HILMAR. Yes, that's how he put it. Naturally I pegged him with a cool look and let him know I'd never been aware of Johan Tønnesen being rich. "Oh," he says, "that's curious. People usually get ahead in America if they have a little something to start with, and your cousin didn't exactly leave here empty-handed."

BERNICK. Hm. Would you do me a favor—

MRS. BERNICK (*troubled*). There, you see, Karsten—

HILMAR. Well, anyway, the man's given me a sleepless night. And there he goes, traipsing about the streets with an innocent air, as if nothing on earth was wrong with him. Why doesn't he just get lost somewhere? It's maddening how some people have more lives than a cat.

MRS. BERNICK. Hilmar, what are you saying?

HILMAR. Oh, nothing, really. But there he's survived railroad accidents and run-ins with California grizzlies and Blackfoot Indians without a scratch. Not even scalped once. Uff! Here they come!

BERNICK (*glancing up the street*). And Olaf's with them!

HILMAR. Why, of course. they have to remind people they belong to the best family in town. Look at all the loafers coming out of the pharmacy to ogle them and swap remarks. This is more than my nerves can take. How any man can hold his standard of idealism high under these circumstances—!

BERNICK. They're heading right here. Now listen, Betty, it's my express desire that you show them every possible courtesy.

MRS. BERNICK. Shall I, Karsten?

BERNICK. Yes, yes, of course. And you too, Hilmar.

We'll hope they won't stay long; and just among us—no innuendoes. We don't want to hurt them in any way.

MRS. BERNICK. Oh, Karsten, you're so magnanimous!

BERNICK. Now, now, that's enough.

MRS. BERNICK. No, but I must thank you. And forgive me for that outburst just now. Really, you had every reason to—

BERNICK. I said, enough! Drop it!

HILMAR. Uff!

(JOHAN TØNNESEN *and* DINA *enter through the garden, followed by* LONA HESSEL *and* OLAF.)

LONA. Good morning, you dear people.

JOHAN. We've been out looking over the old stamping grounds, Karsten.

BERNICK. Yes, so I hear. Lots of changes, um?

LONA. Consul Bernick's great and good works everywhere. We've been up in the park that you gave the town—

BERNICK. Up *there?*

LONA. "Gift of Karsten Bernick," it reads over the entrance. Why, you're the man behind everything around here.

JOHAN. And you have some first-rate ships, too. I met the captain of the *Palm Tree*, an old classmate of mine—

LONA. Yes, and you've built a new school. And I hear you're the prime mover behind the gas works and the water system.

BERNICK. Well, one has to do something for the community one lives in.

LONA. Oh, it's magnificent. But it's also a joy to see how people appreciate you. I don't think I'm especially vain, but I couldn't keep from reminding one or two of those we met that we belonged to this family.

HILMAR. Uff!

LONA. What makes you say "Uff"?

HILMAR. No, I said "Umm"—

LONA. Well, poor thing, that much you're allowed. But you all seem quite alone today.

MRS. BERNICK. Yes, today we're alone.

LONA. As a matter of fact, we met a couple of your moral constabulary up at the market. They seemed to be terribly busy. But you know, we've hardly had any chance to talk yet. Yesterday there were those three railroad builders, and then that pastor—

HILMAR. Schoolmaster.

LONA. He's the pastor to me. But now what do you think of *my* work over these past fifteen years? Hasn't he grown into a strapping boy? You wouldn't recognize the scatter-brain who ran away from home.

HILMAR. Hm—!

JOHAN. Oh, Lona, that's enough bragging.

LONA. Well, all the same, I'm proud of it. Lord, it's the one thing I've done in this world, but it gives me at least some kind of right to exist. Yes, Johan, when I remember how the two of us started out over there, with just our four bare fists—

HILMAR. Hands.

LONA. *I* said fists. Filthy ones at that—

HILMAR. Uff!

LONA. And empty as well.

HILMAR. Empty? Well, I must say—!

LONA. What must you say?

BERNICK. Hm!

HILMAR. I must say—uff! (*He goes out to stand on the garden steps.*)

LONA. What's eating that character?

BERNICK. Oh, never mind about him. He's been rather nervous lately. Wouldn't you like to take a look around the garden? You haven't really seen it yet, and I have an hour free just now.

LONA. Yes, I'd love to. Time and again my thoughts have been with all of you in that garden.

MRS. BERNICK. There've been enormous changes there too, as you'll see.

(BERNICK, MRS. BERNICK *and* LONA HESSEL *go down into the garden, where they are seen intermittently during the following scene.*)

OLAF (*by the garden doorway*). Uncle Hilmar, know what Uncle Johan asked me? He asked if I'd like to go with him to America.

HILMAR. You, you lunkhead! The way you hang on to your mother's skirts—

OLAF. Yes, but I won't any longer. Wait and see, when I grow up—

HILMAR. Oh, bosh! You don't have the backbone it takes to go and—

(*They move down into the garden.*)

JOHAN (*to* DINA, *who has removed her hat and stands in the doorway to the right, shaking the dust from her skirt*). It was quite a warm walk for you.

DINA. Oh, it was a lovely walk. I've never had such a lovely walk.

JOHAN. Don't you take morning walks very often?

DINA. Oh yes, but just with Olaf.

JOHAN. I see. Maybe you'd prefer to go out in the garden than stay in here.

DINA. No, I'd prefer to stay here.

JOHAN. I would, too. All right, so we have an agreement that every morning we'll go for a walk like this.

DINA. No, Mr. Tønnesen, you mustn't do that.

JOHAN. I mustn't? But you promised to.

DINA. Yes, but now as I think about it—you shouldn't go out with me.

JOHAN. Why not?

DINA. You're a stranger here. You can't understand. You see, I'm—

JOHAN. Go on.

DINA. No, I'd rather not talk about it.

JOHAN. Oh, come on now. You certainly can tell me.

DINA. Well, you see, I'm not like the other girls. There's something—something about me. That's why you shouldn't.

JOHAN. But I don't understand the least bit of all this. You haven't done anything wrong, have you?

DINA. *I* haven't, no, but—no, I don't want to talk about this anymore now. You'll hear it soon enough from the others.

JOHAN. Hm.

DINA. But there was something else I really wanted to ask you.

JOHAN. What's that?

DINA. Is it true that it's easy to make something of yourself in America?

JOHAN. No, it's not always so easy, not at all. You usually have to pitch in and work hard at the start.

DINA. Oh, that wouldn't bother me—

JOHAN. You?

DINA. I'm a good worker. I'm strong and healthy, and Aunt Martha's taught me a lot.

JOHAN. Well then, damn it all, come on back with us!

DINA. Oh, now you're just joking. You said that to Olaf, too. But the thing I wanted to know was, if people are very—so very moral over there?

JOHAN. Moral?

DINA. Yes, I mean, if they're as—prim and proper as they are here.

JOHAN. Well, they're certainly not as bad as people here imagine. You don't have to be afraid of that.

DINA. You don't understand. I'd rather they wouldn't be so respectable and moral.

JOHAN. No? How would you have them be?

DINA. I want them to be natural.

JOHAN. Well, in fact, that's just what they are.

DINA. Then it would be the best thing for me if I could go there.

JOHAN. Of course it would! So you have to come back with us.

DINA. No, I don't want to go with you. I'd have to go alone. Oh, I know I'd succeed there; I'd do all right—

BERNICK (*at the foot of the garden steps, with the two ladies*). Wait. Wait, now, Betty dear, I'll get it. You might catch cold.

(*He comes into the room, looking for his wife's shawl.*)

MRS. BERNICK (*from the garden*). Johan, you come along, too. We're going down to the grotto.

BERNICK. No, Johan can stay here. Listen, Dina, take my wife's shawl and go with them. Betty dear, Johan's staying here with me. I want to hear something about the life over there.

MRS. BERNICK. All right, but come along soon. You know where to find us.

(MRS. BERNICK, LONA HESSEL *and* DINA *go down through the garden to the left.* BERNICK *gazes after them a moment, goes to the farther door on the left and closes it, then crosses to* JOHAN *to grasp both his hands, shaking them fervently.*)

BERNICK. Johan, now that we're alone, you must let me thank you.

JOHAN. Oh, come on!

BERNICK. My house and home, my family happiness, my standing in this community—I owe it all to you.

JOHAN. Well, that pleases me, Karsten. So there was some good that came out of that crazy affair.

BERNICK (*gripping his hands again*). Anyway, thank you, thank you! Not one in ten thousand would have done what you did for me.

JOHAN. Sheer nonsense! We were both young and foolish then, weren't we? And one of us had to take the blame—

BERNICK. But rightly it should have been the guilty one.

JOHAN. Now wait! It was quite right at the time that it was the innocent one. After all, I was free, unattached. No parents living. And it was pure joy to shed that grind at the office. On the other hand, you had your old mother still alive, and moreover you'd just gotten secretly engaged to Betty. How would she have taken it, if she'd ever learned—?

BERNICK. True enough, yes. But—

JOHAN. And wasn't it precisely for Betty's sake that you broke off that involvement with Mrs. Dorf? That's why you were there that evening, to break it off—

BERNICK. Yes, that disastrous evening when her drunken husband walked in— Yes, Johan, it was for Betty's sake. But still—for you to be so good-hearted to draw the blame on yourself and leave town—

JOHAN. Stop fussing, Karsten. We agreed on how it should be. No question: you had to be saved, and you were my friend. Oh, how proud I was of that friendship! Here I was, tied down like a poor wage slave; and then you came back, suave and refined, from your grand tour abroad. You'd seen London and Paris both. And yet you picked me as your friend, although I was four years younger. Oh, I understand now, it was because you were courting Betty. But how proud I was! And who wouldn't have been? Who wouldn't have sacrificed himself gladly for you, especially when it meant nothing more than a month's gossip for the town, along with the chance to cut loose into the wide world?

BERNICK. Hm, my dear Johan, quite frankly I should tell you that the story isn't completely forgotten.

JOHAN. Isn't it? Well, what's that to me, when I'm back on my farm over there—

BERNICK. Then you're going back?

JOHAN. Of course.

BERNICK. But I hope, not right away?

JOHAN. As soon as possible. I only came along to humor Lona.

BERNICK. Oh? How's that?

JOHAN. Well, you know, Lona isn't so young anymore, and these last years she's begun to be terribly homesick—though she'd never admit it. (*Smiling.*) How could she dare risk leaving a frivolous scamp like me behind alone, when at age nineteen I was already involved in—

BERNICK. Yes?

JOHAN. Karsten, I have a confession to make that rather embarrasses me.

BERNICK. You didn't tell her all this?

JOHAN. Yes. It was wrong of me, but I couldn't help it. You have no idea what Lona's been to me. You could never stand her; but to me, she's been like a mother. In those first years, when we were so hard pressed over there —the way she worked! And when I lay ill so long and couldn't earn a cent, there was no stopping her: she went out and sang songs in coffee houses—gave lectures that people made fun of—and she wrote a book she's laughed as well as cried over since—all that, just to keep me alive. How could I look at her last winter, wasting away—she, who'd skimped and slaved for me? No, I couldn't do that, Karsten. So I said: Lona, go on home. Don't you worry about *me*; I'm not as frivolous as you think. And so—so she found out.

BERNICK. And how did she take it?

JOHAN. Well, she thought, in truth, since *I* knew I was innocent, that there couldn't be anything against my joining her for the trip back. But rest assured: Lona won't say a word, and *I'll* certainly watch my tongue this time around.

BERNICK. Yes, yes, I trust so.

JOHAN. Here's my hand on it. And now let's stop talking about this old affair. Fortunately, it's the only wild escapade for either of us, I'm sure. Now I'm going to thoroughly enjoy the few days I'll be here. You can't imagine what a marvelous walk we had this morning. Who would have thought that little tomboy who tagged after me and played angels in the theater—! But tell me—whatever happened with her parents?

BERNICK. Oh, I don't have any more to tell you than what I wrote right after you left. You did get those letters, didn't you?

JOHAN. Yes, of course; I have both of them. Then that sot left her?

BERNICK. To be killed in one of his stupors.

JOHAN. *She* died not much later, didn't she? But I suppose, behind the scenes, you did everything you could for her?

BERNICK. She was proud. She never complained, and she accepted nothing.

JOHAN. Anyway, you did the right thing to take Dina in.

BERNICK. Certainly that, yes. Actually, it was Martha who settled it.

JOHAN. Oh, it was Martha? Yes, that's right—Martha. Where's *she* today?

BERNICK. Oh, her? When she's not minding the school, she has her invalids.

JOHAN. So it was Martha who helped her out.

BERNICK. Yes, Martha's always had a special weakness for problems in education; it's why she took her job at the local school. That was monumental stupidity on her part.

JOHAN. Yes, she looked quite exhausted yesterday. I'm worried, too, that her health can't take it.

BERNICK. Oh, as far as health goes, she can take it. But it's unpleasant for *me*. It looks as if her own brother isn't up to supporting her.

JOHAN. Support—? I thought she had her own income—

BERNICK. Not a penny. You must remember what hard times Mother was going through when you left. She went on awhile like that with my help, but of course it was nothing I could sustain over the long run. So, then I agreed to come into the firm; but that was no answer, either.

Finally, I had to take over completely; and when we audited the books, it was clear there was scarcely anything left of Mother's share. So that, when she died soon after, naturally Martha was left out in the cold.

JOHAN. Poor Martha!

BERNICK. Poor? Why? You don't think I'd let her want for anything? Oh no, I dare say I've been a good brother to her. She lives with us here, of course, and eats at our table. Her teacher's salary keeps her nicely in clothes; and as a single woman—what more does she need?

JOHAN. Hm. That isn't the way we think in America.

BERNICK. No, I suppose not—in a high-pressure society like that. But here in our little community, where up to now, thank God, corruption hasn't made any inroads, women are content to assume a decent, modest role in life. Anyhow, it's Martha's own fault; she could have been provided for long ago, if she'd gone after it.

JOHAN. You mean she could have been married?

BERNICK. Yes, she could have been very well connected. She's had several good offers, oddly enough. After all, she's penniless, no longer young, and with all that, a nonentity, really.

JOHAN. A nonentity?

BERNICK. Oh, it's nothing I hold against her. In fact, I wouldn't want her any other way. You can understand—in a big house like ours—that it's always good to have such a dependable person around who'll take on whatever comes along.

JOHAN. Yes, but what about *her?*

BERNICK. Her? What do you mean? Oh, yes; well, she has interests enough of her own. She has me, and Betty, and Olaf, and me. People shouldn't always be thinking of themselves first, especially women. We all have our own communities, large or small, to support and work for. At least *I* do. (*Gesturing toward* KRAP, *who enters, right.*) And there's proof for you. You think I'm caught up here in my own affairs? Far from it. (*Impatiently to* KRAP.) Well?

KRAP (*his voice low, showing him a bundle of papers*). All the sales contracts are in order.

BERNICK. Excellent! Marvelous! And now, Johan—you'll really have to pardon me a moment. (*In an undertone, clasping his hand.*) Thank you, Johan, thank you. And if there's anything I can do for you, don't hesitate—well, you know what I mean. Mr. Krap, let's go.

(*They go into* BERNICK's *study.*)

JOHAN (*briefly gazing after him*). Hm— (*He starts to go down into the garden. Just then* MARTHA BERNICK *enters, right, with a small basket on her arm.*) Well, Martha!

MARTHA BERNICK. Ah—Johan—it's you?

JOHAN. You're out so early?

MARTHA BERNICK. Yes. If you'll wait just a minute, the others will be right along.

(*She starts to go off, left.*)

JOHAN. Why are you always in such a hurry, Martha?

MARTHA BERNICK. I?

JOHAN. Yesterday you seemed to be avoiding me, so I didn't get one word with you, and today—

MARTHA BERNICK. Yes, but—

JOHAN. We used to be always together—as playmates, in the old days.

MARTHA BERNICK. Oh, Johan, that's many, many years ago.

JOHAN. My Lord, it's fifteen years ago, that's all. You think I've changed so much?

MARTHA BERNICK. You? Oh yes, you too, although—

JOHAN. What do you mean?

MARTHA BERNICK. Oh, nothing.

JOHAN. You don't seem exactly overjoyed to see me again.

MARTHA BERNICK. I've waited so long, Johan. *Too* long.

JOHAN. Waited? For me to come?

MARTHA BERNICK. Yes.

JOHAN. And why did you think I'd come?

MARTHA BERNICK. To atone for what you've done.

JOHAN. I?

MARTHA BERNICK. Have you forgotten that a woman died in shame and want because of you? Have you forgotten that, because of you, a growing child had her best years embittered?

JOHAN. How can you say that to me? Martha, hasn't your brother ever—?

MARTHA BERNICK. What?

JOHAN. Hasn't he ever—? Well, I mean, hasn't he ever said one word in my defense?

MARTHA BERNICK. Ah, Johan, you know Karsten and his strict principles.

JOHAN. Hm—yes, of course, I know my old friend Karsten's strict principles. But this is—! Well. I was talking with him just now. I think there's been a definite change in him.

MARTHA BERNICK. How can you say that? He's always been an exemplary man.

JOHAN. Yes, that's not quite what I meant, but let it go. Hm. I'm beginning to understand now how you must have seen me. You've been waiting here for the prodigal to return.

MARTHA BERNICK. Listen, Johan, I'll tell you how I saw you. (*Pointing down into the garden.*) You see her, that girl playing down there on the grass with Olaf? That's Dina. You remember that confused letter you wrote me when you left. You wrote that I should have faith in you. I *have* had faith in you, Johan. All those awful things that were whispered about afterward—must have been done in a daze, without thinking, on impulse—

JOHAN. What do you mean?

MARTHA BERNICK. Oh, you understand me all right—we just won't talk about it any more. But of course you had to get away—and begin a new life. Look, Johan, we were so close as children—well, I've had to substitute for you, here, at home. The duties you forgot to perform here, or couldn't perform, I've done for you. I tell you this so you won't blame yourself for that, too. I've been a mother to that poor, forlorn child and brought her up as best as I could—

JOHAN. And wasted your whole life in the process—

MARTHA BERNICK. It hasn't been wasted. But you've come so late, Johan.

JOHAN. Martha—if I only could tell you— Well, anyhow, let me thank you for being a true friend.

MARTHA BERNICK (*smiles sadly*). Hm— Well, now we've talked it out, Johan. Shh! Someone's coming. Goodbye. I can't stay—

(*She goes out through the farther door to the left.* LONA HESSEL *comes in from the garden, followed by* MRS. BERNICK.)

MRS. BERNICK (*still in the garden*). But, for goodness' sake, Lona, what are you thinking of?

LONA. I tell you, leave me alone! I *am* going to talk with him!

MRS. BERNICK. But it'll make a terrible scandal. Ah, Johan, are you still here?

LONA. Out with you, boy. Don't mope around indoors. Go down in the garden and talk to Dina.

JOHAN. Yes, exactly what I was thinking.

MRS. BERNICK. But—

LONA. John, listen, have you had a good look at Dina?

JOHAN. Yes, I think so.

LONA. Well, just go feast your eyes on her. *That's* something for *you!*

MRS. BERNICK. Lona—!

LONA. Yes, I mean, to look at. Now, out!

JOHAN. Yes, yes, my pleasure entirely!

(*He goes down into the garden.*)

MRS. BERNICK. Lona, you petrify me. You can't possibly be serious?

LONA. Why, of course I am. She's bright and strong and level-headed, right? She's a perfect wife for John. The kind he needs over there, instead of some old half-sister.

MRS. BERNICK. Dina! Dina Dorf! You're not thinking—

LONA. I'm thinking first and foremost of the boy's happiness. And I'll have to help him along; he's not aggressive enough in that respect. He never really has his eye out for girls.

MRS. BERNICK. Him? Johan! Well, I certainly thought we'd had some sorry proof of that—

LONA. Oh, the hell with that stupid story! Where's Karsten gone? I want to talk to him.

MRS. BERNICK. You mustn't, Lona, I'm telling you!

LONA. I will. If the boy takes to her—and she to him—then they're going to have each other. Karsten's such a clever man; he can turn the trick—

MRS. BERNICK. If you think these American crudities will be indulged here—

LONA. Fiddlesticks, Betty—

MRS. BERNICK. —that a man like Karsten, with his strict moral principles—

LONA. Oh, pish! They're not so all-fired strict.

MRS. BERNICK. What did you say!

LONA. I merely said that Karsten isn't more notably moral than other men.

MRS. BERNICK. You can't get over your hate for him, can you? But what is it you want here, when you can't seem to forget—? I don't understand how you can dare face him after the demeaning way you treated him then.

LONA. Yes, Betty, I got out of hand that time.

MRS. BERNICK. And how generously he forgave you—he, a man who's never harmed a living soul! *He* couldn't help it if you went around nursing your hopes. But from that time on, you've hated *me*, too. (*Bursting into tears.*) You've always resented my happiness. And now you've come here to ruin everything for me—by showing the whole town what kind of family I've brought Karsten into.

Yes, I'm the one who has to pay for this, and *that's* what you want. Oh, it's horrible of you!

(*She goes out, sobbing, by the door upstage left.*)

LONA (*looking after her*). Poor Betty!

(BERNICK *enters from his office.*)

BERNICK (*still in the doorway*). Yes, Mr. Krap, yes. That's fine. Excellent. Send four hundred crowns to feed the poor. (*Turns.*) Lona! (*Approaching her.*) By yourself? Isn't Betty coming?

LONA. No. Should I go and get her?

BERNICK. No, no, no, never mind! Oh, Lona, you don't know how I've longed to talk heart-to-heart—to beg your forgiveness.

LONA. Let's not get sentimental, Karsten. It's not our style.

BERNICK. You *must* listen to me, Lona. I know how appearances stand against me, now that you've heard about Dina's mother. But I swear to you it was only a passing infatuation. You're the one I really loved then, honestly and truly.

LONA. Why do you think I came home?

BERNICK. Whatever you have in mind, I implore you not to do anything till I've exonerated myself. Because I can, Lona! At least I can explain.

LONA. Now you're afraid. You say you loved me then. Yes, it's what you kept assuring me in your letters. And maybe it was even true—in a fashion, as long as you were living out there in the great, free world that gave you the courage to think great, free thoughts yourself. Perhaps in me you found a little more character and willpower and independence than most people show around here. And then of course we kept our feelings secret; no one could make fun of your bad taste.

BERNICK. Lona, how can you think—?

LONA. But then when you did come back and heard the ridicule that rained down on me and the laughter at everything that passed for my shortcomings here—

BERNICK. You *were* outspoken then.

LONA. Mostly to shock all the prigs in this town out of their britches and petticoats. And then you met that enchanting young actress—

BERNICK. That was just tomfoolery, nothing more. I swear, not a tenth of the rumors and gossip that went around were true.

LONA. Probably. But then Betty came home, lovely, blossoming, everyone's idol—and after it became known that she'd inherit all her aunt's money, and that I'd get nothing—

BERNICK. Now we're down to cases, Lona! And this time I'll give you the story straight. I wasn't in love with Betty then. I didn't break with you because of some new involvement. It *was* the money. I needed it, I *had* to get hold of it.

LONA. You can say that to my face?

BERNICK. Yes, I can. Lona, listen—

LONA. And yet you wrote me you'd conceived an uncontrollable passion for Betty. You begged my forbearance and pleaded, for Betty's sake, that I stifle everything that had been between us—

BERNICK. I tell you, I had to.

LONA. Then, by the living God, I've no regrets I acted the way I did!

BERNICK. You should know the hard, cold facts of my situation in those days. My mother, you remember, was the head of the firm, but she was totally lacking in any business sense. I was hurriedly called home from Paris; it was a critical period, and I was supposed to put things in order. What did I find? I found something that had to be kept in the closest confidence: that it was as good as ruined, this old, respected firm that had gone through three generations. What else could I do—the son, the only son—but come up with a way to save it?

LONA. So you saved Bernick and Company at a woman's expense.

BERNICK. You know well enough that Betty loved me.

LONA. And as for me?

BERNICK. Believe me, Lona—you would never have been happy with me.

LONA. And did you desert me for the sake of my happiness?

BERNICK. You think I acted as I did out of selfish motives? If I'd only myself to consider, then I would have gloried in the courage to make a fresh start. But you have no conception how a businessman, under the pressure of immense responsibilities, grows to be part of the business he inherits. Do you realize that the lives and fortunes of hundreds—yes, thousands—of people depend on him? Don't you understand that this whole community that you and I call home would have been shaken to its foundations if the firm had gone down?

LONA. Is it also for the sake of the community that, for fifteen years, you've been living a lie?

BERNICK. A lie?

LONA. What does Betty know about all this background to your marriage?

BERNICK. How can you think I'd put her through the pain of these things, to no profitable end?

LONA. Profitable, you say? Oh yes, you're a businessman; you must be an authority on profit. All right, Karsten, listen—now *I'm* going to talk cold, hard facts. Tell me—are you really happy?

BERNICK. In my home life, you mean?

LONA. Of course.

BERNICK. I am, Lona. Oh, it wasn't wasted, that sacrifice you made out of friendship for me. I can say, year by year, I've grown happier. Betty's so kind and accommodating. The way she's learned over the years to adjust herself to my basic needs—

LONA. Hm.

BERNICK. At the start she had any number of exaggerated notions about love. She couldn't get used to the idea that, little by little, it has to subside into a quiet, warm companionship.

LONA. But *now* she goes along with it?

BERNICK. Perfectly. Of course, her daily contact with me could hardly fail to have its tempering influence. People have to learn to moderate their demands on each other if they're going to make their mark in the community they live in. Betty's gradually grown to realize that, which is why our house has become a model for our fellow citizens.

LONA. But these fellow citizens know nothing about the lie?

BERNICK. The lie?

LONA. Yes, the lie you've been living now for fifteen years.

BERNICK. And you call that—?

LONA. I call it a lie. A triple lie. First you lie to me, then you lie to Betty, then you lie to Johan.

BERNICK. Betty's never asked me to speak out.

LONA. Because she knows nothing.

BERNICK. And you wouldn't ask me to. Out of feeling for her, you wouldn't.

LONA. Oh no, they can rake me over with their laughter. I've got a thick skin.

BERNICK. And Johan won't ask, either. He's promised me that.

LONA. But what about you, Karsten? Isn't there something within you that longs to be free of that lie?

BERNICK. You mean, volunteer to sacrifice my family happiness and my place in society!

LONA. What right do you have to that place?

BERNICK. Every day for fifteen years I've earned a portion of that right—by the way I've lived and worked and accomplished.

LONA. Yes, you've worked and accomplished a lot, both for yourself and for others. You're the richest, most powerful man in town; everyone has to yield to your authority, because it seems you haven't one blemish or flaw; your home seems like an ideal home, and your career an ideal career. But all this splendor, yourself included, rests on

quicksand. A moment can come, a word could be spoken
—and you and all your splendor will go down in ruin if
you don't save yourself in time.

BERNICK. Lona, what have you come here for?

LONA. I want to help you put your feet on solid ground,
Karsten.

BERNICK. Revenge! You want revenge on me? I suspected as much. But you won't get away with it! There's
only one person here who can speak the truth, and he'll
keep quiet.

LONA. Johan?

BERNICK. Yes, Johan. If anyone else accuses me, I'll
deny everything. If they try to annihilate me, I'll fight to
the death. But you'll never succeed, I tell you! The only
man who could ruin me won't talk—and he'll soon be
leaving.

(RUMMEL and VIGELAND enter, right.)

RUMMEL. Good morning, good morning, my dear Bernick. You have to come along with us to the Chamber of
Commerce; we're meeting, you know, about the railroad.

BERNICK. I can't. It's impossible right now.

VIGELAND. Really, Mr. Bernick, you must—

RUMMEL. Bernick, you have to. We have people working
against us. That editor, Hammer, and the crowd that backs
the coast route—they're charging private interests are behind the new proposal.

BERNICK. Well, then tell them—

VIGELAND. It doesn't help, what we tell them, Mr. Bernick—

RUMMEL. No, no, you've got to come yourself. Obviously no one would dare suspect you of anything like
that.

LONA. That's for sure!

BERNICK. I'm telling you, I can't. I'm not well. I mean,
wait—let me collect myself.

(RØRLUND enters, right.)

RØRLUND. Beg pardon, Mr. Bernick; as you can see, I'm terribly upset—

BERNICK. Well, what's your trouble?

RØRLUND. I have a question to ask you, Mr. Bernick. Is it with your approval that the young girl who found asylum under your roof shows herself on the public streets in company with a person that—

LONA. What person, Reverend?

RØRLUND. With the person that she, of all people, ought to stay farthest away from?

LONA. Ha ha!

RØRLUND. *Is* it with your approval, Mr. Bernick?

BERNICK (*looking for his hat and gloves*). I don't know anything about it. Sorry, I'm in a rush. I'm due at the Chamber of Commerce.

(HILMAR *enters from the garden and proceeds to the farther door on the left.*)

HILMAR. Betty, Betty, listen!

MRS. BERNICK (*appearing in the doorway*). What is it?

HILMAR. You ought to go down in the garden and put a stop to the philandering of a certain person with that Dina Dorf. It sets my nerves on edge, listening to it.

LONA. Oh? What's this person said?

HILMAR. Oh, simply that he wants her to go off with him to America. Uff!

RØRLUND. Is that possible!

MRS. BERNICK. What did you say?

LONA. But that's a marvelous idea.

BERNICK. Impossible! You didn't hear right.

HILMAR. Then ask him yourself. Here's the pair of them. But just leave me out of it.

BERNICK (*to* RUMMEL *and* VIGELAND). Go on. I'll be along in a moment.

(RUMMEL *and* VIGELAND *go out, right.* JOHAN *and* DINA *come in from the garden.*)

JOHAN. Hurray, Lona, she's coming with us!

MRS. BERNICK. But, Johan—you senseless—!

RØRLUND. Is that a fact! What a monstrous scandal! By what arts of seduction did you—?

JOHAN. Watch it there! What are you saying?

RØRLUND. Answer me, Dina! Is that your aim? Your full and free determination?

DINA. I have to get away from here.

RØRLUND. But with *him*—with *him*!

DINA. Name one other person here with the courage to take me away?

RØRLUND. Well, then you'll also have to know who he is.

JOHAN. Be quiet!

BERNICK. Not one more word!

RØRLUND. That would make me a poor servant of this community whose culture and morals I'm charged with protecting; and I'd be acting indefensibly toward this young girl, in whose education I've also been substantially involved, and who is to me—

JOHAN. Watch your step!

RØRLUND. She's *got* to know! Dina, this is the man who caused all your mother's shame and sorrow.

BERNICK. Mr. Rørlund—!

DINA. Him! (*To* JOHAN.) Is that true?

JOHAN. Karsten, you answer.

BERNICK. Not another word! Enough for today!

DINA. True, then.

RØRLUND. True, true. And more than that. This person that you put your faith in didn't run off empty-handed from home—old Mrs. Bernick's money—Mr. Bernick can bear witness!

LONA. Liar!

BERNICK. Ah—!

MRS. BERNICK. Oh God, oh God!

JOHAN (*making a fist and going for* RØRLUND). And you dare—!

LONA (*restrains him*). Don't hit him, Johan.

RØRLUND. Yes, take it out on me. But the truth is there, and it is the truth. Mr. Bernick's said so himself, and the whole town knows it. Now, Dina, now you know what he is.

(*A short silence.*)

JOHAN (*in an undertone, gripping* BERNICK'S *arm*). Karsten, Karsten, what have you done!

MRS. BERNICK (*softly, in tears*). Oh, Karsten, that I should bring such dishonor on you.

SANDSTAD (*hurrying in, right, and shouting, with his hand still on the doorknob*). Mr. Bernick, you simply have to come now! The whole railroad's hanging by a thread.

BERNICK (*vacantly*). What? I have to what—?

LONA (*gravely and emphatically*). You have to go and be a pillar of society, Karsten.

SANDSTAD. Yes, come on, we need all your moral authority.

JOHAN (*close beside him*). Bernick—the two of us will talk about this tomorrow.

(*He leaves through the garden.* BERNICK, *like an automaton, goes out, right, with* SANDSTAD.)

◄ ACT THREE ►

The garden room in BERNICK's *house.* BERNICK, *with a cane in one hand, enters in a violent rage from the farther room on the left, leaving the door half open behind him.*

BERNICK. There! Now this time for once he'll know I mean business. That's one spanking I think he'll remember. (*To someone inside the room.*) What'd you say—? And I say you're a thoughtless mother! You excuse him and give him leeway for all his bad conduct. *Not* bad conduct? What else can you call it? Slipping out of the house at night, stealing off to sea in a fishing boat, staying out till late the next day, and scaring the life out of me, when I've got a thousand other things to think about. And then the little sneak has the gall to threaten to run away. Well, let him try—! You? No, I don't doubt it. You don't care two straws for his safety. I really think even if he killed himself—! Oh? Yes, but I have work in this world to be carried on. I don't intend to be left childless— No arguments, Betty. It's going to be as I say. He'll not leave this house. (*Listens.*) Shh! Let's keep this quiet.

(KRAP *enters, right.*)

KRAP. Do you have a moment's time, Mr. Bernick?

BERNICK (*tossing the cane aside*). Why, of course. Have you been at the yard?

KRAP. Yes, just now. Hm—

BERNICK. Well? Not anything wrong with the *Palm Tree*, I hope?

KRAP. The *Palm Tree* can sail tomorrow, but—

BERNICK. So it's the *Indian Girl*? I might have known that stiff-necked old—

KRAP. The *Indian Girl* can sail tomorrow, too, but—it's not going to get very far.

BERNICK. What do you mean?

KRAP. Excuse me, Mr. Bernick; that door's ajar, and I think there's someone in there—

BERNICK (*closing the door*). All right. But what is this that nobody's supposed to hear?

KRAP. It's the fact that Aune apparently means to let the *Indian Girl* go down with all hands.

BERNICK. But, merciful God, how can you think—?

KRAP. Can't make sense of it any other way, Mr. Bernick.

BERNICK. Well, tell me, and make it quick—

KRAP. I will. You know yourself how slow things have gone in the yard since we got the new machines and the new untrained workers.

BERNICK. Yes, yes.

KRAP. But this morning when I went down there, I noticed the repairs on the American ship were amazingly far along. The big patch on the hull—you know, where it'd rotted out—

BERNICK. Yes, what about it?

KRAP. Completely repaired—by appearance, anyway. Bottom's sheathed. Looks good as new. I heard Aune himself rigged lights and worked down there all night.

BERNICK. Yes, so—?

KRAP. So I gave it some thought. The men were taking a breakfast break, and I used the opportunity to have a little private look around her, inside and out. Had a hard time getting down in the hold, what with all the cargo; but I saw all I needed to. Funny things are going on, Mr. Bernick.

BERNICK. I can't believe that, Mr. Krap. I can't and won't believe anything like that about Aune.

KRAP. Don't like saying it—but it's the plain truth. I'm telling you, funny things are going on. Been no new timber put in, so far as I could see. Just plugged up and caulked and patched over with plates and tarp and that sort of thing. Pure fake! The *Indian Girl* will never make New York. She'll go to the bottom like a sprung bucket.

BERNICK. That's terrible! But what possibly could be his purpose, do you think?

KRAP. Wants to discredit the machines, most likely. Wants revenge. Wants the old work gang signed back on.

BERNICK. And for this he'll risk all those human lives.

KRAP. He was saying the other day, there are no human beings on the *Indian Girl*—just wild animals.

BERNICK. Well, never mind about that—doesn't he have any idea of the immense amount of capital that would be lost?

KRAP. Aune doesn't take very kindly to big capital, Mr. Bernick.

BERNICK. Quite true. He's an agitator and a trouble-maker. But such an unconscionable act—! You know, Krap, this case will have to be carefully gone into. Not a word about it to anyone. The yard will suffer if this kind of thing gets around.

KRAP. Of course, but—

BERNICK. During the lunch break you must try to get down there again. I have to have absolute proof.

KRAP. I'll get it, Mr. Bernick. But, if you'll pardon my asking, then what will you do?

BERNICK. Report it, naturally. We can't make ourselves accessories to a perfectly obvious crime. I'm not going to have that on my conscience. Besides, it'll make a good impression both on the press and on the public generally, if it's seen that I put all personal interests aside and allow justice to take its course.

KRAP. Very true, Mr. Bernick.

BERNICK. But above all, absolute proof. And in the meantime, silence—

KRAP. Not one word, Mr. Bernick. And you'll have your proof.

(*He goes out through the garden and down the street.*)

BERNICK (*in an undertone*). Outrageous! But no, it's impossible—unthinkable!

(*He is on the verge of entering his office as* HILMAR *comes in from the right.*)

HILMAR. Good morning, Bernick! And congratulations on your victory yesterday at the Chamber of Commerce.

BERNICK. Ah, thank you.

HILMAR. It was a brilliant victory, I hear. A triumph of intelligent public spirit over self-interest and prejudice. Like the French putting down the Arabs. It's remarkable, after that nasty episode here, that you could—

BERNICK. Yes, forget about that—

HILMAR. But the crucial battle hasn't been fought yet.

BERNICK. You mean the railroad?

HILMAR. Yes. You know, I suppose, what that editor Hammer's cooking up?

BERNICK (*tensely*). No! What?

HILMAR. He's latched onto this rumor that's circulating, and he's going to make a feature story out of it.

BERNICK. What rumor?

HILMAR. Obviously the one about all the real estate being snapped up along the branch-line route.

BERNICK. What? You say a rumor like that's going around?

HILMAR. Yes, all over town. I heard it at the club when I stopped by. The word is that one of our local lawyers has been secretly commissioned to buy up all the forest properties, the mineral deposits, the waterfalls—

BERNICK. And they don't say who's behind it?

HILMAR. At the club they thought it must be that some out-of-town syndicate's got wind of what you'd started, and moved fast before the land prices rose— Isn't that odious? Uff!

BERNICK. Odious?

HILMAR. Yes, for strangers to chisel into our territory that way. And for one of our own lawyers to lend himself to anything like that! Now it'll be outsiders that skim off the profits.

BERNICK. But it's just an unverified rumor.

HILMAR. It's being accepted, all the same. And tomorrow or the next day, I'm sure Hammer will see it nailed down as fact. There's a lot of bitterness about it already at the club. I heard a number of them say that, if the rumor proved out, they'd strike their names off the lists.

BERNICK. Impossible!

HILMAR. Really? Why do you suppose all those shop-keepers were so willing to go along with your plans? Don't you think they could smell a little something in it for themselves?

BERNICK. It's impossible, I tell you! We do have *that* much public spirit in our community—

HILMAR. Here? Well, you're an optimist, and you judge others by yourself. But to a pretty sharp observer like myself—there's no one here—excepting ourselves, of course—no one, I tell you, who keeps the banner of the ideal flying high. (*Moving upstage.*) Uff! There, I can see them!

BERNICK. Who?

HILMAR. The two Americans. (*Looks off to the right.*) And who's that with them? God, wouldn't you know, it's the captain of the *Indian Girl*. Uff!

BERNICK. What could they want with *him*?

HILMAR. Oh, they go well together. He's been a slave trader or a pirate, no question; and who knows what those other two have perpetrated in all that time.

BERNICK. It's quite unfair of you to label them that way.

HILMAR. Yes, you're an optimist. But now we've got them on our necks again, so in the nick of time I'll just—

(*He is about to leave by the door left, as* LONA HESSEL *enters, right.*)

LONA. Ah, Hilmar, am I chasing you out of the room?

HILMAR. Of course not. It's just that I'm in a hurry. I want a word with Betty. (*Goes out by the farther door, left.*)

BERNICK (*after a brief pause*). Well, Lona?

LONA. Yes?

BERNICK. How do you rate me today?

LONA. Same as yesterday. One lie more or less—

BERNICK. You've got to listen. Where's Johan?

LONA. He's coming. He was seeing a man about something.

BERNICK. After what you heard yesterday, you can understand that my whole existence will be destroyed if the truth comes to light.

LONA. I understand that.

BERNICK. It ought to be obvious that *I* was never guilty of this crime everyone's talking about.

LONA. That goes without saying. But who was the thief?

BERNICK. There was no thief. There was no money stolen. Not one penny was missing.

LONA. What?

BERNICK. I said, not one penny.

LONA. But the rumors? How did that shameful rumor get around that Johan—?

BERNICK. Lona, I think I can talk to you more freely than anyone else. I won't hide anything from you. I had my share in spreading that rumor.

LONA. You? You could do that to someone who, for your sake, had—

BERNICK. You mustn't judge me without remembering the way things stood at the time. I told you about that yesterday. I came home and found my mother embroiled in a whole mess of foolish ventures. Then all kinds of misfortune struck. It seemed as if there wasn't a calamity that missed us. The business was on the verge of ruin. I swung back and forth from distraction to despair. Lona, I think it was mostly to numb my mind that I began that affair that ended with Johan leaving.

LONA. Hm—

BERNICK. You can well imagine how all kinds of rumors flew after you and he left town. People said, it wasn't his first indiscretion. That Dorf had been given a large sum of money to keep quiet and go his way. Others claimed it was given to *her*. Meanwhile, it was no secret that our firm was having difficulty in meeting its obligations. What was more natural than for the gossip-mongers to put the two rumors together? When she stayed on here, living in poverty, then they maintained he'd taken the money with him to America, and the sums in the rumor grew larger and larger.

LONA. And you, Karsten—?

BERNICK. I seized that rumor like a life raft.

LONA. You helped spread it?

BERNICK. I didn't repudiate it. Our creditors were beginning to press us. It was my job to placate them. That meant dispelling all suspicion of the firm's solidity. We were undergoing temporary readjustments. If they just wouldn't press us—we needed breathing time—everyone would get his due.

LONA. And everyone did?

BERNICK. Yes, Lona, that rumor saved the business and made me the man I am today.

LONA. Then a lie made you the man you are.

BERNICK. Who was hurt by it at the time? It was Johan's plan never to come back.

LONA. You ask who it hurt. Look into your own heart, and tell me if *you* haven't suffered from it.

BERNICK. Look into anyone's heart, and you'll find every individual has at least one dark secret to hide.

LONA. And you call yourselves pillars of society!

BERNICK. Society provides none better.

LONA. Then why go on supporting a society like this? What does it live by? Lies and pretenses—and nothing else. Here you are, the town's leading citizen, well off, happy, enjoying power and honor—you, who've branded an innocent man a criminal.

BERNICK. Don't you think I'm deeply aware of my injustice to him? And don't you think I'm ready to make good on it?

LONA. How? By confessing it?

BERNICK. Is *that* what you want!

LONA. What else could right that kind of injustice?

BERNICK. I'm rich, Lona. Anything Johan asks for—

LONA. Yes, offer him money, and you'll hear his answer.

BERNICK. Do you know his plans?

LONA. No. Since yesterday he's had nothing to say. It's as if all this has made a man of him overnight.

BERNICK. I have to talk to him.

LONA. Well, here he is.

(JOHAN *enters, right.*)

BERNICK (*going toward him*). Johan—!

JOHAN (*shying away*). Let *me* speak. Yesterday morning I gave you my word not to talk.

BERNICK. That's right.

JOHAN. But I wasn't aware then—

BERNICK. Johan, just allow me a word or two to clarify how things stand—

JOHAN. No need. I know exactly how things stand. The firm was in trouble; and since I'd left, you had my defenseless name and reputation at your disposal— Well, I really don't hold that against you; we were young and emptyheaded then. But now I need the truth. You've got to speak out.

BERNICK. And right now I need every scrap of moral credibility. That's why I *can't* speak out.

JOHAN. I'm not greatly bothered by the stories you've circulated about me. It's the other matter you've got to acknowledge. Dina is going to be my wife; and here, here in this town, I want to live and share and build with her.

LONA. That's your plan?

BERNICK. With Dina? As your wife? Here in town!

JOHAN. Yes, right here. I'm staying on just to spite all these liars and backbiters. But for me to win her, you have to vindicate me.

BERNICK. Don't you see that if I acknowledge the one fault, it's the same as confessing the other? You'll say I could prove by our books that no manipulations went on. But I can't. Our books weren't kept so carefully in those days. And even if I could—what would be gained by that? In any event, wouldn't I stand revealed as the man who once saved himself by an untruth, and who for fifteen years let that untruth take root and grow without the least effort to counter it? You've forgotten this community of ours, or else you'd know such a confession would totally destroy me.

JOHAN. I can only repeat that I expect to make Mrs. Dorf's daughter my wife and live with her here in town.

BERNICK (*wiping the sweat from his brow*). Listen, Johan—and you too, Lona. I'm not exactly in the most ordinary circumstances these days. As things stand, if you strike this blow, then you'll ruin me, and not only me, but a future of the greatest promise for this town, which, after all, is your childhood home.

JOHAN. And if I don't strike this blow, then I'll ruin my own future happiness.

LONA. Go on, Karsten.

BERNICK. Listen, now. This all ties in with the railroad project, and that's not as simple a matter as you might suppose. You've undoubtedly heard mention that last year there was some discussion here about a coast line? A lot of influential people backed it, in town and the outlying districts, and in the press especially; but I succeeded in blocking it, because it would have harmed our coastal shipping.

LONA. Do you have interests yourself in coastal shipping?

BERNICK. Yes. But no one dared suspect me on that count. I'm well protected by my good name. Anyway, I could have borne the loss; but the town couldn't. So the decision was for an inland line. Once that was done, I secretly made sure that a branch line could be run out here.

LONA. Why secretly, Karsten?

BERNICK. Have you heard the talk about large acquisitions of forests and mines and waterfalls—?

JOHAN. Yes. It's some syndicate from out of town—

BERNICK. As they stand now, those properties are just about worthless to their different owners; they were sold off for relatively little. If one waited till the branch line was public knowledge, the owners would have inflated the prices out of all reason.

LONA. All right, so—?

BERNICK. Now we come to the part that could be variously interpreted—something that a man in our society could own up to only if he had a spotless name and reputation behind him.

LONA. What?

BERNICK. I'm the one who bought all that land.

LONA. You?

JOHAN. With your own money?

BERNICK. With my own money. If the branch line goes through, I'm a millionaire. If it doesn't, then I'm ruined.

LONA. That's quite a risk, Karsten.

BERNICK. I'm risking my entire fortune on this.

LONA. I'm not thinking of your fortune. But if it comes out that—

BERNICK. That's the point, exactly. With the spotless reputation I've had up till now, I could shoulder the responsibility, carry it through, and say to my fellow citizens: look, this is what I've risked for the good of the community.

LONA. The community?

BERNICK. Yes. And not a single one of them would challenge my integrity.

LONA. Still, there are men here who've acted more openly than you, with no ulterior motives.

BERNICK. Who?

LONA. Rummel, Sandstad and Vigeland, of course.

BERNICK. To gain their support I had to cut them in, too.

LONA. Oh?

BERNICK. They specified a fifth of the profits for their share.

LONA. Ah, these pillars of society!

BERNICK. And isn't it society itself that makes us devious? What would have happened if I hadn't acted in confidence? Everyone would have swarmed in on the project, carved it up, parceled it out, botched and bungled it completely. There's not one man here in town, besides me, who knows how to manage as large an operation as this. In this country generally, it's only families from abroad who have any knack for big business. That's why I have a clear conscience on this score. Only in my hands can these properties have a long-term development that will feed any number of people.

LONA. I guess you're right about that, Karsten.

JOHAN. But I don't know these people of yours, and my whole life's happiness is at stake.

BERNICK. The welfare of this, your birthplace, is also at stake. If anything comes up to cast a shadow on my past record, then all my enemies will join forces to beat me down. In our community a youthful indiscretion is never written off. They'll go over my whole life since then, pull out a thousand little incidents and judge them all in the light of this one disclosure. They'll crush me under the weight of rumor and vilification. I'll have to withdraw from the railroad project; and if I let go of that, it will fail, and I'll be ruined, dead to society.

LONA. Johan, after what you've just heard, you'll have to go and keep quiet.

BERNICK. Yes, yes, Johan, you must!

JOHAN. Yes, I'll go and keep quiet now; but I'll come back, and then I'll talk.

BERNICK. Stay over there, Johan. Say nothing, and I'll see that you get your share—

JOHAN. Keep your money, but give me my name and reputation back.

BERNICK. And sacrifice my own?

JOHAN. That's for you and your community to resolve, if you can. I'm going to marry Dina, and that's final. So— tomorrow I'll be sailing on the *Indian Girl*—

BERNICK. The *Indian Girl*?

JOHAN. Yes. The captain's promised to take me. I'll go over, sell my farm and put my affairs in order. I'll be back in two months.

BERNICK. And you'll speak out then?

JOHAN. Then the guilty one will have to take the blame.

BERNICK. Aren't you forgetting I'll also be blamed for what I'm *not* guilty of?

JOHAN. Who's the one who benefited for fifteen years from that vicious rumor?

BERNICK. I swear, you'll drive me to desperation! If you talk, I'll deny everything! I'll say it's a plot against me. An act of revenge. That you came back here to blackmail me!

LONA. Karsten! No!

BERNICK. I tell you, I'm desperate. And I'm fighting for my life. I'll deny everything, everything!

JOHAN. I have your two letters. I found them in my trunk among my other papers. This morning I reread them. They're quite explicit.

BERNICK. And you'll make them public?

JOHAN. If necessary.

BERNICK. And you'll return in two months?

JOHAN. I hope so. The winds are good. In three weeks I'll be in New York—that is, unless the *Indian Girl* goes down.

BERNICK (*with a start*). Goes down? Why should the *Indian Girl* go down?

JOHAN. No, I hardly expect that.

BERNICK (*barely audible*). Down?

JOHAN. Well, Bernick, now you know what's in store. Meanwhile, you better think it over. Goodbye! My best to Betty, though she's hardly treated me the way a sister should. But I do want to see Martha. She has to tell Dina —she has to promise me—

(*He goes out by the farther door, left.*)

BERNICK (*to himself*). The *Indian Girl*—? (*Rapidly.*) Lona, you *must* stop this!

LONA. You can see yourself, Karsten—I have no more power over him.

(*She follows* JOHAN *into the room, left.*)

BERNICK (*troubled*). Go down—?

(AUNE *enters, right.*)

AUNE. Excuse me, Mr. Bernick, are you free—?

BERNICK (*wheeling angrily*). What do you want?

AUNE. If I might ask you a question, Mr. Bernick.

BERNICK. All right, hurry up. What is it?

AUNE. I wanted to ask if it's certain—dead certain—that I'll be fired from the yard if that *Indian Girl* can't sail tomorrow?

BERNICK. Now what! She *has* to be ready.

AUNE. Yes—of course. But if she isn't—would I get fired?

BERNICK. What's the point of idle questions?

AUNE. I really want to know, Mr. Bernick. Just tell me: would I get fired?

BERNICK. Do I usually keep my word, or not?

AUNE. Then tomorrow I'd lose my place in my own home, and with everyone I care for most. Lose my influence among the workers. Lose all hope of doing a little good for the poor and deprived in society.

BERNICK. Aune, we've been over this before.

AUNE. Then the *Indian Girl* sails.

(*A brief silence.*)

BERNICK. Look, my eyes can't be everywhere. I can't be responsible for everything. I assume you can assure me that the repairs have been carried out to the letter.

AUNE. You gave me a hard deadline, Mr. Bernick.

BERNICK. But you say the repairs are adequate?

AUNE. Of course there's good weather, and it's summer.

(*Another silence.*)

BERNICK. Do you have anything else to say to me?

AUNE. I can't think of anything else, Mr. Bernick.

BERNICK. So then—the *Indian Girl* sails—

AUNE. Tomorrow?

BERNICK. Yes.

AUNE. Right.

(*He nods and goes out.* BERNICK *stands for an instant indecisively; then he paces across to the door as if to call* AUNE *back, but hesitates uneasily with his hand on the doorknob. At that moment the door is opened from outside, and* KRAP *enters.*)

KRAP (*quietly*). Aha, he was here. Has he confessed?

BERNICK. Hm—did you learn anything?

KRAP. What's the need? Couldn't you see the bad conscience in him by the look in his eyes?

BERNICK. Come on now—those things can't be seen. I asked if you'd learned anything?

KRAP. Too late. I couldn't get in. They'd already started hauling the ship out of the dock. But the very fact that they couldn't wait shows clearly—

BERNICK. It shows nothing. Then the inspection's been made?

KRAP. Of course. But—

BERNICK. You see. And no violations?

KRAP. Mr. Bernick, you know perfectly well what inspections are like, especially in a yard with a name as good as ours.

BERNICK. Doesn't matter. We're covered.

KRAP. Mr. Bernick, couldn't you really see, right in Aune's face—?

BERNICK. I'm telling you, Aune's given me an absolute assurance.

KRAP. And I'm telling you it's my moral conviction that—

BERNICK. What does that mean, Mr. Krap? I realize you have a grudge against the man, but if you want to go at him, you ought to choose a better occasion. You know how crucial it is for me—or rather, the company—that the *Indian Girl* sails tomorrow.

KRAP. Very well. As you say. But if we ever hear from *that* ship again—hm!

(VIGELAND *enters, right.*)

VIGELAND. A very good morning to you, Consul Bernick. Do you have a moment?

BERNICK. At your service, Mr. Vigeland.

VIGELAND. I only wanted to hear if we're unanimous that the *Palm Tree* sails tomorrow?

BERNICK. Certainly. That's all settled.

VIGELAND. But the captain just stopped me now to report a gale warning.

KRAP. The barometer's dropped sharply since this morning.

BERNICK. Oh? They're expecting a storm?

VIGELAND. A stiff breeze, anyway. But no headwinds. On the contrary—

BERNICK. Hm. Well, what do you think?

VIGELAND. I think—as I told the captain—that the *Palm Tree* is in the hands of Providence. Besides, she's only crossing the North Sea to start with, and the freight rates right now in England aren't too steep, so—

BERNICK. Yes, it probably would mean a loss to us if we delayed.

VIGELAND. The ship's sound enough, and what's more, she's fully insured. Nothing like the risk with that *Indian Girl*—

BERNICK. How do you mean?

VIGELAND. She's sailing tomorrow, too.

BERNICK. Yes, the company's been rushing the work, and besides—

VIGELAND. Well, if that old crate can ship out—with that crew, in the bargain—it would be pretty sad if we couldn't—

BERNICK. Quite so. I suppose you have the ship's papers on you.

VIGELAND. Yes, here.

BERNICK. Good. Mr. Krap will take care of them inside.

KRAP. If you will. You'll have them right away.

VIGELAND. Thanks. And we'll leave the outcome in the hands of the Almighty.

(*He accompanies* KRAP *into the room downstage left.* RØRLUND *strolls in through the garden.*)

RØRLUND. Ah, Mr. Bernick, at home at this hour of the day?

BERNICK (*deep in thought*). As you see.

RØRLUND. Well, actually I was stopping by to visit your wife. I thought maybe she could use some words of comfort.

BERNICK. I'm sure she can. But I'd like to talk with you a bit, too.

RØRLUND. With pleasure, Mr. Bernick. What's wrong? You look so pale and nervous.

BERNICK. Oh? I do? Well, what else can I be—the way everything's piling up on me just now? All my own business—and then the railroad expansion. Say, tell me something, Mr. Rørlund. Let me ask you a question.

RØRLUND. Of course, Mr. Bernick.

BERNICK. It's a thought that occurred to me. What if a man stood on the brink of a tremendous undertaking that could make an improvement in thousands of lives—and it required the sacrifice of one, single individual—

RØRLUND. How do you mean?

BERNICK. For example, take a man who has it in mind to build a large factory. He knows for sure—all his experience proves—that sooner or later in the running of that factory, human life will be lost.

RØRLUND. Yes, that's more than likely.

BERNICK. Or again, a man who's running a mine. He employs heads of families and young men full of expectations. There isn't the least doubt, is there, that some of them won't make it out with their lives?

RØRLUND. Yes, true enough, unfortunately.

BERNICK. Well. A man like that knows beforehand that the operation he's setting in motion sooner or later is going to claim human life. But it operates for the common good. For every human life it claims, it undoubtedly will benefit thousands of others.

RØRLUND. Aha, you're thinking of the railroad—of all the dangerous tunneling and blasting and such—

BERNICK. Well, all right, I'm thinking of the railroad. And besides—the railroad will bring in factories and mines both. But all the same, don't you think—?

RØRLUND. My dear Mr. Bernick, you're almost too conscientious. I think, if you put this thing in the hands of Providence—

BERNICK. Yes, of course. Providence—

RØRLUND. Then you're blameless. Build your railroad with a clear conscience.

BERNICK. But now, take a specific example. Suppose there's a charge of explosives that has to be set off at a particularly dangerous spot; but unless it's detonated, the railroad can never be built. Suppose the engineer knows it will cost the life of the man that lights the fuse; but it has to be done, and it's the engineer's duty to send a workman out to do it.

RØRLUND. Hm—

BERNICK. I know what you'll say. The great thing would be for the engineer himself to take the match and go and light the fuse. But people don't do such things. So he has to sacrifice a workman.

RØRLUND. No engineer here would ever do that.

BERNICK. No engineer in one of the larger countries would give it a second thought.

RØRLUND. In the larger countries? No, I don't doubt it. In those decadent, unscrupulous societies—

BERNICK. Oh, there's a lot that's good in those societies.

RØRLUND. And you can say that? You, who yourself—?

BERNICK. In large societies you at least have room to evolve a project on a generous scale. They have the courage to sacrifice for a great cause; but here, one's hobbled by all kinds of trivial issues and restrictions.

RØRLUND. Is human life a trivial issue?

BERNICK. When that human life is an obstacle to the welfare of thousands.

RØRLUND. But you're posing quite hypothetical situations, Mr. Bernick! I don't understand you at all today. And then harping on these big societies. Yes, out there— what's a human life worth to them? They rate human life as so much capital. But to my mind, we take a different moral position completely. Look at our foremost shipping magnates. You can't name a single one of them who'd sacrifice a human life for some paltry profit! And then think of those scoundrels in the larger countries who, for the sake of their dividends, send out one unseaworthy ship after another—

BERNICK. I'm not talking about unseaworthy ships!

RØRLUND. But I'm talking about them, Mr. Bernick.

BERNICK. Yes, but what's the point? It's irrelevant. Oh, these timid little qualms! If one of our generals had to lead his men into fire and see them shot, he'd have insomnia for nights. It's not like that elsewhere. You should hear him in there, talking—

RØRLUND. Him? Who? The American—?

BERNICK. That's right. You should hear the way people in America—

RØRLUND. He's inside? And you didn't tell me? I'm going this instant—

BERNICK. It's no use. You won't get anywhere with him.

(JOHAN *enters from the room, left.*)

JOHAN (*calling back through the open door*). Yes, yes, Dina, all right—but I'm not going to give you up. I'll be back, and everything will turn out well for us then.

RØRLUND. Excuse me, but what's that supposed to mean? What is it you want?

JOHAN. I want that girl that you slurred me in front of yesterday to be my wife.

RØRLUND. Your—? And do you really think—?

JOHAN. I want to marry her.

RØRLUND. Well then, you'll find out— (*Crossing to the half-open door.*) Mr. Bernick, if you'd be good enough to be a witness—and you too, Martha. And ask Dina in. (*Sees* LONA HESSEL.) Ah, you're here too?

LONA (*in the doorway*). Shall I also come?

RØRLUND. Any number. The more the better.

(LONA HESSEL, MRS. BERNICK, MARTHA, DINA, *and* HILMAR *enter from the room.*)

MRS. BERNICK. Mr. Rørlund, try as I might, I couldn't stop him—

RØRLUND. I'll stop him, Mrs. Bernick. Dina, you're a thoughtless girl. But I don't greatly blame you. For entirely too long you've lived here without the moral support you need. I blame myself that I haven't given you that support before this.

DINA. Don't say anything now!

MRS. BERNICK. What is all this?

RØRLUND. Now I have to speak, Dina, though your conduct yesterday and today has made it ten times harder for me. But saving you is more important than anything else. You remember I gave you my word. You remember the answer you promised me when I decided the right time had come. Now I can't delay any longer, and so— (*To* JOHAN.) This young girl you've been chasing is my fiancée.

MRS. BERNICK. What's that?

BERNICK. Dina!

JOHAN. She? Your—?

MRS. BERNICK. No, no, Dina!

LONA. Lies!

JOHAN. Dina—is he telling the truth?

DINA (*hesitating a moment*). Yes.

RØRLUND. With that, let's hope all your seducer's wiles will lose their spell. This step that I'm taking here for Dina's well-being, it's my pleasure to announce to our entire community. I devoutly trust it won't be misinterpreted. But now, Mrs. Bernick, I think it's best we take her elsewhere and try to restore peace and equanimity to her mind.

MRS. BERNICK. Yes, come. Oh, Dina, how happy you must be!

(*She leads* DINA *out, left,* RØRLUND *accompanying them.*)

MARTHA BERNICK. Goodbye, Johan. (*She goes out.*)

HILMAR (*in the doorway to the garden*). Hm—I must say, really—!

LONA (*who has been following* DINA *with her eyes*). Don't give up, son. I'll stay here and keep my eye on the Reverend.

(*She goes out, right.*)

BERNICK. You won't sail now with the *Indian Girl*, Johan.

JOHAN. By all means, now!

BERNICK. But you won't be coming back?

JOHAN. I'll be back.

BERNICK. After this? What could you want here after this?

JOHAN. To get my revenge on all of you. Crush as many of you as I can.

(*He goes out right.* VIGELAND *and* KRAP *enter from* BERNICK's *office.*)

VIGELAND. There, the papers are in order now, Mr. Bernick.

BERNICK. Good, good—

KRAP (*quietly*). And it's still definite the *Indian Girl* sails tomorrow?

BERNICK. That's right.

(*He goes into his office.* VIGELAND *and* KRAP *go out right.* HILMAR *is about to follow them, but just then* OLAF's *head appears warily from behind the door, left.*)

OLAF. Uncle! Uncle Hilmar!

HILMAR. Uff, it's you? Why aren't you upstairs? You're in detention.

OLAF (*coming forward a couple of steps*). Shh! Uncle Hilmar, heard the news?

HILMAR. Yes, I heard you had a spanking today.

OLAF (*glowering at his father's office*). He'll never hit me anymore. But have you heard that Uncle Johan's sailing tomorrow for America?

HILMAR. What's that to you? You just get along upstairs again.

OLAF. Maybe I'll go hunting buffalo too, Uncle.

HILMAR. Bosh! A little pipsqueak like you—

OLAF. Yes, you wait and see! You'll find out tomorrow!

HILMAR. Lunkhead!

(*He goes out through the garden.* OLAF *runs back in the room again and closes the door, as he sees* KRAP *entering, right.*)

KRAP (*going to the office door and opening it ajar*). Sorry to bother you again, Mr. Bernick, but there's a fearful storm blowing up. (*He waits a moment; no answer.*) Will the *Indian Girl* still sail?

BERNICK (*after a pause, from within the office*). The *Indian Girl* still sails.

(KRAP *shuts the door and goes out, right.*)

⤳ ACT FOUR ⤶

The garden room in BERNICK's *house. The work table has been removed. It is a stormy afternoon, already growing dark; and the darkness deepens as the action unfolds. A servant is lighting the chandelier. Two maids bring in pots of flowers, lamps and candles, which they place on tables and on sconces along the wall.* RUMMEL, *in white tie and tails, with white gloves, is standing in the room, issuing orders.*

RUMMEL. Just every other candle, Jacob. It shouldn't look too festive; it's meant for a surprise, you know. And all these flowers—? Oh well, let them stay. They can look like the usual—

(BERNICK *enters from his office.*)

BERNICK (*in the doorway*). What's going on?

RUMMEL. Oh-oh, it's you? (*To the servants.*) All right, that's it for now.

(*The man-servant and the maids leave by the door, upstage left.*)

BERNICK (*approaching him*). But, Rummel, what's the meaning of all this?

RUMMEL. It means the proudest moment of your life is at hand. There'll be a procession from the town here tonight, honoring its foremost citizen.

BERNICK. What!

RUMMEL. A parade, with banners and band music! We were going to have torches too, but we can't chance it with this storm in the air. Anyway, there'll be some illuminations; that'll make a choice item for the newspapers.

BERNICK. Listen, Rummel, I don't want any part of this.

RUMMEL. Well, it's too late now. In half an hour they'll be here.

BERNICK. But why didn't you tell me before?

RUMMEL. Exactly because I was afraid you'd object. But I got in touch with your wife, and she allowed me to make some arrangements, and she's taking care of the refreshments.

BERNICK (*listening.*) What's that? They're already coming? I think I hear singing.

RUMMEL (*by the door to the garden*). Singing? Oh, it's just the Americans. It's the *Indian Girl* hauling out to the buoy.

BERNICK. Hauling out! Oh—no, I can't this evening, Rummel. I don't feel well.

RUMMEL. Yes, you look quite miserable. But you've got to brace up there. Hell's fire, man, brace up—you've *got* to! I and Sandstad and Vigeland place the greatest stress on bringing off this occasion well. Our opposition has to be crushed under the greatest possible weight of public opinion. Rumors are flying everywhere. The announcement about our buying up the properties can't be held back a moment longer. It's crucial this evening, and no later— among the songs and toasts and clinking of glasses—in short, in an atmosphere of high celebration—that you let them know what a risk you've run for the good of this community. In such an atmosphere of high celebration— my phrase for it—we can deal masterfully with these people here. But we *have* to have that, or it's not going to work.

BERNICK. Yes, yes, yes—

RUMMEL. Especially when such a delicate and sensitive point is involved. Well, praises be, you've got the reputation that can swing it. But now listen, we better go over this a bit. Young Tønnesen's written a song praising you. It opens beautifully with the words: "Raise high the flag of the ideal." And Mr. Rørlund's going to do the big speech in your honor. Of course, you'll have to respond.

BERNICK. I can't do it tonight, Rummel. Couldn't you—?

RUMMEL. Impossible, even if I wanted to. As you must know, the speech will be especially focused on you. Well, maybe a few words addressed to us, too. I've talked with Vigeland and Sandstad about it. We thought you might respond with a toast to the prosperity of our community. Sandstad will speak a little about the harmony that unites our different social classes; Vigeland will go on to say how desirable it is that this new undertaking not disturb the moral foundations on which we stand; and I thought of making a brief homage in passing to the women, whose contribution, though more humble, is not without significance to the community. But you're not listening—

BERNICK. Yes—yes, of course. But tell me, do you think it's a very heavy sea out there?

RUMMEL. Oh, you're worried about the *Palm Tree*? But she's well insured.

BERNICK. Yes, insured. But—

RUMMEL. And in good condition. That's what counts.

BERNICK. Hm— If something happens to a vessel like that, it doesn't follow necessarily that lives would be lost. The ship and the cargo might go down—and people could lose baggage and papers—

RUMMEL. Hell! Baggage and papers don't matter.

BERNICK. Don't matter! No, no, I only meant— Shh, they're singing again.

RUMMEL. That's from the *Palm Tree*.

(VIGELAND, *enters, right.*)

VIGELAND. Yes, now the *Palm Tree*'s hauling out. Good evening, Mr. Bernick.

BERNICK. As a man who knows the sea, would you still hold that—?

VIGELAND. I hold by Providence, Mr. Bernick. Besides, I went on board myself and passed out a few small tracts that I hope will bring them God's blessings.

(SANDSTAD *and* KRAP *enter, right.*)

SANDSTAD (*still in the doorway*). Well, if she stays afloat, anything will. Ah—good evening, good evening!

BERNICK. Any problems, Mr. Krap?

KRAP. I'm saying nothing, Mr. Bernick.

SANDSTAD. The entire crew of the *Indian Girl* is drunk. I'll be a monkey's uncle if that rabble ever makes it across.

(LONA HESSEL *enters, right.*)

LONA (*to* BERNICK). Well, he's asked me to say goodbye for him.

BERNICK. He's on board already?

LONA. Soon, in any case. I left him outside the hotel.

BERNICK. And his plan is still set?

LONA. Firm as a rock.

RUMMEL (*by the windows*). Damn these new-fangled devices! I can't get the curtains down.

LONA. Down? I thought instead—

RUMMEL. Down first, Miss Hessel. You know what's coming off, don't you?

LONA. Yes, of course. Let me help. (*Grasping the cords.*) I'll ring down the curtain on my brother-in-law—though I'd rather raise it.

RUMMEL. You can do that as well later. When the garden is filled with a host of faces, then the curtains will rise to reveal a surprised and delighted family group. A citizen's home ought to be like a bell jar.

(BERNICK *appears about to say something, then turns quickly and goes into his study.*)

RUMMEL. Well, let's have the last council together. Come along, Mr. Krap; we need your help on a few points of fact.

(*All the men go into* BERNICK's *study.* LONA *has drawn the curtains across the windows and is about to follow suit with the curtain over the glass door, when* OLAF *jumps down on the garden steps from above. He has a bedroll over his shoulder and a bundle in his hand.*)

LONA. Oh my Lord, child, what a fright you gave me!

OLAF (*concealing the bundle*). Auntie, shh!

LONA. Did you jump from the window? Where are you going?

OLAF. Shh, don't say anything. I'm going to Uncle Johan —just down to the pier, that's all—just to say goodbye. Good night, Aunt Lona.

(*He runs out through the garden.*)

LONA. No—wait! Olaf—Olaf!

(JOHAN, *dressed for the voyage, with a bag slung over his shoulder, warily enters through the door, right.*)

JOHAN. Lona!

LONA (*wheeling about*). What! You're back?

JOHAN. There's still a little time. A few minutes. I want to see her just once more. We can't part like this.

(MARTHA BERNICK *and* DINA, *both wearing coats, and the latter with a small valise in her hand, enter from the farther door, left.*)

DINA. I must see him! I must!

MARTHA BERNICK. Yes, and you will, Dina!

DINA. There he is!

JOHAN. Dina!

DINA. Take me with you!

JOHAN. What—?

LONA. You want to—?

DINA. Yes, take me with you! That Rørlund, he wrote

me—and said this evening he's going to tell everyone, publicly—

JOHAN. Dina—you don't love him?

DINA. I've never loved that man. I'd throw myself into the fjord before I'd be engaged to him! Oh, the way he patronized me yesterday with his highflown talk! The way he made me feel he was raising a little nobody up to his level! I won't be patronized anymore. I'm getting out. Can I go with you?

JOHAN. Yes, yes—a thousand times yes!

DINA. I won't be a burden to you for long. Just help me going over. Guide me a little getting started—

JOHAN. Hurray! It'll all work out, Dina.

LONA (*pointing at* BERNICK'*s door*). Shh! Easy, easy.

JOHAN. Dina, I'll wait on you hand and foot!

DINA. Oh, no, you won't. I can take care of myself. I'm sure over there I can. It's just to get away from here. Oh, these women—you don't know. They even wrote me today, instructing me to appreciate my good fortune and reminding me how charitable he's been. From tomorrow on they'd be forever keeping watch over me, to see if I prove myself worthy of everything. It terrifies me, all that respectability!

JOHAN. Tell me, Dina, is that your only reason for leaving? Am I nothing to you?

DINA. Oh, no, Johan—you're more to me than anyone else in the world.

JOHAN. Oh, Dina—!

DINA. Everyone here tells me I ought to loathe and detest you—that it's my duty. But I don't understand this thing about duty. I never will.

LONA. And you don't need to, child!

MARTHA BERNICK. No, you don't. So go with him, as his wife.

JOHAN. Yes, yes!

LONA. What? Let me kiss you, Martha! I wouldn't have expected *that* from *you*.

MARTHA BERNICK. No, I guess not. I didn't expect it myself. But sometime or other I had to let it out. Oh, the way we suffer here from the tyranny of convention, always conforming! Don't put up with it, Dina! Marry him. Let's have something happen that'll break all their rules!

JOHAN. What's your answer, Dina?

DINA. Yes, I'll be your wife.

JOHAN. Dina!

DINA. But first I want to work, become something myself, the way you have. I don't want to be a thing that's just taken along.

LONA. Right. Exactly.

JOHAN. Good. Then I'll wait and hope—

LONA. And you'll win, son! But now, get yourselves on board!

JOHAN. Yes, on board! Ah, Lona, my dear sister—one word, before I leave. Listen—

(*Speaking rapidly to her, he draws her to the back of the room.*)

MARTHA BERNICK. Dina, you lucky girl—let's have a look at you, and a goodbye kiss—for the last time.

DINA. Not the last. No, my dearest Aunt Martha, we'll see each other again.

MARTHA BERNICK. Never! Promise me, Dina—don't ever come back. (*Grasps both her hands and gazes at her.*) Now, you darling girl, go to your happiness—across the sea. Oh, how many times in the schoolroom I've dreamed of being over there! It must be beautiful there—the sky wider, the clouds higher than here, and the air more free overhead—

DINA. Oh, Aunt Martha, someday you'll have to join us.

MARTHA BERNICK. I? Never, never. What I was cut out to be is here; and now I really think I can become everything I was meant for.

DINA. I can't imagine parting from you.

MARTHA BERNICK. Oh, a person can part with quite a bit, Dina. (*Kisses her.*) But you won't ever have to learn that, my dear. Promise me you'll make him happy.

DINA. I won't promise anything. I hate making promises. Things have to go their own way.

MARTHA BERNICK. Yes, yes, of course. Just stay as you are—faithful and true to yourself.

DINA. I will, Aunt Martha.

LONA (*thrusting into her pocket some papers* JOHAN *has given her*). That's fine, just fine, dear boy. But now, get going.

JOHAN. Yes, there's no time to waste now. Goodbye, Lona; thanks for all your love. Goodbye, Martha—and you too, thanks for being a real friend.

MARTHA BERNICK. Goodbye, Johan! Goodbye, Dina! A lifetime's happiness to you both!

(MARTHA BERNICK *and* LONA *propel them toward the garden door.* JOHAN *and* DINA *hurry down through the garden and out.* LONA *shuts the door and pulls the curtain across it.*)

LONA. Now we're alone, Martha. You've lost her; and I, him.

MARTHA BERNICK. You—him?

LONA. Oh, I'd already halfway lost him on the other side. The boy kept longing to stand on his own feet, so I fed him the idea I was homesick.

MARTHA BERNICK. Was that it? Yes, then I understand your return. But he'll want you back, Lona.

LONA. An old stepsister—what would he want with her now? Men will shatter any number of family ties to arrive at happiness.

MARTHA BERNICK. That happens sometimes.

LONA. But we'll stick together, Martha.

MARTHA BERNICK. Can I be a help to you?

LONA. Who else more? We two foster mothers—haven't we, both of us, lost our children? Now we're alone.

MARTHA BERNICK. Yes, alone. So you might as well know —I've loved him more than anything on earth.

LONA. Martha! (*Gripping her arm.*) Is that true?

MARTHA BERNICK. The whole of my life is in those words. I loved him and waited for him. Every summer I waited for him to come. And then he came—but I didn't exist.

LONA. Loved him! But you yourself are the one who put happiness right into his hands.

MARTHA BERNICK. What else could I do, when I loved him? Yes, I've loved him. My entire life has been lived for him, ever since he went away. You're thinking, what grounds did I have for hope? Oh, I believe I had some, all right. But when he came back—then it was as if everything had been wiped out of his memory. I didn't exist.

LONA. It was Dina overshadowing you, Martha.

MARTHA BERNICK. I'm glad she did. When he left here, we were the same age. When I saw him again—oh, that horrible moment—I realized with a shock that now I was ten years older than he. Over there he'd been thriving in the bright, vibrant sunlight, drinking in youth and health with every breath; and meanwhile, here I'd been sitting indoors, spinning and spinning—

LONA. The thread of his happiness, Martha.

MARTHA BERNICK. Yes, it was gold I spun. No bitterness! Isn't it true, Lona, we've been like two good sisters to him.

LONA (*throwing her arms around her*). Martha!

(BERNICK *enters from his office.*)

BERNICK (*to the men inside*). Yes, yes, manage it any way you like. When the time comes, I'm sure I'll— (*Closing the door.*) Ah, you're here? Listen, Martha, you ought to dress up a bit. And tell Betty to do the same. Nothing showy, of course; I don't want that. Just a nice, everyday dress. But hurry up now.

LONA. And a happy, cheerful face, Martha. Let's see your eyes light up.

BERNICK. And let's have Olaf come down, too. I want him by my side.

LONA. Hm. Olaf—

MARTHA BERNICK. I'll give Betty the message.

(*She goes out by the farther door, left.*)

LONA. Well, now the great solemn moment's upon us.

BERNICK (*pacing nervously back and forth*). Yes, quite so.

LONA. A man must feel pleasure and pride at such a moment, I would think.

BERNICK (*looking at her*). Hm!

LONA. The whole town's going to be illuminated, I hear.

BERNICK. Yes, they're thinking along those lines.

LONA. All the civic organizations will be marching here with their banners. Your name will be kindled in letters of fire. Tonight the telegrams will go out all over the country: "Surrounded by his happy family, Consul Karsten Bernick received a tribute from his fellow citizens as one of the pillars of society."

BERNICK. No doubt. And they'll be shouting hurrahs outside, and the crowd will cheer till I show myself at the door, and I'll be compelled to bow and thank them.

LONA. Compelled—?

BERNICK. You think I feel happy at this moment?

LONA. No, I don't think you can feel very happy at all.

BERNICK. Lona, you must despise me.

LONA. Not yet.

BERNICK. You have no right to, either. Not to *despise* me! Lona, you can't imagine how inexpressibly lonely I am here, in this small-minded, stunted community—how with every year I've had to pare down a few more of my hopes for a truly fulfilling existence. What have I accomplished, despite all it seems? Piecework—penny favors. But anything different, anything more wouldn't be tolerated here. If I wanted to move one step ahead of the sentiments and views cried up in the streets this morning, that would be the end of my power. You know what we are—we who've been labeled pillars of society. We're the puppets of society, no more than that.

LONA. Why haven't you seen that before?

BERNICK. Because I've been thinking a good deal lately —since you came back—particularly this evening. Oh, Lona, why didn't I know you better—in the old days?

LONA. What then?

BERNICK. Then I'd never have let you go. And if I'd had you, I wouldn't be in the position I am now.

LONA. And do you ever think what *she* might have been to you—the one you chose instead of me?

BERNICK. I only know she's never been what I've needed most.

LONA. Because you've never shared your lifework with her. You've never had an open and honest relationship with her. You've let her go along reproaching herself for the shame you palmed off on her family.

BERNICK. Yes, yes, yes. It all comes from lies and deceptions.

LONA. Then why don't you quit all the lying and deceiving?

BERNICK. Now? It's too late now, Lona.

LONA. Tell me, Karsten—what satisfaction does fraud and duplicity give you?

BERNICK. None whatsoever. I'll have to go down in ruin, like this whole corrupt society. But there's a generation coming up after us. It's my son that I'm working for. I'm preparing a lifework for *him*. A time will come when truth is rooted in our social structure, and on that he'll build a happier life than his father's.

LONA. Based on a lie? Just think what you're giving your son for a legacy.

BERNICK (*in muted despair*). The legacy I'm giving him is a thousand times worse than you know. But someday the curse has to be lifted. And still—all the same— (*In an outburst.*) How could you bring all this down on my head! But now it's done. I have to go on now. You are *not* going to crush me!

(HILMAR TØNNESEN, *distraught, with a letter in his hand, hurries in, right.*)

HILMAR. But this is— Betty, Betty!

BERNICK. What now? Are they here already?

HILMAR. No, no. But I have to talk to someone right away—

(*He goes out through the farther door, left.*)

LONA. Karsten, you say that we came to crush you. So let me tell you the kind of fiber he's made of, this prodigal son that your moralistic community shuns like the plague. He can get along without you, because he's gone now.

BERNICK. But he'll be back—

LONA. Johan won't ever come back. He's gone for good, and Dina with him.

BERNICK. Won't be back? And Dina went with him?

LONA. Yes, to become his wife. It's their way of giving your self-righteous community a slap in the face, exactly as I once—Oh, well!

BERNICK. Gone—her, too—on the *Indian Girl*—!

LONA. No, he didn't dare trust such a precious cargo to that shifty crew. Johan and Dina sailed on the *Palm Tree*.

BERNICK. Ah! So—all for nothing— (*Paces across to his office door, throws it open and calls in.*) Krap, stop the *Indian Girl*! She mustn't sail tonight!

KRAP (*inside*). The *Indian Girl*'s standing out to sea, Mr. Bernick.

BERNICK (*closes the door and says dully*). Too late—and useless—

LONA. What do you mean?

BERNICK. Nothing, nothing. Let me alone—!

LONA. Hm. Look, Karsten. Johan's asked me to tell you that he's entrusted me with the name and reputation he once loaned you, and that you robbed him of when he was away. Johan will keep quiet; and I can handle the matter any way I want. See, here in my hand I have your two letters.

BERNICK. You have them! And now—now you're going to—this evening—when the procession—

LONA. I didn't come back to expose you. I came to shake you up so you'd speak out of your own free will. It didn't work. So you can stay bogged down in your lie. Look here, I'm tearing up your letters. Take the scraps; they're yours. Now there's no proof against you, Karsten. You're safe now. And you can be happy—if you can.

BERNICK (*deeply shaken*). Lona—why didn't you do that before! Now it's too late. Life is ruined for me now. I can't live my life anymore after today.

LONA. What's happened?

BERNICK. Don't ask— But I *must* live, even so. I *will* live—for Olaf's sake. He'll redeem everything and make it right—

LONA. Karsten—!

(HILMAR *comes hurrying back in.*)

HILMAR. Nobody around. Gone! Betty, too.

BERNICK. What's wrong?

HILMAR. I'm afraid to tell you.

BERNICK. What is it? You've got to tell me!

HILMAR. All right. Olaf's stowed away on the *Indian Girl.*

BERNICK (*jolted*). Olaf—on the *Indian Girl!* No! No!

LONA. Yes, it's true. Now I understand—I saw him jump out of the window.

BERNICK (*at the door to his office, with a desperate cry*). Krap, at all costs, stop the *Indian Girl!*

KRAP (*entering*). Impossible, Mr. Bernick. You can't expect—

BERNICK. We *must* stop her! Olaf's on board!

KRAP. What!

RUMMEL (*coming in from the office*). Olaf's run off? Impossible!

SANDSTAD (*following him*). He'll be returned with the pilot, Mr. Bernick.

HILMAR. No, no; he left me a note. (*Displays a letter.*) He says he'll hide himself in the cargo till they're out to sea.

BERNICK. I'll never see him again!

RUMMEL. Nonsense! A good, stout ship, newly reconditioned—

VIGELAND (*who also has come in*). By your own yard, Mr. Bernick.

BERNICK. I'm telling you, I'll never see him again. I've lost him, Lona, and—now I see—he never really belonged to me. (*Listening.*) What's that?

RUMMEL. Music. The procession's coming.

BERNICK. I can't—I won't see anyone!

RUMMEL. What are you thinking of? That's out of the question.

SANDSTAD. Impossible, Mr. Bernick. Think what's at stake for you.

BERNICK. What does it all matter now? Who do I have to work for now?

RUMMEL. How can you ask that? You have us and the community.

VIGELAND. Yes, just so.

SANDSTAD. And you really shouldn't forget that we—

(MARTHA BERNICK *enters through the farther door, left. Band music can be heard faintly in the distance down the street.*)

MARTHA BERNICK. The procession's coming; but Betty isn't home. I don't understand where she's—

BERNICK. Not home! There, you see, Lona. Whether it's joy or sorrow, she's no support.

RUMMEL. Raise the curtains! Come and help me, Mr. Krap. And you, Mr. Sandstad. What a crying shame that the family can't be together right now. That wasn't the program.

(*The curtains are drawn aside from the windows and door. The entire street is illuminated. On the house opposite is a large, transparent banner, reading: "Long Live Karsten Bernick, Pillar Of Our Society."*)

BERNICK (*recoiling*). Get rid of all that! I don't want to see it! Put it out! Put it out!

RUMMEL. In all due respect, have you lost your mind?

MARTHA BERNICK. What's wrong with him, Lona?

LONA. Shh!

(*She talks to her in a whisper.*)

BERNICK. Get rid of that mockery of a sign, will you! Don't you see, all those lights are tongues stuck out at us!

RUMMEL. Well, this is too much—

BERNICK. Oh, what do *you* know—! But I, I—! They're all tapers in a morgue!

KRAP. Hm—

RUMMEL. Really—you're taking this much too hard.

SANDSTAD. The boy'll get an Atlantic voyage, and then you'll have him back again.

VIGELAND. Just trust in the Almighty, Mr. Bernick.

RUMMEL. And in the ship, Bernick. She's hardly about to sink, you know.

KRAP. Hm—

RUMMEL. Now if she'd been one of those floating coffins you hear about in big countries—

BERNICK. My hair's turning gray overnight, I can feel it.

(MRS. BERNICK, *with a large shawl over her head, comes in from the garden.*)

MRS. BERNICK. Karsten, Karsten, did you hear—?

BERNICK. Yes, I heard. But you—you who see nothing! You, his mother, can't keep an eye on him—!

MRS. BERNICK. Oh, will you listen—!

BERNICK. Why couldn't you watch him? Now I've lost him. Give him back to me, if you can!

MRS. BERNICK. Yes, I can! I have him!

BERNICK. You have him!

THE MEN. Ah!

HILMAR. Well, I thought so.

MRS. BERNICK. You've got him back, Karsten!

LONA. Yes, now win him back, too.

BERNICK. You have him! Is it true, what you're saying? Where is he?

MRS. BERNICK. You can't know that till you've forgiven him.

BERNICK. Forgiven—! But how did you learn—?

MRS. BERNICK. Don't you think a mother notices things? I was worried to death you'd find out. A couple of words he dropped yesterday—and then his room was empty, and his knapsack and clothes missing—

BERNICK. Yes, yes—?

MRS. BERNICK. I ran and got hold of Aune. We went out in his boat. The American ship was just ready to sail. Thank God, we made it in time—got on board—had the hold searched—and found him. Oh, Karsten, you mustn't punish him.

BERNICK. Betty!

MRS. BERNICK. Or Aune either!

BERNICK. Aune? What do you know about him? Is the *Indian Girl* underway again?

MRS. BERNICK. No, that's just it—

BERNICK. Well, go on!

MRS. BERNICK. Aune was just as upset as I was. The search took a long time, it was getting dark, and the pilot started protesting. So Aune took the initiative—in your name—

BERNICK. Yes?

MRS. BERNICK. To delay the sailing till tomorrow.

KRAP. Hm—

BERNICK. How fortunate—I can't tell you—!

MRS. BERNICK. You're not angry?

BERNICK. Oh, Betty, more fortunate than I could have dreamed!

RUMMEL. You're being much too conscientious.

HILMAR. Yes, as soon as there's a little wrangle with the elements—uff!

KRAP (*at the window*). The procession's turning in the garden gate, Mr. Bernick.

BERNICK. Yes, let them come.

RUMMEL. The whole garden's full of people.

SANDSTAD. And the street is packed.

RUMMEL. All the town is here, Bernick. It's really an exhilarating moment.

VIGELAND. Let's take it with a humble mind, Mr. Rummel.

RUMMEL. All the flags are out. What a parade! There comes the program committee, headed by Mr. Rørlund.

BERNICK. I tell you, let them in!

RUMMEL. But look—in this excited frame of mind you're in—

BERNICK. Yes? Well?

RUMMEL. I wouldn't be reluctant to speak some words in your behalf.

BERNICK. No, thanks. Tonight I'll speak for myself.

RUMMEL. But do you know what you ought to say?

BERNICK. Rest easy, Rummel—I know now what I ought to say.

(*The band music has stopped. The door to the garden is thrown open, and* RØRLUND *enters at the head of the committee, accompanied by two hired* SERVANTS, *carrying a covered basket. After them come* TOWNSPEOPLE *of all classes, as many as the room can hold. An enormous crowd, with flags and banners, can be glimpsed out in the garden and on the street.*)

RØRLUND. Most honorable Consul Bernick! I see by the astonishment written on your countenance that we arrive like unbidden guests intruding on your happy family circle, by your peaceful fireside, surrounded by esteemed and industrious friends and fellow citizens. But we come in response to a heartfelt need to pay you homage. This is not the first such occasion; but it *is* the first on such a generous scale. We've many times before brought you our thanks for the strong moral foundation on which you, so to speak, have built our community. This time we particularly honor you as the clear-sighted, tireless, altruistic—may I say, self-sacrificing—fellow citizen who has seized the initiative in an undertaking that will, by all informed opinion, provide a massive infusion into the material prosperity and well-being of this community.

VOICES FROM THE CROWD. Bravo, bravo!

RØRLUND. Consul Bernick, for a number of years now you've furnished our town with a shining example. I'm not alluding here to your exemplary family life, nor to your immaculate moral character in general. These things are most properly praised behind closed doors and not in a civic celebration. But I want to speak instead of your service to the community, which lies open for every eye to see. Well-outfitted ships sail forth from your yards and show the flag on the farthest seas. A sizable and contented staff of workmen look up to you, as to a father. By pioneering new modes of production, you've secured the welfare of hundreds of families. In other words—to an eminent degree, you are the cornerstone of this community.

VOICES. Hear, hear! Bravo!

RØRLUND. And it's exactly this glow of altruism emanating from everything you do that works such incalculable good, especially in these times. You're now on the verge of providing us with a—yes, I won't shrink from using the blunt, prosaic word—a railroad.

MANY VOICES. Bravo! Bravo!

RØRLUND. But this undertaking appears to be encountering difficulties, chiefly prompted by narrow, selfish interests.

VOICES. Hear, hear!

RØRLUND. It has not escaped our notice that certain individuals who are not part of our community have stolen a march on the hardworking people of this area and acquired certain holdings that ought rightfully to benefit our own town.

VOICES. Yes! Yes! Hear, hear!

RØRLUND. This lamentable fact has doubtless come to your attention as well, Consul Bernick. But even so, you are unshakably pursuing your goal, well aware that a patriot must raise his sights beyond his own locality.

DIVERSE VOICES. Hm! No, no! Yes, yes!

RØRLUND. And thus it's man as citizen patriot—man as he ought to be—that we honor in you this evening. May your enterprise evolve into a true and lasting boon to this community! The railroad potentially could prove a way by which we expose ourselves to corrupting elements from without, but it could prove a way of ridding ourselves of them as well. And, as it is, we can hardly keep ourselves free of such undesirable elements. But that we have happily succeeded—if rumor is correct—on this very evening of celebration, in expelling elements of that sort—

VOICES. Shh! Shh!

RØRLUND. —I take to be a lucky omen for this project. The simple fact that I raise this point *here* indicates that we find ourselves in a house where ethical standards rank higher than family ties.

VOICES. Hear, hear! Bravo!

BERNICK (*simultaneously*). May I—

RØRLUND. Just a word or two more, Mr. Bernick. What you've done for this locality, you've certainly not accomplished with the thought in mind of any tangible gain for yourself. But you can hardly refuse to accept a little token of the grateful esteem of your fellow townspeople, least of all at this solemn moment when we stand—as practical men assure us—on the threshold of a new age.

MANY VOICES. Bravo! Hear, hear!

(*He gives a signal to the* SERVANTS, *who bring the basket nearer. During the following, members of the committee take out and present the articles mentioned.*)

RØRLUND. So we take this occasion, Mr. Bernick, to present you with this silver coffee service. May it grace your table when we, in the future as so often in the past, have the pleasure of gathering in this hospitable home. And you too, gentlemen, who have been so unstinting in your support of our leading citizen, we beg you each to accept a little memento. This silver goblet is for you, Mr. Rummel. Many times amid the clinking of cups you've raised an eloquent voice in defense of the civic interests of our community. May you often find worthy opportunities to lift and empty this goblet. To you, Mr. Sandstad, I present this album of photographs of your fellow citizens. Your well-known and celebrated munificence has put you in the enviable position of numbering your friends among every class of society. And to you, Mr. Vigeland, to adorn your private den, may I offer this collection of sermons, printed on vellum and sumptuously bound. Through the seasoning of the years, you've arrived at a profound outlook on life. Your dedication, day by day, to the world's work has gradually been sublimated and ennobled by higher and holier truths. (*Turning to the crowd.*) And now, my friends, long live Consul Bernick and his comrades-in-arms! Three cheers for the pillars of our society!

THE ENTIRE CROWD. Long live Consul Bernick! Long live the pillars of society! Hurrah! Hurrah! Hurrah!

LONA. Happy days, Karsten!

(*An expectant hush.*)

BERNICK (*beginning slowly and thoughtfully to speak*). My fellow citizens—your chairman has stated that we stand this evening on the threshold of a new age—and I hope that's the case indeed. But before it can come, we have to confront the truth—the truth that till this evening has been a total stranger to our community. (*A ripple of surprise runs through the onlookers.*) So I must start by repudiating those words of praise that you, Dr. Rørlund—in the style of such occasions—have showered me with. I don't deserve them, because until today I've been far from altruistic. Even if I haven't always gone after profit, none-theless I'm aware now that a hunger and a craving after power, status and influence has been the driving force behind most of my actions.

RUMMEL (*mutters*). Now what?

BERNICK. I make no apology to you, my fellow citizens, for that. I still believe I deserve a place among the ablest businessmen here in town.

MANY VOICES. Yes, yes, yes!

BERNICK. But what I blame myself for is having often been weak enough to practice duplicity, simply because I knew and feared our community's habit of suspecting ul-terior motives behind everything a man tries to do here. And now I come to a case in point.

RUMMEL (*uneasily*). Hm—hm!

BERNICK. Rumors have been flying about enormous pur-chases of country property. *I* bought that land, all of it, on my own.

VOICES (*in undertones*). What did he say? He did? Ber-nick?

BERNICK. For the time being, I'm holding it. Naturally, I've worked closely with my collaborators, Messrs. Rum-mel, Vigeland and Sandstad, and we've agreed that—

RUMMEL. It's not true! Prove that! Prove it!

VIGELAND. We haven't agreed on anything!

SANDSTAD. Really, this *is* too much—

BERNICK. That's quite true. We haven't agreed yet on what I was just coming to. But I trust these three gentlemen will concur when I announce that tonight I've concluded for myself that these properties should be set up as a public corporation, with shares available to anyone.

MANY VOICES. Hurray! Long live Consul Bernick!

RUMMEL (*quietly to* BERNICK). What a cheap double-cross—!

SANDSTAD (*similarly*). Tricked us, hm—!

VIGELAND. This is one hell of a—! Oh goodness, what am I saying?

THE CROWD (*outside*). Hurrah, hurrah, hurrah!

BERNICK. Gentlemen, silence. I'm not entitled to this applause—because what I've decided now wasn't my original intention. My intention was to retain everything for myself; and it's still my opinion that these properties could best be developed if they're kept together in one man's control. But it's up to you. If you want it that way, I'm willing to manage them to the best of my ability.

VOICES. Yes! Yes! Yes!

BERNICK. But first my fellow townspeople need to know just what I am. Then each of you search his heart, and let's resolve then that, from this night, we'll begin a new age. The old age with its false face, its hypocrisy and its emptiness, its soothing proprieties and craven fears will become nothing more to us than a kind of museum that we'll learn from. And to that museum we'll donate—shall we not, gentlemen?—our coffee service, and the goblet, and the photo album, and the sermon collection printed on vellum and sumptuously bound.

RUMMEL. Why, of course.

VIGELAND (*muttering*). You've taken all the rest, so—

SANDSTAD. Help yourself.

BERNICK. And now to cover my main default to this community. It's been said that certain "undesirable elements" have left us this evening. I can fill out that news a little bit: the man referred to did not leave alone. He was accompanied by his future wife—

LONA (*loudly*). Dina Dorf!

RØRLUND. What!

MRS. BERNICK. No!

(*General commotion.*)

RØRLUND. Gone? Ran off—with him! Impossible!

BERNICK. To marry him, Mr. Rørlund. And I can add a bit more. (*In a whisper.*) Betty, bear up under what's coming next. (*Resoundingly.*) I say: My hat's off to that man, because he selflessly took on another man's crime. My friends and neighbors, I'm through with lies; they've come close to poisoning every fiber of my being. I'll tell you everything. Fifteen years ago, *I* was the guilty one.

MRS. BERNICK (*hushed and shaken*). Karsten!

MARTHA BERNICK (*likewise*). Ah, Johan—!

LONA. At last, you've found yourself!

(*Speechless astonishment among the onlookers.*)

BERNICK. Yes, my friends, I was the guilty one—but *he* went away. All those shabby, false rumors that spread afterward are beyond human power now to retract. But I'm hardly the one to complain of that. Fifteen years ago I went a long way on those rumors. Whether I'm to fall by them now, each of you will have to decide.

RØRLUND. What a thunderbolt! Our leading citizen—! (*Quietly to* MRS. BERNICK.) Oh, Mrs. Bernick, how I do pity you!

HILMAR. What an admission! Really, I must say—!

BERNICK. But don't decide tonight. I ask each one of you to go home—collect yourself—look deep into your own heart. When our minds have all calmed down, we'll see if I've lost or won by talking out. Goodbye. I still have much,

much to repent of—but that concerns my conscience alone. Good night. And away with these garlands. We all must feel that they're out of place here.

RØRLUND. Quite so. (*Quietly to* MRS. BERNICK.) Run away! So, she was totally unworthy of me, after all. (*In an undertone, to the committee.*) Well, gentlemen, after this I think we'd best to make a silent retreat.

HILMAR. Oh, the banner of idealism, how anyone could bear it high after this, I don't know— Uff!

(*The news has meanwhile been whispered from mouth to mouth. The onlookers melt away through the garden.* RUMMEL, SANDSTAD *and* VIGELAND *depart, arguing heatedly in hushed tones.* HILMAR *quietly slips out, right.* BERNICK, MRS. BERNICK, MARTHA BERNICK, LONA *and* KRAP *remain behind in the silent room.*)

BERNICK. Betty, can you forgive me?

MRS. BERNICK (*smiling at him*). Do you know, Karsten, that you've just made me happier than I've been in years?

BERNICK. How—?

MRS. BERNICK. For many years I've thought that you'd once been mine, but I'd lost you. Now I know that you never were mine—but I'm going to win you.

BERNICK (*embracing her*). Oh Betty, you *have* won me! Through Lona I've really come to know you. But let Olaf in now.

MRS. BERNICK. Yes, now you can have him. Mr. Krap—!

(*She speaks inaudibly to him in the background. He goes out the garden door. During the following, one by one, the lights in the houses and the illuminations on the banners are extinguished.*)

BERNICK (*softly*). Thank you, Lona. You've saved what was best in me—and for me.

LONA. That's all I wanted.

BERNICK. Is it? Or isn't it? I can't quite make you out.

LONA. Hm—

BERNICK. So it wasn't hatred? Or revenge? Then why *did* you come back?

LONA. Old friendship doesn't wear away.

BERNICK. Lona!

LONA. When Johan told me about this lie, then I vowed to myself: I want my childhood hero standing free and true.

BERNICK. Oh, how little my miserable self deserved that from you!

LONA. Karsten, if we women responded only to the deserving, well—!

(AUNE *enters with* OLAF *from the garden.*)

BERNICK (*moving toward him*). Olaf!

OLAF. Father, I promise I won't ever again—

BERNICK. Run away?

OLAF. Yes, yes, Father, I promise.

BERNICK. And I promise you, you'll never have reason to. From now on you'll have leave to grow up, not as the executor of *my* lifework, but for the lifework that will be your own.

OLAF. And will I also have leave to be what I want?

BERNICK. Yes.

OLAF. Thank you. Then I don't want to be a pillar of society.

BERNICK. Oh, why not?

OLAF. Because I think it must be so boring.

BERNICK. You just be yourself, Olaf. It'll all follow from that— And you, Aune—

AUNE. I know, Mr. Bernick. I'm fired.

BERNICK. We'll go on together, Aune. And forgive me—

AUNE. How so? The ship didn't sail tonight.

BERNICK. She won't sail tomorrow, either. I gave you too little time. She needs a more careful job.

AUNE. Will do, Mr. Bernick. And with the new machines!

(*He goes out, right.*)

MRS. BERNICK. Now they've all left.

BERNICK. And we're alone. My name isn't up in lights anymore. All the windows are dark.

LONA. Would you want them lit again?

BERNICK. Not for anything on earth. Where have I been? You'd be petrified if you knew. It's as if I were coming back to my senses now after being poisoned. But I feel sure—I *can* be young and strong again. Oh, come closer— come closer in around me. Betty, come! Olaf, my boy, come! And you, Martha—it seems as if all these years I've never really seen you.

LONA. I can well believe it. This society of yours is a bachelors' club. You don't see women.

BERNICK. True, true, and it's exactly why—now don't argue, Lona—you're going to stay right here with Betty and me.

MRS. BERNICK. Yes, Lona, you have to!

LONA. How could I possibly leave all you young people when you're just starting out in life? I wouldn't be a foster mother, then. You and I, Martha, we two old aunts— What are you looking at?

MARTHA BERNICK. The sky's clearing. The light's growing strong over the sea. The *Palm Tree*'s in luck.

LONA. Her luck's on board.

BERNICK. And we—we have a long, hard workday ahead. Especially me. But let it come. As long as you women are close beside me, loyal and true. That's another thing I've learned in the last days: it's you women who are the pillars of society.

LONA. Then it's a pretty flimsy wisdom you've gained,

Karsten. (*Sets her hand firmly on his shoulder.*) No, my dear—the spirit of truth and the spirit of freedom—*those* are the pillars of society.

BERNICK. That's the way. But take special care and pains with it now. There's a lot with us that could stand some careful, painstaking renovation. Well, good night, Aune.

AUNE. Good night, Mr. Bernick. And thank you, thank you!

A DOLL HOUSE

Much—perhaps too much—has been written about the historic influence of *A Doll House* (1879) on the course of Western drama. Making its entrance when the theater was overrun with pseudo-Shakespearean costume pageants and well-carpentered French melodramas, it swept across the serious stages of Europe and America like a cleansing wind from the north. Appealing at first only to the few, often scheduled for special matinees labeled "Not for Children" to keep out the queues of mothers with pinafored daughters, its understated and revolutionary simplicity eventually carried the day in a thousand imitations by several hundred diversely derivative Ibsens, nearly all of whom lacked the transforming deeper purpose of their model. That purpose, his contemporary partisans were sure, was, through an exploratory operation on one complacent, middle-class home, to lay bare the anatomy of a marriage where the wife was no more than a legal infant and her husband's virtual slave.

Certainly, at the time the play was written, Ibsen had strong opinions on the subject of women's rights. In February 1879, when his proposal to the Scandinavian Club in Rome that its female members be granted equal voting rights was narrowly defeated, he made a blistering attack on the male majority, daring them to assert that women were in any way inferior to men in culture, intelligence, knowledge or artistic talent. Nineteen years later, however, in a talk before the Norwegian League for Women's Rights, he took the opportunity to place the matter in the larger context of the artist's freedom and the evolution of the race in general, stating in part: "I am not a member of the Women's Rights League. Whatever I have written has been without any thought of making propaganda. I have been more the poet and less the social philosopher than people generally seem inclined to believe. . . . My task has been the *description of humanity*."

As Ibsen's retrospective emphasis insists, details throughout *A Doll House* release their richer meanings only when freed from the compulsions of propaganda. Early in Act One, for example, when Nora displays her

Christmas purchases—a sword for Ivor, a horse and trumpet for Bob, a doll and doll's bed for Emmy—feminists might choose to focus on the convention-bound assignment of sex roles. Quite rightly so, for the playwright had merely claimed to be less, rather than not at all, the social philosopher. But since by Ibsen's definition to be a poet is most of all to see, we are meant to perceive more comprehensively in this the pattern of a self-fulfilling prophecy: Nora, the doll-child of her father, the doll-wife of her husband, unthinkingly transmitting her doll-identity to her own daughter. And by that generalizing of implication which *is* poetry, this small pattern implies a system, a certain authoritarian set of mind elaborated into a whole culture. Torvald, being a determinist, believes such patterns cannot, must not be broken. ("It's deep in your blood. Yes, these things are hereditary, Nora.") What Nora learns traumatically, through the sudden crisis of the action, is that if the alternative is an intolerable situation ("I've lived by doing tricks for you, Torvald"), then patterns—even those wherein we live and move and have our being—can and must be broken.

Thus, by poetic inference, we are shown that people whose lives are prose and whose actions will never be history, people who may have long been patronized and casually discounted, can pick themselves up out of comfortable humiliation and, by so doing, find unsuspected resources, a whole other personality even, within themselves. Aiming for such universality of reference, Ibsen titled his play *Et dukkehjem*—*A Doll House*, without the possessive 's. Torvald in his way is as humanly undeveloped, as much a doll, as Nora. It is the entire house (*hjem*, home) which is on trial, the total complex of relationships, including husband, wife, children, servants, upstairs and downstairs, that is tested by the visitors that come and go, embodying aspects of the inescapable reality outside. No character is superfluous in the design, nor negligible in performance.

For with this play, the second in the cycle, Ibsen's mature artistic method, his style of metaphoric realism, comes into its own, subsuming the well-made machinery evident in *Pillars of Society*. In that work, plot had, to some degree, manipulated character; from this point on, character,

setting and idea generate plot. Through three consecutive
acts the unchanging walls of the Helmers' apartment take
on the figurative quality of a prison (only *Hedda Gabler* is
as hermetically cut off from the outdoors and the natural
world), and the sense of confinement works silently, increasingly, on both Nora and the audience to prepare the
emotional logic of the final doorslam. Likewise Ibsen's
dedication to realism, the meticulous care with which he
built his characters stroke by stroke until, in his words, he
had penetrated to the last wrinkle of their souls, is the
outward correlative of another kind of caring. Since *A
Doll House*, modern drama has delivered far more brutal,
and brutalized, shocks to its audiences than a wife walking
out on a husband and three small children. The fact that
Ibsen's play can still grip, stir and unsettle stems not so
much from what happens as from the depth of understanding from which its significance was artistically realized and
projected.

THE CHARACTERS

TORVALD HELMER, a lawyer
NORA, his wife
DR. RANK
MRS. LINDE
NILS KROGSTAD, a bank clerk
THE HELMERS' THREE SMALL CHILDREN
ANNE-MARIE, their nurse
HELENE, a maid
A DELIVERY BOY

The action takes place in HELMER's *residence.*

⤙ ACT ONE ⤚

A comfortable room, tastefully but not expensively furnished. A door to the right in the back wall leads to the entryway; another to the left leads to HELMER's *study. Between these doors, a piano. Midway in the left-hand wall a door, and further back a window. Near the window a round table with an armchair and a small sofa. In the right-hand wall, toward the rear, a door, and nearer the foreground a porcelain stove with two armchairs and a rocking chair beside it. Between the stove and the side door, a small table. Engravings on the walls. An* etagère *with china figures and other small art objects; a small bookcase with richly bound books; the floor carpeted; a fire burning in the stove. It is a winter day.*

A bell rings in the entryway; shortly after we hear the door being unlocked. NORA *comes into the room, humming happily to herself; she is wearing street clothes and carries an armload of packages, which she puts down on the table to the right. She has left the hall door open; and through it a* DELIVERY BOY *is seen, holding a Christmas tree and a basket, which he gives to the* MAID *who let them in.*

NORA. Hide the tree well, Helene. The children mustn't get a glimpse of it till this evening, after it's trimmed. (*To the* DELIVERY BOY, *taking out her purse.*) How much?

DELIVERY BOY. Fifty, ma'am.

NORA. There's a crown. No, keep the change. (*The* BOY *thanks her and leaves.* NORA *shuts the door. She laughs softly to herself while taking off her street things. Drawing a bag of macaroons from her pocket, she eats a couple, then steals over and listens at her husband's study door.*) Yes, he's home. (*Hums again as she moves to the table right.*)

HELMER (*from the study*). Is that my little lark twittering out there?

NORA (*busy opening some packages*). Yes, it is.

HELMER. Is that my squirrel rummaging around?

NORA. Yes!

HELMER. When did my squirrel get in?

NORA. Just now. (*Putting the macaroon bag in her pocket and wiping her mouth.*) Do come in, Torvald, and see what I've bought.

HELMER. Can't be disturbed. (*After a moment he opens the door and peers in, pen in hand.*) Bought, you say? All that there? Has the little spendthrift been out throwing money around again?

NORA. Oh, but Torvald, this year we really should let ourselves go a bit. It's the first Christmas we haven't had to economize.

HELMER. But you know we can't go squandering.

NORA. Oh yes, Torvald, we can squander a little now. Can't we? Just a tiny, wee bit. Now that you've got a big salary and are going to make piles and piles of money.

HELMER. Yes—starting New Year's. But then it's a full three months till the raise comes through.

NORA. Pooh! We can borrow that long.

HELMER. Nora! (*Goes over and playfully takes her by the ear.*) Are your scatterbrains off again? What if today I borrowed a thousand crowns, and you squandered them over Christmas week, and then on New Year's Eve a roof tile fell on my head, and I lay there—

NORA (*putting her hand on his mouth*). Oh! Don't say such things!

HELMER. Yes, but what if it happened—then what?

NORA. If anything so awful happened, then it just wouldn't matter if I had debts or not.

HELMER. Well, but the people I'd borrowed from?

NORA. Them? Who cares about them! They're strangers.

HELMER. Nora, Nora, how like a woman! No, but seriously, Nora, you know what I think about that. No debts! Never borrow! Something of freedom's lost—and something of beauty, too—from a home that's founded on borrowing and debt. We've made a brave stand up to now, the two of us; and we'll go right on like that the little while we have to.

NORA (*going toward the stove*). Yes, whatever you say, Torvald.

HELMER (*following her*). Now, now, the little lark's

wings mustn't droop. Come on, don't be a sulky squirrel. (*Taking out his wallet.*) Nora, guess what I have here.

NORA (*turning quickly*).   Money!

HELMER.   There, see. (*Hands her some notes.*) Good grief, I know how costs go up in a house at Christmastime.

NORA.   Ten—twenty—thirty—forty. Oh, thank you, Torvald; I can manage no end on this.

HELMER.   You really will have to.

NORA.   Oh yes, I promise I will! But come here so I can show you everything I bought. And so cheap! Look, new clothes for Ivar here—and a sword. Here a horse and a trumpet for Bob. And a doll and a doll's bed here for Emmy; they're nothing much, but she'll tear them to bits in no time anyway. And here I have dress material and handkerchiefs for the maids. Old Anne-Marie really deserves something more.

HELMER.   And what's in that package there?

NORA (*with a cry*).   Torvald, no! You can't see that till tonight!

HELMER.   I see. But tell me now, you little prodigal, what have you thought of for yourself?

NORA.   For myself? Oh, I don't want anything at all.

HELMER.   Of course you do. Tell me just what—within reason—you'd most like to have.

NORA.   I honestly don't know. Oh, listen, Torvald—

HELMER.   Well?

NORA (*fumbling at his coat buttons, without looking at him*).   If you want to give me something, then maybe you could—you could—

HELMER.   Come on, out with it.

NORA (*hurriedly*).   You could give me money, Torvald. No more than you think you can spare; then one of these days I'll buy something with it.

HELMER.   But Nora—

NORA.   Oh, please, Torvald darling, do that! I beg you, please. Then I could hang the bills in pretty gilt paper on the Christmas tree. Wouldn't that be fun?

HELMER.   What are those little birds called that always fly through their fortunes?

NORA.   Oh yes, spendthrifts; I know all that. But let's do as I say, Torvald; then I'll have time to decide what I really need most. That's very sensible, isn't it?

HELMER (*smiling*). Yes, very—that is, if you actually hung onto the money I give you, and you actually used it to buy yourself something. But it goes for the house and for all sorts of foolish things, and then I only have to lay out some more.

NORA. Oh, but Torvald—

HELMER. Don't deny it, my dear little Nora. (*Putting his arm around her waist.*) Spendthrifts are sweet, but they use up a frightful amount of money. It's incredible what it costs a man to feed such birds.

NORA. Oh, how can you say that! Really, I save everything I can.

HELMER (*laughing*). Yes, that's the truth. Everything you can. But that's nothing at all.

NORA (*humming, with a smile of quiet satisfaction*). Hm, if you only knew what expenses we larks and squirrels have, Torvald.

HELMER. You're an odd little one. Exactly the way your father was. You're never at a loss for scaring up money; but the moment you have it, it runs right out through your fingers; you never know what you've done with it. Well, one takes you as you are. It's deep in your blood. Yes, these things are hereditary, Nora.

NORA. Ah, I could wish I'd inherited many of Papa's qualities.

HELMER. And I couldn't wish you anything but just what you are, my sweet little lark. But wait; it seems to me you have a very—what should I call it?—a very suspicious look today—

NORA. I do?

HELMER. You certainly do. Look me straight in the eye.

NORA (*looking at him*). Well?

HELMER (*shaking an admonitory finger*). Surely my sweet tooth hasn't been running riot in town today, has she?

NORA. No. Why do you imagine that?

HELMER. My sweet tooth really didn't make a little detour through the confectioner's?

NORA. No, I assure you, Torvald—

HELMER. Hasn't nibbled some pastry?

NORA. No, not at all.

HELMER. Not even munched a macaroon or two?

NORA. No, Torvald, I assure you, really—

HELMER. There, there now. Of course I'm only joking.

NORA (*going to the table, right*). You know I could never think of going against you.

HELMER. No, I understand that; and you *have* given me your word. (*Going over to her.*) Well, you keep your little Christmas secrets to yourself, Nora darling. I expect they'll come to light this evening, when the tree is lit.

NORA. Did you remember to ask Dr. Rank?

HELMER. No. But there's no need for that; it's assumed he'll be dining with us. All the same, I'll ask him when he stops by here this morning. I've ordered some fine wine. Nora, you can't imagine how I'm looking forward to this evening.

NORA. So am I. And what fun for the children, Torvald!

HELMER. Ah, it's so gratifying to know that one's gotten a safe, secure job, and with a comfortable salary. It's a great satisfaction, isn't it?

NORA. Oh, it's wonderful!

HELMER. Remember last Christmas? Three whole weeks before, you shut yourself in every evening till long after midnight, making flowers for the Christmas tree, and all the other decorations to surprise us. Ugh, that was the dullest time I've ever lived through.

NORA. It wasn't at all dull for me.

HELMER (*smiling*). But the outcome *was* pretty sorry, Nora.

NORA. Oh, don't tease me with that again. How could I help it that the cat came in and tore everything to shreds.

HELMER. No, poor thing, you certainly couldn't. You wanted so much to please us all, and that's what counts. But it's just as well that the hard times are past.

NORA. Yes, it's really wonderful.

HELMER. Now I don't have to sit here alone, boring myself, and you don't have to tire your precious eyes and your fair little delicate hands—

NORA (*clapping her hands*). No, is it really true, Torvald, I don't have to? Oh, how wonderfully lovely to hear! (*Taking his arm.*) Now I'll tell you just how I've thought we should plan things. Right after Christmas—(*The doorbell rings.*) Oh, the bell. (*Straightening the room up a bit.*) Somebody would have to come. What a bore!

HELMER. I'm not at home to visitors, don't forget.

MAID (*from the hall doorway*). Ma'am, a lady to see you—

NORA. All right, let her come in.

MAID (*to* HELMER). And the doctor's just come too.

HELMER. Did he go right to my study?

MAID. Yes, he did.

> (HELMER *goes into his room. The* MAID *shows in* MRS. LINDE, *dressed in traveling clothes, and shuts the door after her.*)

MRS. LINDE (*in a dispirited and somewhat hesitant voice*). Hello, Nora.

NORA. (*uncertain*). Hello—

MRS. LINDE. You don't recognize me.

NORA. No, I don't know—but wait, I think—(*Exclaiming.*) What! Kristine! Is it really you?

MRS. LINDE. Yes, it's me.

NORA. Kristine! To think I didn't recognize you. But then, how could I? (*More quietly.*) How you've changed, Kristine!

MRS. LINDE. Yes, no doubt I have. In nine—ten long years.

NORA. Is it so long since we met! Yes, it's all of that. Oh, these last eight years have been a happy time, believe me. And so now you've come in to town, too. Made the long trip in the winter. That took courage.

MRS. LINDE. I just got here by ship this morning.

NORA. To enjoy yourself over Christmas, of course. Oh, how lovely! Yes, enjoy ourselves, we'll do that. But take your coat off. You're not still cold? (*Helping her.*) There now, let's get cozy here by the stove. No, the easy chair there! I'll take the rocker here. (*Seizing her hands.*) Yes, now you have your old look again; it was only in that first moment. You're a bit more pale, Kristine—and maybe a bit thinner.

MRS. LINDE. And much, much older, Nora.

NORA. Yes, perhaps a bit older; a tiny, tiny bit; not much at all. (*Stopping short; suddenly serious.*) Oh, but thoughtless me, to sit here, chattering away. Sweet, good Kristine, can you forgive me?

MRS. LINDE. What do you mean, Nora?

NORA (*softly*). Poor Kristine, you've become a widow.

MRS. LINDE.   Yes, three years ago.

NORA.   Oh, I knew it, of course; I read it in the papers. Oh, Kristine, you must believe me; I often thought of writing you then, but I kept postponing it, and something always interfered.

MRS. LINDE.   Nora dear, I understand completely.

NORA.   No, it was awful of me, Kristine. You poor thing, how much you must have gone through. And he left you nothing?

MRS. LINDE.   No.

NORA.   And no children?

MRS. LINDE.   No.

NORA.   Nothing at all, then?

MRS. LINDE.   Not even a sense of loss to feed on.

NORA (*looking incredulously at her*).   But Kristine, how could that be?

MRS. LINDE (*smiling wearily and smoothing her hair*).   Oh, sometimes it happens, Nora.

NORA.   So completely alone. How terribly hard that must be for you. I have three lovely children. You can't see them now; they're out with the maid. But now you must tell me everything—

MRS. LINDE.   No, no, no, tell me about yourself.

NORA.   No, you begin. Today I don't want to be selfish. I want to think only of you today. But there *is* something I must tell you. Did you hear of the wonderful luck we had recently?

MRS. LINDE.   No, what's that?

NORA.   My husband's been made manager in the bank, just think!

MRS. LINDE.   Your husband? How marvelous!

NORA.   Isn't it? Being a lawyer is such an uncertain living, you know, especially if one won't touch any cases that aren't clean and decent. And of course Torvald would never do that, and I'm with him completely there. Oh, we're simply delighted, believe me! He'll join the bank right after New Year's and start getting a huge salary and lots of commissions. From now on we can live quite differently—just as we want. Oh, Kristine, I feel so light and happy! Won't it be lovely to have stacks of money and not a care in the world?

MRS. LINDE. Well, anyway, it would be lovely to have enough for necessities.

NORA. No, not just for necessities, but stacks and stacks of money!

MRS. LINDE (*smiling*). Nora, Nora, aren't you sensible yet? Back in school you were such a free spender.

NORA (*with a quiet laugh*). Yes, that's what Torvald still says. (*Shaking her finger.*) But "Nora, Nora" isn't as silly as you all think. Really, we've been in no position for me to go squandering. We've had to work, both of us.

MRS. LINDE. You too?

NORA. Yes, at odd jobs—needlework, crocheting, embroidery, and such—(*Casually.*) and other things too. You remember that Torvald left the department when we were married? There was no chance of promotion in his office, and of course he needed to earn more money. But that first year he drove himself terribly. He took on all kinds of extra work that kept him going morning and night. It wore him down, and then he fell deathly ill. The doctors said it was essential for him to travel south.

MRS. LINDE. Yes, didn't you spend a whole year in Italy?

NORA. That's right. It wasn't easy to get away, you know. Ivar had just been born. But of course we had to go. Oh, that was a beautiful trip, and it saved Torvald's life. But it cost a frightful sum, Kristine.

MRS. LINDE. I can well imagine.

NORA. Four thousand, eight hundred crowns it cost. That's really a lot of money.

MRS. LINDE. But it's lucky you had it when you needed it.

NORA. Well, as it was, we got it from Papa.

MRS. LINDE. I see. It was just about the time your father died.

NORA. Yes, just about then. And, you know, I couldn't make that trip out to nurse him. I had to stay here, expecting Ivar any moment, and with my poor sick Torvald to care for. Dearest Papa, I never saw him again, Kristine. Oh, that was the worst time I've known in all my marriage.

MRS. LINDE. I know how you loved him. And then you went off to Italy?

NORA. Yes. We had the means now, and the doctors urged us. So we left a month after.

MRS. LINDE. And your husband came back completely cured?

NORA. Sound as a drum!

MRS. LINDE. But—the doctor?

NORA. Who?

MRS. LINDE. I thought the maid said he was a doctor, the man who came in with me.

NORA. Yes, that was Dr. Rank—but he's not making a sick call. He's our closest friend, and he stops by at least once a day. No, Torvald hasn't had a sick moment since, and the children are fit and strong, and I am, too. (*Jumping up and clapping her hands.*) Oh, dear God, Kristine, what a lovely thing to live and be happy! But how disgusting of me—I'm talking of nothing but my own affairs. (*Sits on a stool close by* KRISTINE, *arms resting across her knees.*) Oh, don't be angry with me! Tell me, is it really true that you weren't in love with your husband? Why did you marry him, then?

MRS. LINDE. My mother was still alive, but bedridden and helpless—and I had my two younger brothers to look after. In all conscience, I didn't think I could turn him down.

NORA. No, you were right there. But was he rich at the time?

MRS. LINDE. He was very well off, I'd say. But the business was shaky, Nora. When he died, it all fell apart, and nothing was left.

NORA. And then—?

MRS. LINDE. Yes, so I had to scrape up a living with a little shop and a little teaching and whatever else I could find. The last three years have been like one endless workday without a rest for me. Now it's over, Nora. My poor mother doesn't need me, for she's passed on. Nor the boys, either; they're working now and can take care of themselves.

NORA. How free you must feel—

MRS. LINDE. No—only unspeakably empty. Nothing to live for now. (*Standing up anxiously.*) That's why I couldn't take it any longer out in that desolate hole. Maybe here it'll be easier to find something to do and keep my mind occupied. If I could only be lucky enough to get a steady job, some office work—

NORA. Oh, but Kristine, that's so dreadfully tiring, and you already look so tired. It would be much better for you if you could go off to a bathing resort.

MRS. LINDE (*going toward the window*). I have no father to give me travel money, Nora.

NORA (*rising*). Oh, don't be angry with me.

MRS. LINDE (*going to her*). Nora dear, don't you be angry with me. The worst of my kind of situation is all the bitterness that's stored away. No one to work for, and yet you're always having to snap up your opportunities. You have to live; and so you grow selfish. When you told me the happy change in your lot, do you know I was delighted less for your sakes than for mine?

NORA. How so? Oh, I see. You think maybe Torvald could do something for you.

MRS. LINDE. Yes, that's what I thought.

NORA. And he will, Kristine! Just leave it to me; I'll bring it up so delicately—find something attractive to humor him with. Oh, I'm so eager to help you.

MRS. LINDE. How very kind of you, Nora, to be so concerned over me—doubly kind, considering you really know so little of life's burdens yourself.

NORA. I—? I know so little—?

MRS. LINDE (*smiling*). Well, my heavens—a little needlework and such—Nora, you're just a child.

NORA (*tossing her head and pacing the floor*). You don't have to act so superior.

MRS. LINDE. Oh?

NORA. You're just like the others. You all think I'm incapable of anything serious—

MRS. LINDE. Come now—

NORA. That I've never had to face the raw world.

MRS. LINDE. Nora dear, you've just been telling me all your troubles.

NORA. Hm! Trivia! (*Quietly.*) I haven't told you the big thing.

MRS. LINDE. Big thing? What do you mean?

NORA. You look down on me so, Kristine, but you shouldn't. You're proud that you worked so long and hard for your mother.

MRS. LINDE. I don't look down on a soul. But it *is* true:

I'm proud—and happy, too—to think it was given to me to make my mother's last days almost free of care.

NORA. And you're also proud thinking of what you've done for your brothers.

MRS. LINDE. I feel I've a right to be.

NORA. I agree. But listen to this, Kristine—I've also got something to be proud and happy for.

MRS. LINDE. I don't doubt it. But whatever do you mean?

NORA. Not so loud. What if Torvald heard! He mustn't, not for anything in the world. Nobody must know, Kristine. No one but you.

MRS. LINDE. But what is it, then?

NORA. Come here. (*Drawing her down beside her on the sofa.*) It's true—I've also got something to be proud and happy for. I'm the one who saved Torvald's life.

MRS. LINDE. Saved—? Saved how?

NORA. I told you about the trip to Italy. Torvald never would have lived if he hadn't gone south—

MRS. LINDE. Of course; your father gave you the means—

NORA (*smiling*). That's what Torvald and all the rest think, but—

MRS. LINDE. But—?

NORA. Papa didn't give us a pin. I was the one who raised the money.

MRS. LINDE. You? That whole amount?

NORA. Four thousand, eight hundred crowns. What do you say to that?

MRS. LINDE. But Nora, how was it possible? Did you win the lottery?

NORA (*disdainfully*). The lottery? Pooh! No art to that.

MRS. LINDE. But where did you get it from then?

NORA (*humming, with a mysterious smile*). Hmm, tra-la-la-la.

MRS. LINDE. Because you couldn't have borrowed it.

NORA. No? Why not?

MRS. LINDE. A wife can't borrow without her husband's consent.

NORA (*tossing her head*). Oh, but a wife with a little business sense, a wife who knows how to manage—

MRS. LINDE. Nora, I simply don't understand—

NORA. You don't have to. Whoever said I *borrowed* the

money? I could have gotten it other ways. (*Throwing herself back on the sofa.*) I could have gotten it from some admirer or other. After all, a girl with my ravishing appeal—

MRS. LINDE. You lunatic.

NORA. I'll bet you're eaten up with curiosity, Kristine.

MRS. LINDE. Now listen here, Nora—you haven't done something indiscreet?

NORA (*sitting up again*). Is it indiscreet to save your husband's life?

MRS. LINDE. I think it's indiscreet that without his knowledge you—

NORA. But that's the point: he mustn't know! My Lord, can't you understand? He mustn't ever know the close call he had. It was to *me* the doctors came to say his life was in danger—that nothing could save him but a stay in the south. Didn't I try strategy then! I began talking about how lovely it would be for me to travel abroad like other young wives; I begged and I cried; I told him please to remember my condition, to be kind and indulge me; and then I dropped a hint that he could easily take out a loan. But at that, Kristine, he nearly exploded. He said I was frivolous, and it was his duty as man of the house not to indulge me in whims and fancies—as I think he called them. Aha, I thought, now you'll just have to be saved—and that's when I saw my chance.

MRS. LINDE. And your father never told Torvald the money wasn't from him?

NORA. No, never. Papa died right about then. I'd considered bringing him into my secret and begging him never to tell. But he was too sick at the time—and then, sadly, it didn't matter.

MRS. LINDE. And you've never confided in your husband since?

NORA. For heaven's sake, no! Are you serious? He's so strict on that subject. Besides—Torvald, with all his masculine pride—how painfully humiliating for him if he ever found out he was in debt to me. That would just ruin our relationship. Our beautiful, happy home would never be the same.

MRS. LINDE. Won't you ever tell him?

NORA (*thoughtfully, half smiling*). Yes—maybe sometime, years from now, when I'm no longer so attractive. Don't laugh! I only mean when Torvald loves me less than now, when he stops enjoying my dancing and dressing up and reciting for him. Then it might be wise to have something in reserve—(*Breaking off.*) How ridiculous! That'll never happen— Well, Kristine, what do you think of my big secret? I'm capable of something too, hm? You can imagine, of course, how this thing hangs over me. It really hasn't been easy meeting the payments on time. In the business world there's what they call quarterly interest and what they call amortization, and these are always so terribly hard to manage. I've had to skimp a little here and there, wherever I could, you know. I could hardly spare anything from my house allowance, because Torvald has to live well. I couldn't let the children go poorly dressed; whatever I got for them, I felt I had to use up completely—the darlings!

MRS. LINDE.   Poor Nora, so it had to come out of your own budget, then?

NORA.   Yes, of course. But I was the one most responsible, too. Every time Torvald gave me money for new clothes and such, I never used more than half; always bought the simplest, cheapest outfits. It was a godsend that everything looks so well on me that Torvald never noticed. But it did weigh me down at times, Kristine. It *is* such a joy to wear fine things. You understand.

MRS. LINDE.   Oh, of course.

NORA.   And then I found other ways of making money. Last winter I was lucky enough to get a lot of copying to do. I locked myself in and sat writing every evening till late in the night. Ah, I was tired so often, dead tired. But still it was wonderful fun, sitting and working like that, earning money. It was almost like being a man.

MRS. LINDE.   But how much have you paid off this way so far?

NORA.   That's hard to say, exactly. These accounts, you know, aren't easy to figure. I only know that I've paid out all I could scrape together. Time and again I haven't known where to turn. (*Smiling.*) Then I'd sit here dreaming of a rich old gentleman who had fallen in love with me—

MRS. LINDE.   What! Who is he?

NORA.   Oh, really! And that he'd died, and when his will

was opened, there in big letters it said, "All my fortune shall be paid over in cash, immediately, to that enchanting Mrs. Nora Helmer."

MRS. LINDE. But Nora dear—who *was* this gentleman?

NORA. Good grief, can't you understand? The old man never existed; that was only something I'd dream up time and again whenever I was at my wits' end for money. But it makes no difference now; the old fossil can go where he pleases for all I care; I don't need him or his will—because now I'm free. (*Jumping up.*) Oh, how lovely to think of that, Kristine! Carefree! To know you're carefree, utterly carefree; to be able to romp and play with the children, and to keep up a beautiful, charming home—everything just the way Torvald likes it! And think, spring is coming, with big blue skies. Maybe we can travel a little then. Maybe I'll see the ocean again. Oh yes, it *is* so marvelous to live and be happy!

(*The front doorbell rings.*)

MRS. LINDE (*rising*). There's the bell. It's probably best that I go.

NORA. No, stay. No one's expected. It must be for Torvald.

MAID (*from the hall doorway*). Excuse me, ma'am— there's a gentleman here to see Mr. Helmer, but I didn't know —since the doctor's with him—

NORA. Who is the gentleman?

KROGSTAD (*from the doorway*). It's me, Mrs. Helmer.

(MRS. LINDE *starts and turns away toward the window.*)

NORA (*stepping toward him, tense, her voice a whisper*). You? What is it? Why do you want to speak to my husband?

KROGSTAD. Bank business—after a fashion. I have a small job in the investment bank, and I hear now your husband is going to be our chief—

NORA. In other words, it's—

KROGSTAD. Just dry business, Mrs. Helmer. Nothing but that.

NORA. Yes, then please be good enough to step into the study. (*She nods indifferently as she sees him out by the hall door, then returns and begins stirring up the stove.*)

MRS. LINDE. Nora—who was that man?

NORA. That was a Mr. Krogstad—a lawyer.

MRS. LINDE. Then it really was him.

NORA. Do you know that person?

MRS. LINDE. I did once—many years ago. For a time he was a law clerk in our town.

NORA. Yes, he's been that.

MRS. LINDE. How he's changed.

NORA. I understand he had a very unhappy marriage.

MRS. LINDE. He's a widower now.

NORA. With a number of children. There now, it's burning. (*She closes the stove door and moves the rocker a bit to one side.*)

MRS. LINDE. They say he has a hand in all kinds of business.

NORA. Oh? That may be true; I wouldn't know. But let's not think about business. It's so dull.

(DR. RANK *enters from* HELMER's *study.*)

RANK (*still in the doorway*). No, no, really—I don't want to intrude, I'd just as soon talk a little while with your wife. (*Shuts the door, then notices* MRS. LINDE.) Oh, beg pardon. I'm intruding here too.

NORA. No, not at all. (*Introducing him.*) Dr. Rank, Mrs. Linde.

RANK. Well now, that's a name much heard in this house. I believe I passed the lady on the stairs as I came.

MRS. LINDE. Yes, I take the stairs very slowly. They're rather hard on me.

RANK. Uh-hm, some touch of internal weakness?

MRS. LINDE. More overexertion, I'd say.

RANK. Nothing else? Then you're probably here in town to rest up in a round of parties?

MRS. LINDE. I'm here to look for work.

RANK. Is that the best cure for overexertion?

MRS. LINDE. One has to live, Doctor.

RANK. Yes, there's a common prejudice to that effect.

NORA. Oh, come on, Dr. Rank—you really do want to live yourself.

RANK. Yes, I really do. Wretched as I am, I'll gladly prolong my torment indefinitely. All my patients feel like that. And it's quite the same, too, with the morally sick.

Right at this moment there's one of those moral invalids in there with Helmer—

MRS. LINDE (*softly*). **Ah!**

NORA. Who do you mean?

RANK. Oh, it's a lawyer, Krogstad, a type you wouldn't know. His character is rotten to the root—but even he began chattering all-importantly about how he had to *live*.

NORA. Oh? What did he want to talk to Torvald about?

RANK. I really don't know. I only heard something about the bank.

NORA. I didn't know that Krog—that this man Krogstad had anything to do with the bank.

RANK. Yes, he's gotten some kind of berth down there. (*To* MRS. LINDE.) I don't know if you also have, in your neck of the woods, a type of person who scuttles about breathlessly, sniffing out hints of moral corruption, and then maneuvers his victim into some sort of key position where he can keep an eye on him. It's the healthy these days that are out in the cold.

MRS. LINDE. All the same, it's the sick who most need to be taken in.

RANK (*with a shrug*). Yes, there we have it. That's the concept that's turning society into a sanatorium.

> (NORA, *lost in her thoughts, breaks out into quiet laughter and claps her hands.*)

RANK. Why do you laugh at that? Do you have any real idea of what society is?

NORA. What do I care about dreary old society? I was laughing at something quite different—something terribly funny. Tell me, Doctor—is everyone who works in the bank dependent now on Torvald?

RANK. Is that what you find so terribly funny?

NORA (*smiling and humming*). Never mind, never mind! (*Pacing the floor.*) Yes, that's really immensely amusing: that we—that Torvald has so much power now over all those people. (*Taking the bag out of her pocket.*) Dr. Rank, a little macaroon on that?

RANK. See here, macaroons! I thought they were contraband here.

NORA. Yes, but these are some that Kristine gave me.

MRS. LINDE. What? I—?

NORA. Now, now, don't be afraid. You couldn't possibly know that Torvald had forbidden them. You see, he's worried they'll ruin my teeth. But hmp! Just this once! Isn't that so, Dr. Rank? Help yourself! (*Puts a macaroon in his mouth.*) And you too, Kristine. And I'll also have one, only a little one—or two, at the most. (*Walking about again.*) Now I'm really tremendously happy. Now there's just one last thing in the world that I have an enormous desire to do.

RANK. Well! And what's that?

NORA. It's something I have such a consuming desire to say so Torvald could hear.

RANK. And why can't you say it?

NORA. I don't dare. It's quite shocking.

MRS. LINDE. Shocking?

RANK. Well, then it isn't advisable. But in front of us you certainly can. What do you have such a desire to say so Torvald could hear?

NORA. I have such a huge desire to say—to hell and be damned!

RANK. Are you crazy?

MRS. LINDE. My goodness, Nora!

RANK. Go on, say it. Here he is.

NORA (*hiding the macaroon bag*). Shh, shh, shh!

(HELMER *comes in from his study, hat in hand, overcoat over his arm.*)

NORA (*going toward him*). Well, Torvald dear, are you through with him?

HELMER. Yes, he just left.

NORA. Let me introduce you—this is Kristine, who's arrived here in town.

HELMER. Kristine—? I'm sorry, but I don't know—

NORA. Mrs. Linde, Torvald dear. Mrs. Kristine Linde.

HELMER. Of course. A childhood friend of my wife's, no doubt?

MRS. LINDE. Yes, we knew each other in those days.

NORA. And just think, she made the long trip down here in order to talk with you.

HELMER. What's this?

MRS. LINDE. Well, not exactly—

NORA. You see, Kristine is remarkably clever in office

work, and so she's terribly eager to come under a capable man's supervision and add more to what she already knows—

HELMER. Very wise, Mrs. Linde.

NORA. And then when she heard that you'd become a bank manager—the story was wired out to the papers— then she came in as fast as she could and— Really, Torvald, for my sake you can do a little something for Kristine, can't you?

HELMER. Yes, it's not at all impossible. Mrs. Linde, I suppose you're a widow?

MRS. LINDE. Yes.

HELMER. Any experience in office work?

MRS. LINDE. Yes, a good deal.

HELMER. Well, it's quite likely that I can make an opening for you—

NORA (*clapping her hands*). You see, you see!

HELMER. You've come at a lucky moment, Mrs. Linde.

MRS. LINDE. Oh, how can I thank you?

HELMER. Not necessary. (*Putting his overcoat on.*) But today you'll have to excuse me—

RANK. Wait, I'll go with you. (*He fetches his coat from the hall and warms it at the stove.*)

NORA. Don't stay out long, dear.

HELMER. An hour; no more.

NORA. Are you going too, Kristine?

MRS. LINDE (*putting on her winter garments*). Yes, I have to see about a room now.

HELMER. Then perhaps we can all walk together.

NORA (*helping her*). What a shame we're so cramped here, but it's quite impossible for us to—

MRS. LINDE. Oh, don't even think of it! Good-bye, Nora dear, and thanks for everything.

NORA. Good-bye for now. Of course you'll be back this evening. And you too, Dr. Rank. What? If you're well enough? Oh, you've got to be! Wrap up tight now.

> (*In a ripple of small talk the company moves out into the hall; children's voices are heard outside on the steps.*)

NORA. There they are! There they are! (*She runs to open the door. The children come in with their nurse,* ANNE-

MARIE.) Come in, come in! (*Bends down and kisses them.*)
Oh, you darlings—! Look at them, Kristine. Aren't they
lovely!

RANK.   No loitering in the draft here.

HELMER.   Come, Mrs. Linde—this place is unbearable
now for anyone but mothers.

> (DR. RANK, HELMER, *and* MRS. LINDE *go down
> the stairs.* ANNE-MARIE *goes into the living room
> with the children.* NORA *follows, after closing
> the hall door.*)

NORA.   How fresh and strong you look. Oh, such red
cheeks you have! Like apples and roses. (*The children interrupt her throughout the following.*) And it was so much
fun? That's wonderful. Really? You pulled both Emmy and
Bob on the sled? Imagine, all together! Yes, you're a clever
boy, Ivar. Oh, let me hold her a bit, Anne-Marie. My sweet
little doll baby! (*Takes the smallest from the nurse and
dances with her.*) Yes, yes, Mama will dance with Bob as
well. What? Did you throw snowballs? Oh, if I'd only been
there! No, don't bother, Anne-Marie—I'll undress them myself. Oh yes, let me. It's such fun. Go in and rest; you look
half frozen. There's hot coffee waiting for you on the stove.
(*The nurse goes into the room to the left.* NORA *takes the
children's winter things off, throwing them about, while the
children talk to her all at once.*) Is that so? A big dog
chased you? But it didn't bite? No, dogs never bite little,
lovely doll babies. Don't peek in the packages, Ivar! What
is it? Yes, wouldn't you like to know. No, no, it's an ugly
something. Well? Shall we play? What shall we play? Hide-
and-seek? Yes, let's play hide-and-seek. Bob must hide first.
I must? Yes, let me hide first. (*Laughing and shouting, she
and the children play in and out of the living room and the
adjoining room to the right. At last* NORA *hides under the
table. The children come storming in, search, but cannot
find her, then hear her muffled laughter, dash over to the
table, lift the cloth up and find her. Wild shouting. She
creeps forward as if to scare them. More shouts. Meanwhile, a knock at the hall door; no one has noticed it. Now
the door half opens, and* KROGSTAD *appears. He waits a moment; the game goes on.*)

KROGSTAD.   Beg pardon, Mrs. Helmer—

NORA (*with a strangled cry, turning and scrambling to her knees*).   Oh! What do you want?

KROGSTAD.   Excuse me. The outer door was ajar; it must be someone forgot to shut it—

NORA (*rising*).   My husband isn't home, Mr. Krogstad.

KROGSTAD.   I know that.

NORA.   Yes—then what do you want here?

KROGSTAD.   A word with you.

NORA.   With—? (*To the children, quietly.*) Go in to Anne-Marie. What? No, the strange man won't hurt Mama. When he's gone, we'll play some more. (*She leads the children into the room to the left and shuts the door after them. Then, tense and nervous:*) You want to speak to me?

KROGSTAD.   Yes, I want to.

NORA.   Today? But it's not yet the first of the month—

KROGSTAD.   No, it's Christmas Eve. It's going to be up to you how merry a Christmas you have.

NORA.   What is it you want? Today I absolutely can't—

KROGSTAD.   We won't talk about that till later. This is something else. You do have a moment to spare, I suppose?

NORA.   Oh yes, of course—I do, except—

KROGSTAD.   Good. I was sitting over at Olsen's Restaurant when I saw your husband go down the street—

NORA.   Yes?

KROGSTAD.   With a lady.

NORA.   Yes. So?

KROGSTAD.   If you'll pardon my asking: wasn't that lady a Mrs. Linde?

NORA.   Yes.

KROGSTAD.   Just now come into town?

NORA.   Yes, today.

KROGSTAD.   She's a good friend of yours?

NORA.   Yes, she is. But I don't see—

KROGSTAD.   I also knew her once.

NORA.   I'm aware of that.

KROGSTAD.   Oh? You know all about it. I thought so. Well, then let me ask you short and sweet: is Mrs. Linde getting a job in the bank?

NORA.   What makes you think you can cross-examine me, Mr. Krogstad—you, one of my husband's employees? But since you ask, you might as well know—yes, Mrs. Linde's going to be taken on at the bank. And I'm the one who spoke for her, Mr. Krogstad. Now you know.

KROGSTAD.   So I guessed right.

NORA (*pacing up and down*).   Oh, one does have a tiny bit of influence, I should hope. Just because I am a woman, don't think it means that— When one has a subordinate position, Mr. Krogstad, one really ought to be careful about pushing somebody who—hm—

KROGSTAD.   Who has influence?

NORA.   That's right.

KROGSTAD (*in a different tone*).   Mrs. Helmer, would you be good enough to use your influence on my behalf?

NORA.   What? What do you mean?

KROGSTAD.   Would you please make sure that I keep my subordinate position in the bank?

NORA.   What does that mean? Who's thinking of taking away your position?

KROGSTAD.   Oh, don't play the innocent with me. I'm quite aware that your friend would hardly relish the chance of running into me again; and I'm also aware now whom I can thank for being turned out.

NORA.   But I promise you—

KROGSTAD.   Yes, yes, yes, to the point: there's still time, and I'm advising you to use your influence to prevent it.

NORA.   But Mr. Krogstad, I have absolutely no influence.

KROGSTAD.   You haven't? I thought you were just saying—

NORA.   You shouldn't take me so literally. I! How can you believe that I have any such influence over my husband?

KROGSTAD.   Oh, I've known your husband from our student days. I don't think the great bank manager's more steadfast than any other married man.

NORA.   You speak insolently about my husband, and I'll show you the door.

KROGSTAD.   The lady has spirit.

NORA.   I'm not afraid of you any longer. After New Year's, I'll soon be done with the whole business.

KROGSTAD (*restraining himself*).   Now listen to me, Mrs. Helmer. If necessary, I'll fight for my little job in the bank as if it were life itself.

NORA.   Yes, so it seems.

KROGSTAD.   It's not just a matter of income; that's the

least of it. It's something else— All right, out with it! Look, this is the thing. You know, just like all the others, of course, that once, a good many years ago, I did something rather rash.

NORA. I've heard rumors to that effect.

KROGSTAD. The case never got into court; but all the same, every door was closed in my face from then on. So I took up those various activities you know about. I had to grab hold somewhere; and I dare say I haven't been among the worst. But now I want to drop all that. My boys are growing up. For their sakes, I'll have to win back as much respect as possible here in town. That job in the bank was like the first rung in my ladder. And now your husband wants to kick me right back down in the mud again.

NORA. But for heaven's sake, Mr. Krogstad, it's simply not in my power to help you.

KROGSTAD. That's because you haven't the will to—but I have the means to make you.

NORA. You certainly won't tell my husband that I owe you money?

KROGSTAD. Hm—what if I told him that?

NORA. That would be shameful of you. (*Nearly in tears.*) This secret—my joy and my pride—that he should learn it in such a crude and disgusting way—learn it from you. You'd expose me to the most horrible unpleasantness—

KROGSTAD. Only unpleasantness?

NORA (*vehemently*). But go on and try. It'll turn out the worse for you, because then my husband will really see what a crook you are, and then you'll *never* be able to hold your job.

KROGSTAD. I asked if it was just domestic unpleasantness you were afraid of?

NORA. If my husband finds out, then of course he'll pay what I owe at once, and then we'd be through with you for good.

KROGSTAD (*a step closer*). Listen, Mrs. Helmer—you've either got a very bad memory, or else no head at all for business. I'd better put you a little more in touch with the facts.

NORA. What do you mean?

KROGSTAD. When your husband was sick, you came to

me for a loan of four thousand, eight hundred crowns.

NORA. Where else could I go?

KROGSTAD. I promised to get you that sum——

NORA. And you got it.

KROGSTAD. I promised to get you that sum, on certain conditions. You were so involved in your husband's illness, and so eager to finance your trip, that I guess you didn't think out all the details. It might just be a good idea to remind you. I promised you the money on the strength of a note I drew up.

NORA. Yes, and that I signed.

KROGSTAD. Right. But at the bottom I added some lines for your father to guarantee the loan. He was supposed to sign down there.

NORA. Supposed to? He did sign.

KROGSTAD. I left the date blank. In other words, your father would have dated his signature himself. Do you remember that?

NORA. Yes, I think——

KROGSTAD. Then I gave you the note for you to mail to your father. Isn't that so?

NORA. Yes.

KROGSTAD. And naturally you sent it at once—because only some five, six days later you brought me the note, properly signed. And with that, the money was yours.

NORA. Well, then; I've made my payments regularly, haven't I?

KROGSTAD. More or less. But—getting back to the point —those were hard times for you then, Mrs. Helmer.

NORA. Yes, they were.

KROGSTAD. Your father was very ill, I believe.

NORA. He was near the end.

KROGSTAD. He died soon after?

NORA. Yes.

KROGSTAD. Tell me, Mrs. Helmer, do you happen to recall the date of your father's death? The day of the month, I mean.

NORA. Papa died the twenty-ninth of September.

KROGSTAD. That's quite correct; I've already looked into that. And now we come to a curious thing—(*Taking out a paper.*) which I simply cannot comprehend.

NORA.   Curious thing? I don't know—

KROGSTAD.   This is the curious thing: that your father co-signed the note for your loan three days after his death.

NORA.   How—? I don't understand.

KROGSTAD.   Your father died the twenty-ninth of September. But look. Here your father dated his signature October second. Isn't that curious, Mrs. Helmer? (NORA *is silent.*) Can you explain it to me? (NORA *remains silent.*) It's also remarkable that the words "October second" and the year aren't written in your father's hand, but rather in one that I think I know. Well, it's easy to understand. Your father forgot perhaps to date his signature, and then someone or other added it, a bit sloppily, before anyone knew of his death. There's nothing wrong in that. It all comes down to the signature. And there's no question about *that,* Mrs. Helmer. It really *was* your father who signed his own name here, wasn't it?

NORA (*after a short silence, throwing her head back and looking squarely at him*). No, it wasn't. *I* signed Papa's name.

KROGSTAD.   Wait, now—are you fully aware that this is a dangerous confession?

NORA.   Why? You'll soon get your money.

KROGSTAD.   Let me ask you a question—why didn't you send the paper to your father?

NORA.   That was impossible. Papa was so sick. If I'd asked him for his signature, I also would have had to tell him what the money was for. But I couldn't tell him, sick as he was, that my husband's life was in danger. That was just impossible.

KROGSTAD.   Then it would have been better if you'd given up the trip abroad.

NORA.   I couldn't possibly. The trip was to save my husband's life. I couldn't give that up.

KROGSTAD.   But didn't you ever consider that this was a fraud against me?

NORA.   I couldn't let myself be bothered by that. You weren't any concern of mine. I couldn't stand you, with all those cold complications you made, even though you knew how badly off my husband was.

KROGSTAD.   Mrs. Helmer, obviously you haven't the

vaguest idea of what you've involved yourself in. But I can tell you this: it was nothing more and nothing worse that I once did—and it wrecked my whole reputation.

NORA. You? Do you expect me to believe that you ever acted bravely to save your wife's life?

KROGSTAD. Laws don't inquire into motives.

NORA. Then they must be very poor laws.

KROGSTAD. Poor or not—if I introduce this paper in court, you'll be judged according to law.

NORA. This I refuse to believe. A daughter hasn't a right to protect her dying father from anxiety and care? A wife hasn't a right to save her husband's life? I don't know much about laws, but I'm sure that somewhere in the books these things are allowed. And you don't know anything about it—you who practice the law? You must be an awful lawyer, Mr. Krogstad.

KROGSTAD. Could be. But business—the kind of business we two are mixed up in—don't you think I know about that? All right. Do what you want now. But I'm telling you *this*: if I get shoved down a second time, you're going to keep me company. (*He bows and goes out through the hall.*)

NORA (*pensive for a moment, then tossing her head*). Oh, really! Trying to frighten me! I'm not so silly as all that. (*Begins gathering up the children's clothes, but soon stops.*) But—? No, but that's impossible! I did it out of love.

THE CHILDREN (*in the doorway, left*). Mama, that strange man's gone out the door.

NORA. Yes, yes, I know it. But don't tell anyone about the strange man. Do you hear? Not even Papa!

THE CHILDREN. No, Mama. But now will you play again?

NORA. No, not now.

THE CHILDREN. Oh, but Mama, you promised.

NORA. Yes, but I can't now. Go inside; I have too much to do. Go in, go in, my sweet darlings. (*She herds them gently back in the room and shuts the door after them. Settling on the sofa, she takes up a piece of embroidery and makes some stitches, but soon stops abruptly.*) No! (*Throws the work aside, rises, goes to the hall door and calls out.*) Helene! Let me have the tree in here. (*Goes to the table, left, opens the table drawer, and stops again.*) No, but that's utterly impossible!

MAID (*with the Christmas tree*). Where should I put it, ma'am?

NORA.   There. The middle of the floor.

MAID.   Should I bring anything else?

NORA.   No, thanks. I have what I need.

(*The* MAID, *who has set the tree down, goes out.*)

NORA (*absorbed in trimming the tree*). Candles here—and flowers here. That terrible creature! Talk, talk, talk! There's nothing to it at all. The tree's going to be lovely. I'll do anything to please you, Torvald. I'll sing for you, dance for you—

(HELMER *comes in from the hall, with a sheaf of papers under his arm.*)

NORA.   Oh! You're back so soon?

HELMER.   Yes. Has anyone been here?

NORA.   Here? No.

HELMER.   That's odd. I saw Krogstad leaving the front door.

NORA.   So? Oh yes, that's true. Krogstad was here a moment.

HELMER.   Nora, I can see by your face that he's been here, begging you to put in a good word for him.

NORA.   Yes.

HELMER.   And it was supposed to seem like your own idea? You were to hide it from me that he'd been here. He asked you that, too, didn't he?

NORA.   Yes, Torvald, but—

HELMER.   Nora, Nora, and you could fall for that? Talk with that sort of person and promise him anything? And then in the bargain, tell me an untruth.

NORA.   An untruth—?

HELMER.   Didn't you say that no one had been here? (*Wagging his finger.*) My little songbird must never do that again. A songbird needs a clean beak to warble with. No false notes. (*Putting his arm about her waist.*) That's the way it should be, isn't it? Yes, I'm sure of it. (*Releasing her.*) And so, enough of that. (*Sitting by the stove.*) Ah, how snug and cozy it is here. (*Leafing among his papers.*)

NORA (*busy with the tree, after a short pause*). Torvald!

HELMER.   Yes.

NORA. I'm so much looking forward to the Stenborgs' costume party, day after tomorrow.

HELMER. And I can't wait to see what you'll surprise me with.

NORA. Oh, that stupid business!

HELMER. What?

NORA. I can't find anything that's right. Everything seems so ridiculous, so inane.

HELMER. So my little Nora's come to *that* recognition?

NORA (*going behind his chair, her arms resting on its back*). Are you very busy, Torvald?

HELMER. Oh—

NORA. What papers are those?

HELMER. Bank matters.

NORA. Already?

HELMER. I've gotten full authority from the retiring management to make all necessary changes in personnel and procedure. I'll need Christmas week for that. I want to have everything in order by New Year's.

NORA. So that was the reason this poor Krogstad—

HELMER. Hm.

NORA (*still leaning on the chair and slowly stroking the nape of his neck*). If you weren't so very busy, I would have asked you an enormous favor, Torvald.

HELMER. Let's hear. What is it?

NORA. You know, there isn't anyone who has your good taste—and I want so much to look well at the costume party. Torvald, couldn't you take over and decide what I should be and plan my costume?

HELMER. Ah, is my stubborn little creature calling for a lifeguard?

NORA. Yes, Torvald, I can't get anywhere without your help.

HELMER. All right—I'll think it over. We'll hit on something.

NORA. Oh, how sweet of you. (*Goes to the tree again. Pause.*) Aren't the red flowers pretty—? But tell me, was it really such a crime that this Krogstad committed?

HELMER. Forgery. Do you have any idea what that means?

NORA. Couldn't he have done it out of need?

HELMER. Yes, or thoughtlessness, like so many others.

I'm not so heartless that I'd condemn a man categorically for just one mistake.

NORA. No, of course not, Torvald!

HELMER. Plenty of men have redeemed themselves by openly confessing their crimes and taking their punishment.

NORA. Punishment—?

HELMER. But now Krogstad didn't go that way. He got himself out by sharp practices, and that's the real cause of his moral breakdown.

NORA. Do you really think that would—?

HELMER. Just imagine how a man with that sort of guilt in him has to lie and cheat and deceive on all sides, has to wear a mask even with the nearest and dearest he has, even with his own wife and children. And with the children, Nora—that's where it's most horrible.

NORA. Why?

HELMER. Because that kind of atmosphere of lies infects the whole life of a home. Every breath the children take in is filled with the germs of something degenerate.

NORA (coming closer behind him). Are you sure of that?

HELMER. Oh, I've seen it often enough as a lawyer. Almost everyone who goes bad early in life has a mother who's a chronic liar.

NORA. Why just—the mother?

HELMER. It's usually the mother's influence that's dominant, but the father's works in the same way, of course. Every lawyer is quite familiar with it. And still this Krogstad's been going home year in, year out, poisoning his own children with lies and pretense; that's why I call him morally lost. (Reaching his hands out toward her.) So my sweet little Nora must promise me never to plead his cause. Your hand on it. Come, come, what's this? Give me your hand. There, now. All settled. I can tell you it'd be impossible for me to work alongside of him. I literally feel physically revolted when I'm anywhere near such a person.

NORA (withdraws her hand and goes to the other side of the Christmas tree). How hot it is here! And I've got so much to do.

HELMER (getting up and gathering his papers). Yes, and I have to think about getting some of these read through before dinner. I'll think about your costume, too. And something to hang on the tree in gilt paper, I may even see about that. (*Putting his hand on her head.*) Oh you, my darling little songbird. (*He goes into his study and closes the door after him.*)

NORA (*softly, after a silence*). Oh, really! it isn't so. It's impossible. It must be impossible.

ANNE-MARIE (*in the doorway, left*). The children are begging so hard to come in to Mama.

NORA. No, no, no, don't let them in to me! You stay with them, Anne-Marie.

ANNE-MARIE. Of course, ma'am. (*Closes the door.*)

NORA (*pale with terror*). Hurt my children—! Poison my home? (*A moment's pause; then she tosses her head.*) That's not true. Never. Never in all the world.

⌣⊀ ACT TWO ⊁⌣

Same room. Beside the piano the Christmas tree now stands stripped of ornament, burned-down candle stubs on its ragged branches. NORA's *street clothes lie on the sofa.* NORA, *alone in the room, moves restlessly about; at last she stops at the sofa and picks up her coat.*

NORA (*dropping the coat again*). Someone's coming! (*Goes toward the door, listens.*) No—there's no one. Of course—nobody's coming today, Christmas Day—or tomorrow, either. But maybe—(*Opens the door and looks out.*) No, nothing in the mailbox. Quite empty. (*Coming forward.*) What nonsense! He won't do anything serious. Nothing terrible could happen. It's impossible. Why, I have three small children.

> (ANNE-MARIE, *with a large carton, comes in from the room to the left.*)

ANNE-MARIE. Well, at last I found the box with the masquerade clothes.

NORA. Thanks. Put it on the table.

ANNE-MARIE (*does so*). But they're all pretty much of a mess.

NORA. Ahh! I'd love to rip them in a million pieces!

ANNE-MARIE. Oh, mercy, they can be fixed right up. Just a little patience.

NORA. Yes, I'll go get Mrs. Linde to help me.

ANNE-MARIE. Out again now? In this nasty weather? Miss Nora will catch cold—get sick.

NORA. Oh, worse things could happen— How are the children?

ANNE-MARIE. The poor mites are playing with their Christmas presents, but—

NORA. Do they ask for me much?

ANNE-MARIE. They're so used to having Mama around, you know.

154

NORA. Yes. but Anne-Marie, I *can't* be together with them as much as I was.

ANNE-MARIE. Well, small children get used to anything.

NORA. You think so? Do you think they'd forget their mother if she was gone for good?

ANNE-MARIE. Oh, mercy—gone for good!

NORA. Wait, tell me, Anne-Marie—I've wondered so often—how could you ever have the heart to give your child over to strangers?

ANNE-MARIE. But I had to, you know, to become little Nora's nurse.

NORA. Yes, but how could you *do* it?

ANNE-MARIE. When I could get such a good place? A girl who's poor and who's gotten in trouble is glad enough for that. Because that slippery fish, he didn't do a thing for me, you know.

NORA. But your daughter's surely forgotten you.

ANNE-MARIE. Oh, she certainly has not. She's written to me, both when she was confirmed and when she was married.

NORA (*clasping her about the neck*). You old Anne-Marie, you were a good mother for me when I was little.

ANNE-MARIE. Poor little Nora, with no other mother but me.

NORA. And if the babies didn't have one, then I know that you'd— What silly talk! (*Opening the carton.*) Go in to them. Now I'll have to— Tomorrow you can see how lovely I'll look.

ANNE-MARIE. Oh, there won't be anyone at the party as lovely as Miss Nora. (*She goes off into the room, left.*)

NORA (*begins unpacking the box, but soon throws it aside*). Oh, if I dared to go out. If only nobody would come. If only nothing would happen here while I'm out. What craziness—nobody's coming. Just don't think. This muff—needs a brushing. Beautiful gloves, beautiful gloves. Let it go. Let it go! One, two, three, four, five, six— (*With a cry.*) Oh, there they are! (*Poises to move toward the door, but remains irresolutely standing.* MRS. LINDE *enters from the hall, where she has removed her street clothes.*)

NORA. Oh, it's you, Kristine. There's no one else out there? How good that you've come.

MRS. LINDE. I hear you were up asking for me.

NORA. Yes, I just stopped by. There's something you really can help me with. Let's get settled on the sofa. Look, there's going to be a costume party tomorrow evening at the Stenborgs' right above us, and now Torvald wants me to go as a Neapolitan peasant girl and dance the tarantella that I learned in Capri.

MRS. LINDE. Really, are you giving a whole performance?

NORA. Torvald says yes, I should. See, here's the dress. Torvald had it made for me down there; but now it's all so tattered that I just don't know—

MRS. LINDE. Oh, we'll fix that up in no time. It's nothing more than the trimmings—they're a bit loose here and there. Needle and thread? Good, now we have what we need.

NORA. Oh, how sweet of you!

MRS. LINDE (*sewing*). So you'll be in disguise tomorrow, Nora. You know what? I'll stop by then for a moment and have a look at you all dressed up. But listen, I've absolutely forgotten to thank you for that pleasant evening yesterday.

NORA (*getting up and walking about*). I don't think it was as pleasant as usual yesterday. You should have come to town a bit sooner, Kristine— Yes, Torvald really knows how to give a home elegance and charm.

MRS. LINDE. And you do, too, if you ask me. You're not your father's daughter for nothing. But tell me, is Dr. Rank always so down in the mouth as yesterday?

NORA. No, that was quite an exception. But he goes around critically ill all the time—tuberculosis of the spine, poor man. You know, his father was a disgusting thing who kept mistresses and so on—and that's why the son's been sickly from birth.

MRS. LINDE (*lets her sewing fall to her lap*). But my dearest Nora, how do you know about such things?

NORA (*walking more jauntily*). Hmp! When you've had three children, then you've had a few visits from—from women who know something of medicine, and they tell you this and that.

MRS. LINDE (*resumes sewing; a short pause*). Does Dr. Rank come here every day?

NORA. Every blessed day. He's Torvald's best friend from childhood, and *my* good friend, too. Dr. Rank almost belongs to this house.

MRS. LINDE. But tell me—is he quite sincere? I mean, doesn't he rather enjoy flattering people?

NORA. Just the opposite. Why do you think that?

MRS. LINDE. When you introduced us yesterday, he was proclaiming that he'd often heard my name in this house; but later I noticed that your husband hadn't the slightest idea who I really was. So how could Dr. Rank—?

NORA. But it's all true, Kristine. You see, Torvald loves me beyond words, and, as he puts it, he'd like to keep me all to himself. For a long time he'd almost be jealous if I even mentioned any of my old friends back home. So of course I dropped that. But with Dr. Rank I talk a lot about such things, because he likes hearing about them.

MRS. LINDE. Now listen, Nora; in many ways you're still like a child. I'm a good deal older than you, with a little more experience. I'll tell you something: you ought to put an end to all this with Dr. Rank.

NORA. What should I put an end to?

MRS. LINDE. Both parts of it, I think. Yesterday you said something about a rich admirer who'd provide you with money—

NORA. Yes, one who doesn't exist—worse luck. So?

MRS. LINDE. Is Dr. Rank well off?

NORA. Yes, he is.

MRS. LINDE. With no dependents?

NORA. No, no one. But—

MRS. LINDE. And he's over here every day?

NORA. Yes, I told you that.

MRS. LINDE. How can a man of such refinement be so grasping?

NORA. I don't follow you at all.

MRS. LINDE. Now don't try to hide it, Nora. You think I can't guess who loaned you the forty-eight hundred crowns?

NORA. Are you out of your mind? How could you think such a thing! A friend of ours, who comes here every single day. What an intolerable situation that would have been!

MRS. LINDE. Then it really wasn't him.

NORA. No, absolutely not. It never even crossed my mind for a moment— And he had nothing to lend in those days; his inheritance came later.

MRS. LINDE. Well, I think that was a stroke of luck for you, Nora dear.

NORA. No, it never would have occurred to me to ask Dr. Rank— Still, I'm quite sure that if I had asked him—

MRS. LINDE. Which you won't, of course.

NORA. No, of course not. I can't see that I'd ever need to. But I'm quite positive that if I talked to Dr. Rank—

MRS. LINDE. Behind your husband's back?

NORA. I've got to clear up this other thing; *that's* also behind his back. I've *got* to clear it all up.

MRS. LINDE. Yes, I was saying that yesterday, but—

NORA (*pacing up and down*). A man handles these problems so much better than a woman—

MRS. LINDE. One's husband does, yes.

NORA. Nonsense. (*Stopping.*) When you pay everything you owe, then you get your note back, right?

MRS. LINDE. Yes, naturally.

NORA. And can rip it into a million pieces and burn it up—that filthy scrap of paper!

MRS. LINDE (*looking hard at her, laying her sewing aside, and rising slowly*). Nora, you're hiding something from me.

NORA. You can see it in my face?

MRS. LINDE. Something's happened to you since yesterday morning. Nora, what is it?

NORA (*hurrying toward her*). Kristine! (*Listening.*) Shh! Torvald's home. Look, go in with the children a while. Torvald can't bear all this snipping and stitching. Let Anne-Marie help you.

MRS. LINDE (*gathering up some of the things*). All right, but I'm not leaving here until we've talked this out. (*She disappears into the room, left, as* TORVALD *enters from the hall.*)

NORA. Oh, how I've been waiting for you, Torvald dear.

HELMER. Was that the dressmaker?

NORA. No, that was Kristine. She's helping me fix up my costume. You know, it's going to be quite attractive.

HELMER. Yes, wasn't that a bright idea I had?

NORA. Brilliant! But then wasn't I good as well to give in to you?

HELMER. Good—because you give in to your husband's judgment? All right, you little goose, I know you didn't mean it like that. But I won't disturb you. You'll want to have a fitting, I suppose.

NORA. And you'll be working?

HELMER.   Yes. (*Indicating a bundle of papers.*) See. I've been down to the bank. (*Starts toward his study.*)

NORA.   Torvald.

HELMER (*stops*).   Yes.

NORA.   If your little squirrel begged you, with all her heart and soul, for something—?

HELMER.   What's that?

NORA.   Then would you do it?

HELMER.   First, naturally, I'd have to know what it was.

NORA.   Your squirrel would scamper about and do tricks, if you'd only be sweet and give in.

HELMER.   Out with it.

NORA.   Your lark would be singing high and low in every room—

HELMER.   Come on, she does that anyway.

NORA.   I'd be a wood nymph and dance for you in the moonlight.

HELMER.   Nora—don't tell me it's that same business from this morning?

NORA (*coming closer*).   Yes, Torvald, I beg you, please!

HELMER.   And you actually have the nerve to drag that up again?

NORA.   Yes, yes, you've got to give in to me; you *have* to let Krogstad keep his job in the bank.

HELMER.   My dear Nora, I've slated his job for Mrs. Linde.

NORA.   That's awfully kind of you. But you could just fire another clerk instead of Krogstad.

HELMER.   This is the most incredible stubbornness! Because you go and give an impulsive promise to speak up for him, I'm expected to—

NORA.   That's not the reason, Torvald. It's for your own sake. That man does writing for the worst papers; you said it yourself. He could do you any amount of harm. I'm scared to death of him—

HELMER.   Ah, I understand. It's the old memories haunting you.

NORA.   What do you mean by that?

HELMER.   Of course, you're thinking about your father.

NORA.   Yes, all right. Just remember how those nasty gossips wrote in the papers about Papa and slandered him so cruelly. I think they'd have had him dismissed if the department hadn't sent you up to investigate, and if you hadn't been so kind and open-minded toward him.

HELMER. My dear Nora, there's a notable difference between your father and me. Your father's official career was hardly above reproach. But mine is; and I hope it'll stay that way as long as I hold my position.

NORA. Oh, who can ever tell what vicious minds can invent? We could be so snug and happy now in our quiet, carefree home—you and I and the children, Torvald! That's why I'm pleading with you so—

HELMER. And just by pleading for him you make it impossible for me to keep him on. It's already known at the bank that I'm firing Krogstad. What if it's rumored around now that the new bank manager was vetoed by his wife—

NORA. Yes, what then—?

HELMER. Oh yes—as long as our little bundle of stubbornness gets her way—! I should go and make myself ridiculous in front of the whole office—give people the idea I can be swayed by all kinds of outside pressure. Oh, you can bet I'd feel the effects of that soon enough! Besides—there's something that rules Krogstad right out at the bank as long as I'm the manager.

NORA. What's that?

HELMER. His moral failings I could maybe overlook if I had to—

NORA. Yes, Torvald, why not?

HELMER. And I hear he's quite efficient on the job. But he was a crony of mine back in my teens—one of those rash friendships that crop up again and again to embarrass you later in life. Well, I might as well say it straight out: we're on a first-name basis. And that tactless fool makes no effort at all to hide it in front of others. Quite the contrary—he thinks that entitles him to take a familiar air around me, and so every other second he comes booming out with his "Yes, Torvald!" and "Sure thing, Torvald!" I tell you, it's been excruciating for me. He's out to make my place in the bank unbearable.

NORA. Torvald, you can't be serious about all this.

HELMER. Oh no? Why not?

NORA. Because these are such petty considerations.

HELMER. What are you saying? Petty? You think I'm petty!

NORA. No, just the opposite, Torvald dear. That's exactly why—

HELMER. Never mind. You call my motives petty; then I might as well be just that. Petty! All right! We'll put a stop to this for good. (*Goes to the hall door and calls.*) Helene!

NORA. What do you want?

HELMER (*searching among his papers*). A decision. (*The* MAID *comes in.*) Look here; take this letter; go out with it at once. Get hold of a messenger and have him deliver it. Quick now. It's already addressed. Wait, here's some money.

MAID. Yes, sir. (*She leaves with the letter.*)

HELMER (*straightening his papers*). There, now, little Miss Willful.

NORA (*breathlessly*). Torvald, what was that letter?

HELMER. Krogstad's notice.

NORA. Call it back, Torvald! There's still time. Oh, Torvald, call it back! Do it for my sake—for your sake, for the children's sake! Do you hear, Torvald; do it! You don't know how this can harm us.

HELMER. Too late.

NORA. Yes, too late.

HELMER. Nora dear, I can forgive you this panic, even though basically you're insulting me. Yes, you are! Or isn't it an insult to think that *I* should be afraid of a courtroom hack's revenge? But I forgive you anyway, because this shows so beautifully how much you love me. (*Takes her in his arms.*) This is the way it should be, my darling Nora. Whatever comes, you'll see: when it really counts, I have strength and courage enough as a man to take on the whole weight myself.

NORA (*terrified*). What do you mean by that?

HELMER. The whole weight, I said.

NORA (*resolutely*). No, never in all the world.

HELMER. Good. So we'll share it, Nora, as man and wife. That's as it should be. (*Fondling her.*) Are you happy now? There, there, there—not these frightened dove's eyes. It's nothing at all but empty fantasies— Now you should run through your tarantella and practice your tambourine. I'll go to the inner office and shut both doors, so I won't hear a thing; you can make all the noise you like. (*Turning in the doorway.*) And when Rank comes, just tell him where he can find me. (*He nods to her and goes with his papers into the study, closing the door.*)

NORA (*standing as though rooted, dazed with fright, in a whisper*).   He really could do it. He will do it. He'll do it in spite of everything. No, not that, never, never! Anything but that! Escape! A way out— (*The doorbell rings.*) Dr. Rank! Anything but that! *Anything,* whatever it is! (*Her hands pass over her face, smoothing it; she pulls herself together, goes over and opens the hall door.* DR. RANK *stands outside, hanging his fur coat up. During the following scene, it begins getting dark.*)

NORA.   Hello, Dr. Rank. I recognized your ring. But you mustn't go in to Torvald yet; I believe he's working.

RANK.   And you?

NORA.   For you, I always have an hour to spare—you know that. (*He has entered, and she shuts the door after him.*)

RANK.   Many thanks. I'll make use of these hours while I can.

NORA.   What do you mean by that? While you can?

RANK.   Does that disturb you?

NORA.   Well, it's such an odd phrase. Is anything going to happen?

RANK.   What's going to happen is what I've been expecting so long—but I honestly didn't think it would come so soon.

NORA (*gripping his arm*).   What is it you've found out? Dr. Rank, you have to tell me!

RANK (*sitting by the stove*).   It's all over with me. There's nothing to be done about it.

NORA (*breathing easier*).   Is it you—then—?

RANK.   Who else? There's no point in lying to one's self. I'm the most miserable of all my patients, Mrs. Helmer. These past few days I've been auditing my internal accounts. Bankrupt! Within a month I'll probably be laid out and rotting in the churchyard.

NORA.   Oh, what a horrible thing to say.

RANK.   The thing itself is horrible. But the worst of it is all the other horror before it's over. There's only one final examination left; when I'm finished with that, I'll know about when my disintegration will begin. There's something

I want to say. Helmer with his sensitivity has such a sharp distaste for anything ugly. I don't want him near my sickroom.

NORA.   Oh, but Dr. Rank—

RANK.   I won't have him in there. Under no condition. I'll lock my door to him— As soon as I'm completely sure of the worst, I'll send you my calling card marked with a black cross, and you'll know then the wreck has started to come apart.

NORA.   No, today you're completely unreasonable. And I wanted you so much to be in a really good humor.

RANK.   With death up my sleeve? And then to suffer this way for somebody else's sins. Is there any justice in that? And in every single family, in some way or another, this inevitable retribution of nature goes on—

NORA (*her hands pressed over her ears*).   Oh, stuff! Cheer up! Please—be gay!

RANK.   Yes, I'd just as soon laugh at it all. My poor, innocent spine, serving time for my father's gay army days.

NORA (*by the table, left*).   He was so infatuated with asparagus tips and *pâté de foie gras*, wasn't that it?

RANK.   Yes—and with truffles.

NORA.   Truffles, yes. And then with oysters, I suppose?

RANK.   Yes, tons of oysters, naturally.

NORA.   And then the port and champagne to go with it. It's so sad that all these delectable things have to strike at our bones.

RANK.   Especially when they strike at the unhappy bones that never shared in the fun.

NORA.   Ah that's the saddest of all.

RANK (*looks searchingly at her*).   Hm.

NORA (*after a moment*).   Why did you smile?

RANK.   No, it was you who laughed.

NORA.   No, it was you who smiled, Dr. Rank!

RANK (*getting up*).   You're even a bigger tease than I'd thought.

NORA.   I'm full of wild ideas today.

RANK.   That's obvious.

NORA (*putting both hands on his shoulders*).   Dear, dear Dr. Rank, you'll never die for Torvald and me.

RANK.   Oh, that loss you'll easily get over. Those who go away are soon forgotten.

NORA (*looks fearfully at him*). You believe that?

RANK. One makes new connections, and then—

NORA. Who makes new connections?

RANK. Both you and Torvald will when I'm gone. I'd say you're well under way already. What was that Mrs. Linde doing here last evening?

NORA. Oh, come—you can't be jealous of poor Kristine?

RANK. Oh yes, I am. She'll be my successor here in the house. When I'm down under, that woman will probably—

NORA. Shh! Not so loud. She's right in there.

RANK. Today as well. So you see.

NORA. Only to sew on my dress. Good gracious, how unreasonable you are. (*Sitting on the sofa.*) Be nice now, Dr. Rank. Tomorrow you'll see how beautifully I'll dance; and you can imagine then that I'm dancing only for you—yes, and of course for Torvald, too—that's understood. (*Takes various items out of the carton.*) Dr. Rank, sit over here and I'll show you something.

RANK (*sitting*). What's that?

NORA. Look here. Look.

RANK. Silk stockings.

NORA. Flesh-colored. Aren't they lovely? Now it's so dark here, but tomorrow— No, no, no, just look at the feet. Oh well, you might as well look at the rest.

RANK. Hm—

NORA. Why do you look so critical? Don't you believe they'll fit?

RANK. I've never had any chance to form an opinion on that.

NORA (*glancing at him a moment*). Shame on you. (*Hits him lightly on the ear with the stockings.*) That's for you. (*Puts them away again.*)

RANK. And what other splendors am I going to see now?

NORA. Not the least bit more, because you've been naughty. (*She hums a little and rummages among her things.*)

RANK (*after a short silence*). When I sit here together with you like this, completely easy and open, then I don't know— I simply can't imagine—whatever would have become of me if I'd never come into this house.

NORA (*smiling*). Yes, I really think you feel completely at ease with us.

RANK (*more quietly, staring straight ahead*).   And then to have to go away from it all—

NORA.   Nonsense, you're not going away.

RANK (*his voice unchanged*).   —and not even be able to leave some poor show of gratitude behind, scarcely a fleeting regret—no more than a vacant place that anyone can fill.

NORA.   And if I asked you now for—? No—

RANK.   For what?

NORA.   For a great proof of your friendship—

RANK.   Yes, yes?

NORA.   No, I mean—for an exceptionally big favor—

RANK.   Would you really, for once, make me so happy?

NORA.   Oh, you haven't the vaguest idea what it is.

RANK.   All right, then tell me.

NORA.   No, but I can't, Dr. Rank—it's all out of reason. It's advice and help, too—and a favor—

RANK.   So much the better. I can't fathom what you're hinting at. Just speak out. Don't you trust me?

NORA.   Of course. More than anyone else. You're my best and truest friend, I'm sure. That's why I want to talk to you. All right, then, Dr. Rank: there's something you can help me prevent. You know how deeply, how inexpressibly dearly Torvald loves me; he'd never hesitate a second to give up his life for me.

RANK (*leaning close to her*).   Nora—do you think he's the only one—

NORA (*with a slight start*).   Who—?

RANK.   Who'd gladly give up his life for you.

NORA (*heavily*). I see.

RANK.   I swore to myself you should know this before I'm gone. I'll never find a better chance. Yes, Nora, now you know. And also you know now that you can trust me beyond anyone else.

NORA (*rising, natural and calm*).   Let me by.

RANK (*making room for her, but still sitting*).   Nora—

NORA (*in the hall doorway*).   Helene, bring the lamp in. (*Goes over to the stove.*) Ah, dear Dr. Rank, that was really mean of you.

RANK (*getting up*).   That I've loved you just as deeply as somebody else? Was *that* mean?

NORA.   No, but that you came out and told me. That was quite unnecessary—

RANK. What do you mean? Have you known—?

(*The* MAID *comes in with the lamp, sets it on the table, and goes out again.*)

RANK. Nora—Mrs. Helmer—I'm asking you: have you known about it?

NORA. Oh, how can I tell what I know or don't know? Really, I don't know what to say— Why did you have to be so clumsy, Dr. Rank! Everything was so good.

RANK. Well, in any case, you now have the knowledge that my body and soul are at your command. So won't you speak out?

NORA (*looking at him*).   After that?

RANK. Please, just let me know what it is.

NORA. You can't know anything now.

RANK. I have to. You mustn't punish me like this. Give me the chance to do whatever is humanly possible for you.

NORA. Now there's nothing you can do for me. Besides, actually, I don't need any help. You'll see—it's only my fantasies. That's what it is. Of course! (*Sits in the rocker, looks at him, and smiles.*) What a nice one you are, Dr. Rank. Aren't you a little bit ashamed, now that the lamp is here?

RANK. No, not exactly. But perhaps I'd better go—for good?

NORA. No, you certainly can't do that. You must come here just as you always have. You know Torvald can't do without you.

RANK. Yes, but *you*?

NORA. You know how much I enjoy it when you're here.

RANK. That's precisely what threw me off. You're a mystery to me. So many times I've felt you'd almost rather be with me than with Helmer.

NORA. Yes—you see, there are some people that one loves most and other people that one would almost prefer being with.

RANK. Yes, there's something to that.

NORA. When I was back home, of course I loved Papa most. But I always thought it was so much fun when I could sneak down to the maids' quarters, because they never tried to improve me, and it was always so amusing, the way they talked to each other.

RANK. Aha, so it's *their* place that I've filled.

NORA (*jumping up and going to him*). Oh, dear, sweet Dr. Rank, that's not what I meant at all. But you can understand that with Torvald it's just the same as with Papa—

(*The* MAID *enters from the hall.*)

MAID. Ma'am—please! (*She whispers to* NORA *and hands her a calling card.*)

NORA (*glancing at the card*). Ah! (*Slips it into her pocket.*)

RANK. Anything wrong?

NORA. No, no, not at all. It's only some—it's my new dress—

RANK. Really? But—there's your dress.

NORA. Oh, that. But this is another one—I ordered it— Torvald mustn't know—

RANK. Ah, now we have the big secret.

NORA. That's right. Just go in with him—he's back in the inner study. Keep him there as long as—

RANK. Don't worry. He won't get away. (*Goes into the study.*)

NORA (*to the* MAID). And he's standing waiting in the kitchen?

MAID. Yes, he came up by the back stairs.

NORA. But didn't you tell him somebody was here?

MAID. Yes, but that didn't do any good.

NORA. He won't leave?

MAID. No, he won't go till he's talked with you, ma'am.

NORA. Let him come in, then—but quietly. Helene, don't breathe a word about this. It's a surprise for my husband.

MAID. Yes, yes, I understand— (*Goes out.*)

NORA. This horror—it's going to happen. No, no, no, it can't happen, it mustn't. (*She goes and bolts* HELMER's *door. The* MAID *opens the hall door for* KROGSTAD *and shuts it behind him. He is dressed for travel in a fur coat, boots, and a fur cap.*)

NORA. (*going toward him*). Talk softly. My husband's home.

KROGSTAD. Well, good for him.

NORA. What do you want?

KROGSTAD. Some information.

NORA. Hurry up, then. What is it?

KROGSTAD. You know, of course, that I got my notice.

NORA. I couldn't prevent it, Mr. Krogstad. I fought for you to the bitter end, but nothing worked.

KROGSTAD. Does your husband's love for you run so thin? He knows everything I can expose you to, and all the same he dares to—

NORA. How can you imagine he knows anything about this?

KROGSTAD. Ah, no—I can't imagine it either, now. It's not at all like my fine Torvald Helmer to have so much guts—

NORA. Mr. Krogstad, I demand respect for my husband!

KROGSTAD. Why, of course—all due respect. But since the lady's keeping it so carefully hidden, may I presume to ask if you're also a bit better informed than yesterday about what you've actually done?

NORA. More than you ever could teach me.

KROGSTAD. Yes, I *am* such an awful lawyer.

NORA. What is it you want from me?

KROGSTAD. Just a glimpse of how you are, Mrs. Helmer. I've been thinking about you all day long. A cashier, a night-court scribbler, a—well, a type like me also has a little of what they call a heart, you know.

NORA. Then show it. Think of my children.

KROGSTAD. Did you or your husband ever think of mine? But never mind. I simply wanted to tell you that you don't need to take this thing too seriously. For the present, I'm not proceeding with any action.

NORA. Oh no, really! Well—I knew that.

KROGSTAD. Everything can be settled in a friendly spirit. It doesn't have to get around town at all; it can stay just among us three.

NORA. My husband must never know anything of this.

KROGSTAD. How can you manage that? Perhaps you can pay me the balance?

NORA. No, not right now.

KROGSTAD. Or you know some way of raising the money in a day or two?

NORA. No way that I'm willing to use.

KROGSTAD. Well, it wouldn't have done you any good, anyway. If you stood in front of me with a fistful of bills, you still couldn't buy your signature back.

NORA. Then tell me what you're going to do with it.

KROGSTAD. I'll just hold onto it—keep it on file. There's no outsider who'll even get wind of it. So if you've been thinking of taking some desperate step—

NORA. I have.

KROGSTAD. Been thinking of running away from home—

NORA. I have!

KROGSTAD. Or even of something worse—

NORA. How could you guess that?

KROGSTAD. You can drop those thoughts.

NORA. How could you guess I was thinking of *that*?

KROGSTAD. Most of us think about *that* at first. I thought about it too, but I discovered I hadn't the courage—

NORA (*lifelessly*). I don't either.

KROGSTAD (*relieved*). That's true, you haven't the courage? You too?

NORA. I don't have it—I don't have it.

KROGSTAD. It would be terribly stupid, anyway. After that first storm at home blows out, why, then— I have here in my pocket a letter for your husband—

NORA. Telling everything?

KROGSTAD. As charitably as possible.

NORA (*quickly*). He mustn't ever get that letter. Tear it up. I'll find some way to get money.

KROGSTAD. Beg pardon, Mrs. Helmer, but I think I just told you—

NORA. Oh, I don't mean the money I owe you. Let me know how much you want from my husband, and I'll manage it.

KROGSTAD. I don't want any money from your husband.

NORA. What do you want, then?

KROGSTAD. I'll tell you what. I want to recoup, Mrs. Helmer; I want to get on in the world—and there's where your husband can help me. For a year and a half I've kept myself clean of anything disreputable—all that time struggling with the worst conditions; but I was satisfied, working my way up step by step. Now I've been written right off, and I'm just not in the mood to come crawling back. I tell you, I want to move on. I want to get back in the bank—in a better position. Your husband can set up a job for me—

NORA. He'll never do that!

KROGSTAD. He'll do it. I know him. He won't dare breathe a word of protest. And once I'm in there together with him, you just wait and see! Inside of a year, I'll be the manager's right-hand man. It'll be Nils Krogstad, not Torvald Helmer, who runs the bank.

NORA. You'll never see the day!

KROGSTAD. Maybe you think you can—

NORA. I have the courage now—for *that*.

KROGSTAD. Oh, you don't scare me. A smart, spoiled lady like you—

NORA. You'll see; you'll see!

KROGSTAD. Under the ice, maybe? Down in the freezing, coal-black water? There, till you float up in the spring, ugly, unrecognizable, with your hair falling out—

NORA. You don't frighten me.

KROGSTAD. Nor do you frighten me. One doesn't do these things, Mrs. Helmer. Besides, what good would it be? I'd still have him safe in my pocket.

NORA. Afterwards? When I'm no longer—?

KROGSTAD. Are you forgetting that *I'll* be in control then over your final reputation? (NORA *stands speechless, staring at him.*) Good; now I've warned you. Don't do anything stupid. When Helmer's read my letter, I'll be waiting for his reply. And bear in mind that it's your husband himself who's forced me back to my old ways. I'll never forgive him for that. Good-bye, Mrs. Helmer. (*He goes out through the hall.*)

NORA (*goes to the hall door, opens it a crack, and listens*). He's gone. Didn't leave the letter. Oh no, no, that's impossible too! (*Opening the door more and more.*) What's that? He's standing outside—not going downstairs. He's thinking it over? Maybe he'll—? (*A letter falls in the mailbox; then* KROGSTAD's *footsteps are heard, dying away down a flight of stairs.* NORA *gives a muffled cry and runs over toward the sofa table. A short pause.*) In the mailbox. (*Slips warily over to the hall door.*) It's lying there. Torvald, Torvald—now we're lost!

MRS. LINDE (*entering with the costume from the room, left*). There now, I can't see anything else to mend. Perhaps you'd like to try—

NORA (*in a hoarse whisper*). Kristine, come here.

MRS. LINDE (*tossing the dress on the sofa*). What's wrong? You look upset.

NORA. Come here. See that letter? *There!* Look—through the glass in the mailbox.

MRS. LINDE. Yes, yes, I see it.

NORA. That letter's from Krogstad—

MRS. LINDE. No a—it's Krogstad who loaned you the money!

NORA. Yes, and now Torvald will find out everything.

MRS. LINDE. Believe me, Nora, it's best for both of you.

NORA. There's more you don't know. I forged a name.

MRS. LINDE. But for heaven's sake—?

NORA. I only want to tell you that, Kristine, so that you can be my witness.

MRS. LINDE. Witness? Why should I—?

NORA. If I should go out of my mind—it could easily happen—

MRS. LINDE. Nora!

NORA. Or anything else occurred—so I couldn't be present here—

MRS. LINDE. Nora, Nora, you aren't yourself at all!

NORA. And someone should try to take on the whole weight, all of the guilt, you follow me—

MRS. LINDE. Yes, of course, but why do you think—?

NORA. Then you're the witness that it isn't true, Kristine. I'm very much myself; my mind right now is perfectly clear; and I'm telling you: nobody else has known about this; I alone did everything. Remember that.

MRS. LINDE. I will. But I don't understand all this.

NORA. Oh, how could you ever understand it? It's the miracle now that's going to take place.

MRS. LINDE. The miracle?

NORA. Yes, the miracle. But it's so awful, Kristine. It mustn't take place, not for anything in the world.

MRS. LINDE. I'm going right over and talk with Krogstad.

NORA. Don't go near him; he'll do you some terrible harm!

MRS. LINDE. There was a time once when he'd gladly have done anything for me.

NORA. He?

MRS. LINDE. Where does he live?

NORA. Oh, how do I know? Yes. (*Searches in her pocket.*) Here's his card. But the letter, the letter—!

HELMER (*from the study, knocking on the door*). Nora!

NORA (*with a cry of fear*). Oh! What is it? What do you want?

HELMER.   Now, now, don't be so frightened. We're not coming in. You locked the door—are you trying on the dress?

NORA.   Yes, I'm trying it. I'll look just beautiful, Torvald.

MRS. LINDE (*who has read the card*).   He's living right around the corner.

NORA.   Yes, but what's the use? We're lost. The letter's in the box.

MRS. LINDE.   And your husband has the key?

NORA.   Yes, always.

MRS. LINDE.   Krogstad can ask for his letter back unread; he can find some excuse—

NORA.   But it's just this time that Torvald usually—

MRS. LINDE.   Stall him. Keep him in there. I'll be back as quick as I can. (*She hurries out through the hall entrance.*)

NORA (*goes to* HELMER's *door, opens it, and peers in*). Torvald!

HELMER (*from the inner study*).   Well—does one dare set foot in one's own living room at last? Come on, Rank, now we'll get a look— (*In the doorway.*) But what's this?

NORA.   What, Torvald dear?

HELMER.   Rank had me expecting some grand masquerade.

RANK (*in the doorway*).   That was my impression, but I must have been wrong.

NORA.   No one can admire me in my splendor—not till tomorrow.

HELMER.   But Nora dear, you look so exhausted. Have you practiced too hard?

NORA.   No, I haven't practiced at all yet.

HELMER.   You know, it's necessary—

NORA.   Oh, it's absolutely necessary, Torvald. But I can't get anywhere without your help. I've forgotten the whole thing completely.

HELMER.   Ah, we'll soon take care of that.

NORA.   Yes, take care of me, Torvald, please! Promise me that? Oh, I'm so nervous. That big party— You must give up everything this evening for me. No business—don't even touch your pen. Yes? Dear Torvald, promise?

HELMER.   It's a promise. Tonight I'm totally at your serv-

ice—you little helpless thing. Hm—but first there's one thing
I want to— (*Goes toward the hall door.*)

NORA.   What are you looking for?

HELMER.   Just to see if there's any mail.

NORA.   No, no, don't do that, Torvald!

HELMER.   Now what?

NORA.   Torvald, please. There isn't any.

HELMER.   Let me look, though. (*Starts out. NORA, at the
piano, strikes the first notes of the tarantella. HELMER, at
the door, stops.*) Aha!

NORA.   I can't dance tomorrow if I don't practice with you.

HELMER (*going over to her*).   Nora dear, are you really
so frightened?

NORA.   Yes, so terribly frightened. Let me practice right
now; there's still time before dinner. Oh, sit down and play
for me, Torvald. Direct me. Teach me, the way you always
have.

HELMER.   Gladly, if it's what you want. (*Sits at the
piano.*)

NORA (*snatches the tambourine up from the box, then a
long, varicolored shawl, which she throws around herself,
whereupon she springs forward and cries out:*)   Play for me
now! Now I'll dance!

> (HELMER *plays and* NORA *dances.* RANK *stands be-
> hind* HELMER *at the piano and looks on.*)

HELMER (*as he plays*).   Slower. Slow down.

NORA.   Can't change it.

HELMER.   Not so violent, Nora!

NORA.   Has to be just like this.

HELMER (*stopping*).   No, no, that won't do at all.

NORA (*laughing and swinging her tambourine*).   Isn't that
what I told you?

RANK.   Let me play for her.

HELMER (*getting up*).   Yes, go on. I can teach her more
easily then.

> (RANK *sits at the piano and plays;* NORA *dances
> more and more wildly.* HELMER *has stationed
> himself by the stove and repeatedly gives her
> directions; she seems not to hear them; her hair
> loosens and falls over her shoulders; she does*

not notice, but goes on dancing. MRS. LINDE *enters.*)

MRS. LINDE (*standing dumbfounded at the door*). Ah—!

NORA (*still dancing*). See what fun, Kristine!

HELMER. But Nora darling, you dance as if your life were at stake.

NORA. And it is.

HELMER. Rank, stop! This is pure madness. Stop it, I say!

(RANK *breaks off playing, and* NORA *halts abruptly*).

HELMER (*going over to her*). I never would have believed it. You've forgotten everything I taught you.

NORA (*throwing away the tambourine*). You see for yourself.

HELMER. Well, there's certainly room for instruction here.

NORA. Yes, you see how important it is. You've got to teach me to the very last minute. Promise me that, Torvald?

HELMER. You can bet on it.

NORA. You mustn't, either today or tomorrow, think about anything else but me; you mustn't open any letters—or the mailbox—

HELMER. Ah, it's still the fear of that man—

NORA. Oh yes, yes, that too.

HELMER. Nora, it's written all over you—there's already a letter from him out there.

NORA. I don't know. I guess so. But you mustn't read such things now; there mustn't be anything ugly between us before it's all over.

RANK (*quietly to* HELMER). You shouldn't deny her.

HELMER (*putting his arm around her*). The child can have her way. But tomorrow night, after you've danced—

NORA. Then you'll be free.

MAID (*in the doorway, right*). Ma'am, dinner is served.

NORA. We'll be wanting champagne, Helene.

MAID. Very good, ma'am. (*Goes out.*)

HELMER. So—a regular banquet, hm?

NORA. Yes, a banquet—champagne till daybreak! (*Calling out.*) And some macaroons, Helene. Heaps of them—just this once.

HELMER (*taking her hands*). Now, now, now—no hysterics. Be my own little lark again.

NORA. Oh, I will soon enough. But go on in—and you, Dr. Rank. Kristine, help me put up my hair.

RANK (*whispering, as they go*). There's nothing wrong—really wrong, is there?

HELMER. Oh, of course not. It's nothing more than this childish anxiety I was telling you about. (*They go out, right.*)

NORA. Well?

MRS. LINDE. Left town.

NORA. I could see by your face.

MRS. LINDE. He'll be home tomorrow evening. I wrote him a note.

NORA. You shouldn't have. Don't try to stop anything now. After all, it's a wonderful joy, this waiting here for the miracle.

MRS. LINDE. What is it you're waiting for?

NORA. Oh, you can't understand that. Go in to them; I'll be along in a moment.

> (MRS. LINDE *goes into the dining room.* NORA *stands a short while as if composing herself; then she looks at her watch.*)

NORA. Five. Seven hours to midnight. Twenty-four hours to the midnight after, and then the tarantella's done. Seven and twenty-four? Thirty-one hours to live.

HELMER (*in the doorway, right*). What's become of the little lark?

NORA (*going toward him with open arms*). Here's your lark!

⤙ACT THREE⤚

Same scene. The table, with chairs around it, has been moved to the center of the room. A lamp on the table is lit. The hall door stands open. Dance music drifts down from the floor above. MRS. LINDE *sits at the table, absently paging through a book, trying to read, but apparently unable to focus her thoughts. Once or twice she pauses, tensely listening for a sound at the outer entrance.*

MRS. LINDE (*glancing at her watch*). Not yet—and there's hardly any time left. If only he's not—(*Listening again.*) Ah, there he is. (*She goes out in the hall and cautiously opens the outer door. Quiet footsteps are heard on the stairs. She whispers*:) Come in. Nobody's here.

KROGSTAD (*in the doorway*). I found a note from you at home. What's back of all this?

MRS. LINDE. I just *had* to talk to you.

KROGSTAD. Oh? And it just *had* to be here in this house?

MRS. LINDE. At my place it was impossible; my room hasn't a private entrance. Come in; we're all alone. The maid's asleep, and the Helmers are at the dance upstairs.

KROGSTAD (*entering the room*). Well, well, the Helmers are dancing tonight? Really?

MRS. LINDE. Yes, why not?

KROGSTAD. How true—why not?

MRS. LINDE. All right, Krogstad, let's talk.

KROGSTAD. Do we two have anything more to talk about?

MRS. LINDE. We have a great deal to talk about.

KROGSTAD. I wouldn't have thought so.

MRS. LINDE. No, because you've never understood me, really.

KROGSTAD. Was there anything more to understand—except what's all too common in life? A calculating woman throws over a man the moment a better catch comes by.

MRS. LINDE. You think I'm so thoroughly calculating? You think I broke it off lightly?

KROGSTAD. Didn't you?

MRS. LINDE. Nils—is that what you really thought?

KROGSTAD. If you cared, then why did you write me the way you did?

MRS. LINDE. What else could I do? If I had to break off with you, then it was my job as well to root out everything you felt for me.

KROGSTAD (*wringing his hands*). So that was it. And this —all this, simply for money!

MRS. LINDE. Don't forget I had a helpless mother and two small brothers. We couldn't wait for you, Nils; you had such a long road ahead of you then.

KROGSTAD. That may be; but you still hadn't the right to abandon me for somebody else's sake.

MRS. LINDE. Yes—I don't know. So many, many times I've asked myself if I did have that right.

KROGSTAD (*more softly*). When I lost you, it was as if all the solid ground dissolved from under my feet. Look at me; I'm a half-drowned man now, hanging onto a wreck.

MRS. LINDE. Help may be near.

KROGSTAD. It was near—but then you came and blocked it off.

MRS. LINDE. Without my knowing it, Nils. Today for the first time I learned that it's you I'm replacing at the bank.

KROGSTAD. All right—I believe you. But now that you know, will you step aside?

MRS. LINDE. No, because that wouldn't benefit you in the slightest.

KROGSTAD. Not "benefit" me, hm! I'd step aside anyway.

MRS. LINDE. I've learned to be realistic. Life and hard, bitter necessity have taught me that.

KROGSTAD. And life's taught me never to trust fine phrases.

MRS. LINDE. Then life's taught you a very sound thing. But you do have to trust in actions, don't you?

KROGSTAD. What does that mean?

MRS. LINDE. You said you were hanging on like a half-drowned man to a wreck.

KROGSTAD. I've good reason to say that.

MRS. LINDE. I'm also like a half-drowned woman on a wreck. No one to suffer with; no one to care for.

KROGSTAD. You made your choice.

MRS. LINDE. There wasn't any choice then.

KROGSTAD. So—what of it?

MRS. LINDE. Nils, if only we two shipwrecked people could reach across to each other.

KROGSTAD. What are you saying?

MRS. LINDE. Two on one wreck are at least better off than each on his own.

KROGSTAD. Kristine!

MRS. LINDE. Why do you think I came into town?

KROGSTAD. Did you really have some thought of me?

MRS. LINDE. I have to work to go on living. All my born days, as long as I can remember, I've worked, and it's been my best and my only joy. But now I'm completely alone in the world; it frightens me to be so empty and lost. To work for yourself—there's no joy in that. Nils, give me something—someone to work for.

KROGSTAD. I don't believe all this. It's just some hysterical feminine urge to go out and make a noble sacrifice.

MRS. LINDE. Have you ever found me to be hysterical?

KROGSTAD. Can you honestly mean this? Tell me—do you know everything about my past?

MRS. LINDE. Yes.

KROGSTAD. And you know what they think I'm worth around here.

MRS. LINDE. From what you were saying before, it would seem that with me you could have been another person.

KROGSTAD. I'm positive of that.

MRS. LINDE. Couldn't it happen still?

KROGSTAD. Kristine—you're saying this in all seriousness? Yes, you are! I can see it in you. And do you really have the courage, then—?

MRS. LINDE. I need to have someone to care for; and your children need a mother. We both need each other. Nils, I have faith that you're good at heart—I'll risk everything together with you.

KROGSTAD (gripping her hands). Kristine, thank you, thank you— Now I know I can win back a place in their eyes. Yes—but I forgot—

MRS. LINDE (listening). Shh! The tarantella. Go now! Go on!

KROGSTAD. Why? What is it?

MRS. LINDE. Hear the dance up there? When that's over, they'll be coming down.

KROGSTAD. Oh, then I'll go. But—it's all pointless. Of course, you don't know the move I made against the Helmers.

MRS. LINDE. Yes, Nils, I know.

KROGSTAD. And all the same, you have the courage to—?

MRS. LINDE. I know how far despair can drive a man like you.

KROGSTAD. Oh, if I only could take it all back.

MRS. LINDE. You easily could—your letter's still lying in the mailbox.

KROGSTAD. Are you sure of that?

MRS. LINDE. Positive. But—

KROGSTAD (looks at her searchingly). Is that the meaning of it, then? You'll save your friend at any price. Tell me straight out. Is that it?

MRS. LINDE. Nils—anyone who's sold herself for somebody else once isn't going to do it again.

KROGSTAD. I'll demand my letter back.

MRS. LINDE. No, no.

KROGSTAD. Yes, of course. I'll stay here till Helmer comes down; I'll tell him to give me my letter again—that it only involves my dismissal—that he shouldn't read it—

MRS. LINDE. No, Nils, don't call the letter back.

KROGSTAD. But wasn't that exactly why you wrote me to come here?

MRS. LINDE. Yes, in that first panic. But it's been a whole day and night since then, and in that time I've seen such incredible things in this house. Helmer's got to learn everything; this dreadful secret has to be aired; those two have to come to a full understanding; all these lies and evasions can't go on.

KROGSTAD. Well, then, if you want to chance it. But at least there's one thing I can do, and do right away—

MRS. LINDE (listening). Go now, go, quick! The dance is over. We're not safe another second.

KROGSTAD. I'll wait for you downstairs.

MRS. LINDE. Yes, please do; take me home.

KROGSTAD. I can't believe it; I've never been so happy. (He leaves by way of the outer door; the door between the room and the hall stays open.)

MRS. LINDE (*straightening up a bit and getting together her street clothes*). How different now! How different! Someone to work for, to live for—a home to build. Well, it is worth the try! Oh, if they'd only come! (*Listening.*) Ah, there they are. Bundle up. (*She picks up her hat and coat.* NORA's *and* HELMER's *voices can be heard outside; a key turns in the lock, and* HELMER *brings* NORA *into the hall almost by force. She is wearing the Italian costume with a large black shawl about her; he has on evening dress, with a black domino open over it.*)

NORA (*struggling in the doorway*). No, no, no, not inside! I'm going up again. I don't want to leave so soon.

HELMER. But Nora dear—

NORA. Oh, I beg you, please, Torvald. From the bottom of my heart, *please*—only an hour more!

HELMER. Not a single minute, Nora darling. You know our agreement. Come on, in we go; you'll catch cold out here. (*In spite of her resistance, he gently draws her into the room.*)

MRS. LINDE. Good evening.

NORA. Kristine!

HELMER. Why, Mrs. Linde—are you here so late?

MRS. LINDE. Yes, I'm sorry, but I did want to see Nora in costume.

NORA. Have you been sitting here, waiting for me?

MRS. LINDE. Yes. I didn't come early enough; you were all upstairs; and then I thought I really couldn't leave without seeing you.

HELMER (*removing* NORA's *shawl*). Yes, take a good look. She's worth looking at, I can tell you that, Mrs. Linde. Isn't she lovely?

MRS. LINDE. Yes, I should say—

HELMER. A dream of loveliness, isn't she? That's what everyone thought at the party, too. But she's horribly stubborn—this sweet little thing. What's to be done with her? Can you imagine, I almost had to use force to pry her away.

NORA. Oh, Torvald, you're going to regret you didn't indulge me, even for just a half hour more.

HELMER. There, you see. She danced her tarantella and got a tumultuous hand—which was well earned, although the performance may have been a bit too naturalistic—I mean

it rather overstepped the proprieties of art. But never mind—
what's important is, she made a success, an overwhelming
success. You think I could let her stay on after that and
spoil the effect? Oh no; I took my lovely little Capri girl—
my capricious little Capri girl, I should say—took her under
my arm; one quick tour of the ballroom, a curtsy to every
side, and then—as they say in novels—the beautiful vision
disappeared. An exit should always be effective, Mrs. Linde,
but that's what I can't get Nora to grasp. Phew, it's hot in
here. (*Flings the domino on a chair and opens the door to his
room.*) Why's it dark in here? Oh yes, of course. Excuse me.
(*He goes in and lights a couple of candles.*)

NORA (*in a sharp, breathless whisper*). So?

MRS. LINDE (*quietly*). I talked with him.

NORA. And—?

MRS. LINDE. Nora—you must tell your husband everything.

NORA (*dully*). I knew it.

MRS. LINDE. You've got nothing to fear from Krogstad,
but you have to speak out.

NORA. I won't tell.

MRS. LINDE. Then the letter will.

NORA. Thanks, Kristine. I know now what's to be done.
Shh!

HELMER (*reentering*). Well, then, Mrs. Linde—have you
admired her?

MRS. LINDE. Yes, and now I'll say good night.

HELMER. Oh, come, so soon? Is this yours, this knitting?

MRS. LINDE. Yes, thanks. I nearly forgot it.

HELMER. Do you knit, then?

MRS. LINDE. Oh yes.

HELMER. You know what? You should embroider instead.

MRS. LINDE. Really? Why?

HELMER. Yes, because it's a lot prettier. See here, one
holds the embroidery so, in the left hand, and then one
guides the needle with the right—so—in an easy, sweeping
curve—right?

MRS. LINDE. Yes, I guess that's—

HELMER. But, on the other hand, knitting—it can never
be anything but ugly. Look, see here, the arms tucked in, the
knitting needles going up and down—there's something

Chinese about it. Ah, that was really a glorious champagne they served.

MRS. LINDE. Yes, good night, Nora, and don't be stubborn anymore.

HELMER. Well put, Mrs. Linde!

MRS. LINDE. Good night, Mr. Helmer.

HELMER (*accompanying her to the door*). Good night, good night. I hope you get home all right. I'd be very happy to—but you don't have far to go. Good night, good night. (*She leaves. He shuts the door after her and returns.*) There, now, at last we got her out the door. She's a deadly bore, that creature.

NORA. Aren't you pretty tired, Torvald?

HELMER. No, not a bit.

NORA. You're not sleepy?

HELMER. Not at all. On the contrary, I'm feeling quite exhilarated. But you? Yes, you really look tired and sleepy.

NORA. Yes, I'm very tired. Soon now I'll sleep.

HELMER. See! You see! I was right all along that we shouldn't stay longer.

NORA. Whatever you do is always right.

HELMER (*kissing her brow*). Now my little lark talks sense. Say, did you notice what a time Rank was having tonight?

NORA. Oh, was he? I didn't get to speak with him.

HELMER. I scarcely did either, but it's a long time since I've seen him in such high spirits. (*Gazes at her a moment, then comes nearer her.*) Hm—it's marvelous, though, to be back home again—to be completely alone with you. Oh, you bewitchingly lovely young woman!

NORA. Torvald, don't look at me like that!

HELMER. Can't I look at my richest treasure? At all that beauty that's mine, mine alone—completely and utterly.

NORA (*moving around to the other side of the table*). You mustn't talk to me that way tonight.

HELMER (*following her*). The tarantella is still in your blood, I can see—and it makes you even more enticing. Listen. The guests are beginning to go. (*Dropping his voice.*) Nora—it'll soon be quiet through this whole house.

NORA. Yes, I hope so.

HELMER. You do, don't you, my love? Do you realize—

when I'm out at a party like this with you—do you know why I talk to you so little, and keep such a distance away; just send you a stolen look now and then—you know why I do it? It's because I'm imagining then that you're my secret darling, my secret young bride-to-be, and that no one suspects there's anything between us.

NORA. Yes, yes; oh, yes, I know you're always thinking of me.

HELMER. And then when we leave and I place the shawl over those fine young rounded shoulders—over that wonderful curving neck—then I pretend that you're my young bride, that we're just coming from the wedding, that for the first time I'm bringing you into my house—that for the first time I'm alone with you—completely alone with you, your trembling young beauty! All this evening I've longed for nothing but you. When I saw you turn and sway in the tarantella—my blood was pounding till I couldn't stand it —that's why I brought you down here so early—

NORA. Go away, Torvald! Leave me alone. I don't want all this.

HELMER. What do you mean? Nora, you're teasing me. You will, won't you? Aren't I your husband—?

(*A knock at the outside door.*)

NORA (*startled*). What's that?

HELMER (*going toward the hall*). Who is it?

RANK (*outside*). It's me. May I come in a moment?

HELMER (*with quiet irritation*). Oh, what does he want now? (*Aloud.*) Hold on. (*Goes and opens the door.*) Oh, how nice that you didn't just pass us by!

RANK. I thought I heard your voice, and then I wanted so badly to have a look in. (*Lightly glancing about.*) Ah, me, these old familiar haunts. You have it snug and cozy in here, you two.

HELMER. You seemed to be having it pretty cozy upstairs, too.

RANK. Absolutely. Why shouldn't I? Why not take in everything in life? As much as you can, anyway, and as long as you can. The wine was superb—

HELMER. The champagne especially.

RANK. You noticed that too? It's amazing how much I could guzzle down.

NORA. Torvald also drank a lot of champagne this evening.

RANK. Oh?

NORA. Yes, and that always makes him so entertaining.

RANK. Well, why shouldn't one have a pleasant evening after a well-spent day?

HELMER. Well spent? I'm afraid I can't claim that.

RANK (*slapping him on the back*). But I can, you see!

NORA. Dr. Rank, you must have done some scientific research today.

RANK. Quite so.

HELMER. Come now—little Nora talking about scientific research!

NORA. And can I congratulate you on the results?

RANK. Indeed you may.

NORA. Then they were good?

RANK. The best possible for both doctor and patient—certainty.

NORA (*quickly and searchingly*). Certainty?

RANK. Complete certainty. So don't I owe myself a gay evening afterwards?

NORA. Yes, you're right, Dr. Rank.

HELMER. I'm with you—just so long as you don't have to suffer for it in the morning.

RANK. Well, one never gets something for nothing in life.

NORA. Dr. Rank—are you very fond of masquerade parties?

RANK. Yes, if there's a good array of odd disguises—

NORA. Tell me, what should we two go as at the next masquerade?

HELMER. You little featherhead—already thinking of the next!

RANK. We two? I'll tell you what: you must go as Charmed Life—

HELMER. Yes, but find a costume for *that!*

RANK. Your wife can appear just as she looks every day.

HELMER. That was nicely put. But don't you know what you're going to be?

RANK. Yes, Helmer, I've made up my mind.

HELMER. Well?

RANK. At the next masquerade I'm going to be invisible.

HELMER. That's a funny idea.

RANK. They say there's a hat—black, huge—have you never heard of the hat that makes you invisible? You put it on, and then no one on earth can see you.

HELMER (*suppressing a smile*). Ah, of course.

RANK. But I'm quite forgetting what I came for. Helmer, give me a cigar, one of the dark Havanas.

HELMER. With the greatest pleasure. (*Holds out his case.*)

RANK. Thanks. (*Takes one and cuts off the tip.*)

NORA (*striking a match*). Let me give you a light.

RANK. Thank you. (*She holds the match for him; he lights the cigar.*) And now good-bye.

HELMER. Good-bye, good-bye, old friend.

NORA. Sleep well, Doctor.

RANK. Thanks for that wish.

NORA. Wish me the same.

RANK. You? All right, if you like— Sleep well. And thanks for the light. (*He nods to them both and leaves.*)

HELMER (*his voice subdued*). He's been drinking heavily.

NORA (*absently*). Could be. (HELMER *takes his keys from his pocket and goes out in the hall.*) Torvald—what are you after?

HELMER. Got to empty the mailbox; it's nearly full. There won't be room for the morning papers.

NORA. Are you working tonight?

HELMER. You know I'm not. Why—what's this? Someone's been at the lock.

NORA. At the lock—?

HELMER. Yes, I'm positive. What do you suppose—? I can't imagine one of the maids—? Here's a broken hairpin. Nora, it's yours—

NORA (*quickly*). Then it must be the children—

HELMER. You'd better break them of that. Hm, hm— well, opened it after all. (*Takes the contents out and calls into the kitchen.*) Helene! Helene, would you put out the lamp in the hall. (*He returns to the room, shutting the hall door, then displays the handful of mail.*) Look how it's piled up. (*Sorting through them.*) Now what's this?

NORA (*at the window*). The letter! Oh, Torvald, no!

HELMER. Two calling cards—from Rank.

NORA. From Dr. Rank?

HELMER (*examining them*). "Dr. Rank, Consulting Physician." They were on top. He must have dropped them in as he left.

NORA.   Is there anything on them?

HELMER.   There's a black cross over the name. See? That's a gruesome notion. He could almost be announcing his own death.

NORA.   That's just what he's doing.

HELMER.   What! You've heard something? Something he's told you?

NORA.   Yes. That when those cards came, he'd be taking his leave of us. He'll shut himself in now and die.

HELMER.   Ah, my poor friend! Of course I knew he wouldn't be here much longer. But so soon— And then to hide himself away like a wounded animal.

NORA.   If it has to happen, then it's best it happens in silence—don't you think so, Torvald?

HELMER (*pacing up and down*).   He'd grown right into our lives. I simply can't imagine him gone. He with his suffering and loneliness—like a dark cloud setting off our sunlit happiness. Well, maybe it's best this way. For him, at least. (*Standing still.*) And maybe for us too, Nora. Now we're thrown back on each other, completely. (*Embracing her.*) Oh you, my darling wife, how can I hold you close enough? You know what, Nora—time and again I've wished you were in some terrible danger, just so I could stake my life and soul and everything, for your sake.

NORA (*tearing herself away, her voice firm and decisive*). Now you must read your mail, Torvald.

HELMER.   No, no, not tonight. I want to stay with you, dearest.

NORA.   With a dying friend on your mind?

HELMER.   You're right. We've both had a shock. There's ugliness between us—these thoughts of death and corruption. We'll have to get free of them first. Until then—we'll stay apart.

NORA (*clinging about his neck*).   Torvald—good night! Good night!

HELMER (*kissing her on the cheek*).   Good night, little songbird. Sleep well, Nora. I'll be reading my mail now. (*He takes the letters into his room and shuts the door after him.*)

NORA (*with bewildered glances, groping about, seizing* HELMER'*s domino, throwing it around her, and speaking in short, hoarse, broken whispers*). Never see him again. Never, never. (*Putting her shawl over her head.*) Never see the children either—them, too. Never, never. Oh, the freezing black water! The depths—down— Oh, I wish it were over— He has it now; he's reading it—now. Oh no, no, not yet. Torvald, good-bye, you and the children— (*She starts for the hall; as she does,* HELMER *throws open his door and stands with an open letter in his hand.*)

HELMER. Nora!

NORA (*screams*). Oh—!

HELMER. What is this? You know what's in this letter?

NORA. Yes, I know. Let me go! Let me out!

HELMER (*holding her back*). Where are you going?

NORA (*struggling to break loose*). You can't save me, Torvald!

HELMER (*slumping back*). True! Then it's true what he writes? How horrible! No, no, it's impossible—it can't be true.

NORA. It *is* true. I've loved you more than all this world.

HELMER. Ah, none of your slippery tricks.

NORA (*taking one step toward him*). Torvald—!

HELMER. What *is* this you've blundered into!

NORA. Just let me loose. You're not going to suffer for my sake. You're not going to take on my guilt.

HELMER. No more playacting. (*Locks the hall door.*) You stay right here and give me a reckoning. You understand what you've done? Answer! You understand?

NORA (*looking squarely at him, her face hardening*). Yes. I'm beginning to understand everything now.

HELMER (*striding about*). Oh, what an awful awakening! In all these eight years—she who was my pride and joy—a hypocrite, a liar—worse, worse—a criminal! How infinitely disgusting it all is! The shame! (NORA *says nothing and goes on looking straight at him. He stops in front of her.*) I should have suspected something of the kind. I should have known. All your father's flimsy values— Be still! All your father's flimsy values have come out in you. No religion, no morals, no sense of duty— Oh, how I'm punished for letting him off! I did it for your sake, and you repay me like this.

NORA. Yes, like this.

HELMER. Now you've wrecked all my happiness—ruined my whole future. Oh, it's awful to think of. I'm in a cheap little grafter's hands; he can do anything he wants with me, ask for anything, play with me like a puppet—and I can't breathe a word. I'll be swept down miserably into the depths on account of a featherbrained woman.

NORA. When I'm gone from this world, you'll be free.

HELMER. Oh, quit posing. Your father had a mess of those speeches too. What good would that ever do me if you were gone from this world, as you say? Not the slightest. He can still make the whole thing known; and if he does, I could be falsely suspected as your accomplice. They might even think that I was behind it—that I put you up to it. And all that I can thank you for—you that I've coddled the whole of our marriage. Can you see now what you've done to me?

NORA (*icily calm*). Yes.

HELMER. It's so incredible, I just can't grasp it. But we'll have to patch up whatever we can. Take off the shawl. I said, take it off! I've got to appease him somehow or other. The thing has to be hushed up at any cost. And as for you and me, it's got to seem like everything between us is just as it was—to the outside world, that is. You'll go right on living in this house, of course. But you can't be allowed to bring up the children; I don't dare trust you with them— Oh, to have to say this to someone I've loved so much! Well, that's done with. From now on happiness doesn't matter; all that matters is saving the bits and pieces, the appearance— (*The doorbell rings.* HELMER *starts.*) What's that? And so late. Maybe the worst—? You think he'd—? Hide, Nora! Say you're sick. (NORA *remains standing motionless.* HELMER *goes and opens the door.*)

MAID (*half dressed, in the hall*). A letter for Mrs. Helmer.

HELMER. I'll take it. (*Snatches the letter and shuts the door.*) Yes, it's from him. You don't get it; I'm reading it myself.

NORA. Then read it.

HELMER (*by the lamp*). I hardly dare. We may be ruined, you and I. But—I've got to know. (*Rips open the letter, skims through a few lines, glances at an enclosure, then cries out joyfully.*) Nora! (NORA *looks inquiringly at him.*) Nora! Wait—better check it again— Yes, yes, it's true. I'm saved. Nora, I'm saved!

NORA. And I?

HELMER. You too, of course. We're both saved, both of us. Look. He's sent back your note. He says he's sorry and ashamed—that a happy development in his life—oh, who cares what he says! Nora, we're saved! No one can hurt you. Oh, Nora, Nora—but first, this ugliness all has to go. Let me see— (*Takes a look at the note.*) No, I don't want to see it; I want the whole thing to fade like a dream. (*Tears the note and both letters to pieces, throws them into the stove and watches them burn.*) There—now there's nothing left— He wrote that since Christmas Eve you— Oh, they must have been three terrible days for you, Nora.

NORA. I fought a hard fight.

HELMER. And suffered pain and saw no escape but— No, we're not going to dwell on anything unpleasant. We'll just be grateful and keep on repeating: it's over now, it's over! You hear me, Nora? You don't seem to realize—it's over. What's it mean—that frozen look? Oh, poor little Nora, I understand. You can't believe I've forgiven you. But I have, Nora; I swear I have. I know that what you did, you did out of love for me.

NORA. That's true.

HELMER. You loved me the way a wife ought to love her husband. It's simply the means that you couldn't judge. But you think I love you any the less for not knowing how to handle your affairs? No, no—just lean on me; I'll guide you and teach you. I wouldn't be a man if this feminine helplessness didn't make you twice as attractive to me. You mustn't mind those sharp words I said—that was all in the first confusion of thinking my world had collapsed. I've forgiven you, Nora; I swear I've forgiven you.

NORA. My thanks for your forgiveness. (*She goes out through the door, right.*)

HELMER. No, wait— (*Peers in.*) What are you doing in there?

NORA (*inside*). Getting out of my costume.

HELMER (*by the open door*). Yes, do that. Try to calm yourself and collect your thoughts again, my frightened little songbird. You can rest easy now; I've got wide wings to shelter you with. (*Walking about close by the door.*) How snug and nice our home is, Nora. You're safe here; I'll keep you like a hunted dove I've rescued out of a hawk's claws. I'll bring peace to your poor, shuddering heart. Gradually it'll

happen, Nora; you'll see. Tomorrow all this will look different to you; then everything will be as it was. I won't have
to go on repeating I forgive you; you'll feel it for yourself. How can you imagine I'd ever conceivably want to
disown you—or even blame you in any way? Ah, you don't
know a man's heart, Nora. For a man there's something indescribably sweet and satisfying in knowing he's forgiven his
wife—and forgiven her out of a full and open heart. It's as
if she belongs to him in two ways now: in a sense he's
given her fresh into the world again, and she's become his
wife and his child as well. From now on that's what you'll
be to me—you little, bewildered, helpless thing. Don't be afraid
of anything, Nora; just open your heart to me, and I'll be conscience and will to you both—(NORA *enters in her regular
clothes.*) What's this? Not in bed? You've changed your dress?

NORA.   Yes, Torvald, I've changed my dress.

HELMER.   But why now, so late?

NORA.   Tonight I'm not sleeping.

HELMER.   But Nora dear—

NORA (*looking at her watch*). It's still not so very late.
Sit down, Torvald; we have a lot to talk over. (*She sits at
one side of the table.*)

HELMER.   Nora—what is this? That hard expression—

NORA.   Sit down. This'll take some time. I have a lot to
say.

HELMER (*sitting at the table directly opposite her*). You
worry me, Nora. And I don't understand you.

NORA.   No, that's exactly it. You don't understand me.
And I've never understood you either—until tonight. No,
don't interrupt. You can just listen to what I say. We're
closing out accounts, Torvald.

HELMER.   How do you mean that?

NORA (*after a short pause*). Doesn't anything strike you
about our sitting here like this?

HELMER.   What's that?

NORA.   We've been married now eight years. Doesn't it
occur to you that this is the first time we two, you and I,
man and wife, have ever talked seriously together?

HELMER.   What do you mean—seriously?

NORA.   In eight whole years—longer even—right from our
first acquaintance, we've never exchanged a serious word on
any serious thing.

HELMER. You mean I should constantly go and involve you in problems you couldn't possibly help me with?

NORA. I'm not talking of problems. I'm saying that we've never sat down seriously together and tried to get to the bottom of anything.

HELMER. But dearest, what good would that ever do you?

NORA. That's the point right there: you've never understood me. I've been wronged greatly, Torvald—first by Papa, and then by you.

HELMER. What! By us—the two people who've loved you more than anyone else?

NORA (shaking her head). You never loved me. You've thought it fun to be in love with me, that's all.

HELMER. Nora, what a thing to say!

NORA. Yes, it's true now, Torvald. When I lived at home with Papa, he told me all his opinions, so I had the same ones too; or if they were different I hid them, since he wouldn't have cared for that. He used to call me his doll-child, and he played with me the way I played with my dolls. Then I came into your house—

HELMER. How can you speak of our marriage like that?

NORA (unperturbed). I mean, then I went from Papa's hands into yours. You arranged everything to your own taste, and so I got the same taste as you—or I pretended to; I can't remember. I guess a little of both, first one, then the other. Now when I look back, it seems as if I'd lived here like a beggar—just from hand to mouth. I've lived by doing tricks for you, Torvald. But that's the way you wanted it. It's a great sin what you and Papa did to me. You're to blame that nothing's become of me.

HELMER. Nora, how unfair and ungrateful you are! Haven't you been happy here?

NORA. No, never. I thought so—but I never have.

HELMER. Not—not happy!

NORA. No, only lighthearted. And you've always been so kind to me. But our home's been nothing but a playpen. I've been your doll-wife here, just as at home I was Papa's doll-child. And in turn the children have been my dolls. I thought it was fun when you played with me, just as they thought it fun when I played with them. That's been our marriage, Torvald.

HELMER. There's some truth in what you're saying—under all the raving exaggeration. But it'll all be different after this. Playtime's over; now for the schooling.

NORA. Whose schooling—mine or the children's?

HELMER. Both yours and the children's, dearest.

NORA. Oh, Torvald, you're not the man to teach me to be a good wife to you.

HELMER. And you can say that?

NORA. And I—how am I equipped to bring up children?

HELMER. Nora!

NORA. Didn't you say a moment ago that that was no job to trust me with?

HELMER. In a flare of temper! Why fasten on that?

NORA. Yes, but you were so very right. I'm not up to the job. There's another job I have to do first. I have to try to educate myself. You can't help me with that. I've got to do it alone. And that's why I'm leaving you now.

HELMER (*jumping up*). What's that?

NORA. I have to stand completely alone, if I'm ever going to discover myself and the world out there. So I can't go on living with you.

HELMER. Nora, Nora!

NORA. I want to leave right away. Kristine should put me up for the night—

HELMER. You're insane! You've no right! I forbid you!

NORA. From here on, there's no use forbidding me anything. I'll take with me whatever is mine. I don't want a thing from you, either now or later.

HELMER. What kind of madness is this!

NORA. Tomorrow I'm going home—I mean, home where I came from. It'll be easier up there to find something to do.

HELMER. Oh, you blind, incompetent child!

NORA. I must learn to be competent, Torvald.

HELMER. Abandon your home, your husband, your children! And you're not even thinking what people will say.

NORA. I can't be concerned about that. I only know how essential this is.

HELMER. Oh, it's outrageous. So you'll run out like this on your most sacred vows.

NORA. What do you think are my most sacred vows?

HELMER. And I have to tell you that! Aren't they your duties to your husband and children?

NORA. I have other duties equally sacred.

HELMER. That isn't true. What duties are they?

NORA. Duties to myself.

HELMER. Before all else, you're a wife and a mother.

NORA. I don't believe in that anymore. I believe that, before all else, I'm a human being, no less than you—or anyway, I ought to try to become one. I know the majority thinks you're right, Torvald, and plenty of books agree with you, too. But I can't go on believing what the majority says, or what's written in books. I have to think over these things myself and try to understand them.

HELMER. Why can't you understand your place in your own home? On a point like that, isn't there one everlasting guide you can turn to? Where's your religion?

NORA. Oh, Torvald, I'm really not sure what religion is.

HELMER. What—?

NORA. I only know what the minister said when I was confirmed. He told me religion was this thing and that. When I get clear and away by myself, I'll go into that problem too. I'll see if what the minister said was right, or, in any case, if it's right for me.

HELMER. A young woman your age shouldn't talk like that. If religion can't move you, I can try to rouse your conscience. You do have some moral feeling? Or, tell me— has that gone too?

NORA. It's not easy to answer that, Torvald. I simply don't know. I'm all confused about these things. I just know I see them so differently from you. I find out, for one thing, that the law's not at all what I'd thought—but I can't get it through my head that the law is fair. A woman hasn't a right to protect her dying father or save her husband's life! I can't believe that.

HELMER. You talk like a child. You don't know anything of the world you live in.

NORA. No, I don't. But now I'll begin to learn for myself. I'll try to discover who's right, the world or I.

HELMER. Nora, you're sick; you've got a fever. I almost think you're out of your head.

NORA. I've never felt more clearheaded and sure in my life.

HELMER. And—clearheaded and sure—you're leaving your husband and children?

NORA. Yes.

HELMER. Then there's only one possible reason.

NORA. What?

HELMER. You no longer love me.

NORA. No. That's exactly it.

HELMER. Nora! You can't be serious!

NORA. Oh, this is so hard, Torvald—you've been so kind to me always. But I can't help it. I don't love you anymore.

HELMER (*struggling for composure*). Are you also clear-headed and sure about that?

NORA. Yes, completely. That's why I can't go on staying here.

HELMER. Can you tell me what I did to lose your love?

NORA. Yes, I can tell you. It was this evening when the miraculous thing didn't come—then I knew you weren't the man I'd imagined.

HELMER. Be more explicit; I don't follow you.

NORA. I've waited now so patiently eight long years—for, my Lord, I know miracles don't come every day. Then this crisis broke over me, and such a certainty filled me: *now* the miraculous event would occur. While Krogstad's letter was lying out there, I never for an instant dreamed that you could give in to his terms. I was so utterly sure you'd say to him: go on, tell your tale to the whole wide world. And when he'd done that—

HELMER. Yes, what then? When I'd delivered my own wife into shame and disgrace—!

NORA. When he'd done that, I was so utterly sure that you'd step forward, take the blame on yourself and say: I am the guilty one.

HELMER. Nora—!

NORA. You're thinking I'd never accept such a sacrifice from you? No, of course not. But what good would my protests be against you? That was the miracle I was waiting for, in terror and hope. And to stave that off, I would have taken my life.

HELMER. I'd gladly work for you day and night, Nora —and take on pain and deprivation. But there's no one who gives up honor for love.

NORA. Millions of women have done just that.

HELMER. Oh, you think and talk like a silly child.

NORA. Perhaps. But you neither think nor talk like the

man I could join myself to. When your big fright was over —and it wasn't from any threat against me, only for what might damage you—when all the danger was past, for you it was just as if nothing had happened. I was exactly the same, your little lark, your doll, that you'd have to handle with double care now that I'd turned out so brittle and frail. (*Gets up.*) Torvald—in that instant it dawned on me that for eight years I've been living here with a stranger, and that I'd even conceived three children—oh, I can't stand the thought of it! I could tear myself to bits.

HELMER (*heavily*). I see. There's a gulf that's opened between us—that's clear. Oh, but Nora, can't we bridge it somehow?

NORA. The way I am now, I'm no wife for you.

HELMER. I have the strength to make myself over.

NORA. Maybe—if your doll gets taken away.

HELMER. But to part! To part from you! No, Nora, no —I can't imagine it.

NORA (*going out, right*). All the more reason why it has to be. (*She reenters with her coat and a small overnight bag, which she puts on a chair by the table.*)

HELMER. Nora, Nora, not now! Wait till tomorrow.

NORA. I can't spend the night in a strange man's room.

HELMER. But couldn't we live here like brother and sister—

NORA. You know very well how long that would last. (*Throws her shawl about her.*) Good-bye, Torvald. I won't look in on the children. I know they're in better hands than mine. The way I am now, I'm no use to them.

HELMER. But someday, Nora—someday—?

NORA. How can I tell? I haven't the least idea what'll become of me.

HELMER. But you're my wife, now and wherever you go.

NORA. Listen, Torvald—I've heard that when a wife deserts her husband's house just as I'm doing, then the law frees him from all responsibility. In any case, I'm freeing you from being responsible. Don't feel yourself bound, any more than I will. There has to be absolute freedom for us both. Here, take your ring back. Give me mine.

HELMER. That too?

NORA. That too.

HELMER. There it is.

NORA. Good. Well, now it's all over. I'm putting the keys here. The maids know all about keeping up the house—better than I do. Tomorrow, after I've left town, Kristine will stop by to pack up everything that's mine from home. I'd like those things shipped up to me.

HELMER. Over! All over! Nora, won't you ever think about me?

NORA. I'm sure I'll think of you often, and about the children and the house here.

HELMER. May I write you?

NORA. No—never. You're not to do that.

HELMER. Oh, but let me send you—

NORA. Nothing. Nothing.

HELMER. Or help you if you need it.

NORA. No. I accept nothing from strangers.

HELMER. Nora—can I never be more than a stranger to you?

NORA (*picking up the overnight bag*). Ah, Torvald—it would take the greatest miracle of all—

HELMER. Tell me the greatest miracle!

NORA. You and I both would have to transform ourselves to the point that— Oh, Torvald, I've stopped believing in miracles.

HELMER. But I'll believe. Tell me! Transform ourselves to the point that—?

NORA. That our living together could be a true marriage. (*She goes out down the hall.*)

HELMER (*sinks down on a chair by the door, face buried in his hands*). Nora! Nora! (*Looking about and rising.*) Empty. She's gone. (*A sudden hope leaps in him.*) The greatest miracle—?

(*From below, the sound of a door slamming shut.*)

GHOSTS

As *Hamlet* rests securely on the Elizabethan revenge tragedy and *Waiting for Godot* on the silent film comedies of the 1920s, the intricately figured texture of *Ghosts* (1881) is similarly modeled over the solid, supportive armature of a popular art form. One tends to forget that it is, at its core, a ghost story about five people in a haunted house, told with the sophisticated skill of a master, but nevertheless with the primitive intent of making the listener shudder, glance nervously away from the flickering fire into the enveloping darkness, and then draw closer to the light. That familiar, reassuring image is needful to hold onto, since for the two hours of any genuinely effective performance, the audience is at the mercy of, in James Huneker's words, "the strongest play of the nineteenth century, and also the most harrowing."

But not unrelievedly harrowing. It comes as a surprise to many readers and playgoers to discover, or rediscover, the extent to which *Ghosts* is laced with humor. It is much as if the characters had been virtuosically conceived to range a genre spectrum from near-farce to an intensity of tragic suffering and awareness scarcely equaled in dramatic art. Jacob Engstrand in himself, apart from his sinister function in the design of the whole, is a broadly comic creation of Dickensian verve, sly, unctuously ingratiating, irrepressible, a mock-satanic amalgam of Micawber and Uriah Heep. Pastor Manders is his complement, closer to center, emanating a higher, subtler comedy with his smoke screens of self-protective verbiage, his solicitude for God's opinion on fire insurance, his gradual co-option as silent partner in Engstrand's sporting house for homeless sailors. And Regina stands equivocally at the midpoint of the band of colors, lapped in romantic dreams of Paris, parroting phrasebook French, exuding animal vitality from every pore of her splendid, insouciant figure; but revealed in due time to be only a small, lusterless facet of the cruel indifference of the universe, synonymous with the destiny that waits, coiled to strike, in Mrs. Alving's past and Osvald Alving's brain.

With these two survivors of the original Alving family unit, the hues of the spectrum deepen, and the play modulates into another, immeasurably more somber key. Helene Alving, whose inner evolution is the heart of the dramatic action, has been described as Nora twenty years later, but a Nora who never left her husband, having listened trustingly, not to her own thoughts and feelings, but to the voices of conventional wisdom—her mother and aunt initially, persuading her to make the better match financially in young Lt. Alving; and next, her first love, Manders, who, stricken by fear of scandal when she fled to him distraught after the ravages of her first year of marriage, counseled her to take up her cross and return to her dissolute husband. Thus, the doll house that opened out for Nora into a future, however uncertain, becomes the haunted house upon which, for Mrs. Alving, the past closes in. The past, precisely because it is forever unalterable, a frozen landscape of choices that can never be revived and reversed, is Ibsen's equivalent to what inexorable Fate was for the Greeks. Nothing can amend the eventual retribution of an evaded or misguided choice in the past. This, his starkest of tragic actions, concentrates its object lesson of horrors to put the most urgent premium on the moment and the supreme worth of choosing when it counts: right now, in the present, out of the integrity of one's whole being, in the light of an unflinching regard for all the factors and circumstances involved.

The alternative to striving for such enlightened choice is the state of being ridden by ghosts, the central metaphor that pervades the entire drama. As it is successively re-experienced, that metaphor takes on larger and larger inflections of meaning. Most literally, it warns that, if the effort to choose freely according to the truth of the situation is defaulted, one is subject altogether, rather than only partially, to the dictates of heredity. The worst traits of the parents can then slowly return full force in the children, just as "those two from the greenhouse," Alving and the maid Joanna, come back like phantoms from the dead in Osvald and Regina.

But also false or distorted images of others are specters that strangle life. For years Mrs. Alving had viewed her husband as a virulent but containable blight at Rosenvold.

Now, through newly understanding his thwarted joy in living as it recurs in her son, maimed by inherited venereal disease—"the superbly appropriate symbol of poisoned sexuality," as Brian Johnston notes—she can recognize her early joyless suffering of his advances instilled by a pietistic upbringing as the analogous blight, the poison that she had meant to him. But this past misjudgment is merely her share of still other, greater ghosts of dead beliefs, opinions, doctrines that linger on to afflict mankind. Finally, most expansively, there is a sense in which even the characters themselves seem like apparitions manifesting vast historical forces in collision, as Helene Alving works her innate Hellenic questing intellect out to freedom from its centuries-old domination by the Pauline Christian Manders mentality. Even the world-spirit participates in this remarkable séance called up out of, fundamentally, just five people variously experiencing a day and a night on haunted ground.

THE CHARACTERS

MRS. HELENE ALVING, widow of Captain Alving, late
    Court Chamberlain
OSVALD ALVING, her son, a painter
PASTOR MANDERS
ENGSTRAND, a carpenter
REGINA ENGSTRAND, in service with Mrs. Alving

*The action takes place on Mrs. Alving's country estate
by a large fjord in West Norway.*

⌣(ACT ONE)⌣

A large garden room, with a door in the left-hand wall, and two doors in the wall to the right. In the middle of the room a round table with chairs grouped about it; on the table lie books, magazines, and newspapers. In the left foreground, a window, and next to it a small sofa with a sewing table in front of it. In the background, the room is extended into a somewhat smaller greenhouse, whose walls are great panes of glass. From the right side of the greenhouse, a door leads into the garden. Through the glass walls a somber fjord landscape can be glimpsed, half hidden by the steady rain.

ENGSTRAND *is standing by the garden door. His left leg is partly deformed; under his bootsole he has a wooden block.* REGINA, *with an empty garden syringe in her hand, is trying to keep him from entering.*

REGINA (*in a low voice*). What do you want? Just stay where you are. Why, you're dripping wet.

ENGSTRAND. It's God's own rain, my girl.

REGINA. The devil's rain, it is!

ENGSTRAND. Jeez, how you talk, Regina. (*Hobbles a few steps into the room.*) But now, what I wanted to say—

REGINA. Stop stomping about with that foot, will you! The young master's sleeping upstairs.

ENGSTRAND. Still sleeping? In broad daylight?

REGINA. That's none of your business.

ENGSTRAND. I was out on a binge last night—

REGINA. I can imagine.

ENGSTRAND. Yes, because we mortals are weak, my girl—

REGINA. Yes, so we are.

ENGSTRAND. And temptations are manifold in this world, you see— But for all of that, I was on the job, so help me God, five thirty this morning early.

REGINA. All right now, get out of here. I'm not going to stand around, having a rendezvous with you.

ENGSTRAND. You're not going to have any what?

REGINA. I'm not going to have anyone meeting you here. So—on your way.

ENGSTRAND (*a few steps closer*). Damned if I'll go before I've had my say with you. This afternoon I'll be done with my work down at the schoolhouse, and then I'll rip right back to town by the night boat.

REGINA (*mutters*). Pleasant trip!

ENGSTRAND. Thank you, my girl. Tomorrow they'll be dedicating the orphanage, and there'll probably be all kinds of carrying-on here, with hard liquor, you know. And nobody's going to say about Jacob Engstrand that he can't put temptation behind him.

REGINA. Ha!

ENGSTRAND. Yes, because you know a lot of the best people'll be here tomorrow. Pastor Manders is expected from town.

REGINA. He's coming today.

ENGSTRAND. There, you see. And I'll be damned if he's going to get anything on me.

REGINA. Ah, so *that's* it!

ENGSTRAND. What do you mean, *that?*

REGINA (*looks knowingly at him*). Just what are you out to trick him into this time?

ENGSTRAND. Shh, are you crazy? Would *I* trick the pastor into anything? Oh no, Pastor Manders, he's been much too good to me for that. But it's what I wanted to talk to you about, see—that I'll be leaving for home then, tonight.

REGINA. The sooner the better.

ENGSTRAND. Yes, but I want you along with me, Regina.

REGINA (*open-mouthed*). You want me along—? What did you say?

ENGSTRAND. I'm saying I want you back home with me.

REGINA (*scornfully*). Back home with you? Never. Not a chance!

ENGSTRAND. Oh, we'll see about that.

REGINA. Yes, you can bet we will, all right. *I*, who've been brought up by Mrs. Alving—? Been taken in like one of the family—? *I* should move back with *you*? To a house like that? Pah!

ENGSTRAND. What the devil is this? You trying to cross your own father, you slut?

REGINA (*mutters, without looking at him*). You've always said I had no part of you.

ENGSTRAND. Ahh, never mind about that—

REGINA. How many times haven't you cursed me and called me a—*fi donc!*

ENGSTRAND. So help me God if I've ever used such a dirty word.

REGINA. Oh, I haven't forgotten the word you used.

ENGSTRAND. Yes, but that was only when I had some drink in me—hm. Temptations are manifold in this world, Regina.

REGINA. Ugh!

ENGSTRAND. And when your mother got nasty, see— then I had to find something to needle her with. Always made herself so refined. (*Mimics.*) "Let go of me, Engstrand! Leave me be! I've been three years in service to Chamberlain Alving at Rosenvold!" (*Laughs.*) Jeez, that was something she never could forget—that the captain was made a chamberlain while she was in service there.

REGINA. Poor mother—you bullied the life out of her soon enough.

ENGSTRAND (*with a shrug*). Yes, that's right; I get the blame for everything.

REGINA (*in an undertone, as she turns away*). Ugh—! And that leg.

ENGSTRAND. What did you say, my girl?

REGINA. *Pied de mouton.*

ENGSTRAND. What's that—German?*

REGINA. Yes.

ENGSTRAND. Oh yes, you got some learning out here, and that's going to come in handy now, Regina.

REGINA (*after a short silence*). And what was it you wanted with me in town?

ENGSTRAND. How can you ask what a father wants with his only child? Aren't I a lonely, forsaken widower?

REGINA. Oh, don't give me that garbage. Why do you want me in town?

ENGSTRAND. All right, I'll tell you—I've been thinking of striking into something new.

REGINA (*with a snort*). You've done that so often, and it always goes wrong.

ENGSTRAND. Ah, but this time, Regina, you wait and see! Hell's bells—!

REGINA (*stamps her foot*). Stop swearing!

ENGSTRAND. Sh, sh! Perfectly right you are, my girl! I only wanted to say—I've put by a nice piece of change out of the work on this new orphanage.

REGINA. Have you? Well, that's good for you.

ENGSTRAND. Because what can you spend your money on here, out in the country?

REGINA. Well, so?

---

* "English," in the original, which loses meaning in an English translation.

ENGSTRAND. Yes, so you see, I thought I might put the money into something that'd turn a profit. It was going to be a sort of hotel for seamen—

REGINA. Ugh-ah!

ENGSTRAND. A regular, first-class inn, you understand— not just any old pigsty for sailors. No, damn it all—it's going to be for ship captains and mates and—and real fine people, you understand.

REGINA. And how do I—?

ENGSTRAND. You? You get to help, see. Just for the look of things, if you follow me. There wouldn't be so damn much to do. You can have it just like you want it.

REGINA. I'll bet!

ENGSTRAND. But there've got to be women on the premises, that's clear as day. Because we want a little life in the evenings—singing and dancing and that sort of thing. You have to remember, these are wayfaring seamen on the ocean of life. (*Comes nearer.*) Now don't be stupid and hold yourself back, Regina. What can you come to out here? What good can it do you, all this learning Mrs. Alving's paid out for? You're supposed to take care of the children, I hear, in the new orphanage. Is *that* anything for you, uh? Have you such a hunger to run yourself ragged for the sake of those filthy brats?

REGINA. No, if things go the way *I* want, then— And it could happen, all right. Yes, it could!

ENGSTRAND. What could?

REGINA. None of your business. Is it—quite a bit of money you made out here?

ENGSTRAND. Between this and that, I'd say up to seven, eight hundred crowns.

REGINA. That's not so bad.

ENGSTRAND. It's enough for a start, my girl.

REGINA. Don't you think you might give me some of that money?

ENGSTRAND. No, I don't think I might!

REGINA. Don't you think you could send me at least some cloth for a dress?

ENGSTRAND. Just come with me into town, and you'll have dresses to burn.

REGINA. Pah! I can do as well on my own, if I care to.

ENGSTRAND. No, but it goes better, Regina, with a father's guiding hand. There's a nice house I can get now in Little Harbor Street. They don't want too much money down; and it could make some kind of seamen's home, all right.

REGINA. But I don't want to stay with you! I've got no business with you. Get out!

ENGSTRAND. You wouldn't stay so damn long with me, girl. No such luck—if you know how to show off yourself. A wench as good-looking as you've turned out these last two years—

REGINA. Yes—?

ENGSTRAND. It wouldn't be long before some ship's officer—maybe even a captain—

REGINA. I'm not marrying any of those. Sailors don't have any *savoir-vivre*.

ENGSTRAND. They don't have any what?

REGINA. Let me tell you, I know about sailors. They aren't any sort to marry.

ENGSTRAND. Then forget about getting married. That can pay just as well. (*More confidentially.*) Him—the Englishman—the one with the yacht—he gave three hundred dollars, he did—and she was no better looking than you.

REGINA (*advancing on him*). Get out of here!

ENGSTRAND (*steps back*). Easy now, you don't want to hit me.

REGINA. Don't I! Talk about Mother, and you'll find out. Get out of here, I said! (*She forces him back toward the garden door.*) And no slamming doors; young Mr. Alving—

ENGSTRAND. Yes, he's asleep. It's something all right, how you worry about young Mr. Alving— (*Dropping his voice.*) Ho-ho! It just wouldn't be that *he*—?

REGINA. Out of here, quick! You're all mixed up! No.

not that way. There's Pastor Manders coming. Down the kitchen stairs.

ENGSTRAND (*moving to the right*). All right, I'm going. But you talk with *him* that's coming in. He's the one who'll tell you what a child owes her father. Because, after all, I *am* your father, you know. I can prove it in the parish register.

(*He goes out by the farther door, which* REGINA *has opened, closing it after him. She hurriedly glances at herself in the mirror, fans herself with her handkerchief and straightens her collar, then busies herself with the flowers.* PASTOR MANDERS, *in an overcoat, carrying an umbrella along with a small traveling bag on a strap over his shoulder, comes through the garden door into the greenhouse.*)

MANDERS. Good morning, Miss Engstrand.

REGINA (*turning with a pleasantly surprised look*). Why, Pastor Manders, good morning! The boat's already come?

MANDERS. It just arrived. (*Entering the room.*) It's certainly tedious weather we've been having these days.

REGINA (*following him*). It's a godsend for the farmers, Pastor.

MANDERS. Yes, you're quite right. That's something we townspeople hardly think of. (*He starts taking his overcoat off.*)

REGINA. Oh, let me help you—that's it. My, how wet it is! I'll just hang it up in the hall. And the umbrella, too —I'll leave it open to dry.

(*She goes off with the things through the farther door on the right.* MANDERS *removes his traveling bag and sets it and his hat down on a chair, as* REGINA *returns.*)

MANDERS. Ah, but it's good to be indoors. So— everything's going well out here?

REGINA. Yes, thank you.

MANDERS. But terribly busy, I suppose, getting ready for tomorrow?

REGINA. Oh yes, there's plenty to do.

MANDERS. And, hopefully, Mrs. Alving's at home?

REGINA. Why, of course. She just went upstairs to bring the young master some hot chocolate.

MANDERS. Yes, tell me—I heard down at the pier that Osvald was supposed to have come.

REGINA. He got in the day before yesterday. We hadn't expected him before today.

MANDERS. In the best of health, I hope?

REGINA. Yes, just fine, thank you. But awfully tired after his trip. He came straight from Paris without a break—I mean, he went the whole route without changing trains. I think he's sleeping a little now, so we should talk just a tiny bit softer.

MANDERS. Shh! We'll be so quiet.

REGINA (*as she moves an armchair up to the table*). Please now, do sit down, Pastor, and make yourself comfortable. (*He sits; she slips a footstool under his feet.*) That's it! Is that all right, Pastor?

MANDERS. Just perfect, thank you. (*Regarding her.*) You know, Miss Engstrand, I definitely think you've grown since I saw you last.

REGINA. Do you think so, Pastor? Mrs. Alving says that I've filled out, too.

MANDERS. Filled out—? Well, yes, maybe a little—but acceptably. (*A short pause.*)

REGINA. Shall I tell Mrs. Alving you're here?

MANDERS. Oh, thank you, there's no hurry, my dear child—well, uh—but tell me now, Regina, how's it been going for your father out here?

REGINA. Fairly well, Pastor, thank you.

MANDERS. He was in to see me when he was last in town.

REGINA. Really? He's always so happy when he can talk with you.

MANDERS. And you make it your rule, of course, to look in on him daily.

REGINA. I? Oh, yes, of course—whenever I have some time—

MANDERS. Your father is not very strong in character, Miss Engstrand. He's woefully in need of a guiding hand.

REGINA. Yes, I'm sure of that.

MANDERS. He needs to have someone around him that he can love, and whose judgment carries some weight. He confessed as much quite frankly when he was last up to see me.

REGINA. Yes, he said something like that to me. But I don't know if Mrs. Alving could spare me—especially now, when we've got the new orphanage to manage. And then I'd be so awfully unhappy to leave Mrs. Alving—she's always been so kind to me.

MANDERS. But, my dear girl, a daughter's duty— Naturally, we'd first have to obtain Mrs. Alving's consent.

REGINA. But I don't know if it would do for me, at my age, to keep house for a single man.

MANDERS. What! But, my dear Miss Engstrand, this is your own father we're speaking of!

REGINA. Yes, maybe so, but all the same—you see, if it were a *good* house, with a real gentleman—

MANDERS. But, my dear Regina—

REGINA. One I could care for and look up to, almost like a daughter—

MANDERS. Yes, but my dear child—

REGINA. Because I'd like so much to live in town. Out here it's terribly lonely—and you know yourself, Pastor, what it is to stand alone in the world. And I think I can say that I'm both capable and willing. Mr. Manders, don't you know of a place like that for me?

MANDERS. I? No, I don't, for the life of me.

REGINA. But dear, dear Mr. Manders—you will think of me, in any case, if ever—

MANDERS (*getting up*). Yes, I'll remember, Miss Engstrand.

REGINA. Yes, because if I—

MANDERS. Perhaps you'll be good enough to tell Mrs. Alving I've come.

REGINA. I'll go call her right away, Pastor.

(*She goes out left.* MANDERS *paces back and forth in the room a couple of times, then stands for a moment at the far end of the room, hands behind his back, looking out into the garden. He then returns to the table, picks up a book and looks at the title page, starts, and inspects several others.*)

MANDERS. Hm—aha! Well!

(MRS. ALVING *comes in by the door, left. She is followed by* REGINA, *who immediately goes out by the nearer door to the right.*)

MRS. ALVING (*extending her hand*). So good to see you, Mr. Manders.

MANDERS. Good morning, Mrs. Alving. Here I am, just as I promised.

MRS. ALVING. Always on the dot.

MANDERS. But you can imagine, it was touch and go for me, getting away. All those blessed boards and committees—

MRS. ALVING. All the more kind of you to come so promptly. Now we can get our business done before lunch. But where do you have your bags?

MANDERS (*hurriedly*). My things are down at the general store—I took a room there for tonight.

MRS. ALVING (*repressing a smile*). You can't be persuaded even yet to spend the night here in my house?

MANDERS. No, no, really; thank you so much, but I'll stay down there as usual. It's so convenient to the boat.

MRS. ALVING. Well, you do as you wish. But I really thought instead that two old people like us—

MANDERS. Gracious me, the way you joke! Yes, of course you're in rare spirits today. First the celebration tomorrow, and then you've got Osvald home.

MRS ALVING. Yes, can you imagine how happy I am! It's more than two years since he was home last. And then he's promised to stay with me this whole winter.

MANDERS. No, has he really? That's certainly a nice gesture for a son to make—because there must be other, quite different attractions to life in Rome and Paris, I'm sure.

MRS. ALVING. Yes, but he has his mother here at home, you see. Oh, that dear, blessed boy—he still has room in his heart for me!

MANDERS. It would really be tragic if distance and devotion to anything like art should dull his natural feelings.

MRS. ALVING. You're perfectly right. But there's no chance at all of that with him. Oh, I'm going to be so curious to see if you still recognize him. He'll be down shortly; he's just stretched out to rest a little on the sofa upstairs. But now, my dear Mr. Manders—do sit down.

MANDERS. Thank you. It *is* convenient, then—?

MRS. ALVING. Why, of course. (*She sits at the table.*)

MANDERS. Good. Then let's have a look— (*Goes over to the chair where his bag lies, takes out a sheaf of papers, sits at the opposite side of the table, and searches for a space to lay the papers out.*) Now here, first, we have— (*Breaks off.*) Tell me, Mrs. Alving, where did these books come from?

MRS. ALVING. These books? I'm reading them.

MANDERS. You read this sort of thing?

MRS. ALVING. Yes, of course I do.

MANDERS. Do you feel you've grown any better or happier for this kind of reading?

MRS. ALVING. I think it makes me feel more secure.

MANDERS. That's astonishing. What do you mean?

MRS. ALVING. Well, I find it clarifies and reinforces so many ideas I've been thinking out all to myself. Yes, that's the strange part, Mr. Manders—there's actually nothing really new in these books, nothing beyond what most people think and believe. It's simply that most people don't like to face these things, or what they imply.

MANDERS. Oh, my dear God! You don't seriously consider that most people—?

MRS. ALVING. Yes, I certainly do.

MANDERS. Well, but not here in our society? Not among us?

MRS. ALVING. Yes, definitely—among us, too.

MANDERS. Well, I must say, really—!

MRS. ALVING. But what exactly do you object to in these books?

MANDERS. Object to? You surely don't think I waste my time exploring that kind of publication?

MRS. ALVING. In other words, you know nothing of what you're condemning?

MANDERS. I've read quite enough about these writings to disapprove of them.

MRS. ALVING. Yes, but your own opinion—

MANDERS. My dear Mrs. Alving, there are many circumstances in life where one has to entrust oneself to others. That's the condition of this world, and it's all for the best. How else could society function?

MRS. ALVING. That's true; maybe you're right.

MANDERS. Besides, I wouldn't deny that there's a certain fascination about such writings. And I can't blame you either for wanting to become acquainted with the intellectual currents that, I hear, are quite prevalent in the larger world—where you've let your son wander so long. But—

MRS. ALVING. But—?

MANDERS (dropping his voice). But one needn't talk about it, Mrs. Alving. One doesn't have to recount to all and sundry everything one reads and thinks within one's own four walls.

MRS. ALVING. No, of course not. I agree.

MANDERS. Remember your obligations to the orphanage, which you decided to found at a time when your attitude toward things of the mind and spirit was so very different from now—at least as I see it.

MRS. ALVING. Yes, I admit it, completely. But it was about the orphanage—

MANDERS. It was about the orphanage we wanted to

speak, yes. All the same—prudence, my dear Mrs. Alving! And now, let's turn to business. (*Opens a folder and takes out some papers.*) You see these?

MRS. ALVING. The deeds?

MANDERS. The whole set—in perfect order. You can imagine it hasn't been easy to get them in time. I actually had to apply some pressure. The authorities are almost painfully scrupulous when it comes to decisions. But here they are, in any case. (*Leafing through the papers.*) See, here's the duly recorded conveyance of title of the Solvik farm, said property being part of the Rosenvold estate, together with all buildings newly erected thereon, including the schoolhouse, the staff residence, and the chapel. And here's the official charter for the institution—and the by-laws governing its operation. You see— (*Reads.*) "By-laws governing the Captain Alving Memorial Orphan's Home."

MRS. ALVING (*looking at the papers for a long moment*). So—there it is.

MANDERS. I chose "Captain" for the title, rather than "Court Chamberlain." "Captain" seems less ostentatious.

MRS. ALVING. Yes, whatever you think.

MANDERS. And here you've got the bankbook showing interest on capital reserved to cover the running expenses of the orphanage.

MRS. ALVING. Thank you—but please, won't you hold onto it, for convenience' sake?

MANDERS. Yes, gladly. I think we can leave the money in the bank for a time. It's true, the interest rate isn't very attractive: four percent, with a six-month withdrawal notice. If we could come across a good mortgage later on— naturally, it would have to be a first mortgage, of unquestionable security—then we could reconsider the situation.

MRS. ALVING. Yes, dear Mr. Manders, you know best about all that.

MANDERS. Anyway, I'll keep an eye out. But now there's one more thing I've meant several times to ask you.

MRS. ALVING. And what's that?

MANDERS. Should the orphanage be insured or not?

MRS. ALVING. Why, of course, it has to be insured.

MANDERS. Ah, not too fast, Mrs. Alving. Let's study this question a bit.

MRS. ALVING. Everything I own is insured—buildings, furniture, crops, livestock.

MANDERS. Obviously, when it's your own property. I do the same, naturally. But here, you see, it's a very different matter. This orphanage is going to be, so to say, consecrated to a higher calling.

MRS. ALVING. Yes, but if—

MANDERS. From my personal standpoint, I wouldn't find the slightest objection to insuring us against all eventualities—

MRS. ALVING. No, I wouldn't either.

MANDERS. But how would that sit with the public opinion hereabouts? You know better than I.

MRS. ALVING. Public opinion, hm—

MANDERS. Is there any considerable segment of opinion—I mean, really important opinion—that might take offense?

MRS. ALVING. Well, what do you mean, exactly, by important opinion?

MANDERS. I was thinking mainly of people of such independent and influential position that one could hardly avoid giving their opinions a certain weight.

MRS. ALVING. There are a few like that here who might possibly take offense if—

MANDERS. There, you see! In town we have any number of them. The congregations of other churches, for example. It would be the easiest thing in the world for them to construe this as neither you nor I having adequate faith in Divine Providence.

MRS. ALVING. But, my dear Mr. Manders, as long as you know to your own satisfaction—

MANDERS. Yes, I know, I know—I have my own inner conviction, quite so. But the fact remains that we wouldn't be able to counter a false and damaging impression—and that, in turn, could easily hamper the work of the orphanage.

MRS. ALVING. Well, if that's the case, then—

MANDERS. Also, I can hardly ignore the difficult— I might just as well say, painful—position I'd probably be in myself. Among the best circles in town there's a good deal of interest in the orphanage. After all, it's partly being established to benefit the town as well, and hopefully it's going to have a sizable effect in lowering our local public welfare taxes. But since I've been your adviser in this and made all the business arrangements, I'm afraid those bigots would concentrate all their fire on me—

MRS. ALVING. No, you shouldn't be exposed to that.

MANDERS. Not to mention the charges that would doubtless be leveled against me in certain papers and magazines that—

MRS. ALVING. Enough, Mr. Manders; that settles it.

MANDERS. Then you won't want the insurance?

MRS. ALVING. No, we'll let that be.

MANDERS (*leaning back in his chair*). But now, if there *should* be an accident—one never knows, after all—would you be able to make good the losses?

MRS. ALVING. I can tell you right now, I absolutely wouldn't.

MANDERS. Ah, but you know, Mrs. Alving—then it's a grave responsibility we're taking on.

MRS. ALVING. But what else do you see that we *can* do?

MANDERS. No, that's just the thing: we *can't* do anything else. We shouldn't expose ourselves to unfavorable opinion; and we certainly have no right to stir dissension in the community.

MRS. ALVING. Especially you, as a clergyman.

MANDERS. And also I really do believe that we can depend on a project like this carrying some luck along with it—standing, so to say, under a special protection.

MRS. ALVING. Let's hope so, Mr. Manders.

MANDERS. Then we'll leave things as they are?

MRS. ALVING. Yes, of course.

MANDERS. Right. As you wish. (*Jotting a note.*) No insurance.

MRS. ALVING. It's strange you happened to speak about this just today—

MANDERS. I've often thought to ask you about it—

MRS. ALVING. Because yesterday we nearly had a fire down there.

MANDERS. What!

MRS. ALVING. Well, there wasn't anything to it, really. Some shavings caught fire in the carpenter shop.

MANDERS. Where Engstrand works?

MRS. ALVING. Yes. They say he's often so careless with matches.

MANDERS. He has so much on his mind, that man—so many tribulations. Praise be to God, he's now making a real effort to lead a blameless life, I hear.

MRS. ALVING. Oh? Who's been saying that?

MANDERS. He's assured me of it himself. And he's a capable workman, too.

MRS. ALVING. Why, yes, as long as he's sober—

MANDERS. Ah, that distressing weakness! But he tells me he frequently has to resort to it for the sake of his ailing leg. Last time he was in town, I really was quite moved by him. He stopped in and thanked me so sincerely for getting him this work out here, so he could be together with Regina.

MRS. ALVING. But he hardly ever sees her.

MANDERS. No, he speaks with her every day—he told me that himself.

MRS. ALVING. Yes—well, it's possible.

MANDERS. He feels so positively that he needs someone there who can restrain him when temptation looms. That's what's so engaging about Jacob Engstrand, the way he comes to one so utterly helpless and accuses himself and admits his faults. Just this last time that he talked to me—Mrs. Alving, if it became a vital necessity for him to have Regina home with him again—

MRS. ALVING (*rising impulsively*). Regina!

MANDERS. Then you mustn't set yourself against it.

MRS. ALVING. Yes, I'm decidedly set against it. And besides—Regina will have a position at the orphanage.

MANDERS. But remember, he *is* her father—

MRS. ALVING. I know all too well what kind of father he's been to her. No, she'll never have my blessings to go to him.

MANDERS (*rising*). But my dear Mrs. Alving, don't take it so violently. It's such a pity, the way you misjudge Engstrand. Really, it's as if you were somehow afraid— .

MRS. ALVING (*more calmly*). Never mind about that. I've taken Regina in here, and she'll stay here with me. (*Listens.*) Shh, now! Dear Mr. Manders, let's not talk of this anymore. (*Her face radiating joy.*) Hear that! Osvald's coming downstairs. Now we'll think only of him.

(OSVALD ALVING, *wearing a light overcoat, hat in hand, and smoking a large meerschaum pipe, comes in through the door to the left.*)

OSVALD (*pausing in the doorway*). Oh, I'm sorry—I thought you were in the study. (*Comes in.*) Good morning, Pastor Manders.

MANDERS (*stares at him*). Ah—! That's amazing—!

MRS. ALVING. Yes, what do you think of him, Mr. Manders?

MANDERS. Well, I must say—no, but—is it really—?

OSVALD. Yes, really—the prodigal son, Pastor.

MANDERS. But my dear boy—

OSVALD. Well, the homecoming son, anyway.

MRS. ALVING. Osvald's thinking of the time when you were so against his becoming a painter.

MANDERS. From our human viewpoint, you know, many a step looks doubtful that later turns out— (*Shaking his hand.*) Ah, welcome, welcome back! Imagine, my dear Osvald—may I still call you by your first name?

OSVALD. What else could you think of calling me?

MANDERS. Good. What I meant to say, my dear Osvald—was that you mustn't suppose that I categorically condemn the artist's life. I assume there are quite a few who keep their inner selves uncorrupted even in those circumstances.

OSVALD. Let's hope so.

MRS. ALVING (*beaming with pleasure*). I know one who's kept both his inner and outer selves incorruptible. You only have to look at him, Mr. Manders.

OSVALD (*pacing about the room*). Yes, all right, Mother dear—that's enough.

MANDERS. Completely so—that's undeniable. And you've already begun to make your name. You're often mentioned in the papers—and most favorably, too. Though lately, I should say, there seems to be less.

OSVALD (*near the greenhouse*). I haven't been painting so much lately.

MRS. ALVING. Even artists need a rest now and then.

MANDERS. That I can understand. A time to prepare oneself and gather strength for the great work to come.

OSVALD. Yes. Mother, are we eating soon?

MRS. ALVING. In just half an hour. He certainly has an appetite, thank goodness.

MANDERS. And likes his tobacco, too.

OSVALD. I found Father's pipe upstairs in the bedroom—

MANDERS. Ah, that explains it!

MRS. ALVING. What?

MANDERS. When Osvald came through the door there with that pipe in his mouth, it was as if I saw his father in the flesh.

OSVALD. Really?

MRS. ALVING. Oh, how can you say that? Osvald takes after me.

MANDERS. Yes, but there's a look around the corners of

the mouth, something about the lips, that's the very picture of Alving—especially now that he's smoking.

MRS. ALVING. No, it's nothing like him, not at all. To me, Osvald has more of a minister's look about the mouth.

MANDERS. Yes. Yes, a number of my colleagues have a similar expression.

MRS. ALVING. But put the pipe down, dear. I don't want smoking in this room.

OSVALD (*sets the pipe down*). All right. I only thought I'd try it because I'd once smoked it as a child.

MRS. ALVING. You?

OSVALD. Yes. I was very small then. And I remember going up to Father's room one evening when he was in such a marvelous humor.

MRS. ALVING. Oh, you don't remember anything from those years.

OSVALD. Oh yes, I distinctly remember him taking me on his knee and letting me smoke his pipe. "Smoke, boy," he said, "smoke it for real!" And I smoked for all I was worth, till I felt myself go pale, and the great drops of sweat stood out on my forehead. Then he shook all over with laughter—

MANDERS. That's most peculiar.

MRS. ALVING. I'm sure it's just something that Osvald dreamed.

OSVALD. No, Mother, it was definitely no dream. Because—don't you remember—then you came in and carried me off to the nursery. I was sick then, and I could see you were crying. Did Father often play such tricks?

MANDERS. When he was young he was always full of life—

OSVALD. And still he got so much accomplished—so much that was good and useful, for all that he died so early.

MANDERS. Yes, Osvald Alving—it's a strong and worthy name you've inherited. Well, let's hope it'll inspire you—

OSVALD. It certainly ought to.

MANDERS. And it was good of you to come home for the ceremonies in his honor.

OSVALD. It's the least I could do for Father.

MRS. ALVING. And that he'll remain with me here so long—that's the best of his goodness.

MANDERS. Yes, I hear you're staying all winter.

OSVALD. I'll be staying on indefinitely, Pastor. Oh, it's wonderful to be home again!

MRS. ALVING (*radiant*). Yes, how true!

MANDERS (*looks sympathetically at him*). You were out in the world quite early, Osvald, weren't you?

OSVALD. Yes. I wonder sometimes if it wasn't too early.

MRS. ALVING. Nonsense! There's nothing better for a healthy boy, especially when he's an only child. He shouldn't be kept home and coddled by his mother and father.

MANDERS. That's a highly debatable proposition, Mrs. Alving. A child's rightful place is and always will be his parental home.

OSVALD. I have to agree with Mr. Manders there.

MANDERS. Now- take your own son, for instance. Yes, we can discuss this in front of him. What effect has this had on him? He's grown to age twenty-six or -seven without any chance to experience a normal home life.

OSVALD. Excuse me, Mr. Manders—but you're quite wrong about that.

MANDERS. Really? I thought you'd been moving almost entirely in artistic circles.

OSVALD. I have.

MANDERS. And mainly among the younger artists.

OSVALD. Yes.

MANDERS. But I thought most of those people hadn't the means to start a family and make a home.

OSVALD. It's true that a number of them haven't the means to get married—

MANDERS. Well, that's what I'm saying.

OSVALD. But they can still have a home life. And several of them do—one that's quite normal and pleasant.

(MRS. ALVING, *following attentively, nods but says nothing.*)

MANDERS. But it's not a bachelor life I'm talking about. By home life I mean a family home, where a man lives with his wife and his children.

OSVALD. Yes, or with his children and his children's mother.

MANDERS (*jolted, clasping his hands together*). Merciful God—!

OSVALD. What—?

MANDERS. Lives together with—his children's mother!

OSVALD. Well, would you rather have him abandon her?

MANDERS. But you're talking about illicit relations! About plain, irresponsible free love!

OSVALD. I've never noticed anything particularly irresponsible about the way these people live.

MANDERS. But how is it possible that—that even moderately decent young men or women could accept living in that manner—before the eyes of the world!

OSVALD. But what else can they do? A poor young artist—a poor young girl—and marriage so expensive. What can they do?

MANDERS. What they can do? Well, Mr. Alving, I'll tell you what they can do. They ought to keep each other at a distance right from the start—that's what they ought to do!

OSVALD. You won't get very far with that advice among warm-blooded young people in love.

MRS. ALVING. No, you certainly won't!

MANDERS (*persisting*). And to think the authorities tolerate such things! That it's allowed to go on openly. (*To* MRS. ALVING.) You see what good reason I've had to be concerned about your son. In circles where immorality is flaunted, and even seems to be prized—

OSVALD. Let me tell you something, Pastor. I've been a

frequent Sunday guest in a couple of these so-called unconventional homes—

MANDERS. Sunday, no less!

OSVALD. Yes, the day of rest and relaxation—and yet I've never once heard an offensive word, nor have I ever witnessed anything that could be called immoral. But do you know when and where I *have* met immorality among artists?

MANDERS. No, thank God, I don't!

OSVALD. Well, then let me tell you. I've met it when one or another of our exemplary husbands and fathers—on a trip away from home and out to see a little life—did the artists the honor of dropping in on them in their poor cafés. Then we had our ears opened wide. Those gentlemen could tell us about things and places we never dreamed existed.

MANDERS. What? Are you suggesting that respectable men from here at home would—?

OSVALD. Have you never—when these same respectable men came home from their trips—have you never heard them carrying on about the monstrous immorality abroad?

MANDERS. Why, of course—

MRS. ALVING. I have, too.

OSVALD. Well, you can trust their word for it—they're experts, many of them. (*Clasps his head.*) Oh, that the beautiful freedom of that life—could be made so foul!

MRS. ALVING. You mustn't provoke yourself, Osvald. It's not good for you.

OSVALD. No, you're right, Mother. It's bad for my health. It's this damnable fatigue, you know. Well, I'll go for a little walk now before lunch. I'm sorry, Pastor. You can't share my feelings about this—but it's the way I see it. (*He goes out through the farther door to the right.*)

MRS. ALVING. My poor boy—!

MANDERS. Yes, you can well say that. How far he's strayed! (MRS. ALVING *looks at him, saying nothing.* MANDERS *paces up and down.*) He called himself the prodigal son. Yes, it's sad—sad! (MRS. ALVING *continues to look at him*.) And what do you say to all this?

MRS. ALVING. I say Osvald was right in every word that he said.

MANDERS (*stops short*). Right? Right! With such principles?

MRS. ALVING. Here in my solitude I've come to the same conclusions, Mr. Manders—though I've never dared breathe a word of it. All well and good—my boy can speak for me now.

MANDERS. You're a woman much to be pitied, Mrs. Alving. Now I must talk seriously with you. It's no longer as your business adviser, nor as your and your husband's childhood friend, that I'm standing before you now—but as your priest, exactly as I once did at the most bewildered hour of your life.

MRS. ALVING. And what does my priest have to tell me?

MANDERS. First, let me call up some memories. It's a suitable moment. Tomorrow is the tenth anniversary of your husband's death; tomorrow the memorial will be unveiled in his honor; tomorrow I'll be speaking to all those assembled—but today I want to speak to you alone.

MRS. ALVING. All right, Mr. Manders—speak!

MANDERS. Do you recall how, after barely a year of marriage, you stood on the very edge of the abyss? That you left house and home—deserted your husband—yes, Mrs. Alving, deserted, deserted, and refused to go back to him, for all that he begged and implored you to?

MRS. ALVING. Have you forgotten how unutterably miserable I was that first year?

MANDERS. But this is the very essence of the rebellious spirit, to crave happiness here in this life. What right have we human beings to happiness? No, we must do our duty, Mrs. Alving! And your duty was to stand by that man you once had chosen, and to whom you were joined by a sacred bond.

MRS. ALVING. You know well enough what kind of life Alving led in those days—and the appetites he indulged.

MANDERS. I know quite well the rumors that circulated

about him; and to the extent that those rumors were true, I'd be the last to condone such conduct as his then. But a wife isn't required to be her husband's judge. It was your proper role to bear with a humble heart that cross that a higher will saw fit to lay upon you. But instead, you rebelliously cast away the cross, left the groping soul you should have aided, went off and risked your good name and reputation and—nearly ruined other reputations in the bargain.

MRS. ALVING. Other reputations? Just one, I think you mean.

MANDERS. It was exceedingly thoughtless of you to seek refuge with me.

MRS. ALVING. With our pastor? With an old, close friend?

MANDERS. Yes, for that very reason. You should thank Almighty God that I had the necessary inner strength— that I got you to drop your hysterical plans, and that it was given me to lead you back to the path of duty, and home to your lawful husband.

MRS. ALVING. Yes, Pastor Manders, that certainly was your doing.

MANDERS. I was only a humble instrument directed by a higher power. And that I bent your will to duty and obedience—hasn't that grown as a great blessing, from that time on, in all the days of your life? Didn't it go the way I foretold? Didn't Alving turn away from his depravities, as a man must, and take up a loving and blameless life with you right to the end? Didn't he become a benefactor of the community, and uplift you as well into his own sphere of activities to share them all? And how effectively you shared them, too—that I know, Mrs. Alving; I'll give you *that* credit. But now I come to the next great mistake in your life.

MRS. ALVING. What do you mean?

MANDERS. Just as you once evaded the duties of a wife, you've since evaded those of a mother.

MRS. ALVING. Ah—!

MANDERS. All your life you've been governed by an incorrigible spirit of willfulness. Instinctively you've been drawn to all that's undisciplined and lawless. You never can bear the least constraint. Everything that inconveniences your life you've carelessly and irresponsibly thrown aside—as if it were baggage you could leave behind if you chose. It didn't agree with you to be a wife any longer, so you left your husband. You found it troublesome to be a mother, so you put your child out with strangers.

MRS. ALVING. Yes, it's true—that's what I did.

MANDERS. And for that same reason you've become a stranger to him.

MRS. ALVING. No, no, I'm *not!*

MANDERS. You are. You had to be! And what sort of son have you gotten back? Think well, Mrs. Alving. You were terribly unfair to your husband—you admit as much by raising this monument to him. Now admit as well how unfair you've been to your son; there may still be time to lead him back from the paths of error. Change your ways—and save what's still left to be saved in him. For truly, Mrs. Alving—(*With an admonishing forefinger.*)—you're profoundly guilty as a mother! I've considered it my duty to tell you this.

(*Silence.*)

MRS. ALVING (*deliberately, controlling herself*). You've said your piece, Pastor; and tomorrow you'll be speaking publicly in my husband's memory. Tomorrow I'll make no speeches; but now I want to say something to you, exactly as you've just spoken to me.

MANDERS. Naturally, you want to make excuses for your conduct—

MRS. ALVING. No. Only to tell a few facts.

MANDERS. Well—?

MRS. ALVING. All that you've been saying here about me and my husband and our life together—after, as you put it, you led me back to the path of duty—all this is something you don't know the least thing about at firsthand. From that moment on, you, our dearest friend, never set foot in our house again.

MANDERS. But you and your husband moved out of town right after that.

MRS. ALVING. Yes, and you never came out here to see us while my husband was living. It was business that impelled you to visit me, since you were involved with the orphanage, too.

MANDERS (*in a low, hesitant voice*). Helene—if that's meant as a reproach, then I ask you to consider—

MRS. ALVING. The respect you owed to your calling, yes. And I, after all, was a runaway wife. One can never be careful enough with such reckless women.

MANDERS. Dear—Mrs. Alving, that is a flagrant exaggeration—

MRS. ALVING. Yes, yes, all right, then forget that. I simply wanted to say that when you make judgments on my married life, you're basing them on no more than common gossip.

MANDERS. Granted. Well, what of it?

MRS. ALVING. But now, Mr. Manders, now I'll tell you the truth! I swore to myself that one day you were going to hear it—you alone.

MANDERS. And what, then, is the truth?

MRS. ALVING. The truth is—that my husband died just as dissolute as he'd lived every day of his life.

MANDERS (*groping for a chair*). What did you say?

MRS. ALVING. After nineteen years of marriage, just as dissolute—in his desires, in any case—as he was before you married us.

MANDERS. But these mistakes of his youth, these confusions—dissipations, if you want—you call them a dissolute life?

MRS. ALVING. It's the phrase our doctor used.

MANDERS. I don't understand you.

MRS. ALVING. You don't have to.

MANDERS. It makes my head spin. You mean the whole of your marriage—all those many years together with your husband—were nothing more than a hollow mockery?

MRS. ALVING. Exactly. Now you know.

MANDERS. This—I find this so hard to believe. I can't understand it! It doesn't make sense! But how was it possible to—? How could it be kept a secret?

MRS. ALVING. That was the constant battle I had, day after day. When Osvald was born, I thought things might go better with Alving—but it didn't last long. So then I had to redouble my efforts, fight with a vengeance so no one would know what kind of a man my child's father was. And you know, of course, how charming Alving could be. No one thought anything but good of him. He was one of those people whose lives never detract from their reputations. But then, Mr. Manders—and this you also have to hear—then came the most sickening part of the whole business.

MANDERS. More sickening than what you've told me!

MRS. ALVING. I'd borne with him, even though I knew very well what was going on in secret away from this house. But when the infection came right within our own four walls—

MANDERS. You mean—here!

MRS. ALVING. Yes, here in our own house. In there— (*Pointing to the nearer door on the right.*)—in the dining room, that was where I first discovered it. I had something to get inside, and the door was ajar. I heard the maid come up from the garden with water for the plants—

MANDERS. And—?

MRS. ALVING. A moment later I heard Alving come in after her. I could hear him saying something to her. And then I heard— (*With an abrupt laugh.*) —oh, I can hear it still, as something both so shattering and so ludicrous— my own maid whispering: "Let go of me, Captain Alving! Leave me be!"

MANDERS. How terribly gross and thoughtless of him! Oh, but Mrs. Alving, it was no more than a moment's thoughtlessness, believe me.

MRS. ALVING. I soon learned what to believe. The captain had his way with the girl—and that affair had its after-effects, Pastor Manders.

MANDERS (*as if stunned into stone*). And all that in this house! In this house!

MRS. ALVING. I've endured a lot in this house to keep him home in the evenings—and nights, I had to become his drinking companion as he got sodden over his bottle, holed up in his room. There I had to sit alone with him, forcing myself through his jokes and toasts and all his maundering, abusive talk, and then fight him bare-handed to drag him into bed—

MANDERS (*shaken*). That you were able to bear all that!

MRS. ALVING. I had my little boy, and I bore it for him—at least until that final humiliation, when my own maid—! Then I swore to myself: that was the end! So I took charge of the house—complete charge—over him and everything else. Because now, you see, I had a weapon against him; he couldn't let out a word of protest. It was then I sent Osvald away. He was going on seven and starting to notice things and ask questions, the way children do. All that was too much for me, Manders. I thought the child would be poisoned just breathing this polluted air. That's why I sent him away. And now you can understand, too, why he never set foot in this house as long as his father lived. No one will know what that cost me.

MANDERS. What a trial your life has been!

MRS. ALVING. I could never have gotten through it if it hadn't been for my work. And I *have* worked, I can tell you. All the additions to the property, all the improvements and technical innovations that Alving got fame and credit for—do you think those were *his* doing? *He*, sprawled all day on the sofa, reading old government journals! No, I can tell you as well; it was *I* who got him moving whenever he had his lucid moments; and it was I who had to pull the whole load when he fell back in his old wild ways or collapsed in groveling misery.

MANDERS. And for this man, you're raising a monument!

MRS. ALVING. There's the power of a bad conscience.

MANDERS. A bad—? What do you mean?

MRS. ALVING. It always seemed inevitable to me that the truth would have to come out someday and be believed. So the orphanage was meant to spike all the rumors and dispel the doubts.

MANDERS. Well, you've certainly accomplished that, Mrs. Alving.

MRS. ALVING. And I had still another reason. I didn't want Osvald, my own son, to inherit the least little thing from his father.

MANDERS. Then it's with Alving's money that—?

MRS. ALVING. Yes. The sums I've contributed year after year to the orphanage add up to just the amount—I've figured it out exactly—just the amount that made Lieutenant Alving such a good catch at the time.

MANDERS. Then, if I understand you—

MRS. ALVING. It was my selling price. I don't want that money passing into Osvald's hands. Everything my son inherits will come from me, and no one else.

(OSVALD *enters by the farther door to the right. He has left his hat and overcoat outside.*)

MRS. ALVING (*moving toward him*). You back again, dear?

OSVALD. Yes. What can anyone do outside in this interminable rain? But I hear lunch is ready. That's good news!

(REGINA *enters from the dining room with a package.*)

REGINA. A parcel just came for you, ma'am. (*Handing it to her.*)

MRS. ALVING (*with a quick look at* MANDERS). The choir music for tomorrow, most likely.

MANDERS. Hm—

REGINA. And lunch is served.

MRS. ALVING. Good. We'll be along in a moment; I just want to— (*Starts opening the package.*)

REGINA (*to* OSVALD). Will Mr. Alving have red wine, or white?

OSVALD. Both, Miss Engstrand.

REGINA. *Bien.* Very good, Mr. Alving. (*She goes into the dining room.*)

OSVALD. I better help her uncork the bottles— (*He*

*follows her into the dining room, the door swinging half
shut behind him.)*

MRS. ALVING *(who has unwrapped the package).* Yes,
quite so—it's the choir music, Mr. Manders.

MANDERS *(with folded hands).* How I'll ever be able to
give my speech tomorrow with any conviction—!

MRS. ALVING. Oh, you'll manage all right.

MANDERS *(softly, so as not to be heard in the dining
room).* Yes, we musn't stir up any scandal.

MRS. ALVING *(in a quiet, firm voice).* No. And then this
long, horrible farce will be over. After tomorrow, it will
really seem as if the dead had never lived in this house.
There'll be no one else here but my son and me.

*(From the dining room comes the sound of a chair
knocked over, along with* REGINA's *voice in a sharp whisper.)*

REGINA. Osvald! Are you crazy? Let me go!

MRS. ALVING *(starting in terror).* Ah—!

(She stares distractedly at the half-open door. OSVALD *is
heard to cough within and start humming. A bottle is
uncorked.)*

MANDERS *(shaken).* But what happened, Mrs. Alving?
What was that?

MRS. ALVING *(hoarsely).* Ghosts. Those two from the
greenhouse—have come back.

MANDERS. You mean—! Regina—? Is *she*—?

MRS. ALVING. Yes. Come. Not a word—!

(She grips PASTOR MANDER's *arm and moves falteringly
toward the dining room.)*

⤙ ACT TWO ⤚

The same room. A thick mist still veils the landscape.
MANDERS *and* MRS. ALVING *enter from the dining room.*

MRS. ALVING. Why, you're very welcome, Mr. Manders. (*Speaking into the dining room.*) Aren't you joining us, Osvald?

OSVALD (*from within*). No, thanks; I think I'll go out for a while.

MRS. ALVING. Yes, do that. It's clearing a little now. (*She shuts the dining room door, goes over to the hall door and calls.*) Regina!

REGINA (*from without*). Yes, ma'am.

MRS. ALVING. Go down to the laundry room and help out with the decorations.

REGINA. Very good, ma'am.

(MRS. ALVING *makes certain* REGINA *has gone, then shuts the door.*)

MANDERS. You're sure he can't hear us in there?

MRS. ALVING. Not with the door closed. Anyway, he's going out soon.

MANDERS. I'm still in a daze. I can't understand how I ever managed to devour one morsel of that heavenly meal.

MRS. ALVING (*pacing up and down, suppressing her anxiety*). Nor I, either. But what's to be done?

MANDERS. Yes, what's to be done? Believe me, I just don't know; I'm so utterly inexperienced in such matters.

MRS. ALVING. I'm convinced nothing serious has happened so far.

MANDERS. God forbid! But it's still an unsavory business.

MRS. ALVING. It's just a foolish fancy of Osvald's, you can be sure of that.

MANDERS. Well, as I said, I'm not really up on these things; but it definitely seems to me—

MRS. ALVING. She'll have to get out of this house. Immediately. That's clear as day—

MANDERS. Yes, that's obvious.

MRS. ALVING. But where? We can't simply—

MANDERS. Where? Home to her father, of course.

MRS. ALVING. To whom, did you say?

MANDERS. To her—ah, but of course, Engstrand isn't—! Good Lord, Mrs. Alving, how is this possible? You must be mistaken, really.

MRS. ALVING. Unfortunately, I'm not the least bit mistaken. Joanna had to confess everything to me—and Alving couldn't deny it. There was nothing else to do, then, but have the whole thing hushed up.

MANDERS. Yes, that was essential.

MRS. ALVING. The girl was turned out at once and given a fairly sizable amount to keep quiet. She managed the rest for herself when she got back to town. She revived an old friendship with Engstrand—probably dropped a few hints, I would guess, about all the money she had—and spun him some tale of a foreigner on a yacht berthed here for the summer. So she and Engstrand were married straight off—well, you married them yourself.

MANDERS. But I don't see how—? I distinctly remember when Engstrand came to arrange the wedding. He was so woefully penitent, accusing himself so bitterly of the casual ways he and his fiancée had allowed themselves.

MRS. ALVING. Well, naturally he had to take the blame himself.

MANDERS. But the hypocrisy of the man! And with *me!* I absolutely never would have believed that of Jacob Engstrand. Well, I'll have to be very severe with him; he better be ready for that. And the immorality of such a marriage—all for money! How much did the girl get?

MRS. ALVING. Three hundred dollars.

MANDERS. Yes, can you imagine—to go and get married to a fallen woman for a paltry three hundred dollars!

MRS. ALVING. Then what's your opinion of me, who let herself be married to a fallen man?

MANDERS. God of mercy, what are you saying? A fallen man!

MRS. ALVING. Do you think my husband was any better when I went with him to the altar than Joanna when Engstrand married her?

MANDERS. But—there's a world of difference between you and her—

MRS. ALVING. Much less than a world, I think. There was a considerable difference in price—a paltry three hundred dollars as against a whole fortune.

MANDERS. But there's just no comparison here. After all, you'd listened to the counsels of your own heart, and those of your family.

MRS. ALVING (*not looking at him*). I thought you understood where I'd lost what you call my heart at the time.

MANDERS (*withdrawn*). If I'd understood any such thing, I would never have become a regular visitor in your husband's house.

MRS. ALVING. Anyway, one thing is clear: I never really listened to myself.

MANDERS. Well, to your nearest of kin then, as it's ordained you should: your mother and your two aunts.

MRS. ALVING. Yes, how true. The three of them wrote up my bill of sale. Oh, it's amazing how neatly they figured it out, that it would be stark madness to turn down an offer like that. If Mother could come back and see me now, where all those splendors got me.

MANDERS. No one's responsible for the outcome. At least there's this to be said: your marriage was carried through with every respect for law and order.

MRS. ALVING (*at the window*). Yes, always law and order! I often think they're the root of all our miseries on earth.

MANDERS. Mrs. Alving, that's a sinful thought.

MRS. ALVING. Yes, perhaps it is. But I can't stand it any longer, with all these webs of obligation. I can't stand it! I've got to work my way out to freedom.

MANDERS. What do you mean by that?

MRS. ALVING (*drumming on the windowpane*). I never should have covered up Alving's life. It was all I dared do then—not only for Osvald, but to spare myself. What a coward I was!

MANDERS. Coward?

MRS. ALVING. If people had known anything of what went on, they would have said: "Poor man, it's no wonder he strays at times; his wife ran away, you know."

MANDERS. And they could say that with some right, too.

MRS. ALVING (*looking straight at him*). If I were all I should have been, I would have taken Osvald aside and said: "Listen, my boy, your father was a degenerate human being—"

MANDERS. Good Lord—!

MRS. ALVING. Then I ought to have told him everything— word for word as I've told it to you.

MANDERS. I find you almost frightening, Mrs. Alving.

MRS. ALVING. I'm aware of that. Yes, I'm quite aware! I frighten myself by the thought. (*Coming away from the window.*) That's the coward I am.

MANDERS. And you call it cowardice to do your bounden duty? Have you forgotten that a child should love and honor his father and mother?

MRS. ALVING. Oh, don't let's talk abstractions! Why don't we ask, should Osvald love and honor Captain Alving?

MANDERS. Isn't there something that tells you, as a mother, not to destroy your son's ideals?

MRS. ALVING. Yes, but what of the truth—?

MANDERS. Yes, but what of his ideals—?

MRS. ALVING. Oh—ideals, ideals! If I only weren't the coward I am!

MANDERS. Don't demolish ideals, Mrs. Alving—that can have cruel repercussions. And especially now, with Osvald. He hasn't too many ideals, sad to say—but as far as I can make out, his father is some sort of ideal to him.

MRS. ALVING. Yes, you're right about that.

MANDERS. And the impressions he has you've instilled and nourished yourself, through your letters.

MRS. ALVING. Yes, I felt it was my duty and obligation— so year after year, I've gone on lying to my own child. Oh, what a coward—what a coward I've been!

MANDERS. You've built up a beautiful image in your son's imagination—and that's something you mustn't take lightly.

MRS. ALVING. Hm—who knows how good that's been, after all. But, in any case, I'm not going to have any trifling with Regina. He's not going to get that poor girl in trouble.

MANDERS. Good God, that would be dreadful!

MRS. ALVING. If I knew he was serious about it, and that it would make him happy—

MANDERS. Yes? Then what?

MRS. ALVING. But it wouldn't work out. Regina just isn't the type.

MANDERS. How so? What do you mean?

MRS. ALVING. If I weren't such a wretched coward, then I'd say to him: "Marry her, or live any way you like—but just be honest together."

MANDERS. Heavens above—! A legal marriage, no less! That would be barbarous—! It's unheard of—!

MRS. ALVING. Unheard of, you say? Word of honor, Pastor Manders—haven't you heard that, out here in the country, there are numbers of married couples who are just as closely related?

MANDERS. I really don't understand you.

MRS. ALVING. Oh yes you do, very well.

MANDERS. Well, you mean cases where possibly they—? Yes, unfortunately family life isn't always as pure as it ought to be, that's true. But what you're referring to is hardly ever known—at least, not conclusively. But here, instead—you, the mother, are willing to let your own—!

MRS. ALVING. But I'm not willing. I don't want to encourage it for anything in the world—that's just what I was saying.

MANDERS. No, because you're a coward, as you put it. But if you weren't a coward—! Almighty God—what a monstrous union!

MRS. ALVING. Well, as far as that goes, it's been rumored that we're all descended from a similar union. And who was it who thought up that arrangement, Pastor?

MANDERS. I will not discuss such questions with you, Mrs. Alving—because you're not in the proper state of mind. But, that you can dare call it cowardice on your part—!

MRS. ALVING. You have to understand what I mean by that. I'm anxious and fearful because of the ghosts that haunt me, that I can't get rid of.

MANDERS. Because of—what did you say?

MRS. ALVING. Ghosts. When I heard Regina and Osvald in there, it was as if I was seeing ghosts. But I almost believe we *are* ghosts, all of us, Pastor. It's not only what we inherit from our fathers and mothers that keeps on returning in us. It's all kinds of old dead doctrines and opinions and beliefs, that sort of thing. They aren't alive in us; but they hang on all the same, and we can't get rid of them. I just have to pick up a newspaper, and it's as if I could see the ghosts slipping between the lines. They must be haunting our whole country, ghosts everywhere—so many and thick, they're like grains of sand. And there we are, the lot of us, so miserably afraid of the light.

MANDERS. Ah! So this is the outgrowth of all your

reading. Fine fruit, I must say! Oh, these disgusting, insidious freethinking books!

MRS. ALVING. My dear Mr. Manders, you're wrong. It was you yourself who set me to thinking—and for that I'll always be grateful.

MANDERS. *I?*

MRS. ALVING. Yes, when you made me give in to what you called duty and obligation; when you praised as right and proper what I rebelled against heart and soul as something loathsome—that's when I started going over your teachings, seam by seam. I just wanted to pull out a single thread; but after I'd worked it loose, the whole design fell apart. And then I realized it was only basted.

MANDERS (*quietly, with feeling*). Is that all that was won by the hardest battle of my life?

MRS. ALVING. You mean your most shameful defeat.

MANDERS. It was the greatest victory I've known, Helene—victory over myself.

MRS. ALVING. It was a crime against us both.

MANDERS. That I entreated you by saying, "Woman, go home to your lawful husband," when you came to me distracted, crying, "Here I am, take me!" Was that a crime?

MRS. ALVING. Yes, I think so.

MANDERS. We two don't understand each other.

MRS. ALVING. Not anymore, at least.

MANDERS. Never—never, in even my most secret thoughts, have I seen you as anything but another man's wife.

MRS. ALVING. You believe that?

MANDERS. Helene—!

MRS. ALVING. One forgets so easily.

MANDERS. I don't. I'm the same as I always was.

MRS. ALVING (*shifting her tone abruptly*). Yes, yes, well—let's stop talking about the old days. Now you're up to your ears in boards and committees; and I go around here struggling with ghosts, inside me and outside both.

MANDERS. At least I can help you manage the outer ones. After all the disturbing things I've heard from you today, my conscience won't suffer a defenseless young girl to remain in this house.

MRS. ALVING. It would be best, don't you think, if we could see her established? I mean, decently married.

MANDERS. Undoubtedly. I'd say it's desirable for her in every respect. Regina's already at an age when—of course, I'm really no judge of these things, but—

MRS. ALVING. Regina matured quite early.

MANDERS. Yes, didn't she, though? It's my impression she was unusually well developed physically when I was preparing her for confirmation. But temporarily, in all events, she ought to go home, under her father's supervision—ah, but of course, Engstrand isn't—to think that he—that *he* could conceal the truth from me like that!

(*There is a knock at the hall door.*)

MRS. ALVING. Who can that be? Come in!

(ENGSTRAND, *in his Sunday clothes, appears in the door-way.*)

ENGSTRAND. I beg your pardon most humbly, but—

MANDERS. Aha! Hm—

MRS. ALVING. Oh, it's you, Engstrand.

ENGSTRAND. There were none of the maids about, so I made myself so bold as to give a knock.

MRS. ALVING. Well, all right, come in. You want to talk to me about something?

ENGSTRAND (*coming in*). No, thanks all the same. It was the pastor, actually, I wanted to have a little word with.

MANDERS (*walking up and down*). Oh, yes? You want to talk to me? Is that it?

ENGSTRAND. Yes, I'd be grateful no end—

MANDERS (*stopping in front of him*). Well, may I ask what this is about?

ENGSTRAND. See, it's like this, Pastor; we've gotten paid off down there now—with all thanks to you, ma'am—and now we've finished everything up. And so I was thinking how nice and fitting it'd be if all us honest craftsmen who've been working together all this time—I was thinking, we ought to round things off with a little prayer meeting this evening.

MANDERS. A prayer meeting? Down at the orphanage?

ENGSTRAND. Yes. But of course if the pastor's not agreeable, then—

MANDERS. Oh, it's a splendid thought, but—hm—

ENGSTRAND. I've been holding a few evening prayers down there myself now and then—

MRS. ALVING. You have?

ENGSTRAND. Yes, now and then. Just a little meditation, so to speak. But then I'm a common, ordinary man, with no special gifts, God help me—and so I was thinking, since the pastor was out here—

MANDERS. Now look, Engstrand, first I have to ask you a question. Are you in a proper frame of mind for this kind of meeting? Do you feel your conscience is free and clear?

ENGSTRAND. Oh, Lord help us, Pastor, there's no point going on talking about my conscience.

MANDERS. Ah, but it's exactly what we *are* going to talk about. Well, what's your answer?

ENGSTRAND. My conscience? Yes, that can be pretty nasty at times, it can.

MANDERS. Well, at least you're owning up to it. Now will you tell me, without any subterfuge—just what is your relationship to Regina?

MRS. ALVING (*quickly*). Mr. Manders!

MANDERS (*calming her*). If you'll leave it to me—

ENGSTRAND. To Regina! Jeez, you gave me a turn there! (*Looking at* MRS. ALVING.) There's nothing wrong with Regina, is there?

MANDERS. We hope not. What I mean is, just exactly how are you related to her? You pass for her father, don't you? Well?

ENGSTRAND (*vaguely*). Why—hm—you know, Pastor, this business with me and poor Joanna.

MANDERS. Stop bending the truth. Your late wife told Mrs. Alving everything before she left her service.

ENGSTRAND. But it's supposed to—! She did that, really?

MANDERS. So your secret's out, Engstrand.

ENGSTRAND. And after she swore on a stack of Bibles—!

MANDERS. She swore—!

ENGSTRAND. I mean, she gave me her word. But with such sincerity.

MANDERS. And all these years you've hidden the truth from me. From *me,* who put my absolute trust in you.

ENGSTRAND. Yes, I'm afraid that's just what I've done.

MANDERS. Have I deserved this from you, Engstrand? Haven't I always been ready to help you out in every way, so far as I possibly could? Answer! Haven't I?

ENGSTRAND. There's plenty of times things would've looked pretty bad for me, if it wasn't for Pastor Manders.

MANDERS. And this is the way you pay me back. Get me to make false entries in the parish register, and for years after withhold information you owed as a matter of respect both to me and the plain truth. Your conduct has been unpardonable, Engstrand: and from now on we're through with each other.

ENGSTRAND (*with a sigh*). Well, that's it, I guess.

MANDERS. Yes. Because how can you ever justify yourself?

ENGSTRAND. But how could she go around shaming herself the more by talking about it? If you could just imagine, Pastor, yourself in the same trouble as poor Joanna—

MANDERS. I!

ENGSTRAND. Jeez now, I don't mean the very same. But I mean, supposing you had something to be ashamed of in the eyes of the world, as they say. We menfolk oughtn't to judge a poor woman too hard, Pastor.

MANDERS. But that's not what I'm doing. It's you that I blame.

ENGSTRAND. If I might ask your Reverence one tiny little question—?

MANDERS. Yes, go ahead.

ENGSTRAND. Isn't it right and proper of a man that he raises up the fallen? •

MANDERS. Why, of course.

ENGSTRAND. And isn't a man obliged to keep his word of honor?

MANDERS. Certainly he is, but—

ENGSTRAND. At the time Joanna had her downfall at the hands of that Englishman—or maybe it was an American, or a Russian, or whatever—well, it was then she came back to town. Poor thing, she'd turned me down once or twice already; she only had eyes for the handsome ones, see—and I had this crook in my leg. Yes, you remember, Pastor, how I once took it on myself to go into a dance hall where common seamen were rioting in drink and dissipation, like they say. And when I tried to arouse them to seek out a better life—

MRS. ALVING (*over by the window*). Hm—

MANDERS. Yes, I know, Engstrand; those ruffians threw you downstairs. You've told me that before. Your disability does you great credit.

ENGSTRAND. I'm not priding myself on it, Pastor. But what I wanted to say was that then she came and confessed the whole thing to me, streaming down tears and gnashing her teeth. And I have to say, Pastor, it just about ripped the heart out of me to listen.

MANDERS. All of *that,* Engstrand. Well! Then what?

ENGSTRAND. Yes, so I said to her: that American, he's beating over the seas of the world, he is. And you, Joanna, I said—you've had your downfall, and you're a sinful, fallen creature. But Jacob Engstrand, I said, he stands on two stout legs—yes, I meant it like a manner of speaking, Pastor.

MANDERS. Yes, I quite understand. Go on.

ENGSTRAND. Well, so that's how I raised her up and gave her an honorable marriage, so no one'd ever find out about her wild carrying-on with foreigners.

MANDERS. That was all quite commendable of you. What I cannot approve is that you could bring yourself to accept money—

ENGSTRAND. Money? I? Not a penny.

MANDERS (*with an inquiring glance at* MRS. ALVING). But—?

ENGSTRAND. Oh, yes—just a minute; now I remember. Joanna did have a little odd change, all right—but I wanted nothing of *that*. Faugh! I said: Mammon, that's the wages of sin, it is. We'll take that greasy gold—or banknotes, whatever it was—and heave it back into the American's face, I said. But he was off and gone over the rolling sea, Pastor.

MANDERS. Was that it, my dear Engstrand?

ENGSTRAND. That's right. So I and Joanna agreed that the money ought to be put toward the child's bringing up, and that's where it went; and I can give a true reckoning of every penny.

MANDERS. But that changes things substantially.

ENGSTRAND. That's the way it worked out, Pastor. And I'll be bold enough to say I've been a real father to Regina, as far as it lay in my power—for I have to admit, I'm only a poor, frail mortal.

MANDERS. There, there, Engstrand—

ENGSTRAND. But I will say that I brought up the child and looked after my poor, dear Joanna and made them a home, like the gospel says. But it never would have occurred to me to go up to Pastor Manders, priding myself and making much out of a good deed done in this world. No, when that sort of thing happens to Jacob Engstrand, he keeps it to himself, he does. Though it happens none too often, sorry to say. No, when I come to see Pastor Manders, then it's all I can do just to talk out my sins and errors. Because to say what I said before—my conscience does turn pretty nasty at times.

MANDERS. Give me your hand, Jacob Engstrand.

ENGSTRAND. Oh, Jeez, Pastor—

MANDERS. No fuss now. (*Grasping his hand.*) There!

ENGSTRAND. And if I can dare to beg your pardon, Pastor, most humbly—

MANDERS. You? Quite the contrary, I'm the one who should beg your pardon—

ENGSTRAND. Oh, no, no!

MANDERS. Yes, definitely. And I do, with all my heart. Forgive me that I could so misjudge you. If only I could give you some sign of my sincere regret, and the goodwill I have toward you—

ENGSTRAND. You'd like that, Pastor?

MANDERS. It would please me no end.

ENGSTRAND. Because there's a real good opportunity for that right now. With the bit of honest coin I've put aside from my work out here, I was thinking of founding a kind of seaman's home back in town.

MRS. ALVING. *You?*

ENGSTRAND. Yes, it'd be sort of a refuge for the orphans of the sea, so to speak. Temptations are so manifold for a sailor when he comes wandering ashore. But in this house of mine he could live like under a father's protection, that was my thought.

MANDERS. What do you say to that, Mrs. Alving?

ENGSTRAND. It's not much I have to begin with, Lord knows; but if I could just take hold of a helping hand—

MANDERS. Yes, yes, we have to consider this further. Your project interests me enormously. But now, go on down and get things ready—and light some candles, to give it a ceremonial touch. And then we'll have our devotional hour together, my dear Engstrand, for now I'm sure you're in the right frame of mind.

ENGSTRAND. I really do think so, yes. So good-bye, Mrs. Alving, and thanks for everything. And take good care of Regina for me. (*Brushes a tear from his eye.*) Poor Joanna's child—um, isn't it amazing—but it's just as if that girl had grown a part of my very heart. Yes, sir, and that's a fact. (*He bows and goes out.*)

MANDERS. Well, what do you think of the man now, Mrs. Alving? That's quite a different picture of things we got from him.

MRS. ALVING. Yes, quite so, indeed.

MANDERS. There you see how scrupulously careful one has to be about judging one's fellowman. But it's also a wonderful joy to discover one's made a mistake. Well, what do you say?

MRS. ALVING. I say you are and you always will be a big baby, Manders.

MANDERS. I?

MRS. ALVING (*placing both hands on his shoulders*). And I say I could easily wrap you up in a great, big hug.

MANDERS (*pulling back quickly*). Oh, bless you, no! What an impulse!

MRS. ALVING (*with a smile*). Oh, don't be afraid of me.

MANDERS (*by the table*). You sometimes have the most outrageous way of expressing yourself. Now I first want to collect these documents together and put them in my bag. (*Doing so.*) There now. And so good-bye for the moment. Keep your eye on Osvald when he comes back. I'll be looking in on you later.

(*He takes his hat and goes out by the hall door.* MRS. ALVING *sighs, gazes a moment out of the window, straightens the room up a bit and starts into the dining room, then stops with a stifled cry in the doorway.*)

MRS. ALVING. Osvald! Are you still at the table?

OSVALD (*from the dining room*). I'm just finishing my cigar.

MRS. ALVING. I thought you'd gone for a walk.

OSVALD. In such weather?

(*The chink of a glass and decanter.* MRS. ALVING *leaves the door open and settles down with her knitting on the sofa by the window.*)

OSVALD. Wasn't that Pastor Manders who left just now?

MRS. ALVING. Yes, he went down to the orphanage.

OSVALD. Hm.

(*Again, the chink of glass and decanter.*)

MRS. ALVING (*with an anxious glance*). Osvald dear, you ought to go easy with the liqueur. It's strong.

OSVALD. It keeps the dampness out.

MRS. ALVING. Wouldn't you rather come in here with me?

OSVALD. But I can't smoke in there.

MRS. ALVING. Now you know a cigar is all right.

OSVALD. Oh, well, then I'll come in. Just a tiny drop more—ah, there. (*He enters, smoking his cigar, and shuts the door after him. Short silence.*) Where'd the pastor go?

MRS. ALVING. I told you, he went down to the orphanage.

OSVALD. Oh yes, that's right.

MRS. ALVING. You shouldn't go on sitting at the table so long, Osvald.

OSVALD (*holding his cigar behind his back*). But I think it's so cozy, Mother. (*Patting and fondling her.*) Imagine—what it is for me, coming home, to sit at my mother's own table, in my mother's room, and enjoy her delectable meals.

MRS. ALVING. My dear, dear boy!

OSVALD (*somewhat impatiently, walking about and smoking*). And what else am I going to do here? I can't accomplish anything—

MRS. ALVING. Can't you?

OSVALD. In all this murk? Not a glimmer of sunlight the whole day long? (*Pacing about.*) Oh, this—! This not being able to work—!

MRS. ALVING. Perhaps it wasn't such a good idea for you to come home.

OSVALD. No, Mother, that was essential.

MRS. ALVING. Because I'd ten times rather give up the joy of having you home with me, if it meant that you—

OSVALD (*stops by the table*). Now tell me, Mother—is it really such a great joy for you to have me home?

MRS. ALVING. What a question to ask!

OSVALD (*crumbling a newspaper*). I should have thought it hardly mattered to you whether I was here or not.

MRS. ALVING. You have the heart to say that to your mother, Osvald?

OSVALD. But you lived without me very well before.

MRS. ALVING. Yes, I've lived without you—that's true.

(*Silence. The twilight gradually deepens.* OSVALD *paces the floor, back and forth. He has set his cigar down.*)

OSVALD (*stops by* MRS. ALVING). Do you mind if I sit beside you on the sofa?

MRS. ALVING (*making room for him*). Please sit down, dear.

OSVALD (*sitting*). There's something I have to tell you, Mother.

MRS. ALVING (*nervously*). What?

OSVALD (*staring ahead into space*). Because I can't go on bearing it any longer.

MRS. ALVING. Bearing what? What is it?

OSVALD (*as before*). I couldn't bring myself to write you about it; and ever since I came home—

MRS. ALVING (*gripping his arm*). But, Osvald, what *is* it?

OSVALD. All yesterday and today I've been trying to drive these thoughts away—and free myself. But it doesn't work.

MRS. ALVING (*rising*). You've got to speak out, Osvald!

OSVALD (*drawing her down on the sofa again*). Sit still, and I'll try to tell you— I've been complaining so about my tiredness after the trip here—

MRS. ALVING. Yes? Well?

OSVALD. But that isn't what's wrong with me, not any ordinary tiredness—

MRS. ALVING (*starts to rise*). Osvald, you're not ill!

OSVALD (*draws her down again*). Sit still, Mother. Just be calm about it. I'm not exactly ill—at least not ill in the ordinary sense. (*Puts his hands to his head.*) Mother, it's my mind that's broken down—out of control—I'll never be able to work again! (*Hands over his face, he throws himself down in her lap and bursts into deep sobs.*)

MRS. ALVING (*pale and trembling*). Osvald! Look at me! No, no, it isn't true.

OSVALD (*looks up despairingly*). Never able to work again! Never—never! It's like a living death! Mother, can you imagine anything as horrible?

MRS. ALVING. My poor boy! How did this awful thing happen to you?

OSVALD (*sitting up again*). That's just what I don't understand. I can't figure it out. I've never lived a wild life—not in any respect. You have to believe me, Mother—that's something I've never done!

MRS. ALVING. I believe you, Osvald.

OSVALD. And yet it's come on me—this horrible thing!

MRS. ALVING. Oh, but dearest, it's going to be all right. It's no more than nervous exhaustion, believe me.

OSVALD (*heavily*). That's what I thought at first—but it's not so.

MRS. ALVING. Tell me everything, right from the start.

OSVALD. Yes, I want to.

MRS. ALVING. When did you first notice anything?

OSVALD. It was just after my last visit home, and I'd returned to Paris. I began having such tremendous pains in my head—mostly toward the back, it seemed. It felt like a tight iron band squeezing me from my neck up—

MRS. ALVING. Go on.

OSVALD. At first I thought they were nothing more than the old, familiar headaches I've been bothered by ever since I was little.

MRS. ALVING. Yes, yes—

OSVALD. But I soon found out: that wasn't it. I couldn't work any longer. I wanted to start a new large painting, but it was as if all my talents had flown, and all my strength was paralyzed; I couldn't focus any of my thoughts; everything swam—around and around. Oh, it was a terrifying state to be in! Finally I sent for a doctor—and through him I discovered the truth.

MRS. ALVING. What do you mean?

OSVALD. He was one of the foremost doctors down there. He had me describe exactly what I was feeling; and then he began asking me a whole lot of questions that didn't seem to bear at all. I couldn't grasp what he was after—

MRS. ALVING. So—?

OSVALD. At last he said: Right from your birth, your whole system has been more or less worm-eaten. The actual expression he used was *vermoulu*.

MRS. ALVING (*anxiously*). What did he mean by that?

OSVALD. I didn't understand either, so I asked him to be more specific. And then that old cynic said— (*Clenching his fist*). Oh—!

MRS. ALVING. What—?

OSVALD. He said: The sins of the fathers are visited upon the children.

MRS. ALVING (*slowly stands up*). The sins of the fathers—!

OSVALD. I almost hit him in the face.

MRS. ALVING (*moving across the room*). The sins of the fathers—

OSVALD (*smiles sadly*). Yes, can you imagine? Of course I assured him that was absolutely out of the question. But do you think he gave way? No, he had his mind made up; and it was only when I brought out your letters and translated all the parts to him that dealt with Father—

MRS. ALVING. What then—?

OSVALD. Well, then naturally he had to admit he'd been on the wrong track; and that's when I learned the truth—the incredible truth: that this beautiful, soul-stirring life with my young artist friends was something I should never have entered. It was too much for my strength. So—everything's my own fault.

MRS. ALVING. Osvald, no! You mustn't believe that!

OSVALD. There was no other way to explain it, he said. *That's* the worst of it. The whole of my life ruined beyond repair—all because of my own carelessness. So much that I wanted to do in this world—I don't dare think of it anymore—I'm not *able* to think of it. Oh, if I only could live my life over—and wipe out what I've done!

(*He throws himself face down on the sofa.* MRS. ALVING *wrings her hands and walks silently back and forth, locked in inner struggle. After a moment,* OSVALD *looks up, propping himself on his elbows.*)

OSVALD. If it had only *been* something inherited—something that wasn't my fault. But this! In a shameful, mindless, trivial way, to have thrown away health, happiness, a world of possibility—my future, my life—!

MRS. ALVING. No, no, my own dearest—it can't be! (*Bending over him.*) Things aren't as desperate as you think.

OSVALD. Oh, you don't know— (*Leaps to his feet.*) And then all the pain that I'm causing you, Mother! How often I could almost hope and wish you wouldn't care for me so much.

MRS. ALVING. Oh, Osvald, my only boy! You're all I have in this world, and all I care to have.

OSVALD (*grasps both her hands and kisses them*). Yes, yes, now I see. When I'm home I see it so well. And it's part of what weighs on me— Anyway, now you know the whole story. And let's not talk about it anymore today. I can't bear thinking about it very long. (*Walking about the room.*) Give me something to drink, Mother!

MRS. ALVING. To drink? What do you want to drink now?

OSVALD. Oh, anything. You must have some cold punch in the house.

MRS. ALVING. Oh, but Osvald dear—!

OSVALD. Don't refuse me that, Mother. Be good now! I've got to have something to drown all these gnawing thoughts.

(*Goes into the greenhouse.*) And how—how dark it is here!

(MRS. ALVING *goes over to the bellpull, right, and rings.*)

OSVALD. And this interminable rain. Week after week it can go on; whole months at a time. In all my visits home, I never once remember seeing the sun shine.

MRS. ALVING. Osvald—you're thinking of leaving me!

OSVALD. Hm— (*Sighs deeply.*) I'm not thinking of anything. I can't think of anything! (*In a low tone.*) I've given that up.

REGINA (*entering from the dining room*). You rang, ma'am?

MRS. ALVING. Yes, bring the lamp in.

REGINA. Right away, ma'am. It's already lit. (*Goes out.*)

MRS. ALVING (*going over to* OSVALD). Osvald, don't keep anything from me.

OSVALD. I won't, Mother. (*Moves to the table.*) I've told you a lot, I think.

(REGINA *comes in with the lamp and sets it on the table.*)

MRS. ALVING. Yes, and Regina, you might bring us a half bottle of champagne.

REGINA. Yes, ma'am. (*Goes out again.*)

OSVALD (*clasping* MRS. ALVING *about the neck*). That's the way it should be. I knew you wouldn't let your boy go thirsty.

MRS. ALVING. Ah, my poor dear Osvald—how could I refuse you anything now?

OSVALD (*buoyantly*). Is that true, Mother? You mean it?

MRS. ALVING. Mean what—?

OSVALD. That you won't refuse me *any*thing?

MRS. ALVING. But Osvald dear—

OSVALD. Shh!

(REGINA *returns with a half bottle of champagne and two glasses on a tray, which she sets down on the table.*)

REGINA. Should I open it—?

OSVALD. No, thanks, I'll do it.

(REGINA *goes out again.*)

MRS. ALVING (*seating herself at the table*). What did you mean—that I shouldn't refuse you?

OSVALD (*busy opening the bottle*). First a glass—maybe two.

(*The cork pops; he fills one glass and is about to pour the second.*)

MRS. ALVING (*holds her hand over it*). Thanks—not for me.

OSVALD. Well, for me then. (*He drains the glass, refills it, drains it again, then sits down at the table.*)

MRS. ALVING (*expectantly*). Well?

OSVALD (*not looking at her*). Say, tell me—I thought you and Mr. Manders looked so strange—hm, so quiet during lunch.

MRS. ALVING. You noticed that?

OSVALD. Yes. Hm— (*A short silence.*) Tell me, what do you think of Regina?

MRS. ALVING. What do I think?

OSVALD. Yes, isn't she splendid?

MRS. ALVING. Osvald dear, you don't know her as well as I do—

OSVALD. So—?

MRS. ALVING. It's too bad Regina lived at home for so long. I should have taken her in earlier.

OSVALD. Yes, but she's magnificent to look at, isn't she, Mother?

MRS. ALVING. Regina has a good many serious flaws—

OSVALD. Oh, but what does that matter? (*He drinks again.*)

MRS. ALVING. Even so, I'm fond of her; and I'm responsible for her. I wouldn't for the world want anything to hurt her.

OSVALD (*springing to his feet*). Mother, Regina's my only hope!

MRS. ALVING (*rising*). What do you mean by that?

OSVALD. I can't bear this anguish all by myself.

MRS. ALVING. But you have your mother to help you bear it, don't you?

OSVALD. Yes, I thought so—and that's why I came home to you. But it won't work that way. I can see; it won't work. I can't make a life out here.

MRS. ALVING. Osvald!

OSVALD. I have to live differently, Mother. So I will have to leave you. I don't want you to see all this.

MRS. ALVING. Oh, my miserable child! But, Osvald, when you're sick as you are—

OSVALD. If it were only the illness, I'd stay with you, Mother—I would. For you're my best friend in this world.

MRS. ALVING. Yes, it's true; I am, aren't I?

OSVALD (*striding restlessly about*). But it's all the torment, agony, remorse—and the great deathly fear. Oh—this hideous fear!

MRS. ALVING (*following him*). Fear? What fear? What do you mean?

OSVALD. Oh, don't ask me anymore about it. I don't know. I can't describe it to you.

(MRS. ALVING *crosses to the bell-pull, right, and rings.*)

OSVALD. What do you want?

MRS. ALVING. I want my boy to be happy, that's what. He mustn't go around brooding. (*To* REGINA, *who has appeared at the door.*) More champagne. A whole bottle.

(REGINA *goes.*)

OSVALD. Mother!

MRS. ALVING. Don't you think, in the country too, we know how to live?

OSVALD. Isn't she magnificent-looking? The figure she has! And the glow of her health!

MRS. ALVING. Sit down, Osvald, and let's have a quiet talk.

OSVALD (*sits*). You wouldn't know this, Mother, but I have a wrong to make right with Regina.

MRS. ALVING. You!

OSVALD. Or a little indiscretion—you might call it. Quite innocent, actually. When I was home last—

MRS. ALVING. Yes?

OSVALD. She asked me so many times about Paris, and I told her bits and pieces about the life down there. And I remember that one day I chanced to say, "Wouldn't you like to go there yourself?"

MRS. ALVING. Well?

OSVALD. I could see her blushing all shades of red, and then she said, "Yes, I'd very much like to." "All right," I said, "I expect that can be arranged"—or something like that.

MRS. ALVING. Oh?

OSVALD. Of course I forgot the whole thing completely; but then the day before yesterday I happened to ask her if she was glad I'd be staying so long at home this time—

MRS. ALVING. Yes?

OSVALD. And she gave me such a peculiar look and said, "But what about my trip to Paris?"

MRS. ALVING. Her trip!

OSVALD. And then I got it out of her that she'd taken the whole thing seriously, that she'd been thinking of me all this while, and that she'd even started to learn some French—

MRS. ALVING. So that's why—

OSVALD. Mother—when I saw her there in front of me, that splendid girl, so alive with health and beauty—it was as if I'd never noticed her before—but now she was standing there as if her arms were simply waiting to take me in—

MRS. ALVING. Osvald!

OSVALD. Then it struck me that in her was my salvation, because I saw how the joy of life was in her.

MRS. ALVING (*with a start*). The joy of life—? Is there salvation in that?

REGINA (*entering from the dining room with a bottle of champagne*). I'm sorry for taking so long, but I had to go down in the cellar— (*Sets the bottle down on the table.*)

OSVALD. And get one more glass.

REGINA (*looks at him in surprise*). But Mrs. Alving has her glass.

OSVALD. Yes, but bring one for yourself, Regina.

(REGINA *looks startled and flashes a quick, shy glance at* MRS. ALVING.)

OSVALD. Well?

REGINA (*her voice low and hesitant*). Is that your wish, Mrs. Alving—?

MRS. ALVING. Get the glass, Regina.

(REGINA *goes out into the dining room.*)

OSVALD (*his eyes following her*). Can you see the way she walks? So firm and fearless.

MRS. ALVING. Osvald, this can't happen—!

OSVALD. The thing is settled. You must see that. There's no use denying it.

(REGINA *returns with an empty glass in her hands.*)

OSVALD. Sit down, Regina.

(REGINA *looks uncertainly at* MRS. ALVING.)

MRS. ALVING. Sit down.

(REGINA *sits on a chair by the dining-room door, still holding the empty glass in her hand.*)

MRS. ALVING. What were you saying, Osvald, about the joy of life?

OSVALD. Yes, the joy of life, Mother—you don't know much about that here at home. I never feel it here.

MRS. ALVING. Not even with me?

OSVALD. Not when I'm home. But how could you understand that?

MRS. ALVING. Oh, yes, yes. I think I'm beginning to understand—now.

OSVALD. That—and the joy of work. Yes, they're really the same thing, basically. But no one understands that here, either.

MRS. ALVING. Maybe you're right. Go on, I want to hear more of this.

OSVALD. I mean, here everyone's brought up to believe that work is a curse and a punishment, and that life is a miserable thing that we're best off to be out of as soon as possible.

MRS. ALVING. A vale of tears, yes. And we ingeniously manage to make it that.

OSVALD. But they won't hear of such things down there. Nobody abroad believes in that sort of outlook anymore. Down there, simply to be alive in the world is held for a kind of miraculous bliss. Mother, have you noticed how everything I've painted is involved with this joy of life? Always and invariably, the joy of life. With light and sun and holiday scenes—and faces radiant with human content. That's why I'm afraid to stay on at home with you.

MRS. ALVING. Afraid? What are you afraid of here with me?

OSVALD. I'm afraid that everything that's most alive in me will degenerate into ugliness here.

MRS. ALVING (*looking fixedly at him*). Would *that* happen, do you think?

OSVALD. I'm sure it would. Live here the same as down there—and it still wouldn't be the same life.

MRS. ALVING (*who has been listening intently, rises, her eyes large and thoughtful*). Now I see how it all fits together.

OSVALD. What do you see?

MRS. ALVING. I see it now, for the first time. And now I can speak.

OSVALD (*getting up*). I don't understand you, Mother.

REGINA (*who has also gotten up*). Shouldn't I go?

MRS. ALVING. No, stay here. Now I can speak. Now, my son, you have to know everything—and then you can choose. Osvald! Regina!

OSVALD. Quiet! The pastor—

MANDERS (*entering by the hall door*). Well, we've really had a heart-warming session together.

OSVALD. We also.

MANDERS. Engstrand needs help with his seaman's home. Regina will have to move back and accommodate him—

REGINA. No, thank you, Pastor.

MANDERS (*just noticing her*). What—? Here—with a glass in your hand!

REGINA (*hurriedly putting the glass down*). *Pardon*—!

OSVALD. Regina's leaving with me, Pastor.

MANDERS. Leaving—with you!

OSVALD. Yes, as my wife—if she wants that.

MANDERS. Merciful heavens—!

REGINA. It wasn't my doing, Mr. Manders.

OSVALD. Or she'll stay here if I stay.

REGINA (*involuntarily*). Here!

MANDERS. You petrify me, Mrs. Alving.

MRS. ALVING. Neither one nor the other will happen— because now I can speak out freely.

MANDERS. But you can't do that! No, no, no!

MRS. ALVING. I both can and will. And without demolishing any ideals.

OSVALD. Mother, what is it you're hiding from me?

REGINA (*listening*). Mrs. Alving! Listen! People are shouting out there. (*She goes into the greenhouse and looks out.*)

OSVALD (*moving toward the window, left*). What's going on? What's that light in the sky?

REGINA (*cries out*). The orphanage—it's burning!

MRS. ALVING (*hurrying to the window*). Burning!

MANDERS. Burning? Impossible. I was just down there.

OSVALD. Where's my hat? Oh, never mind—! Father's orphanage—! (*He runs out through the garden door.*)

MRS. ALVING. My shawl, Regina! It's all ablaze!

MANDERS. How awful! Mrs. Alving, this is God's fiery judgment on a wayward house!

MRS. ALVING. Yes, no doubt. Come along, Regina.

(*She and* REGINA *hurry out the hall door.*)

MANDERS (*clasping his hands together*). And then—no insurance! (*He follows them out.*)

⤙ ACT THREE ⤚

The room as before. All the doors stand open. The lamp is still burning on the table. It is dark outside, with only a faint red glow in the background to the left. MRS. ALVING, with a large shawl over her head, is standing in the greenhouse, gazing out. REGINA, also with a shawl about her, stands slightly behind her.

MRS. ALVING. Completely burned out—right to the ground.

REGINA. It's burning still in the basement.

MRS. ALVING. Why Osvald doesn't come up—? There's nothing to save.

REGINA. Should I go down to him with his hat?

MRS. ALVING. He hasn't even got his hat?

REGINA (*pointing into the hall*). No, it's hanging in there.

MRS. ALVING. Oh, leave it be. He has to come up soon. I'll look for him myself. (*She goes into the garden.*)

MANDERS (*entering from the hall*). Isn't Mrs. Alving here?

REGINA. She just went into the garden.

MANDERS. This is the most frightful night I've ever experienced.

REGINA. Yes, it's a terrible catastrophe, isn't it, Pastor?

MANDERS. Oh, don't speak of it! I can hardly think of it even.

REGINA. But how could it have happened—?

MANDERS. Don't ask me, Miss Engstrand. How should I know? You're not also going to—? Isn't it enough that your father—?

REGINA. What about him?

MANDERS. He's got me completely confused.

ENGSTRAND (*entering from the hall*). Pastor—!

MANDERS (*turning away, appalled*). Are you after me even here!

ENGSTRAND. Yes, God strike me dead, but I have to—! Good grief, what a mess this is, Pastor!

MANDERS (*pacing back and forth*). Dreadful, dreadful!

REGINA. What's going on?

ENGSTRAND. Oh, it was on account of this here meeting, see? (*In an undertone.*) Now we've got the old bird snared, my girl. (*Aloud.*) And to think it's all my fault that it's Pastor Manders' fault for something like this!

MANDERS. But I assure you, Engstrand—

ENGSTRAND. But there was nobody besides the pastor who messed around with the candles down there.

MANDERS (*stopping*). Yes, that's what you say. But I absolutely cannot remember ever having a candle in my hand.

ENGSTRAND. And I saw so plainly how the pastor took that candle and pinched it out with his fingers and flicked the tip of the wick down into those shavings.

MANDERS. You saw me do that?

ENGSTRAND. Plain as day, I saw it.

MANDERS. I just don't understand it. It's never been a habit of mine to snuff a candle in my fingers.

ENGSTRAND. Yes, it did look pretty sloppy to me, all right. But could it really do that much damage, Pastor?

MANDERS (*walking restlessly back and forth*). Oh, don't ask me.

ENGSTRAND (*walking along with him*). And then your Reverence hadn't insured it either, had you?

MANDERS (*keeps walking*). No, no, no—you heard me.

ENGSTRAND (*keeps following him*). Not insured. And then to go straight over and set the whole works afire. Lord love us—what awful luck!

MANDERS (*wiping the sweat from his brow*). Yes, you can say that again, Engstrand.

ENGSTRAND. And to think it would happen to a charitable institution that was meant to serve the whole community, so to speak. The papers'll handle you none too gently, Pastor, I can bet.

MANDERS. No, that's just what I've been thinking about. That's almost the worst part of the whole business— all these vicious attacks and innuendoes—! Oh, it's too upsetting to think about!

MRS. ALVING (*coming from the garden*). I can't pull him away from the embers.

MANDERS. Ah, you're back, Mrs. Alving.

MRS. ALVING. So you got out of making your speech, Mr. Manders.

MANDERS. Oh, I would have been only too glad—

MRS. ALVING (*her voice subdued*). It's best that it went like this. This orphanage was never made for anyone's benefit.

MANDERS. You think it wasn't?

MRS. ALVING. You think it was?

MANDERS. It was a frightful misfortune, in any case.

MRS. ALVING. Let's discuss it purely as a business arrangement—Are you waiting for the pastor, Engstrand?

ENGSTRAND (*by the hall door*). Well, actually I was.

MRS. ALVING. Then sit down and rest a moment.

ENGSTRAND. Thanks. I can stand all right.

MRS. ALVING (*to* MANDERS.) I suppose you'll be leaving by the steamer?

MANDERS. Yes. It goes an hour from now.

MRS. ALVING. Would you be so good as to take all the

papers back with you. I don't want to hear another word about this thing. I've got other matters to think about—

MANDERS. Mrs. Alving—

MRS. ALVING. I'll shortly be sending you power of attorney to settle everything however you choose.

MANDERS. I'll be only too glad to take care of it. Of course the original terms of the bequest will have to be changed completely now, I'm afraid.

MRS. ALVING. That's understood.

MANDERS. Just offhand, it strikes me that I might arrange it so the Solvik property is made over to the parish. The land itself can hardly be written off as worthless; it can always be put to some use or other. And the interest on the balance of capital in the bank—I could probably apply that best to support some project or other that might be considered of benefit to the town.

MRS. ALVING. Whatever you wish. The whole thing's utterly indifferent to me now.

ENGSTRAND. Think of my seaman's home, Pastor!

MANDERS. Yes, definitely, that's a possibility. Well, it will bear some investigation.

ENGSTRAND. The hell with investigating—oh, Jeez!

MANDERS (*with a sigh*). And then too, unfortunately I have no idea how long I'll be able to handle these affairs— or if public opinion won't force me to drop them. That depends entirely on the results of the inquest into the fire.

MRS. ALVING. What are you saying?

MANDERS. And those results aren't predictable in advance.

ENGSTRAND (*approaching him*). Oh yes, they are! Because here's old Jacob Engstrand, right beside you.

MANDERS. Yes, but—?

ENGSTRAND (*lowering his voice*). And Jacob Engstrand's not the man to go back on a worthy benefactor in his hour of need, as the expression goes.

MANDERS. Yes, but my dear fellow—how can you—?

ENGSTRAND. Jacob Engstrand's sort of like your guardian angel, Pastor, see?

MANDERS. No, no, that I absolutely cannot accept.

ENGSTRAND. Oh, it's how it's going to be, anyway. It's not like somebody here hasn't taken the blame for somebody else before, you know.

MANDERS. Jacob! (*Grasps his hand.*) You're a rare individual. Well, you're going to have every bit of help you need for your seaman's home, you can count on that.

(ENGSTRAND *tries to thank him, but is overcome by emotion.*)

MANDERS (*slipping the strap of his traveling bag over his shoulder*). Well, time to be off. We can travel together.

ENGSTRAND (*by the dining-room door*). Come along with me, wench! You'll live soft as a yoke in an egg.

REGINA (*tossing her head*). Merci! (*She goes out in the hall and fetches* MANDERS' *overcoat and umbrella.*)

MANDERS. Good-bye, Mrs. Alving. And may the spirit of law and order soon dwell again in this house.

MRS. ALVING. Good-bye, Manders. (*She goes into the greenhouse as she notices* OSVALD *coming in through the garden door.*)

ENGSTRAND (*as he and* REGINA *help* MANDERS *on with his coat*). Good-bye, my girl. And if you're ever in any trouble, well, you know where to find Jacob Engstrand. (*Quietly.*) Little Harbor Street, hm—! (*To* MRS. ALVING *and* OSVALD.) And my house for wayfaring seamen—that's going to be known as "Captain Alving's Home," yes. And if I get to run that house after my own devices, I think I can promise you it'll be truly worthy of that great man's memory, bless him.

MANDERS (*in the doorway*). Hm—hm! Come along, my dear Engstrand. Good-bye, good-bye!

(*He and* ENGSTRAND *go out the hall door.*)

OSVALD (*going toward the table*). What is this house he was speaking of?

MRS. ALVING. It's some sort of home that he and the pastor want to establish.

OSVALD. It'll burn up like all this here.

MRS. ALVING. Why do you say that?

OSVALD. Everything will burn. There'll be nothing left in memory of Father. And here I'm burning up, too.

(REGINA *stares perplexed at him.*)

MRS. ALVING. Osvald! Poor boy, you shouldn't have stayed down there so long.

OSVALD (*sitting at the table*). I guess you're right.

MRS. ALVING. Let me dry your face, dear; you're dripping wet.

OSVALD (*gazing indifferently into space*). Thank you, Mother.

MRS. ALVING. Aren't you tired, Osvald? Perhaps you could sleep?

OSVALD (*anxiously*). No, no—not sleep! I never sleep; I only pretend to. (*Dully.*) That comes soon enough.

MRS. ALVING (*looking worriedly at him*). You know, dearest, you really are ill.

REGINA (*tensely*). Is Mr. Alving ill?

OSVALD (*impulsively*). And shut all the doors! This racking fear—!

MRS. ALVING. Shut them, Regina.

(REGINA *shuts the doors and remains standing by the hall door.* MRS. ALVING *removes her shawl;* REGINA *does the same.*)

MRS. ALVING (*draws a chair over beside* OSVALD *and sits by him*). There, now I'll sit with you—

OSVALD. Yes, do that. And Regina must stay here too. I always want her close to me. You'll give me your help, Regina—won't you?

REGINA. I don't understand—

MRS. ALVING. Help?

OSVALD. Yes—when it's needed.

MRS. ALVING. Osvald, don't you have your mother to give you help?

OSVALD. You? (*Smiles.*) No, Mother, that kind of help you'd never give me (*With a mournful laugh.*) You! Ha, ha! (*Looks soberly at her.*) Although you're the obvious choice. (*Vehemently.*) Regina, why are you so reserved toward me? Why can't you call me Osvald?

REGINA (*softly*). I don't think Mrs. Alving would like it.

MRS. ALVING. You'll have every right to soon—so won't you sit down with us here?

(*After a moment,* REGINA *sits down with shy dignity at the other side of the table.*)

And now, my poor, troubled boy, I'm going to take all this weight off your mind—

OSVALD. You, Mother?

MRS. ALVING. Everything you call the agony of remorse and self-reproach.

OSVALD. Do you think you can?

MRS. ALVING. Yes, Osvald, now I can. You were speaking earlier about the joy of life; and as you said those words, it was as if a new light had been shed over the whole of my life.

OSVALD (*shaking his head*). I don't understand this.

MRS. ALVING. You should have known your father when he was just a young lieutenant. *He* had the joy of life, he did!

OSVALD. Yes, I know.

MRS. ALVING. It was like a holiday just to look at him. And all the energy, the unquenchable power that was in him!

OSVALD. Well—?

MRS. ALVING. And then, so full of that very joy, this child—because he *was* like a child then, really—had to make a life here in a mediocre town that had no joys to offer—only distractions. He had to get along here with no real goal in life—only a routine job to hold down. He never found any activity he could throw himself in heart and soul—only business affairs. He never had one single friend with the slightest sense of what the joy of life can mean—no one but drifters and drunkards—

OSVALD. Mother—!

MRS. ALVING. And finally the inevitable happened.

OSVALD. The inevitable?

MRS. ALVING. You said yourself, earlier this evening, what would happen to you if you stayed at home.

OSVALD. You're saying that Father—?

MRS. ALVING. Your poor father never found any outlet for the overpowering joy of life that he had. And I'm afraid I couldn't make his home very festive, either.

OSVALD. You, too?

MRS. ALVING. They'd drilled me so much in duty and things of that kind that I went on here all too long putting my faith in them. Everything resolved into duties—*my* duties, and *his* duties, and—I'm afraid I made this home unbearable for your poor father.

OSVALD. Why didn't you ever write me any of this?

MRS. ALVING. I've never seen it before as anything I could mention to you—his son.

OSVALD. And how, then, did you see it?

MRS. ALVING (*slowly*). I only saw the one thing: that your father was a ravaged man before you were born.

OSVALD (*with a strangled cry*). Ah—! (*He stands up and goes to the window.*)

MRS. ALVING. And then day after day I had only one thought on my mind: that Regina in reality belonged here in this house—just as much as my own son.

OSVALD (*wheeling about*). Regina—!

REGINA (*brought shaken to her feet, in a choked voice*). I—!

MRS. ALVING. Yes, now you both know.

OSVALD. Regina!

REGINA (*to herself*). So that's what she was.

MRS. ALVING. Your mother was decent in many ways, Regina.

REGINA. Yes, but she was that kind, all the same. Well, I sometimes thought so, but—then, Mrs. Alving, if you don't mind, may I leave right away, at once?

MRS. ALVING. Do you really want to, Regina?

REGINA. Yes, of course I want to.

MRS. ALVING. Naturally you can do as you wish, but—

OSVALD (*going over to* REGINA). Leave now? But you belong here.

REGINA. *Merci*, Mr. Alving—yes, I guess I can call you Osvald now. But it's certainly not the way I wanted to.

MRS. ALVING. Regina, I haven't been straightforward with you—

REGINA. That's putting it mild! If I'd known that Osvald was sick, why— And now that there isn't a chance of anything serious between us— No, I really can't stay out in the country and run myself ragged for invalids.

OSVALD. Not even for someone this close to you?

REGINA. Not on your life, I can't! A poor girl's only got her youth; she'd better use it—or else she'll find herself barefoot at Christmas before she knows it. And I've got this joy of life too, Mrs. Alving—in *me!*

MRS. ALVING. Yes, I'm afraid so. Only don't throw yourself away, Regina.

REGINA. Oh, things go as they go. If Osvald takes after his father, then I take after my mother, I guess. May I ask, Mrs. Alving, if Pastor Manders knows all this about me?

MRS. ALVING. Pastor Manders knows everything.

REGINA (*busy putting on her shawl*). Then I really better see if I can catch the boat out of here as quick as I can. The pastor's so nice to deal with, and I definitely think I've got just as much right to some of that money as he does—that rotten carpenter.

MRS. ALVING. You're quite welcome to it, Regina.

REGINA (*looking sharply at her*). You know, Mrs. Alving, you could have raised me as a gentleman's daughter—

and I would've been a lot better off. (*Tossing her head.*) But, hell—what's the difference! (*With a bitter glance at the unopened bottle.*) I'll get my champagne in society yet, just see if I don't.

MRS. ALVING. If you ever need a home, Regina, you can come to me.

REGINA. No, thank you, ma'am. Pastor Manders'l look out for me, all right. And if things really go wrong, I still know a house where I'll do just fine.

MRS. ALVING. Where?

REGINA. In "Captain Alving's Home."

MRS. ALVING. Regina—I can see now—you'll go to your ruin!

REGINA. Ahh, ffft! *Adieu.* (*She curtsies and goes out the hall door.*)

OSVALD (*standing at the window, looking out*). Has she gone?

MRS. ALVING. Yes.

OSVALD (*murmuring to himself*). I think it's insane, all this.

MRS. ALVING (*goes over behind him, placing her hands on his shoulders*). Osvald, dear—has this disturbed you terribly?

OSVALD (*turning his face toward her*). All that about Father, you mean?

MRS. ALVING. Yes, about your poor father. I'm afraid it's been too much of a shock for you.

OSVALD. Why do you think so? It came as quite a surprise, of course; but basically it can hardly make any difference to me.

MRS. ALVING (*withdrawing her hands*). No difference! That your father was so enormously unhappy!

OSVALD. Naturally I can feel sympathy for him as for any human being, but—

MRS. ALVING. Nothing more—for your own father—!

OSVALD (*impatiently*). Yes, Father—Father! I never

knew a father. My only memory of him is that he once got me to vomit.

MRS. ALVING. That's a dreadful thought! Surely a child ought to feel some love for his father, no matter what.

OSVALD. When that child has nothing to thank him for? Hasn't even known him? Do you really hang on to that old superstition—you, so enlightened in everything else?

MRS. ALVING. And is that just a superstition—!

OSVALD. Yes, you must realize that, Mother. It's one of these ideas that materialize in the world for a while, and then—

MRS. ALVING (*with a shudder*). Ghosts!

OSVALD (*pacing the floor*). Yes, you could very well call them ghosts.

MRS. ALVING (*in an outcry*). Osvald—you don't love me either!

OSVALD. I know you, at least—

MRS. ALVING. Yes, I know—but is that all?

OSVALD. And I know how much you care for me, and I have to be grateful to you for that. And you can be especially useful to me, now that I'm ill.

MRS. ALVING. Yes, I can, Osvald, can't I? Oh, I could almost bless this illness that forced you home to me, because it's made me see you're really not mine; you still have to be won.

OSVALD (*impatiently*). Yes, yes, yes, that's all just a manner of speaking. You have to remember I'm a sick man, Mother. I can't be concerned very much with others; I have enough just thinking about myself.

MRS. ALVING (*softly*). I'll be patient and forebearing.

OSVALD. And cheerful, Mother!

MRS. ALVING. Yes, dearest, you're right. (*Going over to him.*) Now have I taken away all your remorse and self-reproach?

OSVALD. Yes, you have. But who'll take away the fear?

MRS. ALVING. The fear?

OSVALD (*pacing about the room*). Regina would have done it for the asking.

MRS. ALVING. I don't understand. What is all this about fear—and Regina?

OSVALD. Is it very late, Mother?

MRS. ALVING. It's nearly morning. (*Looking out through the greenhouse.*) There's the first light of dawn already on the mountains. It's going to be clear, Osvald! In a little while you'll see the sun.

OSVALD. I look forward to that. Oh, there can be so much still to look forward to, and live for—!

MRS. ALVING. I'm sure there will be!

OSVALD. And even though I can't work, I'll—

MRS. ALVING. Oh, my dearest, you'll find yourself working again so soon. Because now you won't have these worrisome, depressing thoughts to brood on any longer.

OSVALD. Yes, it was good that you could rid me of all those fantasies of mine. And now, if I can only face this one thing more— (*Sits down on the sofa.*) Mother, we have to talk together—

MRS. ALVING. Yes, let's. (*She pushes an armchair over by the sofa and sits beside him.*)

OSVALD. And meanwhile the sun will rise. And by then, you'll know—and I won't have this fear any longer.

MRS. ALVING. Tell me, what will I know?

OSVALD (*not listening*). Mother, didn't you say earlier this evening that there wasn't anything in the world you wouldn't do for me if I asked you?

MRS. ALVING. Why, yes, of course!

OSVALD. And you meant it, Mother?

MRS. ALVING. That you can depend on. You're my one and only boy; I have nothing else to live for but you.

OSVALD. All right, then listen. You have a strong, resilient mind, I know that. I want you to sit very quiet as I tell this.

MRS. ALVING. But what is it that's so terrible—?

OSVALD. You mustn't scream. Do you hear? Promise

me that? We're going to sit and speak of it quietly. Mother, promise me?

MRS. ALVING. Yes, yes, I promise—just tell me!

OSVALD. Well, then you've got to realize that all this about tiredness—and my incapacity for thinking in terms of my work—isn't the real illness—

MRS. ALVING. What is the real illness?

OSVALD. The one that I inherited, the illness—(*Points to his forehead and speaks very softly.*)—that's seated here.

MRS. ALVING (*nearly speechless*). Osvald! No—no!

OSVALD. Don't scream; I can't bear it. Yes, it sits in here and waits. And any day, at any time, it can strike.

MRS. ALVING. Oh, how horrible—!

OSVALD. Just stay calm. So, that's how things are with me.

MRS. ALVING (*springing to her feet*). It's not true, Osvald! It's impossible! It can't be!

OSVALD. I had one attack down there. It soon passed off—but when I found out how things stood with me, then this anxiety took hold, racking me like a cold fever; and with that, I started home here to you as fast as I could.

MRS. ALVING. So that's the fear—!

OSVALD. Yes, I can't tell you how excruciating it is. Oh, if it only had been some ordinary disease that would kill me— I'm not so afraid of dying, though I want to live as long as I can.

MRS. ALVING. Yes, yes, Osvald, you must!

OSVALD. But the thought of it *is* excruciating. To revert back to a helpless child again. To have to be fed, to have to be—oh, it's unspeakable.

MRS. ALVING. My child has his mother to nurse him.

OSVALD (*leaps up*). No, never! That's just what I won't have! I can't abide the thought of lying here like that for years—turning old and gray. And in the meantime you might die before me. (*Sits in* MRS. ALVING's *chair.*) Because the doctor said it needn't be fatal at once. He called it a kind of "softening of the brain"—some phrase like that. (*Smiles sadly.*) I think that expression sounds so nice. It always makes me think of cherry-red velvet draperies—something soft to stroke.

MRS. ALVING (*screams*). Osvald!

OSVALD (*leaps up again and paces the floor*). And now you've taken Regina away from me! If I'd only had her. She would have helped me out, I'm sure.

MRS. ALVING (*going over to him*). My dear boy, what do you mean? Is there any help in this world that I wouldn't willingly give you?

OSVALD. After I'd recovered from the attack down there, the doctor told me that, when it struck again—and it *would* strike—there'd be no more hope.

MRS. ALVING. That he could be so heartless—

OSVALD. I demanded it of him. I told him I had certain arrangements to make. (*With a shy smile.*) And so I had. (*Brings out a small box from his inner breast pocket.*) Mother, you see this?

MRS. ALVING. What's that?

OSVALD. Morphine pills.

MRS. ALVING (*looks at him in horror*). Osvald—my child!

OSVALD. I've saved up twelve of them—

MRS. ALVING (*snatching at it*). Give me the box, Osvald!

OSVALD. Not yet, Mother. (*He returns the box to his pocket.*)

MRS. ALVING. I can't live through this!

OSVALD. You'll have to. If I'd had Regina here now, I'd have told her what state I was in—and asked for her help with this one last thing. She'd have helped me, I'm positive of that.

MRS. ALVING. Never!

OSVALD. If this horrible thing struck me down, and she saw me lying there like an infant child, helpless, and beyond help, lost, hopeless—incurable—

MRS. ALVING. Regina never would have done that!

OSVALD. Yes, she would have. Regina was so wonderfully lighthearted. She soon would have gotten tired of tending an invalid like me.

MRS. ALVING. Then thank God Regina's not here!

OSVALD. So now, Mother, you've got to give me that help.

MRS. ALVING (*in a loud outcry*). I!

OSVALD. What more obvious choice than you?

MRS. ALVING. I! Your mother!

OSVALD. Exactly the reason.

MRS. ALVING. I, who gave you life!

OSVALD. I never asked you for life. And what is this life you gave me? I don't want it! You can take it back!

MRS. ALVING. Help! Help! (*She runs out into the hall.*)

OSVALD (*right behind her*). Don't leave me! Where are you going?

MRS. ALVING (*in the hall*). To get the doctor, Osvald! Let me out!

OSVALD (*also in the hall*). You don't leave. And no one comes in.

(*The sound of a key turning in a lock.*)

MRS. ALVING (*coming in again*). Osvald—Osvald—my child!

OSVALD (*following her*). Have you no mother-love for me at all—to see me suffer this unbearable fear!

MRS. ALVING (*after a moment's silence, controlling her voice*). Here's my hand on it.

OSVALD. Then you will—?

MRS. ALVING. If it becomes necessary. But it won't be necessary. No, no, that's simply impossible!

OSVALD. Well, that we can hope. And now let's live together as long as we can. Thank you, Mother.

(*He settles down in the armchair that* MRS. ALVING *had moved over to the sofa. The day is breaking; the lamp still burns on the table.*)

MRS. ALVING. Now do you feel all right?

OSVALD. Yes.

MRS. ALVING (*bending over him*). What a fearful nightmare this has been for you, Osvald—but it was all a dream. Too much excitement—it hasn't been good for you. But now you can have your rest, at home with your mother near, my own, my dearest boy. Anything you want you can have, just like when you were a little child. There now, the pain is over. You see how quickly it went. Oh, I knew it would— And look, Osvald, what a lovely day we'll have. Bright sunlight. Now you really can see your home.

(*She goes to the table and puts out the lamp. Sunrise. The glaciers and peaks in the background shine in the brilliant light of morning. With his back toward the distant view,* OSVALD *sits motionless in the armchair.*)

OSVALD (*abruptly*). Mother, give me the sun.

MRS. ALVING (*by the table, looks at him, startled*). What did you say?

OSVALD (*repeats in a dull monotone*). The sun. The sun.

MRS. ALVING (*moves over to him*). Osvald, what's the matter?

(OSVALD *appears to crumple inwardly in the chair; all his muscles loosen; the expression leaves his face; and his eyes stare blankly.*)

MRS. ALVING (*shaking with fear*). What is it? (*In a shriek.*) Osvald! What's wrong! (*Drops to her knees beside him and shakes him.*) Osvald! Osvald! Look at me! Don't you know me?

OSVALD (*in the same monotone*). The sun—the sun.

MRS. ALVING (*springs to her feet in anguish, tears at her hair with both hands and screams*). I can't bear this! (*Whispers as if paralyzed by fright.*) I can't bear it!

Never! (*Suddenly.*) Where did he put them? (*Her hand skims across his chest.*) Here! (*She shrinks back several steps and shrieks.*) No, no, no!—Yes!—No, no! (*She stands a few steps away from him, her fingers thrust into her hair, staring at him in speechless horror.*)

OSVALD (*sitting motionless, as before*). The sun—the sun.

AN ENEMY OF THE PEOPLE

The day after completing *An Enemy of the People* (1882), Ibsen wrote his publisher in Copenhagen, stating that "I am still uncertain as to whether I should call it a comedy or a straight drama. It has many of the traits of comedy, but it also is based on a serious idea." The playwright's doubts directly reflect the play's structure, which derives in more or less equal measure from both its comic form and its underlying idea.

Comedy from the Greeks to the present has played endless, ingenious variations on one basic, inexhaustible plot. As Northrop Frye notes, that plot pits an insistent force of vitality, usually a pair of young lovers, against an outworn, rigidified, established society. The characters that embody that vitality, by their actions, expose the rulers of society as impostors, since they have forgotten, in the process of defending their vested interests in the status quo, that the law of life is change, succession, regeneration.

In *An Enemy of the People* the status quo is represented by the spa, the mineral baths that are the mainstay of the town's prosperity. Its water system, conveying all the heady triumphs of nineteenth-century technology and entrepreneurial capitalism, was designed, when properly functioning, to be a source of health and well-being. But also since, by the Bible that Ibsen's childhood was steeped in, water and the spirit are commensurable, the water system is analogous to the moral and spiritual ideas that, by rights, should freely circulate in the community and the civilization it exemplifies.

When pollution is discovered in the system, the arrogant refusal of the establishment to listen to dissenting expertise in the rush for profits stands exposed. The lines are soon drawn between that minority advocating further change to rectify past errors and that majority willing to cover up the pollution, and ready to discredit, and if necessary destroy, its discoverers. The spa is run by an invisible board of directors, for which Mayor Stockmann, with his comical rigidities and his more ominous flair for intimidation and expedient maneuver, is the managerial front. His name,

Peter, identifies him as the unyielding rock upon which orthodoxy rests.

The mayor's headstrong, impulsive, exuberant adversary is his younger brother Thomas, the doubter, the skeptic who cannot accept the opinions of others, but must ascertain the truth for himself. Around him a small nucleus of progressive-minded young people has cohered; but by Act Five, it has almost completely melted away, Hovstad and Billing having proved themselves impostors, traitors to their rhetoric, through defection to the establishment. The exception, Horster, Ibsen emphasized, must be conceived and cast as a young man, counter to stock images of Norwegian sea captains; and he and Petra must be depicted as strongly drawn to each other, evoking in the midst of Stockmann's final, beleaguered but unbowed isolation a promise of the classic comedic resolution of the life-forwarding union of young lovers.

The doctor has been isolated, it turns out, not by an unpopular fact, the contamination of the baths, but by a serious idea, expressed of course too sweepingly with his typically intemperate gusto. In defiance of the democratic dogma, the minority, he claims, is always right, for those who think and create on history's evolving frontiers, those pioneers of today's unsettling change that becomes tomorrow's truth, must always be the few. (Ibsen's own version of the idea: "That man is right who is most in league with the future.") However put, whether explicitly proclaimed as in the stirring theatrical tour de force of Act Four, or translated into the overall action that systematically strips the protagonist of all class or factional alliances, all naive illusions of belonging, down to the tiny minority of his likeminded own, this idea, fully as much as the comedic conflict, fuels and propels the drama.

But what remains with readers and audience is less likely to be plot structure or thematic idea than a character and an attitude, the infectiously buoyant fighting spirit of Thomas Stockmann. The actor-director Stanislavsky found in that character the most congenial of all his roles, and it helped lead him to the intuitive essence of the actor's art, the method of building credible character from within. "From the intuition of feelings I passed naturally to the inner image with all its peculiarities and details: the short-sighted eyes that spoke so eloquently of his inner blindness to human faults, the childlike and youthful manner of movement, the friendly relations with his children and family, the happiness, the joking and play, the gregariousness and attractiveness which forced all who came in touch with him to become purer and better, and to show the best sides of their nature in his presence. From the intuition of feelings I went to the outer image, and the soul and body of Stockmann-Stanislavsky became one organically."

More than anything, for Stanislavsky the appeal and the secret of playing Stockmann lay in his love of, and feeling for, truth. It buoyed the familial openness so warmly celebrated above, and when faced by the consensual betrayal of truth, it roused him to the wrath of an Old Testament prophet. In short, it made his life integral, high-purposed, all of one positive piece. Kierkegaard's words, "purity of heart is to will one thing," could be his motto. No later protagonist in the cycle would similarly enjoy his guiltless and undivided mind.

THE CHARACTERS

DR. THOMAS STOCKMANN, staff physician at the municipal baths

MRS. STOCKMANN, his wife

PETRA, their daughter, a teacher

EILIF
MORTEN } their sons, aged 12 and 10

PETER STOCKMANN, the doctor's older brother, mayor, police chief, chairman of the board of the municipal baths, etc.

MORTEN KIIL, master tanner; Mrs. Stockmann's foster-father

HOVSTAD, editor of the *People's Courier*

BILLING, his assistant on the paper

CAPTAIN HORSTER

ASLAKSEN, a printer

PARTICIPANTS IN A PUBLIC MEETING: men of all social ranks, several women, and a gang of schoolboys

The action takes place in a coastal town in southern Norway.

◁ ACT ONE ▷

Evening. DR. STOCKMANN's *living room, simply but at-*
tractively furnished and decorated. In the side wall to the
right are two doors, the farther one leading out to the hall,
and the nearer into the DOCTOR's *study. In the facing wall,*
directly opposite the hall door, is a door to the family's
living quarters. At the middle of this wall stands the stove;
closer in the foreground, a sofa with a mirror above it,
and in front of these, an oval table covered by a cloth. On
the table a lamp, shaded and lit. In the back wall, an open
door to the dining room. The table is set for dinner within,
with a lit lamp on it.

BILLING, *napkin under his chin, sits at the table inside.*
MRS. STOCKMANN *is standing by the table, passing him a*
plate with a large slice of roast beef. The other places at
the table are empty; the settings are in disorder, as after a
meal.

MRS. STOCKMANN. Well, if you come an hour late, Mr.
Billing, then you have to accept cold food.

BILLING (*eating*). It tastes simply marvelous—just perfect.

MRS. STOCKMANN. Because you know how precise my
husband is about keeping his regular mealtime—

BILLING. Doesn't bother me in the least. In fact, I
really think food tastes best to me when I can eat like
this, alone and undisturbed.

MRS. STOCKMANN. Yes, well—just so you enjoy it

283

—(*Turns, listening, toward the hall door.*) Now that must be Hovstad coming.

BILLING. Probably.

(PETER STOCKMANN *enters, wearing an overcoat and the official hat of his mayor's office. He carries a walking stick.*)

MAYOR STOCKMANN. A most pleasant good evening, my dear Katherine.

MRS. STOCKMANN (*comes into the living room*). Why, good evening! So it's you? How nice that you stopped up to see us.

MAYOR STOCKMANN. I was just passing by, so— (*With a glance toward the dining room.*) Ah, but it seems you have company already.

MRS. STOCKMANN (*somewhat embarrassed*). No, no— he was quite unexpected. (*Hurriedly.*) Won't you step in and join him for a bite?

MAYOR STOCKMANN. I? No, thank you. Good heavens, hot food at night! Not with *my* digestion.

MRS. STOCKMANN. Oh, but just this once—

MAYOR STOCKMANN. No, really, that's kind of you; but I'll stick to my bread and butter and tea. It's healthier in the long run—and a bit more economical, too.

MRS. STOCKMANN (*smiling*). Now you mustn't think that Thomas and I live so lavishly, either.

MAYOR STOCKMANN. Not *you,* Katherine. *That* never crossed my mind. (*Points toward the* DOCTOR'*s study.*) I suppose he isn't home?

MRS. STOCKMANN. No, he went for a little walk after dinner—he and the boys.

MAYOR STOCKMANN. How healthy is that, I wonder? (*Listening.*) That ought to be him.

MRS. STOCKMANN. No, I don't think it is. (*A knock at the door.*) Come in!

(HOVSTAD *enters from the hall.*)

MRS. STOCKMANN. Ah, so it's Mr. Hovstad—

HOVSTAD. Yes, you'll have to excuse me, but I got held up at the printer's. Good evening, Mr. Mayor.

MAYOR STOCKMANN (*bowing rather stiffly*). Mr. Hovstad. Here on business, I suppose?

HOVSTAD. Partly. It's about something going in the paper.

MAYOR STOCKMANN. I'm not surprised. I hear my brother's become a very active contributor to the *People's Courier*.

HOVSTAD. Yes, he deigns to write for the *Courier* whenever he has a little plain speaking to do about this and that.

MRS. STOCKMANN (*to* HOVSTAD). But won't you—? (*Points toward the dining room.*)

MAYOR STOCKMANN. Oh, well now, I can hardly blame him for writing for the sort of readers who'd give him the best reception. And of course, personally, you know, I haven't the least cause for any ill will toward your paper, Mr. Hovstad.

HOVSTAD. No, I wouldn't think so.

MAYOR. On the whole, there's a fine spirit of tolerance in this town of ours—a remarkable public spirit. And that stems, of course, from our having a great common concern that binds us all together—a concern that involves to the same high degree every right-minded citizen—

HOVSTAD. The spa, yes.

MAYOR STOCKMANN. Exactly. We have our great, new, magnificent installation, the spa. Mark my words, Mr. Hovstad—these baths will become the very life-principle of our town. Unquestionably!

MRS. STOCKMANN. That's what Thomas says, too.

MAYOR STOCKMANN. Why, it's simply extraordinary the way this place has revived in the past two years! People here have some money again. There's life, excitement! Land and property values are rising every day.

HOVSTAD. And unemployment's down.

MAYOR STOCKMANN. Yes, that too. The taxes for public welfare have been cut by a comfortable margin for the propertied classes, and will be still more if we can only have a really good summer this year—hordes of visitors— masses of invalids who can give the baths a reputation.

HOVSTAD. And that's the prospect, I hear.

MAYOR STOCKMANN. The outlook is very auspicious. Every day, inquiries coming in about accommodations and the like.

HOVSTAD. Well, then the doctor's article ought to be quite timely.

MAYOR STOCKMANN. Has he been writing something again?

HOVSTAD. This is something he wrote last winter: a recommendation of the baths, and a report on the health-promoting character of the life here. But I held the article back at the time.

MAYOR STOCKMANN. There was a flaw in it somewhere, I suppose?

HOVSTAD. No, that's not it. I thought it was better to wait till now, in the spring, when people start planning their summer vacations—

MAYOR STOCKMANN. Quite right. Absolutely right, Mr. Hovstad.

MRS. STOCKMANN. Yes, Thomas spares nothing when the baths are involved.

MAYOR STOCKMANN. Well, he *is* on the staff, after all.

HOVSTAD. Yes, and then he's the one, too, who really originated the idea.

MAYOR STOCKMANN. He *did?* Really? Yes, I do occasionally hear that certain people hold that opinion. But I still had an impression that *I* also played some modest part in this enterprise.

MRS. STOCKMANN. Yes, Thomas says that always.

HOVSTAD. No one denies that, Mr. Mayor. You got the thing moving and put it into practical reality—we all know that. I only meant that the idea came from the doctor first.

MAYOR STOCKMANN. Yes, my brother's had more than enough ideas in his time, I'm afraid. But when there's something to be done, it's another sort of man that's called for, Mr. Hovstad. And I really had thought that, at least here, in this house—

MRS. STOCKMANN. But, my dear Peter—

HOVSTAD. Sir, how can you possibly think—?

MRS. STOCKMANN. Mr. Hovstad, do go in and take some refreshment. My husband's sure to be back any moment.

HOVSTAD. Thank you; just a bite, maybe. (*He goes into the dining room.*)

MAYOR STOCKMANN (*dropping his voice*). It's curious with these people of peasant stock: they never can learn any tact.

MRS. STOCKMANN. But why let that bother you? It's not worth it. Can't you and Thomas share the honor, like brothers?

MAYOR STOCKMANN. Yes, it would seem so; but it isn't everyone who can be satisfied with his share, apparently.

MRS. STOCKMANN. Oh, nonsense! You and Thomas get along splendidly together. (*Listening.*) There, now I think we have him. (*Goes over and opens the hall door.*)

DR. STOCKMANN (*laughing and raising commotion outside*). Look, Katherine—you've got another guest here. Isn't this a treat, eh? There we are, Captain Horster; hang your coat up on the peg. Oh, that's right—you don't wear a coat. Imagine, Katherine, I met him on the street, and he almost didn't want to come up.

(CAPTAIN HORSTER *enters and greets* MRS. STOCKMANN. DR. STOCKMANN *appears in the doorway.*)

In you go, boys. They're ravenous all over again! Come on, Captain Horster; now you're going to have some roast beef—

(*He propels* HORSTER *into the dining room;* EILIF *and* MORTEN *follow after.*)

MRS. STOCKMANN. But, Thomas, don't you see—?

DR. STOCKMANN (*turning by the door*). Oh, it's you, Peter! (*Goes over to shake hands.*) Well, this *is* a pleasure.

MAYOR STOCKMANN. I'm afraid I have to be going in just a moment—

DR. STOCKMANN. Rubbish! There's hot toddy on the table now, any minute. You haven't forgotten the toddy, Katherine?

MRS. STOCKMANN. Of course not. The water's boiling. (*She goes into the dining room.*)

MAYOR STOCKMANN. Toddy, too—!

DR. STOCKMANN. Yes, have a seat, so we can get comfortable.

MAYOR STOCKMANN. Thank you, I never take part in toddy parties.

DR. STOCKMANN. But this isn't a party.

MAYOR STOCKMANN. Well, it looks to me— (*Glancing toward the dining room.*) It's astonishing how they put all that food away.

DR. STOCKMANN (*rubbing his hands*). Yes, isn't it wonderful to watch young people eat? Endless appetites—just as it ought to be! They've got to have food—for strength! They're the ones who'll put a kick in the future, Peter.

MAYOR STOCKMANN. May I ask what, here, needs a "kick put in it," in your manner of speaking?

DR. STOCKMANN. Well, you better ask the young ones that—when the time comes. We don't see it, of course. Naturally. A pair of old fogies like you and me—

MAYOR STOCKMANN. Now really! That's a very peculiar term—

DR. STOCKMANN. Oh, you mustn't take things so literally with me, Peter. Because you know, I've been feeling so buoyant and happy. I can't tell you how lucky I feel to be part of this life that's budding and bursting out everywhere. What an amazing age we live in! It's as if a whole new world were rising around us.

MAYOR STOCKMANN. You really believe that?

DR. STOCKMANN. Of course you can't see it as well as I can. You've lived in the midst of it all your life, and that dulls the impression. But I, who've been stuck all these many years in my little limbo up north, hardly ever seeing a stranger with a fresh idea to share—to me, it's as if I'd been plunked down in the middle of a swarming metropolis.

MAYOR STOCKMANN. Hm—metropolis—

DR. STOCKMANN. Oh, I'm well aware this is small scale compared with a lot of other places. But there's life here— a promise, an immensity of things to work and fight for; and *that's* what's important. (*Calls.*) Katherine, didn't the mailman come?

MRS. STOCKMANN (*from the dining room*). No, not today.

DR. STOCKMANN. And then to make a good living, Peter! That's something you learn to appreciate when you've been getting along, as we have, on starvation wages—

MAYOR STOCKMANN. Oh, come—

DR. STOCKMANN. You can just imagine how tight things were for us up there, yes, many times. And now we can live like kings! Today, for instance, we had roast beef for dinner, and we had some more for supper. Don't you want a piece? Or, anyway, let me show it to you. Come here—

MAYOR STOCKMANN. No, definitely not—

DR. STOCKMANN. Well, then come over here. Look, we bought a new tablecloth.

MAYOR STOCKMANN. Yes, so I noticed.

DR. STOCKMANN. And we got a lampshade. See? It's all out of Katherine's savings. And it makes the room so cozy, don't you think? Just stand right here—no, no, no, not there. Just—so! Look, how the light concentrates there where it falls. Really, I find that quite elegant. Don't you?

MAYOR STOCKMANN. Yes, if you can allow yourself luxuries like that—

DR. STOCKMANN. Oh yes. I can allow myself that. Katherine says I'm now earning almost as much as we spend.

MAYOR STOCKMANN. Almost—!

DR. STOCKMANN. But a man of science ought to live with a little style. I'm sure the average district judge spends more in a year than I do.

MAYOR STOCKMANN. Yes, I expect so! A district judge, a superior magistrate—

DR. STOCKMANN. Well, an ordinary businessman then. That kind of man spends a lot more—

MAYOR STOCKMANN. It's a matter of circumstances.

DR. STOCKMANN. In any case, I honestly don't waste anything on luxuries, Peter. But I don't feel I can deny myself the gratification of having people in. You see, I need that. Having been shut out for so long—for me it's a necessity of life to spend time with high-spirited, bold young people, with adventurous minds and a wealth of energy—and that's what they are, all of them sitting and savoring their food in there. I wish you knew Hovstad a bit better—

MAYOR STOCKMANN. Yes, come to think of it, Hovstad told me he'll be printing another of your articles.

DR. STOCKMANN. Of *my* articles?

MAYOR STOCKMANN. Yes, about the baths. Something you wrote last winter.

DR. STOCKMANN. Oh yes, that! No, I don't want that in right now.

MAYOR STOCKMANN. No? It strikes me this is just the opportune time.

DR. STOCKMANN. Yes, you might be right—under ordinary circumstances— (*He paces about the room.*)

MAYOR STOCKMANN (*following him with his eyes*). What's extraordinary about the circumstances now?

DR. STOCKMANN (*stops*). Peter, I swear, at this moment I can't tell you—anyway, not this evening. There could be something quite extraordinary about the circumstances— or it might be nothing at all. It could well be that it's just imagination.

MAYOR STOCKMANN. I have to confess, it sounds very mysterious. Is anything wrong? Something I'm excluded from? I would assume that I, as chairman of the board of the municipal baths—

DR. STOCKMANN. And I would assume that—oh, come on, Peter, let's not fly at each other like this.

MAYOR STOCKMANN. Heaven forbid! I'm not in the habit of flying at people, as you put it. But I most definitely must insist that all necessary steps be taken and carried out in a businesslike manner by the legally constituted authorities. I can't condone any sly or underhanded activities.

DR. STOCKMANN. When have I ever been sly or underhanded?

MAYOR STOCKMANN. You have an inveterate tendency to go your own way, in any case. And in a well-ordered society, that's nearly as inexcusable. The individual has to learn to subordinate himself to the whole—or, I should say, to those authorities charged with the common good.

DR. STOCKMANN. Possibly. But what in thunder does that have to do with me?

MAYOR STOCKMANN. Because, my dear Thomas, it's this you seem never to want to learn. But watch out; someday you're going to pay for it—sooner or later. Now I've told you. Good-bye.

DR. STOCKMANN. Are you stark, raving mad? You're completely on the wrong track—

MAYOR STOCKMANN. That's not my custom. And now, if I may excuse myself— (*With a bow toward the dining room.*) Good night, Katherine. Good night, gentlemen. (*Goes out.*)

MRS. STOCKMANN (*coming into the living room*). He's gone?

DR. STOCKMANN. Yes, and in a foul humor.

MRS. STOCKMANN. Oh, Thomas dear, what did you do to him this time?

DR. STOCKMANN. Nothing at all. He can't demand that I settle accounts with him before the time comes.

MRS. STOCKMANN. What accounts do you have to settle with him?

DR. STOCKMANN. Hm, don't ask me, Katherine. It's odd that the mailman hasn't come.

(HOVSTAD, BILLING, *and* HORSTER *have risen from the*

table and come into the living room. EILIF *and* MORTEN *follow after a moment.*)

BILLING (*stretching his arms*). Ah, a meal like that and, ye gods, you feel like a new man!

HOVSTAD. The mayor wasn't in his best spirits tonight.

DR. STOCKMANN. It's his stomach; he has bad digestion.

HOVSTAD. I'm sure it was mainly us from the *Courier* he couldn't digest.

MRS. STOCKMANN. You were getting on rather well with him, I thought.

HOVSTAD. Oh yes, but it's nothing more than an armistice.

BILLING. That's it! That's the word for it.

DR. STOCKMANN. We have to remember, Peter's a lonely man. Poor fellow, he has no home to give him comfort— just business, business. And all that damn weak tea he's always sloshing down. Well, now, pull up your chairs to the table, boys! Katherine, don't we get any toddy?

MRS. STOCKMANN (*going toward the dining room*). I'm just bringing it.

DR. STOCKMANN. And you sit here on the sofa by me, Captain Horster. A rare guest like you—please, sit down, everyone.

(*The men seat themselves at the table.* MRS. STOCKMANN *comes back with a tray, holding a hotplate, glasses, decanters, and the like.*)

MRS. STOCKMANN. There now. This is arrack, and here's rum, and cognac. So just help yourselves.

DR. STOCKMANN (*taking a glass*). Oh, I think we'll manage! (*While the toddy is mixed.*) And let's have the cigars. Eilif, I'm sure you know where the box is. And, Morten, you can fetch my pipe. (*The boys go into the room on the right.*) I have a suspicion that Eilif sneaks a cigar now and then—but I play innocent. (*Calls.*) And my smoking cap too, Morten! Katherine, can't you tell him where I left it? Ah, he's got it! (*The boys bring in the various items.*) Help yourselves, everybody. I'll stick to my pipe. This one's taken me through a lot of dirty weather on my rounds up north. (*Clinking glasses.*) Skoal! Ah, it's a lot better sitting here, snug and warm.

MRS. STOCKMANN (*sits and starts knitting*). Are you sailing soon, Captain Horster?

HORSTER. I think we'll be ready by next week.

MRS. STOCKMANN. And you'll be going to America then?

HORSTER. That's the intention, yes.

BILLING. But then you can't vote in the new town election.

HORSTER. There's an election coming up?

BILLING. Didn't you know?

HORSTER. No, I don't bother with such things.

BILLING. But you *are* concerned about public affairs, aren't you?

HORSTER. No. I don't understand them.

BILLING. Even so, a person at least ought to vote.

HORSTER. People who don't understand, too?

BILLING. Understand? What do you mean by that? Society's like a ship: all hands have to stand to the wheel.

HORSTER. Maybe on land; but at sea it wouldn't work too well.

HOVSTAD. It's remarkable how most sailors are so little concerned with what happens on land.

BILLING. Very strange.

DR. STOCKMANN. Sailors are like birds of passage: north, south, wherever they are is home. But it's why the rest of us have to be all the more effective, Mr. Hovstad. Anything of general interest in tomorrow's *Courier?*

HOVSTAD. No local items. But I was thinking of running your article the day after tomorrow—

DR. STOCKMANN. Hell's bells, that article! No, listen, you'll have to wait on that.

HOVSTAD. Oh? We have so much space right now, and it seems like the opportune moment—

DR. STOCKMANN. Yes, yes, you're probably right; but you'll have to wait all the same—

(PETRA, *wearing a hat and coat, comes in from the hall, with a stack of exercise books under her arm.*)

PETRA. Good evening.

DR. STOCKMANN. That's you, Petra? Good evening.

(*Greetings all around.* PETRA *takes off her hat and coat and leaves them, with the books, on a chair by the door.*)

PETRA. And here you all sit partying while I'm out slaving away.

DR. STOCKMANN. Well, now it's your party, too.

BILLING. Can I fix you a little drink?

PETRA (*coming to the table*). Thanks, I'll do it myself. You always make it too strong. Oh, Father, by the way, I have a letter for you. (*Goes over to the chair where her things are.*)

DR. STOCKMANN. A letter! Who from?

PETRA (*searching in her coat pocket*). I got it from the mailman as I was just going out—

DR. STOCKMANN (*gets up and goes toward her*). And you don't bring it till now!

PETRA. I really hadn't the time to run up again. Here it is.

DR. STOCKMANN (*seizing the letter*). Let me see, let me see, child. (*Looks at the envelope.*) Yes, that's it—!

MRS. STOCKMANN. Is *this* the one you've been so impatient for?

DR. STOCKMANN. Exactly. I must take it straight in and —where can I find a light, Katherine? Is there no lamp in my room again?

MRS. STOCKMANN. The lamp is lit and standing on your desk.

DR. STOCKMANN. Good, good. Excuse me a minute— (*Goes into his study to the right.*)

PETRA. Mother, what do you suppose that is?

MRS. STOCKMANN. I don't know. These last days he's been asking constantly about the mailman.

BILLING. Most likely some patient out of town—

PETRA. Poor Father, he's taking on too much work. (*Mixing a drink.*) Ooh, this'll be good!

HOVSTAD. Were you teaching night school again today?

PETRA (*sipping her glass*). Two hours.

BILLING. And four hours mornings at the Institute—

PETRA (*sitting by the door*). Five hours.

MRS. STOCKMANN. And papers to correct in the evening, I see.

PETRA. A whole batch, yes.

HORSTER. It looks like you take on your own full share.

PETRA. Yes, but that's fine. You feel so delectably tired afterward.

BILLING. You like that?

PETRA. Yes. Then you sleep so well.

MORTEN. You must be horribly wicked, Petra.

PETRA. Wicked?

MORTEN. Yes, when you work so hard. Mr. Rørland says that work is a punishment for our sins.

EILIF (*snorts*). Pah, how stupid you are, to believe that stuff.

MRS. STOCKMANN. Now, now, Eilif!

BILLING (*laughing*). Oh, marvelous!

HOVSTAD. You'd rather not work so hard, Morten?

MORTEN. No, I wouldn't.

HOVSTAD. Yes, but what do you want to be in life?

MORTEN. Best of all, I want to be a Viking.

EILIF. But then you'd have to be a pagan.

MORTEN. Well, so then I'll be a pagan!

BILLING. I'm with you, Morten! Exactly what I say!

MRS. STOCKMANN (*making signals*). No, you don't really, Mr. Billing.

BILLING. Ye gods, yes—! I *am* a pagan, and proud of it. Just wait, we'll all be pagans soon.

MORTEN. And can we then do anything we want?

BILLING. Well, you see, Morten—

MRS. STOCKMANN. Now, in you go, boys, both of you. I'm sure you've got homework for tomorrow.

EILIF. *I* could stay a little longer—

MRS. STOCKMANN. Oh no, you can't. The two of you, out!

(*The boys say good night and go into the room to the left.*)

HOVSTAD. Do you really think it could hurt the boys to hear these things?

MRS. STOCKMANN. Well, I don't know. But I don't like it.

PETRA. Oh, Mother, I think you're just being silly.

MRS. STOCKMANN. Yes, that's possible; but I don't like it—not here at home.

PETRA. Oh, there's so much hypocrisy, both at home and in school. At home we have to keep quiet, and in school we have to stand there and lie to the children.

HORSTER. You have to lie?

PETRA. Yes, don't you know, we have to teach them all kinds of things we don't believe in ourselves?

BILLING. Yes, that's for certain.

PETRA. If I only had the means, then I'd start a school myself, and things would be different there.

BILLING. Pah, the means—!

HORSTER. Well, if that's your idea, Miss Stockmann, I'll gladly provide you the facilities. My father's old place has been standing nearly empty; there's a huge dining room on the ground floor—

PETRA (*laughing*). Oh, thank you! But nothing'll come of it, I'm sure.

HOVSTAD. No, I think Miss Petra's more apt to go in for journalism. Incidentally, have you had time to look over that English story you promised to translate for us?

PETRA. No, not yet. But I'll get it to you in time.

(DR. STOCKMANN *comes in from his study, the open letter in his hand.*)

DR. STOCKMANN (*waving the letter*). Well, let me tell you, here's news for the town!

BILLING. News?

MRS. STOCKMANN. What sort of news?

DR. STOCKMANN. A great discovery, Katherine!

HOVSTAD. Really?

MRS. STOCKMANN. That you've made?

DR. STOCKMANN. My own, yes. (*Pacing back and forth.*) Now let them come around the way they do, saying it's just whims and wild fantasies. But they better watch out! (*With a laugh.*) They're going to watch out, I think!

PETRA. But, Father, tell what it is!

DR. STOCKMANN. Yes, all right, just give me time, and you'll learn everything. If I only had Peter here now! There you see how we human beings can go around, passing judgments as blind as moles—

HOVSTAD. What do you mean by that, Doctor?

DR. STOCKMANN (*stops by the table*). It's the general opinion, isn't it, that our town is a healthy place?

HOVSTAD. Why, of course.

DR. STOCKMANN. A most outstandingly healthy place, as a matter of fact—a place to be glowingly recommended to sick and well alike—

MRS. STOCKMANN. But, Thomas, dear—

DR. STOCKMANN. And recommend it we have, and praised it to the skies. I've written endlessly in the *Courier* and in pamphlets—

HOVSTAD. All right, so?

DR. STOCKMANN. This establishment, the baths, that's

been called the "main artery" of the town, and its "nerve center," and—who the hell knows what else—

BILLING. "The pulsating heart of our town" I once, in a moment of exuberance, went so far as to—

DR. STOCKMANN. Oh yes, that too. But do you know what they are in reality, these great, splendid, celebrated baths that have cost such a lot of money—you know what they are?

HOVSTAD. No, what are they?

MRS. STOCKMANN. What?

DR. STOCKMANN. The whole setup's a pesthole.

PETRA. The baths, Father!

MRS. STOCKMANN (*simultaneously*). Our baths!

HOVSTAD (*likewise*). But, Doctor—

BILLING. Simply incredible!

DR. STOCKMANN. It's a whited sepulcher, the whole establishment—poisoned, you hear me! A health hazard in the worst way. All that pollution up at Mølledal—all that reeking waste from the mill—it's seeped into the pipes feeding the pump-room; and the same damn poisonous slop's been draining out on the beach as well.

HORSTER. You mean in the bathing area?

DR. STOCKMANN. Exactly.

HOVSTAD. How can you be so certain of all this, Doctor?

DR. STOCKMANN. I've investigated the facts as scrupulously as possible. Oh, I've had suspicions for quite a while. Last year there were a number of unusual cases among the visitors here—typhoid and gastritis—

MRS. STOCKMANN. That's right, there were.

DR. STOCKMANN. At the time we assumed the visitors had brought their maladies with them. But later, over the past winter, I began having second thoughts; so I set out to analyze the water with the best means available.

MRS. STOCKMANN. So *that's* what you've been so involved in!

DR. STOCKMANN. Yes, involved—you can well say that, Katherine. But here, of course, I lacked the necessary scientific equipment, so I sent samples of both the drinking water and the seawater to the university for a strict laboratory analysis.

HOVSTAD. And this you've just gotten?

DR. STOCKMANN (*showing the letter*). This is it! There's irrefutable proof of the presence of decayed organic matter in the water—millions of bacteria. It's positively injurious to health, for either internal or external use.

MRS. STOCKMANN. What a godsend that you found out in time!

DR. STOCKMANN. You can say that again.

HOVSTAD. And what do you plan to do now, Doctor?

DR. STOCKMANN. To see things set to rights, of course.

HOVSTAD. Can that be done?

DR. STOCKMANN. It's got to be. Otherwise, the baths are totally useless—ruined. But there's no need for that. I'm quite clear about what actions have to be taken.

MRS. STOCKMANN. But, Thomas dear, why have you made such a secret of all this?

DR. STOCKMANN. Maybe I should have run out in the streets, blabbering about it before I had sure proof. No thanks, I'm not that crazy.

PETRA. But to us at home—

DR. STOCKMANN. Not to one living soul! But tomorrow you can run over to the Badger—

MRS. STOCKMANN. Really, Thomas—!

DR. STOCKMANN. All right then, your grandfather. Yes, this'll stand the old boy on his ear. He's always thought I'm a bit unhinged—oh yes, and a lot more think the same, I'm aware. But now these good people are going to find out—! (*Walks about, rubbing his hands.*) What a stir this'll make in town, Katherine! You can't imagine. The whole water system has to be relaid.

HOVSTAD (*rising*). The whole water system—?

DR. STOCKMANN. Well, obviously. The intake's too low; it's got to be placed much higher up.

PETRA. So you were right, after all.

DR. STOCKMANN. Ah, you remember that, Petra? I wrote a protest when they were just starting construction. But nobody would listen to me then. Well, now you can bet I'll pour on the heat—yes, because naturally I've written a report for the board of directors. It's been lying in my drawer a whole week; I've just been waiting for this. (*Waving the letter.*) But now it'll be sent right off. (*Goes into his study and returns with a sheaf of papers.*) See here! Four closely written pages! And a covering letter. A newspaper, Katherine—something to wrap this in! Good, that's it. Give it to—to— (*Stamps his foot.*) —what the hell's her name? The maid! Well, give it to her and tell her to take it straight to the mayor.

(MRS. STOCKMANN *takes the packet and goes out through the dining room.*)

PETRA. What do you think Uncle Peter will say, Father?

DR. STOCKMANN. What should he say? Undoubtedly he has to be glad that a fact of such importance is brought to light.

HOVSTAD. May I have permission to run a little item on your discovery in the *Courier?*

DR. STOCKMANN. I'd be most gratified if you would.

HOVSTAD. The public should hear about this, and the sooner the better.

DR. STOCKMANN. Absolutely.

MRS. STOCKMANN (*returning*). She's gone with it.

BILLING. So help me, Doctor, you're the foremost citizen of this town!

DR. STOCKMANN (*walks about, looking pleased*). Oh, come on—really, I haven't done anything more than my duty. I've been a lucky treasure-hunter, and that's it. All the same—

BILLING. Hovstad, don't you think this town owes Doctor Stockmann a parade?

HOVSTAD. I'll come out for it, in any case.

BILLING. And I'll put it up to Aslaksen.

DR. STOCKMANN. No, my dear friends, please—forget all this nonsense. I don't want any ceremonies. And if the board tries to vote me a raise in salary, I won't take it. Katherine, I'm telling you this—I won't take it.

MRS. STOCKMANN. That's only right, Thomas.

PETRA (*raising her glass*). Skoal, Father!

HOVSTAD *and* BILLING. Skoal, skoal, Doctor!

HORSTER (*clinking glasses with him*). May this bring you nothing but joy.

DR. STOCKMANN. Thank you. Dear friends, thank you! My heart is so full of happiness—! Ah, what a blessing it is to feel that you've done some service for your own home town and your fellow citizens. Hurrah, Katherine!

(*He wraps both hands around her neck and whirls about the room with her; she screams and struggles against him. Laughter, applause, and cheers for the* DOCTOR. *The* BOYS *poke their heads in at the door.*)

⤙ ACT TWO ⤚

The DOCTOR's *living room. The dining-room door is closed. It is morning.* MRS. STOCKMANN, *with a sealed letter in her hand, enters from the dining room, goes across to the door of the* DOCTOR's *study, and peers inside.*

MRS. STOCKMANN. Are you in, Thomas?

DR. STOCKMANN (*from within*). Yes, I just got back. (*Entering.*) Is there something?

MRS. STOCKMANN. Letter from your brother. (*Hands it to him.*)

DR. STOCKMANN. Ah, let's see. (*Opens the envelope and reads.*) "The enclosed manuscript is returned herewith—" (*Reads on in an undertone.*) Hm—

MRS. STOCKMANN. What does he say?

DR. STOCKMANN (*slips the papers in his pocket*). Only that he'll be stopping up around noon sometime.

MRS. STOCKMANN. You *must* remember not to go out, then.

DR. STOCKMANN. Oh, that's no problem. I've finished my calls for the morning.

MRS. STOCKMANN. I'm terribly curious to know how he takes it.

DR. STOCKMANN. You'll see, he's not going to like it that I made the discovery, and he didn't.

MRS. STOCKMANN. Yes, doesn't that worry you?

DR. STOCKMANN. Oh, basically he'll be pleased, you can imagine. All the same—Peter's so damned nervous that somebody besides himself might do this town a little good.

MRS. STOCKMANN. But, you know what, Thomas— that's why you ought to be nice and share the honors with him. Couldn't it get around that he was the one who put you on the track—?

DR. STOCKMANN. Fine, as far as I'm concerned. If I can just get this thing cleared up—

(*Old* MORTEN KIIL *sticks in his head at the hall door, looks about inquisitively, and shakes with silent laughter.*)

MORTEN KIIL (*slyly*). Is is—is it true?

MRS. STOCKMANN (*moving toward him*). Father—it's you!

DR. STOCKMANN. Why, Father-in-law, good morning, good morning!

MRS. STOCKMANN. Oh, but aren't you coming in?

MORTEN KIIL. Yes, if it's true—if not, I'm leaving—

DR. STOCKMANN. If what's true?

MORTEN KIIL. This wild story about the waterworks. Is that true?

DR. STOCKMANN. Of course it's true. But how did *you* hear about it?

MORTEN KIIL (*entering*). Petra flew in on her way to school—

DR. STOCKMANN. Oh, did she?

MORTEN KIIL. Oh yes, and she told me. I thought she was just making a fool of me; but that isn't like Petra, either.

DR. STOCKMANN. You don't mean that!

MORTEN KIIL. Oh, you can't trust anybody. You can be made a fool of before you know it. It really is true, though?

DR. STOCKMANN. Yes, irrefutably. Now, please, have a seat, Father. (*Pressing him down onto the sofa.*) Isn't this a real piece of luck for the town?

MORTEN KIIL (*stifling his laughter*). Luck for the town?

DR. STOCKMANN. Yes, that I made this discovery in the nick of time—

MORTEN KIIL (*as before*). Yes, yes, yes! But I'd never have dreamed that you'd play your monkeyshines on your own brother.

DR. STOCKMANN. Monkeyshines!

MRS. STOCKMANN. But, Father—

MORTEN KIIL (*rests his hands and chin on the handle of his cane and winks slyly at the* DOCTOR). How was it now? You're saying that some animals got loose in the water-pipes?

DR. STOCKMANN. Yes, bacteria.

MORTEN KIIL. And there are lots of those animals in there, Petra said. A huge crowd of them.

DR. STOCKMANN. Up in the millions, most likely.

MORTEN KIIL. But no one can see them—wasn't that it?

DR. STOCKMANN. You can't *see* them, of course not.

MORTEN KIIL (*chuckling to himself*). Damned if this isn't the best one you've pulled off yet.

DR. STOCKMANN. What do you mean?

MORTEN KIIL. But you'll never get the mayor believing anything like that.

DR. STOCKMANN. Well, we'll see.

MORTEN KIIL. You think he's that crazy?

DR. STOCKMANN. I hope the whole town will be that crazy.

MORTEN KIIL. The whole town! Yes, that's not impossible. It'd serve them right—and show them up. They think they're so much smarter than us old boys. They hounded me out of the town council. That's right, I'm telling you, like a dog they hounded me out, they did. But now they're going to get it. You just go on and lay your monkeyshines on them, Stockmann.

DR. STOCKMANN. Yes, but—

MORTEN KIIL. Make monkeys out of them, I say. (*Getting up.*) If you can work it so the mayor and his cronies get their ears pinned back, right then and there I'll donate a hundred crowns to the poor.

DR. STOCKMANN. You're very generous.

MORTEN KIIL. Yes, of course I've got little enough to spare, you understand. But if you can do that, I'll remember the poor next Christmas with a good fifty crowns.

(HOVSTAD *comes in from the hall.*)

HOVSTAD. Good morning! (*Stopping.*) Oh, excuse me—

DR. STOCKMANN. No, come in, come in.

MORTEN KIIL (*chuckling again*). Him! Is he in on this too?

HOVSTAD. What do you mean?

DR. STOCKMANN. Why, of course he is.

MORTEN KIIL. I might have guessed it. It's going into the paper. You're really the limit, Stockmann. Well, now you two get together; I'm leaving.

DR. STOCKMANN. No, stay a while, Father.

MORTEN KIIL. No, I'm leaving. And scheme up all the monkeyshines you can. You damn well aren't going to lose by it!

(*He goes, accompanied by* MRS. STOCKMANN.)

DR. STOCKMANN (*laughing*). What do you think—the old man doesn't believe a word of this about the water system.

HOVSTAD. Oh, was it *that*—?

DR. STOCKMANN. Yes, that's what we were talking about. And I suppose you're here for the same.

HOVSTAD. That's right. Do you have just a moment, Doctor?

DR. STOCKMANN. As long as you like.

HOVSTAD. Have you heard anything from the mayor?

DR. STOCKMANN. Not yet. He's stopping by later.

HOVSTAD. I've been thinking a good deal about this business since last evening.

DR. STOCKMANN. Oh?

HOVSTAD. For you, as a doctor and a scientist, this

condition in the water system is something all to itself. I mean, it hasn't occurred to you that it's interrelated with a lot of other things.

DR. STOCKMANN. How so? Here, let's sit down. No, on the sofa there.

(HOVSTAD *sits on the sofa, and* STOCKMANN *in an armchair on the other side of the table.*)

DR. STOCKMANN. Well? You were thinking—?

HOVSTAD. You said yesterday that the polluted water came from impurities in the soil.

DR. STOCKMANN. Yes, beyond any doubt it comes from that poisoned swamp up at Mølledal.

HOVSTAD. If you'll pardon me, Doctor, I think it comes from another swamp altogether.

DR. STOCKMANN. What sort?

HOVSTAD. The swamp where our whole community lies rotting.

DR. STOCKMANN. What the deuce is that supposed to mean, Mr. Hovstad?

HOVSTAD. Little by little every activity in this town has passed into the hands of a little clique of politicians—

DR. STOCKMANN. Come on now, they're not all of them politicians.

HOVSTAD. No, but those who aren't politicians are their friends and camp followers. All the rich in town, and the old established names—they're the powers that rule our lives.

DR. STOCKMANN. Yes, but then those people have a great deal of competence and vision.

HOVSTAD. Did they show competence and vision when they laid the water mains where they are now?

DR. STOCKMANN. No, of course that was an enormous piece of stupidity. But that'll be straightened out now.

HOVSTAD. You think it'll go so smoothly?

DR. STOCKMANN. Smoothly or not—it's going to go through.

HOVSTAD. Yes, if the press steps in.

DR. STOCKMANN. That won't be necessary, really. I'm positive that my brother—

HOVSTAD. Excuse me, Doctor; but I'm telling you that I plan to take this matter up.

DR. STOCKMANN. In the paper?

HOVSTAD. Yes. When I took over the *Courier*, it was my intention to break up that ring of pig-headed reactionaries who hold all the power.

DR. STOCKMANN. But you've told me yourself what the outcome was: you nearly wrecked the paper over them.

HOVSTAD. Yes, that time we had to back down, it's true. There was some risk that the baths might never have been constructed if those men had fallen. But now we have the baths, and the high and mighty are expendable now.

DR. STOCKMANN. Expendable, yes; but we still owe them a great debt.

HOVSTAD. And we'll acknowledge that, in all fairness. But a journalist of my radical leanings can't let an opportunity like this go by. The myth of the infallibility of the ruling class has to be shattered. It has to be rooted out, like any other superstition.

DR. STOCKMANN. I fully agree with you there, Mr. Hovstad. If it's a superstition, then out with it!

HOVSTAD. Of course I'm rather loath to involve the mayor, since he *is* your brother. But certainly you believe as I do, that the truth comes before anything else.

DR. STOCKMANN. No question of that. (*In an outburst.*) Yes, but—but—!

HOVSTAD. You mustn't think badly of me. I'm no more self-seeking or power-hungry than most people.

DR. STOCKMANN. But—whoever said you were?

HOVSTAD. I come from a poor family, as you know; and I've had ample opportunity to observe what the most pressing need is among the lower classes. Doctor, it's to play some part in directing our public life. That's the thing that develops skills and knowledge and self-respect—

DR. STOCKMANN. I understand absolutely—

HOVSTAD. Yes—and so I think a journalist is terribly remiss if he neglects the least opportunity for the liberation of the powerless, oppressed masses. Oh, I know—those on top are going to label this agitation, among other things; but they can say what they please. So long as my conscience is clear, then—

DR. STOCKMANN. That's it, yes! That's it, Mr. Hovstad. But all the same—damn it—! (*A knock at the door.*) Come in!

(ASLAKSEN, *the printer, appears at the hall door. He is plainly but respectably dressed in black, with a white, somewhat wrinkled cravat; he holds gloves and a high silk hat in his hand.*)

ASLAKSEN (*bowing*). Pardon me, Doctor, for intruding like this—

DR. STOCKMANN (*rises*). Well, now—it's Mr. Aslaksen!

ASLAKSEN. That's right, Doctor.

HOVSTAD (*getting up*). Were you looking for me, Aslaksen?

ASLAKSEN. No, I didn't think to meet you here. No, it was the doctor himself—

DR. STOCKMANN. Well, what can I do for you?

ASLAKSEN. Is it true, what I heard from Mr. Billing, that you're of a mind to get us a better water system?

DR. STOCKMANN. Yes, for the baths.

ASLAKSEN. Of course; I understand. Well, then I'm here to say, I'm throwing my full support behind you in this.

HOVSTAD (*to the* DOCTOR). You see!

ASLAKSEN. Because it might just come in handy to have us small businessmen in back of you. We make up pretty much of a solid majority in this town—that is, when we *choose* to. And it's always good to have the majority with you, Doctor.

DR. STOCKMANN. That's undoubtedly true. But I can hardly believe that any special measures are going to be needed here. With something as clear-cut as this, it would seem to me—

ASLAKSEN. Oh, it could be a good thing all the same. Because I know these local authorities. The ones that run things don't take too kindly to propositions coming from the outside. And so I was thinking it wouldn't be out of the way if we staged a little demonstration.

HOVSTAD. That's the idea.

DR. STOCKMANN. You say, a demonstration? Just how would you plan to demonstrate?

ASLAKSEN. Naturally with great moderation, Doctor. I always make every effort for moderation. Because moderation is a citizen's chief virtue—in *my* opinion, anyway.

DR. STOCKMANN. You're certainly well known for it, Mr. Aslaksen.

ASLAKSEN. Yes, I think that's not too much to say. And this question of the water system, it's immensely important to us little businessmen. The baths show every sign of becoming like a miniature gold mine for this town. It's the baths that'll give us all a living, and especially us home owners. That's why we want to support this operation in every possible way. And since I'm now chairman of the Home Owners Council—

DR. STOCKMANN. Yes—?

ASLAKSEN. And since, moreover, I'm a representative of the Temperance Union—you knew, Doctor, did you not, that I am a temperance worker?

DR. STOCKMANN. Yes, that follows.

ASLAKSEN. Well—so it's quite obvious that I come in contact with a wide variety of people. And since I'm known for being a sober, law-abiding citizen, as you yourself said, Doctor, I've acquired a certain influence in this town—just a little position of power—if I may say so myself.

DR. STOCKMANN. I'm well aware of that, Mr. Aslaksen.

ASLAKSEN. So you see—it would be a small matter for me to work up a tribute, in a pinch.

DR. STOCKMANN. A tribute?

ASLAKSEN. Yes, a kind of tribute of thanks from the townspeople to you, for having advanced such a vital interest for the community. It goes without saying that it's got to be phrased with all due moderation, so it doesn't offend the authorities, or anyone else in power. And if we just watch ourselves *there,* then I don't think anyone will object, do you?

HOVSTAD. So, even if they didn't like it too well—

ASLAKSEN. No, no, no! No affronts to the authorities, Mr. Hovstad. No collisions with people so much involved in our lives. I've had enough of that in my time; and no good ever comes of it, either. But a citizen's sober and honest opinions are not to be scorned by any man.

DR. STOCKMANN (*shaking his hand*). My dear Mr. Aslaksen, I can't tell you how deeply it pleases me to find so much sympathy among my fellow citizens. It makes me so happy—so happy! Listen, why not a little glass of sherry, what?

ASLAKSEN. Many thanks, but no. I never indulge in spirits.

DR. STOCKMANN. Well, then a glass of beer—what do you say to that?

ASLAKSEN. Thanks again, Doctor, but I never partake so early in the day. Just now I want to get around town and talk to some of the home owners and prepare their reactions.

DR. STOCKMANN. That's exceptionally kind of you, Mr. Aslaksen. But I simply can't get it through my head that all these measures are going to be necessary. I think the matter could very well take care of itself.

ASLAKSEN. Authorities tend to need goading, Doctor Stockmann—though, on my soul, I don't mean to be critical of them—!

HOVSTAD. We'll go after them in the paper tomorrow, Aslaksen.

ASLAKSEN. But without violence, Mr. Hovstad. Proceed in moderation, or you'll never get anywhere. You can trust my word on that, because I've gleaned my experience in the school of life. Well, then—I'll say good-bye to you, Doctor. Now you know that, in any event, we small businessmen stand behind you, like a wall. You've got the solid majority on your side, Doctor.

DR. STOCKMANN. Thank you for that, Mr. Aslaksen. (*Shaking his hand.*) Good-bye, good-bye!

ASLAKSEN. Will you be coming along to the pressroom, Mr. Hovstad?

HOVSTAD. I'll be in later. I still have a bit more to do.

ASLAKSEN. Very good.

(*He bows and leaves.* DR. STOCKMANN *accompanies him into the hall.*)

HOVSTAD (*as the* DOCTOR *re-enters*). Well, what do you say now, Doctor? Don't you think it's about time to stir up and air out all the stale, spineless inertia in this town?

DR. STOCKMANN. You're referring to Aslaksen?

HOVSTAD. Yes, I am. He's one of them who's sunk in the swamp—good a man as he is in some other ways. He's what most of them are around here: they go along tacking and trimming from this side to that. With all their scruples and second thoughts, they never dare strike out for anything.

DR. STOCKMANN. But to me Aslaksen seemed so thoroughly well-intentioned.

HOVSTAD. There's something I value more—and that's standing your ground as a strong, self-reliant man.

DR. STOCKMANN. I agree with you there entirely.

HOVSTAD. That's why I want to take this opportunity now and see if I can't force some of these models of intention to make men of themselves for once. The worship of authority in this town has to be uprooted. This inexcusable lapse of judgment about the water system has to be driven home to every eligible voter.

DR. STOCKMANN. All right. If you think it's best for the community, then go ahead. But not before I've talked with my brother.

HOVSTAD. Meanwhile, I'm writing an editorial to have on hand. And if the mayor doesn't get after this thing—

DR. STOCKMANN. Oh, but how can you think he wouldn't?

HOVSTAD. It's quite thinkable. And, if so—?

DR. STOCKMANN. Well, then I promise you—listen—then you can print my report—complete and uncut.

HOVSTAD. May I? Your word on that?

DR. STOCKMANN (*hands him the manuscript*). Here it is. Take it along. It can't hurt if you read it through; and you can give it back to me later.

HOVSTAD. Very good; I'll do that. Good-bye then, Doctor.

DR. STOCKMANN. Good-bye, good-bye. Yes, you'll see now, it'll all go smoothly, Mr. Hovstad. Very smoothly.

HOVSTAD. Hm—we'll see. (*He bows and goes out by the hall door.*)

DR. STOCKMANN (*goes over to the dining room and looks in*). Katherine—! Oh, are you back, Petra?

PETRA (*entering*). Yes, I just came from school.

MRS. STOCKMANN (*entering*). He's still not been in?

DR. STOCKMANN. Peter? No. But I had a long talk with Hovstad. He's very much excited by the discovery I've made. Its repercussions go a lot farther, apparently, than I thought at first. So he's put his paper at my disposal, if it comes to that.

MRS. STOCKMANN. Do you think it will come to that?

DR. STOCKMANN. Oh, of course not. But all the same, it's a heady feeling to know you've got the independent liberal press on your side. Yes, and guess what? I also had a visit from the chairman of the Home Owners Council.

MRS. STOCKMANN. Oh? And what did he want?

DR. STOCKMANN. To support me, as well. They'll all support me, if things get rough. Katherine—do you know what I have backing me up?

MRS. STOCKMANN. Backing you up? No, what do you have?

DR. STOCKMANN. The solid majority.

MRS. STOCKMANN. Really. And that's a good thing, is it, Thomas?

DR. STOCKMANN. Well, I should hope it's a good thing! (*Paces up and down, rubbing his hands together.*) My Lord, how gratifying it is to stand like this, joined together in brotherhood with your fellow citizens.

PETRA. And then to accomplish so much that's fine and useful, Father!

DR. STOCKMANN. And for one's own birthplace in the bargain.

MRS. STOCKMANN. There's the bell.

DR. STOCKMANN. That's got to be him. (*A knock at the door.*) Come in!

MAYOR STOCKMANN (*entering from the hall*). Good morning.

DR. STOCKMANN. Good to see you, Peter!

MRS. STOCKMANN. Morning, Peter. How's everything with you?

MAYOR STOCKMANN. Just so-so, thank you. (*To the* DOCTOR.) Yesterday, after office hours, I received a report from you, discussing the condition of the water at the baths.

DR. STOCKMANN. Yes. Have you read it?

MAYOR STOCKMANN. I have.

DR. STOCKMANN. What have you got to say about it?

MAYOR STOCKMANN (*glancing at the others*). Hm—

MRS. STOCKMANN. Come along, Petra.

(*She and* PETRA *go into the room on the left.*)

MAYOR STOCKMANN (*after a moment*). Was it necessary to press all these investigations behind my back?

DR. STOCKMANN. Well, as long as I didn't have absolute proof, then—

MAYOR STOCKMANN. And now you think you do?

DR. STOCKMANN. You must be convinced of that yourself.

MAYOR STOCKMANN. Is it your object to put this document before the board of directors by way of an official recommendation?

DR. STOCKMANN. Of course. Something has to be done about this. And fast.

MAYOR STOCKMANN. As usual, in your report you let your language get out of hand. You say, among other things, that what we're offering our summer visitors is guaranteed poison.

DR. STOCKMANN. But, Peter, how else can you describe it? You've got to realize—this water *is* poison for internal *or* external use! And it's foisted on poor, suffering creatures who turn to us in good faith and pay us exorbitant fees to gain their health back again!

MAYOR STOCKMANN. And then you arrive at the conclusion, by your line of reasoning, that we have to build a sewer to drain off these so-called impurities from Mølledal, and that all the water mains have to be relaid.

DR. STOCKMANN. Well, do you see any other way out? I don't.

MAYOR STOCKMANN. I invented a little business this morning down at the town engineer's office. And in a half-joking way, I brought up these proposals as something we perhaps ought to take under advisement at some time in the future.

DR. STOCKMANN. Some time in the future!

MAYOR STOCKMANN. He smiled at my whimsical extravagance—naturally. Have you gone to the trouble of estimating just what these proposed changes would cost? From the information I received, the expenditure would probably run up into several hundred thousand crowns.

DR. STOCKMANN. As high as that?

MAYOR STOCKMANN. Yes. But that's not the worst. The work would extend over at least two years.

DR. STOCKMANN. Two years? Two full years?

MAYOR STOCKMANN. At the least. And meanwhile what do we do with the baths? Shut them down? Yes, we'll have to. Do you really think anyone would make the effort to come all the distance here if the rumor got out that the water was contaminated?

DR. STOCKMANN. Yes, but Peter, that's what it is.

MAYOR STOCKMANN. And then all this happens now—just now, when the baths were being recognized. Other towns in this area have the same resources for development as health resorts. Don't you think they'll leap at the chance to attract the whole flow of tourists to them? No question of it. And there we are, left stranded. We'll most likely have to abandon the whole costly enterprise; and then you'll have ruined the town you were born in.

DR. STOCKMANN. I—ruined—!

MAYOR STOCKMANN. It's through the baths alone that this town has any future to speak of. You can see that just as plain as I can.

DR. STOCKMANN. But then what do you think ought to be done?

MAYOR STOCKMANN. From your report I'm unable to persuade myself that the condition of the baths is as critical as you claim.

DR. STOCKMANN. Look, if anything, it's worse! Or it'll be that by summer, when the warm weather comes.

MAYOR STOCKMANN. Once again. I think you're exaggerating considerably. A capable doctor must know the right steps to take—he should be able to control toxic elements, and to treat them if they make their presence too obvious.

DR. STOCKMANN. And then—? What else—?

MAYOR STOCKMANN. The water system for the baths as it now stands is simply a fact and clearly has to be accepted as such. But in time the directors will more than likely agree to take under consideration to what extent—depending on the funds available—they can institute certain improvements.

DR. STOCKMANN. And you can think I'd play along with that kind of trickery!

MAYOR STOCKMANN. Trickery?

DR. STOCKMANN. Yes, it's a trick—a deception, a lie, an out-and-out crime against the public and society at large!

MAYOR STOCKMANN. As I've already observed, I've not yet persuaded myself that there's any real impending danger here.

DR. STOCKMANN. Yes, you have! There's no alternative. My report is perfectly accurate, I know that! And you're very much aware of it, Peter, but you won't admit it. You're the one who got the baths and the water system laid out where they are today; and it's *this*—it's this hellish miscalculation that you won't concede. Pah! You don't think I can see right through you?

MAYOR STOCKMANN. And even if it were true? Even if I seem a bit overanxious about my reputation, it's all for the good of the town. Without moral authority I could hardly guide and direct affairs in the way I believe serves the general welfare. For this reason—among many others—it strikes me as imperative that your report not be submitted to the board of directors. It has to be withheld for the common good. Then, later, I'll bring the matter up for discussion, and we'll do the very best we can, as quietly as possible. But nothing—not the slightest word of this catastrophe must leak out to the public.

DR. STOCKMANN. My dear Peter, there's no stopping it now.

MAYOR STOCKMANN. It must and it will be stopped.

DR. STOCKMANN. I'm telling you, it's no use. Too many people know already.

MAYOR STOCKMANN. Know already! Who? Not those fellows from the *Courier*—?

DR. STOCKMANN. Why, of course they know. The independent liberal press is going to see that you do your duty.

MAYOR STOCKMANN (*after a short pause*). You're an exceptionally thoughtless man, Thomas. Haven't you considered the consequences that can follow for you?

DR. STOCKMANN. Consequences? For me?

MAYOR STOCKMANN. For you and your family as well.

DR. STOCKMANN. What the devil does *that* mean?

MAYOR STOCKMANN. I think, over the years, I've proved a helpful and accommodating brother to you.

DR. STOCKMANN. Yes, you have, and I'm thankful to you for that.

MAYOR STOCKMANN. I'm not after thanks. Because, in part, I was forced into it—for my own sake. I always hoped I could keep you in check somewhat if I helped better your economic status.

DR. STOCKMANN. What? Just for your own sake—!

MAYOR STOCKMANN. In part, I said. It's embarrassing for a public servant when his closest relative goes and compromises himself again and again.

DR. STOCKMANN. And that's what you think I do?

MAYOR STOCKMANN. Yes, unfortunately you do, without your knowing it. You have a restless, unruly, combative nature. And then this unhappy knack of bursting into print on all kinds of likely and unlikely subjects. You're no sooner struck by an idea than right away you have to scribble a newspaper article on it, or a whole pamphlet even.

DR. STOCKMANN. Well, but isn't it a citizen's duty to inform the public if he comes on a new idea?

MAYOR STOCKMANN. Oh, the public doesn't need new ideas. The public is served best by the good, old, time-tested ideas it's always had.

DR. STOCKMANN. That's putting it plainly!

MAYOR STOCKMANN. I have to talk to you plainly for once. Up till now I've always tried to avoid that because I know how irritable you are; but now I'm telling you the truth, Thomas. You have no conception how much you injure yourself with your impetuosity. You complain about the authorities and, yes, the government; you rail against them—and insist you're being passed over and persecuted. But what can you expect—someone as troublesome as you.

DR. STOCKMANN. Ah—so I'm troublesome, too?

MAYOR STOCKMANN. Yes, Thomas, you're a very troublesome man to work with. I know from experience. You show no consideration at all. You seem to forget completely that I'm the one you can thank for your post here as staff physician at the baths—

DR. STOCKMANN. I was the inevitable choice—I and nobody else! I was the first to see that this town could become a flourishing spa; and I was the *only* one who could see it then. I stood alone fighting for that idea for years; and I wrote and wrote—

MAYOR STOCKMANN. Unquestionably. But the right moment hadn't arrived yet. Of course you couldn't judge that from up there in the wilds. But when the opportune time came, and I—and a few others—took the matter in hand—

DR. STOCKMANN. Yes, and bungled the whole magnificent plan. Oh yes, it's really coming out now what a brilliant crew you've been!

MAYOR STOCKMANN. All that's coming out, to my mind, is your usual hunger for a good fight. You want to attack your superiors—it's your old pattern. You can't stand any authority over you; you resent anyone in a higher position and regard him as a personal enemy—and then one weapon's as good as another to use. But now I've acquainted you with the vital interests at stake here for this whole town—and, naturally, for me as well. And so I'm warning you, Thomas, I'll be adamant about the demand I am going to make of you.

DR. STOCKMANN. What demand?

MAYOR STOCKMANN. Since you've been so indiscreet as to discuss this delicate issue with outsiders, even though it should have been kept secret among the directors, it of course can't be hushed up now. All kinds of rumors will go flying around, and the maliciously inclined will dress them up with trimmings of their own. It'll therefore be necessary that you publicly deny these rumors.

DR. STOCKMANN. I! How? I don't understand.

MAYOR STOCKMANN. We can expect that, after further investigation, you'll arrive at the conclusion that things are far from being as critical or dangerous as you'd first imagined.

DR. STOCKMANN. Ah—you expect that!

MAYOR STOCKMANN. Moreover, we expect that you'll support and publicly affirm your confidence in the present directors to take thorough and conscientious measures, as necessary, to remedy any possible defects.

DR. STOCKMANN. But that's utterly out of the question for me, as long as they try to get by with patchwork. I'm telling you that, Peter; and it's my unqualified opinion—!

MAYOR STOCKMANN. As a member of the staff, you're not entitled to any personal opinions.

DR. STOCKMANN (*stunned*). Not entitled—?

MAYOR STOCKMANN. As a staff member, I said. As a private person—why, that's another matter. But as a subordinate official at the baths, you're not entitled to express any opinions that contradict your superiors.

DR. STOCKMANN. That's going too far! I, as a doctor, a man of science, aren't entitled to—!

MAYOR STOCKMANN. What's involved here isn't a purely scientific problem. It's a mixture of both technical and economic considerations.

DR. STOCKMANN. I don't care what the hell it is! I want the freedom to express myself on any problem under the sun!

MAYOR STOCKMANN. Anything you like—except for the baths. We forbid you that.

DR. STOCKMANN (*shouting*). You forbid—! You! A crowd of—!

MAYOR STOCKMANN. *I* forbid it—*I,* your supervisor. And when I forbid you, then you obey.

DR. STOCKMANN (*controls himself*). Peter—if you weren't my brother—

PETRA (*flinging the door open*). You don't have to take this, Father!

MRS. STOCKMANN (*following her*). Petra, Petra!

MAYOR STOCKMANN. Ah, an ear to the keyhole.

MRS. STOCKMANN. You were so loud, we couldn't avoid—

PETRA. Oh, but I was there, listening.

MAYOR STOCKMANN. Well, I'm just as glad, really—

DR. STOCKMANN (*approaching him*). You were talking to me about forbidding and obeying—?

MAYOR STOCKMANN. You forced me to adopt that tone.

DR. STOCKMANN. So you want me to stand up in public and confess I'm a liar?

MAYOR STOCKMANN. We find it absolutely essential that you make a public statement along the lines I've indicated.

DR. STOCKMANN. And what if I don't—obey?

MAYOR STOCKMANN. Then we ourselves will issue a statement to soothe the public.

DR. STOCKMANN. Very well. But then I'll attack you in print. I'll stand my ground. I'll prove that I'm right, and you're wrong. And then what will you do?

MAYOR STOCKMANN. Then I won't be able to prevent your dismissal.

DR. STOCKMANN. What—!

PETRA. Father—dismissal!

MRS. STOCKMANN. Dismissal!

MAYOR STOCKMANN. You'll be dismissed from the staff. I'll find myself obliged to see you put on immediate notice and suspended from all activities involving the baths.

DR. STOCKMANN. And you'll dare that!

MAYOR STOCKMANN. You're the one playing the dare-devil.

PETRA. Uncle, this is a shameful way to treat a man like Father!

MRS. STOCKMANN. Will you please be quiet, Petra!

MAYOR STOCKMANN (*regarding* PETRA). Ah, so we've already learned to voice opinions. Yes, naturally. (*To* MRS. STOCKMANN.) Katherine, I expect you're the most sensible member of this household. Use whatever influence you have over your husband, and make him understand what effect this will have on both his family—

DR. STOCKMANN. My family concerns no one else but me.

MAYOR STOCKMANN. As I was saying, on both his family and the town he lives in.

DR. STOCKMANN. I'm the one who really wants the best for the town! I want to expose failings that'll come to light sooner or later anyway. That ought to show that I love this town.

MAYOR STOCKMANN. Yes, by setting out in blind spite to cut off our major source of revenue.

DR. STOCKMANN. That source is poisoned, man! Are you crazy! We live by marketing filth and corruption. The whole affluence of this community has its roots in a lie!

MAYOR STOCKMANN. Sheer fantasy—or something worse. Any man who could hurl such nauseating charges at his own home town must be an enemy of society.

DR. STOCKMANN (*going for him*). You dare—!

MRS. STOCKMANN (*throws herself between them*). Thomas!

PETRA (*seizing her father by the arm*). Easy, Father!

MAYOR STOCKMANN. I don't have to subject myself to violence. Now you've been warned. Just consider what you owe yourself and your family. Good-bye. (*He leaves.*)

DR. STOCKMANN (*pacing up and down*). And I have to take this treatment! In my own house, Katherine! What do you say to that!

MRS. STOCKMANN. Of course it's humiliating, Thomas—

PETRA. Oh, what I could do to Uncle—!

DR. STOCKMANN. It's my own fault. I should have faced them down long ago—shown my teeth—and bit back! Call *me* an enemy of society! So help me God, I'm not going to swallow that!

MRS. STOCKMANN. But, Thomas dear, your brother does have the power—

DR. STOCKMANN. Yes, but I'm in the right!

MRS. STOCKMANN. The right? Ah, what does it help to be in the right if you don't have any power?

PETRA. Mother, no—why do you talk like that?

DR. STOCKMANN. You mean it doesn't help in a free society to be on the side of right? Don't be absurd, Katherine. And besides—don't I have the independent liberal press to lead the way—and the solid majority behind me? There's power enough in them, I'd say!

MRS. STOCKMANN. But Thomas, for heaven's sake—surely you're not thinking of—

DR. STOCKMANN. Thinking of what?

MRS. STOCKMANN. Of setting yourself up against your brother.

DR. STOCKMANN. What in hell do you want me to do? Abandon everything that's true and right?

PETRA. Yes, I'd ask the same.

MRS. STOCKMANN. But it won't do you the least bit of good. If they won't, they won't.

DR. STOCKMANN. Oh ho, Katherine, just give me time! You'll see, I'll push this fight through to the end.

MRS. STOCKMANN. Yes, maybe you'll just push yourself out of your job—that's what you'll do.

DR. STOCKMANN. Then anyway I'll have done my duty to the people—to society. Though they call me its enemy!

MRS. STOCKMANN. And to your family, Thomas? To us at home? You think that's doing your duty to those who depend on you?

PETRA. Oh, stop always thinking of us first of all, Mother.

MRS. STOCKMANN. Yes, it's easy for *you* to talk. If need be, you can stand on your own feet. But remember the boys, Thomas. And think of yourself a little, and of me—

DR. STOCKMANN. You must be utterly mad, Katherine! If I had to crawl like an abject coward to Peter and his damned cohorts—do you think I'd ever know one moment's happiness for the rest of my life?

MRS. STOCKMANN. I don't know about that. But God preserve us from the kind of happiness we'll share if you press your defiance. You'll be back again where you started—no position, no assured income. I thought we'd had enough of that in the old days. Remember that, Thomas; and think of what lies ahead.

DR. STOCKMANN (*clenching his fists and writhing in inner conflict*). And this is how these bureaucrats can clamp down on a plain, honest man! It's despicable, Katherine, isn't it?

MRS. STOCKMANN. Yes, they've acted shamefully toward you, of course. But, my Lord, there's so much injustice that people have to bear with in this world— There are the boys, Thomas! Look at them! What'll become of them? No, no, you wouldn't have the heart—

(*As she speaks,* EILIF *and* MORTEN *come in, carrying their schoolbooks.*)

DR. STOCKMANN. The boys—! (*Suddenly resolved.*) I don't care if all the world caves in, I'm not going to lick the dust. (*He heads for his study.*)

MRS. STOCKMANN (*following him*). Thomas—what are you doing?

DR. STOCKMANN (*at the door*). I want the chance to look my boys straight in the eyes when they've grown up to be free men. (*He goes within.*)

MRS. STOCKMANN (*bursting into tears*). Oh, God help us all!

PETRA. Father—he's wonderful! He's not giving in.

(*The boys, in bewilderment, ask what has happened;* PETRA *signals them to be quiet.*)

⌣ ACT THREE ⌢

The editorial office of the People's Courier. *At the back, left, is the entrance door; to the right in the same wall is another door, through which one can see the pressroom. In the wall to the right, a third door. At the center of the room is a large table covered with papers, newspapers, and books. In the foreground at the left a window and, next to it, a writing desk with a high stool. A couple of armchairs are drawn up by the table; several other chairs along the walls. The room is barren and cheerless, the furnishings old, the armchairs grimy and torn. In the pressroom two typesetters can be seen at work, and, beyond them, a handpress in operation.*

HOVSTAD *is seated at the desk, writing. After a moment* BILLING *enters from the right, the* DOCTOR'S *manuscript in his hand.*

BILLING. Well, that's really something—!

HOVSTAD (*writing*). Did you read it all?

BILLING (*lays the manuscript on the desk*). I'll say I did.

HOVSTAD. He makes a pretty sharp statement, doesn't he?

BILLING. Sharp? Ye gods, it's pulverizing! Every word hits home like a sledgehammer.

HOVSTAD. Yes, but that crowd isn't going to come down at one blow.

BILLING. That's true. But then we'll keep on hitting them—blow upon blow, till their whole leadership crumbles. When I sat in there reading this, it was exactly as if I could see the revolution breaking like the dawn.

HOVSTAD (*turning*). Shh! Don't say that so Aslaksen hears.

BILLING (*dropping his voice*). Aslaksen's a chicken-livered coward; there's no spine in the man. But this time you'll carry your own will through, uh? Right? You'll run the doctor's article?

HOVSTAD. Yes, if only the mayor doesn't give in—

BILLING. That'd be boring as hell.

HOVSTAD. Well, fortunately, no matter what happens, we can make something out of the situation. If the mayor won't buy the doctor's proposal, then he gets the small businessmen down on his neck—the Home Owners Council and that sort. And if he does buy it, he'll fall out with a whole host of the big stockholders in the baths, the ones who've been his best supporters up to now—

BILLING. Yes, that's right; they'll have to kick in a lot of new capital—

HOVSTAD. You bet they will! And then the ring is broken, see. And day after day in the paper we'll keep drumming it into the public that the mayor's incompetent on one score after another, and that all the elective offices in town—the whole administration—ought to be placed in the hands of the liberals.

BILLING. Ye gods, that's the living truth! I see it—I can see it! We're right on the verge of a revolution!

(*A knock at the door.*)

HOVSTAD. Shh! (*Calls out.*) Come in!

(DR. STOCKMANN *enters by the door at the back, left.*)

HOVSTAD (*goes to meet him*). Ah, here's the doctor. Well?

DR. STOCKMANN. Roll your presses, Mr. Hovstad!

HOVSTAD. Then it's come to that?

BILLING. Hurray!

DR. STOCKMANN. I said, roll your presses. Yes, it's come to that. But now they'll get what they're asking for. Now it's war in this town, Mr. Billing!

BILLING. War to the knife, I hope! Lay into them, Doctor!

DR. STOCKMANN. This article's only the beginning. My head's already brimming with ideas for four or five more pieces. Where do I find Aslaksen?

BILLING (*shouting into the pressroom*). Aslaksen, come here a minute!

HOVSTAD. Four or five more pieces, you say? On the same subject?

DR. STOCKMANN. No, not by a long shot. No, they're on totally different topics. But they all originate from the water system and the sewers. One thing leads to another, you know. It's the way it is when you start patching up an old building. Precisely like that.

BILLING. Ye gods, but that's the truth. You find out you'll never be done with it till you've torn down the whole rotten structure.

ASLAKSEN (*comes in from the pressroom*). Torn down! You don't plan to tear down the baths, Doctor?

HOVSTAD. Not at all. Don't get frightened.

DR. STOCKMANN. No, that was something else entirely. Well, what do you say about my article, Mr. Hovstad?

HOVSTAD. I think it's a pure masterpiece—

DR. STOCKMANN. Yes, isn't it—? Well, I'm most gratified, most gratified.

HOVSTAD. It's so clear and readable; you don't have to be a specialist at all to follow the argument. I daresay you'll have every reasonable man on your side.

ASLAKSEN. And all the moderates, too?

BILLING. Moderates and immoderates both—well, I mean, practically the entire town.

ASLAKSEN. Then we might take a chance on running it.

DR. STOCKMANN. Yes, I should think so!

HOVSTAD. It'll go in tomorrow morning.

DR. STOCKMANN. Good grief, it better; we can't waste a single day. Look, Mr. Aslaksen, I know what I wanted to ask you: would you give the manuscript your personal attention?

ASLAKSEN. I certainly will.

DR. STOCKMANN. Handle it like gold. No misprints; every word is vital. I'll stop back in again later; maybe I could glance over the proofs. Oh, I can't tell you how I'm dying to see this thing in print—delivered—

BILLING. Delivered—like a lightning-bolt!

DR. STOCKMANN. —addressed to the judgment of every thinking man. Ah, you can't imagine what I've been subjected to today. They've threatened me from all sides; they've tried to deprive me of my most fundamental human rights—

HOVSTAD. Of your rights!

DR. STOCKMANN. They've tried to humiliate me, and turn me into a jellyfish, and make me deny my deepest and holiest convictions for private profit.

BILLING. Ye gods, that's unforgivable.

HOVSTAD. Oh well, you have to expect anything from that crowd.

DR. STOCKMANN. But with me it's not going to work: they're going to get it, spelled out in black and white. I'm going to drop anchor right here at the *Courier* and rake them with broadsides: a fresh article every day—

ASLAKSEN. Yes, but now listen—

BILLING. Hurray! It's war—war!

DR. STOCKMANN. I'll smash them into the ground and shatter them! I'll wreck their defenses in the eyes of every fair-minded man! That's what I'll do!

ASLAKSEN. But do it temperately, Doctor. War, yes—in moderation.

BILLING. No, no! Don't spare the dynamite!

DR. STOCKMANN (*continues, unruffled*). Because now, you see, this isn't simply a matter of sewers and water mains anymore. No, it's the whole society that has to be purged and disinfected—

BILLING. That's the remedy!

DR. STOCKMANN. All these lunkheads in the old generation have to be dumped. And that means: no matter *who* they are! I've had such endless vistas opening up for me today. I haven't quite clarified it yet, but I'm working it out. My friends, we have to go forth and search out fresh, young standard-bearers; we have to have new commanders for all our outposts.

BILLING. Hear, hear!

DR. STOCKMANN. And if we only can stick together, everything will go off smoothly. The entire revolution will be launched as trim as a ship down the ways. Don't you think so?

HOVSTAD. For my part, I think we now have every prospect of seeing community control put right where it belongs.

ASLAKSEN. And if we just move ahead in moderation, I can't believe there's likely to be any danger.

DR. STOCKMANN. Who the hell cares about danger! Whatever I do will be done in the name of truth, for the sake of my conscience.

HOVSTAD. You're a man who deserves support, Doctor.

ASLAKSEN. Yes, that's a fact: the doctor's a true friend to the town, and a real friend to society.

BILLING. Ye gods, Aslaksen; Doctor Stockmann is the people's friend!

ASLAKSEN. I can imagine the Home Owners Council may pick that up as a slogan.

DR. STOCKMANN (*moved, pressing their hands*). Thank you, thank you, my dear, unfailing friends—it's so heartening to hear you say these things—my esteemed brother called me something quite different. Well, I swear he's going to get it back, with interest! But now I've got to look in on a patient, poor devil. I'll stop by again, as I said. Don't forget to look out for my manuscript, Mr. Aslaksen—and, whatever you do, don't cut any exclamation points. If anything, put a few more in! Fine, fine! Good-bye till later, good-bye, good-bye!

(*Amid mutual farewells, he is escorted to the door and departs.*)

HOVSTAD. He can be an exceptionally useful man for us.

ASLAKSEN. As long as he limits himself to the baths. But if he goes further, then it wouldn't be politic to join forces with him.

HOVSTAD. Hm, that all depends—

BILLING. You're always so damn fearful, Aslaksen.

ASLAKSEN. Fearful? Yes, as far as the local authorities go, I'm fearful, Mr. Billing. Let me tell you, it's something I've learned in the school of experience. But put me in the arena of national politics, opposed to the government itself, and then you'll see if I'm fearful.

BILLING. No, you're certainly not. But that's exactly where you're so inconsistent.

ASLAKSEN. I'm a man of conscience, that's the thing. As long as you attack the government, you can't do any real damage to society. You see, the men on that level, they aren't affected—they just ride it out. But the *local* authorities, *they* can be ousted; and then you might wind up with a lot of bunglers in power, who could do enormous damage to the property owners, among others.

HOVSTAD. But how about self-government as part of a citizen's education—don't you care about that?

ASLAKSEN. When a man has material assets at stake, he can't go thinking of everything.

HOVSTAD. Then I hope I'm never burdened with material assets.

BILLING. Hear, hear!

ASLAKSEN (*smiles*). Hm. (*Pointing at the desk.*) In that editor's chair, right there, your predecessor, Councilman Stengaard, used to sit.

BILLING (*spits*). Pah! That renegade.

HOVSTAD. I'm no double-dealer—and I never will be.

ASLAKSEN. A politician has to keep all possibilities open, Mr. Hovstad. And you, Mr. Billing—I think you better take a reef or two in your sails, now that you've put in for a job in the town clerk's office.

BILLING. I—!

HOVSTAD. *You* have, Billing?

BILLING. Yes, uh—you can damn well imagine I only did it to needle the establishment.

ASLAKSEN. Well, it's no business of mine, of course. But when I get labeled fearful and inconsistent in my stand, there's one thing I want to emphasize: my political record is available to all comers. I've never changed my position, except that I've become more moderate. My heart belongs to the people, always; but I can't deny that my reason disposes me toward the authorities—I mean, only the local ones, that is.

(*He goes into the pressroom.*)

BILLING. Shouldn't we call it quits with him, Hovstad?

HOVSTAD. You know any other printer who'll extend us credit for paper and labor costs?

BILLING. It's damnable that we don't have any capital.

HOVSTAD (*sitting at the desk*). Yes, if we only had that—

BILLING. How about approaching Stockmann?

HOVSTAD (*leafing through some papers*). What use would there be in that? He has nothing.

BILLING. No, but he's got a good man backing him: old Morten Kiil—the one they call the Badger.

HOVSTAD (*writing*). How can you know for sure *he* has anything?

BILLING. Ye gods, of course he does! And some part of it has to come to the Stockmanns. He's got to make provision—at least for the children.

HOVSTAD (*half turning*). Are you figuring on *that*?

BILLING. Figuring? I never figure on anything.

HOVSTAD. That's wise. And you'd better not figure on that job with the town, because I can promise you—you won't get it.

BILLING. Don't you think I've known that all along? There's nothing I'd welcome more than not getting it. A rejection like that really kindles your fighting spirit—it's almost like an infusion of fresh gall, and that's exactly what you need in an anthill like this, where hardly anything ever happens to really stir you up.

HOVSTAD (*continues writing*). How true, how true.

BILLING. Well—they'll soon be hearing from *me!* Now I'll go in and write that appeal to the Home Owners Council. (*He goes into the room to the right.*)

HOVSTAD (*sits at the desk, chews the end of his pen and says slowly*). Hm—so that's how it is. (*A knock at the door.*) Come in!

(PETRA *enters by the door at the back, left.*)

HOVSTAD (*getting up*). Oh, it's you? What are you doing here?

PETRA. You'll have to excuse me—

HOVSTAD (*pulls an armchair forward*). Won't you sit?

PETRA. No, thanks—I can't stay.

HOVSTAD. Is it something from your father that—?

PETRA. No, it's something from me. (*Takes a book out of her coat pocket.*) Here's that English story.

HOVSTAD. Why are you giving it back?

PETRA. Because I don't want to translate it.

HOVSTAD. But you promised me, definitely—

PETRA. Well, I hadn't read it then. And of course you haven't read it either.

HOVSTAD. No. You know I don't understand English; but—

PETRA. All right, that's why I wanted to tell you that you'll have to find somebody else. (*Lays the book on the table.*) This could never be used in the *Courier*.

HOVSTAD. Why not?

PETRA. It's totally opposed to everything you stand for.

HOVSTAD. Well, actually—

PETRA. You still don't understand me. It shows how a supernatural power, watching over the so-called good people of this world, arranges everything for the best in their lives—and how all the so-called wicked get their punishment.

HOVSTAD. But that's fair enough. It's exactly what the public wants.

PETRA. And do you want to be the one who feeds the public that sort of thing? You don't believe a word of it yourself. You know perfectly well things don't happen like that in reality.

HOVSTAD. You're perfectly right; but then an editor can't always do what he might prefer. You often have to bow to public opinions in lesser matters. After all, politics is the main thing in life—for a newspaper, in any event. And if I want to lead people toward greater liberation and progress, then I mustn't scare them away. When they find a moral story like this in the back pages, they're more willing to accept what we print up front—they feel more secure.

PETRA. Oh, come! You wouldn't be so tricky and lay snares for your readers. You're not a spider.

HOVSTAD (*smiles*). Thank you for thinking so well of me. No, it really was Billing's scheme, and not mine.

PETRA. Billing's!

HOVSTAD. Yes. At any rate, he was speaking of it just the other day. It's Billing who's been so hot about getting that story in; I don't know the book.

PETRA. But how could Billing, with his liberal attitude—?

HOVSTAD. Oh, Billing is a many-sided man. Now I hear he's out for a job in the town clerk's office.

PETRA. I don't believe it, Hovstad. How could he ever conform himself to that?

HOVSTAD. That's something you'll have to ask him.

PETRA. I never would have thought it of Billing.

HOVSTAD (*looks more sharply at her*). You wouldn't? Does it surprise you so?

PETRA. Yes. Or maybe not, really. Oh, honestly, I don't know—

HOVSTAD. We journalists don't amount to much, Miss Stockmann.

PETRA. You actually mean that?

HOVSTAD. It's what I think sometimes.

PETRA. Yes, in your normal day-to-day existence—I can understand that well enough. But now that you're lending a hand in a great cause—

HOVSTAD. This matter of your father, you mean?

PETRA. Exactly. Now I think you must feel like a man who's more valuable than most.

HOVSTAD. Yes, I feel something of that today.

PETRA. Yes, you do, don't you? Oh, it's a glorious calling you've chosen! To pioneer the way for embattled truths and daring new insights—or simply to stand up fearlessly for a man who's been wronged—

HOVSTAD. Especially when that man who's been wronged is—hm—I don't quite know how to put it—

PETRA. When he's so direct and honest, you mean?

HOVSTAD (*in a softer voice*). No, I meant—especially when he's your father.

PETRA (*startled*). It's *that!*

HOVSTAD. Yes, Petra—Miss Petra.

PETRA. Is *that* the main thing for you? Not the issue itself? Not the truth? Not my father's compassion for life?

HOVSTAD. Why, yes—of course, that too.

PETRA. No, thanks, Mr. Hovstad; you betrayed yourself. And now I'll never trust you again, in anything.

HOVSTAD. How can you be so hard on me, when it's mostly for your own sake—?

PETRA. What I'm mad at you about is you haven't played fair with Father. You've talked to him as if the truth and the good of the community lay closest to your heart. You've made fools of both him and me. You're not the man you pretend to be. And for that I'll never forgive you—never!

HOVSTAD. You shouldn't be so bitter, Miss Petra—paticularly right now.

PETRA. Why not now?

HOVSTAD. Because your father can't dispense with my help.

PETRA (*scanning him*). And you're that kind, too? So!

HOVSTAD. No, no, I'm not. I don't know what brought that on. You have to believe me.

PETRA. I know what I have to believe. Good-bye.

ASLAKSEN (*entering from the pressroom, brusquely and cryptically*). God Almighty, Hovstad— (*Sees* PETRA.) Oh, what a mess—

PETRA. There's the book; you can give it to somebody else. (*Goes toward the entrance door.*)

HOVSTAD (*following her*). But, Miss Petra—

PETRA. Good-bye. (*She leaves.*)

ASLAKSEN. Mr. Hovstad, listen!

HOVSTAD. Yes, all right, what is it?

ASLAKSEN. The mayor's out there in the pressroom.

HOVSTAD. You say, the mayor?

ASLAKSEN. Yes, he wants to talk to you. He came in the back entrance—didn't want to be seen, I guess.

HOVSTAD. What's this all about? No, wait, I'll go—

(*He crosses to the door of the pressroom, opens it, and beckons the* MAYOR *in.*)

HOVSTAD. Keep an eye out, Aslaksen, so nobody—

ASLAKSEN. I understand— (*Goes into the pressroom.*)

MAYOR STOCKMANN. I imagine you hardly expected to see me here, Mr. Hovstad.

HOVSTAD. No, I really hadn't.

MAYOR STOCKMANN (*looking about*). You've certainly made yourself quite comfortable here. Very nice.

HOVSTAD. Oh—

MAYOR STOCKMANN. And now I come along unceremoniously and monopolize your time.

HOVSTAD. By all means, Mr. Mayor; I'm at your service. But please, let me take your things— (*Sets the* MAYOR'*s hat and stick on a chair.*) Won't you have a seat?

MAYOR STOCKMANN (*sitting at the table*). Thank you.
(HOVSTAD *likewise sits at the table.*)

MAYOR STOCKMANN. I've gone through—really a most troublesome episode today, Mr. Hovstad.

HOVSTAD. Yes? Oh well, with all the cares that the mayor has—

MAYOR STOCKMANN. It involves the staff physician at the baths.

HOVSTAD. You mean, the doctor?

MAYOR STOCKMANN. He's penned a kind of report to the board of directors, alleging that the baths have certain deficiencies.

HOVSTAD. He has?

MAYOR STOCKMANN. Yes, didn't he tell you—? I thought he said—

HOVSTAD. Oh yes, that's true. He made some mention of it—

ASLAKSEN (*entering from the pressroom*). I need to have that manuscript—

HOVSTAD (*vexed*). Hm, it's there on the desk.

ASLAKSEN (*locating it*). Good.

MAYOR STOCKMANN. But look—that's *it,* exactly—

ASLAKSEN. Yes, that's the doctor's article, Mr. Mayor.

HOVSTAD. Oh, is *that* what you were talking about?

MAYOR STOCKMANN. None other. What do you think of it?

HOVSTAD. I'm really no expert, and I've barely skimmed through it.

MAYOR STOCKMANN. Still, you're going to print it.

HOVSTAD. A man of his reputation I can hardly refuse—

ASLAKSEN. I have no say at all in this paper, Mr. Mayor.

MAYOR STOCKMANN. Naturally.

ASLAKSEN. I only print what's put in my hands.

MAYOR STOCKMANN. Quite properly.

ASLAKSEN. So, if you'll pardon me— (*Goes toward the pressroom.*)

MAYOR STOCKMANN. No, just a minute, Mr. Aslaksen. With your permission, Mr. Hovstad—

HOVSTAD. My pleasure.

MAYOR STOCKMANN. You're a sober-minded and thoughtful man, Mr. Aslaksen.

ASLAKSEN. I'm glad Your Honor holds that opinion.

MAYOR STOCKMANN. And a man of influence in many circles.

ASLAKSEN. That's mostly among the little people.

MAYOR STOCKMANN. The small taxpayers are the great majority—here, as elsewhere.

ASLAKSEN. That's the truth.

MAYOR STOCKMANN. And I don't doubt that you know the general sentiment among most of them. Am I right?

ASLAKSEN. Yes, I daresay I do, Mr. Mayor.

MAYOR STOCKMANN. Well—if there's such a worthy spirit of self-sacrifice prevailing among the town's less affluent citizens, then—

ASLAKSEN. How's that?

HOVSTAD. Self-sacrifice?

MAYOR STOCKMANN. It's a beautiful token of community spirit, an exceptionally beautiful token. I was close to saying that I wouldn't have expected it. But you know the feelings of these people far better than I.

ASLAKSEN. Yes, but, Your Honor—

MAYOR STOCKMANN. And as a matter of fact, it's no small sacrifice this town will be asked to bear.

HOVSTAD. The town?

ASLAKSEN. But I don't follow— It's the baths—!

MAYOR STOCKMANN. At a tentative estimate, the changes that our staff physician finds desirable run up to a couple of hundred thousand crowns.

ASLAKSEN. That's a lot of money, but—

MAYOR STOCKMANN. Of course it'll be necessary for us to take out a municipal loan.

HOVSTAD (*rises*). It can't be your intention for the town to—

ASLAKSEN. Not out of property taxes! Out of the empty pockets of the home owners!

MAYOR STOCKMANN. Well, my dear Mr. Aslaksen, where else would the capital come from?

ASLAKSEN. The men who own the baths can raise it.

MAYOR STOCKMANN. The owners find themselves in no position to extend themselves further than they are already.

ASLAKSEN. Is that quite definite, Mr. Mayor?

MAYOR STOCKMANN. I've ascertained it for a fact. So if one wants all these elaborate changes, the town itself will have to pay for them.

ASLAKSEN. But hell and damnation—excuse me, sir!— but this is a totally different picture, Mr. Hovstad.

HOVSTAD. It certainly is.

MAYOR STOCKMANN. The worst part of it is that we'll be forced to shut down the baths for a two-year period.

HOVSTAD. Shut down? Completely?

ASLAKSEN. For two years!

MAYOR STOCKMANN. Yes, the work has to take that long—at the least.

ASLAKSEN. But, God Almighty, we'll never last that out, Mr. Mayor! What'll we home owners live on in the meantime?

MAYOR STOCKMANN. Unhappily, it's extremely difficult to answer that, Mr. Aslaksen. But what do you want us to do? You think we'll get a single summer visitor here if anyone goes around posing suppositions that the water is polluted, that we're living in a pesthole, that the whole town—

ASLAKSEN. And it's all just supposition?

MAYOR STOCKMANN. With the best will in the world, I haven't been able to persuade myself otherwise.

ASLAKSEN. Yes, but then it's absolutely indefensible of Dr. Stockmann—begging your pardon, Mr. Mayor, but—

MAYOR STOCKMANN. It's distressingly true, what you imply, Mr. Aslaksen. I'm afraid my brother's always been a reckless man.

ASLAKSEN. And in spite of this, you want to go on supporting him, Mr. Hovstad!

HOVSTAD. But how could anyone have suspected—?

MAYOR STOCKMANN. I've drawn up a brief statement of the relevant facts, as they might appear to a disinterested observer; and I've suggested therein how any possible deficiencies might well be covered without exceeding the current budget for the baths.

HOVSTAD. Do you have this statement with you, Mr. Mayor?

MAYOR STOCKMANN (*groping in his pocket*). Yes, I took it along just in case—

ASLAKSEN (*abruptly*). Oh, my God, there he is!

MAYOR STOCKMANN. Who? My brother?

HOVSTAD. Where—where!

ASLAKSEN. Coming through the pressroom.

MAYOR STOCKMANN. How embarrassing! I don't want to run up against him here, and I still have things to talk to you about.

HOVSTAD (*pointing toward the door at the right*). Step in there for a moment.

MAYOR STOCKMANN. But—?

HOVSTAD. It's just Billing in there.

ASLAKSEN. Quick, Your Honor! He's coming!

MAYOR STOCKMANN. Yes, all right, but try to get rid of him fast.

(*He goes out the door, right, as* ASLAKSEN *opens and closes it for him.*)

HOVSTAD. Look like you're doing something, Aslaksen.

(*He sits and starts to write.* ASLAKSEN *rummages in a pile of papers on a chair to the right.*)

DR. STOCKMANN (*entering from the pressroom*). Here I am again. (*Puts down his hat and stick.*)

HOVSTAD (*writing*). Already, Doctor? Get going on what we were talking about, Aslaksen. We can't waste time today.

DR. STOCKMANN (*to* ASLAKSEN). I gather, no proofs as yet.

ASLAKSEN (*without turning*). How could you expect that, Doctor?

DR. STOCKMANN. No, no, I'm just impatient—you have to understand. I won't have a moment's peace till I see it in print.

HOVSTAD. Hm—it's bound to be a good hour still. Don't you think so, Aslaksen?

ASLAKSEN. Yes, I'm afraid so.

DR. STOCKMANN. My dear friends, that's quite all right; I'll come back. I'll gladly come back twice, if necessary. With anything so important—the welfare of this whole town—it's no time to take it easy. (*Starts to go, then pauses and returns.*) Oh, listen—there's still something I want to mention to you.

HOVSTAD. Sorry, but couldn't we some other time—?

DR. STOCKMANN. I can say it in two seconds. It's simply this—when people read my article in the paper tomorrow and find out as well that I've spent the whole winter in seclusion, working for the good of the town—

HOVSTAD. Yes, but Doctor—

DR. STOCKMANN. I know what you'll say. You don't think it was any more than my blasted duty—ordinary civic responsibility. Well, of course; I know that just as well as you do. But my fellow townspeople, you see— bless their souls, they hold such a high regard for me—

ASLAKSEN. Yes, the people have held you in the highest regard—up till now, Doctor.

DR. STOCKMANN. Yes, and it's just the reason I'm afraid that— What I'm trying to say is this: my article, if it affects the people—especially the deprived classes—as an incitement to take the future affairs of the town into their own hands—

HOVSTAD (*getting up*). Hm, Doctor, I don't want to mislead you—

DR. STOCKMANN. Aha—I thought there was something brewing! But I won't hear of it. So if they go preparing anything—

HOVSTAD. Such as?

DR. STOCKMANN. Oh, anything of the kind—a parade or a banquet or a testimonial award or whatever, then you promise me by all that's holy to get it quashed. And you too, Mr. Aslaksen; you hear me!

HOVSTAD. Pardon me, Doctor, but we'd better tell you the unvarnished truth right now—

(MRS. STOCKMANN, *in hat and coat, comes in by the entrance door, back left.*)

MRS. STOCKMANN (*seeing the* DOCTOR). I thought so!

HOVSTAD (*going toward her*). Mrs. Stockmann, you too?

DR. STOCKMANN. Katherine, what the deuce are you doing here?

MRS. STOCKMANN. You know very well what I want.

HOVSTAD. Won't you have a seat? Or perhaps—

MRS. STOCKMANN. Thanks, but don't bother. And please, don't be offended that I'm here to fetch Stockmann; because I'm the mother of three children, I want you to know.

DR. STOCKMANN. Oh, bosh! We know all that.

MRS. STOCKMANN. Well, it really doesn't seem as if you're thinking much of your wife and children these days, or else you wouldn't have gone on this way, hurling us all into perdition.

DR. STOCKMANN. Are you utterly insane. Katherine? Does a man with a wife and children have no right to proclaim the truth—no right to be an effective citizen—or to serve the town he lives in?

MRS. STOCKMANN. All those things—in moderation, Thomas!

ASLAKSEN. I agree. Moderation in all things.

MRS. STOCKMANN. That's why you wrong us terribly, Mr. Hovstad, when you inveigle my husband out of house and home and down here to make a fool of himself in this.

HOVSTAD. I don't make fools of people—

DR. STOCKMANN. Fools! Nobody fools *me!*

MRS. STOCKMANN. Oh yes, they do. I know you're the smartest man in town, but you're so very easy to fool, Thomas. (*To* HOVSTAD.) And just consider that he'll lose his job at the baths if you print what he's written—

ASLAKSEN. What!

HOVSTAD. Yes, but you know, Doctor—

DR. STOCKMANN (*laughing*). Just let them try! Oh, no— they won't dare. Because, you see, I've got the solid majority behind me.

MRS. STOCKMANN. Yes, that's the trouble, exactly. An ugly lot like that behind you.

DR. STOCKMANN. Balderdash, Katherine! Go home and take care of your house and let me take care of society. How can you be so scared, when I'm so secure and happy? (*Walks up and down, rubbing his hands.*) Truth and the people will win the battle, you can count on that. Oh, I can see all the liberal-minded citizens everywhere gathering into a victorious army—! (*Stops by a chair.*) What—what the hell is *this?*

ASLAKSEN (*looking over*). Ow-ah!

HOVSTAD (*likewise*). Hm—!

DR. STOCKMANN. Here we see the summit of authority. (*He takes the* MAYOR'S *hat delicately between his finger-tips and holds it high.*)

MRS. STOCKMANN. The mayor's hat!

DR. STOCKMANN. And here's the scepter of command, too. How in blazes—?

HOVSTAD. Well, uh—

DR. STOCKMANN. Ah, I get it! He's been here to coax you over. Ho ho, he knew right where to come. And then he caught sight of me in the pressroom. (*Explodes with laughter.*) Did he run, Mr. Aslaksen?

ASLAKSEN (*hurriedly*). Oh yes, Doctor, he ran off.

DR. STOCKMANN. Ran away from his stick and his— My eye! Peter never runs from anything. But where the devil have you put him? Ah—inside, of course. Now you watch this, Katherine!

MRS. STOCKMANN. Thomas—please—!

ASLAKSEN. Watch yourself, Doctor!

(DR. STOCKMANN *sets the* MAYOR's *hat on his head and takes his stick; he then goes over, throws open the door, and raises his hand in salute. The* MAYOR *comes in, red with anger.* BILLING *enters behind him.*)

MAYOR STOCKMANN. What's the meaning of this rowdyism?

DR. STOCKMANN. Some respect, if you will, Peter. I'm the authority in town now. (*He parades up and down.*)

MRS. STOCKMANN (*nearly in tears*). Thomas, no!

MAYOR STOCKMANN (*following him*). Give me my hat and my stick!

DR. STOCKMANN. If you're the police chief, then I'm the mayor. I'm in charge of the whole town, see!

MAYOR STOCKMANN. I'm telling you, take off that hat. Remember, that's an insignia of office!

DR. STOCKMANN. Pah! Do you think the waking lion of the people's strength is going to be scared of a hat? Yes, because you better know: tomorrow we're making a revolution in town. You threatened me with my dismissal, but now I'm dismissing you—from all your public offices. You don't think I can? Oh yes, you'll see. I've got the ascendant forces of society on my side. Hovstad and Billing will thunder in the *People's Courier;* and Aslaksen will take the field, leading the whole Home Owners Council—

ASLAKSEN. I won't do it, Doctor.

DR. STOCKMANN. Why, of course you will—

MAYOR STOCKMANN. Ah, but perhaps, even so, Mr. Hovstad will be joining this rebellion?

HOVSTAD. No, Mr. Mayor.

ASLAKSEN. No, Mr. Hovstad isn't so crazy that he'd go and wreck both himself and the paper for the sake of a mere surmise.

DR. STOCKMANN (*looking about*). What's going on here?

HOVSTAD. You've presented your case in a false light, Doctor; and that's why I can't support it.

BILLING. No, after what the mayor was good enough to tell me in there—

DR. STOCKMANN. False! You can leave that to me. Just print my article. I can take care of defending it.

HOVSTAD. I'm not printing it. I cannot and will not and dare not print it.

DR. STOCKMANN. You dare not? What kind of rot is that? You're the editor, aren't you? And it's the editors who run the press, I hope!

ASLAKSEN. No, it's the readers, Doctor.

MAYOR STOCKMANN. Thankfully, yes.

ASLAKSEN. It's public opinion, the informed citizens, the home owners, and all the rest—they're the ones that run the press.

DR. STOCKMANN (*comprehending*). And all these powers I have against me?

ASLAKSEN. That's right. If your article is printed, it'll mean absolute ruin for this town.

DR. STOCKMANN. I see.

MAYOR STOCKMANN. My hat and my stick!

(DR. STOCKMANN *removes the hat and sets it, along with the stick, on the table.*)

MAYOR STOCKMANN (*reclaiming them both*). That was a sudden end to your first term in office.

DR. STOCKMANN. It's not the end yet. (*To* HOVSTAD.)

Then there's no possibility of getting my article in the *Courier?*

HOVSTAD. None whatever. Partly out of regard for your family.

MRS. STOCKMANN. Oh, never mind about this family, Mr. Hovstad.

MAYOR STOCKMANN (*takes a sheet of paper from his pocket*). For the protection of the public, it will be sufficient if this goes in. It's an authorized statement. If you will.

HOVSTAD (*taking the sheet*). Good. We'll insert it right away.

DR. STOCKMANN. But not mine! People think they can stifle me and choke off the truth! But it won't go as smooth as you think. Mr. Aslaksen, would you take my manuscript and issue it at once as a pamphlet—at my expense—under my own imprint. I'll want four hundred copies; no, five—six hundred I'll need.

ASLAKSEN. Even if you gave me its weight ·in gold, I couldn't put my plant to that use, Doctor. I wouldn't dare, in view of public opinion. You won't get that printed anywhere in this town.

DR. STOCKMANN. Then give it back.

HOVSTAD (*hands him the manuscript*). There.

DR. STOCKMANN (*picks up his hat and stick*). It's coming out, no matter what. I'll hold a mass meeting and read it aloud. All my fellow townspeople are going to hear the voice of truth.

MAYOR STOCKMANN. There's not an organization in town that'll rent you a hall for such a purpose.

ASLAKSEN. Not one. I'm positive of that.

BILLING. Ye gods, no!

MRS. STOCKMANN. But this is shameful. Why do they all turn against you, these men?

DR. STOCKMANN (*furiously*). I'll tell you why! It's because all the so-called men in this town are old women—like you. They all just think of their families and never the common good.

MRS. STOCKMANN (*taking his arm*). Then I'll show them a—an old woman who can be a man for once. I'm standing with you, Thomas!

DR. STOCKMANN. That was well said, Katherine. And, by God, I'll get this out! If I can't rent a hall, then I'll hire a drummer to walk the town with me, and I'll cry out the truth on every street corner.

MAYOR STOCKMANN. You're not going to act like a raving maniac!

DR. STOCKMANN. Yes, I am!

ASLAKSEN. In this whole town, you won't get one solitary man to go with you.

BILLING. Ye gods, I'll say you won't!

MRS. STOCKMANN. Don't give in, Thomas. I'll ask the boys to go with you.

DR. STOCKMANN. That's a marvelous idea!

MRS. STOCKMANN. Morten would love to do it; and Eilif—he'll go along.

DR. STOCKMANN. Yes, and Petra too! And you yourself, Katherine!

MRS. STOCKMANN. No, no, that's not for me. But I'll stand at the window and watch you; that I'll do.

DR. STOCKMANN (*throws his arms about her and kisses her*). Thanks for that! And now, gentlemen, let's try our steel. I'd just like to see if conniving hypocrisy can gag the mouth of a patriot who's out to clean up society!

(*He and* MRS. STOCKMANN *leave by the entrance door, back left.*)

MAYOR STOCKMANN (*gravely shaking his head*). Now he's driven her crazy, too.

⌐◄ ACT FOUR ►¬

A large, old-fashioned room in CAPTAIN HORSTER's *house. Double doors, standing open at the back, lead to an anteroom. Spaced along the wall, left, are three windows. At the middle of the opposite wall a platform has been prepared, with a small table; on it are two candles, a water carafe, a glass, and a bell. The room is mainly illuminated by wall lamps between the windows. In the left foreground stands a table with candles on it, and a chair. Farther forward at the right is a door, with several chairs beside it.*

There is a large assemblage of TOWNSPEOPLE *from all levels of society. Scattered among them are a few* WOMEN *and some* SCHOOLBOYS. *More and more people gradually crowd in from the rear, until the room is full.*

A CITIZEN (*to another, as he jostles against him*). Are you here too, Lamstad?

SECOND CITIZEN. I never miss a public meeting.

THIRD CITIZEN. I hope you brought along your whistle?

SECOND CITIZEN. You bet I did. And you?

THIRD CITIZEN. Of course. Skipper Evensen has a whopping big horn he said he'd bring.

SECOND CITIZEN. He's a character, that Evensen.

(*Laughter among the group.*)

FOURTH CITIZEN (*joining them*). Say, tell me, what's going on here tonight?

346

SECOND CITIZEN. It's Dr. Stockmann; he's giving a speech against the mayor.

FOURTH CITIZEN. But the mayor's his brother.

FIRST CITIZEN. What of it? The doctor isn't afraid.

THIRD CITIZEN. Yes, but he's all wrong. The *Courier* said so.

SECOND CITIZEN. Yes, he really must be this time, because nobody'll rent him a hall—neither the Home Owners Council nor the civic club.

FIRST CITIZEN. Even the hall at the baths wouldn't have him.

SECOND CITIZEN. Well, that you can imagine.

A MAN (*in another group*). Who are we backing in this?

ANOTHER MAN (*next to him*). Just watch Aslaksen and do what he does.

BILLING (*with a portfolio under his arm, forcing his way through the crowd*). Excuse me, gentlemen! If you'll let me by, please? I'm covering this for the *Courier*. Thank you so much! (*He sits at the table on the left.*)

A WORKMAN. Who's he?

ANOTHER WORKMAN. You don't know *him?* That's Billing—writes for Aslaksen's paper.

(CAPTAIN HORSTER *conducts* MRS. STOCKMANN *and* PETRA *in through the door to the right.* EILIF *and* MORTEN *follow.*)

HORSTER. I was thinking the family could sit here. If anything should happen, you could slip out quietly.

MRS. STOCKMANN. Do you think there'll be a disturbance?

HORSTER. You never can tell—with so many people. But sit down and rest easy.

MRS. STOCKMANN (*sitting*). How kind of you to offer Thomas this room.

HORSTER. When nobody else would, then—

PETRA (*who also has seated herself*). And it was brave of you, too, Captain Horster.

HORSTER. Oh, I don't think it took much courage for that.

(HOVSTAD *and* ASLAKSEN *make their way forward at the same time, but separately, through the crowd.*)

ASLAKSEN (moves across to HORSTER). Hasn't the doctor come yet?

HORSTER. He's waiting inside.

(*A flurry of activity by the doorway in back.*)

HOVSTAD (*to* BILLING). Here's the mayor. Look!

BILLING. Ye gods, he showed up after all!

(*The* MAYOR *proceeds quietly through the crowd, exchanging polite greetings, and then stations himself by the wall, left. After a moment* DR. STOCKMANN *enters through the door to the right. He is dressed in a black frock coat with a white tie. There is scattered, hesitant applause, which is met by subdued hissing. The room grows silent.*)

DR. STOCKMANN (*in an undertone*). How do you feel, Katherine?

MRS. STOCKMANN. Oh, I'm all right. (*Lowering her voice.*) Now, Thomas, don't fly off the handle.

DR. STOCKMANN. I can manage myself, you know that. (*Looks at his watch, then ascends the platform and bows.*) It's already a quarter past—so I'd like to begin— (*Taking his manuscript out.*)

ASLAKSEN. First, we really ought to elect a chairman.

DR. STOCKMANN. No, that's quite unnecessary.

SEVERAL VOICES (*shouting*). Yes, yes!

MAYOR STOCKMANN. I also submit that we ought to elect a moderator.

DR. STOCKMANN. But I've called this meeting to present a lecture, Peter!

MAYOR STOCKMANN. The doctor's lecture is likely to arouse some contrary opinions.

MORE VOICES FROM THE CROWD. A chairman! A moderator!

HOVSTAD. The will of the people seems to demand a chairman.

DR. STOCKMANN (*restraining himself*). All right, then, let the will of the people rule.

ASLAKSEN. Would the mayor agree to accept the chair?

THREE GENTLEMEN (*applauding*). Bravo! Bravo!

MAYOR STOCKMANN. For certain self-evident reasons, I must decline. But luckily we have in our midst a man whom I think we can all accept. I'm referring to the chairman of the Home Owners Council, Mr. Aslaksen.

MANY VOICES. Yes, yes! Aslaksen! Hurray for Aslaksen!

(DR. STOCKMANN *puts away his manuscript and leaves the platform.*)

ASLAKSEN. If my fellow townspeople express their confidence in me, I cannot refuse—

(*Applause and shouts of approval.* ASLAKSEN *mounts the platform.*)

BILLING (*writing*). So—"Mr. Aslaksen chosen by acclamation—"

ASLAKSEN. And since I'm standing here now in this role, permit me to say a few brief words. I am a man of peace and quiet who's dedicated himself to prudent moderation and to—and to moderate prudence; everyone who knows me can attest to that.

MANY VOICES. Right! You said it, Aslaksen!

ASLAKSEN. I've learned in life's school of experience that moderation is the most rewarding of all virtues for the citizen—

MAYOR STOCKMANN. Hear, hear!

ASLAKSEN. And, moreover, that prudence and temperance are what serve society best. Therefore, I would urge the estimable gentleman who convened this meeting that he make every effort to stay within the bounds of moderation.

A DRUNK (*near the door*). To the Temperance Union, skoal!

A VOICE. Shut the hell up!

MANY VOICES. Sh, sh!

ASLAKSEN. No interruptions, gentlemen! Does anyone have something to say?

MAYOR STOCKMANN. Mr. Chairman!

ASLAKSEN. The chair recognizes the mayor.

MAYOR STOCKMANN. Considering my close relationship, which you all know, to the present staff physician of the baths, I would very much have wished not to express myself here this evening. But my official connection with the baths, and a due regard for the crucial interests of this town, compel me to present a proposal. I think it safe to assume that not a single citizen here tonight would find it desirable that exaggerated and unreliable charges about the sanitary conditions of the baths should gain currency abroad.

MANY VOICES. No, no, no! Of course not! We protest!

MAYOR STOCKMANN. I therefore move that this gathering refuse to permit the staff physician to read or otherwise report on his version of the matter.

DR. STOCKMANN (*infuriated*). Refuse permission—What's that?

MRS. STOCKMANN (*coughing*). Hm, hm!

DR. STOCKMANN (*controls himself*). Permission refused —all right.

MAYOR STOCKMANN. In my statement to the *People's Courier*, I've acquainted the public with the pertinent facts, so that every right-minded citizen can easily form his own judgment. You'll see there that the doctor's proposal— besides being a vote of no confidence in the leadership of this town—would actually mean afflicting our local tax-payers with a needless expenditure of at least a hundred thousand crowns.

(*Cries of outrage and the sound of whistles.*)

ASLAKSEN (*ringing the bell*). Quiet, gentlemen! Allow me to second the mayor's proposal. It's *my* opinion, also, that the doctor's agitation has an ulterior motive. He talks about the baths, but it's a revolution he's after. He wants to put the government into different hands. No one doubts the doctor's honest intentions; Lord knows there's no divided opinion on that. I'm also a friend of self-determination by the people—as long as it doesn't hit the taxpayer too hard. But that exactly would be the case here; and it's why I'll be damned—excuse me—if I can go along with Dr. Stockmann in this. You can pay too much, even for gold; that's *my* opinion.

(*Lively approval from all sides.*)

HOVSTAD. Likewise I feel obligated to clarify my own position. Dr. Stockmann's agitation seemed at first to be winning a good deal of acceptance, and I supported it as impartially as I could. But then we began to sense that we'd let ourselves be misled by a false interpretation—

DR. STOCKMANN. False—!

HOVSTAD. A less reliable interpretation, then. The mayor's statement has proved that. I hope no one here tonight would challenge my liberal sentiments; the *Courier*'s policy on our great political issues is well known to all of you. Still, I've learned from men of wisdom and experience that in purely local matters a paper ought to move with a certain caution.

ASLAKSEN. I agree perfectly.

HOVSTAD. And, in the matter in question, it's now indisputable that Dr. Stockmann has the will of the majority against him. But an editor's first and foremost responsibility—what is that, gentlemen? Isn't it to work in collaboration with his readers? Hasn't he received something on the order of an unspoken mandate to strive actively and unceasingly on behalf of those who share his beliefs? Or maybe I'm wrong in this?

MANY VOICES. No, no, no! He's right.

HOVSTAD. It's been a bitter struggle for me to break with a man in whose home I've lately been a frequent guest—a man who, until today, could bask in the undivided esteem of the community—a man whose only fault, or whose greatest fault at least, is that he follows his heart more than his head.

SOME SCATTERED VOICES. That's true! Hurray for Dr. Stockmann!

HOVSTAD. But my duty to society compelled me to break with him. And then there's another consideration that prompts me to oppose him and, if possible, to deter him from the ominous course he's chosen: namely, consideration for his family—

DR. STOCKMANN. Stick to the sewers and water mains!

HOVSTAD. —consideration for his wife and his distressed children.

MORTEN. Is that us, Mother?

MRS. STOCKMANN. Hush!

ASLAKSEN. I hereby put the mayor's proposal to a vote.

DR. STOCKMANN. Never mind that! It's not my intention to speak tonight of all that squalor in the baths. No, you're going to hear something quite different.

MAYOR STOCKMANN (*muttering*). Now what?

THE DRUNK (*from the main doorway*). I'm a taxpayer! And, therefore, so I got rights to an opinion! And I have the sotted—solid and incomprehensible opinion that—

SEVERAL VOICES. Quiet over there!

OTHERS. He's drunk! Throw him out!

(*The* DRUNK *is ejected.*)

DR. STOCKMANN. Do I have the floor?

ASLAKSEN (*ringing the bell*). Dr. Stockmann has the floor!

DR. STOCKMANN. If it had been only a few days ago that anyone had tried to gag me like this tonight—I'd have fought for my sacred human rights like a lion! But it doesn't matter to me now. Because now I have greater things to discuss.

(*The* CROWD *presses in closer around him;* MORTEN KIIL *becomes visible among them.*)

DR. STOCKMANN (*continuing*). I've been thinking a lot these past few days—pondering so many things that finally my thoughts began running wild—

MAYOR STOCKMANN (*coughs*). Hm—!

DR. STOCKMANN. But then I got everything in place again, and I saw the whole structure so distinctly. It's why I'm here this evening. I have great disclosures to make, my friends! I'm going to unveil a discovery to you of vastly different dimension than this trifle that our water system is polluted and that our health spa is built on a muckheap.

MANY VOICES (*shouting*). Don't talk of the baths! We won't listen! Enough of that!

DR. STOCKMANN. I've said I'd talk about the great discovery I've made these last few days: the discovery that all the sources of our spiritual life are polluted, and that our entire community rests on a muckheap of lies.

STARTLED VOICES (*in undertones*). What's he saying?

MAYOR STOCKMANN. Of all the insinuations—

ASLAKSEN (*his hand on the bell*). The speaker is urged to be moderate.

DR. STOCKMANN. I've loved my birthplace as much as any man can. I was barely grown when I left here; and distance and deprivation and memory threw a kind of enchantment over the town, and the people, too.

(*Scattered applause and cheers.*)

For many years, then, I practiced in the far north, at the dead end of nowhere. When I came in contact with some of the people who lived scattered in that waste of rocks, I many times thought it would have done those poor starved creatures more good if they'd gotten a veterinary instead of someone like me.

(*Murmuring among the crowd.*)

BILLING (*setting down his pen*). Ye gods, why I never heard such—!

HOVSTAD. That's an insult to the common man!

DR. STOCKMANN. Just a minute—! I don't think anyone could ever say that I'd forgotten my home town up there. I brooded on my egg like an eider duck; and what I hatched—was the plan for the baths.

(*Applause and objections.*)

And finally, at long last, when fate relented and allowed me to come back home—my friends, then it seemed as though I had nothing left to wish for in this world. No, I did have one wish: a fierce, insistent, burning desire to contribute to the best of my town and my people.

MAYOR STOCKMANN (*gazing into space*). It's a funny way to—hm.

DR. STOCKMANN. And so I went around, exulting in my blind happiness. But yesterday morning—no, actually it was the night before last—the eyes of my spirit were opened wide, and the first thing I saw was the consummate stupidity of the authorities—

(*Confusion, outcries, and laughter.* MRS. STOCKMANN *coughs vigorously.*)

MAYOR STOCKMANN. Mr. Chairman!

ASLAKSEN (*ringing his bell*). By the powers vested in me—!

DR. STOCKMANN. It's petty to get hung up on a word, Mr. Aslaksen! I only mean that it came to me then what a consummate mess our local leaders had made out of the baths. Our leaders are one group that, for the life of me, I can't stand. I've had enough of that breed in my days. They're like a pack of goats in a stand of new trees—they strip off everything. They get in a free man's way wherever he turns—and I really don't see why we shouldn't exterminate them like any other predator—

(*Tumult in the room.*)

MAYOR STOCKMANN. Mr. Chairman, can you let such a statement pass?

ASLAKSEN (*his hand on the bell*). Doctor—!

DR. STOCKMANN. I can't imagine why I've only now taken a really sharp look at these gentlemen, because right before my eyes almost daily I've had a superb example— my brother Peter—slow of wit and thick of head—

(*Laughter, commotion, and whistles.* MRS. STOCKMANN *coughs repeatedly.* ASLAKSEN *vehemently rings his bell.*)

THE DRUNK (*who has gotten in again*). Are you referring to me? Yes, my name's Pettersen all right—but I'll fry in hell, before—

ANGRY VOICES. Out with that drunk! Throw him out!

(*Again the* DRUNK *is ejected.*)

MAYOR STOCKMANN. Who was that person?

A BYSTANDER. I don't know him, Your Honor.

ANOTHER. He's not from this town.

A THIRD. It must be that lumber dealer from over in— (*The rest is inaudible.*)

ASLAKSEN. The man was obviously muddled on Munich beer. Go on, Dr. Stockmann, but try to be more temperate.

DR. STOCKMANN. So then, my friends and neighbors, I'll say nothing further about our leading citizens. If, from what I've just said, anyone imagines that I'm out to get those gentlemen here this evening, then he's wrong—most emphatically wrong. Because I nourish a benign hope that all those mossbacks, those relics of a dying world of thought, are splendidly engaged in digging their own graves—they don't need a doctor's aid to speed them off the scene. And besides, *they're* not the overwhelming menace to society; *they're* not the ones most active in poisoning our spiritual life and polluting the very ground we stand on; *they're* not the most insidious enemies of truth and freedom in our society.

SHOUTS FROM ALL SIDES. Who, then! Who are they? Name them!

DR. STOCKMANN. Yes, you can bet I'll name them! Because *that's* exactly my great discovery yesterday. (*Raising his voice.*) The most insidious enemy of truth and freedom among us is the solid majority. Yes, the damned, solid, liberal majority—that's it! Now you know.

(*Wild turmoil in the room. Almost all those present are shouting, stamping, and whistling. Several elderly gentlemen exchange sly glances and appear to be amused.* EILIF *and* MORTEN *move threateningly toward the* SCHOOLBOYS, *who are making a disturbance.* ASLAKSEN *rings his bell and calls for order. Both* HOVSTAD *and* BILLING *are talking, without being heard. Finally quiet is restored.*)

ASLAKSEN. As chairman, I urge the speaker to withdraw his irresponsible comments.

DR. STOCKMANN. Not a chance, Mr. Aslaksen. It's that same majority in our community that's stripping away my freedom and trying to keep me from speaking the truth.

HOVSTAD. The majority is always right.

BILLING. And it acts for truth. Ye gods!

DR. STOCKMANN. The majority is never right. I say, never! That's one of those social lies that any free man who thinks for himself has to rebel against. Who makes up the majority in any country—the intelligent, or the stupid? I think we've got to agree that, all over this whole wide earth, the stupid are in a fearsomely overpowering majority. But I'll be damned to perdition if it's part of the eternal plan that the stupid are meant to rule the intelligent!

(*Commotion and outcries.*)

Oh yes, you can shout me down well enough, but you can't refute me. The majority has the might—unhappily —but it lacks the *right*. The right is with me, and the other few, the solitary individuals. The minority is always right.

(*Renewed turmoil.*)

HOVSTAD (*laughs*). So, in a couple of days, the doctor's turned aristocrat.

DR. STOCKMANN. I've told you I'm not going to waste any words on that wheezing, little, narrow-chested pack of reactionaries. The tide of life has already passed them by. But I'm thinking of the few, the individuals among us, who've mastered all the new truths that have been germinating. Those men are out there holding their positions like outposts, so far in the vanguard that the solid majority hasn't even begun to catch up—and *there's* where they're fighting for truths too newly born in the world's consciousness to have won any support from the majority.

HOVSTAD. Well, and now he's a revolutionist!

DR. STOCKMANN. Yes, you're damn right I am, Mr. Hovstad! I'm fomenting a revolution against the lie that only the majority owns the truth. What are these truths the majority flocks around? They're the ones so ripe in age they're nearly senile. But, gentlemen, when a truth's grown that old, it's gone a long way toward becoming a lie.

(*Laughter and jeers.*)

Oh yes, you can believe me as you please; but truths aren't at all the stubborn old Methuselahs people imagine. An ordinary, established truth lives, as a rule—let's say—some seventeen, eighteen, at the most twenty years; rarely more.

But those venerable truths are always terribly thin. Even so, it's only *then* that the majority takes them up and urges them on society as wholesome spiritual food. But there isn't much nutriment in that kind of diet, I promise you; and as a doctor, I know. All these majority-truths are like last year's salt meat—like rancid, tainted pork. And there's the cause of all the moral scurvy that's raging around us.

ASLAKSEN. It strikes me that the distinguished speaker has strayed rather far from his text.

MAYOR STOCKMANN. I must agree with the chairman's opinion.

DR. STOCKMANN. You're out of your mind, Peter! I'm sticking as close to the text as I can. Because this is exactly what I'm talking about: that the masses, the crowd, this damn solid majority—that *this* is what I say is poisoning our sources of spiritual life and defiling the earth under our feet.

HOVSTAD. And the great liberal-minded majority does this because they're reasonable enough to honor only basic, well-accepted truths?

DR. STOCKMANN. Ah, my dear Mr. Hovstad, don't talk about basic truths! The truths accepted by the masses now are the ones proclaimed basic by the advance guard in our grandfathers' time. We fighters on the frontiers today, we no longer recognize them. There's only one truth that's basic in my belief: that no society can live a healthy life on the bleached bones of that kind of truth.

HOVSTAD. Instead of standing there rambling on in the blue, it might be interesting to describe some of those bleached bones we're living on.

(*Agreement from various quarters.*)

DR. STOCKMANN. Oh, I could itemize a whole slew of abominations; but to start with, I'll mention just one recognized truth that's actually a vicious lie, though Mr. Hovstad and the *Courier* and all the *Courier's* devotees live on it.

HOVSTAD. That being—?

DR. STOCKMANN. That being the doctrine inherited from your ancestors, which you mindlessly disseminate far and wide—the doctrine that the public, the mob, the masses are the vital core of the people—in fact, that they *are* the people—and that the common man, the inert, unformed component of society, has the same right to admonish and approve, to prescribe and to govern as the few spiritually accomplished personalities.

BILLING. Well, I'll be—

HOVSTAD (*simultaneously, shouting*). Citizens, did you hear that!

ANGRY VOICES. Oh, we're not the people, uh? So, only the accomplished rule!

A WORKMAN. Out with a man who talks like that!

OTHERS. Out the door! Heave him out!

A MAN (*yells*). Evensen, blow the horn!

(*Deep blasts on a horn are heard; whistles and furious commotion in the room.*)

DR. STOCKMANN (*when the noise has subsided a bit*). Now just be reasonable! Can't you stand hearing the truth for a change? I never expected you all to agree with me on the spot. But I really did expect that Mr. Hovstad would admit I'm right, after he'd simmered down a little. Mr. Hovstad claims to be a freethinker—

STARTLED VOICES (*in undertones*). What was that? A freethinker? Hovstad a freethinker?

HOVSTAD (*loudly*). Prove it, Dr. Stockmann! When have I said that in print?

DR. STOCKMANN (*reflecting*). No, by God, you're right—you've never had the courage. Well, I don't want to put you in hot water. Let's say I'm the freethinker then. Because I'm going to demonstrate scientifically that the *Courier*'s leading you shamelessly by the nose when they say that you—the public, the masses—are the vital core of the people. You see, that's just a journalistic lie! The masses are no more than the raw material out of which a people is shaped.

(*Mutterings, laughter, and disquiet in the room.*)

Well, isn't that a fact throughout all the rest of life? What about the difference between a thoroughbred and a hybrid animal? Look at your ordinary barnyard fowl. What meat can you get off such scrawny bones? Not much! And what kind of eggs does it lay? Any competent crow or raven could furnish about the same. But now take a purebred Spanish or Japanese hen, or a fine pheasant or turkey—there's where you'll see the difference! Or again with dogs, a family we humans so closely resemble. First, think of an ordinary stray dog—I mean, one of those nasty, ragged, common mongrels that run around the streets, and spatter the walls of houses. Then set that stray alongside a poodle whose pedigree runs back through a distinguished line to a house where fine food and harmonious voices and music have been the rule. Don't you think the mentality of that poodle will have developed quite differently from the stray's? Of course it will! A young pedigreed poodle can be raised by its trainer to perform the most incredible feats. Your common mongrel couldn't learn such things if you stood him on his head.

(*Tumult and derision generally.*)

A CITIZEN (*shouting*). Now you're making us into dogs, uh?

ANOTHER MAN. We're not animals, Doctor!

DR. STOCKMANN. Oh yes, brother, we *are* animals! We're the best animals, all in all, that any man could wish for. But there aren't many animals of quality among us. There's a terrible gap between the thoroughbreds and the mongrels in humanity. And what's amusing is that Mr. Hovstad totally agrees with me as long as we're talking of four-legged beasts—

HOVSTAD. Well, but they're a class by themselves.

DR. STOCKMANN. All right. But as soon as I extend the law to the two-legged animals, Mr. Hovstad stops cold. He doesn't dare think his own thoughts any longer, or follow his ideas to a logical conclusion. So he turns the whole doctrine upside down and declares in the *Courier* that the barnyard fowl and the mongrel dog—that *these* are the real paragons of the menagerie. But that's how it always goes as long as conformity is in your system, and you haven't worked through to a distinction of mind and spirit.

HOVSTAD. I make no claim of any kind of distinction. I was born of simple peasants, and I'm proud that my roots run deep in those masses that he despises.

NUMEROUS WOMEN. Hurray for Hovstad! Hurray, hurray!

DR. STOCKMANN. The kind of commonness I'm talking of isn't only found in the depths: it teems and swarms all around us in society—right up to the top. Just look at your own neat and tidy mayor. My brother Peter's as good a common man as any that walks on two feet—

(*Laughter and hisses.*)

MAYOR STOCKMANN. I protest against these personal allusions.

DR. STOCKMANN (*unruffled*). —and that's not because he's descended, just as I am, from a barbarous old pirate from Pomerania or thereabouts—because so we are—

MAYOR STOCKMANN. A ridiculous fiction. I deny it!

DR. STOCKMANN. —no, he's that because he thinks what the higher-ups think and believes what they believe. The people who do that are the spiritually common men. And that's why my stately brother Peter, you see, is in fact so fearfully lacking in distinction—and consequently so narrowminded.

MAYOR STOCKMANN. Mr. Chairman—!

HOVSTAD. So you have to be distinguished to be liberal-minded in this country. That's a completely new insight.

(*General laughter.*)

DR. STOCKMANN. Yes, that's also part of my new discovery. And along with it goes the idea that broadmindedness is almost exactly the same as morality. That's why I say it's simply inexcusable of the *Courier*, day in and day out, to promote the fallacy that it's the masses, the solid majority, who stand as the guardian of tolerance and morality—and that degeneracy and corruption of all kinds are a sort of by-product of culture, filtering down to us like all the pollution filtering down to the baths from the tanneries up at Mølledal.

(*Turmoil and interruptions.*)

DR. STOCKMANN (*unfazed, laughing in his enthusiasm*).

And yet this same *Courier* can preach that the deprived masses must be raised to greater cultural opportunities. But, hell's bells—if the *Courier's* assumption holds true, then raising the masses like that would be precisely the same as plunging them smack into depravity! But luckily it's only an old wives' tale—this inherited lie that culture demoralizes. No, it's ignorance and poverty and ugliness in life that do the devil's work! In a house that isn't aired and swept every day—my wife Katherine maintains that the floors ought to be scrubbed as well, but that's debatable—anyway—I say in a house like that, within two or three years, people lose all power for moral thought and action. Lack of oxygen dulls the conscience. And there must be a woeful dearth of oxygen in the houses of this town, it seems, if the entire solid majority can numb their consciences enough to want to build this town's prosperity on a quagmire of duplicity and lies.

ASLAKSEN. It's intolerable—such a gross attack on a whole community.

A GENTLEMAN. I move the chairman rule the speaker out of order

FURIOUS VOICES Yes, yes! That's right Out of order

DR. STOCKMANN (*vehemently*). Then I'll cry out the truth from every street corner. I'll write to newspapers in other towns! The entire country'll learn what's happened here!

HOVSTAD. It almost looks like the doctor's determined to destroy this town

DR STOCKMANN. Yes, I love my home town so much I'd rather destroy it than see it flourishing on a lie.

ASLAKSEN. That's putting it plain.

(*Tumult and whistling.* MRS. STOCKMANN *coughs in vain; the* DOCTOR *no longer hears her.*)

HOVSTAD (*shouting above the noise*). Any man who'd destroy a whole community must be a public enemy!

DR. STOCKMANN (*with mounting indignation*). What's the difference if a lying community gets destroyed! It ought to be razed to the ground, I say! Stamp them out like vermin, everyone who lives by lies! You'll contaminate this entire nation in the end, till the land itself deserves to be destroyed. And if it comes to that even, then I say with all my heart: let this whole land be destroyed, let its people all be stamped out!

A MAN. That's talking like a real enemy of the people!

BILLING. Ye gods, but *there's* the people's voice!

THE WHOLE CROWD (*shrieking*). Yes, yes, yes! He's an enemy of the people! He hates his country! He hates all his people!

ASLAKSEN. Both as a citizen and as a human being, I'm profoundly shaken by what I've had to listen to here. Dr. Stockmann has revealed himself in a manner beyond anything I could have dreamed. I'm afraid that I have to endorse the judgment just rendered by my worthy fellow citizens; and I propose that we ought to express this judgment in a resolution, as follows: "This meeting declares that it regards Dr. Thomas Stockmann, staff physician at the baths, to be an enemy of the people."

(*Tumultuous cheers and applause. Many onlookers close in around the* DOCTOR, *whistling at him.* MRS. STOCKMANN *and* PETRA *have risen.* MORTEN *and* EILIF *are fighting with the other* SCHOOLBOYS, *who have also been whistling. Several grown-ups separate them.*)

DR. STOCKMANN (*to the hecklers*). Ah, you fools—I'm telling you—

ASLAKSEN (*ringing his bell*). The doctor is out of order! A formal vote is called for; but to spare personal feelings, it ought to be a secret ballot. Do you have any blank paper, Mr. Billing?

BILLING. Here's some blue and white both—

ASLAKSEN (*leaving the platform*). Fine. It'll go faster that way. Cut it in slips—yes, that's it. (*To the gathering.*) Blue means no, white means yes. I'll go around myself and collect the votes.

(*The* MAYOR *leaves the room.* ASLAKSEN *and a couple of other citizens circulate through the crowd with paper slips in their hats.*)

A GENTLEMAN (*to* HOVSTAD). What's gotten into the doctor? How should we take this?

HOVSTAD. Well, you know how hot-headed he is.

ANOTHER GENTLEMAN (*to* BILLING). Say, you've visited there off and on. Have you noticed if the man drinks?

BILLING. Ye gods, I don't know what to say. When anybody stops in, there's always toddy on the table.

A THIRD GENTLEMAN. No, I think at times he's just out of his mind.

FIRST GENTLEMAN. I wonder if there isn't a strain of insanity in the family?

BILLING. It's quite possible.

A FOURTH GENTLEMAN. No, it's pure spite, that's all. Revenge for something or other.

BILLING. He was carrying on about a raise at one time—but he never got it.

ALL THE GENTLEMEN (*as one voice*). Ah, there's the answer!

THE DRUNK (*within the crowd*). Let's have a blue one! And—let's have a white one, too!

CRIES. There's that drunk again! Throw him out!

MORTEN KIIL (*approaching the* DOCTOR). Well, Stockmann, now you see what your monkeyshines come to?

DR. STOCKMANN. I've done my duty.

MORTEN KIIL. What was that you said about the tanneries at Mølledal?

DR. STOCKMANN. You heard it. I said all the pollution came from them.

MORTEN KIIL. From *my* tannery, too?

DR. STOCKMANN. I'm afraid your tannery's the worst of them.

MORTEN KIIL. You're going to print *that* in the papers?

DR. STOCKMANN. I'm sweeping nothing under the carpet.

MORTEN KIIL. That could cost you plenty, Stockmann. (*He leaves.*)

A FAT GENTLEMAN (*going up to* HORSTER, *without greeting the ladies*). Well, Captain, so you lend out your house to enemies of the people?

HORSTER. I think I can dispose of my property, sir, as I see fit.

THE MAN. So you'll certainly have no objection if I do the same with mine.

HORSTER. What do you mean?

THE MAN. You'll hear from me in the morning. (*He turns and leaves.*)

PETRA (*to* HORSTER). Doesn't he own your ship?

HORSTER. Yes, that was Mr. Vik.

ASLAKSEN (*ascends the platform with ballots in hand and rings for order*). Gentlemen, let me make you acquainted with the outcome. All of the votes with one exception—

A YOUNG MAN. That's the drunk!

ASLAKSEN. All of the votes, with the exception of an intoxicated man, are in favor of this assembly of citizens declaring the staff physician of the baths, Dr. Thomas Stockmann, an enemy of the people. (*Shouts and gestures of approval.*) Long live our ancient and glorious community! (*More cheers.*) Long live our capable and effective mayor, who so loyally has suppressed the ties of family! (*Cheers.*) This meeting is adjourned. (*He descends from the platform.*)

BILLING. Long live the chairman!

THE ENTIRE CROWD. Hurray for Aslaksen!

DR. STOCKMANN. My hat and coat, Petra. Captain, have you room for several passengers to the New World?

HORSTER. For you and your family, Doctor, we'll make room.

DR. STOCKMANN (*as* PETRA *helps him on with his coat*). Good. Come, Katherine! Come on, boys!

(*He takes his wife by the arm.*)

MRS. STOCKMANN (*dropping her voice*). Thomas, dear, let's leave by the back way.

DR. STOCKMANN. No back ways out, Katherine. (*Raising his voice.*) You'll be hearing from the enemy of the people before he shakes this dust off his feet! I'm not as meek as one certain person; I'm not saying, "I forgive them, because they know not what they do."

ASLAKSEN (*in an outcry*). That's a blasphemous comparison, Dr. Stockmann!

BILLING. That it is, so help me— It's a bit much for a pious man to take.

A COARSE VOICE. And then he threatened us, too!

HEATED VOICES. Let's smash his windows for him! Dunk him in the fjord!

A MAN (*in the crowd*). Blast your horn, Evensen! Honk, honk!

(*The sound of the horn; whistles and wild shrieks. The* DOCTOR *and his family move toward the exit,* HORSTER *clearing the way for them.*)

THE WHOLE CROWD (*howling after them*). Enemy! Enemy! Enemy of the people!

BILLING (*organizing his notes*). Ye gods, I wouldn't drink toddy at the Stockmanns' tonight!

(*The crowd surges toward the exit; the noise diffuses outside; from the street the cry continues*: "*Enemy! Enemy of the people!*")

⤙ ACT FIVE ⤚

DR. STOCKMANN's *study. Bookcases and cabinets filled with various medicines line the walls. In the back wall is a door to the hall; in the foreground, left, the door to the living room. At the right, opposite, are two windows, with all their panes shattered. In the middle of the room is the* DOCTOR's *desk, covered with books and papers. The room is in disorder. It is morning.* DR. STOCKMANN, *in a dressing gown, slippers, and a smoking cap, is bent down, raking under one of the cabinets with an umbrella; after some effort, he sweeps out a stone.*

DR. STOCKMANN (*calling through the open living-room door*). Katherine, I found another one.

MRS. STOCKMANN (*from the living room*). Oh, I'm sure you'll find a lot more yet.

DR. STOCKMANN (*adding the stone to a pile of others on the table*). I'm going to preserve these stones as holy relics. Eilif and Morten have got to see them every day; and when they're grown, they'll inherit them from me. (*Raking under a bookcase.*) Hasn't—what the hell's her name—the maid—hasn't she gone for the glazier yet?

MRS. STOCKMANN (*enters*). Of course, but he said he didn't know if he could come today.

DR. STOCKMANN. More likely he doesn't dare.

MRS. STOCKMANN. Yes, Randina thought he was afraid of what the neighbors might say. (*Speaking into the living room.*) What do you want, Randina? Oh yes. (*Goes out and comes back immediately.*) Here's a letter for you, Thomas.

DR. STOCKMANN. Let me see. (*Opens it and reads.*) Of course.

MRS. STOCKMANN. Who's it from?

DR. STOCKMANN. The landlord. He's giving us notice.

MRS. STOCKMANN. Is that true! He's such a decent man—

DR. STOCKMANN (*reading on in the letter*). He doesn't dare not to, he says. It pains him to do it, but he doesn't dare not to—in fairness to his fellow townspeople—a matter of public opinion—not independent—can't affront certain powerful men—

MRS. STOCKMANN. You see, Thomas.

DR. STOCKMANN. Yes, yes, I see very well. They're cowards, all of them here in town. Nobody dares do anything, in fairness to all the others. (*Hurls the letter on the table.*) But that's nothing to us, Katherine. We're off for the New World now—

MRS. STOCKMANN. But, Thomas, is that really the right solution, to emigrate?

DR. STOCKMANN. Maybe I ought to stay here, where they've pilloried me as an enemy of the people, branded me, smashed in my windows! And look at this, Katherine; they even tore my black trousers.

MRS. STOCKMANN. Oh, no—and they're the best you have!

DR. STOCKMANN. One should never wear his best trousers when he goes out fighting for truth and freedom. It's not that I'm so concerned about the trousers, you understand; you can always mend them for me. But what grates is that mob setting on me bodily as if they were my equals—by God, that's the thing I can't bear!

MRS. STOCKMANN. Yes, they've abused you dreadfully in this town, Thomas. But do we have to leave the country entirely because of *that*?

DR. STOCKMANN. Don't you think the common herd is just as arrogant in other towns as well? Why, of course—

it's all one and the same. Ahh, shoot! Let the mongrels yap; they're not the worst. The worst of it is that everyone the country over is a slave to party. But *that's* not the reason—it's probably no better in the free United States; I'm sure they have a plague of solid majorities and liberal public opinions and all the other bedevilments. But the scale there is so immense, you see. They might kill you, but they don't go in for slow torture; they don't lock a free soul in the jaws of a vise, the way they do here at home. And, if need be, there's space to get away. (*Pacing the floor.*) If I only knew of some primeval forest, or a little South Sea island at a bargain price—

MRS. STOCKMANN. But, Thomas, think of the boys.

DR. STOCKMANN (*stopping in his tracks*). You are remarkable, Katherine! Would you rather they grew up in a society like ours? You saw yourself last night that half the population are raging maniacs; and if the other half haven't lost their reason, it's because they're such mutton-heads they haven't any reason to lose.

MRS. STOCKMANN. Yes, but dear, you're so intemperate in your speech.

DR. STOCKMANN. Look! Isn't it true, what I'm saying? Don't they turn every idea upside down? Don't they scramble right and wrong up completely? Don't they call everything a lie that I know for the truth? But the height of insanity is that here you've got all these full-grown liberals going round in a bloc and deluding themselves and the others that they're independent thinkers! Did you ever hear the like of it, Katherine?

MRS. STOCKMANN. Yes, yes, it's all wrong of course, but—

(PETRA *enters from the living room.*)

MRS. STOCKMANN. You're back from school already?

PETRA. Yes. I got my notice.

MRS. STOCKMANN. Your notice.

DR. STOCKMANN. You, too!

PETRA. Mrs. Busk gave me my notice, so I thought it better to leave at once.

DR. STOCKMANN. You did the right thing!

MRS. STOCKMANN. Who would have thought Mrs. Busk would prove such a poor human being!

PETRA. Oh, Mother, she really isn't so bad. It was plain to see how miserable she felt. But she said she didn't dare not to. So I got fired.

DR. STOCKMANN (*laughs and rubs his hands*). She didn't dare not to, either. Oh, that's charming.

MRS. STOCKMANN. Well, after that awful row last night—

PETRA. It was more than just that. Father, listen now!

DR. STOCKMANN. What?

PETRA. Mrs. Busk showed me no less than three letters she'd gotten this morning.

DR. STOCKMANN. Anonymous, of course?

PETRA. Yes.

DR. STOCKMANN. Because they don't *dare* sign their names, Katherine.

PETRA. And two of them stated that a gentleman who's often visited this household had declared in the club last night that I had extremely free ideas on various matters—

DR. STOCKMANN. And that you didn't deny, I hope.

PETRA. No, you know that. Mrs. Busk has some pretty liberal ideas herself, when it's just the two of us talking. But with this all coming out about me, she didn't dare keep me on.

MRS. STOCKMANN. And to think—it was one of our regular visitors! You see, Thomas, there's what you get for your hospitality.

DR. STOCKMANN. We won't go on living in a pigsty like this. Katherine, get packed as soon as you can. Let's get out of here, the quicker the better.

MRS. STOCKMANN. Be quiet—I think there's someone in the hall. Have a look, Petra.

PETRA (*opening the door*). Oh, is it you, Captain Horster? Please, come in.

HORSTER (*from the hall*). Good morning. I thought I ought to stop by and see how things stand.

DR. STOCKMANN (*shaking his hand*). Thanks. That certainly is kind of you.

MRS. STOCKMANN. And thank you, Captain Horster, for helping us through last night.

PETRA. But how did you ever make it home again?

HORSTER. Oh, no problem. I can handle myself pretty well; and they're mostly a lot of hot air, those people.

DR. STOCKMANN. Yes, isn't it astounding, this bestial cowardice? Come here, and I'll show you something. See, here are all the stones they rained in on us. Just look at them! I swear, there aren't more than two respectable paving blocks in the whole pile; the rest are nothing but gravel—only pebbles. And yet they stood out there, bellowing, and swore they'd hammer me to a pulp. But action—action—no, you don't see much of that in this town!

HORSTER. I'd say this time that was lucky for you, Doctor.

DR. STOCKMANN. Definitely. But it's irritating, all the same; because if it ever comes to a serious fight to save this country, you'll see how public opinion is all for ducking the issue, and how the solid majority runs for cover like a flock of sheep. That's what's so pathetic when you think of it; it makes me heartsick— Damn it all, no—this is sheer stupidity; they've labeled me an enemy of the people, so I better act like one.

MRS. STOCKMANN. You never could be that, Thomas.

DR. STOCKMANN. Don't count on it, Katherine. To be called some ugly name hurts like a stabbing pain in the lung. And that damnable label—I can't shake it off; it's fixed itself here in the pit of my stomach, where it sits and rankles and corrodes like acid. And there's no magnesia to work against that.

PETRA. Oh, Father, you should just laugh at them.

HORSTER. People will come around in their thinking, Doctor.

MRS. STOCKMANN. As sure as you're standing here, they will.

DR. STOCKMANN. Yes, maybe after it's too late. Well, they've got it coming! Let them stew in their own mess and rue the day they drove a patriot into exile. When are you sailing, Captain Horster?

HORSTER. Hm—as a matter of fact, that's why I stopped by to talk to you—

DR. STOCKMANN. Oh, has something gone wrong with the ship?

HORSTER. No. But it looks like I won't sail with her.

PETRA. You haven't been fired, have you?

HORSTER (*smiles*). Yes, exactly.

PETRA. You, too.

MRS. STOCKMANN. See there, Thomas.

DR. STOCKMANN. And all this for the truth! Oh, if only I could have foreseen—

HORSTER. Now, don't go worrying about me; I'll find a post with some shipping firm out of town.

DR. STOCKMANN. And there we have Mr. Vik—a merchant, a man of wealth, independent in every way—! What a disgrace!

HORSTER. He's quite fair-minded otherwise. He said himself he'd gladly have retained me if he dared to—

DR. STOCKMANN. But he didn't dare? No, naturally!

HORSTER. It's not so easy, he was telling me, when you belong to a party—

DR. STOCKMANN. There's a true word from the merchant prince. A political party—it's like a sausage grinder; it grinds all the heads up together into one mash, and then it turns them out, link by link, into fatheads and meatheads!

MRS. STOCKMANN. Thomas, really!

PETRA (*to* HORSTER). If you just hadn't seen us home, things might not have gone like this.

HORSTER. I don't regret it.

PETRA (*extending her hand to him*). Thank you!

HORSTER (*to the* DOCTOR). So, what I wanted to say was, if you're still serious about leaving, then I've thought of another plan—

DR. STOCKMANN. Excellent. If we can only clear out of here fast—

MRS. STOCKMANN. Shh! Didn't someone knock?

PETRA. It's Uncle, I'll bet.

DR. STOCKMANN. Aha! (*Calls.*) Come in!

MRS. STOCKMANN. Thomas dear, you must promise me—

(*The* MAYOR *enters from the hall.*)

MAYOR STOCKMANN (*in the doorway*). Oh, you're occupied. Well, then I'd better—

DR. STOCKMANN. No, no, come right in.

MAYOR STOCKMANN. But I wanted to speak to you alone.

MRS. STOCKMANN. We'll go into the living room for a time.

HORSTER. And I'll come by again later.

DR. STOCKMANN. No, you go in with them, Captain Horster. I need to hear something more about—

HORSTER. Oh yes, I'll wait then.

(*He accompanies* MRS. STOCKMANN *and* PETRA *into the living room. The* MAYOR *says nothing, but glances at the windows.*)

DR. STOCKMANN. Maybe you find it a bit drafty here today? Put your hat on.

MAYOR STOCKMANN. Thank you, if I may. (*Does so.*) I think I caught cold last night. I was freezing out there—

DR. STOCKMANN. Really? It seemed more on the warm side to me.

MAYOR STOCKMANN. I regret that it wasn't within my power to curb those excesses last evening.

DR. STOCKMANN. Do you have anything else in particular to say to me?

MAYOR STOCKMANN (*taking out a large envelope*). I have this document for you from the board of directors.

DR. STOCKMANN. It's my notice?

MAYOR STOCKMANN. Yes, effective today. (*Places the envelope on the table.*) This pains us deeply, but—to be quite candid—we didn't dare not to, in view of public opinion.

DR. STOCKMANN (*smiles*). Didn't dare? Seems as though I've already heard those words today.

MAYOR STOCKMANN. I suggest that you face your position clearly. After this, you mustn't count on any practice whatsoever here in town.

DR. STOCKMANN. To hell with the practice! But how can you be so sure?

MAYOR STOCKMANN. The Home Owners Council is circulating a resolution, soliciting all responsible citizens to dispense with your services. And I venture to say that not one single householder will risk refusing to sign. Quite simply, they wouldn't dare.

DR. STOCKMANN. I don't doubt it. But what of it?

MAYOR STOCKMANN. If I could give you some advice, it would be that you leave this area for a while—

DR. STOCKMANN. Yes, I've been half thinking of just that.

MAYOR STOCKMANN. Good. Then, after you've had some six months, more or less, to reconsider things, if on mature reflection you find yourself capable of a few words of apology, acknowledging your mistakes—

DR. STOCKMANN. Then maybe I could get my job back, you mean?

MAYOR STOCKMANN. Perhaps. It's not at all unlikely.

DR. STOCKMANN. Yes, but public opinion? You could hardly dare, in that regard.

MAYOR STOCKMANN. Opinion tends to go from one extreme to another. And to be quite honest, it's especially important to us to get a signed statement to that effect from you.

DR. STOCKMANN. Yes, wouldn't you lick your chin-choppers for that! But, damnation, don't you remember what I already said about that kind of foxy game?

MAYOR STOCKMANN. Your position was much more favorable then. You could imagine then that you had the whole town in back of you—

DR. STOCKMANN. Yes, and I feel now as if the whole town's on my back— (*Flaring up.*) But even if the devil and his grandmother were riding me—never! Never, you hear me!

MAYOR STOCKMANN. A family provider can't go around risking everything the way you do. You can't risk it, Thomas!

DR. STOCKMANN. Can't risk! There's just one single thing in this world a free man can't risk; and do you know what that is?

MAYOR STOCKMANN. No.

DR. STOCKMANN. Of course not. But *I'll* tell you. A free man can't risk befouling himself like a savage. He doesn't dare sink to the point that he'd like to spit in his own face.

MAYOR STOCKMANN. This all sounds highly plausible; and if there weren't another prior explanation for your stubborn arrogance—but then of course, there is—

DR. STOCKMANN. What do you mean by *that?*

MAYOR STOCKMANN. You understand perfectly well. But as your brother and as a man of some discernment, let me advise you not to build too smugly on prospects that might very well never materialize.

DR. STOCKMANN. What in the world are you driving at?

MAYOR STOCKMANN. Are you actually trying to make me believe you're ignorant of the terms of Morten Kiil's will?

DR. STOCKMANN. I know that the little he has is going to a home for destitute craftsmen. But how does that apply to me?

MAYOR STOCKMANN. First of all, the amount under discussion is far from little. Morten Kiil is a rather wealthy man.

DR. STOCKMANN. I hadn't the slightest idea—!

MAYOR STOCKMANN. Hm—really? And you hadn't any idea, either, that a considerable part of his fortune will pass to your children, with you and your wife enjoying the interest for life. He hasn't told you that?

DR. STOCKMANN. Not one blessed word of it! Quite the contrary, he goes on fuming endlessly about the outrageously high taxes he pays. But how do you know this for sure, Peter?

MAYOR STOCKMANN. I have it from a totally reliable source.

DR. STOCKMANN. But, my Lord, then Katherine's provided for—and the children too! I really must tell her—(*Shouts.*) Katherine, Katherine!

MAYOR STOCKMANN (*restraining him*). Shh, don't say anything yet!

MRS. STOCKMANN (*opening the door*). What is it?

DR. STOCKMANN. Nothing, dear. Go back inside.

(MRS. STOCKMANN *shuts the door.*)

DR. STOCKMANN (*pacing the floor*). Provided for! Just imagine—every one of them, provided for. And for life! What a blissful feeling, to know you're secure!

MAYOR STOCKMANN. Yes, but that's precisely what you aren't. Morten Kiil can revise his will any time he pleases.

DR. STOCKMANN. But, my dear Peter, he won't do that. The Badger's enraptured by the way I've gone after you and your smart friends.

MAYOR STOCKMANN (*starts and looks penetratingly at him*). Aha, that puts a new light on things.

DR. STOCKMANN. What things?

MAYOR STOCKMANN. So this whole business has been a collusion. These reckless, violent assaults you've aimed, in the name of truth, at our leading citizens were—

DR. STOCKMANN. Yes—were what?

MAYOR STOCKMANN. They were nothing more than a calculated payment for a piece of that vindictive old man's estate.

DR. STOCKMANN (*nearly speechless*). Peter—you're the cheapest trash I've known in all my days.

MAYOR STOCKMANN. Between us, everything is through.

Your dismissal is irrevocable—for now we've got a weapon against you. (*He goes.*)

DR. STOCKMANN. Why, that scum—aaah! (*Shouts.*) Katherine! Scour the floors where he's been! Have her come in with a pail—that girl—whozzis, damn it—the one with the smudgy nose—

MRS. STOCKMANN (*in the living-room doorway*). Shh, Thomas. Shh!

PETRA (*also in the doorway*). Father, Grandpa's here and wonders if he can speak to you alone.

DR. STOCKMANN. Yes, of course he can. (*By the door.*) Come in.

(MORTEN KIIL *enters. The* DOCTOR *closes the door after him.*)

DR. STOCKMANN. Well, what is it? Have a seat.

MORTEN KIIL. Won't sit. (*Looking about.*) You've made it very attractive here today, Stockmann.

DR. STOCKMANN. Yes, don't you think so?

MORTEN KIIL. Really attractive. And fresh air, too. Today you've got enough of that oxygen you talked about yesterday. You must have a marvelous conscience today, I imagine.

DR. STOCKMANN. Yes, I have.

MORTEN KIIL. I can imagine. (*Tapping his chest.*) But do you know what *I* have here?

DR. STOCKMANN. Well, I'm hoping a marvelous conscience, too.

MORTEN KIIL. Pah! No, it's something better than that. (*He takes out a thick wallet, opens it, and displays a sheaf of papers.*)

DR. STOCKMANN (*stares at him, amazed*). Shares in the baths.

MORTEN KIIL. They weren't hard to get today.

DR. STOCKMANN. And you were out buying—?

MORTEN KIIL. As many as I could afford.

DR. STOCKMANN. But, my dear Father-in-law—with everything at the baths in jeopardy!

MORTEN KIIL. If you go back to acting like a reasonable man, you'll soon get the baths on their feet again.

DR. STOCKMANN. You can see yourself, I'm doing all I can; but the people are crazy in this town.

MORTEN KIIL. You said yesterday that the worst pollution came from my tannery. But now if that *is* true, then my grandfather and my father before me and I myself over numbers of years have been poisoning this town right along, like three angels of death. You think I can rest with that disgrace on my head?

DR. STOCKMANN. I'm afraid you'll have to learn how.

MORTEN KIIL. No thanks. I want my good name and reputation. People call me the Badger, I've heard. A badger's a kind of pig, isn't it? They're not going to be right about that. Never. I want to live and die a clean human being.

DR. STOCKMANN. And how are you going to do that?

MORTEN KIIL. You'll make me clean, Stockmann.

DR. STOCKMANN. I!

MORTEN KIIL. Do you know where I got the money to buy these shares? No, you couldn't know that, but now I'll tell you. It's the money Katherine and Petra and the boys will be inheriting from me someday. Yes, because, despite everything, I've laid a little aside, you see.

DR. STOCKMANN (*flaring up*). So you went out and spent Katherine's money for *those!*

MORTEN KIIL. Yes, now the money's completely bound up in the baths. And now I'll see if you're really so ranting, raging mad after all, Stockmann. Any more about bugs and such coming down from my tannery, it'll be exactly the same as cutting great strips out of Katherine's skin, and Petra's, and the boys'. But no normal man would do that—he'd *have* to be mad.

DR. STOCKMANN (*pacing back and forth*). Yes, but I *am* a madman; I *am* a madman!

MORTEN KIIL. But you're not so utterly out of your senses as to flay your wife and children.

DR. STOCKMANN (*stopping in front of him*). Why

couldn't you talk with me before you went out and bought all that worthless paper?

MORTEN KIIL. When a thing's been done, it's best to hang on.

DR. STOCKMANN (*paces the room restlessly*). If only I weren't so certain in this—! But I'm perfectly sure I'm right.

MORTEN KIIL (*weighing the wallet in his hand*). If you keep on with this foolishness, then these aren't going to be worth much, will they? (*He replaces the wallet in his pocket.*)

DR. STOCKMANN. Damn it, science should be able to provide some counter-agent, some kind of germicide—

MORTEN KIIL. You mean something to kill those little animals?

DR. STOCKMANN. Yes, or else make them harmless.

MORTEN KIIL. Couldn't you try rat poison?

DR. STOCKMANN. Oh, that's nonsense! But—everyone says this is all just imagination. Well, why not? Let them have what they want! Stupid, mean little mongrels—didn't they brand me enemy of the people? And weren't they spoiling to tear the clothes off my back?

MORTEN KIIL. And all the windows they broke for you.

DR. STOCKMANN. And I do have family obligations! I must talk this over with Katherine; she's very shrewd in these things.

MORTEN KIIL. Good. You pay attention to a sensible woman's advice.

DR. STOCKMANN (*turning on him*). And you, too—how could you make such a mess of it! Gambling with Katherine's money; tormenting me with this horrible dilemma! When I look at you, I could be seeing the devil himself—!

MORTEN KIIL. I think I'd better be going. But by two o'clock I want your answer: yes—or no. If it's no, the stock gets willed to charity—and right this very day.

DR. STOCKMANN. And what does Katherine get then?

MORTEN KIIL. Not a crumb.

(*The hall door is opened.* HOVSTAD and ASLAKSEN *come into view, standing outside.*)

MORTEN KIIL. Well, will you look at *them?*

DR. STOCKMANN (*staring at them*). *What—!* You still dare to come around here?

HOVSTAD. Of course we do.

ASLAKSEN. You see, we've something to talk with you about.

MORTEN KIIL (*in a whisper*). Yes or no—by two o'clock.

ASLAKSEN (*glancing at* HOVSTAD). Aha!

(MORTEN KIIL *leaves.*)

DR. STOCKMANN. Well now, what do you want? Cut it short.

HOVSTAD. I can easily realize your bitterness toward us for the posture we took at last night's meeting—

DR. STOCKMANN. You call that a posture! Yes, that was a lovely posture! I call it spinelessness, like a bent old woman—holy God!

HOVSTAD. Call it what you will, we couldn't do otherwise.

DR. STOCKMANN. You didn't *dare,* you mean. Isn't that right?

HOVSTAD. Yes, if you like.

ASLAKSEN. But why didn't you pass us the word beforehand? Just the least little hint to Hovstad or me.

DR. STOCKMANN. A hint? What about?

ASLAKSEN. The reason why.

DR. STOCKMANN. I simply don't understand you.

ASLAKSEN (*nods confidentially*). Oh, yes, you do, Dr. Stockmann.

HOVSTAD. Let's not make a mystery out of it any longer.

DR. STOCKMANN (*looking from one to the other*). What in sweet blazes *is* this—!

ASLAKSEN. May I ask—hasn't your father-in-law been combing the town to buy up stock in the baths?

DR. STOCKMANN. Yes, he's bought a few shares today; but—?

ASLAKSEN. It would have been more clever if you'd gotten someone else to do it—someone less closely related.

HOVSTAD. And you shouldn't have moved under your own name. No one had to know the attack on the baths came from you. You should have brought me in on it, Doctor.

DR. STOCKMANN (*stares blankly in front of him; a light seems to dawn on him, and he says as if thunderstruck*). It's unbelievable! Do these things happen?

ASLAKSEN (*smiles*). Why, of course they do. But they only happen when you use finesse, if you follow me.

HOVSTAD. And they go better when a few others are involved. The risk is less for the individual when the responsibility is shared.

DR. STOCKMANN (*regaining his composure*). In short, gentlemen, what is it you want?

ASLAKSEN. Mr. Hovstad can best—

HOVSTAD. No, Aslaksen, you explain.

ASLAKSEN. Well, it's this—that now that we know how it all fits together, we thought we might venture to put the *People's Courier* at your disposal.

DR. STOCKMANN. Ah, so now you'll venture? But public opinion? Aren't you afraid there'll be a storm raised against us?

HOVSTAD. We're prepared to ride out the storm.

ASLAKSEN. And you should be prepared for a quick reversal in position, Doctor. As soon as your attack has served its purpose—

DR. STOCKMANN. You mean as soon as my father-in-law and I have cornered all the stock at a dirt-cheap price—?

HOVSTAD. I suppose it's mostly for scientific purposes that you want control of the baths.

DR. STOCKMANN. Naturally. It was for scientific purposes that I got the old Badger in with me on this. So we'll tinker a bit with the water pipes and dig around a little on the beach, and it won't cost the town half a crown. That ought to do it, don't you think? Hm?

HOVSTAD. I think so—as long as you've got the *Courier* with you.

ASLAKSEN. The press is a power in a free society, Doctor.

DR. STOCKMANN. How true. And so's public opinion. Mr. Aslaksen, I assume you'll take care of the Home Owners Council?

ASLAKSEN. The Home Owners Council and the Temperance Union both. You can count on that.

DR. STOCKMANN. But, gentlemen—it embarrasses me to mention it, but—*your* compensation—?

HOVSTAD. Preferably, of course, we'd like to help you for nothing, as you can imagine. But the *Courier*'s on shaky legs these days; it's not doing too well; and to shut the paper down now when there's so much to work for in the larger political scene strikes me as insupportable.

DR. STOCKMANN. Clearly. That would be a hard blow for a friend of the people like you. (*In an outburst.*) But *I'm* an enemy of the people! (*Lunges about the room.*) Where do I have my stick? Where in hell is that stick?

HOVSTAD. What's this?

ASLAKSEN. You're not going to—?

DR. STOCKMANN (*stops*). And what if I didn't give you one iota of my shares? We tycoons aren't so free with our money, don't forget.

HOVSTAD. And don't *you* forget that this matter of shares can be posed in two different lights.

DR. STOCKMANN. Yes, you're just the man for that. If I don't bail out the *Courier,* you'll put a vile construction on it all. You'll hound me down—set upon me—try to choke me off like a dog chokes a hare!

HOVSTAD. That's the law of nature. Every animal has to struggle for survival.

ASLAKSEN. We take our food where we can find it, you know.

DR. STOCKMANN. Then see if you can find yours in the gutter! (*Striding about the room.*) Because now we're going to learn, by God, who's the strongest animal among the three of us! (*Finds his umbrella and flourishes it.*) Hi, look out—!

HOVSTAD. Don't hit us!

ASLAKSEN. Watch out with that umbrella!

DR. STOCKMANN. Out of the window with you, Hovstad.

HOVSTAD (*by the hall door*). Have you lost your mind?

DR. STOCKMANN. Out of the window, Aslaksen! I said, jump! Don't be the last to go.

ASLAKSEN (*running around the desk*). Moderation, Doctor! I'm out of condition—I'm not up to this— (*Shrieks.*) Help! Help!

(MRS. STOCKMANN, PETRA, and HORSTER *enter from the living room.*)

MRS. STOCKMANN. My heavens, Thomas, what's going on in here?

DR. STOCKMANN (*swinging his umbrella*). Jump, I'm telling you! Into the gutter!

HOVSTAD. This is unprovoked assault! Captain Horster, I'm calling you for a witness. (*He scurries out down the hall.*)

ASLAKSEN (*confused*). If I just knew the layout here— (*Sneaks out through the living-room door.*)

MRS. STOCKMANN (*holding onto the* DOCTOR). Now you control yourself, Thomas!

DR. STOCKMANN (*flings the umbrella away*). Damn, they got out of it after all!

MRS. STOCKMANN. But what did they want you for?

DR. STOCKMANN. You can hear about it later. I have other things to think about now. (*Goes to the desk and writes on a visiting card.*) See, Katherine. What's written here?

MRS. STOCKMANN. "No," repeated three times. Why is that?

DR. STOCKMANN. You can hear about that later, too. (*Holding the card out.*) Here, Petra, tell Smudgy-face to run over to the Badger's with this, quick as she can. Hurry!

(PETRA *leaves with the card by the hall door.*)

Well, if I haven't had visits today from all the devil's envoys, I don't know what. But now I'll sharpen my pen into a stiletto and skewer them; I'll dip it in venom and gall; I'll sling my inkstand right at their skulls!

MRS. STOCKMANN. Yes, but we're leaving here, Thomas.

(PETRA *returns.*)

DR. STOCKMANN. Well?

PETRA. It's on its way.

DR. STOCKMANN. Good. Leaving, you say? The hell we are! We're staying here where we are, Katherine!

PETRA. We're staying?

MRS. STOCKMANN. In this town?

DR. STOCKMANN. Exactly. This is the battleground; here's where the fighting will be; and here's where I'm going to win! As soon as I've got my trousers patched, I'm setting out to look for a house. We'll need a roof over our heads by winter.

HORSTER. You can share mine.

DR. STOCKMANN. I can?

HORSTER. Yes, perfectly well. There's room enough, and I'm scarcely ever home.

MRS. STOCKMANN. Oh, how kind of you, Horster.

PETRA. Thank you!

DR. STOCKMANN (*shaking his hand*). Many, many thanks! So that worry is over. Now I can make a serious start right today. Oh, Katherine, it's endless, the number of things that need looking into here! And it's lucky I have so much time now to spend—yes, because, I meant to tell you, I got my notice from the baths—

MRS. STOCKMANN (*sighing*). Ah me, I've been expecting it.

DR. STOCKMANN. And then they want to take my practice away, too. Well, let them! I'll keep the poor people at least—the ones who can't pay at all; and, Lord knows, they're the ones that need me the most. But, by thunder, they'll have to hear me out. I'll preach to them in season and out of season, as someone once said.

MRS. STOCKMANN. But, dear, I think you've seen how much good preaching does.

DR. STOCKMANN. You really are preposterous, Katherine. Should I let myself be whipped from the field by public opinion and the solid majority and other such barbarities? No, thank you! Besides, what I want is so simple and clear and basic. I just want to hammer into the heads of these mongrels that the so-called liberals are the most insidious enemies of free men—that party programs have a way of smothering every new, germinal truth—that acting out of expediency turns morality and justice into a hollow mockery, until it finally becomes monstrous to go on living. Captain Horster, don't you think I could get people to recognize that?

HORSTER. Most likely. I don't understand much about such things.

DR. STOCKMANN. Don't you see—let me explain! The party leaders have to be eradicated—because a party leader's just like a wolf, an insatiable wolf that needs so and so many smaller animals to feed off per annum, if he's going to survive. Look at Hovstad and Aslaksen! How many lesser creatures haven't they swallowed up—or they maul and mutilate them till they can't be more than home owners and subscribers to the *Courier!* (*Sitting on the edge of the desk.*) Ah, come here, Katherine—look at that sunlight, how glorious, the way it streams in today. And how wonderful and fresh the spring air is.

MRS. STOCKMANN. Yes, if we only could live on sunlight and spring air, Thomas.

DR. STOCKMANN. Well, you'll have to skimp and save a

bit here and there—it'll turn out. That's my least concern. No, what's worse is that I don't know any man who's free-spirited enough to carry my work on after me.

PETRA. Oh, don't think of that, Father; you've lots of time. Why, look—the boys, already.

(EILIF and MORTEN *come in from the living room.*)

MRS. STOCKMANN. Did you get let out early?

MORTEN. No. We had a fight with some others at recess—

EILIF. That isn't true; it was the others that fought us.

MORTEN. Yes, and so Mr. Rørland said we'd better stay home for a few days.

DR. STOCKMANN (*snapping his fingers and jumping down off the desk*). I've got it! So help me, I've got it! You'll never set foot in school again.

THE BOYS. No more school?

MRS. STOCKMANN. But, Thomas—

DR. STOCKMANN. I said, never! I'll teach you myself—by that, I mean, you won't learn a blessed fact—

THE BOYS. Hurray!

DR. STOCKMANN. But I'll make you into free-spirited and accomplished men. Listen, you have to help me, Petra.

PETRA. Yes, of course I will.

DR. STOCKMANN. And the school—that'll be held in the room where they assailed me as an enemy of the people. But we have to be more. I need at least twelve boys to begin with.

MRS. STOCKMANN. You'll never get them from this town.

DR. STOCKMANN. Let's see about that. (*To the* BOYS.) Don't you know any boys off the street—regular little punks—

MORTEN. Sure, I know lots of them!

DR. STOCKMANN. So, that's fine. Bring around a few samples. I want to experiment with mongrels for a change. There might be some fantastic minds out there.

MORTEN. But what'll we do when we've become free-spirited and accomplished men?

DR. STOCKMANN. You'll drive all the wolves into the Far West, boys!

(EILIF *looks somewhat dubious;* MORTEN *jumps about and cheers.*)

MRS. STOCKMANN. Ah, just so those wolves aren't hunting you anymore, Thomas.

DR. STOCKMANN. Are you utterly mad, Katherine! Hunt *me* down! Now, when I'm the strongest man in town!

MRS. STOCKMANN. The strongest—now?

DR. STOCKMANN. Yes, I might go further and say that now I'm one of the strongest men in the whole world.

MORTEN. You mean it?

DR. STOCKMANN (*lowering his voice*). Shh, don't talk about it yet—but I've made a great discovery.

MRS. STOCKMANN. What, again?

DR. STOCKMANN. Yes, why not! (*Gathers them around him and speaks confidentially.*) And the essence of it, you see, is that the strongest man in the world is the one who stands most alone.

MRS. STOCKMANN (*smiling and shaking her head*). Oh, Thomas, Thomas—!

PETRA (*buoyantly, gripping his hands*). Father!

THE WILD DUCK

The dramatist's language of space and time, his artful selection and modulation of setting, can hardly be overestimated in its distinctive contribution to the world of an Ibsen play. Through a shift of scene, a change of light, a momentary accent on an object or an item of furniture conferred by a gesture or a passing remark, the inanimate speaks, becomes histrionic, enters into a running commentary on the dialogue and the gathering meaning of the action.

In *The Wild Duck* (1884), for example, the two settings are curiously congruent. In Act One, set in a wealthy industrialist's town house, Haakon Werle's dimly lit study-office dominates the foreground, while to the rear one sees a brilliantly illuminated salon. The remaining four acts take place in the financially straitened Ekdal residence, a large studio loft, naturally rather than artificially lit by a skylight, with photographic equipment conspicuously in view; and, presently disclosed, a spacious garret room mysteriously stocked with various small animals, withered Christmas trees, cupboards of old books, and its most prized inhabitant, a crippled but thriving wild duck.

In both instances the bisected set segregates what has been well termed "a foreground, fallen reality of prosaic work and a compensatory background." The boldly committed effort of mind and will that gave the personality of a Thomas Stockmann its integrity, its courage to be, is absent here, along with, as well, the flatter tone of a civics lesson in the preceding play. Instead, we have modern man, on average, as intrinsically self-divided, split between the unremitting pressures of a utilitarian existence and that more remote, rich and strange plenitude of life sensed to be beyond the daily struggle for survival or, in Werle's case, for further aggrandizement. Neither inner regeneration within the system, such as Bernick experiences, nor reform incited from without, as Dr. Stockmann prescribes, can remedy this condition, though Ibsen represents both of these as imperative waystages in clearing away society's lies and delusions. Rather, the dissociated individual is a function of the present historical and evolutionary development of civilization, either a demoralizing impasse to be passively suffered, as in this drama, or a challenge to be actively combatted, as Stockmann would doubtless conceive it.

From the significant spatial division in the two settings, and its extension, like a fault line, through a number of the character's lives, an appropriate abundance of thematic antitheses radiate out, any one of which suggests a basis for interpreting the play: such oppositions as truth versus the vital lie, physical versus spiritual blindness, the literalism of the camera versus the mystery of the wild duck, complete candor versus discreet forgetfulness as competing policies for marriage. Or, again, the polarity of the child and the adult, which puts yet another construction on the dual, complementary settings.

For the Ekdal household is a kind of private playground for displaced children, supervised by Gina and Relling. An atmosphere of otherworldly wonder suffuses it, proceeding from the toy forest and miniature menagerie of Old Ekdal's second childhood, and from Hedwig's adolescent, yet poetically profound daydream of her surroundings as the depths of the sea. Conversely, the Werle establishment, into which the Ekdals venture only to suffer humiliation and defeat, stands as the citadel of the adult world, guarded by its sharp practices and tactical appraisals of useful and nonuseful people. "In becoming civilized," Ibsen wrote in his working notes for *The Wild Duck*, "man undergoes the same change as when a child grows up. Instinct weakens, but the powers of logical thought are developed. Adults have lost the ability to play with dolls." The Ekdal garret is the refuge of instinct, the primordial yearning for the wild duck's domain of the marshes, the woods, the sky and the sea, while Werle's study is an armory of hard business logic—just as "becoming civilized" in this context means a restrictive business civilization whose compensations consist of banquets, Tokay, photograph albums and an unwelcome piano recital. At the time of *A Doll House* Ibsen had his heroine firmly set aside childish things. Now he finds it a more inclusive truth, in a play pierced by memories of his own childhood, to acknowledge "the mind of the child in the spirit of the adult."

The resulting fusion of a seasoned realism with a child-like receptivity to the insights of fairy tale and myth is the very heart of Ibsen's later style. And what becomes method for the dramatist forms a common bond among his protagonists, as Hugo von Hofmannsthal perceived: "Before these people begin to suffer in [the adult world] they have nearly all experienced a confused, almost dreamlike childhood in a kind of enchanted forest from which they emerge insatiably homesick and peculiarly insulated, like Parzival riding out into the world dressed as a fool and with the experience of a small child . . . For children's eyes give things a form which we strive in vain to recapture. Commonplace events become fabulous or heroic, in the same way that dread, fever or genius transform them." The tragedy of this tragicomedy is that, even in Gregers, there is a confused, hurt, vengeful child, transforming those "great, miraculous beings" he sees around him into weapons against his father, blindly, in a fever—a deadly "moralistic fever," by Relling's diagnosis. Its triumph is that the author transforms them all—adults, children, persecutors, victims—into a world whose events are simultaneously commonplace, fabulous and, once experienced, not to be forgotten.

THE CHARACTERS

HAAKON WERLE, wholesale merchant and millowner
GREGERS WERLE, his son
OLD EKDAL
HJALMAR EKDAL, his son, a photographer
GINA EKDAL, Hjalmar's wife
HEDVIG, their daughter, aged fourteen
MRS. SØRBY, housekeeper for the elder Werle
RELLING, a doctor
MOLVIK, a former divinity student
GRAABERG, a bookkeeper
PETTERSEN, manservant to the elder Werle
JENSEN, a hired waiter
A FAT MAN
A BALD-HEADED MAN
A NEARSIGHTED MAN
SIX OTHER MEN, dinner guests at Werle's
OTHER HIRED SERVANTS

The first act takes place in WERLE's *house; the following four acts in* HJALMAR EKDAL's *studio.*

ACT ONE

At WERLE'S *house. A richly and comfortably furnished study, with bookcases and upholstered furniture, a writing table, with papers and reports, in the middle of the floor, and green-shaded lamps softly illuminating the room. In the rear wall, open folding doors with curtains drawn back disclose a large, fashionable room, brightly lit by lamps and candelabra. In the right foreground of the study, a small private door leads to the offices. In the left foreground, a fireplace filled with glowing coals, and further back a double door to the dining room.*

WERLE'S *manservant,* PETTERSEN, *in livery, and* JENSEN, *a hired waiter, in black, are straightening up the study. In the larger room two or three other hired waiters are moving about, putting things in order and lighting more candles. In from the dining room come laughter and the hum of many voices in conversation; a knife clinks upon a glass; silence; a toast is made; cries of "Bravo," and the hum of conversation resumes.*

PETTERSEN (*lighting a lamp by the fireplace and putting on the shade*). Ah, you hear that, Jensen. Now the old boy's up on his feet, proposing a long toast to Mrs. Sørby.

JENSEN (*moving an armchair forward*). Is it really true what people say, that there's something between them?

PETTERSEN. Lord knows.

JENSEN. I've heard he was a real goat in his day.

PETTERSEN. Could be.

JENSEN. But they say it's his son he's throwing this party for.

PETTERSEN. Yes. His son came home yesterday.

JENSEN. I never knew before that old Werle had any son.

PETTERSEN. Oh yes, he's got a son. But he spends all his time up at the works in Hoidal. He hasn't been in town all the years I've served in this house.

A HIRED WAITER (*in the door to the other room*). Say, Pettersen, there's an old guy here who—

PETTERSEN (*muttering*). What the hell—somebody coming now!

> (*Old* EKDAL *appears from the right through the inner room. He is dressed in a shabby overcoat with a high collar, woolen gloves, and in his hand, a cane and a fur cap; under his arm is a bundle wrapped in brown paper. He has a dirty, reddish-brown wig and a little gray moustache.*)

PETTERSEN (*going toward him*). Good Lord, what do *you* want in here?

EKDAL (*at the door*). Just have to get into the office, Pettersen.

PETTERSEN. The office closed an hour ago, and—

EKDAL. Heard that one at the door, boy. But Graaberg's still in there. Be nice, Pettersen, and let me slip in that way. (*Pointing toward the private entrance.*) I've gone that way before.

PETTERSEN. All right, go ahead, then. (*Opens the door.*) But don't forget now—take the other way out; we have guests.

EKDAL. Got you—hmm! Thanks, Pettersen, good old pal! Thanks. (*To himself.*) Bonehead! (*He goes into the office;* PETTERSEN *shuts the door after him.*)

JENSEN. Is *he* on the office staff too?

PETTERSEN. No, he's just someone who does copying on the outside when it's needed. Still, in his time he was well up in the world, old Ekdal.

JENSEN. Yes, he looks like he's been a little of everything.

PETTERSEN. Oh yes. He was a lieutenant once, if you can imagine.

JENSEN. Good Lord—him a lieutenant!

PETTERSEN. So help me, he was. But then he went into the lumber business or something. They say he must have pulled some kind of dirty deal on the old man once, for the two of them were running the Hoidal works together then. Oh, I know good old Ekdal, all right. We've drunk

many a schnapps and bottle of beer together over at
Eriksen's.

JENSEN. He can't have much money for standing
drinks.

PETTERSEN. My Lord, Jensen, you can bet it's me that
stands the drinks. I always say a person ought to act refined toward quality that's come down in life.

JENSEN. Did he go bankrupt, then?

PETTERSEN. No, worse than that. He was sent to jail.

JENSEN. To jail!

PETTERSEN. Or maybe it was the penitentiary. (*Laughter
from the dining room.*) Hist! They're leaving the table.

> (*The dining room door is opened by a pair of
> servants inside.* MRS. SØRBY, *in conversation
> with two gentlemen, comes out. A moment later
> the rest of the guests follow, among them
> WERLE. Last of all come HJALMER EKDAL and
> GREGERS WERLE.*)

MRS. SØRBY (*to the servant, in passing*). Pettersen, will
you have coffee served in the music room.

PETTERSEN. Yes, Mrs. Sørby.

> (*She and the two gentlemen go into the inner
> room and exit to the right.* PETTERSEN *and* JEN-
> SEN *leave in the same way.*)

A FAT GUEST (*to a balding man*). Phew! That dinner—
that was a steep bit of work!

THE BALD-HEADED GUEST. Oh, with a little good will a
man can do wonders in three hours.

THE FAT GUEST. Yes, but afterward, my dear fellow,
afterward.

A THIRD GUEST. I hear we can sample coffee and liqueur
in the music room.

THE FAT GUEST. Fine! Then perhaps Mrs. Sørby will
play us a piece.

THE BALD-HEADED GUEST (*in an undertone*). Just so Mrs.
Sørby doesn't play us to pieces.

THE FAT GUEST. Oh, now really, Berta wouldn't punish
her old friends, would she? (*They laugh and enter the inner
room.*)

WERLE (*in a low, depressed tone*). I don't think anyone noticed it, Gregers.

GREGERS. What?

WERLE. Didn't you notice it either?

GREGERS. What should I have noticed?

WERLE. We were thirteen at the table.

GREGERS. Really? Were we thirteen?

WERLE (*with a glance at* HJALMAR EKDAL). Yes—our usual number is twelve. (*To the others*). Be so kind, gentlemen.

(*He and those remaining, except* HJALMAR *and* GREGERS, *go out to the rear and right.*)

HJALMAR (*who has heard the conversation*). You shouldn't have sent me the invitation, Gregers.

GREGERS. What! The party's supposed to be for *me*. And then I'm not supposed to have my best and only friend—

HJALMAR. But I don't think your father likes it. Ordinarily I never come to this house.

GREGERS. So I hear. But I had to see you and talk with you, for I'm sure to be leaving soon again. Yes, we two old classmates, we've certainly drifted a long way apart. You know, we haven't seen each other now in sixteen—seventeen years.

HJALMAR. Has it been so long?

GREGERS. Yes, all of that. Well, how have you been? You look well. You're almost becoming stout.

HJALMAR. Hm, stout is hardly the word, though I probably look more of a man than I did then.

GREGERS. Yes, you do. The outer man hasn't suffered.

HJALMAR (*in a gloomier tone*). Ah, but the inner man! Believe me, he has a different look. You know, of course how everything went to pieces for me and my family since you and I last saw each other.

GREGERS (*dropping his voice*). How's it going for your father now?

HJALMAR. Oh, Gregers, let's not talk about that. My poor, unhappy father naturally lives at home with me. He's got no one else in the whole world to turn to. But this all is so terribly hard for me to talk about, you know. Tell me, instead, how you've found life up at the mine.

GREGERS. Marvelously solitary, that's what—with a good chance to mull over a great many things. Come on, let's be comfortable.

(*He sits in an armchair by the fire and urges* HJALMAR *down into another by its side.*)

HJALMAR. (*emotionally*). In any case, I'm grateful that you asked me here, Gregers, because it proves you no longer have anything against me.

GREGERS (*astonished*). How could you think that I had anything against you?

HJALMAR. In those first years you did.

GREGERS. Which first years?

HJALMAR. Right after that awful misfortune. And it was only natural you should. It was just by a hair that your own father escaped being dragged into this—oh, this loathsome business.

GREGERS. And that's why I had it in for you? Whoever gave you that idea?

HJALMAR. I know you did, Gregers; it was your father himself who told me.

GREGERS (*startled*). Father! I see. Hm—is that why I never heard from you—not a single word?

HJALMAR. Yes.

GREGERS. Not even when you went out and became a photographer.

HJALMAR. Your father said it wasn't worth writing you—about anything.

GREGERS (*looking fixedly ahead*). No, no, maybe he was right there— But tell me, Hjalmar—do you find yourself reasonably content with things as they are?

HJALMAR (*with a small sigh*). Oh, I suppose I do. What else can I say? At first, you can imagine, it was all rather strange for me. They were such completely different expectations that I came into. But then everything was so different. That immense, shattering misfortune for Father —the shame and the scandal, Gregers—

GREGERS (*shaken*). Yes, yes. Of course.

HJALMAR. I couldn't dream of going on with my studies; there wasn't a penny to spare. On the contrary, debts instead—mainly to your father, I think—

GREGERS. Hm—

HJALMAR. Anyway, I thought it was best to make a clean break—and cut all the old connections. It was your father especially who advised me to; and since he'd already been so helpful to me—

GREGERS. He had?

HJALMAR. Yes, you knew that, didn't you? Where could *I* get the money to learn photography and fit out a studio and establish myself? I can tell you, that all adds up.

GREGERS. And all that Father paid for?

HJALMAR. Yes, Gregers, didn't you know? I understood him to say that he'd written you about it.

GREGERS. Not a word saying *he* was the one. Maybe he forgot. We've never exchanged anything but business letters. So that was Father, too—!

HJALMAR. That's right. He never wanted people to know, but he was the one. And he was also the one who put me in a position to get married. Or perhaps—didn't you know that either?

GREGERS. No, not at all. (*Takes him by the arm.*) But Hjalmar, I can't tell you how all this delights me—and disturbs me. Perhaps I've been unfair to my father—in certain ways. Yes, for all this does show good-heartedness, doesn't it? It's almost a kind of conscience—

HJALMAR. Conscience?

GREGERS. Yes, or whatever you want to call it. No, I can't tell you how glad I am to hear this about my father. So you're married, then, Hjalmar. That's further than I'll ever go. Well, I hope you're happy as a married man?

HJALMAR. Oh, absolutely. She's as capable and fine a wife as any man could wish for. And she's not entirely without culture, either.

GREGERS (*a bit surprised*). No, I'm sure she's not.

HJALMAR. No. Life is a teacher, you see. Associating with me every day—and then there are one or two gifted people who visit us regularly. I can tell you, you wouldn't recognize Gina now.

GREGERS. Gina?

HJALMAR. Yes, Gregers, had you forgotten her name is Gina?

GREGERS. Whose name is Gina? I haven't the faintest idea—

HJALMAR. But don't you remember, she was here in this very house a while—in service?

GREGERS (*looking at him*). You mean Gina Hansen—?

HJALMAR. Yes, of course. Gina Hansen.

GREGERS. Who was housekeeper for us that last year of Mother's illness?

HJALMAR. Exactly. But my dear Gregers, I know for sure that your father wrote you about my marriage.

GREGERS (*who has gotten up*). Yes, of course he did. But not that— (*Walks about the floor.*) Yes, wait a minute— it may well be, now that I think of it. My father's letters are always so brief. (*Sits on chair arm.*) Listen, tell me, Hjalmar—this is interesting—how did you come to know Gina?—your wife, I mean.

HJALMAR. Oh, it was all very simple. Gina didn't stay long here in the house; there was so much confusion— your mother's sickness and all. Gina couldn't stand it, so she just up and left. That was the year before your mother died—or maybe it was the same year.

GREGERS. It was the same year. And I was up at the works at the time. But what then?

HJALMAR. Well, then Gina lived at home with her mother, a Mrs. Hansen, a very capable, hardworking woman who ran a little restaurant. She also had a room for rent, a very pleasant, comfortable room.

GREGERS. And you were lucky enough to find it?

HJALMAR. Yes. Actually it was your father who suggested it to me. And it was there, you see—there that I really got to know Gina.

GREGERS. And then your engagement followed?

HJALMAR. Yes. Young people fall in love so easily— hm—

GREGERS (*getting up and pacing about a little*). Tell me —when you became engaged—was it *then* that my father got you to—I mean, was it then that you started in learning photography?

HJALMAR. That's right. I wanted to get on and set up a home as soon as possible, and both your father and I decided that this photography idea was the most feasible one. And Gina thought so too. Yes, and you see, there was another inducement, a lucky break, in that Gina had already taken up retouching.

GREGERS. That worked out wonderfully all around.

HJALMAR (*pleased, getting up*). Yes, isn't that so? Don't you think it's worked out wonderfully all around?

GREGERS. Yes, I must say. My father has almost been a kind of providence to you.

HJALMAR (*with feeling*). He didn't abandon his old friend's son in a time of need. You see, he does have a heart.

MRS. SØRBY (*entering with* WERLE *on her arm*). No more nonsense, my dear Mr. Werle. You mustn't stay in there any longer, staring at all those lights; it's doing you no good.

WERLE (*freeing his arm from hers and passing his hand over his eyes*). Yes, I guess you're right about that.

(PETTERSEN *and* JENSEN *enter with trays.*)

MRS. SØRBY (*to the guests in the other room*). Gentlemen, please—if anyone wants a glass of punch, he must take the trouble to come in here.

THE FAT GUEST (*comes over to* MRS. SØRBY). But really, is it true you've abolished our precious smoking privilege?

MRS. SØRBY. Yes. Here in Mr. Werle's sanctum, it's forbidden.

THE BALD-HEADED GUEST. When did you pass these drastic amendments to the cigar laws, Mrs. Sørby?

MRS. SØRBY. After the last dinner—when there were certain persons here who let themselves exceed all limits.

THE BALD-HEADED GUEST. And my dear Berta, one isn't permitted to exceed the limits, even a little bit?

MRS. SØRBY. Not in any instance, Mr. Balle.

(*Most of the guests have gathered in the study;
the waiters are proffering glasses of punch.*)

WERLE (*to* HJALMAR, *over by a table*). What is it you're poring over, Ekdal?

HJALMAR. It's only an album, Mr. Werle.

THE BALD-HEADED GUEST (*who is wandering about*). Ah, photographs! Yes, of course, that's just the thing for you.

THE FAT GUEST (*seated in an armchair*). Haven't you brought along some of your own?

HJALMAR. No, I haven't.

THE FAT GUEST. You really should have. It's so good for the digestion to sit and look at pictures.

THE BALD-HEADED GUEST. And then it always adds a morsel to the entertainment, you know.

A NEARSIGHTED GUEST. And all contributions are gratefully received.

MRS. SØRBY. These gentlemen mean that if one's invited for dinner, one must also work for the food, Mr. Ekdal.

THE FAT GUEST. Where the larder's superior, *that* is pure joy.

THE BALD-HEADED GUEST. My Lord, it's all in the struggle for existence—

MRS. SØRBY. How right you are! (*They continue laughing and joking.*)

GREGERS (*quietly*). You should talk with them, Hjalmar.

HJALMAR (*with a shrug*). What could I talk about?

THE FAT GUEST. Don't you think, Mr. Werle, that Tokay compares favorably as a healthful drink for the stomach?

WERLE (*by the fireplace*). The Tokay you had today I can vouch for in any case; it's one of the very, very finest years. But you recognized that well enough.

THE FAT GUEST. Yes, it had a remarkably delicate flavor.

HJALMAR (*tentatively*). Is there some difference between the years?

THE FAT GUEST (*laughing*). Oh, that's rich!

WERLE (*smiling*). It certainly doesn't pay to offer you a noble wine.

THE BALD-HEADED GUEST. Tokay wines are like photographs, Mr. Ekdal—sunshine is of the essence. Isn't that true?

HJALMAR. Oh yes, light is very important.

MRS. SØRBY. Exactly the same as with court officials—who push for their place in the sun too, I hear.

THE BALD-HEADED GUEST. Ouch! That was a tired quip.

THE NEARSIGHTED GUEST. The lady's performing—

THE FAT GUEST. And at our expense. (*Frowning.*) Mrs. Sørby, Mrs. Sørby!

MRS. SØRBY. Yes, but it certainly is true now that the years can vary enormously. The old vintages are the finest.

THE NEARSIGHTED GUEST. Do you count me among the old ones?

MRS. SØRBY. Oh, far from it.

THE BALD-HEADED GUEST. Ha, you see! But what about *me,* Mrs. Sørby—?

THE FAT GUEST. Yes, and me! What years would you put us among?

MRS. SØRBY. I would put you all among the sweet years, gentlemen. (*She sips a glass of punch; the guests laugh and banter with her.*)

WERLE. Mrs. Sørby always finds a way out—when she wants to. Pass your glasses, gentlemen. Pettersen, take care of them. Gregers, I think we'll have a glass together. (GREGERS *does not stir.*) Won't you join us, Ekdal? I had no chance to remember you at the table.

(GRAABERG, *the bookkeeper, peers out from the door to the offices.*)

GRAABERG. Beg pardon, Mr. Werle, but I can't get out.

WERLE. What, are you locked in again?

GRAABERG. Yes, and Flakstad's left with the keys—

WERLE. Well, then, go through here.

GRAABERG. But there's someone else—

WERLE. All right, all right, both of you. Don't be shy.

(GRAABERG *and old* EKDAL *come out from the office.*)

WERLE (*involuntarily*). Oh no!

(*The laughter and small talk die among the guests.* HJALMAR *starts at the sight of his father, sets down his glass, and turns away toward the fireplace.*)

EKDAL (*without looking up, but bowing slightly to each side and mumbling*). Beg your pardon. It's the wrong way. Door locked—door locked. Beg pardon. (*He and* GRAABERG *exit in back to the right.*)

WERLE (*between his teeth*). That damned Graaberg!

GREGERS (*with open mouth, staring at* HJALMAR). But it couldn't have been—!

THE FAT GUEST. What's going on? Who was that?

GREGERS. Oh, no one. Only the bookkeeper and somebody else.

THE NEAR SIGHTED GUEST (*to* HJALMAR). Did *you* know him?

HJALMAR. I don't know—I didn't notice—

THE FAT GUEST (*getting up*). What in thunder's wrong? (*He goes over to some others, who are talking.*)

MRS. SØRBY (*whispering to the waiter*). Slip something to him outside, something really fine.

PETTERSEN (*nodding*). I'll see to it. (*He goes out.*)

GREGERS (*in a shocked undertone*). Then it really was him!

HJALMAR. Yes.

GREGERS. And yet you stood here and denied you knew him!

HJALMAR (*whispering fiercely*). But how could I—!

GREGERS. Be recognized by your father?

HJALMAR (*painfully*). Oh, if you were in my place, then—

(*The hushed conversations among the guests now mount into a forced joviality.*)

THE BALD-HEADED GUEST (*approaching* HJALMAR *and* GREGERS *amiably*). Ah ha! You over here, polishing up old memories from your student years? Well? Won't you smoke, Mr. Ekdal? Have a light? Oh, that's right, we're not supposed to—

HJALMAR. Thanks, I couldn't—

THE FAT GUEST. Haven't you got a neat little poem to recite for us, Mr. Ekdal? In times past you did that so nicely.

HJALMAR. I'm afraid I can't remember any.

THE FAT GUEST. Oh, that's a shame. Well, Balle, what can we find to do? (*The two men cross the floor into the other room and go out.*)

HJALMAR (*somberly*). Gregers—I'm going! When a man's had a hammer blow from fate on his head—you understand. Say good night to your father for me.

GREGERS. Yes, of course. Are you going straight home?

HJALMAR. Yes, why?

GREGERS. Well, I may pay you a visit later.

HJALMAR. No, you mustn't. Not to my home. My house is a sad one, Gregers—especially after a brilliant occasion like this. We can always meet somewhere in town.

MRS. SØRBY (*who has approached; in a low voice*). Are you going, Ekdal?

HJALMAR. Yes.

MRS. SØRBY. Greet Gina.

HJALMAR. Thank you.

MRS. SØRBY. And tell her I'll stop by to see her one day soon.

HJALMAR. Yes, Thanks. (*To* GREGERS.) Stay here. I'd

rather disappear without any fuss. (*He strolls around the floor, then into the other room and out to the right.*)

MRS. SØRBY (*quietly to the waiter, who has returned*). Well, did the old man get something to take home?

PETTERSEN. Sure. I slipped him a bottle of cognac.

MRS. SØRBY. Oh, you could have found something better.

PETTERSEN. Not at all, Mrs. Sørby. He knows nothing better than cognac.

THE FAT GUEST (*in the doorway, holding a score of music*). How about the two of us playing something, Mrs. Sørby?

MRS. SØRBY. All right. Let's.

> (*The guests shout approval.* MRS. SØRBY *and the others exit right, through the inner room.* GREGERS *remains standing by the fireplace.* WERLE *looks for something on the writing table, seeming to wish that* GREGERS *would leave; when he fails to stir,* WERLE *crosses toward the door.*)

GREGERS. Father, won't you wait a moment?

WERLE (*pausing*). What is it?

GREGERS. I must have a word with you.

WERLE. Can't it wait till we're alone?

GREGERS. No, it can't, because it just might occur that we never are alone.

WERLE (*coming closer*). What does *that* mean?

> (*Distant piano music is heard from the music room during the following conversation.*)

GREGERS. How could anyone here let that family decay so pitifully?

WERLE. You're referring to the Ekdals, no doubt.

GREGERS. Yes, I mean the Ekdals. Lieutenant Ekdal was once so close to you.

WERLE. Yes, worse luck, he was all too close; and for that I've paid a price these many years. He's the one I can thank for putting something of a blot on my good name and reputation.

GREGERS (*quietly*). Was *he* really the only guilty one?

WERLE. Who else do you mean!

GREGERS.   You and he were both in on buying that big stand of timber—

WERLE.   But it was Ekdal, wasn't it, who made the survey of the sections—that incompetent survey? He was the one who carried out all the illegal logging on state property. In fact, he was in charge of the whole operation up there. I had no idea of what Lieutenant Ekdal was getting into.

GREGERS.   Lieutenant Ekdal himself had no idea of what he was getting into.

WERLE.   Very likely. But the fact remains that he was convicted and I was acquitted.

GREGERS.   Yes, I'm aware that no proof was found.

WERLE.   Acquittal is acquittal. Why do you rake up this ugly old story that's given me gray hair before my time? Is this what you've been brooding about all those years up there? I can assure you, Gregers—here in town the whole business has been forgotten long ago—as far as I'm concerned.

GREGERS.   But that miserable Ekdal family!

WERLE.   Seriously, what would you have me do for these people? When Ekdal was let out, he was a broken man, beyond any help. There are people in this world who plunge to the bottom when they've hardly been winged, and they never come up again. Take my word for it, Gregers; I've done everything I could, short of absolutely compromising myself and arousing all kinds of suspicion and gossip—

GREGERS.   Suspicion—? So that's it.

WERLE.   I've gotten Ekdal copying jobs from the office, and I pay him much, much more than his work is worth—

GREGERS (*without looking at him*).   Hm. No doubt.

WERLE.   You're laughing? Maybe you think what I'm saying isn't true? There's certainly nothing to show in my books; I don't record such payments.

GREGERS (*with a cold smile*).   No. I'm sure that certain payments are best left unrecorded.

WERLE (*surprised*).   What do you mean by *that*?

GREGERS (*plucking up his courage*).   Did you record what it cost you to have Hjalmar Ekdal study photography?

WERLE.   I? Why should I?

GREGERS.   I know now it was you who paid for that. And now I know, too, that it was you who set him up so comfortably in business.

WERLE. Well, and I suppose this still means that I've done nothing for the Ekdals! I can assure you, those people have already cost me enough expense.

GREGERS. Have you recorded any of the expenses?

WERLE. Why do you ask that?

GREGERS. Oh, there are reasons. Listen, tell me—the time when you developed such warmth for your old friend's son —wasn't that just when he was planning to marry?

WERLE. How the devil—how, after so many years, do you expect me—?

GREGERS. You wrote me a letter then—a business letter, naturally; and in a postscript it said, brief as could be, that Hjalmar Ekdal had gotten married to a Miss Hansen.

WERLE. Yes, that's right; that was her name.

GREGERS. But you never said that this Miss Hansen was Gina Hansen—our former housekeeper.

WERLE (*with a derisive, yet uneasy laugh*). No, it just never occurred to me that you'd be so very interested in our former housekeeper.

GREGERS. I wasn't. But—(*Dropping his voice.*) there were others in the house who were quite interested in her.

WERLE. What do you mean by that? (*Storming at him.*) You're not referring to me!

GREGERS (*quietly but firmly*). Yes, I'm referring to you.

WERLE. And you dare—! You have the insolence—! How could he, that ungrateful dog, that—photographer; how could he have the gall to make such insinuations?

GREGERS. Hjalmar hasn't breathed a word of it. I don't think he has the shadow of a doubt about all this.

WERLE. Then where did you get it from? Who could have said such a thing?

GREGERS. My poor, unhappy mother said it—the last time I saw her.

WERLE. Your mother! Yes, I might have guessed. She and you—you always stuck together. It was she who, right from the start, turned your mind against me.

GREGERS. No. It was everything she had to suffer and endure until she broke down and died so miserably.

WERLE. Oh, she had nothing to suffer and endure—no more, at least, than so many others. But you can't get anywhere with sick, high-strung people. I've certainly learned that. Now you're going around suspecting that sort of thing, digging up all manner of old rumors and slanders against your own father. Now listen, Gregers, I really think that at your age you could occupy yourself more usefully.

GREGERS. Yes, all in due time.

WERLE. Then your mind might be clearer than it seems to be now. What can it lead to, you up there at the works, slaving away year in and year out like a common clerk, never taking a penny over your month's salary. It's pure stupidity.

GREGERS. Yes, if only I were so sure of that.

WERLE. I understand you well enough. You want to be independent, without obligation to me. But here's the very opportunity for you to become independent, your own man in every way.

GREGERS. So? And by what means—?

WERLE. When I wrote you that it was essential you come to town now, immediately—hmm—

GREGERS. Yes. What is it you really want of me? I've been waiting all day to find out.

WERLE. I'm suggesting that you come into the firm as a partner.

GREGERS. I! In your firm? As a partner?

WERLE. Yes. It wouldn't mean we'd need to be together much. You could take over the offices here in town, and then I'd move up to the mill.

GREGERS. You *would*?

WERLE. Yes. You see, I can't take on work now the way I once could. I have to spare my eyes, Gregers; they're beginning to fail.

GREGERS. They've always been weak.

WERLE. Not like this. Besides—circumstances may make it desirable for me to live up there—at least for a while.

GREGERS. I never dreamed of anything like this.

WERLE. Listen, Gregers, there are so very many things that keep us apart, and yet, you know—we're father and son still. I think we should be able to reach some kind of understanding.

GREGERS. Just on the surface, is that what you mean?

WERLE. Well, at least that would be something. Think it over, Gregers. Don't you think it ought to be possible? Eh?

GREGERS (*looking at him coldly*). There's something behind all this.

WERLE. How so?

GREGERS. It might be that somehow you're using me.

WERLE. In a relationship as close as ours, one can always be of use to the other.

GREGERS. Yes, so they say.

WERLE. I'd like to have you home with me now for a while. I'm a lonely man, Gregers; I've always felt lonely—all my life through, but particularly now when the years are beginning to press me. I need to have someone around—

GREGERS. You have Mrs. Sørby.

WERLE. Yes, I do—and she's become, you might say, almost indispensable. She's witty, even-tempered; she livens up the house—and that's what I need so badly.

GREGERS. Well, then, you've got everything the way you want it.

WERLE. Yes, but I'm afraid it can't go on. The world is quick to make inferences about a woman in her position. Yes, I was going to say, a man doesn't gain by it either.

GREGERS. Oh, when a man gives dinner parties like yours, he can certainly take a few risks.

WERLE. Yes, Gregers, but what about her? I'm afraid she won't put up with it much longer. And even if she did—even if, out of her feeling for me, she ignored the gossip and the backbiting and so on—do you still think, Gregers, you with your sharp sense of justice—

GREGERS (*cutting him off*). Tell me short and sweet just one thing. Are you planning to marry her?

WERLE. And if I *were* planning such a thing—what then?

GREGERS. Yes, that's what I'm asking. What then?

WERLE. Would you be so irreconcilably set against it?

GREGERS. No, not at all. Not in any way.

WERLE. Well, I really didn't know whether, perhaps out of regard for your dead mother's memory—

GREGERS. I am not high-strung.

WERLE. Well, you may or may not be, but in any case you've taken a great load off my mind. I'm really very happy that I can count on your support in this.

GREGERS (*staring intently at him*). Now I see how you want to use me.

WERLE. Use you! That's no way to talk!

GREGERS. Oh, let's not be squeamish in our choice of words. At least, not when it's man to man. (*He laughs*

brusquely.) So that's it! That's why I—damn it all!—had
to make my personal appearance in town. On account of
Mrs. Sørby, family life is in order in this house. Tableau of
father with son! That's something new, all right!

WERLE. How dare you speak in that tone!

GREGERS. When has there ever been family life here?
Never, as long as I can remember. But *now*, of course,
there's need for a little of that. For who could deny what a
fine impression it would make to hear that the son—on the
wings of piety—came flying home to the aging father's
wedding feast. What's left then of all the stories about what
the poor dead woman suffered and endured? Not a scrap.
Her own son ground them to dust.

WERLE. Gregers—I don't think there's a man in this
world you hate as much as me.

GREGERS. I've seen you at too close quarters.

WERLE. You've seen me with your mother's eyes. (*Dropping his voice.*) But you should remember that those eyes
were—clouded at times.

GREGERS (*faltering*). I know what you mean. But who
bears the guilt for Mother's fatal weakness? You, and all
those—! The last of them was that female that Hjalmar
Ekdal was fixed up with when you had no more—ugh!

WERLE (*shrugs*). Word for word, as if I were hearing
your mother.

GREGERS (*paying no attention to him*). . . . and there he
sits right now, he with his great, guileless, childlike mind
plunged in deception—living under the same roof with that
creature, not knowing that what he calls his home is built
on a lie. (*Coming a step closer.*) When I look back on all
you've done, it's as if I looked out over a battlefield with
broken human beings on every side.

WERLE. I almost think the gulf is too great between us.

GREGERS (*bows stiffly*). So I've observed; therefore I'll
take my hat and go.

WERLE. You're going? Out of this house?

GREGERS. Yes. Because now at last I can see a mission to
live for.

WERLE. What mission is that?

GREGERS. You'd only laugh if you heard it.

WERLE. A lonely man doesn't laugh so easily, Gregers.

GREGERS (*pointing toward the inner room*). Look—your

gentleman friends are playing blindman's buff with Mrs.
Sørby. Good night and goodbye.

> (*He goes out at the right rear. Laughter and*
> *joking from the company, which moves into*
> *view in the inner room.*)

WERLE (*muttering contemptuously after* GREGERS). Huh!
Poor fool—and he says he's not high-strung!

◁ ACT TWO ▷

HJALMAR EKDAL's *studio. The room, which is fairly spacious, appears to be a loft. To the right is a sloping roof with great panes of glass, half hidden by a blue curtain. In the far right corner is the entrance; nearer on the same side, a door to the living room. Similarly, at the left there are two doors, and between these an iron stove. At the back is a wide double door, designed to slide back to the sides. The studio is simply but comfortably furnished and decorated. Between the right-hand doors, slightly away from the wall, stands a sofa beside a table and some chairs; on the table is a lighted lamp with a shade; by the stove an old armchair. Photographic apparatus and equipment of various sorts are set up here and there in the room. At the left of the double doors stands a bookcase containing a few books, small boxes and flasks of chemicals, various tools, implements, and other objects. Photographs and such small articles as brushes, paper, and the like lie on the table.*

GINA EKDAL *sits on a chair by the table, sewing.* HEDVIG *sits on the sofa, hands shading her eyes, thumbs in her ears, reading a book.*

GINA (*having glanced over several times at* HEDVIG, *as if with anxiety*). Hedvig! (HEDVIG *does not hear.*)

GINA (*louder*). Hedvig!

HEDVIG (*removing her hands and looking up*). Yes, Mother?

GINA. Hedvig dear, you mustn't sit and read anymore.

HEDVIG. Oh, but Mother, can't I please read a little longer? Just a little!

GINA. No, no—you must set the book down. Your father doesn't like it; *he* never reads in the evening.

HEDVIG (*closing the book*). No, Daddy's no great one for reading.

GINA (*lays her sewing aside and takes a pencil and a small*

411

notebook from the table). Do you remember how much we spent for butter today?

HEDVIG. It was one sixty-five.

GINA. That's right. (*Making a note.*) It's awful how much butter gets used in this house. And then so much for smoked sausage, and for cheese—let me see—(*Making more notes.*) and so much for ham—hmm. (*Adds.*) Yes, that adds right up to—

HEDVIG. And then there's the beer.

GINA. Yes, of course. (*Makes another note.*) It mounts up —but it can't be helped.

HEDVIG. Oh, but you and I had no hot food for dinner, 'cause Daddy was out.

GINA. No, and that's to the good. What's more, I also took in eight crowns fifty for photographs.

HEDVIG. No! Was it that much?

GINA. Exactly eight crowns fifty.

    (*Silence.* GINA *again picks up her sewing.* HEDVIG
    takes paper and pencil and starts to draw, shad-
    ing her eyes with her left hand.)

HEDVIG. Isn't it something to think that Daddy's at a big dinner party at old Mr. Werle's?

GINA. You can't really say that he's at old Mr. Werle's. It was his son who sent him the invitation. (*After a pause.*) We have nothing to do with old Mr. Werle.

HEDVIG. I can hardly wait for Daddy to come home. He promised he'd ask Mrs. Sørby about bringing me a treat.

GINA. Yes, you can bet there are lots of treats to be had in *that* house.

HEDVIG (*again drawing*). Besides, I'm a little hungry, too.

    (*Old* EKDAL, *with a bundle of papers under his*
    arm and another bundle in his coat pocket,
    comes in through the hall door.)

GINA. My, but you're late today, Grandfather.

EKDAL. They'd locked the office. Had to wait for Graaberg. And then I had to go through—uhh.

GINA. Did they give you something new to copy, Grandfather?

EKDAL. This whole pile. Just look.

GINA. That's fine.

HEDVIG. And you've got a bundle in your pocket, too.

EKDAL. Oh? Nonsense; that's nothing. (*Puts his cane away in the corner.*) Here's work for a good spell, Gina, this here. (*Pulls one of the double doors slightly open.*) Shh! (*Peers into the room a moment, then carefully closes the door again.*) He, he! They're sound asleep, the lot of them. And she's bedded down in the basket all on her own. He, he!

HEDVIG. Are you sure she won't be cold in the basket, Grandpa?

EKDAL. What a thought! Cold? In all that straw? (*Goes toward the farther door on the left.*) I'll find some matches in here, eh?

GINA. The matches are on the bureau.

(EKDAL *goes into his room.*)

HEDVIG. It's wonderful that Grandpa got all that copying to do.

GINA. Yes, poor old Father; he'll earn himself a little pocket money.

HEDVIG. And he also won't be able to sit the whole morning down in that horrid Mrs. Eriksen's café.

GINA. That too, yes. (*A short silence.*)

HEDVIG. Do you think they're still at the dinner table?

GINA. Lord only knows; it may well be.

HEDVIG. Just think, all the lovely food Daddy's eaten! I'm sure he'll be happy and content when he comes. Don't you think so, Mother?

GINA. Of course. Imagine if we could tell him now that we'd rented out the room.

HEDVIG. But that's not necessary tonight.

GINA. Oh, it could well come in handy, you know. It's no good to us as it is.

HEDVIG. No, I mean it's not necessary because tonight Daddy's feeling good. It's better we have news about the room some other time.

GINA (*looking over at her*). Are you glad when you have something nice to tell your father when he comes home at night?

HEDVIG. Yes, for things here are pleasanter then.

GINA (*reflecting*). Well, there's something to that.

(*Old* EKDAL *comes in again and starts out through the nearer door to the left.*)

GINA (*half turning in her chair*).   Does Grandfather want something from the kitchen?

EKDAL.   I do, yes. Don't stir. (*He goes out.*)

GINA.   He never fusses with the fire out there. (*After a moment.*) Hedvig, go see what he's doing.

> (EKDAL *reenters with a small jug of steaming water.*)

HEDVIG.   Are you after hot water, Grandpa?

EKDAL.   Yes, I am. Need it for something. Have to write, and the ink is caked thick as porridge—hmm.

GINA.   But you ought to have supper first, Grandfather. It's all set and waiting in there.

EKDAL.   Never mind about the supper, Gina. Terribly busy, I tell you. I don't want anybody coming into my room— nobody. Hmm. (*He goes into his room.* GINA *and* HEDVIG *exchange glances.*)

GINA (*lowering her voice*).   Where do you figure he's gotten money?

HEDVIG.   He must have got it from Graaberg.

GINA.   Not a chance. Graaberg always sends the pay to me.

HEDVIG.   Maybe he got a bottle somewhere on credit.

GINA.   Poor Grandpa, no one'll give him credit.

> (HJALMAR EKDAL, *wearing an overcoat and a gray felt hat, enters from the right.*)

GINA (*dropping her sewing and getting up*).   Ah, Hjalmar, here you are!

HEDVIG (*jumping up at the same time*).   At last you're home, Daddy!

HJALMAR (*putting his hat down*).   Yes, most of them were leaving.

HEDVIG.   So early?

HJALMAR.   Yes, it was only a dinner party. (*Starts to remove his overcoat.*)

GINA.   Let me help you.

HEDVIG.   Me too.

> (*They take off his coat;* GINA *hangs it up on the rear wall.*)

HEDVIG.   Were there many there, Daddy?

HJALMAR. Oh no, not many. We were some twelve, fourteen people at the table.

GINA. And you got to talk with every one of them?

HJALMAR. Oh yes, a little, though Gregers rather monopolized me.

GINA. Is Gregers ugly as ever?

HJALMAR. Well, he doesn't look any better. Isn't the old man home?

HEDVIG. Yes, Grandpa's inside, writing.

HJALMAR. Did he say anything?

GINA. No, what should he say?

HJALMAR. Didn't he mention anything of—I thought I heard that he'd been with Graaberg. I'll go in and have a word with him.

GINA. No, no, don't bother.

HJALMAR. Why not? Did he say he wouldn't see me?

GINA. He doesn't want anyone in there this evening.

HEDVIG (*making signals*). Uh—uh!

GINA (*not noticing*). He's already been out here and gotten hot water.

HJALMAR. Aha! Is he—?

GINA. Yes, exactly.

HJALMAR. Good Lord, my poor old white-haired father! Well, let him be, enjoying life's pleasures as he may.

(*Old* EKDAL *in a bathrobe, smoking a pipe, enters from his room.*)

EKDAL. Home, eh? Thought it was your voice I heard.

HJALMAR. I just arrived.

EKDAL. You didn't see me at all, did you?

HJALMAR. No, but they said you'd been through—so I thought I'd follow after.

EKDAL. Hm, good of you, Hjalmar. Who were they, all those people?

HJALMAR. Oh, different sorts. There was Flor—he's at the court—and Balle and Kaspersen and, uh—I forget his name, but people at court, all of them—

EKDAL (*nodding*). Listen to that, Gina! He travels only in the best circles.

GINA. Yes, it's real elegant in that house now.

HEDVIG. Did the court people sing, Daddy? Or give readings?

HJALMAR. No, they just babbled away. Of course they wanted *me* to recite for them, but I couldn't see that.

EKDAL. You couldn't see that, eh?

GINA. That you could easily have done.

HJALMAR. Never. One mustn't be a doormat for every passing foot. (*Walking about the room.*) At least, that's not my way.

EKDAL. No, no, that's not for Hjalmar.

HJALMAR. I don't know why I should always provide the entertainment, when I'm out in society so rarely. Let the others make an effort. There those fellows go from one banquet to the next, eating and drinking day in and day out. So let them do their tricks in return for all the good food they get.

GINA. But you didn't say that there?

HJALMAR (*humming*). Um—um—um—they were told a thing or two.

EKDAL. Right to the nobility!

HJALMAR. I don't see why not. (*Casually.*) Later we had a little quibble about Tokay.

EKDAL. Tokay, you mean? That's a fine wine, that.

HJALMAR (*coming to a halt*). On occasion. But I must tell you that not all years are equally good. Everything depends strictly on how much sun the grapes have had.

GINA. Really? Oh, Hjalmar, you know everything.

EKDAL. And they could argue about that?

HJALMAR. They tried to. But then they were informed that it's exactly the same with court officials. Among them as well, all years are not equally fine—it was said.

GINA. The things you think of!

EKDAL. He—he! So you served that up to them, eh?

HJALMAR. Smack between the eyes they got it.

EKDAL. Hear, Gina! He laid that one smack between the eyes of the nobility.

GINA. Just think, smack between the eyes.

HJALMAR. That's right. But I don't want a lot of talk about this. One doesn't speak of such things. Everything really went off in the most friendly spirit, naturally. They're all pleasant, genial people. How could I hurt their feelings? Never!

EKDAL. But smack between the eyes—

HEDVIG (*ingratiatingly*). How nice to see you in evening clothes, Daddy. You look so well in them.

HJALMAR. Yes, don't you think so? And this one here really fits very well. It's almost as if it were made for me. A bit snug under the arms, maybe—help me, Hedvig. (*Takes off the coat.*) I'd rather wear my jacket. What did you do with my jacket, Gina?

GINA. Here it is. (*Brings the jacket and helps him into it.*)

HJALMAR. There! Now don't forget to give Molvik his coat back first thing in the morning.

GINA (*putting it away*). I'll take care of it.

HJALMAR (*stretching*). Ah, but this feels much more comfortable. This kind of free and easy dress suits my whole personality better. Don't you think so, Hedvig?

HEDVIG. Yes, Daddy.

HJALMAR. And when I pull my necktie out into a pair of flowing ends—so! Look! What then?

HEDVIG. Yes, it goes so well with your moustache and your long, curly hair.

HJALMAR. Curly? I wouldn't say it's that. I'd call it wavy.

HEDVIG. Yes, but it *is* so curly.

HJALMAR. No—wavy.

HEDVIG (*after a moment, tugs at his sleeve*). Daddy!

HJALMAR. What is it?

HEDVIG. Oh, you know what.

HJALMAR. No, I don't. Honestly.

HEDVIG (*laughing fretfully*). Come on, Daddy, don't tease me any longer.

HJALMAR. But what is it, then?

HEDVIG (*shaking him*). Silly! Out with it, Daddy. You know—all the treats you promised me.

HJALMAR. Oh—no! How did I ever forget that?

HEDVIG. No, you can't fool me. Shame on you! Where have you hidden it?

HJALMAR. So help me if I didn't forget. But wait a minute! I've got something else for you, Hedvig. (*Goes over and rummages in his coat pockets.*)

HEDVIG (*jumping and clapping her hands*). Oh, Mother, Mother!

GINA. You see, if you're only patient enough, then—

HJALMAR (*returning with a piece of paper*). See, here we have it.

HEDVIG. That? But that's just a piece of paper.

HJALMAR. It's the bill of fare, the complete bill of fare. Here it says "menu"; that means "bill of fare."

HEDVIG. Don't you have anything else?

HJALMAR. I forgot to bring anything else, I tell you. But take my word for it: it's bad business, this doting on sugar candy. Now, if you'll sit down at the table and read the menu aloud, I'll describe for you just how each dish tasted. How's that, Hedvig?

HEDVIG (*swallowing her tears*). Thanks. (*She sits, but does not read.* GINA *makes gestures at her, which* HJALMAR *notices.*)

HJALMAR (*pacing about the floor*). What incredible things a family breadwinner is asked to remember; and if he forgets even the tiniest detail—immediately he's met with sour faces. Well, he has to get used to that, too. (*Pauses at the stove beside* EKDAL.) Have you looked inside this evening, Father?

EKDAL. Oh, that you can be sure of. She's gone into the basket.

HJALMAR. No! Into the basket? Then she's begun to get used to it.

EKDAL. Yes. You see, it was just as I predicted. But now there are some little things to do—

HJALMAR. Some improvements, eh?

EKDAL. But they've got to be done, you know.

HJALMAR. All right, let's talk a bit about the improvements, Father. Come, we'll sit here on the sofa.

EKDAL. Very good. Umm—think I'll fill my pipe first. Needs cleaning, too. Hmm. (*He goes into his room.*)

GINA (*smiling at* HJALMAR). Clean his pipe!

HJALMAR. Ah, now, Gina, let him be. Poor shipwrecked old man. Yes, the improvements—it's best we get those off our hands tomorrow.

GINA. Tomorrow you won't have time, Hjalmar—

HEDVIG (*interrupting*). Oh yes, he will, Mother!

GINA. Remember those prints that need retouching. They've been called for so many times already.

HJALMAR. Oh yes, those prints again. They'll be finished in no time. Did any new orders come in?

GINA. No such luck. For tomorrow, I have nothing except those two portrait sittings you know about.

HJALMAR. Nothing else? Ah, well, if people won't even try, then naturally—

GINA. But what else can I do? I've put ads in the papers time and again.

HJALMAR. Yes, ads, ads—you see what a help they are. And of course nobody's been to look at the spare room either?

GINA. No, not yet.

HJALMAR. That was to be expected. If one doesn't keep wide awake—Gina, you've simply got to pull yourself together.

HEDVIG (*going to him*). Let me bring you your flute, Daddy.

HJALMAR. No, no flute. I want no pleasures in this world. (*Pacing about.*) Ah, yes, work—I'll be deep in work tomorrow; there'll be no lack of *that*. I'll sweat and slave as long as my strength holds out—

GINA. But Hjalmar dear, I didn't mean it that way.

HEDVIG. Can't I get you a bottle of beer, then?

HJALMAR. Absolutely not. There's nothing I need. (*Stopping.*) Beer? Did you say beer?

HEDVIG (*vivaciously*). Yes, Daddy, lovely cool beer.

HJALMAR. Well—if you really insist, I suppose you could bring in a bottle.

GINA. Yes, do that. Then we'll have it cozy.

(HEDVIG *runs toward the kitchen door.* HJALMAR *by the stove stops her, gazes at her, clasps her about the head and hugs her to him.*)

HJALMAR. Hedvig! Hedvig!

HEDVIG (*with tears of joy*). Oh, my dearest Daddy!

HJALMAR. No, don't call me that. There I sat, helping myself at a rich man's table, gorging myself with all good things—! I could at least have remembered—

GINA (*sitting at the table*). Oh, nonsense, Hjalmar.

HJALMAR. Yes, I could! But you mustn't be too hard on me. You both know I love you anyway.

HEDVIG (*throwing her arms around him*). And we love you too, so much!

HJALMAR. And if I should seem unreasonable at times, then—good Lord—remember that I am a man assailed by a host of cares. Ah, yes! (*Drying his eyes.*) No beer at a time like this. Bring me my flute. (HEDVIG *runs to the bookcase and fetches it.*) Thank you. There—so. With flute in hand, and you two close by me—ah!

> (HEDVIG *sits at the table by* GINA, HJALMAR *walks back and forth, then forcefully begins to play a Bohemian folk dance, but in a slow elegaic tempo with sentimental intonation. After a moment he breaks off the melody and extends his left hand to* GINA.)

HJALMAR (*with feeling*).   So what if we skimp and scrape along under this roof, Gina—it's still our home. And I'll say this: it's good to be here. (*He starts playing again; immediately there comes a knock on the hall door.*)

GINA (*getting up*).   Shh, Hjalmar. I think someone's there.

HJALMAR (*returning the flute to the bookcase*).   What, again! (GINA *goes over and opens the door.*)

GREGERS WERLE (*out in the hallway*).   Excuse me—

GINA (*drawing back slightly*).   Oh!

GREGERS.   But doesn't Mr. Ekdal, the photographer, live here?

GINA.   Yes, that's right.

HJALMAR (*going toward the door*).   Gregers! Is it really you? Well, come right in.

GREGERS (*entering*).   I said I was going to drop in on you.

HJALMAR.   But tonight? Have you left the party?

GREGERS.   Left both party and family home. Good evening, Mrs. Ekdal. I don't know whether you recognize me?

GINA.   Oh yes. Young Mr. Werle is not so hard to recognize.

GREGERS.   No. I look like my mother, and you remember her, no doubt.

HJALMAR.   Did you say you'd left your home?

GREGERS.   Yes, I've moved into a hotel.

HJALMAR.   I see. Well, now that you've come, take off your things and sit down.

GREGERS.   Thank you. (*Removes his overcoat. He is dressed now in a simple grey suit of somewhat rustic cut.*)

HJALMAR.   Here, on the sofa. Make yourself at home.

> (GREGERS *sits on the sofa,* HJALMAR *on a chair at the table.*)

GREGERS (*looking around*). So this is where you work, then, Hjalmar. And you live here as well.

HJALMAR. This is the studio, as you can see—

GINA. There's more room in here, so we like it better.

HJALMAR. We had a better place before; but this apartment has one great advantage: it has such wonderful adjoining rooms—

GINA. And so we have a room on the other side of the hall that we can rent out.

GREGERS (*to* HJALMAR). Ah, then you have lodgers, too.

HJALMAR. No, not yet. It's not that easy, you know. One has to keep wide awake. (*To* HEDVIG.) But how about that beer?

(HEDVIG *nods and goes into the kitchen.*)

GREGERS. So that's your daughter, then?

HJALMAR. Yes, that's Hedvig.

GREGERS. An only child?

HJALMAR. She's the only one, yes. She's the greatest joy of our lives, and—(*Lowering his voice.*) also our deepest sorrow, Gregers.

GREGERS. What do you mean?

HJALMAR. Yes. You see, there's the gravest imminent danger of her losing her sight.

GREGERS. Going blind!

HJALMAR. Yes. So far only the first signs are present, and things may go well for a while. All the same, the doctor has warned us. It will come inevitably.

GREGERS. What a dreadful misfortune! How did this happen?

HJALMAR (*sighing*). Heredity, most likely.

GREGERS (*startled*). Heredity?

GINA. Hjalmar's mother also had bad eyes.

HJALMAR. Yes, so my father says. I don't remember her.

GREGERS. Poor child. And how is she taking it?

HJALMAR. Oh, you can well imagine, we haven't the heart to tell her. She suspects nothing. She's carefree, gay, and singing like a tiny bird, she's fluttering into life's eternal night. (*Overcome.*) Oh, it's a brutal blow for me, Gregers.

(HEDVIG *brings in beer and glasses on a tray, which she sets down on the table.*)

HJALMAR (*stroking her head*).   Thanks. Thanks, Hedvig.

> (HEDVIG *puts her arms around his neck and whispers in his ear.*)

HJALMAR.   No. No bread and butter now. (*Looking over.*) Or maybe Gregers will have a piece?

GREGERS (*making a gesture of refusal*).   No. No, thanks.

HJALMAR (*his tone still mournful*).   Well, you can bring in a little anyway. If you have a crust, that would be fine. And please, put enough butter on, too.

> (HEDVIG *nods contentedly and returns to the kitchen.*)

GREGERS (*after following her with his eyes*).   In every other respect she looks so strong and healthy.

GINA.   Yes, thank God, she's got nothing else wrong with her.

GREGERS.   She'll certainly look like you when she grows up, Mrs. Ekdal. How old is she now?

GINA.   Hedvig is almost fourteen exactly; her birthday's the day after tomorrow.

GREGERS.   Rather tall for her age.

GINA.   Yes, she's shot right up this past year.

GREGERS.   Nothing like the growth of a child to show us how old we're getting. How long is it you've been married now?

GINA.   We've been married now for—yes, near fifteen years.

GREGERS.   No, truly! Has it been that long?

GINA (*looking at him, becoming wary*).   Yes, no doubt about it.

HJALMAR.   That's right. Fifteen years, short a few months. (*Changing the subject.*) They must have been long years for you, Gregers, up there at the works.

GREGERS.   They were long while I was living them—but now I scarcely know what became of the time.

> (*Old* EKDAL *enters from his room, without his pipe, but with his old military cap on his head; his walk is a bit unsteady.*)

EKDAL.   There, now, Hjalmar. Now we can settle down and talk about that—umm. What was it again?

HJALMAR (*going toward him*).   Father, someone is here. Gregers Werle. I don't know if you remember him.

EKDAL (*regarding* GREGERS, *who has gotten up*).   Werle? That's the son, isn't it? What does he want with me?

HJALMAR.   Nothing; it's me he's come to see.

EKDAL.   Well, then nothing's up, eh?

HJALMAR.   No, of course not.

EKDAL (*swinging his arms*).   It's not that I'm scared of anything, you know, but—

GREGERS (*going over to him*).   I just want to greet you from your old hunting grounds, Lieutenant Ekdal.

EKDAL.   Hunting grounds?

GREGERS.   Yes, up there around the Hoidal works.

EKDAL.   Oh, up there. Yes, I was well known there once.

GREGERS.   In those days you were a tremendous hunter.

EKDAL.   So I was. Still am, maybe. You're looking at my uniform. I ask nobody permission to wear it in here. As long as I don't walk in the streets with it— (HEDVIG *brings a plate of buttered bread, which she places on the table.*)

HJALMAR.   Sit down, Father, and have a glass of beer. Help yourself, Gregers.

> (EKDAL *stumbles, muttering, over to the sofa.*
> GREGERS *sits on the chair nearest him,* HJALMAR
> *on the other side of* GREGERS. GINA *sits near
> the table and sews;* HEDVIG *stands beside her
> father.*)

GREGERS.   Do you remember, Lieutenant Ekdal, when Hjalmar and I would come up to visit you summers and at Christmas?

EKDAL.   Did you? No, no, no, I don't recall. But I'll tell you something: I've been a first-rate hunter. Bear— I've shot them, too. Shot nine in all.

GREGERS (*looking sympathetically at him*).   And now you hunt no more.

EKDAL.   Oh, I wouldn't say *that*, boy. Get some hunting in now and then. Yes, but not that kind there. The woods, you see—the woods, the woods— (*Drinks.*) How do the woods look up there?

GREGERS.   Not so fine as in your time. They've been cut into heavily.

EKDAL.   Cut into? (*More quietly, as if in fear.*) It's a dangerous business, that. It catches up with you. The woods take revenge.

HJALMAR (*filling his glass*).   Here, a little more, Father.

GREGERS.   How can a man like you—such an outdoorsman—live in the middle of a stuffy city, cooped up in these four walls?

EKDAL (*half laughs and glances at* HJALMAR).   Oh, it's not so bad here. Not bad at all.

GREGERS.   But all those other things, the very roots of your soul—that cool, sweeping breeze, that free life of the moors and forests, among the animals and birds—?

EKDAL (*smiling*).   Hjalmar, should we show him?

HJALMAR (*quickly and a bit embarrassed*).   No, no, Father, not tonight.

GREGERS.   What's that he wants to show me?

HJALMAR.   Oh, it's only a sort of—you can see it some other time.

GREGERS (*speaking again to* EKDAL).   Yes, my point was this, Lieutenant Ekdal, that now you might as well return with me to the works, for I'm sure to be leaving very soon. Without a doubt, you could get some copying to do up there; and here you've nothing in the world to stir your blood and make you happy.

EKDAL (*staring at him, astonished*).   I have nothing, nothing at all—!

GREGERS.   Of course you have Hjalmar, but then again, he has his own. And a man like you, who's always felt himself so drawn to whatever is free and wild—

EKDAL (*striking the table*).   Hjalmar, now he's *got* to see it!

HJALMAR.   But Father, is it worth it now? It's dark, you know—

EKDAL.   Nonsense! There's moonlight. (*Getting up.*) I say he's got to see it. Let me by. Come and help me, Hjalmar!

HEDVIG.   Oh yes, do that, Father!

HJALMAR (*getting up*).   Well—all right.

GREGERS (*to* GINA).   What's this all about?

GINA.   Oh, you really mustn't expect anything special.

> (EKDAL *and* HJALMAR *have gone to the back wall to push aside the two halves of the double door;* HEDVIG *helps her grandfather, while* GREG-

ERS *remains standing by the sofa and* GINA *sits, imperturbably sewing. The doorway opens on an extensive, irregular loft room with many nooks and corners, and two separate chimney shafts ascending through it. Clear moonlight streams through skylights into certain parts of the large room; others lie in deep shadow.*)

EKDAL (*to* GREGERS). All the way over here, please.

GREGERS (*going over to them*). What *is* it, then?

EKDAL. See for yourself—hmm.

HJALMAR (*somewhat self-conscious*). All this belongs to Father, you understand.

GREGERS (*peering in at the doorway*). So you keep poultry, Lieutenant Ekdal!

EKDAL. I'll say we keep poultry! They're roosting now; but you just ought to see our poultry by daylight!

HEDVIG. And then there's a—

EKDAL. Shh, shh—don't say anything yet.

GREGERS. And you've got pigeons too, I see.

EKDAL. Oh yes, it might just be we've got some pigeons. They have their nesting boxes up there under the eaves; pigeons like to perch high, you know.

HJALMAR. They're not ordinary pigeons, all of them.

EKDAL. Ordinary! No, I should say not! We have tumblers, and we have a couple of pouters also. But look here! Can you see that hutch over there by the wall?

GREGERS. Yes. What do you use that for?

EKDAL. The rabbits sleep there at night, boy.

GREGERS. Well, so you have rabbits too?

EKDAL. Yes, what the devil do you think we have but rabbits! He asks if we have rabbits, Hjalmar! Hmm! But now listen, this is really something! This is it! Out of the way, Hedvig. Stand right here—that's it—and look straight down there. Do you see a basket there with straw in it?

GREGERS. Yes, and there's a bird nesting in the basket.

EKDAL. Hmm! "A bird"—

GREGERS. Isn't it a duck?

EKDAL (*hurt*). Yes, of course it's a duck.

HJALMAR. But what *kind* of duck?

HEDVIG. It's not just any old duck—

EKDAL. Shh!

GREGERS.   And it's no exotic breed, either.

EKDAL.   No, Mr.—Werle, it's not any exotic breed—because it's a wild duck.

GREGERS.   No, is it really? A wild duck?

EKDAL.   Oh yes, that's what it is. That "bird" as you said —that's a wild duck. That's our wild duck, boy.

HEDVIG.   *My* wild duck—I own it.

GREGERS.   And it can survive up here indoors? And do well?

EKDAL.   You've got to understand, she's got a trough of water to splash around in.

HJALMAR.   Fresh water every other day.

GINA (*turning to* HJALMAR).   Hjalmar dear, it's freezing cold in here now.

EKDAL.   Hmm, let's close up, then. Doesn't pay to disturb their rest either. Lend a hand, Hedvig dear. (HJALMAR *and* HEDVIG *push the double doors together*.) Another time you can get a proper look at her. (*Sits in the armchair by the stove.*) Oh, they're most curious, the wild ducks, you know.

GREGERS.   But how did you capture it, Lieutenant Ekdal?

EKDAL.   Didn't capture it myself. There's a certain man here in town we can thank for it.

GREGERS (*starts slightly*).   That man—it wouldn't be my father?

EKDAL.   Exactly right—your father. Hmm.

HJALMAR.   It was odd you were able to guess that, Gregers.

GREGERS.   Well, you said before that you owed Father for so many different things, so I thought here too—

GINA.   But we didn't get the duck from Mr. Werle himself—

EKDAL.   We might just as well thank Haakon Werle for her anyhow, Gina. (*To* GREGERS.) He was out in his boat—follow me?—and he shot for her, but he sees so bad now, your father, that—hm—he only winged her.

GREGERS.   I see. She took some shot in her body.

HJALMAR.   Yes, some one, two—three pieces.

HEDVIG.   She got it under the wing, and so she couldn't fly.

GREGERS.   Ah, so she dived right for the bottom, eh?

EKDAL (*sleepily, with a thick voice*).   You can bet on that. They always do, the wild ducks—streak for the bottom,

deep as they can get, boy—bite right into the weeds and
sea moss—and all that devil's beard that grows down there.
And then they never come up again.

GREGERS. But Lieutenant Ekdal, *your* wild duck came up
again.

EKDAL. He had such a remarkably clever dog, your
father. And that dog—he dove down and brought her up.

GREGERS (*turning to* HJALMAR). And then you got her
here.

HJALMAR. Not directly. First she went home to your
father's, but there she didn't do well, so Pettersen got his
orders to put an end to her—

EKDAL (*half asleep*). Hm—yes, Pettersen—that bonehead—

HJALMAR (*speaking more softly*). That's the way we got
her, you see. Father knows Pettersen a bit and when he
heard all this about the wild duck, he arranged to have her
handed over to us.

GREGERS. And now she's absolutely thriving in that attic
room.

HJALMAR. Yes, it's incredible. She's gotten fat. I think
she's been in there so long, too, that she's forgotten her old
wild life, and that's what it all comes down to.

GREGERS. You're certainly right there, Hjalmar. Just don't
let her ever catch sight of the sea and the sky— But I
mustn't stay any longer, for I think your father's asleep.

HJALMAR. Oh, don't bother about that.

GREGERS. But incidentally—you said you had a room for
rent, a free room?

HJALMAR. Yes. Why? Do you know someone, perhaps—?

GREGERS. Could I take that room?

HJALMAR. You?

GINA. No, not *you*, Mr. Werle—

GREGERS. Could I take the room? If so, I'll move in
first thing in the morning.

HJALMAR. By all means, with the greatest pleasure—

GINA. No, but Mr. Werle, it's not at all the room for *you*.

HJALMAR. But Gina, how can you say that?

GINA. Oh, the room isn't large enough, or light enough,
and—

GREGERS. That really doesn't matter, Mrs. Ekdal.

HJALMAR. I think it's a very pleasant room, and it's not
badly furnished, either.

GINA. But remember those two who live right below.

GREGERS. What two are those?

GINA. Oh, one of them's been a private tutor—

HJALMAR. That's Molvik, from the university.

GINA. And then there's a doctor named Relling.

GREGERS. Relling? I know him somewhat. He practiced a while up in Hoidal.

GINA. They're a pretty wild pair, those fellows. They go out on the town evenings and then come home in the dead of night, and they're not always so—

GREGERS. One gets used to that soon enough. I'm hoping things will go for me the same as with the wild duck—

GINA. Well, I think you ought to sleep on it first, anyway.

GREGERS. You're not very anxious to have me in the house, Mrs. Ekdal.

GINA. Goodness, what makes you think that?

HJALMAR. Yes, Gina, this is really peculiar of you. (*To* GREGERS.) But tell me, do you expect to stay here in town for a while?

GREGERS (*putting on his overcoat*). Yes, now I expect to stay on.

HJALMAR. But not at home with your father? What do you plan to do with yourself?

GREGERS. Yes, if I only knew that—then I'd be doing all right. But when one carries the cross of a name like Gregers—"Gregers"—and then "Werle" coming after— have you ever heard anything so disgusting?

HJALMAR. Oh, I don't agree at all.

GREGERS. Ugh! Phew! I feel I'd like to spit on any man with a name like that. But once you have to bear that cross of being Gregers—Werle in this world, as I do—

HJALMAR (*laughing*). If you weren't Gregers Werle, who would you want to be?

GREGERS. If I could choose, above all else I'd like to be a clever dog.

GINA. A dog!

HEDVIG (*involuntarily*). Oh no!

GREGERS. Yes. A really fantastic, clever dog, the kind that goes to the bottom after wild ducks when they dive under and bite fast into the weeds down in the mire.

HJALMAR. You know, Gregers—I can't follow a word you're saying.

GREGERS. Never mind. There's really nothing very remarkable in it. But tomorrow morning, early, I'll be moving in. (*To* GINA.) I won't be any trouble to you; I do everything for myself. (*To* HJALMAR.) The rest we can talk over tomorrow. Good night, Mrs. Ekdal. (*Nods to* HEDVIG.) Good night.

GINA. Good night, Mr. Werle.

HEDVIG. Good night.

HJALMAR (*who has lit a lamp*). Just a minute. I'd better light your way; it's quite dark on the stairs.

(GREGERS *and* HJALMAR *go out through the hall.*)

GINA (*gazing into space, her sewing in her lap*). Wasn't that a queer business, his wanting to be a dog?

HEDVIG. I'll tell you something, Mother—it seemed to me he meant something else by th..t.

GINA. What else could he mean?

HEDVIG. I don't know—but it was just as if he meant something else from what he said, all the time.

GINA. Do you think so? It was strange, all right.

HJALMAR (*coming back*). The light was still lit. (*Putting out the lamp and setting it down.*) Ah, at last one can get a bite to eat. (*Beginning on the bread and butter.*) Well, now you see, Gina—if you simply keep wide awake, then—

GINA. What do you mean, wide awake?

HJALMAR. Well, it was lucky, then, that we got the room rented out for a while at last. And think—to a person like Gregers—a good old friend.

GINA. Yes. I don't know what to say. I don't.

HEDVIG. Oh, Mother, you'll see. It'll be fun.

HJALMAR. You really are peculiar. Before you were so eager to rent, and now you don't like it.

GINA. Yes, Hjalmar, if it could only have been somebody else. What do you think the old man will say?

HJALMAR. Old Werle? This doesn't concern him.

GINA. But you can sure bet that something has come up between them, since the son is moving out. You know how those two get along together.

HJALMAR. Yes, that may well be, but—

GINA. And now maybe the old man thinks it's you that's behind—

HJALMAR. He can think that as much as he likes! Old

Werle has done a tremendous amount for me. God knows, I'm aware of that. But even so, I can't make myself eternally dependent on him.

GINA.   But Hjalmar dear, that can have its effect on Grandfather. He may now lose that miserable little income he gets from Graaberg.

HJALMAR.   I could almost say, so much the better! Isn't it rather humiliating for a man like me to see his gray-haired father go around like an outcast? But now time is gathering to a ripeness, I think. (*Takes another piece of bread and butter.*) Just as sure as I've got a mission in life, I'm going to carry it out!

HEDVIG.   Oh yes, Daddy! Do!

GINA.   Shh! Don't wake him up.

HJALMAR (*more quietly*).   I *will* carry it out, I tell you. There will come a day when— And that's why it's good we got the room rented out, for now I'm more independently fixed. Any man *must* be that, who's got a mission in life. (*Over by the armchair; emotionally.*) Poor old white-haired Father—lean on your Hjalmar. He has broad shoulders— powerful shoulders, in any case. One fine day you'll wake up and—(*To* GINA.) You do believe that, don't you?

GINA (*getting up*).   Yes, of course I do. But first let's see about getting him to bed.

HJALMAR.   Yes, let's do that.

(*Gently they lift up the old man.*)

⤙ ACT THREE ⤚

HJALMAR EKDAL's *studio. It is morning. Daylight streams through the large window in the sloping roof; the curtain is drawn back.*

HJALMAR *is sitting at the table, busy retouching a photograph; many other pictures lie in front of him. After a moment* GINA, *wearing a hat and coat, enters by the hall door; she has a covered basket on her arm.*

HJALMAR. Back so soon, Gina?

GINA. Oh yes. Got to keep moving. (*She sets the basket on a chair and takes her coat off.*)

HJALMAR. Did you look in on Gregers?

GINA. Um-hm, I certainly did. Looks real nice in there. The moment he came, he got his room in beautiful shape.

HJALMAR. Oh?

GINA. Yes. He wanted to do everything himself, he said. So he starts building a fire in the stove, and the next thing he's closed down the damper so the whole room is full of smoke. Phew! What a stink, enough to—

HJALMAR. Oh no!

GINA. But that's not the best part! So then he wants to put it out, so he empties his whole water pitcher into the stove and now the floor's swimming in the worst muck.

HJALMAR. That's a nuisance.

GINA. I got the janitor's wife to come and scrub up after him, the pig; but it'll be unfit to live in till afternoon.

HJALMAR. What's he doing with himself in the meantime?

GINA. Thought he'd take a little walk, he said.

HJALMAR. I was in to see him for a moment too—after you left.

GINA. I heard that. You asked him for lunch.

HJALMAR. Just the tiniest little midday snack, you understand. It's the very first day—we could hardly avoid it. You always have something in the house.

GINA. I'll see what I can find.

431

HJALMAR. But now don't make it too skimpy. Because Relling and Molvik are dropping in too, I think. I just met Relling on the stairs, you see, so of course I had to—

GINA. Oh? Must we have those two also?

HJALMAR. Good Lord, a couple of sandwiches more or less; what's the difference?

EKDAL (*opening his door and looking in*). Say, listen, Hjalmar— (*Noticing* GINA.) Oh, well.

GINA. Is there something Grandfather wants?

EKDAL. Oh no. Let it be. Hmm. (*Goes in again.*)

GINA (*picking up the basket*). Keep a sharp eye on him so he doesn't go out.

HJALMAR. Oh yes, I'll do that. Listen, Gina, a little herring salad would be awfully good—because Relling and Molvik were out on a binge last night.

GINA. Just so they don't come before I'm ready—

HJALMAR. Not a chance. Take your time.

GINA. That's fine, then—and meanwhile you can get a little work done.

HJALMAR. Can't you see how I'm working! I'm working for all I'm worth!

GINA. Because then you'll have *those* off your hands, you know. (*She carries the basket out to the kitchen.* HJALMAR *sits for a while, tinting the photograph in a glum and listless manner.*)

EKDAL (*peeks in, peers about the studio, and whispers*). Are you busy, boy?

HJALMAR. Of course. I'm sitting here struggling with these pictures—

EKDAL. Oh well, don't bother. If you're so busy, then— Hm! (*He reenters his room, leaving the door ajar.*)

HJALMAR (*continues a moment in silence, then puts down the brush and goes over to the door*). Father, are *you* busy?

EKDAL (*grumbling from within*). When you're busy—I'm busy too. Huh!

HJALMAR. Yes, of course. (*Returns to his work.*)

EKDAL (*a moment later, coming in again*). Hm. Well, now, Hjalmar, I'm really not *that* busy.

HJALMAR. I thought you had copying to do.

EKDAL. Oh, the devil! Can't he, Graaberg, wait a day or two? I'm sure it's no matter of life or death.

HJALMAR. No, and you're no slave, either.

EKDAL. And then there was that other business inside—

HJALMAR. Yes, that's just it. Maybe you want to go in? Shall I open it up for you?

EKDAL. Wouldn't be a bad idea, really?

HJALMAR (*getting up*). And then we'd have *that* off our hands.

EKDAL. Yes, exactly. And it has to be ready first thing tomorrow. But it *is* tomorrow, isn't it?

HJALMAR. It certainly is tomorrow.

> (HJALMAR *and* EKDAL *each push back one of the double doors. Within, morning sunlight shines through the skylights. A few doves fly back and forth; others perch, cooing, on the rafters. Chickens cackle now and then from back in the loft.*)

HJALMAR. There, now you can get in, Father.

EKDAL (*going in*). Aren't you coming along?

HJALMAR. Well, you know what—I almost think—(*Sees* GINA *in the kitchen doorway.*) I? No, I haven't the time; I've got to work. But that means our new mechanism—

> (*He pulls a cord; inside a curtain descends, its lower portion composed of a strip of old sailcloth, the upper part being a piece of worn-out fishnetting. By this means, the floor of the loft is rendered invisible.*)

HJALMAR (*returning to the table*). That's that. Now at last I can work in peace for a while.

GINA. Is he in there, romping around again?

HJALMAR. Isn't that better than having him run down to Mrs. Eriksen's? (*Sitting.*) Is there anything you want? You look so—

GINA. I only wanted to ask, do you think we can set the lunch table in here?

HJALMAR. Well, we haven't any portraits scheduled that early, have we?

GINA. No. I don't expect anybody except that couple who want to be taken together.

HJALMAR. Why the devil can't they be taken together some other day?

GINA. Now, Hjalmar dear, I've got them booked for during your midday nap.

HJALMAR. Well, that's fine, then. So we'll eat in here.

GINA. All right. But there's no hurry about setting the table; you can certainly use it a while longer.

HJALMAR. Oh, it's obvious I'm using the table as much as I can!

GINA. Because then you'll be free later on, you know. (*She goes back into the kitchen. A short pause.*)

EKDAL (*at the door to the loft, behind the net*). Hjalmar!

HJALMAR. Well?

EKDAL. 'Fraid we'll have to move the water trough after all.

HJALMAR. Yes, that's what I've been saying all along.

EKDAL. Hm—hm—hm. (*Disappears from the doorway.*)

(HJALMAR *works a bit, glances toward the loft, and half rises.* HEDVIG *enters from the kitchen.*)

HJALMAR (*hurriedly sitting again*). What do you want?

HEDVIG. I was just coming in to you, Father.

HJALMAR (*after a moment*). You seem to be kind of snooping around. Are you checking up, maybe?

HEDVIG. No, not at all.

HJALMAR. What's Mother doing out there now?

HEDVIG. Oh, she's half through the herring salad. (*Going over to the table.*) Don't you have some little thing I could help you with, Daddy?

HJALMAR. Oh no. It's better just to leave me alone with all this—so long as my strength holds out. Nothing to worry about, Hedvig—if only your father can keep his health—

HEDVIG. Oh, Daddy, no. That's horrid; you mustn't talk like that. (*She wanders about a little, stops by the loft doorway, and looks in.*)

HJALMAR. What's he trying to do now?

HEDVIG. It must be a new pathway up to the water trough.

HJALMAR. He can't possibly rig that up on his own! And I'm condemned to sit here—!

HEDVIG (*going to him*). Let *me* take the brush, Daddy. I know I can.

HJALMAR. Oh, nonsense, you'll only ruin your eyes.

HEDVIG. No such thing. Give me the brush.

HJALMAR (*getting up*). Well, it'll only be for a minute or two.

HEDVIG. Pooh! How could that hurt me? (*Takes the brush.*) There now. (*Sitting.*) And here's one to go by.

HJALMAR. But don't ruin your eyes! Hear me? I won't take the blame; you can take the blame yourself—you hear me?

HEDVIG (*at work retouching*). Yes, yes, sure I will.

HJALMAR. You're wonderfully clever, Hedvig. Just for a couple of minutes now.

> (*He slips around the edge of the curtain into the loft.* HEDVIG *sits at her work.* HJALMAR *and* EKDAL *are heard arguing inside.*)

HJALMAR (*appearing behind the net*). Hedvig, just hand me the pliers from the shelf. And the chisel, please. (*Turning over his shoulder.*) Yes, now you'll see, Father. Will you give me a chance to show you the way I mean! (HEDVIG *fetches the desired tools from the bookcase and passes them in to him.*) Ah, thanks. See, dear, it was a good thing I came. (*He vanishes from the doorway; sounds of carpentry and bantering are heard.* HEDVIG *remains, looking in at them. A moment later, a knock at the hall door; she fails to notice it.*)

GREGERS (*bareheaded, and without his overcoat, enters, hesitating slightly at the door*). Hm—

HEDVIG (*turning and going toward him*). Good morning. Please come in.

GREGERS. Thanks. (*Looking at the loft.*) You seem to have workmen in the house.

HEDVIG. No, that's only Father and Grandfather. I'll go tell them.

GREGERS. No, no, don't bother. I'd rather wait a bit. (*He sits on the sofa.*)

HEDVIG. It's so messy here— (*Starts to remove the photographs.*)

GREGERS. Oh, they can stay. Are those some pictures that have to be finished?

HEDVIG. Yes, it's a little job I'm helping Daddy with.

GREGERS. Please don't let me disturb you.

HEDVIG. All right. (*She gathers her materials around her*

and sets to work again; GREGERS *meanwhile regards her in silence.*)

GREGERS. Did the wild duck sleep well last night?

HEDVIG. Yes, I'm sure she did, thanks.

GREGERS (*turning toward the loft*). It looks so very different by daylight than it did by moonlight.

HEDVIG. Yes, it can change so completely. In the morning it looks different from in the afternoon; and when it rains it's different from when it's clear.

GREGERS. Have you noticed that?

HEDVIG. Sure. You can't help it.

GREGERS. And do you like it in there with the wild duck, too?

HEDVIG. Yes, whenever I can be there—

GREGERS. But of course you don't have much free time; you do go to school, don't you?

HEDVIG. No, not anymore. Daddy's afraid I'll hurt my eyes.

GREGERS. Oh. Then he tutors you himself.

HEDVIG. Daddy's promised to, but he hasn't found time for that yet.

GREGERS. But isn't there anyone else to help you a little?

HEDVIG. Sure, there's Mr. Molvik, but he isn't always exactly, really—well—

GREGERS. He gets drunk, eh?

HEDVIG. He *certainly* does.

GREGERS. Well, then you do have time to yourself. And inside—I'll bet in there it's just like a world of its own—am I right?

HEDVIG. Oh, completely! And then there are so many wonderful things.

GREGERS. Really?

HEDVIG. Yes, big cupboards with books in them; and lots of the books have pictures.

GREGERS. Ah!

HEDVIG. And then there's an old cabinet with drawers and compartments, and a huge clock with figures that are supposed to come out. But the clock doesn't go anymore.

GREGERS. Even time doesn't exist in there—with the wild duck.

HEDVIG. Yes. And then there's an old watercolor set and things like that. And then all the books.

GREGERS. And of course you read the books?

HEDVIG. Oh yes, whenever I can. But they're mostly in English, and I don't understand that. But then I look at the pictures. There's one just enormous book called *Harryson's History of London*; it must be a hundred years old, and it's got ever so many pictures in it. At the front there's a picture of Death with an hourglass and a girl. I think that's horrible. But then there are all the other pictures of churches and castles and streets and great ships sailing on the ocean.

GREGERS. But tell me, where did all these rare things come from!

HEDVIG. Oh, an old sea captain lived here once, and he brought them home. They called him "the flying Dutchman" —and that's the strangest thing, because he wasn't a Dutchman at all.

GREGERS. No?

HEDVIG. No. But then he didn't come back finally, and he left all these things behind.

GREGERS. Listen, tell me—when you sit in there and look at pictures, don't you ever want to go out and see the real world all for yourself?

HEDVIG. No, never! I'm going to stay at home always and help Daddy and Mother.

GREGERS. You mean finishing photographs?

HEDVIG. No, not just that. Most of all, I'd like to learn how to engrave pictures like those in the English books.

GREGERS. Hm. What does your father say to that?

HEDVIG. I don't think he likes it. Daddy's so funny about such things. Just think, he talks about me learning basket-making and wickerwork! But I don't see anything in *that*.

GREGERS. Oh no, I don't either.

HEDVIG. But Daddy's right when he says that if I'd learned how to make baskets, I could have made the new basket for the wild duck.

GREGERS. You could have, yes—and that really was up to you.

HEDVIG. Yes, because it's *my* wild duck.

GREGERS. Yes, of course it is.

HEDVIG. Uh-huh, I own it. But Daddy and Grandpa can borrow it as much as they want.

GREGERS. Oh? What do they do with it?

HEDVIG. Oh, they look after it and build things for it and so on.

GREGERS. I can well imagine. The wild duck rules supreme in there, doesn't she?

HEDVIG. Yes, she does, and that's because she's a *real* wild bird. And then it's so sad for her; the poor thing has no one to turn to.

GREGERS. No family, like the rabbits—

HEDVIG. No. Even the chickens have all the others that they were baby chicks with, but she's so completely apart from any of her own. So you see, everything is so really mysterious about the wild duck. There's no one who knows her, and no one who knows where she's come from, either.

GREGERS. And actually, she's been in the depths of the sea.

HEDVIG (*glances at him, suppresses a smile, and asks*). Why did you say "depths of the sea"?

GREGERS. What else should I say?

HEDVIG. You could have said "bottom of the sea"—or "the ocean's bottom"?

GREGERS. But couldn't I just as well say "depths of the sea"?

HEDVIG. Sure. But to me it sounds so strange when someone else says "depths of the sea."

GREGERS. But why? Tell me why?

HEDVIG. No, I won't. It's something so stupid.

GREGERS. It couldn't be. Now tell me why you smiled.

HEDVIG. That was because always, when all of a sudden —in a flash—I happen to think of that in there, it always seems to me that the whole room and everything in it is called "the depths of the sea"! But that's all so stupid.

GREGERS. Don't you dare say that.

HEDVIG. Oh yes, because it's only an attic.

GREGERS. Are you so sure of that?

HEDVIG (*astonished*). That it's an attic!

GREGERS. Yes. Do you know that for certain?

(HEDVIG, *speechless, stares at him open-mouthed.*
GINA *enters from the kitchen with a tablecloth.*)

GREGERS (*getting up*). I'm afraid I've come too early for you.

GINA. Oh, you can find yourself a spot; it's almost ready now. Clear the table, Hedvig.

(HEDVIG *puts away the materials; during the following dialogue, she and* GINA *set the table.* GREGERS *settles in the armchair and pages through an album.*)

GREGERS. I hear you do retouching, Mrs. Ekdal.

GINA (*with a side-glance*). Um, yes, I do that.

GREGERS. That's really very lucky.

GINA. Why "lucky"?

GREGERS. With Hjalmar a photographer, I mean.

HEDVIG. Mother does photography, too.

GINA. Oh yes, I even got taught in *that* art.

GREGERS. So we might say it's you who runs the business.

GINA. Yes, when my husband hasn't the time himself—

GREGERS. He finds himself so taken up with his old father, I suppose.

GINA. Yes, and then it's no kind of thing for a man like Hjalmar to go taking portraits of your common average.

GREGERS. I agree; but once he's chosen this line of work, then—

GINA. Mr. Werle, you must realize that my husband is not just any old photographer.

GREGERS. Well, naturally; but even so—

(*A shot is fired in the loft.*)

GREGERS (*jumping up*). What's that!

GINA. Uff, now they're shooting again.

GREGERS. They shoot, also?

HEDVIG. They go hunting.

GREGERS. What! (*Going to the loft doorway.*) Have you gone hunting, Hjalmar?

HJALMAR (*behind the net*). Are you here? I didn't realize; I was so occupied— (*To* HEDVIG.) And you, you didn't tell us. (*Comes into the studio.*)

GREGERS. Do you go shooting in the loft?

HJALMAR (*producing a double-barreled pistol*). Oh, only with this here.

GINA. Yes, some day you and Grandfather'll have an accident with that there gun.

HJALMAR (*annoyed*). I believe I've remarked that this type of firearm is called a pistol.

GINA. I don't see that that makes it any better.

GREGERS. So you've turned out a "hunter" as well. Hjalmar?

HJALMAR. Just a little rabbit hunt, now and then. It's mainly for Father's sake, you understand.

GINA. Men are so funny, really; they've always got to have their little diversities.

HJALMAR (*angrily*). That's right, yes—they always have to have their little diversions.

GINA. Yes, that's just what I was saying.

HJALMAR. Oh, well! (*To* GREGERS.) So that's it, and then we're very lucky in the way the loft is placed—nobody can hear us when we're shooting. (*Puts the pistol on the highest bookshelf.*) Don't touch the pistol, Hedvig! One barrel's still loaded, don't forget.

GREGERS (*peering through the netting*). You've got a hunting rifle too, I see.

HJALMAR. Yes, that's Father's old rifle. It won't shoot anymore; something's gone wrong with the lock. But it's a lot of fun to have anyway, because we can take it all apart and clean it and grease it and put it together again— Of course, it's mostly Father who fools around with that sort of thing.

HEDVIG (*crossing to* GREGERS). Now you can really see the wild duck.

GREGERS. I was just now looking at her. She seems to drag one wing a little.

HJALMAR. Well, no wonder; she took a bad wound.

GREGERS. And then she limps a little. Isn't that so?

HJALMAR. Maybe just a tiny bit.

HEDVIG. Yes, that was the foot the dog bit her in.

HJALMAR. But she hasn't a thing wrong with her otherwise; and that's simply remarkable when you think that she's had a charge of shot in her body and been held by the teeth of a dog—

GREGERS (*with a glance at* HEDVIG). And been in the depths of the sea—so long.

HEDVIG (*smiling*). Yes.

GINA (*arranging the table*). Oh, that sacred duck—there's been crucifixes enough made for her.

HJALMAR. Hm. Are you nearly ready?

GINA. Yes, right away. Hedvig, now you can come and help me.

(GINA *and* HEDVIG *exit into the kitchen.*)

HJALMAR (*in an undertone*). I don't think it's so good that you stand there, watching my father. He doesn't like it. (GREGERS *comes away from the loft doorway.*) And it's better, too, that I close up before the others come. (*Shooing away the menagerie with his hands.*) Hssh! Hssh! Go 'way now! (*With this he raises the curtain and draws the double doors together.*) I invented these contraptions myself. It's really great fun to have such things around to take care of and fix when they get out of whack. And besides, it's absolutely necessary, you know; Gina doesn't go for rabbits and chickens out here in the studio.

GREGERS. Of course not. And I suppose it *is* your wife who manages here?

HJALMAR. My general rule is to delegate the routine matters to her, and that leaves me free to retire to the living room to think over more important things.

GREGERS. And what sort of things are these, Hjalmar?

HJALMAR. I've been wondering why you haven't asked me that before. Or maybe you haven't heard about my invention.

GREGERS. Invention? No.

HJALMAR. Oh? Then you haven't? Well, no, up there in that waste and wilderness—

GREGERS. Then you've really invented something!

HJALMAR. Not completely invented it yet, but I'm getting very close. You must realize that when I decided to dedicate my life to photography, it wasn't my idea to spend time taking pictures of a lot of nobodies.

GREGERS. Yes, that's what your wife was just now saying.

HJALMAR. I swore that if I devoted my powers to the craft, I would then exalt it to such heights that it would become both an art and a science. That's when I decided on this amazing invention.

GREGERS. And what does this invention consist of? What's its purpose?

HJALMAR. Yes, Gregers, you mustn't ask for details like that yet. It takes time, you know. And you mustn't think it's vanity that's driving me, either. I'm certainly not working for myself. Oh no, it's my life's mission that stands before me day and night.

GREGERS. What life's mission is that?

HJALMAR. Remember the silver-haired old man?

GREGERS. Your poor father. Yes, but actually what can you do for him?

HJALMAR. I can raise his self-respect from the dead—by restoring the Ekdal name to dignity and honor.

GREGERS. So that's your life's work.

HJALMAR. Yes. I am going to rescue that shipwrecked man. That's just what he suffered—shipwreck—when the storm broke over him. When all those harrowing investigations took place, he wasn't himself anymore. That pistol, there—the one we use to shoot rabbits with—it's played a part in the tragedy of the Ekdals.

GREGERS. Pistol! Oh?

HJALMAR. When he was sentenced and facing prison, he had that pistol in his hand—

GREGERS. You mean he—!

HJALMAR. Yes. But he didn't dare. He was a coward. That shows how broken and degraded he'd become by then. Can you picture it? He, a soldier, a man who'd shot nine bears and was directly descended from two lieutenant colonels—I mean, one after the other, of course. Can you picture it, Gregers?

GREGERS. Yes, I can picture it very well.

HJALMAR. Well, I can't. And then that pistol intruded on our family history once again. When he was under lock and key, dressed like a common prisoner—oh, those were agonizing times for me, you can imagine. I kept the shades of both my windows drawn. When I looked out, I saw the sun shining the same as ever. I couldn't understand it. I saw the people going along the street, laughing and talking of trivial things. I couldn't understand it. I felt all creation should be standing still, like during an eclipse.

GREGERS. I felt that way when my mother died.

HJALMAR. During one of those times Hjalmar Ekdal put a pistol to his own breast.

GREGERS. You were thinking of—

HJALMAR. Yes.

GREGERS. But you didn't shoot?

HJALMAR. No. In that critical moment I won a victory

over myself. I stayed alive. But you can bet it takes courage to choose life in those circumstances.

GREGERS. Well, that depends on your point of view.

HJALMAR. Oh, absolutely. But it was all for the best, because now I've nearly finished my invention; and then Dr. Relling thinks, just as I do, that they'll let Father wear his uniform again. I want only that one reward.

GREGERS. So it's really the uniform that he——?

HJALMAR. Yes, that's what he really hungers and craves for. You've no idea how that makes my heart ache. Every time we throw a little family party—like my birthday, or Gina's, or whatever—then the old man comes in, wearing that uniform from his happier days. But if there's even a knock at the door, he goes scuttering back in his room fast as the old legs will carry him. You see, he doesn't dare show himself to strangers. What a heartrending spectacle for a son!

GREGERS. Approximately when do you think the invention will be finished?

HJALMAR. Oh, good Lord, don't hold me to a timetable. An invention, that's something you can hardly dictate to. It depends a great deal on inspiration, on a sudden insight—and it's nearly impossible to say in advance when that will occur.

GREGERS. But it *is* making progress?

HJALMAR. Of course it's making progress. Every single day I think about my invention. I'm brimming with it. Every afternoon, right after lunch, I lock myself in the living room where I can meditate in peace. But it's no use driving me; it simply won't work. Relling says so too.

GREGERS. And you don't think all those contraptions in the loft distract you and scatter your talents?

HJALMAR. No, no, no, on the contrary. You mustn't say that. I can't always go around here, brooding over the same nerve-racking problems. I need some diversion to fill in the time. You see, inspiration, the moment of insight—when that comes, nothing can stop it.

GREGERS. My dear Hjalmar, I suspect you've got a bit of the wild duck in you.

HJALMAR. Of the wild duck? What do you mean?

GREGERS. You've plunged to the bottom and clamped hold of the seaweed.

HJALMAR. I suppose you mean that near-fatal shot that brought down Father—and me as well?

GREGERS. Not quite that. I wouldn't say you're wounded; but you're wandering in a poisonous swamp, Hjalmar. You've got an insidious disease in your system, and so you've gone to the bottom to die in the dark.

HJALMAR. Me? Die in the dark! You know what, Gregers —you'll really have to stop that talk.

GREGERS. But never mind. I'm going to raise you up again. You know, I've found my mission in life, too. I found it yesterday.

HJALMAR. Yes, that may well be; but you can just leave me out of it. I can assure you that—apart from my quite understandable melancholy—I'm as well off as any man could wish to be.

GREGERS. And your thinking so is part of the sickness.

HJALMAR. Gregers, you're my old friend—please—don't talk any more about sickness and poison. I'm not used to that kind of conversation. In my house nobody talks to me about ugly things.

GREGERS. That's not hard to believe.

HJALMAR. Yes, because it isn't good for me. And there's no swamp air here, as you put it. In a poor photographer's house, life is cramped; I know that. My lot is a poor one—but, you know, I'm an inventor. And I'm the family breadwinner, too. *That's* what sustains me through all the pettiness. Ah, here they come with the lunch.

> (GINA *and* HEDVIG *bring in bottles of beer, a decanter of brandy, glasses, and the like. At the same time,* RELLING *and* MOLVIK *enter from the hall. Neither wears a hat or overcoat;* MOLVIK *is dressed in black.*)

GINA (*setting things down on the table*). Well, the two of them—right on time.

RELLING. Molvik was positive he could smell that herring salad, and there was just no holding him back. 'Morning for the second time, Ekdal.

HJALMAR. Gregers, I'd like you to meet Mr. Molvik. And Dr.—ah, but don't you know Relling?

GREGERS. Yes, slightly.

RELLING. Well, Mr. Werle junior. Yes, we've had a few

run-ins together up at the Hoidal works. You've just moved in, haven't you?

GREGERS. I moved in this morning.

RELLING. And Molvik and I live downstairs; so you're not very far from a doctor and a priest, if you ever have need of such.

GREGERS. Thanks; that could happen. After all, we had thirteen at the table last night.

HJALMAR. Oh, don't start in on ugly subjects again!

RELLING. You don't have to worry, Hjalmar; Lord knows this doesn't involve you.

HJALMAR. I hope not, for my family's sake. But let's sit down and eat and drink and be merry.

GREGERS. Shouldn't we wait for your father?

HJALMAR. No, he'll have his lunch sent in to him later. Come now!

> (*The men sit at the table, eating and drinking.* GINA *and* HEDVIG *go in and out, serving the food.*)

RELLING. Last night Molvik was tight as a tick, Mrs. Ekdal.

GINA. Oh? Last night again?

RELLING. Didn't you hear him when I finally brought him home?

GINA. No, can't say I did.

RELLING. That's lucky—because Molvik was revolting last night.

GINA. Is that so, Molvik?

MOLVIK. Let's draw a veil over last night's activities. They have no bearing on my better self.

RELLING (*to* GREGERS). All of a sudden he's possessed by an impulse; and then I have to take him out on a bat. You see, Mr. Molvik is demonic.

GREGERS. Demonic?

RELLING. Molvik is demonic, yes.

GREGERS. Hm.

RELLING. And demonic natures aren't made to go through life on the straight and narrow; they've got to take detours every so often. Well—and you're still sticking it out there at that dark, hideous mill.

GREGERS. I've stuck it out till now.

RELLING. And did you ever serve that "summons" you were going around with?

GREGERS. Summons? (*Understanding him.*) Oh, that.

HJALMAR. Were you serving summonses, Gregers?

GREGERS. Nonsense.

RELLING. Oh, but he was, definitely. He went around to all the cotters' cabins and tendered something he called "Summons to the Ideal."

GREGERS. I was young then.

RELLING. You're right, there. You were very young. And that summons to the ideal—it wasn't ever honored during my time up there.

GREGERS. Nor later, either.

RELLING. Well, I guess you've learned enough to cut down your expectations a bit.

GREGERS. Never—when I meet a man who's a real man.

HJALMAR. Yes, that seems quite reasonable to me. A little butter, Gina.

RELLING. And then a piece of pork for Molvik.

MOLVIK. Ugh, no pork!

(*There is a knock on the loft door.*)

HJALMAR. Open it, Hedvig; Father wants to get out.

(HEDVIG *goes to open the door a little; old* EKDAL *enters with a fresh rabbit skin. He closes the door after him.*)

EKDAL. Good morning, gentlemen. Good hunting today. Shot a big one.

HJALMAR. And you went ahead and skinned it without waiting for me!

EKDAL. Salted it, too. It's nice tender meat, this rabbit meat. And it's so sweet. Tastes like sugar. Enjoy your food, gentlemen! (*He goes into his room.*)

MOLVIK (*getting up*). Pardon—I, I can't—got to go downstairs right—

RELLING. Drink soda water, man!

MOLVIK (*rushing out the hall door*). Ugh—ugh!

RELLING (*to* HJALMAR). Let's empty a glass to the old hunter.

HJALMAR (*clinking glasses with him*). Yes, to the gallant sportsman on the brink of the grave.

RELLING. To the old, gray-haired—(*Drinks.*) Tell me something, is it gray hair he's got, or is it white?

HJALMAR. It's really a little of both. But as a matter of fact, he's scarcely got a hair on his head.

RELLING. Well, fake hair will take you through life, good as any. You know, Ekdal, you're really a very lucky man. You have your high mission in life to fight for—

HJALMAR. And I am fighting for it, too.

RELLING. And then you've got this clever wife of yours, padding around in her slippers and waggling her hips and keeping you neat and cozy.

HJALMAR. Yes, Gina—(*Nodding at her.*) you're a good companion for life's journey, you are.

GINA. Oh, don't sit there deprecating me.

RELLING. And what about your Hedvig, Ekdal?

HJALMAR (*stirred*). My child, yes! My child above all. Hedvig, come here to me. (*Caresses her head.*) What day is tomorrow, dear?

HEDVIG (*shaking him*). Oh, don't talk about it, Daddy!

HJALMAR. It's like a knife turning in my heart when I think how bare it's all going to be, just the tiniest celebration out in the loft—

HEDVIG. Oh, but that will be just wonderful!

RELLING. And wait till that marvelous invention comes to the world, Hedvig!

HJALMAR. Ah, yes—then you'll see! Hedvig, I've resolved to make your future secure. As long as you live, you'll live in style. I'll assure you of something, one way or another. That will be the poor inventor's sole reward.

HEDVIG (*whispering, with her arms around his neck*). Oh, you dear, dear Daddy!

RELLING (*to* GREGERS). Well, now, isn't it good for a change to be sitting around a well-spread table in a happy family circle?

HJALMAR. Yes, I really prize these hours around the table.

GREGERS. I, for my part, don't thrive in marsh gas.

RELLING. Marsh gas?

HJALMAR. Oh, don't start that rubbish again!

GINA. Lord knows there isn't any marsh gas here, Mr. Werle; every blessed day I air the place out.

GREGERS (*leaving the table*). You can't air out the stench I mean.

HJALMAR. Stench!

GINA. What about that, Hjalmar!

RELLING. Beg pardon—but it wouldn't be you who brought that stench in with you from the mines up there?

GREGERS. It's just like you to call what I'm bringing into this house a stench.

RELLING (*crossing over to him*). Listen, Mr. Werle junior, I've got a strong suspicion that you're still going around with the uncut version of that "Summons to the Ideal" in your back pocket.

GREGERS. I've got it written in my heart.

RELLING. I don't care where the devil you've got it; I wouldn't advise you to play process-server here as long as I'm around.

GREGERS. And what if I do anyway?

RELLING. Then you'll go head first down the stairs, that's what.

HJALMAR (*getting up*). Come, now, Relling!

GREGERS. Yes, just throw me out—

GINA (*coming between them*). You can't do that, Relling. But I'll tell you this, Mr. Werle—that you, who made all that mess with your stove, have no right to come to me talking about smells.

(*A knock at the hall door.*)

HEDVIG. Mother, somebody's knocking.

HJALMAR. Wouldn't you know, it's open house!

GINA. I'll go— (*She crosses and opens the door, gives a start, shudders and shrinks back.*) Uff! Oh no!

(*Old* WERLE, *in a fur coat, steps into the room.*)

WERLE. Excuse me, but I think my son is living in this house.

GINA (*catching her breath*). Yes.

HJALMAR (*coming closer*). If Mr. Werle will be so good as to—

WERLE. Thanks, I'd just like to talk with my son.

GREGERS. Yes, why not? Here I am.

WERLE. I'd like to talk with you in your room.

GREGERS. In my room—fine—(*Starts in.*)

GINA. No. Good Lord, that's in no condition for—

WERLE. Well, out in the hall, then. This is just between us.

HJALMAR. You can talk here, Mr. Werle. Come into the living room, Relling.

(HJALMAR *and* RELLING *go out to the right;*
GINA *takes* HEDVIG *with her into the kitchen.*)

GREGERS (*after a brief interval*). Well, now it's just the two of us.

WERLE. You dropped a few remarks last night— And since you've now taken a room with the Ekdals, I must assume that you're planning something or other against me.

GREGERS. I'm planning to open Hjalmar Ekdal's eyes. He's going to see his situation just as it is—that's all.

WERLE. Is *that* the mission in life you talked about yesterday?

GREGERS. Yes. You haven't left me any other.

WERLE. Am I the one that spoiled your mind, Gregers?

GREGERS. You've spoiled my entire life. I'm not thinking of all that with Mother. But you're the one I can thank for my going around, whipped and driven by this guilt-ridden conscience.

WERLE. Ah, it's your conscience that's gone bad.

GREGERS. I should have taken a stand against you when the trap was laid for Lieutenant Ekdal. I should have warned him, for I had a pretty good idea what was coming off.

WERLE. Yes, you really should have spoken up then.

GREGERS. I didn't dare; I was so cowed and frightened. I was unspeakably afraid of you—both then and for a long time after.

WERLE. That fright seems to be over now.

GREGERS. It is, luckily. The harm done to old Ekdal, both by me and—others, can never be undone; but Hjalmar I can free from all the lies and evasions that are smothering him here.

WERLE. You believe you'd be doing him good by that?

GREGERS. That's what I believe.

WERLE.   Maybe you think Ekdal's the kind of man who'll thank you for that friendly service?

GREGERS.   Yes! He *is* that kind of man.

WERLE.   Hmm—we'll see.

GREGERS.   And besides—if I'm ever to go on living, I'll have to find a cure for my sick conscience.

WERLE.   It'll never be sound. Your conscience has been sickly from childhood. It's an inheritance from your mother, Gregers—the only inheritance she left you.

GREGERS (*with a wry half-smile*).   You've never been able to accept the fact, have you, that you calculated wrong when you thought she'd bring you a fortune?

WERLE.   Let's not get lost in irrelevancies. Then you're still intent on this goal of putting Ekdal on what you suppose is the right track?

GREGERS.   Yes, I'm intent on that.

WERLE.   Well, then I could have saved myself the walk up here. For there's no point in asking if you'll move back home with me?

GREGERS.   No.

WERLE.   And you won't come into the business either?

GREGERS.   No.

WERLE.   Very well. But since I'm now planning a second marriage, the estate, of course, will be divided between us.

GREGERS (*quickly*).   No, I don't want that.

WERLE.   You don't want it?

GREGERS.   No, I wouldn't dare, for the sake of my conscience.

WERLE (*after a pause*).   You going back to the works again?

GREGERS.   No. I consider that I've retired from your service.

WERLE.   But what are you going to do, then?

GREGERS.   Simply carry out my life's mission; nothing else.

WERLE.   Yes, but afterwards? What will you live on?

GREGERS.   I have some of my salary put aside.

WERLE.   Yes, that won't last long!

GREGERS.   I think it will last my time.

WERLE.   What do you mean by that?

GREGERS.   I'm not answering any more.

WERLE. Good-bye then, Gregers.

GREGERS. Good-bye.

(*Old* WERLE *goes out.*)

HJALMAR (*peering out*). Has he gone?

GREGERS. Yes.

(HJALMAR *and* RELLING *come in.* GINA *and* HEDVIG
also return from the kitchen.)

RELLING. There's one lunch gone to the dogs.

GREGERS. Put your things on, Hjalmar; you've got to take
a long walk with me.

HJALMAR. Yes, gladly. What did your father want? Was it
anything to do with me?

GREGERS. Just come. We have some things to talk over.
I'll go and get my coat. (*He leaves by the hall door.*)

GINA. You mustn't go out with him, Hjalmar.

RELLING. No, don't go. Stay where you are.

HJALMAR (*getting his hat and overcoat*). But why? When
a childhood friend feels a need to open his mind to me in
private—

RELLING. But damn it all! Can't you see the man's mad,
crazy, out of his skull!

GINA. Yes, that's the truth, if you'd listen. His mother, off
and on, had those same conniption fits.

HJALMAR. That's just why he needs a friend's watchful
eye on him. (*To* GINA.) Be sure dinner's ready in plenty of
time. See you later. (*Goes out the hall door.*)

RELLING. It's really a shame that fellow didn't go straight
to hell down one of the Hoidal mines.

GINA. Mercy—why do you say that?

RELLING (*muttering*). Oh, I've got my reasons.

GINA. Do you think Gregers Werle is really crazy?

RELLING. No, worse luck. He's no crazier than most people. But he's got a disease in his system all the same.

GINA. What is it that's wrong with him?

RELLING. All right, I'll tell you, Mrs. Ekdal. He's suffering from an acute case of moralistic fever.

GINA. Moralistic fever?

HEDVIG. Is that a kind of disease?

RELLING. Oh yes, it's a national disease, but it only

breaks out now and then. (*Nodding to* GINA.) Thanks for lunch. (*He goes out through the hall door.*)

GINA (*walking restlessly around the room*). Ugh, that Gregers Werle—he was always a cold fish.

HEDVIG (*standing by the table, looking searchingly at her*). This is all so strange to me.

⸺⟨ ACT FOUR ⟩⸺

HJALMAR EKDAL's *studio. A photograph has just been taken; a portrait camera covered with a cloth, a stand, a couple of chairs, a console table, among other things, stand well out in the room. Late afternoon light; it is near sunset; somewhat later it begins to grow dark.*

GINA *is standing in the hall doorway with a plate-holder and a wet photographic plate in her hand, talking with someone outside.*

GINA. Yes, that's definite. When I promise something, I keep my word. On Monday the first dozen will be ready. Good-bye. Good-bye. (*Footsteps are heard descending the stairs.* GINA *closes the door, puts the plate into the holder, and slips both back into the covered camera.*)

HEDVIG (*coming in from the kitchen*). Are they gone?

GINA (*tidying up*). Yes, thank goodness, at last I'm rid of them.

HEDVIG. But why do you suppose Daddy isn't home yet?

GINA. Are you sure he's not below with Relling?

HEDVIG. No, he's not there. I ran down the back stairs just now and asked.

GINA. And his dinner's standing and getting cold, too.

HEDVIG. Just imagine—Daddy's always sure to be on time for dinner.

GINA. Oh, he'll be right along, you'll see.

HEDVIG. Oh, I wish he would come! Everything's so funny around here.

GINA (*calling out*). There he is!

(HJALMAR *comes in by the hall door.*)

HEDVIG (*running toward him*). Daddy! Oh, we've waited ages for you!

GINA (*eyeing him*). You've been out pretty long, Hjalmar.

HJALMAR (*without looking at her*). I've been a while, yes.

(*He takes off his overcoat.* GINA *and* HEDVIG *start to help him; he waves them away.*)

GINA.   Did you eat with Werle, maybe?

HJALMAR (*hanging his coat up*).   No.

GINA (*going toward the kitchen*).   I'll bring your dinner in, then.

HJALMAR.   No, the dinner can wait. I don't want to eat now.

HEDVIG (*coming closer*).   Don't you feel well, Daddy?

HJALMAR.   Well? Oh yes, well enough. We had an exhausting walk, Gregers and I.

GINA.   You shouldn't do that, Hjalmar; you're not used to it.

HJALMAR.   Hm. There are a lot of things a man's got to get used to in this world. (*Walking about the room a bit.*) Did anyone come while I was out?

GINA.   No one but that engaged couple.

HJALMAR.   No new orders?

GINA.   No, not today.

HEDVIG.   You'll see, there'll be some tomorrow, Daddy.

HJALMAR.   I certainly hope so, because tomorrow I'm going to throw myself into my work—completely.

HEDVIG.   Tomorrow! But don't you remember what day tomorrow is?

HJALMAR.   Oh yes, that's right. Well, the day after tomorrow, then. From now on, I'm doing everything myself; I just want to be left alone with all the work.

GINA.   But Hjalmar, what's the point of that? It'll only make your life miserable. Let me handle the photographing, and then you'll be free to work on the invention.

HEDVIG.   And free for the wild duck, Daddy—and for all the chickens and rabbits—

HJALMAR.   Don't talk to me about that rubbish! Starting tomorrow I shall never again set foot in that loft.

HEDVIG.   Yes, but Daddy, you promised me tomorrow there'd be a celebration.

HJALMAR.   Hm, that's true. Well, the day after, then. That infernal wild duck—I'd almost like to wring its neck!

HEDVIG (*crying out*).   The wild duck!

GINA.   What an idea!

HEDVIG (*shaking him*).   Yes, but Daddy—it's my wild duck!

HJALMAR. That's why I won't do it. I haven't the heart—for your sake, Hedvig, I haven't the heart. But deep inside me I feel I ought to. I shouldn't tolerate under my roof a creature that's been in that man's hands.

GINA. My goodness, just because Grandfather got her from that worthless Pettersen—

HJALMAR (*pacing the floor*). There are certain claims—what should I call them—ideal claims, let's say—a kind of summons that a man can't put aside without damaging his soul.

HEDVIG (*following him*). But think—the wild duck—the poor wild duck!

HJALMAR (*stopping*). You heard me say I'd spare it—for your sake. It won't be hurt, not a hair on its—well, anyway, I'll spare it. After all, there are greater missions than that to take on. But now, Hedvig, you ought to go out for your walk; the light's about right for your eyes.

HEDVIG. No, I don't want to go out now.

HJALMAR. Yes, go on. You seem to be blinking your eyes so. All these fumes in here aren't good for you; the air here under this roof is bad.

HEDVIG. All right, then, I'll run down the back stairs and take a little walk. My coat and hat? Oh, they're in my room. Daddy—promise you won't hurt the wild duck while I'm out.

HJALMAR. There won't be a feather ruffled on its head. (*Drawing her to him.*) You and I, Hedvig—we two! Now run along, dear.

(HEDVIG *nods to her parents and goes out through the kitchen.*)

HJALMAR (*walking around without looking up*). Gina.

GINA. Yes?

HJALMAR. From tomorrow on—or let's say the day after tomorrow—I'd prefer to keep the household accounts myself.

GINA. You want to keep the household accounts, too?

HJALMAR. Yes, or budget the income, in any case.

GINA. Lord love us, there's nothing to that.

HJALMAR. One wouldn't think so. It seems to me you can make our money stretch remarkably far. (*Stopping and looking at her.*) How *is* that?

GINA. Hedvig and I, we don't need much.

HJALMAR. Is it true that Father gets such good pay for the copying he does for Werle?

GINA. I don't know how good it is. I don't know rates for such things.

HJALMAR. Well, what does he get, just roughly? Tell me!

GINA. It's never the same. I suppose it's roughly what he costs us, with a little pocket money thrown in.

HJALMAR. What he costs us! That's something you've never told me before!

GINA. No, I never could. You were always so happy thinking he got everything from you.

HJALMAR. And instead it comes from Mr. Werle.

GINA. Oh, but he's got plenty to spare, that one.

HJALMAR. Let's have the lamp lit!

GINA (*lighting it*). And then we can't know if it really is the old man; it could well be Graaberg—

HJALMAR. Why try to put me off with Graaberg?

GINA. No, I don't know. I just thought—

HJALMAR. Hm!

GINA. You know it wasn't me that got Grandfather the copying. It was Berta, that time she came here.

HJALMAR. Your voice sounds so shaky.

GINA (*putting the shade on the lamp*). It does?

HJALMAR. And then your hands are trembling. Or aren't they?

GINA (*firmly*). Say it straight out, Hjalmar. What is it he's gone and said about me?

HJALMAR. Is it true—can it possibly be that—that there was some kind of involvement between you and Mr. Werle while you were in service there?

GINA. That's not true. Not then, there wasn't. Werle was after me, all right. And his wife thought there was something to it, and she made a big fuss and bother, and she roasted me coming and going, she did—so I quit.

HJALMAR. But then what!

GINA. Yes, so then I went home. And Mother—well, she wasn't all you took her to be, Hjalmar; she ran on telling me one thing and another, because Werle was a widower by then.

HJALMAR. Yes. And then!

GINA. Well, you might as well know it all. He didn't give up till he had his way.

HJALMAR (*with a clap of his hands*). And this is the mother of my child! How could you keep that hidden from me!

GINA. Yes, I did the wrong thing; I really should have told you long ago.

HJALMAR. Right at the start, you mean—so I could have known what sort you are.

GINA. But would you have married me anyway?

HJALMAR. How can you think that?

GINA. No. But that's why I didn't dare say anything then. Because I'd come to be so terribly in love with you, as you know. And then how could I make myself utterly miserable—

HJALMAR (*walking about*). And this is my Hedvig's mother! And then to know that everything I see around me—(*Kicking at a table.*) my whole home—I owe to a favored predecessor. Ah, that charmer Werle!

GINA. Do you regret the fourteen, fifteen years we've lived together?

HJALMAR (*stopping in front of her*). Tell me—don't you every day, every hour, regret this spider web of deception you've spun around me? Answer me that! Don't you really go around in a torment of remorse?

GINA. Hjalmar dear, I've got so much to think about just with the housework and the day's routine—

HJALMAR. Then you never turn a critical eye on your past!

GINA. No. Good Lord, I'd almost forgotten that old affair.

HJALMAR. Oh, this dull, unfeeling content! To me there's something outrageous about it. Just think—not one regret!

GINA. But Hjalmar, tell me now—what would have happened to you if you hadn't found a wife like me?

HJALMAR. Like you—!

GINA. Yes, because I've always been a bit more hardheaded and resourceful than you. Well, of course I'm a couple of years older.

HJALMAR. What would have happened to me?

GINA. You were pretty bad off at the time you met me; you can't deny that.

HJALMAR. "Pretty bad off" you call it. Oh, you have no idea what a man goes through when he's deep in misery and despair—especially a man of my fiery temperament.

GINA. No, that may be. And I shouldn't say nothing about it, either, because you turned out such a good-hearted husband as soon as you got a house and home—and now we've made it so snug and cozy here, and pretty soon both Hedvig and I could begin spending a little on food and clothes.

HJALMAR. In the swamp of deception, yes.

GINA. Ugh, that disgusting creature, tracking his way through our house!

HJALMAR. I also thought this home was a good place to be. That was a pipe dream. Now where can I find the buoyancy I need to carry my invention into reality? Maybe it'll die with me; and then it'll be your past, Gina, that killed it.

GINA (*close to tears*). No, you mustn't ever say such things, Hjalmar. All my days I've only wanted to do what's best for you!

HJALMAR. I wonder—what happens now to the breadwinner's dream? When I lay in there on the sofa pondering my invention, I had a hunch it would drain my last bit of strength. I sensed that the day I took the patent in my hand— that would be the day of—departure. And it was my dream that then *you* would go on as the departed inventor's prosperous widow.

GINA (*drying her eyes*). No, don't say that, Hjalmar. Lord knows I never want to see the day I'm a widow.

HJALMAR. Oh, what does it matter? Everything's over and done with now. Everything!

     (GREGERS *cautiously opens the hall door and looks
        in.*)

GREGERS. May I come in?

HJALMAR. Yes, do.

GREGERS (*advancing with a beaming countenance, hands outstretched as if to take theirs*). Now, you dear people—! (*Looks from one to the other, then whispers to* HJALMAR.) But isn't it done, then?

HJALMAR (*resoundingly*). It's done.

GREGERS. It is?

HJALMAR. I've just known the bitterest hour of my life.

GREGERS. But also the most exalted, I think.

HJALMAR. Well, anyway, it's off our hands for the moment.

GINA. God forgive you, Mr. Werle.

GREGERS (*with great surprise*). But I don't understand this.

HJALMAR. What don't you understand?

GREGERS. With this great rapport—the kind that forges a whole new way of life—a life, a companionship in truth with no more deception—

HJALMAR. Yes, I know, I know all that.

GREGERS. I was really positive that when I came through that door I'd be met by a transfigured light in both your faces. And what do I see instead but this gloomy, heavy, dismal—

GINA. How true. (*She removes the lampshade.*)

GREGERS. You don't want to understand me, Mrs. Ekdal. No, no, you'll need time— But you yourself, Hjalmar? You must have gained a sense of high purpose out of this great unburdening.

HJALMAR. Yes, naturally. That is—more or less.

GREGERS. Because there's nothing in the world that compares with showing mercy to a sinner and lifting her up in the arms of love.

HJALMAR. Do you think a man can recover so easily from the bitter cup I've just emptied!

GREGERS. Not an ordinary man, no. But a man like you—!

HJALMAR. Good Lord, yes, I know that. But you mustn't be driving me, Gregers. You see, these things take time.

GREGERS. You've *lots* of the wild duck in you, Hjalmar.

(RELLING *has entered through the hall door.*)

RELLING. Aha! The wild duck's flying again, eh?

HJALMAR. Yes, the wounded trophy of old Werle's hunt.

RELLING. Old Werle? Is it him you're talking about?

HJALMAR. Him and—all of us.

RELLING (*under his breath to* GREGERS). The devil take you!

HJALMAR. What'd you say?

RELLING. I merely expressed my heartfelt desire that this quack would cut out for home. If he stays here, he's just the man to ruin you both.

GREGERS. They won't be ruined, Mr. Relling. Regarding Hjalmar, I'll say nothing. We know him. But she, too, surely, in the depths of her being, has something authentic, something sincere.

GINA (*near tears*). Well, if I *was* that, why didn't you leave me alone?

RELLING (*to* GREGERS). Would it be nosy to ask what you're really trying to do in this house?

GREGERS. I want to establish a true marriage.

RELLING. Then you don't think Ekdal's marriage is good enough as it is?

GREGERS. It's about as good a marriage as most, unfortunately. But it isn't yet a *true* marriage.

HJALMAR. You don't believe in ideals in life, Relling.

RELLING. Nonsense, sonny boy! Excuse me, Mr. Werle, but how many—in round numbers—how many "true marriages" have you seen in your time?

GREGERS. I believe I've hardly seen a single one.

RELLING. And I likewise.

GREGERS. But I've seen innumerable marriages of the opposite kind. And I've had a chance to see at close range what such a marriage can destroy in two people.

HJALMAR. A man's whole moral foundation can crumble under his feet; that's the dreadful thing.

RELLING. Well, I've never really exactly been married, so I'm no judge of these things. But I do know this, that the child is part of the marriage too. And you've got to leave the child in peace.

HJALMAR. Ah, Hedvig! My poor Hedvig!

RELLING. Yes, you'll please see that Hedvig's left out of it. You're both grown people; you're free, God knows, to slop up your private lives all you want. But I tell you, you've got to be careful with Hedvig, or else you might do her some serious harm.

HJALMAR. Harm!

RELLING. Yes, or she could do harm to herself—and possibly others as well.

GINA. But how can you know that, Relling?

HJALMAR. There's no immediate threat to her eyes, is there?

RELLING. This has nothing to do with her eyes. Hedvig's arrived at a difficult age. She's open to all kinds of erratic ideas.

GINA. You know—she is at that! She's begun to fool around something awful with the fire in the kitchen stove.

She calls it playing house afire. I'm often scared she *will* set the house on fire.

RELLING.   See what I mean? I knew it.

GREGERS (*to* RELLING).   But how do you explain something like that?

RELLING (*brusquely*).   Her voice is changing, junior.

HJALMAR.   As long as the child has *me*! As long as I'm above the sod.

(*A knock is heard at the door.*)

GINA.   Shh, Hjalmar, someone's in the hall. (*Calling out.*) Come on in!

(MRS. SØRBY, *wearing street clothes, enters.*)

MRS. SØRBY.   Good evening!

GINA (*going toward her*).   Is it you, Berta!

MRS. SØRBY.   Oh yes, it's me. But perhaps I came at an awkward time?

HJALMAR.   Oh, not at all; a messenger from *that* house—

MRS. SØRBY (*to* GINA).   As a matter of fact, I'd hoped that I wouldn't find your menfolk in at this hour, so I ran over just to have a word with you and say good-bye.

GINA.   Oh? Are you going away?

MRS. SØRBY.   Yes, tomorrow, early—up to Hoidal. Mr. Werle left this afternoon. (*Casually to* GREGERS.) He sends his regards.

GINA.   Just think!

HJALMAR.   So Mr. Werle has left? And you're following him?

MRS. SØRBY.   Yes, what do you say to that, Ekdal?

HJALMAR.   I say watch out.

GREGERS.   Let me explain. My father is marrying Mrs. Sørby.

HJALMAR.   He's marrying her!

GINA.   Oh, Berta, it's come at last!

RELLING (*his voice quavering slightly*).   This really can't be true.

MRS. SØRBY.   Yes, my dear Relling, it's completely true.

RELLING.   You want to marry again?

MRS. SØRBY.   Yes, so it seems. Werle has gotten a special license, and we're going to have a very quiet wedding up at the works.

GREGERS. So I ought to wish you happiness, like a good stepson.

MRS. SØRBY. Thank you, if you really mean it. I'm hoping it will bring us happiness, both Werle and me.

RELLING. That's a reasonable hope. Mr. Werle never gets drunk—as far as *I* know; and he's certainly not given to beating up his wives the way the late horse doctor did.

MRS. SØRBY. Oh, now let Sørby rest in peace. He did have some worthy traits, you know.

RELLING. Old Werle's traits are worth rather more, I'll bet.

MRS. SØRBY. At least he hasn't wasted the best that's in him. Any man who does *that* has to take the consequences.

RELLING. Tonight I'm going out with Molvik.

MRS. SØRBY. You shouldn't, Relling. Don't do it—for my sake.

RELLING. What else is left? (*To* HJALMAR.) If you'd care to, you could come too.

GINA. No, thanks. Hjalmar never goes dissipating.

HJALMAR (*in an angry undertone*). Can't you keep quiet!

RELLING. Good-bye, Mrs.—Werle. (*He goes out the hall door.*)

GREGERS (*to* MRS. SØRBY). It would seem that you and Dr. Relling know each other quite intimately.

MRS. SØRBY. Yes, we've known each other for many years. At one time something might have developed between us.

GREGERS. It was certainly lucky for you that it didn't.

MRS. SØRBY. Yes, that's true enough. But I've always been wary of following my impulses. After all, a woman can't just throw herself away.

GREGERS. Aren't you even a little bit afraid that I'll drop my father a hint about this old friendship?

MRS. SØRBY. You can be sure I've told him myself.

GREGERS. Oh?

MRS. SØRBY. Your father knows every last scrap of gossip that holds any grain of truth about me. I told him all of those things; it was the first thing I did when he made his intentions clear.

GREGERS. Then I think you're more frank than most people.

MRS. SØRBY. I've always been frank. In the long run, it's the best thing for us women to be.

HJALMAR. What do you say to that, Gina?

GINA. Oh, women are all so different. Some live one way and some live another.

MRS. SØRBY. Well, Gina, I do think it's wisest to handle things as I have. And Werle, for his part, hasn't held back anything either. Really, it's this that's brought us so close together. Now he can sit and talk to me as freely as a child. He's never had that chance before. He, a healthy, vigorous man, had to spend his whole youth and all his best years hearing nothing but sermons on his sins. And generally those sermons were aimed at the most imaginary failings—at least from what *I* could see.

GINA. Yes, that's just as true as you say.

GREGERS. If you women are going to explore this subject, I'd better leave.

MRS. SØRBY. You can just as well stay, for that matter; I won't say another word. But I did want you to understand that I haven't done anything sly or in any way underhanded. I suppose it looks like I've had quite a nice piece of luck, and that's true enough, up to a point. But, anyway, what I mean is that I'll not be taking any more than I give. One thing I'll never do is desert him. And I can be useful to him and care for him now better than anyone else after he's helpless.

HJALMAR. After he's helpless?

GREGERS (*to* MRS. SØRBY). All right, don't talk about that here.

MRS. SØRBY. No need to hide it any longer, much as he'd like to. He's going blind.

HJALMAR (*astounded*). He's going blind? But that's peculiar. Is he going blind too?

GINA. Lots of people do.

MRS. SØRBY. And you can imagine what that means for a businessman. Well, I'll try to make my eyes do for his as well as I can. But I mustn't stay any longer; I've so much to take care of now. Oh yes, I was supposed to tell you this, Ekdal—that if there's anything Werle can do for you, please just get in touch with Graaberg.

GREGERS. That offer Hjalmar Ekdal will certainly decline.

MRS. SØRBY. Come, now, I don't think that in the past he's—

GINA. No, Berta, Hjalmar doesn't need to take anything from Mr. Werle now.

HJALMAR (*slowly and ponderously*). Would you greet your future husband from me and say that I intend very shortly to call on his bookkeeper, Graaberg—

GREGERS. What! Is that what you want?

HJALMAR. To call on his bookkeeper Graaberg, as I said, to request an itemized account of what I owe his employer. I shall repay this debt of honor— (*Laughs.*) That's a good name for it, "debt of honor"! But never mind. I shall repay every penny of it, with five percent interest.

GINA. But Hjalmar dear, God knows we don't have the money for that.

HJALMAR. Will you tell your husband-to-be that I'm working away relentlessly at my invention. Would you tell him that what keeps my spirits up through this grueling ordeal is the desire to be quit of a painful burden of debt. That's why I'm making my invention. The entire proceeds will be devoted to shedding my monetary ties with your imminent partner.

MRS. SØRBY. Something has really happened in this house.

HJALMAR. Yes, it certainly has.

MRS. SØRBY. Well, good-bye, then. I still have a little more to talk about with you, Gina, but that can keep till another time. Good-bye.

> (HJALMAR *and* GREGERS *silently nod;* GINA *accompanies* MRS. SØRBY *to the door.*)

HJALMAR. Not across the threshold, Gina!

> (MRS. SØRBY *leaves;* GINA *closes the door behind her.*)

HJALMAR. There, now, Gregers—now I've got that pressing debt off my hands.

GREGERS. You will soon, anyway.

HJALMAR. I believe my attitude could be called correct.

GREGERS. You're the man I always thought you were.

HJALMAR. In certain circumstances it's impossible not to feel the summons of the ideal. As the family provider, you know, I've got to writhe and groan beneath it. Believe you me, it's really no joke for a man without means to try and pay off a long-standing debt over which the dust of oblivion, so to speak, had fallen. But it's got to be, all the same; my human self demands its rights.

GREGERS (*laying one hand on his shoulder*). Ah, Hjalmar —wasn't it a good thing I came?

HJALMAR. Yes.

GREGERS. Getting a clear picture of the whole situation—wasn't that a good thing?

HJALMAR (*a bit impatiently*). Of course it was good. But there's one thing that irks my sense of justice.

GREGERS. What's that?

HJALMAR. It's the fact that—oh, I don't know if I dare speak so freely about your father.

GREGERS. Don't hold back on my account.

HJALMAR. Well, uh—you see, I find something so irritating in the idea that I'm not the one, he's the one who's going to have the true marriage.

GREGERS. How can you say such a thing!

HJALMAR. But it's true. Your father and Mrs. Sørby are entering a marriage based on complete trust, one that's wholehearted and open on both sides. They haven't bottled up any secrets from each other; there isn't any reticence between them; they've declared—if you'll permit me—a mutual forgiveness of sins.

GREGERS. All right. So what?

HJALMAR. Yes, but that's the whole thing, then. You said yourself that the reason for all these difficulties was the founding of a true marriage.

GREGERS. But that marriage is a very different sort, Hjalmar. You certainly wouldn't compare either you or her with those two—well, you know what I mean.

HJALMAR. Still, I can't get over the idea that there's something in all this that violates my sense of justice. It really seems as if there's no just order to the universe.

GINA. Good Lord, Hjalmar, you mustn't say such things.

GREGERS. Hm, let's not start on that question.

HJALMAR. But then, on the other hand, I can definitely make out what seems to be the meticulous hand of fate. He's going blind.

GINA. Oh, that's not for sure.

HJALMAR. That is indisputable. Anyway, we oughtn't to

doubt it, because it's precisely this fact that reveals the just retribution. Years back he abused the blind faith of a fellow human being—

GREGERS. I'm afraid he's done that to many others.

HJALMAR. And now a pitiless, mysterious something comes and claims the old man's eyes in return.

GINA. What a horrible thing to say! It really frightens me.

HJALMAR. It's useful sometimes to go down deep into the night side of existence.

(HEDVIG, *in her hat and coat, comes in, happy and breathless, through the hall door.*)

GINA. Back so soon?

HEDVIG. Yes, I got tired of walking, and it was just as well, 'cause then I met someone down at the door.

HJALMAR. That must have been Mrs. Sørby.

HEDVIG. Yes.

HJALMAR (*pacing back and forth*). I hope that's the last time you'll see her.

(*Silence.* HEDVIG *glances timidly from one to the other, as if trying to read their feelings.*)

HEDVIG (*coaxingly, as she approaches*). Daddy.

HJALMAR. Well—what is it, Hedvig?

HEDVIG. Mrs. Sørby brought along something for me.

HJALMAR (*stopping*). For you?

HEDVIG. Yes. It's something meant for tomorrow.

GINA. Berta's always brought some little gift for your birthday.

HJALMAR. What is it?

HEDVIG. No, you can't know that yet, because Mother has to bring it to me in bed first thing in the morning.

HJALMAR. Oh, all this conspiracy that I'm left out of!

HEDVIG (*hurriedly*). Oh, you can see it all right. It's a big letter. (*She takes the letter out of her coat pocket.*)

HJALMAR. A letter, too?

HEDVIG. Well, it's only the letter. I guess the rest will come later. But just think—a letter! I've never gotten a real letter before. And on the outside there, it says "Miss." (*She reads.*) "Miss Hedvig Ekdal." Just think—that's me.

HJALMAR. Let me see the letter.

HEDVIG (*handing it over*). See, there.

HJALMAR. That's old Werle's writing.

GINA. Are you positive, Hjalmar?

HJALMAR. See for yourself.

GINA. Oh, how would I know?

HJALMAR. Hedvig, mind if I open the letter—and read it?

HEDVIG. Sure. If you want to, go right ahead.

GINA. No, not tonight, Hjalmar. It's meant for tomorrow.

HEDVIG (*softly*). Oh, won't you let him read it! It's got to be something good, and then Daddy'll be happy and things will be pleasant again.

HJALMAR. May I open it, then?

HEDVIG. Yes, please do, Daddy. It'll be fun to find out what it is.

HJALMAR. Good. (*He opens the envelope, takes out a sheet of paper, and reads it through with growing bewilderment.*) Now what's this all about?

GINA. But what does it say?

HEDVIG. Oh yes, Daddy—tell us!

HJALMAR. Be quiet. (*He reads it through once more, turns pale, then speaks with evident restraint.*) This is a deed of gift, Hedvig.

HEDVIG. Honestly? What am I getting?

HJALMAR. Read for yourself.

(HEDVIG *goes over to the lamp and reads for a moment.*)

HJALMAR (*clenching his fists, in almost a whisper*). The eyes! The eyes—and now that letter!

HEDVIG (*interrupting her reading*). Yes, but I think the gift is for Grandfather.

HJALMAR (*taking the letter from her*). Gina—do you understand this?

GINA. I know nothing at all about it. Just tell me.

HJALMAR. Mr. Werle writes Hedvig to say that her old grandfather needn't trouble himself any longer with copying work, but that henceforth he can draw one hundred crowns a month from the office—

GREGERS. Aha!

HEDVIG. One hundred crowns, Mother! I read that.

GINA. That'll be nice for Grandfather.

HJALMAR. One hundred crowns, as long as he needs it. That means till death, of course.

GINA. Well, then he's provided for, poor dear.

HJALMAR. But there's more. You didn't read far enough, Hedvig. Afterwards this gift passes over to you.

HEDVIG. To me! All of it?

HJALMAR. You're assured the same income for the rest of your life, he writes. Hear that, Gina?

GINA. Yes, of course I heard.

HEDVIG. Imagine me getting all that money! (*Shaking* HJALMAR.) Daddy, Daddy, aren't you glad?

HJALMAR (*disengaging himself*). Glad! (*Walking about the room.*) Ah, what vistas—what perspectives it offers me. Hedvig is the one, she's the one he remembers so bountifully.

GINA. Of course, because it's Hedvig's birthday.

HEDVIG. And anyway, you'll have it, Daddy. You know that I'll give all the money to you and Mother.

HJALMAR. To Mother, yes! There we have it.

GREGERS. Hjalmar, this is a trap that's been set for you.

HJALMAR. You think it could be another trap?

GREGERS. When he was here this morning, he said, "Hjalmar Ekdal is not the man you think he is."

HJALMAR. Not the man—!

GREGERS. "You'll find that out," he said.

HJALMAR. Find out if I could be bought off for a price, eh—!

HEDVIG. But Mother, what's this all about?

GINA. Go and take your things off.

(HEDVIG, *close to tears, goes out the kitchen door.*)

GREGERS. Yes, Hjalmar—now we'll see who's right, he or I.

HJALMAR (*slowly tearing the paper in half and putting both pieces on the table*). That is my answer.

GREGERS. What I expected.

HJALMAR (*going over to* GINA, *who is standing by the stove, and speaking quietly*). And now no more pretenses. If that thing between you and him was all over when you—came to be so terribly in love with me, as you put it—then why did he give us the means to get married?

GINA. Maybe he thought he could come and go here.

HJALMAR. Is that all? Wasn't he afraid of a certain possibility?

GINA. I don't know what you mean.

HJALMAR. I want to know if—your child has the right to live under my roof.

GINA (*draws herself up, her eyes flashing*). And you can ask that?

HJALMAR. Just answer me this: does Hedvig belong to me—or? Well!

GINA (*regarding him with chill defiance*). I don't know.

HJALMAR (*with a slight quaver*). You don't know!

GINA. How would *I* know that? A woman of my sort—

HJALMAR (*softly, turning from her*). Then I have nothing more to do in this house.

GREGERS. You must think about this, Hjalmar.

HJALMAR (*putting on his overcoat*). There's nothing to think about for a man like me.

GREGERS. Oh, there's so very much to think about. You three have got to stay together if you're ever going to win through to a self-sacrificial, forgiving spirit.

HJALMAR. I don't want that. Never, never! My hat! (*Takes his hat.*) My home is down in ruins around me. (*Breaks into tears.*) Gregers, I have no child!

HEDVIG (*who has opened the kitchen door*). What are you saying! (*Running toward him.*) Daddy, Daddy!

GINA. Now look!

HJALMAR. Don't come near me, Hedvig! Keep away. I can't bear seeing you. Oh, the eyes! Goodbye. (*Starts for the door.*)

HEDVIG (*clinging fast to him and shrieking*). Oh no! Oh no! Don't leave me.

GINA (*crying out*). Look out for the child, Hjalmar! Look out for the child!

HJALMAR. I won't. I can't. I've got to get out—away from all this! (*He tears himself loose from* HEDVIG *and goes out through the hall door.*)

HEDVIG (*with desperate eyes*). He's left us, Mother! He's left us! He'll never come back again!

GINA. Now don't cry, Hedvig. Daddy's coming back.

HEDVIG (*throws herself, sobbing, on the sofa*). No, no, he'll never come home to us again.

GREGERS. Will you believe I've wanted everything for the best, Mrs. Ekdal?

GINA. Yes, I think I believe that—but God have mercy on you all the same.

HEDVIG (*lying on the sofa*). I think I'll die from all this. What did I do to him? Mother, you've got to make him come home!

GINA. Yes, yes, yes, just be calm, and I'll step out and look for him. (*Putting on her coat.*) Maybe he's gone down to Relling's. But now don't you lie there, wailing away. Will you promise?

HEDVIG (*sobbing convulsively*). Yes, I'll be all right—if only Daddy comes back.

GREGERS (*to* GINA, *about to leave*). Wouldn't it be better, though, to let him fight through his painful battle first?

GINA. Oh, he can do that later. First of all, we've got to comfort the child. (*She goes out the hall door.*)

HEDVIG (*sitting up and drying her tears*). Now you have to tell me what it's all about. Why does Daddy not want to see me anymore?

GREGERS. That's something you mustn't ask until you're big and grown-up.

HEDVIG (*catching her breath*). But I can't go on being so horribly unhappy till I'm big and grown-up. I bet I know what it is. Perhaps I'm really not Daddy's child.

GREGERS (*disturbed*). How could that ever be?

HEDVIG. Mother could have found me. And now maybe Daddy's found out. I've read about these things.

GREGERS. Well, but if that was the—

HEDVIG. Yes, I think he could love me even so. Or maybe more. The wild duck was sent us as a present too, and I'm terribly fond of it, all the same.

GREGERS (*divertingly*). Of course, the wild duck, that's true. Let's talk a bit about the wild duck, Hedvig.

HEDVIG. The poor wild duck. He can't bear to see her again, either. Imagine, he wanted to wring her neck!

GREGERS. Oh, he certainly wouldn't do that.

HEDVIG. No, but that's what he said. And I think it was awful for Daddy to say, because each night I make a prayer for the wild duck and ask that she be delivered from death and everything evil.

GREGERS (*looking at her*). Do you always say your prayers at night?

HEDVIG. Uh-huh.

GREGERS. Who taught you that?

HEDVIG. I taught myself, and that was once when Daddy was so sick and had leeches on his neck, and then he said he was in the jaws of death.

GREGERS. Oh yes?

HEDVIG. So I said a prayer for him when I went to bed. And I've kept it up ever since.

GREGERS. And now you pray for the wild duck, too?

HEDVIG. I thought it was best to put the wild duck in, because she was ailing so at the start.

GREGERS. Do you say morning prayers, too?

HEDVIG. No, not at all.

GREGERS. Why not morning prayers as well?

HEDVIG. In the morning it's light, and so there's nothing more to be afraid of.

GREGERS. And the wild duck you love so much—your father wants to wring her neck.

HEDVIG. No. He said it would be the best thing for him if he did, but for my sake he would spare her; and that was good of Daddy.

GREGERS (*coming closer*). But what if you now, of your own free will, sacrificed the wild duck for *his* sake.

HEDVIG (*springing up*). The wild duck!

GREGERS. What if you, in a sacrificing spirit, gave up the dearest thing you own and know in the whole world?

HEDVIG. Do you think that would help?

GREGERS. Try it, Hedvig.

HEDVIG (*softly, with shining eyes*). Yes, I'll try it.

GREGERS. And the strength of mind, do you think you have it?

HEDVIG. I'll ask Grandpa to shoot the wild duck for me.

GREGERS. Yes, do that. But not a word to your mother about all this!

HEDVIG. Why not?

GREGERS. She doesn't understand us.

HEDVIG. The wild duck? I'll try it tomorrow, early.

(GINA *comes in through the hall door*.)

HEDVIG (*going toward her*). Did you find him, Mother?

GINA. No. But I heard he'd looked in downstairs and gotten Relling along.

GREGERS. Are you sure of that?

GINA. Yes, I asked the janitor's wife. And Molvik was with them, she said.

GREGERS. And this, right when his mind needs nothing so much as to wrestle in solitude—!

GINA (*taking off her coat*). Oh, men are strange ones, they are. God knows where Relling has led him! I ran over to Mrs. Eriksen's café, but they weren't there.

HEDVIG (*struggling with her tears*). Oh, what if he never comes back again!

GREGERS. He *will* come back. I'll get a message to him tomorrow, and then you'll see just how quick he comes. Believe that, Hedvig, and sleep well. Good night. (*He goes out the hall door.*)

HEDVIG (*throwing herself, sobbing, into* GINA's *arms*). Mother, Mother!

GINA (*pats her on the back and sighs*). Ah, me, Relling was right. That's the way it goes when these crazy people come around, summoning up their ideals.

⤙ ACT FIVE ⤚

HJALMAR EKDAL's *studio. A cold, gray morning light filters in; wet snow lies on the huge panes of the skylight.* GINA, *wearing a pinafore, comes in from the kitchen, carrying a feather duster and a cleaning cloth, and makes for the living room door. At the same moment* HEDVIG *rushes in from the hallway.*

GINA (*stopping*). Well?

HEDVIG. You know, Mother, I'm pretty sure he's down at Relling's—

GINA. There, you see!

HEDVIG. 'Cause the janitor's wife said she heard Relling had two others with him when he came in last night.

GINA. That's about what I thought.

HEDVIG. But it's still no good if he won't come up to us.

GINA. At least I can go down there and talk with him.

(EKDAL, *in dressing gown and slippers, smoking a pipe, appears in the doorway to his room.*)

EKDAL. Say, Hjalmar— Isn't Hjalmar home?

GINA. No, he's gone out, I guess.

EKDAL. So early? In a raging blizzard like this? Oh, well, never mind; I'll take my morning walk alone, that's all.

(*He pulls the loft door ajar,* HEDVIG *helping him. He goes in; she closes up after him.*)

HEDVIG (*lowering her voice*). Just think, Mother, when Grandpa finds out that Daddy's leaving us.

GINA. Go on, Grandpa won't hear anything of the kind. It was a real stroke of providence he wasn't here yesterday in all that racket.

473

HEDVIG.   Yes, but—

(GREGERS *comes in the hall entrance.*)

GREGERS.   Well? Had any reports on him?

GINA.   He should be down at Relling's, they tell me.

GREGERS.   With Relling! Did he really go out with those fellows?

GINA.   Apparently.

GREGERS.   Yes, but he who needed so much to be alone to pull himself together—!

GINA.   Yes, just as you say.

(RELLING *enters from the hall.*)

HEDVIG (*going toward him*).   Is Daddy with you?

GINA (*simultaneously*).   Is he there?

RELLING.   Yes, of course he is.

HEDVIG.   And you never told us!

RELLING.   Oh, I'm a beast. But first of all, I had that other beast to manage—you know, the demonic one, him—and then, next, I fell so sound asleep that—

GINA.   What's Hjalmar been saying today?

RELLING.   He's said absolutely nothing.

HEDVIG.   Hasn't he talked at all?

RELLING.   Not a blessed word.

GREGERS.   No, no, I can well understand that.

GINA.   But what's he doing, then?

RELLING.   He's laid out on the sofa, snoring.

GINA.   Oh? Yes, Hjalmar's great at snoring.

HEDVIG.   He's asleep? Can he sleep?

RELLING.   Well, so it seems.

GREGERS.   It's conceivable—when all that strife of spirit has torn him.

GINA.   And then he's never been used to roaming around the streets at night.

HEDVIG.   Maybe it's a good thing that he's getting some sleep, Mother.

GINA.   I think so too. But then it's just as well we don't rouse him too soon. Thanks a lot, Relling. Now I've got to clean and straighten up here a bit, and then— Come and help me, Hedvig.

(GINA *and* HEDVIG *disappear into the living room.*)

GREGERS (*turning to* RELLING). Have you an explanation for the spiritual upheaval taking place within Hjalmar Ekdal?

RELLING. For the life of me, I can't remember any spiritual upheaval in him.

GREGERS. Wait! At a time of crisis like this, when his life has been recast? How can you believe that a rare personality like Hjalmar—?

RELLING. Pah! Personality—him! If he's ever had a tendency toward anything so abnormal as what you call personality, it was ripped up, root and vine, by the time he was grown, and that's a fact.

GREGERS. That's rather surprising—with all the loving care he had as a child.

RELLING. From those two 'warped, hysterical maiden aunts, you mean?

GREGERS. I want to tell you they were women who always summoned themselves to the highest ideals—yes, now of course you'll start mocking me again.

RELLING. No, I'm hardly in a mood for that. Besides, I'm well informed here; he's regurgitated any amount of rhetoric about his "twin soul-mothers." I really don't believe he has much to thank them for. Ekdal's misfortune is that in his circle he's always been taken for a shining light—

GREGERS. And isn't he, perhaps, exactly that? In his heart's core, I mean?

RELLING. I've never noticed anything of the kind. His father thinks so—but that's nothing; the old lieutenant's been a fool all his life.

GREGERS. He has, all his life, been a man with a childlike awareness; and that's something you just don't understand.

RELLING. Oh, sure! But back when our dear, sweet Hjalmar became a student of sorts, right away he got taken up by his classmates as the great beacon of the future. Oh, he was good-looking, the lout—pink and white—just the way little moon-eyed girls like boys. And then he had that excitable manner and that heart-winning tremor in his voice, and he was so cute and clever at declaiming other people's poems and ideas—

GREGERS (*indignantly*). Is it Hjalmar Ekdal you're speaking of that way?

RELLING. Yes, with your permission. That's an inside look at him, this idol you're groveling in front of.

GREGERS. I really didn't think I was utterly blind.

RELLING. Well, you're not far from it. Because you're a sick man, you are. You know that.

GREGERS. There you're right.

RELLING. Oh yes. Your case has complications. First there's this virulent moralistic fever; and then something worse—you keep going off in deliriums of hero worship; you always have to have something to admire that's outside of yourself.

GREGERS. Yes, I certainly have to look for it outside myself.

RELLING. But you're so woefully wrong about these great miraculous beings you think you see and hear around you. You've simply come back to a cotter's cabin with your summons to the ideal; there's no one but fugitives here.

GREGERS. If you've got no higher estimate of Hjalmar Ekdal than this, how can you ever enjoy seeing him day after day?

RELLING. Good Lord, I *am* supposed to be some kind of doctor, I'm ashamed to say. Well, then I ought to look after the poor sick people I live with.

GREGERS. Oh, come! Is Hjalmar Ekdal sick, too?

RELLING. Most of the world is sick, I'm afraid.

GREGERS. And what's your prescription for Hjalmar?

RELLING. My standard one. I try to keep up the life-lie in him.

GREGERS. The life-lie? I don't think I heard—

RELLING. Oh yes, I said the life-lie. The life-lie, don't you see—that's the animating principle of life.

GREGERS. May I ask what kind of lie has infected Hjalmar?

RELLING. No, thanks, I don't betray secrets like that to quacks. You'd just be able to damage him all the more for me. My method is tested, though. I've also used it on Molvik. I made him "demonic." That was my remedy for him.

GREGERS. Then he isn't demonic?

RELLING. What the devil does it mean to be demonic? That's just some hogwash I thought up to keep life going in him. If I hadn't done that, the poor innocent mutt would have given in years ago to self-contempt and despair. And then take the old lieutenant! But he really discovered his own cure himself.

GREGERS. Lieutenant Ekdal? How so?

RELLING. Well, what do you think of this bear hunter going into a dark loft to stalk rabbits? There isn't a happier sportsman in the world than the old man when he's prowling around in that junkyard. Those four or five dried-out Christmas trees he's got—to him they're like all the green forests of Hoidal; the hens and the rooster—they're the game birds up in the fir tops; and the rabbits hopping across the floor—they're the bears that call up his youth again, out in the mountain air.

GREGERS. Poor, unhappy old Ekdal, yes. He certainly had to pare down his early ideals.

RELLING. While I remember it, Mr. Werle junior—don't use that exotic word *ideals*. Not when we've got a fine native word—*lies*.

GREGERS. You're implying the two have something in common?

RELLING. Yes, about like tetanus and lockjaw.

GREGERS. Dr. Relling, I won't rest till I've gotten Hjalmar out of your clutches.

RELLING. So much the worse for him. Deprive the average man of his life-lie and you've robbed him of happiness as well. (*To* HEDVIG, *entering from the living room.*) Well, little wild-duck mother, now I'll go down and see if Papa's still lying and pondering his marvelous invention. (*He goes out the hall door.*)

GREGERS (*approaching* HEDVIG). I can see by your face that it's not fulfilled.

HEDVIG. What? Oh, about the wild duck. No.

GREGERS. Your courage failed you when the time came to act, I suppose.

HEDVIG. No, it's not exactly that. But when I woke up this morning early and thought of what we talked about, then it seemed so strange to me.

GREGERS. Strange?

HEDVIG. Yes, I don't know—Last night, right at the time, there was something so beautiful about it, but after I'd slept and then thought it over, it didn't seem like so much.

GREGERS. Ah, no, you couldn't grow up here without some taint in you.

HEDVIG. I don't care about that; if only Daddy would come up, then——

GREGERS. Oh, if only your eyes were really open to what makes life worth living—if only you had the true, joyful, courageous spirit of self-sacrifice, *then* you'd see him coming up to you. But I still have faith in you. (*He goes out the hall door.*)

> (HEDVIG *wanders across the room, then starts into the kitchen. At that moment a knock comes on the loft door,* HEDVIG *goes over and opens it a space;* EKDAL *slips out, and she slides it shut again.*)

EKDAL. Hm, a morning walk alone is no fun at all.

HEDVIG. Don't you want to go hunting, Grandpa?

EKDAL. The weather's no good for hunting. Awfully dark in there; you can hardly see ahead of you.

HEDVIG. Don't you ever want to shoot at anything but rabbits?

EKDAL. Aren't rabbits good enough, eh?

HEDVIG. Yes, but the wild duck, say?

EKDAL. Ha, ha! You're afraid I'll shoot the wild duck for you? Never in this world, dear. Never!

HEDVIG. No, you couldn't do that. It must be hard to shoot wild ducks.

EKDEL. Couldn't? I certainly could!

HEDVIG. How would you go about it, Grandpa?—I don't mean with *my* wild duck, but with others.

EKDAL. I'd be sure to shoot them in the breast, understand; that's the safest. And then they've got to be shot *against* the feathers, you see—not *with* the feathers.

HEDVIG. They die then, Grandpa?

EKDAL. Oh yes, they do indeed—if you shoot them right. Well, got to go in and clean up. Hm—you understand—hm. (*He goes into his room.*)

> (HEDVIG *waits a moment, glances at the living room door, goes to the bookcase, stands on tiptoe, takes down the double-barreled pistol from the shelf and looks at it.* GINA, *with duster and cloth, comes in from the living room.* HEDVIG *hastily sets down the pistol, unnoticed.*)

GINA. Don't mess with your father's things, Hedvig.

HEDVIG (*leaving the bookcase*). I was just straightening up a little.

GINA. Go out in the kitchen instead and make sure the coffee's still hot; I'll take a tray along to him when I go down.

> (HEDVIG *goes out;* GINA *begins to dust and clean up the studio. After a moment the hall door is cautiously opened, and* HJALMAR *peers in. He wears his overcoat, but no hat. He is unwashed, with tousled, unruly hair; his eyes are dull and inert.*)

GINA (*standing rooted with duster in hand, looking at him*). Don't tell me, Hjalmar—are you back after all?

HJALMAR (*steps in and answers in a thick voice*). I'm back—but only for one moment.

GINA. Oh yes, I'm sure of that. But my goodness—what a sight you are!

HJALMAR. Sight?

GINA. And then your good winter coat! Well, it's done for.

HEDVIG (*at the kitchen door*). Mother, should I— (*Seeing* HJALMAR, *giving a squeal of delight, and running toward him.*) Oh, Daddy, Daddy!

HJALMAR (*turning from her and waving her off*). Get away! Get away! (*To* GINA.) Make her get away from me, will you!

GINA (*in an undertone*). Go in the living room, Hedvig.

(HEDVIG *silently goes out.*)

HJALMAR (*with a busy air, pulling out the table drawer*). I must have my books along. Where are my books?

GINA. What books?

HJALMAR. My scientific works, of course—the technical journals I use for my invention.

GINA (*looking over the bookshelves*). Are these them, the ones without covers?

HJALMAR. Yes, exactly.

GINA (*putting a stack of booklets on the table*). Could I get Hedvig to cut the pages for you?

HJALMAR. Nobody has to cut pages for me. (*A short silence.*)

GINA. Then it's definite that you're moving out, Hjalmar?

HJALMAR (*rummaging among the books*). Yes, that would seem to me self-evident.

GINA. I see.

HJALMAR. How could I go on here and have my heart shattered every hour of the day!

GINA. God forgive you for thinking so badly of me.

HJALMAR. Show me proof—

GINA. I think *you're* the one to show proof.

HJALMAR. After your kind of past? There are certain claims—I'd like to call them ideal claims—

GINA. But Grandfather? What'll happen to him, poor dear?

HJALMAR. I know my duty; that helpless old soul leaves with me. I'm going downtown and make arrangements— hm— (*Hesitantly.*) Did anybody find my hat on the stairs?

GINA. No. Have you lost your hat?

HJALMAR. I had it on, naturally, when I came in last night; I'm positive of that. But today I couldn't find it.

GINA. My Lord, where did you go with those two stumblebums?

HJALMAR. Oh, don't bother me with petty questions. Do you think I'm in a mood to remember details?

GINA. I just hope you didn't catch cold, Hjalmar. (*She goes out into the kitchen.*)

HJALMAR (*muttering to himself in exasperation, as he empties the table drawer*). You're a sneak, Relling! A barbarian, that's what! Oh, snake in the grass! If I could just get someone to strangle you! (*He puts some old letters to one side, discovers the torn deed of the day before, picks it up and examines the pieces. He hurriedly puts them down as* GINA *enters.*)

GINA (*setting a breakfast tray on the table*). Here's a drop of something hot, if you care for it. And there's some bread and butter and a little salt meat.

HJALMAR (*glancing at the tray*). Salt meat? Never under this roof! Of course I haven't enjoyed going without food for nearly twenty-four hours; but that doesn't matter— My notes! My unfinished memoirs! Where can I find my journal and my important papers? (*Opens the living room door, then draws back.*) There she is again!

GINA. Well, goodness, the child has to be somewhere.

HJALMAR. Come out. (*He stands aside, and* HEDVIG, *terrified, comes into the studio.*)

HJALMAR (*with his hand on the doorknob, says to* GINA). These last moments I'm spending in my former home, I'd like to be free from intruders—(*Goes into the living room.*)

HEDVIG (*rushing to her mother, her voice hushed and trembling*). Does he mean me?

GINA. Stay in the kitchen, Hedvig. Or, no—go into your own room instead. (*Speaking to* HJALMAR *as she goes in to him.*) Just a minute, Hjalmar. Don't muss up the bureau like that; I know where everything is. (HEDVIG *stands for a moment as if frozen by fright and bewilderment, biting her lips to keep the tears back; then she clenches her fists convulsively.*)

HEDVIG (*softly*). The wild duck. (*She steals over and takes the pistol from the shelf, sets the loft door ajar, slips in and draws the door shut after her.* HJALMAR *and* GINA *start arguing in the living room.*)

HJALMAR (*reenters with some notebooks and old loose papers, which he lays on the table*). Oh, what good is that traveling bag! I've got a thousand things to take with me.

GINA (*following with the traveling bag*). So leave everything else for the time being, and just take a shirt and a pair of shorts with you.

HJALMAR. Phew! These agonizing preparations! (*Takes off his overcoat and throws it on the sofa.*)

GINA. And there's your coffee getting cold, too.

HJALMAR. Hm. (*Unthinkingly takes a sip and then another.*)

GINA. The hardest thing for you will be to find another room like that, big enough for all the rabbits.

HJALMAR. What! Do I have to take all the rabbits with me, too?

GINA. Yes, Grandfather couldn't live without the rabbits, I'm sure.

HJALMAR. He's simply got to get used to it. The joys of life *I* have to renounce are higher than rabbits.

GINA (*dusting the bookcase*). Should I put your flute in the traveling bag?

HJALMAR. No. No flute for me. But give me the pistol!

GINA. You want your pistol along?

HJALMAR. Yes. My loaded pistol.

GINA (*looking for it*). It's gone. He must have taken it inside.

HJALMAR. Is he in the loft?

GINA. Of course he's in the loft.

HJALMAR. Hm—lonely old man. (*He takes a piece of bread and butter, eats it, and finishes the cup of coffee.*)

GINA. Now if we only hadn't rented the room, you could have moved in there.

HJALMAR. I should stay on under the same roof as—! Never! Never!

GINA. But couldn't you put up in the living room just for a day or two? You've got everything you need in there.

HJALMAR. Never within these walls!

GINA. Well, how about down with Relling and Molvik?

HJALMAR. Don't mention those barbarians' names! I can almost lose my appetite just thinking about them. Oh no, I've got to go out in sleet and snow—tramp from house to house and seek shelter for Father and me.

GINA. But you haven't any hat, Hjalmar! You've lost your hat.

HJALMAR. Oh, those two vermin, wallowing in sin! The hat will have to be bought. (*Taking another piece of bread and butter.*) Someone's got to make arrangements. I certainly don't intend to risk my life. (*Looking for something on the tray.*)

GINA. What are you looking for?

HJALMAR. Butter.

GINA. Butter's coming right up. (*Goes into the kitchen.*)

HJALMAR (*calling after her*). Oh, never mind; I can just as easily eat dry bread.

GINA (*bringing in a butter dish*). Look. It's fresh today. (*She passes him another cup of coffee. He sits on the sofa, spreads more butter on the bread, eats and drinks a moment in silence.*)

HJALMAR. Could I—without being annoyed by anybody —anybody at all—put up in the living room just for a day or two?

GINA. Yes, of course you could, if you want to.

HJALMAR. Because I can't see any possibility of getting all Father's things out in one trip.

GINA. And then there's this, too, that you've first got to tell him you're not living with us any longer.

HJALMAR (*pushing the coffee cup away*). That too, yes. All these intricate affairs to unravel. I've got to clear my thinking; I need a breathing spell; I can't shoulder all these burdens in one day.

GINA. No, and not when the weather's like it is out.

HJALMAR (*picking up* WERLE's *letter*). I see this letter's still kicking around.

GINA. Yes, *I* haven't touched it.

HJALMAR. This trash is nothing to me—

GINA. Well, I'm not going to use it for anything.

HJALMAR. All the same, there's no point in throwing it around helter-skelter. In all the confusion of my moving, it could easily—

GINA. I'll take good care of it, Hjalmar.

HJALMAR. First and foremost, the deed of gift is Father's; it's really his affair whether or not he wants to use it.

GINA (*sighing*). Yes, poor old Father—

HJALMAR. Just for safety's sake—where would I find some paste?

GINA (*going to the bookcase*). Here's the pastepot.

HJALMAR. And then a brush.

GINA. Here's a brush, too. (*Bringing both.*)

HJALMAR (*taking a pair of scissors*). A strip of paper down the back, that's all. (*Cutting and pasting.*) Far be it from me to take liberties with another's property—least of all, a penniless old man's. No, nor with—the other person's. There, now. Let it lie a while. And when it's dry, then take it away. I don't want to set eyes on that document again. Ever!

(GREGERS *enters from the hall.*)

GREGERS (*somewhat surprised*). What? You're sitting here, Hjalmar?

HJALMAR (*springing up*). I was overcome by fatigue.

GREGERS. Still, you've had breakfast, I see.

HJALMAR. The body asserts its claims now and then.

GREGERS. What have you decided to do?

HJALMAR. For a man like me there's only one way open.
I'm in the process of assembling my most important things.
But that takes time, don't you know.

GINA (*a bit impatient*). Should I get the room ready for
you, or should I pack your bag?

HJALMAR (*after a vexed glance at* GREGERS). Pack—
and get the room ready!

GINA (*taking the traveling bag*). All right, then I'll put
in the shirt and the rest. (*She goes into the living room,
shutting the door behind her.*)

GREGERS (*after a short silence*). I never dreamed that
things would end like this. Is it really necessary for you to
leave house and home?

HJALMAR (*pacing restlessly about*). What would you have
me do? I wasn't made to be unhappy, Gregers. I've got to
have it snug and secure and peaceful around me.

GREGERS. But why can't you, then? Give it a try. Now
I'd say you have solid ground to build on—so make a fresh
start. And don't forget you have your invention to live for,
too.

HJALMAR. Oh, don't talk about the invention. That seems
such a long way off.

GREGERS. Oh?

HJALMAR. Good Lord, yes. What would you really have
me invent? Other people have invented so much already. It
gets more difficult every day—

GREGERS. And you've put so much work in it.

HJALMAR. It was that dissolute Relling who got me
started.

GREGERS. Relling?

HJALMAR. Yes, he was the one who first made me aware
that I had a real talent for inventing something in photography.

GREGERS. Aha—that was Relling!

HJALMAR. Oh, I was so blissfully happy as a result. Not
so much from the invention itself, but because Hedvig believed in it—believed in it with all the power and force of a
child's mind. Yes, in other words, fool that I am, I've gone
around imagining that she believed in it.

GREGERS. You can't really think that Hedvig could lie
to you!

HJALMAR. Now I can think anything. It's Hedvig that

ruins it all. She's managed to blot the sun right out of my life.

GREGERS. Hedvig! You mean Hedvig? How could she ever do that?

HJALMAR (*without answering*). How inexpressibly I loved that child! How inexpressibly happy I was whenever I came home to my poor rooms and she came flying to meet me with those sweet, fluttering eyes. I was so unspeakably fond of her—and so I dreamed and deluded myself into thinking that she, too, was fond of me beyond words.

GREGERS. Can you call *that* just a delusion?

HJALMAR. How can I tell? I can't get anything out of Gina; and besides, she has no feeling at all for the ideal phase of these complications. But with you, Gregers, I feel impelled to open my mind. There's this horrible doubt—maybe Hedvig never really, truly has loved me.

GREGERS. She may perhaps give you proof that she has. (*Listening.*) What's that? I thought I heard the wild duck cry.

HJALMAR. The duck's quacking. Father's in the loft.

GREGERS. Is he? (*His face radiates joy.*) I tell you, you may yet have proof that your poor, misjudged Hedvig loves you!

HJALMAR. Oh, what proof could she give me? I don't dare hope to be reassured from that quarter.

GREGERS. Hedvig's completely free of deceit.

HJALMAR. Oh, Gregers, that's just what I can't be sure of. Who knows what Gina and this Mrs. Sørby have whispered and gossiped about in all the times they've sat here? And Hedvig uses her ears, you know. Maybe the deed of gift wasn't such a surprise, after all. In fact, I seemed to get that impression.

GREGERS. What is this spirit that's gotten into you?

HJALMAR. I've had my eyes opened. Just wait—you'll see; the deed of gift is only the beginning. Mrs. Sørby has always cared a lot for Hedvig, and now she has the power to do what she wants for the child. They can take her away from me any time they like.

GREGERS. You're the last person in the world Hedvig would leave.

HJALMAR. Don't be too sure of that. If they stand beckoning her with all they have—? Oh, I who've loved her so inexpressibly! I who'd find my highest joy in taking her tenderly by the hand and leading her as one leads a child terrified of the dark through a huge, empty room! I can feel it now with such gnawing certainty; the poor photographer up in this attic has never meant much to her. She's merely been clever to keep on a good footing with him till the right time came.

GREGERS. You really don't believe that, Hjalmar.

HJALMAR. The worst thing is precisely that I don't know what to believe—that I'll never know. But can you honestly doubt that it's just what I'm saying? (*With a bitter laugh.*) Oh, you trust too much in the power of ideals, my dear Gregers! Suppose the others come with their hands full of riches and call out to the child: Leave him. Life waits for you here with us—

GREGERS (*quickly*). Yes, then what?

HJALMAR. If I asked her then: Hedvig, are you willing to give up life for me? (*Laughs derisively.*) Yes, thanks—you'd hear all right what answer I'd get!

(*A pistol shot is heard in the loft.*)

GREGERS (*with a shout of joy*). Hjalmar!

HJALMAR. Hear that. He's got to go hunting as well.

GINA (*coming in*). Oh, Hjalmar, it sounds like Grandfather's shooting up the loft by himself.

HJALMAR. I'll take a look—

GREGERS (*animated and exalted*). Wait now! Do you know what that was?

HJALMAR. Of course I know.

GREGERS. No, you don't know. But *I* do. That was the proof!

HJALMAR. What proof?

GREGERS. That was a child's sacrifice. She's had your father shoot the wild duck.

HJALMAR. Shoot the wild duck!

GINA. No, really—!

HJALMAR. What for?

GREGERS. She wanted to sacrifice to you the best thing she had in the world, because she thought then you'd have to love her again.

HJALMAR (*stirred, gently*). Ah, that child!

GINA. Yes, the things she thinks of!

GREGERS. She only wants your love again, Hjalmar; she felt she couldn't live without it.

GINA (*struggling with tears*). There you are, Hjalmar.

HJALMAR. Gina, where's she gone?

GINA (*sniffling*). Poor thing. I guess she's out in the kitchen.

HJALMAR (*going over and flinging the kitchen door open*). Hedvig, come! Come here to me! (*Looking about.*) No, she's not there.

GINA. Then she's in her own little room.

HJALMAR (*out of sight*). No, she's not there either. (*Coming back in.*) She may have gone out.

GINA. Yes, you didn't want her around anywhere in the house.

HJALMAR. Oh, if only she comes home soon—so I can just let her know—! Things will work out now, Gregers— for now I really believe we can start life over again.

GREGERS (*quietly*). I knew it; through the child everything rights itself.

(EKDAL *appears at the door to his room; he is in full uniform, absorbed in buckling his sword.*)

HJALMAR (*astonished*). Father! Are you there?

GINA. Were you out gunning in your room?

EKDAL (*approaching angrily*). So you've been hunting alone, eh, Hjalmar?

HJALMAR (*baffled and anxious*). Then it wasn't you who fired a shot in the loft?

EKDAL. Me, shoot? Hm!

GREGERS (*shouting to* HJALMAR). She's shot the wild duck herself!

HJALMAR. What is all this! (*Rushes to the loft doors, throws them open, looks in and cries:*) Hedvig!

GINA (*running to the door*). Lord, what now!

HJALMAR (*going in*). She's lying on the floor!

GREGERS. Hedvig, on the floor! (*Follows* HJALMAR *in.*)

GINA (*simultaneously*). Hedvig! (*Going into the loft.*) No, no, no!

EKDAL. Ha, ha! So she's a hunter, too.

(HJALMAR, GINA, *and* GREGERS *drag* HEDVIG *into the studio; her right hand hangs down and her fingers curve tightly around the pistol.*)

HJALMAR (*distraught*). The pistol's gone off. She's wounded herself. Call for help! Help!

GINA (*running into the hall and calling downstairs*). Relling! Relling! Dr. Relling, come up as quick as you can!

(HJALMAR *and* GREGERS *lay* HEDVIG *down on the sofa.*)

EKDAL (*hushed*). The woods take revenge.

HJALMAR (*on his knees by her*). She's just coming to now. She's coming to now—oh yes, yes.

GINA (*who has returned*). Where is she wounded? I can't see anything—

(RELLING *hurries in, and right after him,* MOLVIK, *who is without vest or tie, his dress coat open.*)

RELLING. What's going on here?

GINA. They say Hedvig shot herself.

HJALMAR. Come here and help.

RELLING. Shot herself! (*He shoves the table to one side and begins to examine her.*)

HJALMAR (*kneeling still, looking anxiously up at him*). It can't be serious? Huh, Relling? She's hardly bleeding. It can't be serious?

RELLING. How did this happen?

HJALMAR. Oh, how do I know—

GINA. She wanted to shoot the wild duck.

RELLING. The wild duck?

HJALMAR. The pistol must have gone off.

RELLING. Hm. I see.

EKDAL. The woods take revenge. But I'm not scared, even so. (*He goes into the loft, shutting the door after him.*)

HJALMAR. But Relling—why don't you say something?

RELLING. The bullet's entered her breast.

HJALMAR. Yes, but she's coming to!

RELLING. You can see for yourself that Hedvig is dead.

GINA (*breaking into tears*). Oh, my child, my child!

GREGERS (*hoarsely*). In the depths of the sea—

HJALMAR (*jumping up*). No, no, she *must* live! Oh, in God's name, Relling—just for a moment—just enough so I can tell her how inexpressibly I loved her all the time!

RELLING. It's reached the heart. Internal hemorrhage. She died on the spot.

HJALMAR. And I drove her from me like an animal! And she crept terrified into the loft and died out of love for me.

(*Sobbing.*) Never to make it right again! Never to let her know—! (*Clenching his fists and crying to heaven.*) Oh, you up there—if you *do* exist. Why have you done this to me!

GINA. Hush, hush, you mustn't say those terrible things. We just didn't deserve to keep her, I guess.

MOLVIK. The child isn't dead; she sleepeth.

RELLING. Rubbish!

HJALMAR (*becoming calm, going over to the sofa to stand, arms folded, looking at* HEDVIG). There she lies, so stiff and still.

RELLING (*trying to remove the pistol*). She holds it so tight, so tight.

GINA. No, no, Relling, don't break her fingers. Let the gun be.

HJALMAR. She should have it with her.

GINA. Yes, let her. But the child shouldn't lie displayed out here. She ought to go into her own little room, she should. Give me a hand, Hjalmar.

(HJALMAR *and* GINA *lift* HEDVIG *between them.*)

HJALMAR (*as they carry her off*). Oh, Gina, Gina, how can you bear it!

GINA. We must try to help each other. For now she belongs to us both, you know.

MOLVIK (*outstretching his arms and mumbling*). Praise be to God. Dust to dust, dust to dust—

RELLING (*in a whisper*). Shut up, you fool; you're drunk.

(HJALMAR *and* GINA *carry the body out through the kitchen door.* RELLING *closes it after them.* MOLVIK *steals out the hall door.*)

RELLING (*going over to* GREGERS). Nobody's ever going to sell me the idea that this was an accident.

GREGERS (*who has stood in a convulsive fit of horror*). Who can say how this awful thing happened?

RELLING. There are powder burns on her blouse. She must have held the pistol right at her breast and fired.

GREGERS. Hedvig did not die in vain. Did you notice how grief freed the greatness in him?

RELLING. The grief of death brings out greatness in almost everyone. But how long do you think this glory will last with *him*?

GREGERS. I should think it would last and grow all his life.

RELLING. In less than a year little Hedvig will be nothing more to him than a pretty theme for recitations.

GREGERS. You dare say that about Hjalmar Ekdal!

RELLING. We'll be lectured on this when the first grass shows on her grave. Then you can hear him spewing out phrases about "the child torn too soon from her father's heart," and you'll have your chance to watch him souse himself in conceit and self-pity. Wait and see.

GREGERS. If you're right, and I'm wrong, then life isn't worth living.

RELLING. Oh, life would be good in spite of all, if we only could have some peace from these damned shysters who come badgering us poor people with their "summons to the ideal."

GREGERS (*staring straight ahead*). In that case, I'm glad my destiny is what it is.

RELLING. Beg pardon—but what *is* your destiny?

GREGERS (*about to leave*). To be the thirteenth man at the table.

RELLING. Oh, go to hell.

ROSMERSHOLM

In the medieval form of allegory known as the *psycho-machia*, personified virtues and vices met on the battlefield of the human mind to wage war for the soul of man. In *Rosmersholm* (1886), although the density of observed reality precludes anything so abstract as allegory and the playwright scrupulously refrains from labeling the combatants as virtues and vices, something similar occurs. In the most eminent country house of its district in Norway four characters—the ruthless conservative, Kroll, the calculating liberal, Mortensgaard, the superstitious Mrs. Helseth and the flashily learned Ulrik Brendel—concentrate their forces, influences or mere presences on two finer, more sensitive minds, with the intent, conscious or unconscious, of determining the soul and tendency of the age.

The two delicately poised focal characters immediately impress us as sympathetically attractive, in appearance, in manner, in the grace of their responsiveness to others. John Rosmer is an aristocrat by birth, the last of a long line of churchmen, military officers and public servants who have set the tone of society in the region for generations. Rebecca West is aristocratic in another sense more crucial to Ibsen's hopes for the future: self-schooled and refined beyond her origins into a manifest nobility of character, mind and spirit. Through an almost entirely retrospective action, this initial favorable impression is put to an acid test that eats away the present surface to reveal the past, hidden, ugly truth with which any idealistic program for the ennoblement of man must contend.

The first layer of subsurface disclosure is best summarized by Ibsen himself, in a letter that gives *Rosmersholm* still more the look of a modern *psychomachia* whose protagonists are clashing faculties within one mind: "The play deals with the struggle which all serious-minded human beings must wage within themselves to bring their lives into harmony with their convictions. The different spiritual functions do not develop evenly or comparably in any one person. The acquisitive instinct rushes on from one conquest to another. The moral consciousness—

conscience—is, however, very conservative. It has its roots deep in tradition and in the past generally. Hence the conflict within the individual." If Rosmer embodies moral conservatism, tradition, the past, Rebecca acts from, and including, the time of her arrival at Rosmersholm by acquisitive instinct. Just as earlier with Dr. West she acquired what Kroll dismisses as "some kind of sense of the latest theories in various fields," she proceeds to acquire favor, trust, ascendancy with the Rosmers—stages of active intellectual and social climbing that her present well-settled charm belies.

But Rebecca is more than an *arriviste*. The acid eats on, skillfully applied by Kroll, who will stop at nothing to retain Rosmer in the conservative camp by discrediting the resident liberalizing influence that has captured him. For, far from acting simply as an adventuress, Rebecca has come to Rosmersholm, in Maurice Valency's phrase, like a secret agent of the Third Empire, the next great era of cultural-historical evolution into which Western civilization is moving. Toward the end of joining and, if necessary, reindoctrinating the man of her choice to serve this vast purpose, she will use everything she has, likewise stopping at nothing. To what extreme she *has* in fact gone to gain Rosmer, Kroll is resolved to submit to his old friend's already tender conscience.

The accurate name for that extreme was supplied by Strindberg in an article on the play: psychic murder. Rebecca's entrée at Rosmersholm was secured by her bewitching appeal not merely to Kroll and Rosmer, but also to the latter's troubled, melancholy wife Beata, who becomes morbidly infatuated with this siren from traditionally pagan Finmark and insists on installing her as, in effect, a live-in companion. Shortly after, Rebecca finds herself overcome by a sudden storm of passion for Rosmer, which soon finds the means to Beata's removal justified by the end of rescuing an exceptional mind from a stultifying marriage. Through precisely what powers of suggestion the psychic murder is carried out can be left to the text; but even after a year of mourning, Beata's presence persists wraithlike in the house, another of Ibsen's vampiric ghosts, like the night-riding White Horses that, by local legend, appear to foretell imminent death in the household.

Independent now of Kroll's stratagems, the restoring acid etches in still deeper contours of the past, left unconfessed, only hinted at by Rebecca's involuntary responses. Her real name is her mother's, Gamvik; her birth, illegitimate. Later, she was adopted by the district health officer, Dr. West; and not knowing, or perhaps, as Freud suggests in a brief, penetrating study, half suspecting that he is in truth her father, she becomes his mistress, setting herself beyond the good and evil of traditional morality. This original Oedipal superseding of the mother with the father, Freud argues, is repeated, then, with Beata and Rosmer. But if Freud is correct, is Rebecca's amoral assertion of absolute freedom no more than a repetition compulsion? And is her final decision the last, unfree toll of that compulsion, a death for a death, or the ultimate, free merging of the acquisitive with the moral faculty toward the emerging Third Empire? As *Rosmersholm* attests, Ibsen stands as one of the greatest masters of human psychology—not least because the psychological questions he raises are explored, not for their own sake alone, but as part of a larger world-view.

THE CHARACTERS

JOHN ROSMER, master of Rosmersholm, former pastor of the parish

REBECCA WEST, in residence at Rosmersholm

DR. KROLL, Rosmer's brother-in-law, a headmaster

ULRIK BRENDEL

PETER MORTENSGAARD

MRS. HELSETH, housekeeper at Rosmersholm

The action takes place at Rosmersholm, an old manor house on the outskirts of a small town by a fjord in West Norway.

⌣(ACT ONE)⌣

The living room at Rosmersholm, spacious, old-fashioned and comfortable. Downstage right, against the wall, is a tiled heating stove decorated with fresh-cut birch boughs and wild flowers. Farther back, a door. In the rear wall, double doors opening on the entry hall. In the lefthand wall, a window, and downstage from this, a stand with flowers and plants. Near the stove, a table, along with a sofa and armchairs. Around the walls hang portraits, both old and more recent, of clergymen, military officers and public officials in uniform. The window is open; likewise the doors to the hall, and the front door to the house. Outside, an avenue of huge, ancient trees is visible, leading out to the estate. The twilight of a summer evening, after sundown.

REBECCA WEST *is sitting in an armchair by the window, crocheting a large, white, woolen shawl which is almost finished. Every now and then she glances expectantly out the window through the flowers. Some moments later* MRS. HELSETH *enters, right*

MRS. HELSETH. Shouldn't I begin setting the table a bit for supper, miss?

REBECCA. Yes, do that. Mr. Rosmer ought to be back any time now.

MRS. HELSETH. Isn't it terribly drafty there, miss?

REBECCA. Yes, somewhat. Maybe you could close the window.

(MRS. HELSETH *goes over and shuts the doors to the hall, then crosses to the window.*)

MRS. HELSETH (*looking out before closing it*). But isn't that the pastor coming now?

REBECCA (*quickly*). Where? (*Rises.*) Yes, that's him. (*Behind the curtain.*) Stand back. Don't let him see us.

MRS. HELSETH (*stepping back into the room*). Look at that, miss—he's beginning to use the old mill-path again.

REBECCA. He took the mill-path the day before yesterday, too. (*Peering out between the curtain and the window sash.*) But now let's see—

MRS. HELSETH. Will he dare go over the footbridge?

REBECCA. That's what I want to see. (*Pause.*) No, he's turning back. Taking the upper path again today. (*Leaves the window.*) The long way round.

MRS. HELSETH. But, my heavens, it must be hard for the pastor to set foot on that bridge. Not *there*, after what happened—

REBECCA (*gathers up her crocheting*). At Rosmersholm they cling to their dead.

MRS. HELSETH. To my mind, miss, it's the dead that cling to Rosmersholm.

REBECCA (*looking at her*). The dead?

MRS. HELSETH. Yes, it's, so to say, as if they couldn't quite tear themselves free from the ones that stay on.

REBECCA. Where did you get that notion?

MRS. HELSETH. Well, I mean, otherwise you wouldn't have this white horse that comes.

REBECCA. Mrs. Helseth, what exactly is all this about a white horse?

MRS. HELSETH. Oh, why talk about it? Anyway, you don't believe in such things.

REBECCA. Do *you* believe in it?

MRS. HELSETH (*goes over and shuts the window*). Oh, I'm not going to make a fool of myself, miss. (*Looks out.*) Wait—isn't that the pastor down on the mill-path again?

REBECCA (*looking out*). Down there? (*Goes to the window.*) No, that's Dr. Kroll!

MRS. HELSETH. Of course, it's the headmaster.

REBECCA. Why, how delightful! You'll see, he's coming to visit us.

MRS. HELSETH. Right over the footbridge *he* goes—even though she was flesh and blood to him, and his own sister. Well, I'll go in and set the supper table, miss.

(*She goes out, right.* REBECCA *stands briefly at the window, then smiles and nods a greeting to the visitor. It begins to grow dark.*)

REBECCA (*crosses right to the door and calls within*). Oh, Mrs. Helseth, please could you put something a little extra-special on the table. You must know what the headmaster really likes.

MRS. HELSETH (*from within*). Oh, yes, miss. I'll do that.

REBECCA (*opening the doors to the hall*). Well, how long it's been—! My dear Dr. Kroll, I'm so glad to see you!

KROLL (*in the hall, laying down his walking stick*). Thank you. I'm not calling at a bad time, then?

REBECCA. You? That's no way to talk.

KROLL (*coming in*). Charming as ever. (*Glances about.*) I suppose Rosmer's up in his room?

REBECCA. No, he's out for a walk. He's been gone a bit longer than usual. But he'll surely be here any moment. (*Gesturing toward the sofa.*) Won't you sit down and wait?

KROLL (*sets down his hat*). Why, thank you. (*Sits and surveys the room.*) My, but you've made the old place bright and inviting. Flowers everywhere.

REBECCA Mr. Rosmer loves having fresh-cut flowers around.

KROLL. And I think you do, as well.

REBECCA. Yes, I find them so delightfully calming. At one time we had to give up that pleasure.

KROLL (*nodding sadly*). Poor Beata couldn't bear the scent.

REBECCA. Nor the colors, either. She was—disturbed by them.

KROLL. I well remember. (*In a lighter vein.*) So, how are things going out here?

REBECCA. In the usual quiet way. One day like another. And how are things at home? Your wife—?

KROLL. Ah, my dear Miss West, let's not discuss my situation. There's always something in a family that isn't quite right. Especially in the times we're living in now.

REBECCA (*sitting, after a moment, in an armchair by the sofa*). It's your summer vacation, and yet you haven't been out even once to see us. Why not?

KROLL. Well, I don't want to haunt your doorstep—

REBECCA. If you only knew how we've missed you—

KROLL. And besides, I've been away—

REBECCA. Yes, for a couple of weeks. I understand you've been making the rounds at political meetings?

KROLL (*nods*). And what do you say to that? Would you ever have thought, in my old age, that I'd become a political agitator? Hm?

REBECCA (*smiling*). Now, Dr. Kroll, you've always been something of an agitator.

KROLL. Well, yes, for my own private amusement. But from now on, it'll be in dead earnest. Do you ever read any of those radical newspapers?

REBECCA. Why, yes, I can't deny that—

KROLL. My dear Miss West, no need to make excuses. Not in your case.

REBECCA. No, that's how I feel. I've got to stay in touch. Keep informed.

KROLL. In any event, I certainly wouldn't expect you, as a

woman, to be involved in this civil dissension—civil war is more like it—that's raging here. But—then you've already read how these "defenders of the people" have gratified themselves by smearing me. The vile abuse they've dared to stoop to?

REBECCA. Yes, but I must say, you bit back pretty sharply.

KROLL. You bet I did, if I say so myself. And now that I've tasted blood, they're going to learn that I'm not a man who just smiles and turns the other cheek— (*Breaking off.*) Oh, but, listen—let's not get into that melancholy business this evening.

REBECCA. No, of course not, Dr. Kroll.

KROLL. I'd rather hear more about how you've been managing alone here at Rosmersholm, now that our poor Beata—

REBECCA. I've been managing very nicely, thank you. There's a great emptiness after her passing, of course, in so many ways. A sense of sorrow and loss—naturally. But otherwise—

KROLL. Do you plan to stay on? More or less permanently, I mean?

REBECCA. Oh, I really haven't given much thought to it, either way. I've become so very much a part of this place, I almost feel I belong to it.

KROLL. And you do. I quite agree.

REBECCA. And as long as Mr. Rosmer finds I can give him any support or comfort—why, then no doubt I'll be staying, I suppose.

KROLL (*regards her with feeling*). You know, there's something awe-inspiring about a woman who can sacrifice the whole of her youth to other people.

REBECCA. What else have I got to live for?

KROLL. First, you went through that endless ordeal with your foster father, caring for him after he was paralyzed and so irrational—

REBECCA. You know, Dr. West wasn't that irrational up north in Finmark. It was those dreadful ocean voyages that ruined his health. But after we moved down here—yes, there were a couple of hard years before he passed on.

KROLL. Weren't they harder still for you, the years that followed?

REBECCA. Oh, you mustn't say that! When I was so very fond of Beata—and she, poor dear, was so pitifully in need of care and a little tenderness.

KROLL. Bless you for remembering her so kindly.

REBECCA (*moving a bit closer*). Dear Dr. Kroll, you said that with such warmth of feeling, I can't believe you harbor any bitterness toward me.

KROLL. Bitterness? What do you mean?

REBECCA. Well, it wouldn't be at all surprising if you found it quite painful to see me, an outsider, running things at Rosmersholm.

KROLL. But what on earth—?

REBECCA. But you don't. (*Seizes his hand.*) Thank you, Dr. Kroll! All my thanks for that.

KROLL. But how on earth could you ever imagine I would?

REBECCA. I began getting a bit uneasy when you came out to see us so rarely.

KROLL. Then you've been absolutely off on the wrong track, Miss West. Besides—nothing really has changed here. It was you, and you alone, who managed the household in that last unhappy period of Beata's life.

REBECCA. I was only a kind of agent acting in her name.

KROLL. Well, no matter. You know, Miss West—for my part, I wouldn't have the least objection if you— But I suppose it isn't quite proper to speak of it yet.

REBECCA. What isn't?

KROLL. If it could work out for you to fill the empty place—

REBECCA. I have the place I want, Dr. Kroll.

KROLL. Functionally, yes; but not—

REBECCA (*interrupting him, in deep earnest*). For shame, Dr. Kroll. How can you joke about these things?

KROLL. Ah, well, our good John Rosmer no doubt feels he's had more than his fill of married life. But, even so—

REBECCA. You know—I really have to smile at you.

KROLL. And yet— Tell me, Miss West, if you'll pardon my asking—just how old are you?

REBECCA. Past twenty-nine, I'm ashamed to say. I'm almost thirty.

KROLL. Um-hm. And Rosmer—he's how old? Let me see, he's five years younger than I, so he's a good forty-three. That seems to me very suitable.

REBECCA. Why, yes, of course. Thoroughly suitable. Will you join us for supper this evening?

KROLL. Yes, thank you. I was intending to stay awhile. There's a matter I have to discuss with our mutual friend. And to keep you from getting any more silly ideas, Miss West, I guess I'll have to stop out here more regularly, just like old times.

REBECCA. Oh, yes, please do! (*Clasping his hands.*) And thank you so much! You *are* the soul of kindness.

KROLL (*brusquely*). Am I? That's a lot more than I ever hear at home.

(JOHN ROSMER *enters, right.*)

REBECCA. Mr. Rosmer! Look who's here!

ROSMER. Mrs. Helseth told me.

(KROLL *has gotten up, and* ROSMER *takes his hand.*)

ROSMER (*quietly, with suppressed emotion*). My dear Kroll, welcome back to this house. (*Placing his hands on* KROLL's *shoulders and looking into his eyes.*) My dear old friend! I was sure someday things would straighten out between us.

KROLL. But, my dear man, did you also have this crazy illusion that we were at odds?

REBECCA (*to* ROSMER). Yes, how wonderful that it was just an illusion.

ROSMER. Was it really that, Kroll? But then why have you been avoiding us?

KROLL (*his voice muted and somber*). Because I didn't want to intrude here as a living reminder of those unhappy years—and of her—who drowned in the millrace.

ROSMER. That was considerate of you. But then you've always been thoughtful. Still, it was hardly necessary to stay away on that account. Come on, let's get settled on the sofa. (*They sit.*) No, I don't find it painful at all to think about Beata. We talk of her every day. To us, it's as if she's still part of the house.

KROLL. You really feel that.

REBECCA (*lighting the lamp*). Yes, we really do.

ROSMER. It's quite natural. We both cared for her so deeply. And both Rebec—both Miss West and I know inwardly that we did everything in our power for that poor, afflicted soul. We've nothing to reproach ourselves for. It's why I can feel there's something calm and sustaining in the thought of Beata now.

KROLL. You dear, wonderful people! From now on, I must come by and look in on you every day.

REBECCA (*sits in an armchair*). Let's see now that you keep that promise.

ROSMER (*hesitating somewhat*). I wish, Kroll, that—we'd never had any break between us. As long as we've known each other, you've been the one person I've always turned to for advice. Ever since my university days.

KROLL. I know; that's something that means a great deal to me. Why, is there anything in particular now—?

ROSMER. There's so much that I'd really like to talk out with you, without any reservations. Straight from the heart.

REBECCA. Yes, how true, Mr. Rosmer! I think that would be so good—just two old friends—

KROLL. Oh, believe me, I have even more to talk over with you. I suppose you've heard that I've gone actively into politics.

ROSMER. Yes, so I heard. How did that come about?

KROLL. I had to, Rosmer—like it or not. It's no longer possible to look on like an idle bystander. Now, with these radicals coming so dangerously into power, it's high time to— That's why I've prodded our little circle of friends there in town to close their ranks. I tell you, the time is ripe.

REBECCA (*with a faint smile*). Yes, in fact, isn't it even a bit too late?

KROLL. Undoubtedly it would have been better if we could have stemmed the tide at some earlier point. But who could have foreseen what was coming? Not I, for one. (*Rising and pacing about the room.*) Yes, but now I've had my eyes opened. Because now that revolutionary spirit has insinuated itself even into the school.

ROSMER. The school? You don't mean into *your* school?

KROLL. Yes, exactly. Into my own school. And what do you think! It's come to my attention that the boys in the senior class—or, at least, a number of them—have been meeting in a secret society for more than six months, and they've been following Mortensgaard's paper!

REBECCA. The *Daily Beacon*.

KROLL. Yes, what do you think of that intellectual diet for our future national leaders? But the saddest part of it is that it's all the brightest students who've ganged up in this conspiracy against me. It's only the numskulls at the foot of the class who've kept out of it.

REBECCA. This really upsets you, then?

KROLL. Of course! To see my life work thwarted and contravened. (*More quietly.*) I could almost say: well, it will all work itself out—except that I'm only now coming to the worst of it. (*Glancing about.*) There wouldn't be anyone listening at the door?

REBECCA. Certainly not.

KROLL. Then you might as well know that this dissent and rebellion has infiltrated my own house. My own peaceful home. It's disrupted the harmony of my family life.

ROSMER (*gets up*). Your own home—! What do you mean?

REBECCA (*going over to* KROLL). But, my dear Dr. Kroll, what's happened?

KROLL. Could you imagine that my own children—? All right, in brief, it's Laurits who's the ringleader of the conspiracy in school. And Hilda has embroidered a red slipcase to hide her copies of the *Beacon* in.

ROSMER. I never would have dreamed—that, in *your* family—

KROLL. No, whoever could have dreamed of it? In my house, where order and obedience have always ruled—where until now we've only known a perfect unity of will—

REBECCA. How does your wife take all this?

KROLL. That's the most astounding part of it. All her born days, she's shared my opinions and backed my views in everything, large and small—and now she actually favors the children's side in point after point. And she even blames *me* for what's happened. She says I browbeat the children—as if it wasn't sometimes necessary to— Well, that's the kind of trouble I've got at home. But of course I talk about it as little as possible. That sort of thing is best covered up. (*Moving about the room.*) Ah, yes, yes, yes.

(*He stops by the window, hands behind his back, and gazes out.* REBECCA *goes over to* ROSMER.)

REBECCA (*softly and quickly, to escape* KROLL'*s notice*). Tell him!

ROSMER. Not tonight.

REBECCA. Yes, now.

(*She crosses over and adjusts the lamp.*)

KROLL (*returning from the window*). So, my dear Rosmer, now you know how the spirit of the age has cast its shadow over both my personal and professional lives. And this insidious, corrupting, destructive spirit of the age—shouldn't I fight it with every weapon at my command? Yes, that's what I plan to do—by writing, as well as by speaking out.

ROSMER. You really think you can accomplish anything that way?

KROLL. At least I'll be doing my duty as a citizen. And to my mind, every true patriot who believes in fighting the good fight has an obligation to do the same. In fact—that's the reason behind my coming out here tonight.

ROSMER. But what do you mean? How can I—?

KROLL. You're going to help your old friends. Do like the rest of us. Lend a hand as much as you can.

REBECCA. But, Dr. Kroll, you know Mr. Rosmer's distaste for that sort of thing.

KROLL. Then he's got to overcome his distaste. You ought to be with us, Rosmer, and instead you're sitting out here and burying yourself in your historical research. God knows, I have the highest respect for genealogies and such —but unfortunately these just aren't the times for such pursuits. You have no conception of the way things are going in this country. There's scarcely one single idea that hasn't been stood on its head. It'll be a long, hard battle, getting all these heresies rooted out again.

ROSMER. I agree. But that kind of work just isn't for me.

REBECCA. Besides, I really think Mr. Rosmer has come to see life in a larger perspective than before.

KROLL (*jarred*). Larger—?

REBECCA. Yes, or freer, perhaps. Less biased.

KROLL. What's that supposed to mean? Rosmer—you surely aren't so weak as to be impressed by those demagogues winning a victory that's no more than temporary and accidental?

ROSMER. Oh, you know well enough how little I understand politics. But I really believe the individual, in these past few years, has begun to show a bit more independence in his thinking.

KROLL. And you take that, on face value, as a good thing! But, my friend, you're making a big mistake. Just look at what passes for ideas currently among the radicals, both out here and in town. It doesn't diverge by a single hair from the wisdom preached in the *Daily Beacon*.

REBECCA. Yes, Mortensgaard has enormous influence in these parts.

KROLL. Yes, can you imagine! A man with his tainted past. A person fired from his teaching post for moral turpitude—! That he can set himself up as a leader of the people. And make it! He's actually made it! He's going to expand his paper, I hear. I have it on good authority that he's looking for a capable co-editor.

REBECCA. I'm surprised you and your friends haven't launched an opposition paper.

KROLL. That's exactly our next move. Today we bought the *County Herald*. The money part of it wasn't any problem. But— (*Turning to* ROSMER.) —and here's my real purpose in coming out here. The management, the editorial direction, you see—that's the rub. Tell me, Rosmer—don't you feel compelled to take it on, for the good of the cause?

ROSMER (*in sudden alarm*). Me?

REBECCA. You're not serious!

KROLL. That you're averse to public meetings, and the kind of rough-and-tumble that goes on there, is understandable enough. But an editor's activities, being more removed, or, should I say—

ROSMER. No, no, Kroll, you mustn't ask this of me.

KROLL. I'd like very much to take a stab at it myself. But it's simply beyond me. I'm overloaded already with any number of things to do—while you, on the other hand, since you're not professionally involved anymore— And of course the rest of us would help you as much as we could.

ROSMER. I can't, Kroll. I'm just not up to it.

KROLL. Not up to it? You said the same thing when your father got you this parish—

ROSMER. I was right. It's why I resigned my ministry.

KROLL. Oh, if you're only as able an editor as you were a pastor, we won't complain.

ROSMER. My dear Kroll—once and for all, I tell you, I won't do it.

KROLL. Well, in any case, you *will* let us use your name.

ROSMER. My name?

KROLL. Why, merely the name John Rosmer would be an asset to the paper. The rest of us are rather well known as strong party men. I hear I'm even being muckraked now as a raging fanatic. So, with our own names on the masthead, we couldn't count on the paper having much impact on the poor, muddled masses. You, on the other hand—you've always kept yourself above the struggle. Your noble, forebearing nature, your scrupulous mind, your unassailable integrity are known and prized by everyone in this county. Then there's the honor and respect you've retained from your time in the ministry. And, to top it off, there's the aura of the old family name.

ROSMER. Oh, the family name—

KROLL (*gesturing toward the portraits*). The Rosmers of Rosmersholm—churchmen and officers. Trusted public servants. All of them, men of unfailing dedication. And that line, for nearly two hundred years, has held forth here, in this very house, as the foremost family of the county. (*Lays his hand on* ROSMER'*s shoulder.*) Rosmer—you owe it to yourself and the heritage of your ancestors to join in defending all those things that, up till now, have been held sacred in our society. (*Turning.*) What do *you* say, Miss West?

REBECCA (*with a small, rippling laugh*). Dr. Kroll—all this strikes me as ridiculous beyond words.

KROLL. What? Ridiculous!

REBECCA. Yes. Because now I'll tell you exactly why—

ROSMER. No, no—just drop it! Not yet!

KROLL (*looking from one to the other*). But, my dear friends, what in the world— (*Breaks off.*) Hm!

(MRS. HELSETH *enters, right.*)

MRS. HELSETH. There's a man waiting out on the back steps. He says he'd like to greet the pastor.

ROSMER (*relieved*). I see. All right, invite him in.

MRS. HELSETH. Here, in the living room?

ROSMER. Of course.

MRS. HELSETH. But he hardly looks the type you'd want in your living room.

REBECCA. Then how does he look, Mrs. Helseth?

MRS. HELSETH. Like not very much, miss.

ROSMER. Did he say his name?

MRS. HELSETH. Yes, I think he said he was called Hekman, or something like that.

ROSMER. I don't know anyone by that name.

MRS. HELSETH. And he said he was also called Uldrik.

ROSMER. (*with a start*). Ulrik Hetman! Was that it?

MRS. HELSETH. Yes. It was Hetman.

KROLL. That name sounds familiar.

REBECCA. Of course. It's the name he used to write under, that curious man—

ROSMER (*to* KROLL). It's Ulrik Brendel's pen name, remember?

KROLL. Now I do, yes. That impostor Ulrik Brendel.

REBECCA. So he's still alive.

ROSMER. I believe he was touring with some theatrical company.

KROLL. The last I heard of him, he was in the workhouse.

ROSMER. Ask him in, Mrs. Helseth.

MRS. HELSETH. Whatever you say, sir. (*She goes out.*)

KROLL. Can you actually tolerate that man in your living room?

ROSMER. At one time he was my tutor, you know.

KROLL. Yes, I know that he came here and filled your head full of radical notions, till your father drove him out of the door with a horsewhip.

ROSMER (*with an edge of bitterness*). Even in his own home, Father had to play the major.

KROLL. You should thank him in his grave for that. Well!

(MRS. HELSETH *ushers* ULRIK BRENDEL *in the door, right, then withdraws, shutting it behind him. He is an imposing figure, with gray hair and beard, a bit emaciated, but virile and vigorous nonetheless. His dress is that of a common tramp: a threadbare overcoat, battered shoes, no visible shirt. He wears old black gloves and carries a soft, well soiled hat under his arm and a walking stick in one hand. At first he hesitates, then crosses briskly over to* KROLL, *with his free hand extended.*)

BRENDEL. Good evening, John.

KROLL. Beg pardon—

BRENDEL. Had you ever expected to see me again? And here, within these odious walls?

KROLL. I beg your pardon. (*Pointing.*) There—

BRENDEL (*turns*). Of course. There we have him. John—my boy—you, whom I loved the most—!

ROSMER (*taking his hand*). My old teacher.

BRENDEL. In spite of certain memories, I couldn't pass by Rosmersholm without paying you a fleeting visit.

ROSMER. You're cordially welcome here now. Rest assured of that.

BRENDEL. Ah, and this captivating lady—? (*Bows.*) Your esteemed wife, of course.

ROSMER. Miss West.

BRENDEL. A close relative, no doubt. And yonder stranger—? A fellow prelate, I observe.

ROSMER. Dr. Kroll, headmaster of our preparatory school.

BRENDEL. Kroll? Kroll? Wait now. Didn't you study philology in your student days?

KROLL. Why, naturally.

BRENDEL. *Donnerwetter!* I knew you then.

KROLL. I beg your pardon—

BRENDEL. Weren't you—

KROLL. I beg your pardon—

BRENDEL. —one of those bullyboys of virtue that had me booted out of the Debating Club?

KROLL. It's quite possible. But I disavow any closer connection.

BRENDEL. I see! *Nach Belieben, Herr Doktor.* It's all the same to me. Ulrik Brendel remains the man he is, no matter what.

REBECCA. You're on your way into town, Mr. Brendel?

BRENDEL. You have hit the bull's-eye, your ladyship. At certain intervals I'm compelled to strike a blow for survival. I do it with reluctance; but—*enfin!*—necessity is absolute.

ROSMER. But, my dear Mr. Brendel, won't you allow me to help you? I mean, there must be something or other—

BRENDEL. Ah! What a suggestion! Do you want to traduce the ties that bind us? Never, John—never!

ROSMER. But what were you intending to do in town? Believe me, you won't find it so easy—

BRENDEL. You leave that to me, my boy. The die is cast. You see me poised before you on the threshold of a portentous journey, more so than all my earlier forays together. (*To* KROLL.) Might I ask the Herr Professor—*unter uns*—if there happens to be a passably decent, respectable and commodious meeting hall in your worthy town.

KROLL. The Workmen's Union Hall is the largest.

BRENDEL. And does the learned doctor have any accredited standing in this no doubt most useful organization?

KROLL. I have nothing whatsoever to do with them.

REBECCA (*to* BRENDEL). You'll have to get in touch with Peter Mortensgaard.

BRENDEL. *Pardon, madame*—but who is this idiot?

ROSMER. What makes you take him for an idiot?

BRENDEL. Can't I hear at once, from the name, that he's a plebeian?

KROLL. I didn't expect *that* answer.

BRENDEL. However, I shall stifle my distaste. Nothing else to do. If one stands—as I do—poised on the turning point of his life— It's settled. I'll establish contact with the individual—open direct negotiations—

ROSMER. Seriously, are you really standing at a turning point?

BRENDEL. Don't you know by now, my boy, that Ulrik Brendel is serious wherever he takes his stand? Yes, the time has come to put on the new man—to cast off that delicate reticence I've displayed till now.

ROSMER. How will you—?

BRENDEL. I shall take hold of life with a fiery hand. Forge on. Thrust upward. Our spirits are breathing at long last the age of the tempestuous solstice. And now I want to lay my wisp of dust on the altar of liberation.

KROLL. *You*, too—?

BRENDEL (*to them all*). Has the present company any intimate knowledge of my scattered writings?

KROLL. No, I frankly have to admit that, uh—

REBECCA. I've read quite a few. My foster father owned them.

BRENDEL. Beautiful lady—then you've wasted your time. Let me tell you, they're less than trash.

REBECCA. Oh?

BRENDEL. The ones you've read, yes. No man, no woman —no one knows my greatest works—except myself.

REBECCA. Why so?

BRENDEL. Because they remain unwritten.

ROSMER. But, my dear Mr. Brendel—

BRENDEL. You recall, *mein Johannes*, that I'm something of a sybarite. *Ein Feinschmecker*. And have been, all my days. I love to savor things in solitude. Because then my pleasure doubles, yes, ten times over. So you see—whenever golden dreams poured over me and engulfed me—whenever new ideas unfolded, dazzlingly and boundlessly within me, lifting me to the heights on their soaring wings—then I formed them into poems, visions, images. I mean, into their equivalents, you understand.

ROSMER. Oh, yes.

BRENDEL. The ecstasies I've relished in my time, John! The mysterious beatitude of creation—or, again, its equivalent—the plaudits, the acclaim, the celebrity, the laurel crowns—all these I've gathered in my grateful hands, trembling with joy. In my most secret imaginings, I've known such exaltation—that my mind goes reeling into space.

KROLL. Hm—

ROSMER. But nothing written down?

BRENDEL. Not a word. It's always sickened me, that slave's labor of being my own secretary. And then, why should I profane my own ideals, when I can enjoy them in their purity, all to myself? But now they're going on the block. Truly—I feel just like a mother giving her budding daughters into their bridegrooms' arms. But I'll sacrifice them, nevertheless, on the altar of liberation. A series of well-devised lectures, throughout the country—!

REBECCA (*with animation*). How generous of you, Mr. Brendel! You're giving the best you have.

ROSMER. All you have.

REBECCA (*looks meaningfully at* ROSMER). How many of us would do that? Would *dare* to?

ROSMER (*returning her look*). Who knows?

BRENDEL. My audience is moved. That cheers my heart and restores my will. With this, I can press into action. But one thing, still— (*To* KROLL.) Herr Preceptor, can you inform me—is there a Temperance Society in town? I mean, for total abstention! There has to be.

KROLL. Indeed there is. And I, its president, am at your service.

BRENDEL. Ah, how could I mistake you! Well, it's not impossible that I'll look in on you then, and enroll for the span of a week.

KROLL. Excuse me—but we don't take members by the week.

BRENDEL. À la bonheur, Herr Pedagogue. Ulrik Brendel will not foist himself on such a conclave. But I mustn't prolong my presence in this house, so rich in memories. I'm off to town, and the choice of suitable lodgings. I trust one can find a respectable hotel.

REBECCA. Won't you have a little warming drink before you go?

BRENDEL. Warming in what way, gracious lady?

REBECCA. Oh, a cup of tea, or—

BRENDEL. I thank my bountiful hostess. However, I can impose no longer on private hospitality. (*With a flourish of his hand.*) Farewell, my masters—and madame! (*Starts for the door, then turns.*) Oh, by the way, John—Pastor Rosmer—for the sake of our old-time friendship, could you do your former tutor a service?

ROSMER. Of course. With all my heart.

BRENDEL. Good. Then loan me—for a day or two—a clean dress shirt.

ROSMER. Is that all?

BRENDEL. You see, I'm journeying on foot—for the moment. My baggage is being forwarded.

ROSMER. Why, yes. But is there nothing else?

BRENDEL. Ah, you know what—maybe you could spare me an old, worn topcoat?

ROSMER. Yes, yes, certainly.

BRENDEL. And if there were a pair of passable boots to match—

ROSMER. Don't worry, we'll turn up something. As soon as we have your address, we'll send them on.

BRENDEL. Absolutely not! No inconveniences on my account. I'll just take these few bagatelles along.

ROSMER. All right. If you'll come upstairs with me, then.

REBECCA. No, let me. Mrs. Helseth and I can do it.

BRENDEL. I could never allow this distinguished lady to—

REBECCA. Oh, bosh! Come along, Mr. Brendel.

(*She goes out, right.*)

ROSMER (*detaining* BRENDEL). Tell me—isn't there anything else I can help you with.

BRENDEL. In point of fact, I can't imagine *what*. Oh, blast it! Yes, now that I think of it—John, would you possibly have eight crowns on you?

ROSMER. Let's have a look. (*Opens his wallet.*) Here's a couple of ten-crown notes.

BRENDEL. Oh, well, never mind. I'll take those. Can always break them in town. And thanks the while. Don't forget, that's two tens I owe you. Good night, John, my own dear boy! And to you, honored sir!

(*He goes out, right, where* ROSMER, *after taking leave of him, shuts the door.*)

KROLL. God of mercy! So that's the Ulrik Brendel that people once thought would be a force in this world.

ROSMER (*quietly*). At least he's had the courage to live life on his own terms. I think that's no small thing to have done.

KROLL. What? His kind of life? I almost think that man could muddle your ideas even now.

ROSMER. Oh, no. I finally have my thinking all straightened out.

KROLL. I only hope you're right, Rosmer. You're so awfully impressionable.

ROSMER. Let's sit down. I'd like to talk to you.

KROLL. Go right ahead.

(*They settle down on the sofa.*)

ROSMER (*after a brief pause*). We have it nice and comfortable here, don't you think?

KROLL. Yes, nice, comfortable—and peaceful. You've made yourself a home here. And I've lost mine.

ROSMER. Oh, don't say that. What's divided now will soon heal together.

KROLL. Never. Never. The lance has broken in the wound. Nothing will ever be the same.

ROSMER. Listen, Kroll. The two of us have been close now for so many, many years. Do you think it's conceivable that anything could disrupt our friendship?

KROLL. I don't know what on earth could ever come between us. But why do you bring that up?

ROSMER. The fact that you place such importance on people holding precisely the same views.

KROLL. Well, yes. But then our two outlooks hardly differ at all—on the key issues, anyway.

ROSMER (*softly*). That's—no longer true.

KROLL (*starts to rise*). What's this?

ROSMER (*restraining him*). No, Kroll, stay. Please.

KROLL. What's going on? I don't understand you. Speak out!

ROSMER. It's a new summer that's entered my spirit. A way of seeing that's fresh—and young again. And that's why I stand now—

KROLL. Where? Where do you stand?

ROSMER. There, where your children stand.

KROLL. You? You! But that's impossible! You stand—*where* did you say?

ROSMER. With Laurits and Hilda, on their side.

KROLL (*bowing his head*). An apostate. John Rosmer, an apostate.

ROSMER. I ought to have felt so glad—so richly content, practicing what you call apostasy. But I suffered painfully all the same. Because I knew only too well what bitter sorrow it would mean for you.

KROLL. Rosmer—Rosmer! I'll never get over this. (*Looks sadly at him.*) Oh, that even you could give yourself over to the forces of decadence and corruption that are undermining our miserable country.

ROSMER. It's the forces of liberation I want to give myself to.

KROLL. Oh, I know about that! That's what they call it, both the pied pipers and the fools that get led astray. But do you really think there's any liberation to be found in the spiritual poison that's filtering through our whole society?

ROSMER. I'm not committed to the spirit that destroys. Not to any faction. I want to bring people together from all sides. As many as I can reach, as honestly as I can. I want to live and use all my vital energies toward that one end: the creation of a true democracy in this land.

KROLL. Don't we have democracy enough! For my part, I think we're all on our way down into the muck and mire, where only the lowest of the low can thrive.

ROSMER. Exactly why I want democracy to assume its rightful role.

KROLL. What role?

ROSMER. To elevate all our countrymen into noblemen.

KROLL. All of them—!

ROSMER. As many as possible, anyway.

KROLL. Through what means?

ROSMER. By liberating their minds and tempering their wills.

KROLL. You're a dreamer, Rosmer. Will *you* liberate them? And temper them?

ROSMER. No, I can only try to rouse them. As for doing it—that's their job.

KROLL. And you think they can?

ROSMER. Yes.

KROLL. Through their own power?

ROSMER. Precisely. Through their own power. There is no other.

KROLL (*rising*). Is that language that befits a man of God?

ROSMER. I am no longer a man of God.

KROLL. Yes, but—the faith of your childhood—?

ROSMER. Is gone now.

KROLL. You don't—!

ROSMER (*rises*). I've given it up. I *had* to give it up, Kroll.

KROLL. I see. Yes, of course. One follows from the other. I suppose that was why you resigned from the church?

ROSMER. Yes. When I finally got my thinking straightened out—when I understood beyond any doubt that this was no temporary crisis, but rather something I never again could, or would, shake off—then I left.

KROLL. So that's been festering in you all this time. And we—your friends—were kept in the dark about it. Rosmer, Rosmer—how could you hide the dismal truth from us?

ROSMER. Because I felt it was a problem that concerned no one but me. And I didn't want to cause you and my other friends any unnecessary pain. I thought I could go on living here as before: quiet, tranquil, content. I wanted to read—to immerse myself in all those works that once had been closed books to me—to open my entire life to that great world of truth and freedom that's come to me now like a revelation.

KROLL. Apostasy! It's stamped on every word. But why are you confessing your secret? Why now, of all times?

ROSMER. You drove me to it, Kroll.

KROLL. I—drove you—!

ROSMER. When I heard how violent you'd been at those political meetings—and read about all those brutal speeches you were making—all those vicious attacks and derisive remarks you hurled at anybody who opposed you— Oh, Kroll, that you, you could become like that. Then my duty was clear. Humanity is being defiled by this struggle we're in. We need peace and joy and reconciliation filling our souls. That's why I've taken this step now, to proclaim myself openly—yes, and to test my own powers. Couldn't you—from your side—meet me halfway in that?

KROLL. Never in my life will I compromise with the subversive elements in society.

ROSMER. Then let's at least fight with honorable weapons, since we *have* to come to that.

KROLL. He who isn't with me in such matters of life and death, I can recognize no longer. And I owe him no consideration.

ROSMER. Does that include me?

KROLL. You're the one who broke with me, Rosmer.

ROSMER. But *is* this a break—between us?

KROLL. Us! This is a break with everyone who's stood by you in the past. Now you can take the consequences.

(REBECCA *comes in, right, opening the door wide.*)

REBECCA. So, he's on his way now to his great, sacrificial feast. And now we can have our supper. Dr. Kroll, won't you—?

KROLL (*taking his hat*). Good night, Miss West. I don't belong in this house any more.

REBECCA (*agitated*). What is it? (*Shuts the door and approaches them.*) Have you told him—?

ROSMER. He knows now.

KROLL. We're not letting you go, Rosmer. We'll force you back with us again.

ROSMER. I'll never come back.

KROLL. We'll see about that. You're not a man who can stand alone.

ROSMER. I'm not so completely alone, you know. There are two of us to bear the solitude.

KROLL. Ah—! (*A suspicion flashes through him.*) That, too. Beata's words—!

ROSMER. Beąta—?

KROLL (*rejecting the thought*). No, no—that's indecent. Forgive me.

ROSMER. What? What is?

KROLL. Let's drop it. It's—inconceivable! Forgive me. Goodbye.

(*He moves toward the double doors to the hall.*)

ROSMER (*following him*). Kroll! We can't end what's between us like this. I'm coming to see you tomorrow.

KROLL (*turning in the doorway*). Don't you set foot in my house!

(*He takes his stick and goes.* ROSMER *stands a moment in the open doorway, then closes the doors and goes over to the table.*)

ROSMER. Never mind, Rebecca. We'll weather it out, you and I. We two faithful friends.

REBECCA. What do you suppose he was thinking of when he said: "It's inconceivable"?

ROSMER. Don't give it a second thought, my dear. He didn't know what he was thinking. But I'll visit him in the morning. Good night.

REBECCA. You want to turn in so early? Even after this?

ROSMER. Exactly as usual. I feel so relieved, now that it's over. You can see—I'm quite calm. And you mustn't let it upset you either. Good night.

REBECCA. Good night, John dear. Sleep well.

(ROSMER *goes out by the hall door; his footsteps are heard going up the stairs.* REBECCA *crosses and pulls a bell rope near the stove. After a moment,* MRS. HELSETH *enters right.*)

REBECCA. Clear the table, would you, Mrs. Helseth. The pastor's not having supper—and Dr. Kroll's gone home.

MRS. HELSETH. The headmaster gone? Was something the matter with him?

REBECCA (*picks up her crocheting*). He said he felt a terrible storm coming on—

MRS. HELSETH. That *is* strange. Because there's not a cloud in the sky tonight.

REBECCA. As long as he doesn't meet the white horse. I'm afraid we may hear soon now from one of those ghostly beings.

MRS. HELSETH. Lord love you, miss! Don't talk that way. It's awful.

REBECCA. There, there, now—

MRS. HELSETH (*in a hushed voice*). You really believe, miss, that there's somebody here who's marked to go?

REBECCA. Oh, of course not. But there are so many different kinds of white horses in this world, Mrs. Helseth. Well, good night. I'm going to my room.

MRS. HELSETH. Good night, miss.

(REBECCA, *carrying her crochet-work, goes out, right.*)

MRS. HELSETH (*turns down the lamp, shaking her head and muttering*). Oh, my—glory be! That Miss West. The things she can think to say.

⤳(ACT TWO)↢

JOHN ROSMER'S *study. Entrance door in the side wall, left. In the background a doorway, with drapes drawn aside, leading into* ROSMER'S *bedroom. A window at the right, and in front of it a desk covered with books and papers. Bookshelves and cabinets around the walls. Austere furnishings. An old-fashioned settee with a table in front of it, downstage left.* ROSMER, *wearing a smoking jacket, is seated in a high-backed chair at the desk. He is leafing through a periodical, cutting the pages and browsing in it here and there. A knock at the door, left.*

ROSMER (*without turning*). Come in.

(REBECCA WEST *enters, wearing a dressing gown.*)

REBECCA. Good morning.

ROSMER (*continuing to read*). Good morning, my dear. Did you want something?

REBECCA. I only wanted to know if you'd slept well.

ROSMER. Oh, a lovely, sound sleep. No dreams. (*Turns.*) And you?

REBECCA. Oh, yes, thanks. Near morning, anyway.

ROSMER. I haven't felt so light-hearted in I don't know how long. It was certainly good to have talked this out.

REBECCA. Yes, John, you shouldn't have held back so long.

523

ROSMER. I can't understand myself that I could be such a coward.

REBECCA. Well, it wasn't really cowardice—

ROSMER. Yes, yes, it was. At bottom I can see, there was some cowardice there.

REBECCA. How much more courageous of you, then, to break with them. (*Sitting down beside him on a chair by the desk.*) But now I want to tell you something I've done —and, please, don't be angry with me.

ROSMER. Angry? My dear, why would you think that—?

REBECCA. Yes, because it was a bit presumptuous of me maybe, but—

ROSMER. Well, tell me then.

REBECCA. Last evening, when Ulrik Brendel was leaving —I gave him a note of—some two or three lines to take to Mortensgaard.

ROSMER (*somewhat uneasily*). But, Rebecca dear— Well, what did you write?

REBECCA. I wrote he'd be doing you a real favor if he looked out for that poor man a little and helped him in any way possible.

ROSMER. My dear, that you shouldn't have done. You've only hurt Brendel by that. And Mortensgaard—he's one man I just don't want to be involved with. You know the trouble I had with him once.

REBECCA. But don't you think now might be a very good time to renew your relationship with him?

ROSMER. I? With Mortensgaard? Why so?

REBECCA. Because you can hardly be secure now—with this breach between you and your friends.

ROSMER (*looks at her and shakes his head*). Do you actually think Kroll or any of the others would want to take revenge? That they'd try to—?

REBECCA. In their first fit of rage—who knows? It seems to me, considering the way he took it—

ROSMER. Oh, you still ought to know him better than that. Kroll's a man of principle, to the core. I'll go into town this afternoon and talk to him. I'll talk with all of them. You'll see how it'll all pass over—

(MRS. HELSETH *enters, left.*)

REBECCA (*rises*). What is it, Mrs. Helseth?

MRS. HELSETH. Dr. Kroll is downstairs in the hall.

ROSMER (*quickly getting up*). Kroll!

REBECCA. I don't believe it—!

MRS. HELSETH. He asks if he might come up and speak with the pastor.

ROSMER (*to* REBECCA). What did I say! Why, of course he can. (*Goes to the door and calls down the stairs.*) Come right up, my friend! You couldn't be more welcome!

(ROSMER *stands holding the door open.* MRS. HELSETH *leaves.* REBECCA *draws the drapes across the doorway in back, then straightens up the room here and there.* DR. KROLL, *hat in hand, comes in.*)

ROSMER (*with quiet feeling*). I knew it just couldn't be the last time—

KROLL. Today I see things in a totally different light than yesterday.

ROSMER. Yes, you must. And you do, Kroll, don't you? Now, after you've reflected—

KROLL. You misunderstand me completely. (*Places his hat on the table by the settee.*) It's essential that I talk to you alone.

ROSMER. Why shouldn't Miss West—?

REBECCA. No, no, Mr. Rosmer. I'll go.

KROLL (*surveying her up and down*). And I ought to beg your pardon, Miss West, for stopping by so early in the day—and surprising you before you had time to—

REBECCA (*startled*). Why not? Do you find anything wrong in my wearing a dressing gown around this house?

KROLL. Heavens, no! I haven't the least idea what the local customs are now at Rosmersholm.

ROSMER. Kroll—you're like another person today!

REBECCA. If you'll excuse me, Dr. Kroll.

(*She goes out, left.*)

KROLL. With your permission— (*He sits on the settee.*)

ROSMER. Yes, let's sit down in confidence and have a good talk. (*He takes a chair opposite* KROLL.)

KROLL. I haven't shut my eyes since yesterday. I lay awake all night, thinking and thinking.

ROSMER. And what's your verdict today?

KROLL. This will take some time, Rosmer. Let me begin with a kind of prelude. I can give you a little news about Ulrik Brendel.

ROSMER. Did he come to see you?

KROLL. No. He found himself lodgings in a cheap tavern, among the dregs of society, naturally. He drank, and stood drinks, as long as he had anything left. Then he started assailing the entire company present as barbarian scum, in which, of course, he was quite correct. But their response was to beat him soundly and heave him in the gutter.

ROSMER. So he really is incorrigible, then.

KROLL. He'd also pawned your coat. But that was redeemed for him. Can you guess by whom?

ROSMER. You, perhaps?

KROLL. No. By the princely Mr. Mortensgaard.

ROSMER. I see.

KROLL. I heard tell that Mr. Brendel's first social call was made on that "idiot" and "plebeian."

ROSMER. That appears to have been lucky for him—

KROLL. Quite so. (*Leans closer to* ROSMER *across the table.*) But now we're getting into something that, for our old—I mean, our former friendship's sake, I ought to warn you about.

ROSMER. And what's that, Kroll?

KROLL. It's that there seems to be some kind of game going on behind your back in this house.

ROSMER. Why do you think so? You don't mean Reb— Miss West?

KROLL. Yes, precisely. And I can perfectly understand it, from her point of view. She's been accustomed for so long now to running things in this house. But, even so—

ROSMER. My dear Kroll, you couldn't be more mistaken. She and I—we keep no secrets from each other. About anything.

KROLL. Has she told you she's been corresponding with the editor of the *Beacon*?

ROSMER. Oh, you mean that little note she sent with Brendel?

KROLL. So you know about that. And do you approve of her courting that scandalmonger who tries to pillory me week after week, both as an educator and as a public figure?

ROSMER. Really, Kroll, I'm sure she never thought of that aspect of it. And besides, she's as free to act on her own as I am.

KROLL. So? Well, I guess that goes along with this new direction you've taken. I can assume, then, that Miss West stands where you do.

ROSMER. She does. The two of us have been working this through together.

KROLL (*looks at him and slowly shakes his head*). How blind and beguiled you are!

ROSMER. I? Why do you say that?

KROLL. Because I dare not—*will* not think the worst. No, no—let me finish! You really do value my friendship, don't you, Rosmer? And my respect?

ROSMER. That question hardly needs an answer.

KROLL. But there are other questions that do—that demand a full explanation on your part. Would you object if I held a sort of inquest—?

ROSMER. Inquest?

KROLL. Yes, to ask you about a few matters that might stir up some painful memories. You see, this apostasy of yours—or this liberation, as you put it—is bound up with so much else that you really must clarify for me, simply for your own sake.

ROSMER. You can ask about anything. I've nothing to hide.

KROLL. Tell me, then—what do you honestly believe was the underlying motive for Beata to take her own life?

ROSMER. Can you be in any doubt about that? Or rather —can there be any accounting for what a sick, agonized, unbalanced mind may do?

KROLL. Are you positive that Beata really was so unbalanced? The doctors agreed, at any rate, that her case was open to interpretation.

ROSMER. If the doctors had ever seen her the way I did so many times, day and night, they wouldn't have had any doubts.

KROLL. I had none, either, then.

ROSMER. No, sad to say, it was impossible to have any doubts. I've told you about that wild sensual passion she couldn't control—and expected me to respond to. Oh, she could be terrifying! And then, in her last years, those torments of self-reproach that hadn't the slightest basis in fact.

KROLL. Yes, after she learned she could never have children.

ROSMER. Can you imagine—such fits of anguish over something that wasn't at all her fault—! You call that sanity?

KROLL. Hm. Do you remember if you had any books in the house then, on marriage and the way it's been changing today—in certain advanced quarters?

ROSMER. I remember Miss West loaned me a book like that. She inherited Dr. West's library, as you know. But, my dear Kroll, you surely don't imagine we'd be careless enough to expose an unstable mind to that sort of thing.

I'd swear to high heaven, we're not to blame. It was her own overstrung nerves that took her over the edge.

KROLL. One thing I can tell you, in any case. When poor Beata put an end to her tortured, exhausted life, she did it so you could be happy—and free to live—as you wished.

ROSMER (*half rising out of his chair*). What do you mean by that?

KROLL. Listen to me quietly, Rosmer. Because now I can speak about this. Twice in that last year she came to see me, to pour out the dread and despair she was feeling.

ROSMER. About what you just told me?

KROLL. No. The first time, she came by and announced that you were on the verge of apostasy—planning to break with the faith of your fathers.

ROSMER (*heatedly*). What you're saying, Kroll, is impossible! Simply impossible! You've got to be mistaken.

KROLL. Why?

ROSMER. Because as long as Beata lived, I kept all this turmoil and doubt bottled up inside of me. I was fighting it out alone, in utter silence. I don't even think that Rebecca—

KROLL. Rebecca?

ROSMER. All right—Miss West. It's so much easier to say Rebecca.

KROLL. So I've noticed.

ROSMER. Don't you see, it's just inconceivable that Beata could get that idea. And why wouldn't she talk to me about it. But she never did. Never a word.

KROLL. Poor thing—she begged and implored me to talk to you.

ROSMER. Then why didn't you?

KROLL. How could I have a moment's doubt, then, that she was mentally ill? Such an accusation against a man like you! And then she came by again—about a month later. This time she seemed more calm. But as she was leaving, she said: "They can look for the white horse soon now at Rosmersholm."

ROSMER. Yes, the white horse—she spoke about it so often.

KROLL. And then when I tried to divert her from those morbid thoughts, she only answered: "I don't have much time. Because now John has to marry Rebecca, at once."

ROSMER (*almost speechless*). What did you say—? I marry—!

KROLL. It was a Thursday afternoon. That Saturday evening she threw herself from the footbridge into the mill-race.

ROSMER And you didn't warn us—!

KROLL. You know yourself how she'd make those remarks about not having long to live.

ROSMER. I know. But still—you *should* have warned us!

KROLL. I realized that. But then it was too late.

ROSMER. But why, in all this time—? Why have you suppressed all this?

KROLL. What earthly good would it serve to come here and distress you even further? Obviously, I took everything she said to be sheer delusion—up to last night.

ROSMER. But not anymore?

KROLL. Didn't Beata see quite clearly when she said you were deserting the faith you were raised in?

ROSMER (*staring into space*). Yes, that I can't understand. It's beyond all comprehension.

KROLL. Incomprehensible or not—it's a fact. And I ask you now, Rosmer—how much truth is there in her other charge? That last one, I mean.

ROSMER. Charge? *Was* it a charge?

KROLL. Perhaps you didn't notice the precise wording. She was going to depart, she said—why? Well?

ROSMER. So I could marry Rebecca—

KROLL. Not quite her language. Beata expressed it differently. She said: "I don't have much time. Because now John *has* to marry Rebecca, *at once.*"

ROSMER (*looks at him a moment, then rises*). Now I understand you, Kroll.

KROLL. Well, what's your answer?

ROSMER (*his voice quietly controlled throughout*). To anything so insulting—? The only proper answer would be to show you the door.

KROLL (*getting up*). As you say.

ROSMER (*planting himself in front of him*). Now you listen to me. For more than a year—ever since Beata died —Rebecca West and I have lived alone here at Rosmersholm. In all that time you've known Beata's charge against us. But not for one instant have I observed that you took the least exception to Rebecca and me living together this way.

KROLL. I didn't realize till yesterday evening that an atheist had been cohabiting with a—a freethinker.

ROSMER. Ah—! Then you don't believe nobility of character can exist among atheists and freethinkers? Or that a love of morality can function in them as strong as a natural drive?

KROLL. I set no great store by any morality that isn't rooted in the faith of the church.

ROSMER. And that goes for Rebecca and me, too? In our relationship?

KROLL. I can hardly exempt the two of you from my sense that there's no sizable gap separating free thought from—hm!

ROSMER. From what?

KROLL. From free love—if you insist.

ROSMER (*softly*). And you have no shame, saying that to me! You, who've known me from my earliest childhood.

KROLL. Exactly my point. I know how easily you can be molded by the people around you. And this Rebecca of yours—all right, Miss West—we really don't know very much about her. In short, Rosmer—I'm not giving up on you. And for your part, you must try to save yourself before it's too late.

ROSMER. Save myself—? How—?

(MRS. HELSETH *appears at the door, left, and looks in.*)

ROSMER. What do you want?

MRS. HELSETH. It was to ask Miss West to come downstairs—

ROSMER. Miss West isn't up here.

MRS. HELSETH. No? (*Glancing about.*) But that's strange. (*She goes.*)

ROSMER. You were saying—?

KROLL. Listen. What went on here in secret while Beata lived—and what may still go on here—is nothing I care to look into. You were terribly unhappy in your marriage. And, to some extent, that excuses you.

ROSMER. Oh, how little you really know me—

KROLL. Don't interrupt. What I'm saying is—if this relationship with Miss West is going to continue, then it's imperative for you to be discreet about this backsliding— this tragic betrayal of your faith she's led you into. Let me speak! Let me speak! I'm saying, if this madness has to go on, then think and believe and trust in anything you want, for God's sake—anything. But keep your beliefs to yourself. These are totally private matters, after all. There's no need to shout them from the rooftops.

ROSMER. But I do need to free myself from a situation that's false and ambiguous.

KROLL. Remember, you have a duty to your family traditions, Rosmer. Since time out of mind, Rosmersholm has been a kind of citadel of ceremony and order—of a delicate regard for everything that's sanctioned and upheld by the best in society. The whole district has drawn its style from Rosmersholm. If it ever was rumored around that you yourself had shattered what I might call the ruling idea of the Rosmers, it would create the most devastating and hopeless confusion.

ROSMER. I can't see it that way, Kroll. It seems to me I have an overriding obligation to shed a little light and happiness here, where the Rosmer family has sown gloom and darkness far, far too long.

KROLL (*looks at him sternly*). Yes, wouldn't that be a worthy challenge for the last of the family line! Pass it up, Rosmer. It's not the work you were cut out for. You were made to live quietly, among books.

ROSMER. Yes, perhaps. But I want to take part, for once now, in the battle of life.

KROLL. The battle of life—you know what that would mean for you? A fight to the finish with all your friends.

ROSMER (*in a low voice*). They can't all be as fanatical as you.

KROLL. You're an innocent soul, Rosmer. You have no experience of the world. You have no conception of the storm that's going to break over you.

(MRS. HELSETH *looks in at the door, left.*)

MRS. HELSETH. Miss West wants me to ask—

ROSMER. What is it?

MRS. HELSETH. There's someone downstairs who'd like a word with the pastor.

ROSMER. The man who was here last night?

MRS. HELSETH. No, it's that Mortensgaard.

ROSMER. Mortensgaard?

KROLL. Aha! So we've come to that! Already!

ROSMER. Why does he want me? Why didn't you send him away?

MRS. HELSETH. Miss West said I should ask if he might come up.

ROSMER. Tell him somebody's here—

KROLL (*to* MRS. HELSETH). You can admit him.

(MRS. HELSETH *leaves.*)

KROLL (*takes his hat*). I'm quitting the field—for the moment. But the decisive battle is yet to come.

ROSMER. As I live and breathe, Kroll—I have nothing to do with Mortensgaard.

KROLL. I don't believe you any more. On anything. In no respect can I trust you after this. Now it's war to the knife. We'll have to see that you're put out of commission.

ROSMER. Oh, Kroll, how far—and how low you've fallen.

KROLL. I? You should talk! Remember Beata!

ROSMER. Back to *that* again.

KROLL. No. The mystery of the mill-race you'll have to resolve in your own conscience—if you still have one.

(PETER MORTENSGAARD *enters quietly and imperturbably at the left. He is a small, lean man with thin reddish hair and beard.*)

KROLL (*hatred in his glance*). Ah, the *Beacon*. And burning at Rosmersholm. (*Buttoning his coat.*) Well, that leaves me no doubt about the course I have to take.

MORTENSGAARD (*amiably*). The *Beacon* will always be shining to light Dr. Kroll on his way.

KROLL. Yes, you're a monument to good will. Actually, I believe there's a commandment reminding us not to bear false witness against our neighbor—

MORTENSGAARD. The headmaster hardly needs to instruct me in the commandments.

KROLL. Not even the seventh?

ROSMER. Kroll—!

MORTENSGAARD. If I had such a need, my obvious choice would be the pastor.

KROLL (*with veiled scorn*). The pastor? Yes, no question that Pastor Rosmer's the obvious choice in *that* department. To your mutual profit, gentlemen! (*He goes out, slamming the door behind him.*)

ROSMER (*remains staring at the door and speaks to himself*). So—then that's it. (*Turns.*) Tell me, Mr. Mortensgaard, what brings you out here to see me?

MORTENSGAARD. It was actually Miss West I came to see.

I thought I ought to thank her for the good letter she sent me yesterday.

ROSMER. I know she wrote you. Did you get to talk with her?

MORTENSGAARD. Yes, a little. (*With a faint smile.*) I hear viewpoints are shifting on certain issues here at Rosmersholm.

ROSMER. My views have shifted a great deal. I could almost say—about everything.

MORTENSGAARD. Miss West told me. And that's why she thought I ought to stop up and talk with you a bit about this.

ROSMER. About what, Mr. Mortensgaard?

MORTENSGAARD. Would you allow me to make a statement in the *Beacon* that you've rethought your position— and allied yourself with the liberal and progressive cause?

ROSMER. Certainly you may. In fact, I specifically request you to.

MORTENSGAARD. Then I'll run it in tomorrow morning's edition. That'll make a story of some consequence: Pastor Rosmer of Rosmersholm enlisting to fight for enlightenment in *both* senses now.

ROSMER. I'm not sure I understand you.

MORTENSGAARD. I'm saying, in effect, that it raises the moral tone of our party whenever we gain a supporter of high Christian principles.

ROSMER (*somewhat surprised*). You don't know—? Miss West didn't tell you that, too?

MORTENSGAARD. What, Pastor? She didn't have time. She said I could get the rest straight from you up here.

ROSMER. Well, then I ought to explain that my self-liberation is categorical. Across the board. I've cut all my ties with the church. Its doctrines mean nothing to me now.

MORTENSGAARD (*gazing at him in astonishment*). No! If the moon fell out of the sky, I wouldn't be more—! You, of all people—!

ROSMER. Yes, I stand now where you've stood for so long. You can report that tomorrow in the *Beacon*.

MORTENSGAARD. That, too? No, my dear Pastor—excuse me, but that side of it is hardly worth mentioning.

ROSMER. Not worth mentioning?

MORTENSGAARD. I mean, not immediately.

ROSMER. But I don't understand—

MORTENSGAARD. Yes, you see, Pastor—you're probably not up on all the fine points of this the way I am. But if you've really come over to the liberal cause, and if—as Miss West says—you want to take part in the movement—then I'm sure your intention is to lend whatever support you can to both.

ROSMER. Yes, I want to very much.

MORTENSGAARD. Well, then let me just tell you that if you bring your break with the church out in the open, you'll have tied your hands right at the start.

ROSMER. You think so?

MORTENSGAARD. Yes, there won't be much you can accomplish hereabouts, you can be certain of that. And besides—we've got enough freethinkers as it is. I almost said, we have more than we know what to do with. What the party needs is Christian elements—something everyone has to respect. *That's* where our shortage is. The best advice for you is to stay close-mouthed about anything that doesn't concern the public. At least, that's my opinion.

ROSMER. I see. So you couldn't risk involving yourself with me if I openly confessed my apostasy?

MORTENSGAARD (*shaking his head*). I couldn't chance it, Pastor. Lately I've made it a rule never to support anything or anyone who's got it in for the church.

ROSMER. Have you been turning back to the church, then?

MORTENSGAARD. That's beside the point.

ROSMER. Oh, I see. Yes, now I understand you.

MORTENSGAARD. Pastor—you should remember that I, more than most, have had my freedom of action curbed.

ROSMER. Curbed by what?

MORTENSGAARD. By the fact that I'm a marked man.

ROSMER. Ah—that's true.

MORTENSGAARD. A marked man, Pastor. You above all should remember that. Because it was you, primarily, who set the mark on me.

ROSMER. If I'd stood then where I do now, I would have treated your misconduct more sensitively.

MORTENSGAARD. I agree that you would. But it's too late now. You've branded me once and for all. Marked me for life. You don't quite realize what those words mean. But maybe soon now, Pastor, you'll know that pain yourself.

ROSMER. I?

MORTENSGAARD. Yes. You don't imagine that Kroll and his crowd will ever forgive a defection like yours. And I hear the *County Herald* is calling for blood. It might well be that you become a marked man, too.

ROSMER. I think my private life is above reproach, Mr. Mortensgaard. There's nothing there to attack.

MORTENSGAARD (*with a slight smile*). That's a sweeping statement, Pastor.

ROSMER. Perhaps. But I feel it's justified.

MORTENSGAARD. Even if you probed your own conduct as carefully as you once probed mine?

ROSMER. You speak so strangely. What are you alluding to? Something in particular?

MORTENSGAARD. Yes, there *is* something. Just one little thing. But it could prove quite unsavory if any of the foul-minded opposition got wind of it.

ROSMER. Would you be good enough to tell me what that is?

MORTENSGAARD. You can't guess?

ROSMER. Not at all. I haven't any idea.

MORTENSGAARD. Well, then, let me tell you. I have in my possession a curious letter that was written here at Rosmersholm.

ROSMER. You mean Miss West's. Is that so curious?

MORTENSGAARD. No, there's nothing curious about that one. But I once had another letter from this house.

ROSMER. Also from Miss West?

MORTENSGAARD. No, Pastor.

ROSMER. Well, from whom, then? From whom?

MORTENSGAARD. From the late Mrs. Rosmer.

ROSMER. From my wife! *You* had a letter from my wife?

MORTENSGAARD. That's right.

ROSMER. When?

MORTENSGAARD. Shortly before she died. It must be a year and a half since then. And it's *that* letter I find so curious.

ROSMER. You know, of course, that my wife was mentally ill at the time.

MORTENSGAARD. I know there were many who thought so. But, to my mind, there was no sign of it in the letter. When I say the letter was curious, I mean in a different way.

ROSMER. And what on earth did my poor wife find to write you about?

MORTENSGAARD. I have it at home. She begins by saying, in effect, that she lives in a constant terror. There are so many malicious people in these parts, she writes. And they only think about how they can injure and hurt you.

ROSMER. Me?

MORTENSGAARD. So she says. And then, most curious of all— Should I go on, Pastor?

ROSMER. Yes, everything! Don't hold back.

MORTENSGAARD. Then she begged and beseeched me to be magnanimous. She said she knew it was her husband who got me dismissed from my teaching job. So she fervently implored me not to take revenge.

ROSMER. How did she think you could take revenge?

MORTENSGAARD. According to the letter, if I should hear rumors about anything disreputable going on at Rosmersholm, I mustn't put any stock in them, because they'd only be the work of spiteful people out to make you miserable.

ROSMER. Is that in the letter?

MORTENSGAARD. You can read it yourself, at your convenience.

ROSMER. But I don't understand—! What sort of vicious rumors was she imagining?

MORTENSGAARD. First, that you'd repudiated your childhood faith. She denied that most emphatically—then. And, secondly—hm—

ROSMER. Yes?

MORTENSGAARD. Well, secondly, she writes—and it's a bit confused here—that she knows of no illicit relationship at Rosmersholm. That no wrong has ever been committed against her. And if rumors to that effect should circulate, she begs me not to report them in the *Beacon*.

ROSMER. Did she name any names?

MORTENSGAARD. No.

ROSMER. Who brought you this letter?

MORTENSGAARD. I promised not to say. It was hand-delivered to me one evening, after dark.

ROSMER. If you'd made inquiries at the time, you would have learned that my poor, unhappy wife wasn't exactly of sound mind.

MORTENSGAARD. I did make inquiries, Pastor. But I must say, I didn't get quite *that* impression.

ROSMER. No? But why are you telling me now about this old, confused letter?

MORTENSGAARD. As a warning for you, Pastor Rosmer, to be exceedingly cautious.

ROSMER. In my private life, you mean?

MORTENSGAARD. Yes. You have to remember that you're not invulnerable any more.

ROSMER. You persist in the assumption that I have something to hide.

MORTENSGAARD. I don't know why a man of liberal persuasion shouldn't be entitled to live as full a life as possible. But, as I said, from now on just be careful. If there's talk of anything that flies in the face of public sentiment, then you can be sure that the whole liberal movement here will suffer for it. Goodbye, Pastor Rosmer.

ROSMER. Goodbye.

MORTENSGAARD. I'll go directly to the pressroom and put the great news in the *Beacon*.

ROSMER. Put it all in.

MORTENSGAARD. I'll put in everything that our good public needs to know.

(*He bows and departs.* ROSMER *remains standing in the doorway as* MORTENSGAARD *goes down the stairs. The sound of the front door closing.*)

ROSMER (*calls softly from the doorway*). Rebecca! Re— Hm. (*Aloud.*) Mrs. Helseth—isn't Miss West down there?

MRS. HELSETH (*from the downstairs hall*). No, sir, she's not here.

(*The drapes to the rear are drawn aside.* REBECCA *appears in the bedroom doorway.*)

REBECCA. John.

ROSMER (*turns*). What! Were you in my bedroom? What were you doing in there?

REBECCA (*going over to him*). I was listening.

ROSMER. No, but, Rebecca—how could you!

REBECCA. Why shouldn't I? He was so snide—about my dressing gown—

ROSMER. Ah, so you were listening, too, when Kroll—?

REBECCA. Yes. I wanted to hear what his scheme was.

ROSMER. I would have told you.

REBECCA. You wouldn't have told me quite everything. And certainly not in his words.

ROSMER. Then you heard it all?

REBECCA. Just about, I think. I had to go downstairs a moment when Mortensgaard came.

ROSMER. And then back up again—

REBECCA. John dear, don't be annoyed.

ROSMER. You do whatever you think right and proper. You have full freedom of action— But what about all this, Rebecca—? Oh, I don't think I've ever needed you so much as now.

REBECCA. And yet we've both been expecting something like this to happen.

ROSMER. No, no—not like this.

REBECCA. Not like this?

ROSMER. Of course I knew sooner or later our pure and beautiful friendship might be twisted and distorted. Not by Kroll. I never would have thought that of him. But by all the others with their dirty minds and prying eyes. Oh, yes—I had good reason to keep our relationship so well concealed. It was a dangerous secret.

REBECCA. Oh, why care what the others think! We know, between us, we haven't done anything wrong.

ROSMER. Nothing wrong? Yes, I believed that for myself —until today. But now—now, Rebecca—

REBECCA. Yes, what now?

ROSMER. How can I account for Beata's horrible accusation?

REBECCA (*vehemently*). Oh, stop talking about Beata! Don't think of Beata any more! Here you've finally been freeing yourself from her. Because she's dead!

ROSMER. Since I've heard these things, I have the eerie sense that she's come alive again.

REBECCA. Oh, no—you mustn't, John! You mustn't!

ROSMER. Yes, I'm telling you. We have to try to get to the bottom of this. How could she arrive at that fatal misconception?

REBECCA. You're not starting to doubt that she was nearly insane, are you?

ROSMER. Yes—that's exactly what I can't be so sure of anymore. And besides—even if she was—

REBECCA. If she was? Yes, then what?

ROSMER. I mean—then where can we find the immediate cause that drove her sick mind into madness?

REBECCA. Oh, what good is there in going around, brooding about these things?

ROSMER. I can't help it, Rebecca. I can't ignore this rankling doubt, no matter how much I'd like to.

REBECCA. But that could be dangerous, always to be circling about the same morbid question.

ROSMER (*walking restlessly about, deep in thought*). Somehow or other, I must have revealed my feelings. She must have noticed how much happier I was after *you* came here to live.

REBECCA. But, dear, even if she did—

ROSMER. For one thing—it couldn't escape her that we shared the same books. And that we sought each other out and talked over all the new developments. But I just don't understand. I was so careful to protect her. When I look back on it, I don't think, to save my life, I could have done more to shield her from our involvement. Or, am I wrong, Rebecca?

REBECCA. No, it's true, absolutely.

ROSMER. And you did, too. And still—! Oh, this is hideous to think about! So she must have been moving about this place—sick with her passion—silent, always silent—observing everything—and misjudging everything.

REBECCA (*her hands clenched*). I never should have come to Rosmersholm.

ROSMER. Imagine what she was suffering in that silence! All the ugliness her sick brain must have invented about us. Did she never say anything to you that might have warned you?

REBECCA (*looking startled*). To me! You think I would have stayed here one day longer then?

ROSMER. No, no, of course not. Oh, what a battle she must have fought. And fought it alone, Rebecca. Desperately and totally alone. And then, finally, that piercing accusation of her victory—in the mill-race—

(*He throws himself down in the chair by the desk, propping his elbows on the desk top and burying his face in his hands.*)

REBECCA (*approaching him hesitantly from behind*). John, tell me now. If it were in your power to call Beata back—to you—to Rosmersholm—would you do it?

ROSMER. Oh, how do I know what I'd do or not do? All my thoughts keep revolving about this one thing—that can never be altered.

REBECCA. You were just starting to live, John. You *had* started already. In every way, you'd freed yourself from so much. You were feeling so relaxed and happy—

ROSMER. I was, yes—I really was. And now, this overwhelming burden—

REBECCA (*standing behind him, her arms on the back of his chair*). How lovely it was when we'd sit down there in the living room in the twilight—and help each other make the plans that would change our lives. You wanted to plunge into the stream of life—the living stream of the life of our time, you called it. You wanted to go like a liberator from house to house, winning minds and wills to your vision and creating a new nobility—in wider and wider circles around you. Noblemen.

ROSMER. Happy noblemen.

REBECCA. Yes—happy.

ROSMER. Because it's joy that ennobles the mind, Rebecca.

REBECCA. But don't you think—suffering, too? Great sorrow?

ROSMER. Yes—if one can only get through it. Over it. Transcend it.

REBECCA. That's what *you* have to do.

ROSMER (*sadly shaking his head*). I'll never transcend this—completely. There'll always be a lingering doubt. A question. I'll never again be able to relish the one thing that makes it so marvelously sweet to be alive.

REBECCA (*leaning over the back of the chair, softly*). And what's that, John?

ROSMER (*looking up at her*). The calm joy of innocence.

REBECCA (*steps back*). Yes. Innocence.

(*A short pause.*)

ROSMER (*one elbow on the desk, supporting his head on his hand and gazing straight ahead*). And the way she must have pieced it together. How methodically she built the pattern. First, she began doubting my faith—though how could she have known at the time? But she did. And then it grew into a certainty. And after that—yes, then it was easy enough for her to find all the rest of it credible. (*Sits up in the chair and runs his hands through his hair.*) Oh, all these wild speculations! I'll never be rid of them. I can feel that. I just know it. All of a sudden, they'll swarm in on me, reminding me of the dead.

REBECCA. Like the white horse of Rosmersholm.

ROSMER. Yes. Rushing out of the darkness. Out of the silence.

REBECCA. Yes because of that brain-sick fantasy, you'll turn your back on the stream of life you were just beginning to master.

ROSMER. Of course it's hard. Hard, Rebecca. But it isn't my choice to make. How could I ever hope to overcome the past?

REBECCA (*behind the chair*). By forming new relationships.

ROSMER (*startled, glancing up*), New relationships?

REBECCA. Yes, new relationships to the outside world. Live, work, accomplish things. Don't sit around brooding over insoluble mysteries.

ROSMER (*getting up*). New relationships. (*Walks across the room, pauses by the door, then returns*). A question occurs to me. Haven't you put the same question to yourself, Rebecca?

REBECCA (*breathing heavily*). If you'll—tell me—what it is.

ROSMER. How do you think *our* relationship will fare after today?

REBECCA. I think our friendship will stand—against all odds.

ROSMER. That isn't quite what I mean. The thing that drew us together from the start—that binds us so closely to each other—the belief we share that a man and a woman can live together simply as friends—

REBECCA. Yes, yes—so?

ROSMER. I mean that a relationship like that—like ours —isn't it best adapted to a life that's quiet and serene—?

REBECCA. Go on!

ROSMER. But now all I can see ahead of me is a life of struggle and unrest and fierce passions. Because I *will* live my own life, Rebecca! I will not be beaten into the ground by any disquieting thoughts. I won't have my way of life dictated, either by the living or—anyone else.

REBECCA. No, no—don't let it happen! To your utmost, John, make yourself free! A free man!

ROSMER. But you know then what I'm thinking? Don't you know? Don't you see how I can liberate myself best from all those rankling memories—from the whole sad past?

REBECCA. How?

ROSMER. By overpowering it with a new, living reality.

REBECCA (*groping for the chair back*). A living—? What—?

ROSMER (*approaching her*). Rebecca—if I asked you now—would you be my wife?

REBECCA (*speechless a moment, then cries out in joy*). Your wife! Your—! I!

ROSMER. Yes. Let's try. The two of us will be one. There mustn't be an empty place for the dead any longer.

REBECCA. I—in Beata's place—!

ROSMER. Then she's out of the picture. Completely out. Gone forever.

REBECCA (*her voice soft and tremulous*). Do you think so, John?

ROSMER. It has to be so! It has to! I can't—I won't go through life with a corpse on my back. Help me cast it off, Rebecca. And then let's drown all these memories in joy, in freedom, in passion. For me, you'll be the only wife I ever had.

REBECCA (*controlling herself*). Don't speak of this ever again. I'll never be your wife.

ROSMER. What! Never! Oh, don't you think you could come to love me? Isn't there already a touch of love in our friendship?

REBECCA (*pressing her hands over her ears as if in fright*). Don't talk that way, John! Don't say these things!

ROSMER (*gripping her arm*). Yes, there *is* a world of promise in our relationship. And I can see in your face you feel the same. Don't you, Rebecca?

REBECCA (*again calm and collected*). Now, listen. I'm telling you—if you go on like this, I'll have to leave Rosmersholm.

ROSMER. Leave! You! You can't do that. It's impossible.

REBECCA. It's still more impossible for me to marry you. Never on earth can I do that.

ROSMER (*looks at her, surprised*). You say "can." And you say it so strangely. Why can't you?

REBECCA (*takes both his hands*). My dear friend—both for your sake and mine—don't ask why. (*Releasing him.*) Accept it, John. (*She goes toward the door on the left.*)

ROSMER. From now on I'll have no other question to ask but—why?

REBECCA (*turns and regards him*). Then it's all over.

ROSMER. Between you and me?

REBECCA. Yes.

ROSMER. It can never be over between us two. You'll never leave Rosmersholm.

REBECCA (*her hand on the doorknob*). No, I expect I won't. But if you ever ask me again, it'll be over all the same.

ROSMER. Over? Why so—?

REBECCA. Yes, because then I'll go the same way Beata went. Now you know, John.

ROSMER. Rebecca—!

REBECCA (*in the doorway, with a slow nod*). Now you know. (*She goes out.*)

ROSMER (*stares blankly at the closed door and says to himself*). But I don't—understand—

ᴧ ACT THREE ᴫ

The living room at Rosmersholm. The window and hall doors are open. Outside, morning sunlight. REBECCA WEST, *dressed as in Act One, is standing at the window, watering and arranging the flowers. Her crocheting lies in an armchair.* MRS. HELSETH *is moving about, dusting the furniture with a feather duster.*

REBECCA (*after a short silence*). Mr. Rosmer's staying up there so late today. It's strange.

MRS. HELSETH. Oh, he's done that often enough. He'll be down soon, I'm sure.

REBECCA. Have you seen him already?

MRS. HELSETH. Just for a moment. When I brought up the coffee, he was in his bedroom, getting dressed.

REBECCA. I'm asking because yesterday he wasn't feeling too well.

MRS. HELSETH. Yes, he looked a bit off. I wonder if he and his brother-in-law didn't have some kind of falling out?

REBECCA. What do you suppose happened?

MRS. HELSETH. I wouldn't know. Maybe it's that Mortensgaard, setting them against each other.

REBECCA. It's possible. You know this Peter Mortensgaard at all?

548

MRS. HELSETH. No, thanks! How could you think so, miss? A type like him!

REBECCA. You mean because he runs that dreadful paper?

MRS. HELSETH. Oh, it's more than that. You must have heard, miss, that he had a child by a married woman whose husband had left her.

REBECCA. I've heard tell of it. But that must have been long before I came here.

MRS. HELSETH. Oh, Lord, yes. He was young as could be, then. She should have had better sense than him. And he was all for marrying her, too, but then he couldn't get permission. He's had to pay the price, all right. But, my stars, how that Mortensgaard has come up in the world. There's no end of people chasing after *him*.

REBECCA. I hear many of the poor go straight to him whenever they're in trouble.

MRS. HELSETH. And not just the poor, either—

REBECCA (*glancing obliquely at her*). Oh?

MRS. HELSETH (*by the sofa, dusting and cleaning briskly*). Some of the people you'd least expect, miss.

REBECCA (*rearranging the flowers*). Well, that's just a notion of yours, Mrs. Helseth. *You* can't know that for sure.

MRS. HELSETH. You don't think so, miss? Oh, yes, I can. Because—let me tell you—I once took a letter to Mortensgaard myself.

REBECCA (*turns*). No—did you?

MRS. HELSETH. Yes, so help me. And a letter written right here, at Rosmersholm.

REBECCA. Really, Mrs. Helseth.

MRS. HELSETH. Yes, I swear, it's true. And fine paper it was written on, with fine red sealing wax on the envelope, too.

REBECCA. And you were charged to deliver it? Well, my dear Mrs. Helseth, then it's not hard to guess who sent it.

MRS. HELSETH. No?

REBECCA. Obviously, it was something poor Mrs. Rosmer, in her illness—

MRS. HELSETH. You said it, miss. I didn't.

REBECCA. But what was the letter about? No, of course —you couldn't know that.

MRS. HELSETH. And suppose I did know that, just by chance.

REBECCA. Did she tell you?

MRS. HELSETH. No, not likely. But when Mortensgaard read it, he started questioning me, up, down and sideways, until I could pretty well guess what it said.

REBECCA. And what *did* it say? Oh, dear Mrs. Helseth, please tell me!

MRS. HELSETH. No, miss. Not for anything in this world.

REBECCA. Oh, you could tell me. We're such good friends.

MRS. HELSETH. God help me if I told you anything about *that*, miss. All I can say is that it was something awful they went and got that poor sick woman to believe.

REBECCA. Who did?

MRS. HELSETH. Evil people, Miss West. Evil people.

REBECCA. Evil—?

MRS. HELSETH. Yes, I could say that again. Real evil people it must have been.

REBECCA. Who do you suppose it was?

MRS. HELSETH. Oh, I have my suspicions. But, God knows, my lips are sealed. Even if there *is* a certain lady in town—hm!

REBECCA. I can see you mean Mrs. Kroll.

MRS. HELSETH. Yes, she's one of a kind, she is. She's always looked down her nose at me. And she's never had any love lost for you, either.

REBECCA. Do you think Mrs. Rosmer was in her right mind when she wrote that letter to Mortensgaard?

MRS. HELSETH. The mind's a peculiar thing, miss. But I don't think she was that far gone.

REBECCA. But she certainly seemed incoherent when she found out she couldn't have children. That's what unbalanced her.

MRS. HELSETH. Yes, she took it awfully hard, poor dear.

REBECCA (*picks up her crocheting and sits in the chair by the window*). But, after all—don't you think it may have been best for Mr. Rosmer that way?

MRS. HELSETH. Which way, miss?

REBECCA. That there were no children. Hm?

MRS. HELSETH. Oh, I don't know what to say.

REBECCA. Yes, it was the best thing for him, believe me. Mr. Rosmer isn't cut out to deal with crying children.

MRS. HELSETH. Children never cry at Rosmersholn, miss.

REBECCA (*looking at her*). Never cry?

MRS. HELSETH. Here in this house children have never been known to cry as long as anyone can remember.

REBECCA. That's strange.

MRS. HELSETH. Yes, isn't it? But it's in the family. And there's another strange thing. When they grow up, they never laugh. Never, as long as they live.

REBECCA. How extraordinary—

MRS. HELSETH. Have you ever once seen or heard the Pastor laugh?

REBECCA. No, come to think of it, you must be right. But around here in general, people don't laugh very much, it seems to me.

MRS. HELSETH. No, they don't. People say it started at Rosmersholm. And then it more or less spread out from here, like some sort of plague, I suppose.

REBECCA. You're a very wise woman, Mrs. Helseth.

MRS. HELSETH. Oh, you mustn't make fun of me, miss. (*Listens.*) Shh—the Pastor's coming down. He doesn't like my dusting in here.

(*She goes out the door, right.* ROSMER, *with hat and stick in hand, comes in from the hall.*)

ROSMER. Good morning, Rebecca.

REBECCA. Good morning, my dear. (*A pause, as she crochets.*) You're going out?

ROSMER. Yes.

REBECCA. It's such marvelous weather.

ROSMER. You didn't look in on me this morning.

REBECCA. No— I didn't. Not today.

ROSMER. You won't be doing that anymore?

REBECCA. Oh, I don't know yet.

ROSMER. Is there any mail?

REBECCA. The *County Herald* came.

ROSMER. The *County Herald*—!

REBECCA. It's there on the table.

ROSMER (*putting down his hat and stick*). Anything in it about—?

REBECCA. Yes.

ROSMER. And you didn't send it up—

REBECCA. You'd read it soon enough.

ROSMER. Let's see. (*Takes the paper and reads it, standing at the table.*) What! ". . . impossible to warn too strongly about spineless deserters . . ." (*Looking at her.*) They call me a deserter, Rebecca.

REBECCA. They don't mention names.

ROSMER. What's the difference? (*Reading on.*) ". . . secret traitors to the good cause . . . the arrogance of Judas-goats who reveal their apostasy as soon as they sense the opportune and—profitable moment has come . . . the fair name of a noble family wantonly defiled . . . in the expectation that those momentarily in power will surely provide a suitable reward." (*Putting down the paper on the table.*) And that's what they write about me. People who've known me so long and well. They don't believe it themselves. There isn't a word of truth in it, and they know it—and still they write it.

REBECCA. There's more to come.

ROSMER (*picks up the paper again*). ". . . unseasoned judgment the sole excuse . . . demoralizing influence—possibly extending into areas that, at present, we prefer to withhold from public comment or criticism . . ." (*Looks at her.*) What's this?

REBECCA. An allusion to me, apparently.

ROSMER (*lays the paper down*). Rebecca—this is the work of men without honor.

REBECCA. Yes, I don't think Mortensgaard can teach them anything.

ROSMER (*pacing about*). This *has* to be redeemed. All the best in humanity will go down if this sort of thing is condoned. It's got to be stopped! Oh, how happy—how happy I'd be if I could kindle a little light in all this barbarous darkness.

REBECCA (*rises*). Yes, how true! You'd have something great and glorious to live for then.

ROSMER. Think, if I could rouse them to self-awareness. Bring them to repent and feel ashamed of themselves. Teach them to come together in tolerance—in love, Rebecca.

REBECCA. Yes, just put all your talents into that, and you'll see—you'll win!

ROSMER. I think it can all work out. Oh, what joy it would be then to live. No more brutal conflicts. Only friendly competition. All eyes converging on the same goal. Every will, every mind striving onward and upward—each following out its own natural path. Happiness for all—created through all. (*Coming to the window, he gazes at the view outside, starts, and says sorrowfully.*) Ah! But not through me.

REBECCA. Not—? Not through you?

ROSMER. And not *for* me, either.

REBECCA. Oh, John, don't give in to your doubts.

ROSMER. Happiness, Rebecca dear—more than anything, happiness is a calm, sure sense of being guiltless.

REBECCA (*staring straight ahead*). Yes, always this guilt—

ROSMER. Oh, you don't understand it. But I—

REBECCA. You least of all!

ROSMER (*pointing out the window*). The mill-race.

REBECCA. Oh, John—!

(MRS. HELSETH *looks in the door, right.*)

MRS. HELSETH. Miss. West!

REBECCA. Later, later. Not now.

MRS. HELSETH. Just a word, miss.

(REBECCA *goes over to the door.* MRS. HELSETH *tells her something. They converse a moment in whispers.* MRS. HELSETH *nods and leaves.*)

ROSMER (*uneasily*). Anything concerning me?

REBECCA. No, only the housework— You ought to get out in the fresh air, John. A good, long walk is what you need.

ROSMER (*taking his hat*). Yes, come on. We'll go together.

REBECCA. No, I can't right now. You go alone. But do try to shake off these heavy thoughts. Promise me.

ROSMER. I may never be rid of them, I'm afraid.

REBECCA. How can anything so groundless have such power over you—!

ROSMER. I'm afraid this is more than groundless. I've lain awake pondering it all night. Maybe Beata really saw the truth.

REBECCA. What truth?

ROSMER. When she believed that I loved you, Rebecca.

REBECCA. Truth—in *that?*

ROSMER (*sets his hat down on the table*). The question I've been wrestling with is—whether the two of us weren't deceiving ourselves all the time when we called this bond between us friendship.

REBECCA. You mean we could just as well have called it—?

ROSMER. Love. Yes, exactly. Even when Beata was living, I was always thinking of you—and longing only for you. It was with you that I had this tranquil, buoyant happiness, above and beyond all desire. If we really think about it, Rebecca—our life together began the way two children fall in love, secretly and sweetly. No demands, and no dreams. Didn't you feel that way, too? Tell me.

REBECCA (*struggling for self-control*). Oh—I don't know how to answer.

ROSMER. And it's this intense inner life, with and for each other, that we took for friendship. No, our relationship has been a spiritual marriage—perhaps from the very start. So the guilt is mine. I had no right to it—no right, for Beata's sake.

REBECCA. No right to a happy life. You believe that, John?

ROSMER. She saw our relationship through the eyes of *her* love—and judged it by the same measure. Naturally. There's no other judgment she could come to.

REBECCA. But then why blame yourself for her distortions?

ROSMER. For love of me—her own kind of love—she threw herself into the mill-race. That fact is indisputable, Rebecca. And I'll never get over it.

REBECCA. Oh, don't think of anything but the great, shining mission you've set for your life!

ROSMER (*shaking his head*). That can never be carried out. Not by me. Not after what I know now.

REBECCA. Why not by you?

ROSMER. Because victory is impossible for any cause that's rooted in guilt.

REBECCA (*in an outburst*). Oh, all these doubts, scruples, anxieties—they're the ancestral curse of the family! Around here they say the dead haunt the living in the shape of white horses. I think this is something like that.

ROSMER. Possibly. But what's the difference if I can't escape them? And believe me, Rebecca, it's just as I say. Any cause that aims to win a lasting victory—needs a leader who's free of guilt and full of joy.

REBECCA. Is happiness so very essential to *you*, John?

ROSMER. Happiness? Yes—it is.

REBECCA. To you, who can never laugh?

ROSMER. Never mind. I can assure you, I have an enormous capacity for being happy.

REBECCA. Now, you must take your walk, dear. A long one—nice and long. You hear me? See, there's your hat. And your stick.

ROSMER (*accepting both*). Thanks. You won't be coming?

REBECCA. No, no, I can't just now.

ROSMER. All right. But you'll be with me, anyway.

(*He goes out through the doorway to the hall.* REBECCA *remains a moment, watching his departure from behind one of the open doors. Then she moves across to the door, right.*)

REBECCA (*opens the door and speaks in an undertone*). All right, Mrs. Helseth. You can let him in now.

(*She goes over toward the window. A moment later* KROLL *enters, right. He bows silently and formally, keeping his hat in his hand.*)

KROLL. He's gone, then?

REBECCA. Yes.

KROLL. Is he usually out quite long?

REBECCA. Oh, yes. But today he's more unpredictable. So, if you'd rather not meet him—

KROLL. No, no. It's you I want to talk to. You alone.

REBECCA. Then we'd better use our time. Please, sit down.

(*She sits in the armchair by the window.* KROLL *seats himself on a chair beside her.*)

KROLL. Miss West—I doubt if you can realize how deeply and sorely it pains me—this change in John Rosmer.

REBECCA. We expected it would be like that—at first.

KROLL. Only at first?

REBECCA. Mr. Rosmer was certain that sooner or later you'd join him.

KROLL. I?

REBECCA. You and all his other friends.

KROLL. Ah, there, you see! That's how bad his judgment is when it comes to situations and people in real life.

REBECCA. Besides—now that he feels it necessary to liberate himself across the board—

KROLL. Yes, but that's precisely what I *don't* believe.

REBECCA. What *do* you believe?

KROLL. I believe *you're* the one behind all this.

REBECCA. That idea comes from your wife, Dr. Kroll.

KROLL. It's quite immaterial where it comes from. What matters is the strong suspicion I have—an uncommonly strong suspicion, I might say—when I examine and piece together everything you've done from the day you arrived here.

REBECCA (*looks at him*). I seem to remember a time once when you had an uncommonly strong *faith* in me. An *ardent* faith, I could almost say.

KROLL (*softly*). Who couldn't you bewitch—if you tried?

REBECCA. You think I tried to—!

KROLL. Yes, you did. I'm no longer so foolish as to imagine there were any feelings involved in the game you played. You simply wanted to work your way in at Rosmersholm. Embed yourself here. And I could help you along. I see that now.

REBECCA. You must have forgotten that it was Beata who begged and cajoled me to come here and live.

KROLL. Yes, after you bewitched her as well. Or would you call it friendship—what she came to feel about you? It verged on idolatry—blind worship. And it degenerated into —what can I say? Into a kind of desperate infatuation. Yes, that's the right phrase for it.

REBECCA. You'd do well to remember your sister's condition. As for myself, I don't think I could be described as overexcitable in any way.

KROLL. No, you're certainly not. Which makes you all the more dangerous to those you want to gain power over. It's so easy for you to act by deliberate calculation—precisely because you are so cold-blooded.

REBECCA. Cold-blooded? Are you quite sure about that?

KROLL. I'm positive now. Otherwise you couldn't have gone on here year after year, pursuing your goal so relentlessly. Yes, well—you've got what you wanted. You have him and the whole estate in your power. But, to attain all that, you didn't hesitate to make him miserable.

REBECCA. That's not true. I'm not the one. It's you yourself who've made him miserable.

KROLL. Have I?

REBECCA. Yes, by leading him to think he was to blame for Beata's horrible death.

KROLL. So that got through to him, then?

REBECCA. You should know that. A mind as sensitive as his—

KROLL. I thought a liberated spirit, so-called, could rise above any such scruples. But there we are! Ah, well—I expected as much, I guess. For a descendant of the men looking down on us here—it's not so likely he could break away from those generations on generations of the family line.

REBECCA (*looking down thoughtfully*). John Rosmer has very deep family roots. No doubt about that.

KROLL. Yes, and you might have considered that, if you had any real compassion for him. But I guess that kind of feeling is beyond you. Your two backgrounds are worlds apart.

REBECCA. What backgrounds do you mean?

KROLL. I mean your family background. Your pedigree—Miss West.

REBECCA. I see. Well, it's perfectly true—I come from very humble stock. But even so—

KROLL. I wasn't alluding to rank and status. It's your moral background I had in mind.

REBECCA. Moral—? I don't see—?

KROLL. The facts surrounding your birth.

REBECCA. What do you mean!

KROLL. I only mean, they account for all your behavior.

REBECCA. I don't understand this. You'd better explain yourself!

KROLL. I hardly think you need an explanation. Because otherwise it would seem peculiar, letting yourself be adopted by Dr. West—

REBECCA (*rises*). Of course. Now I understand.

KROLL. —and taking his name. Your mother's name was Gamvik.

REBECCA (*walking across the room*). My father's name was Gamvik, Dr. Kroll.

KROLL. Your mother's occupation must have brought her into frequent contact with the public health officer of the district.

REBECCA. That's right.

KROLL. And then, just after your mother died—he takes you in with him. He treats you harshly. And yet you stay on. You're aware that he's not going to leave you one penny. In fact, all you got was a crate of books. And still you stay on with him. Put up with him. Take care of him, right to the end.

REBECCA (*by the table, looking disdainfully at him*). And all that I did for him you explain by something immoral—something criminal about my birth?

KROLL. What you did for him I ascribe to instincts any daughter couldn't help but feel. As I say, I take all your behavior to be a consequence of your birth.

REBECCA (*heatedly*). But in everything you say there's not one word of truth! And I can prove it! Dr. West wasn't living in Finmark before I was born.

KROLL. Beg pardon, Miss West, but he arrived there the previous year. I've established that fact.

REBECCA. And I say you're wrong! Absolutely wrong!

KROLL. You said a couple of days ago you were twenty-nine. Nearly thirty.

REBECCA. Oh? Did I say that?

KROLL. Yes, you did. And on that basis, I'd calculate—

REBECCA. Wait! Don't bother calculating. Because I can just as well tell you right now: I'm a year older than I claim to be.

KROLL (*smiling skeptically*). Really? That's news. How did that come about?

REBECCA. When I passed twenty-five—and I was still unmarried—I felt I was simply getting too old. So I began dropping a year.

KROLL. You? A liberated woman? Do you nourish prejudices about the right age for marriage?

REBECCA. I know, it's stupid—and ridiculous. But there are always a few loose ends that we can't bind up. We're all like that.

KROLL. Perhaps. But my computations may be right, after all. Because Dr. West was in the district for a short stay a year before he took the practice.

REBECCA (*in an outcry*). That isn't true!

KROLL. Isn't it?

REBECCA. No. Or Mother would have mentioned it.

KROLL. She didn't?

REBECCA. No, never. Nor Dr. West, either. Not once.

KROLL. Couldn't that be because they both had good reason to skip a year. Just as you did, Miss West. Maybe it's a family idiosyncrasy.

REBECCA (*walks about, clenching and wringing her hands*). It's impossible. You must want me to believe this. It's simply not true, that's all. It can't be! No, never—!

KROLL (*rises*). But, my dear Miss West—why in heaven's name are you so upset? Really, you frighten me! What do you expect me to think—?

REBECCA. Nothing. You don't have to think anything.

KROLL. Then you certainly have to explain to me why you find this fact—or possibility—so disturbing.

REBECCA (*composing herself*). It's simple enough, Dr. Kroll. I have no desire that people think of me as illegitimate.

KROLL. I see. All right, let's accept that explanation—for the time being. But then you seem to retain a certain—prejudice on that score, too.

REBECCA. Yes, I guess so.

KROLL. Well, I presume it's much the same with the greater part of what you call your "liberation." You've read your way through a whole slew of new ideas and opinions. You've acquired some kind of sense of the latest theories in various fields—theories that seem to overturn certain axioms that we've always taken to be hard and fast. But it's all remained on an intellectual plane with you, Miss West. It's never entered your blood.

REBECCA (*reflectively*). Perhaps you're right.

KROLL. Yes, just put yourself to the test, and you'll see! And if that's how it stands with you, one can well surmise how it must be with John Rosmer. It's pure, unadulterated madness—it's rushing headlong into disaster—for *him* to come out openly and proclaim himself an apostate! Imagine it—a man of his delicacy of mind—exiled and persecuted by the one circle of friends he has. Exposed to remorseless attack from the very best people in society. He's the last man on earth who could stand up to that.

REBECCA. He *must* stand up to it! It's too late for him to pull back now.

KROLL. It's not too late at all. Not by any means. Whatever's gone on here can be covered up—or at least explained away as no more than a momentary lapse, however
regrettable that may be. But—there's one expedient that's
absolutely vital.

REBECCA. What's that?

KROLL. You must get him to legalize the relationship,
Miss West.

REBECCA. His relationship with me?

KROLL. Yes. You have to get him to do that.

REBECCA. You just can't free yourself from the idea that
our relationship needs to be—legalized, as you put it?

KROLL. I don't want to involve myself any further in these
affairs. But I do have a strong impression that the most
easily broken of all the so-called conventions are the
ones—hm.

REBECCA. Governing the relations between a man and a
woman, you mean?

KROLL. Yes, frankly speaking. It seems so to me.

REBECCA (*meanders across the room and gazes out the
window*). I nearly said—I hope you're right, Dr. Kroll.

KROLL. What do you mean by that? You say it so
strangely.

REBECCA. Oh, forget it. Let's not talk about it anymore.
Ah—he's coming back.

KROLL. Already! Then I'll be leaving.

REBECCA (*crossing toward him*). No, stay. There's something you ought to hear.

KROLL. Not now. I don't think I can bear to see him.

REBECCA. Please—stay! Do that. Or you'll be sorry later.
It's the last time I'll ask you for anything.

KROLL (*looks at her in wonderment and puts down his
hat*). All right, Miss West. Whatever you say.

(*Silence for a moment. Then* ROSMER *enters from the
hall.*)

ROSMER (*sees* KROLL *and stops in the doorway*). What! *You're* here?

REBECCA. Rosmer dear, he didn't intend to meet you.

KROLL (*involuntarily*). "Dear"?

REBECCA. Yes, Dr. Kroll. John and I use terms of endearment. It's that "relationship" of ours.

KROLL. Was *this* what you wanted me to hear?

REBECCA. That—and a few other things.

ROSMER (*approaching him*). Why did you come here today?

KROLL. I wanted to try one last time to stop you and win you back.

ROSMER (*pointing at the newspaper*). After what's been written *there?*

KROLL. I didn't write it.

ROSMER. Did you make any move to stop it?

KROLL That would be indefensible meddling within my own party. Besides, it was beyond my control.

REBECCA (*tears the paper up, crumples the pieces and throws them behind the stove*). There! Now it's out of sight. Let it be out of mind, too. Because there won't be any more of that kind of thing, John.

KROLL. Yes, if you'd only use your influence.

REBECCA. Come, dear, let's sit down. All three of us. Then I'll tell you everything.

ROSMER (*sitting automatically*). What's come over you, Rebecca? This ominous calm—what is it?

REBECCA. The calm of decision. (*Sits.*) You sit, too, Dr. Kroll.

(KROLL *settles down on the sofa.*)

ROSMER. Decision, you say. What decision?

REBECCA. I want to give you back what you need to live your life. You'll have the joy of innocence again.

ROSMER. What does that mean!

REBECCA. I'll just explain something. That should be enough.

ROSMER. Well?

REBECCA. When I came down here from Finmark—together with Dr. West—I felt as if a new, great, wide world was opening up for me. The Doctor had taught me so much—so many different things that were all I knew about life then. (*Struggling inwardly, and barely audible.*) And then—

KROLL. And then?

ROSMER. But, Rebecca—I know all this.

REBECCA (*pulling herself together*). Yes, yes—of course, you're right. You probably do.

KROLL (*looking sharply at her*). Maybe it's better I go.

REBECCA. No, you stay here, Dr. Kroll. (*To* ROSMER.) Yes, you see, that was it—I wanted to be part of this new age that was dawning—and in on all the new ideas. One day Dr. Kroll told me that Ulrik Brendel had had such a powerful influence over you at the time you were a boy. I thought it might be possible for me to continue what he'd started.

ROSMER. You had a secret motive in coming here—!

REBECCA. I wanted the two of us to go forward in freedom. Always onward. Pioneering the future. But—between you and the fullness of freedom was always this dark, insurmountable barrier.

ROSMER. What barrier?

REBECCA. I mean that you never could grow into freedom, John, except in the sparkling sunlight. But there you were, stifling and withering away in that desolate marriage of yours.

ROSMER. You've never talked like that to me about my marriage before.

REBECCA. No, I didn't dare; I thought it would frighten you.

KROLL (*nods to* ROSMER). You hear that?

REBECCA (*going on*). Then I saw the way out for you. The only way out. And so I acted.

ROSMER. Acted how?

KROLL. You don't mean that—!

REBECCA. Yes, John. (*Getting up.*) No, stay there. You, too, Dr. Kroll. It's time to say this. It wasn't you, John. You're innocent. I was the one who lured—who managed to lure Beata into the maze—

ROSMER (*springs to his feet*). Rebecca!

KROLL (*gets up from the sofa*). Into the maze!

REBECCA. The maze—that led to the mill-race. Now you know, both of you.

ROSMER (*as if numbed*). But I don't understand—! What is she saying? I don't understand a word—!

KROLL. Ah, yes, my friend. I'm beginning to.

ROSMER. But what did you do? What could you ever have said to her? There was nothing to say. Nothing!

REBECCA. She was made to realize that you were set upon working yourself free from all your old hidebound attitudes.

ROSMER. Yes, but I wasn't at the time.

REBECCA. I knew you would be soon.

KROLL (*nods to* ROSMER). Aha!

ROSMER. And then? What else? I want to know everything now.

REBECCA. A short while after that—I begged and implored her to let me leave Rosmersholm.

ROSMER. Why—then?

REBECCA. I didn't want to go. I wanted to stay right here. But I told her, it was probably best for all of us—if I went away in time. I indicated to her that, if I stayed much longer—it could be—it could be that—anything could happen.

ROSMER. You said—and did that?

REBECCA. Yes, John.

ROSMER. It's what you meant by having "acted"?

REBECCA (*in a broken voice*). What I meant, yes.

ROSMER (*after a pause*). Have you confessed everything now, Rebecca?

REBECCA. Yes.

KROLL. Not quite.

REBECCA (*looking at him, terrified*). What else is there?

KROLL. Didn't you finally suggest to Beata that it was necessary—not just best, but necessary—for your sake and Rosmer's, that you should go away somewhere—as soon as possible? Well?

REBECCA (*in an undertone, indistinctly*). Maybe I said something like that.

ROSMER (*sinks into the armchair by the window*). And sick as she was, poor Beata went and believed all that web of lies and deceit. Believed without question. Unshakably. (*Looking up at* REBECCA.) And she never turned to me. Never said a word. Oh, Rebecca—I can see in your face— you advised her not to.

REBECCA. She'd gotten it into her head that a childless wife had no right to be here. And then she convinced herself that her duty to you was to step aside for somebody else.

ROSMER. And you—you did nothing to discourage that idea?

REBECCA. No.

ROSMER. Maybe you even reinforced it? Answer! Didn't you?

REBECCA. She could have understood me that way, I guess. .

ROSMER. Yes, yes—she bowed to your will in everything. And gave up her place. (*Springs to his feet.*) How could— how could you play this hideous game?

REBECCA. I felt it was a choice between two lives, John.

ROSMER (*with austere authority*). What right did *you* have to make that choice?

REBECCA (*fervently*). You think I went through all this with ice in my veins? That I calculated every move! I was a different woman then than I am now, standing here, telling about it. Anyway, I think a person can be of two wills about something. I wanted Beata out of here, one way or another. But even so, I never dreamed it could happen. With every step ahead that I gambled on, it was as if something inside me cried out: "No further! Not one step further!" And yet I *couldn't* stop. I *had* to try for a tiny bit more. Just the least little bit. And then again—and always again—until it happened. That's the way these things *do* happen.

(*A short silence.*)

ROSMER (*to* REBECCA). And what do you think will happen to *you?* Now, after this?

REBECCA. What happens to me doesn't matter. It isn't very important.

KROLL. Not even a word of remorse. Don't you feel any?

REBECCA (*coolly disdainful*). Excuse me, Dr. Kroll—but that's nobody else's business. I have to settle that with myself.

KROLL (*to* ROSMER). And it's this woman you live under the same roof with—on intimate terms. (*Looking around at the portraits.*) Oh, if those departed could only see us now!

ROSMER. Are you going into town?

KROLL (*taking his hat*). Yes. The sooner the better.

ROSMER (*likewise taking his hat*). Then I'll go with you.

KROLL. You will! Yes, I thought we hadn't quite lost you.

ROSMER. Come on, Kroll! Let's go!

(*They go out together down the hall without looking at* REBECCA. *After a moment* REBECCA *moves warily over to the window and peers out through the flowers.*)

REBECCA (*speaking quietly to herself*). Again, not by the bridge—but around, by the high path. Never across the mill-race. Never.

(*She crosses and pulls the bell rope.* MRS. HELSETH *enters a moment later from the right.*)

MRS. HELSETH. What is it, miss?

REBECCA. Mrs. Helseth, would you be good enough to have my trunk brought down from the attic?

MRS. HELSETH. Your trunk?

REBECCA. Yes, you know—the brown sealskin one.

MRS. HELSETH. Of course. But, my Lord, miss—you're not leaving?

REBECCA. Yes, Mrs. Helseth, I'm going away now.

MRS. HELSETH. Now? This instant?

REBECCA. As soon as I'm packed.

MRS. HELSETH. Well, I've never heard the like! But you'll come back soon, won't you, miss?

REBECCA. I'll never come back.

MRS. HELSETH. Never! But, my stars, how will we ever get on at Rosmersholm with you gone, miss? And now, with the poor Pastor so nicely settled again.

REBECCA. Yes, but I had a fright today, Mrs. Helseth.

MRS. HELSETH. A fright! Sweet Jesus—what was it?

REBECCA. I thought I saw something like a glimpse of white horses.

MRS. HELSETH. White horses! In broad daylight?

REBECCA. Oh, they come at all hours—the white horses of Rosmersholm. (*Her tone changing.*) So—speaking of the trunk, Mrs. Helseth—

MRS. HELSETH. Yes. Yes, the trunk.

(*Together, they go out, right.*)

⋎ ACT FOUR ⋋

The living room at Rosmersholm. It is late evening. A lamp, covered by a shade, is burning on the table. REBECCA WEST *stands by the table, packing some small articles in a valise. Her cloak, hat, and the white crocheted shawl are hanging over the back of the sofa.* MRS. HELSETH *enters, right.*

MRS. HELSETH (*her voice hushed and her manner constrained*). Well, all your things are down now, miss. They're out in the kitchen hall.

REBECCA. Good. And the coach is ordered?

MRS. HELSETH. Yes. He wants to know when he should be here.

REBECCA. I think about eleven o'clock. The steamer sails at midnight.

MRS. HELSETH (*hesitating a little*). But the Pastor? Suppose he's not home by then?

REBECCA. I'll be leaving anyway. If I don't get to see him, you can tell him I'll write. A long letter. Tell him that.

MRS. HELSETH. Well, I guess it'll do—just to write. But, poor Miss West—I really think you should try to talk to him one more time.

REBECCA. Yes, maybe. Or again, maybe not.

MRS. HELSETH. Oh, that I should live to see this! I never would have thought it!

REBECCA. What would you have thought, Mrs. Helseth?

MRS. HELSETH. Well, I honestly thought Pastor Rosmer had more to him than this.

REBECCA. More to him?

MRS. HELSETH. Yes, by the life of me, I did.

REBECCA. But, my dear Mrs. Helseth, what do you mean?

MRS. HELSETH. I mean, to do what's right and decent, miss. He shouldn't get out of it *that* way, no.

REBECCA (*looks at her*). Now listen, Mrs. Helseth. Tell me straight—why do you think I'm leaving?

MRS. HELSETH. Good Lord, miss, I expect because you *have* to. Oh, my, my, my! But, really, I think he's not doing right, the Pastor. Mortensgaard you could excuse, because her husband was still alive—so they couldn't get married, much as they wanted to. But now, the Pastor—hm!

REBECCA (*with a faint smile*). Could you actually believe something like that about me and Pastor Rosmer?

MRS. HELSETH. No, never! I mean—not before today.

REBECCA. But today—?

MRS. HELSETH. You know—after all those ugly stories I heard they wrote about him in the papers—

REBECCA. Aha!

MRS. HELSETH. In my opinion, any man who can go over to Mortensgaard's religion—why, I swear, he could do anything.

REBECCA. Well, perhaps so. But then how about me? What do you say about me?

MRS. HELSETH. Oh, goodness, miss—I don't see much point in blaming you. I mean, it's none too easy for a single woman to stand a man off. We're only human, all of us, Miss West.

REBECCA. True enough, Mrs. Helseth. We're all only human— Do you hear something?

MRS. HELSETH (*softly*). Lord love us—I think he's coming right now.

REBECCA (*starting*). You don't mean—! (*With determination.*) Well, then, let's face it.

(ROSMER *enters from the hall.*)

ROSMER (*sees her valise and traveling clothes and turns to* REBECCA). What does this mean?

REBECCA. I'm leaving.

ROSMER. Now?

REBECCA. Yes. (*To* MRS. HELSETH.) Eleven o'clock, tell him.

MRS. HELSETH. Very good, miss. (*Goes out, right.*)

ROSMER (*after a short pause*). Where are you going, Rebecca?

REBECCA. North, by the steamer.

ROSMER. North? Why up north?

REBECCA. It's where I came from.

ROSMER. But you have no ties up there now.

REBECCA. I have none down here, either.

ROSMER. What are your plans?

REBECCA. I don't know. I just want to end all this.

ROSMER. End this?

REBECCA. Rosmersholm has broken me.

ROSMER (*suddenly absorbed*). You mean that?

REBECCA. Broken me, utterly and completely. When I first came here, my spirit was strong and fresh and afraid of nothing. Now I'm worn down by an alien law. After today I don't think I'll have nerve enough left for anything.

ROSMER. Why not? What is this law you're talking about—?

REBECCA. My dear, *that's* nothing we need to discuss now. What went on between you and Kroll?

ROSMER. We've made peace.

REBECCA. I see. So that's what it's come to.

ROSMER. He invited all our old circle of friends to meet at his house. They made me recognize that this work of ennobling the minds of men—that it's quite beyond me. And besides, it's a hopeless dream in any case. I'm giving it up.

REBECCA. Yes, well—maybe it's best that way.

ROSMER. Is *that* what you say—and believe—now?

REBECCA. It's the belief I've come to—in the past few days.

ROSMER. You're lying, Rebecca.

REBECCA. Lying—!

ROSMER. Yes, you're lying. You've never believed in me. You never believed I could carry this battle through to victory.

REBECCA. I believed we two could do it together.

ROSMER. That's not true. You believed you could make something great out of your own life. And that you could use me along the way. That I could serve your purpose. *That's* what you believed.

REBECCA. John, listen—

ROSMER (*sits disconsolately on the sofa*). Oh, what's the use! I see through the whole thing now. I've been like putty in your hands.

REBECCA. John, listen. Let's have this out. It'll be the last time. (*Sitting in a chair by the sofa.*) I was thinking I'd write you about all of this—after I'd arrived up north. But I guess it's better that you get to hear it now.

ROSMER. You have still more to confess?

REBECCA. Yes, the crux of everything.

ROSMER. The crux—?

REBECCA. What you've never even suspected. The thing that pulls the whole picture together.

ROSMER (*shaking his head*). I don't understand any of this.

REBECCA. It's perfectly true that I once tried every trick I knew to gain an entrée here at Rosmersholm. Because I had a sense I could make out well enough here. One way or another—you know.

ROSMER. And you succeeded. You got what you wanted.

REBECCA. I think I could have gotten anything—in those days. I still had the fearless free will I was born with. I never knew second thoughts. No one could stop me. But then it began—the thing that crushed my will at last—and filled my life with a wretched fear.

ROSMER. What began? Speak so I can understand.

REBECCA. It came over me—this wild, uncontrollable desire—! Oh, John—!

ROSMER. Desire? You—! For what?

REBECCA. For you.

ROSMER (*tensing to spring up*). What's that!

REBECCA (*restraining him*). Don't get up, dear. You must listen.

ROSMER. And you're telling me—that you loved me—in that way!

REBECCA. I thought it was the meaning of "to love"— then. I did think that that was love. But it wasn't. It was just what I said. It was wild, uncontrollable desire.

ROSMER (*with difficulty*). Rebecca—is this really you— *you*, sitting here, telling me this?

REBECCA. Don't you believe me, John?

ROSMER. And out of this—and under its power it was, that—you "acted," as you call it.

REBECCA. It came over me like a storm at sea. Like one of those storms we have sometimes up north in the winters. It takes you—and sweeps you along with it—for as long as it lasts. You don't think of resisting.

ROSMER. And so it swept poor Beata into the mill-race.

REBECCA. Yes. It was mortal combat between the two of us.

ROSMER. You were clearly the strongest at Rosmersholm. Stronger than Beata and me together.

REBECCA. I knew enough of you to realize there was no way through to you until you were set free, outwardly—as well as inwardly.

ROSMER. I can't puzzle you out, Rebecca. You yourself —and the way you've behaved—it's all an insoluble mystery to me. All right, now I *am* free—inwardly and outwardly. You've reached the very goal you posed for yourself from the start. And yet—!

REBECCA. I've never been further from my goal than now.

ROSMER. And yet—when I asked you yesterday—begged you to become my wife, then you cried out, almost in terror, that it could never be.

REBECCA. I cried out in despair, John.

ROSMER. Why?

REBECCA. Because Rosmersholm has stolen my strength. It's crippled my courage and smothered my will. The time is over for me when I could dare anything. I've lost the power to act, John.

ROSMER. Tell me, how did that happen?

REBECCA. Through living with you.

ROSMER. But how? How?

REBECCA. After I was alone with you here—and you'd become what you really are—

ROSMER. Yes, yes?

REBECCA. Because you were never fully yourself so long as Beata lived—

ROSMER. I'm afraid that's true.

REBECCA. But when I began living here together with you—in peace—in solitude—when you gave me all your thoughts unreservedly—and all your feelings, so delicate, so fine, exactly as you felt them—*then* the great change took place. Very slowly, you understand. Almost imperceptibly—but in the end overwhelming me, to the depths of my soul.

ROSMER. *What* change, Rebecca?

REBECCA. All that other—that unbearable sensual desire —ebbed out of me, far, far away. All those turbulent passions quieted down and grew still. A profound inner peace descended on me—a tranquillity, like an island of sleeping birds, up north, under the midnight sun.

ROSMER. Oh, if I could have had some hint of all this!

REBECCA. It's best as it is. Yesterday—when you asked me to be your wife—such a joy surged up in me—

ROSMER. Yes, it did, Rebecca! I could feel it.

REBECCA. For just a moment, I forgot myself—and my old, impetuous will began struggling again to be free. But it hasn't the strength anymore—no staying power.

ROSMER. How do you explain this change in you?

REBECCA. The Rosmer way of life—or *your* way of life, in any case. It's infected my will.

ROSMER. Infected—?

REBECCA. And left it an invalid. A slave to laws that never had mattered to me before. You—our life together— has ennobled my mind—

ROSMER. Oh, if I could believe that!

REBECCA. You don't have to doubt it. The Rosmer way of life ennobles. But— (*Shaking her head.*) —but—but—

ROSMER. But what?

REBECCA. But it kills happiness.

ROSMER. You mean that, Rebecca?

REBECCA. At least, for me.

ROSMER. But how can you be so certain? If I asked you again—? Begged you to reconsider—

REBECCA. Oh, my dear—don't ever touch on this again. It's impossible—! Because you might as well know, John, that I have—something in my past.

ROSMER. More than what you've told me?

REBECCA. Something more and quite different.

ROSMER (*with a wan smile*). Isn't it odd, Rebecca. You

know, I've had a suspicion along that line from time to time.

REBECCA. You have! And yet—in spite of it—?

ROSMER. I never accepted it. I only played with it—as a conjecture, you know.

REBECCA. If you want, I'll tell you all about that as well.

ROSMER (*recoiling*). No, no! Don't say a word. Whatever it is, let me forget about it.

REBECCA. But I can't forget.

ROSMER. Oh, Rebecca—!

REBECCA. *That's* the awful part of it, John. Now, when I'm offered all the joy of life with open arms—I've changed, so that my own past seals me off from it.

ROSMER. Your past is dead, Rebecca. It has no hold on you anymore. No connection with you. You're a different person now.

REBECCA. Oh, my dearest, that's only empty talk. What about innocence? How can I get *that* back?

ROSMER (*sadly*). Innocence—

REBECCA. Innocence, yes. The ground of all joy and contentment. Wasn't that the very teaching you wanted to bring to life in all those noble, happy human beings of the future?

ROSMER. Don't remind me of *that*. It was only a half-baked dream, Rebecca. A harebrained notion I don't believe in anymore. Human beings can't be ennobled from without.

REBECCA (*quietly*). You don't think, even by selfless love?

ROSMER (*reflectively*). Yes, of course that's the one great hope. About the most magnificent thing in life, I guess—if it really exists. (*Writhing restlessly.*) But how can I ever resolve this question? Or fathom it, even?

REBECCA. You don't believe me, John?

ROSMER. Oh, Rebecca—how *can* I wholly believe in

you? You've gone around here, hiding and covering up such unspeakable things! And now you come forth with this new idea. If there's any motive behind it—just say it right out. Is there something, maybe, that you want to gain by it? You know I'll gladly do anything I can for you.

REBECCA (*wringing her hands*). Oh, this murderous doubt—! John—John—!

ROSMER. Yes, it's appalling, isn't it? But I can't overcome it. I'll never be able to free myself from this doubt. Never know for sure that your love is sound and true.

REBECCA. But doesn't something deep inside you recognize that I've been through a transformation! And that it's come from you—and only you!

ROSMER. Oh, Rebecca—I've lost faith in any power of mine to transform people. I have no faith in myself any more. I believe neither in you nor in me.

REBECCA (*looking at him somberly*). Then how will you be able to live?

ROSMER. Well, I don't know. I have no idea. I'm not sure I *can* live. And I really don't know what on earth is worth living for.

REBECCA. Oh, but—life renews itself. Let's hold it close, John. We're out of it soon enough.

ROSMER (*leaps restlessly to his feet*). Then give me my faith again! My faith in *you*, Rebecca! Faith in your love! Proof! I've got to have proof!

REBECCA. Proof? How can I give you proof—!

ROSMER. You *must*! (*Pacing the floor.*) I can't bear this desolation—this awful nothingness—this—this—

(*A sharp knock on the hall door.*)

REBECCA (*up from her chair, startled*). Ah—who's that!

(*The door opens.* ULRIK BRENDEL *comes in. He is wearing a dress shirt, a black coat and a pair of good boots into which his trousers are tucked. Otherwise he is dressed as before. He appears confused.*)

ROSMER. Oh, is it you, Mr. Brendel?

BRENDEL. John, my boy! It's hello—and goodbye.

ROSMER. Where are you going so late?

BRENDEL. Downhill.

ROSMER. What—?

BRENDEL. I'm homeward bound, my beloved disciple. I've grown homesick for the great void.

ROSMER. Something's happened to you, Mr. Brendel. What is it?

BRENDEL. So you observe a transformation? Yes—quite so. When I last set foot in this salon, I stood before you as a man of substance, jingling my well-filled pockets.

ROSMER. Hm! I don't quite understand—

BRENDEL. But on this night what you see is a deposed monarch on the ash heap of his gutted palace.

ROSMER. If there's anything I can help you with—

BRENDEL. You've conserved within you the heart of a child, John. Could you extend me a loan?

ROSMER. Why, yes, gladly.

BRENDEL. Could you spare me an ideal or two?

ROSMER. What did you say?

BRENDEL. A couple of cast-off ideals. You'd do me a good deed, then. For I'm wiped out, dear boy. Flat broke.

REBECCA. Didn't you give your lecture?

BRENDEL. No, enchanting lady. Can you imagine? Precisely as I stood prepared to disgorge my horn of plenty, I made the embarrassing discovery that I'm bankrupt.

REBECCA. But all your unwritten works—?

BRENDEL. For twenty-five years I've sat like a miser on his chest of gold. And then yesterday—when I opened it up to take out the treasure—there was nothing. The teeth of time had ground it to dust. To nothing at all. *Garnichts*.

ROSMER. Are you positive of that?

BRENDEL. Not a particle of doubt, my laddie. The President's convinced me of that.

ROSMER. The President?

BRENDEL. Well, His Excellency, then. *Ganz nach Belieben.*

ROSMER. Who would that be?

BRENDEL. Peter Mortensgaard, of course.

ROSMER. What?

BRENDEL (*with an air of mystery*). Shh, shh, shh! Peter Mortensgaard is lord and master of the future. Never before have I stood in a more august presence. Peter Mortensgaard has a property of omnipotence. He can do anything he wants.

ROSMER. Oh, don't you believe it!

BRENDEL. Ah, yes, my boy! Because Peter Mortensgaard never wants anything more than what he can do. Peter Mortensgaard is wholly capable of a life without ideals. And *that*, you see—*that*, essentially, is the great secret of successful action. It's the sum of all worldly wisdom. *Basta!*

ROSMER (*quietly*). I understand now—why you're leaving here poorer than you came.

BRENDEL. *Bien!* Then follow the *Beispiel* of your old teacher. Erase everything he ever once imprinted on your brain. Build not your castle on the shifting sand. And beware—and take care—before you build on this lovely creature who sows sweetness in your life.

REBECCA. You mean me?

BRENDEL. Yes, my seductive mermaid.

REBECCA. And why am I not fit to build on?

BRENDEL (*moves a step closer*). My impression is that my former pupil has a life work to carry through to victory.

REBECCA. So—?

BRENDEL. His victory is assured. But—please observe—on one immutable condition.

REBECCA. Which is—?

BRENDEL (*taking her gently by the wrist*). That the woman who loves him will gladly go out in the kitchen and lop off her delicate, pink-and-white little finger—*here*— right at the middle joint. Moreover, that the aforesaid loving lady, just as gladly, cuts off her incomparably formed left ear. (*Releases her and turns to* ROSMER.) Farewell, John, my conquering hero!

ROSMER. Are you leaving now? In the dark of night?

BRENDEL. The dark of night is best. Peace be with you.

(*He goes out. There is silence for a moment in the room.*)

REBECCA (*breathing heavily*). Oh, this air—! It's suffocating in here!

(*She goes to the window, opens it, and remains standing there.*)

ROSMER (*sitting in the armchair by the stove*). There's no way around it, Rebecca. I can see that now. You've got to go away.

REBECCA. Yes, I don't see any other choice.

ROSMER. Then let's use the brief time we have. Come over here and sit by me.

REBECCA (*crossing to sit on the sofa*). What do you want, John?

ROSMER. First, to tell you, you needn't have any worries about your future.

REBECCA (*smiles*). Hm. *My* future.

ROSMER. I provided for all contingencies a long while ago. Whatever happens, you'll be taken care of.

REBECCA. Oh, John dear—even that!

ROSMER. You could have anticipated as much.

REBECCA. It's been ages since I've thought about such things.

ROSMER. Yes, of course—you couldn't imagine we wouldn't be going on just as we always have.

REBECCA. Yes, it's what I expected.

ROSMER. I, too. But if I shouldn't be around—

REBECCA. Oh, John—you'll live longer than I will.

ROSMER. It's in my power to dispose of this wretched life as I choose.

REBECCA. What do you mean! You're not thinking of—!

ROSMER. Does that seem so strange to you? After this crushing, humiliating defeat I've suffered. And *I* was going to carry my life work through to victory—? Here I've fled the field—before the battle even started!

REBECCA. Take up the struggle again, John! If you really try—you'll see, you'll win. You'll ennoble souls by the hundreds—and thousands. But you must try!

ROSMER. Oh, Rebecca—when I've lost faith in my own life work?

REBECCA. But your work already has proved itself. You've ennobled one person at least—me, for as long as I live.

ROSMER. Yes—if I could only believe you.

REBECCA (*wringing her hands*). Oh, but, John—isn't there anything, anything that would make you believe me?

ROSMER (*starting, as if in dread*). Don't press this, Rebecca! That's enough! Let's not talk about it!

REBECCA. Oh, but it's just what we must talk about. Is there anything you know that could overcome your doubt? Because I don't know of anything at all.

ROSMER. So much the better for you. For us both.

REBECCA. No, no, no—I won't be satisfied with that. If you know of anything that would acquit me in your eyes, I demand as my right that you speak.

ROSMER (*as if inwardly compelled, against his own will*). All right, let's see then. You say you're filled with a great selfless love. That through me your spirit has been ennobled. Is that it? Is that how you figure things? Shall we audit that figure? Hm?

REBECCA. I'm prepared to.

ROSMER. When?

REBECCA. Whenever you like. The sooner, the better.

ROSMER. Then would you show me, Rebecca—right

now, tonight—if you—for my sake— (*Breaks off*). Oh, no, no, no!

REBECCA. Yes, John! Yes, yes! Tell me, and you'll see.

ROSMER. Have you the courage—and the will—gladly, as Ulrik Brendel said—for my sake, now, tonight—gladly —to go the same way Beata went?

REBECCA (*rising slowly from the sofa, in a whisper*). John—!

ROSMER. Yes, that's the question that's going to haunt me—after you've left this house. There won't be an hour in the day that I don't come back to it. Oh, I have an image of you, so clear in my mind's eye—standing out on the bridge—there, at the center. Now you're leaning out over the railing! Swaying, spellbound, out—and down toward the swirling water, the mill-race! No! You pull back. You don't dare—what *she* dared.

REBECCA. But what if I had the courage? And I could dare it gladly? What then?

ROSMER. Then I'd have to trust in you. I'd recover my faith in my life work. Faith in my power to ennoble the human spirit. And faith in the capability of the human spirit to be ennobled.

REBECCA (*slowly picks up her shawl, throws it over her head, and says with great calm*). Then I'll give you back your faith.

ROSMER. Have you the courage and will—for that, Rebecca?

REBECCA. That you have to judge tomorrow—or later— whenever my body is recovered.

ROSMER (*gripping his head in his hands*). There's a hideous fascination about this—!

REBECCA. I don't want to lie down there—any longer than necessary. Take care that they find me.

ROSMER (*springs to his feet*). But this is—it's insanity! Either leave—or stay here! I take you on your word this one time more.

REBECCA. Empty talk, John. No more quaking and running away. How can you ever believe me on my word of honor after today?

ROSMER. But I don't want to see you defeated.

REBECCA. There'll be no defeat.

ROSMER. Yes, there will. You'll never be able to follow Beata.

REBECCA. You don't think so?

ROSMER. Never. You're not like Beata. You're not driven by a warped view of life.

REBECCA. But my outlook is shaped by Rosmersholm—*now*. For the stain of my sin—I have to atone.

ROSMER (*looks fixedly at her*). Have you come to *that?*

REBECCA. Yes.

ROSMER (*with determination*). I see. Well, *I* hold by our liberated view of life. There is no higher judgment than ours, so we have to carry out justice ourselves.

REBECCA (*misinterpreting him*). Yes. Yes, that too. My going will save all that's best in you.

ROSMER. There's nothing in me left to save.

REBECCA. No, there is. But as for me—from now on, I'd be no better than a sea-troll, hanging like a dead weight on the ship that's carrying you forward. I have to go overboard. Or perhaps I should waste out my days up here, dragging a crippled life after me? Or brooding on the happiness my past has cost me? No, I'm leaving the game, John.

ROSMER. If you go—then I'll go with you.

REBECCA (*smiles almost imperceptibly, gazes at him, and says slowly*). Yes, come with me—and be my witness—

ROSMER. I said, I'll go with you.

REBECCA. Out to the bridge, yes. You never set foot on it, that I know.

ROSMER. You've noticed that?

REBECCA (*in a sorrowful, broken voice*). Yes. I knew, then, that my love was hopeless.

ROSMER. Rebecca—I lay my hand, now, upon your head. (*Doing so.*) And take you in marriage as my own true wife.

REBECCA (*holding both his hands and bowing her head against his chest*). Thank you, John. (*Releasing him.*) And now I go—gladly.

ROSMER. Man and wife should go together.

REBECCA. Just to the bridge, John.

ROSMER. And out to the center. As far as you go—I'll go, too. Now I have the will.

REBECCA. Are you perfectly certain—that this is the best way for you?

ROSMER. I'm sure it's the only way.

REBECCA. And what if you're deceiving yourself? If it's only a delusion? One of those white horses of Rosmersholm?

ROSMER. It's always possible. Because we'll never be free of them—we of this house.

REBECCA. Stay then, John!

ROSMER. The husband must go with his wife, as the wife with the husband.

REBECCA. But tell me this first: is it you who go with me, or I who go with you?

ROSMER. We'll never sift to the bottom of that.

REBECCA. Still, I would like to know.

ROSMER. We follow each other, Rebecca. I, you—and you, me.

REBECCA. It seems that way.

ROSMER. For now we two are one.

REBECCA. Yes. Now we're one. Come! We'll go then—gladly.

(*They go out hand in hand down the hall and outside, turning off to the left. The door stands open after them. The room remains empty a moment. Then* MRS. HELSETH *opens the door, right.*)

MRS. HELSETH. Miss—the carriage is— (*Glances about.*) Not there? Out together, at this hour? Well, really—I must say—! Hm! (*Going out in the hall, looking around, and coming back in.*) Not in the garden. Ah, no. No. (*Goes to the window and peers out.*) Oh, sweet Jesus! Over there, the white—! My Lord, it's them, both, on the bridge! God have mercy on the sinful creatures! Embracing each other like that! (*Screams.*) Oh! Falling—both of them! Into the water. Help! Help! (*Her knees shaking, she holds on tremulously to the back of a chair, barely able to form her words.*) No. No help now—the dead wife—she's taken them.

THE LADY
FROM THE SEA

"With changed surroundings and with one's mind developed, there is an increase in one's cravings and longings and desires. A man or a woman who has reached the top desires the secrets of the future, a share in the life of the future, and communication with distant planets. Everywhere limitation."

As he approached the composition of *The Lady from the Sea* (1888) Ibsen himself could justifiably feel he had reached a certain summit of achievement and recognition. Following the publication of *Rosmersholm*, his most savagely attacked drama, *Ghosts*, had been triumphantly staged by the Meininger, the most admired theater company in Europe; and after its reception in Berlin, its author had been hailed at a testimonial dinner as the foremost literary figure of the age.

The play that grew out of the working notes excerpted above, and elsewhere below, represents what a view from the summit might imply: a kind of watershed in Ibsen's later work. It is pivotal in that sequence which he later acknowledged to extend from *A Doll House* to *When We Dead Awaken*. The dramas preceding it have chiefly figurative titles and deal predominantly with the individual as the pressure point of the world-process, a vector of what Manders calls the *åndelige strømninger*, the intellectual and spiritual currrents of the time. The dramas that follow have mainly proper names as titles (including *Bygmester Solness*, as *The Master Builder* is designated in Norwegian); and, without losing sight of the earlier evolutionary theme, they deal repeatedly with the relationship of the ego and the self. Here, in a work whose protagonist is agitated to the brink of insanity with cravings, longings and desires, the latter concern is explored on the largest geographic scale of metaphor, through the opposition of the land and its limitations to the sea and its unfathomable mystery.

"People akin to the sea. Bound by the sea. Dependent on the sea. Must return to it. One fish species forms a basic link in the evolutionary series. Do rudiments of it still remain in the human mind? In the minds of certain individuals?"

Ellida Wangel is one such mind. Living in a tiny, provincial town by the Moldefjord, she is both landlocked in a rootless marriage with the local physician and spellbound by the sea, whose fluctuating moods suffused her lonely, impressionable childhood. Only daughter of a lighthouse keeper and a mother who died insane, she was irresistibly drawn as a young girl to the first mate of an American ship, a Finn whose talk conjured protean images of sea-creatures and whose sea-eyes mesmerized her. One day, in an obscure quarrel, the mate killed his captain; and before taking flight, he brought her to Bratthammer, the headland near the lighthouse, and, removing a ring from her finger and one from his, linked them together and cast them out into the ocean in a symbolic wedding.

Years pass. She considers the infatuation outgrown, a thing of the past, and enters a marriage of convenience with the kind and honest Wangel, who gratefully ensures that the housework will continue in the hands of his older daughter, Bolette. Two years later, thoughts of the strange seaman return obsessively, and in time she bears a short-lived son, whose eyes, resembling his, are changeable like the sea. Horrified that she has somehow been cohabiting with, and impregnated by, this phantom lover, she bans her husband from her bed and, over the next three years, exists in a torment of instability assuaged by Wangel's drugs and by long daily swims that are like wishful rites of purification.

This, briefly, is the background of Ellida's malaise. The present action of the play recounts its first frank confession, its feverish crisis and its decisive cure. When the Stranger returns with his implacable claim on Ellida, and Wangel adamantly opposes him, only to discover what he must lose of himself to win her, the stage is set for a conflict that resonates with all the contrasting values of land and sea: the fixed against the fluid, the defined against the indefinable, the predictable against the unknown, compromise with limitation against the promise of fulfillment, the laws of contract against the unaccountable affinities of the life force. And, not least among these, the conscious, volitional ego against the tidal flow of the unconscious in the self.

"The sea possesses a power to affect one's moods which operates like the power of the will. The sea can hypnotize. Nature at large can do this. The great secret is the dependence of the will on 'the will-less'."

Ellida's cure furnishes a classic case history for modern psychotherapy, but her immersion in the intuitive, will-less hyperaesthesia of the total self conveys Ibsen's art into the border zone of parapsychology. The Stranger's conjectural possession of Wangel's body to father a child by Wangel, his materialization "large as life" before her eyes, her seeming precognitive sense of his presence before he arrives are all paranormal phenomena, whereof Wangel perhaps speaks for Ibsen in saying: "I neither believe nor disbelieve. I simply don't know. So I leave it open." An appropriate working premise for a restless pioneer who had written to the cataloguer of the species masochist, the Austrian novelist Sacher-Masoch: "In these times every work of creative writing should attempt to move the frontier markers."

THE CHARACTERS

DR. WANGEL, district physician
ELLIDA WANGEL, his second wife
BOLETTE } daughters by
HILDA } his first
          } marriage
ARNHOLM, headmaster of a school
LYNGSTRAND
BALLESTED
A STRANGER
YOUNG PEOPLE OF THE TOWN
TOURISTS AND SUMMER VISITORS

The action takes place during the summer in a small town on a fjord in northern Norway.

↶ ACT ONE ↷

DR. WANGEL'S *house. A spacious veranda to the left, with a garden to the front and side of the house. Below the veranda, a flagpole. In the garden to the right, an arbor, containing a table and chairs. A hedge with a small gate in the background. Beyond the hedge, a path along the shore, lined by trees. Through the trees the fjord can be seen, with high peaks and mountain ranges in the distance. It is a warm, brilliantly clear summer morning.*

BALLESTED, *middle-aged, wearing an old velvet jacket and a broad-brimmed artist's hat, stands under the flagpole, adjusting the ropes. The flag lies on the ground. Not far from him is an easel with canvas in place. Beside it on a campstool are brushes, a palette, and a paint-box.*

BOLETTE WANGEL *comes out through the open door to the veranda. She is carrying a large vase of flowers, which she sets down on the table.*

BOLETTE. Well, Ballested—can you get it to work?

BALLESTED. Why, certainly, miss. It's nothing, really. If you'll pardon the question—are you expecting visitors today?

BOLETTE. Yes, we expect Mr. Arnholm here this morning. He arrived in town last night.

BALLESTED. Arnholm? But wait—wasn't his name Arnholm, the man who was tutor here some years ago?

BOLETTE. Yes, that's the man.

BALLESTED. I see. So he's back in these parts again.

BOLETTE. That's why we want the flag up.

BALLESTED. Well, that makes sense, I guess.

(BOLETTE *goes back into the house. After a moment* LYNGSTRAND *comes down the road from the right and stops, interested, as he catches sight of the easel and painting materials. He is a slender young man, poorly but neatly dressed, and has a rather frail appearance.*)

LYNGSTRAND (*from the other side of the hedge*). Good morning.

BALLESTED (*turning*). What—! Good morning. (*Runs up the flag.*) There—she's off. (*Fastens the rope and begins busying himself at the easel.*) Good morning, sir. I really don't believe I've had the pleasure—

LYNGSTRAND. You must be a painter.

BALLESTED. Naturally. And why shouldn't I be a painter?

LYNGSTRAND. Yes, I can see you are. Would it be all right if I just stopped in a moment?

BALLESTED. Maybe you'd like to look at it?

LYNGSTRAND. Yes, I really would, very much.

BALLESTED. Oh, there's nothing remarkable to see yet. But please, if you want to, come in.

LYNGSTRAND. Thank you. (*He enters through the gate.*)

BALLESTED (*painting*). It's the fjord there between those islands that I'm trying to get.

LYNGSTRAND. Yes, I see.

BALLESTED. But the figure's still lacking. In this town there's not a model to be found.

LYNGSTRAND. Is there going to be a figure as well?

BALLESTED. Yes. In here by this rock in the foreground, there'll be a mermaid lying, half dead.

LYNGSTRAND. Why half dead?

BALLESTED. She's wandered in from the sea and can't find her way out again. And so, you see, she lies here, expiring in the tide pools.

LYNGSTRAND. Yes, of course.

BALLESTED. It was the lady of this house who gave me the idea.

LYNGSTRAND. What will you call the painting when it's finished?

BALLESTED. I've thought of calling it "The Dying Mermaid."

LYNGSTRAND. Very effective. You certainly can make something fine out of this.

BALLESTED (*looking at him*). A fellow craftsman, perhaps?

LYNGSTRAND. A painter, you mean?

BALLESTED. Yes.

LYNGSTRAND. No, I'm not that. But I'm going to be a sculptor. My name is Hans Lyngstrand.

BALLESTED. So you're going to be a sculptor? Yes, yes, sculpture's one of the better arts, too—quite elegant. I think I've seen you a couple of times on the street. Have you been in town very long?

LYNGSTRAND. No, I've been here only two weeks. But if I can manage it, I'd like to stay the whole summer.

BALLESTED. And savor the ocean bathing, hm?

LYNGSTRAND. Yes, I need to build up my strength a little.

BALLESTED. Not in delicate health, I hope.

LYNGSTRAND. Yes, my health's been a bit uncertain. But it's nothing really serious. It's my chest—just some trouble getting my breath.

BALLESTED. Pah—that's nothing! All the same, you still ought to see a good doctor.

LYNGSTRAND. I was thinking of Dr. Wangel, if I have the chance.

BALLESTED. Yes, do that. (*Looks off to the left.*) There's another steamer, jammed full of people. It's incredible how many more tourists have been coming here these last few years.

LYNGSTRAND. Yes, it seems like pretty heavy traffic to me.

BALLESTED. And with all the summer visitors, too. I'm often afraid our town's going to lose its character with all these strangers around.

LYNGSTRAND. Were you born here?

BALLESTED. No, I wasn't. But I've accli—acclimatized myself. I've grown attached to the place—time and habit, I guess.

LYNGSTRAND. Then you've lived here quite a while?

BALLESTED. Oh, some seventeen, eighteen years. I came with Skive's Theater Company. But then we ran into financial problems, and the company broke up and scattered to the winds.

LYNGSTRAND. But you stayed on.

BALLESTED. I stayed. And I did rather well for myself. Actually, in those days I was mainly a scene painter, if you want to know.

(BOLETTE *comes out with a rocking chair, which she sets down on the veranda.*)

BOLETTE (*speaking toward the room within*). Hilda— see if you can find the embroidered footstool for Father.

LYNGSTRAND (*going over to the veranda to greet her*). Good morning, Miss Wangel!

BOLETTE (*by the railing*). Oh my, is it you, Mr. Lyngstrand? Good morning. Excuse me a moment—I just have to— (*Goes within.*)

BALLESTED. Do you know the family?

LYNGSTRAND. Not really. I've only met the girls here and there in company. And then I talked a while with Mrs. Wangel at the last concert in the park. She said I was welcome to come and call on them.

BALLESTED. Ah, you know what—you ought to cultivate that connection.

LYNGSTRAND. Yes, I was thinking of making a visit. Sort of a courtesy call, you might say. Now if I could only find some excuse—

BALLESTED. Some—what? Excuse! (*Glances off to the left.*) Damnation! (*Gathering his things together.*) The steamer's already docked. I'm due at the hotel. It might be some of the new arrivals will need me. Actually, if you want to know, I'm working as a barber and a hairdresser, too.

LYNGSTRAND. You're really very versatile.

BALLESTED. In small towns you have to know how to ac—acclimatize yourself in various fields. If you ever need anything in the way of hair preparations—a little pomade or something, then ask for Ballested, the dance instructor.

LYNGSTRAND. Dance instructor—?

BALLESTED. Director of the Wind Ensemble, if you like. We're giving a concert in the park this evening. Good-bye—good-bye!

(*He carries his painting materials through the garden gate and goes off to the left.* HILDA *comes out with the footstool.* BOLETTE *brings more flowers.* LYNGSTRAND *nods to* HILDA *from below in the garden.*)

HILDA (*by the railing, without returning his greeting*). Bolette said that you'd ventured inside today.

LYNGSTRAND. Yes, I took the liberty of coming inside just a little.

HILDA. Have you had your morning walk already?

LYNGSTRAND. Oh, no—I didn't get very far today.

HILDA. Did you have a swim then?

LYNGSTRAND. Yes, I was in for a short while. I saw your mother down there. She went into her bathhouse.

HILDA. Who did?

LYNGSTRAND. Your mother.

HILDA. You don't say. (*She places the footstool in front of the rocking chair.*)

BOLETTE (*breaking in*). Did you see anything of Father's boat out on the fjord?

LYNGSTRAND. Yes, I thought I saw a sailboat heading inshore.

BOLETTE. That must be Father. He's been on a sick call out in the islands. (*She straightens up the table.*)

LYNGSTRAND (*taking one step up the stairs to the veranda*). How marvelous, with all these flowers—!

BOLETTE. Yes, doesn't it look nice?

LYNGSTRAND. Oh, it looks lovely. It looks as if there were a holiday in the house.

HILDA. That's just what it is.

LYNGSTRAND. I thought as much. It has to be your father's birthday today.

BOLETTE (*warningly to* HILDA). Uh-uh!

HILDA (*paying no attention*). No, Mother's.

LYNGSTRAND. Oh, it's your mother's?

BOLETTE (*in a low, angry voice*). Really, Hilda—!

HILDA (*likewise*). Leave me alone! (*To* LYNGSTRAND) I suppose you'll be going home for lunch now?

LYNGSTRAND (*stepping down off the stairs*). Yes, I guess I better get something to eat.

HILDA. You must find it a pretty good life at the hotel.

LYNGSTRAND. I'm not living at the hotel any longer. It was too expensive.

HILDA. Where are you living now?

LYNGSTRAND. I'm boarding up at Mrs. Jensen's.

HILDA. Which Mrs. Jensen?

LYNGSTRAND. The midwife.

HILDA. Pardon me, Mr. Lyngstrand—but I'm really much too busy to—

LYNGSTRAND. Oh, I know I shouldn't have said that.

HILDA. Said what?

LYNGSTRAND. What I said.

HILDA (*measuring him with a cool look*). I absolutely don't understand you.

LYNGSTRAND. No, no. Well, then I'll be saying good-bye to you both for now.

BOLETTE (*coming forward to the stairs*). Good-bye, good-bye, Mr. Lyngstrand. You really must excuse us today. But some other time—when you really can stay a while—and if you'd like to—then you must stop by again and see Father and—and the rest of us.

LYNGSTRAND. Oh, thank you. I'd like that very much. (*He bows and goes out by the gate. As he passes along the road to the left, he nods and smiles again up to the veranda.*)

HILDA (*in an undertone*). Adieu, monsieur! Do give my best to Mother Jensen.

BOLETTE (*softly, shaking her by the arm*). Hilda—! You naughty child! Are you crazy! He could have heard you!

HILDA. Ffft! Who cares!

BOLETTE (*looking off to the right*). There's Father.

(DR. WANGEL, *dressed for travel and carrying a small bag, comes up the footpath from the left.*)

WANGEL. So, my little girls, you have me back! (*He comes in through the gate.*)

BOLETTE (*going toward him across the garden*). Oh, how lovely that you're here.

HILDA (*also going down to him*). Are you taking the rest of the day off, Father?

WANGEL. Oh, no, I'll still have to go down to the office for a spell. Say, do you know if Arnholm's come?

BOLETTE. Yes, he arrived last night. We had word from the hotel.

WANGEL. Then you haven't seen him yet?

BOLETTE. No. But he's sure to be out here this morning.

WANGEL. Yes, he undoubtedly will.

HILDA (*tugging at him*). Father, now you must look around.

WANGEL (*glancing over at the veranda*). Yes, child, I can see. It's really quite festive.

BOLETTE. Yes, don't you think we've made it attractive?

WANGEL. Well, I should say so! Are—are we alone here, just the three of us?

HILDA. Yes, she went in—

BOLETTE (*hurriedly*). Mother's in swimming.

WANGEL (*looks fondly at* BOLETTE *and pats her head, then says somewhat hesitantly*). But listen, you girls—do you want to leave all these things here, like this, all day long? And the flag up, too, all day?

HILDA. Oh, but Father, of course! What else do you think!

WANGEL. Hm—all right, but you see—

BOLETTE (*nodding and winking at him*). Can't you imagine how we went and did all this for Mr. Arnholm's sake. When such a good old friend comes back to visit you the very first time—

HILDA (*smiling and shaking him*). Just think—he used to be Bolette's tutor, Father!

WANGEL (*with a half smile*). What a pair of sly ones you are! Well, after all—it's only natural that we go on remembering her, although she's no longer with us. But even so—Hilda, see here. (*Handing over his bag.*) This goes down to the office. No, children—I don't like this. It just isn't right, you understand. Every year we shouldn't have to— Well, what can one say! I don't know that it'll ever be different.

HILDA (*starts through the garden, left, with the bag, then stops and turns, pointing*). See that man there, walking this way? That must be your tutor.

BOLETTE (*following her gaze*). Him? (*Laughs.*) Oh, you are the limit! You think that decrepit specimen is Arnholm!

WANGEL. Not so fast, there. So help me if it isn't him—! Yes, it most certainly is!

BOLETTE (*staring, hushed in astonishment*). My Lord, yes, I think you're right—!

(ARNHOLM, *in elegant morning dress, with gold-rimmed glasses and a thin cane, appears on the path from the right. He looks rather tired, as if overworked. Approaching the garden he waves a friendly greeting and enters through the gate.*)

WANGEL (*going toward him*). Welcome, my dear old friend! Welcome back to the old grounds!

ARNHOLM. Thank you, Dr. Wangel! Many, many thanks. (*They shake hands and walk up through the garden together.*) And these are the children! (*Taking their hands and looking at them.*) Why, I can hardly recognize them.

WANGEL. No, I'm not surprised.

ARNHOLM. Oh, well—perhaps Bolette. Yes, Bolette I would have known.

WANGEL. Just barely, I imagine. It's been nine, ten years now since you saw her last. Ah, yes, a great deal has changed here since then.

ARNHOLM (*looking around*). As a matter of fact, I was thinking just the opposite. Except that the trees have grown considerably—and an arbor has been built over there—

WANGEL. Oh, no, if you mean outwardly—

ARNHOLM (*with a smile*). And then not to mention that now you have two grown-up, marriageable daughters in the house.

WANGEL. Oh, there's only one who's marriageable yet.

HILDA (*in an undertone*). Father, honestly!

WANGEL. But now I think we'll set ourselves up on the veranda. It's cooler than here. If you will.

ARNHOLM. Thank you, Doctor.

(*They mount the stairs,* WANGEL *motioning* ARNHOLM *into the rocking chair.*)

WANGEL. There now. You just sit perfectly quiet and relax. Because, really, you look quite done in from the trip.

ARNHOLM. Oh, that's nothing. In these surroundings here—

BOLETTE (*to* WANGEL). Shouldn't we bring you some

soda water and lemonade? And perhaps you'd like it inside? It's going to be very hot out.

WANGEL. Yes, do that, girls. Some soda water and lemonade. And then maybe a little cognac.

BOLETTE. Cognac, too?

WANGEL. Just a little. In case somebody wants it.

BOLETTE. All right, then. Hilda, you go down to the office with the bag.

(BOLETTE *goes into the house, closing the door after her.* HILDA *takes the bag and goes through the garden around the house to the left.*)

ARNHOLM (*who has followed* BOLETTE *with his eyes*). What an attractive— How attractively your two daughters have turned out!

WANGEL (*sitting*). Yes, don't you think?

ARNHOLM. Why, Bolette is simply astonishing. And Hilda, too. But—about yourself, now, Doctor. Have you decided to stay here permanently?

WANGEL. Yes, so it seems. After all, I was born and raised in these parts, as they say. And then I had those years of marvelous happiness here with her—who was taken from us so soon. And who you remember from your time here, Arnholm.

ARNHOLM. Yes—yes.

WANGEL. And now I've been made happy again by my second wife. I must say, in the sum of things, fate's been kind to me.

ARNHOLM. But no children in your second marriage?

WANGEL. We had a little boy about two, two and a half years ago. But we didn't keep him long. He died when he was some four, five months old.

ARNHOLM. Is your wife not home today?

WANGEL. Oh, yes, she'll be along any time. She went down for a swim. It's her regular practice now, every day—and in all sorts of weather.

ARNHOLM. Not for reasons of health, I hope.

WANGEL. No, not exactly. Although she's definitely

shown signs of nervousness in the past two years. Off and on, I mean. I really can't make out just what the trouble is. But this bathing in the sea—it's become almost the one ruling passion of her life.

ARNHOLM. I remember something of the kind from before.

WANGEL (*with an almost imperceptible smile*). That's right, you know Ellida from the time you were teaching out at Skjoldvik.

ARNHOLM. Of course. She often visited the rectory where I boarded. And then I nearly always saw her whenever I was out at the lighthouse visiting her father.

WANGEL. I can tell you, the life out there has left its mark on her. The people in town here can't understand her. They call her "the lady from the sea."

ARNHOLM. They do?

WANGEL. Yes. So, if you would—talk to her now about the old days, Arnholm. It would do her a world of good.

ARNHOLM (*looking skeptically at him*). Have you really any reason to think so?

WANGEL. I'm sure of it.

ELLIDA'S VOICE (*from the garden, off to the right*). Are you there, Wangel?

WANGEL (*rising*). Yes, dear.

(ELLIDA WANGEL, *wearing a large, light robe, her hair wet and falling loose over her shoulders, comes through the trees near the arbor.* ARNHOLM *gets up.*)

WANGEL (*smiling and reaching his hands out toward her*). Well, there's our mermaid!

ELLIDA (*moving quickly to the veranda and taking his hands*). Thank goodness you're here! When did you come?

WANGEL. Just now. Only a moment ago. (*Gesturing toward* ARNHOLM.) But aren't you going to greet an old acquaintance—?

ELLIDA (*holding her hand out to* ARNHOLM). So, we finally got you here. Welcome! And forgive me that I wasn't home—

ARNHOLM. Don't mention it. No standing on ceremony—

WANGEL. Was the water nice and fresh today?

ELLIDA. Fresh! Good Lord, this water's never fresh. So stale and tepid. Ugh! The water's sick here in the fjord.

ARNHOLM. Sick?

ELLIDA. Yes, it's sick. And I think it makes people sick, too.

WANGEL (*smiling*). Well, you're a fine testimonial for a summer resort.

ARNHOLM. It seems more likely to me, Mrs. Wangel, that you have a peculiar tie to the sea and everything connected with it.

ELLIDA. Oh, yes, it's possible. At times I almost think so— But just look, how festive the girls have made things in your honor!

WANGEL (*embarrassed*). Hm— (*Looks at his watch.*) Now I will have to run—

ARNHOLM. Is this really in my honor—?

ELLIDA. Obviously. We don't have displays like this every day. Phew! It's stifling under this roof! (*Going down into the garden.*) Come on over here. At least there's the semblance of a breeze. (*She settles herself in the arbor.*)

ARNHOLM (*following after*). The air here seems quite refreshing to me.

ELLIDA. Yes, you're used to that foul city air. I've heard it's just dreadful there in the summer.

WANGEL (*who also has gone down into the garden*). Ellida dear—now it's up to you to entertain our friend for a while.

ELLIDA. You have work to do?

WANGEL. Yes, I have to go down to my office. And then I want to change my clothes. But I won't be long—

ARNHOLM (*sitting down in the arbor*). Don't rush yourself, Doctor. I'm sure your wife and I will find much to talk about.

WANGEL (*nods*). I'm counting on that. Well—till later, then. (*He goes out through the garden to the left.*)

ELLIDA (*after a short pause*). Isn't it lovely to sit here?

ARNHOLM. I think it's lovely now.

ELLIDA. We call this place the summerhouse. *My* summerhouse, because I had it built. Or rather Wangel did—for my sake.

ARNHOLM. Do you often sit here?

ELLIDA. Yes, most of the day.

ARNHOLM. I suppose, with the children?

ELLIDA. No, the children—they keep to the veranda.

ARNHOLM. And Wangel?

ELLIDA. Oh, Wangel goes back and forth. First he's here with me, and then he's over with them.

ARNHOLM. Is it you who want it like that?

ELLIDA. I think all parties concerned prefer it that way. We can talk across to each other—whenever we have something to say.

ARNHOLM (*after a moment's thought*). The last time we saw each other—out at Skjoldvik, I mean—hm—it seems so long ago now—

ELLIDA. It's all of ten years since you came out to see us.

ARNHOLM. Yes, about that. But when I remember you out there at the lighthouse—! "The pagan"—as the old priest used to call you, because your father gave you the name of a ship instead of a proper Christian name—

ELLIDA. Well—?

ARNHOLM. The last thing I'd ever have believed was that I would see you again down here, as Mrs. Wangel.

ELLIDA. No, at that time Wangel wasn't yet— The girls' mother was still alive then. Their real mother, I mean.

ARNHOLM. Yes, I understand. But even if that hadn't been— Even if he'd been quite unattached—I never would have imagined that this could happen.

ELLIDA. Nor I, either. Not for anything—then.

ARNHOLM. Wangel is such a good man. So honest. So genuinely kind toward everyone—

ELLIDA (*with warm affection*). Yes, he is!

ARNHOLM. But to me, the two of you seem different as night and day.

ELLIDA. You're right. We are.

ARNHOLM. Well, but how did this happen then? How did it happen!

ELLIDA. Oh, Arnholm, don't ask me that. I'd never be able to explain it. And even if I could, you'd never understand one particle of it.

ARNHOLM. Hm. (*His voice dropping slightly.*) Have you ever told your husband anything about me? I mean, about that futile gesture I once let myself be charmed into?

ELLIDA. Certainly not! I've said nothing at all to him about—what you mean.

ARNHOLM. I'm glad. Because I've been feeling a bit oppressed by the idea that—

ELLIDA. You needn't be. I've only told him what's perfectly true, that I was very fond of you, and that you were the best and truest friend I had up there.

ARNHOLM. Thank you. But tell me then—why did you never write me after I left?

ELLIDA. I thought it might be painful for you to hear from someone who—who couldn't respond as you wanted. It seemed to me rather like reopening a wound.

ARNHOLM. Hm—yes, yes, you may be right.

ELLIDA. But why did you never write yourself?

ARNHOLM (*regarding her with a half-reproachful smile*). I make the overtures? Maybe arouse suspicion of trying to start things up again? After the kind of rejection I got?

ELLIDA. Yes, I can understand. But has there never been any other involvement since?

ARNHOLM. Never. I've stayed faithful to my memories.

ELLIDA (*half joking*). Oh, nonsense! Let the old memories go. You should be thinking instead of becoming a happily married man.

ARNHOLM. That'll have to be soon then. You realize I've already passed thirty-seven?

ELLIDA. Well, all the more reason to hurry up. (*She is silent a moment, then speaks in a low, serious voice.*) But listen, Arnholm—I want to tell you something now that I couldn't have mentioned then to save my life.

ARNHOLM. What's that?

ELLIDA. When you made what you just called your futile gesture—there was no other answer I *could* have given you.

ARNHOLM. I know you only had friendship to offer. I know that.

ELLIDA. But you didn't know that my whole being and all my thoughts were directed elsewhere at the time.

ARNHOLM. At the time!

ELLIDA. Yes.

ARNHOLM. But that's impossible! You're mistaken about the time! You hardly knew Wangel then.

ELLIDA. I don't mean Wangel.

ARNHOLM. You don't—? But up in Skjoldvik—I can't recall one single, solitary person you could possibly have been interested in.

ELLIDA. No, I can imagine. Because it was all so utterly insane.

ARNHOLM. But then you must tell me more about this!

ELLIDA. Oh, it's enough for you to know I wasn't free then. And you know that now.

ARNHOLM. But if you *had* been free—?

ELLIDA. Yes?

ARNHOLM. Would you have answered my letter differently?

ELLIDA. How do I know? When Wangel came, I answered differently.

ARNHOLM. Then what's the good of telling me you weren't free?

ELLIDA (*rising with a troubled, anxious air*). Because I've got to confide in someone. No, no, don't get up.

ARNHOLM. Your husband knows nothing of this?

ELLIDA. I let him know from the first that I'd once set my heart on somebody else. He never asked to know more, and we've never discussed it since. After all, it was nothing but madness. And it was over before it started. That is—more or less.

ARNHOLM (*rises*). More or less? Not definitely!

ELLIDA. Yes, yes, definitely! Good Lord, Arnholm, it's not what you're thinking at all. It's something so incomprehensible, I don't know how to begin telling you. You'd only believe I was ill—or out of my mind.

ARNHOLM. My dear Ellida—there's no other way: you've got to tell me everything.

ELLIDA. All right! At least I can try. How would you, as a reasonable man, presume to account for— (*Looks away and breaks off.*) Wait a while. Someone's coming.

(LYNGSTRAND *appears on the road to the left and enters the garden. He is wearing a flower in his lapel and carries a large, colorful bouquet wrapped in paper and silk ribbons. He stops, with a hesitant, uncertain look, by the veranda.*)

ELLIDA (*coming forward in the arbor*). Are you looking for the girls, Mr. Lyngstrand?

LYNGSTRAND (*turning*). Oh, are you there, Mrs. Wangel? (*Bows and approaches.*) No, actually not. Not for the girls. For you, Mrs. Wangel. You suggested that I might come and call on you—

ELLIDA. I certainly did. You're always welcome here.

LYNGSTRAND. Thank you. And since it just so happens that you're having a celebration here today—

ELLIDA. Ah, you know about that?

LYNGSTRAND. Oh, yes. That's why I'd like to take the liberty of presenting you, Mrs. Wangel, with this— (*He bows and offers the bouquet.*)

ELLIDA (*smiling*). But my dear Mr. Lyngstrand, wouldn't it be better if you gave those beautiful flowers to

Mr. Arnholm directly? Because, you see, it's really for his sake that—

LYNGSTRAND (*looking indecisively at them both*). Pardon me—but I don't know this gentleman. This is—I brought it for a birthday present.

ELLIDA. Birthday? Then you're mistaken, Mr. Lyngstrand. It's no one's birthday here today.

LYNGSTRAND (*smiling broadly*). Oh, I know it is. But I never thought it was such a secret.

ELLIDA. Just what do you know?

LYNGSTRAND. That it's your birthday, Mrs. Wangel.

ELLIDA. Mine?

ARNHOLM (*looks inquiringly at her*). Today? No, it can't be.

ELLIDA (*to* LYNGSTRAND). Whatever gave you that idea?

LYNGSTRAND. It was Hilda who let it slip. I stopped by here a moment earlier today, and I happened to ask the girls why all the decorations, the flowers, the flag—

ELLIDA. Yes, and—?

LYNGSTRAND. And so Hilda answered: "Because today it's Mother's birthday."

ELLIDA. Mother's—! I see.

ARNHOLM. Aha! (*Exchanges an understanding look with* ELLIDA.) Well, Mrs. Wangel, since the young man already knows—

ELLIDA. Yes, now that you know, of course—

LYNGSTRAND (*presenting the bouquet again*). If you'll permit me to offer my very best wishes—

ELLIDA (*taking the flowers*). Thank you very much. Please, come and sit for a moment, Mr. Lyngstrand.

(ELLIDA, ARNHOLM, *and* LYNGSTRAND *sit down in the arbor.*)

ELLIDA. This business—about my birthday—it was supposed to have been a secret, Mr. Arnholm.

ARNHOLM. Yes, I'm sure of that. It wasn't for us outsiders.

ELLIDA (*laying the bouquet aside*). Yes, quite so. Not for outsiders.

LYNGSTRAND. I promise I won't tell a living soul.

ELLIDA. Oh, it's really not that important. But how are things going for you? I think you're looking better now than you did.

LYNGSTRAND. Yes, I believe I'm doing quite well. And then next year, if maybe I can get to the south of Europe—

ELLIDA. And you will, the girls tell me.

LYNGSTRAND. Yes, because I have a patron in Bergen who'll back me. And he's agreed to help me next year.

ELLIDA. How did you get to know him?

LYNGSTRAND. Ah, that was a rare piece of luck. I went to sea once on one of his ships.

ELLIDA. Really? So you had the sea in your blood?

LYNGSTRAND. No, not at all. But when my mother died, my father didn't want me lolling around the house any longer, so he packed me off to sea. Then on the home trip we went down in the English Channel. Yes, and that was lucky for me.

ARNHOLM. How so?

LYNGSTRAND. Well, because it was through the shipwreck that I got the condition here in my chest. I stayed so long in the icy waters before they pulled me out that I had to quit the sea. Yes, it was really my good fortune.

ARNHOLM. You believe that?

LYNGSTRAND. Yes. Because this condition is hardly dangerous. And now I can be a sculptor, which I want more than anything else. Imagine—a chance to work in that beautiful clay, to feel it so supple under your fingers, and to model it into form.

ELLIDA. What kind of form? Mermen and mermaids? Or the old Vikings—?

LYNGSTRAND. No, nothing like that. As soon as I'm able, I want to try for a large work—a group, as they call it.

ELLIDA. Oh, yes. But what will this group portray?

LYNGSTRAND. It'll be based on something out of my own experience.

ARNHOLM. Good—stay close to that.

ELLIDA. But what will it be?

LYNGSTRAND. Well, my idea was to have the figure of a young woman, a sailor's wife, stretched out, lying in a strangely troubled sleep. And she would be dreaming, too. I really believe I can develop it so you can actually see that she's dreaming.

ARNHOLM. But isn't there more to the idea?

LYNGSTRAND. Oh, yes, there'll be one other figure. A kind of specter, you might say. It would be her husband, that she'd been unfaithful to while he was away. And he's been drowned at sea.

ARNHOLM. What—?

ELLIDA. He's been drowned?

LYNGSTRAND. Yes. He was drowned on a voyage. But then the strange thing is that he comes home all the same. It's night, and now he stands there over her bed, looking down at her. He'll stand there, dripping wet, like a man dragged out of the sea.

ELLIDA (*leaning back in her chair*). What an astonishing conception! (*Shuts her eyes.*) Yes, I can see it as clear as crystal.

ARNHOLM. But how on earth, Mr.—Mr.—! You said it was something you'd experienced yourself.

LYNGSTRAND. That's right. I did experience all this—at least up to a point.

ARNHOLM. You witnessed a dead man that—

LYNGSTRAND. Well now, I didn't mean experience, strictly speaking. Not actuality. But something very much like it—

ELLIDA (*with lively anticipation*). Tell me more—all you can—about this! I want to know everything.

ARNHOLM (*smiling*). Yes, this is just the thing for you. It has the spell of the sea.

ELLIDA. What was it, Mr. Lyngstrand?

LYNGSTRAND. We were to sail for home from a town called Halifax when, as it happened, the boatswain took sick, and we had to leave him behind in the hospital there. So we signed on an American as a replacement. This new boatswain—

ELLIDA. The American?

LYNGSTRAND. Yes. One day he borrowed a stack of old newspapers from the captain, and he used to read them by the hour. He said he wanted to learn Norwegian.

ELLIDA. Yes? And then!

LYNGSTRAND. Then one evening we were running in a tremendous gale. All the crew were on deck—except the boatswain and me. He'd turned his ankle so he couldn't walk on it, and I was on the sick list, laid up in my bunk. Well, so he was sitting there in the forecastle, reading in one of those old papers again—

ELLIDA. Yes! Go on!

LYNGSTRAND. Then all of a sudden I heard him give out almost a kind of howl. And when I looked at him, I could see that his face had gone chalk-white. Then he twisted and tore the paper in his hands and ripped it to a thousand little pieces. But he did it all so quietly, so quietly.

ELLIDA. Did he say anything? Did he speak?

LYNGSTRAND. Not at first. But after a time he said, as if to himself: "Married. To another man. While I was away."

ELLIDA (closing her eyes, in a near whisper). He said that?

LYNGSTRAND. Yes. And, you know—he said it in perfect Norwegian. He must have a rare gift for learning languages, that man.

ELLIDA. And then what? What happened after?

LYNGSTRAND. Well, then came this incredible thing that I'll never forget as long as I live. For he went on, again very quietly, and said: "But she's mine, and mine she'll always be. And if I go home and fetch her, she'll have to go off with me, even if I came as a drowned man up out of the dark sea."

ELLIDA (*pouring herself a glass of water, her hand trembling*). Phew—how humid it is today—!

LYNGSTRAND. And he said that with such a power of will, I thought he'd be the man to do it, too.

ELLIDA. Do you have any idea—what became of this man?

LYNGSTRAND. Oh, I'm sure he's no longer alive.

ELLIDA (*quickly*). Why do you think so?

LYNGSTRAND. Well, because we went down in the Channel right after. I got away in the longboat with the captain and five others. The mate went with the dinghy, along with the American and another man.

ELLIDA. And nothing's been heard of them since?

LYNGSTRAND. No, not a word. My patron mentioned it again just recently in a letter. But that's exactly why I feel such an urge to turn all this into a work of art. I can see the unfaithful wife so vividly in my mind. And then the avenger, drowned, and yet coming back from the sea. I can picture them both so clearly.

ELLIDA. And I, too. (*Rising.*) Come, let's go in. Or better, down to Wangel. I think it's stifling here. (*She goes out of the arbor.*)

LYNGSTRAND (*who likewise has risen*). For my part, I'll have to be saying good-bye. This was only meant for a short visit on account of your birthday.

ELLIDA. As you wish. (*Giving him her hand.*) Good-bye, and thank you for the flowers.

(LYNGSTRAND *bows and leaves through the gate and off to the left.*)

ARNHOLM (*rises and goes over to* ELLIDA). It's plain to see this has struck you to the heart, Ellida.

ELLIDA. Yes, that's a good way of putting it—although—

ARNHOLM. But, after all, is it really any more than you should have expected?

ELLIDA (*staring at him*). Expected!

ARNHOLM. Yes, I'd say so.

ELLIDA. Expect someone to return again——! Return like that!

ARNHOLM. What in the world——! Is it that crazy sculptor's story——?

ELLIDA. Perhaps he's not so crazy, Arnholm.

ARNHOLM. Is it this nonsense about a dead man that's shaken you so? And I was thinking——

ELLIDA. What?

ARNHOLM. I was thinking, of course, that you were simply putting on an act. That actually you were sitting here suffering because you'd discovered that a family ritual was being kept secret from you. That your husband and his children had a private life that you weren't part of.

ELLIDA. Oh, no. That's as it has to be. I have no right to demand that my husband be mine and mine alone.

ARNHOLM. I'd say you have that right.

ELLIDA. Yes. But, even so, I don't. That's the point. I also have a life—that the others aren't part of.

ARNHOLM. You! (*Lowering his voice.*) Does that mean——? Do you—not really love your husband?

ELLIDA. Yes, yes! With all my heart, I've learned to love him! And that's just what makes it so terrible—so baffling—so utterly inconceivable——!

ARNHOLM. Now you *must* tell me your troubles, freely and openly, Ellida! Will you do that?

ELLIDA. Oh, my dear friend, I can't. Not now, in any case. Perhaps later.

(BOLETTE *comes out on the veranda and down into the garden.*)

BOLETTE. Father's back from the office. Couldn't we all sit inside?

ELLIDA. Yes, let's do that.

(WANGEL, *in fresh clothes, comes with* HILDA *around the house from the left.*)

WANGEL. There! Now I'm totally at your service! How about a nice glass of something cool to drink?

ELLIDA. Just a moment. (*She goes into the arbor and gets the bouquet.*)

HILDA. Oh, look! What lovely flowers! Where did you get them?

ELLIDA. From Mr. Lyngstrand, dear.

HILDA (*startled*). From Lyngstrand?

BOLETTE (*uneasily*). Was Lyngstrand here—again?

ELLIDA (*with a half smile*). Yes. He stopped by with these. For a birthday present, you know.

BOLETTE (*glancing at* HILDA). Oh—!

HILDA (*under her breath*). The beast!

WANGEL (*painfully embarrassed, to* ELLIDA). Uh—yes, you see—I should explain, Ellida, my dear—dearest—

ELLIDA (*interrupting*). Come along, girls! We can put my flowers in water with the others. (*She goes up onto the veranda.*)

BOLETTE (*softly to* HILDA). She really *is* kind at heart.

HILDA (*in an angry whisper*). Flimflam! She's just bewitching Father.

WANGEL (*on the veranda, presses* ELLIDA's *hand*). Thank you! Thank you for that, Ellida!

ELLIDA (*arranging the flowers*). Nonsense. Shouldn't I play my part too in celebrating—Mother's birthday?

ARNHOLM. Hm!

(*He goes up and joins* WANGEL *and* ELLIDA. BOLETTE *and* HILDA *remain below in the garden.*)

⤙ ACT TWO ⤚

In a local park, high on a wooded hill behind the town. A cairn of stones and a weather vane stand in the near background. Large stones, serving as seats, are grouped about the cairn and in the foreground. Far below, the outer fjord can be seen in the distance, with islands and jutting headlands. The open sea is not visible. It is one of the light summer nights of the north. There is a red-gold tinge to the twilight sky and over the mountain peaks far off on the horizon. The sound of four-part singing drifts faintly up the hill from the right. Young men and women from the town come in couples up from the right and, conversing casually, pass the cairn and go out, left. A moment later BALLESTED *appears, guiding a party of foreign tourists with their ladies. He is loaded down with shawls and traveling bags.*

BALLESTED (*pointing upward with his stick*). *Sehen Sie, meine Herrschaften—dort* over there *liegt eine andere* hill. *Das willen wir* also *besteigen, und so herunter—* (*He continues in French and leads the group out to the left.*)

(HILDA *comes briskly up the slope on the right, stops and looks back. After a moment* BOLETTE *comes up after her.*)

BOLETTE. But, Hilda, why should we run away from Lyngstrand?

HILDA. Because I can't stand climbing hills like that. So slow! Look! Look at him, creeping along!

616

BOLETTE. Oh, you know how sickly he is.

HILDA. Do you think it's very serious?

BOLETTE. Yes, I think so, definitely.

HILDA. He was in to see Father this afternoon. I'd give anything to know what Father thinks.

BOLETTE. He told me it was a hardening of the lungs— or something like that. And Father said he hasn't too long to live.

HILDA. No! He said that? Imagine—I guessed the same, exactly.

BOLETTE. But, for heaven's sake now, don't show anything.

HILDA. Oh, what an idea! (*Lowering her voice.*) There, now Hans has finally made it. Hans—doesn't he just look like his name should be Hans?

BOLETTE (*whispers*). Will you behave yourself! You're going to get it!

(LYNGSTRAND *comes in from the right, carrying a parasol*).

LYNGSTRAND. You girls will have to forgive me that I can't go as fast as you can.

HILDA. Did you get yourself a parasol too, now?

LYNGSTRAND. It's your mother's. She said I should use it for a stick. I forgot to bring one.

BOLETTE. Are they down there still? Father and the others?

LYNGSTRAND. Yes. Your father stopped in at the restaurant a moment, and the others are sitting outside, listening to the music. But your mother said they'll be up later.

HILDA (*stands staring at him*). You really look tired now.

LYNGSTRAND. Yes, I almost think I'm a bit tired out. I really do believe I'll have to sit down a while. (*He sits on a stone in the foreground, right.*)

HILDA (*standing in front of him*). Did you know there's going to be a dance later, down by the bandstand?

LYNGSTRAND. Yes, I heard some talk about that.

HILDA. Don't you think it's fun, going dancing?

BOLETTE (*who has begun picking wild flowers in the heather*). Now, Hilda—let Mr. Lyngstrand get his breath.

LYNGSTRAND (*to* HILDA). Yes, I'm sure I'd love dancing—if I only could.

HILDA. You've never learned?

LYNGSTRAND. No, I haven't, actually—but that's not what I meant. I meant, I can't because of my chest.

HILDA. Because of what you call your "condition"?

LYNGSTRAND. Yes, that's it.

HILDA. Does having your "condition" make you very unhappy?

LYNGSTRAND. Oh, no, I can't really say that. (*Smiles.*) Because I think it's why people are always being so kind and considerate—and so charitable to me.

HILDA. Yes, and then it's not at all serious, either.

LYNGSTRAND. No, not in the least. Your father was quite reassuring on that.

HILDA. Then as soon as you're able to travel, it'll pass off.

LYNGSTRAND. Oh, yes. It'll pass off.

BOLETTE (*with flowers*). Here you are, Mr. Lyngstrand —these go in your buttonhole.

LYNGSTRAND. Ah, thank you so much! This is really too kind of you.

HILDA (*looking downward to the right*). They're coming up the path.

BOLETTE (*also looking down*). If they only know where to turn off. No, they're missing it.

LYNGSTRAND (*gets up*). I'll run down to the bend and call them.

HILDA. You'll really have to shout.

BOLETTE. No, it's not worth it. You'll only tire yourself out again.

LYNGSTRAND. Oh, it's easy going downhill. (*He hurries off to the right.*)

HILDA. Yes—downhill. (*Looking after him.*) He's even jumping! And it never occurs to him that he's got to climb back up again.

BOLETTE. Poor thing—

HILDA. If Lyngstrand proposed to you, would you accept him?

BOLETTE. Are you out of your mind?

HILDA. I mean, naturally, if he didn't have this condition in his chest. And if he weren't going to die so soon. Would you have him then?

BOLETTE. I think you better have him.

HILDA. Not on your life! He doesn't have a pin to his name. He hasn't even got enough to live on himself.

BOLETTE. Then why are you so taken up with him?

HILDA. Oh, I'm interested in his disease, that's all.

BOLETTE. I've never noticed you pitying him for that.

HILDA. I don't, either. But I think it's fascinating.

BOLETTE. What?

HILDA. To watch him and to get him to say it isn't serious and that he's going to travel abroad and be an artist. He really believes every bit of it, and it fills him with such a joy. And yet it's all going to come to nothing, absolutely nothing. Because he won't live long enough. When I think of it, it seems so thrilling.

BOLETTE. Thrilling!

HILDA. Yes, I do think it's thrilling. That's my privilege.

BOLETTE. Hilda, you really are a nasty brat!

HILDA. That's what I want to be. Just for spite! (*Looking down.*) Well, at last! Arnholm doesn't like all this climbing. (*Turns.*) That's for sure. You know what I saw about Arnholm at lunch?

BOLETTE. What?

HILDA. He's beginning to lose his hair—right up here, in the middle of his head.

BOLETTE. What nonsense! It's not true.

HILDA. Oh, yes. And then he has wrinkles here around

his eyes. Oh, Bolette, how could you have had such a crush on him when he was your tutor!

BOLETTE (*smiling*). Yes, would you believe it? I remember crying my heart out once because he said he thought Bolette was an ugly name.

HILDA. Imagine! (*Looking down again.*) Well, will you look at that! There goes our "lady from the sea," babbling away to Arnholm. Father's all by himself. Hm—I wonder if those two don't have eyes for each other.

BOLETTE. You should be ashamed of yourself, really! How can you stand there and talk about her like that? Just when we were getting along so well—

HILDA. That's right—dream on, my little goose! Oh, no, we'll never get along with her, never. She's not our kind. And we're not hers, either. God knows why Father ever dragged her into the house—! I wouldn't be surprised if, one fine day, she was to go quite mad.

BOLETTE. Mad! How'd you get that idea?

HILDA. Oh, it's not so inconceivable. After all, her mother went crazy. She died insane, I know that.

BOLETTE. Good grief, what you don't have your nose in! But just don't go around talking about it. Try to be good now—for Father's sake. Do you hear me, Hilda?

(WANGEL, ELLIDA, ARNHOLM, *and* LYNGSTRAND *come up from the right.*)

ELLIDA (*pointing off into the distance*). It lies out there.

ARNHOLM. That's right. It must be in that direction.

ELLIDA. Out there, the sea.

BOLETTE (*to* ARNHOLM). Don't you think it's pretty up here?

ARNHOLM. I think it's magnificent. The view's superb.

WANGEL. Yes, I expect you've never been up here before.

ARNHOLM. No, never. I think in my time it was nearly inaccessible. Not even a footpath then.

WANGEL. And no park, either. This has all come about in the last few years.

BOLETTE. The view is even more marvelous over there from Lodskoll.

WANGEL. Perhaps we should go there, Ellida?

ELLIDA (*sitting down on a stone to the right*). Thanks, but not for me. You others can go. I don't mind sitting here for a while.

WANGEL. Well, then I'll stay with you. The girls can show Arnholm around.

BOLETTE. Would you like to go with us, Mr. Arnholm?

ARNHOLM. Yes, very much. Is there a path over there too?

BOLETTE. Oh, yes. A fine, wide path.

HILDA. The path's so wide, two people can easily go arm in arm.

ARNHOLM (*lightly*). Can I believe that, my little Hilda? (*To* BOLETTE.) Shall the two of us see if she's right?

BOLETTE (*suppressing a smile*). All right. Let's. (*They go out, left, arm in arm.*)

HILDA (*to* LYNGSTRAND). Shall we go too—?

LYNGSTRAND. Arm in arm—?

HILDA. Well, why not? Suits me.

LYNGSTRAND (*takes her arm and laughs delightedly*). This really is droll!

HILDA. Droll—?

LYNGSTRAND. I mean, it looks exactly as if we were engaged.

HILDA. You've never gone strolling before with a girl on your arm, Mr. Lyngstrand? (*They go out to the left.*)

WANGEL (*standing by the cairn*). So, Ellida dear, now we have time to ourselves—

ELLIDA. Yes, come and sit here by me.

WANGEL (*sitting*). How free and calm it is. Now we can talk a little.

ELLIDA. What about?

WANGEL. About you. And about our life together. I see all too well that it can't go on like this.

ELLIDA. What would you have instead?

WANGEL. Full confidence between us. A closeness of man and wife—like the old days.

ELLIDA. Oh, I wish it could be! But it's impossible.

WANGEL. I think I understand. From certain remarks you've dropped now and then, I think I know.

ELLIDA (*passionately*). But you don't! Don't say you understand—!

WANGEL. And yet, I do. Ellida, you're such an honest person. So loyal.

ELLIDA. Yes—loyal.

WANGEL. Any relationship in which you could feel secure and happy would have to be complete and unreserved.

ELLIDA (*looking tensely at him*). And so?

WANGEL. You were never made to be a man's second wife.

ELLIDA. Why do you say that—now?

WANGEL. I've often had my misgivings. Today made it clear. The children celebrating the birthday anniversary— you saw me as a kind of accomplice. And—well, a man's memories can't be erased. Not mine, anyway. I'm not like that.

ELLIDA. I know that. Oh, I know it so well.

WANGEL. But you're mistaken, all the same. For you it's almost as if the children's mother were still alive. As if she were there, invisible, among us. You think my feelings are divided equally between you and her. It's that thought that unsettles you. You find something almost immoral in our relationship. And that's why you no longer can—or no longer want to live with me as a wife.

ELLIDA (*rising*). Is this how you see it, Wangel? Like this?

WANGEL. Yes, today I finally saw the whole thing, down to the bottom.

ELLIDA. Down to the bottom, you say. Oh, don't be too sure.

WANGEL (*rising*). I know quite well there's still more to it.

ELLIDA (*anxiously*). More?

WANGEL. Yes. The fact is, you can't bear these surroundings. The mountains oppress and weigh down your spirit. There's not enough light for you here. Not enough space. Not enough strength and sweep to the wind.

ELLIDA. You're right. Night and day, winter and summer, I feel it—this overpowering homesickness for the sea.

WANGEL. Ellida dear, I know that. (*Putting his hand on her head.*) It's why the poor sick child will be going back home again.

ELLIDA. What do you mean?

WANGEL. Just what I said. We're moving away.

ELLIDA. Away!

WANGEL. Yes. Away somewhere by the open sea. Someplace where you can find a true home after your own heart.

ELLIDA. Oh, don't even think of it! It's impossible. You'd never be happy anywhere on earth but here.

WANGEL. Let that take care of itself. Besides—do you think I could live here happily—without you?

ELLIDA. But I'm here. And I'll stay here. I'm yours.

WANGEL. Are you mine, Ellida?

ELLIDA. Oh, don't talk about this other. Here's where you have everything you live for. Your whole lifework is right here.

WANGEL. I said, let that take care of itself. We're moving. Going somewhere out there. It's all settled now, Ellida.

ELLIDA. But what do you think we'll gain by that?

WANGEL. You'll regain your health and your peace of mind.

ELLIDA. By some remote chance. But what of you? Think of yourself. What would you gain?

WANGEL. You, back again.

ELLIDA. But you can't! No, no, you can't do that, Wangel! That's just what's so terrible—and so desolating to think about.

WANGEL. It's worth the risk. If you're going around thinking like this, then there's really no other solution for you than—a move. And the sooner, the better. It's all settled, you hear.

ELLIDA. No! In heaven's name then, I'd better tell you everything straight out—just as it is.

WANGEL. Yes, if you only would!

ELLIDA. I don't want you unhappy for my sake. Especially when it won't get us anywhere.

WANGEL. You gave me your word now that you'll tell me everything—just as it is.

ELLIDA. I will, as best I can. And as much as I understand it. Come here and sit by me.

(*They sit on the stones.*)

WANGEL. Well, Ellida? So—?

ELLIDA. That day when you came out to the lighthouse and asked if I'd be yours—you spoke to me so openly and so honestly about your first marriage. It had been so very happy, you said.

WANGEL. And it was.

ELLIDA. Yes, dear, I believe you. That's not why I bring it up now. I only want to remind you that, on my side also, I was straightforward with you. I told you quite frankly that once in my life I had loved someone else. That it had developed into—into a kind of engagement between us.

WANGEL. A kind of—?

ELLIDA. Yes, something of the sort. Well, it lasted no time at all, hardly. He went away. And so I took it as over and done with. I told you all that.

WANGEL. But, Ellida dear, why drag this up? Really, it has nothing to do with me. And I've never so much as asked you once who he was.

ELLIDA. No, you haven't. You're always so considerate of me.

WANGEL (*smiling*). Oh, in any case—I think I could more or less guess the name.

ELLIDA. The name!

WANGEL. Up there around Skjoldvik there weren't so many to choose from. As a matter of fact, there was actually only one choice—

ELLIDA. You're thinking it was—Arnholm.

WANGEL. Well, wasn't it?

ELLIDA. No.

WANGEL. It wasn't? Well, then I'm really at a loss.

ELLIDA. Do you remember once in late autumn a large American ship that put in to Skjoldvik for repairs?

WANGEL. Yes, I remember very well. They found the captain in his cabin one morning, murdered. I went out myself and did the postmortem.

ELLIDA. That's right, you did.

WANGEL. It was the mate, supposedly, who killed him.

ELLIDA. Who can tell! It was never proved.

WANGEL. There's not much doubt about it, all the same. Why else should he go off and drown himself?

ELLIDA. He didn't drown himself. He shipped out, to the north.

WANGEL (*surprised*). How do you know?

ELLIDA (*with an effort*). You see—it was the mate that I was—engaged to.

WANGEL (*springing up*). What are you saying! Impossible!

ELLIDA. Yes—but true. He was the one.

WANGEL. But, Ellida, how on earth—! How could you do such a thing! Get engaged to someone like him! A total stranger—! What was his name?

ELLIDA. At that time he called himself Freeman. Later, in his letters, he signed himself Alfred Johnston.

WANGEL. And where was he from?

ELLIDA. From Finmark, he said. But actually he was

born in Finland and came to Norway as a child—with his father, I think.

WANGEL. A Quain, then.

ELLIDA. Yes, I guess that's what they're called.

WANGEL. What else do you know about him?

ELLIDA. Only that he went to sea quite young. And that he'd made some long voyages.

WANGEL. Nothing else?

ELLIDA. No. We never talked of his past.

WANGEL. What did you talk of?

ELLIDA. Mainly about the sea.

WANGEL. Ah—! About the sea.

ELLIDA. About the storms and the calms. The dark nights at sea. And the sea in the sparkling sunlight, that too. But mostly we talked of whales and dolphins, and of the seals that would lie out on the skerries in the warm noon sun. And then we spoke of the gulls and the eagles and every kind of seabird you can imagine. You know—it's strange, but when we talked in such a way, then it seemed to me that all these creatures belonged to him.

WANGEL. And you yourself—?

ELLIDA. Yes, I almost felt that I belonged among them, too.

WANGEL. I see. So that's how you got engaged.

ELLIDA. Yes. He said I must.

WANGEL. Must? Had you no will of your own?

ELLIDA. Not when he was near. Oh—afterward I thought it was utterly incomprehensible.

WANGEL. Were you often together with him?

ELLIDA. No, not very often. One day he came out for a look around the lighthouse. That's how we met. And later we saw each other occasionally. But then came this thing with the captain, and he had to leave.

WANGEL. Yes, tell me a bit more about that.

ELLIDA. It was early one morning, just getting light—when I had a message from him. In it he said that I should meet him out at Bratthammer—you know, that headland between the lighthouse and Skjoldvik.

WANGEL. Of course—I remember it well.

ELLIDA. I was to go there right away, he wrote, because he had to speak to me.

WANGEL. And you went?

ELLIDA. Yes, I had to. Well, he told me then that he'd stabbed the captain that night.

WANGEL. He said it himself! Confessed!

ELLIDA. Yes. But he'd only done what was necessary and right, he said.

WANGEL. Necessary and right? Then why did he kill him?

ELLIDA. He wouldn't discuss it. Only that it was nothing for me to hear.

WANGEL. And you believed him, on his word alone?

ELLIDA. I never thought to doubt him. Well, anyway he had to get away. But just before he was to say good-bye— you'll never guess what he did.

WANGEL. Well, tell me.

ELLIDA. He took a key-ring out of his pocket, and then pulled a ring that he'd always worn from his finger. I also had a little ring, and he took that too. He slipped both of them together onto the key-ring—and then he said that we two would marry ourselves to the sea.

WANGEL. Marry—?

ELLIDA. Yes, that's what he said. And then he threw the rings together, with all his strength, as far as he could out in the ocean.

WANGEL. And you, Ellida? You accepted all this?

ELLIDA. Yes, can you imagine—I felt then as if it were fated to be. But then, thank God—he went away!

WANGEL. And when he'd gone—?

ELLIDA. Oh, I came to my senses soon enough—and saw how mad and meaningless it had all been.

WANGEL. But you mentioned some letters before. So you *have* heard from him since.

ELLIDA. Yes, I've heard from him. First I got a few short lines from Archangel. He wrote only that he was going on to America. And he enclosed an address where I could write him.

WANGEL. And did you?

ELLIDA. At once. I wrote, of course, that everything had to be ended between us. That he was no longer to think of me, just as I would never again think of him.

WANGEL. And he wrote back, even so?

ELLIDA. Yes, he wrote back.

WANGEL. And what did he say to your terms?

ELLIDA. Not a word. It was as if I'd never broken with him at all. His answer was cool and calm, that I should wait for him. When he could provide for me, he would let me know, and then I should come to him at once.

WANGEL. So he wouldn't let you go?

ELLIDA. No. I wrote him again. Almost word for word the same as before—but in even stronger terms.

WANGEL. Did he give up then?

ELLIDA. Oh, no, nothing like that. He wrote as calmly as ever. Not a word that I'd broken it off. Then I realized it was useless, so I never wrote him again.

WANGEL. Or heard from him, either?

ELLIDA. Yes, I had three more letters from him. He wrote me once from California, and another time from China. The last letter I had was from Australia. He said then that he was going to the gold mines. I haven't heard from him since.

WANGEL. That man has had an unearthly power over you, Ellida.

ELLIDA. Yes. Yes, he's horrible!

WANGEL. But you mustn't think of him anymore. Never! My dearest Ellida, promise me that! Now we have to try a better cure for you. Fresher air than here in the fjords. The sting of the salt sea breeze. What do you say?

ELLIDA. Oh, don't talk about it! Or think of it even! There's no help for me there. I can feel it in my bones—I won't get rid of this out there either.

WANGEL. Of what? Just what do you mean?

ELLIDA. I mean the horror. The fantastic hold on my mind—

WANGEL. But you *have* gotten rid of it. Long ago. When you broke with him. It's over and done with now.

ELLIDA (*springing to her feet*). No, that's just the thing, it isn't.

WANGEL. Not over!

ELLIDA. No, Wangel—it's not over. And I'm afraid it never will be.

WANGEL (*in a strangled voice*). Are you saying, then, that in your heart of hearts, you'll never be able to forget this man?

ELLIDA. I *had* forgotten him. But suddenly one day it was as if he returned.

WANGEL. When was that?

ELLIDA. About three years ago now—or a little more. It was while I was carrying the child.

WANGEL. Ah—then! Yes, now I begin to understand.

ELLIDA. No, dear, you're wrong! This thing that's happened to me—oh, I don't think it can ever be understood.

WANGEL (*looking sorrowfully at her*). To think—that here you've gone for three whole years loving another man. Another man. Not me—but somebody else!

ELLIDA. Oh, you're so absolutely wrong. I love no one else but you.

WANGEL (*quietly*). Why, then, in all this time, have you not wanted to live with me as my wife?

ELLIDA. Because of the terror I feel of him, of the stranger.

WANGEL. Terror—?

ELLIDA. Yes, terror. A terror so huge that only the sea could hold it. All right, I'll tell you, Wangel—

(The young people of the town come back from the left, nod as they pass and go out to the right. Along with them come ARNHOLM, BOLETTE, HILDA, *and* LYNGSTRAND.*)*

BOLETTE *(as they go by).* Well, are you still enjoying the view?

ELLIDA. Yes, it's so cool and nice up here.

ARNHOLM. We've decided to go dancing.

WANGEL. Very good. We'll be down right away.

HILDA. See you soon then.

ELLIDA. Mr. Lyngstrand—oh, just a moment.

*(*LYNGSTRAND *stops.* ARNHOLM, BOLETTE, *and* HILDA *go out to the right.)*

ELLIDA *(to* LYNGSTRAND*).* Are you going dancing, too?

LYNGSTRAND. No, Mrs. Wangel, I don't think I should.

ELLIDA. Yes, you'd better be careful. That chest trouble—you're not fully over it, you know.

LYNGSTRAND. Not entirely, no.

ELLIDA *(somewhat hesitantly).* How long can it be now since you made that trip—?

LYNGSTRAND. When I got this condition?

ELLIDA. Yes, the voyage you told about this morning.

LYNGSTRAND. Oh, I guess that was around—let me see—yes, it's a good three years ago now.

ELLIDA. Three years.

LYNGSTRAND. Or a shade more. We left America in February, and we went down in March. It was the equinoctial gales that finished us off.

ELLIDA *(looking at* WANGEL*).* So it was at that time—

WANGEL. But, Ellida dear—?

ELLIDA. Well, don't let us keep you, Mr. Lyngstrand. Go on now. But don't dance.

LYNGSTRAND. No, I'll just look on. *(He goes out, right.)*

WANGEL. Ellida, why did you question him about the voyage?

ELLIDA. Johnston was with him on board, I'm positive of that.

WANGEL. Why do you think so?

ELLIDA (*without answering*). It was then that he learned I'd married someone else while he was away. And then—at that same moment, this thing came over me.

WANGEL. This terror?

ELLIDA. Yes. Sometimes, suddenly, I can see him standing large as life in front of me. Or actually—a little to one side. He never looks at me. He's simply there.

WANGEL. How does he seem to look?

ELLIDA. Exactly as I saw him last.

WANGEL. Ten years ago?

ELLIDA. Yes, out at Bratthammer. And clearest of all I can see the stickpin he wore, with a great blue-white pearl in it. That pearl is like the eye of a dead fish. And it seems to be staring at me.

WANGEL. In God's name—! Ellida, you're ill—much more than I thought. Or than you can possibly know.

ELLIDA. Yes! Yes, help me! I feel it's tightening—tightening around me. More and more.

WANGEL. And you've been going about in this state for three whole years, bearing your suffering in secret, without confiding in me.

ELLIDA. But I couldn't tell you! Not till now, not till I had to—for your sake. If I'd confessed all this to you, I'd also have had to tell you—what's unspeakable.

WANGEL. Unspeakable—?

ELLIDA (*averting her face*). No, no, no! Don't talk! Just one other thing, then I'm through. Wangel—how can we ever fathom this—this—mystery about the child's eyes—?

WANGEL. My dearest Ellida, I promise you, that was nothing but your own imagination. The child had exactly the same eyes as all other normal children.

ELLIDA. He did not! And you can't see it! His eyes changed color with the sea. When the fjord lay still in the sunlight, his eyes were like that. And in the storms, too—oh, I saw it well enough, even if you didn't.

WANGEL (*indulgently*). Well—so be it. But even so—what then?

ELLIDA (*quietly, coming closer*). I've seen eyes like that before.

WANGEL. When? And where?

ELLIDA. Out on Bratthammer—ten years ago.

WANGEL (*stepping back*). What do you—?

ELLIDA (*whispers, with a shudder*). The child had the stranger's eyes.

WANGEL (*with an involuntary cry*). Ellida—!

ELLIDA (*clasping her hands in misery about her head*). Now you can understand why I never again *want*—why I never again *dare* to live with you as your wife! (*She turns quickly and runs off down the hill to the right.*)

WANGEL (*hurrying after her and calling*). Ellida—Ellida! My poor, miserable Ellida!

⤙ ACT THREE ⤚

A remote corner of DR. WANGEL's *garden. It is a damp, marshy place, overshadowed by large old trees. To the right the edge of a stagnant pond is visible. A low picket fence separates the garden from the footpath and the fjord in the background. Beyond the fjord on the horizon, high peaks and mountain ranges. It is late afternoon, near evening.* BOLETTE *sits, sewing, on a stone bench to the left. On the bench lie a couple of books and a sewing basket.* HILDA *and* LYNGSTRAND, *both with fishing rods, walk along the edge of the pond.*

HILDA (*making a sign to* LYNGSTRAND). Don't move! There, I can see a big one.

LYNGSTRAND (*looking*). Where?

HILDA (*pointing*). Can't you see—down there. And there! Holy God, look at that one! (*Peering off through the trees.*) Ahh! Here he comes to scare them away.

BOLETTE (*glancing up*). Who's coming?

HILDA. Your tutor, ma'am.

BOLETTE. My—?

HILDA. Well, I'll bet you he's never been *mine*.

(ARNHOLM *comes through the trees from the right.*)

ARNHOLM. Are there fish in the pond now?

HILDA. Yes, some enormously old carp.

ARNHOLM. Really? So the old carp are still alive?

HILDA. Yes, they're tough, all right. But we're going to pull in a few of them.

ARNHOLM. You'd probably do better out by the fjord.

LYNGSTRAND. No, the pond is—I think it's more mysterious.

HILDA. Yes, it's more thrilling here. Have you been in the water?

ARNHOLM. Moments ago. I'm just now coming from the bathhouse.

HILDA. You stick close to the shore, I guess.

ARNHOLM. Yes, I'm not very much of a swimmer.

HILDA. Can you swim on your back?

ARNHOLM. No.

HILDA. I can. (*To* LYNGSTRAND.) Let's try over there on the other side.

(*They go around the pond off to the right.*)

ARNHOLM (*going closer to* BOLETTE). Sitting all by yourself, Bolette?

BOLETTE. Oh, yes, I do that quite often.

ARNHOLM. Isn't your mother here in the garden?

BOLETTE. No, she's gone for a walk with Father.

ARNHOLM. How is she this afternoon?

BOLETTE. I'm not quite sure. I forgot to ask.

ARNHOLM. What are the books you have there?

BOLETTE. Oh, one of them's something on plant life. And the other's a geography book.

ARNHOLM. Do you like reading that sort of thing?

BOLETTE. Yes, when I can find time for it. But I have to put the housework first.

ARNHOLM. But doesn't your mother—your stepmother—help you with that?

BOLETTE. No, that's up to me. I had to look after it the two years that Father was alone. And it's gone on that way since.

ARNHOLM. But you're as fond of reading as ever.

BOLETTE. Yes, I read every book I can get hold of and that I think I can learn from. One wants so much to know something about the world. Because here we live so completely cut off from everything that's going on. Well, almost completely.

ARNHOLM. Now, Bolette, you mustn't say that.

BOLETTE. It's true. I don't think we live very differently from the carp down there in the pond. They have the fjord so close to them, and there the shoals of great, wild fish go streaking in and out. But these poor, tame pet fish know nothing of that, and they'll never be part of that life.

ARNHOLM. I hardly think they'd do very well out there.

BOLETTE. As well as here, I expect.

ARNHOLM. Besides, you really can't say you're so very removed from life here. Not in the summer, at least. Nowadays it seems like this place is a rendezvous for the whole live world. Almost *the* social capital for tourists.

BOLETTE (*smiling*). Oh, yes, since you're here only as one of the tourists, it's easy enough for you to make fun of us.

ARNHOLM. I make fun—? What gives you that idea?

BOLETTE. Oh, because all that rendezvous and tourist capital talk is something you've heard in town. They always say things like that.

ARNHOLM. Well, as a matter of fact—so I've noticed.

BOLETTE. But actually there's not a word of truth in it. Not for us year-round people. What good is it to us if the great, strange world goes by on its way up to see the midnight sun? We never go along. We never see the midnight sun. Oh, no, we live our snug little lives out here, in our fish pond.

ARNHOLM (*sitting down beside her*). Tell me, Bolette— I'm wondering, as you go about your life here, isn't there something—I mean some definite thing—that you long for?

BOLETTE. Yes—perhaps.

ARNHOLM. And what's that? Tell me.

BOLETTE. Mostly to get away.

ARNHOLM. That most of all?

BOLETTE. Yes. And afterward, a chance to learn. To get to know something about—just everything.

ARNHOLM. In those days when I was tutoring you, your father often said you'd be going on to the university.

BOLETTE. Oh, poor Father—he says so many things. But when it comes right down to it—there's no real willpower in him.

ARNHOLM. Yes. I'm afraid you're right; there isn't. But have you ever spoken to him about it? I mean, quite seriously and unequivocally?

BOLETTE. No, I haven't exactly.

ARNHOLM. But you know, you absolutely should. Before it's too late, Bolette. Why haven't you?

BOLETTE. Oh, I suppose it's because there's no real willpower in me, either. That's one trait I've picked up from him.

ARNHOLM. Hm—don't you think you're being unfair to yourself?

BOLETTE. I wish I were, but—no. Besides, Father has so little time to think of me and my future. And not much interest, either. That kind of thing he'd rather avoid, if he possibly can. Because he's so involved with Ellida—

ARNHOLM. Involved—? How—?

BOLETTE. I mean, he and my stepmother— (*Breaking off.*) Father and Mother have their own world, you can see that.

ARNHOLM. Well, so much the better, then, if you get away from here.

BOLETTE. Yes, but I don't think I have any right to go—to leave Father.

ARNHOLM. But, Bolette dear, you're going to have to someday, anyway. So I'd say, the sooner the better.

BOLETTE. Oh, I guess it's the only thing. I ought to think of myself, too. Try to get some kind of work. When

Father goes, I'll have no one to turn to. But poor Father—
I dread leaving him.

ARNHOLM. Dread—?

BOLETTE. Yes, for his sake.

ARNHOLM. But, good Lord, your stepmother! She'll be
with him.

BOLETTE. That's true. But she simply hasn't any grasp
of all those things that Mother took on so well. There's so
much this one just doesn't see. Or maybe doesn't want to
see—or bother with. I don't know which it is.

ARNHOLM. Hm. I think I know what you mean.

BOLETTE. Poor Father—he's weak in certain respects.
Perhaps you've noticed it yourself. Then too, he hasn't
enough work to fill up his time. And she's so incapable of
giving him any support. But that's partly his own fault.

ARNHOLM. How so?

BOLETTE. Oh, Father only wants to see happy faces
around him. There has to be sunshine and joy in the
house, he says. So I'm afraid that many times he's given
her medicine that in the long run does her no good.

ARNHOLM. Do you really think so?

BOLETTE. I can't think anything else. She acts so strange
at times. (*Heatedly.*) But it does seem so unfair that I
should have to stay on here at home! It's really no earthly
use to Father. And I have obligations to myself, too.

ARNHOLM. You know, Bolette—we have to talk all this
over more fully.

BOLETTE. Oh, that's not going to help any. I'm just
fated to stay in my fish pond, that's all.

ARNHOLM. Nonsense! It depends completely on you.

BOLETTE (*suddenly buoyant*). You really think so?

ARNHOLM. Yes, I know so. The whole thing is there,
right in your own hands.

BOLETTE. Oh, if that could be true—! Would you
maybe put in a good word for me with Father?

ARNHOLM. Of course. But first of all I want to speak
frankly and freely with you, Bolette. (*Glancing off to the*

left.) Shh! Don't give it away. We'll come back to this later.

(ELLIDA *appears from the left, hatless, with a large scarf thrown over her head and shoulders.*)

ELLIDA (*nervously animated*). It's lovely here! Simply beautiful!

ARNHOLM (*getting up*). Have you been out walking?

ELLIDA. Yes, a long, long glorious walk through the hills with Wangel. And now we're going out for a sail.

BOLETTE. Won't you sit down?

ELLIDA. No, thanks. I won't sit.

BOLETTE (*moving along the bench*). There's plenty of room.

ELLIDA. No, no, no—I won't sit. Won't sit.

ARNHOLM. That walk certainly did you good. You look so elated.

ELLIDA. Oh, I feel so marvelously well! So indescribably happy! And safe! So safe— (*Looking off to the left.*) What's that big steamer coming in there?

BOLETTE (*rises and looks out*). It must be the large English one.

ARNHOLM. It's putting in by the buoy. Does it usually stop here?

BOLETTE. Just half an hour. It goes farther on up the fjord.

ELLIDA. And then tomorrow—out again. Out on the great open sea. Straight over the sea. Imagine—just to be on board! If one could! If only one could!

ARNHOLM. Have you never taken a long sea voyage, Mrs. Wangel?

ELLIDA. Never at all. Only these short trips here in the fjord.

BOLETTE (*with a sigh*). Ah, yes, we have to make do with dry land.

ARNHOLM. Well, after all, it's our natural home.

ELLIDA. I don't believe that in the slightest.

ARNHOLM. But—we belong to the land, no?

ELLIDA. No. I don't believe it. I believe that, if only mankind had adapted itself from the start to a life on the sea—or perhaps *in* the sea—then we would have become something much different and more advanced than we are now. Both better—and happier.

ARNHOLM. You really believe that?

ELLIDA. I don't see why not. I've often discussed it with Wangel.

ARNHOLM. Yes, and he—?

ELLIDA. He thinks it's entirely possible.

ARNHOLM (*playfully*). Well—maybe. But what's done is done. So once and for all we took the wrong turn and became land animals, instead of sea creatures. Considering the circumstances, it's a little late now to amend the error.

ELLIDA. Yes, there's the unhappy truth. And I think people have some sense of it, too. They bear it about inside them like a secret sorrow. And I can tell you—there, in that feeling, is the deepest source of all the melancholy in man. Yes—I'm sure of it.

ARNHOLM. But, my dear Mrs. Wangel—I never got the impression humanity was so very melancholy. Quite the contrary, I think the majority take life for the best, as it comes—and with a great, quiet, instinctive joy.

ELLIDA. Oh no, that isn't true. The joy—it's much like our joy in these long, light summer days and nights. It has the hint in it of dark times to come. And that hint is what throws a shadow over our human joy—like the drifting clouds with their shadows over the fjord. Everything lies there so bright and blue—and then all of a sudden—

ARNHOLM. You shouldn't give way to these sad thoughts now. A moment ago you were so gay, so elated—

ELLIDA. Yes. Yes, so I was. Oh, this—I'm so stupid. (*Looking around uneasily.*) If Wangel would only come. He promised me he would, definitely. But he still hasn't come. He must have forgotten. Oh, my dear Arnholm, please, try to find him for me, won't you?

ARNHOLM. Yes, gladly.

ELLIDA. Tell him he has to come right away. Because now I can't see him—

ARNHOLM. Can't see him—?

ELLIDA. Oh, you wouldn't understand. When he's not near me, then often I can't remember how he looks. And then it's as if I'd lost him for good. It's a horrible feeling. Please, go! (*She walks aimlessly about by the pond.*)

BOLETTE (*to* ARNHOLM). I'll go with you. You won't know where—

ARNHOLM. Don't bother. I'll manage—

BOLETTE (*in an undertone*). No, no, I'm worried. I'm afraid he's gone on the ship.

ARNHOLM. Afraid?

BOLETTE. Yes, he likes to see if there are people he knows. And then there's the bar on board—

ARNHOLM. Oh, yes. Well, come on then.

(*He and* BOLETTE *go off, left.* ELLIDA *stands a moment, staring down into the pond. Intermittently she speaks in broken whispers to herself. Outside, on the path behind the fence, a* STRANGER, *dressed for traveling, comes from the left. He has bushy, reddish hair and a beard. He has a Scotch tam on his head and a musette bag on a strap over his shoulder. The* STRANGER *walks slowly along the fence, scanning the garden. When his eyes fall on* ELLIDA, *he stops and stares at her with an intense, probing gaze.*)

STRANGER (*in a low voice*). Good evening, Ellida!

ELLIDA (*turning with a cry*). Oh, my love—you've come at last!

STRANGER. Yes, at last.

ELLIDA (*looks with astonishment and terror at him*). Who are you? What do you want here?

STRANGER. You know well enough.

ELLIDA (*starting*). What's that! Why are you speaking to me. Who are you looking for?

STRANGER. I've been looking for you.

ELLIDA (*with a shudder*). Ah—! (*Stares at him, falters back and breaks out in a half-stifled cry.*) The eyes! The eyes!

STRANGER. Well—you're finally beginning to know me again? I knew you at once, Ellida.

ELLIDA. The eyes! Don't look at me like that! I'll cry for help!

STRANGER. Shh, shh! Don't be afraid. I won't hurt you.

ELLIDA (*her hands over her eyes*). I said, don't look at me that way!

STRANGER (*leaning his arms on the fence*). I came on the English ship.

ELLIDA (*glancing fearfully at him*). What do you want of me?

STRANGER. I promised you I'd return as soon as I could—

ELLIDA. Go! Go away! Don't ever come back—ever! I wrote you that everything was over between us! Completely! You know that!

STRANGER (*unperturbed, not answering her*). I wanted to come before this. But I couldn't. Now, at last, I'm able. And so you have me, Ellida.

ELLIDA. What is it you want of me? What are you thinking of? What have you come here for?

STRANGER. You must know that I've come to take you.

ELLIDA (*wincing in fright*). To take me! Is that your idea!

STRANGER. Why, of course.

ELLIDA. But—you must know that I'm married.

STRANGER. Yes, I know.

ELLIDA. And yet—even so, you've come here to—to take me!

STRANGER. That's what I'm doing.

ELLIDA (*pressing her fists to her head*). Oh, it's monstrous! It's horrible—horrible!

STRANGER. Do you think you won't come?

ELLIDA (*in confusion*). Don't look at me that way!

STRANGER. I'm asking if you don't want to come.

ELLIDA. No, no, no! I don't! Never! I don't want to, I

tell you! I neither can nor will! (*More quietly.*) Nor dare to.

STRANGER (*climbing over the fence and entering the garden*). All right, Ellida—then let me just say one thing to you before I move on.

ELLIDA (*tries to run, but cannot, and stands as if paralyzed by fright, supporting herself against a tree by the pond*). Don't touch me! Stay away from me! Not—nearer! Don't touch me, you hear!

STRANGER (*cautiously coming a few steps closer*). You needn't be afraid of me, Ellida.

ELLIDA (*covering her eyes with her hands*). Don't look at me like that!

STRANGER. Don't be afraid. Don't be afraid.

(DR. WANGEL *comes through the garden from the left.*)

WANGEL (*still half hidden by the trees*). Well, you've been waiting a mighty long while for me.

ELLIDA (*rushes to him and clings tightly to his arm, crying out*). Oh, Wangel—save me. Save me—if you can!

WANGEL. Ellida—what in God's name—!

ELLIDA. Save me, Wangel! Can't you see him? He's standing right over there!

WANGEL. That man? (*Approaching him.*) If I may—who are you? And why are you here in the garden?

STRANGER (*indicating* ELLIDA *with a nod*). I want to talk to her.

WANGEL. I see. So it was you— (*To* ELLIDA.) I heard some stranger had been up at the house, asking for you.

STRANGER. Yes, it was me.

WANGEL. And what do you want with my wife? (*Turning.*) Do you know him, Ellida?

ELLIDA (*quietly, wringing her hands*). Do I know him? Yes, yes!

WANGEL (*brusquely*). Well?

ELLIDA. It's him, Wangel! He's the man! The one I told you about—!

WANGEL. What? What did you say? (*Turning.*) Are you the Johnston who once—

STRANGER. You can call me Johnston—it's all right with me. But that's not my name.

WANGEL. It's not?

STRANGER. Not any longer, no.

WANGEL. And what is it you want with my wife? Because you know, of course, that the lighthouse keeper's daughter has been married for some time now. And I guess you must also know whom she's married to.

STRANGER. I've known for more than three years.

ELLIDA (*in suspense*). How did you find out?

STRANGER. I was on my way home to you, when I came on an old newspaper—one from these parts—and it told there about the wedding.

ELLIDA (*staring into space*). The wedding—so that was it—

STRANGER. I found it so strange. Because those rings in the sea—they were a wedding, too, Ellida.

ELLIDA (*hiding her face in her hands*). Ah—!

WANGEL. How dare you!

STRANGER. Had you forgotten?

ELLIDA (*feeling his eyes on her*). Stop looking at me like that!

WANGEL (*moving up to him*). Better deal with me, not her. All right, to the point—since you know the situation, what business do you have around here? Why have you sought out my wife?

STRANGER. I promised Ellida I'd come to her as soon as I could.

WANGEL. Ellida—again!

STRANGER. And Ellida promised faithfully to wait till I came.

WANGEL. I hear you calling my wife by her first name. That kind of familiarity isn't appreciated around here.

STRANGER. I understand. But, after all, she belongs to me first—

WANGEL. To you! Still—!

ELLIDA (*retreating behind* WANGEL). Oh—! He'll never let go!

WANGEL. To you! You say she belongs to you!

STRANGER. Did she tell you anything about the two rings? Mine and Ellida's?

WANGEL. She did. But what of it? She put an end to that long ago. You've had her letters. You should know.

STRANGER. Ellida and I both agreed that joining our rings would have all the binding force of an actual marriage.

ELLIDA. But I don't want it, you hear me! I never want to see you again! Keep your eyes off me! I don't want this!

WANGEL. You must be crazy if you think you can come here and base your rights on such adolescent games.

STRANGER. It's true, I have no rights—in your sense.

WANGEL. Then what do you intend to do? You certainly can't imagine you could take her away from me forcibly—against her will?

STRANGER. No. What good would that be? If Ellida goes off with me, she'll have to come of her own free will.

ELLIDA (*with a start, crying out*). My own free will—!

WANGEL. How can you think—!

ELLIDA (*to herself*). My own free will—!

WANGEL. You must be out of your head! Get on your way. We've nothing more to do with you.

STRANGER (*looking at his watch*). It's almost time for me to be on board again. (*Approaching a step.*) Well, Ellida—I've kept my promise. (*Closer still.*) I've kept the word I gave you.

ELLIDA (*shrinking aside*). Oh, don't—don't touch me!

STRANGER. And now you've got till tomorrow night to think it over.

WANGEL. There's nothing here to think over. Let's see you clear out!

STRANGER (*still to* ELLIDA). I'll be going up the fjord now with the ship. Tomorrow night I'll come by here again—and I'll look for you. You must wait for me here in the garden. Because I'd rather settle this matter with you alone, you understand?

ELLIDA (*in a low, tremulous voice*). Oh, you hear that, Wangel?

WANGEL. Don't worry. I think we can forestall that visit.

STRANGER. Good-bye until then, Ellida. Till tomorrow night.

ELLIDA (*imploringly*). No, no—not tomorrow night! Not ever again!

STRANGER. And if, by that time, you've made up your mind to follow me over the sea—

ELLIDA. Don't look at me that way!

STRANGER. Then be ready to leave right away.

WANGEL. Go up to the house, Ellida!

ELLIDA. I can't. Oh, help me! Save me, Wangel!

STRANGER. Because you have to remember one thing: if you don't go with me tomorrow, it's all over.

ELLIDA (*trembling as she looks at him*). All over? Forever?

STRANGER (*nods*). It can never be altered then, Ellida. I'll never be back in these parts again. You won't see me anymore. Or hear from me, either. Never. Then I'll be dead and gone from you forever.

ELLIDA (*her breathing labored*). Oh—!

STRANGER. So think over carefully what you'll do. Good-bye. (*Goes to the fence, climbs over, stops and says.*) Yes, Ellida—be ready to travel tomorrow night. I'm coming to take you away. (*He goes slowly and calmly off down the path to the right.*)

ELLIDA (*looking after him a moment*). He said, of my

own free will! Imagine—he said I should go with him of my own free will.

WANGEL. Don't get upset. He's gone now—and you won't see him anymore.

ELLIDA. How can you say that? He's coming back to-morrow night.

WANGEL. Let him come. He's not seeing you, at any rate.

ELLIDA (*shaking her head*). Ah, Wangel, don't think you can stop him.

WANGEL. Oh, yes, dear, I can—just leave it to me.

ELLIDA (*deep in thought, not hearing him*). After he's been here tomorrow night—and after he's sailed off to sea with the ship—

WANGEL. Yes?

ELLIDA. I wonder if he'll never—never come back?

WANGEL. Ellida dear, that you can be quite sure of. What would he be doing here afterward? Now that he's heard from your own lips that you've no more interest in him at all. That closes the case.

ELLIDA (*to herself*). Tomorrow, then. Or never.

WANGEL. And even if he did come back—

ELLIDA. Then what?

WANGEL. Then it's within our power to render him harmless.

ELLIDA. Don't you believe it.

WANGEL. I'm telling you, we have that power! If you can't have peace from him any other way, he's going to pay for the murder of the captain.

ELLIDA (*passionately*). No! No, not that! We know nothing about the captain's murder! Nothing at all!

WANGEL. We don't know? He confessed to you himself!

ELLIDA. No, nothing of that! If you say anything, I'll deny it. Don't cage him in! He belongs to the open sea. He belongs out there.

WANGEL (*gazes at her and says slowly*). Ah, Ellida—Ellida!

ELLIDA (*clinging to him passionately*). Oh, my dearest own—save me from that man!

WANGEL (*gently freeing himself*). Come! Come with me!

(LYNGSTRAND *and* HILDA, *both with fishing rods, appear from the right by the pond.*)

LYNGSTRAND (*goes quickly up to* ELLIDA). You know what, Mrs. Wangel—it's the most amazing thing!

WANGEL. What is?

LYNGSTRAND. Just think—we saw the American.

WANGEL. The American?

HILDA. Yes, I saw him, too.

LYNGSTRAND. He passed up behind the garden and then onto that big English steamer.

WANGEL. How do you know this man?

LYNGSTRAND. I once went to sea with him. I was positive he'd been drowned—and there he was, live as could be.

WANGEL. You know anything more about him?

LYNGSTRAND. No. But he must have come back to have revenge on his faithless wife.

WANGEL. What did you say?

HILDA. Lyngstrand's going to make him into a piece of sculpture.

WANGEL. I don't understand one word—

ELLIDA. You can hear it all later.

(ARNHOLM *and* BOLETTE *come along the path from the left outside the fence.*)

BOLETTE (*to those in the garden*). Come and see! It's the English steamer sailing up the fjord.

(*A large steamer glides slowly by in the distance.*)

LYNGSTRAND (*to* HILDA, *near the fence*). Tonight he'll be standing over her.

HILDA (*nods*). Over the faithless wife—yes.

LYNGSTRAND. Imagine—as midnight strikes.

HILDA. I think it's just thrilling.

ELLIDA (*watching the ship*). Tomorrow, then—

WANGEL. And then, never again.

ELLIDA (*in a low, uncertain voice*). Oh, Wangel—save me from myself.

WANGEL (*looking anxiously at her*). Ellida—I feel something behind this.

ELLIDA. Yes. You can feel the undertow.

WANGEL. The undertow—?

ELLIDA. That man is like the sea.

(*She goes slowly and pensively out through the garden to the left.* WANGEL *walks uneasily beside her, observing her searchingly.*)

⤙ ACT FOUR ⤚

DR. WANGEL's *conservatory. Doors right and left. In the rear wall, between the two windows, a glass door, open, leading out to the veranda. Beyond, some of the garden can be seen. A sofa and table in the left foreground. To the right a piano, and farther back a large flower stand. In the center of the room, a round table with chairs grouped about it. On the table a blossoming rose tree, and various potted plants elsewhere around the room. It is morning.*

By the table to the left, BOLETTE *sits on the sofa, occupied with some embroidery.* LYNGSTRAND *is seated on a chair at the upper end of the table. Below in the garden* BALLESTED *sits painting.* HILDA *stands next to him, looking on.*

LYNGSTRAND (*sits for a time in silence, his arms resting on the table, studying the way* BOLETTE *works*). It must really be very hard to sew a border like that, Miss Wangel.

BOLETTE. Oh, no, it's not so difficult—if you just keep your counting straight—

LYNGSTRAND. Counting? You mean you're counting as well?

BOLETTE. Yes, the stitches. See here.

LYNGSTRAND. Why, of course! That's amazing! You know, it's almost a kind of art. Can you also sketch?

BOLETTE. Oh, yes—if I can copy something.

LYNGSTRAND. Otherwise, no?

BOLETTE. Otherwise no.

LYNGSTRAND. Then it's not a real art, after all.

BOLETTE. No, I guess it's mostly a kind of—handiwork.

LYNGSTRAND. But I do think that you could maybe learn an art.

BOLETTE. When I haven't any talent?

LYNGSTRAND. In spite of that—if you were to spend your time in the company of a real, authentic artist—

BOLETTE. You think I could learn from him?

LYNGSTRAND. I don't mean learn in the conventional sense. But I think it would dawn on you little by little— almost like a kind of miracle, Miss Wangel.

BOLETTE. That would be something.

LYNGSTRAND (*after a moment*). Have you ever thought imminently—I mean—have you ever thought deeply and seriously about marriage, Miss Wangel?

BOLETTE (*giving him a quick glance*). About—? No.

LYNGSTRAND. I have.

BOLETTE. Oh? Have you really?

LYNGSTRAND. Oh, yes. I think very often about things like that. Most of all, about marriage. And then, of course, I've read about it, too, in quite a few books. I think that marriage has to be accounted almost a kind of miracle. The way a woman little by little makes herself over until she becomes like her husband.

BOLETTE. Takes on his interests, you mean?

LYNGSTRAND. Yes, exactly!

BOLETTE. Well, but his powers too? His skills, and his talents?

LYNGSTRAND. Hm—yes, I wonder if all that couldn't as well—

BOLETTE. Then perhaps you also believe that whatever a man has studied, or thought out for himself—that this, too, can become a part of his wife?

LYNGSTRAND. That too, yes. Little by little, almost miraculously. But I'm quite sure it can only happen in a marriage that's faithful and loving and truly happy.

BOLETTE. Has it ever occurred to you that perhaps a man could also be absorbed that way, over into his wife? Become like her, I mean?

LYNGSTRAND. A man? No, I never thought of that.

BOLETTE. But why couldn't it work as well one way as the other?

LYNGSTRAND. No, because a man has his vocation to live for. And that's the thing that makes a man strong and stable, Miss Wangel. He has a calling in life, you see.

BOLETTE. All men? Every last one?

LYNGSTRAND. Oh, no. I was thinking particularly of artists.

BOLETTE. Do you think it's right for an artist to go and get married?

LYNGSTRAND. Yes, of course I think so. If he can find someone that he cares for deeply—

BOLETTE. All the same, I think he'd do best simply to live for his art alone.

LYNGSTRAND. Well, naturally he will. But he can do that just as well if he's also married.

BOLETTE. Yes, but what about her?

LYNGSTRAND. Her? Who?

BOLETTE. The one that he marries. What's she going to live for?

LYNGSTRAND. She'll live for his art, also. I think that a woman must feel a profound happiness in that.

BOLETTE. Hm—I wonder really—

LYNGSTRAND. Oh, yes, that you can believe. Not only from all the honor and esteem that she'll win through him—because I think that ought to be reckoned about the least of it. But that she can help him to create—that she can ease his work for him by being there and making him comfortable and taking care of him and seeing that his life is really enjoyable. I think that must be thoroughly satisfying for a woman.

BOLETTE. Why, you have no idea how self-centered you are!

LYNGSTRAND. I—self-centered! My Lord in heaven, if you only knew me a little better—! (*Leaning closer to her.*) Miss Wangel, once I'm gone—and I will be soon enough—

BOLETTE (*looking compassionately at him*). Please, don't start thinking sad thoughts.

LYNGSTRAND. There's nothing so sad about that.

BOLETTE. What do you mean then?

LYNGSTRAND. I'll be leaving now in about a month's time. First from here, and then, soon after, I'll be traveling south.

BOLETTE. Oh, I see. Of course.

LYNGSTRAND. Miss Wangel, will you think of me then, every so often?

BOLETTE. Yes, of course I will.

LYNGSTRAND (*happily*). Promise me that!

BOLETTE. Yes, I promise.

LYNGSTRAND. By all that's holy—Bolette?

BOLETTE. By all that's holy. (*In a changed tone.*) But what can it come to, really? It won't lead to anything at all.

LYNGSTRAND. How can you say that! For me it will be so beautiful to know that you're here at home, thinking of me.

BOLETTE. Yes, but what else?

LYNGSTRAND. Well, beyond that I really don't know exactly—

BOLETTE. Nor I either. It has so much working against it. Everything works against it, I think.

LYNGSTRAND. But miracles can happen, you know. A marvelous spell of good fortune—something like that. Because I really believe that luck is with me.

BOLETTE (*vivaciously*). Yes, that's right! You believe it, don't you!

LYNGSTRAND. I believe it unshakably, beyond all doubt. And then—in a few years—when I come home again as a famous sculptor, comfortably fixed, in the fullness of health—

BOLETTE. Yes. Yes, that's what we're hoping for you.

LYNGSTRAND. You can count on it. If only you'll think warm, faithful thoughts of me while I'm away in the south. And now I have your word for that.

BOLETTE. You have my word. (*Shaking her head.*) But it can never lead anywhere, all the same.

LYNGSTRAND. Oh, yes, at the least it's sure to do one thing—make my work as an artist go easier and faster.

BOLETTE. You really think so?

LYNGSTRAND. Yes, I can feel it intuitively. And then I should think it would be quite exhilarating for you, too— out here so remote from everything—to know secretly that you were helping me to create.

BOLETTE (*looks at him*). And you, for your part—?

LYNGSTRAND. I—?

BOLETTE (*glancing out toward the garden*). Shh! Talk about something else. Mr. Arnholm's coming.

(ARNHOLM *comes into view below in the garden from the left. He stops and speaks with* BALLESTED *and* HILDA.)

LYNGSTRAND. Are you fond of your old teacher, Bolette?

BOLETTE. Fond of him?

LYNGSTRAND. Yes, I mean, do you think a lot of him?

BOLETTE. Why, of course. He's been wonderful to have as an adviser and a friend. He never fails to be helpful whenever he can be.

LYNGSTRAND. But isn't it surprising that he's never married?

BOLETTE. You think it's so very surprising?

LYNGSTRAND. Yes. Because they tell me he's quite well off.

BOLETTE. I suppose he is. But then it hasn't been so easy for him to find someone who'll have him.

LYNGSTRAND. Why?

BOLETTE. Well, almost all the young girls he knows have been his students. He says that himself.

LYNGSTRAND. So—what's the difference?

BOLETTE. But, my Lord, you don't go marrying someone who's been your teacher!

LYNGSTRAND. Don't you think that a young girl can fall in love with her teacher?

BOLETTE. Not after she's really grown up.

LYNGSTRAND. What an amazing idea!

BOLETTE (*warning him*). Shh, shh, shh!

(BALLESTED *has, in the meantime, been gathering his things together; he carries them off to the right in the garden,* HILDA *helping him.* ARNHOLM *comes up onto the veranda and enters the room.*)

ARNHOLM. Good morning, my dear Bolette. Good morning, Mr.—Mr.—hm!

(*He looks irritated and nods coolly to* LYNGSTRAND, *who gets up and bows.*)

BOLETTE (*rising and going to* ARNHOLM). Good morning, Mr. Arnholm.

ARNHOLM. How's everything here today?

BOLETTE. Just fine, thank you.

ARNHOLM. I suppose your stepmother's down swimming again today?

BOLETTE. No, she's up in her room.

ARNHOLM. Not feeling well?

BOLETTE. I don't know. She's locked herself in.

ARNHOLM. Hm—has she?

LYNGSTRAND. Mrs. Wangel had a horrible shock from that American yesterday.

ARNHOLM. What do you know about that?

LYNGSTRAND. I told Mrs. Wangel that I'd seen him go walking large as life past the garden.

ARNHOLM. Oh, I see.

BOLETTE (*to* ARNHOLM). You and Father were certainly up late last night.

ARNHOLM. Yes, rather late. We got into a serious discussion.

BOLETTE. Did you get to talk a little about me and my plans?

ARNHOLM. No, Bolette dear. I hadn't a chance—he was completely caught up in something else.

BOLETTE (*sighs*). Ah, yes—he always is.

ARNHOLM (*gives her a meaningful look*). But later today the two of us will have to talk some more about all this. Where's your father now? Gone out, perhaps?

BOLETTE. Oh, no, he must be down at the office. Let me go fetch him.

ARNHOLM. Please don't. I'd just as soon go down there.

BOLETTE (*hearing sounds to the left*). Wait a bit, Mr. Arnholm. I think that's Father on the stairs. Yes. I guess he's been up to see her.

(DR. WANGEL *comes in through the door, left.*)

WANGEL (*shaking hands with* ARNHOLM). Well, my friend—you're here already? It was good of you to come so early. I want to talk some more with you.

BOLETTE (*to* LYNGSTRAND). Maybe we should go out in the garden a while with Hilda?

LYNGSTRAND. Oh, I'd like to, very much.

(*He and* BOLETTE *go down into the garden and out through the trees in the background.*)

ARNHOLM (*having followed them with his eyes, turns to* WANGEL). Do you know that young man fairly well?

WANGEL. No, not at all.

ARNHOLM. But then what do you think of him hanging around the girls so much?

WANGEL. Does he? I really hadn't noticed.

ARNHOLM. Seems to me, you ought to keep an eye on him.

WANGEL. Yes, you're entirely right. But, my Lord, what

can a poor man do? The girls are so used to looking after themselves. They can't be told anything, by me or Ellida.

ARNHOLM. Not by her, either?

WANGEL. No. Besides, I can hardly expect her to get mixed up in these matters. They're beyond her competence. (*Breaking off.*) But we're not here to talk about that. Tell me—have you thought anymore about this business—about everything I told you?

ARNHOLM. I've thought of nothing else since I left you last night.

WANGEL. And what do you think ought to be done?

ARNHOLM. I think that you, as a doctor, must know far better than I.

WANGEL. Oh, if you only knew how hard it is for a doctor to prescribe for someone he loves! And then this is no ordinary illness. No ordinary doctor can help here—and no ordinary medicines.

ARNHOLM. How is she today?

WANGEL. I was up to see her just now, and she seemed quite calm. But behind all her moods there's something mysterious that I just can't fathom. And then she's so erratic—so elusive—so thoroughly unpredictable.

ARNHOLM. That goes with the morbid state of her mind.

WANGEL. Only in part. If you come right down to it, she was born that way. Ellida's one of the sea people. There's the crux of it.

ARNHOLM. What do you really mean by that?

WANGEL. Haven't you ever noticed that the people who live out close by the sea are almost like a race to themselves? It's as though they lived the sea's own life. There's the surge of the waves—the ebb and the flow—in their thoughts and their feelings both. And they never can be transplanted. Oh, I should have remembered that. It was a plain sin against Ellida to take her away from there and bring her inland.

ARNHOLM. You've come to that conclusion?

WANGEL. Yes, more and more I have. But I should have seen it from the start. Oh, basically I knew it, all right.

But I didn't want to look at it. Because I loved her so much, you see. So first and foremost I thought of myself. I was just inexcusably selfish then!

ARNHOLM. Hm—any man would be a bit selfish under those circumstances. As a matter of fact, that's a flaw I don't think I've noticed in you, Doctor.

WANGEL (*pacing about restlessly*). Oh, yes! And I've gone on being selfish, too. I'm so very much older than she is. I should have been something of a father to her—and a guide. I should have done my best toward helping her mind develop and grow. But unhappily nothing came of it. I hadn't the willpower for it. I wanted her just as she was. But then she grew worse and worse. And here I was, not knowing what I should do. (*Quieter.*) That was why, in my perplexity, I wrote you and asked you here for a visit.

ARNHOLM (*staring astounded at him*). What! Is that why you wrote?

WANGEL. Yes. But don't give it away.

ARNHOLM. But of all things—what earthly good did you expect of me? I don't understand.

WANGEL. That's not surprising. You see, I was off on the wrong track. I thought that Ellida had once set her heart on you—and that secretly she still cared for you a little. I thought maybe it would do her good to see you again and talk of home and the old days.

ARNHOLM. It was your wife, then, that you meant when you wrote that there was someone here thinking of me and—and perhaps longing to see me.

WANGEL. Yes, who else?

ARNHOLM (*quickly*). No, no, that's all right. I just hadn't understood.

WANGEL. It's not at all surprising, as I said. I was completely on the wrong track.

ARNHOLM. And you say that you're selfish!

WANGEL. Oh, I have a lot to atone for. I felt I shouldn't neglect anything that could possibly ease her mind a little.

ARNHOLM. How can you explain the power this stranger has over her?

WANGEL. Well—there may be aspects of the problem that just don't admit explanation.

ARNHOLM. You mean something that *can't* be explained, inherently—and permanently.

WANGEL. Something that can't, anyway—by what we know now.

ARNHOLM. Then you believe in such things.

WANGEL. I neither believe nor disbelieve. I simply don't know. So I leave it open.

ARNHOLM. Yes, but tell me one thing: this peculiar, grim insistence of hers about the child's eyes—

WANGEL (*fiercely*). I don't believe one word of it! I won't believe anything like that! It's pure imagination on her part—and nothing else.

ARNHOLM. Did you notice the man's eyes when you saw him yesterday?

WANGEL. Of course I did.

ARNHOLM. And you found no such resemblance?

WANGEL (*evasively*). Well, my Lord—what can I say? There wasn't much light when I saw him. And then I've always heard so much about that resemblance from Ellida—I really don't know if I was able to see him objectively.

ARNHOLM. Well, that's quite possible. But the other thing then. That all this anxiety and unrest came over her at exactly the time the stranger seems to have been on his voyage home?

WANGEL. Yes, you know—that's also something she must have dreamed up overnight. It never came on her as suddenly—all at once—as she's claiming now. Ever since she heard from this young Lyngstrand that Johnston—or Freeman—or whatever he's called—that he was on his way here three years ago in March, she's honestly believed that all her mental turmoil dates from that very month.

ARNHOLM. You mean it doesn't?

WANGEL. Not by any means. There were ample warning signs long before that time. It *is* true that—as it happens—

just in March three years ago, she had a rather violent siege of it—

ARNHOLM. Well, then—!

WANGEL. Yes, but that could easily be a sign of what she was going through, of her condition then. She was expecting at the time.

ARNHOLM. So—signs against signs.

WANGEL (*knitting his hands*). And then not to be able to help her! Not to know what to say! Not to see the way out!

ARNHOLM. If only you could bring yourself to move away and live elsewhere. Someplace where she'd be able to feel more at home.

WANGEL. Oh, don't you think I've suggested that, too? I proposed that we move back to Skjoldvik. But she won't.

ARNHOLM. Not even there?

WANGEL. No. She doesn't see any use to that. And maybe she's right.

ARNHOLM. Hm—you think so?

WANGEL. Yes. What's more—on second thought—I really don't know how I could carry through with it. For the girls' sakes, I scarcely think I could justify a move into such isolation. After all, they have to live where there are at least some prospects for a decent marriage.

ARNHOLM. Marriage? Are you already so concerned about that?

WANGEL. Well, my Lord—I do have to think about it! But then, on the other hand again, there's my poor, sick Ellida—! Ah, my dear Arnholm—in many ways, I really feel caught between fire and water.

ARNHOLM. You hardly need to worry about Bolette— (*Breaking off.*) I wonder where she's—where they've gone? (*He goes to the open door and looks out.*)

WANGEL (*over by the piano*). I'd gladly make any sacrifice for all three of them—if I only knew what.

(ELLIDA *comes through the door on the left.*)

ELLIDA (*hurriedly to* WANGEL). You mustn't go out this morning.

WANGEL. No, of course not. I'll stay home with you. (*Gesturing toward* ARNHOLM, *who approaches them.*) But aren't you going to greet our friend?

ELLIDA (*turning*). Oh, you're here, Mr. Arnholm. (*Gives him her hand.*) Good morning.

ARNHOLM. Good morning, Mrs. Wangel. Not taking your swim today?

ELLIDA. No, no! Don't even mention it. But won't you sit down just a moment?

ARNHOLM. No, thank you—not now. (*Looks at* WANGEL.) I promised the girls I'd meet them in the garden.

ELLIDA. Well, goodness knows if you'll find them. I never know where they've gone.

WANGEL. Oh, now, they're sure to be down by the pond.

ARNHOLM. Well, I guess I can follow their trail. (*He nods and crosses the veranda into the garden and off, right.*)

ELLIDA. What time is it, Wangel?

WANGEL (*looking at his watch*). A little after eleven.

ELLIDA. A little after. And at eleven—or half-past eleven tonight, the steamer will come. Oh, to be done with it!

WANGEL (*going closer to her*). Ellida dear—there's one thing I want to ask you about.

ELLIDA. What is it?

WANGEL. The night before last—up there in the park— you said, in these last three years, you'd seen him so often before you, large as life.

ELLIDA. Yes, that's true. I have.

WANGEL. But how did you see him?

ELLIDA. How did I see him—?

WANGEL. I mean—how did he look when you saw him?

ELLIDA. But you know yourself, Wangel, how he looks.

WANGEL. Did he look just like that in these visions of yours?

ELLIDA. Yes, exactly.

WANGEL. But how did it happen, then, that you didn't recognize him at once?

ELLIDA (*with a start*). I didn't?

WANGEL. No. You said yourself, later, that you didn't have any idea at first who this stranger was.

ELLIDA (*struck with wonder*). Yes, actually—you're right! But isn't that odd, Wangel? Imagine—that I didn't know him at once.

WANGEL. It was only by the eyes, you said—

ELLIDA. Yes—the eyes! The eyes!

WANGEL. But at the park you said he always appeared to you the way he looked when you parted—out there, ten years ago.

ELLIDA. I said that?

WANGEL. Yes.

ELLIDA. Then he must have looked about the same in those days as he does now.

WANGEL. No. Walking back, the night before last, you gave me quite a different picture of him. You said he had no beard ten years ago. He was dressed quite differently, too. And then the stickpin with the pearl—the man yesterday had nothing like that.

ELLIDA. No, that's right.

WANGEL (*looks searchingly at her*). Try to think back now, Ellida. Or—maybe you can't remember any longer how he looked when he stood with you on Bratthammer?

ELLIDA (*concentrating with her eyes closed*). Not very clearly. No—today I can't at all. Isn't that strange?

WANGEL. Not so strange, actually. There's a new image in you now, shaped out of reality—and it's eclipsing the old one so you can't see it anymore.

ELLIDA. Do you think so, Wangel?

WANGEL. Yes. And it's shutting out the sick fantasies, too. It's a good thing the reality came.

ELLIDA. Good? You call it good?

WANGEL. Yes. The fact that it came—may well be the cure you've needed.

ELLIDA (*sitting down on the sofa*). Wangel—come and sit here by me. I have to tell you all that's on my mind.

WANGEL. Yes, my dear, please do. (*He sits on a chair on the other side of the table.*)

ELLIDA. It was really a stroke of misfortune—for both of us—that we two, of all people, had to come together.

WANGEL (*startled*). What are you saying!

ELLIDA. Oh, yes—it was. And that was only natural. It could only end in misfortune—considering the way that we came together.

WANGEL. What was so wrong about the way we—!

ELLIDA. Now listen, Wangel—there's no need for us going around any longer, lying to ourselves—and to each other.

WANGEL. We're doing what! Lying?

ELLIDA. Yes. Or anyway, concealing the truth. Because the truth—the plain, simple truth is that you came out there and—and bought me.

WANGEL. Bought—! You say—bought!

ELLIDA. Oh, I wasn't one particle better than you. I met your offer—and sold myself to you.

WANGEL (*gives her a pained look*). Ellida—how can you be so heartless?

ELLIDA. But what else can I call it? You couldn't bear the emptiness in your house any longer. You were out after a new wife—

WANGEL. And a new mother for the children, Ellida.

ELLIDA. Perhaps that too—on the side. Although you had no idea if I'd fit that role. You'd no more than seen me, and talked a bit with me a couple of times. Then you wanted me, and so—

WANGEL. Yes, you can put it that way, if you choose.

ELLIDA. And I, on my side—I was helpless then, not knowing which way to turn—and so utterly alone. It was such good sense to accept your offer—since you proposed maintaining me for life.

WANGEL. It never struck me in terms of maintainance. I asked you, in all honesty, if you'd be willing to share with me and the children the little I had.

ELLIDA. Yes, so you did. But the point is, I never should have accepted. Never, for any price! I never should have sold myself! The meanest work—the poorest conditions would have been better—if I'd chosen them myself, by my own free will!

WANGEL (*rising*). Then these five, six years we've lived together—have they been such a total waste?

ELLIDA. Oh, you mustn't think that, Wangel! I've lived as well here with you as anyone could hope for. But I didn't come into your house by my own free will. That's the thing.

WANGEL (*studying her*). Not by your own free will!

ELLIDA. No. I didn't go with you freely.

WANGEL (*quietly*). Ah—I remember those words—from yesterday.

ELLIDA. Everything came together in those words—like a beam of light—and I can see things now, as they are.

WANGEL. What do you see?

ELLIDA. I see that this life we're living with each other—is really no marriage at all.

WANGEL (*bitterly*). What you say is true enough. The life we have *now* is no marriage.

ELLIDA. Nor earlier, either. Never. Not from the very start. (*Gazing into space.*) The first—*that* one might have been full and complete.

WANGEL. The first? What first do you mean?

ELLIDA. Mine—with him.

WANGEL (*stares bewildered at her*). I absolutely don't understand you.

ELLIDA. Oh, Wangel—let's not lie to each other. Or to ourselves, either.

WANGEL. All right! Go on.

ELLIDA. You see—we can never get away from one thing: that a promise freely given is just as binding as a marriage license.

WANGEL. But what in God's name—!

ELLIDA (*rising impetuously*). I want to be free to leave you, Wangel.

WANGEL. Ellida—! Ellida—!

ELLIDA. Yes, yes—give me my freedom! You have to believe me—things aren't going to change. Not after the way we met and married.

WANGEL (*mastering his feelings*). Have we really come to this point?

ELLIDA. We had to. There was no other way.

WANGEL (*looking sorrowfully at her*). Then all we've shared hasn't won you to me. You've never belonged to me—never.

ELLIDA. Oh, Wangel—if only I could love you as much as I want to! As completely as you deserve! But now I can tell—it's not going to be.

WANGEL. Divorce, then? That's what you want? An absolute divorce?

ELLIDA. You understand me so little. I'm not concerned about the formalities. This isn't a matter of outward things. What I want is simply that the two of us agree, of our own free will, to release each other.

WANGEL (*bitterly, nodding slowly*). Dissolve the contract—hm?

ELLIDA. Exactly. Dissolve the contract.

WANGEL. And then what, Ellida? Afterward? Have you thought over what lies ahead of us then? How life might turn out both for you and for me?

ELLIDA. That doesn't matter. Life will take care of itself. What I'm begging and pleading for, Wangel, is all that's important. Let me go free! Give me my full freedom back!

WANGEL. Ellida, this is a fearful thing you're asking. At least give me some time to collect my thoughts and come to a decision. Let's talk it over some more. And give yourself time to consider what you're doing.

ELLIDA. There isn't the time for that. I must have my freedom today.

WANGEL. Why so soon?

ELLIDA. Because he'll be here tonight.

WANGEL (*with a start*). He! Coming! What's this stranger got to do with it?

ELLIDA. I want to be free, completely, when I go to him.

WANGEL. And what—what good will that do you?

ELLIDA. I won't hide behind the fact of being another man's wife. I won't claim that I have no choice—because then there'd be no decision made.

WANGEL. You talk of choice! Choice, Ellida! Choice in this thing!

ELLIDA. Yes, I must have freedom of choice. Choice either way. To send him away alone—or, as well, to go with him.

WANGEL. Do you know what you're saying? To go with him! To put your whole fate in his hands!

ELLIDA. But I put my whole fate in your hands—without any question.

WANGEL. That's true. But he! He's a total stranger! You hardly know him.

ELLIDA. But I think I knew you even less—and still I went off with you.

WANGEL. At least at that time you knew something of what kind of life you'd be taking on. But here, with him? Just consider! What do you know about him? Nothing! Not even who he is—or what he is.

ELLIDA (*staring into space*). It's true. But that's exactly the horror of it.

WANGEL. Yes—well, it *is* horrible.

ELLIDA. And it's also why, it seems to me, I've got to face it.

WANGEL (*looking at her*). Because you find it horrible?

ELLIDA. Yes. Precisely.

WANGEL (*comes closer*). Tell me, Ellida—what do you really mean when you speak of the horror?

ELLIDA (*after a moment's thought*). It's something that—that terrifies and attracts.

WANGEL. Attracts, too?

ELLIDA. Attracts most of all—I think.

WANGEL (*deliberately*). Ellida—you belong to the sea.

ELLIDA. That's part of the horror.

WANGEL. And part of the horror in you. You both terrify—and attract.

ELLIDA. You think so, Wangel?

WANGEL. I've really never known you—at least, to any depth. I'm beginning to see that now.

ELLIDA. Then you have to set me free! Completely free from whatever's yours! I'm not the person you took me for. Now you can see it yourself. We can separate now as friends—by our own free choice.

WANGEL (*heavily*). It might be best for us both—if we parted—but even so, I just can't! You have for me this same horrifying spell, Ellida, this attraction—that's so powerful in you.

ELLIDA. You can say that?

WANGEL. Let's try to get through this day resolutely—with calm in our spirits. I don't dare let you go or free you today. I can't take that liberty. Not for your sake, Ellida. I have my right and my duty to defend you.

ELLIDA. Defend me? Against what? There's no threat here from the outside. The horror goes deeper, Wangel. The horror—is the force of attraction in my own mind. And what can you do about that?

WANGEL. I can steady and strengthen you to fight against it.

ELLIDA. Yes—if I want to fight it.

WANGEL. You don't want to?

ELLIDA. That's it—I don't know!

WANGEL. It will all be settled tonight, Ellida—

ELLIDA (*in an outburst*). Yes, to think—! The decision so near! And for the rest of my life!

WANGEL. And tomorrow—

ELLIDA. Yes, tomorrow! By then the future I was meant for may have been ruined!

WANGEL. You were meant for—?

ELLIDA. A whole, full life of freedom ruined, wasted—for me—and maybe for him.

WANGEL (*in a lower tone, gripping her by the wrist*). Ellida—do you love this stranger?

ELLIDA. Do I—? Oh, how do I know! I only know that for me he has a terrifying attraction, and that—

WANGEL. And that—?

ELLIDA (*tearing herself away*). That I think I belong with him.

WANGEL (*bowing his head*). I begin to understand nearly everything.

ELLIDA. And how can you help against this? What do you prescribe for me?

WANGEL (*looks sadly at her*). Tomorrow—he'll be gone. This misfortune will have blown over. And then I'll be willing to let you go free. We'll dissolve the contract then, Ellida.

ELLIDA. Oh, Wangel—! Tomorrow—then it's too late!

WANGEL (*looking out toward the garden*). The children! We ought to spare them at least—while we can.

(ARNHOLM, BOLETTE, HILDA, and LYNGSTRAND *appear in the garden.* LYNGSTRAND *excuses himself and goes out left. The others come into the room.*)

ARNHOLM. We've been making some marvelous plans—

HILDA. We'll be going out on the fjord tonight, and—

BOLETTE. No, don't say anything!

WANGEL. We've been making some plans here, too.

ARNHOLM. Oh—really?

WANGEL. Tomorrow Ellida's going away to Skjoldvik—for a while.

BOLETTE. Going away—?

ARNHOLM. Why, that's a fine idea, Mrs. Wangel.

WANGEL. She wants to go home again. Home to the sea.

HILDA (*darting several steps toward* ELLIDA). You're going? You're leaving us!

ELLIDA (*alarmed*). But, Hilda! What's got into you?

HILDA (*controlling herself*). Oh, it's nothing. (*Under her breath, turning away.*) Go! Go on then!

BOLETTE (*anxiously*). Father—I can see it in your face. You're going away, too—to Skjoldvik.

WANGEL. No, certainly not! I may be out there at times—

BOLETTE. But you'll come back to us—?

WANGEL. I'll be here, too.

BOLETTE. Yes, at times!

WANGEL. My dear child, it has to be. (*He crosses the room.*)

ARNHOLM (*in a whisper to* BOLETTE). We'll talk this over later. (*He follows* WANGEL. *They talk quietly together by the door.*)

ELLIDA (*to* BOLETTE, *her voice lowered*). What was that with Hilda? She looked so upset.

BOLETTE. Haven't you ever noticed what it is that Hilda longs for day and night?

ELLIDA. Longs for?

BOLETTE. Ever since you came to this house.

ELLIDA. No. No, what's that?

BOLETTE. One small expression of love from you.

ELLIDA. Ah—! Then—I do have some purpose here?

(*She clasps her hands tight over her head and stares intently off into space, as if riddled by conflicting thoughts and feelings.* WANGEL *and* ARNHOLM *come forward in hushed conversation.* BOLETTE *goes over and glances into the room to the right, then opens the door wide.*)

BOLETTE. Father dear—the food's on the table—if you'd like to—

WANGEL (*with forced composure*). Is it, dear? That's good. Arnholm, please! Now we'll go drink a parting cup to the health of—of our "lady from the sea."

(*They move toward the door on the right.*)

✠ ACT FIVE ✠

The far corner of DR. WANGEL's *garden by the carp pond. The deepening twilight of a summer night.* ARNHOLM, BOLETTE, LYNGSTRAND, *and* HILDA, *in a boat, are punting along the bank from the left.*

HILDA. See, we can easily jump ashore from here!

ARNHOLM. No, no, don't!

LYNGSTRAND. I can't jump, Hilda.

HILDA. And you, Arnholm, can't you jump either?

ARNHOLM. I'd rather pass it up.

BOLETTE. Then let's put in by the bathhouse steps.

(They pole off to the right. At the same time BALLESTED *appears on the footpath from the right, carrying music scores and a French horn. He waves to those in the boat, turns and talks to them. Their answers are heard farther and farther off in the distance.)*

BALLESTED. What did you say—? Yes, that's right—for the English steamer. It's her last trip of the year. But if you want to relish the music, you better not wait too long. *(Shouts.)* What? *(Shaking his head.)* Can't hear you!

*(*ELLIDA, *with a shawl over her head, comes in from the left, followed by* DR. WANGEL.*)*

WANGEL. But, Ellida dear—I tell you, there's still plenty of time.

ELLIDA. No, no—there isn't! He can come any moment.

BALLESTED (*outside the garden fence*). Well, good evening, Doctor! Good evening, Mrs. Wangel!

WANGEL (*becoming aware of him*). Oh, is that you? Are we having music tonight?

BALLESTED. Yes. The Wind Ensemble's going to make itself heard. There's no shortage of festivities these days. Tonight we're saluting the English ship.

ELLIDA. The English ship! Has she been sighted?

BALLESTED. Not yet. But she slips her way in, you know—between the islands. There's no sign of her—and then, suddenly, there she is.

ELLIDA. Yes—that's just the way it is.

WANGEL (*half to* ELLIDA). Tonight's the last voyage. And then—no more.

BALLESTED. A doleful thought, Doctor. But all the more reason, as I say, for making a celebration. Ah, me! These delightful summer days will soon be over. The sea-lanes will soon be locked in ice—as the old tragedy has it.

ELLIDA. The sea-lanes locked—yes.

BALLESTED. How sad to think. We've been summer's happy children now for weeks and months. It's hard to reconcile oneself with the dark days coming. Yes, I mean, it is at first. Because, you know, people learn to accli—acclimatize themselves, Mrs. Wangel. Yes, they really do.

(*He bows and goes out left.*)

ELLIDA (*looking out across the fjord*). Oh, this agonizing suspense! This feverish last half hour before the decision.

WANGEL. Then you definitely do want to talk to him yourself?

ELLIDA. I have to talk to him myself. It's the only way I can make a free choice.

WANGEL. You have no choice, Ellida. You haven't the right. I won't permit it.

ELLIDA. You can't keep me from choosing. Neither you nor anyone else. You can forbid me to go with him—if I choose that. You can hold me here by force—against my will. That you can do. But that I choose—choose from the depths of my being—choose him, and not you—if I have to—*that* you can never prevent.

WANGEL. No, you're right. I can't prevent you.

ELLIDA. So I have nothing at all to stop me. Not one earthly tie here at home. I've been so completely without roots in this house, Wangel. I have no place with the children—in their hearts, I mean. I never have. When I go—if I go—either with him tonight, or to Skjoldvik tomorrow—I won't even have a key to give up, or a set of instructions to leave behind about anything at all. That's how rootless—how totally outside of things I've been from the moment I came.

WANGEL. You wanted it that way yourself.

ELLIDA. No, I didn't. I had no wants this way or that. I've simply left everything just as it was on the day I arrived. It was you, and nobody else, who wanted it like that.

WANGEL. I tried to do what was best for you.

ELLIDA. Yes, Wangel—I know you did! But these things retaliate on us; they take revenge. Now I have nothing to hold me here—no foundation—no support—no impulse toward everything that should have been our dearest common bonds.

WANGEL. Yes, that's clear enough. So you'll have your freedom from tomorrow on. You can live your own life then.

ELLIDA. My own life, you call it! Oh, no, the real thread of my life snapped when I came here to live with you. (*Clenching her fists in a tremor of fear.*) And now, tonight—in half an hour, he'll be here, the man I broke faith with, the man whose word I should have kept sacred, as he kept mine. He's coming to ask me—this one last time—to start my life over—to live a life out of my own truth—the life that terrifies and attracts—and that I *can't* give up, not of my own free will!

WANGEL. Exactly why you need me, as your husband—and your doctor—to assume that power, and act in your own behalf.

ELLIDA. Yes, Wangel, I understand very well. Oh, don't think there aren't times when I'm sure there'd be peace and security for me in taking refuge completely in you—and trying to defy all the tempting, treacherous powers. But I can't. No, no—I can't do it!

WANGEL. Come, Ellida—let's walk up and down by the shore for a while.

ELLIDA. I'd like to. But I don't dare. He said I should wait for him here.

WANGEL. Come along. You have plenty of time.

ELLIDA. You think so?

WANGEL. More than enough, yes.

ELLIDA. Let's walk a bit then.

(*They go off in the foreground to the right. As they depart,* ARNHOLM *and* BOLETTE *appear by the upper bank of the pond.*)

BOLETTE (*noticing the others leaving*). Look—!

ARNHOLM (*softly*). Shh—let them go.

BOLETTE. Have you any idea what's been happening between them the last few days?

ARNHOLM. Have you noticed anything?

BOLETTE. I'll say!

ARNHOLM. Something special?

BOLETTE. Oh, this and that. Haven't you?

ARNHOLM. Oh, I really don't know—

BOLETTE. Yes, you know all right. But you won't come out with it.

ARNHOLM. I think it'll be good for your stepmother to take that little trip.

BOLETTE. You think so?

ARNHOLM. Yes, I'm wondering if it wouldn't be a good thing for all parties if she could get away now and then?

BOLETTE. If she goes home to Skjoldvik tomorrow, she'll never come back here again to us.

ARNHOLM. But, Bolette dear, where did you ever get that notion?

BOLETTE. I'm absolutely convinced. You just wait! You'll see—she won't come back again. At least, not while Hilda and I are around the house.

ARNHOLM. Hilda, too?

BOLETTE. Well, with Hilda it might work out. She's still not much more than a child. And then I think, underneath, she really worships Ellida. But with me, it's another story. A stepmother who's hardly much older than oneself—

ARNHOLM. Bolette—for you it might not be so long before you could get away.

BOLETTE (*fervently*). You mean it! Then you've talked it over with Father?

ARNHOLM. Yes, I've done that.

BOLETTE. Well—and what did he say?

ARNHOLM. Hm—of course, right now your father's so absorbed in other things—

BOLETTE. Yes, that's what I told you before.

ARNHOLM. But I did get this much out of him: that you mustn't be counting on any help from him.

BOLETTE. None—!

ARNHOLM. He made his situation quite clear to me. Something of that order, he felt, would be totally out of the realm of possibility for him.

BOLETTE (*reproachfully*). And you can simply stand there and tease me.

ARNHOLM. I'm not teasing at all, Bolette. It's completely up to you whether or not you can break away.

BOLETTE. You say it's up to me?

ARNHOLM. That is, if you really want to enter the world—and learn about everything that interests you most—share in whatever you've longed for here at home—and live a more ample life. What do you say, Bolette?

BOLETTE (*clasping her hands*). My God in heaven—!

But—it's all so impossible. If Father won't or can't, then—Because there's no one else I can turn to.

ARNHOLM. Couldn't you accept a helping hand from your old—I mean, your former teacher?

BOLETTE. From you, Mr. Arnholm! You'd be willing to—?

ARNHOLM. To stand by you? Yes, with all my heart. In both word and deed. You can rely on that. So—do you agree? Well? Is it a bargain?

BOLETTE. A bargain! To leave—to see the world—to learn what life really is! It's like some beautiful, unattainable dream.

ARNHOLM. But it all can come true for you now—if you'll try for it.

BOLETTE. So much happiness—it's breathtaking! And you'll help me to it. But—tell me, is it right to take such a gift from a stranger?

ARNHOLM. From me, Bolette, you certainly can. Whatever you need.

BOLETTE (*seizing his hands*). Yes, I almost believe I can! I don't know why it is, but— (*In an outburst of feeling.*)—oh, I could both laugh and cry for joy! I feel so happy. Oh—so I *am* going to live, after all. I was beginning to feel so afraid that life would pass me by.

ARNHOLM. That's nothing you have to fear. But now you must tell me very frankly—if there's anything—anything to bind you here.

BOLETTE. Bind me? No, there isn't.

ARNHOLM. No one in particular?

BOLETTE. No one at all. Well, I mean—Father, of course, in a way. And Hilda, too. But—

ARNHOLM. Well—you'd be leaving your father sooner or later. And Hilda will be going her own way, too, before long. It's only a question of time, that's all. But otherwise you've no other ties? No other kind of relationship?

BOLETTE. No, nothing. So I can just as well leave as I wish.

ARNHOLM. Well, if that's the case—then you must leave with me.

BOLETTE (*clapping her hands*). Oh, God—I can't believe it!

ARNHOLM. Because I hope you have full confidence in me?

BOLETTE. Why, of course.

ARNHOLM. And you feel quite safe in trusting yourself and your future in my hands? You do, don't you?

BOLETTE. Naturally! Why shouldn't I? How can you ask? You're my old teacher—I mean, my teacher from the old days.

ARNHOLM. Not only that. That aspect of it I'd just as soon forget. But—well—anyway you're free, Bolette. There are no ties binding you. So I'm asking you then—if you'd—you'd be willing to join yourself to me—for life.

BOLETTE (*recoiling, startled*). Oh—what are you saying?

ARNHOLM. For the rest of your life, Bolette. If you'll be my wife.

BOLETTE (*half to herself*). No, no, no! This is impossible. Quite impossible.

ARNHOLM. Does it really seem so utterly impossible to you that—?

BOLETTE. But you don't mean—you can't mean what you're saying, Mr. Arnholm! (*Looking at him.*) Or—anyway— Is that what you meant when you offered to do so much for me?

ARNHOLM. Now listen to me a minute. I've surprised you considerably, I guess.

BOLETTE. How could something like this—from you—how could it not surprise me?

ARNHOLM. Perhaps you're right. Of course you didn't—and couldn't—know that it was for your sake I made the trip here.

BOLETTE. You came here—for my sake!

ARNHOLM. Yes. Last spring I got a letter from your

father. There were some lines in it that gave me the idea—hm—that your memories of me were a little more than—just friendly.

BOLETTE. How could Father write like that!

ARNHOLM. He didn't mean it at all that way. But I persuaded myself into imagining that a young girl was going around the house here, yearning for me to return— No, Bolette, now don't interrupt! And you have to understand—when someone like me, who's past the pride of his youth, has that kind of belief—or illusion—it makes a powerful impression. From then on, there grew in me a warm—and grateful affection for you. I felt I had to come to you—see you again—and tell you that I shared those feelings which I'd dreamed myself into believing you felt for me.

BOLETTE. But now you know it wasn't true! That it was a mistake!

ARNHOLM. It's no help, Bolette. Your image—as I carry it within me—will always be colored now by those mistaken emotions. Maybe you can't understand all this. But it's the way it is.

BOLETTE. Anything like this I never would have believed possible.

ARNHOLM. But now that you know it is—what do you say, Bolette? Won't you promise yourself in—in marriage to me?

BOLETTE. But, Mr. Arnholm, to me it's simply unthinkable. You were my teacher. I can't imagine ever being in any other kind of relationship to you.

ARNHOLM. Well, all right—if you really don't think you can— But, in any case, the old relationship is still unchanged.

BOLETTE. What do you mean?

ARNHOLM. Naturally, I stand by my offer, just the same. I'll make sure that you get out and see something of the world—study what interests you—and have a secure and independent life. And I'll see that your future's taken care of. I want you to know you'll always find me a staunch, reliable friend.

BOLETTE. But—Mr. Arnholm—that's all become quite impossible now.

ARNHOLM. Is that impossible, too?

BOLETTE. Yes, isn't that obvious! After what you've told me here—and the answer I gave you—oh, how could you think me capable of helping myself at your expense! There's absolutely nothing I can take from you—nothing after this!

ARNHOLM. You mean you'd rather stay here at home and watch life slipping away from you?

BOLETTE. Oh, that's too horribly depressing to think about!

ARNHOLM. You want to throw away your chance to see the outside world and be part of everything you've longed for? To know there's so infinitely much to life—and that, after all, you've never really experienced any of it? Think well on what you're doing, Bolette.

BOLETTE. Yes, yes—you're very right, Mr. Arnholm.

ARNHOLM. And then, when your father's no longer here—maybe to stand alone and helpless in the world. Or else to have to give yourself to another man for whom you—quite possibly—might also feel no affection.

BOLETTE. Oh, yes—I can see quite well how true it is—everything you say. But still—! Or—perhaps—

ARNHOLM (*quickly*). Well?

BOLETTE (*looking irresolutely at him*). Perhaps it isn't so utterly impossible, after all—

ARNHOLM. What, Bolette?

BOLETTE. It might do, then—to try what—what you suggested.

ARNHOLM. You mean that perhaps you'd be willing to—? That at least you'd give me the satisfaction of being able to help you as a friend?

BOLETTE. No, no! That's absolutely impossible! No—Mr. Arnholm—if, instead, you'll take me—

ARNHOLM. Bolette! Then you will?

BOLETTE. Yes—I think—I want that.

ARNHOLM. Then you *will* be my wife?

BOLETTE. Yes. If you still think that—that you want me.

ARNHOLM. If I still—! (*Seizes her hand.*) Oh, thank you—thank you, Bolette! All this that you've said—these doubts you've had—they don't frighten me. If I don't have you wholeheartedly now, I'll find the ways to win you. Oh, Bolette, how I'll treasure you!

BOLETTE. Now I can live in the world, in the midst of life. You promised me that.

ARNHOLM. And I'll keep my word.

BOLETTE. And I can study anything I want.

ARNHOLM. I'll teach you, just as I used to. Remember that last school year—?

BOLETTE (*musing quietly*). Imagine—to be free—and to come out—into the unknown. And not to worry about the future, or scrimping to get along—

ARNHOLM. No, you won't have to waste your thoughts like that anymore. Which ought to be quite a relief in itself, don't you think?

BOLETTE. Yes, definitely.

ARNHOLM (*putting his arms around her waist*). Ah, wait till you see how easy and comfortable we'll be with each other. And how competently we'll manage things together, Bolette!

BOLETTE. Yes, I'm beginning to think—I really believe— this is going to work. (*Looks off to the right and hurriedly frees herself.*) Ah! Don't say anything yet!

ARNHOLM. Dear, what is it?

BOLETTE. Oh, it's that poor— (*Pointing.*) See, there.

ARNHOLM. Is it your father—?

BOLETTE. No, it's that young sculptor. He's over there walking with Hilda.

ARNHOLM. Oh, Lyngstrand. What's the matter with him?

BOLETTE. Well, you know how frail and sickly he is.

ARNHOLM. Yes, if it isn't all in his mind.

BOLETTE. No, it's serious enough. He can't live much longer. But maybe it's the best thing for him.

ARNHOLM. How could *that* be the best thing?

BOLETTE. Well, because—because nothing could ever come of his art, anyway. Let's go before they get here.

ARNHOLM. With the greatest pleasure, dearest. Let's.

(HILDA *and* LYNGSTRAND *appear by the pond.*)

HILDA. Hey—hey! Won't your majesties wait for us?

ARNHOLM. We'd rather stay in the lead.

(*He and* BOLETTE *go out to the left.*)

LYNGSTRAND (*laughs quietly*). It's really delightful here around this hour. Humanity comes in couples. Everyone's two by two.

HILDA (*looking after them*). I could almost swear that he's been courting her.

LYNGSTRAND. Really? Have you noticed something?

HILDA. Oh, yes. It's not too difficult—if you've got eyes in your head.

LYNGSTRAND. Bolette wouldn't have him. I'm positive of that.

HILDA. No. She thinks he's beginning to look horribly old. And also that he's going to be bald soon.

LYNGSTRAND. Those aren't the only reasons. She wouldn't have him, anyhow.

HILDA. How do you know that?

LYNGSTRAND. Because there's someone else she's promised to give her thoughts to.

HILDA. Just her thoughts?

LYNGSTRAND. While he's away, yes.

HILDA. Oh, in other words, it's *you* that she's going to go thinking about!

LYNGSTRAND. Well, it might just be.

HILDA. Did she promise you that?

LYNGSTRAND. Yes, just think—she promised me that! But you mustn't ever tell her you know.

HILDA. Oh, so help me God, I'll be quiet as the grave.

LYNGSTRAND. I think it's awfully kind of her.

HILDA. And when you come back here again—will you get engaged to her? And marry her?

LYNGSTRAND. No, that wouldn't be too good a match. I don't dare think about marrying for the first few years. And when I finally do arrive, then I expect she'll probably be too old for me.

HILDA. But all the same, you want to have her going around thinking about you?

LYNGSTRAND. Well, it's very necessary for me. You know, as an artist. And it's easy enough for her to do, when she hasn't any real vocation in life, anyhow. But it's kind of her, all the same.

HILDA. Do you believe you can work better on your art if you know Bolette's up here thinking about you?

LYNGSTRAND. Yes, I'm convinced of it. To know that someplace on this earth there's a young woman of rare breeding, living quietly in her dreams—of me—why, I think that must be so—so— Well, I really don't know what to call it.

HILDA. You mean—thrilling?

LYNGSTRAND. Thrilling? Yes, it's thrilling; you could call it that. Or something like it. (*Looks at her a moment.*) You're so perceptive, Hilda. Amazingly perceptive. When I come home again, you'll be about the same age your sister is now. Maybe then you'll look like her as well. And maybe you'll have gotten her temperament, too. Almost as if you and she had grown together—in one form, so to speak.

HILDA. Would that please you?

LYNGSTRAND. I really don't know. Yes, I guess it would. But now—for this summer—I'd prefer you to be just yourself alone. Exactly what you are.

HILDA. You like me best that way?

LYNGSTRAND. Yes, I like you very well that way.

HILDA. Hm—tell me—as an artist, do you think it's right for me always to wear these light summer dresses?

LYNGSTRAND. Yes, I think they're just the thing for you.

HILDA. Do you find the bright colors becoming on me?

LYNGSTRAND. Very becoming on you, at least to my taste.

HILDA. But tell me—as an artist—how do you think I'd look in black?

LYNGSTRAND. In black, Hilda?

HILDA. Yes, all in black. Do you think it would set me off well?

LYNGSTRAND. Black really isn't quite the thing for summer. Although you certainly would look striking in black. Especially with your complexion.

HILDA (*gazing into the distance*). In black right up to the neck. Black ruffles. Black gloves. And a long black veil hanging down behind.

LYNGSTRAND. If you were to dress up like that, Hilda— I'd wish myself into a painter—and I'd paint you as a young, beautiful, grieving widow.

HILDA. Or a young, grieving bride.

LYNGSTRAND. Yes, that would be even better. But you can't really want to dress like that?

HILDA. It's hard to say. But I think it's thrilling.

LYNGSTRAND. Thrilling?

HILDA. Thrilling to think of, yes. (*Points suddenly out to the left.*) Oh, look there!

LYNGSTRAND (*following her stare*). The English steamer! And she's already docked.

(WANGEL *and* ELLIDA *appear by the pond.*)

WANGEL. No, Ellida, I tell you—you're wrong! (*Notices the others.*) Well, are you two here? What's the word, Mr. Lyngstrand—she's not in sight yet, is she?

LYNGSTRAND. The English ship?

WANGEL. What else!

LYNGSTRAND (*pointing*). She's right there, Doctor.

ELLIDA. Ah—! I knew it.

WANGEL. Already come!

LYNGSTRAND. Like a thief in the night, you could say. Gliding soundlessly in—

WANGEL. You better take Hilda down to the pier. Hurry up! She'll want to hear the music.

LYNGSTRAND. Yes, we were just now leaving, Doctor.

WANGEL. We may come along later. In a little while.

HILDA (*whispering to* LYNGSTRAND). See, still another couple.

(*She and* LYNGSTRAND *go out through the garden to the left. During what follows, the music of a brass band is heard far off out on the fjord.*)

ELLIDA. He's come! He's here! Yes, yes—I can feel that.

WANGEL. You'd best go inside, Ellida. Let me talk to him alone.

ELLIDA. Oh—it's impossible! Impossible, I tell you! (*Crying out.*) Oh—there he is, Wangel!

(*The* STRANGER *appears from the left and stops on the footpath outside the fence.*)

STRANGER (*bowing*). Good evening. So you see I'm back, Ellida.

ELLIDA. Yes. The hour has come.

STRANGER. Are you ready to leave, or not?

WANGEL. You can see yourself that she's not.

STRANGER. I'm not talking about traveling clothes and that sort of thing—or whether her trunks are packed. Everything she needs on the trip I have with me on board. I've also reserved her a cabin. (*To* ELLIDA.) I'm asking, then, if you're ready to come with me—of your own free will?

ELLIDA. Oh, don't ask me! You mustn't!

(*A ship's bell sounds in the distance.*)

STRANGER. They're ringing the first warning. Now you've got to say yes or no.

ELLIDA (*wringing her hands*). To decide! Decide for the rest of my life! And never the chance to go back!

STRANGER. Never! In half an hour it'll be too late.

ELLIDA (*with a shy, inquiring look*). Why are you so determined not to let me go?

STRANGER. Don't you feel, as I do, that we belong together?

ELLIDA. You mean, because of the promise?

STRANGER. Promises bind no one. Neither man nor woman. I don't let you go—because I can't.

ELLIDA (*in a low, tremulous voice*). Why didn't you come before?

WANGEL. Ellida!

ELLIDA (*in an outburst*). Oh—this power that charms and tempts and allures me—into the unknown! All the force of the sea is in this man!

(*The* STRANGER *climbs over the fence.*)

ELLIDA (*retreating behind* WANGEL). What is it? What do you want?

STRANGER. I can see it and I can hear it in you, Ellida—it will be me that you choose in the end.

WANGEL (*steps toward him*). My wife has no choice in this. I'll both decide—and defend—where she's concerned. Yes, defend! If you don't clear out of here—out of this country—and never come back—then you better know what you're in for!

ELLIDA. No, no, Wangel! Don't!

STRANGER. What will you do to me?

WANGEL. I'll have you arrested—as a criminal! Right now, before you board ship! I know all about the murder up at Skjoldvik.

ELLIDA. Oh, Wangel—how can you—?

STRANGER. I was prepared for that. And so— (*Draws a revolver from his breast pocket.*)—so I provided myself with this.

ELLIDA (*flinging herself in front of* WANGEL). No— don't kill him! Kill me instead!

STRANGER. I'm not killing either of you, so don't get

excited. This is for my own use. I want to live and die a free man.

ELLIDA (*in a rising tumult of feeling*). I have to say this—and say it so he can hear! Yes, you can lock me in here! You've got the power and the means! And that's what you want to do! But my mind—my thoughts—all my longing dreams and desires—those you can never constrain! They'll go raging and hunting out—into the unknown that I was made for—and that you've shut out for me!

WANGEL (*in quiet pain*). I see it so well, Ellida. Inch by inch you're slipping away from me. This hunger for the boundless, the infinite—the unattainable—will finally drive your mind out completely into darkness.

ELLIDA. Oh, yes, yes—I feel it—like black, soundless wings hanging over me!

WANGEL. It's not going to come to that. There's no other way to save you. At least, not that I can see. And so—so I agree that—our contract's dissolved. Right now, this moment. Now you can choose your own path—in full freedom.

ELLIDA (*stares at him briefly as if struck dumb*). Is that true—true—what you're saying? You mean it—with all your heart?

WANGEL. Yes, I mean it—with all my miserable heart.

ELLIDA. Then you *can*—? You can let this *be?*

WANGEL. Yes, I can. Because I love you so much.

ELLIDA (*her voice soft and tremulous*). Have I grown so close—and so dear to you?

WANGEL. With the years and the living together, yes.

ELLIDA (*striking her hands together*). And I—who've been so blind!

WANGEL. Your thoughts have gone other ways. But now—now you're entirely free from me—my life—my world. Now you can pick up the thread of your own true existence again. Because now you can choose in freedom—on your own responsibility.

ELLIDA (*hands to her head, staring blankly at* WANGEL). In freedom—responsible to myself! Responsible? How this—transforms everything!

(*The ship's bell rings again.*)

STRANGER. Ellida, listen! It's ringing for the last time now. Come!

ELLIDA (*turns, looks fixedly at him, and speaks in a firm voice*). I could never go with you after this.

STRANGER. Never!

ELLIDA (*holding tight to* WANGEL). No—I'll never leave you now!

WANGEL. Ellida—Ellida!

STRANGER. Then it's over?

ELLIDA. Yes. Over forever.

STRANGER. I see. There's something stronger here than my will.

ELLIDA. Your will hasn't a shred of power over me now. To me you've become a dead man who came up out of the sea—and who's drifting back down again. There's no terror in you now. And no attraction.

STRANGER. Good-bye, then. (*He vaults over the fence.*) From now on, you're nothing more than—a shipwreck I barely remember. (*Goes out to the left.*)

WANGEL (*looks at her a moment*). Ellida, your mind is like the sea—it ebbs and flows. What brought the change?

ELLIDA. Oh, don't you understand that the change came—that it *had* to come—when I could choose in freedom?

WANGEL. And the unknown—it doesn't attract you anymore?

ELLIDA. It neither terrifies nor attracts. I've been able to see deep into it—and I could have plunged in, if I'd wanted to. I could have chosen it now. And that's why, also, I could reject it.

WANGEL. I begin to understand you—little by little. You think and feel in images—and in visions. Your longing and craving for the sea—your attraction toward him, toward this stranger—these were the signs of an awakened, growing rage for freedom in you. Nothing else.

ELLIDA. Oh, I don't know what to say. Except that

you've been a good doctor for me. You found, and you dared to use the right treatment—the only one that could help me.

WANGEL. Yes—when it comes to extreme cases, we doctors have to risk desperate remedies. But now—will you be coming back to me, Ellida?

ELLIDA. Yes, my dear, faithful Wangel—I'm coming back to you now. I can now, because I come to you freely—and on my own.

WANGEL (*regarding her warmly*). Ellida! Ellida! Ah—to think that now we can live wholly for one another—

ELLIDA. And with the shared memories of our lives. Yours—and mine.

WANGEL. Yes, darling, we will.

ELLIDA. And with our two children, Wangel.

WANGEL. You call them *ours!*

ELLIDA. They're not mine—but I'll win them to me.

WANGEL. Ours—! (*Joyfully and quickly kissing her hands.*) Oh—how can I thank you for that one word!

(HILDA, BALLESTED, LYNGSTRAND, ARNHOLM, *and* BOLETTE *come from the left into the garden. At the same time a number of the young people of the town, along with summer visitors, come along the footpath outside.*)

HILDA (*in a whisper to* LYNGSTRAND). Why, she and Father—they look as if they're just engaged!

BALLESTED (*having overheard*). But it's summertime, little one.

ARNHOLM (*glancing at* WANGEL *and* ELLIDA). There, she's casting off now—for England.

BOLETTE (*going to the fence*). Here's the place to see her best.

LYNGSTRAND. The last sailing of the year.

BALLESTED. The sea-lanes will soon be locked in ice, as the poet says. It's sad, Mrs. Wangel. And now we'll lose you, too, for a while. Tomorrow, I hear, you're off for Skjoldvik.

WANGEL. No, not anymore. We changed our minds this evening.

ARNHOLM (*looking from one to the other*). No—really!

HILDA (*goes to* ELLIDA). You'll stay with us, after all?

ELLIDA. Yes, Hilda dear—if you'll have me.

HILDA (*struggling between joy and tears*). Oh—if I'll have—what an idea!

ARNHOLM (*to* ELLIDA). Well, this is quite a surprise—!

ELLIDA (*smiling gravely*). You see, Mr. Arnholm—you remember, we talked about it yesterday. Once you've really become a land animal, then there's no going back again—into the sea. Or the life that belongs to the sea, either.

BALLESTED. But that's just how it is with my mermaid.

ELLIDA. Yes, much the same.

BALLESTED. Except for the difference—that the mermaid dies of it. But people, human beings—they can acclam—acclimatize themselves. Yes, yes—that's the thing, Mrs. Wangel. They can ac-cli-matize themselves.

ELLIDA. Yes, they can, Mr. Ballested—once they're free.

WANGEL. And responsible, Ellida.

ELLIDA (*quickly takes his hand*). How very true!

(*The great steamer glides silently out over the fjord. The music can be heard closer in toward shore.*)

HEDDA GABLER

Enough parallels exist between the unhappy heroine of *Hedda Gabler* (1890) and Ellida Wangel in the play immediately preceding to indicate that Ibsen was impelled to take a second look, in another context, at a single provocative set of relationships. Both women are depicted as restively enduring the limbo of an emotionally detached marriage to a dependable, unexciting husband chosen more for acceptability than for love. Both have their conditions complicated by the lack of any real responsibilities or clear direction in their self-absorbed lives. Each woman is then perilously unbalanced by the sudden reawakening of a former involvement, through the return of a virile, undomesticated male with a strong romantic aura, who speaks to the heart of her being with a bewilderingly intimate authority.

In other crucial respects, however, the two plays stand in marked contrast. The crisis of *The Lady from the Sea* is enveloped, and its outcome forecast, by its outdoor ambience of summer sunlight and the magical white nights of the north, amplified by four-part singing and distant band music coming across the open waters of the fjord. Its successor runs its taut course in a wholly enclosed interior space where sunlight is contested and repelled like a hostile invader. The vacant sky outside, in turn, has the sole function of receiving Hedda's randomly fired bullets; no verbal image could convey so tellingly both Hedda's bitter duel of honor with the universe and the general aimlessness of her existence. Indeed, the most characteristic sound effect in *Hedda Gabler*, counter to the harmony of music, is the harsh eruption of pistol shots, from which much in the design of the play takes its cue. Those shots, like Spanish exclamation points, punctuate the tentative beginning and the disastrous end of Hedda's aristocratic war with the bourgeois world. And, like the shots, the dialogue throughout is as staccato and stichomythic as the amenities of polite discourse will allow. No declamatory arias here in deliciously fulsome praise of the pillars of society, nor speculative excursions on the question of whether man should revert to the sea. Nothing is extraneous to the relentless coil of constricting circumstance that seals Hedda's fate.

The inhabitants of the play similarly take cues from the tone of the setting: the mansion of the late widow Falk, where the unaired rooms smell faintly and ominously of lavender and dried roses (death and beauty close combined), and where accordingly the true emotional atmosphere is—all elegance of scale and furnishings to the contrary—in T.S. Eliot's line, smaller and drier than the will. The seven characters divide more or less equally into two groups, the first of which Ibsen himself defined succinctly: "Jørgen Tesman, his old aunts and the faithful servant Berta together form a picture of complete unity. They think alike, they share the same memories and have the same outlook on life. To Hedda they appear like a strange and hostile power, aimed at her very being. In a performance of the play the harmony that exists between them must be conveyed." The Tesman group represents the dominant bourgeois society, whose middle-class goals and values they wholeheartedly accept. Basically good, warmly outgoing, dutiful, unimaginative, they share one common unifying motivation: to be useful, to help one another. Thea Elvsted, who begins the play courageously if tremulously alone, in time gravitates into their ranks by proving her usefulness to Tesman's work. If this seems a reductive compromise, Ibsen's notes remind us of "an unconscious futurity in her"; Thea at least serves the unfolding potential of mankind.

The remaining three characters also share a common motivation, but one which acts to divide them: each is out for his or her own self-realization—Brack, the suave geometer of marital triangles through erotic intrigue; Løvborg, the cultural historian as secular prophet, through recognition of the preeminence of his work; and Hedda, most convoluted, most inwardly torn, desiring something of both, guardedly exposing her sensual strain with Brack, deviously imposing her sterile will to power on the productive, vulnerable Løvborg.

"Hedda—Gabler!" as Løvborg whispers with a certain awe, thereby dismissing the mere technicality of her marriage. No neat formulation can sum her up, though scores, hundreds have tried. George Bernard Shaw's is no better nor worse than most: "Though she has imagination and an intense appetite for beauty, she has no conscience, no conviction: with plenty of cleverness, energy and personal fascination, she remains mean, envious, insolent, cruel in protest against others' happiness, fiendish in her dislike of inartistic people and things; a bully in reaction to her own cowardice." And at once the impulse leaps to supply a corrective, to assert overlooked traits that will render her complexity more justly. Hedda has invited portrayal as high tragedy, as pyrotechnic melodrama, as absurdist farce, as psychopathological document, as Marxist indictment, as feminist tract. She has been sentimentalized into a "good person," a misunderstood victim, and trivialized into a transvestite self-portrait of the artist. Faced with all these partial perspectives, one should begin by simply reaffirming her irreducible, many-sided humanity and, as well, the truth of an observation by Henry James on Ibsen: "His subject is always, like the subjects of all first-rate men, primarily an idea." The idea is incarnate in, not a role, but the entire play, and only attention to the ensemble of which Hedda is but one part will reveal it.

THE CHARACTERS

GEORGE TESMAN, research fellow in cultural history
HEDDA TESMAN, his wife
MISS JULIANA TESMAN, his aunt
MRS. ELVSTED
JUDGE BRACK
EILERT LØVBORG
BERTA, the TESMAN's maid

The action takes place in TESMAN'*s residence in the fashionable part of town.*

⤙ ACT ONE ⤚

A large, attractively furnished drawing room, decorated in dark colors. In the rear wall, a wide doorway with curtains drawn back. The doorway opens into a smaller room in the same style as the drawing room. In the right wall of the front room, a folding door that leads to the hall. In the left wall opposite, a glass door, with curtains similarly drawn back. Through the panes one can see part of an overhanging veranda and trees in autumn colors. In the foreground is an oval table with tablecloth and chairs around it. By the right wall, a wide, dark porcelain stove, a high-backed armchair, a cushioned footstool, and two taborets. In the right-hand corner, a settee with a small round table in front. Nearer, on the left and slightly out from the wall, a piano. On either side of the doorway in back, étagères with terra-cotta and majolica ornaments. Against the back wall of the inner room, a sofa, a table, and a couple of chairs can be seen. Above this sofa hangs a portrait of a handsome, elderly man in a general's uniform. Over the table, a hanging lamp with an opalescent glass shade. A number of bouquets of flowers are placed about the drawing room in vases and glasses. Others lie on the tables. The floors in both rooms are covered with thick carpets. Morning light. The sun shines in through the glass door.

*   MISS JULIANA TESMAN, wearing a hat and carrying a parasol, comes in from the hall, followed by* BERTA, *who holds a bouquet wrapped in paper.* MISS TESMAN *is a lady around sixty-five with a kind and good-natured look, nicely but simply dressed in a gray tailored suit.* BERTA *is a maid somewhat past middle age, with a plain and rather provincial appearance.*

MISS TESMAN (*stops close by the door, listens, and says softly*). Goodness, I don't think they're even up yet!

BERTA (*also softly*). That's just what I said, Miss Juliana.

695

Remember how late the steamer got in last night. Yes, and afterward! My gracious, how much the young bride had to unpack before she could get to bed.

MISS TESMAN. Well, then—let them enjoy a good rest. But they must have some of this fresh morning air when they do come down. (*She goes to the glass door and opens it wide.*)

BERTA (*by the table, perplexed, with the bouquet in her hand*). I swear there isn't a bit of space left. I think I'll have to put it here, miss. (*Places the bouquet on the piano.*)

MISS TESMAN. So now you have a new mistress, Berta dear. Lord knows it was misery for me to give you up.

BERTA (*on the verge of tears*). And for me, miss! What can I say? All those many blessed years I've been in your service, you and Miss Rina.

MISS TESMAN. We must take it calmly, Berta. There's really nothing else to do. George needs you here in this house, you know that. You've looked after him since he was a little boy.

BERTA. Yes, but miss, I'm all the time thinking of her, lying at home. Poor thing—completely helpless. And with that new maid! She'll never take proper care of an invalid, that one.

MISS TESMAN. Oh, I'll manage to teach her. And most of it, you know, I'll do myself. So you mustn't be worrying over my poor sister.

BERTA. Well, but there's something else too, miss. I'm really so afraid I won't please the young mistress.

MISS TESMAN. Oh, well—there might be something or other at first—

BERTA. Because she's so very particular.

MISS TESMAN. Well, of course. General Gabler's daughter. What a life she had in the general's day! Remember seeing her out with her father—how she'd go galloping past in that long black riding outfit, with a feather in her hat?

BERTA. Oh yes—I remember! But I never would have dreamed then that she and George Tesman would make a match of it.

MISS TESMAN. Nor I either. But now, Berta—before I forget: from now on, you mustn't say George Tesman. You must call him Doctor Tesman.

BERTA. Yes, the young mistress said the same thing—

last night, right after they came in the door. Is that true
then, miss?

MISS TESMAN. Yes, absolutely. Think of it, Berta—they
gave him his doctor's degree. Abroad, that is—on this
trip, you know. I hadn't heard one word about it, till he told
me down on the pier.

BERTA. Well, he's clever enough to be anything. But I
never thought he'd go in for curing people.

MISS TESMAN. No, he wasn't made that kind of doctor.
(*Nods significantly.*) But as a matter of fact, you may soon
now have something still greater to call him.

BERTA. Oh, really! What's that, miss?

MISS TESMAN (*smiling*). Hm, wouldn't you like to know!
(*Moved.*) Ah, dear God—if only my poor brother could look
up from his grave and see what his little boy has become!
(*Glancing about.*) But what's this, Berta? Why, you've taken
all the slipcovers off the furniture—?

BERTA. Madam told me to. She doesn't like covers on
chairs, she said.

MISS TESMAN. Are they going to make this their regular
living room, then?

BERTA. It seems so—with her. For his part—the doctor
—he said nothing.

> (GEORGE TESMAN *enters the inner room from the
> right, singing to himself and carrying an empty,
> unstrapped suitcase. He is a youngish-looking
> man of thirty-three, medium sized, with an open,
> round, cheerful face, blond hair and beard. He
> is somewhat carelessly dressed in comfortable
> lounging clothes.*)

MISS TESMAN. Good morning, good morning, George!

TESMAN (*in the doorway*). Aunt Julie! Dear Aunt Julie!
(*Goes over and warmly shakes her hand.*) Way out here—
so early in the day—uh?

MISS TESMAN. Yes, you know I simply had to look in on
you a moment.

TESMAN. And that without a decent night's sleep.

MISS TESMAN. Oh, that's nothing at all to me.

TESMAN. Well, then you did get home all right from
the pier? Uh?

MISS TESMAN. Why, of course I did—thank goodness.

Judge Brack was good enough to see me right to my door.

TESMAN. We were sorry we couldn't drive you up. But you saw for yourself—Hedda had all those boxes to bring along.

MISS TESMAN. Yes, that was quite something, the number of boxes she had.

BERTA (*to* TESMAN). Should I go in and ask Mrs. Tesman if there's anything I can help her with?

TESMAN. No, thanks, Berta—don't bother. She said she'd ring if she needed anything.

BERTA (*going off toward the right*). All right.

TESMAN. But wait now—you can take this suitcase with you.

BERTA (*taking it*). I'll put it away in the attic. (*She goes out by the hall door.*)

TESMAN. Just think, Aunt Julie—I had that whole suitcase stuffed full of notes. You just can't imagine all I've managed to find, rummaging through archives. Marvelous old documents that nobody knew existed—

MISS TESMAN. Yes, you've really not wasted any time on your wedding trip, George.

TESMAN. I certainly haven't. But do take your hat off, Auntie. Here—let me help you—uh?

MISS TESMAN (*as he does so*). Goodness—this is exactly as if you were still back at home with us.

TESMAN (*turning the hat in his hand and studying it from all sides*). My—what elegant hats you go in for!

MISS TESMAN. I bought that for Hedda's sake.

TESMAN. For Hedda's sake? Uh?

MISS TESMAN. Yes, so Hedda wouldn't feel ashamed of me if we walked down the street together.

TESMAN (*patting her cheek*). You think of everything, Aunt Julie! (*Laying the hat on a chair by the table.*) So—look, suppose we sit down on the sofa and have a little chat 'till Hedda comes. (*They settle themselves. She puts her parasol on the corner of the sofa.*)

MISS TESMAN (*takes both of his hands and gazes at him*). How wonderful it is having you here, right before my eyes again, George! You—dear Jochum's own boy!

TESMAN. And for me too, to see you again, Aunt Julie! You, who've been father and mother to me both.

MISS TESMAN. Yes, I'm sure you'll always keep a place in your heart for your old aunts.

TESMAN. But Auntie Rina—hm? Isn't she any better?

MISS TESMAN. Oh no—we can hardly expect that she'll ever be better, poor thing. She lies there, just as she has all these years. May God let me keep her a little while longer! Because otherwise, George, I don't know what I'd do with my life. The more so now, when I don't have you to look after.

TESMAN (*patting her on the back*). There, there, there—

MISS TESMAN (*suddenly changing her tone*). No, but to think of it, that now you're a married man! And that it was *you* who carried off Hedda Gabler. The beautiful Hedda Gabler! Imagine! She, who always had so many admirers!

TESMAN (*hums a little and smiles complacently*). Yes, I rather suspect I have several friends who'd like to trade places with me.

MISS TESMAN. And then to have such a wedding trip! Five —almost six months—

TESMAN. Well, remember, I used it for research, too. All those libraries I had to check—and so many books to read!

MISS TESMAN. Yes, no doubt. (*More confidentially; lowering her voice.*) But now listen, George—isn't there something —something special you have to tell me?

TESMAN. From the trip?

MISS TESMAN. Yes.

TESMAN. No, I can't think of anything beyond what I wrote in my letters. I got my doctor's degree down there —but I told you that yesterday.

MISS TESMAN. Yes, of course. But I mean—whether you have any kind of—expectations—?

TESMAN. Expectations?

MISS TESMAN. My goodness, George—I'm your old aunt!

TESMAN. Why, naturally I have expectations.

MISS TESMAN. Ah!

TESMAN. I have every expectation in the world of becoming a professor shortly.

MISS TESMAN. Oh, a professor, yes—

TESMAN. Or I might as well say, I'm sure of it. But, Aunt Julie—you know that perfectly well yourself.

MISS TESMAN (*with a little laugh*). That's right, so I do.

(*Changing the subject.*) But we were talking about your trip. It must have cost a terrible amount of money.

TESMAN. Well, that big fellowship, you know—it took us a good part of the way.

MISS TESMAN. But I don't see how you could stretch it enough for two.

TESMAN. No, that's not so easy to see—uh?

MISS TESMAN. And especially traveling with a lady. For I hear tell that's much more expensive.

TESMAN. Yes, of course—it's a bit more expensive. But Hedda just had to have that trip. She *had* to. There was nothing else to be done.

MISS TESMAN. No, no, I guess not. A honeymoon abroad seems to be the thing nowadays. But tell me—have you had a good look around your house?

TESMAN. You can bet I have! I've been up since daybreak.

MISS TESMAN. And how does it strike you, all in all?

TESMAN. First-rate! Absolutely first-rate! Only I don't know what we'll do with the two empty rooms between the back parlor and Hedda's bedroom.

MISS TESMAN (*laughing again*). Oh, my dear George, I think you can use them—as time goes on.

TESMAN. Yes, you're quite right about that, Aunt Julie! In time, as I build up my library—uh?

MISS TESMAN. Of course, my dear boy. It was your library I meant.

TESMAN. I'm happiest now for Hedda's sake. Before we were engaged, she used to say so many times there was no place she'd rather live than here, in Secretary Falk's town house.

MISS TESMAN. Yes, and then to have it come on the market just after you'd sailed.

TESMAN. We really have had luck, haven't we?

MISS TESMAN. But expensive, George dear! You'll find it expensive, all this here.

TESMAN (*looks at her, somewhat crestfallen*). Yes, I suppose I will.

MISS TESMAN. Oh, Lord, yes!

TESMAN. How much do you think? Approximately? Hm?

MISS TESMAN. It's impossible to say till the bills are all in.

TESMAN. Well, fortunately Judge Brack has gotten me quite easy terms. That's what he wrote Hedda.

MISS TESMAN. Don't worry yourself about that, dear. I've also put up security to cover the carpets and furniture.

TESMAN. Security? Aunt Julie, dear—you? What kind of security could *you* give?

MISS TESMAN. I took out a mortgage on our pension.

TESMAN (*jumping up*). What! On your—and Auntie Rina's pension!

MISS TESMAN. I saw nothing else to do.

TESMAN (*standing in front of her*). But you're out of your mind, Aunt Julie! That pension—it's all Aunt Rina and you have to live on.

MISS TESMAN. Now, now—don't make so much of it. It's only a formality; Judge Brack said so. He was good enough to arrange the whole thing for me. Just a formality, he said.

TESMAN. That's all well enough. But still—

MISS TESMAN. You'll be drawing your own salary now. And, good gracious, if we have to lay out a bit, just now at the start—why, it's no more than a pleasure for us.

TESMAN. Oh, Aunt Julie—you never get tired of making sacrifices for me!

MISS TESMAN (*rises and places her hands on his shoulders*). What other joy do I have in this world than smoothing the path for you, my dear boy? You, without father or mother to turn to. And now we've come to the goal, George! Things may have looked black at times; but now, thank heaven, you've made it.

TESMAN. Yes, it's remarkable, really, how everything's turned out for the best.

MISS TESMAN. Yes—and those who stood against you—who wanted to bar your way—they've gone down. They've fallen, George. The one most dangerous to you—he fell farthest. And he's lying there now, in the bed he made—poor, misguided creature.

TESMAN. Have you heard any news of Eilert? I mean, since I went away.

MISS TESMAN. Only that he's supposed to have brought out a new book.

TESMAN. What's that? Eilert Løvborg? Just recently, uh?

MISS TESMAN. So they say. But considering everything, it

can hardly amount to much. Ah, but when *your* new book comes out—it'll be a different story, George! What will it be about?

TESMAN. It's going to treat the domestic handicrafts of Brabant in the Middle Ages.

MISS TESMAN. Just imagine—that you can write about things like that!

TESMAN. Actually, the book may take quite a while yet. I have this tremendous collection of material to put in order, you know.

MISS TESMAN. Yes, collecting and ordering—you do that so well. You're not my brother's son for nothing.

TESMAN. I look forward so much to getting started. Especially now, with a comfortable home of my own to work in.

MISS TESMAN. And most of all, dear, now that you've won her, the wife of your heart.

TESMAN (*embracing her*). Yes, yes, Aunt Julie! Hedda— that's the most beautiful part of it all! (*Glancing toward the doorway.*) But I think she's coming—uh?

> (HEDDA *enters from the left through the inner room. She is a woman of twenty-nine. Her face and figure show breeding and distinction; her complexion is pallid and opaque. Her steel gray eyes express a cool, unruffled calm. Her hair is an attractive medium brown, but not particularly abundant. She wears a tasteful, rather loose-fitting gown.*)

MISS TESMAN (*going to meet* HEDDA). Good morning, Hedda dear—how good to see you!

HEDDA (*holding out her hand*). Good morning, my dear Miss Tesman! Calling so early? This *is* kind of you.

MISS TESMAN (*slightly embarrassed*). Well—did the bride sleep well in her new home?

HEDDA. Oh yes, thanks. Quite adequately.

TESMAN. Adequately! Oh, I like that, Hedda! You were sleeping like a stone when I got up.

HEDDA. Fortunately. But of course one has to grow accustomed to anything new, Miss Tesman—little by little. (*Looking toward the left.*) Oh! That maid has left the door open—and the sunlight's just flooding in.

MISS TESMAN (*going toward the door*). Well, we can close it.

HEDDA. No, no—don't! (*To* TESMAN.) There, dear, draw the curtains. It gives a softer light.

TESMAN (*by the glass door*). All right—all right. Look, Hedda—now you have shade and fresh air both.

HEDDA. Yes, we really need some fresh air here, with all these piles of flowers— But—won't you sit down, Miss Tesman?

MISS TESMAN. Oh no, thank you. Now that I know that everything's fine—thank goodness—I will have to run along home. My sister's lying there waiting, poor thing.

TESMAN. Give her my very, very best, won't you? And say I'll be looking in on her later today.

MISS TESMAN. Oh, you can be sure I will. But what do you know, George—(*Searching in her bag.*)—I nearly forgot. I have something here for you.

TESMAN. What's that, Aunt Julie? Hm?

MISS TESMAN (*brings out a flat package wrapped in newspaper and hands it to him*). There, dear. Look.

TESMAN (*opening it*). Oh, my—you kept them for me, Aunt Julie! Hedda! That's really touching! Uh!

HEDDA (*by the* étagère *on the right*). Yes, dear, what is it?

TESMAN. My old bedroom slippers! My slippers!

HEDDA. Oh yes. I remember how often you spoke of them during the trip.

TESMAN. Yes, I missed them terribly. (*Going over to her.*) Now you can see them, Hedda!

HEDDA (*moves toward the stove*). Thanks, but I really don't care to.

TESMAN (*following her*). Imagine—Auntie Rina lay and embroidered them, sick as she was. Oh, you couldn't believe how many memories are bound up in them.

HEDDA (*at the table*). But not for me.

MISS TESMAN. I think Hedda is right, George.

TESMAN. Yes, but I only thought, now that she's part of the family—

HEDDA (*interrupting*). We're never going to manage with this maid, Tesman.

MISS TESMAN. Not manage with Berta?

TESMAN.   But dear—why do you say that? Uh?

HEDDA (*pointing*).   See there! She's left her old hat lying out on a chair.

TESMAN (*shocked; dropping the slippers*).   But Hedda—!

HEDDA.   Suppose someone came in and saw it.

TESMAN.   Hedda—that's Aunt Julie's hat!

HEDDA.   Really?

MISS TESMAN (*picking it up*).   That's right, it's mine. And what's more, it certainly is not old—Mrs. Tesman.

HEDDA.   I really hadn't looked closely at it, Miss Tesman.

MISS TESMAN (*putting on the hat*).   It's actually the first time I've had it on. The very first time.

TESMAN.   And it's lovely, too. Most attractive!

MISS TESMAN.   Oh, it's hardly all that, George. (*Looks about.*) My parasol—? Ah, here. (*Takes it.*) For that's mine too. (*Murmurs.*) Not Berta's.

TESMAN.   New hat and new parasol! Just imagine, Hedda!

HEDDA.   Quite charming, really.

TESMAN.   Yes, aren't they, uh? But Auntie, take a good look at Hedda before you leave. See how charming *she* is!

MISS TESMAN.   But George dear, there's nothing new in that. Hedda's been lovely all her life. (*She nods and starts out, right.*)

TESMAN (*following her*).   But have you noticed how plump and buxom she's grown? How much she's filled out on the trip?

HEDDA (*crossing the room*).   Oh, do be quiet—!

MISS TESMAN (*who has stopped and turned*).   Filled out?

TESMAN.   Of course, you can't see it so well when she has that dressing gown on. But I, who have the opportunity to—

HEDDA (*by the glass door, impatiently*).   Oh, you have no opportunity for anything!

TESMAN.   It must have been the mountain air, down in the Tyrol—

HEDDA (*brusquely interrupting*).   I'm exactly as I was when I left.

TESMAN.   Yes, that's your claim. But you certainly are not. Auntie, don't you agree?

MISS TESMAN (*gazing at her with folded hands*).   Hedda is lovely—lovely—lovely. (*Goes up to her, takes her head in both hands, bends it down and kisses her hair.*) God bless and keep Hedda Tesman—for George's sake.

HEDDA (*gently freeing herself*). Oh—! Let me go.

MISS TESMAN (*with quiet feeling*). I won't let a day go by without looking in on you two.

TESMAN. Yes, please do that, Aunt Julie! Uh?

MISS TESMAN. Good-bye—good-bye!

> (*She goes out by the hall door.* TESMAN *accompanies her, leaving the door half open. He can be heard reiterating his greetings to Aunt Rina and his thanks for the slippers. At the same time,* HEDDA *moves about the room, raising her arms and clenching her fists as if in a frenzy. Then she flings back the curtains from the glass door and stands there, looking out. A moment later* TESMAN *comes back, closing the door after him.*)

TESMAN (*retrieving the slippers from the floor*). What are you standing and looking at, Hedda?

HEDDA (*again calm and controlled*). I'm just looking at the leaves—they're so yellow—and so withered.

TESMAN (*wraps up the slippers and puts them on the table*). Yes, well, we're into September now.

HEDDA (*once more restless*). Yes, to think—that already we're in—in September.

TESMAN. Didn't Aunt Julie seem a bit strange? A little—almost formal? What do you suppose was bothering her? Hm?

HEDDA. I hardly know her at all. Isn't that how she usually is?

TESMAN. No, not like this, today.

HEDDA (*leaving the glass door*). Do you think this thing with the hat upset her?

TESMAN. Oh, not very much. A little, just at the moment, perhaps—

HEDDA. But really, what kind of manners has she—to go throwing her hat about in a drawing room! It's just not proper.

TESMAN. Well, you can be sure Aunt Julie won't do it again.

HEDDA. Anyhow, I'll manage to smooth it over with her.

TESMAN. Yes, Hedda dear, I wish you would!

HEDDA. When you go in to see them later on, you might ask her out for the evening.

TESMAN. Yes, I'll do that. And there's something else you could do that would make her terribly happy.

HEDDA. Oh?

TESMAN. If only you could bring yourself to speak to her warmly, by her first name. For my sake, Hedda? Uh?

HEDDA. No, no—don't ask me to do that. I told you this once before. I'll try to call her "Aunt." That should be enough.

TESMAN. Oh, all right. I was only thinking, now that you belong to the family—

HEDDA. Hm—I really don't know— (*She crosses the room to the doorway.*)

TESMAN (*after a pause*). Is something the matter, Hedda? Uh?

HEDDA. I'm just looking at my old piano. It doesn't really fit in with all these other things.

TESMAN. With the first salary I draw, we can see about trading it in on a new one.

HEDDA. No, not traded in. I don't want to part with it. We can put it there, in the inner room, and get another here in its place. When there's a chance, I mean.

TESMAN (*slightly cast down*). Yes, we could do that, of course.

HEDDA (*picks up the bouquet from the piano*). These flowers weren't here when we got in last night.

TESMAN. Aunt Julie must have brought them for you.

HEDDA (*examining the bouquet*). A visiting card. (*Takes it out and reads it.*) "Will stop back later today." Can you guess who this is from?

TESMAN. No. Who? Hm?

HEDDA. It says "Mrs. Elvsted."

TESMAN. No, really? Sheriff Elvsted's wife. Miss Rysing, she used to be.

HEDDA. Exactly. The one with the irritating hair that she was always showing off. An old flame of yours, I've heard.

TESMAN (*laughing*). Oh, that wasn't for long. And it was before I knew you, Hedda. But imagine—that she's here in town.

HEDDA. It's odd that she calls on us. I've hardly seen her since we were in school.

TESMAN. Yes, I haven't seen her either—since God knows when. I wonder how she can stand living in such an out-of-the-way place. Hm?

HEDDA (*thinks a moment, then bursts out*). But wait—isn't it somewhere up in those parts that he—that Eilert Løvborg lives?

TESMAN. Yes, it's someplace right around there. (BERTA *enters by the hall door.*)

BERTA. She's back again, ma'am—that lady who stopped by and left the flowers an hour ago. (*Pointing.*) The ones you have in your hand, ma'am.

HEDDA. Oh, is she? Good. Would you ask her to come in.

> (BERTA *opens the door for* MRS. ELVSTED *and goes out.* MRS. ELVSTED *is a slender woman with soft, pretty features. Her eyes are light blue, large, round, and somewhat prominent, with a startled, questioning look. Her hair is remarkably light, almost a white-gold, and unusually abundant and wavy. She is a couple of years younger than* HEDDA. *She wears a dark visiting dress, tasteful, but not quite in the latest fashion.*)

HEDDA (*going to greet her warmly*). Good morning, my dear Mrs. Elvsted. How delightful to see you again!

MRS. ELVSTED (*nervously; struggling to control herself*). Yes, it's a very long time since we last met.

TESMAN (*gives her his hand*). Or since *we* met, uh?

HEDDA. Thank you for your beautiful flowers—

MRS. ELVSTED. Oh, that's nothing—I would have come straight out here yesterday afternoon, but then I heard you weren't at home—

TESMAN. Have you just now come to town? Uh?

MRS. ELVSTED. I got in yesterday toward noon. Oh, I was in desperation when I heard that you weren't at home.

HEDDA. Desperation! Why?

TESMAN. But my dear Mrs. Rysing—Mrs. Elvsted, I mean—

HEDDA. You're not in some kind of trouble?

MRS. ELVSTED. Yes, I am. And I don't know another living soul down here I can turn to.

HEDDA (*putting the bouquet down on the table*). Come, then—let's sit here on the sofa—

MRS. ELVSTED. Oh, I can't sit down. I'm really too much on edge!

HEDDA. Why, of course you can. Come here.

(*She draws* MRS. ELVSTED *down on the sofa and sits beside her.*)

TESMAN. Well? What is it, Mrs. Elvsted?

HEDDA. Has anything particular happened at home?

MRS. ELVSTED. Yes, that's both it—and not it. Oh, I do want so much that you don't misunderstand me—

HEDDA. But then the best thing, Mrs. Elvsted, is simply to speak your mind.

TESMAN. Because I suppose that's why you've come. Hm?

MRS. ELVSTED. Oh yes, that's why. Well, then, I have to tell you—if you don't already know—that Eilert Løvborg's also in town.

HEDDA. Løvborg—!

TESMAN. What! Is Eilert Løvborg back! Just think, Hedda!

HEDDA. Good Lord, I can hear.

MRS. ELVSTED. He's been back all of a week's time now. A whole week—in this dangerous town! Alone! With all the bad company that's around.

HEDDA. But my dear Mrs. Elvsted, what does *he* have to do with you?

MRS. ELVSTED (*glances anxiously at her and says quickly*). He was the children's tutor.

HEDDA. Your children's?

MRS. ELVSTED. My husband's. I have none.

HEDDA. Your stepchildren's, then.

MRS. ELVSTED. Yes.

TESMAN. (*somewhat hesitantly*). But was he—I don't know quite how to put it—was he sufficiently—responsible in his habits for such a job? Uh?

MRS. ELVSTED. In these last two years, there wasn't a word to be said against him.

TESMAN. Not a word? Just think of that, Hedda!

HEDDA. . I heard it.

MRS. ELVSTED. Not even a murmur, I can assure you! Nothing. But anyway—now that I know he's here—in this big city—and with so much money in his hands—then I'm just frightened to death for him.

TESMAN. But why didn't he stay up there where he was? With you and your husband? Uh?

MRS. ELVSTED. After the book came out, he just couldn't rest content with us.

TESMAN. Yes, that's right—Aunt Julie was saying he'd published a new book.

MRS. ELVSTED. Yes, a great new book, on the course of civilization—in all its stages. It's been out two weeks. And now it's been bought and read so much—and it's made a tremendous stir—

TESMAN. Has it really? It must be something he's had lying around from his better days.

MRS. ELVSTED. Years back, you mean?

TESMAN. I suppose.

MRS. ELVSTED. No, he's written it all up there with us. Now—in this last year.

TESMAN. That's marvelous to hear. Hedda! Just imagine!

MRS. ELVSTED. Yes, if only it can go on like this!

HEDDA. Have you seen him here in town?

MRS. ELVSTED. No, not yet. I had such trouble finding out his address. But this morning I got it at last.

HEDDA (*looks searchingly at her*). I must say it seems rather odd of your husband—

MRS. ELVSTED (*with a nervous start*). Of my husband—! What?

HEDDA. To send you to town on this sort of errand. Not to come and look after his friend himself.

MRS. ELVSTED. No, no, my husband hasn't the time for that. And then I had—some shopping to do.

HEDDA (*with a slight smile*). Oh, that's different.

MRS. ELVSTED (*getting up quickly and uneasily*). I beg you, please, Mr. Tesman—be good to Eilert Løvborg if he comes to you. And he will, I'm sure. You know—you were such good friends in the old days. And you're both doing the same kind of work. The same type of research—from what I can gather.

TESMAN. We were once, at any rate.

MRS. ELVSTED. Yes, and that's why I'm asking you, please—you too—to keep an eye on him. Oh, you will do that, Mr. Tesman—promise me that?

TESMAN. I'll be only too glad to, Mrs. Rysing—

HEDDA. Elvsted.

TESMAN. I'll certainly do everything in my power for Eilert. You can depend on that.

MRS. ELVSTED. Oh, how terribly kind of you! (*Pressing his hands.*) Many, many thanks! (*Frightened.*) He means so much to my husband, you know.

HEDDA (*rising*). You ought to write him, dear. He might not come by on his own.

TESMAN. Yes, that probably would be the best, Hedda? Hm?

HEDDA. And the sooner the better. Right now, I'd say.

MRS. ELVSTED (*imploringly*). Oh yes, if you could!

TESMAN. I'll write him this very moment. Have you got his address, Mrs.—Mrs. Elvsted?

MRS. ELVSTED. Yes. (*Takes a slip of paper from her pocket and hands it to him.*) Here it is.

TESMAN. Good, good. Then I'll go in— (*Looking about.*) But wait—my slippers? Ah! Here. (*Takes the package and starts to leave.*)

HEDDA. Write him a really warm, friendly letter. Nice and long, too.

TESMAN. Don't worry, I will.

MRS. ELVSTED. But please, not a word that I asked you to!

TESMAN. No, that goes without saying. Uh? (*Leaves by the inner room, to the right.*)

HEDDA (*goes over to* MRS. ELVSTED, *smiles, and speaks softly*). How's that! Now we've killed two birds with one stone.

MRS. ELVSTED. What do you mean?

HEDDA. Didn't you see that I wanted him out of the room?

MRS. ELVSTED. Yes, to write the letter—

HEDDA. But also to talk with you alone.

MRS. ELVSTED (*confused*). About this same thing?

HEDDA. Precisely.

MRS. ELVSTED (*upset*). But Mrs. Tesman, there's nothing more to say! Nothing!

HEDDA. Oh yes, but there is. There's a great deal more— I can see that. Come, sit here—and let's speak openly now, the two of us. (*She forces* MRS. ELVSTED *down into the armchair by the stove and sits on one of the taborets.*)

MRS. ELVSTED (*anxiously glancing at her watch*). But Mrs. Tesman, dear—I was just planning to leave.

HEDDA. Oh, you can't be in such a rush— Now! Tell me a little about how things are going at home.

MRS. ELVSTED. Oh, that's the last thing I'd ever want to discuss.

HEDDA. But with me, dear—? After all, we were in school together.

MRS. ELVSTED. Yes, but you were a class ahead of me. Oh, I was terribly afraid of you then!

HEDDA. Afraid of me?

MRS. ELVSTED. Yes, terribly. Because whenever we met on the stairs, you'd always pull my hair.

HEDDA. Did I really?

MRS. ELVSTED. Yes, and once you said you would burn it off.

HEDDA. Oh, that was just foolish talk, you know.

MRS. ELVSTED. Yes, but I was so stupid then. And, anyway, since then—we've drifted so far—far apart from each other. We've moved in such different circles.

HEDDA. Well, let's try now to come closer again. Listen, at school we were quite good friends, and we called each other by our first names—

MRS. ELVSTED. No, I'm sure you're mistaken.

HEDDA. Oh, I couldn't be! I remember it clearly. And that's why we have to be perfectly open, just as we were. (*Moves the stool nearer* MRS. ELVSTED.) There now! (*Kissing her cheek.*) You have to call me Hedda.

MRS. ELVSTED (*pressing and patting her hands*). Oh, you're so good and kind—! It's not at all what I'm used to.

HEDDA. There, there! And I'm going to call you my own dear Thora.

MRS. ELVSTED. My name is Thea.

HEDDA. Oh yes, of course. I meant Thea. (*Looks at her compassionately.*) So you're not much used to goodness or kindness, Thea? In your own home?

MRS. ELVSTED. If only I had a home! But I don't. I never have.

HEDDA (*glances quickly at her*). I thought it had to be something like that.

MRS. ELVSTED (*gazing helplessly into space*). Yes—yes—yes.

HEDDA. I can't quite remember now—but wasn't it as a housekeeper that you first came up to the Elvsteds?

MRS. ELVSTED. Actually as a governess. But his wife—his first wife—she was an invalid and mostly kept to her bed. So I had to take care of the house too.

HEDDA. But finally you became mistress of the house yourself.

MRS. ELVSTED (*heavily*). Yes, I did.

HEDDA. Let me see—about how long ago was that?

MRS. ELVSTED. That I was married?

HEDDA. Yes.

MRS. ELVSTED. It's five years now.

HEDDA. That's right. It must be.

MRS. ELVSTED. Oh, these five years—! Or the last two or three, anyway. Oh, if you only knew, Mrs. Tesman—

HEDDA (*gives her hand a little slap*). Mrs. Tesman! Now, Thea!

MRS. ELVSTED. I'm sorry; I'll try— Yes, if you could only understand—Hedda—

HEDDA (*casually*). Eilert Løvborg has lived up there about three years too, hasn't he?

MRS. ELVSTED (*looks at her doubtfully*). Eilert Løvborg? Yes—he has.

HEDDA. Had you already known him here in town?

MRS. ELVSTED. Hardly at all. Well, I mean—by name, of course.

HEDDA. But up there—I suppose he'd visit you both?

MRS. ELVSTED. Yes, he came to see us every day. He was tutoring the children, you know. Because, in the long run, I couldn't do it all myself.

HEDDA. No, that's obvious. And your husband—? I suppose he often has to be away?

MRS. ELVSTED. Yes, you can imagine, as sheriff, how much traveling he does around in the district.

HEDDA (*leaning against the chair arm*). Thea—my poor, sweet Thea—now you must tell me everything—just as it is.

MRS. ELVSTED. Well, then you have to ask the questions.

HEDDA. What sort of man is your husband, Thea? I mean—you know—to be with. Is he good to you?

MRS. ELVSTED (*evasively*). He believes he does everything for the best.

HEDDA. I only think he must be much too old for you. More than twenty years older, isn't he?

MRS. ELVSTED (*irritated*). That's true. Along with everything else. I just can't stand him! We haven't a single thought in common. Nothing at all—he and I.

HEDDA. But doesn't he care for you all the same—in his own way?

MRS. ELVSTED. Oh, I don't know what he feels. I'm no more than useful to him. And then it doesn't cost much to keep me. I'm inexpensive.

HEDDA. That's stupid of you.

MRS. ELVSTED (*shaking her head*). It can't be otherwise. Not with him. He really doesn't care for anyone but himself—and maybe a little for the children.

HEDDA. And for Eilert Løvborg, Thea.

MRS. ELVSTED (*looking at her*). Eilert Løvborg! Why do you think so?

HEDDA. But my dear—it seems to me, when he sends you all the way into town to look after him— (*Smiles almost imperceptibly.*) Besides, it's what you told my husband.

MRS. ELVSTED (*with a little nervous shudder*). Really? Yes, I suppose I did. (*In a quiet outburst.*) No—I might as well tell you here and now! It's bound to come out in time.

HEDDA. But my dear Thea—?

MRS. ELVSTED. All right, then! My husband never knew I was coming here.

HEDDA. What! Your husband never knew—

MRS. ELVSTED. Of course not. Anyway, he wasn't at home. Off traveling somewhere. Oh, I couldn't bear it any longer, Hedda. It was impossible! I would have been so alone up there now.

HEDDA. Well? What then?

MRS. ELVSTED. So I packed a few of my things together —the barest necessities—without saying a word. And I slipped away from the house.

HEDDA. ~~Right then and there?~~

MRS. ELVSTED. Yes, and took the train straight into town.

HEDDA. But my dearest girl—that you could dare to do such a thing!

MRS. ELVSTED (*rising and walking about the room*). What else could I possibly do!

HEDDA. But what do you think your husband will say when you go back home?

MRS. ELVSTED (*by the table, looking at her*). Back to *him*?

HEDDA. Yes, of course.

MRS. ELVSTED. I'll never go back to him.

HEDDA (*rising and approaching her*). You mean you've left, in dead earnest, for good?

MRS. ELVSTED. Yes. There didn't·seem anything else to do.

HEDDA. But—to go away so openly.

MRS. ELVSTED. Oh, you can't keep a thing like that secret.

HEDDA. But what do you think people will say about you, Thea?

MRS. ELVSTED. God knows they'll say what they please. (*Sitting wearily and sadly on the sofa.*) I only did what I had to do.

HEDDA (*after a short silence*). What do you plan on now? What kind of work?

MRS. ELVSTED. I don't know yet. I only know I have to live here, where Eilert Løvborg is—if I'm going to live at all.

HEDDA (*moves a chair over from the table, sits beside her, and strokes her hands*). Thea dear—how did this—this friendship—between you and Eilert Løvborg come about?

MRS. ELVSTED. Oh, it happened little by little. I got some kind of power, almost, over him.

HEDDA. Really?

MRS. ELVSTED. He gave up his old habits. Not because I'd asked him to. I never dared do that. But he could tell they upset me, and so he dropped them.

HEDDA (*hiding an involuntary, scornful smile*). My dear little Thea—just as they say—you rehabilitated him.

MRS. ELVSTED. Well, he says so, at any rate. And he—on his part—he's made a real human being out of me.

Taught me to think—and understand so many things.

HEDDA. You mean he tutored you also?

MRS. ELVSTED. No, not exactly. But he'd talk to me—talk endlessly on about one thing after another. And then came the wonderful, happy time when I could share in his work! When I could help him!

HEDDA. Could you really?

MRS. ELVSTED. Yes! Whenever he wrote anything, we'd always work on it together.

HEDDA. Like two true companions.

MRS. ELVSTED (*eagerly*). Companions! You know, Hedda—that's what he said too! Oh, I ought to feel so happy—but I can't. I just don't know if it's going to last.

HEDDA. You're no more sure of him than that?

MRS. ELVSTED (*despondently*). There's a woman's shadow between Eilert Løvborg and me.

HEDDA (*looks at her intently*). Who could that be?

MRS. ELVSTED. I don't know. Someone out of his—his past. Someone he's really never forgotten.

HEDDA. What has he said—about this!

MRS. ELVSTED. It's only once—and just vaguely—that he touched on it.

HEDDA. Well! And what did he say!

MRS. ELVSTED. He said that when they broke off she was going to shoot him with a pistol.

HEDDA (*with cold constraint*). That's nonsense! Nobody behaves that way around here.

MRS. ELVSTED. No. And that's why I think it must have been that redheaded singer that at one time he—

HEDDA. Yes, quite likely.

MRS. ELVSTED. I remember they used to say about her that she carried loaded weapons.

HEDDA. Ah—then of course it must have been her.

MRS. ELVSTED (*wringing her hands*). But you know what, Hedda—I've heard that this singer—that she's in town again! Oh, it has me out of my mind—

HEDDA (*glancing toward the inner room*). Shh! Tesman's coming. (*Gets up and whispers.*) Thea—keep all this just between us.

MRS. ELVSTED (*jumping up*). Oh yes! In heaven's name—!

(GEORGE TESMAN, *with a letter in his hand, enters from the right through the inner room.*)

TESMAN. There, now—the letter's signed and sealed.

HEDDA. That's fine. I think Mrs. Elvsted was just leaving. Wait a minute. I'll go with you to the garden gate.

TESMAN. Hedda, dear—could Berta maybe look after this?

HEDDA (*taking the letter*). I'll tell her to.

(BERTA *enters from the hall.*)

BERTA. Judge Brack is here and says he'd like to greet you and the Doctor, ma'am.

HEDDA. Yes, ask Judge Brack to come in. And, here— put this letter in the mail.

BERTA (*takes the letter*). Yes, ma'am.

(*She opens the door for* JUDGE BRACK *and goes out.* BRACK *is a man of forty-five, thickset, yet well-built, with supple movements. His face is roundish, with a distinguished profile. His hair is short, still mostly black, and carefully groomed. His eyes are bright and lively. Thick eyebrows; a moustache to match, with neatly clipped ends. He wears a trimly tailored walking suit, a bit too youthful for his age. Uses a monocle, which he now and then lets fall.*)

JUDGE BRACK (*hat in hand, bowing*). May one dare to call so early?

HEDDA. Of course one may.

TESMAN (*shakes his hand*). You're always welcome here. (*Introducing him.*) Judge Brack—Miss Rysing—

HEDDA. Ah—!

BRACK (*bowing*). I'm delighted.

HEDDA (*looks at him and laughs*). It's really a treat to see you by daylight, Judge!

BRACK. You find me—changed?

HEDDA. Yes. A bit younger, I think.

BRACK. Thank you, most kindly.

TESMAN. But what do you say for Hedda, uh? Doesn't she look flourishing? She's actually—

HEDDA. Oh, leave me out of it! You might thank Judge Brack for all the trouble he's gone to—

BRACK. Nonsense—it was a pleasure—

HEDDA. Yes, you're a true friend. But here's Thea, standing here, aching to get away. Excuse me, Judge; I'll be right back.

(*Mutual good-byes.* MRS. ELVSTED *and* HEDDA *go out by the hall door.*)

BRACK. So—is your wife fairly well satisfied, then—?

TESMAN. Yes, we can't thank you enough. Of course— I gather there's some rearrangement called for here and there. And one or two things are lacking. We still have to buy a few minor items.

BRACK. Really?

TESMAN. But that's nothing for you to worry about. Hedda said she'd pick up those things herself. Why don't we sit down, hm?

BRACK. Thanks. Just for a moment. (*Sits by the table.*) There's something I'd like to discuss with you, Tesman.

TESMAN. What? Oh, I understand! (*Sitting.*) It's the serious part of the banquet we're coming to, uh?

BRACK. Oh, as far as money matters go, there's no great rush—though I must say I wish we'd managed things a bit more economically.

TESMAN. But that was completely impossible! Think about Hedda, Judge! You, who know her so well— I simply couldn't have her live like a grocer's wife.

BRACK. No, no—that's the trouble, exactly.

TESMAN. And then—fortunately—it can't be long before I get my appointment.

BRACK. Well, you know—these things can often hang fire.

TESMAN. Have you heard something further? Hm?

BRACK. Nothing really definite— (*Changing the subject.*) But incidentally—I do have one piece of news for you.

TESMAN. Well?

BRACK. Your old friend Eilert Løvborg is back in town.

TESMAN. I already know.

BRACK. Oh? How did you hear?

TESMAN. She told me. The lady that left with Hedda.

BRACK. I see. What was her name again? I didn't quite catch it—

TESMAN. Mrs. Elvsted.

BRACK.   Aha—Sheriff Elvsted's wife. Yes—it's up near them he's been staying.

TESMAN.   And, just think—what a pleasure to hear that he's completely stable again!

BRACK.   Yes, that's what they claim.

TESMAN.   And that he's published a new book, uh?

BRACK.   Oh yes!

TESMAN.   And it's created quite a sensation.

BRACK.   An extraordinary sensation.

TESMAN.   Just imagine—isn't that marvelous? He, with his remarkable talents—I was so very afraid that he'd really gone down for good.

BRACK.   That's what everyone thought.

TESMAN.   But I've no idea what he'll find to do now. How on earth can he ever make a living? Hm?

> (*During the last words,* HEDDA *comes in by the hall door.*)

HEDDA (*to* BRACK, *laughing, with a touch of scorn*).   Tesman always goes around worrying about how people are going to make a living.

TESMAN.   My Lord—it's poor Eilert Løvborg, we're talking of, dear.

HEDDA (*glancing quickly at him*).   Oh, really? (*Sits in the armchair by the stove and asks casually.*) What's the matter with him?

TESMAN.   Well—he must have run through his inheritance long ago. And he can't write a new book every year. Uh? So I was asking, really, what's going to become of him.

BRACK.   Perhaps I can shed some light on that.

TESMAN.   Oh?

BRACK.   You must remember that he does have relatives with a great deal of influence.

TESMAN.   Yes, but they've washed their hands of him altogether.

BRACK.   They used to call him the family's white hope.

TESMAN.   They used to, yes! But he spoiled all that himself.

HEDDA.   Who knows? (*With a slight smile.*) He's been rehabilitated up at the Elvsteds—

BRACK.   And then this book that he's published—

TESMAN. Oh, well, let's hope they really help him some way or other. I just now wrote to him. Hedda dear, I asked him out here this evening.

BRACK. But my dear fellow, you're coming to my stag party this evening. You promised down on the pier last night.

HEDDA. Had you forgotten, Tesman?

TESMAN. Yes, I absolutely had.

BRACK. For that matter, you can rest assured that he'd never come.

TESMAN. What makes you say that, hm?

BRACK (*hesitating, rising and leaning on the back of the chair*). My dear Tesman—and you too, Mrs. Tesman—I can't, in all conscience, let you go on without knowing something that—that—

TESMAN. Something involving Eilert—?

BRACK. Both you and him.

TESMAN. But my dear Judge, then tell us!

BRACK. You must be prepared that your appointment may not come through as quickly as you've wished or expected.

TESMAN (*jumping up nervously*). Has something gone wrong? Uh?

BRACK. It may turn out that there'll have to be a competition for the post—

TESMAN. A competition! Imagine, Hedda!

HEDDA (*leaning further back in the chair*). Ah, there— you see!

TESMAN. But with whom! You can't mean—?

BRACK. Yes, exactly. With Eilert Løvborg.

TESMAN (*striking his hands together*). No, no—that's completely unthinkable! It's impossible! Uh?

BRACK. Hm—but it may come about, all the same.

TESMAN. No, but, Judge Brack—that would just be incredibly inconsiderate toward me! (*Waving his arms.*) Yes, because—you know—I'm a married man! We married on my prospects, Hedda and I. We went into debt. And even borrowed money from Aunt Julie. Because that job—my Lord, it was as good as promised to me, uh?

BRACK. Easy now—I'm sure you'll get the appointment. But you will have to compete for it.

HEDDA (*motionless in the armchair*). Just think, Tesman —it will be like a kind of championship match.

TESMAN. But Hedda dearest, how can you take it so calmly!

HEDDA (*as before*). I'm not the least bit calm. I can't wait to see how it turns out.

BRACK. In any case, Mrs. Tesman, it's well that you know now how things stand. I mean—with respect to those little purchases I hear you've been threatening to make.

HEDDA. This business can't change anything.

BRACK. I see! Well, that's another matter. Good-bye. (*To* TESMAN.) When I take my afternoon walk, I'll stop by and fetch you.

TESMAN. Oh yes, please do—I don't know where I'm at.

HEDDA (*leaning back and reaching out her hand*). Good-bye, Judge. And come again soon.

BRACK. Many thanks. Good-bye now.

TESMAN (*accompanying him to the door*). Good-bye, Judge! You really must excuse me—

(BRACK *goes out by the hall door.*)

TESMAN (*pacing about the room*). Oh, Hedda—one should never go off and lose oneself in dreams, uh?

HEDDA (*looks at him and smiles*). Do *you* do *that*?

TESMAN. No use denying it. It was living in dreams to go and get married and set up house on nothing but expectations.

HEDDA. Perhaps you're right about that.

TESMAN. Well, at least we have our comfortable home, Hedda! The home that we always wanted. That we both fell in love with, I could almost say. Hm?

HEDDA (*rising slowly and wearily*). It was part of our bargain that we'd live in society—that we'd keep a great house—

TESMAN. Yes, of course—how I'd looked forward to that! Imagine—seeing you as a hostess—in our own select circle of friends! Yes, yes—well, for a while, we two will just have to get on by ourselves, Hedda. Perhaps have Aunt Julie here now and then. Oh, you—for you I wanted to have things so—so utterly different—!

HEDDA. Naturally this means I can't have a butler now.

TESMAN. Oh no—I'm sorry, a butler—we can't even talk about that, you know.

HEDDA. And the riding horse I was going to have—

TESMAN (*appalled*). Riding horse!

HEDDA. I suppose I can't think of that anymore.

TESMAN. Good Lord, no—that's obvious!

HEDDA (*crossing the room*). Well, at least I have one thing left to amuse myself with.

TESMAN (*beaming*). Ah, thank heaven for that! What is it, Hedda? Uh?

HEDDA (*in the center doorway, looking at him with veiled scorn*). My pistols, George.

TESMAN (*in fright*). Your pistols!

HEDDA (*her eyes cold*). General Gabler's pistols. (*She goes through the inner room and out to the left.*)

TESMAN (*runs to the center doorway and calls after her*). No, for heaven's sake, Hedda darling—don't touch those dangerous things! For my sake, Hedda! Uh?

⌁(ACT TWO)⌁

The rooms at the TESMANS', *same as in the first act, except that the piano has been moved out, and an elegant little writing table with a bookcase put in its place. A smaller table stands by the sofa to the left. Most of the flowers have been removed.* MRS. ELVSTED's *bouquet stands on the large table in the foreground. It is afternoon.*

HEDDA, *dressed to receive callers, is alone in the room. She stands by the open glass door, loading a revolver. The match to it lies in an open pistol case on the writing table.*

HEDDA (*looking down into the garden and calling*). Good to see you again, Judge!

BRACK (*heard from below, at a distance*). Likewise, Mrs. Tesman!

HEDDA (*raises the pistol and aims*). And now, Judge, I'm going to shoot you!

BRACK (*shouting from below*). No-no-no! Don't point that thing at me!

HEDDA. That's what comes of sneaking in the back way. (*She fires.*)

BRACK (*nearer*). Are you out of your mind—!

HEDDA. Oh, dear—I didn't hit you, did I?

BRACK (*still outside*). Just stop this nonsense!

HEDDA. All right, you can come in, Judge.

> (JUDGE BRACK, *dressed for a stag party, enters through the glass door. He carries a light overcoat on his arm.*)

BRACK. Good God! Are you still playing such games? What are you shooting at?

HEDDA. Oh, I was just shooting into the sky.

BRACK (*gently taking the pistol out of her hand*). Permit me. (*Looks at it.*) Ah, this one—I know it well. (*Glancing around.*) Where's the case? Ah, here. (*Puts the pistol away and shuts the case.*) We'll have no more of that kind of fun today.

HEDDA. Well, what in heaven's name do you want me to do with myself?

BRACK. You haven't had any visitors?

HEDDA (*closing the glass door*). Not a single one. All of our set are still in the country, I guess.

BRACK. And Tesman isn't home either?

HEDDA (*at the writing table, putting the pistol case away in a drawer*). No. Right after lunch he ran over to his aunts. He didn't expect you so soon.

BRACK. Hm— I should have realized. That was stupid of me.

HEDDA (*turning her head and looking at him*). Why stupid?

BRACK. Because in that case I would have stopped by a little bit—earlier.

HEDDA (*crossing the room*). Well, you'd have found no one here then at all. I've been up in my room dressing since lunch.

BRACK. And there's not the least little crack in the door we could have conferred through.

HEDDA. You forgot to arrange it.

BRACK. Also stupid of me.

HEDDA. Well, we'll just have to settle down here—and wait. Tesman won't be back for a while.

BRACK. Don't worry, I can be patient.

> (HEDDA *sits in the corner of the sofa.* BRACK *lays his coat over the back of the nearest chair and sits down, keeping his hat in his hand. A short pause. They look at each other.*)

HEDDA. Well?

BRACK (*in the same tone*). Well?

HEDDA. I spoke first.

BRACK (*leaning slightly forward*). Then let's have a nice little cozy chat, Mrs. Hedda.

HEDDA (*leaning further back on the sofa*). Doesn't it seem like a whole eternity since the last time we talked together? Oh, a few words last night and this morning—but they don't count.

BRACK. You mean, like this—between ourselves? Just the two of us?

HEDDA. Well, more or less.

BRACK. There wasn't a day that I didn't wish you were home again.

HEDDA. And I was wishing exactly the same.

BRACK. You? Really, Mrs. Hedda? And I thought you were having such a marvelous time on this trip.

HEDDA. Oh, you can imagine!

BRACK. But that's what Tesman always wrote.

HEDDA. Oh, him! There's nothing he likes better than grubbing around in libraries and copying out old parchments, or whatever you call them.

BRACK (*with a touch of malice*). But after all, it's his calling in life. In good part, anyway.

HEDDA. Yes, that's true. So there's nothing wrong with it— But what about *me*! Oh, Judge, you don't know— I've been so dreadfully bored.

BRACK (*sympathetically*). You really mean that? In all seriousness?

HEDDA. Well, you can understand—! To go for a whole six months without meeting a soul who knew the least bit about our circle. No one that one could talk to about our kind of things.

BRACK. Ah, yes— I think that would bother me too.

HEDDA. But then the most unbearable thing of all—

BRACK. What?

HEDDA. To be everlastingly together with—with one and the same person—

BRACK (*nodding in agreement*). Morning, noon, and night —yes. At every conceivable hour.

HEDDA. I said "everlastingly."

BRACK. All right. But with our good friend Tesman, I really should have thought—

HEDDA. My dear Judge, Tesman is—a specialist.

BRACK. Undeniably.

HEDDA. And specialists aren't at all amusing to travel with. Not in the long run, anyway.

BRACK. Not even—the specialist that one *loves*.

HEDDA. Ugh—don't use that syrupy word!

BRACK (*startled*). What's that, Mrs. Hedda!

HEDDA (*half laughing, half annoyed*). Well, just try it yourself! Try listening to the history of civilization morning, noon, and—

BRACK. Everlastingly.

HEDDA. Yes! Yes! And then all this business about domestic crafts in the Middle Ages—! That really is just too revolting!

BRACK (*looks searchingly at her*). But tell me—I can't see how it ever came about that—? Hm—

HEDDA. That George Tesman and I could make a match?

BRACK. All right, let's put it that way.

HEDDA. Good Lord, does it seem so remarkable?

BRACK. Well, yes—and no, Mrs. Hedda.

HEDDA. I really had danced myself out, Judge. My time was up. (*With a slight shudder.*) Ugh! No, I don't want to say that. Or think it, either.

BRACK. You certainly have no reason to.

HEDDA. Oh—reasons— (*Watching him carefully.*) And George Tesman—he is, after all, a thoroughly acceptable choice.

BRACK. Acceptable and dependable, beyond a doubt.

HEDDA. And I don't find anything especially ridiculous about him. Do you?

BRACK. Ridiculous? No-o-o, I wouldn't say that.

HEDDA. Hm. Anyway, he works incredibly hard on his research! There's every chance that, in time, he could still make a name for himself.

BRACK (*looking at her with some uncertainty*). I thought you believed, like everyone else, that he was going to be quite famous some day.

HEDDA (*wearily*). Yes, so I did. And then when he kept pressing and pleading to be allowed to take care of me—I didn't see why I ought to resist.

BRACK. No. From that point of view, of course not—

HEDDA. It was certainly more than my other admirers were willing to do for me, Judge.

BRACK (*laughing*). Well, I can't exactly answer for all the others. But as far as I'm concerned, you know that I've always cherished a—a certain respect for the marriage bond. Generally speaking, that is.

HEDDA (*bantering*). Oh, I never really held out any hopes for *you*.

BRACK. All I want is to have a warm circle of intimate friends, where I can be of use one way or another, with the freedom to come and go as—as a trusted friend—

HEDDA.   Of the man of the house, you mean?

BRACK (*with a bow*).   Frankly—I prefer the lady. But the man, too, of course, in his place. That kind of—let's say, triangular arrangement—you can't imagine how satisfying it can be all around.

HEDDA.   Yes, I must say I longed for some third person so many times on that trip. Oh—those endless tête-à-têtes in railway compartments—!

BRACK.   Fortunately the wedding trip's over now.

HEDDA (*shaking her head*).   The trip will go on—and on. I've only come to one stop on the line.

BRACK.   Well, then what you do is jump out—and stretch yourself a little, Mrs. Hedda.

HEDDA.   I'll never jump out.

BRACK.   Never?

HEDDA.   No. Because there's always someone on the platform who—

BRACK (*with a laugh*).   Who looks at your legs, is that it?

HEDDA.   Precisely.

BRACK.   Yes, but after all—

HEDDA (*with a disdainful gesture*).   I'm not interested. I'd rather keep my seat—right here, where I am. Tête-à-tête.

BRACK.   Well, but suppose a third person came on board and joined the couple.

HEDDA.   Ah! That's entirely different.

BRACK.   A trusted friend, who understands—

HEDDA.   And can talk about all kinds of lively things—

BRACK.   Who's not in the least a specialist.

HEDDA (*with an audible sigh*).   Yes, that would be a relief.

BRACK (*hearing the front door open and glancing toward it*). The triangle is complete.

HEDDA (*lowering her voice*).   And the train goes on.

> (GEORGE TESMAN, *in a gray walking suit and a soft felt hat, enters from the hall. He has a good number of unbound books under his arm and in his pockets.*)

TESMAN (*going up to the table by the corner settee*). Phew! Let me tell you, that's hot work—carrying all these. (*Setting the books down.*) I'm actually sweating, Hedda. And what's this—you're already here, Judge? Hm? Berta didn't tell me.

BRACK (*rising*). I came in through the garden.

HEDDA. What are all these books you've gotten?

TESMAN (*stands leafing through them*). They're new publications in my special field. I absolutely need them.

HEDDA. Your special field?

BRACK. Of course. Books in his special field, Mrs. Tesman.

(BRACK *and* HEDDA *exchange a knowing smile.*)

HEDDA. You need still more books in your special field?

TESMAN. Hedda, my dear, it's impossible ever to have too many. You have to keep up with what's written and published.

HEDDA. Oh, I suppose so.

TESMAN (*searching among the books*). And look—I picked up Eilert Løvborg's new book too. (*Offering it to her.*) Maybe you'd like to have a look at it? Uh?

HEDDA. No, thank you. Or—well, perhaps later.

TESMAN. I skimmed through some of it on the way home.

HEDDA. Well, what do you think of it—as a specialist?

TESMAN. I think it's amazing how well it holds up. He's never written like this before. (*Gathers up the books.*) But I'll take these into the study now. I can't wait to cut the pages—! And then I better dress up a bit. (*To* BRACK.) We don't have to rush right off, do we? Hm?

BRACK. No, not at all. There's ample time.

TESMAN. Ah, then I'll be at my leisure. (*Starts out with the books, but pauses and turns in the doorway.*) Oh, incidentally, Hedda—Aunt Julie won't be by to see you this evening.

HEDDA. She won't? I suppose it's that business with the hat?

TESMAN. Don't be silly. How can you think that of Aunt Julie? Imagine—! No, it's Auntie Rina—she's very ill.

HEDDA. She always is.

TESMAN. Yes, but today she really took a turn for the worse.

HEDDA. Well, then it's only right for her sister to stay with her. I'll have to bear with it.

TESMAN. But you can't imagine how delighted Aunt Julie was all the same—because you'd filled out so nicely on the trip!

HEDDA (*under her breath; rising*). Oh, these eternal aunts!

TESMAN. What?

HEDDA (*going over to the glass door*). Nothing.

TESMAN. All right, then. (*He goes through the inner room and out, right.*)

BRACK. What were you saying about a hat?

HEDDA. Oh, it's something that happened with Miss Tesman this morning. She'd put her hat down over there on the chair. (*Looks at him and smiles.*) And I pretended I thought it was the maid's.

BRACK (*shaking his head*). But my dear Mrs. Hedda, how could you do that! Hurt that fine old lady!

HEDDA (*nervously, pacing the room*). Well, it's—these things come over me, just like that, suddenly. And I can't hold back. (*Throws herself down in the armchair by the stove.*) Oh, I don't know myself how to explain it.

BRACK (*behind the armchair*). You're not really happy—that's the heart of it.

HEDDA (*gazing straight ahead*). And I don't know why I ought to be—happy. Or maybe you can tell me why?

BRACK. Yes—among other things, because you've gotten just the home you've always wanted.

HEDDA (*looks up at him and laughs*). You believe that story too?

BRACK. You mean there's nothing to it?

HEDDA. Oh yes—there's something to it.

BRACK. Well?

HEDDA. There's this much to it, that I used Tesman as my escort home from parties last summer—

BRACK. Unfortunately—I was going in another direction then.

HEDDA. How true. Yes, you had other directions to go last summer.

BRACK (*laughing*). For shame, Mrs. Hedda! Well—so you and Tesman—?

HEDDA. Yes, so one evening we walked by this place. And Tesman, poor thing, was writhing in torment, because he couldn't find anything to say. And I felt sorry for a man of such learning—

BRACK (*smiling skeptically*). Did you? Hm—

HEDDA. No, I honestly did. And so—just to help him off the hook—I came out with some rash remark about this lovely house being where I'd always wanted to live.

BRACK. No more than that?

HEDDA. No more that evening.

BRACK. But afterward?

HEDDA. Yes, my rashness had its consequences, Judge.

BRACK. I'm afraid our rashness all too often does, Mrs. Hedda.

HEDDA. Thanks! But don't you see, it was this passion for the old Falk mansion that drew George Tesman and me together! It was nothing more than that, that brought on our engagement and the marriage and the wedding trip and everything else. Oh yes, Judge—I was going to say, you make your bed and then you lie in it.

BRACK. But that's priceless! So actually you couldn't care less about all this?

HEDDA. God knows, not in the least.

BRACK. But even now? Now that we've made it somewhat comfortable for you here?

HEDDA. Ugh—all the rooms seem to smell of lavender and dried roses. But maybe that scent was brought in by Aunt Julie.

BRACK (*laughing*). No, I think it's a bequest from the late Mrs. Falk.

HEDDA. Yes, there's something in it of the odor of death. It's like a corsage—the day after the dance. (*Folds her hands behind her neck, leans back in her chair, and looks at him.*) Oh, my dear Judge—you can't imagine how horribly I'm going to bore myself here.

BRACK. But couldn't you find some goal in life to work toward? Others do, Mrs. Hedda.

HEDDA. A goal—that would really absorb me?

BRACK. Yes, preferably.

HEDDA. God only knows what that could be. I often wonder if— (*Breaks off.*) But that's impossible too.

BRACK. Who knows? Tell me.

HEDDA. I was thinking—if I could get Tesman to go into politics.

BRACK (*laughing*). Tesman! No, I can promise you—politics is absolutely out of his line.

HEDDA. No, I can believe you. But even so, I wonder if I could get him into it?

BRACK. Well, what satisfaction would you have in that, if he can't succeed? Why push him in that direction?

HEDDA. Because, I've told you, I'm bored! (*After a pause.*) Then you think it's really out of the question that he could ever be a cabinet minister?

BRACK. Hm—you see, Mrs. Hedda—to be anything like that, he'd have to be fairly wealthy to start with.

HEDDA (*rising impatiently*). Yes, there it is! It's this tight little world I've stumbled into— (*Crossing the room.*) That's what makes life so miserable! So utterly ludicrous! Because that's what it *is*.

BRACK. I'd say the fault lies elsewhere.

HEDDA. Where?

BRACK. You've never experienced anything that's really stirred you.

HEDDA. Anything serious, you mean.

BRACK. Well, you can call it that, if you like. But now perhaps it's on the way.

HEDDA (*tossing her head*). Oh, you mean all the fuss over that wretched professorship! But that's Tesman's problem. I'm not going to give it a single thought.

BRACK. No, that isn't—ah, never mind. But suppose you were to be confronted now by what—in rather elegant language—is called your most solemn responsibility. (*Smiling.*) A new responsibility, Mrs. Hedda.

HEDDA (*angrily*). Be quiet! You'll never see me like that!

BRACK (*delicately*). We'll discuss it again in a year's time —at the latest.

HEDDA (*curtly*). I have no talent for such things, Judge. I won't have responsibilities!

BRACK. Don't you think you've a talent for what almost every woman finds the most meaningful—

HEDDA (*over by the glass door*). Oh, I told you, be quiet! I often think I have talent for only one thing in life.

BRACK (*moving closer*). And what, may I ask, is that?

HEDDA (*stands looking out*). Boring myself to death. And that's the truth. (*Turns, looks toward the inner room, and laughs.*) See what I mean! Here comes the professor.

BRACK (*in a low tone of warning*). Ah-ah-ah, Mrs. Hedda!

> (GEORGE TESMAN, *dressed for the party, with hat and gloves in hand, enters from the right through the inner room.*)

TESMAN. Hedda—there's been no word from Eilert Løvborg, has there? Hm?

HEDDA. No.

TESMAN. Well, he's bound to be here soon then. You'll see.

BRACK. You really believe he'll come?

TESMAN. Yes, I'm almost positive of it. Because I'm sure they're nothing but rumors, what you told us this morning.

BRACK. Oh?

TESMAN. Yes. At least Aunt Julie said she couldn't for the world believe that he'd stand in my way again. Can you imagine that!

BRACK. So, then everything's well and good.

TESMAN (*putting his hat with the gloves inside on a chair to the right*). Yes, but I really would like to wait for him as long as possible.

BRACK. We have plenty of time for that. There's no one due at my place till seven or half past.

TESMAN. Why, then we can keep Hedda company for a while. And see what turns up. Uh?

HEDDA (*taking* BRACK's *hat and coat over to the settee*). And if worst comes to worst, Mr. Løvborg can sit and talk with me.

BRACK (*trying to take his things himself*). Ah, please, Mrs. Tesman—! What do you mean by "worst," in this case?

HEDDA. If he won't go with you and Tesman.

TESMAN (*looks doubtfully at her*). But Hedda dear—is it quite right that he stays with you here? Uh? Remember that Aunt Julie isn't coming.

HEDDA. No, but Mrs. Elvsted is. The three of us can have tea together.

TESMAN. Oh, well, that's all right.

BRACK (*smiling*). And that might be the soundest plan for him too.

HEDDA. Why?

BRACK. Well, really, Mrs. Tesman, you've made enough pointed remarks about my little bachelor parties. You've always said they're only fit for men of the strictest principles.

HEDDA. But Mr. Løvborg is surely a man of principle now. After all, a reformed sinner—

(BERTA *appears at the hall door.*)

BERTA. Ma'am, there's a gentleman here who'd like to see you—

HEDDA. Yes, show him in.

TESMAN (*softly*). I'm sure it's him! Just think!

> (EILERT LØVBORG *enters from the hall. He is lean and gaunt, the same age as* TESMAN, *but looks older and rather exhausted. His hair and beard are dark brown, his face long and pale, but with reddish patches over the cheekbones. He is dressed in a trim black suit, quite new, and holds dark gloves and a top hat in his hand. He hesitates by the door and bows abruptly. He seems somewhat embarrassed.*)

TESMAN (*crosses over and shakes his hand*). Ah, my dear Eilert—so at last we meet again!

EILERT LØVBORG (*speaking in a hushed voice*). Thanks for your letter, George! (*Approaching* HEDDA.) May I shake hands with you too, Mrs. Tesman?

HEDDA (*taking his hand*). So glad to see you, Mr. Løvborg. (*Gesturing with her hand.*) I don't know if you two gentlemen—?

LØVBORG (*bowing slightly*). Judge Brack, I believe.

BRACK (*reciprocating*). Of course. It's been some years—

TESMAN (*to* LØVBORG, *with his hands on his shoulders*). And now, Eilert, make yourself at home, completely! Right, Hedda? I hear you'll be settling down here in town again? Uh?

LØVBORG. I plan to.

TESMAN. Well, that makes sense. Listen—I just got hold of your new book. But I really haven't had time to read it yet.

LØVBORG. You can save yourself the bother.

TESMAN. Why? What do you mean?

LØVBORG. There's very little to it.

TESMAN. Imagine—you can say that!

BRACK. But it's won such high praise, I hear.

LØVBORG. That's exactly what I wanted. So I wrote a book that everyone could agree with.

BRACK. Very sound.

TESMAN. Yes, but my dear Eilert—!

LØVBORG. Because now I want to build up my position again—and try to make a fresh start.

TESMAN (*somewhat distressed*). Yes, that is what you want, I suppose. Uh?

LØVBORG (*smiling, puts down his hat and takes a thick manila envelope out of his pocket*). But when this comes out—George Tesman—you'll have to read it. Because this is the real book—the one that speaks for my true self.

TESMAN. Oh, really? What sort of book is that?

LØVBORG. It's the sequel.

TESMAN. Sequel? To what?

LØVBORG. To the book.

TESMAN. The one just out?

LØVBORG. Of course.

TESMAN. Yes, but my dear Eilert—that comes right down to our own time!

LØVBORG. Yes, it does. And this one deals with the future.

TESMAN. The future! But good Lord, there's nothing we know about that!

LØVBORG. True. But there are one or two things worth saying about it all the same. (*Opens the envelope.*) Here, take a look—

TESMAN. But that's not your handwriting.

LØVBORG. I dictated it. (*Paging through the manuscript.*) It's divided into two sections. The first is about the forces shaping the civilization of the future. And the second part, here—(*Paging further on.*) suggests what lines of development it's likely to take.

TESMAN. How extraordinary! It never would have occurred to me to write about anything like that.

HEDDA (*at the glass door, drumming on the pane*). Hm—no, of course not.

LØVBORG (*puts the manuscript back in the envelope and lays it on the table*). I brought it along because I thought I might read you a bit of it this evening.

TESMAN. Ah, that's very good of you, Eilert; but this evening— (*Glancing at* BRACK.) I'm really not sure that it's possible—

LØVBORG. Well, some other time, then. There's no hurry.

BRACK. I should explain, Mr. Løvborg—there's a little party at my place tonight. Mostly for Tesman, you understand.

LØVBORG (*looking for his hat*). Ah—then I won't stay—

BRACK. No, listen—won't you give me the pleasure of having you join us?

LØVBORG (*sharply and decisively*). No, I can't. Thanks very much.

BRACK. Oh, nonsense! Do that. We'll be a small, select group. And you can bet we'll have it "lively," as Mrs. Hed —Mrs. Tesman says.

LØVBORG. I don't doubt it. But nevertheless—

BRACK. You could bring your manuscript with you and read it to Tesman there, at my place. I have a spare room you could use.

TESMAN. Why, of course, Eilert—you could do that, couldn't you? Uh?

HEDDA (*intervening*). But dear, if Mr. Løvborg simply doesn't want to! I'm sure Mr. Løvborg would much prefer to settle down here and have supper with me.

LØVBORG (*looking at her*). With you, Mrs. Tesman!

HEDDA. And with Mrs. Elvsted.

LØVBORG. Ah. (*Casually.*) I saw her a moment this afternoon.

HEDDA. Oh, did you? Well, she'll be here soon. So it's almost essential for you to stay, Mr. Løvborg. Otherwise, she'll have no one to see her home.

LØVBORG. That's true. Yes, thank you, Mrs. Tesman— I'll be staying, then.

HEDDA. Then let me just tell the maid—

> (*She goes to the hall door and rings.* BERTA *enters.*
> HEDDA *talks to her quietly and points toward
> the inner room.* BERTA *nods and goes out again.*)

TESMAN (*at the same time, to* LØVBORG). Tell me, Eilert —is it this new material—about the future—that you're going to be lecturing on?

LØVBORG. Yes.

TESMAN. Because I heard at the bookstore that you'll be giving a lecture series here this autumn.

LØVBORG. I intend to. I hope you won't be offended, Tesman.

TESMAN. Why, of course not! But—?

LØVBORG. I can easily understand that it makes things rather difficult for you.

TESMAN (*dispiritedly*). Oh, I could hardly expect that for my sake you'd—

LØVBORG. But I'm going to wait till you have your appointment.

TESMAN. You'll wait! Yes, but—but—you're not competing for it, then? Uh?

LØVBORG. No. I only want to win in the eyes of the world.

TESMAN. But, my Lord—then Aunt Julie was right after all! Oh yes—I knew it all along! Hedda! Can you imagine— Eilert Løvborg won't stand in our way!

HEDDA (*brusquely*). Our way? Leave me out of it.

(*She goes up toward the inner room where* BERTA *is putting a tray with decanters and glasses on the table.* HEDDA *nods her approval and comes back again.* BERTA *goes out.*)

TESMAN (*at the same time*). But you, Judge—what do you say to all this? Uh?

BRACK. Well, I'd say that victory and honor—hm—after all, they're very sweet—

TESMAN. Yes, of course. But still—

HEDDA (*regarding* TESMAN *with a cold smile*). You look as if you'd been struck by lightning.

TESMAN. Yes—something like it—I guess—

BRACK. That's because a thunderstorm just passed over us, Mrs. Tesman.

HEDDA (*pointing toward the inner room*). Won't you gentlemen please help yourselves to a glass of cold punch?

BRACK (*looking at his watch*). A parting cup? That's not such a bad idea.

TESMAN. Marvelous, Hedda! Simply marvelous! The way I feel now, with this weight off my mind—

HEDDA. Please, Mr. Løvborg, you too,

LØVBORG (*with a gesture of refusal*). No, thank you. Not for me.

BRACK. Good Lord, cold punch—it isn't poison, you know.

LØVBORG. Perhaps not for everyone.

HEDDA. I'll keep Mr. Løvborg company a while.

TESMAN. All right, Hedda dear, you do that.

(*He and* BRACK *go into the inner room, sit down, drink punch, smoke cigarettes, and talk animatedly during the following.* LØVBORG *remains standing by the stove.* HEDDA *goes to the writing table.*)

HEDDA (*slightly raising her voice*). I can show you some photographs, if you like. Tesman and I traveled through the Tyrol on our way home.

(*She brings over an album and lays it on the table by the sofa, seating herself in the farthest corner.* EILERT LØVBORG *comes closer, stops and looks at her. Then he takes a chair and sits down on her left, his back toward the inner room.*)

HEDDA (*opening the album*). You see this view of the mountains, Mr. Løvborg. That's the Ortler group. Tesman's labeled them underneath. Here it is: "The Ortler group, near Meran."

LØVBORG (*whose eyes have never left her, speaking in a low, soft voice*). Hedda—Gabler!

HEDDA (*with a quick glance at him*). Ah! Shh!

LØVBORG (*repeating softly*). Hedda Gabler!

HEDDA (*looks at the album*). Yes, I used to be called that. In those days—when we two knew each other.

LØVBORG. And from now on—for the rest of my life—I have to teach myself not to say Hedda Gabler.

HEDDA (*turning the pages*). Yes, you have to. And I think you ought to start practicing it. The sooner the better, I'd say.

LØVBORG (*resentment in his voice*). Hedda Gabler married? And to George Tesman!

HEDDA. Yes—that's how it goes.

LØVBORG. Oh, Hedda, Hedda—how could you throw yourself away like that!

HEDDA (*looks at him sharply*). All right—no more of that!

LØVBORG. What do you mean?

(TESMAN *comes in and over to the sofa.*)

HEDDA (*hears him coming and says casually*). And this one, Mr. Løvborg, was taken from the Val d'Ampezzo. Just look at the peaks of those mountains. (*Looks warmly up at* TESMAN.) Now what were those marvelous mountains called, dear?

TESMAN. Let me see. Oh, those are the Dolomites.

HEDDA. Why, of course! Those are the Dolomites, Mr. Løvborg.

TESMAN. Hedda dear—I only wanted to ask if we shouldn't bring in some punch anyway. At least for you, hm?

HEDDA. Yes, thank you. And a couple of *petits fours*, please.

TESMAN. No cigarettes?

HEDDA. No.

TESMAN. Right.

(*He goes through the inner room and out to the
right.* BRACK *remains sitting inside, keeping his
eye from time to time on* HEDDA *and* LØVBORG.)

LØVBORG (*softly, as before*). Answer me, Hedda—how could you go and do such a thing?

HEDDA (*apparently immersed in the album*). If you keep on saying Hedda like that to me, I won't talk to you.

LØVBORG. Can't I say Hedda even when we're alone?

HEDDA. No. You can think it, but you mustn't say it like that.

LØVBORG. Ah, I understand. It offends your—love for George Tesman.

HEDDA (*glances at him and smiles*). Love? You *are* absurd!

LØVBORG. Then you don't love him!

HEDDA. I don't expect to be unfaithful, either. I'm not having any of that!

LØVBORG. Hedda, just answer me one thing—

HEDDA. Shh!

(TESMAN, *carrying a tray, enters from the inner
room.*)

TESMAN. Look out! Here come the goodies. (*He sets the tray on the table.*)

HEDDA. Why do you do the serving?

TESMAN (*filling the glasses*). Because I think it's such fun to wait on you, Hedda.

HEDDA. But now you've poured out two glasses. And you know Mr. Løvborg doesn't want—

TESMAN. Well, but Mrs. Elvsted will be along soon.

HEDDA. Yes, that's right—Mrs. Elvsted—

TESMAN. Had you forgotten her? Uh?

HEDDA. We've been so caught up in these. (*Showing him a picture.*) Do you remember this little village?

TESMAN. Oh, that's the one just below the Brenner Pass! It was there that we stayed overnight—

HEDDA. And met all those lively summer people.

TESMAN. Yes, that's the place. Just think—if we could have had *you* with us, Eilert! My! (*He goes back and sits beside* BRACK.)

LØVBORG. Answer me just one thing, Hedda—

HEDDA. Yes?

LØVBORG. Was there no love with respect to me, either? Not a spark—not one glimmer of love at all?

HEDDA. I wonder, really, was there? To me it was as if we were two true companions—two very close friends. (*Smiling.*) You, especially, were so open with me.

LØVBORG. You wanted it that way.

HEDDA. When I look back on it now, there was really something beautiful and fascinating—and daring, it seems to me, about—about our secret closeness—our companionship that no one, not a soul, suspected.

LØVBORG. Yes, Hedda, that's true! Wasn't there? When I'd come over to your father's in the afternoon—and the general sat by the window reading his papers—with his back to us—

HEDDA. And we'd sit on the corner sofa—

LØVBORG. Always with the same illustrated magazine in front of us—

HEDDA. Yes, for the lack of an album.

LØVBORG. Yes, Hedda—and the confessions I used to make—telling you things about myself that no one else knew of then. About the way I'd go out, the drinking, the madness that went on day and night, for days at a time. Ah, what power was it in you, Hedda, that made me tell you such things?

HEDDA. You think it was some kind of power in me?

LØVBORG. How else can I explain it? And all those— those devious questions you asked me—

HEDDA. That you understood so remarkably well—

LØVBORG. To think you could sit there and ask such questions! So boldly.

HEDDA. Deviously, please.

LØVBORG. Yes, but boldly, all the same. Interrogating me about—all that kind of thing!

HEDDA. And to think you could answer, Mr. Løvborg.

LØVBORG. Yes, that's exactly what I don't understand— now, looking back. But tell me, Hedda—the root of that bond between us, wasn't it love? Didn't you feel, on your part, as if you wanted to cleanse and absolve me—when I brought those confessions to you? Wasn't that it?

HEDDA. No, not quite.

LØVBORG. What was your power, then?

HEDDA. Do you find it so very surprising that a young girl—if there's no chance of anyone knowing—

LØVBORG. Yes?

HEDDA. That she'd like some glimpse of a world that—

LØVBORG. That—?

HEDDA. That she's forbidden to know anything about.

LØVBORG. So that was it?

HEDDA. Partly. Partly that, I guess.

LØVBORG. Companionship in a thirst for life. But why, then, couldn't it have gone on?

HEDDA. But that was your fault.

LØVBORG. You broke it off.

HEDDA. Yes, when that closeness of ours threatened to grow more serious. Shame on you, Eilert Løvborg! How could you violate my trust when I'd been so—so bold with my friendship?

LØVBORG (clenching his fists). Oh, why didn't you do what you said! Why didn't you shoot me down!

HEDDA. I'm—much too afraid of scandal.

LØVBORG. Yes, Hedda, you're a coward at heart.

HEDDA. A terrible coward. (Changing her tone.) But that

was lucky for you. And now you're so nicely consoled at the Elvsteds'.

LØVBORG. I know what Thea's been telling you.

HEDDA. And perhaps you've been telling her all about us?

LØVBORG. Not a word. She's too stupid for that sort of thing.

HEDDA. Stupid?

LØVBORG. When it comes to those things, she's stupid.

HEDDA. And I'm a coward. (*Leans closer, without looking him in the eyes, and speaks softly*). But there *is* something now that I can tell you.

LØVBORG (*intently*). What?

HEDDA. When I didn't dare shoot you—

LØVBORG. Yes?

HEDDA. That wasn't my worst cowardice—that night.

LØVBORG (*looks at her a moment, understands, and whispers passionately*). Oh, Hedda! Hedda Gabler! Now I begin to see it, the hidden reason why we've been so close! You and I—! It was the hunger for *life* in you—

HEDDA (*quietly, with a sharp glance*). Careful! That's no way to think!

> (*It has begun to grow dark. The hall door is opened from without by* BERTA.)

HEDDA (*clapping the album shut and calling out with a smile*). Well, at last! Thea dear—please come in!

> (MRS. ELVSTED *enters from the hall. She is in evening dress. The door is closed behind her.*)

HEDDA (*on the sofa, stretching her arms out toward her*). Thea, my sweet—I thought you were never coming!

> (*In passing,* MRS. ELVSTED *exchanges light greetings with the gentlemen in the inner room, then comes over to the table and extends her hand to* HEDDA. LØVBORG *has gotten up. He and* MRS. ELVSTED *greet each other with a silent nod.*)

MRS. ELVSTED. Perhaps I ought to go in and talk a bit with your husband?

HEDDA. Oh, nonsense. Let them be. They're leaving soon.

MRS. ELVSTED. They're leaving?

HEDDA. Yes, for a drinking party.

MRS. ELVSTED (*quickly, to* LØVBORG). But you're not?

LØVBORG. No.

HEDDA. Mr. Løvborg—is staying with us.

MRS. ELVSTED (*taking a chair, about to sit down beside him*). Oh, it's so good to be here!

HEDDA. No, no, Thea dear! Not there! You have to come over here by me. I want to be in the middle.

MRS. ELVSTED. Any way you please.

(*She goes around the table and sits on the sofa to* HEDDA's *right.* LØVBORG *resumes his seat.*)

LØVBORG (*after a brief pause, to* HEDDA). Isn't she lovely to look at?

HEDDA (*lightly stroking her hair*). Only to look at?

LØVBORG. Yes. Because we two—she and I—we really *are* true companions. We trust each other completely. We can talk things out together without any reservations—

HEDDA. Never anything devious, Mr. Løvborg?

LØVBORG. Well—

MRS. ELVSTED (*quietly, leaning close to* HEDDA). Oh, Hedda, you don't know how happy I am! Just think—he says that I've inspired him.

HEDDA (*regarding her with a smile*). Really, dear; did he say that?

LØVBORG. And then the courage she has, Mrs. Tesman, when it's put to the test.

MRS. ELVSTED. Good heavens, me! Courage!

LØVBORG. Enormous courage—where I'm concerned.

HEDDA. Yes, courage—yes! If one only had that.

LØVBORG. Then what?

HEDDA. Then life might still be bearable. (*Suddenly changing her tone.*) But now, Thea dearest—you really must have a nice cold glass of punch.

MRS. ELVSTED. No, thank you. I never drink that sort of thing.

HEDDA. Well, then you, Mr. Løvborg.

LØVBORG. Thanks, not for me either.

MRS. ELVSTED. No, not for him either!

HEDDA (*looking intently at him*). But if I insist?

LØVBORG. Makes no difference.

HEDDA (*with a laugh*). Poor me, then I have no power over you at all?

LØVBORG. Not in that area.

HEDDA. But seriously, I think you ought to, all the same. For your own sake.

MRS. ELVSTED. But Hedda—!

LØVBORG. Why do you think so?

HEDDA. Or, to be more exact, for others' sakes.

LØVBORG. Oh?

HEDDA. Otherwise, people might get the idea that you're not very bold at heart. That you're not really sure of yourself at all.

MRS. ELVSTED (*softly*). Oh, Hedda, don't—!

LØVBORG. People can think whatever they like, for all I care.

MRS. ELVSTED (*happily*). Yes, that's right!

HEDDA. I saw it so clearly in Judge Brack a moment ago.

LØVBORG. What did you see?

HEDDA. The contempt in his smile when you didn't dare join them for a drink.

LØVBORG. Didn't dare! Obviously I'd rather stay here and talk with you.

MRS. ELVSTED. That's only reasonable, Hedda.

HEDDA. But how could the judge know that? And besides, I noticed him smile and glance at Tesman when you couldn't bring yourself to go to their wretched little party.

LØVBORG. Couldn't! Are you saying I couldn't?

HEDDA. *I'm* not. But that's the way Judge Brack sees it.

LØVBORG. All right, let him.

HEDDA. Then you won't go along?

LØVBORG. I'm staying here with you and Thea.

MRS. ELVSTED. Yes, Hedda—you can be sure he is!

HEDDA (*smiles and nods approvingly at* LØVBORG). I see. Firm as a rock. True to principle, to the end of time. There, that's what a man ought to be! (*Turning to* MRS. ELVSTED *and patting her.*) Well, now, didn't I tell you that, when you came here so distraught this morning—

LØVBORG (*surprised*). Distraught?

MRS. ELVSTED (*terrified*). Hedda—! But Hedda—!

HEDDA. Can't you see for yourself? There's no need at

all for your going around so deathly afraid that— (*Changing her tone.*) There! Now we can all enjoy ourselves!

LØVBORG (*shaken*). What is all this, Mrs. Tesman?

MRS. ELVSTED. Oh, God, oh, God, Hedda! What are you saying! What are you doing!

HEDDA. Not so loud. That disgusting judge is watching you.

LØVBORG. So deathly afraid? For my sake?

MRS. ELVSTED (*in a low moan*). Oh, Hedda, you've made me so miserable!

LØVBORG (*looks intently at her a moment, his face drawn*). So that's how completely you trusted me.

MRS. ELVSTED (*imploringly*). Oh, my dearest—if you'll only listen—!

LØVBORG (*takes one of the glasses of punch, raises it, and says in a low, hoarse voice*). Your health, Thea! (*He empties the glass, puts it down, and takes the other.*)

MRS. ELVSTED (*softly*). Oh, Hedda, Hedda—how could you want such a thing!

HEDDA. Want it? I? Are you crazy?

LØVBORG. And your health too, Mrs. Tesman. Thanks for the truth. Long live truth! (*Drains the glass and starts to refill it.*)

HEDDA (*laying her hand on his arm*). All right—no more for now. Remember, you're going to a party.

MRS. ELVSTED. No, no, no!

HEDDA. Shh! They're watching you.

LØVBORG (*putting down his glass*). Now, Thea—tell me honestly—

MRS. ELVSTED. Yes!

LØVBORG. Did your husband know that you followed me?

MRS. ELVSTED (*wringing her hands*). Oh, Hedda—listen to him!

LØVBORG. Did you have it arranged, you and he, that you should come down into town and spy on me? Or maybe he got you to do it himself? Ah, yes—I'm sure he needed me back in the office! Or maybe he missed my hand at cards?

MRS. ELVSTED (*softly, in anguish*). Oh, Eilert, Eilert—!

LØVBORG (*seizing his glass to fill it*). Skoal to the old sheriff, too!

HEDDA (*stopping him*). That's enough. Don't forget, you're giving a reading for Tesman.

LØVBORG (*calmly, setting down his glass*). That was stupid of me, Thea. I mean, taking it like this. Don't be angry at me, my dearest. You'll see—you and all the others —that if I stumbled and fell—I'm back on my feet again now! With your help, Thea.

MRS. ELVSTED (*radiant with joy*). Oh, thank God—!

> (BRACK, *in the meantime, has looked at his watch. He and* TESMAN *stand up and enter the drawing room.*)

BRACK (*takes his hat and overcoat*). Well, Mrs. Tesman, our time is up.

HEDDA. I suppose it is.

LØVBORG (*rising*). Mine too, Judge.

MRS. ELVSTED (*softly pleading*). Oh, Eilert—don't!

HEDDA (*pinching her arm*). They can hear you!

MRS. ELVSTED (*with a small cry*). Ow!

LØVBORG (*to* BRACK). You were kind enough to ask me along.

BRACK. Oh, then you *are* coming, after all?

LØVBORG. Yes, thank you.

BRACK. I'm delighted—

LØVBORG (*putting the manila envelope in his pocket, to* TESMAN). I'd like to show you one or two things before I turn this in.

TESMAN. Just think—how exciting! But Hedda dear, how will Mrs. Elvsted get home? Uh?

HEDDA. Oh, we'll hit on something.

LØVBORG (*glancing toward the ladies*). Mrs. Elvsted? Don't worry, I'll stop back and fetch her. (*Coming nearer.*) Say about ten o'clock, Mrs. Tesman? Will that do?

HEDDA. Yes. That will do very nicely.

TESMAN. Well, then everything's all set. But you mustn't expect *me* that early, Hedda.

HEDDA. Dear, you stay as long—just as long as you like.

MRS. ELVSTED (*with suppressed anxiety*). Mr. Løvborg —I'll be waiting here till you come.

LØVBORG (*his hat in his hand*). Yes, I understand.

BRACK. So, gentlemen—the excursion train is leaving! I hope it's going to be lively, as a certain fair lady puts it.

HEDDA. Ah, if only that fair lady could be there, invisible—!

BRACK. Why invisible?

HEDDA. To hear a little of your unadulterated liveliness, Judge.

BRACK (*laughs*). I wouldn't advise the fair lady to try.

TESMAN (*also laughing*). Hedda, you are the limit! What an idea!

BRACK. Well, good night. Good night, ladies.

LØVBORG (*bowing*). About ten o'clock, then.

> (BRACK, LØVBORG, *and* TESMAN *go out the hall door. At the same time,* BERTA *enters from the inner room with a lighted lamp, which she sets on the drawing room table, then goes out the same way.*)

MRS. ELVSTED (*having risen, moving restlessly about the room*). Hedda—Hedda—what's going to come of all this?

HEDDA. At ten o'clock—he'll be here. I can see him now —with vine leaves in his hair—fiery and bold—

MRS. ELVSTED. Oh, how good that would be!

HEDDA. And then, you'll see—he'll be back in control of himself. He'll be a free man, then, for the rest of his days.

MRS. ELVSTED. Oh, God—if only he comes as you see him now!

HEDDA. He'll come back like that, and no other way! (*Gets up and goes closer.*) Go on and doubt him as much as you like. *I* believe in him. And now we'll find out—

MRS. ELVSTED. There's something behind what you're doing, Hedda.

HEDDA. Yes, there is. For once in my life, I want to have power over a human being.

MRS. ELVSTED. But don't you have that?

HEDDA. I don't have it. I've never had it.

MRS. ELVSTED. Not with your husband?

HEDDA. Yes, what a bargain *that* was! Oh, if you only could understand how poor I am. And you're allowed to be so rich! (*Passionately throws her arms about her.*) I think I'll burn your hair off, after all!

MRS. ELVSTED. Let go! Let me go! I'm afraid of you, Hedda!

BERTA (*in the doorway to the inner room*).   Supper's waiting in the dining room, ma'am.

HEDDA.   All right, we're coming.

MRS. ELVSTED.   No, no, no! I'd rather go home alone! Right away—now!

HEDDA.   Nonsense! First you're going to have tea, you little fool. And then—ten o'clock—Eilert Løvborg comes—with vine leaves in his hair.

> (*She drags* MRS. ELVSTED, *almost by force, toward the doorway.*)

⎯⟨ ACT THREE ⟩⎯

The same rooms at the TESMANS'. *The curtains are down across the doorway to the inner room, and also across the glass door. The lamp, shaded and turned down low, is burning on the table. The door to the stove stands open; the fire has nearly gone out.*

MRS. ELVSTED, *wrapped in a large shawl, with her feet up on a footstool, lies back in the armchair close by the stove.* HEDDA, *fully dressed, is asleep on the sofa, with a blanket over her. After a pause,* MRS. ELVSTED *suddenly sits straight up in the chair, listening tensely. Then she sinks wearily back again.*

MRS. ELVSTED (*in a low moan*). Not yet—oh, God—oh, God—not yet!

(BERTA *slips in cautiously by the hall door. She holds a letter in her hand.*)

MRS. ELVSTED (*turns and whispers anxiously*). Yes? Has anyone come?

BERTA (*softly*). Yes, a girl just now stopped by with this letter.

MRS. ELVSTED (*quickly, reaching out her hand*). A letter! Give it to me!

BERTA. No, it's for the Doctor, ma'am.

MRS. ELVSTED. Oh.

BERTA. It was Miss Tesman's maid that brought it. I'll leave it here on the table.

MRS. ELVSTED. Yes, do.

BERTA (*putting the letter down*). I think I'd best put out the lamp. It's smoking.

MRS. ELVSTED. Yes, put it out. It'll be daylight soon.

BERTA (*does so*). It's broad daylight already, ma'am.

MRS. ELVSTED. It's daylight! And still no one's come—!

BERTA. Oh, mercy—I knew it would go like this.

MRS. ELVSTED. You knew?

BERTA. Yes, when I saw that a certain gentleman was back here in town—and that he went off with them. We've heard plenty about that gentleman over the years.

MRS. ELVSTED. Don't talk so loud. You'll wake Mrs. Tesman.

BERTA (*looks toward the sofa and sighs*). Goodness me— yes, let her sleep, poor thing. Should I put a bit more on the fire?

MRS. ELVSTED. Thanks, not for me.

BERTA. All right. (*She goes quietly out the hall door.*)

HEDDA (*wakes as the door shuts and looks up*). What's that?

MRS. ELVSTED. It was just the maid—

HEDDA (*glancing about*). In here—? Oh yes, I remember now. (*Sits up on the sofa, stretches, and rubs her eyes.*) What time is it, Thea?

MRS. ELVSTED (*looking at her watch*). It's after seven.

HEDDA. When did Tesman get in?

MRS. ELVSTED. He isn't back.

HEDDA. Not back yet?

MRS. ELVSTED (*getting up*). No one's come in.

HEDDA. And we sat here and waited up for them till four o'clock—

MRS. ELVSTED (*wringing her hands*). And *how* I've waited for him!

HEDDA (*yawns, and speaks with her hand in front of her mouth*). Oh, dear—we could have saved ourselves the trouble.

MRS. ELVSTED. Did you get any sleep?

HEDDA. Oh yes. I slept quite well, I think. Didn't you?

MRS. ELVSTED. No, not at all. I couldn't, Hedda! It was just impossible.

HEDDA (*rising and going toward her*). There, there, now! There's nothing to worry about. It's not hard to guess what happened.

MRS. ELVSTED. Oh, what? Tell me!

HEDDA. Well, it's clear that the party must have gone on till all hours—

MRS. ELVSTED. Oh, Lord, yes—it must have. But even so—

HEDDA. And then, of course, Tesman didn't want to come home and make a commotion in the middle of the night.

(*Laughs.*) Probably didn't care to show himself, either—so full of his party spirits.

MRS. ELVSTED. But where else could he have gone?

HEDDA. He must have gone up to his aunts' to sleep. They keep his old room ready.

MRS. ELVSTED. No, he can't be with them. Because he just now got a letter from Miss Tesman. It's over there.

HEDDA. Oh? (*Looking at the address.*) Yes, that's Aunt Julie's handwriting, all right. Well, then he must have stayed over at Judge Brack's. And Eilert Løvborg—he's sitting with vine leaves in his hair, reading away.

MRS. ELVSTED. Oh, Hedda, you say these things, and you really don't believe them at all.

HEDDA. You're such a little fool, Thea.

MRS. ELVSTED. That's true; I guess I am.

HEDDA. And you really look dead tired.

MRS. ELVSTED. Yes, I feel dead tired.

HEDDA. Well, you just do as I say, then. Go in my room and stretch out on the bed for a while.

MRS. ELVSTED. No, no—I still wouldn't get any sleep.

HEDDA. Why, of course you would.

MRS. ELVSTED. Well, but your husband's sure to be home now soon. And I've got to know right away—

HEDDA. I'll call you the moment he comes.

MRS. ELVSTED. Yes? Promise me, Hedda?

HEDDA. You can count on it. Just go and get some sleep.

MRS. ELVSTED. Thanks. I'll try. (*She goes out through the inner room.*)

> (HEDDA *goes over to the glass door and draws the curtains back. Bright daylight streams into the room. She goes over to the writing table, takes out a small hand mirror, regards herself and arranges her hair. She then goes to the hall door and presses the bell. After a moment,* BERTA *enters.*)

BERTA. Did you want something, ma'am?

HEDDA. Yes, you can build up the fire. I'm freezing in here.

BERTA. Why, my goodness—we'll have it warm in no time. (*She rakes the embers together and puts some wood on, then stops and listens.*) There's the front doorbell, ma'am.

HEDDA. Go see who it is. I'll take care of the stove.

BERTA. It'll be burning soon. (*She goes out the hall door.*)

> (HEDDA *kneels on the footstool and lays more wood on the fire. After a moment,* GEORGE TESMAN *comes in from the hall. He looks tired and rather serious. He tiptoes toward the doorway to the inner room and is about to slip through the curtains.*)

HEDDA (*at the stove, without looking up*). Good morning.

TESMAN (*turns*). Hedda! (*Approaching her.*) But what on earth—! You're up so early? Uh?

HEDDA. Yes, I'm up quite early today.

TESMAN. And I was so sure you were still in bed sleeping. Isn't that something, Hedda!

HEDDA. Not so loud. Mrs. Elvsted's resting in my room.

TESMAN. Was Mrs. Elvsted here all night?

HEDDA. Well, no one returned to take her home.

TESMAN. No, I guess that's right.

HEDDA (*shuts the door to the stove and gets up*). So—did you enjoy your party?

TESMAN. Were you worried about me? Hm?

HEDDA. No, that never occurred to me. I just asked if you'd had a good time.

TESMAN. Oh yes, I really did, for once. But more at the beginning, I'd say—when Eilert read to me out of his book. We got there more than an hour too soon—imagine! And Brack had so much to get ready. But then Eilert read to me.

HEDDA (*sitting at the right-hand side of the table*). Well? Tell me about it—

TESMAN (*sitting on a footstool by the stove*). Really, Hedda—you can't imagine what a book that's going to be! I do believe it's one of the most remarkable things ever written. Just think!

HEDDA. Yes, I don't mean the book—

TESMAN. But I have to make a confession, Hedda. When he'd finished reading—I had such a nasty feeling—

HEDDA. Nasty?

TESMAN. I found myself envying Eilert, that he was able to write such a book. Can you imagine, Hedda!

HEDDA. Oh yes, I can imagine!

TESMAN. And then how sad to see—that with all his gifts—he's still quite irreclaimable.

HEDDA. Don't you mean that he has more courage to live than the others?

TESMAN. Good Lord, no—I mean, he simply can't take his pleasures in moderation.

HEDDA. Well, what happened then—at the end?

TESMAN. I suppose I'd have to say it turned into an orgy, Hedda.

HEDDA. Were there vine leaves in his hair?

TESMAN. Vine leaves? Not that I noticed. But he gave a long, muddled speech in honor of the woman who'd inspired his work. Yes, that was his phrase for it.

HEDDA. Did he give her name?

TESMAN. No, he didn't. But it seems to me it has to be Mrs. Elvsted. Wait and see!

HEDDA. Oh? Where did you leave him?

TESMAN. On the way here. We broke up—the last of us —all together. And Brack came along with us too, to get a little fresh air. And then we did want to make sure that Eilert got home safe. Because he really had a load on, you know.

HEDDA. He must have.

TESMAN. But here's the curious part of it, Hedda. Or perhaps I should say, the distressing part. Oh, I'm almost ashamed to speak of it—for Eilert's sake—

HEDDA. Yes, go on—

TESMAN. Well, as we were walking toward town, you see, I happened to drop back a little behind the others. Only for a minute or two—you follow me?

HEDDA. Yes, yes, so—?

TESMAN. And then when I was catching up with the rest of them, what do you think I found on the sidewalk? Uh?

HEDDA. Oh, how should I know!

TESMAN. You mustn't breathe a word to anyone, Hedda— you hear me? Promise me that, for Eilert's sake. (*Takes a manila envelope out of his coat pocket.*) Just think—I found this.

HEDDA. Isn't that what he had with him yesterday?

TESMAN. That's right. It's the whole of his precious, irreplaceable manuscript. And he went and lost it—without even noticing. Can you imagine, Hedda! How distressing—

HEDDA.　But why didn't you give it right back to him?

TESMAN.　No, I didn't dare do that—in the state he was in—

HEDDA.　And you didn't tell any of the others you'd found it?

TESMAN.　Of course not. I'd never do that, you know—for Eilert's sake.

HEDDA.　Then there's no one who knows you have Eilert Løvborg's manuscript?

TESMAN.　No. And no one must ever know, either.

HEDDA.　What did you say to him afterwards?

TESMAN.　I had no chance at all to speak with him. As soon as we reached the edge of town, he and a couple of others got away from us and disappeared. Imagine!

HEDDA.　Oh? I expect they saw him home.

TESMAN.　Yes, they probably did, I suppose. And also Brack went home.

HEDDA.　And where've you been carrying on since then?

TESMAN.　Well, I and some of the others—we were invited up by one of the fellows and had morning coffee at his place. Or a post-midnight snack, maybe—uh? But as soon as I've had a little rest—and given poor Eilert time to sleep it off, then I've got to take this back to him.

HEDDA (*reaching out for the envelope*).　No—don't give it back! Not yet, I mean. Let me read it first.

TESMAN.　Hedda dearest, no. My Lord, I can't do that.

HEDDA.　You can't?

TESMAN.　No. Why, you can just imagine the anguish he'll feel when he wakes up and misses the manuscript. He hasn't any copy of it, you know. He told me that himself.

HEDDA (*looks searchingly at him*).　Can't such a work be rewritten? I mean, over again?

TESMAN.　Oh, I don't see how it could. Because the inspiration, you know—

HEDDA.　Yes, yes—that's the thing, I suppose. (*Casually.*) Oh, by the way—there's a letter for you.

TESMAN.　No, really—?

HEDDA (*handing it to him*).　It came early this morning.

TESMAN.　Dear, from Aunt Julie! What could that be? (*Sets the envelope on the other taboret, opens the letter, skims through it, and springs to his feet.*) Oh, Hedda—she says poor Auntie Rina's dying!

HEDDA. It's no more than we've been expecting.

TESMAN. And if I want to see her one last time, I've got to hurry. I'll have to hop right over.

HEDDA (*suppressing a smile*). Hop?

TESMAN. Oh, Hedda dearest, if you could only bring yourself to come with me! Think of it!

HEDDA (*rises and dismisses the thought wearily*). No, no, don't ask me to do such things. I don't want to look on sickness and death. I want to be free of everything ugly.

TESMAN. Yes, all right, then— (*Dashing about.*) My hat—? My overcoat—? Oh, in the hall— I do hope I'm not there too late, Hedda! Hm?

HEDDA. Oh, if you hurry—

(BERTA *appears at the hall door.*)

BERTA. Judge Brack's outside, asking if he might stop in.

TESMAN. At a time like this! No, I can't possibly see him now.

HEDDA. But I can. (*To* BERTA.) Ask the judge to come in.

(BERTA *goes out.*)

HEDDA (*quickly, in a whisper*). Tesman, the manuscript! (*She snatches it from the taboret.*)

TESMAN. Yes, give it here!

HEDDA. No, no, I'll keep it till you're back.

(*She moves over to the writing table and slips it in the bookcase.* TESMAN *stands flustered, unable to get his gloves on.* BRACK *enters from the hall.*)

HEDDA. Well, aren't you the early bird.

BRACK. Yes, wouldn't you say so? (*To* TESMAN.) Are you off and away too?

TESMAN. Yes, I absolutely have to get over to my aunts'. Just think—the invalid one, she's dying.

BRACK. Good Lord, she is? But then you mustn't let me detain you. Not at a moment like this—

TESMAN. Yes, I really must run— Good-bye! Good-bye! (*He goes hurriedly out the hall door.*)

HEDDA. It would seem you had quite a time of it last night, Judge.

BRACK. I've not been out of my clothes yet, Mrs. Hedda.

HEDDA. Not you, either?

BRACK. No, as you can see. But what's Tesman been telling you about our night's adventures?

HEDDA. Oh, some tedious tale. Something about stopping up somewhere for coffee.

BRACK. Yes, I know all about the coffee party. Eilert Løvborg wasn't with them, I expect?

HEDDA. No, they'd already taken him home.

BRACK. Tesman, as well.

HEDDA. No, but he said some others had.

BRACK (*smiles*). George Tesman is really a simple soul, Mrs. Hedda.

HEDDA. God knows he's that. But was there something else that went on?

BRACK. Oh, you might say so.

HEDDA. Well, now! Let's sit down, Judge; you'll talk more easily then.

(*She sits at the left-hand side of the table, with* BRACK *at the long side, near her.*)

HEDDA. So?

BRACK. I had particular reasons for keeping track of my guests—or, I should say, certain of my guests, last night.

HEDDA. And among them Eilert Løvborg, perhaps?

BRACK. To be frank—yes.

HEDDA. Now you really have me curious—

BRACK. You know where he and a couple of the others spent the rest of the night, Mrs. Hedda?

HEDDA. Tell me—if it's fit to be told.

BRACK. Oh, it's very much fit to be told. Well, it seems they showed up at a quite animated soiree.

HEDDA. Of the lively sort.

BRACK. Of the liveliest.

HEDDA. Do go on, Judge—

BRACK. Løvborg, and the others also, had advance invitations. I knew all about it. But Løvborg had begged off, because now, of course, he was supposed to have become a new man, as you know.

HEDDA. Up at the Elvsteds', yes. But he went anyway?

BRACK. Well, you see, Mrs. Hedda—unfortunately the spirit moved him up at my place last evening—

HEDDA. Yes, I hear that he *was* inspired there.

BRACK. To a very powerful degree, I'd say. Well, so his mind turned to other things, that's clear. We males, sad to say—we're not always so true to principle as we ought to be.

HEDDA. Oh, I'm sure you're an exception, Judge. But what about Løvborg—?

BRACK. Well, to cut it short—the result was that he wound up in Mademoiselle Diana's parlors.

HEDDA. Mademoiselle Diana's?

BRACK. It was Mademoiselle Diana who was holding the soiree. For a select circle of lady friends and admirers.

HEDDA. Is she a redhaired woman?

BRACK. Precisely.

HEDDA. Sort of a—singer?

BRACK. Oh yes—she's that too. And also a mighty huntress—of men, Mrs. Hedda. You've undoubtedly heard about her. Løvborg was one of her ruling favorites—back there in his palmy days.

HEDDA. And how did all this end?

BRACK. Less amicably, it seems. She gave him a most tender welcoming, with open arms, but before long she'd taken to fists.

HEDDA. Against Løvborg?

BRACK. That's right. He accused her or her friends of having robbed him. He claimed that his wallet was missing —along with some other things. In short, he must have made a frightful scene.

HEDDA. And what did it come to?

BRACK. It came to a regular free-for-all, the men and the women both. Luckily the police finally got there.

HEDDA. The police too?

BRACK. Yes. But it's likely to prove an expensive little romp for Eilert Løvborg. That crazy fool.

HEDDA. So?

BRACK. He apparently made violent resistance. Struck one of the officers on the side of the head and ripped his coat. So they took him along to the station house.

HEDDA. Where did you hear all this?

BRACK. From the police themselves.

HEDDA (*gazing straight ahead*). So that's how it went. Then he had no vine leaves in his hair.

BRACK. Vine leaves, Mrs. Hedda?

HEDDA (*changing her tone*). But tell me, Judge—just why do you go around like this, spying on Eilert Løvborg?

BRACK. In the first place, it's hardly a matter of no concern to me, if it's brought out during the investigation that he'd come direct from my house.

HEDDA. There'll be an investigation—?

BRACK. Naturally. Anyway, that takes care of itself. But I felt that as a friend of the family I owed you and Tesman a full account of his nocturnal exploits.

HEDDA. Why, exactly?

BRACK. Well, because I have a strong suspicion that he'll try to use you as a kind of screen.

HEDDA. Oh, how could you ever think such a thing!

BRACK. Good Lord—we're really not blind, Mrs. Hedda. You'll see! This Mrs. Elvsted, she won't be going home now so quickly.

HEDDA. Well, even supposing there were something between them, there are plenty of other places where they could meet.

BRACK. Not one single home. From now on, every decent house will be closed to Eilert Løvborg.

HEDDA. So mine ought to be too, is that what you mean?

BRACK. Yes. I'll admit I'd find it more than annoying if that gentleman were to have free access here. If he came like an intruder, an irrelevancy, forcing his way into—

HEDDA. Into the triangle?

BRACK. Precisely. It would almost be like turning me out of my home.

HEDDA (*looks at him with a smile*). I see. The one cock of the walk—that's what you want to be.

BRACK (*nodding slowly and lowering his voice*). Yes, that's what I want to be. And that's what I'll fight for—with every means at my disposal.

HEDDA (*her smile vanishing*). You can be a dangerous person, can't you—in a tight corner.

BRACK. Do you think so?

HEDDA. Yes, now I'm beginning to think so. And I'm thoroughly grateful—that you have no kind of hold over me.

BRACK (*with an ambiguous laugh*). Ah, yes, Mrs. Hedda—perhaps you're right about that. If I had, then who knows just what I might do?

HEDDA. Now you listen here, Judge! That sounds too much like a threat.

BRACK (*rising*). Oh, nothing of the kind! A triangle, after all—is best fortified and defended by volunteers.

HEDDA. There we're agreed.

BRACK. Well, now that I've said all I have to say, I'd better get back to town. Good-bye, Mrs. Hedda. (*He goes toward the glass door.*)

HEDDA (*rising*). Are you going through the garden?

BRACK. Yes, I find it's shorter.

HEDDA. Yes, and then it's the back way, too.

BRACK. How true. I have nothing against back ways. At certain times they can be rather piquant.

HEDDA. You mean, when somebody's sharpshooting?

BRACK (*in the doorway, laughing*). Oh, people don't shoot their tame roosters!

HEDDA (*also laughing*). I guess not. Not when there's only one—

(*Still laughing, they nod good-bye to each other. He goes. She shuts the door after him, then stands for a moment, quite serious, looking out. She then goes over and glances through the curtains to the inner room. Moves to the writing table, takes* LØVBORG's *envelope from the bookcase, and is about to page through it, when* BERTA's *voice is heard loudly in the hall.* HEDDA *turns and listens. She hurriedly locks the envelope in the drawer and lays the key on the inkstand.* EILERT LØVBORG, *with his overcoat on and his hat in his hand, throws open the hall door. He looks confused and excited.*)

LØVBORG (*turned toward the hall*). And I'm telling you, I have to go in! I will, you hear me! (*He shuts the door, turns, sees* HEDDA, *immediately gains control of himself and bows.*)

HEDDA (*at the writing table*). Well, Mr. Løvborg, it's late to call for Thea.

LØVBORG. Or rather early to call on you. You must forgive me.

HEDDA. How did you know she was still with me?

LØVBORG. They said at her lodgings that she'd been out all night.

HEDDA (*goes to the center table*). Did you notice anything in their faces when they said that?

LØVBORG (*looking at her inquiringly*). Notice anything?

HEDDA. I mean, did it look like they had their own thoughts on the matter?

LØVBORG (*suddenly understanding*). Oh yes, that's true! I'm dragging her down with me! Actually, I didn't notice anything. Tesman—I don't suppose he's up yet?

HEDDA. No, I don't think so.

LØVBORG. When did he get in?

HEDDA. Very late.

LØVBORG. Did he tell you anything?

HEDDA. Well, I heard you'd had a high time of it out at Judge Brack's.

LØVBORG. Anything else?

HEDDA. No, I don't think so. As a matter of fact, I was terribly sleepy—

(MRS. ELVSTED *comes in through the curtains to the inner room.*)

MRS. ELVSTED (*running toward him*). Oh, Eilert! At last—!

LØVBORG. Yes, at last. And too late.

MRS. ELVSTED (*looking anxiously at him*). What's too late?

LØVBORG. Everything's too late now. It's over with me.

MRS. ELVSTED. Oh no, no—don't say that!

LØVBORG. You'll say the same thing when you've heard—

MRS. ELVSTED. I won't hear anything!

HEDDA. Maybe you'd prefer to talk with her alone. I can leave.

LØVBORG. No, stay—you too. Please.

MRS. ELVSTED. But I tell you, I don't want to hear anything!

LØVBORG. It's nothing about last night.

MRS. ELVSTED. What is it, then—?

LØVBORG. It's simply this, that from now on, we separate.

MRS. ELVSTED. Separate!

HEDDA (*involuntarily*). I knew it!

LØVBORG. Because I have no more use for you, Thea.

MRS. ELVSTED. And you can stand there and say that! No more use for me! Then I'm not going to help you now, as I have? We're not going to go on working together?

LØVBORG. I have no plans for any more work.

MRS. ELVSTED (*in desperation*). Then what will I do with my life?

LØVBORG. You must try to go on living as if you'd never known me.

MRS. ELVSTED. But I can't do that!

LØVBORG. You must try to, Thea. You'll have to go home again—

MRS. ELVSTED (*in a fury of protest*). Never! No! Where you are, that's where I want to be! I won't be driven away like this! I'm going to stay right here—and be together with you when the book comes out.

HEDDA (*in a tense whisper*). Ah, yes—the book!

LØVBORG (*looks at her*). My book and Thea's—for that's what it is.

MRS. ELVSTED. Yes, that's what I feel it is. And that's why I have the right, as well, to be with you when it comes out. I want to see you covered with honor and respect again. And the joy—I want to share the joy of it with you too.

LØVBORG. Thea—our book's never coming out.

HEDDA. Ah!

MRS. ELVSTED. Never coming out!

LØVBORG. *Can* never come out.

MRS. ELVSTED (*with anguished foreboding*). Eilert—what have you done with the manuscript?

HEDDA (*watching him intently*). Yes, the manuscript—?

MRS. ELVSTED. Where is it!

LØVBORG. Oh, Thea—don't ask me that.

MRS. ELVSTED. Yes, yes, I have to know. I've got a right to know, this minute!

LØVBORG. The manuscript—well, you see—I tore the manuscript into a thousand pieces.

MRS. ELVSTED (*screams*). Oh no, no—!

HEDDA (*involuntarily*). But that just isn't—!

LØVBORG (*looks at her*). Isn't so, you think?

HEDDA (*composing herself*). All right. Of course; if you say it yourself. But it sounds so incredible—

LØVBORG. It's true, all the same.

MRS. ELVSTED (*wringing her hands*). Oh, God—oh, God, Hedda—to tear his own work to bits!

LØVBORG. I've torn my own life to bits. So why not tear up my life's work as well—

MRS. ELVSTED. And you did this thing last night!

LØVBORG. Yes, you heard me. In a thousand pieces. And scattered them into the fjord. Far out. At least there, there's clean salt water. Let them drift out to sea—drift with the tide and the wind. And after a while, they'll sink. Deeper and deeper. As I will, Thea.

MRS. ELVSTED. Do you know, Eilert, this thing you've done with the book—for the rest of my life it will seem to me as if you'd killed a little child.

LØVBORG. You're right. It was like murdering a child.

MRS. ELVSTED. But how could you do it—! It was my child too.

HEDDA (*almost inaudible*). Ah, the child—

MRS. ELVSTED (*breathes heavily*). Then it *is* all over. Yes, yes, I'm going now, Hedda.

HEDDA. But you're not leaving town, are you?

MRS. ELVSTED. Oh, I don't know myself what I'll do. Everything's dark for me now. (*She goes out the hall door.*)

HEDDA (*stands waiting a moment*). You're not going to take her home, then, Mr. Løvborg?

LØVBORG. I? Through the streets? So people could see that she'd been with me?

HEDDA. I don't know what else may have happened last night. But is it so completely irredeemable?

LØVBORG. It won't just end with last night—I know that well enough. But the thing is, I've lost all desire for that kind of life. I don't want to start it again, not now. It's the courage and daring for life—that's what she's broken in me.

HEDDA (*staring straight ahead*). To think that pretty little fool could have a man's fate in her hands. (*Looks at him*) But still, how could you treat her so heartlessly?

LØVBORG. Oh, don't say it was heartless!

HEDDA. To go ahead and destroy what's filled her whole being for months and years! That's not heartless?

LØVBORG. To you, Hedda—I can tell the truth.

HEDDA. The truth?

LØVBORG. Promise me first—give me your word that what I tell you now, you'll never let Thea know.

HEDDA. You have my word.

LØVBORG. Good. I can tell you, then, that what I said here just now isn't true.

HEDDA. About the manuscript?

LØVBORG. Yes. I didn't tear it up—or throw it in the fjord.

HEDDA. No, but—where is it, then?

LØVBORG. I've destroyed it all the same, Hedda. Utterly destroyed it.

HEDDA. I don't understand.

LØVBORG. Thea said that what I've done, for her was like killing a child.

HEDDA. Yes—that's what she said.

LØVBORG. But killing his child—that's not the worst thing a father can do.

HEDDA. *That's* not the worst?

LØVBORG. No. I wanted to spare Thea the worst.

HEDDA. And what's that—the worst?

LØVBORG. Suppose now, Hedda, that a man—in the early morning hours, say—after a wild, drunken night, comes home to his child's mother and says: "Listen—I've been out to this place and that—here and there. And I had our child with me. In this place and that. And I lost the child. Just lost it. God only knows what hands it's come into. Or who's got hold of it."

HEDDA. Well—but when all's said and done—it was only a book—

LØVBORG. Thea's pure soul was in that book.

HEDDA. Yes, I understand.

LØVBORG. Well, then you can understand that for her and me there's no future possible any more.

HEDDA. What do you intend to do?

LØVBORG. Nothing. Just put an end to it all. The sooner the better.

HEDDA (*coming a step closer*). Eilert Løvborg—listen to me. Couldn't you arrange that—that it's done beautifully?

LØVBORG.   Beautifully? (*Smiles.*) With vine leaves in my hair, as you used to dream in the old days—

HEDDA.   No. I don't believe in vine leaves any more. But beautifully, all the same. For this once—! Good-bye! You must go now—and never come here again.

LØVBORG.   Good-bye, then. And give my best to George Tesman. (*He turns to leave.*)

HEDDA.   No, wait. I want you to have a souvenir from me.

> (*She goes to the writing desk and opens the drawer and the pistol case, then comes back to* LØVBORG *with one of the pistols.*)

LØVBORG (*looks at her*).   That? Is that the souvenir?

HEDDA (*nods slowly*).   Do you recognize it? It was aimed at you once.

LØVBORG.   You should have used it then.

HEDDA.   Here! Use it now.

LØVBORG (*puts the pistol in his breast pocket*).   Thanks.

HEDDA.   And beautifully, Eilert Løvborg. Promise me that!

LØVBORG.   Good-bye, Hedda Gabler.

> (*He goes out the hall door.* HEDDA *listens a moment at the door. Then she goes over to the writing table, takes out the envelope with the manuscript, glances inside, pulls some of the sheets half out and looks at them. She then goes over to the armchair by the stove and sits, with the envelope in her lap. After a moment, she opens the stove door, then brings out the manuscript.*)

HEDDA (*throwing some of the sheets into the fire and whispering to herself*).   Now I'm burning your child, Thea! You, with your curly hair! (*Throwing another sheaf in the stove.*) Your child and Eilert Løvborg's. (*Throwing in the rest.*) Now I'm burning—I'm burning the child.

⤙ ACT FOUR ⤚

The same rooms at the TESMANS'. *It is evening. The draw-ing room is in darkness. The inner room is lit by the hanging lamp over the table. The curtains are drawn across the glass door.* HEDDA, *dressed in black, is pacing back and forth in the dark room. She then enters the inner room, moving out of sight toward the left. Several chords are heard on the piano. She comes in view again, returning into the drawing room.* BERTA *enters from the right through the inner room with a lighted lamp, which she puts on the table in front of the settee in the draw-ing room. Her eyes are red from crying, and she has black ribbons on her cap. She goes quietly and discreetly out to the right.* HEDDA *moves to the glass door, lifts the curtains aside slightly, and gazes out into the darkness.*

Shortly after, MISS TESMAN, *in mourning, with a hat and veil, comes in from the hall.* HEDDA *goes toward her, extending her hand.*

MISS TESMAN. Well, Hedda, here I am, all dressed in mourning. My poor sister's ordeal is finally over.

HEDDA. As you see, I've already heard. Tesman sent me a note.

MISS TESMAN. Yes, he promised he would. But all the same I thought that, to Hedda—here in the house of life —I ought to bear the news of death myself.

HEDDA. That was very kind of you.

MISS TESMAN. Ah, Rina ought not to have passed on just now. This is no time for grief in Hedda's house.

HEDDA (*changing the subject*). She had a peaceful death, then, Miss Tesman?

MISS TESMAN. Oh, she went so calmly, so beautifully. And so inexpressibly happy that she could see George once again. And say good-bye to him properly. Is it possible that he's still not home?

763

HEDDA. No, he wrote that I shouldn't expect him too early. But won't you sit down?

MISS TESMAN. No, thank you, my dear—blessed Hedda. I'd love to, but I have so little time. I want to see her dressed and made ready as best as I can. She should go to her grave looking her finest.

HEDDA. Can't I help you with something?

MISS TESMAN. Oh, you mustn't think of it. This is nothing for Hedda Tesman to put her hands to. Or let her thoughts dwell on, either. Not at a time like this, no.

HEDDA. Ah, thoughts—they're not so easy to control—

MISS TESMAN (*continuing*). Well, there's life for you. At my house now we'll be sewing a shroud for Rina. And here, too, there'll be sewing soon, I imagine. But a far different kind, praise God!

(GEORGE TESMAN *enters from the hall.*)

HEDDA. Well, at last! It's about time.

TESMAN. Are you here, Aunt Julie? With Hedda? Think of that!

MISS TESMAN. I was just this minute leaving, dear boy. Well, did you get done all you promised you would?

TESMAN. No, I'm really afraid I've forgotten half. I'll have to run over and see you tomorrow. My brain's completely in a whirl today. I can't keep my thoughts together.

MISS TESMAN. But George dear, you mustn't take it that way.

TESMAN. Oh? Well, how should I, then?

MISS TESMAN. You should rejoice in your grief. Rejoice in everything that's happened, as I do.

TESMAN. Oh yes, of course. You're thinking of Auntie Rina.

HEDDA. It's going to be lonely for you, Miss Tesman.

MISS TESMAN. For the first few days, yes. But it won't be for long, I hope. I won't let dear Rina's little room stand empty.

TESMAN. No? Who would you want to have in it? Hm?

MISS TESMAN. Oh, there's always some poor invalid in need of care and attention.

HEDDA. Would you really take another burden like that on yourself?

MISS TESMAN. Burden! Mercy on you, child—it's been no burden for me.

HEDDA. But now, with a stranger—

MISS TESMAN. Oh, you soon make friends with an invalid. And I do so much need someone to live for—I, too. Well, thank God, in this house as well, there soon ought to be work that an old aunt can turn her hand to.

HEDDA. Oh, forget about us—

TESMAN. Yes, think how pleasant it could be for the three of us if—

HEDDA. If—?

TESMAN (*uneasily*). Oh, nothing. It'll all take care of itself. Let's hope so. Uh?

MISS TESMAN. Ah, yes. Well, I expect you two have things to talk about. (*Smiles.*) And perhaps Hedda has something to tell you, George. Good-bye. I'll have to get home now to Rina. (*Turning at the door.*) Goodness me, how strange! Now Rina's both with me and with poor dear Jochum as well.

TESMAN. Yes, imagine that, Aunt Julie! Hm?

(MISS TESMAN *goes out the hall door.*)

HEDDA (*follows* TESMAN *with a cold, probing look*). I almost think you feel this death more than she.

TESMAN. Oh, it's not just Auntie Rina's death. It's Eilert who has me worried.

HEDDA (*quickly*). Any news about him?

TESMAN. I stopped up at his place this afternoon, thinking to tell him that the manuscript was safe.

HEDDA. Well? Didn't you see him then?

TESMAN. No, he wasn't home. But afterward I met Mrs. Elvsted, and she said he'd been here early this morning.

HEDDA. Yes, right after you left.

TESMAN. And apparently he said he'd torn his manuscript up. Uh?

HEDDA. Yes, he claimed that he had.

TESMAN. But good Lord, then he must have been completely demented! Well, then I guess you didn't dare give it back to him, Hedda, did you?

HEDDA. No, he didn't get it.

TESMAN. But you did tell him we had it, I suppose?

HEDDA. No. (*Quickly.*) Did you tell Mrs. Elvsted anything?

TESMAN. No, I thought I'd better not. But you should have said something to him. Just think, if he goes off in desperation and does himself some harm! Give me the manuscript, Hedda! I'm taking it back to him right away. Where do you have it?

HEDDA (*cold and impassive, leaning against the armchair*). I don't have it anymore.

TESMAN. You don't have it! What on earth do you mean by that?

HEDDA. I burned it—the whole thing.

TESMAN (*with a start of terror*). Burned it! Burned Eilert Løvborg's manuscript!

HEDDA. Stop shouting. The maid could hear you.

TESMAN. Burned it! But my God in heaven—! No, no, no—that's impossible!

HEDDA. Yes, but it's true, all the same.

TESMAN. But do you realize what you've done, Hedda! It's illegal disposition of lost property. Just think! Yes, you can ask Judge Brack; he'll tell you.

HEDDA. It would be wiser not mentioning this—either to the judge or to anyone else.

TESMAN. But how could you go and do such an incredible thing! Whatever put it into your head? What got into you, anyway? Answer me! Well?

HEDDA (*suppressing an almost imperceptible smile*). I did it for your sake, George.

TESMAN. For my sake!

HEDDA. When you came home this morning and told about how he'd read to you—

TESMAN. Yes, yes, then what?

HEDDA. Then you confessed that you envied him this book.

TESMAN. Good Lord, I didn't mean it literally.

HEDDA. Never mind. I still couldn't bear the thought that anyone should eclipse you.

TESMAN (*in an outburst of mingled doubt and joy*). Hedda—is this true, what you say! Yes, but—but—I never dreamed you could show your love like this. Imagine!

HEDDA. Well, then it's best you know that—that I'm

going to— (*Impatiently, breaking off.*) No, no—you ask your Aunt Julie. She's the one who can tell you.

TESMAN. Oh, I'm beginning to understand you, Hedda! (*Claps his hands together.*) Good heavens, no! Is it actually *that*! Can it be? Uh?

HEDDA. Don't shout so. The maid can hear you.

TESMAN. The maid! Oh, Hedda, you're priceless, really! The maid—but that's Berta! Why, I'll go out and tell her myself.

HEDDA (*clenching her fists in despair*). Oh, I'll die— I'll die of all this!

TESMAN. Of what, Hedda? Uh?

HEDDA. Of all these—absurdities—George.

TESMAN. Absurdities? What's absurd about my being so happy? Well, all right—I guess there's no point in my saying anything to Berta.

HEDDA. Oh, go ahead—why not that, too?

TESMAN. No, no, not yet. But Aunt Julie will have to hear. And then, that you've started to call me George, too! Imagine! Oh, Aunt Julie will be so glad—so glad!

HEDDA. When she hears that I burned Eilert Løvborg's book—for your sake?

TESMAN. Well, as far as that goes—this thing with the book—of course, no one's to know about that. But that you have a love that burns for me, Hedda—Aunt Julie can certainly share in that! You know, I wonder, really, if things such as this are common among young wives? Hm?

HEDDA. I think you should ask Aunt Julie about that, too.

TESMAN. Yes, I definitely will, when I have the chance.

(MRS. ELVSTED, *dressed as on her first visit, with hat and coat, comes in the hall door.*)

MRS. ELVSTED (*greets them hurriedly and speaks in agitation*). Oh, Hedda dear, don't be annoyed that I'm back again.

HEDDA. Has something happened, Thea?

TESMAN. Something with Eilert Løvborg? Uh?

MRS. ELVSTED. Yes, I'm so terribly afraid he's met with an accident.

HEDDA (*seizing her arm*). Ah—you think so!

TESMAN. But, Mrs. Elvsted, where did you get that idea?

MRS. ELVSTED. Well, because I heard them speaking of him at the boardinghouse, just as I came in. Oh, there are the most incredible rumors about him in town today.

TESMAN. Yes, you know, I heard them too! And yet I could swear that he went right home to bed last night. Imagine!

HEDDA. Well—what did they say at the boardinghouse?

MRS. ELVSTED. Oh, I couldn't get anything clearly. They either didn't know much themselves, or else— They stopped talking when they saw me. And I didn't dare to ask.

TESMAN (*restlessly moving about*). Let's hope—let's hope you misunderstood them, Mrs. Elvsted!

MRS. ELVSTED. No, no, I'm sure they were talking of him. And then I heard them say something or other about the hospital, or—

TESMAN. The hospital!

HEDDA. No—but that's impossible!

MRS. ELVSTED. Oh, I'm so deathly afraid for him now. And later I went up to his lodging to ask about him.

HEDDA. But was that very wise to do, Thea?

MRS. ELVSTED. What else could I do? I couldn't bear the uncertainty any longer.

TESMAN. But didn't you find him there either? Hm?

MRS. ELVSTED. No. And no one had any word of him. He hadn't been in since yesterday afternoon, they said.

TESMAN. Yesterday! Imagine them saying that!

MRS. ELVSTED. I think there can only be one reason— something terrible must have happened to him!

TESMAN. Hedda dear—suppose I went over and made a few inquiries—?

HEDDA. No, no—don't you get mixed up in this business.

> (JUDGE BRACK, *with hat in hand, enters from the hall,* BERTA *letting him in and shutting the door after him. He looks grave and bows silently.*)

TESMAN. Oh, is that you, Judge? Uh?

BRACK. Yes, it's imperative that I see you this evening.

TESMAN. I can see that you've heard the news from Aunt Julie.

BRACK. Among other things, yes.

TESMAN. It's sad, isn't it? Uh?

BRACK. Well, my dear Tesman, that depends on how you look at it.

TESMAN *(eyes him doubtfully)*. Has anything else happened?

BRACK. Yes, as a matter of fact.

HEDDA *(intently)*. Something distressing, Judge?

BRACK. Again, that depends on how you look at it, Mrs. Tesman.

MRS. ELVSTED *(in an uncontrollable outburst)*. Oh, it's something about Eilert Løvborg!

BRACK *(glancing at her)*. Now how did you hit upon that, Mrs. Elvsted? Have you, perhaps, heard something already—?

MRS. ELVSTED *(in confusion)*. No, no, nothing like that —but—

TESMAN. Oh, for heaven's sake, tell us!

BRACK *(with a shrug)*. Well—I'm sorry, but—Eilert Løvborg's been taken to the hospital. He's dying.

MRS. ELVSTED *(crying out)*. Oh, God, oh, God—!

TESMAN. To the hospital! And dying!

HEDDA *(involuntarily)*. All so soon—!

MRS. ELVSTED *(wailing)*. And we parted in anger, Hedda!

HEDDA *(in a whisper)*. Thea—be careful, Thea!

MRS. ELVSTED *(ignoring her)*. I have to see him! I have to see him alive!

BRACK. No use, Mrs. Elvsted. No one's allowed in to see him.

MRS. ELVSTED. Oh, but tell me, at least, what happened to him! What is it?

TESMAN. Don't tell me he tried to—! Uh?

HEDDA. Yes, he did, I'm sure of it.

TESMAN. Hedda—how can you say—!

BRACK *(his eyes steadily on her)*. Unhappily, you've guessed exactly right, Mrs. Tesman.

MRS. ELVSTED. Oh, how horrible!

TESMAN. Did it himself! Imagine!

HEDDA. Shot himself!

BRACK. Again, exactly right, Mrs. Tesman.

MRS. ELVSTED *(trying to control herself)*. When did it happen, Mr. Brack?

BRACK. This afternoon. Between three and four.

TESMAN. But good Lord—where did he do it, then? Hm?

BRACK (*hesitating slightly*). Where? Why—in his room, I suppose.

MRS. ELVSTED. No, that can't be right. I was there between six and seven.

BRACK. Well, somewhere else, then. I don't know exactly. I only know he was found like that. Shot—in the chest.

MRS. ELVSTED. What a horrible thought! That he should end that way!

HEDDA (*to* BRACK). In the chest, you say.

BRACK. Yes—I told you.

HEDDA. Not the temple?

BRACK. In the chest, Mrs. Tesman.

HEDDA. Well—well, the chest is just as good.

BRACK. Why, Mrs. Tesman?

HEDDA (*evasively*). Oh, nothing—never mind.

TESMAN. And the wound is critical, you say? Uh?

BRACK. The wound is absolutely fatal. Most likely, it's over already.

MRS. ELVSTED. Yes, yes, I can feel that it is! It's over! All over! Oh, Hedda—!

TESMAN. But tell me now—how did you learn about this?

BRACK (*brusquely*). One of the police. Someone I talked to.

HEDDA (*in a clear, bold voice.*) At last, something truly done!

TESMAN (*shocked*). My God, what are you saying, Hedda!

HEDDA. I'm saying there's beauty in all this.

BRACK. Hm, Mrs. Tesman—

TESMAN. Beauty! What an idea!

MRS. ELVSTED. Oh, Hedda, how can you talk about beauty in such a thing?

HEDDA. Eilert Løvborg's settled accounts with himself. He's had the courage to do what—what had to be done.

MRS. ELVSTED. Don't you believe it! It never happened like that. When he did this, he was in a delirium!

TESMAN. In despair, you mean.

HEDDA. No, he wasn't. I'm certain of that.

MRS. ELVSTED. But he was! In delirium! The way he was when he tore up our book.

BRACK (*startled*). The book? His manuscript, you mean? He tore it up?

MRS. ELVSTED. Yes. Last night.

TESMAN (*in a low whisper*). Oh, Hedda, we'll never come clear of all this.

BRACK. Hm, that's very strange.

TESMAN (*walking about the room*). To think Eilert could be gone like that! And then not to have left behind the one thing that could have made his name live on.

MRS. ELVSTED. Oh, if it could only be put together again!

TESMAN. Yes, imagine if that were possible! I don't know what I wouldn't give—

MRS. ELVSTED. Perhaps it can, Mr. Tesman.

TESMAN. What do you mean?

MRS. ELVSTED (*searching in the pockets of her dress*). Look here. I've kept all these notes that he used to dictate from.

HEDDA (*coming a step closer*). Ah—!

TESMAN. You've kept them, Mrs. Elvsted! Uh?

MRS. ELVSTED. Yes, here they are. I took them along when I left home. And they've stayed right here in my pocket—

TESMAN. Oh, let me look!

MRS. ELVSTED (*hands him a sheaf of small papers*). But they're in such a mess. All mixed up.

TESMAN. But just think, if we could decipher them, even so! Maybe the two of us could help each other—

MRS. ELVSTED. Oh yes! At least, we could try—

TESMAN. We can do it! We *must*! I'll give my whole life to this!

HEDDA. You, George. Your life?

TESMAN. Yes. Or, let's say, all the time I can spare. My own research will have to wait. You can understand, Hedda. Hm! It's something I owe to Eilert's memory.

HEDDA. Perhaps.

TESMAN. And so, my dear Mrs. Elvsted, let's see if we can't join forces. Good Lord, there's no use brooding over what's gone by. Uh? We must try to compose our thoughts as much as we can, in order that—

MRS. ELVSTED.   Yes, yes, Mr. Tesman, I'll do the best I can.

TESMAN.   Come on, then. Let's look over these notes right away. Where shall we sit? Here? No, in there, in the back room. Excuse us, Judge. You come with me, Mrs. Elvsted.

MRS. ELVSTED.   Dear God—if only we can do this!

(TESMAN *and* MRS. ELVSTED *go into the inner room. She takes off her hat and coat. They both sit at the table under the hanging lamp and become totally immersed in examining the papers.* HEDDA *goes toward the stove and sits in the armchair. After a moment,* BRACK *goes over by her.*)

HEDDA (*her voice lowered*).   Ah, Judge—what a liberation it is, this act of Eilert Løvborg's.

BRACK.   Liberation, Mrs. Hedda? Well, yes, for him; you could certainly say he's been liberated—

HEDDA.   I mean for me. It's liberating to know that there can still actually be a free and courageous action in this world. Something that shimmers with spontaneous beauty.

BRACK (*smiling*).   Hm—my dear Mrs. Hedda—

HEDDA.   Oh, I already know what you're going to say. Because you're a kind of specialist too, you know, just like— Oh, well!

BRACK (*looking fixedly at her*).   Eilert Løvborg meant more to you than you're willing to admit, perhaps even to yourself. Or am I wrong about that?

HEDDA.   I won't answer that sort of question. I simply know that Eilert Løvborg's had the courage to live life after his own mind. And now—this last great act, filled with beauty! That he had the strength and the will to break away from the banquet of life—so young.

BRACK.   It grieves me, Mrs. Hedda—but I'm afraid I have to disburden you of this beautiful illusion.

HEDDA.   Illusion?

BRACK.   One that, in any case, you'd soon be deprived of.

HEDDA.   And what's that?

BRACK.   He didn't shoot himself—of his own free will.

HEDDA.   He didn't—!

BRACK.   No. This whole affair didn't go off quite the way I described it.

HEDDA (*in suspense*). You've hidden something? What is it?

BRACK. For poor Mrs. Elvsted's sake, I did a little editing here and there.

HEDDA. Where?

BRACK. First, the fact that he's already dead.

HEDDA. In the hospital?

BRACK. Yes. Without regaining consciousness.

HEDDA. What else did you hide?

BRACK. That the incident didn't occur in his room.

HEDDA. Well, that's rather unimportant.

BRACK. Not entirely. Suppose I were to tell you that Eilert Løvborg was found shot in—in Mademoiselle Diana's boudoir.

HEDDA (*half rises, then sinks back again*). That's impossible, Judge! He wouldn't have gone there again today!

BRACK. He was there this afternoon. He went there, demanding something he said they'd stolen from him. Kept raving about a lost child—

HEDDA. Ah—so that was it—

BRACK. I thought perhaps that might be his manuscript. But, I hear now, he destroyed that himself. So it must have been his wallet.

HEDDA. I suppose so. Then, there—that's where they found him.

BRACK. Yes, there. With a discharged pistol in his breast pocket. The bullet had wounded him fatally.

HEDDA. In the chest—yes.

BRACK. No—in the stomach—more or less.

HEDDA (*stares up at him with a look of revulsion*). That too! What is it, this—this curse—that everything I touch turns ridiculous and vile?

BRACK. There's something else, Mrs. Hedda. Another ugly aspect to the case.

HEDDA. What's that?

BRACK. The pistol he was carrying—

HEDDA (*breathlessly*). Well! What about it!

BRACK. He must have stolen it.

HEDDA (*springs up*). Stolen! That's not true! He didn't!

BRACK. It seems impossible otherwise. He must have stolen it—shh!

(TESMAN *and* MRS. ELVSTED *have gotten up from
the table in the inner room and come into the
drawing room.*)

TESMAN (*with both hands full of papers*).   Hedda dear—
it's nearly impossible to see in there under that overhead
lamp. You know?

HEDDA.   Yes, I know.

TESMAN.   Do you think it would be all right if we used
your table for a while? Hm?

HEDDA.   Yes, I don't mind. (*Quickly.*) Wait! No, let me
clear it off first.

TESMAN.   Oh, don't bother, Hedda. There's plenty of
room.

HEDDA.   No, no, let me just clear it off, can't you? I'll
put all this in by the piano. There!

(*She has pulled out an object covered with sheet
music from under the bookcase, adds more
music to it, and carries the whole thing into
the inner room and off left.* TESMAN *puts the
scraps of paper on the writing table and moves
the lamp over from the corner table. He and*
MRS. ELVSTED *sit down and go on with their
work.* HEDDA *comes back.*)

HEDDA (*behind* MRS. ELVSTED'*s chair, gently ruffling her
hair*).   Well, my sweet little Thea—how is it going with
Eilert Løvborg's monument?

MRS. ELVSTED (*looking despondently up at her*).   Oh, dear
—it's going to be terribly hard to set these in order.

TESMAN.   It's got to be done. There's just no alternative.
Besides, setting other people's papers in order—it's exactly
what I can do best.

(HEDDA *goes over by the stove and sits on one of
the taborets.* BRACK *stands over her, leaning on
the armchair.*)

HEDDA (*whispering*).   What did you say about the pistol?

BRACK (*softly*).   That he must have stolen it.

HEDDA.   Why, necessarily, that?

BRACK.   Because every other explanation would seem impossible, Mrs. Hedda.

HEDDA. I see.

BRACK (*glancing at her*). Of course, Eilert Løvborg was here this morning. Wasn't he?

HEDDA. Yes.

BRACK. Were you alone with him?

HEDDA. Yes, briefly.

BRACK. Did you leave the room while he was here?

HEDDA. No.

BRACK. Consider. You didn't leave, even for a moment.

HEDDA. Well, yes, perhaps, just for a moment—into the hall.

BRACK. And where did you have your pistol case?

HEDDA. I had it put away in—

BRACK. Yes, Mrs. Hedda?

HEDDA. It was lying over there, on the writing table.

BRACK. Have you looked since to see if both pistols are there?

HEDDA. No.

BRACK. No need to. I saw the pistol. Løvborg had it on him. I knew it immediately, from yesterday. And other days too.

HEDDA. Do you have it, maybe?

BRACK. No, the police have it.

HEDDA. What will they do with it?

BRACK. Try to trace it to the owner.

HEDDA. Do you think they'll succeed?

BRACK (*bending over her and whispering*). No, Hedda Gabler—as long as I keep quiet.

HEDDA (*looking at him anxiously*). And if you don't keep quiet—then what?

BRACK (*with a shrug*). Counsel could always claim that the pistol was stolen.

HEDDA (*decisively*). I'd rather die!

BRACK (*smiling*). People *say* such things. But they don't *do* them.

HEDDA (*without answering*). And what, then, if the pistol wasn't stolen. And they found the owner. What would happen?

BRACK. Well, Hedda—there'd be a scandal.

HEDDA. A scandal!

BRACK. A scandal, yes—the kind you're so deathly afraid of. Naturally, you'd appear in court—you and Mademoiselle

Diana. She'd have to explain how the whole thing occurred. Whether it was an accident or homicide. Was he trying to pull the pistol out of his pocket to threaten her? Is that why it went off? Or had she torn the pistol out of his hand, shot him, and slipped it back in his pocket again? It's rather like her to do that, you know. She's a powerful woman, this Mademoiselle Diana.

HEDDA.   But all that sordid business is no concern of mine.

BRACK.   No. But you'll have to answer the question: why did you give Eilert Løvborg the pistol? And what conclusions will people draw from the fact that you did give it to him?

HEDDA (*her head sinking*).   That's true. I hadn't thought of that.

BRACK.   Well, luckily there's no danger, as long as I keep quiet.

HEDDA.   So I'm in your power, Judge. You have your hold over me from now on.

BRACK (*whispers more softly*).   My dearest Hedda—believe me—I won't abuse my position.

HEDDA.   All the same, I'm in your power. Tied to your will and desire. Not free. Not free, then! (*Rises impetuously.*) No—I can't bear the thought of it. Never!

BRACK (*looks at her half mockingly*).   One usually manages to adjust to the inevitable.

HEDDA (*returning his look*).   Yes, perhaps so. (*She goes over to the writing table. Suppressing an involuntary smile, she imitates* TESMAN's *intonation.*) Well? Getting on with it, George? Uh?

TESMAN.   Goodness knows, dear. It's going to mean months and months of work, in any case.

HEDDA (*as before*).   Imagine that! (*Runs her hand lightly through* MRS. ELVSTED's *hair.*). Don't you find it strange, Thea? Here you are, sitting now beside Tesman—just as you used to sit with Eilert Løvborg.

MRS. ELVSTED.   Oh, if I could only inspire your husband in the same way,

HEDDA.   Oh, that will surely come—in time.

TESMAN.   Yes, you know what, Hedda—I really think I'm beginning to feel something of the kind. But you go back and sit with Judge Brack.

HEDDA. Is there nothing the two of you need from me now?

TESMAN. No, nothing in the world. (*Turning his head.*) From now on, Judge, you'll have to be good enough to keep Hedda company.

BRACK (*with a glance at* HEDDA). I'll take the greatest pleasure in that.

HEDDA. Thanks. But I'm tired this evening. I want to rest a while in there on the sofa.

TESMAN. Yes, do that, dear. Uh?

> (HEDDA *goes into the inner room, pulling the curtains closed after her. Short pause. Suddenly she is heard playing a wild dance melody on the piano.*)

MRS. ELVSTED (*starting up from her chair*). Oh—what's that?

TESMAN (*running to the center doorway*). But Hedda dearest—don't go playing dance music tonight! Think of Auntie Rina! And Eilert, too!

HEDDA (*putting her head out between the curtains*). And Auntie Julie. And all the rest of them. From now on I'll be quiet. (*She closes the curtains again.*)

TESMAN (*at the writing table*). She can't feel very happy seeing us do this melancholy work. You know what, Mrs. Elvsted—you must move in with Aunt Julie. Then I can come over evenings. And then we can sit and work there. Uh?

MRS. ELVSTED. Yes, perhaps that would be best—

HEDDA. I can hear everything you say, Tesman. But what will I do evenings over here?

TESMAN (*leafing through the notes*). Oh, I'm sure Judge Brack will be good enough to stop by and see you.

BRACK (*in the armchair, calling out gaily*). I couldn't miss an evening, Mrs. Tesman! We'll have great times here together, the two of us!

HEDDA (*in a clear, ringing voice*). Yes, you can hope so, Judge, can't you? You, the one cock of the walk—

> (*A shot is heard within.* TESMAN, MRS. ELVSTED, *and* BRACK *start from their chairs.*)

TESMAN. Oh, now she's fooling with those pistols again.

(*He throws the curtains back and runs in.* MRS. ELVSTED *follows.* HEDDA *lies, lifeless, stretched out on the sofa. Confusion and cries.* BERTA *comes in, bewildered, from the right.*)

TESMAN (*shrieking to* BRACK). Shot herself! Shot herself in the temple! Can you imagine!

BRACK (*in the armchair, prostrated*). But good God! People don't *do* such things!

THE MASTER BUILDER

The Master Builder (1892) is iridescently imbued through-out with the quality that J. R. R. Tolkien once declared essential to any work of successful fantasy, an "arresting strangeness." Halvard Solness, a distinguished architect at the peak of his career, keeps his hard-driven staff of three in forced servitude by literally spellbinding the young woman who does his bookkeeping. To the family doctor he confesses that this emotional hostage, Kaja Fosli, came to be employed by him through telepathic powers of sugges-tion. His duty-ridden wife, Aline, who resents his long train of female admirers, dresses perpetually, perhaps vin-dictively, in black, not as we learn for the sake of their twin sons, dead in infancy in the aftermath of the fire that consumed their first home, but for the nine conflagrated dolls she retained into marriage, carrying them under her heart like little unborn children.

Into this airless prison of enslaved and exhausted ener-gies comes an unanticipated and breezily refreshing caller from the seventh play of the cycle, the now grown, younger daughter of Dr. Wangel, her entrance again seem-ingly in telepathic response to Solness' troubled thoughts. Almost immediately she relates a strange story, of how ten years ago to the day, following the dedication of a newly completed church, Solness, its builder, in the privacy of her father's home, had kissed her, a girl of no more than thirteen, many, many times and promised her a kingdom in a decade's time, which she has punctually arrived to col-lect. Solness, who denies her allegation vehemently, is gradually persuaded that, in some mysterious way, the episode did occur. They then proceed to converse like conspiratorial children in a secret language, an idiom of encoded images of castles in the air, dreams of falling, helpers and servers, trolls, devils, towers and princesses. And as they talk, the burdens of the master builder's past and present melt away before an influx of resurgent vitality and creative purpose.

From no more than this, one can grasp why many of the play's interpreters have found it a case less of arresting strangeness than of arrested development, the by-product of a late-blooming, foolish-fond infatuation of its sixty-four-year-old author. Unfortunately, still the most prevalent view of *The Master Builder* takes it as thinly disguised autobiography. Critics who would scarcely dare offer an explication of *Othello* featuring Desdemona as Anne Hathaway close the book on *The Master Builder* after equating Solness with Ibsen, Hilda Wangel with the pianist Hildur Andersen (ignoring the first appearance of the character three years before Ibsen's young protégé attracted his interest), and Solness' three kinds of building with Ibsen's hypothesized three styles of drama—conveniently overlooking the absurdity of the playwright ever construing *Ghosts* or *Rosmersholm* as "homes for happy human beings." As with all major writers, certain highly speculative connections exist between Ibsen's experience and the inner workings of his mind and imagination; but the easy reduction of questions of meaning to the record of one vanished, late-nineteenth-century life is an evasion of the ideas and insights in the play that are the real source of its enduring relevance.

What approaches are warranted, then, to the play's audacious blend of realism and occultism, fantasy and fact? At least three. First of all, *The Master Builder* presents a penetrating, objective psychological study of character in crisis, of a man at the top of his profession experiencing the vertigo of the male climacteric. In realistic terms, the play can be seen and staged as a portrait in depth of a proto-Art Nouveau architect, one of those forerunners of modernism who, through their work, attacked the blight of the Victorian city and inspired later architects of the Art Nouveau generation of Hosta, Guimard, Endell and Hoffmann. When Solness successively represents his extrasensory encounters as madness to Herdal, Aline and Hilda, he is himself adopting this naturalistic perspective and thereby establishing it in the play.

Secondly, *The Master Builder* is a profoundly subjective inquiry into the creative process, utilizing techniques the theater would presently recognize as expressionistic. Without ever breaking with verisimilitude, the characters are—as they tend to be in Ibsen's final dramas—aspects of the mind, interacting components of the psyche. The three earthly helpers and servers, Brovik, Ragnar and Kaja, for example, seen at curtain rise slaving over ledgers and drafting tables, from this perspective are exactly as described earlier: the artist's imprisoned energies awaiting the entrance of what Hilda symbolizes, that which classic poetry designated more simply as the Muse.

When Hilda disdains Solness' offer to work, like Kaja, in the ledger, she sets herself above the practical world's concern with profit and loss, success and its cost, and reveals herself in league with the spirit realm. The third valid approach to *The Master Builder* finds that realm not illusory, not madness, but transcendentally real. Its gateway is what Solness calls the troll within; for, though the word " 'troll' suggests dark layers of infra-human, even, as in *Peer Gynt*, obscene instinct," G. Wilson Knight observes, "it is this element in the psyche that makes contact with the spirit-powers." Solness' true blasphemy and nemesis is, perhaps, that he converts the rare powers bestowed upon his larger self into cat's-paws for his ego and its ambition to ascend beyond earthly limit to "the impossible." Truths beyond, within, outside the self—the play blends all three into a lyrical and seamless unity.

THE CHARACTERS

HALVARD SOLNESS, Master Builder
ALINE SOLNESS, his wife
DR. HERDAL, the family doctor
KNUT BROVIK, former architect, now assistant to SOLNESS
RAGNAR BROVIK, his son, a draftsman
KAJA FOSLI, his niece, a bookkeeper
MISS HILDA WANGEL
SOME LADIES
A CROWD IN THE STREET

The action takes place in and around SOLNESS's *house.*

$\smile\!\!\prec$ ACT ONE $\succ\!\!\smile$

A plainly furnished workroom in SOLNESS's *house. Folding doors in the wall to the left lead to the entryway. To the right is a door to the inner rooms. In the rear wall a door stands open on the drafting room. Downstage left, a desk with books, papers, and writing materials. Upstage, beyond the folding doors, a stove. In the right-hand corner, a sofa with a table and a couple of chairs. On the table, a carafe of water and a glass. A smaller table with a rocker and an armchair in the right foreground. Lights for working lit over the drafting room table, on the table in the corner, and on the desk.*

In the drafting room KNUT BROVIK *and his son* RAGNAR *are sitting, busy with blueprints and calculations. At the desk in the workroom* KAJA FOSLI *stands, writing in a ledger.* KNUT BROVIK *is a gaunt old man with white hair and beard. He wears a rather threadbare but well-preserved black coat, glasses, and a white muffler somewhat yellowed by age.* RAGNAR BROVIK *is in his thirties, well-dressed, blond, with a slight stoop.* KAJA FOSLI *is a delicate young girl of twenty some years, trimly dressed, but rather sickly in appearance. She is wearing a green eyeshade. All three work on for a time in silence.*

KNUT BROVIK (*suddenly stands up from the drafting table, as if in fright, his breathing heavy and labored as he comes forward into the doorway*). No, I can't go on much longer!

KAJA (*moves over to him*). Are you feeling quite bad tonight, Uncle?

BROVIK. Oh, I think it gets worse every day.

RAGNAR (*having risen and approached them*). Father, you'd better go home. Try to get some sleep—

BROVIK (*impatiently*). Take to my bed, hm? You want to have me suffocate for good!

KAJA. Go out for a little walk, then.

RAGNAR. Yes, go on. I'll walk with you.

BROVIK (*vehemently*). I won't go till he's back! Tonight I'm putting it straight up to—(*With suppressed resentment.*) to him—to the chief.

KAJA (*upset*). Oh no, Uncle—please, let it wait!

RAGNAR. Yes, Father, wait a while!

BROVIK (*struggling for breath*). Uhh—uhh! I haven't much time to wait.

KAJA (*listening*). Shh! I hear him down on the stairs. (*All three return to work. Short silence.*)

> (HALVARD SOLNESS *comes in from the entry hall. He is a middle-aged man, strong and forceful, with close-cropped, curly hair, a dark moustache and thick, dark eyebrows. His jacket, gray-green with wide lapels, is buttoned, with the collar turned up. On his head is a soft gray felt hat, and under his arm a couple of portfolios.*)

SOLNESS (*by the door, pointing at the drafting room and whispering*). Are they gone?

KAJA (*softly, shaking her head*). No. (*She removes the eyeshade.* SOLNESS *crosses the room, tosses his hat on a chair, sets the folios on the sofa table and then comes back toward the desk.* KAJA *steadily continues writing, but seems nervous and ill at ease.*)

SOLNESS (*aloud*). What's that you're putting down there, Miss Fosli?

KAJA (*with a start*). Oh, it's just something that—

SOLNESS. Here, let me see. (*Bends over her, pretending to examine the ledger, and whispers.*) Kaja?

KAJA (*softly, as she writes*). Yes.

SOLNESS. Why do you always take off that shade when I'm around?

KAJA (*as before*). You know it makes me look so ugly.

SOLNESS (*smiling*). And you don't want that, do you, Kaja?

KAJA (*half glancing up at him*). Not for all the world. Not for *you* to see.

SOLNESS (*lightly stroking her hair*). Poor, poor little Kaja—

KAJA (*ducking her head*). Shh—they can hear you!

(SOLNESS *strolls across the room to the right, turns,
and pauses at the drafting room door.*)

SOLNESS. Has anyone been in to see me?

RAGNAR (*getting up*). Yes, the young couple that want to build out at Løvstrand.

SOLNESS (*growling*). Oh, them. Well, they can wait. I'm not quite clear on the plans yet.

RAGNAR (*coming forward and rather hesitantly*). They did want so badly to have those drawings soon.

SOLNESS (*as before*). Good God—they all want that!

BROVIK (*looking up*). They said they had such a longing to move into their own place.

SOLNESS. All right, all right—we know that! So they'll make do with anything—any kind of a—a roost. Just a peg to hang their hats. But not a home. No—no, thanks! They can go find somebody else. Tell them that when they come again.

BROVIK (*pushing his glasses up on his forehead and staring at him in amazement*). Find somebody else? You'd turn that commission down?

SOLNESS (*impatiently*). Yes, damn it all, yes! If that's how it's going to be— It's better than slapping a shack together. (*Exploding.*) What do I know about these people!

BROVIK. They're good solid people. Ragnar knows them. He's like one of the family. Very solid people.

SOLNESS. Ahh, solid—solid! That's not what I mean. Lord—don't *you* understand me either? (*Sharply.*) I'll have nothing to do with strangers. They can find anyone they please, for all I care!

BROVIK (*rising*). Seriously, you mean that?

SOLNESS (*sullenly*). Yes—for once. (*He paces across the room.*)

(BROVIK *exchanges a look with* RAGNAR, *who makes
a warning gesture. He then comes into the workroom.*)

BROVIK. May I have a word or two with you?

SOLNESS. Gladly.

BROVIK (*to* KAJA). Kaja, go inside a while.

KAJA (*uneasily*). Oh, but Uncle—

BROVIK. Do as I say, child. And close the door after you.

(KAJA *goes reluctantly into the drafting room and, with a fearful and imploring look at* SOLNESS, *shuts the door.*)

BROVIK (*dropping his voice*).   I don't want the poor children knowing how sick I am.

SOLNESS.   Yes, you're looking quite done in these days.

BROVIK.   It's almost over with me. My strength—it's less every day.

SOLNESS.   Sit down, rest a bit.

BROVIK.   Thanks—may I?

SOLNESS (*adjusting the armchair*).   Here, please. Well?

BROVIK (*having seated himself with difficulty*).   Yes, well, it's Ragnar; he's on my mind. What's going to happen with him?

SOLNESS.   Your son, he can stay on here with me, naturally, as long as he wants.

BROVIK.   But that's just the thing: it's not what he wants. He thinks he can't—now, any longer.

SOLNESS.   Well, I'd say he's got a very nice salary. But if he's out for a little more, I wouldn't be averse to—

BROVIK.   No, no, it isn't that! (*Impatiently.*) But he needs a chance to work on his own.

SOLNESS (*not looking at him*).   Do you think Ragnar has really enough talent for that?

BROVIK.   Don't you see, *that's* the worst of it. That I'm beginning to have my doubts about the boy. For you've never said so much as—as one word of encouragement about him. But then I think it can't be any other way—he *must* have the talent.

SOLNESS.   Well, but he hasn't learned anything yet—nothing basic. Nothing but drafting.

BROVIK (*looking at him with veiled hatred, his voice hoarse*).   You hadn't learned anything either, back when you worked for me. But you got along all right. (*Breathing heavily.*) Pushed your way up. Cut the ground out from under me—and so many others.

SOLNESS.   Well—I had luck on my side.

BROVIK.   True enough. Everything was on your side. But you can't have the heart, then, to let me die—without seeing what Ragnar can do. And then, I'd like so much to see them married—before I'm gone.

SOLNESS (*sharply*). Is she the one who wants that?

BROVIK. Not so much Kaja. But Ragnar talks of it every day. (*Beseeching him.*) You must—you *must* help him get some independent work now! I've got to see something the boy has done. You hear me!

SOLNESS (*angrily*). What the hell—you think I can pull down commissions out of the moon for him!

BROVIK. He could have a fine commission right now. A big piece of work.

SOLNESS (*surprised and disconcerted*). He could?

BROVIK. If you'd give permission.

SOLNESS. What work is that?

BROVIK (*hesitating a bit*). He could build that house at Løvstrand.

SOLNESS. That! But I'm building that!

BROVIK. Oh, but you have no more interest in it.

SOLNESS (*flaring up*). No interest! Me! Who says so?

BROVIK. You said it yourself just now.

SOLNESS. Oh, don't listen to what I—say. Would they give Ragnar that job?

BROVIK. Yes. He knows the family. And then, just for fun, he's worked out the plans and the estimate, the whole thing—

SOLNESS. And they like the plans? Those people—?

BROVIK. Yes. So if you'd just go over them and give your approval, then—

SOLNESS. Then they'd invite Ragnar to build their home.

BROVIK. They really liked what he wants to do. They thought it was completely new and different—that's what they said.

SOLNESS. Aha! New! Modern! None of the old-fashioned stuff I build!

BROVIK. They thought it was something—different.

SOLNESS (*with suppressed bitterness*). And they came here to Ragnar—while I was out!

BROVIK. They came to see you—and also to ask if you'd be willing to give up—

SOLNESS (*erupting*). Give up! I!

BROVIK. That is, if you found Ragnar's plans—

SOLNESS. I—give up for your son!

BROVIK. Give up the commission, they meant.

SOLNESS. Oh, it's one and the same. (*With a wry laugh.*)

So that's it! Halvard Solness—he ought to start giving up now! Make room for youth. For even the youngest. Just make room! Room! Room!

BROVIK. Good Lord, there's room enough here for more than one man—

SOLNESS. There's not that much room here anymore. But, never mind—I'm not giving up! I never give ground. Not voluntarily. Never in this world, never!

BROVIK (*rising with effort*). And I—must I give up life without hope? Without joy? Without faith and trust in Ragnar? Without seeing a single one of his works? Is that it?

SOLNESS (*half turning away, in a whisper*). Don't ask any more now.

BROVIK. Yes, answer me. Shall I go into death so poor?

SOLNESS (*after an inner struggle, he speaks at last in a low but firm voice*). You have to face death the best you can.

BROVIK. Then that's it. (*He walks away.*)

SOLNESS (*following him, half in desperation*). Don't you see—what else can I do! I'm made the way I am! I can't change myself over!

BROVIK. No, no, I guess you can't. (*Stumbles and halts by the sofa table.*) May I have a glass of water?

SOLNESS. Please. (*Pours and hands him the glass.*)

BROVIK. Thanks. (*Drinks and sets the glass down.*)

SOLNESS (*going over and opening the door to the drafting room*). Ragnar—come take your father home.

> (RAGNAR *quickly gets up. He and* KAJA *come into the workroom.*)

RAGNAR. Father, what is it?

BROVIK. Give me your arm. Then we'll go.

RAGNAR. All right. You get your things too, Kaja.

SOLNESS. Miss Fosli will have to stay on a moment—I've a letter to be written.

BROVIK (*looking at* SOLNESS). Good night. Sleep well—if you can.

SOLNESS. Good night.

> (BROVIK *and* RAGNAR *leave by way of the entry hall.* KAJA *goes over to the desk.* SOLNESS *stands, head bent, to the right by the armchair.*)

KAJA (*hesitating*). *Is* there a letter—?

SOLNESS (*brusquely*). Of course not. (*With a fierce look at her.*) Kaja!

KAJA (*frightened, softly*). Yes?

SOLNESS (*decisively, beckoning her*). Over here! Quick!

KAJA (*reluctantly*). Yes.

SOLNESS (*as before*). Closer!

KAJA (*obeying*). What do you want of me?

SOLNESS (*looking at her a moment*). Are you at the root of all this?

KAJA. No, no, don't believe that!

SOLNESS. But marriage—that's what you want now.

KAJA (*quietly*). Ragnar and I have been engaged four or five years, and so—

SOLNESS. So you think it just can't go on forever—isn't that it?

KAJA. Ragnar and Uncle tell me I must—so I think I'll have to give in.

SOLNESS (*more gently*). Kaja, don't you really care a little for Ragnar too?

KAJA. I cared very much for Ragnar once—before I came here to you.

SOLNESS. But no more? Not at all?

KAJA (*passionately, extending her clasped hands out toward him*). Oh, you know I care now for one, only one! Nobody else in this whole world. I'll never care for anyone else!

SOLNESS. Yes, you say that. And then you desert me all the same. Leave me to struggle with everything alone.

KAJA. But couldn't I stay on with you even if Ragnar—?

SOLNESS. No, no, that's out of the question. If Ragnar goes out on his own, he'll be needing you himself.

KAJA (*wringing her hands*). Oh, I don't see how I *can* ever part from you! It's just so completely impossible.

SOLNESS. Then try to rid Ragnar of these stupid ideas. Marry him as much as you like—(*Changing his tone.*) Well, I mean—don't let him throw over a good job here with me. Because—then I can keep *you* too, Kaja dear.

KAJA. Oh yes, how lovely that would be, if only we could manage it!

SOLNESS (*caressing her head with both hands and whisper-*

ing). Because I can't be without you. You understand? I've got to have you close to me every day.

KAJA (*shivering with excitement*).   Oh, God! God!

SOLNESS (*kissing her hair*).   Kaja—Kaja!

KAJA (*sinks down before him*).   Oh, how good you are to me! How incredibly good you are!

SOLNESS (*intensely*).   Get up! Get up now, I—I hear someone coming!

> (*He helps her up. She falters over to the desk.*
> MRS. SOLNESS *enters by the door on the right.
> She looks thin and careworn, but traces of form-
> er beauty still show. Blonde ringlets. Dressed
> stylishly, entirely in black. Speaks rather slowly
> in a plaintive voice.*)

MRS. SOLNESS (*in the doorway*).   Halvard!

SOLNESS (*turning*).   Oh, is it you, dear—?

MRS. SOLNESS (*with a glance at* KAJA).   I'm afraid I'm intruding.

SOLNESS.   Not a bit. Miss Fosli has one short letter to write.

MRS. SOLNESS.   Yes—I see that.

SOLNESS.   What did you want me for, Aline?

MRS. SOLNESS.   I just wanted to say that Dr. Herdal's in the living room. Maybe you could join us, Halvard?

SOLNESS (*looks suspiciously at her*).   Hm—is the doctor so anxious to talk with me?

MRS. SOLNESS.   No, not exactly anxious. He stopped by to see me, but he'd like to say hello to you too.

SOLNESS (*laughing to himself*).   Yes, I can imagine. Well, then you'd better ask him to wait a while.

MRS. SOLNESS.   And you'll look in on him later?

SOLNESS.   Possibly. Later—later, dear. In a while.

MRS. SOLNESS (*glancing again at* KAJA).   Don't forget now, Halvard. (*She leaves, closing the door after her.*)

KAJA (*softly*).   Oh, my Lord—she must think the worst of me!

SOLNESS.   Oh, certainly not. No more than usual, anyway. Still, it's best if you go now, Kaja.

KAJA.   Yes, I've *got* to go now.

SOLNESS (*sternly*).   And then you'll settle up that business for me—you hear!

KAJA. Oh, if only it were just up to *me*, then—

SOLNESS. Listen, I want it settled! Tomorrow the latest!

KAJA (*apprehensively*). If it doesn't work out, then I'd rather break off with him.

SOLNESS (*explosively*). Break off with him! Are you crazy, completely! You'd break it off?

KAJA (*in desperation*). Yes. I have to—have to stay here with you! I can't ever leave you! Ever! That's impossible!

SOLNESS (*in an outburst*). But damn it—Ragnar! Ragnar's the one that I—

KAJA (*looking at him with terrified eyes*). Is it more for Ragnar's sake that—that you—?

SOLNESS (*checking himself*). Of course not! Oh, you don't see what I mean either. (*Gently and softly.*) Obviously, it's you that I need here. You above all, Kaja. But that's precisely why you have to make Ragnar hang onto his job. There, there—run along home now.

KAJA. All right—good night, then.

SOLNESS. Good night. (*As she starts out.*) Oh, wait—are Ragnar's drawings in there?

KAJA. Yes, I don't think he took them along.

SOLNESS. See if you can locate them for me. I could give them a look maybe, after all.

KAJA (*in delight*). Oh yes, please do!

SOLNESS. For your sake, Kaja, my sweet. Now let's have them in a hurry, you hear?

(KAJA *runs into the drafting room, rummages anxiously in the table drawer, pulls out a portfolio and brings it.*)

KAJA. All the drawings are here.

SOLNESS. Fine. Lay them over there on the table.

KAJA (*does so*). Good night. (*Imploringly.*) And please— think well of me.

SOLNESS. Oh, you know I do, always. Good night, my dear little Kaja. (*Glancing to the right.*) Go on now—go!

(MRS. SOLNESS *and* DR. HERDAL *enter through the door on the right. He is a plump, elderly man with a round, complacent face, smooth shaven; he has light, thinning hair, and gold spectacles.*)

MRS. SOLNESS (*standing in the doorway*).   Halvard, I can't keep the doctor any longer.

SOLNESS.   Well, come in, then.

MRS. SOLNESS (*to* KAJA, *who is dimming the desk lamp*). All finished with the letter, Miss Fosli?

KAJA (*confused*).   The letter—?

SOLNESS.   Yes, it was very short.

MRS. SOLNESS.   I'm sure it was terribly short.

SOLNESS.   You may as well leave, Miss Fosli. And be here on time in the morning.

KAJA.   I certainly will. Good night, Mrs. Solness. (*She goes out by the hall door.*)

MRS. SOLNESS.   You've certainly been in luck, Halvard, to have gotten hold of that girl.

SOLNESS.   Oh yes. She's useful in all kinds of ways.

MRS. SOLNESS.   She looks it.

HERDAL.   A clever bookkeeper, too?

SOLNESS.   Well—she's had a lot of experience these past two years. And then she's willing and eager to take on anything.

MRS. SOLNESS.   Yes, that must be such a great comfort—

SOLNESS.   It is—especially when one's so used to doing without.

MRS. SOLNESS (*in a tone of mild reproach*).   Can *you* really say *that,* Halvard?

SOLNESS.   Ah, my dear Aline, no, no. I beg your pardon.

MRS. SOLNESS.   Don't trouble yourself. Well, Doctor, so you'll stop in again later and have some tea with us?

HERDAL.   As soon as I've made that house call, I'll be back.

MRS. SOLNESS.   Thank you. (*She goes out the door right.*)

SOLNESS.   Are you pressed for time, Doctor?

HERDAL.   No, not a bit.

SOLNESS.   May I have a few words with you?

HERDAL.   Yes, by all means.

SOLNESS.   Then let's sit down. (*He motions the doctor toward the rocker, and after seating himself in the armchair, looks at him sharply.*) Tell me—did you notice anything about Aline?

HERDAL.   Just now, you mean, when she was here?

SOLNESS.   Yes. With respect to me. Did you notice anything?

HERDAL (*smiling*). Well, really—one could hardly help noticing that your wife—hm—

SOLNESS. Go on.

HERDAL. That your wife doesn't think very much of this Miss Fosli.

SOLNESS. Nothing else? I could tell that myself.

HERDAL. And, after all, it's not so very surprising.

SOLNESS. What?

HERDAL. That she isn't exactly pleased that you enjoy another woman's company every day.

SOLNESS. That's true, you're right—and so is Aline. But it can't be changed.

HERDAL. Couldn't you hire a man instead?

SOLNESS. Just anyone off the street? No, thanks—that isn't the way I work.

HERDAL. But what if your wife—? When she *is* so delicate, what if she can't endure this thing?

SOLNESS. Even so—I'm tempted to say it can't make a bit of difference. I've got to keep Kaja Fosli. Nobody else will do.

HERDAL. Nobody else?

SOLNESS (*curtly*). No, nobody else.

HERDAL (*draws his chair in closer*). If I may, Mr. Solness, I'd like to ask you something, just between us.

SOLNESS. Yes, go ahead.

HERDAL. Women, you know—in certain areas they do have a painfully keen intuition—

SOLNESS. That they do. So—?

HERDAL. Well. All right, then. If your wife simply can't bear this Kaja Fosli—

SOLNESS. Yes, what then?

HERDAL. Hasn't she perhaps some tiny grounds for this instinctive dislike?

SOLNESS (*looks at him and rises*). Aha!

HERDAL. Now don't get excited. But really—hasn't she?

SOLNESS (*his voice clipped and decisive*). No.

HERDAL. Not the slightest grounds?

SOLNESS. Nothing, except her own suspicious mind.

HERDAL. I realize you've known a good many women in your life.

SOLNESS. I have, yes.

HERDAL. And thought very well of some of them, too.

SOLNESS. Oh yes, that also.

HERDAL. But in this case—there's nothing of that kind involved?

SOLNESS. No. Nothing whatever—on my side.

HERDAL. But on hers?

SOLNESS. I don't think you've any right to ask about that, Doctor.

HERDAL. We were discussing your wife's intuition.

SOLNESS. We were, yes. And for that matter—(*Dropping his voice.*) Aline's intuition, as you call it—you know, to a certain extent it's proved itself.

HERDAL. There—see!

SOLNESS. Dr. Herdal—let me tell you a strange story. That is, if you don't mind listening.

HERDAL. I like listening to strange stories.

SOLNESS. Ah, that's good. I guess you remember how I took on Knut Brovik and his son here—that time when the old man nearly went under.

HERDAL. I vaguely remember, yes.

SOLNESS. Because, you know, they're really a clever pair, those two. They've got ability, each in his own way. But then the son went out and got engaged. And then, of course, he was all for getting married—and launching his own career as a builder. Because the young people today, that's all they ever think about.

HERDAL (*laughing*). Yes, they have this bad habit of pairing off.

SOLNESS. Well, but *I* can't be bothered by that. You see, I need Ragnar—and the old man as well. He has a real knack for calculating stresses, cubic content—all that damned detail work.

HERDAL. Of course, that's important too.

SOLNESS. Yes, it is. But Ragnar, he felt he wanted and he had to be out on his own. There just wasn't any reasoning with him.

HERDAL. Even so, he stayed on with you.

SOLNESS. Yes, but now listen to what happened. One day she came in, this Kaja Fosli, on some errand for them. First time she'd ever been here. And when I saw those two, how completely wrapped up in each other they were, then the thought struck me: suppose I could get her here in the office, then maybe Ragnar would stay put too.

HERDAL. That was reasonable enough.

SOLNESS. But I didn't breathe a word of any of this then —just stood looking at her—every ounce of me wishing that I had her here. I made a little friendly conversation about one thing or another. And then she went away.

HERDAL. So?

SOLNESS. But the next day, in the late evening, after old Brovik and Ragnar had gone, she came by to see me again, acting as if we'd already struck a bargain.

HERDAL. Bargain? What about?

SOLNESS. About precisely what I'd been standing there wishing before—even though I hadn't uttered a word of it.

HERDAL. That *is* strange.

SOLNESS. Yes, isn't it? So she wanted to know what her job would be—and whether she'd be starting the very next morning. Things like that.

HERDAL. Don't you think she did that to be with her fiancé?

SOLNESS. I thought so too, at first. But no, that wasn't it. From the moment she came here to work, she started drifting away from him.

HERDAL. And over to you?

SOLNESS. Yes, completely. If I look at her when her back is turned, I can tell she feels it. She trembles and quivers if I even come near her. What do you make of it?

HERDAL. Hm—it's easy enough to explain.

SOLNESS. Well, but the rest of it, then? The fact that she thought I'd told her what I had only wished and willed—all in silence, inwardly. To myself. What do you say about that? Can you explain such a thing, Dr. Herdal?

HERDAL. No, I wouldn't attempt to.

SOLNESS. I thought as much. That's why I've never cared to discuss it till now. But you see, as time goes on, I'm finding it such a damned nuisance. Here, day after day, I have to keep on pretending that I'm— And then, poor girl, it's not fair to her. (*Furiously.*) But I can't help it! If she runs off—then Ragnar will follow, out on his own.

HERDAL. And you haven't told your wife this whole story.

SOLNESS. No.

HERDAL. Why in the world haven't you?

SOLNESS (*looking intently at him, his voice constrained*).

Because I feel that there's almost a kind of beneficial self-torment in letting Aline do me an injustice.

HERDAL (*shaking his head*). I don't understand one blessed word of this.

SOLNESS. Yes, don't you see—it's rather like making a small payment on a boundless, incalculable debt—

HERDAL. To your wife?

SOLNESS. Yes. And it always eases the mind a bit. Then you can breathe more freely for a while, you know.

HERDAL. God help me if I understand a word—

SOLNESS (*breaking in, and again getting up*). Yes, all right —so we won't speak of it anymore, then. (*He meanders across the room, comes back, and stops by the table. Looks at the doctor with a quiet smile.*) Now you really think you've done a neat job of drawing me out, hm, Doctor?

HERDAL (*somewhat upset*). Drawing you out? Mr. Solness, I'm still very much in the dark.

SOLNESS. Oh, come now—confess. Because really, you know, it's been so obvious to me!

HERDAL. *What's* so obvious to you?

SOLNESS (*slowly, in an undertone*). That behind this genial manner, you're keeping your eye on me.

HERDAL. Am I! Why on earth should I do that?

SOLNESS. Because you think I'm— (*Explosively.*) Oh, damn it! You think the same as Aline about me.

HERDAL. But what does she think of you, then?

SOLNESS. She's begun to think that I'm—I'm somewhat ill.

HERDAL. Ill! You! She's never breathed a word of it to me. What is it that's wrong with you, then?

SOLNESS (*leans over the back of the chair and whispers*). Aline's got the idea that I'm mad. *That's* what she thinks.

HERDAL (*rising*). But my dear Mr. Solness—!

SOLNESS. Yes, on my soul she does! And she has you thinking the same. Oh, I tell you, Doctor—I can see it in you so clear, so clear. Because I'm not so easily fooled, I'm not, I can tell you that.

HERDAL (*stares at him, amazed*). I've never, Mr. Solness —never had the least inkling of anything like this.

SOLNESS (*with a skeptical smile*). Really? Not at all?

HERDAL. No, never! And your wife certainly hasn't either—I'd almost swear to that.

SOLNESS. Well, you'd better not. Because, you know, maybe, in a way—maybe she's not so far off.

HERDAL. Look, I'm telling you now, really—!

SOLNESS (*breaking in, with a sweep of his hand*). All right there, Doctor—then let's not go on with this. Each to his own, that's the best. (*His tone changes to quiet amusement.*) But now listen, Doctor—hm—

HERDAL. Yes?

SOLNESS. If you don't think, then, that I'm, somehow—ill—or crazy or mad and that sort of thing—

HERDAL. Then what, hm?

SOLNESS. Then I guess you must imagine that I'm a very happy man.

HERDAL. Is *that* no more than imagination?

SOLNESS (*with a laugh*). Oh no, not a chance! God forbid! Just think—to be Solness, the master builder! Halvard Solness! Oh, thanks a lot!

HERDAL. Yes, I must say, to *me* it seems that you've had luck with you to an incredible degree.

SOLNESS (*masking a wan smile*). So I have. Can't complain of that.

HERDAL. First, that hideous old robbers' den burned down for you. And that was really a stroke of luck.

SOLNESS (*seriously*). It was Aline's family home that burned—don't forget.

HERDAL. Yes, for *her* it must have been a heavy loss.

SOLNESS. She hasn't recovered right to this day. Not in all these twelve–thirteen years.

HERDAL. What followed after, that must have been the worst blow for her.

SOLNESS. The two together.

HERDAL. But you yourself—*you* rose from those ashes. You began as a poor boy from the country—and now you stand the top man in your field. Ah, yes, Mr. Solness, you've surely had luck on your side.

SOLNESS (*glancing nervously at him*). Yes, but that's exactly why I've got this horrible fear.

HERDAL. Fear? For having luck on your side?

SOLNESS. It racks me, this fear—it racks me, morning and night. Because someday things have to change, you'll see.

HERDAL. Oh, rot! Where's this change coming from?

SOLNESS (*with firm conviction*).   From the young.

HERDAL.   Hah! The young! I'd hardly say that you're ob-solete. No, you've probably never been better established than you are now.

SOLNESS.   The change is coming. I can sense it. And I feel that it's coming closer. Someone or other will set up the cry: Step back for *me!* And all the others will storm in after, shaking their fists and shouting: Make room—make room—make room! Yes, Doctor, you better look out. Some-day youth will come here, knocking at the door—

HERDAL (*laughing*).   Well, good Lord, what if they do?

SOLNESS.   What if they do? Well, then it's the end of Sol-ness, the master builder.

(*A knock at the door to the left.*)

SOLNESS (*with a start*).   What's that? Did you hear it?

HERDAL.   Somebody's knocking.

SOLNESS (*loudly*).   Come in!

> (HILDA WANGEL *enters from the hall. She is of medium height, supple and well-formed. Slight sunburn. Dressed in hiking clothes, with short-ened skirt, sailor blouse open at the throat, and a little sailor hat. She has a knapsack on her back, a plaid in a strap, and a long alpenstock.*)

HILDA (*goes directly to* SOLNESS, *her eyes shining with hap-piness*).   Good evening!

SOLNESS (*looking hesitantly at her*).   Good evening—

HILDA (*laughing*).   I almost think you don't recognize me!

SOLNESS.   No—really—I must say, just at the moment—

HERDAL (*coming over*).   But I recognize you, young lady—

HILDA (*delighted*).   Oh no! It's you, that—?

HERDAL.   That's right, it's me. (*To* SOLNESS.) We met up at one of the mountain lodges last summer. (*To* HILDA.) What happened to all those other ladies?

HILDA.   Oh, they went off down the west slope.

HERDAL.   They didn't quite like all our fun in the eve-nings.

HILDA.   No, they certainly didn't.

HERDAL (*shaking his finger at her*).   Of course, we can't quite say you didn't flirt with us a bit.

HILDA. I'd a lot rather do that than sit knitting knee socks with all the old hens.

HERDAL (*laughing*). I couldn't agree with you more!

SOLNESS. Did you just get in town this evening?

HILDA. Yes, just now.

HERDAL. All by yourself, Miss Wangel?

HILDA. Of course!

SOLNESS. Wangel? Is your name Wangel?

HILDA (*looks at him with amused surprise*). Well, I should hope so.

SOLNESS. Then aren't you the daughter of the public health officer up at Lysanger?

HILDA (*still amused*). Sure. Whose daughter did you think I was?

SOLNESS. Ah, so that's where we met, up there. The summer I went up and built a tower on the old church.

HILDA (*more serious*). Yes, it was then.

SOLNESS. Well, that's a long time back.

HILDA (*her eyes fixed on him*). It's exactly ten years to the day.

SOLNESS. I'd swear you weren't any more than a child then.

HILDA (*carelessly*). Around twelve—thirteen, maybe.

HERDAL. Is this the first time you've been here in town, Miss Wangel?

HILDA. Yes, that's right.

SOLNESS. And you probably don't know anyone, hm?

HILDA. No one but you. Yes, and of course your wife.

SOLNESS. Then you know *her* too?

HILDA. Just slightly. We were together a few days at that health resort.

SOLNESS. Ah, up *there*.

HILDA. She told me please to visit her if I ever came down into town. (*Smiles.*) Even though she really didn't have to.

SOLNESS. Funny she never spoke of it—

(HILDA *puts her stick down by the stove, slips off the knapsack, and sets it and the plaid on the sofa.* DR. HERDAL *tries to assist.* SOLNESS *stands, gazing at her.*)

HILDA (*going up to him*). So now, if I may, I'd like to stay here overnight.

SOLNESS. I'm sure that can be arranged.

HILDA. 'Cause I haven't any other clothes, except what I've got on. Oh, and a set of underthings in my knapsack. But they better be washed. They're real grimy.

SOLNESS. Oh, well, that's easy to manage. Just let me speak to my wife—

HERDAL. Then I'll go on to my house call.

SOLNESS. Yes, do that. And stop back again later.

HERDAL (*playfully, with a glance at* HILDA). Oh, you can bet I will! (*Laughing.*) You read the future all right, Mr. Solness!

SOLNESS. How so?

HERDAL. Youth *did* come along, knocking at your door.

SOLNESS (*buoyantly*). Yes, but that was something else completely.

HERDAL. Oh yes, yes. Definitely!

> (*He goes out the hall door.* SOLNESS *opens the door
> on the right and calls into the room beyond.*)

SOLNESS. Aline! Would you come in here, please. There's a Miss Wangel to see you.

MRS. SOLNESS (*appearing at the door*). Who did you say? (*Sees* HILDA.) Oh, is it you, then? (*Goes over and takes her hand.*) So you've come to town after all.

SOLNESS. Miss Wangel's just arrived. And she's wondering if she might stay here overnight.

MRS. SOLNESS. Here with us? Why, of course.

SOLNESS. To get her clothes fixed up a bit, you know.

MRS. SOLNESS. I'll do what I can for you. It's no more than my duty. Is your trunk on the way?

HILDA. I haven't any trunk.

MRS. SOLNESS. Well, it'll all work out, I guess. Now if you'll just make yourself at home here with my husband a while, I'll see about getting a room comfortable for you.

SOLNESS. Can't we give up one of the nurseries? They're all ready and waiting.

MRS. SOLNESS. Oh yes. We've more than enough room there. (*To* HILDA.) Just sit down and rest a bit. (*She goes out, right.*)

(HILDA, *her hands behind her back, wanders
around the room, looking at one thing and another.* SOLNESS *stands in front of the table, his
hands also behind his back, following her with
his eyes.*)

HILDA (*stops and looks at him*). You have several nurseries?

SOLNESS. There are three nurseries in the house.

HILDA. That's plenty. You must have an awful lot of children.

SOLNESS. No. We have no children. But now you can be
the child here for a while.

HILDA. Yes, for tonight. There won't be a peep out of me.
I'm going to try to sleep like a stone.

SOLNESS. Yes, you're pretty tired, I'll bet.

HILDA. Oh no! But, after all— You know it is so ravishing just to lie and dream.

SOLNESS. Do you often dream at night?

HILDA. Oh yes! Nearly always.

SOLNESS. What do you dream about most?

HILDA. I won't tell you, not tonight. Some other time—
maybe. (*She starts wandering about the room again, stops
at the desk, and fingers the books and papers a little.*)

SOLNESS (*approaching her*). Something you're looking for?

HILDA. No, it's only to see all this here. (*Turning.*) But
I shouldn't, maybe?

SOLNESS. Yes, go ahead.

HILDA. Is it you that writes in this big ledger?

SOLNESS. No, that's the bookkeeper.

HILDA. A woman?

SOLNESS (*smiles*). Of course.

HILDA. Someone you have working here?

SOLNESS. Yes.

HILDA. Is she married?

SOLNESS. No, she's single.

HILDA. I see.

SOLNESS. But I understand she's getting married now
quite soon.

HILDA. That's very nice—for her.

SOLNESS. But not so nice for me. Because then I'll have
no one to help me.

HILDA. Can't you find somebody else who's just as good?

SOLNESS. Maybe you'd like to stay here and—and write in the ledger?

HILDA (*giving him a dark look*). Yes, wouldn't that suit you! No, thanks—we're not having any of that. (*She strolls across the room again and settles into the rocker.* SOLNESS *follows her over to the table.* HILDA *goes on in the same tone.*) Because there are plenty of other things to be done around here. (*Looks up at him, smiling.*) Don't you think so too?

SOLNESS. Why, of course. First of all, I expect you'll want to tour the shops and do yourself up in style.

HILDA (*amused*). No, somehow I think I'll pass that up.

SOLNESS. Oh?

HILDA. Yes—since, you see, I'm completely broke.

SOLNESS (*laughing*). No trunk, or money either!

HILDA. Nothing of both. But shoot! What's the difference, anyway?

SOLNESS. Ah, I really like you for that!

HILDA. Only for that?

SOLNESS. Among other things. (*Sits in the armchair.*) Is your father still living?

HILDA. Yes, still living.

SOLNESS. And are you thinking of studying here now?

HILDA. No, that's not what I'd thought.

SOLNESS. But you *are* staying here for some time, I suppose?

HILDA. Depends how things go. (*A pause, while she sits rocking and looking at him half seriously, half with a suppressed smile. She then takes off her hat and places it on the table before her.*) Mr. Solness?

SOLNESS. Yes?

HILDA. Are you very forgetful?

SOLNESS. Forgetful? No, not as far as *I* know.

HILDA. But do you absolutely not want to talk to me about what happened up there?

SOLNESS (*with a momentary start*). Up at Lysanger? (*Carelessly.*) Well, there's not much to talk about, I'd say.

HILDA (*gazing reproachfully at him*). How can you sit there and say that!

SOLNESS. All right, *you* tell me about it then.

HILDA. When the tower was finished, we had a big function in town.

SOLNESS. Yes, that's one day I won't soon forget.

HILDA (*smiling*). Won't you? So good of you!

SOLNESS. Good?

HILDA. They had music in the churchyard. And there were hundreds and hundreds of people. We schoolgirls were all dressed in white, and we had flags, all of us.

SOLNESS. Oh yes, the flags—I remember them, all right.

HILDA. Then you climbed straight up the scaffolding, straight to the very top—and you had a great wreath with you—and you hung it up high on the weather vane.

SOLNESS (*interrupting brusquely*). I did that back in those days. It's an old custom.

HILDA. It was so wonderfully thrilling to stand below, looking up at you. What if he slipped and fell—he, the master builder himself!

SOLNESS (*as if thrusting the subject aside*). Yes, all right, that could have happened too. Because one of those little devils in white—how she carried on, screaming up at me—

HILDA (*eyes sparkling in delight*). "Hurray for Mr. Solness, the master builder!" Yes!

SOLNESS. Waving her flag and flourishing it till my—my head nearly spun at the sight of it.

HILDA (*growing more quiet and serious*). That little devil —that was *me*.

SOLNESS (*peering fixedly at her*). I'm sure of that now.

HILDA (*vivacious again*). It was so terribly thrilling and lovely. I'd never dreamt that anywhere in the world there was a builder who could build a tower so high. And then, that you could stand there right at the top, large as life! And that you weren't the least bit dizzy! That's what made me so—almost dizzy to realize.

SOLNESS. What makes you so sure I wasn't—?

HILDA (*deprecatingly*). Oh, honestly—come on! I felt it within me. How else could you stand up there singing?

SOLNESS (*stares astonished at her*). Singing? I sang?

HILDA. Yes, really you did.

SOLNESS (*shaking his head*). I've never sung a note in my life.

HILDA. Yes, you were singing then. It sounded like harps in the air.

SOLNESS (*thoughtfully*). It's something very peculiar—this.

HILDA (*silent a moment, then looking at him and speaking softly*). But then—afterwards—came the *real* thing.

SOLNESS. The real thing?

HILDA (*her vivacity kindling again*). Oh, now I don't have to remind you of that!

SOLNESS. Better give me a little reminder there, too.

HILDA. Don't you remember a big banquet for you at the club?

SOLNESS. Of course. That must have been the same afternoon—because I left the next morning.

HILDA. And after the club, you were asked home to our place for the evening.

SOLNESS. You're right, Miss Wangel. Amazing how you can keep all these details clear in your mind.

HILDA. Details! Oh, you! I suppose it was just another detail that I was alone in the room when you came in?

SOLNESS. Were you?

HILDA (*not answering him*). You didn't call me any little devil then.

SOLNESS. No, I guess not.

HILDA. You said I was lovely in my white dress—and that I looked like a little princess.

SOLNESS. I'm sure you did, Miss Wangel. And then, feeling the way I did that day, so light and free—

HILDA. And then you said that when I grew up, I could be *your* princess.

SOLNESS (*with a short laugh*). Really—I said that too?

HILDA. Yes, you did. And when I asked how long I should wait, then you said you'd come back in ten years, like a troll, and carry me off—to Spain or someplace. And there you promised to buy me a kingdom.

SOLNESS (*as before*). Well, after a good meal one's not in a mood to count pennies. But did I really *say* all that?

HILDA (*laughing softly*). Yes, and you also said what the kingdom would be called.

SOLNESS. Oh? What?

HILDA. It was going to be the Kingdom of Orangia, you said.

SOLNESS. Ah, that's a delectable name.

HILDA. No, I didn't like it at all. It was as if you were out to make fun of me.

SOLNESS. But I hadn't the slightest intention to.

HILDA. No, it wouldn't seem so—not after what you did next—

SOLNESS. What on earth did I do next?

HILDA. Well, this is really the limit if you've even forgotten *that*! A thing like that I think anybody ought to remember.

SOLNESS. All right, just give me a tiny hint, then, maybe —hm?

HILDA (*looking intently at him*). You caught me up and kissed me, Mr. Solness.

SOLNESS (*open-mouthed, getting up*). I *did*!

HILDA. Oh yes, that you did. You held me in both your arms and bent me back and kissed me—many times.

SOLNESS. But, my dear Miss Wangel—!

HILDA (*rising*). You can't deny it, can you?

SOLNESS. Yes, I most emphatically do deny it!

HILDA (*looking scornfully at him*). I see. (*She turns and walks slowly over close by the stove and remains standing motionless, face averted from him, hands behind her back. A short pause.*)

SOLNESS (*going cautiously over behind her*). Miss Wangel—? (HILDA *stays silent, not moving.*) Don't stand there like a statue. These things you've been saying—you must have dreamed them. (*Putting his hand on her arm.*) Now listen— (HILDA *moves her arm impatiently.* SOLNESS *appears struck by a sudden thought.*) Or else—wait a minute! There's something strange in back of all this, you'll see! (*In a hushed but emphatic voice.*) This all must have been in my thoughts. I must have willed it. Wished it. Desired it. And so— Doesn't that make sense? (HILDA *remains still.* SOLNESS *speaks impatiently.*) Oh, all right, for God's sake—so I *did* the thing too!

HILDA (*turning her head a bit, but without looking at him*). Then you confess?

SOLNESS. Yes. Whatever you please.

HILDA. That you threw your arms around me?

SOLNESS. All right!

HILDA. And bent me back.

SOLNESS. Way over back.

HILDA. And kissed me.

SOLNESS. Yes, I did it.

HILDA. Many times?

SOLNESS. As many as you ever could want.

HILDA (*whirling about to face him, the sparkle once again in her delighted eyes*). There, you see—I did get it out of you in the end!

SOLNESS (*with a thin smile*). Yes—imagine my forgetting something like that.

HILDA (*sulking a little once more, moving away from him*). Oh, you've kissed a good many in your time, I think.

SOLNESS. No, you mustn't think that of me.

(HILDA *sits in the armchair.* SOLNESS *stands leaning on the rocking chair, watching her closely.*)

SOLNESS. Miss Wangel?

HILDA. Yes.

SOLNESS. How was it, now? What went on next—with us?

HILDA. Nothing else went on. You know that well enough. Because then all the others came in, and—ffft!

SOLNESS. That's right. The others came. And I could forget that too.

HILDA. Oh, you haven't forgotten a thing. You're just a little ashamed. Nobody forgets this kind of thing.

SOLNESS. No, it wouldn't seem likely.

HILDA (*looking at him, vivacious again*). Or maybe you've even forgotten what day it was?

SOLNESS. What day—?

HILDA. Yes, what day you hung the wreath on the tower? Well? Quick, say it!

SOLNESS. Hm—I guess I've forgotten the actual date. I only know it was ten years ago. Sometime in the fall.

HILDA (*nodding her head slowly several times*). It was ten years ago. The nineteenth of September.

SOLNESS. Ah, yes, it must have been about then. So you've remembered that too! (*Hesitates.*) But wait a minute—! Yes —today it's also the nineteenth of September.

HILDA. Yes, it is. And the ten years are up. And you didn't come—as you promised me.

SOLNESS. Promised you? Threatened, don't you mean?

HILDA. It never struck me as some kind of threat.

SOLNESS. Well, teased that I would, then.

HILDA. Is that all you wanted? To tease me?

SOLNESS. Well, or to joke a bit with you, then! Lord knows I don't remember. But it must have been something like that—for you were only a child at the time.

HILDA. Oh, maybe I wasn't so much of a child either. Not quite the little kitten you thought.

SOLNESS (*looks searchingly at her*). Did you really in all seriousness get the idea I'd be coming back?

HILDA (*hiding a rather roguish smile*). Of course! That's what I expected.

SOLNESS. That I'd come to your home and carry you off with me?

HILDA. Just like a troll, yes.

SOLNESS. And make you a princess?

HILDA. It's what you promised.

SOLNESS. And give you a kingdom, too?

HILDA (*gazing at the ceiling*). Why not? After all, it didn't have to be the everyday, garden-variety kingdom.

SOLNESS. But something else that was just as good.

HILDA. Oh, at least just as good. (*Glancing at him.*) If you could build the highest church tower in the world, it seemed to me you certainly should be able to come up with some kind of kingdom, too.

SOLNESS. (*shaking his head*). I just can't figure you out, Miss Wangel.

HILDA. You can't? I think it's so simple.

SOLNESS. No, I can't make out whether you mean all you say—or whether you're just having some fun—

HILDA (*smiles*). Fooling around—and teasing, maybe. I too?

SOLNESS. Exactly. Making fools—of both of us. (*Looking at her.*) How long have you known I was married?

HILDA. Right from the start. Why do you ask about *that*?

SOLNESS (*casually*). Oh, nothing—just wondered. (*Lowering his voice, with a straight look at her.*) Why have you come?

HILDA. I want my kingdom. Time's up.

SOLNESS (*laughing in spite of himself*). You are the limit!

HILDA (*gaily*). Give us the kingdom, come on! (*Drumming with her fingers.*) One kingdom, on the line!

SOLNESS (*pushing the rocking chair closer and sitting*). Seriously now—why have you come? What do you really want to do here?

HILDA. Oh, to begin with, I want to go around and look at everything you've built.

SOLNESS. That'll keep you going a while.

HILDA. Yes, you've built such an awful lot.

SOLNESS. I have, yes. Mainly these later years.

HILDA. Many more church towers? Enormously high ones?

SOLNESS. No, I don't build any church towers now. Nor churches either.

HILDA. What *do* you build then?

SOLNESS. Homes for human beings.

HILDA (*reflectively*). Couldn't you put a small—a small church tower up over the homes as well?

SOLNESS (*with a start*). What do you mean by that?

HILDA. I mean—something pointing—free, sort of, into the sky. With a weather vane way up in the reeling heights.

SOLNESS (*musing*). How odd that you should say that. It's exactly what, most of all, I've wanted.

HILDA (*impatiently*). But why don't you do it, then!

SOLNESS (*shaking his head*). Because people won't have it.

HILDA. Imagine—not to want that!

SOLNESS (*more lightly*). But I'm building a new home now —right opposite this.

HILDA. For yourself?

SOLNESS. Yes. It's almost ready. And it has a tower.

HILDA. A high one?

SOLNESS. Yes.

HILDA. Very high?

SOLNESS. People are bound to say, too high. At least for a home.

HILDA. I'll be out looking at that tower first thing in the morning.

SOLNESS (*sitting with his hand propping his cheek, gazing at her*). Miss Wangel, tell me—what's your name? Your first name, I mean?

HILDA. You know—it's Hilda.

SOLNESS (*as before*). Hilda? So?

HILDA. You don't remember *that*? You called me Hilda yourself—the day when you acted up.

SOLNESS. I did that, too?

HILDA. But then you said "little Hilda," and I didn't care for that.

SOLNESS. So, Miss Hilda, you didn't care for that.

HILDA. Not at such a time, no. But—Princess Hilda—that's going to sound quite nice, I think.

SOLNESS. No doubt. Princess Hilda of—of that kingdom, what was it called?

HILDA. Ish! I'm through with that stupid kingdom! I want a different one, completely.

SOLNESS (*who has leaned back in his chair, goes on studying her*). Isn't it strange—? The more I think about it, the more it seems to me that all these years I've been going around tormented by—hm—

HILDA. By what?

SOLNESS. By a search for something—some old experience I thought I'd forgotten. But I've never had an inkling of what it could be.

HILDA. You should have tied a knot in your handkerchief, Mr. Solness.

SOLNESS. Then I'd only wind up puzzling over what the knot might mean.

HILDA. Yes, there's even that kind of troll in the world too.

SOLNESS (*slowly gets up*). It's really so good that you've come to me now.

HILDA (*with a probing look*). Is it?

SOLNESS. I've been so alone here—and felt so utterly helpless watching it all. (*Dropping his voice.*) I should tell you —I've begun to grow afraid—so awfully afraid of the young.

HILDA (*sniffing scornfully*). Pooh! Are the young anything to fear!

SOLNESS. Decidedly. That's why I've locked and bolted myself in. (*Mysteriously.*) Wait and see, the young will come here, thundering at the door! Breaking in on me!

HILDA. Then I think you should go out and open your door to the young.

SOLNESS. Open the door?

HILDA. Yes. Let them come in to you—as friends.

SOLNESS. No, no, no! The young—don't you see, they're retribution—the spearhead of change—as if they came marching under some new flag.

HILDA (*rises, looks at him, her lips trembling as she speaks*). Can you find a use for *me*, Mr. Solness?

SOLNESS. Oh, of course I can! Because I feel that you've come, too, almost—under some new flag. And then it's youth against youth—!

(DR. HERDAL *comes in by the hall door.*)

HERDAL. So? You and Miss Wangel still here?

SOLNESS. Yes. We've had a great many things to talk about.

HILDA. Both old and new.

HERDAL. Oh, have you?

HILDA. Really, it's been such fun. Because Mr. Solness— he's got just a fantastic memory. He remembers the tiniest little details in a flash.

(MRS. SOLNESS *enters by the door to the right.*)

MRS. SOLNESS. All right, Miss Wangel, your room's all ready for you now.

HILDA. Oh, how kind of you.

SOLNESS (*to his wife*). Nursery?

MRS. SOLNESS. Yes, the middle one. But first we ought to have a bite to eat, don't you think?

SOLNESS (*nodding to* HILDA). So Hilda sleeps in the nursery, then.

MRS. SOLNESS (*looking at him*). Hilda?

SOLNESS. Yes, Miss Wangel's name is Hilda. I knew her when she was small.

MRS. SOLNESS. No, did you really, Halvard? Well—shall we? Supper's waiting.

(*She takes* DR. HERDAL's *arm and they go out, right.*
HILDA *meanwhile gathers up her hiking gear.*)

HILDA (*softly and quickly to* SOLNESS). Is that true, what you said? *Can* you find a use for me?

SOLNESS (*taking her things away from her*). You're the one person I've needed the most.

HILDA (*clasping her hands and looking at him with wondering eyes full of joy*). Oh, you beautiful, big world—!

SOLNESS (*tensely*). What—?

HILDA. Then I have my kingdom!

SOLNESS (*involuntarily*). Hilda—!

HILDA (*her lips suddenly trembling again*). *Almost*—that's what I meant.

(*She goes out to the right, with* SOLNESS *following.*)

⌒ᴠ ACT TWO ⟩⌒

An attractively furnished small living room in SOLNESS's
*house. A glass door in the back wall opens on the veranda
and garden. Diagonally cutting the right-hand corner is a
broad bow window with flower stands before it. The left-
hand corner is similarly cut by a wall containing a door
papered to match. In each of the side walls, an ordinary
door. In the right foreground, a console table and a large
mirror. Flowers and plants richly displayed. In the left
foreground, a sofa, along with table and chairs. Further
back, a bookcase. Out in the room in front of the bow
window, a little table and a couple of chairs. It is early
in the morning.*

SOLNESS *is sitting at the little table with* RAGNAR
BROVIK'S *portfolio open before him. He is leafing through
the drawings and now and then looks sharply at one.*
MRS. SOLNESS *moves silently about with a small watering
can, freshening the flowers. She wears black, as before.
Her hat, coat, and parasol lie on a chair by the mirror.
Unnoticed by her,* SOLNESS *follows her several times with
his eyes. Neither of them speaks.*

KAJA FOSLI *comes quietly in by the door on the left.*

SOLNESS (*turns his head and speaks with careless indifference*). Oh, is that you?

KAJA. I just wanted to tell you I'm here.

SOLNESS. Yes, that's fine. Isn't Ragnar there too?

KAJA. No, not yet. He had to wait a bit for the doctor.
But he'll be along soon to find out—

SOLNESS. How's the old man getting on?

KAJA. Poorly. He's so very sorry, but he can't leave his
bed today.

SOLNESS. Of course not. He mustn't stir. But you go on to
your work.

KAJA. Yes. (*Pauses at the door.*) Will you want to speak
to Ragnar when he gets in?

SOLNESS. No—I've nothing special to say.

(KAJA *goes out again to the left.* SOLNESS *continues to sit and leaf through the drawings.*)

MRS. SOLNESS (*over by the plants*). I wonder if he won't die now, he too.

SOLNESS (*looking at her*). He—and who else?

MRS. SOLNESS (*not answering*). Yes, old Brovik—he's going to die now too, Halvard. You wait and see.

SOLNESS. Aline dear, couldn't you do with a little walk?

MRS. SOLNESS. Yes, I really suppose I could. (*She goes on tending the flowers.*)

SOLNESS (*bent over the drawings*). Is she still sleeping?

MRS. SOLNESS (*looking at him*). Is it Miss Wangel you're sitting there thinking about?

SOLNESS (*casually*). I just happened to remember her.

MRS. SOLNESS. Miss Wangel's been up for hours.

SOLNESS. Oh, she has?

MRS. SOLNESS. When I looked in, she was busy arranging her things. (*She goes to the mirror and begins slowly putting her hat on.*)

SOLNESS (*after a short silence*). So we did find use for one of the nurseries after all, Aline.

MRS. SOLNESS. Yes, we did.

SOLNESS. And I think that's better really, than all of them standing empty.

MRS. SOLNESS. You're right—that emptiness, it's horrible.

SOLNESS (*closes the portfolio, rises, and approaches her*). You're only going to see *this,* Aline—that from now on things'll go better for us. Much pleasanter. Life will be easier—especially for you.

MRS. SOLNESS (*looking at him*). From now on?

SOLNESS. Yes, believe me, Aline—

MRS. SOLNESS. You mean— because *she's* come?

SOLNESS (*restraining himself*). I mean, of course, once we're in the new house.

MRS. SOLNESS (*taking her coat*). Yes, do you think so, Halvard? That things will go better there?

SOLNESS. I'm sure of it. And you, don't you have the same feeling?

MRS. SOLNESS. I feel absolutely nothing about the new house.

SOLNESS (*dejected*). Well, that's certainly hard for me to hear. It's mostly for your sake that I built it. (*He makes a motion toward helping her on with her coat.*)

MRS. SOLNESS (*evading him*). As it is, you do all too much for my sake.

SOLNESS (*rather heatedly*). No, no, Aline, don't talk like that! I can't stand hearing you say such things.

MRS. SOLNESS. All right, then I won't say them, Halvard.

SOLNESS. But I swear I'm right. You'll see, it'll go so well for you over there.

MRS. SOLNESS. Oh, Lord—so well for me—!

SOLNESS (*eagerly*). Oh yes, it will! Just trust that it will. Because over there—you'll see, there'll be so very much to remind you of your own old home—

MRS. SOLNESS. Of what was Mother and Father's—that burned to the ground.

SOLNESS (*gently*). Yes, my poor Aline. That was a terrible blow for you.

MRS. SOLNESS (*breaking out in lamentation*). You can build as much as you ever want, Halvard—but for *me* you can never build up a real home again.

SOLNESS (*pacing across the room*). Then, for God's sake, let's not discuss it anymore.

MRS. SOLNESS. We don't ordinarily discuss it at all. Because you only push it aside—

SOLNESS (*stops short and looks at her*). Do I? And why should I do that? Push it aside?

MRS. SOLNESS. Oh, don't you think I know you, Halvard? You want so much to spare me—to find excuses for me, all that you can.

SOLNESS (*eyes wide in amazement*). For *you*! Is it you—yourself you're talking of, Aline?

MRS. SOLNESS. Yes, it has to be me, of course.

SOLNESS (*involuntarily, to himself*). That, too!

MRS. SOLNESS. After all, with the old house—it couldn't have happened otherwise. Once disaster's on the wind, then—

SOLNESS. Yes, you're right. There's no running away from trouble—they say.

MRS. SOLNESS. But it's the horror after the fire—*that's* the thing! That, that, that!

SOLNESS (*vehemently*). Don't think about it, Aline!

MRS. SOLNESS. Oh, but it's what I have to think about, exactly that. And finally talk about for once, too. Because I don't see how I can bear it any longer. And then, never the least chance to forgive myself—!

SOLNESS (*exclaiming*). Yourself!

MRS. SOLNESS. Yes, you know I had my duties on both sides—both to you and to the babies. I should have made myself strong. Not let fear take hold of me so. Or grief either, because my old home had burned. (*Wringing her hands.*) Oh, if I'd only been strong enough, Halvard!

SOLNESS (*softly, moved, coming closer*). Aline—you must promise me never to think these thoughts again. Promise me now.

MRS. SOLNESS. Good heavens—promise! Promise! Anyone can promise—

SOLNESS (*clenching his fists and crossing the room*). Oh, how hopeless it is! Never a touch of sun! Not the least glimmer of light in this home!

MRS. SOLNESS. This is no home, Halvard.

SOLNESS. No, that's true enough. (*Heavily.*) And God knows if you're not right that it'll be no better for us in the new place.

MRS. SOLNESS. It can never be different. Just as empty—just as barren—there as here.

SOLNESS (*fiercely*). But why in the world did we build it, then? Tell me that?

MRS. SOLNESS. No, that answer you'll have to find in yourself.

SOLNESS (*glancing at her suspiciously*). What do you mean by *that*, Aline?

MRS. SOLNESS. What do I mean?

SOLNESS. Yes, damn it—! You said it so strangely—as if you were holding something back.

MRS. SOLNESS. No, I can assure you—

SOLNESS (*coming closer*). Ah, thanks a lot! I know what I know. I've got eyes and ears, Aline, don't forget.

MRS. SOLNESS. But what's this about? What is it?

SOLNESS (*planting himself in front of her*). Aren't you out to discover some sly, hidden meaning in the most innocent thing I say?

MRS. SOLNESS. *I*, you say? *I* do that?

SOLNESS (*laughing*). Of course that's only natural, Aline

—when you've got a sick man around to deal with—

MRS. SOLNESS (*anxiously*). Sick? Are you ill, Halvard?

SOLNESS (*in an outburst*). Half mad, then. A crazy man. Anything you want to call me.

MRS. SOLNESS (*groping for a chair and sitting*). Halvard—for God's sake—!

SOLNESS. But you're wrong, both of you. Both you and the doctor. It's no such thing with me. (*He paces back and forth, MRS. SOLNESS following him anxiously with her eyes, until he goes over and speaks quietly to her.*) In fact, there's nothing the matter with me at all.

MRS. SOLNESS. No, of course not. But what is it, then, that's upsetting you?

SOLNESS. It's this, that I often feel that I'm going to sink under this awful burden of debt—

MRS. SOLNESS. Debt? But you're not in debt to anyone, Halvard.

SOLNESS (*softly, with emotion*). Infinitely in debt to you —to you, Aline—to you.

MRS. SOLNESS (*rising slowly*). What's back of all this? Might as well tell me right now.

SOLNESS. But nothing's back of it. I've never done anything against you—not that I've ever known. And yet—there's this sense of some enormous guilt hanging over me, crushing me down.

MRS. SOLNESS. A guilt toward *me*?

SOLNESS. Toward you most of all.

MRS. SOLNESS. Then you are—ill, after all, Halvard.

SOLNESS (*wearily*). I suppose so—something like that. (*Looks toward the door to the right, as it opens.*) Ah! But it's brightening up.

> (HILDA WANGEL *comes in. She has made some changes in her clothes and let down her skirt.*)

HILDA. Good morning, Mr. Solness!

SOLNESS (*nodding*). Sleep well?

HILDA. Beautifully! Like a child in a cradle. Oh—I lay and stretched myself like—like a princess.

SOLNESS (*smiling a little*). Quite comfortable, then.

HILDA. I'll say.

SOLNESS. And I suppose you dreamed?

HILDA. Oh yes. But that was awful.

SOLNESS. So?

HILDA. Yes, 'cause I dreamed I was falling over a terribly high, steep cliff. *You* ever dream such things?

SOLNESS. Oh yes—now and then—

HILDA. It's wonderfully thrilling—just to fall and fall.

SOLNESS. It makes my blood run cold.

HILDA. You pull your legs up under you while you fall?

SOLNESS. Of course, as high as possible.

HILDA. Me too.

MRS. SOLNESS (*taking her parasol*). I've got to go down into town now, Halvard. (*To* HILDA.) And I'll try to pick up a few of the things you need.

HILDA (*about to throw her arms around her*). Oh, Mrs. Solness, you're a dear! You're really too kind—terribly kind—

MRS. SOLNESS (*deprecatingly, freeing herself*). Oh, not at all. It's simply my duty, so I'm quite happy to do it.

HILDA (*piqued and pouting*). Actually, I don't see any reason why I can't go out myself—with my clothes all neat again. Why can't I?

MRS. SOLNESS. To tell the truth, I rather think people would be staring at you a bit.

HILDA (*sniffing*). Pooh! Is that all? But that's fun.

SOLNESS (*with suppressed bad temper*). Yes, but you see people might get the idea that *you* were mad too.

HILDA. Mad? Are there so many mad people in town here?

SOLNESS (*points at his forehead*). Here's one, at least.

HILDA. You—Mr. Solness!

MRS. SOLNESS. Oh, Halvard, really!

SOLNESS. You mean you haven't noticed *that*?

HILDA. No, I certainly have not. (*Reflects a moment and laughs a little.*) Well, maybe in just one thing.

SOLNESS. Ah, hear that, Aline?

MRS. SOLNESS. What sort of thing, Miss Wangel?

HILDA. I'm not saying.

SOLNESS. Oh yes, come on!

HILDA. No thanks—I'm not *that* crazy.

MRS. SOLNESS. When Miss Wangel and you are alone, I'm sure she'll tell you, Halvard.

SOLNESS. Oh—you think so?

MRS. SOLNESS. Why, of course. After all, you've known

her so well in the past. Ever since she was a child—you tell me. (*She goes out by the door on the left.*)

HILDA (*after a brief pause*). Does your wife not like me at all?

SOLNESS. Does it seem so to you?

HILDA. Couldn't you see it yourself?

SOLNESS (*evasively*). These last years Aline's become very shy around people.

HILDA. Has she really?

SOLNESS. But if only you got to know her well— Because underneath, she's so kind—so good—such a fine person—

HILDA (*impatiently*). But if she *is* all that—why does she run on so about duty!

SOLNESS. Duty?

HILDA. Yes. She said she'd go out and buy me some things because that was her *duty*. Oh, I can't stand that mean, ugly word!

SOLNESS. Why not?

HILDA. No, it sounds so cold and sharp and cutting. Duty, duty, duty! Don't you feel it too? As if it's made to cut.

SOLNESS. Hm—never thought of it, really.

HILDA. But it's true! And if she's so kind—the way you say—why would she put it like that?

SOLNESS. But, my Lord, what would you want her to say?

HILDA. She could have said she'd do it because she liked me a lot. Something like that she could have said. Something really warm and straight from the heart—you know?

SOLNESS (*looking at her*). Is *that* what you'd want?

HILDA. Yes, just that. (*She strolls around the room, stopping at the bookcase and examining the books.*)

HILDA. You have an awful lot of books.

SOLNESS. Oh, I've picked up a fair number.

HILDA. Do you read them all, too?

SOLNESS. I used to try, in the old days. Do *you* do much reading?

HILDA. No, never! At least, not now. I can't connect with them anymore.

SOLNESS. It's exactly the same for me.

(HILDA *wanders about a little, stops by the small table, opens the portfolio and turns over some sketches.*)

HILDA. Did you do all these designs?

SOLNESS. No, they're done by a young man I've had helping me.

HILDA. Someone you've been teaching.

SOLNESS. Oh yes, I guess he's learned something from me, all right.

HILDA (*sitting*). Then he must be quite clever, hm? (*Studies one of the sketches a moment.*) Isn't he?

SOLNESS. Oh, could be worse. For *my* work, though—

HILDA. Oh yes! He must be dreadfully clever.

SOLNESS. You think you can see it in the drawings?

HILDA. Ffft! These scribbles! But if he's been studying with *you*, then—

SOLNESS. Oh, for that matter, there've been plenty of others who've studied with me, and none of them have ever come to much.

HILDA (*looks at him, shaking her head*). For the life of me, I don't understand how you can be so stupid.

SOLNESS. Stupid? You really think I'm so stupid?

HILDA. Yes, really I do. When you can take time to go on teaching these fellows—

SOLNESS (*with a start*). Well, why not?

HILDA (*rising, half serious, half laughing*). Oh, come on, Mr. Solness! What's the point of it? Nobody but you should have a right to build. You should be all alone in that. Have the field to yourself. Now you know.

SOLNESS (*involuntarily*). Hilda—!

HILDA. Well?

SOLNESS. What on earth gave you that idea?

HILDA. Am I so very wrong, then?

SOLNESS. No, that's not it. But let me tell you something.

HILDA. What?

SOLNESS. Here, in my solitude and silence—endlessly— I've been brooding on that same idea.

HILDA. Well, it seems only natural to me.

SOLNESS (*looks rather sharply at her*). And I'm sure you've already noticed it.

HILDA. No, not a bit.

SOLNESS. But before—when you said you thought I was— unbalanced, there was one thing—

HILDA. Oh, I was thinking of something quite different.

SOLNESS. What do you mean, different?

HILDA. Never you mind, Mr. Solness.

SOLNESS (*crossing the room*). All right—have it your way. (*Stops at the bow window.*) Come over here, and I'll show you something.

HILDA (*approaching*). What's that?

SOLNESS. You see—out there in the garden—?

HILDA. Yes?

SOLNESS (*pointing*). Right above that big quarry?

HILDA. The new house, you mean?

SOLNESS. The one under construction, yes. Nearly finished.

HILDA. I think it's got a very high tower.

SOLNESS. The scaffolding's still up.

HILDA. That's your new house?

SOLNESS. Yes.

HILDA. The one you're about to move into?

SOLNESS. Yes.

HILDA (*looking at him*). Are there nurseries in that house too?

SOLNESS. Three, same as here.

HILDA. And no children.

SOLNESS. Not now—nor ever.

HILDA (*half smiling*). So, isn't that just what I said—?

SOLNESS. Namely—?

HILDA. Namely, that you are a little—sort of mad, after all.

SOLNESS. Was that what you were thinking of?

HILDA. Yes, of all those empty nurseries I slept in.

SOLNESS (*dropping his voice*). We did have children— Aline and I.

HILDA (*looking intently at him*). You did—?

SOLNESS. Two little boys. Both the same age.

HILDA. Twins.

SOLNESS. Yes, twins. That's some eleven, twelve years ago now.

HILDA (*cautiously*). And both of them are—? The twins— they're not with you anymore?

SOLNESS (*with quiet feeling*). We had them only about three weeks. Not even that. (*In an outburst.*) Oh, Hilda, how amazingly lucky for me that you've come! Now at last I've got someone I can talk to.

HILDA. You can't talk with—*her*?

SOLNESS. Not about this. Not the way I want to and need

to. (*Heavily*.) And there's so much else I can never talk out.

HILDA (*her voice subdued*). Was that all you meant when you said you needed me?

SOLNESS. Mostly that, I guess. Yesterday, anyhow. To-day I'm not so sure— (*Breaking off*.) Come here, Hilda, and let's get settled. Sit there on the sofa—then you can look out in the garden. (HILDA *sits in the corner of the sofa*. SOLNESS *draws over a chair*.) Would you care to hear about it?

HILDA. Yes, I like listening to you.

SOLNESS (*sitting*). Then I'll give you the whole story.

HILDA. Now I'm looking at both the garden and you, Mr. Solness. So tell me. Please!

SOLNESS (*pointing out the bow window*). Over on that ridge there—where you see the new house—

HILDA. Yes.

SOLNESS. That's where Aline and I lived in those early years. There was an old house up there then, one that had belonged to her mother—and then passed on to us. And this whole enormous garden came with it.

HILDA. Did that house have a tower too?

SOLNESS. No, not at all. From the outside it was an ugly, dark, overgrown packing case. And yet, for all that, it was snug and cozy enough inside.

HILDA. Did you tear the old crate down, then?

SOLNESS. No, it burned.

HILDA. To the ground?

SOLNESS. Yes.

HILDA. Was it a terrible loss for you?

SOLNESS. Depends how you look at it. As a builder, the fire put me in business—

HILDA. Well, but—?

SOLNESS. We'd just had the two little boys at the time—

HILDA. The poor little twins, yes.

SOLNESS. They'd come so plump and healthy into life. And every day you could see them growing.

HILDA. Babies grow fast at the start.

SOLNESS. There was nothing finer in the world to see than Aline, lying there, holding those two— But then it came, the night of the fire—

HILDA (*excitedly*). What happened? Go on! Was anyone burned?

SOLNESS. No, not that. They were all rescued out of the house—

HILDA. Well, but then what—?

SOLNESS. The fright shook Aline to the core. The alarms —getting out of the house—and all the confusion—the whole thing at night, in the freezing cold to boot. They had to be carried out just as they lay—both she and the babies.

HILDA. And they didn't survive?

SOLNESS. Oh, *they* pulled through it all right. But Aline came down with fever—and it affected her milk. Nurse them herself, she had to do that. It was her duty, she said. And both of our little boys, they—(*Knotting his hands.*) they —oh!

HILDA. They couldn't take that as well.

SOLNESS. No, they couldn't take that as well. It's how we lost them.

HILDA. It must have been terribly hard for you.

SOLNESS. Hard enough for me—but ten times harder for Aline. (*Clenching his fists in suppressed fury.*) Oh, why do such things have to happen in life! (*Brusquely and firmly.*) From the day I lost them, I never wanted to build another church.

HILDA. And the church tower in our town—you disliked doing that?

SOLNESS. Very much. I remember when it was finished how relieved I felt.

HILDA. *I* remember too.

SOLNESS. And now I'll never build those things anymore —never! No church towers, or churches.

HILDA (*nodding slowly*). Only houses for people to live in.

SOLNESS. Homes for human beings, Hilda.

HILDA. But homes with high towers and spires on them.

SOLNESS. If possible. (*In a lighter tone.*) Anyhow—as I said before—the fire put me in business. As a builder, I mean.

HILDA. Why don't you call yourself an architect like the others?

SOLNESS. Never went through the training. Almost all I know I've had to find out for myself.

HILDA. But still you've made a success.

SOLNESS. Out of the fire, yes. I subdivided nearly the

whole garden into small lots, where I could build exactly the way I wanted. And after that, things really began to move for me.

HILDA (*looking at him searchingly*). How happy you must be—with the life you've made.

SOLNESS (*darkly*). Happy? You say it too? Same as all the others.

HILDA. Yes, you have to be, I really think so. If you just could stop thinking about the little twins—

SOLNESS (*slowly*). The little twins—they're not so easy to forget, Hilda.

HILDA (*with some uncertainty*). They really still bother you? After so many years?

SOLNESS (*regarding her steadily, without answering*). A happy man, you said—

HILDA. Yes, but aren't you—I mean, otherwise?

SOLNESS (*continues to look at her*). When I told you all that about the fire—

HILDA. Yes?

SOLNESS. Did nothing strike you then—nothing special?

HILDA (*puzzling a moment*). No. Was there something special?

SOLNESS (*quietly stressing his words*). By means of that fire, and that alone, I won my chance to build homes for human beings. Snug, cozy, sunlit homes, where a father and mother and a whole drove of children could live safe and happy, feeling what a sweet thing it is to be alive in this world. And mostly, knowing they belonged to each other— in the big things and the small.

HILDA (*animated*). Yes, but isn't it really a joy for you then, to create these beautiful homes?

SOLNESS. The price, Hilda. The awful price I've had to pay for that chance.

HILDA. But can you never get over that?

SOLNESS. No. For this chance to build homes for others, I've had to give up—absolutely give up any home of my own —a real home, I mean, with children.

HILDA (*delicately*). But did you have to? Absolutely, that is?

SOLNESS (*slowly nodding*). That was the price for my famous luck. Luck—hm. This good luck, Hilda—it couldn't be bought for less.

HILDA (*as before*).   But still, mightn't it all work out?

SOLNESS.   Never in this world. Never. That also comes out of the fire. And Aline's sickness after.

HILDA (*looks at him with an enigmatic expression*).   And so you go and build all these nurseries.

SOLNESS (*seriously*).   Have you ever noticed, Hilda, how the impossible—how it seems to whisper and call to you?

HILDA (*reflecting*).   The impossible? (*Vivaciously.*) Oh yes! *You* know it too?

SOLNESS.   Yes.

HILDA.   Then I guess there's—something of a troll in you as well?

SOLNESS.   Why a troll?

HILDA.   Well, what would *you* call it, then?

SOLNESS (*getting up*).   Hm, yes, could be. (*Furiously.*) But why shouldn't the troll be in me—the way things go for me all the time, in everything! In everything!

HILDA.   What do you mean?

SOLNESS (*hushed and inwardly stirred*).   Pay attention to what I tell you, Hilda. All I've been given to do, to build and shape into beauty, security, a good life—into even a kind of splendor—(*Knotting his fists.*) Oh, how awful just to think of it—!

HILDA.   What's so awful?

SOLNESS.   That I've got to make up for it all. Pay up. Not with money, but with human happiness. And not just my own happiness. With others', too. You understand, Hilda! That's the price my name as an artist has cost me—and others. And every single day I've got to look on here and see that price being paid for me again and again—over and over and over, endlessly!

HILDA (*rises, looking intently at him*).   Now you're thinking of—of her.

SOLNESS.   Yes, mostly of Aline. Because Aline—she had her lifework too—just as I had mine. (*His voice trembles.*) But *her* lifework had to be cut down, crushed, broken to bits, so that mine could win through to—to some kind of great victory. Aline, you know—she had a talent for building too.

HILDA.   She! For building?

SOLNESS (*shaking his head*).   Not houses and towers and spires—the kind of thing I do—

HILDA.   What, then?

SOLNESS (*gently, with feeling*). For building up the souls of children, Hilda. Building those souls up to stand on their own, poised, in beautiful, noble forms—till they'd grown into the upright human spirit. *That's* what Aline had a talent for. And now, there it lies, all of it—unused and useless forever. And for what earthly reason. Just like charred ruins after a fire.

HILDA. Yes, but even if this were so—?

SOLNESS. It *is* so! It *is*! I know.

HILDA. Well, but in any case it's not *your* fault.

SOLNESS (*fixing his eyes on her and nodding slowly*). Ah, you see—that's the enormous, ugly riddle—the doubt that gnaws at me day and night.

HILDA. That?

SOLNESS. Put it this way. Suppose it *was* my fault, in some sense.

HILDA. You! For the fire?

SOLNESS. For everything, the whole business. And yet, perhaps—completely innocent all the same.

HILDA (*looks at him anxiously*). Mr. Solness—when you can talk like that, then it sounds like you are—ill, after all.

SOLNESS. Hm—I don't think I'll ever be quite sound in that department.

> (RAGNAR BROVIK *cautiously opens the small corner*
> *door at the left.* HILDA *crosses the room.*)

RAGNAR (*on seeing* HILDA). Oh—excuse me, Mr. Solness. (*He starts to leave.*)

SOLNESS. No, no, don't go. Let's be done with it.

RAGNAR. Yes, if we only could!

SOLNESS. Your father's no better, I hear.

RAGNAR. He's going downhill fast now. And that's why I'm begging you, please—give me a good word or two, just something on one of the drawings for Father to read before he—

SOLNESS (*explosively*). Stop talking to me about those drawings of yours!

RAGNAR. Have you looked them over?

SOLNESS. Yes—I have.

RAGNAR. And they're worthless? And no doubt I'm worthless too?

SOLNESS (*evasively*). You stay on here with me, Ragnar.

You'll get everything the way you want it. You can marry Kaja then and have it easy—happy even. Just don't think about doing your own building.

RAGNAR.   Oh, sure, I should go home and tell that to my father. Because I promised to. *Shall* I tell him that—before he dies?

SOLNESS (*with a groan*).   Oh, tell him—tell him—don't ask me what to say! Anything. Better still to say nothing. (*In an outburst.*) I can't do any more than I'm doing, Ragnar.

RAGNAR.   May I take along my drawings, then?

SOLNESS.   Yes, take them—help yourself! They're on the table.

RAGNAR (*going to the table*).   Thanks.

HILDA (*putting her hand on the portfolio*).   No, no, leave them.

SOLNESS.   Why?

HILDA.   Because *I* want to see them too.

SOLNESS.   But you've already— (*To* RAGNAR.) All right, then, just leave them.

RAGNAR.   Gladly.

SOLNESS.   And go right home to your father.

RAGNAR.   Yes, I really ought to.

SOLNESS (*with an air of desperation*).   Ragnar—don't ask me for what I can't give! You hear, Ragnar? You mustn't!

RAGNAR.   No, no. Excuse me— (*He bows and goes out through the corner door.* HILDA *goes over and sits on a chair by the mirror.*)

HILDA (*looking angrily at* SOLNESS).   That was really mean of you.

SOLNESS.   You think so too?

HILDA.   Yes, it was terribly mean. And hard and wicked and cruel.

SOLNESS.   You don't know my side of it.

HILDA.   All the same. No, you shouldn't be like that.

SOLNESS.   You were only just now saying that no one but me should be allowed to build.

HILDA.   *I* can say that—but *you* mustn't.

SOLNESS.   But I can, most of all—when I've paid such a price for my recognition.

HILDA.   That's right—with what you think of as the comfortable life—that sort of thing.

SOLNESS.   And my inner peace in the bargain.

HILDA (*rising*). Inner peace! (*Intensely.*) Yes, yes, you're right! Poor Mr. Solness—you imagine that—

SOLNESS (*with a quiet laugh*). Sit down again, Hilda—if you want to hear something funny.

HILDA (*expectantly, sitting down*). Well?

SOLNESS. It sounds like such a ridiculous little thing. You see, the whole business revolves about no more than a crack in a chimney.

HILDA. Nothing else?

SOLNESS. No; at least, not at the start. (*He moves a chair closer to* HILDA *and sits.*)

HILDA (*impatiently, tapping her knee*). So—the crack in the chimney!

SOLNESS. I'd noticed that tiny opening in the flue long, long before the fire. Every time I was up in the attic, I checked to see that it was still there.

HILDA. And was it?

SOLNESS. Yes. Because no one else knew.

HILDA. And you said nothing?

SOLNESS. No. Nothing.

HILDA. Never thought of fixing the flue, either?

SOLNESS. I thought, yes—but never got to it. Every time I wanted to start repairing it, it was exactly as if a hand were there, holding me back. Not today, I'd think. Tomorrow. So nothing came of it.

HILDA. But why did you keep on postponing?

SOLNESS. Because I went on thinking. (*Slowly, in an undertone.*) Through that little black opening in the chimney I could force my way to success—as a builder.

HILDA (*looking straight ahead of her*). That must have been thrilling.

SOLNESS. Irresistible, almost. Completely irresistible. Because the whole thing, then, seemed so easy and obvious to me. I wanted it to happen on some winter's day, a little before noon. I'd be out with Aline for a drive in the sleigh. The people at home would have fires blazing in the stoves—

HILDA. Yes, because the day should be bitterly cold—

SOLNESS. Yes, quite raw. And they'd want it snug and warm for Aline when she got in.

HILDA. Because I'm sure her temperature's normally low.

SOLNESS. It is, you know. So then, driving home it was, that we were supposed to see the smoke.

HILDA. Only the smoke?

SOLNESS. The smoke first. But when we'd pull in at the garden gate, there the old packing case would stand, a roaring inferno. At least, that's how I wanted it.

HILDA. Oh, but if it only could have gone that way!

SOLNESS. Yes, you can say that well enough, Hilda.

HILDA. But wait a minute, Mr. Solness—how can you be so sure the fire started from that little crack in the chimney?

SOLNESS. I can't, not at all. In fact, I'm absolutely certain it had nothing whatever to do with the fire.

HILDA. What!

SOLNESS. It's been proved without a shadow of a doubt that the fire broke out in a clothes closet, in quite another part of the house.

HILDA. Then what's the point in all this sitting and mooning around about a cracked chimney!

SOLNESS. You mind if I go on talking a bit, Hilda?

HILDA. No, if only you'll talk sense—

SOLNESS. I'll try. (*He moves his chair in closer.*)

HILDA. So—go on then, Mr. Solness.

SOLNESS (*confidingly*). Don't you believe with me, Hilda, that there are certain special, chosen people who have a gift and power and capacity to *wish* something, *desire* something, *will* something—so insistently and so—so inevitably —that at last it *has* to be theirs? Don't you believe that?

HILDA (*with an inscrutable look in her eyes*). If that's true, then we'll see someday—if *I'm* one of the chosen.

SOLNESS. It's not one's self alone that makes great things. Oh no—the helpers and servers—they've got to be with you if you're going to succeed. But they never come by themselves. One has to call on them, incessantly—within oneself, I mean.

HILDA. What are these helpers and servers?

SOLNESS. Oh, we can talk about that some other time. Let's stay with the fire now.

HILDA. Don't you think the fire still would have come— even if you hadn't wished it?

SOLNESS. If old Knut Brovik had owned the house, it never would have burned down so conveniently for him—I'm positive of that. Because he doesn't know how to call on the helpers, or the servers either. (*Gets up restlessly.*) So you see, Hilda—it *is* my fault that the twins had to die. And isn't it my fault, too, that Aline's never become the woman she could have and should have been? And wanted to be, more than anything?

HILDA. Yes, but if it's really these helpers and servers, then—?

SOLNESS. Who called for the helpers and servers? I did! And they came and did what I willed. (*In rising agitation.*) That's what all the nice people call "having the luck." But I can tell you what this luck feels like. It feels as if a big piece of skin had been stripped, right here, from my chest. And the helpers and servers go on flaying the skin off other people to patch *my* wound. But the wound never heals—never! Oh, if you knew how sometimes it leeches and burns.

HILDA (*looking at him attentively*). You *are* ill, Mr. Solness. Very ill, I almost think.

SOLNESS. Insane. You can say it. It's what you mean.

HILDA. No, I don't think you've lost your reason.

SOLNESS. *What*, then? Out with it!

HILDA. I'm wondering if maybe you didn't enter life with a frail conscience.

SOLNESS. A frail conscience? What in hell's name does that mean?

HILDA. I mean your conscience is very fragile. Over-refined, sort of. It isn't made to struggle with things—to pick up what's heavy and bear it.

SOLNESS (*growling*). Hm! And what kind of conscience do you recommend?

HILDA. I could wish that your conscience was—well, quite robust.

SOLNESS. Oh? Robust? And I suppose *you* have a robust conscience?

HILDA. Yes, I think so. I've never noticed it wasn't.

SOLNESS. I'd say you've never had a real test to face up to, either.

HILDA (*with tremulous lips*). Oh, it wasn't so easy to leave Father, when I'm so terribly fond of him.

SOLNESS. Come on! Just for a month or two—

HILDA. I'm never going home again.

SOLNESS. Never? Why did you leave home, then?

HILDA (*half serious, half teasing*). You still keep forgetting that the ten years are up?

SOLNESS. Nonsense. Was something wrong there at home? Hm?

HILDA (*fully serious*). It was inside me, something goading and driving me here. Coaxing and luring me, too.

SOLNESS (*eagerly*). That's it! That's it, Hilda! There's a troll in you—same as in me. It's that troll in us, don't you see—that's what calls on the powers out there. And then we *have* to give in—whether we want to or not.

HILDA. I almost believe you're right, Mr. Solness.

SOLNESS (*walking about the room*). Oh, Hilda, there are so many devils one can't see loose in the world!

HILDA. Devils, too?

SOLNESS (*stops*). Good devils and bad devils. Blond devils and black-haired ones. And if only you always knew if the light or the dark ones had you! (*Pacing about; with a laugh.*) Wouldn't it be simple then!

HILDA (*her eyes following him*). Or if you had a really strong conscience, brimming with health—so you could dare what you most wanted.

SOLNESS (*stopping by the console table*). Still, I think most people, in this respect, are just as weak as I am.

HILDA. Probably.

SOLNESS (*leaning against the table*). In the sagas— Ever done any reading in the old sagas?

HILDA. Oh yes! In the days when I used to read books—

SOLNESS. In the sagas it tells about Vikings that sailed to foreign countries and plundered and burned and killed the men—

HILDA. And captured the women—

SOLNESS. And carried them off—

HILDA. Took them home in their ships—

SOLNESS. And treated them like—like the worst of trolls.

HILDA (*looking straight ahead with half-veiled eyes*). I think that must have been thrilling.

SOLNESS (*with a short, deep laugh*). Capturing women, hm?

HILDA. *Being* captured.

SOLNESS (*studying her a moment*). I see.

HILDA (*as if breaking the train of thought*). But what are you getting at with all these Vikings, Mr. Solness?

SOLNESS. Just that there's your robust conscience—in *those* boys! When they got back home, they went on eating and drinking and living lighthearted as children. And the women as well! They soon had no urge, most of them, ever to give up their men. Does that make sense to you, Hilda?

HILDA. Those women make perfect sense to me.

SOLNESS. Aha! Perhaps you could go and do likewise?

HILDA. Why not?

SOLNESS. Live, of your own free will, with a barbarian like that?

HILDA. If it was a barbarian that I really loved—

SOLNESS. But *could* you ever love one?

HILDA. My Lord, you don't just plan whom you're going to love.

SOLNESS (*gazing thoughtfully at her*). No—I suppose it's the troll within that decides.

HILDA (*half laughing*). Yes, and all those enchanting little devils—your friends. The blond and the black-haired both.

SOLNESS (*with quiet warmth*). Then I'll ask that the devils choose tenderly for you, Hilda.

HILDA. For me they've already chosen. Now and forever.

SOLNESS (*looks at her probingly*). Hilda—you're like some wild bird of the woods.

HILDA. Hardly. I don't go hiding away under bushes.

SOLNESS. No. No, there's more in you of the bird of prey.

HILDA. More that—perhaps. (*With great vehemence.*) And why not a bird of prey? Why shouldn't I go hunting as well? Take the spoil I'm after? If I can once set my claws in it and have my own way.

SOLNESS. Hilda—you know what you are?

HILDA. Yes, I'm some strange kind of bird.

SOLNESS. No. You're like a dawning day. When I look at you—then it's as if I looked into the sunrise.

HILDA. Tell me, Mr. Solness—are you quite sure that you've never called for me? Within yourself, I mean?

SOLNESS (*slowly and softly*). I almost think I must have.

HILDA. What did you want with me?

SOLNESS. You, Hilda, are youth.

HILDA (*smiles*). Youth that you're so afraid of?

SOLNESS (*nodding slowly*). And that, deep within me, I'm so much hungering for.

(HILDA *rises, goes over to the small table, and takes up* RAGNAR BROVIK's *portfolio*.)

HILDA (*holding the portfolio out toward him*). Then, about these drawings—

SOLNESS (*sharply, waving them aside*). Put those things away! I've seen enough of them.

HILDA. Yes, but you've got to write your comment on them.

SOLNESS. Write a comment! Never!

HILDA. But now, with that poor old man near death! Can't you do him and his son a kindness before they're parted? And maybe later he could build from these drawings.

SOLNESS. Yes, that's exactly what he would do. The young pup's made sure of that.

HILDA. But, my Lord, if that's all—then can't you tell a little white lie?

SOLNESS. A lie? (*Furious.*) Hilda—get away with those damned drawings!

HILDA (*pulls back the portfolio a bit*). Now, now, now—don't bite me. You talk about trolls. I think you're acting like a troll yourself. (*Glancing about.*) Where's your pen and ink?

SOLNESS. Haven't got any.

HILDA (*going toward the door*). But out there where that girl works—

SOLNESS. Hilda, stay here—! You said I could lie a little. Well, I guess, for the old man's sake, I could manage it. I did beat him down in his time—and broke him—

HILDA. Him too?

SOLNESS. I had to have room for myself. But this Ragnar —he mustn't be given the least chance to rise.

HILDA. Poor boy, his chances are slim enough—if he simply hasn't got it in him—

SOLNESS (*comes closer, looks at her and whispers*). If Ragnar Brovik gets his chance, he'll hammer me to the ground. Break me—same as I broke his father.

HILDA. Break you? Can he do that?

SOLNESS. You bet he can! He's all the youth that's waiting to come thundering at my door—to do away with master builder Solness.

HILDA (*with a quietly reproachful look*). And so you'll still try to lock him out. For shame, Mr. Solness!

SOLNESS. It's cost me heart's blood enough to fight my battle. And then—the helpers and servers, I'm afraid they won't obey me anymore.

HILDA. Then you'll have to get along on your own, that's all.

SOLNESS. Hopeless, Hilda. The change, it's coming. Maybe a little sooner, maybe later. But the retribution—it's inescapable.

HILDA (*pressing her hands to her ears in fright*). Don't say those things! You want to kill me? You want to take what's even more than my life?

SOLNESS. And what's that?

HILDA. I want to see you great. See you with a wreath in your hand—high, high up on a church tower! (*Calm again.*) So—out with your pencil. You do have a pencil on you?

SOLNESS (*brings one out with his pocket sketchbook*). Here's one.

HILDA (*puts the portfolio down on the table*). Good. Now let's get settled here, Mr. Solness, the two of us.

(SOLNESS *sits at the table.* HILDA, *behind him, leans over the back of his chair.*)

HILDA. And now let's write on these drawings—something really warm and nice—for this stupid Roar—or whoever he is.

SOLNESS (*writes a few lines, then turns his head and looks up at her*). Tell me one thing, Hilda.

HILDA. Yes?

SOLNESS. If you've really been waiting for me all these ten years—

HILDA. Then what?

SOLNESS. Why didn't you write to me? I could have answered you then.

HILDA (*hurriedly*). No, no, no! That's just what I didn't want.

SOLNESS. Why not?

HILDA. I was afraid then the whole thing'd be ruined— But we should be writing on the drawings, Mr. Solness.

SOLNESS. Yes, of course.

HILDA (*bends forward, watching as he writes*). Something

heartfelt and kind. Oh, how I hate—how I hate this Roald—

SOLNESS (*writing*). Have you never really loved anyone, Hilda?

HILDA (*harshly*). What did you say?

SOLNESS. Have you never loved anyone?

HILDA. Anyone else. Is that what you mean?

SOLNESS (*glancing up at her*). Anyone else, yes. You never have—in ten whole years? Never?

HILDA. Oh yes, now and then. When I was really furious at you for not coming.

SOLNESS. So you did care for others too?

HILDA. A little bit—for a week or so. Oh, honestly, Mr. Solness, you ought to know that kind of thing.

SOLNESS. Hilda—what are you here for?

HILDA. Don't waste time talking. That poor old man could easily be dying on us.

SOLNESS. Answer me, Hilda. What do you want from me?

HILDA. I want my kingdom.

SOLNESS. Hm—

> (*He gives a quick glance toward the door on the left and resumes writing on the drawings. At the same moment* MRS. SOLNESS *enters; she has several packages with her.*)

MRS. SOLNESS. I brought along a little something here for you, Miss Wangel. They'll send the big parcels out later.

HILDA. Oh, how wonderfully kind of you!

MRS. SOLNESS. No more than my duty, that's all.

SOLNESS (*reading over his comments*). Aline.

MRS. SOLNESS. Yes?

SOLNESS. Did you notice if she—if the bookkeeper's out there?

MRS. SOLNESS. Oh, *she's* there, don't worry.

SOLNESS (*sliding the drawings back in the portfolio*). Hm—

MRS. SOLNESS. She's right at her desk, as she always is— whenever *I* go through the room.

SOLNESS (*getting up*). Then I'll give her this, and tell her that—

HILDA (*taking the portfolio from him*). Oh no, let me have the pleasure. (*Goes toward the door, then turns.*) What's her name?

SOLNESS. Miss Fosli.

HILDA. Ah, that's much too cold! I mean her first name.

SOLNESS. Kaja—I think.

HILDA (*opens the door and calls*). Kaja, come in here! Hurry up! The master builder wants to speak to you.

(KAJA FOSLI *appears at the door.*)

KAJA (*looking fearfully at him*). Here I am—?

HILDA (*handing her the portfolio*). See here, Kaja— you can have this now. The master builder's written his opinion.

KAJA. Oh, at last!

SOLNESS. Get it to old Brovik soon as you can.

KAJA. I'll go right over with it.

SOLNESS. Yes, go on. Now Ragnar can do some building.

KAJA. Oh, can he stop by and thank you for all—?

SOLNESS (*sharply*). I want no thanks! Tell him that, with my respects.

KAJA. Yes, I'll—

SOLNESS. And tell him as well that hereafter I won't be needing his services. Nor yours, either.

KAJA (*her voice low and quavering*). Nor mine, either?

SOLNESS. You'll have other things to think about now. A lot to do. And that's only right. So run along home with the drawings, Miss Fosli. Quick! Hear me?

KAJA (*as before*). Yes, Mr. Solness. (*She goes out.*)

MRS. SOLNESS. My, what scheming eyes she has.

SOLNESS. She? That poor little fool.

MRS. SOLNESS. Oh—I see just what I see, Halvard. Are you really letting them go?

SOLNESS. Yes.

MRS. SOLNESS. Her too?

SOLNESS. Isn't that the way you wanted it?

MRS. SOLNESS. But to get rid of *her*—? Oh, well, Halvard, I'm sure you have one in reserve.

HILDA (*playfully*). As for me, I just can't function behind a desk.

SOLNESS. There, there, now—it'll all work out, Aline. Don't think of anything now except moving into the new home—as soon as you can. We'll be hanging the wreath up this evening—(*Turning to* HILDA.) way up high at the top of the tower. What do you say to that, Miss Hilda?

HILDA (*gazing at him with sparkling eyes*). It'll be so marvelous seeing you high up there again!

SOLNESS. Me!

MRS. SOLNESS. For heaven's sake, Miss Wangel, what are you thinking of! My husband—who gets so dizzy!

HILDA. He dizzy? Impossible!

MRS. SOLNESS. Oh yes, it's true, though.

HILDA. But I've seen him myself, right at the top of a high church tower!

MRS. SOLNESS. Yes, I've heard people talk about that. But it's so completely impossible—

SOLNESS (*forcefully*). Impossible—yes, impossible! But all the same I stood there!

MRS. SOLNESS. Oh, Halvard, how can you say that? You can't even bear going out on the second-story balcony here. You've always been like that.

SOLNESS. Maybe this evening you'll see something new.

MRS. SOLNESS (*terrified*). No, no, no, I hope to God I never see that! I'm getting in touch with the doctor right away. He'll know how to stop you from this.

SOLNESS. But Aline—!

MRS. SOLNESS. Yes, because you know you're sick, Halvard. This only proves it! God—oh, God! (*She goes hurriedly out to the right.*)

HILDA (*looking intently at him*). *Is* it true, or isn't it?

SOLNESS. That I get dizzy?

HILDA. That my master builder dares not—and *can* not climb as high as he builds?

SOLNESS. Is that the way you see it?

HILDA. Yes.

SOLNESS. I think soon I won't have a corner in me safe from you.

HILDA (*looking toward the bow window*). So then, up. Right up there.

SOLNESS (*coming closer*). In the topmost room of the tower—that's where you could live, Hilda—live like a princess.

HILDA (*ambiguously; half playing, half serious*). Sure, it's what you promised.

SOLNESS. Did I really?

HILDA. Oh, come on, Mr. Solness! You said I'd be a princess—and you'd give me a kingdom. So you went and—well?

SOLNESS (*warily*). Are you quite positive this isn't some kind of dream—some fantasy that's taken hold of you?

HILDA (*caustically*). Meaning you didn't do it, hm?

SOLNESS. I hardly know myself. (*Dropping his voice.*) But one thing I know for certain—that I—

HILDA. That you—? Go on!

SOLNESS. That I *ought* to have done it.

HILDA (*exclaiming spiritedly*). *You* could never be dizzy!

SOLNESS. So we'll hang the wreath this evening—Princess Hilda.

HILDA (*with a wry face*). Over your new home, yes.

SOLNESS. Over the new house—that'll never be home for me. (*He goes out by the garden door.*)

HILDA (*looks straight ahead with a veiled look, whispering to herself. The only words heard are:*) Terribly thrilling—

⌐ ACT THREE ⌐

A large, broad veranda, part of SOLNESS's *house. A portion of the house, with a door leading onto the veranda, is visible left. A railing along the veranda to the right. Far back at the end of the veranda, steps lead down to the garden below. Huge old trees in the garden spread their branches over the veranda and toward the house. Through the trees at the far right, a glimpse of the lower structure of the new house, scaffolding rising around the base of the tower. In the background, the garden is bordered by an old wooden fence. Beyond the fence, a street with small, low, dilapidated houses. The evening sky is streaked with sunlit clouds.*

On the veranda a garden bench stands along the wall of the house, and in front of the bench a long table. On the other side of the table are an armchair and some stools. All the furniture is wickerwork.

MRS. SOLNESS, *wrapped in a large white crepe shawl, sits resting in the armchair and gazing off to the right. After a moment* HILDA WANGEL *comes up the steps from the garden. She is dressed the same as before and is wearing her hat. On her blouse she has a little bouquet of small common flowers.*

MRS. SOLNESS (*turning her head slightly*). Have you had a walk in the garden, Miss Wangel?

HILDA. Yes, I've been having a look around.

MRS. SOLNESS. And found some flowers too, I see.

HILDA. Oh yes! They're just growing thick in through the bushes.

MRS. SOLNESS. Oh, are they really? Still? I hardly ever get down there, you know.

HILDA (*approaching*). Honestly? You don't run down to the garden every day?

MRS. SOLNESS (*with a faint smile*). I don't "run" any place, not anymore.

HILDA. Well, but don't you go down even once in a while and visit all those lovely things?

MRS. SOLNESS. It's grown so strange to me, all of it. I'm almost frightened of seeing it again.

HILDA. Your own garden!

MRS. SOLNESS. I don't feel it's mine anymore.

HILDA. What's *that* mean—?

MRS. SOLNESS. No, no, it isn't. Not what it used to be, in Mother and Father's time. They've taken so much of the garden away, it's painful, Miss Wangel. Can you imagine— they've cut it up and built houses for strangers. People I don't know. And they can sit at their windows and look in on me.

HILDA (*her face lighting up*). Mrs. Solness?

MRS. SOLNESS. Yes?

HILDA. May I stay here a while with you?

MRS. SOLNESS. Yes, of course, if you want to.

HILDA (*moving a stool over to the armchair and sitting*). Ah—you can sit and really sun yourself here, like a cat.

MRS. SOLNESS (*laying her hand gently on* HILDA's *neck*). It's kind of you to want to sit with me. I thought you'd be going in to my husband.

HILDA. What would I want with him?

MRS. SOLNESS. To help him, I thought.

HILDA. No, thanks. Besides, he's not in. He's over there with the workmen. But he looked so ferocious I didn't dare speak to him.

MRS. SOLNESS. Oh, underneath he's so mild and soft-hearted.

HILDA. *Him!*

MRS. SOLNESS. You hardly know him yet, Miss Wangel.

HILDA (*looking at her warmly*). Are you happy to be moving into the new place?

MRS. SOLNESS. I *should* be happy. It's what Halvard wants—

HILDA. Oh, but not just for that reason.

MRS. SOLNESS. Oh yes, Miss Wangel. For that's no more than my duty, giving in to him. But it isn't always so easy forcing your thoughts to obey.

HILDA. I'm sure it can't be.

MRS. SOLNESS.   Believe me, it's not. When one's no better a person than I am, then—

HILDA.   You mean, when one's gone through all the sorrow you have—

MRS. SOLNESS.   How did you hear of that?

HILDA.   Your husband told me.

MRS. SOLNESS.   With me he hardly ever mentions those things. Yes, I've been through more than my share in life, Miss Wangel.

HILDA (*regarding her sympathetically and slowly nodding*). Poor Mrs. Solness. First you had the fire—

MRS. SOLNESS (*with a sigh*).   Yes. Everything of mine burned.

HILDA.   And then what was worse followed.

MRS. SOLNESS (*looks questioningly at her*).   Worse?

HILDA.   The worst of all.

MRS. SOLNESS.   What do you mean?

HILDA (*softly*).   You lost your two little boys.

MRS. SOLNESS.   Oh, *them,* yes. Yes, you see, that's something quite different, that. That was an act of Providence, you know. And there one can only bow one's head and submit. And be grateful.

HILDA.   And are you?

MRS. SOLNESS.   Not always, I'm afraid. I know very well it's my duty. But all the same, I *can't.*

HILDA.   Of course not. That's only natural.

MRS. SOLNESS.   And time and again I have to remind myself that it was a just punishment for me—

HILDA.   Why?

MRS. SOLNESS.   Because I wasn't staunch enough under misfortune.

HILDA.   But I don't see that—

MRS. SOLNESS.   Oh no, no, Miss Wangel. Don't talk anymore to me about the two little boys. We can only be happy for them. Because they're well off—so well off now. No, it's the small losses in life that strike at your heart. Losing all of those things that other people value at next to nothing.

HILDA (*laying her arms on* MRS. SOLNESS's *knee and looking up at her fondly*).   Dear Mrs. Solness—wnat sort of things? Tell me.

MRS. SOLNESS.   As I say—just little things. There were all the old portraits on the walls that burned. And all the old silk dresses. They'd been in the family for ever so long, generations—they burned. And all Mother's and Grandmother's lace—that burned too. And just think—their jewels! (*Heavily.*) And then, all the dolls.

HILDA. The dolls?

MRS. SOLNESS (*choking with tears*). I had nine beautiful dolls.

HILDA. And they burned also?

MRS. SOLNESS. All of them. Oh, that was hard—so hard for me.

HILDA. Were they dolls that you'd had put away, ever since you were little?

MRS. SOLNESS. Not put away. I and the dolls had gone on living together.

HILDA. After you'd grown up?

MRS. SOLNESS. Yes, long after that.

HILDA. After you were married, too?

MRS. SOLNESS. Oh yes. As long as he didn't see them, then— But then, poor things, they were all burned up. No one ever thought about saving *them*. Oh, it's so sad to remember. Now you mustn't laugh at me, Miss Wangel.

HILDA. I'm not laughing a bit.

MRS. SOLNESS. Because, you see, in a way there was life in them too. I used to carry them under my heart. Just like little unborn children.

> (DR. HERDAL, *with his hat in his hands, comes out through the door and spots* MRS. SOLNESS *and* HILDA.)

DR. HERDAL. So you're out here, Mrs. Solness, catching yourself a cold, hm?

MRS. SOLNESS. It seems so nice and warm here today.

DR. HERDAL. All right. But is something the matter? I got a note from you.

MRS. SOLNESS (*getting up*). Yes, there's something I have to talk to you about.

DR. HERDAL. Fine. Perhaps we'd better go in, then. (*To* HILDA.) Still dressed for climbing mountains, hm?

HILDA (*gaily, rising*). That's right—full gear! But I won't be climbing and breaking my neck today. We two are going to stay quietly down below and watch, Doctor.

DR. HERDAL. Watch what?

MRS. SOLNESS (*to* HILDA, *in a low, frightened voice*).   Shh, shh—for God's sake! He's coming. Just try and get him out of this wild idea. And then, do let's be friends, Miss Wangel. Can't we be?

HILDA (*throwing her arms impetuously around* MRS. SOLNESS).   Oh—if we only could!

MRS. SOLNESS (*gently disengaging herself*).   Oh-oh-oh! There he is, Doctor. We've got to talk.

DR. HERDAL.   Is this about *him*?

MRS. SOLNESS.   Of course it is. Just come inside.

> (*She and* DR. HERDAL *enter the house. A moment after,* SOLNESS *comes up the steps from the garden. A serious look comes over* HILDA'S *face.*)

SOLNESS (*glancing toward the door of the house, carefully being closed from within*).   Have you noticed something, Hilda—that the moment I come, she goes?

HILDA.   I've noticed that the moment you come, you *make* her go.

SOLNESS.   Maybe so. But I can't help that. (*Scrutinizing her.*) Are you cold, Hilda? You rather look it to me.

HILDA.   I've just come up out of a tomb.

SOLNESS.   Now what's that mean?

HILDA.   That I've been chilled right to the bone, Mr. Solness.

SOLNESS (*slowly*).   I think I understand—

HILDA.   What do you want here now?

SOLNESS.   I caught sight of you from over there.

HILDA.   But then you must have seen her too, hm?

SOLNESS.   I knew she'd leave immediately if I came.

HILDA.   Is it very hard on you, that she keeps on avoiding you like this?

SOLNESS.   In a way it's almost a relief.

HILDA.   That you don't have her right under your eyes?

SOLNESS.   Yes.

HILDA.   And you're not always seeing how she broods over this business of the children?

SOLNESS.   Yes. Mostly that.

> (HILDA *saunters across the veranda with her hands behind her back, takes a stance at the railing, and looks out over the garden.*)

SOLNESS (*after a short pause*). Did you talk with her quite a while? (*Hilda remains motionless, without answering.*) I'm asking, did you talk quite a while? (HILDA *says nothing.*) What did she talk about, Hilda? (HILDA *stays silent.*) Poor Aline! It was the twins, I suppose. (HILDA *shudders nervously, then quickly nods several times.*) She'll never get over it. Never in this world. (*Coming closer.*) Now you're standing there like a statue again. The same as last night.

HILDA (*turns and looks at him with great, serious eyes*). I'm going away.

SOLNESS (*sharply*). Away!

HILDA. Yes.

SOLNESS. But I won't let you!

HILDA. What can I do here now?

SOLNESS. Just *be* here, Hilda!

HILDA (*looking him up and down*). Sure, thanks a lot. You know it wouldn't stop there.

SOLNESS (*wildly*). So much the better.

HILDA (*with intensity*). I just *can't* hurt somebody I *know!* Or take away something that's really hers—

SOLNESS. Who wants you to?

HILDA. A stranger, yes. Because that's different, completely! Someone I never laid eyes on. But somebody I've gotten close to—! No, not that! Never!

SOLNESS. But what have I ever suggested?

HILDA. Oh, master builder, you know so well what would happen. And that's why I'm going away.

SOLNESS. And what'll become of me when you're gone. What'll I have to live for then? Afterwards?

HILDA (*with the inscrutable look in her eyes*). There's no real problem for you. You have your duties to her. Live for those duties.

SOLNESS. Too late. These powers—these—these—

HILDA. Devils—

SOLNESS. Yes, devils! And the troll inside me too—they've sucked all the lifeblood out of her. (*With a desperate laugh.*) They did it to make me happy! Successful! And now she's dead—thanks to me. And I'm alive, chained to the dead. (*In anguish.*) I—I, who can't go on living without joy in life!

(HILDA *goes around the table and sits on the bench
with her elbows on the table and her head
propped in her hands.*)

HILDA (*after watching him a while*).   What are you building next?

SOLNESS (*shaking his head*).   Don't think I'll build much
more now.

HILDA.   No more warm, happy homes for mothers and
fathers—and droves of children?

SOLNESS.   Who knows if there'll be any use for such
homes in the future.

HILDA.   Poor master builder! And you who've gone all
these ten years and put your life into—nothing but that.

SOLNESS.   Yes, you might as well say it, Hilda.

HILDA (*in an outburst*).   Oh, it's just so senseless, really,
so senseless—the whole thing!

SOLNESS.   What whole thing?

HILDA.   Not daring to take hold of one's own happiness.
Of one's own life! Just because someone you know is there,
standing in the way.

SOLNESS.   Someone you have no right to leave.

HILDA.   Who knows if you really don't have a right. And
still, all the same— Oh, to sleep the whole business away!
(*She lays her arms down flat on the table, rests her head
on her hands, and shuts her eyes.*)

SOLNESS (*turning the armchair and sitting by the table*).
Was yours a warm, happy home—up there with your father,
Hilda?

HILDA (*motionless, answering as if half asleep*).   I only
had a cage.

SOLNESS.   And you won't go back in?

HILDA (*as before*).   Wild birds never like cages.

SOLNESS.   They'd rather go hunting in the open sky—

HILDA (*still as before*).   Birds of prey like hunting best—

SOLNESS (*letting his eyes rest on her*).   Oh, to have had
the Viking spirit—

HILDA (*in her usual voice, opening her eyes, but not moving*). And the other? Say what that was!

SOLNESS.   A robust conscience.

(HILDA *sits up on the bench, vivacious once more.*

Her eyes again have their happy, sparkling look.)

HILDA (*nods to him*). I know what you're going to build next!

SOLNESS. Then you know more than I do, Hilda.

HILDA. Yes, master builders—they're really so dumb.

SOLNESS. All right, what's it going to be?

HILDA (*nods again*). The castle.

SOLNESS. What castle?

HILDA. *My* castle, of course.

SOLNESS. Now you want a castle?

HILDA. Let me ask you—don't you owe me a kingdom?

SOLNESS. If I listen to you, I do.

HILDA. So. You owe me this kingdom, then. And who ever heard of a kingdom without a castle!

SOLNESS (*more and more animated*). Yes, they usually do go together.

HILDA. Good. So build it for me! Right now!

SOLNESS (*laughing*). Is everything always "right now"?

HILDA. That's right! Because the ten years, they're up—and I'm not going to wait any longer. So, come on, Mr. Solness—fork over the castle!

SOLNESS. It's not easy owing you anything, Hilda.

HILDA. You should've thought of that before. It's too late now. Come on—(*Drumming on the table.*) one castle on the table! It's *my* castle! I want it *now*!

SOLNESS (*more serious, leaning nearer her, with his arms on the table*). What sort of castle did you imagine for yourself, Hilda?

HILDA (*her expression veiling itself more and more, as if she were peering deep within herself; then, slowly*). My castle must stand up—very high up—and free on every side. So I can see far—far out.

SOLNESS. And I suppose it'll have a high tower?

HILDA. A terribly high tower. And at the highest pinnacle of the tower there'll be a balcony. And out on that balcony I'll stand—

SOLNESS (*instinctively clutching his forehead*). How you can want to stand at those dizzy heights—!

HILDA. Why not! I'll stand right up there and look down on the others—the ones who build churches. And homes for mothers and fathers and droves of children. And you must come up and look down on them too.

SOLNESS (*his voice low*). Will the master builder be allowed to come up to the princess?

HILDA. If he wants to.

SOLNESS (*lower still*). Then I think he'll come.

HILDA (*nods*). The master builder—he'll come.

SOLNESS. But never build anymore—poor master builder.

HILDA (*full of life*). Oh, but he will! We two, we'll work together. And that way we'll build the loveliest—the most beautiful thing anywhere in the world.

SOLNESS (*caught up*). Hilda—tell me, what's that!

HILDA (*looks smilingly at him, shakes her head a little, purses her lips, and speaks as if to a child*). Master builders, they are very—very stupid people.

SOLNESS. Of course they're stupid. But tell me what it is! What's the world's most beautiful thing that we're going to build together?

HILDA (*silent a moment, then says, with an enigmatic look in her eyes*). Castles in the air.

SOLNESS. Castles in the air?

HILDA (*nodding*). Yes, castles in the air! You know what a castle in the air is?

SOLNESS. It's the loveliest thing in the world, you say.

HILDA (*rising impatiently, with a scornful gesture of her hand*). Why, yes, of course! Castles in the air—they're so easy to hide away in. And easy to build too. (*Looking contemptuously at him.*) Especially for builders who have a—dizzy conscience.

SOLNESS (*getting up*). From this day on we'll build together, Hilda.

HILDA (*with a skeptical smile*). A real castle in the air?

SOLNESS. Yes. One with solid foundations.

> (RAGNAR BROVIK *comes out of the house. He carries a large green wreath with flowers and silk ribbons.*)

HILDA (*in an outcry of joy*). The wreath! Oh, that'll be magnificent!

SOLNESS (*surprised*). Are you bringing the wreath, Ragnar?

RAGNAR. I promised the foreman I would.

SOLNESS (*relieved*). Oh. Then I suppose your father's better?

RAGNAR. No.

SOLNESS. Didn't he get a lift from what I wrote?

RAGNAR. It came too late.

SOLNESS. Too late!

RAGNAR. When she got back with it, he was in a coma. He'd had a stroke.

SOLNESS. But go home to him, then! Look after your father!

RAGNAR. He doesn't need me anymore.

SOLNESS. But you need to be with him.

RAGNAR. *She's* sitting by his bed.

SOLNESS (*somewhat uncertain*). Kaja?

RAGNAR (*giving him a dark look*). Yes—Kaja, yes.

SOLNESS. Go home, Ragnar, to both of them. Let *me* have the wreath.

RAGNAR (*suppresses a mocking smile*). You don't mean you're going to—

SOLNESS. I'll take it down myself, thanks. (*Takes the wreath from him.*) And go along home. We won't be needing you today.

RAGNAR. I'm aware that you won't be needing me permanently. But today I'm staying.

SOLNESS. Well, then stay, if—you're so anxious to.

HILDA (*at the railing*). Mr. Solness—I'll stand here and watch you.

SOLNESS. Watch me!

HILDA. It'll be terribly thrilling.

SOLNESS (*in an undertone*). We'll talk about that later, Hilda. (*He goes, with the wreath, down the steps and off through the garden.*)

HILDA (*looking after him, then turning to* RAGNAR). It seems to me you might at least have thanked him.

RAGNAR. Thanked him? Should I have thanked *him*?

HILDA. Yes, you absolutely should have!

RAGNAR. If anything, it's probably you I should thank.

HILDA. Why do you say that?

RAGNAR (*without answering*). But just look out for yourself, miss. Because, actually, you hardly know him yet.

HILDA (*fiercely*). Oh, I know him the best!

RAGNAR (*with a bitter laugh*). Thank him, when he's held

me down year after year! He, who made my own father doubt me. Made me doubt myself— And all that, just so he could—

HILDA (*as if surmising something*). He could—? Say it out!

RAGNAR. So he could keep her with him.

HILDA (*with a start toward him*). The girl at the desk!

RAGNAR. Yes.

HILDA (*threateningly, with fists clenched*). It isn't true! You're lying about him!

RAGNAR. I didn't want to believe it either, before today— when she said it herself.

HILDA (*as if beside herself*). *What* did she say! I've got to know! Now! Right now!

RAGNAR. She said he'd taken possession of her mind— completely. That all her thoughts are caught up in him, only him. She says she'll never let him go—that she wants to stay here where *he* is—

HILDA (*her eyes flashing*). She won't be allowed to!

RAGNAR (*searchingly*). Who won't allow her?

HILDA (*quickly*). *He* won't either.

RAGNAR. Oh no—I understand everything now. From here on she could only be, shall we say—an inconvenience.

HILDA. You understand nothing—when you can talk like that! No, *I'll* tell you why he kept her.

RAGNAR. Why?

HILDA. So he could keep *you.*

RAGNAR. Did he tell you that?

HILDA. No, but it's true! It *must* be true! (*Wildly.*) I will—I *will* have it that way!

RAGNAR. But just the moment you come by—is when he drops her.

HILDA. *You*—you're the one he dropped. What do you think he cares about strange girls like her?

RAGNAR (*reflectively*). You suppose he's really been afraid of me all along?

HILDA. Him afraid? I wouldn't be so conceited if I were you.

RAGNAR. Oh, I think he's suspected for a long time that I had it in me all right. Besides—*afraid*—that's exactly what he is, you know.

HILDA. Him! Oh, don't give me that!

RAGNAR. In certain ways he's afraid—this great master builder. When it comes to stealing other people's happiness in life—like my father's and mine—there he's not afraid. But if it's a matter of climbing up a measly piece of scaffolding—watch him take God's own sweet time getting around to it!

HILDA. Oh, if you'd only seen him as I did once—way, high up in the spinning sky!

RAGNAR. You've seen that?

HILDA. Of course I have. How proud and free he looked, standing there, tying the wreath to the weather vane!

RAGNAR. I heard that he'd once gone up—just that once in his lifetime. Among us younger men, talking about it— it's almost a legend now. But no power on earth could get him to do it again.

HILDA. He'll do it again today.

RAGNAR (scornfully). Sure—tell me another!

HILDA. We're going to see it!

RAGNAR. Neither you nor I will ever see that.

HILDA (in a frenzy). I will see it! I will and I must see it!

RAGNAR. But he's not going to do it. He simply doesn't dare. He's got this disability now, and that's it.

(MRS. SOLNESS comes out on the veranda.)

MRS. SOLNESS. (looking about). Isn't he here? Where has he gone?

RAGNAR. Mr. Solness is down with the men.

HILDA. He took the wreath over.

MRS. SOLNESS (terrified). He took the wreath! Oh, God, no! Brovik—go down to him! Try to get him back up here!

RAGNAR. Should I say you'd like to speak with him?

MRS. SOLNESS. Oh yes, dear, do that. No, no—don't say I'd like anything! You can say that somebody's here—and he should come at once.

RAGNAR. Good. I'll take care of it, Mrs. Solness. (He goes down the steps and out through the garden.)

MRS. SOLNESS. Oh, Miss Wangel, you can't imagine how anxious I am about him.

HILDA. But is there anything here, really, to be so frightened about?

MRS. SOLNESS. Of course. It's obvious. Suppose he goes

through with this seriously—and tries to climb that scaffolding?

HILDA (*thrilled*). You think he might?

MRS. SOLNESS. One just never knows what he'll come up with. He could easily do anything.

HILDA. Ah, so you do think that he's—somewhat—?

MRS. SOLNESS. I don't know what to think about him anymore. The doctor's been telling me so much now, and when I put it all together with one thing and another that I've heard him say—

(DR. HERDAL *opens the door and looks out.*)

DR. HERDAL. Isn't he coming right up?

MRS. SOLNESS. Yes, I guess so. In any case, I've sent after him.

DR. HERDAL (*approaching*). But I think you'd better go in, Mrs. Solness—

MRS. SOLNESS. No, no. I'll stay out here and wait for Halvard.

DR. HERDAL. Yes, but some ladies are here asking for you—

MRS. SOLNESS. Good grief, that too? And right at this moment!

DR. HERDAL. They say they absolutely must see the ceremony.

MRS. SOLNESS. Oh, well, I suppose I ought to go in to them after all. It *is* my duty.

DR. HERDAL. Can't you just invite them to move on?

MRS. SOLNESS. No, that wouldn't do. Now that they're here, it's my duty to make them welcome. (*To* HILDA.) But you stay here a while—until he comes.

DR. HERDAL. And try to hold him here talking as long as possible—

MRS. SOLNESS. Yes, do try, Miss Wangel, dear. Hold him, as hard as you can.

HILDA. Aren't you the one who ought to be doing that?

MRS. SOLNESS. Lord, yes—it's my duty, I know. But when you have duties in so many directions, then—

DR. HERDAL (*looking toward the garden*). There he comes!

MRS. SOLNESS. Oh, my—and I have to go in!

DR. HERDAL (*to* HILDA). Don't say anything about my being here.

HILDA. Don't worry. I'm sure I can find something else to talk to him about.

MRS. SOLNESS. And hold him, no matter what. I'm sure *you* can do it best.

(MRS. SOLNESS *and* DR. HERDAL *go into the house.* HILDA *remains standing on the veranda.* SOLNESS *comes up the steps from the garden.*)

SOLNESS. I hear someone wants me.

HILDA. Yes, I'm the someone, Mr. Solness.

SOLNESS. Oh, it's you, Hilda. I was afraid it'd be Aline and the doctor.

HILDA. You're pretty easily frightened, I guess!

SOLNESS. You think so?

HILDA. Yes, people say you're afraid to go clambering around—like up on scaffolds.

SOLNESS. Well, that's a special case.

HILDA. But you *are* afraid—it's true, then?

SOLNESS. Yes, I am.

HILDA. Afraid of falling and killing yourself?

SOLNESS. No, not that.

HILDA. What, then?

SOLNESS. Afraid of retribution, Hilda.

HILDA. Of retribution? (*Shaking her head.*) I don't follow that.

SOLNESS. Sit down and I'll tell you something.

HILDA. Yes, do! Right now! (*She sits on a stool by the railing and looks expectantly at him.*)

SOLNESS (*tosses his hat on the table*). You know that I first started out with building churches.

HILDA (*nods*). I know that, of course.

SOLNESS. Because, you see, as a boy I came from a pious home out in the country. That's why the building of churches seemed to me the noblest thing I could do with my life.

HILDA. Go on.

SOLNESS. And I think I can say that I built those poor country churches in so honest and warm and fervent a spirit that—that—

HILDA. That—what?

SOLNESS. Well, that I feel He should have been pleased with me.

HILDA. He? Who's "He"?

SOLNESS. He who was to have the churches, of course. He whose honor and glory they served.

HILDA. I see! But are you sure that—that He wasn't—well, pleased with you?

SOLNESS (*scoffingly*). He pleased with me! What are you saying, Hilda? He who turned the troll in me loose to stuff its pockets. He who put on call, right around the clock for me, all these—these—

HILDA. Devils—

SOLNESS. Yes—both kinds. Oh no, I pretty well got the idea that He wasn't pleased with me. (*Mysteriously.*) Actually, that's why He had the old house burn.

HILDA. That was why—?

SOLNESS. Yes, don't you see? He wanted me to have the chance to become a complete master in my own realm—and enhance His glory with still greater churches. At first I didn't understand what He was after—but then, all at once, it dawned on me.

HILDA. When was that?

SOLNESS. When I was building the church tower in Lysanger.

HILDA. I thought so.

SOLNESS. For you see, Hilda, up in those strange surroundings I used to go around musing and pondering inside myself. And I saw then, clearly, why He'd taken my children from me. It was to keep me from becoming attached to anything else. I was only to be a master builder, nothing else. And all my life through, I was to go on building for Him. (*Laughs.*) But that never got very far.

HILDA. What did you do then?

SOLNESS. First, I searched my heart—tested myself—

HILDA. And then?

SOLNESS. Then I did the impossible. I no less than He.

HILDA. The impossible?

SOLNESS. I'd never in my life been able to climb straight up to a great height. But that day I could.

HILDA (*jumping up*). Yes, yes, you could!

SOLNESS. And when I stood right up at the very top, hanging the wreath, I said to Him: Hear me, Thou Almighty! From this day on, I'll be a free creator—free in my own realm, as you are in yours.

HILDA (*with great, luminous eyes*). That was the singing I heard in the air!

SOLNESS. Yes—but His mill went right on grinding.

HILDA. What do you mean by *that*?

SOLNESS (*looking despondently at her*). This building homes for human beings—it's not worth a bent pin, Hilda!

HILDA. You really feel that now?

SOLNESS. Yes, because now I see it. Human beings don't know how to use these homes of theirs. Not for being happy in. And I couldn't have found use for a home like that either—if I'd had one. (*With a quiet, bitter laugh.*) So that's the sum total, as far as far back as I can see. Nothing really built. And nothing sacrificed for the chance to build, either. Nothing, nothing—it all comes to nothing.

HILDA. Then will you never build anything again?

SOLNESS (*animated*). Why, I'm just now beginning!

HILDA. With what? What'll you build? Tell me now!

SOLNESS. The one thing human beings can be happy in— that's what I'm building now.

HILDA (*looking intently at him*). Master builder—you mean our castles in the air.

SOLNESS. Castles in the air, yes.

HILDA. I'm afraid you'd be dizzy before we got halfway up.

SOLNESS. Not if I went hand in hand with you, Hilda.

HILDA (*with a touch of suppressed resentment*). Only with me? Won't we have company?

SOLNESS. Who else?

HILDA. Oh, her—that Kaja at the desk. Poor thing—don't you want her along too?

SOLNESS. Ah, so she was the subject of Aline's little talk.

HILDA. Is it true, or isn't it?

SOLNESS (*hotly*). I wouldn't answer a question like that! You'll have to trust me, absolutely!

HILDA. For ten years I've trusted you utterly—utterly—

SOLNESS. You'll have to keep on trusting me.

HILDA. Then let me see you high and free, up there!

SOLNESS (*wearily*). Oh, Hilda—I'm not up to that every day.

HILDA (*passionately*). I want you to! I want that! (*Im-*

ploring.) Just once more, master builder! Do the impossible again!

SOLNESS (*looking deep into her eyes*). If I did try it, Hilda, I'd stand up there and talk to Him the same as before.

HILDA (*with mounting excitement*). What would you say to Him?

SOLNESS. I'd say: Hear me, Almighty God—you must judge me after your own wisdom. But from now on, I'll build only what's most beautiful in all this world—

HILDA (*enraptured*). Yes—yes—yes!

SOLNESS. Build it together with a princess that I love—

HILDA. Oh, tell Him that! Tell Him!

SOLNESS. Yes. And then I'll say to Him: I'm going down now and throw my arms about her and kiss her—

HILDA. —many times! Say that!

SOLNESS. —many, many times, I'll say.

HILDA. And then—?

SOLNESS. Then I'll swing my hat in the air—and come down to earth, here—and do as I said.

HILDA (*with outstretched arms*). Now I see you again as if there was singing in the air!

SOLNESS (*looks at her with bowed head*). How did you ever become what you are, Hilda?

HILDA. How have you made me into what I am?

SOLNESS (*decisively*). The princess shall have her castle.

HILDA (*jubilant, clapping her hands*). Oh, Mr. Solness—! My lovely, lovely castle. Our castle in the air!

SOLNESS. On a solid foundation.

> (*Out in the street, faintly visible through the trees, a* CROWD OF PEOPLE *has gathered. Distant music of a brass band is heard from behind the new house.* MRS. SOLNESS, *with a fur stole around her neck,* DR. HERDAL, *with her white shawl on his arm, and several* LADIES *come out onto the veranda.* RAGNAR BROVIK *comes up at the same time from the garden.*)

MRS. SOLNESS (*to* RAGNAR). There'll be music too?

RAGNAR. Yes. They're from the Building Trades Association. (*To* SOLNESS.) I'm supposed to tell you from the foreman that he's ready to go up now with the wreath.

SOLNESS (*taking his hat*). Good. I'll go down myself.

MRS. SOLNESS (*anxiously*). What are you going to do there, Halvard?

SOLNESS (*brusquely*). I've got to be down below with the men.

MRS. SOLNESS. Yes, down below. Please, stay down below.

SOLNESS. Don't I always—as a normal rule? (*He goes down the steps and off across the garden.*)

MRS. SOLNESS (*calling after him from the railing*). But you must tell the man to be careful climbing! Promise me, Halvard.

DR. HERDAL (*to* MRS. SOLNESS). You see, I was right. He's forgotten all about that craziness.

MRS. SOLNESS. Oh, what a relief! We've had men fall there twice now, and both times they were killed on the spot. (*Turning to* HILDA.) Thank you so much, Miss Wangel, for taking hold of him like that. I'm sure I never could have managed it.

DR. HERDAL (*roguishly*). You know, Miss Wangel—you have a gift for taking hold of a man that you shouldn't hide!

> (MRS. SOLNESS *and* DR. HERDAL *move across to the* LADIES, *who stand nearer the steps, looking out over the garden.* HILDA *remains standing at the railing in the foreground.* RAGNAR *goes over to her.*)

RAGNAR (*with stifled laughter, dropping his voice*). Miss Wangel—do you see all the young people, down there in the street?

HILDA. Yes.

RAGNAR. They're my fellow students, come for a look at the master.

HILDA. Why do they want to look at *him*?

RAGNAR. They want to see him afraid to climb up on his own house.

HILDA. So, that's what the boys want!

RAGNAR (*with seething scorn*). He's kept us down so long —now we're going to see him have the pleasure of keeping himself down.

HILDA. You're not going to see it. Not today.

RAGNAR (*smiling*). Really? And where will we see him!

HILDA. High—high up by the weather vane, that's where.

RAGNAR (*laughs*). Him! Oh, you bet!

HILDA. His will—is to climb straight to the top. And that's where you'll see him, too.

RAGNAR. His *will*, yes, sure—that I believe. But he simply can't do it. His head would be swimming before he was even halfway up. He'd have to crawl down again on his hands and knees.

DR. HERDAL (*pointing*). Look! There goes the foreman up the ladder.

MRS. SOLNESS. And he's got the wreath to carry, too. Oh, if he'll only take care.

RAGNAR (*crying out in astonishment*). But it's—!

HILDA (*in an outburst of joy*). It's the master builder himself!

MRS. SOLNESS (*with a shriek of terror*). Yes, it's Halvard! Oh, my God! Halvard! Halvard!

DR. HERDAL. Shh. Don't shout at him!

MRS. SOLNESS (*half distracted*). I'll go to him. Get him down again!

DR. HERDAL (*restraining her*). All of you—don't move!

HILDA (*motionless, following* SOLNESS *with her eyes*). He's climbing and climbing. Always higher. Always higher! Look! Just look!

RAGNAR (*breathlessly*). Now he's got to turn back. It's all he can do.

HILDA. He's climbing and climbing. He's almost there.

MRS. SOLNESS. Oh, I'll die of fright. I can't bear to look.

DR. HERDAL. Then don't watch him.

HILDA. There he is, on the highest planks! Straight to the top!

DR. HERDAL. Nobody move—you hear me!

HILDA (*exulting with quiet intensity*). At last! At last! Now I can see him great and free again.

RAGNAR (*nearly speechless*). But this is—

HILDA. All these ten years I've seen him like this. How strong he stands! Terribly thrilling, after all. Look at him! Now he's hanging the wreath on the vane!

RAGNAR. I feel like I'm seeing something here that's—that's impossible.

HILDA. Yes, it's the impossible, now, that he's doing! (*With the inscrutable look in her eyes.*) Do you see anyone up there with him?

RAGNAR. There's nobody else.

HILDA. Yes, there's someone he's struggling with.

RAGNAR. You're mistaken.

HILDA. You don't hear singing in the air, either?

RAGNAR. It must be the wind in the treetops.

HILDA. I hear the singing—a tremendous music! (*Crying out in wild exultation.*) Look, look! He's waved his hat! He's waving to us down here! Oh, wave—wave back up to him again—because now, now, it's fulfilled! (*Snatches the white shawl from the doctor, waves it, and calls out.*) Hurray for master builder Solness!

DR. HERDAL. Stop! Stop! In God's name—!

> (*The* LADIES *on the veranda wave their handkerchiefs, and shouts of "Hurray" fill the street below. Suddenly they are cut short, and the* CROWD *breaks into a cry of horror. A human body, along with some planks and splintered wood, is indistinctly seen plunging down between the trees.*)

MRS. SOLNESS AND THE LADIES (*as one*). He's falling! He's falling!

> (MRS. SOLNESS *sways and sinks back in a faint; the* LADIES *catch her up amid cries and confusion. The* CROWD *in the street breaks the fence down and storms into the garden.* DR. HERDAL *also rushes down below. A short pause.*)

HILDA (*stares fixedly upward and speaks as if petrified*). *My* master builder.

RAGNAR (*leans, trembling, against the railing*). He must have been smashed to bits. Killed on the spot.

ONE OF THE LADIES (*as* MRS. SOLNESS *is carried into the house*). Run down to the doctor—

RAGNAR. I can't move—

ANOTHER LADY. Call down to someone, then!

RAGNAR (*trying to call*). How is it? Is he alive?

A VOICE (*down in the garden*). Mr. Solness is dead.

OTHER VOICES (*nearer*). His whole head's been crushed— He fell right into the quarry.

HILDA (*turns to* RAGNAR *and says quietly*). I can't see him up there anymore.

RAGNAR. How horrible this is. And so, after all—he really couldn't do it.

HILDA (*as if out of a hushed, dazed triumph*). But he went straight, straight to the top. And I heard harps in the air. (*Swings the shawl up overhead and cries with wild intensity.*) My—my master builder!

LITTLE EYOLF

Like *The Lady from the Sea*, its counterpart in atmosphere and topography of six years previous, *Little Eyolf* (1894) confronts the universal human problem of coping with the anguish of personal loss. In the earlier play what was lost forever was less a person than an *idée fixe*, an unshakable eidetic image of what a completely fulfilling romantic love should be. Ellida's torturous yet liberating choice restores her to an intact and waiting family; renouncing the Stranger is both a self-integrative act and a reconciliation to life within a human scale of values. In *Little Eyolf*, however, what dies is not illusory, but cruelly real: an only child. There is, or seems to be, no reconciliation possible for a loss so abrupt, senseless, unanswerable. Moreover, in the aftermath of the shock, the father and mother are driven apart in guilt and recrmination. The family unit, including as well the hitherto sustaining presence and now imminent departure of the husband's half-sister, is strained to the utmost. The action of *Little Eyolf* is deeper, fuller, more majestic in its basic rhythms than its predecessor, for what must be accommodated is not life, but death—"death," and, continuing in the words of Joseph Campbell, "disintegration, dismemberment, and the crucifixion of our heart with the passing of the forms we love."

The physical death that occurs before our ears, offstage in one of the most vivid and affecting dramatic climaxes Ibsen ever wrote, is echoed by another, symbolic death which we hear about only much later. It occupies one more of those strange stories that recur throughout the latter half of the cycle, and it bears directly on the other configuration given to the play's central concern: the anguish of the threatened loss of the object of a devouring sensual passion. A strong eroticism is an intermittently surfacing undercurrent in almost all of the plays (excepting *Pillars of Society* and *An Enemy of the People*), but in *Little Eyolf eros* assumes co-equal importance with *thanatos* in what, for the period, was an unusually explicit presentation of a woman's unsatisfied sexuality. For just as Alfred Allmers feels most acutely the loss of Eyolf, Rita feels most fearfully the loss of her husband, not to a rival, but to the directives arising out of a mystical experience.

Allmers, we learn, has been some ten weeks away on a walking tour in the mountains—in ten years of marriage, significantly, the first period of more than a day he has spent apart from his consumingly possessive wife. Unremittingly in "the infinite solitude" of the vast moraines, "in an understanding and a communion" with sunrises, mountain peaks, stars, he comes at length to the desolate shore of an immense lake. Striking off in a side valley, he becomes lost, delirious in the pathless night, skirting precipices, sensing without fear death traveling companionably alongside him, until at dawn he descends safely on the farther shore. Allmers' account is hallucinatory, dreamlike. It is, in fact, the ancient, archetypal dream of passing from one shore to another, signifying a momentous decision, a transition to a new plane of existence, a spiritual death of the insatiably desiring ego and a rebirth in terms of a self merely subsisting in the cosmic life force.

Immediately it must be stressed that Ibsen is not proclaiming Allmers an exemplar of nature's noblemen by virtue of this experience. It simply provides one of the grounds on which the action of the drama proceeds and is studied, as Eyolf's similarly irrational death provides the other, in vertical tension with it: mountain peaks and sea depths, self-transcendence and submersion in ego, exaltation and despair. The play asks, how well do we creatures of a middle state measure up between these extremes of human potential? At first sight, the judgment on the two principals seems quietly but mercilessly unsparing. Rita has private income enough—the "gold and green forests"—to indulge a *folie à deux*, a point on which Shaw builds an eloquent argument of Fabian accusation. Allmers wavers between renunciation of his wife's manifold physical charms as well as his projected magnum opus, *On Human Responsibility*, and the resurgent ego of conceiving Eyolf's future education, transferred from books to life, as an extension of himself. Moreover, he proves himself, besides being capable of a love and grief worthy of respect (Ibsen's dramatic economy does not repeat the portrait of Hjalmar Ekdal), to be weak, mean-spirited, caustic and vain. These

and other defects of Allmers' character Herman Weigand
has elaborated into a one-sidedly negative fusillade of
1920s-style debunking.

The thematic use of setting, which the older schools of
social and character criticism mainly ignored, offers a clue
to a more inclusive interpretation which does not violate
the entire tone and the conclusion of the play. Through its
three acts the drama moves from elevation, to depression,
to elevation of terrain. Act Two, the locus of the most
acrid recrimination, is crucial. Here we are shown that
traumatic grief, like an ocean storm, may bring all manner
of sea wrack to the surface. But the play implicitly counsels, let it come, get it out, go through it to the bitter end
and beyond, where greater meanings wait in the deprived
lives of others, the spirit world, the mountain peaks and
the stars. *Little Eyolf*, like one of its commanding images,
the water lily, floats on the sensuous and hazardous surface, while it stems from the farthest depths.

THE CHARACTERS

ALFRED ALLMERS, landed proprietor, man of letters, formerly a part-time teacher
RITA ALLMERS, his wife
EYOLF, their child, nine years old
ASTA ALLMERS, Alfred's younger half-sister
BORGHEJM, an engineer
THE RAT-WIFE

The action takes place on ALLMERS' *estate beside the fjord, a dozen or more miles out from the town.*

~~~✦ ACT ONE ✦~~~

*An attractive, elegantly decorated garden room, filled with
furniture, flowers and plants. In the background, open
glass doors leading to a veranda, with a wide prospect of
the fjord beyond. Steep wooded hills in the distance. In
each of the side walls, a door, the one to the right being a
double door set farther back. On the near right, a sofa with
soft bolsters and throw rugs. Chairs and a small table next
to the sofa. On the near left, a large table with armchairs
around it. An open valise lies on the table. The scene is
bathed in the warm sunlight of an early summer morning.*

RITA ALLMERS *is standing by the table, facing left, unpacking the valise. She is a blond, good-looking, full-
bodied woman, brimming with vitality, about thirty years
old. She wears a brightly colored morning dress.*

After a moment ASTA ALLMERS *enters by the right-hand
door, dressed in a light-brown summer outfit, with hat,
jacket and parasol. Under one arm she holds a fair-sized,
locked portfolio. She is slim, of medium height, with dark
hair and deep, serious eyes; twenty-five years old.*

ASTA (*in the doorway*). Good morning, Rita dear.

RITA (*turns her head and nods a greeting*). No, is that
you, Asta! Out from town so early? All the way out here?

ASTA (*laying her things on a chair by the door*). Yes, I
had such a sense of uneasiness. I felt I *had* to come and

look in on little Eyolf today. And you, too. (*Sets the portfolio down on the table by the sofa.*) So I took the steamer out.

RITA (*smiling at her*). And did you happen to meet one of your special friends on board? Just by accident, I mean.

ASTA (*quietly*). No, not anyone I knew at all. (*Noticing the valise.*) But, Rita—what's that?

RITA (*continuing to unpack*). Alfred's suitcase. Don't you recognize it?

ASTA (*joyously, coming closer*). What! Alfred's home?

RITA. Yes, can you imagine—a complete surprise. He came on the night train.

ASTA. Oh, so *that's* what I was feeling. *That's* what drew me out here! And he didn't send a letter ahead? Not even a card?

RITA. Not a word.

ASTA. Nor a telegram, either?

RITA. Oh, yes, an hour before he arrived. Just the cold, bare facts. (*She laughs.*) That's his style, Asta, isn't it?

ASTA. Yes, very much. He doesn't like excitement.

RITA. But it was all the more delectable, getting him back that way.

ASTA. Um, I can well imagine.

RITA. A whole two weeks before I expected him!

ASTA. And everything's all right with him? He's not depressed?

RITA (*snaps the valise shut and smiles at her*). He looked completely transformed when he came in through the door.

ASTA. Not the least bit tired, even?

RITA. Oh yes, I'm sure he was tired. Dead tired. But, poor dear, he went most of the way on foot.

ASTA. And then the mountain air may have been too raw for him.

RITA. I doubt it. I haven't heard him cough once.

ASTA. Well, there, you see! So it really was the best thing possible—the doctor coaxing him into that trip.

RITA. Yes, now that it's finally over— But, Asta, believe me, this has been a horrible time for me. I've never wanted to speak about it. And then you hardly ever came out to see me—

ASTA. Yes, I certainly haven't done right by you. But—

RITA. Now, never mind—you had the school there in town. (*Smiles.*) And our road-builder—of course, he was away, too.

ASTA. Oh, stop it, Rita!

RITA. All right. Forget the road-builder— Ah, but how lost I've felt without Alfred! How empty—like a desert! Oh, it was as if this house were an open grave—!

ASTA. Now, really! What's it been—six, seven weeks—?

RITA. Yes, but you have to remember, Alfred's never been away from me before. Not even so much as overnight. Never, in all these ten years—

ASTA. No, but that's exactly why I think it was high time he got away a bit this year. He should have had a hiking trip in the mountains every summer. That's what he needed.

RITA (*with a half-smile*). Oh, yes, it's well enough for you to talk. If I were as—as level-headed as you, I'd probably have let him go before this. Perhaps. But I felt I didn't dare, Asta! I had a sense that I'd never get him back again. That's something you can understand, can't you?

ASTA. No. But that's undoubtedly because I have no one to lose.

RITA (*with a teasing smile*). No one at all—really—?

ASTA. Not that *I* know of. (*Changing the subject.*) But tell me, Rita—where is Alfred? Still sleeping?

RITA. Oh, hardly. He was up early as usual today.

ASTA. Then he couldn't have been so dead tired after all.

RITA. Oh, last night he was. When he got in. But now he's had Eyolf in there with him for more than an hour.

ASTA. That poor, pale little boy! Is he going to start his perpetual studying again?

RITA (*with a shrug*). It's how Alfred wants it, you know.

ASTA. Yes, but I think you ought to put your foot down, Rita.

RITA (*somewhat impatiently*). No—honestly—I can't get involved in that. Alfred understands these things so much better than I. And besides, what would you want Eyolf to do? He can't run around and play—like other children.

ASTA (*firmly*). I'll talk to Alfred about this.

RITA. Yes, dear, you do that— Ah, here we are—

(ALFRED ALLMERS, *in a summer suit, enters through the door on the left, leading* EYOLF *by the hand. He is a lean, slightly built man of thirty-six or thirty-seven, with mild eyes and thin, brown hair and beard. His face has a serious and thoughtful look.* EYOLF *wears a suit cut like a uniform, with gold braid and brass buttons with lions on them. He is lame and walks with a crutch under his left arm, the leg on that side being paralyzed. He is underweight and appears sickly, but has beautiful, intelligent eyes.*)

ALLMERS (*releases* EYOLF *and goes happily across to extend both hands to* ASTA). Asta! Dearest Asta! Here, already! How wonderful to see you so soon!

ASTA. I felt I had to— Welcome home again!

ALLMERS (*shaking her hands*). Thanks for coming!

RITA. Doesn't he look marvelous?

ASTA (*gazing intently at him*). Splendid! Simply splendid! His eyes are so alive! Yes, you must have written a great deal out there. (*Joy welling up in her.*) Maybe you even finished the book, Alfred?

ALLMERS (*shrugs*). The book—? Oh, *that*—

ASTA. Yes, I felt it would practically write itself if you could only get away.

ALLMERS. I felt the same. But, you know—that's not the way it went. I didn't write one single line on the book.

ASTA. You didn't write—!

RITA. Of course! I couldn't understand why there was so much blank paper in your bag.

ASTA. But, Alfred dear, what did you do in all that time?

ALLMERS (*smiles*). Just walked and thought and thought.

RITA (*placing her arm across his shoulders*). A little, now and then, about us here at home?

ALLMERS. Yes, you can be sure of that. Very much. Every day.

RITA (*releasing him*). So, then eveything's well and good.

ASTA. But nothing written on the book? And still you can look so happy and content? You're not like that usually. Not when your work's going badly, I mean.

ALLMERS. You're right. Because you see, I've been so stupid in the past. Thinking—that's the best part of us. What finds its way onto paper is scarcely important.

ASTA (*exclaims*). Scarcely important!

RITA (*with a laugh*). You must be out of your mind, Alfred!

EYOLF (*looking trustfully up at him*). Oh but, Papa, what *you* write—that's important.

ALLMERS (*smiles and strokes his hair*). Yes, yes, if *you* say so— But mark my words—there'll be someone coming in time who'll do it better.

EYOLF. What do you mean, someone? Oh, tell me!

ALLMERS. Just wait. He'll come, sure enough, and announce himself.

EYOLF. And then what will you do?

ALLMERS (*seriously*). I'll go up in the mountains again—

RITA. Oh, Alfred, don't carry on!

ALLMERS. Up on the heights, on the great barrens.

EYOLF. Papa, don't you think I'll soon be strong enough that I can go with you?

ALLMERS (*his feelings painful*). Oh, perhaps, yes—my little boy.

EYOLF. Because I think that would be great if I could go mountain-climbing, too.

ASTA (*changing the subject*). My, how nice and neat you're dressed today, Eyolf!

EYOLF. Yes, don't you think so, Auntie?

ASTA. Oh, yes. Is it for Papa's sake that you're wearing the new clothes?

EYOLF. Yes, I asked Mama if I could. Because I wanted Papa to see me in them.

ALLMERS (*quietly to* RITA). You shouldn't have gotten him a suit like that.

RITA (*softly*). Oh, but he kept plaguing me. Interminably. He didn't give me a moment's peace.

EYOLF. And guess what, Papa—Borghejm bought me a bow and arrow. And taught me to shoot with it, too.

ALLMERS. Ah now, that's really your kind of thing, Eyolf.

EYOLF. And when he comes again next time, I'm going to ask him to teach me to swim.

ALLMERS. Swim! But why do you want to do that!

EYOLF. Because all the boys down at the shore, they can swim. I'm the only one who can't.

ALLMERS (*moved, taking him in his arms*). You'll have the chance to learn everything you want. Anything you like.

EYOLF. Yes, you know what I'd like most of all, Papa?

ALLMERS. No. Tell me.

EYOLF. Most of all, I want to learn to be a soldier.

ALLMERS. Oh, little Eyolf, there are so many other things better than that.

EYOLF. Yes, but when I'm big, then I *have* to be a soldier. You know that now.

ALLMERS (*clenching his fists*). Yes, yes, yes, we'll see—

ASTA (*sitting by the table at the left*). Eyolf! Come over here, and I'll tell you something.

EYOLF (*going up to her*). What's that, Auntie?

ASTA. You know what, Eyolf—I've seen the Rat-Wife.

EYOLF. What! You saw the Rat-Wife! Oh, you're just teasing me!

ASTA. No, it's true. I saw her yesterday.

EYOLF. Where did you see her?

ASTA. I saw her on the road, outside town.

ALLMERS. I saw her too, upcountry somewhere.

RITA (*seated on the sofa*). Maybe we'll get to see her too, Eyolf.

EYOLF. Isn't it strange, Auntie, that she's called the Rat-Wife?

ASTA. She's simply called that because she goes around the countryside, driving away all the rats.

ALLMERS. Actually, I believe her name is Varg.

EYOLF. Varg? That means a wolf, doesn't it?

ALLMERS (*patting him on the head*). So, you know *that* too, Eyolf?

EYOLF (*thoughtfully*). Then maybe it's really true that she's a werewolf at night. Do you think so, Papa?

ALLMERS. Oh no, I don't believe that. But now you should go out and play a little in the garden.

EYOLF. Don't you think I'd better take some books with me?

ALLMERS. No, from now on, no books. Go down to the shore, with the other boys.

EYOLF (*embarrassed*). No, Papa, I don't want to go play with those boys today.

ALLMERS. Why not?

EYOLF. Oh, because I have these clothes on.

ALLMERS (*frowning*). You mean they make fun of—of your nice clothes!

EYOLF (*evasively*). No, they don't dare. Because then I'd hit them.

ALLMERS. Well—what, then—?

EYOLF. But they're so mean, those boys. And they say that I can never be a soldier.

ALLMERS (*repressing his anger*). Why would they say that?

EYOLF. They're probably jealous of me. You know, Papa, they're so poor, they have to go barefoot.

ALLMERS (*in a low, choked voice*). Oh, Rita—it's nothing but heartache, all this!

RITA (*rises, soothingly*). There, there, now!

ALLMERS (*ominously*). But those boys are going to learn someday who's master down at the shore!

ASTA (*listening*). Someone's knocking.

EYOLF. It must be Borghejm.

RITA. Come in!

(*The* RAT-WIFE *slips silently in through the door on the right. She is a tiny, thin, wizened figure, old and gray-haired, with sharp, probing eyes, wearing an old-fashioned, flowered dress and a black, hooded cape. In one hand she has a large red umbrella and a black bag hanging on a string over her arm.*)

EYOLF (*gripping* ASTA's *dress, softly*). Auntie! It must be her!

RAT-WIFE (*curtsying at the door*). My apologies for intruding—but are the master and mistress bothered by anything gnawing away here in the house?

ALLMERS. Are we—? No, I don't think so.

RAT-WIFE. Because otherwise it'd be all my pleasure to help them get rid of it.

RITA. Yes, yes, we understand. But we don't have anything like that.

RAT-WIFE. That *is* a shame. Because I'm just off around

the country now. And who knows when I'll be back in these parts—? Oh, I'm so tired!

ALLMERS (*pointing toward a chair*). Yes, you look it.

RAT-WIFE. A body never ought to get tired of doing good by those poor little creatures, hated and hunted down so cruelly. But it takes every bit of your strength.

RITA. Won't you sit and rest for a moment?

RAT-WIFE. Ah, thanks no end. (*Settles down on a chair between the door and the sofa.*) Because all night I've been out working.

ALLMERS. Have you?

RAT-WIFE. Yes, over to the islands. (*Chuckling.*) The people, they had to send for me all right. They didn't like it at all, but there was no other choice. They had to smile and bite the sour apple. (*Looks at* EYOLF *and nods.*) Sour apple, little sir. Sour apple.

EYOLF (*involuntarily, and somewhat shyly*). Why did they have to—?

RAT-WIFE. What?

EYOLF. To bite it?

RAT-WIFE. Oh, because they hadn't any more to feed on. Because of the rats and all the little rat babies, you can imagine, young sir.

RITA. Ugh! The poor people— Were there all *that* many?

RAT-WIFE. Yes, the place crept and crawled with them. (*With a quietly amused laugh.*) Up in the beds they scampered and scuttled the whole night long. They plopped down in the milk pails. And every which way over the floors they went, whisking and rustling.

EYOLF (*to* ASTA, *in an undertone*). I'll never go out there, Auntie.

RAT-WIFE. But then *I* came—and one more. And we took them all away with us—the sweet little creatures. We got rid of them, every one.

EYOLF (*with a shriek*). Papa—look, look!

RITA. Good Lord, Eyolf!

ALLMERS. What's wrong?

EYOLF (*pointing*). There's something squirming in the bag!

RITA (*shrinks to the left and screams*). Oh, no! Get her out, Alfred!

RAT-WIFE (*laughing*). Oh, my dearest lady, nothing to be afraid of in this little ragamuffin.

ALLMERS. But what *is* it, anyway?

RAT-WIFE. It's only Mopseman. (*Untying the bag.*) Come, little friend. Up, out of the dark, dearie.

(*A small dog with a wide black snout sticks its head up out of the bag. The* RAT-WIFE *nods and beckons to* EYOLF.)

RAT-WIFE. No fear, my little wounded soldier. Come closer. He won't bite. Come and pet him. Come on!

EYOLF (*clings to* ASTA). No, I don't dare.

RAT-WIFE. Wouldn't the young gentleman say he has a kind and loving countenance?

EYOLF (*pointing in amazement*). *That*, there!

RAT-WIFE. Yes, him.

EYOLF (*barely audibly, staring riveted at the dog*). I think he has the most horrible—countenance I've ever seen.

RAT-WIFE (*closing the bag*). Oh, we'll see, we'll see about that.

EYOLF (*moves involuntarily nearer, then crosses and lightly strokes the bag*). But still he's—beautiful. He's beautiful.

RAT-WIFE (*in a gentle voice*). But now he's so tired and weary, poor dear. So bone-tired he is. (*Looks at* ALLMERS.) Because, as you must know, sir, it drains your strength—that sort of game.

ALLMERS. What sort of game?

RAT-WIFE. The lure-game.

ALLMERS. Ah, is it the dog luring the rats then?

RAT-WIFE (*nods*). Mopseman and I. We work together. It goes slick as a whistle—to look at, anyway. I put a string through his collar, and then I lead him three times around the house—and play on my Jew's harp. And when they hear *that*, they have to come up from the cellars and down from the lofts and out of their holes—all those blessed little creatures.

EYOLF. Then does he bite them to death?

RAT-WIFE. Oh, far from it! No, we go down to the boat, he and I. And so they follow us—both the grown and the little hobbly ones, too.

EYOLF (*tense with excitement*). And then what—? Tell me!

RAT-WIFE. Then we shove off from land; and I scull with one oar and play on my mouth-harp. And Mopseman, he swims after me. (*With glistening eyes.*) And all those scuttly, scampering things, they follow and follow us out to the deep waters. Yes, because they *have* to!

EYOLF. Why do they *have* to?

RAT-WIFE. Just because they don't *want* to. Because they're so sickly afraid of the water—they have to go out in it.

EYOLF. Do they drown then?

RAT-WIFE. Every last one. (*More softly.*) And then they have it as still and as nice and dark as they ever could wish for—little beauties. Down there they sleep such a sweet, long sleep—all of them that people hate and persecute. (*Rises.*) Yes, in the old days I didn't need any Mopseman. I did my luring myself. All alone.

EYOLF. What did you lure?

RAT-WIFE. Men. One, mostly.

EYOLF (*in suspense*). Oh, tell me, who was it?

RAT-WIFE (*laughs*). It was my own true love, little heartbreaker!

EYOLF. Where is he now?

RAT-WIFE (*curtly*). Down under, with all the rats. (*Her tone mild again.*) But now I've got to get off and busy again. Always on the go. (*To* RITA.) Does Madame have no use for me at all today? Because then I could do it on the spot.

RITA. Thank you, there's nothing pressing, really.

RAT-WIFE. Oh well, my dear lady—you never know. If your graces notice anything here that nibbles and gnaws— and creeps and crawls—then you just call on me and Mopseman. Goodbye, goodbye, many thousand goodbyes.

(*She goes out by the door, right.*)

EYOLF (*quietly and triumphantly to* ASTA). Think, Auntie—*I've* seen the Rat-Wife too!

(RITA *goes out on the veranda and fans herself with her handkerchief. Shortly after,* EYOLF *slips out unnoticed through the door, right.*)

ALLMERS (*picking up the portfolio from the table by the sofa*). Is this your portfolio, Asta?

ASTA. Yes. I have a few of the old letters in it.

ALLMERS. Oh, the family letters—

ASTA. You remember asking me to sort them out while you were away?

ALLMERS (*gives her a pat on the head*). You're a wonder! You found time for *that*, too.

ASTA. Oh yes. I did it partly out here and partly in town at my place.

ALLMERS. Thanks, dear. Find anything interesting in them?

ASTA (*offhandedly*). Oh—you know, there's always something or other you find in old papers. (*In a subdued, serious tone.*) The ones in the folio there are letters to Mother.

ALLMERS. Well, those, of course, you must keep.

ASTA (*with an effort*). No. I want you to look through them, too, Alfred. Sometime—later in life. But I don't have the key with me today.

ALLMERS. Doesn't matter, Asta dear. Because I'd never read your mother's letters anyway.

ASTA (*fixes her eyes on him*). Then sometime—on a quiet evening—I'll tell you something about what's in them.

ALLMERS. Yes, that you could do. But hold onto your mother's letters. You haven't too many mementos of her.

(*He gives* ASTA *the portfolio. She takes it and places it on the chair under her hat and parasol.* RITA *comes back into the room.*)

RITA. Ugh, that old hag! I swear, she brings the smell of corpses with her.

ALLMERS. Yes, she *was* rather sinister.

RITA. I thought I was going to be sick while she was in the room.

ALLMERS. All the same, I can understand that power of attraction she talked about. The solitude in the mountains, up in those vast moraines, has something like it.

ASTA (*looking keenly at him*). What is this thing that's happened with you, Alfred?

ALLMERS (*smiling*). With me?

ASTA. Yes, something has. Like a transformation, almost. Rita's noticed it, too.

RITA. Yes, I saw it as soon as you came. But it's for the good, isn't it, Alfred?

ALLMERS. It *should* be. It's got to, and it will, be for the good.

RITA (*impetuously*). You had some kind of experience on that trip. Don't deny it! I can read it ail over you!

ALLMERS (*shaking his head*). Nothing at all—outwardly. But—

RITA (*avidly*). But—?

ALLMERS. Inwardly, it's true— I've been through a minor upheaval.

RITA. Oh, God—!

ALLMERS (*soothingly, stroking her head*). All for the best, Rita dear. Don't worry.

RITA (*sitting on the sofa*). You better tell us about this right away. Everything.

ALLMERS (*turning to* ASTA). All right, let's sit, Asta. I'll try to tell this as well as I can.

(*He settles down on the sofa beside* RITA. ASTA *pulls up a chair and sits near him. A brief pause.*)

RITA (*looks at him expectantly*). Well—?

ALLMERS (*gazing straight ahead*). When I think back on my life—and my lot—these last ten, eleven years, it seems almost like a fairy tale to me, or a dream. Don't you think so, Asta?

ASTA. Yes, in many ways.

ALLMERS (*as before*). When I think of what the two of us were once, Asta, A pair of penniless orphans—

RITA (*impatiently*). Oh, but that's so far back.

ALLMERS (*not hearing her*). And now here I am, in comfort and style—having been able to follow my calling—to work and study, all just as I wished. (*Reaching out his hand.*) And every bit of this incredible, great good fortune —we owe to you, Rita, my dearest.

RITA (*half irritated, half amused, slaps his hand*). Now, enough of that nonsense.

ALLMERS. I mention it only by way of introduction—

RITA. Then skip the introductions!

ALLMERS. Rita—you mustn't suppose it was the doctor's advice that drove me up into the mountains.

ASTA. It wasn't?

RITA. What drove you, then?

ALLMERS. It was because I found no peace in working any more.

RITA. No peace! But, dear, who was it disturbed you?

ALLMERS (*shaking his head*). No person. I simply had a

feeling that I was in effect misusing—or—no, neglecting my best talents. That I was squandering my time.

ASTA (*wide-eyed*). By writing your book?

ALLMERS (*nods*). Because I must have more talents than *that*. I should be able to do one or two other things as well.

RITA. Is *that* what was bothering you so much?

ALLMERS. Yes, mainly.

RITA. And that's why you've been so dissatisfied with yourself lately. And with all of us, too. Yes, because you certainly were, Alfred!

ALLMERS (*gazing straight ahead*). I sat there, bent over the table, writing day after day. Many times half the night, too. Writing and writing on that massive tome on *Human Responsibility*. Hm!

ASTA (*placing her hand on his arm*). But, dear—you know that book is your life's work.

RITA. Yes, you've said that often enough.

ALLMERS. So I thought—in all the time since I first grew up. (*His eyes kindling.*) And then, Rita dear, you gave me the chance to start in on it.

RITA. Rubbish!

ALLMERS (*smiling at her*). You with your gold and green forests—

RITA (*half laughing, half displeased*). Any more of your foolishness, and I'll hit you.

ASTA (*looking uneasily at him*). But, Alfred, the book?

ALLMERS. It seemed to fade away into the distance. My thoughts, more and more, were on the higher duties that claimed me.

RITA (*radiantly, grasping his hand*). Alfred!

ALLMERS. Thoughts of Eyolf, Rita.

RITA (*cast down, releasing his hand*). Oh—Eyolf.

ALLMERS. Poor little Eyolf's grown deeper and deeper

into me. Ever since that awful fall from the table. And particularly since we've known it was incurable—

RITA (*intently*). But you've done everything you could for him, Alfred!

ALLMERS. As a teacher, yes. But not as a father. And it's a father I want to be to Eyolf from now on.

RITA (*looking at him, shaking her head*). I really don't understand you.

ALLMERS. I mean I'll try with all my power to ease what can't be cured in him any way I can.

RITA. But, dear—thank heaven, I don't think it's anything *he* feels so deeply.

ASTA (*emotionally*). Oh, but Rita, he does.

ALLMERS. Yes, you can be positive he feels it deeply.

RITA (*impatiently*). But, dearest—what more can you do for him?

ALLMERS. I want to see if I can kindle all the rich possibilities dawning in that child's mind. All the tentative nobility in him I want to help to grow—and blossom and bear fruit. (*With more and more fervor, getting up.*) And I'll do more than that! I'll help him bring his dreams in harmony with what he's capable of. Because now they're *not*. All his ambitions are bent on what, for the rest of his life, can only be out of his reach. But I'll mold his mind toward happiness.

(*He paces back and forth across the room.* ASTA *and* RITA *follow him with their eyes.*)

RITA. You shouldn't take these things so hard, Alfred.

ALLMERS (*stops by the table on the left and regards them*). Eyolf will take up my life's work. If he wants to. Or he can choose something that's all his own. Maybe that's better— Well, in any case, I'm done with mine.

RITA (*rising*). But, Alfred dearest—can't you work for yourself and for Eyolf both?

ALLMERS. No, I can't. That's impossible! I can't divide myself here. So I'll stand aside. Eyolf will be the fulfillment of our family line. And I'll find my new life's work in preparing him toward that end.

ASTA (*having gotten up, goes to him*). What a fearfully hard struggle this must have cost you, Alfred.

ALLMERS. Yes, it has. Here at home I never could have managed it. Never could have forced myself to that renunciation. Never here, at home.

RITA. Was that why you went off this summer?

ALLMERS (*his eyes glowing*). Yes! I went up into the infinite solitude. And watched the sunrise shining on the mountain peaks. Felt myself closer to the stars. Almost in an understanding and a communion with them. And then I could do it.

ASTA (*looking at him sadly*). But the book on *Human Responsibility*—you won't ever write any more on it?

ALLMERS. No, never, Asta. I tell you, I can't split myself between two callings. But I'll follow human responsibility through—in my own life.

RITA (*with a smile*). Do you really think you can maintain such high objectives here at home?

ALLMERS (*taking her hand*). With you to help me, I can. (*Extending his other hand.*) And with you too, Asta.

RITA (*withdraws her hand*). With both of us. Then you *can* divide yourself.

ALLMERS. But, my dearest Rita—!

(RITA *moves from him and stands in the garden doorway. There is a quick, light knocking on the door, left.* BORGHEJM, *the engineer, comes in briskly. He is a young man in his early thirties, with an open, confident expression and erect carriage.*)

BORGHEJM. Good morning, good morning, Mrs. Allmers. (*Stops, delighted at seeing* ALLMERS.) Well, look here! Already home again, Mr. Allmers?

ALLMERS (*shaking his hand*). Yes, I got in last night.

RITA (*gaily*). His parole was revoked, Mr. Borghejm.

ALLMERS. Come on, Rita, that's not true—

RITA (*moving closer*). Why, of course it's true. He's being recommitted.

BORGHEJM. You hold your husband on such a tight leash, Mrs. Allmers?

RITA. I hold by my rights. Besides, everything has to come to an end.

BORGHEJM. Oh, not everything—I hope. Good morning, Miss Allmers.

ASTA (*coolly*). Good morning.

RITA (*looking at* BORGHEJM). You say, not everything?

BORGHEJM. Oh, I absolutely believe there has to be *something* in this world that doesn't have an end.

RITA. You must be thinking of love—and suchlike.

BORGHEJM (*warmly*). I'm thinking of everything that's lovely!

RITA. And that has no end. Yes, let's think on that. Hope on it, all of us.

ALLMERS (*coming over to them*). You'll be finished soon with your road construction out here?

BORGHEJM. I *am* finished. Finished up yesterday. It's gone on long enough. But, thank God, *that* came to an end.

RITA. And that's what you're so jubilant about?

BORGHEJM. Oh, I am, absolutely!

RITA. Well, I must say—

BORGHEJM. What, Mrs. Allmers?

RITA. It's not very nice of you, Mr. Borghejm.

BORGHEJM. Really? Why not?

RITA. Because from now on you probably won't be out in these parts too often.

BORGHEJM. No, that's true. I hadn't thought of that.

RITA. Well, once in a while you'll have to visit us anyway.

BORGHEJM. No, unfortunately that'll be impossible for me for quite some time now.

RITA. Oh? Why so?

BORGHEJM. I've just landed a big new assignment that I'll have to light into right away.

ALLMERS. No, really? (*Presses his hand.*) That pleases me enormously.

RITA. Congratulations, Mr. Borghejm!

BORGHEJM. Shh! I'm not supposed to breathe a word about it yet. But I can't hold back! It's a huge road job—up north. Through the mountains—with some fantastic problems involved! (*Fervently.*) Ah, what a marvelous world—and what a piece of luck, to be a road-builder!

RITA (*smiles at him roguishly*). Is it simply highway engineering that's brought you out here in such wild spirits today?

BORGHEJM. No, not just that. There are so many bright, beckoning prospects opening up for me.

RITA (*as before*). Ah, then maybe there's something even lovelier in store?

BORGHEJM (*glancing toward* ASTA). Who knows? They say good fortune comes in torrents. (*Turns to* ASTA.) Miss Allmers, shouldn't we have a little walk together? Like old times?

ASTA (*quickly*). No, no thanks. Not now. Not today.

BORGHEJM. Oh, come on! Just a little walk! I feel I have so much to say to you before I go.

RITA. That you can't talk about openly yet?

BORGHEJM. Hm, it all depends—

RITA. You know, you might try whispering it. (*In a low voice.*) Asta, go with him.

ASTA. But, Rita—

BORGHEJM (*beseeching her*). Miss Asta—remember, it'll be our last walk—for a long, long·time.

ASTA (*taking her hat and parasol*). All right, let's walk a little around the garden then.

BORGHEJM. Ah, thank you—thank you!

ALLMERS. And while you're there, keep an eye on Eyolf.

BORGHEJM. Yes, Eyolf, that's right! Where *is* Eyolf today? I brought something for him.

ALLMERS. He's playing somewhere down there.

BORGHEJM. Oh, really? So he's started to play now? He used to just sit indoors and read.

ALLMERS. That's over and done with. He's going to be a real outdoor boy now.

BORGHEJM. That's the right idea! Out in the open with him, too, poor boy. God Almighty, what is there better in this blessed world to do than play? Seems to me this whole life is a kind of game. Miss Asta—let's go!

(BORGHEJM *and* ASTA *leave by the veranda and down through the garden.*)

ALLMERS (*stands, looking after them*). Well, Rita—you think there's something between those two?

RITA. I don't know what to say. At one time I thought so. But Asta's grown so unfathomable—lately I don't know what to make of her.

ALLMERS. Really, has she? While I've been gone?

RITA. Yes, the last couple of weeks.

ALLMERS. And you think she isn't interested in him now?

RITA. Not seriously. Not in any committed way. I don't think so. (*Looks probingly at him.*) Would you feel put out if she was?

ALLMERS. Hardly put out. But it certainly would make me uneasy—

RITA. Uneasy?

ALLMERS. Well, you have to remember I'm responsible for Asta. For her life's happiness.

RITA. Responsible—come on! Asta's grown up now. She's capable of choosing for herself, I should think.

ALLMERS. Yes, let's hope so, Rita.

RITA. For my part, I know absolutely nothing against Borghejm.

ALLMERS. No, dear—I don't, either. The reverse, if anything. But still—

RITA (*continuing*). And I'd be so happy to see the two of them get together.

ALLMERS (*displeased*). Oh? Why, particularly?

RITA (*with mounting emotion*). Because then she'd have to go off with him, far away! And she wouldn't be coming out here to us anymore, ever!

ALLMERS (*staring amazed at her*). What! You want to be rid of Asta!

RITA. Yes, Alfred, yes!

ALLMERS. But, why on earth—?

RITA (*flinging her arms passionately around his neck*). Yes, because at last then I'd have you for myself alone! Except—not even *then!* Not all to myself! (*Bursts into racking sobs.*) Oh, Alfred, Alfred—I *can't* let you go.

ALLMERS (*gently disengaging himself*). But, Rita darling —be reasonable!

RITA. No, I don't care at all to be reasonable! I only care about you! Only you in this whole world! (*Throwing her arms again around his neck.*) You—you—only you!

ALLMERS. Let go, let go—you're choking me—!

RITA (*releasing him*). Oh, I'd love that! (*Regards him with flashing eyes.*) Oh, if you knew how I've hated you—!

ALLMERS. Hated me—!

RITA. Yes—when you sat in there by yourself and pored over your work—till late, late into the night. (*Fretfully.*) So late—and long, Alfred. Oh, how I hated your work!

ALLMERS. But now that's all over.

RITA (*laughs bitterly*). That's right! And now you're involved in something worse.

ALLMERS (*appalled*). Worse! You don't mean our child?

RITA (*vehemently*). Yes, I do. I say he's the worse for us. Because the child's more than a book; he's a live human being. (*In a rising fury.*) But I won't take it, Alfred! I won't take it—I'm telling you!

ALLMERS (*staring fixedly at her, in a low voice*). At times I'm almost afraid of you, Rita.

RITA (*darkly*). I'm often afraid of myself. And that's why you mustn't stir up the evil in me.

ALLMERS. In God's name—do I do that?

RITA. Yes, you do—when you mutilate the holiest thing between us.

ALLMERS (*heatedly*). Rita, you're forgetting. It's your own child—our only child we're talking about.

RITA. The child's only half mine. (*In another outcry.*) But I want *you* for myself! Mine, all mine! It's my right to have that from you!

ALLMERS (*shrugs his shoulders*). Ah, Rita dear, it's no good demanding things. Everything's got to come freely.

RITA (*looking tensely at him*). And from now on you can't do that?

ALLMERS. No, I can't. I have to share myself between you and Eyolf.

RITA. But if Eyolf had never been born? Then what?

ALLMERS (*evasively*). Well, that's different. Then I'd only have you to think of.

RITA (*her voice low and tremulous*). Then I could wish I'd never borne him.

ALLMERS (*flaring up*). Rita! You don't know what you're saying!

RITA (*shaking with emotion*). The unspeakable pain it cost me to bring him into this world. But I suffered it joyfully, for your sake.

ALLMERS (*warmly*). Yes, yes, I know that.

RITA (*unequivocally*). But that part of it has to end. I have a life to live. Together with you. Completely with you! I can't go on here, just being Eyolf's mother. Just that, and nothing more, I tell you, I won't! I *can't!* I want to be everything to you, Alfred! Everything!

ALLMERS. But you *are* that, Rita. Through our child—

RITA. Oh—sentimental gush! That's all it is. No, don't try to hand me that. I was made to *become* a mother—but not to *be* one, that's all. You have to take me the way I am, Alfred.

ALLMERS. And you were so fond of Eyolf before.

RITA. I felt so sorry for him. Because you let him shift for himself—as long as he read his eyes out. You hardly gave him a second glance.

ALLMERS (*nods slowly*). No, I was blind. It wasn't time for me yet—

RITA (*looking at him*). But now it is—?

ALLMERS. Yes, now, at last. Now I see that the highest mission I have in this world is to be a true father to Eyolf.

RITA. And to *me?* What will you be to *me?*

ALLMERS (*gently*). I'll go on loving you. From the depths of my soul. (*He tries to take her hand.*)

RITA (*evading him*). I don't care about the depths of your soul. I want you—every part of you—alone—the way I had you in those first, sweet, ravenous weeks. (*Fiercely.*) I'm not making do with leftovers, Alfred! Never!

ALLMERS (*mildly*). I think surely there must be enough happiness for all three of us here, Rita.

RITA (*with scorn*). Then you don't ask for much. (*Sitting by the table on the left.*) Listen—

ALLMERS (*approaching*). Well? What is it?

RITA (*looks up at him with a faint gleam in her eyes*). When I got your telegram last night—

ALLMERS. Yes?

RITA. I dressed myself in white—

ALLMERS. Yes, I saw you were wearing white when I came in.

RITA. I'd let down my hair—

ALLMERS. Your thick, fragrant hair—

RITA. So it streamed down my neck and my back—

ALLMERS. I saw that. I saw it. Oh, you were beautiful, Rita!

RITA. There were rose-red shades on both the lamps. And we were alone, just you and I. The only ones awake in the entire house. And there was champagne on the table.

ALLMERS. I didn't have any.

RITA (*with a bitter look*). How true. (*Laughs sharply.*) "The champagne was there, but you touched it not"—as the poem goes. (*She rises from the armchair and walks wearily across to sit, half reclining, on the sofa.*)

ALLMERS (*going over to stand in front of her*). I was so absorbed in serious thoughts. I'd determined we ought to talk about our future, Rita. Above all, about Eyolf.

RITA (*smiles*). Which you did, my dear.

ALLMERS. No, I never managed to. Because you began undressing.

RITA. Yes, and all the time you talked about Eyolf. Remember? You asked how his digestion was.

ALLMERS (*looks reproachfully at her*). Rita—!

RITA. And then you lay down in bed. And slept like a baby.

ALLMERS (*shaking his head*). Rita—Rita!

RITA (*lying back full length and gazing up at him*). Well, Alfred—?

ALLMERS. Yes?

RITA. "The champagne was there, but you touched it not."

ALLMERS (*his voice hardening*). No, I didn't touch it.

(*He moves away from her to stand in the doorway to the garden.* RITA *lies motionless for a time, her eyes closed.*)

RITA (*springs abruptly to her feet*). But let me tell you something, Alfred.

ALLMERS (*turning*). Yes?

RITA. Don't grow too sure of yourself!

ALLMERS. Sure?

RITA. Don't get too complacent! Don't presume that you *have* me!

ALLMERS (*approaching her*). And what does *that* mean?

RITA (*lips trembling*). I've never once considered being unfaithful to you, Alfred! Not for a moment!

ALLMERS. I know that, Rita. I know you so well.

RITA (*with smoldering eyes*). But if you abandon me—!

ALLMERS. Abandon—! I don't follow you.

RITA. Oh, you don't know what things could be roused in me if—

ALLMERS. If—?

RITA. If I discovered one day you no longer cared for me—loved me the way you once did.

ALLMERS. But, my dearest Rita—human beings change over the years—and we have to as well—just like everyone else.

RITA. Not me! And I don't want to hear of you changing, either. I couldn't bear that, Alfred. I want to keep you all to myself.

ALLMERS (*looks at her uneasily*). You have such a jealous temperament—

RITA. I can't make myself over. (*Ominously.*) If you divide yourself between me and anyone else—

ALLMERS. Then what—?

RITA. I'll have my revenge on you, Alfred!

ALLMERS. With what?

RITA. I don't know. Oh yes, I know!

ALLMERS. Well?

RITA. I'll throw my life away—

ALLMERS. Throw away your life!

RITA. I'll do it. I'll throw myself in the arms of—of the first man who comes along.

ALLMERS (*looks warmly at her, shaking his head*). You wouldn't ever, Rita—you with your pride and honor and devotion.

RITA (*drapes her arms round his neck*). Oh, you have no idea how far I could go if you—if you tried to be rid of me.

ALLMERS. Be rid of you, Rita? How can you say things like that!

RITA (*half laughing, releases him*). I could set a trap for him, you know—that road-builder in the garden.

ALLMERS (*relieved*). Ah, thank God—you're joking.

RITA. Not at all. Why shouldn't it be him, as well as anyone?

ALLMERS. Well, because he's already involved.

RITA. All the better! Then I'll have taken him from someone else. That's the very thing Eyolf's done to me.

ALLMERS. You can't mean our little Eyolf's done *that?*

RITA (*pointing her finger at him*). See there! See! The moment you mention Eyolf's name, you get weak and your voice trembles. (*Threateningly, clenching her fists.*) Oh, I'm almost tempted to wish—ah!

ALLMERS (*regarding her anxiously*). Wish what, Rita—?

RITA (*fervently, moving away*). No, no, no—I won't tell you! Never!

ALLMERS (*following her*). Rita! I beg you—for your sake and mine, don't be tempted into anything evil.

(BORGHEJM *and* ASTA *come up from the garden. Both have a close rein on their emotions and look somber and dispirited.* ASTA *remains outside on the veranda.* BORGHEJM *comes into the room.*)

BORGHEJM. Well—Miss Allmers and I have had our last walk together.

RITA (*looks at him, surprised*). Oh? There won't be a longer trip afterward?

BORGHEJM. Yes, for me.

RITA. For you alone?

BORGHEJM. Yes, for me alone.

RITA (*with a quick, dark look at* ALLMERS). Hear that, Alfred. (*Turning to* BORGHEJM.) I'll bet it's the evil eye that's played tricks on you here.

BORGHEJM (*studying her*). The evil eye?

RITA (*nods*). Yes.

BORGHEJM. You believe in the evil eye, Mrs. Allmers?

RITA. Yes, I've begun to believe in the evil eye recently. Mainly in the evil eye of a child.

ALLMERS (*shocked, in a whisper*). Rita—how can you—!

RITA (*huskily*). If I'm vile and evil, Alfred, it's *your* doing.

(*Confused shouts and cries are heard from far off, down by the water.*)

BORGHEJM (*going to the doorway*). What's the excitement—?

RITA. Look, all those people running out on the pier.

ALLMERS. What *is* this? (*Glances out.*) It must be that gang of boys up to something again.

BORGHEJM (*calling down from the railing*). Hey, you boys down there! What's going on?

(*Several answering voices can be heard, mingled and indistinct.*)

RITA. What do they say?

BORGHEJM. They say, there's a child that's drowned.

ALLMERS. A child drowned.

ASTA (*uneasily*). A little boy, they say.

ALLMERS. Oh, they all know how to swim.

RITA (*cries out in fright*). Where's Eyolf!

ALLMERS. Calm down. Eyolf's playing in the garden.

ASTA. No, he isn't. Not in the garden—

RITA (*throwing her arms up*). Oh, if it just isn't *him!*

BORGHEJM (*listens and then calls down*). You say it's whose child?

(*A babble of indistinct voices.* BORGHEJM *and* ASTA *let out stifled cries and rush down through the garden.*)

RITA (*in a paroxysm of dread*). Shh, be quiet! Let me hear what they're saying! (*She reels back into the room with a rending shriek of pain.*)

ALLMERS (*following her*). What did they say?

RITA (*sinking down by the armchair on the left*). They said, "The crutch is floating!"

ALLMERS (*as if frozen*). No! No! No!

RITA (*hoarsely*). Eyolf! Eyolf! Oh, but they *have* to save him!

ALLMERS (*in near delirium*). They *must!* Such a dear life! So dear! So dear! (*He dashes down through the garden.*)

⤙ ACT TWO ⤚

A little wooded glen on ALLMERS' *land, down by the shore. Huge old trees on the left form a leafy canopy over the scene. Across the hillside in the background a brook spills down to lose itself among stones on the edge of the wood. To the right there are only scattered trees, through which the fjord can be glimpsed. In the foreground the corner of a boathouse can be seen, with a beached boat next to it. Under the old trees to the left stands a table with a bench and a couple of chairs, all built out of light birchwood. It is an overcast, dark day, with rolling clouds of mist.*

ALFRED ALLMERS, *dressed as before, is seated on the bench, his arms resting on the table. His hat lies in front of him. He gazes impassively and vacuously out over the water.*

After some moments ASTA ALLMERS *comes down the path through the woods. She is carrying a raised umbrella.*

ASTA (*going quietly and warily up to him*). You shouldn't be sitting down here in this wet weather, Alfred.

(ALLMERS *nods slowly without answering.* ASTA *shuts her umbrella.*)

ASTA. I've been looking for you for hours.

ALLMERS (*tonelessly*). Thank you.

ASTA (*moving a chair to sit beside him*). Have you been sitting here long? All this while?

ALLMERS (*does not answer, then finally speaks*). No, I can't fathom it. It seems totally impossible—this thing.

ASTA (*lays her hand on his arm in sympathy*). Poor Alfred.

ALLMERS (*stares at her*). Then is this really true, Asta? Or have I gone mad? Or am I just dreaming? Oh, if only it was a dream! Think, how marvelous, if I woke now!

ASTA. And if only I could wake you.

ALLMERS (*gazing out over the water*). How cruel it looks today, the fjord—lying so heavy and full of sleep—blue-gray—with flakes of gold—reflecting the rainclouds.

ASTA (*imploringly*). Oh, Alfred, don't sit staring out at the fjord!

ALLMERS (*not hearing her*). On the surface, yes. But in the depths—*there*—the undertow pulls—

ASTA (*fearfully*). Oh, for God's sake—don't think about that!

ALLMERS (*gazes gently at her*). You probably believe that he's lying right out there? But he's not, Asta. You mustn't believe that. For you have to remember how fast the current runs here. Straight out to sea.

ASTA (*slumps across the table, sobbing, face buried in her hands*). Oh God—oh God!

ALLMERS (*heavily*). So little Eyolf's gone so far—far away from us all now.

ASTA (*looks up at him beseechingly*). Oh, Alfred, don't talk like that!

ALLMERS. Why, you can figure it out for yourself, you're so clever— In twenty-eight, twenty-nine hours— Let me see—let me see—

ASTA (*stops her ears and shrieks*). Alfred—!

ALLMERS (*grinding his fists against the table*). Well, can you find a meaning in any of this?

ASTA (*looking at him*). In what?

ALLMERS. In this blow that's been dealt Rita and me.

ASTA. Meaning?

ALLMERS (*impatiently*). Yes, I said meaning. Because there has to be some meaning in it. Life, existence—fate can't be so utterly meaningless as all that.

ASTA. Oh, Alfred, who can speak with certainty on these things?

ALLMERS (*with a bitter laugh*). No, no; I think you're right about that. Perhaps it's all pure chance—and things just happen, like a ship drifting without a rudder. It's entirely possible. At least, that's the way it seems.

ASTA (*lost in thought*). But suppose it only seems—?

ALLMERS (*hotly*). Oh? Maybe *you* can figure it out for me? Because I can't. (*More temperately.*) There's Eyolf, just on the threshold of a spiritually aware existence. A being with such infinite possibilities. So richly endowed. The pride and joy of my life-to-be. And then all it needs is for a crazy old woman to come along—and display a dog in a bag—

ASTA. But we have no idea what really happened—

ALLMERS. Yes, we know. The boys saw her row out over the fjord. They saw Eyolf standing alone, far out on the pier. Saw him stare after her—and grow dizzy. (*His voice quavering.*) And then he fell forward—and was gone.

ASTA. Yes, yes. But still—

ALLMERS. She pulled him into the depths; you can be sure of that.

ASTA. But, dear—why should she?

ALLMERS. Of course—*that's* the point! Why should she? There's no reprisal behind it. Nothing to atone for, I mean. Eyolf had never done her any harm. He'd never mocked her—or thrown stones at her dog. He'd never even set eyes on her or the dog before yesterday. So, it's no kind of reprisal. It's baseless, that's all. Completely meaningless, Asta. And nonetheless, it serves the order of the world.

ASTA. Have you talked about these things with Rita?

ALLMERS (*shakes his head*). I feel I can talk about them more easily with you. (*Sighing.*) As with everything else.

(ASTA *takes her sewing materials and a small paper parcel out of her pocket.* ALLMERS *sits watching her vacantly.*)

ALLMERS. What have you got there, Asta?

ASTA (*picking up his hat*). A little black crepe.

ALLMERS. Oh, what's the point of that?

ASTA. Rita asked me to. May I?

ALLMERS. Yes. All right.

(*She sews the crepe on the hat.*)

ALLMERS (*gazing at her*). Where's Rita now?

ASTA. She's walking a bit in the garden. Borghejm's with her.

ALLMERS (*slightly taken aback*). Really? Is he out here again today?

ASTA. Yes. He arrived on the train at noon.

ALLMERS. I hardly expected that.

ASTA (*sewing*). He was so fond of Eyolf.

ALLMERS. Borghejm's the soul of devotion, Asta.

ASTA (*with quiet warmth*). Yes, he *is* devoted. No doubt about it.

ALLMERS (*his eyes fixed on her*). You do care for him, don't you?

ASTA. Yes, I do.

ALLMERS. But still you can't make up your mind to—?

ASTA (*breaking in*). Oh, Alfred dear, let's not talk about *that!*

ALLMERS. Well, but just tell me why you can't—?

ASTA. Stop it! I ask you, please! Don't cross-examine me. It's all so painful. There. The hat's done.

ALLMERS. Thank you.

ASTA. Now the left arm.

ALLMERS. That, too?

ASTA. Yes, it's customary.

ALLMERS. Well—then go ahead.

(*She moves closer and begins to sew.*)

ASTA. Hold your arm still. I don't want to prick you.

ALLMERS (*half smiling*). It's like old times.

ASTA. Yes, isn't it?

ALLMERS. When you were a little girl, you'd sit like this and mend my clothes.

ASTA. I tried to, anyway.

ALLMERS. The very first thing you sewed for me—was black crepe, too.

ASTA. Oh?

ALLMERS. Around my student cap. When Father died.

ASTA. I sewed *then*? Funny, I don't remember that.

ALLMERS. Oh my, you were so small at the time.

ASTA. Yes—I was.

ALLMERS. And then two years later—when we lost your mother, you sewed a wide black band for *my* arm, too.

ASTA. It only seemed proper.

ALLMERS (*patting her hand*). Yes, yes, quite so, Asta. And then when we were left alone in the world, we both— Are you all through?

ASTA. Yes. (*Gathering up her sewing things.*) That was really a beautiful time for us, Alfred. The two of us alone.

ALLMERS. Yes, wasn't it? For all the hard work.

ASTA. That *you* did.

ALLMERS (*more animated*). Oh, you did as much, in your way. (*Smiles.*) My dear, faithful—Eyolf.

ASTA. Oh! Don't remind me about that silly business with the name.

ALLMERS. Well, if you'd been a boy, you would have been called Eyolf.

ASTA. Yes, *if*. But then when you went to college— (*Smiles involuntarily.*) Imagine, that you could be so childish.

ALLMERS. You think *I* was childish!

ASTA. Yes, it seems so to me, really, looking back on it. You were embarrassed you didn't have a brother. Only a sister.

ALLMERS. No, it was you. *You* were embarrassed.

ASTA. Oh yes, I was, a little bit maybe. And I guess I felt sorry for you—

ALLMERS. Yes, you must have. So you hunted up those old clothes I had as a boy—

ASTA. Those nice Sunday clothes, yes. You remember the blue blouse and the knee pants.

ALLMERS (*his eyes lingering on her*). I remember so well the way you dressed up and walked around in them.

ASTA. That was only when we were at home alone.

ALLMERS. And how serious and self-important we were. And I always called you Eyolf.

ASTA. Alfred, you've never told any of this to Rita, have you?

ALLMERS. Oh, I think I did tell her once.

ASTA. No, Alfred, how could you!

ALLMERS. Well, you know—a man tells his wife everything—nearly.

ASTA. Yes, I suppose so.

ALLMERS (*as if waking with a start, strikes his forehead and jumps up*). Oh! That I can sit here and—

ASTA (*rises, looking anxiously at him*). What's wrong?

ALLMERS. He'd almost left me. Left me completely.

ASTA. Eyolf!

ALLMERS. I've been sitting here, living in memories. And he wasn't there.

ASTA. Oh, but Alfred—little Eyolf was behind everything.

ALLMERS. No, he wasn't. He'd slipped out of my mind. Out of my thoughts. I lost sight of him a moment while we sat talking together. Totally forgot him that whole time.

ASTA. Oh, but you can't be grieving every moment. You need some rest.

ALLMERS. No, no, no—that's just what I don't need. I don't deserve it. Have no right to it. Or heart for it, either. (*Walking agitatedly toward the right.*) I only want my thoughts out there, where he lies drifting down in the depths.

ASTA (*pursues him and holds him fast*). Alfred—Alfred! Don't go to the fjord!

ALLMERS. I've got to go out to him! Let go of me, Asta! I'm taking the boat.

ASTA (*screams*). You hear me, not the fjord!

ALLMERS (*yielding*). No, no—I won't. Just leave me alone.

ASTA (*leading him back to the table*). You *have* to give your thoughts some rest, Alfred. Come here and sit down.

ALLMERS (*starting to sit on the bench*). Very well—whatever you say.

ASTA. No, don't sit there.

ALLMERS. Yes, let me.

ASTA. No, don't! Because you'll only keep staring at the— (*Forces him down in a chair facing left.*) That's it. Now you're set. (*Seats herself on the bench.*) So, let's go on talking a bit.

ALLMERS (*with an audible sigh*). It was good to forget the pain and sorrow for a moment.

ASTA. You *have* to, Alfred.

ALLMERS. But don't you think I'm terribly callous and weak—to be able to?

ASTA. Oh, no. Because it's simply impossible to go on circling back over the same ground.

ALLMERS. Well, for me, it's impossible. Before you came down, I was sitting here, and I can't begin to tell you how I was agonizing over this rending, gnawing grief—

ASTA. Yes?

ALLMERS. And then, would you believe it, Asta—? Hm—

ASTA. Well?

ALLMERS. In the midst of my agony I caught myself wondering what we were going to have for dinner today.

ASTA (*soothingly*). Yes, if only you found some rest in that—

ALLMERS. Well, you know—it did seem to rest me somehow. (*Extends his hand across the table to her.*) How fortunate it is that I have you, Asta. I'm so happy for that. Happy—even in grief.

ASTA (*looking seriously at him*). You should be happy above all that you have Rita.

ALLMERS. Well, of course. But Rita and I aren't family. It's not like having a sister.

ASTA (*tensely*). You mean that, Alfred?

ALLMERS. Yes, *our* family is quite unique. (*Half jokingly.*) For one thing, we've always had names that begin with vowels. You remember how often we talked about that? And all our relatives—they're all equally poor. And all of us have the same sort of eyes.

ASTA. You think mine are—?

ALLMERS. No, you take after your mother, completely. You're not like the rest of us at all. Not even like Father. But still—

ASTA. Still—?

ALLMERS. Yes, I think that living together has shaped us both in each other's image. Inwardly, I mean.

ASTA (*strongly moved*). Oh, don't say that, Alfred, ever. I'm the one who's been shaped by you. And it's to you that I owe everything—everything that's fine in this life.

ALMERS (*shaking his head*). You owe me nothing, Asta. Quite the reverse—

ASTA. I owe everything to you! You must realize that. No sacrifice has been too great for you—

ALLMERS (*interrupting*). Oh, really—sacrifice! That's a bit much—I've no more than loved you, Asta. Ever since you were a little child. (*After a short pause.*) And then, too, I always felt I had so many wrongs to set right.

ASTA (*surprised*). Wrongs! You?

ALLMERS. Not exactly on my part. But—

ASTA (*tensely*). But—?

ALLMERS. On Father's.

ASTA (*half rising from the bench*). Father's! (*Sitting again.*) What do you mean by that?

ALLMERS. Father wasn't always very good to you.

ASTA (*impulsively*). Oh, don't say that!

ALLMERS. Yes, because it's true. He didn't love you. Not the way he should have.

ASTA (*evasively*). No, maybe not the way he loved *you.* That's understandable.

ALLMERS. And he was often hard on your mother. In those last years, anyway.

ASTA (*softly*). Mother was so very much younger than he, you have to remember that.

ALLMERS. You think they really didn't get along together?

ASTA. Perhaps not.

ALLMERS. Yes, but still— Father otherwise was so gentle and kindhearted—so considerate toward everyone—

ASTA (*quietly*). And then Mother wasn't always what she ought to be.

ALLMERS. Your mother wasn't!

ASTA. Perhaps not always.

ALLMERS. To Father, you mean?

ASTA. Yes.

ALLMERS. I never noticed anything like that.

ASTA (*rises, struggling against tears*). Oh, Alfred dear— those who are gone—let them rest. (*She crosses toward the right.*)

ALLMERS (*standing*). Yes, let them rest. (*Wringing his hands.*) But those who're gone—won't let *us* rest. Day or night.

ASTA (*looks at him sympathetically*). But time will heal everything, Alfred.

ALLMERS (*gazing helplessly at her*). Yes, you believe that too, don't you? But how I'll ever get through these terrible first days— (*Hoarsely.*) —I have no idea.

ASTA (*imploringly, placing her hands on his shoulders*). Go up to Rita. Oh, please, do it—

ALLMERS (*wrenches away from her*). No, no, no—don't say *that!* Because, don't you realize, I can't! (*More calmly.*) Just let me stay here with you.

ASTA. Yes, I won't leave you.

ALLMERS (*seizes her hand and holds it tight*). Thank you. (*Looking out over the fjord a moment.*) Where's my little Eyolf gone now? (*Smiles sadly at her.*) Can you tell me that—my big, wise Eyolf? (*Shakes his head.*) No one on earth can tell me that. I only know the one horrible truth, that I no longer have him.

ASTA (*glances up left and withdraws her hand*). They're coming.

(MRS. ALLMERS *and* BORGHEJM *appear, as she leads the way and he follows down the path through the woods. She wears a dark dress, with a black veil over her head. He carries an umbrella under one arm.*)

ALLMERS (*going to meet her*). How are you, Rita?

RITA (*walking past him*). Oh, don't ask.

ALMERS. Why have you come here?

RITA. Just looking for you. What have you been doing?

ALLMERS. Nothing special. Asta came down to talk.

RITA. Yes, but before she came. You've been away from me all morning.

ALLMERS. I've been sitting here, looking out over the water.

RITA. Ugh—how can you!

ALLMERS (*impatiently*). I'd rather be alone right now!

RITA (*pacing restlessly about*). And then to sit there, glued to the same spot!

ALLMERS. I have no earthly reason to move.

RITA. *I* can't settle down any place. Least of all here—with the fjord pressing in.

ALLMERS. That's exactly it—the fjord's so close.

RITA (*to* BORGHEJM). Don't you think he should go up with the rest of us?

BORGHEJM (*to* ALLMERS). It would be better for you, I think.

ALLMERS. No, no—let me be where I am.

RITA. Then I'll stay with you, Alfred.

ALLMERS. All right, then. You stay too, Asta.

ASTA (*whispers to* BORGHEJM). Let them be by themselves.

BORGHEJM (*with an understanding look*). Miss Allmers—shall we walk out a ways—along the shore? For the very last time?

ASTA (*taking her umbrella*). Yes, let's. Just a little walk.

(ASTA *and* BORGHEJM *go off together behind the boathouse.* ALLMERS *meanders about for a moment, then sits on a rock under the trees in the left foreground.* RITA *approaches and stands facing him, her hands clasped, hanging down in front of her.*)

RITA. Can you realize it, Alfred—that we've lost Eyolf?

ALLMERS (*looking down sorrowfully at the ground*). We'll have to learn to realize it.

RITA. I can't. And I'll have that horrible sight with me the rest of my life.

ALLMERS (*glancing up*). What sight? What have you seen?

RITA. I didn't see it myself. Just heard them telling it. Oh—!

ALLMERS. Come on, out with it.

RITA. I took Borghejm along with me down to the pier—

ALLMERS. Why down there?

RITA. To question the boys about exactly what happened.

ALLMERS. We know all that.

RITA. We learned some more.

ALLMERS. Well?

RITA. It isn't true that he disappeared instantly.

ALLMERS. They're saying that now?

RITA. Yes. They say they could see him lying on the bottom. Deep down in the clear water.

ALLMERS (*through clenched teeth*). And they didn't save him!

RITA. I guess they couldn't.

ALLMERS. They could swim—all of them. Did they say how he was lying when they saw him?

RITA. Yes. They said he lay on his back. With his eyes wide open.

ALLMERS. Eyes open. But quite still?

RITA. Yes, quite still. And then something came and pulled him away. It was an undertow, they said.

ALLMERS (*nodding slowly*). Then *that* was the last they saw of him.

RITA (*choked with tears*). Yes.

ALLMERS (*in a low voice*). And no one ever—ever will see him again.

RITA (*wailing*). Day and night I'll see him the way he was lying down there.

ALLMERS. With those big open eyes.

RITA (*shudders*). Yes, with those big open eyes. I see them! I can see them there!

ALLMERS (*rises slowly and looks quietly but ominously at her*). And were they evil, those eyes, Rita?

RITA (*turning pale*). Evil—!

ALLMERS (*moving in close to her*). Were they evil eyes, staring up? Up from the depths?

RITA (*shrinking back*). Alfred—!

ALLMERS (*moves after her*). Answer me that! Were they a child's evil eyes?

RITA (*screams*). Alfred! Alfred!

ALLMERS. Now it's come true—what you wished for,

RITA. *I!* What did *I* wish?

ALLMERS. That Eyolf wasn't here.

RITA. I've never on my life wished that! For Eyolf not to come between us—that's all I wanted.

ALLMERS. Well—from now on, he won't anymore.

RITA (*softly, staring straight ahead*). Maybe now, most of all. (*With a start.*) Oh, that awful sight!

ALLMERS (*nodding*). The child's evil eyes, yes.

RITA (*in anguish, recoiling*). Let me be, Alfred! I'm afraid of you! I've never seen you like this before.

ALLMERS (*with a hard, cold look*). Grief makes us vile and ugly.

RITA (*fearful, but still defiant*). I feel the same thing.

(ALLMERS *crosses right and looks out over the fjord.* RITA *seats herself at the table. A short pause.*)

ALLMERS (*over his shoulder toward her*). You never cared for him wholeheartedly. Never!

RITA (*with cool self-command*). Eyolf would never give himself wholeheartedly to me.

ALLMERS. Because you didn't want it.

RITA. Oh, yes, I wanted it very much. But someone stood in the way. Right from the start.

ALLMERS (*turning*). You mean I did?

RITA. Oh no. Not at the start.

ALLMERS (*going closer*). Who, then?

RITA. His aunt.

ALLMERS. Asta?

RITA. Yes. She managed to block my way.

ALLMERS. You mean that, Rita?

RITA. Yes. Asta—she captured him—right from the time it happened—that horrible fall.

ALLMERS. If she did do that, it was out of love.

RITA (*in a fury*). Exactly! I can't stand sharing anything with someone else! Not in love!

ALLMERS. *We* should have shared him together in love.

RITA (*looks disdainfully at him*). We? Oh, basically you never had any real love for him, either.

ALLMERS (*stunned*). *I* never—!

RITA. No, you didn't. First, you were so caught up in that book of yours—on responsibility.

ALLMERS (*forcefully*). Yes, I was. But I sacrificed the book—for Eyolf's sake.

RITA. Not out of any love for him.

ALLMERS. Then why, in your opinion?

RITA. Because of the self-doubt eating away at you. You'd begun to question whether you really had any great mission to live for in this world.

ALLMERS (*probingly*). That was something you saw in me?

RITA. Oh yes—little by little. And so you hungered for something new to fill the void. I guess *I* wasn't enough any more.

ALLMERS. That's the law of change, Rita.

RITA. And it's why you wanted to make a child prodigy out of poor little Eyolf.

ALLMERS. That isn't it. I wanted to help him become a happy human being. No more than that.

RITA. But not out of love for him. Look into yourself. (*Somewhat shyly.*) And face everything you've buried—and hidden away.

ALLMERS (*evading her eyes*). There's something you're not admitting.

RITA. You too.

ALLMERS (*gazes thoughtfully at her*). If it's what you're thinking, then our child never really belonged to either of us.

RITA. No. Not in the fullness of love.

ALLMERS. And yet we go on grieving so bitterly for him.

RITA (*bitingly*). Yes, isn't it a curious thing? To go on grieving this way over a little boy who was a passing stranger.

ALLMERS (*in a choked cry*). Oh, don't call him a stranger!

RITA (*shaking her head sadly*). We never won him over, Alfred. Not I. Nor you either.

ALLMERS (*his hands working*). And now it's too late! Too late!

RITA. And so totally hopeless—all of it.

ALLMERS (*flaring in sudden rage*). *You're* the guilty one!

RITA (*rises*). I?

ALLMERS. Yes, *you! You're* to blame that he became— what he was! It's *your* fault that he couldn't save himself in the water.

RITA (*with a gesture of aversion*). Alfred—you're *not* going to put this on *me!*

ALLMERS (*growing more and more distraught*). Yes, yes, I do! It was you who left that helpless baby all to himself on the table.

RITA. He was lying so snugly on the pillows. And sleeping so soundly. And you'd promised to watch out for him.

ALLMERS. Yes, I had. (*His voice dropping.*) But then you came—you, you—luring me in to you.

RITA (*regards him defiantly*). Oh, let's say instead, you forgot the child and everything else.

ALLMERS (*with stifled fury*). Yes, that's true. (*Huskily.*) I forgot the child—in your arms.

RITA (*agitated*). Alfred! Alfred—that's hateful of you!

ALLMERS (*quietly, clenching his fists*). In that hour you put the mark of death on little Eyolf.

RITA (*wildly*). You too! You too—in that case!

ALLMERS. Oh yes—you can hold me accountable, too—if you want. We've both sinned. So there *was* retribution in Eyolf's death, all the same.

RITA. Retribution?

ALLMERS (*regaining his composure*). Yes. A judgment on you and me. Now we've got what we deserved. While he was alive, our secret, cowardly remorse made us draw away from him. We couldn't stand to see it—that thing he had to drag about—

RITA (*softly*). The crutch.

ALLMERS. Yes, exactly. And what we're going around now, calling our pain and our grief—is the pang of conscience. Nothing more.

RITA (*stares desolately at him*). I think this can only end in despair—in madness for both of us. Because we can never—never make it right again.

ALLMERS (*in a reverie*). I dreamed of Eyolf last night. I could see him walking up from the pier. He could run just like the other boys. Nothing had happened to him. Not the least harm. The ghastly truth was only a dream—that's what I thought. Oh, how I thanked and blessed— (*Checks himself.*) —Hm—

RITA (*her eyes on him*). Whom?

ALLMERS (*evasively*). Whom—?

RITA. Yes, that you thanked and blessed?

ALLMERS (*deprecatingly*). I said I was only dreaming—

RITA. One you don't believe in yourself?

ALLMERS. Anyhow, it's the way I felt. I was asleep, of course.

RITA (*reproachfully*). You shouldn't have destroyed my faith, Alfred.

ALLMERS. Would it have been right of me to have let you go through life in self-delusion?

RITA. That would have been better for me. I would have had something to hold onto, then. Now, I don't know where I'm at.

ALLMERS (*watching her closely*). And if you could choose now— If you could follow Eyolf down to where he is—?

RITA. Yes? Go on.

ALLMERS. If you had full certainty that you'd find him again—know him—understand him—?

RITA. Yes, yes? Go on.

ALLMERS. Would you then, of your own free will, make the leap across to him? Of your own free will, give up everything here? Renounce life on this earth? Would you, Rita?

RITA (*softly*). You mean, here and now?

ALLMERS. Yes, now, today. This very hour. Answer me. Would you?

RITA (*haltingly*). Oh, I don't know, Alfred. No—I think I'd want to stay on here a while with you.

ALLMERS. For my sake?

RITA. Yes, just for your sake.

ALLMERS. But then afterward? Would you—? Tell me!

RITA. Oh, how can I say? No, I *couldn't* leave you. Never! Never!

ALLMERS. But now, suppose I went to Eyolf? And suppose you were completely certain you'd meet both him and me there. Then would you come over to us?

RITA. Of course I would. Oh yes, gladly! So gladly! But—

ALLMERS. Yes?

RITA (*in a low moan*). I couldn't do it—I feel sure of that. No, no, I absolutely couldn't! Not for all the glories of heaven!

ALLMERS. Neither could I.

RITA. No, it's true, isn't it, Alfred? You couldn't, either.

ALLMERS. No. We belong to this life of earth, we, the living.

RITA. Yes, the only happiness we can understand is here.

ALLMERS (*darkly*). Oh, happiness—happiness—

RITA. You mean that happiness—that we'll never find it again. (*Gazes inquiringly at him.*) But what if—? (*Fervently.*) No, no—I don't dare say it! Or think it even.

ALLMERS. Yes, say it. Rita, say it.

RITA (*tentatively*). Couldn't we try to—? Shouldn't it be possible—that we could forget him?

ALLMERS. Forget Eyolf.

RITA. Forget the pain and remorse, I mean.

ALLMERS. That's what you want?

RITA. Yes. If possible. (*In an outburst.*) Because this thing—I can't bear it much longer! Oh, can't we find anything to help us forget!

ALLMERS (*shakes his head*). Like what?

RITA. Couldn't we try going on a long trip?

ALLMERS. Leaving home? But you're never at ease anywhere else but here.

RITA. Well, then can't we have lots of people in? Hold open house. Throw ourselves into something to numb the pain.

ALLMERS. That's no kind of life for me. No—I'd be better off to take up my work again.

RITA (*caustically*). Your work? The wall you keep putting up between us?

ALLMERS (*slowly, looking rigidly at her*). From now on, there'll always be a wall between us.

RITA. Why?

ALLMERS. Who knows if the great, wide eyes of a child aren't on us day and night.

RITA (*hushed, with a shiver*). Alfred—that's a terrible thought!

ALLMERS. Our love's been like a raging fire. But it has to be snuffed out now.

RITA (*moving toward him*). Snuffed out!

ALLMERS (*harshly*). It already had been—in one of us.

RITA (*as if turned to stone*). You dare say that to me!

ALLMERS (*more gently*). It's dead, Rita. But in what I feel for you, and together with you—the guilt and the self-reproach—I can see something like a rebirth—

RITA (*violently*). Oh, rebirth—who cares about that!

ALLMERS. Rita!

RITA. I'm a warm-blooded human being! I don't go around here half asleep—with fish blood in my veins. (*Clenching her fists.*) And then, to be locked up for a lifetime—in miseries and regrets! Locked up with someone who's no longer mine, mine, mine!

ALLMERS. One day it had to end like this, Rita.

RITA. But like *this!* What began in such a storm of passion for us!

ALLMERS. I had no passionate feelings for you at the start.

RITA. What did you feel for me then?

ALLMERS. Terror.

RITA. I can understand that. But then what did I do to change you?

ALLMERS (*in a near whisper*). You were so incredibly beautiful, Rita.

RITA (*her eyes probing him*). And that was all? Confess, Alfred. Was that all?

ALLMERS (*struggling with himself*). No—there *was* something else.

RITA (*impetuously*). I can guess what it was! It was "my gold, and my green forests," as you put it. Wasn't that it, Alfred?

ALLMERS. Yes.

RITA (*gazes with deep reproach at him*). But how—how could you!

ALLMERS. I had Asta to think of.

RITA (*fiercely*). Asta, yes! (*Bitterly.*) So it was Asta, really, who brought us together.

ALLMERS. She knew nothing about it. She doesn't suspect it even now.

RITA (*dismissively*). But it was Asta, nevertheless! (*With a disdainful smile and sidelong glance.*) Or, no—it was little Eyolf. Little Eyolf, right?

ALLMERS. Eyolf—?

RITA. Yes, didn't you use to call her Eyolf? It seems to me you confessed that once—in a private moment. (*Coming closer.*) Do you remember it, Alfred—that wildly beautiful hour.

ALLMERS (*recoiling, as if in dread*). I remember nothing! I won't remember!

RITA (*pursuing him*). It was during that hour—when your other little Eyolf became crippled.

ALLMER (*heavily, bracing himself against the table*). Retribution.

RITA (*ominously*). Yes, retribution.

(ASTA *and* BORGHEJM *reappear by the boathouse. She carries some water lilies in one hand.*)

RITA (*outwardly controlled*). Well, Asta—did you and Mr. Borghejm get everything talked out?

ASTA. Yes, pretty much so. (*She sets down her umbrella and places the flowers on a chair.*)

BORGHEJM. Miss Allmers has been very reserved on our walk.

RITA. No, has she? Well, Alfred and I have talked out enough together to—

ASTA (*looking tensely at them*). What—?

RITA. To last us the rest of our lives, I'd say. (*Changing her tone.*) But come, let's all go up to the house now.

From this time on, we're going to need company around us. Alfred and I can't weather this alone.

ALLMERS. Yes, go on ahead, you two. (*Turns.*) But, Asta, I want to have a word with you first.

RITA (*looks at him*). Oh? All right, then you come with me, Mr. Borghejm.

(RITA *and* BORGHEJM *depart up the path through the* woods.)

ASTA (*anxiously*). Alfred, what's wrong?

ALLMERS (*darkly*). Simply that I can't go on here any longer.

ASTA. Here? With Rita, you mean?

ALLMERS. Yes. Rita and I can't continue living together.

ASTA (*shaking him by the arm*). Alfred—don't say such a terrible thing!

ALLMERS. What I'm saying is true. We're making each other vicious and ugly.

ASTA (*pained*). Oh, I never—never suspected it.

ALLMERS. I had no idea of it, either, before today.

ASTA. And now you want—well, what exactly do you want, Alfred?

ALLMERS. I want to get away completely. As far as possible from all this.

ASTA. And be totally alone in the world?

ALLMERS (*nodding*). Yes. Like in the old days.

ASTA. But you're not made to stand alone.

ALLMERS. Oh, yes. I managed to once.

ASTA. Once, yes. But you had me with you then.

ALLMERS (*trying to take her hand*). Yes. And it's you, Asta, I want to come home to again.

ASTA (*evading him*). To me? No, Alfred, no! That's quite impossible.

ALLMERS (*looking at her sadly*). So Borghejm *is* between us?

ASTA (*insistently*). No, no, he's not! You're wrong about that!

ALLMERS. Good. Then I'll come to you—my dear, dear sister. I *have* to come back—back home to you, to be cleansed and raised up from my life with—

ASTA (*appalled*). Alfred—you're degrading Rita!

ALLMERS. I've already degraded her. But not in this. Oh, Asta, don't you remember—the kind of life we shared, you and I. Wasn't it like one high holy day from first to last?

ASTA. Yes, it was like that. But we can't relive those days.

ALLMERS (*bitterly*). You mean that marriage has spoiled me for good?

ASTA (*calmly*). No, I don't mean that.

ALLMERS. Well, then we'll both live again as we did.

ASTA (*with resolution*). Alfred, we *can't* do that.

ALLMERS. Yes, we can. A love between brother and sister—

ASTA (*impatiently*). Is what?

ALLMERS. Is the only relationship that isn't bound by the law of change.

ASTA (*trembling, her voice faint*). But if that relationship turned out—

ALLMERS. Turned out—?

ASTA. Not to be *our* relationship?

ALLMERS (*staring stunned at her*). Not ours? What do you mean by that?

ASTA. It's best I tell you straight out, Alfred, now.

ALLMERS. Yes, yes, tell me!

ASTA. The letters to Mother—in the portfolio—

ALLMERS. Yes?

ASTA. You have to read them—when I've gone.

ALLMERS. Why?

ASTA (*with difficulty*). Because then you'll see that—

ALLMERS. Go on!

ASTA. That I have no right to bear—your father's name.

ALLMERS (*shaken*). Asta! You don't mean—!

ASTA. Read the letters. Then you'll see. And understand. And maybe forgive Mother—for what she did.

ALLMERS (*clutches his forehead*). I can't comprehend this. It's too much, Asta—then you aren't—

ASTA. You're not my brother, Alfred.

ALLMERS (*quickly, with a tinge of defiance, looking at her*). Well, does that alter anything in our relationship? Essentially, no.

ASTA (*shaking her head*). It alters everything, Alfred. Our relationship isn't brother and sister.

ALLMERS. No, but it's just as sacred. And it always will be.

ASTA. Don't forget—it's bound now to the law of change —as you called it a moment ago.

ALLMERS (*gives her a searching look*). You mean that—?

ASTA (*softly, with warmth*). Don't say another word. My dear, dear Alfred. (*Taking the flowers from the chair.*) You see these water lilies?

ALLMERS (*slowly nodding*). They're the kind that shoot up—from the farthest depths.

ASTA. I picked them from the tarn—there, where it flows out into the fjord. (*Extending them.*) Will you have them, Alfred?

ALLMERS (*accepts them*). Thank you.

ASTA (*her eyes filling with tears*). They're a last greeting to you from—from little Eyolf.

ALLMERS (*looking at her*). From Eyolf out there? Or from you?

ASTA (*in a hushed voice*). From us both. (*Taking her umbrella.*) Come along back up to Rita. (*She goes up the path through the woods.*)

ALLMERS (*takes his hat and whispers sorrowfully*). Asta. Eyolf. Little Eyolf—! (*He follows her up the path.*)

⤙ ACT THREE ⤚

A stretch of high ground, densely covered with shrubs and bushes, in ALLMERS' *garden. In the background a steep cliff guarded by a railing, with a flight of steps descending on the left. An expansive view out over the fjord, which lies far below. A flagstaff with halyards, but without a flag, stands by the railing. In the right foreground is a summer-house screened by creepers and wild vines. A bench outside. It is a late summer evening, with twilight gathering in a clear sky.*

ASTA *is sitting on the bench, her hands in her lap. She wears a light coat and a hat, with her parasol beside her and a small traveling bag on a strap over her shoulder.*

BORGHEJM *comes up into view in the left background. He also has a traveling bag slung from a shoulder strap. Over his arm he carries a rolled-up flag.*

BORGHEJM (*catching sight of* ASTA). Ah, so here's where you're keeping yourself?

ASTA. I'm just enjoying the view for the last time.

BORGHEJM. A good thing I took a look up here, too.

ASTA. Were you trying to find me?

BORGHEJM. Yes. I wanted very much to say goodbye to you—for now. But, I hope, not permanently.

ASTA (*smiles faintly*). You don't give up, do you?

BORGHEJM. A road-builder can't afford to.

ASTA. Did you see anything of Alfred? Or Rita?

BORGHEJM. Yes, I saw them both.

ASTA. Together?

BORGHEJM. No, they were apart.

ASTA. What are you doing with the flag?

BORGHEJM. Mrs. Allmers asked me to come up and raise it.

ASTA. Raise the flag, now?

BORGHEJM. To half mast. She wants it flying day and night, she said.

ASTA (*sighs*). Poor Rita. And poor Alfred.

BORGHEJM (*occupied with the flag*). Do you really have the heart to go off and leave them? I ask, because I see you're dressed for travel.

ASTA (*in a low voice*). I *have* to leave.

BORGHEJM. Well, if you *have* to—

ASTA. And you're going tonight, too?

BORGHEJM. I have to, as well. I'll be taking the train. How about you?

ASTA. No. I'm going in by steamer.

BORGHEJM (*glances at her*). On our separate ways, then.

ASTA. Yes.

(*She sits and watches as he raises the flag halfway up the mast. After he finishes, he crosses to her.*)

BORGHEJM. Asta—you have no idea how I've grieved over little Eyolf.

ASTA (*looking up at him*). Yes, I'm sure you have.

BORGHEJM. It pains me so. Because basically grief isn't something that comes naturally to me.

ASTA (*lifting her eyes to the flag*). But it will pass away in time—altogether. All the sorrows.

BORGHEJM. All? You believe that?

ASTA. Like a summer storm. Wait till you're far, far from here, you'll see—

BORGHEJM. It'll have to be more than that.

ASTA. And then you have that great, new road project, also.

BORGHEJM. But no one to help me on with it.

ASTA. Oh, why, of course you have.

BORGHEJM (*shaking his head*). No one. No one to share the joy with. For it's the joy that matters most.

ASTA. Not the struggle and frustration?

BORGHEJM. Pah—one can always overcome that part of it alone.

ASTA. But the joy—you feel that has to be shared?

BORGHEJM. Yes, for what pleasure is there in being happy otherwise?

ASTA. True. I guess that's right.

BORGHEJM. Well, of course you can go on for a spell just being happy inside yourself. But it doesn't last long. No, joy—it takes two for that.

ASTA. Always just two? Never more? Never a crowd?

BORGHEJM. Well, you see—that becomes another sort of experience, then— Asta—don't you really think you could settle on sharing joy and happiness—as well as struggle and frustration with one—one particular person?

ASTA. I tried that—once.

BORGHEJM. *You?*

ASTA. Yes, all that while when my brother—when Alfred and I were living together.

BORGHEJM. Oh yes, your brother. But that's something quite different. I'd say there's more a kind of peace in that than happiness.

ASTA. Anyway, it was beautiful.

BORGHEJM. See there—even *that* seemed beautiful to you. But suppose now— What if he hadn't been your brother?

ASTA (*impelled to rise, but remains sitting*). Then, obviously, we wouldn't have lived together. Because I was a child then. And he was hardly more.

BORGHEJM (*after a moment*). *Was* it so very beautiful—that time?

ASTA. Yes. You can't imagine.

BORGHEJM. Did you really feel buoyed up and happy to be alive then?

ASTA. Oh, yes, so much. Incredibly so.

BORGHEJM. Tell me a little more about it, Asta.

ASTA. They were such small things, really.

BORGHEJM. Such as—? What?

ASTA. Such as the time when Alfred took his exams—and he ranked so high. Or when he began to work his way up, post by post, in one school or another. Or when he'd be writing on an article. And he'd read it to me. And then later get it published in some journal.

BORGHEJM. Yes, I'm sure that must have been a lovely, placid life. A brother and sister, sharing their joys. (*Shakes his head.*) I can't understand how your brother could let you go, Asta.

ASTA (*stanching her emotions*). Alfred got married.

BORGHEJM. Wasn't that hard on you?

ASTA. Of course, at first. I thought, with this one thing I've lost him for good.

BORGHEJM. But happily, that wasn't so.

ASTA. No.

BORGHEJM. But still—how could he do it? I mean, get married. When he could have kept you all for himself.

ASTA (*gazing into space*). He was bound by the law of change, I guess.

BORGHEJM. The law of change?

ASTA. That's Alfred's term for it.

BORGHEJM. Pah—that must be a stupid law! I don't believe one particle of it.

ASTA (*getting up*). Maybe in time you'll come to believe in it.

BORGHEJM. Not a chance! (*Urgently.*) But now listen, Asta! Be reasonable now—for once. I mean, about this business—

ASTA (*breaking in*). Oh, no, no—don't let's start on that again!

BORGHEJM (*continuing in the same tone*). Yes, Asta—I can't let you go so easily. Now your brother has everything exactly the way he wants it. He can live his life content without you. He doesn't need you at all. And then this— this thing that's changed your whole position out here overnight—

ASTA (*starts*). What do you mean by that?

BORGHEJM. The loss of the child. What else?

ASTA (*recovering her poise*). Little Eyolf's gone, yes.

BORGHEJM. So what more, actually, do you have to do here? You don't have to look after that poor little boy any longer. No duties—no responsibilities here at all—

ASTA. Oh, please, Mr. Borghejm—don't press me so hard!

BORGHEJM. Why, I'd be crazy if I didn't try to the limit. One of these days I'll be leaving town. I may not get to see you before I go. I may not get to see you again for the longest time. And who knows what could happen in between?

ASTA (*smiling gravely*). Are you afraid of the law of change, after all?

BORGHEJM. No, definitely not. (*With a bitter laugh.*) And there's nothing going to change, anyway. Not with you, I mean. For you don't care very much for me, I can tell that.

ASTA. I do, and you know it.

BORGHEJM. Well, but not *enough*, by a long shot. Not the way I'd like it. (*More vehemently.*) My Lord, Asta— you couldn't be more wrong about this! Just beyond to- morrow and the next day, perhaps the joy of a whole lifetime lies waiting for us. And we're passing it up! Aren't we going to regret that someday, Asta?

ASTA (*quietly*). I don't know. But we have to let it lie, that's all.

BORGHEJM (*steadying himself as he looks at her*). Then I have to build my roads alone?

ASTA (*warmly*). Oh, if only I could be with you doing that! Help you in the struggle. Share the satisfaction—

BORGHEJM. Would you—if you could?

ASTA. Yes, I would.

BORGHEJM. But you *can't?*

ASTA (*eyes downcast*). Would you be content with just *half* of me?

BORGHEJM. No. I want you whole and undivided.

ASTA (*looks at him and says softly*). Then I can't.

BORGHEJM. Then goodbye, Miss Allmers.

(*He is on the verge of leaving, when* ALLMERS *comes up into view in the left background.* BORGHEJM *pauses.*)

ALLMERS (*from the top of the steps, points down and speaks quietly*). Is Rita there, in the summerhouse?

BORGHEJM. No. Just Miss Allmers up here.

(ALLMERS *approaches.*)

ASTA (*moving toward him*). Shall I go down and look for her? Maybe get her to come up?

ALLMERS (*blocking her path*). No, no, no—let her be. (*To* BORGHEJM.) Is it you that raised the flag?

BORGHEJM. Yes. Mrs. Allmers asked me to. It's why I came up here.

ALLMERS. And you're leaving tonight.

BORGHEJM. Yes. Tonight I'm leaving for good.

ALLMERS (*with a glance at* ASTA). Well provided with good companionship, I hope.

BORGHEJM (*shakes his head*). I'm traveling alone.

ALLMERS (*surprised*). Alone?

BORGHEJM. Very much alone.

ALLMERS (*preoccupied*). I see.

BORGHEJM. And to live alone, too.

ALLMERS. There's something monstrous about living alone. It chills me to the marrow—

ASTA. Oh, but Alfred, you aren't alone.

ALLMERS. There can be something monstrous in *that* too, Asta.

ASTA (*heartsick*). Don't talk that way! Or think it, even!

ALLMERS (*not hearing her*). But if you're not leaving with—? If there's nothing to hold you—why won't you stay on here with me—and Rita?

ASTA (*edgily*). No, I can't. I simply have to move back into town now.

ALLMERS. But only into town, Asta. You hear me!

ASTA. Yes.

ALLMERS. And promise you'll be out here soon again.

ASTA (*hurriedly*). No, no, that's more than I dare promise for a while, anyway.

ALLMERS. Fine. Have it your way. So we'll meet there in town.

ASTA. But, Alfred, you *must* stay home now with Rita!

ALLMERS (*turns to* BORGHEJM, *without responding*). You know, it might turn out best for you, after all, to be traveling alone.

BORGHEJM (*irritably*). And what brings you to say that!

ALLMERS. Sure, because you can never know whom you might just happen to meet. In transit.

ASTA (*involuntarily*). Alfred!

ALLMERS. The right one to share the journey. Before it's too late. Too late.

ASTA (*softly, trembling*). Alfred! Alfred!

BORGHEJM (*looking from one to the other*). What's going on? I don't understand—

(RITA *comes in view up the steps in the left background.*)

RITA (*fretfully*). Why is it you've all left me?

ASTA (*crossing to meet her*). You said you'd like to be alone—

RITA. Yes, but I'm frightened to be. It's growing so terribly dark. I feel there are great, wide eyes watching me!

ASTA (*with gentle sympathy*). Suppose there were, Rita? Those eyes you shouldn't be frightened of.

RITA. How can you say that! Not frightened!

ALLMERS (*urgently*). Asta, I beg you—by all powers on earth—stay here—with Rita!

RITA. Yes! And with Alfred, too! Please, Asta, do that!

ASTA (*inwardly struggling*). Oh, I can't tell you how much I'd like to—

RITA. Well, then do it! Alfred and I can't go through our sorrow and loss alone.

ALLMERS (*grimly*). Better say, our gnawing pangs of remorse.

RITA. Oh, no matter what you call it—we can't bear it alone. Oh, Asta, I implore you, please—stay here and help us! Take Eyolf's place—

ASTA (*shivers*). Eyolf's—

RITA. Yes, couldn't she, Alfred?

ALLMERS. If she can and will.

RITA. After all, you called her your little Eyolf once. (*Seizing her hand.*) From now on, you'll be *our* Eyolf, Asta, the same as you were before.

ALLMERS (*hiding his feelings*). Stay—and share life with us, Asta. With Rita. With me. Me—your brother.

ASTA (*now resolved, pulling back her hand*). No. I can't. (*Turning.*) When does the boat sail, Borghejm?

BORGHEJM. Any moment now.

ASTA. Then I'll be on board. Will you be there with me?

BORGHEJM (*checking a surge of delight*). Will I? Yes, yes, yes!

ASTA. Then let's go.

RITA (*slowly*). Ah, so that's it. Well, then of course you can't stay with us.

ASTA (*throwing her arms about her*). Thanks for everything, Rita! (*Goes over and grasps* ALLMERS' *hand.*) Alfred —goodbye! A thousand, thousand goodbyes!

ALLMERS (*low, intently*). What is this, Asta? It looks like you're running away.

ASTA (*in stifled anguish*). Yes, Alfred—I am running away.

ALLMERS. Running—from me?

ASTA (*whispers*). From you—and from myself.

ALLMERS (*shaken*). Ah—!

(ASTA *hurries across to and down the steps in the background.* BORGHEJM *waves his hat and follows her.* RITA *leans against the entrance to the summerhouse.* ALLMERS, *in great inward agitation, proceeds to the railing and stands there, gazing down. A pause.*)

ALLMERS (*turns, speaking with willed self-possession*). The steamer's coming now. See, Rita. There.

RITA. I don't dare look.

ALLMERS. Don't dare?

RITA. No. Because it has eyes. One red. And one green. Great glowing eyes.

ALLMERS. Oh, that's only the lights.

RITA. From now on they're eyes. For me. Staring and staring out of the darkness. And into the darkness, too.

ALLMERS. Now it's putting in to tie up.

RITA. Where's it putting in tonight?

ALLMERS (*moving toward her*). As usual, at the pier.

RITA (*straightens up*). How can it tie up *there?*

ALLMERS. It has to.

RITA. But that's where Eyolf—! How can they dock it there, those people?

ALLMERS. Yes, life is merciless, Rita.

RITA. Human beings are heartless. They don't care. Not for the living, nor the dead.

ALLMERS. You're right. Life goes its own way—exactly as if nothing at all had happened.

RITA (*staring straight ahead*). Nothing, in fact, *has* happened. Not to the others. Only to the two of us.

ALLMERS (*the pain reviving*). Yes, Rita—what did it come to, your bearing him in tears and anguish? Because now he's gone again—without a trace.

RITA. Only the crutch was saved.

ALLMERS (*heatedly*). Enough! I don't want to hear that word!

RITA (*ruefully*). Oh, I can't stand the thought that we've lost him forever.

ALLMERS (*coldly, bitterly*). You could dispense with him all too well while he lived. You could go most of the day without seeing him.

RITA. That was because I knew I could see him anytime I wanted.

ALLMERS. Yes, it's how we wasted the short time we had together with little Eyolf.

RITA (*listening, in dread*). Alfred, hear it! Now it's tolling again!

ALLMERS (*peering down below*). That's the steamer. It's about to cast off.

RITA. Oh, it isn't that bell I mean. I've heard it all day, tolling in my ears. There it is again!

ALLMERS (*crosses to her*). You're mistaken, Rita.

RITA. No, I can hear it distinctly. It's like a death knell. Slowly, slowly. And always the same words.

ALLMERS. Words? What words?

RITA (*her head nodding the beat*). "The-crutch is-float-ing. The-crutch is-float-ing." I'm sure you must hear it, too.

ALLMERS (*shakes his head*). I hear nothing. There's nothing to hear.

RITA. Say what you will. I can hear it perfectly.

ALLMERS (*looking out over the railing*). They're on board now, Rita. The ship's heading in toward town.

RITA. How can you not hear it! "The-crutch is-float-ing. The-crutch—"

ALLMERS (*moving toward her*). Don't stand there, straining your ears for something that doesn't exist. I'm saying that Asta and Borghejm are on board now. Already underway. Asta's gone.

RITA (*looking warily at him*). So I guess you'll soon be gone, too, Alfred?

ALLMERS (*brusquely*). What do you mean by *that!*

RITA. That you'll be joining your sister.

ALLMERS. Did Asta say anything?

RITA. No. But you said yourself, it was Asta that—that brought us together.

ALLMERS. Yes, but you, you made me yours—by the life we've come to share.

RITA. Even though, to your mind, I'm not—not so— enthrallingly beautiful anymore.

ALLMERS. Perhaps the law of change can still hold us together.

RITA (*slowly nodding*). There *is* something changing in me now. It's such a painful feeling.

ALLMERS. Painful?

RITA. Yes, like something giving birth.

ALLMERS. That's it. Or a resurrection. A passage into a higher life.

RITA (*gazing blankly straight ahead*). Yes—with the loss of all, all of life's happiness.

ALLMERS. The loss—that's the heart of the victory.

RITA (*explosively*). Oh, fine phrases! Great God, we're still human beings born of earth.

ALLMERS. We've some part of the sea and the stars in us too, Rita.

RITA. Maybe you. Not me.

ALLMERS. Oh, yes. *You*, more than you realize.

RITA (*moving a step toward him*). Listen, Alfred—couldn't you think of taking your work up again?

ALLMERS. The work you hate?

RITA. I'm reconciled to it now. I'm willing to share you with the book.

ALLMERS. Why?

RITA. Simply to keep you here with me. Close by.

ALLMERS. Oh, I'm so little help to you, Rita.

RITA. But maybe I could help you.

ALLMERS. To do my work, you mean?

RITA. No. To live your life.

ALLMERS (*shakes his head*). I don't think I have any life worth living.

RITA. Well, to bear life, then.

ALLMERS (*half to himself, somberly*). I expect we'd both be better off if we separated.

RITA (*scrutinizing him*). Where would you go then? To Asta, perhaps?

ALLMERS. No. Never anymore to Asta.

RITA. Where, then?

ALLMERS. Up into the solitude.

RITA. Into the mountains? Is that it?

ALLMERS. Yes.

RITA. But that's pure fantasy, Alfred. You couldn't live up there.

ALLMERS. All the same, it's where I'm drawn to be now—up there.

RITA. Why? I want to know!

ALLMERS. Sit down, and I'll tell you something curious.

RITA. Something up there, that happened to you?

ALLMERS. Yes.

RITA. That you didn't tell Asta and me?

ALLMERS. Yes.

RITA. Oh, you're so close-mouthed about everything. You shouldn't be.

ALLMERS. If you'll sit down there, I'll tell you.

RITA. Yes, yes—I want to hear!

(*She seats herself on the bench by the summerhouse.*)

ALLMERS. I was all alone up there, in the middle of the high mountains. I came to the shore of an immense, desolate mountain lake. And I had to get across that lake. But I couldn't, because there wasn't a boat or a single human being in sight.

RITA. Yes? So?

ALLMERS. So I struck off on my own into a side valley. That way I thought I'd make it up through the foothills and between the mountains. And then descend and be on the far side of the lake.

RITA. Ah, so then you got lost for sure.

ALLMERS. Yes. I got all turned around. Because there was no road, no path, nothing. I walked the whole day. And the whole night, too. And finally I was convinced that I'd never see a human being again.

RITA. Or us, here at home? Oh, how your thoughts must have dwelled on us.

ALLMERS. No—they didn't.

RITA. No?

ALLMERS. No. It was so strange. Both you and Eyolf had faded far, far away from me. And Asta, too.

RITA. But what were you thinking of then?

ALLMERS. I stopped thinking. I kept dragging myself on along the precipices—relishing the peace and security of the nearness of death.

RITA (*jumping to her feet*). Oh, don't use such words for anything so awful!

ALLMERS. It's the way I felt. Not the slightest fear. It seemed to me that death and I were walking together, like two good traveling companions. Everything seemed so natural—so very simple, at the time. In my family, you see, people rarely live to be old—

RITA. Oh, don't talk like that, Alfred! After all, you came out of it alive.

ALLMERS. Yes, suddenly I was in the clear. On the other side of the lake.

RITA. It must have been a horrifying night for you, Alfred. But now, looking back, you won't admit it to yourself.

ALLMERS. That night I rose to a decision. That's when I turned back and came straight home. To Eyolf.

RITA (*hushed*). Too late.

ALLMERS. Yes. And then when—my companion came and took him—I felt his terror in everything. In all—that we still don't dare to give up. We're so earthbound, both of us, Rita.

RITA (*with a flicker of joy*). Yes, that's so! For you, too! (*Moving toward him.*) Oh, let's just live our lives out together, as long as we can!

ALLMERS (*with a shrug*). Live our lives out, yes. But with nothing to fill them. Waste and emptiness altogether, everywhere I look.

RITA (*anxiously*). Oh, sooner or later you'll leave me, Alfred! I can sense it. And I can see it in you, too. You're going to leave me.

ALLMERS. You mean, with my traveling companion?

RITA. No, I mean something worse. You'll go of your own free will. Because you think it's only here, with me, that you have nothing to live for. Answer me! Isn't that what you're thinking?

ALLMERS (*staring fixedly at her*). And suppose I was—?

(*A raucous clamor of angry, heated voices is heard rising from far below.* ALLMERS *goes to the railing.*)

RITA. What's going on? (*Exclaims.*) Oh, you'll see, they've found him!

ALLMERS. He won't ever be found.

RITA. But what is it, then?

ALLMERS (*returning*). Just a brawl—as usual.

RITA. Down on the shore?

ALLMERS. Yes. All those shore houses ought to be leveled. Now the men are back home—drunk, naturally. Battering their children. Can you hear the boys crying! And the women howling for someone to help them—

RITA. Well, shouldn't we send someone down to help them?

ALLMERS (*in cold fury*). Help those who didn't help Eyolf! No, let them go under—as they let him go under!

RITA. That's no way to talk! Or think, either!

ALLMERS. I can't think in other terms. All those shanties ought to be torn down.

RITA. Then what's to become of all those poor people?

ALLMERS. They can find someplace else.

RITA. And the children?

ALLMERS. Is it of any great matter where they die off?

RITA (*quietly, with reproach*). You're forcing yourself to be callous, Alfred.

ALLMERS (*fiercely*). It's my right to be callous after this. And my duty.

RITA. Your duty?

ALLMERS. To Eyolf. He mustn't lie unavenged. That's the long and short of it, Rita! I'm telling you! Think it over. Have that whole area razed to the ground—when I'm gone.

RITA (*with a probing look*). When you're gone?

ALLMERS. Yes, it'll give you something, at least, to fill out your life. And you've got to have that.

RITA (*reaching a conclusion*). You're quite right. I'll need that. But can you guess what I'll be doing—after you're gone?

ALLMERS. No, what?

RITA (*slowly and decisively*). As soon as you've left me, I'm going down to the shore and bring all those poor, mistreated children back up with me into this house. All those rowdy boys—

ALLMERS. What will you do with them here?

RITA. Learn to love them.

ALLMERS. *You?*

RITA. Yes. From the day you leave, they'll be staying here, all of them—as if they were my own.

ALLMERS (*shocked*). In our little Eyolf's place?

RITA. Yes, in our little Eyolf's place. They'll live in Eyolf's rooms. They'll read his books. Play with his toys. They'll sit in turn on his chair at the table.

ALLMERS. This sounds like utter madness! I don't know a single person in this world less equipped for something like this than you.

RITA. Then I'll have to educate myself for it. Train and develop myself.

ALLMERS. If you're dead serious about this—everything you speak of—then you must have undergone a change.

RITA. It's true, Alfred. You took care of that. You've made an empty place inside me. I'll have to try to fill it with something. Something in the shape of love.

ALLMERS (*thoughtful for a moment, then looks at her*). Actually, we've never done much for those poor people down there.

RITA. We've done nothing for them.

ALLMERS. Hardly even given them a thought.

RITA. A sympathetic thought, anyway.

ALLMERS. We who had "the gold and the green forests."

RITA. We closed our hands to them. And our hearts too.

ALLMERS (*nods*). So it's hardly surprising, perhaps, that they wouldn't risk their lives to save Eyolf.

RITA (*quietly*). If you consider, Alfred—are you so sure that—that we would have risked our own?

ALLMERS (*dismissing the thought uneasily*). You mustn't ever doubt *that*, Rita!

RITA. We *are* so earthbound, you know.

ALLMERS. What do you actually think you can do for all those mistreated children?

RITA. I suppose, if anything, I'll see if I can lighten—and refine their lives.

ALLMERS. If you can do that, then Eyolf wasn't born in vain.

RITA. Or taken from us in vain, either.

ALLMERS (*regarding her fixedly*). One thing you better be clear about, Rita—it isn't love that's behind this.

RITA. No, it isn't. At least, not yet.

ALLMERS. Then, really, what is it?

RITA (*somewhat diffidently*). You know, you've talked so often with Asta about human responsibility—

ALLMERS. About the book you hated.

RITA. I still hate it. But I sat and listened while you talked. And now I want to try myself to carry it on—in my own way.

ALLMERS (*shakes his head*). It's not for the sake of that unfinished book—

RITA. No, I have a second reason.

ALLMERS. What?

RITA (*softly, with a sad smile*). I want to win my pardon from those great, open eyes.

ALLMERS (*touched, gazing at her*). Maybe I could join you? And help you, Rita?

RITA. Would you?

ALLMERS. Yes—if I only knew how.

RITA (*hesitantly*). But then, of course, you'd have to stay here.

ALLMERS (*in a low voice*). Let's see if it can't work.

RITA (*almost inaudibly*). Let's try, Alfred.

(*Both are silent. Then* ALLMERS *goes over to the flagstaff and runs the flag up to the top.* RITA *stands by the summerhouse, quietly watching him.*)

ALLMERS (*returning*). There's a hard day's work ahead of us, Rita.

RITA. You'll see—every now and then, a Sabbath stillness will come over us.

ALLMERS (*gently, moved*). And then maybe we'll sense the spirits, visiting.

RITA (*whispers*). Spirits?

ALLMERS (*as before*). Yes. Then perhaps they'll be around us—those we've lost.

RITA (*slowly nodding*). Our little Eyolf. And your big Eyolf, too.

ALLMERS (*looking into space*). It may be that we still, now and then—on our way through life—will have glimpses of them.

RITA. Where should we look, Alfred—?

ALLMERS (*his eyes fixed on her*). Upward.

RITA (*nodding in agreement*). Yes, yes—upward.

ALLMERS. Upward—toward the mountain peaks. Toward the stars. And toward that great silence.

RITA (*extending her hand to his*). Thank you!

JOHN GABRIEL BORKMAN

How to understand and account adequately for the prodigious dynamism of the nineteenth century? A playwright of ambition and vision, with a strong sense of history, might well pose that question. How sum up and objectify in the art of drama the gist of an age of such discoveries, innovations, progress, expansion, disruption, dashed hopes, mass miseries, extravagant dreams? Perhaps through a series of representative portraits of those who served as the most characteristic vehicles of the century's advance, its promise and its unfulfillment.

Of necessity the sequence would have to include the man of ideas. Never before had conceptions and concepts been so important, the former because every invention which accelerated the transforming of a natural, organic environment into a mechanized, industrial economy had begun in some individual mind; the latter because that very acceleration demanded new philosophies and ideologies to rationalize the dislocation of the present from the past. Enter Alfred Allmers.

Likewise inevitable, possibly holding priority of dramatic interest, would be the man converting ideas into material forms, in the larger sense the builder of the nineteenth century, specifically exemplified by the residential architect, striving to keep pace with a burgeoning population that, in an unprecedented leap, had more than doubled in Europe within the century. For Halvard Solness, a leading role.

Ideas, their execution—but what of rewards? The rugged individualists and robber barons of the era worked so intensively not for the joy of achievement alone, but also for certain typical satisfactions. Light amusements, of course, like watching naked beauties revolve on turntables at the Folies-Bergère and other variety halls. Since, however, these were men seriously impressed with themselves, only a marble portrait bust would suffice, equating them with the sages of Greece and the emperors of Rome. Arnold Rubek on stage.

Nonetheless, one representative figure, the weightiest and most consequential, is still lacking from the related group of four final plays within the larger cycle; and in *John Gabriel Borkman* (1896) Ibsen examines his character and his world. That was the financier, who, with his gift, approaching genius, for the deployment of venture capital, stood behind the nineteenth-century proliferation of ideas and inventions into whole sectors of new industry; and whose interests in banking and trade were girdling the globe, binding it together in a single system of international payments. Unlike Shaw or Brecht, Ibsen's study of the finance capitalist is unconnected with any program for restructuring society. Instead, more like Shakespeare and Molière, he accepts the organization of society as it is, and lets the lives that result speak for themselves.

The foreign name John, Ibsen told his physician, was meant to imply the man of big business, an association with the British origins of the Industrial Revolution, and the name of the archangel Gabriel to suggest his touch of genius. (Considering Ibsen's interest at the time in things English, evidenced also in Fanny Wilton of enigmatic background, there may also be an overtone of Dante Gabriel Rossetti and a metallic touch of the poet.) Indeed, Borkman is alone among Ibsen's major characters to have a lordly sweep of three names, the first two, "John Gabriel," having been known once throughout the country, even as the king's.

For Borkman *was*, in a double sense, a king. Once, in the world of fact, he savored a power as great as any monarch's; and his personal gauge of reference is Napoleon, that titan of the will to power that haunted the dream life of the nineteenth century from Julien Sorel and Raskolnikov on. (Titled after its hero, Dostoevsky's novel of crime and punishment had lately appeared in Norway and was much admired by Ibsen.) Thus, like an emperor in exile, Borkman waits—to his mind quite reasonably, knowing his own competence—for a deputation to restore him to financial command from his private Elba, that insulation from others that protects his megalomania from utter collapse. The Nietzschean syndrome of the financier as superman proves to be nothing other than the romantic ego grown hard-shelled through its willed isolation, much as Lewis Mumford has described it: "Deprived of society, the ego loses any confining sense of its own proper dimensions: it swings between insignificance and infinity, between self-annihilation and world-conquest; between the hidden sorrows of Werther and the visible triumphs of Napoleon; between the desperation of suicide and the arrogance of godhead."

Borkman is restrained from suicide not merely by the vital lie of an imaginary rescuing delegation, but also by the one real, enduring romance he has known, with his second kingdom underground. The earth is like glass beneath his feet, and the miner's son can see clairvoyantly the cold arms, the winding veins of precious metals reaching longingly out to him, entreating release into the daylight and the service of mankind. The brilliance of Ibsen's portrayal of the psychology of the great financier lies with an empathic insight into his driving motivation, beneath the clichés of greed and profit, status and domination, in the authentic subterranean poetry of its obsessional roots— and, at the same time, a strict reckoning of the devastating price in human wreckage he exacts. By converting Ella, the woman he loves, into capital for career advancement, by contracting a loveless marriage with her sister Gunhild, by repelling his son Erhard into a short-term loan of other, outstretched arms, warm and practiced, belonging to Fanny Wilton, Borkman has, in fact, entered his cold kingdom, which he rules beyond fear of challenge or possibility of escape.

THE CHARACTERS

JOHN GABRIEL BORKMAN, formerly president of a bank
GUNHILD BORKMAN, his wife
ERHART BORKMAN, their son, a student
MISS ELLA RENTHEIM, Mrs. Borkman's twin sister
MRS. FANNY WILTON
VILHELM FOLDAL, part-time clerk in a government office
FRIDA FOLDAL, his daughter
MRS. BORKMAN'S MAID

The action takes place during a winter evening on the Rentheim family estate near the capital city.

⚊⊰ ACT ONE ⊱⚊

MRS. BORKMAN's *living room, furnished in old-fashioned, faded elegance. In the background is an open sliding door, leading into a garden room with windows and a glass door. Through these, a view into the garden, where a snowstorm swirls in the dusk. In the wall to the right, the entry door from the hall. Further forward, a large old iron stove with a fire burning in it. On the left, set back somewhat, a single, smaller door. In front of this on the same side, a window hung with heavy curtains. Between the window and the door, a sofa covered in horsehair, and in front of it, a table with a cloth on it. On the table, a lighted lamp with a shade. Near the stove, a high-backed armchair.*

MRS. GUNHILD BORKMAN *is seated on the sofa, crocheting. She is an elderly woman, cold and distinguished in appearance, with a stiff bearing and impassive features. Her abundant hair has turned iron-gray; her hands are delicate and translucent. She wears a thick, dark silk dress that once was stylish, but now is somewhat frayed and worn, and a woolen shawl over her shoulders.*

For a short while she sits erect and immobile at her crocheting. Then from outside comes the sound of bells on a passing sleigh. She listens, her eyes lighting up with joy.

MRS. BORKMAN (*in an involuntary whisper*). Erhart! At last!

(*She rises and gazes out through the curtains; then, with a look of disappointment, she settles again on the sofa at* her work. *Some moments later the* MAID *enters from the hall with a visiting card on a small tray.*)

MRS. BORKMAN (*quickly*). Was it Mr. Erhart after all?

MAID. No, ma'am. But there's a lady here—

MRS. BORKMAN (*setting her crocheting aside*). Oh, Mrs. Wilton, then—

MAID (*approaching*). No, it's a strange lady—

MRS. BORKMAN (*takes the card*). Let me see— (*Reads it, rises abruptly, and fixes her eyes on the* MAID.) Are you quite certain this is for me?

MAID. Yes, I understood it was meant for you.

MRS. BORKMAN. She asked to speak to Mrs. Borkman?

MAID. That's right, ma'am.

MRS. BORKMAN (*brusquely, with resolution*). Good. Then say that I'm at home.

(*The* MAID *opens the door for the stranger and goes out.* MISS ELLA RENTHEIM *enters the room. She resembles her sister in appearance, but her face has more of suffering than of hardness in its expression. Its former great beauty and character is still clearly evident. Her thick hair, now turned silvery white, is swept back in natural waves from her forehead. She is dressed in black velvet, with a hat and fur-lined coat of the same material. The two sisters stand in silence for a moment as they look probingly at each other. Each is apparently waiting for the other to speak first.*)

ELLA (*hesitating by the door*). You look quite surprised to see me, Gunhild.

MRS. BORKMAN (*standing stiffly upright between the sofa and the table, steadying her fingertips against the cloth*). Aren't you mistaken? The manager of the estate lives in the annex, you know.

ELLA. I'm not here to see the manager today.

MRS. BORKMAN. Did you want me for something?

ELLA. Yes. I need a few words with you.

MRS. BORKMAN (*moving toward her*). Well—then have a seat.

ELLA. Thank you; I can just as well stand for the moment.

MRS. BORKMAN. Whatever you like. But at least open your coat a bit.

ELLA (*unbuttoning her coat*). Yes, it's terribly warm in here.

MRS. BORKMAN. I'm always freezing.

ELLA (*stands for a time looking at her, with her arms resting on the back of the armchair*). Well—Gunhild, it's nearly eight years now since we saw each other last.

MRS. BORKMAN (*coldly*). Or since we've spoken, at any rate.

ELLA. Since we've spoken; yes, that's better. Because you must have seen me at times—when I made my yearly visit to the manager.

MRS. BORKMAN. I think, once or twice.

ELLA. I've also had a glimpse of you a few times. There, in the window.

MRS. BORKMAN. That must have been through the curtains. You have sharp eyes, Ella. (*Hard and caustic.*) But the last time we *spoke* together—that was here in this room—

ELLA (*defensively*). Yes, yes, I know, Gunhild!

MRS. BORKMAN. The week before he—before he was released.

ELLA (*walking away toward the back*). Oh, don't start on *that!*

MRS. BORKMAN (*in a firm but muted voice*). It was the week before he—Borkman was set free again.

ELLA (*coming forward*). Oh, yes, yes, yes! I haven't forgotten that time! But it's simply too heartbreaking to think about—even to dwell on for one instant—oh!

MRS. BORKMAN (*dully*). And yet the mind can never stop brooding on it alone. (*In an outburst, striking her hands together.*) No, I can't understand it! I never will! I can't comprehend how anything like this—anything so appalling could overwhelm one family! And, that it's *our* family! A family so distinguished! Why did it have to strike *us!*

ELLA. Oh, Gunhild—there were many, many besides *our* family struck down by that blow.

MRS. BORKMAN. Yes, but all those others don't concern me especially. It was only a little money, or some papers, that they lost. But for *us*—! For me! And for Erhart— no more than a child then! (*With rising passion.*) What shame for us, the innocent! What dishonor! The ugly, stupefying dishonor! And then, everything in ruins!

ELLA (*cautiously*). Tell me, Gunhild—how is he bearing it?

MRS. BORKMAN. Erhart, you mean?

ELLA. No, he himself. How is he bearing it?

MRS. BORKMAN (*with contempt*). Do you think I'd ask?

ELLA. Ask? You shouldn't have to ask—

MRS. BORKMAN (*stares at her, astonished*). You really believe I consort with him? Or cross his path? Or lay eyes on him?

ELLA. Not even that!

MRS'. BORKMAN. A man for five years in prison! (*Buries her face in her hands.*) Oh, such a vile disgrace! (*In a surge of fury.*) And to think what the name John Gabriel Borkman once used to mean! No, no, no, I never want to see him again! Never!

ELLA (*regarding her briefly*). You have a hard heart, Gunhild.

MRS. BORKMAN. Toward him, yes.

ELLA. He's still your husband.

MRS. BORKMAN. Didn't he tell the court that *I* was the one who began his ruin? That I needed too much money—?

ELLA (*gently*). But wasn't there some truth in that?

MRS. BORKMAN. But that's just the way he wanted it! Everything had to be so impossibly luxurious—

ELLA. I'm aware of that. It's exactly why you should have held back—which you certainly didn't do.

MRS. BORKMAN. How could I know it wasn't his—the money he gave me to squander? And that he squandered, too—ten times beyond what I spent!

ELLA (*quietly*). Well, I guess his position required it—in good part, anyway.

MRS. BORKMAN (*scornfully*). Yes, I always heard that we had to "set the style." So he set the style all right—to a fault! Drove a four-in-hand—as if he were a king. Let people bow and scrape to him, as if to a king. (*With a laugh.*) And they called him by his forename—all through the country—exactly like the king himself. "John Gabriel. John Gabriel." They all knew "John Gabriel" for a great man then.

ELLA. He *was* a great man then.

MRS. BORKMAN. Yes, outwardly. But never one single word to let me know what his real position was. Never an inkling of where he got his funds.

ELLA. No, no—the others never suspected either.

MRS. BORKMAN. Oh, forget about the others. But he was duty-bound to tell *me* the truth. And he never did! He only lied—lied interminably to me—

ELLA (*interrupting*). Certainly not, Gunhild! He may have concealed things. But he surely didn't lie.

MRS. BORKMAN. Yes, call it what you will; it's one and the same— And then it shattered. Everything. All that splendor overthrown.

ELLA (*to herself*). Everything shattered—for him—and for others.

MRS. BORKMAN (*draws herself up grimly*). But I can tell you this, Ella—I'm not giving in! I'll find my way through to restitution. You can take my word for it!

ELLA (*tensely*). Restitution? What do you mean by that?

MRS. BORKMAN. Restitution for my name and honor and fortune! For the whole of my desolated life, that's what I mean! I have somebody to turn to, you know! Someone who'll cleanse everything that—that Borkman tarnished.

ELLA. Gunhild! Gunhild!

MRS. BORKMAN (*with swelling emotion*). There's an avenger living! One who'll make up for all his father's wrongs against me!

ELLA. Erhart.

MRS. BORKMAN. Yes, Erhart—my own good son! He'll find the way to restore the family, the house, our name. Everything that *can* be restored. And maybe something more.

ELLA. And just how do you expect that to happen?

MRS. BORKMAN. It'll come about in its own way. I don't know exactly *how*. But I know that it *will* and it *must* happen someday. (*Looks inquisitively at her.*) But Ella— isn't this the same, essentially, as what you've been thinking ever since he was a child?

ELLA. No, I really can't say it is.

MRS. BORKMAN. It isn't? Then why did you take him in, when the storm broke over—over our house?

ELLA. You couldn't manage things yourself, Gunhild.

MRS. BORKMAN. No—that's right, I couldn't. And his father—he was legally incompetent—there where he sat— so nicely protected—

ELLA (*infuriated*). Oh, how can you talk like that—! *You!*

MRS. BORKMAN (*with a venomous expression*). And how could *you* bring yourself to take in a child of—of John Gabriel! Absolutely as if that child were yours. Take him from *me*—to go home with you—and to keep him, year after year, till the boy was nearly grown. (*Regarding her distrustfully.*) What did you really do it for, Ella? Why did you keep him?

ELLA. I came to love him so much—

MRS. BORKMAN. More than I—his mother!

ELLA (*evasively*). That's beyond me to say. And then, of course, Erhart was rather frail as a child—

MRS. BORKMAN. Erhart—frail!

ELLA. Yes, I thought so—at the time, anyhow. And the air out there on the west coast is so much milder than here, you know.

MRS. BORKMAN (*with a wry smile*). Hm. Is it really? (*Breaking off.*) Yes, you truly have done a great deal for Erhart. (*Her tone alters.*) Well, it's understandable; you could well afford it. (*Smiles.*) You've been so lucky, Ella. You got back everything of yours untouched.

ELLA (*hurt*). I had nothing to do with that, believe me. I hadn't any suspicion—not till long, long after—that the securities made over to me at the bank—that they'd been spared—

MRS. BORKMAN. Oh, well, I can't fathom such things! I'm only saying that you were lucky. (*Looks questioningly at her.*) But when you set about, all on your own, to bring up Erhart for me—what was your motive in that?

ELLA (*looking at her*). My motive—?

MRS. BORKMAN. Yes, you must have had a motive. What did you want to make of him? Make out of him, I mean.

ELLA (*slowly*). I wanted to open a path for Erhart to be happy here on earth.

MRS. BORKMAN (*scornfully*). Pah! People of our standing have better things to do than think about happiness.

ELLA. What else—in your opinion?

MRS. BORKMAN (*regards her solemnly*). Erhart has an obligation, before all else, to achieve a brilliance of such height and scope that not one person in this country will still recall the shadow his father cast over me—and over my son.

ELLA (*incisively*). Tell me, Gunhild—is that the aim Erhart himself has for his own life—?

MRS. BORKMAN (*startled*). Well, let's hope so!

ELLA. Or isn't it rather an aim that you've imposed on him?

MRS. BORKMAN (*brusquely*). Erhart and I always share the same goals.

ELLA (*slowly and sadly*). Are you so very sure of your son, then, Gunhild?

MRS. BORKMAN (*secretly exulting*). Yes, thank God, I am. You can be positive of that!

ELLA. Then, I think, at heart you must feel you've been lucky after all. In spite of everything.

MRS. BORKMAN. Oh, I do—in that respect. But, every other moment, you see, the rest of it comes sweeping over me like a tempest.

ELLA (*her tone changing*). Tell me—and you might as well right away, since it's actually why I've come—

MRS. BORKMAN. What?

ELLA. Something I feel I have to talk to you about— Tell me, Erhart doesn't live out here with—with the family?

MRS. BORKMAN (*sharply*). Erhart *can't* live out here with me. He's got to live in town—

ELLA. He wrote me that.

MRS. BORKMAN. He's got to, because of his studies. But every evening he stops out and visits me for a while.

ELLA. Then perhaps I could see him? And speak to him right now?

MRS. BORKMAN. He hasn't come yet. But I expect him any minute.

ELLA. But, Gunhild—I'm sure he's here. I hear him walking upstairs.

MRS. BORKMAN (*with a quick upward glance*). Up in the salon?

ELLA. Yes. I've heard him walking there ever since I came.

MRS. BORKMAN (*averting her eyes*). That's not Erhart, Ella.

ELLA (*puzzled*). Not Erhart? (*Surmising.*) Who is it then?

MRS. BORKMAN. It's him.

ELLA (*quietly, with stifled grief*). Borkman! John Gabriel!

MRS. BORKMAN. That's how he walks, up and down. Back and forth. From morning to night. Day in and day out.

ELLA. Of course I've heard rumors about—things—

MRS. BORKMAN. No doubt. There must be a lot of rumors about us.

ELLA. Erhart has hinted of it. In his letters. That his father kept mainly to himself—up there. And you, alone down here.

MRS. BORKMAN. Yes. We've lived like that, Ella. Ever since they released him, and sent him home to me. All these eight long years.

ELLA. But I've never thought it could really be true. Or possible—!

MRS. BORKMAN (*nods*). It's true. And it can never be different.

ELLA (*looking at her*). It must be a horrible existence, Gunhild.

MRS. BORKMAN. More than horrible. I can't bear it much longer.

ELLA. I understand.

MRS. BORKMAN. Always hearing his footsteps up there. From early morning till far into the night. And so loud, as if they were here in this room!

ELLA. Yes, it's strange how the sound carries.

MRS. BORKMAN. Often I have the feeling that I have a sick wolf pacing his cage up in the salon. Right over my head. (*Listens, then whispers.*) Hear that, Ella! Listen! Back and forth—back and forth, the wolf pacing.

ELLA (*hesitatingly*). Couldn't things be different, Gunhild?

MRS. BORKMAN (*with a disdainful gesture*). He's never made one move in that direction.

ELLA. Couldn't you make the first move, then?

MRS. BORKMAN (*incensed*). I? After all I've suffered from him! No thanks! Let the wolf go on roaming his cage.

ELLA. It's too warm for me in here. If I may, I'll take my coat off after all.

MRS. BORKMAN. Yes, I asked you before—

(ELLA *removes her hat and coat, laying them on a chair by the hall door.*)

ELLA. Don't you ever run into him outside the house?

MRS. BORKMAN (*with a bitter laugh*). Out in society, you mean?

ELLA. I mean, when he's out for some air. On a path in the woods, or—

MRS. BORKMAN. He never goes out.

ELLA. Not even at dusk.

MRS. BORKMAN. Never.

ELLA (*touched*). He can't even face that?

MRS. BORKMAN. Apparently not. He has his great cape and his hat hanging in the closet. In the hall, you know—

ELLA (*to herself*). The one we played in when we were little—

MRS. BORKMAN (*nodding*). And every so often—late in the evening—I hear him coming down—to put on his things and go out. But then he stops, usually halfway down the stairs—and turns back. Back to the salon.

ELLA (*softly*). Don't any of his old friends ever stop up to see him?

MRS. BORKMAN. He has no old friends.

ELLA. He had so many, once.

MRS. BORKMAN. Hm! He found a very nice way to shed them. He became an expensive friend to have, this John Gabriel.

ELLA. Yes, I guess you're right.

MRS. BORKMAN (*heatedly*). Nevertheless, I must say it's mean, cheap, petty, and contemptible to lay so much weight on any minor losses they may have suffered through him. It was only money, after all.

ELLA (*not answering*). So he lives up there quite alone. In isolation.

MRS. BORKMAN. Yes, that's about it. I hear there's an old clerk or copyist who stops up to see him occasionally.

ELLA. Oh yes. That would be Foldal, most likely. I know they were friends in their early years.

MRS. BORKMAN. Yes, I believe so. I know nothing about him, otherwise. He was never part of our set. When we had one—

ELLA. But *now* he comes out to Borkman?

MRS. BORKMAN. Yes, he's not fastidious. But naturally he only comes after dark.

ELLA. This Foldal—he was among the ones who had losses when the bank failed.

MRS. BORKMAN (*indifferently*). I do seem to remember that he lost some money also. But it was quite insignificant.

ELLA (*stressing her words slightly*). It was everything he had.

MRS. BORKMAN (*smiles*). Well, but, my Lord—what he had: that was next to nothing. Hardly worth mentioning.

ELLA. It never was mentioned, was it, at the trial—by Foldal?

MRS. BORKMAN. Furthermore, I can tell you that Erhart has amply compensated for any pittance he may have lost.

ELLA (*surprised*). Erhart? How has he managed that?

MRS. BORKMAN. He's been looking after Foldal's younger daughter. And helping to educate her—so she can make something of herself and be independent someday. That's certainly more than her father ever could have done for her.

ELLA. Yes, her father must be starving along, I can imagine.

MRS. BORKMAN. And then Erhart's arranged music lessons for her. She's already so practiced at it that she can go up—up to him in the salon and play for him.

ELLA. So he still loves music?

MRS. BORKMAN. Oh, I suppose so. He's got the piano you sent out—when he was expected home—

ELLA. And she plays on that?

MRS. BORKMAN. Yes, just now and then. In the evenings. Erhart took care of that, too.

ELLA. The poor girl has to travel all the way out here? And then back to town again?

MRS. BORKMAN. Not at all. Erhart's settled it that she stays with a lady here in the neighborhood. A Mrs. Wilton—

ELLA (*fascinated*). Mrs. Wilton!

MRS. BORKMAN. A very rich woman. Not anyone you know.

ELLA. I've heard the name. Mrs. Fanny Wilton, I believe—

MRS. BORKMAN. Yes, exactly—

ELLA. Erhart's written about her in several of his letters. Is she living out here now?

MRS. BORKMAN. Yes, she rented a house and moved out from town a while ago.

ELLA (*hesitating a bit*). They say that she's divorced.

MRS. BORKMAN. Her husband's been dead for several years.

ELLA. Yes, but they were divorced. He divorced her.

MRS. BORKMAN. He deserted her, actually. The fault certainly wasn't on her side.

ELLA. Do you know her fairly well, Gunhild?

MRS. BORKMAN. Why, yes, of course. She lives quite near and looks in on me every so often.

ELLA. You like her?

MRS. BORKMAN. She's exceptionally understanding. And remarkably clear in her perceptions.

ELLA. Of people, you mean?

MRS. BORKMAN. Particularly of people. She's made a thorough study of Erhart. Really profound—into his very soul. And consequently, she idolizes him—which is only reasonable.

ELLA (*slyly*). So perhaps she knows Erhart even more intimately than she knows you.

MRS. BORKMAN. Yes, they got together quite a bit in town. Before she moved out here.

ELLA (*impulsively*). And still she moved from town—?

MRS. BORKMAN (*starts and looks narrowly at her*). Still! What do you mean by that?

ELLA (*evasively*). Oh, now really—by that?

MRS. BORKMAN. You said it in such a peculiar way. You did mean something, Ella!

ELLA (*meeting her eyes directly*). Yes, it's true, Gunhild. I meant something, all right.

MRS. BORKMAN. Well then, out with it!

ELLA. First of all *this:* that I feel I also have a certain kind of right to Erhart. Or maybe you don't agree?

MRS. BORKMAN (*gazing about the room*). My gracious —after the amounts you've spent on him—

ELLA. Oh, that's no reason, Gunhild. But because I love him—

MRS. BORKMAN (*smiles scornfully*). My son? Can you love him? You? In spite of everything?

ELLA. Yes, I can, in spite of everything. And I do. I love Erhart—as much as I could ever love anyone—now, at my age.

MRS. BORKMAN. Yes, yes, all right—

ELLA. So you see, that's why I get upset the instant I see anything threatening him.

MRS. BORKMAN. Threatening Erhart! Well, but what threatens him? Or *who* does?

ELLA. You, to start with—in *your* way—

MRS. BORKMAN. I!

ELLA. And then this Mrs. Wilton, too—she frightens me.

MRS. BORKMAN (*stares at her, momentarily speechless*). How can you think anything of the kind about Erhart! About my own son! He, with his great mission to fulfill!

ELLA (*disdainfully*). Oh, come, his mission—!

MRS. BORKMAN (*furiously*). How dare you take that arrogant tone!

ELLA. Do you suppose that a young person of Erhart's

age—healthy and exuberant—do you suppose that he'll go out and sacrifice himself—for anything like a "mission"?

MRS. BORKMAN (*tenaciously*). Erhart will! I know it for a fact!

ELLA (*shaking her head*). You neither know it nor believe it, Gunhild.

MRS. BORKMAN. Don't I!

ELLA. It's only something you dream about. Because if you didn't have that to cling to, you're afraid you'd give way to total despair.

MRS. BORKMAN. Yes, then I'd really be in despair. (*Fiercely.*) And perhaps that's what you'd like to see most, Ella!

ELLA (*her head held high*). Yes, I would—if you can't liberate yourself except by victimizing Erhart.

MRS. BORKMAN (*threateningly*). You want to come between us! Between mother and son! *You!*

ELLA. I want to free him from your power—your control—your domination.

MRS. BORKMAN (*triumphantly*). You've lost your chance! You had him in your net—right up to his fifteenth year. But now, you see, I've won him back!

ELLA. Then I'll win him again from you! (*In a rasping, near whisper.*) The two of us, we've already fought like savages once for a man!

MRS. BORKMAN (*looks at her, gloatingly*). Yes, and *I* was victorious.

ELLA (*with a mocking smile*). Do you still think that victory won you anything?

MRS. BORKMAN (*somberly*). No—that's God's own truth.

ELLA. You won't win anything this time, either.

MRS. BORKMAN. Won't win, by asserting a mother's power over her boy!

ELLA. No, because it's only *power* over him that you want.

MRS. BORKMAN. And you?

ELLA (*with warmth*). I want his affections—his soul—his whole heart—!

MRS. BORKMAN (*explosively*). You won't get them again, ever in this world!

ELLA (*eyeing her*). You've seen to that?

MRS. BORKMAN (*smiles*). Yes. I've indulged that privilege. Couldn't you read that in his letters?

ELLA (*slowly nods*). Yes. His last letters have been you, completely.

MRS. BORKMAN (*baiting her*). I've made use of these eight years—while I've had him under my eyes, you see.

ELLA (*with restraint*). What have you told him about me? If it's proper to discuss?

MRS. BORKMAN. Oh, it's quite proper to.

ELLA. Then discuss it!

MRS. BORKMAN. I've merely told him the truth.

ELLA. Well?

MRS. BORKMAN. I've everlastingly impressed upon him that he must please be sure to remember that it's you we have to thank for the fact that we can live as decently as we do. Or that we *can* live at all.

ELLA. No more than that?

MRS. BORKMAN. Oh, such knowledge festers. It does in me.

ELLA. But it's hardly different from what Erhart knew before.

MRS. BORKMAN. When he came back home to me, he imagined that you did all this out of a kind heart. (*Looks vindictively at her.*) Now he doesn't think that any longer.

ELLA. What does he think now?

MRS. BORKMAN. He thinks the truth. I asked him how he could explain why Aunt Ella never came to visit us—

ELLA (*interrupting*). He knew why already!

MRS. BORKMAN. Now he knows even better. You'd made him believe that it was to spare me—and him, upstairs.

ELLA. And it was.

MRS. BORKMAN. Erhart doesn't believe a word of it anymore.

ELLA. What have you gotten him to believe about me?

MRS. BORKMAN. He believes the truth: that you're ashamed of us—and you despise us. Or maybe you don't? Didn't you once intend to take him away from me altogether? Think, Ella. You're sure to remember.

ELLA (*shrugging it off*). That was at the worst of the scandal—when the case was in court. I no longer cherish that thought.

MRS. BORKMAN. It wouldn't profit you if you did. Then what would become of his mission? No, thank you! It's me Erhart needs—not you. And so he's the same as dead for you! And you for him!

ELLA (*coldly determined*). We'll see. Because now I'm staying here.

MRS. BORKMAN (*staring at her*). At this house?

ELLA. Yes.

MRS. BORKMAN. Here—with us? Overnight?

ELLA. I'm staying here all the rest of my days, if it's so granted.

MRS. BORKMAN (*composing herself*). Yes, yes, Ella—of course, the house is yours.

ELLA. Oh, stop—!

MRS. BORKMAN. Everything in it is yours. The chair I sit on is yours. The bed I lie on, tossing sleeplessly, belongs to you. The food we eat we get thanks to you.

ELLA. There's no other way of doing things. Borkman can't have property in his own name. In no time someone would come and take possession of it.

MRS. BORKMAN. I'm aware of that. We have to bear with living on your mercy and charity.

ELLA (*coldly*). I can't help your seeing it that way, Gunhild.

MRS. BORKMAN. No, you can't. When will you want us to move?

ELLA (*looking at her*). To move?

MRS. BORKMAN (*excitedly*). Yes, you certainly don't imagine that I'll remain living here under the same roof with you! I'd rather go to the poorhouse, or take to the roads!

ELLA. All right. Then let me have Erhart—

MRS. BORKMAN. Erhart! My only son? My child?

ELLA. Yes. Because in that case I'll go right back home.

MRS. BORKMAN (*after a brief deliberation, firmly*). Erhart himself can choose between us.

ELLA (*looking doubtfully at her*). Let *him* choose? But —can you risk that, Gunhild?

MRS. BORKMAN (*with a hard laugh*). Can I risk—my boy choosing between his mother and you! Why, yes, I'll risk that.

ELLA (*listening*). Is someone coming? I think I hear—

MRS. BORKMAN. That's probably Erhart—

(*There is a brisk knock on the hall door, which then is opened right away.* MRS. WILTON, *wearing an evening gown under her winter coat, comes in. The* MAID, *having had no time to announce her, follows her in, looking bewildered.* MRS. WILTON *is a singularly handsome woman, with a ripe figure, somewhere in her thirties. She has full, red, smiling lips, mischievous eyes, and rich, dark hair.*)

MRS. WILTON. Mrs. Borkman, dear, good evening!

MRS. BORKMAN (*somewhat dryly*). Good evening, Mrs. Wilton. (*To the* MAID, *pointing to the garden room.*) Take the lamp in there out and light it.

(*The* MAID *fetches the lamp and goes out with it.*)

MRS. WILTON (*seeing* ELLA). Oh, excuse me—you have guests—

MRS. BORKMAN. Only my sister, Ella Rentheim, who's visiting—

(ERHART BORKMAN *comes storming through the half-opened door, flinging it back. He is a young man, elegantly dressed, with gay, sparkling eyes. He shows early signs of a moustache.*)

ERHART (*radiating delight, as he pauses on the threshold*). What's this! Has Aunt Ella come? (*He rushes up*

to her, seizing her hands.) Aunt Ella! No, is it possible!
Are *you* here?

ELLA (*throwing her arms about him*). Erhart! My dear,
sweet boy. My, how big you've grown! Oh, it does me
good to see you again!

MRS. BORKMAN (*sharply*). What does this mean, Erhart? Hiding yourself out in the hall.

MRS. WILTON (*hurriedly*). Erhart—Mr. Borkman arrived with me.

MRS. BORKMAN (*gauging him with her eyes*). So, Erhart. You don't come first to your mother?

ERHART. I only had to stop by Mrs. Wilton's for a
second—to pick up Frida.

MRS. BORKMAN. You have Miss Foldal along, too?

MRS. WILTON. Yes, we've left her waiting in the entryway.

ERHART (*calling out through the doorway*). Just go
right up, Frida.

(*A pause.* ELLA *studies* ERHART. *He appears self-conscious
and rather impatient; his face assumes a tense, colder expression. The* MAID *comes in with the lighted lamp for the
garden room, then withdraws, closing the door behind
her.*)

MRS. BORKMAN (*with constrained politeness*). Well,
Mrs. Wilton—if you'd like to settle down here for the
evening, why—

MRS. WILTON. Thank you ever so much, Mrs. Borkman,
dear—but I don't see how I can. We've got another
invitation. We're expected down at Mr. Hinkel's.

MRS. BORKMAN (*looking at her*). We? Which "we" do
you mean?

MRS. WILTON (*laughing*). Well, really I just mean
myself. But I was delegated by the ladies of the house to
bring along Mr. Borkman—if I happened to set eyes on
him.

MRS. BORKMAN. And you happened to, as I can see.

MRS. WILTON. Yes, fortunately. Since he was so accommodating as to look in on me—for little Frida's sake.

MRS. BORKMAN (*dryly*). But, Erhart—I had no idea you were acquainted with this family—the Hinkels.

ERHART (*vexed*). No, I'm really not acquainted with them at all. (*Continues somewhat impatiently.*) You know very well yourself, Mother, the people I do or don't know.

MRS. WILTON. Oh, pish! One soon gets acquainted in *that* house! Gay, amusing, hospitable people. And teeming with young ladies.

MRS. BORKMAN (*emphatically*). If I know my son, Mrs. Wilton, that's scarcely the proper company for him.

MRS. WILTON. But, my gracious, dear, he's young himself, you know!

MRS. BORKMAN. Yes, luckily he's young. With those people he'd have to be.

ERHART (*masking his impatience*). Yes, yes, yes, Mother—it's self-evident that I have no business going down to the Hinkels' this evening. Naturally, I'll be staying here with you and Aunt Ella.

MRS. BORKMAN. I was sure you would, dear.

ELLA. No, Erhart—don't stay away on my behalf—

ERHART. Why, certainly, Aunt Ella; there's nothing more to discuss. (*Looks hesitantly at* MRS. WILTON.) But how can we explain it? Will it be acceptable? After all, you've already told them "yes" for me.

MRS. WILTON (*vivaciously*). What nonsense! Why shouldn't it be acceptable? When I make my way down into that room after room of shimmering festivities— lonely and abandoned—can you picture it?— Why, then I'll have to tell them "no"—for you.

ERHART (*grudgingly*). Well, if you honestly think it'll be acceptable—

MRS. WILTON (*dismissing it lightly*). I've said a great many "yeses" and "noes" in my time—for myself. And how could you leave your aunt, when she's only now just come? For shame, Monsieur Erhart—is that any way for a son to behave?

MRS. BORKMAN (*piqued*). For a son?

MRS. WILTON. Well, for a foster son, then, Mrs. Borkman.

MRS. BORKMAN. Yes, you ought to add that.

MRS. WILTON. Oh, I think one has more to thank a good foster mother for than one's real mother.

MRS. BORKMAN. Was that your own experience?

MRS. WILTON. Regrettably. I hardly even knew my mother. But if I'd had such a good foster mother, then perhaps I wouldn't have turned out as—as wicked as people say I am. (*To* ERHART.) So you stay snug at home now with mama and your aunt—and drink tea! (*To the ladies.*) Good-bye, good-bye, Mrs. Borkman, dear. Good-bye, Miss Rentheim!

(*The ladies bow silently. She goes toward the door.*)

ERHART (*following her*). Shouldn't I escort you partway—?

MRS. WILTON (*by the door, motioning him away*). Not one step. I'm very well accustomed to making my way along. (*Standing in the doorway, eyeing him and nodding.*) But now you better watch out, Mr. Borkman—I'm warning you.

ERHART. Why must I watch out?

MRS. WILTON (*roguishly*). Because when I'm going down the road—lonely and abandoned, as I said—then I'll try to cast a spell on you.

ERHART (*laughing*). Oh, I see! You're going to try *that* again.

MRS. WILTON (*half seriously*). Yes, so you be careful. When I'm going along, I'll talk to myself—right out of my innermost secret will, and I'll say: "Erhart Borkman, take your hat this instant!"

MRS. BORKMAN. And do you think he will?

MRS. WILTON (*laughing*). Oh, absolutely; he'll pick up his hat like a shot. And then I'll say: "Put on your overcoat nicely, Erhart Borkman. And the galoshes! Don't you dare forget your galoshes! And then, follow after me! Tenderly. Tenderly. Tenderly."

ERHART (*with forced gaiety*). Yes, you can depend on me.

MRS. WILTON (*her forefinger uplifted*). Tenderly! Tenderly! Good night!

(*She laughs, nods to the ladies, and shuts the door after her.*)

MRS. BORKMAN. Does she really perform such tricks?

ERHART. Oh, of course not. How can you think so? It's only a joke. (*Breaking off.*) But let's not talk now about Mrs. Wilton. (*He presses* ELLA *to sit in the armchair by the stove and stands looking at her briefly.*) Imagine your taking the long trip here, Aunt Ella. And now, in the dead of winter!

ELLA. In the end I just couldn't put it off, Erhart.

ERHART. Oh? Why was that?

ELLA. I had to come in for a consultation with the doctors.

ERHART. Well, that's good.

ELLA (*smiles*). You think that's good?

ERHART. That you finally decided to, I mean.

MRS. BORKMAN (*from the sofa, coldly*). Ella, are you ill?

ELLA. You know very well I'm ill.

MRS. BORKMAN. Well, I know you've been semi-invalid for a good many years.

ERHART. The whole time I stayed with you I kept telling you that you ought to be seeing a doctor.

ELLA. Oh, up where I live, there's nobody I have any confidence in. Besides, it didn't bother me so much then.

ERHART. You're feeling worse now?

ELLA. Oh yes, dear; I've taken something of a turn for the worse.

ERHART. But nothing dangerous, though?

ELLA. Well, that's all in the way one takes it.

ERHART (*warmly*). Yes, but now listen, Aunt Ella—then you mustn't make the trip home again so soon.

ELLA. No, I don't intend to, either.

ERHART. You've got to stay here in town. Because here you have all the best doctors to choose from.

ELLA. Yes, that was my thought when I left home.

ERHART. Then you should try to find some really nice accommodations—in some quiet, cozy pension.

ELLA. I checked in this morning at the old place where I've stayed before.

ERHART. Oh yes, *there* you can be comfortable.

ELLA. All the same, I don't think I'll be staying there.

ERHART. Really? Why not?

ELLA. No, I decided differently when I came out here.

ERHART (*puzzled*). Oh—? You decided—?

MRS. BORKMAN (*crocheting, without looking up*). Your aunt wants to live here on her estate, Erhart.

ERHART (*glancing from one to the other*). Here? With us! With all of us! Is that true, Aunt Ella?

ELLA. Yes, that's my decision now.

MRS. BORKMAN (*as before*). Everything here is your aunt's, you know.

ELLA. So I'll be staying on here, Erhart. At first, anyway. For a time. I'll make my own provisions, over in the annex—

ERHART. That's the right idea. There are always rooms standing empty over there. (*Suddenly animated.*) But actually, Aunt Ella—aren't you pretty tired after your trip?

ELLA. Oh, I'm a bit tired, yes.

ERHART. Well, then I think you ought to go off early to bed.

ELLA (*regards him with a smile*). So I shall.

ERHART (*fervently*). Because then we could talk more freely tomorrow—or another day. About everything possible. You and Mother and I. Wouldn't that be much better, Aunt Ella?

MRS. BORKMAN (*vehemently, rising from the sofa*). Erhart—I can see by your look that you want to leave me!

ERHART (*unsettled*). What do you mean?

MRS. BORKMAN. You want to go on to—to the Hinkels' place!

ERHART (*involuntarily*). Oh, that! (*Composing himself.*) Well, do you think I ought to sit here, keeping Aunt Ella up until way into the night? She *is* ill, Mother. Remember that.

MRS. BORKMAN. You want to go to the Hinkels', Erhart!

ERHART (*impatiently*). Well, but good Lord, Mother—I don't see how I can very well pass it up. What do you say, Aunt Ella?

ELLA. It's best if you'll act in complete freedom, Erhart.

MRS. BORKMAN (*turns on her menacingly*). You want to tear him from me!

ELLA (*rising*). Yes, Gunhild, if I only could!

(*Music is heard overhead.*)

ERHART (*writhing as if in pain*). Oh, I can't take this anymore! (*He peers about him.*) Where'd I leave my hat? (*To* ELLA.) Do you know that music upstairs?

ELLA. No. What is it?

ERHART. It's the *Danse Macabre*. The Dance of Death. Don't you know the Dance of Death, Aunt Ella?

ELLA (*smiles sorrowfully*). Not yet, Erhart.

ERHART (*to* MRS. BORKMAN). Mother—I appeal to you, please—do let me go!

MRS. BORKMAN (*looks sternly at him*). From your mother? You want that?

ERHART. I'll be coming out again—maybe tomorrow.

MRS. BORKMAN (*in passionate agitation*). You want to leave me! To be out with those strangers! With—with— no, I won't even think of it!

ERHART. There are so many shimmering lights down there. And young, happy faces. And there's music there, Mother!

MRS. BORKMAN (*pointing up toward the ceiling*). Upstairs there's also music, Erhart.

ERHART. Yes, it's that music *there*—that's what's hounding me out of this house.

ELLA. Can't you allow your father a little chance to forget himself?

ERHART. Yes, I can. I can allow it a thousand times over—if I just don't have to hear it myself.

MRS. BORKMAN (*looks reprovingly at him*). Be strong, Erhart! Strong, my son! Don't ever forget you have a great mission!

ERHART. Oh, Mother—don't make those phrases! I wasn't created to be a missionary! Good night, Aunt Ella. Good night, Mother.

(*He hurries out down the hall.*)

MRS. BORKMAN (*after a short silence*). You've retaken him soon enough, at any rate, Ella.

ELLA. I wish I dared believe that.

MRS. BORKMAN. But you're not going to hold him for long, you'll see.

ELLA. Thanks to you?

MRS. BORKMAN. To me, or—to her, that other one.

ELLA. Better her than you.

MRS. BORKMAN (*nodding slowly*). I understand that. I say the same. Better her than you.

ELLA. Whatever the end result for him—

MRS. BORKMAN. That scarcely matters now, I think.

ELLA (*taking her coat over her arm*). For the first time in our lives, we two twin sisters are of one mind. Good night, Gunhild. (*Goes out down the hall.*)

(*The music swells in sound from overhead.*)

MRS. BORKMAN (*stands quietly a moment, gives a start, recoils and whispers involuntarily*). The wolf howling again. The sick wolf. (*She stays standing a moment, then hurls herself down on the floor, writhing and moaning, and whispers in anguish.*) Erhart! Erhart—be true to me! Oh, come home and help your mother! I can't bear this life any longer!

⤙ ACT TWO ⤚

The former grand salon upstairs in the Rentheim house. The walls are covered with old tapestries, depicting hunting scenes, shepherds and shepherdesses, in faded, mottled colors. In the wall to the left, a sliding door, and closer in the foreground, a piano. In the left rear corner, an unframed door decorated with tapestry to blend with the background. At the middle of the right-hand wall, a large carved oak desk, with many books and papers. Further forward on the same side, a sofa, along with a table and chairs. All the furniture is in austere Empire style. On the desk and table, lighted lamps.

JOHN GABRIEL BORKMAN *is standing by the piano, his hands clasped behind his back, listening to* FRIDA FOLDAL, *who sits playing the last measures of the* Danse Macabre. BORKMAN *is a man in his sixties, of medium height, strongly and compactly built. His appearance is distinguished, with a finely chiseled profile, piercing eyes, and curling, grayish-white hair and beard. He is dressed in a black, somewhat old-fashioned suit, with a white necktie.* FRIDA FOLDAL *is a good-looking, pale girl of fifteen, with a rather tired, strained expression; she wears a cheap, light-colored dress. The music comes to an end. Silence.*

BORKMAN. Can you guess where I first heard such music as this?

FRIDA (*looking up at him*). No, Mr. Borkman.

BORKMAN. It was down in the mines.

FRIDA (*not understanding*). You did? In the mines?

967

BORKMAN. I'm a miner's son, as I guess you know. Or maybe you didn't know that?

FRIDA. No, Mr. Borkman.

BORKMAN. A miner's son. And my father took me down with him sometimes, into the mines. Down there the metal sings.

FRIDA. Really? It sings.

BORKMAN (*nods*). When the ore is loosened. The hammer blows that loosen it—they're like the midnight bell that strikes and sets it free. And so the metal sings—for joy—in its way.

FRIDA. Why does it do that, Mr. Borkman?

BORKMAN. It wants to come up into daylight and serve mankind. (*He paces back and forth across the salon, his hands still behind his back.*)

FRIDA (*sits and waits for a moment, then looks at her watch and gets up*). Pardon me, Mr. Borkman—but I'm afraid I have to go now.

BORKMAN (*stopping in front of her*). You're going so soon?

FRIDA (*putting her music away in a folder*). Yes, I really have to. (*Visibly embarrassed.*) I've been engaged for this evening elsewhere.

BORKMAN. Elsewhere, meaning a party?

FRIDA. Yes.

BORKMAN. And you're going to give them a concert?

FRIDA (*biting her lip*). No—I'm going to play for the dancing.

BORKMAN. Only for dancing?

FRIDA. Yes, they want to dance after supper.

BORKMAN (*stands, looking at her*). Do you like to play for dances? Around in different houses?

FRIDA (*putting on her winter coat*). Yes, when I can get an engagement— It always brings in a little something.

BORKMAN. Is *that* what you think about most while you sit playing for the dancers?

FRIDA. No. I mostly think how sad it is that I can't join in the dancing myself.

BORKMAN (*nods*). That's precisely what I wanted to know. (*Walks restlessly about the salon.*) Yes, yes, yes— this thing that one can't join in oneself, that hurts the most. (*Stops.*) But then there *is* something that evens it up for you, Frida.

FRIDA (*looks curiously at him*). What's that, Mr. Borkman?

BORKMAN. The sense that you've got ten times more music in you than in all the dancers put together.

FRIDA (*smiles diffidently*). Oh, that's far from certain.

BORKMAN (*admonishing her with upraised forefinger*). Don't ever be so foolish as to doubt yourself!

FRIDA. But, good heavens, if nobody knows it—?

BORKMAN. As long as *you* know it, then that's enough. Where is it you're playing this evening?

FRIDA. Over at Mr. Hinkel's.

BORKMAN (*gives her an abrupt, penetrating look*). Mr. Hinkel's, you say!

FRIDA. Yes.

BORKMAN (*with a bitter smile*). Do guests come to that man's house? Can he get people to visit him?

FRIDA. Yes, lots of people are coming, from what Mrs. Wilton says.

BORKMAN (*heatedly*). But what kind of people? Can you tell me that?

FRIDA (*a bit apprehensively*). No, I really don't know. Oh, for one—I do know young Mr. Borkman's going.

BORKMAN (*jarred*). Erhart! My son?

FRIDA. Yes, he'll be there.

BORKMAN. How do you know that?

FRIDA. He said so himself. Just an hour ago.

BORKMAN. Is he out here today?

FRIDA. Yes, he's been at Mrs. Wilton's the whole afternoon.

BORKMAN (*probingly*). Do you know if he stopped here, too? If he was in to speak with anyone downstairs, I mean?

FRIDA. Yes, he was in seeing Mrs. Borkman a while.

BORKMAN (*stung*). Aha—I might have known.

FRIDA. But there was also a strange lady with her, I think.

BORKMAN. Oh? Was there? Ah well, I expect people do visit her every so often.

FRIDA. Should I tell your son, if I meet him later, that he ought to come up to see you, too?

BORKMAN (*brusquely*). Don't say anything! I expressly forbid it! People who want to look in on me can find their way by themselves. I beg from no one.

FRIDA. No, no, then I won't say anything. Good night, Mr. Borkman.

BORKMAN (*roams about the room and growls*). Good night.

FRIDA. Do you suppose I could run down the spiral staircase? It's quicker.

BORKMAN. Oh, good grief—run down whatever stairs you like, for all I care. Good night to you!

FRIDA. Good night, Mr. Borkman.

(*She leaves through the little tapestry door in the left background.* BORKMAN, *deep in thought, goes over to the piano, about to close it, then lets it be. He gazes at all the emptiness surrounding him and starts pacing up and down the floor from the corner by the piano to the corner in the right background—disquieted and restless, ceaselessly back and forth. Finally he goes over to the desk, listens in the direction of the sliding door, quickly picks up a hand-mirror, studies himself in it, and adjusts his necktie. There is a knock on the sliding door.* BORKMAN *hears it, glances hastily toward the door, but remains silent. A moment later, the knock sounds again, louder this time.*)

BORKMAN (*standing by the desk, his left hand resting on its top, his right thrust in the breast of his coat*). Come in!

(VILHELM FOLDAL *warily enters the room. He is a bent, worn man with mild blue eyes and long, thin gray hair falling down over his coat collar. He has a portfolio under his arm, a soft felt hat in one hand and large horn-rimmed glasses, which he pushes up on his forehead.*)

BORKMAN (*changes his stance and regards his visitor with a half-disappointed, half-gratified expression*). Oh, it's only you.

FOLDAL. Good evening, John Gabriel. Yes, quite so, it's me.

BORKMAN (*with a severe look*). By the way, I think you're rather late.

FOLDAL. Well, the distance isn't exactly short, you know. Especially for someone on foot.

BORKMAN. But why do you always walk, Vilhelm? You're right by the streetcar.

FOLDAL. It's healthier to walk. And then there's the carfare saved. Well, has Frida been up to play for you lately?

BORKMAN. She left only this minute. You didn't meet her outside?

FOLDAL. No, I haven't set eyes on her for a long time. Not since she started living at this Mrs. Wilton's.

BORKMAN (*sits on the sofa and motions with a wave of his hand toward a chair*). You're welcome to a seat, Vilhelm.

FOLDAL (*perching on the edge of a chair*). Many thanks. (*Looks at him in dejection.*) Oh, you can't imagine how lonely I feel since Frida left home.

BORKMAN. Oh, come—you've got more in reserve.

FOLDAL. God knows I do. Five in the lot. But Frida was the only one that understood me a little. (*Shakes his head dolefully.*) The others can't understand me at all.

BORKMAN (*somberly, staring into space and drumming his fingers on the table*). No, that's a fact. *That's* the curse that we, the exceptional, the chosen human beings have to bear. The masses—all the gray average—they don't understand us, Vilhelm.

FOLDAL (*resignedly*). Understanding can take care of itself. With a little patience, one can always wait a bit longer for that. (*His voice chokes with tears.*) But there's something more bitter still.

BORKMAN (*fiercely*). Nothing's more bitter than that!

FOLDAL. Yes, there is, John Gabriel. I've just had a domestic scene—before I came out here.

BORKMAN. Really? Why?

FOLDAL (*in an outburst*). My family—they have contempt for me.

BORKMAN (*incensed*). Contempt—!

FOLDAL (*wiping his eyes*). I've been sensing it for a long time. But today it really came out.

BORKMAN (*after a pause*). You made a decidedly poor choice when you married.

FOLDAL. I scarcely had any choice. And besides—one has an urge to get married when one starts getting on in years. And then being so distressed, so down at the heels as I was then—

BORKMAN (*springing up angrily*). Is that a recrimination against me! A reproof—!

FOLDAL (*anxiously*). No, for God's sake, John Gabriel—!

BORKMAN. Yes, you've been brooding about all the trouble that struck the bank—!

FOLDAL (*reassuringly*). But I don't blame *you* for *that!* I swear—!

BORKMAN (*resumes his seat, grumbling*). Well, that's good.

FOLDAL. Also, you mustn't think it's my wife I'm complaining about. She hasn't much refinement, poor thing, it's true. But, all the same, she does pretty well. No, it's the children—

BORKMAN. I'm not surprised.

FOLDAL. Because the children—you see, they have more culture. And make more demands on life.

BORKMAN (*looks sympathetically at him*). And that's why your young ones have contempt for you, Vilhelm?

FOLDAL (*shrugging his shoulders*). I haven't made much of a career, you see. No getting around that—

BORKMAN (*drawing closer and laying his hand on* FOLDAL'*s arm*). Don't they know that you wrote a tragedy when you were young?

FOLDAL. Yes, they know that, of course. But it doesn't seem to make any particular impression on them.

BORKMAN. Then they're insensitive. Because your tragedy is good. I believe that unshakably.

FOLDAL (*brightening*). Yes, don't you feel there's a lot that's good in it, John Gabriel? Lord love me, if I only could get it staged—! (*He eagerly opens the portfolio and shuffles the papers in it.*) Look here! Now let me show you something I revised—

BORKMAN. You have it with you?

FOLDAL. Yes, I brought it along. It's such a long time now since I read it to you. So I thought it might divert you to hear an act or two—

BORKMAN (*waving him off as he gets up*). No, no, it can better wait till another time.

FOLDAL. Yes, yes, as you like.

(BORKMAN *paces back and forth across the room.* FOLDAL *packs away his manuscript again.*)

BORKMAN (*stopping in front of him*). You were right in what you were just saying—that you hadn't made a career. But I promise you this, Vilhelm, that once the hour of restitution strikes for me—

FOLDAL (*starts to rise*). Ah, thank you—!

BORKMAN (*motioning him down*). If you'll just stay seated, please. (*With mounting fervor.*) When the hour of restitution strikes for me—when they realize that they can't dispense with me—when they come up to me here in this room—and eat crow and beg me to take the reins of the bank again—! The new bank that they've founded— and can't direct— (*He poses by the desk as before and strikes his chest.*) *Here's* where I'll stand and greet them! And all over this land they'll ask and they'll learn what terms John Gabriel Borkman sets before he'll— (*Stops abruptly and stares at* FOLDAL.) You're giving me such a doubtful look! Maybe you don't think they'll come? That they *must—must—must* come to me one of these days? You don't think so!

FOLDAL. Why, God knows I do, John Gabriel, yes.

BORKMAN (*sitting again on the sofa*). I believe that, unshakably. I *know*—with absolute certainty—that they'll come. If I didn't have that certainty—then I would have put a bullet through my head long ago.

FOLDAL (*in alarm*). Oh, no, don't ever say—!

BORKMAN (*exultantly*). But they'll come! They're coming! You wait! Any day, any hour, I can expect them here. And, as you can see, I hold myself in readiness to welcome them.

FOLDAL (*with a sigh*). If only they'd get here soon.

BORKMAN (*restlessly*). Yes, old friend, time passes; the years pass; life—oh, no—I mustn't think about that! (*Looking at him.*) You know what I feel like sometimes?

FOLDAL. What?

BORKMAN. I feel like a Napoleon, maimed in his first battle.

FOLDAL (*touching his portfolio*). I know that feeling.

BORKMAN. Oh yes, well, that's on a smaller scale.

FOLDAL (*quietly*). My little world of poetry has tremendous worth to *me*, John Gabriel.

BORKMAN (*heatedly*). Yes, but I, who could have made millions! All the mines I could have controlled! Drilling new shafts, endlessly! Waterfalls! Stone quarries! Trade routes and shipping lines, girdling the globe. And all of these, I alone should have managed!

FOLDAL. Yes, I know that. There wasn't a thing you wouldn't take on.

BORKMAN (*kneading his hands*). And now I have to sit here like a wounded eagle and watch the others pass me by—and snatch it away from me, piece by piece!

FOLDAL. Likewise for me.

BORKMAN (*paying him no attention*). Just think. How close I was to my goal! If I'd only had eight days' respite to cover myself. All the deposits would have been replaced. All the securities I'd used so audaciously would have been back again, lying in the vault as before. That entire enormous stock pool was within a hair's breadth of existence. Nobody would have lost a share—

FOLDAL. My Lord, yes—how incredibly close you were—

BORKMAN (*with stifled fury*). And then I met with betrayal. Right on the brink of success! (*Looks at him.*) Do you know what I consider to be the most despicable crime a man can commit?

FOLDAL. No, tell me.

BORKMAN. It isn't murder. Nor robbery, nor housebreaking. Not even perjury. Most cases of that kind are directed against people one hates or is indifferent to, people of no concern.

FOLDAL. But the most despicable crime, John Gabriel—?

BORKMAN (*emphatically*). Is to abuse the trust of a friend.

FOLDAL (*somewhat skeptically*). Yes, but listen—

BORKMAN (*bristling*). What are you getting at! I can read it in your face. But it's not true. The investors who kept their securities in the bank would have gotten them all back. To the last decimal point! No, I'm telling you— the most despicable crime a man can commit is to betray a friend's correspondence—to publish to the whole wide world what was entrusted to one single person only, in confidence, like a whisper in an empty, dark, locked room. The man who can resort to such means is cankered and poisoned to the core with the morality of a loan shark. And I had that sort of friend. And he's the one who ruined me.

FOLDAL. I can guess who you mean.

BORKMAN. There wasn't one facet of my business affairs that I didn't lay open to him. And then the moment arrived when he turned the weapons against me that I'd put in his hands myself.

FOLDAL. I never could understand why he— Well, there were a lot of various rumors at the time, of course.

BORKMAN. What rumors? What were they? Tell me. I

didn't hear anything. I went right away into—into isolation. What were they gossiping about, Vilhelm?

FOLDAL. You were supposed to be made a cabinet minister, they said.

BORKMAN. They offered me a post. But I turned it down.

FOLDAL. So you weren't blocking him there.

BORKMAN. Oh no; that's not why he betrayed me.

FOLDAL. Well, then I simply can't understand—

BORKMAN. I might as well tell you, Vilhelm.

FOLDAL. Yes?

BORKMAN. You see, there was—a woman involved.

FOLDAL. A woman? But, John Gabriel—?

BORKMAN (*breaking off*). Oh, never mind—enough of these old, idiotic stories— Well, neither of us made the cabinet.

FOLDAL. But he rose to the heights.

BORKMAN. And I went to the depths.

FOLDAL. Oh, it's a terrible tragedy—

BORKMAN (*nodding to him*). I guess, almost as terrible as yours, when I stop to think of it.

FOLDAL (*innocently*). Yes, at least as terrible.

BORKMAN (*with a quiet laugh*). But from another perspective, it's really a kind of comedy, too.

FOLDAL. A comedy? This?

BORKMAN. Yes, the way it seems to be developing now. No, this really is something—

FOLDAL. What?

BORKMAN. You say you didn't meet Frida when you came?

FOLDAL. No.

BORKMAN. While the two of us sit here, she's sitting down there playing dances for the man that betrayed and ruined me.

FOLDAL. I hadn't any inkling of that.

BORKMAN. Yes, she took her music and went straight from me to—to that mansion.

FOLDAL (*apologetically*). Ah yes, poor child—

BORKMAN. And can you guess whom she's playing for—among others?

FOLDAL. Who?

BORKMAN. My son.

FOLDAL. What!

BORKMAN. Yes, what do you make of it, Vilhelm? My son down there in the throngs of dancers tonight. Isn't that, just as I say, a comedy?

FOLDAL. Well, but he certainly doesn't know any of this.

BORKMAN. Of what?

FOLDAL. He certainly doesn't know how *he*—this, uh—

BORKMAN. You can say the name. I can stand hearing it now.

FOLDAL. I'm sure your son doesn't realize the connection, John Gabriel.

BORKMAN (*grimly, drumming on the table*). He knows it—as sure as I'm sitting here.

FOLDAL. But can you conceive, then, his *ever* wanting to enter that house!

BORKMAN (*shaking his head*). My son, I suppose, doesn't see things the way I do. I'm willing to swear that he sides with my enemies! Undoubtedly he thinks, as they do, that Hinkel only acted damn well as a responsible attorney when he went and betrayed me.

FOLDAL. But—who could have given him that idea?

BORKMAN. Who? Are you forgetting who brought him up? First his aunt—from when he was six, seven years old. And since then—his mother!

FOLDAL. I think you're being unfair to them.

BORKMAN (*heatedly*). I'm never unfair to anyone! Those two have incited him against me, I'm telling you!

FOLDAL (*indulgently*). Yes, of course, I guess they have.

BORKMAN (*full of indignation*). Oh, these women! They corrupt and distort our lives! They completely botch up our destinies—our paths to glory.

FOLDAL. Not all of them!

BORKMAN. Really? Name me one single one who's any good!

FOLDAL. No, that's the problem. The ones I know—they're just no good.

BORKMAN (*snorts scornfully*). Well, then what's the point! So good women exist—but you never know them!

FOLDAL (*with warmth*). Yes, but, John Gabriel, all the same there *is* a point. It's such a blessed and consoling thought to realize that somewhere, out there around us, far away—*there* the true woman is waiting to be found.

BORKMAN (*shifting restlessly on the sofa*). Oh, cut that poetical rot!

FOLDAL (*looks at him, deeply wounded*). You call my most sacred faith poetical rot?

BORKMAN (*curtly*). I do, yes! It's the cause of your never having gotten anywhere in life. If you could only rinse your mind of all that, I could still help you get on your feet—and to move ahead.

FOLDAL (*smoldering inwardly*). Ah, you can't do that.

BORKMAN. I *can*, when I come back in power again.

FOLDAL. But that's an awfully remote possibility.

BORKMAN (*vehemently*). Maybe you think the time will never come? I want an answer!

FOLDAL. I don't know how to answer you.

BORKMAN (*rises, cold and imposing, and motions toward the door*). Then I no longer have any use for you.

FOLDAL (*springing up from his chair*). No use—!

BORKMAN. If you don't believe that my fate will change—

FOLDAL. But I can't believe against all reason! You're asking for full restitution—

BORKMAN. Go on! Go on!

FOLDAL. I know I never took my degree, but I've read *that* much law in my day—

BORKMAN (*quickly*). You mean it's impossible?

FOLDAL. There's no precedent for it.

BORKMAN. There *are* no precedents for exceptional men.

FOLDAL. The law doesn't make such allowances.

BORKMAN (*caustically*). You're no poet, Vilhelm.

FOLDAL (*impulsively clasping his hands*). You say that in all seriousness?

BORKMAN (*dismissing the matter*). We're only wasting each other's time. You better not come again.

FOLDAL. Then you want me to leave you alone.

BORKMAN (*without looking at him*). I've no more use for you.

FOLDAL (*gently*). No, no, no; I guess not.

BORKMAN. All this time, you've been lying to me.

FOLDAL (*shaking his head*). I never lied, John Gabriel.

BORKMAN. Haven't you sat here, lying hope and faith and trust into me?

FOLDAL. Those weren't lies as long as you believed in my talent. As long as you believed in me, I believed in you.

BORKMAN. Then we've practiced mutual deception on each other. And perhaps deceived ourselves—both of us.

FOLDAL. But isn't that the very basis of friendship, John Gabriel?

BORKMAN (*smiles wryly*). Quite so. To deceive—is friendship. You're right. I've had the experience once already.

FOLDAL (*looking at him*). No talent for poetry. And you could say that to me so callously.

BORKMAN (*tempering his voice*). Well, I'm no specialist in that field.

FOLDAL. More perhaps than you realize.

BORKMAN. I?

FOLDAL (*quietly*). Yes, you. Because I've had my own doubts from time to time, you know. The dreadful doubt— that I've botched my whole life up for the sake of a fantasy.

BORKMAN. When you doubt yourself, then you've lost your footing.

FOLDAL. That's why it was so heartening to come here for your support, because you believed. (*Taking his hat.*) But now you seem like a stranger to me.

BORKMAN. As you seem to me.

FOLDAL. Good night, John Gabriel.

BORKMAN. Good night, Vilhelm.

(FOLDAL *goes out to the left.* BORKMAN *stands for some moments and gazes at the closed door; he makes a gesture as if he would call* FOLDAL *back, but then reconsiders and begins to walk up and down the floor, his hands behind his back. He then stops at the sofa table and puts out the lamp. The salon now is in semidarkness. Shortly thereafter, a knock is heard on the tapestry door.*)

BORKMAN (*by the table, starts, turns and asks loudly*). Who's knocking?

(*No answer. Another knock.*)

BORKMAN (*frozen in place*). Who is that? Come in!

(ELLA RENTHEIM, *with a lighted candle in her hand, appears in the doorway. She is wearing a black dress as before, with her coat thrown loosely over her shoulders.*)

BORKMAN (*staring at her*). Who are you? What do you want with me?

ELLA (*shutting the door after her and coming closer*). It's me, John Gabriel. (*She sets down the candle on the piano and remains beside it.*)

BORKMAN (*stands and gazes at her as if thunderstruck; in a faint whisper*). Is that—is it Ella? Ella Rentheim?

ELLA. Yes—it's "your" Ella—as you used to call me. Once. So many—so many years ago.

BORKMAN (*as before*). Yes, it's you, Ella—I see that now.

ELLA. You still recognize me?

BORKMAN. Yes, I'm beginning to now—

ELLA. The years have worn and withered me, Borkman. Don't you think so?

BORKMAN (*uneasily*). You're somewhat changed. At first glance, anyway—

ELLA. I don't have the dark curls tumbling down my back anymore. Those curls you once liked to wind around your fingers.

BORKMAN (*briskly*). Right! Now I see, Ella. You've changed your hair style.

ELLA (*with a sad smile*). Exactly. It's the hair style that does it.

BORKMAN (*changing the subject*). I never knew you were here, in this part of the country.

ELLA. I've only just arrived.

BORKMAN. Why did you make that trip—now, in winter?

ELLA. You're going to hear why.

BORKMAN. Is it something you want from *me?*

ELLA. You, as well. But if we're going to talk about that, I'll have to begin far back.

BORKMAN. You must be tired.

ELLA. Yes, tired.

BORKMAN. Won't you sit? There—on the sofa.

ELLA. Yes, thank you. I need to.

(*She goes over to the right and seats herself in the near corner of the sofa.* BORKMAN *stands by the table, his hands behind his back, and studies her. Short silence.*)

ELLA. It's ages since the two of us met face to face, John Gabriel.

BORKMAN (*somberly*). A long, long time. With all that wretchedness in between.

ELLA. A whole lifetime between. A lifetime wasted.

BORKMAN (*looks sharply at her*). Wasted!

ELLA. Yes, just that. For us both.

BORKMAN (*in a cold, businesslike tone*). I don't rate my life wasted as yet.

ELLA. Well, what about *mine?*

BORKMAN. There you can only blame yourself, Ella.

ELLA (*with a tremor*). And *you* can say *that!*

BORKMAN. You could very well have been happy without me.

ELLA. You think so?

BORKMAN. If you'd resolved to.

ELLA (*bitterly*). Yes, I'm perfectly aware that there was someone else waiting to marry me—

BORKMAN. But you turned him away—

ELLA. Yes, I did.

BORKMAN. Time after time you turned him away. Year after year—

ELLA (*scornfully*). You mean, year after year I turned away from my happiness?

BORKMAN. You could just as well have been happy with him. And *I* would have been saved, then.

ELLA. You—?

BORKMAN. Yes. Then you would have saved me, Ella.

ELLA. How do you mean?

BORKMAN. He thought I was behind your refusals—your constant rejection. So he took revenge. He could do that so easily—since he had all those ill-considered, confidential letters of mine in his possession. He used them—and that put an end to me, for a time, at least. You see, all that was your doing, Ella!

ELLA. That's right, John Gabriel—if we really get down to cases, it seems *I* owe a debt to *you.*

BORKMAN. You can take it that way. I know thoroughly well how much I need to thank you for. You bought the estate, this entire property, at the auction, and turned it completely over to me and—your sister. You took in Erhart—and cared for him in every way—

ELLA. As long as I was allowed to—

BORKMAN. By your sister, yes. I've never intruded in these domestic questions. As I was saying, I know what you've sacrificed for me and for your sister. But then, you were *able* to. And you have to remember that *I* was the one who put you in that position.

ELLA (*heatedly*). You're enormously mistaken, John Gabriel! It was the deep warmth of my feeling for Erhart— and for you, too—it was *that* alone that moved me.

BORKMAN (*interrupting*). My dear, let's not get into feelings and such. I only mean that, if you acted the way you did, I was the one who gave you the power to do so.

ELLA (*smiles*). Hm, the power, the power—

BORKMAN (*incensed*). Yes, the power, exactly! When the great, decisive blow was poised to fall—when I couldn't spare friends or family—when I had to take, and did take, the millions that were entrusted to me—then I spared everything of yours, everything you owned and held—although I could have borrowed it, and used it, like all the rest.

ELLA (*with icy calm*). That's undoubtedly true, John Gabriel.

BORKMAN. It is. And that's why, when they came and took me, they found all your securities undisturbed in the bank vault.

ELLA (*scrutinizing him*). I've many times thought about that. Just why did you spare my holdings? And only mine?

BORKMAN. Why?

ELLA. Yes, why? Tell me.

BORKMAN (*with harsh disdain*). I suppose you think it was so I could have something to fall back on—if anything went wrong?

ELLA. Oh, no—you didn't think that way in those days, I'm sure.

BORKMAN. Never! I was so utterly confident of victory.

ELLA. Yes, but why then—?

BORKMAN (*shrugging his shoulders*). Good Lord, Ella— it's not so easy to remember motives from twenty years ago. I only remember that when I was alone then, struggling in silence with all the vast projects that would be set in motion, it seemed to me almost as if I were a voyager in the air. I walked the sleepless nights, inflating a huge balloon that would sail out over a shadowy, perilous ocean.

ELLA (*smiling*). You, who never doubted your victory.

BORKMAN (*impatiently*). Men are like that, Ella. They both doubt and believe at the same time. (*Gazing into space.*) And that's probably why I didn't want you and what you owned with me in the balloon.

ELLA (*intently*). Why? Tell me why?

BORKMAN (*not looking at her*). One doesn't care to take all that's dearest along on a journey like that.

ELLA. You had what was dearest to you on board. Your own future life.

BORKMAN. One's life isn't always what's dearest.

ELLA (*breathlessly*). Was that how you felt then?

BORKMAN. I think so.

ELLA. That *I* was dearest of all to you?

BORKMAN. Yes, I have—something of that impression.

ELLA. And yet that was years after you'd abandoned me—and married—someone else!

BORKMAN. You say I abandoned you? You know well enough there were higher incentives—well, *other* incentives—that impelled me. Without his aid, I would have gotten nowhere.

ELLA (*controlling herself*). So you abandoned me for—higher incentives.

BORKMAN. I couldn't get on without his help. And he set *you* as his price.

ELLA. And you paid the price. In full. Without a murmur.

BORKMAN. I had no choice. It was win or go under.

ELLA (*her voice trembling, as she looks at him*). Is it really true what you say—that I was dearest in this world to you then?

BORKMAN. Both then and after—long, long after.

ELLA. And still you traded me away. Bargained your rightful love to another man. Sold my love for a—for a bank presidency.

BORKMAN (*somberly, bowed down*). The necessity was overwhelming, Ella.

ELLA (*rises from the sofa, quivering with passion*). Criminal!

BORKMAN (*starting, then recovering his composure*). I've heard the word before.

ELLA. Oh, don't think I mean any law of the land you've broken! The use you made of all these stocks and bonds, or whatever—what do you think I care about that! If I could have been standing beside you when· everything went to pieces—

BORKMAN (*tensely*). Then what, Ella?

ELLA. Believe me, I would have borne it so gladly with you. The shame, the ruin—all of it I would have helped you bear—

BORKMAN. Would you have had the will to? And the courage?

ELLA. The will and the courage both. Because then, you see, I knew nothing about your great, intolerable crime—

BORKMAN. Which? What do you mean?

ELLA. I mean the crime that's beyond all forgiveness—

BORKMAN (*staring at her*). You're out of your senses.

ELLA (*advancing on him*). You're a murderer! You've committed the supreme, mortal sin!

BORKMAN (*backing toward the piano*). You're raving, Ella!

ELLA. You've killed the capacity to love in me. (*Approaching him.*) Can you understand what that means? In the Bible it speaks of a mysterious sin for which there *is* no forgiveness. I've never known before what that could be. Now I know. The great unforgivable sin is—to murder the love in a human being.

BORKMAN. And that's what you say I've done?

ELLA. You've done that. I've never truly realized before this evening exactly what it was that happened to me. That you abandoned me and turned instead to Gunhild—I took that as no more than a simple lack of constancy on your part, and the result of heartless calculation on hers. I almost think I despised you a little—in spite of everything. But *now* I see it! You abandoned the woman you *loved!* Me, me, me! The dearest that you had in this world you were ready to sign away for profit. It's a double murder you're guilty of! Murder of your own soul, and of mine!

BORKMAN (*with cold self-control*). How well I recognize that overbearing passion in you, Ella. I suppose it's very natural for you to see this the way you do. You're a woman. And so it seems, to your mind, that nothing else in the world exists or matters.

ELLA. Yes, nothing else.

BORKMAN. Only what touches your own heart.

ELLA. Only that! Only that! Yes.

BORKMAN. But you have to remember that I'm a man. As a woman, to me you were the dearest in the world. But in the last analysis, any woman can be replaced by another.

ELLA (*regarding him with a smile*). Was that your experience when you took Gunhild to marry?

BORKMAN. No. But my life's work helped me to bear *that*, too. All the sources of power in this country I wanted at my command. The earth, the mountains, the forests, the sea—I wanted to subjugate all the riches they held, and carve out a kingdom for myself, and use it to further the well-being of so many thousands of others.

ELLA (*lost in memory*). I know. All those many evenings that we talked about your plans—

BORKMAN. Yes, I could talk with you, Ella.

ELLA. I used to joke about your projects and ask if you wanted to wake all the slumbering spirits of the gold.

BORKMAN (*nods*). I remember the phrase. (*Slowly.*) All the slumbering spirits of the gold.

ELLA. But you didn't take it for a joke. You said: "Yes, yes, Ella; that's exactly what I want."

BORKMAN. And it was. If only I once could get my foot in the stirrup—and that depended then on this one man. He was able and willing to ensure my control of the bank—if, in return—

ELLA. Yes! If, in return, you gave up the woman you loved—and who loved you beyond expression—

BORKMAN. I knew his unbounded passion for you—and that no other condition would satisfy his—

ELLA. So you came to terms.

BORKMAN (*fervently*). Yes, Ella, I did! Because the rage for power was so relentless in me, don't you see? I came to terms. I *had* to. And he helped me halfway up toward the enticing heights I longed for. I climbed and climbed. Year upon year, I climbed—

ELLA. And I was erased from your life.

BORKMAN. But even so, he toppled me into the abyss. Because of you, Ella.

ELLA (*after a brief, reflective silence*). John Gabriel— doesn't it seem to you as if there's been a kind of curse on our whole relationship?

BORKMAN (*looks at her*). A curse?

ELLA. Yes. Don't you think so?

BORKMAN (*uneasily*). Yes. But why, really—? (*In an outburst.*) Oh, Ella—I scarcely know any longer who's right—you or I!

ELLA. You're the guilty one. You put to death all the natural joy in me.

BORKMAN (*anxiously*). Don't say that, Ella.

ELLA. All the joy a woman should know, at least. From the time your image began to fade in me, I've lived as if under an eclipse. Through all those years it's grown harder and harder—and finally impossible—for me to love any living creature. Not people, nor animals, nor plants. Only that one—

BORKMAN. Which one?

ELLA. Erhart, of course.

BORKMAN. Erhart—?

ELLA. Your son, John Gabriel.

BORKMAN. Has he meant all that to you, actually?

ELLA. Why else do you think I took him in, and kept him as long as I could? Why?

BORKMAN. I thought it was out of compassion. Like all the rest you've done.

ELLA (*reflecting powerful inner feeling*). Compassion, you say! (*With a laugh.*) I've never known any compassion—since you left me. I'm wholly incapable of that. If a poor, starving child came into my kitchen, freezing and weeping, and begged for a little food, then I left it up to my cook. I never felt any urge to take the child in myself, warm it at my own hearth, and enjoy sitting by, watching it eat its fill. And I was never like that in my youth; I remember so clearly. It's you who've made this sterile, empty desert within me—and around me, too.

BORKMAN. Except for Erhart.

ELLA. Yes, except for your son. But for all else, all that lives and moves. You've cheated me of a mother's joy and happiness in life. And of a mother's cares and tears as well. And maybe that's been the hardest loss.

BORKMAN. You'd say so, Ella?

ELLA. Who knows? A mother's cares and tears are perhaps what I've needed most. (*With still stronger feeling.*) But I couldn't reconcile myself to that loss. And that's why I took Erhart in. Won him completely. Won all of the warm, trusting heart of a child—until—oh!

BORKMAN. Until what?

ELLA. Until his mother—his physical mother, I mean—took him from me.

BORKMAN. He had to leave you, to live here in town.

ELLA (*wringing her hands*). Yes, but I can't stand the desolation! The emptiness! The loss of your son's heart!

BORKMAN (*a malignant look in his eyes*). Hm—I'm sure you haven't lost it, Ella. It's not easy to lose one's heart to anyone down below—on the ground floor.

ELLA. I've lost Erhart here. And *she's* won him back. Or

someone else has. That's clear enough from the letters he writes to me now and then.

BORKMAN. Are you here, then, to take him home with you?

ELLA. If that were only possible—!

BORKMAN. It's perfectly possible, if it's really what you want. You *do* have the first and greatest claim on him.

ELLA. Oh, claim, claim! What does a claim mean here? If he's not mine by his own free will, then I can't have him. And I must! I must have my child's heart now—whole and intact!

BORKMAN. You have to remember that Erhart's into his twenties. You could hardly figure on retaining his heart intact, as you put it, for very long.

ELLA (*with a sad smile*). It wouldn't have to be for very long.

BORKMAN. No? I would have thought, if you wanted something, you'd want it to the end of your days.

ELLA. I do. But that's why I say it wouldn't have to be for long.

BORKMAN (*startled*). What does that mean?

ELLA. You knew, of course, that I've been ill for the past few years?

BORKMAN. You have?

ELLA. You didn't know?

BORKMAN. No, actually not—

ELLA (*looks at him, surprised*). Erhart hasn't told you that?

BORKMAN. I honestly can't remember at the moment.

ELLA. Perhaps he's never mentioned me at all?

BORKMAN. Oh, I know he's talked about you. But the fact is, it's so seldom I see anything of him. Hardly ever. There's someone down below who keeps him away from me. Far away, you understand.

ELLA. You're positive of that?

BORKMAN. I know it for certain. (*Changing his tone.*) But Ella—you say you've been ill!

ELLA. Yes, I have. This past autumn it got so much worse, I decided I'd better come in and see some specialists.

BORKMAN. And have you seen them already?

ELLA. Yes, this morning.

BORKMAN. What did they say?

ELLA. They gave complete confirmation of what I'd long suspected—

BORKMAN. Well?

ELLA (*in a calm monotone*). The illness I have is terminal.

BORKMAN. Oh, you mustn't believe anything of the kind!

ELLA. It's an illness for which there's no help or cure. The doctors don't know any treatment. They just let it run its course. There's nothing they can do to arrest it. Just alleviate the pain a little, perhaps. And, of course, that's always something.

BORKMAN. But it can last for a long time still, believe me.

ELLA. It might possibly last out the winter, I've been told.

BORKMAN (*without thinking*). Well—the winters here are long.

ELLA (*quietly*). In any case, long enough for *me*.

BORKMAN (*animatedly, avoiding the subject*). But what on earth could have caused this illness? You've lived such a healthy, regular life—? What could have caused it?

ELLA (*looking at him*). The doctors concluded that perhaps, at some time, I'd undergone a severe emotional upheaval.

BORKMAN (*flaring up*). Emotional upheaval! Ah yes, I understand. It has to be *me* that's to blame!

ELLA (*with rising inner agitation*). It's too late to argue that now. But I *must* have the child of my heart, my one and only again, before I go! It's too inexpressibly mournful to think that I have to leave all that life is—leave the sun, the light, and the air, without leaving here behind me one single person who'll think of me and remember me warmly and tenderly—the way a son thinks, remembering the mother he's lost.

BORKMAN (*after a short pause*). Take him, Ella—if you can win him.

ELLA (*exhilarated*). You'll consent to it? *Can* you?

BORKMAN (*somberly*). Yes. It isn't much of a sacrifice. Because he's really not mine to give.

ELLA. Thank you, thank you for the sacrifice, even so! But then I've just one thing more to ask you for. Something big for me, John Gabriel.

BORKMAN. Well then, tell me.

ELLA. You may find it childish of me—and won't understand—

BORKMAN. Go on—tell me!

ELLA. Soon now, when I'm gone, there'll be a considerable inheritance—

BORKMAN. Yes, I would guess so.

ELLA. It's my intention to let it all go to Erhart.

BORKMAN. Well, you really have no one who's closer.

ELLA (*with warmth*). No, certainly no one closer than he.

BORKMAN. No one of your own family. You're the last of the line.

ELLA (*nodding slowly*). Yes, that's it, exactly. When I die, the Rentheim name dies as well. And to me, that's a torturing thought. To be erased from existence—even to one's very name—

BORKMAN (*incensed*). Ah—I see what you're after!

ELLA (*passionately*). Don't let it happen! Let Erhart carry on the name!

BORKMAN (*looking fiercely at her*). I quite understand. You want to spare my son the weight of his father's name. So that's it.

ELLA. No, never! I would have borne your name myself gladly, with pride, together with you! But a mother who's about to die— A name binds more than you could believe, John Gabriel.

BORKMAN (*coldly and proudly*). All right, Ella. I'll be man enough to bear my name alone.

ELLA (*grasping and pressing his hands*). Thank you, thank you! Now everything's made up between us. Yes, yes, I hope that's so! You've redeemed as much as you could. For when I'm gone, Erhart Rentheim will live on after me.

(*The tapestry door is thrown open.* MRS. BORKMAN, *with her large shawl over her head, stands in the doorway.*)

MRS. BORKMAN (*convulsively agitated*). Never in all eternity will Erhart take that name!

ELLA (*shrinking back*). Gunhild!

BORKMAN (*grimly threatening*). No one's permitted to come up here to me!

MRS. BORKMAN (*advancing a step*). I permit myself that.

BORKMAN (*moving toward her*). What do you want of me?

MRS. BORKMAN. I want to fight for you. Protect you from the evil powers.

BORKMAN. The worst of those powers are in yourself, Gunhild.

MRS. BORKMAN (*harshly*). Whatever you say. (*Menacingly.*) But *I* say, he'll carry on his father's name—and bear it high again, in honor. And I'll be his mother—I alone! My son's heart will belong to me. To me, and no one else.

(*She leaves through the tapestry door, closing it behind her.*)

ELLA (*shaken and distraught*). John Gabriel—Erhart's bound to go down in this storm. There's got to be some understanding between you and Gunhild. We must go down to her at once.

BORKMAN (*looks at her*). We? I, as well, you mean?

ELLA. You and I both.

BORKMAN (*shaking his head*). She's hard, Ella. Hard as the metal I once dreamed of tunneling out of the mountains.

ELLA. Then try—just try, now!

(BORKMAN *does not answer, as he stands looking at her, full of doubt.*)

❧ ACT THREE ❧

MRS. BORKMAN's *living room. The lamp is still burning on the table by the sofa. The garden room to the rear is now dark.* MRS. BORKMAN, *with the shawl over her head, enters through the hall door, profoundly shaken. She goes to the window and draws the curtain aside slightly; then she crosses over to sit in the armchair by the stove, but immediately springs to her feet again and goes to the bellpull and rings. For a moment she stands, waiting by the sofa. No one comes. She rings again, this time more violently. After some moments the* MAID *enters from the hall. She looks sleepy and ill-tempered and appears to have dressed in haste.*

MRS. BORKMAN (*impatiently*). What's become of you, Malene? I had to ring twice!

MAID. Yes, ma'am, I heard you.

MRS. BORKMAN. And still you didn't come.

MAID (*petulantly*). Well, I had to throw on a few clothes first, I guess.

MRS. BORKMAN. Yes, you dress yourself up properly. And then you've got to run over right away and fetch my son.

MAID (*staring at her in amazement*). Me—fetch Mr. Erhart?

MRS. BORKMAN. Yes. Just tell him he has to come home to me at once. That I have to speak with him.

MAID (*sullenly*). Then I guess I better go wake the coachman in the annex.

MRS. BORKMAN. Why?

MAID. So he can harness the sleigh. It's been an awful snowstorm tonight.

MRS. BORKMAN. Oh, that's nothing. Hurry up and go! It's only around the corner.

MAID. No, but, ma'am, that's not just around the corner.

MRS. BORKMAN. Why, of course it is. Don't you know where Mr. Hinkel's place is?

MAID (*sarcastically*). Oh, I see—is *that* where Mr. Erhart is tonight?

MRS. BORKMAN (*puzzled*). Where else would he be?

MAID (*suppressing a smile*). Oh, I only thought he was over where he usually is.

MRS. BORKMAN. Where do you mean?

MAID. At that Mrs. Wilton's, as they call her.

MRS. BORKMAN. Mrs. Wilton's? My son isn't there so often.

MAID (*under her breath*). There's some say he's there every day.

MRS. BORKMAN. That's a pack of nonsense, Malene. Now go over to Mr. Hinkel's and see that you get hold of him.

MAID (*tossing her head*). Oh, all right; I'm going.

(*She is on the verge of going out down the hall, when at that instant the hall door opens, and* ELLA RENTHEIM *and* BORKMAN *appear on the threshold.*)

MRS. BORKMAN (*recoils a step*). What does this mean?

MAID (*terrified, impulsively clasping her hands*). In Jesus' name!

MRS. BORKMAN (*whispering to her*). Tell him to come directly, at once!

MAID (*quietly*). Yes, ma'am.

(ELLA *and, behind her,* BORKMAN *come into the room. The*

MAID *steals around in back of them and out the door, shutting it after her. A brief silence.*)

MRS. BORKMAN (*again controlled, turning to* ELLA). What does he want in my room down here?

ELLA. He wants to try and reach some understanding with you, Gunhild.

MRS. BORKMAN. He's never tried to before.

ELLA. He wants to this evening.

MRS. BORKMAN. The last time we faced each other— was in court. When I was summoned to give an explanation—

BORKMAN (*approaching closer*). And tonight I'm the one who'll give an explanation.

MRS. BORKMAN (*looking at him*). You!

BORKMAN. Not about my offense. The whole world knows about that.

MRS. BORKMAN (*with a bitter sigh*). Yes, how true. The whole world knows.

BORKMAN. But it doesn't know why I committed it. Why I *had* to commit it. People don't understand that I had to because I was myself—John Gabriel Borkman—and no one else. That's what I want to try and explain to you.

MRS. BORKMAN (*shaking her head*). It's no use. Intentions acquit no one. Nor impulses, either.

BORKMAN. They can acquit a man in his own eyes.

MRS. BORKMAN (*with a gesture of dismissal*). Oh, let's be done with all this! I've pondered all those dark dealings of yours to the limit.

BORKMAN. So have I. Through five endless years in my cell—and elsewhere—I've had time enough for that. And with eight years in the salon upstairs, I've had more than enough time. I've retried the whole case—all to myself. I've reopened the proceedings again and again. I've been my own prosecutor, my own defender, and my own judge. More impartially than anybody else would be—that I'll wager. I've walked the floor up there, turning every detail of my actions over and over in my mind. I've scrutinized them backward and forward just as unsparingly and remorselessly as any lawyer. And the verdict I continually arrive at is this: that the only one I've committed an offense against—is myself.

MRS. BORKMAN. Not against me? Or your son?

BORKMAN. You and he are included in what I mean by myself.

MRS. BORKMAN. And what of those hundreds of others—the ones they say you ruined?

BORKMAN (*more intensely*). I had the power! And the relentless voices within me! The buried millions lay everywhere, deep in the mountains, all over the country, crying out to me, crying out to be freed! But not one of all the others heard. Only I, alone.

MRS. BORKMAN. Yes, to brand the name Borkman with dishonor.

BORKMAN. Who knows, if the others had had the power, whether they wouldn't have acted just as I did?

MRS. BORKMAN. No one, no one besides you could have done the same.

BORKMAN. Maybe not. But then that was because they lacked my abilities. And if they *had* done it, they couldn't have done it with *my* vision. The action would have to be different. In short, I've acquitted myself.

ELLA (*in a softly appealing tone*). Oh, how can you speak so surely, John Gabriel?

BORKMAN (*nodding*). Acquitted myself to *that* extent. But then comes the great, crushing self-accusation.

MRS. BORKMAN. What's that?

BORKMAN. I've holed myself away up there and wasted eight priceless years of my life! The very day I was released, I should have moved out into reality—iron-hard, dreamless reality! I should have begun at the bottom and raised myself up to the heights again—higher than ever before—in spite of what intervened.

MRS. BORKMAN. Oh, it would just be the same life all over again—believe me.

BORKMAN (*shakes his head and regards her with a didactic air*). Nothing new ever happens. But whatever has happened never repeats itself, either. It's the eye that transforms the action. The newborn eye transforms the old action. (*Breaking off.*) Ahh, you don't understand that.

MRS. BORKMAN (*brusquely*). No, I don't understand it.

BORKMAN. Yes, that's the curse, exactly: that I've never found understanding in any human soul.

ELLA (*looking at him*). Never, John Gabriel?

BORKMAN. With one exception—perhaps. Long, long ago, in the days when I didn't think I needed understanding. But since then, never, with anyone! I've had no one attentive enough to be near at hand, encouraging me— rousing me like a morning bell—urging me on once more to do inspired work. And confirming to me that I've done nothing irretrievable.

MRS. BORKMAN (*laughs contemptuously*). So—you need outside confirmation of that?

BORKMAN (*with gathering resentment*). Yes, when the whole world hisses in unison that I'm a man lost beyond recall, then I have moments when I'm almost ready to believe it myself. (*Lifting his head.*) But then my inner-most consciousness rises triumphant again. And that acquits me!

MRS. BORKMAN (*regarding him bitterly*). Why did you never come and ask me for what you call understanding?

BORKMAN. What use would it have been—coming to you!

MRS. BORKMAN (*with a gesture of dismissal*). You've never loved anything outside yourself—and that's the essence of it.

BORKMAN (*with pride*). I've loved power—

MRS. BORKMAN. Power, yes!

BORKMAN. The power to create human happiness for vast multitudes around me.

MRS. BORKMAN. You once had the power to make *me* happy. Have you used it for that?

BORKMAN (*not looking at her*). Someone very often has to go down—in a shipwreck.

MRS. BORKMAN. And your own son! Have you used your power, have you lived and labored, to make *him* happy?

BORKMAN. I don't know him.

MRS. BORKMAN. Yes, that's true. You don't even know him.

BORKMAN (*harshly*). You—you, his mother, took care of that.

MRS. BORKMAN (*regards him with an imperious air*). Oh, you have no idea what I've taken care of!

BORKMAN. You?

MRS. BORKMAN. Yes, I—I alone.

BORKMAN. Tell me.

MRS. BORKMAN. I've shaped your final reputation.

BORKMAN (*with a short, dry laugh*). My final reputation? Come now! That sounds as though I were already dead.

MRS. BORKMAN (*stressing her words*). And you are.

BORKMAN (*slowly*). Yes, maybe you're right. (*Flaring up.*) But no, no! Not yet! I've come so close, so close to it. But now I'm awake. Revived again. Life still reaches ahead of me. I can see that new and radiant life still waits there, beckoning. And you'll see it as well. You, too.

MRS. BORKMAN (*raising her hand*). No more dreams of life! Rest quietly where you lie.

ELLA (*appalled*). Gunhild! Gunhild, how could you—!

MRS. BORKMAN (*not listening to her*). I'll raise a monument over your grave.

BORKMAN. A memorial to shame, I suppose?

MRS. BORKMAN (*with swelling emotion*). Oh no, it won't be a marker of stone or metal. And no one will have a chance to carve a slurring inscription on the monument I'll raise. It will be as if a living fence, a woven hedge of trees and bushes was planted thick, thick around your buried life. All the dark of the past will be screened away; and all remembrance of John Gabriel Borkman will vanish into oblivion.

BORKMAN (*hoarsely and cuttingly*). And *that* work of love you'll carry out?

MRS. BORKMAN. Not through my own efforts. That's beyond me. But I've trained an assistant who'll focus his life on this one thing. His life will be so pure and brilliant and exalted that all your own grubbing in the dark will be wiped from this earth!

BORKMAN (*in grim warning*). If it's Erhart you mean, you better say so right now.

MRS. BORKMAN (*looking him straight in the eye*). Yes, it's Erhart. My son, that you're willing to relinquish—in penance for your failings.

BORKMAN (*with a glance at* ELLA). In penance for my greatest sin.

MRS. BORKMAN (*dismissing the thought*). A sin only against a stranger. Remember the sin against *me*! (*Looking exultantly at them both.*) But he won't listen to you! When I cry out to him in my need, then he'll come! For it's with *me* he wants to be! With me, and nobody else— (*Abruptly listens, then cries.*) There, I hear him! He's here—he's here! Erhart!

(ERHART BORKMAN *bursts open the hall door and comes into the room. He is wearing an overcoat and a hat on his head.*)

ERHART (*pale and anxious*). Mother—what in God's name—! (*He sees* BORKMAN, *standing by the doorway to the garden room, starts, and takes off his hat. A brief pause.*) What do you want me for, Mother? What happened?

MRS. BORKMAN (*stretching out her arms toward him*). I want to see you, Erhart! I want to have you with me—always!

ERHART (*stammering*). Have me—? Always! What do you mean?

MRS. BORKMAN. To have you! I want to have you—because there's someone trying to take you from me!

ERHART (*falls back a step*). Ah—then you know?

MRS. BORKMAN. Yes. But *you* know, too?

ERHART (*surprised, looking at her*). Do *I* know? Why, naturally—

MRS. BORKMAN. So! Plotting—behind my back! Erhart, Erhart!

ERHART (*quickly*). Mother, tell me, what is it you know?

MRS. BORKMAN. I know everything. I know that your aunt's come here to take you away from me.

ERHART. Aunt Ella!

ELLA. Oh, listen to *me* a while first, Erhart!

MRS. BORKMAN (*continuing*). She wants me to give you over to her. She wants to assume your mother's place, Erhart! She wants you to be her son hereafter, and not mine. She wants you to inherit everything she owns, and to drop your own name for hers instead!

ERHART. Aunt Ella, is all this true?

ELLA. Yes, it's true.

ERHART. I didn't know any of this till now. Why do you want me back with you?

ELLA. Because I feel I'm losing you here.

MRS. BORKMAN (*harshly*). Losing him to me—yes! And that's just as it ought to be.

ELLA (*looks imploringly at him*). Erhart, I can't afford to lose you. You must be aware that I'm a lonely—dying woman.

ERHART. Dying—?

ELLA. Yes, dying. Will you stay with me to the end? Commit yourself wholly to me—as if you were my own child—?

MRS. BORKMAN (*breaking in*). And abandon your mother and perhaps your mission in life as well? Do you want that, Erhart?

ELLA. I'm condemned to die. Answer me, Erhart.

ERHART (*warmly, moved*). Aunt Ella—you've been good to me beyond words. With you I was able to grow up in as much carefree happiness as I think any child could have known—

MRS. BORKMAN. Erhart, Erhart!

ELLA. What a blessing that you still feel that way!

ERHART. But I can't sacrifice myself for you now. It's impossible for me simply to give myself over to being a son to you—

MRS. BORKMAN (*triumphantly*). Ah, I knew it! You won't get him! You won't get him, Ella!

ELLA (*heavily*). I see. You *have* won him back.

MRS. BORKMAN. Yes, yes—he's mine, and he'll stay mine! It's true, isn't it, Erhart—the two of us still have a long way to go together?

ERHART (*struggling with himself*). Mother—I might just as well tell you right now—

MRS. BORKMAN (*tensely*). Yes?

ERHART. It's only a short distance more we'll be going together, you and I.

MRS. BORKMAN (*as if physically struck*). What does *that* mean?

ERHART (*mustering his courage*). My God, Mother— I'm young! The air here in this room—I feel it's going to smother me completely.

MRS. BORKMAN. Here—with me!

ERHART. Yes, here with you, Mother!

ELLA. Then come with me, Erhart!

ERHART. Oh, Aunt Ella, it's not one shade better with you. It would be different there. But not better. Not for me. It's roses and lavender—stale indoor air, exactly like here.

MRS. BORKMAN (*shaken, but with composure reestablished*). The air is stale here, you say?

ERHART (*with mounting impatience*). Oh, I don't know what else to call it. All this morbid concern about me, this—this idolatry, or whatever it is. I can't take it any longer!

MRS. BORKMAN (*with a look of profound solemnity*). Are you forgetting what you've dedicated your life to, Erhart?

ERHART (*vehemently*). Oh, you mean what *you've* dedicated my life to! You've been my will! I've never been allowed to have one of my own. But I won't wear these chains any longer! I'm young! You've got to remember that, Mother. (*With a polite, respectful glance at* BORK-MAN.) I can't dedicate my life to someone else's atonement—no matter who that someone may be.

MRS. BORKMAN (*gripped by a gathering dread*). Who is it that's changed you, Erhart?

ERHART (*caught*). Who—? Couldn't it be that, all on my own, I—

MRS. BORKMAN. No, no, no! There's some strange power that's over you. You're not under your mother's influence anymore. Nor your—your foster mother's, either.

ERHART (*with effortful defiance*). I know my own strength now, Mother. And my own will, too!

BORKMAN (*approaching* ERHART). Then perhaps my time has finally come.

ERHART (*with a distant, formal courtesy*). What—? What do you mean, sir?

MRS. BORKMAN (*contemptuously*). Yes, and I'd certainly like to hear.

BORKMAN (*continues calmly*). Listen, Erhart—would you consider going in with your father? No man can find restitution through somebody's else's career. That's just an empty dream that's been spun for you here—down in this stale indoor air. Even if you could manage to live a life like all the saints put together, it wouldn't help me one particle.

ERHART (*deferentially*). That's just as you say.

BORKMAN. Yes, it is. And it wouldn't help either if I let myself wilt away in penance and contrition. I've tried to nurse myself along through all these years on hopes and dreams; but they've done me no earthly good. And now I want to shed my dreams.

ERHART (*bowing slightly*). And what—what will you do, sir?

BORKMAN. Reestablish myself, that's what. Begin from the bottom again. It's only by his present and his future that a man can expiate the past. By work—by unremitting work for everything that, in my youth, meant more to me than life itself. And that means now a thousand times more. Erhart—would you go in with your father and help me win this new life?

MRS. BORKMAN (*raising her hand in warning*). Don't do it, Erhart!

ELLA (*warmly*). Yes, yes, do it! Oh, help him, Erhart!

MRS. BORKMAN. And that's *your* advice? You—alone and dying—

ELLA. It doesn't matter about me.

MRS. BORKMAN. Yes, just so *I'm* not the one who takes him from you.

ELLA. Precisely, Gunhild.

BORKMAN (*to* ERHART). What do you say?

ERHART (*painfully distressed*). Father, I can't, not now. It's totally impossible.

BORKMAN. Well, what *do* you want then?

ERHART (*in a blaze of emotion*). I'm young! I want my chance to live, for once! I want to live my own life!

ELLA. But not to give up a few short months to lighten the last days of an unhappy life.

ERHART. As much as I wish to, Aunt Ella, I can't.

ELLA. Not for someone who loves you beyond words?

ERHART. As I live and breathe, I tell you—I can't.

MRS. BORKMAN (*looking intensely at him*). And your mother can't hold you now, either?

ERHART. Mother, I'll always love you. But I can't continue living for you alone. Because that isn't life for me.

BORKMAN. Then why not come in with me! Because life is work, Erhart. Come, let's the two of us take life on and work together!

ERHART (*passionately*). Yes, but I don't *want* to work now! Because I'm young! I've never known what that meant before, but now I feel it surging through every fiber of me. I *will* not work! Just live, live, live!

MRS. BORKMAN (*with a cry of premonition*). Erhart—
what will you live for?

ERHART (*his eyes kindling*). For happiness, Mother!

MRS. BORKMAN. And where do you think you can find
that?

ERHART. I've found it already!

MRS. BORKMAN (*in a shriek*). Erhart—!

(ERHART *strides quickly over to the hall door and opens
it.*)

ERHART (*calls*). Fanny—you can come in now.

(MRS. WILTON, *in her winter coat, appears in the doorway.*)

MRS. BORKMAN (*her hands upraised*). Mrs. Wilton—!

MRS. WILTON (*rather shyly, with a questioning glance
at* ERHART). Can I then—?

ERHART. Yes, now you can. I've said everything.

(MRS. WILTON *enters the room,* ERHART *closing the door
after her. She bows politely to* BORKMAN, *who silently returns the greeting. A brief pause.*)

MRS. WILTON (*in a subdued, but firm voice*). So the
words have been said. Then I guess I stand here as
someone who's inflicted a great catastrophe on this house.

MRS. BORKMAN (*slowly, looking rigidly at her*). You've
shattered the last remnants of what I had to live for. (*In
an outburst.*) But this—this is all so utterly impossible!

MRS. WILTON. I understand very well, Mrs. Borkman,
that this must seem impossible to you.

MRS. BORKMAN. Yes, you must be able to see that
yourself, that it's impossible.

MRS. WILTON. Implausible, utterly implausible—I'd prefer to call it that. But, nevertheless, it *is.*

MRS. BORKMAN (*turning*). Are you completely serious
about this, Erhart?

ERHART. This is happiness to me, Mother. The greatest,
loveliest happiness of life. I can't tell you more than that.

MRS. BORKMAN (*to* MRS. WILTON, *wringing her hands*).

Oh, the way you've inveigled and seduced my unfortunate son!

MRS. WILTON (*tossing her head proudly*). I've done nothing of the kind.

MRS. BORKMAN. Oh, haven't you!

MRS. WILTON. No. Neither inveigled nor seduced him. Erhart's come to me of his own free will. And I've met him freely halfway.

MRS. BORKMAN (*eyeing her up and down with contempt*). Yes! Oh yes, that I can well believe!

MRS. WILTON (*restraining herself*). Mrs. Borkman— there are forces in human life that you seem to know singularly little of.

MRS. BORKMAN. What forces, might I ask?

MRS. WILTON. The forces that impel two people to unite their lives indissolubly—without fearing the consequences.

MRS. BORKMAN (*smiles*). I thought you were already indissolubly united—to someone else.

MRS. WILTON (*curtly*). That someone deserted me.

MRS. BORKMAN. But he's still living, they say.

MRS. WILTON. He's dead to *me*.

ERHART (*incisively*). Yes, Mother, for Fanny he's dead. Moreover, this other man has nothing to do with me.

MRS. BORKMAN (*looking severely at him*). You know about him, then—this other man.

ERHART. Yes, I know. I know all about it, completely!

MRS. BORKMAN. And even so, you say it has nothing to do with you?

ERHART (*with airy disdain*). I can only tell you, it's happiness I want! I'm young! I want to live, live, live!

MRS. BORKMAN. Yes, you're young, Erhart. Much too young for this.

MRS. WILTON. Don't think, Mrs. Borkman, I haven't told him just that. I've laid out my whole life story for him. I've reminded him repeatedly that I'm a full seven years older than he—

ERHART (*interrupting*). Oh, look, Fanny—I knew that at the start.

MRS. WILTON. But nothing, nothing does any good.

MRS. BORKMAN. Really? Not at all? Then why didn't you dismiss him flat? Close your house to him? You know, you could have done that in good time.

MRS. WILTON (*looks at her and says softly*). I simply couldn't, Mrs. Borkman.

MRS. BORKMAN. Why not?

MRS. WILTON. Because my happiness was at stake in him, too.

MRS. BORKMAN (*scornfully*). Hm—happiness, happiness—

MRS. WILTON. I've never before known what happiness is in life. And I can't possibly turn it away, just because it came so late.

MRS. BORKMAN. And how long do you think this happiness will endure?

ERHART (*interrupting*). Short or long, Mother—what's the difference?

MRS. BORKMAN (*furious*). What a blind fool you are! Can't you see where all this is leading?

ERHART. I don't want to consider the future. Or be farsighted in any direction! I just want the chance to live my own life for once!

MRS. BORKMAN (*pained*). And you call that life, Erhart!

ERHART. Yes, don't you see how lovely she is?

MRS. BORKMAN (*clenching her fists*). And *this* burden of shame, then, I'll have to bear, too.

BORKMAN (*from the back of the room, brusquely incisive*). Ha! You're well practiced in that sort of thing, Gunhild!

ELLA (*imploringly*). John Gabriel—!

ERHART (*similarly*). Father—!

MRS. BORKMAN. Here I'm condemned to go on day by day, seeing my son with a—a—

ERHART (*breaking in fiercely*). You'll see nothing like that, Mother—rest assured! I'm not staying here any longer.

MRS. WILTON (*briskly and decisively*). We're going away, Mrs. Borkman.

MRS. BORKMAN (*turning pale*). Going away! Together, I suppose?

MRS. WILTON (*nods*). I'm traveling south, yes. Abroad. Together with a young girl. And Erhart's going with us.

MRS. BORKMAN. With you—and a young girl?

MRS. WILTON. Yes. It's that little Frida Foldal that I took into my house. I want her to go abroad and develop her music.

MRS. BORKMAN. So you're taking her with you.

MRS. WILTON. Yes. I could hardly send the child down there all on her own.

MRS. BORKMAN (*suppressing a smile*). What do *you* say to *that,* Erhart?

ERHART (*somewhat ill at ease, with a shrug*). Well, Mother—if that's how Fanny wants it to be, then—

MRS. BORKMAN (*coldly*). When will this entourage be leaving, might I ask?

MRS. WILTON. We're departing immediately, tonight. My sleigh is waiting—over at the Hinkels'.

MRS. BORKMAN (*scanning her*). I see—so that was the evening party.

MRS. WILTON (*smiling*). Yes, no one but Erhart and me. And Frida, of course.

MRS. BORKMAN. And where is she now?

MRS. WILTON. Sitting in the sleigh, waiting.

ERHART (*painfully embarrassed*). Mother—I hope you understand—? I wanted to spare you—spare everyone—all of this.

MRS. BORKMAN (*looks at him, deeply injured*). You would have left me without saying good-bye?

ERHART. Yes. I thought it was best that way. Best on

both sides. Everything was ready to go. Our bags were packed. But then when you sent that message for me, well— (*Reaches his hands out toward her.*) Good-bye then, Mother.

MRS. BORKMAN (*averting herself, with a gesture of repulsion*). Don't touch me!

ERHART (*gently*). Is that your last word?

MRS. BORKMAN (*austerely*). Yes.

ERHART (*turning*). And good-bye to you, Aunt Ella.

ELLA (*pressing his hands*). Good-bye, Erhart! Live your life—and be as happy—just as happy as you can!

ERHART. Thanks, Aunt Ella. (*Bows to* BORKMAN.) Good-bye, Father. (*Whispers to* MRS. WILTON.) Let's get away now, the quicker the better.

MRS. WILTON (*softly*). Yes, let's.

MRS. BORKMAN (*with a malevolent smile*). Mrs. Wilton —do you think you're very wise, taking that young girl along with you?

MRS. WILTON (*returns the smile, half ironically, half seriously*). Men are so variable, Mrs. Borkman. And women likewise. When Erhart is finished with me—and I with him—then it'll be good for both of us that he, poor boy, has someone to fall back on.

MRS. BORKMAN. But you yourself?

MRS. WILTON. Oh, I'll arrange for myself, don't worry. Good-bye, all of you!

(*She bows slightly and goes out the hall door.* ERHART *stands a moment as though faltering; then he turns and follows her.*)

MRS. BORKMAN (*her folded hands dropping*). Childless.

BORKMAN (*as if awakening into resolution*). Out into the storm alone then! My hat! My coat! (*He moves rapidly toward the door.*)

ELLA (*in terror, stopping him*). John Gabriel, where are you going?

BORKMAN. Out in the storm of life, you hear. Let go, Ella!

ELLA (*gripping him tightly*). No, no, I won't let you go out. You're ill. I can see that.

BORKMAN. I said, let me go! (*He tears himself loose and goes out down the hall.*)

ELLA (*in the doorway*). Help me to hold him, Gunhild!

MRS. BORKMAN (*remains standing in the middle of the room; cold and hard*). There's nobody in this world that I'm going to hold. Let them all leave me. This one and that. As far—as far as ever they want. (*Suddenly, with a rending cry.*) Erhart, don't go!

(*She rushes with outstretched arms toward the door.* ELLA RENTHEIM *stops her.*)

⤙ ACT FOUR ⤚

A stretch of open ground outside the main building, which lies to the right. One of its corners, including a flight of stone steps leading to the entrance door, projects out. Extending across the background near the edge of the open land, steep slopes covered with fir trees. To the left, scattered trees, the beginnings of a small woods. The snowstorm has ended, but the earth is deeply buried under the new-fallen snow. The fir branches hang heavy under its weight. The night is dark with scudding clouds. Occasionally a pale glimmer of the moon shines through. The surroundings are visible only in the faint light reflected by the snow.

BORKMAN, MRS. BORKMAN, *and* ELLA RENTHEIM *are standing on the steps.* BORKMAN *leans wearily against the wall of the house. He has an old-fashioned cape thrown over his shoulders and holds a soft gray felt hat in one hand, a thick, gnarled walking stick in the other.* ELLA *carries her coat on her arm.* MRS. BORKMAN's *large shawl has slipped down about her neck, leaving her hair uncovered.*

ELLA (*barring* MRS. BORKMAN's *path*). Don't go after him, Gunhild!

MRS. BORKMAN (*panic-stricken*). Out of my way, you! He mustn't leave me!

ELLA. I tell you, it's totally useless! You'll never catch up to him.

MRS. BORKMAN. I don't care; let me go, Ella! I'll scream

after him down the road. He's got to hear his mother's cry!

ELLA. He can't hear you. He's already sitting in the sleigh—

MRS. BORKMAN. No, no—he couldn't have reached the sleigh!

ELLA. He's been in the sleigh for some time, believe me!

MRS. BORKMAN (*in desperation*). If he's in the sleigh, then he's sitting by her, by her—her!

BORKMAN (*laughs darkly*). Then he won't likely hear his mother scream.

MRS. BORKMAN. No—then he won't hear. (*Listens.*) Shh! What's that?

ELLA (*also listening*). That sounds like sleigh bells—

MRS. BORKMAN (*with a stifled moan*). It's *her* sleigh!

ELLA. It could be somebody else's—

MRS. BORKMAN. No, no, it's Mrs. Wilton's sleigh! Those silver bells, I know them. Listen! Now they're driving right past us—at the foot of the hill.

ELLA (*hurriedly*). Gunhild, if you want to call to him, do it *now!* Maybe he still might— (*The sleigh bells sound close at hand within the woods.*) Quick, Gunhild! They're down there below us right now!

MRS. BORKMAN (*stands indecisively a moment; then stiffens, hard and cold*). No, I won't cry after him. Let Erhart Borkman go from me—far, far off into what he now calls life and happiness.

(*The sound fades in the distance.*)

ELLA (*after a moment*). You can't hear them anymore.

MRS. BORKMAN. To me they sounded like funeral bells.

BORKMAN (*with dry, hushed laughter*). Ah—they're not ringing for *me* yet.

MRS. BORKMAN. But for *me.* And for him that left me.

ELLA (*nodding pensively*). Who knows, Gunhild—they could be ringing in life and happiness for him, after all.

MRS. BORKMAN (*with a start; stares at her*). Life and happiness—?

ELLA. For a brief while, anyway.

MRS. BORKMAN. Would you wish him life and happiness —with *her?*

ELLA (*fervently*). Yes, I would, from the bottom of my heart!

MRS. BORKMAN (*coldly*). You must be richer than I, then, in the power to love.

ELLA (*looking far off*). Maybe it's lack of love that nourishes the power.

MRS. BORKMAN (*fastens her eyes on her*). If that's so, Ella—then I'll soon be as rich as you.

(*She turns and goes into the house.* ELLA *stands a moment, looking with concern at* BORKMAN; *then she lays her hand lightly on his shoulder.*)

ELLA. John, do come inside. You, too.

BORKMAN (*as if awakening*). I?

ELLA. Yes. You can't take this raw winter air—you're showing the cold, John. Come on now; go in with me. Inside, where it's warm.

BORKMAN (*angrily*). You mean, up in that salon again?

ELLA. No, downstairs instead, with her.

BORKMAN (*seething with rage*). I'll never set foot under that roof again.

ELLA. But where will you go then? It's late in the night, John.

BORKMAN (*puts on his hat*). First of all, I want to go out and have a look at my buried treasures.

ELLA (*regarding him anxiously*). John—I don't understand you!

BORKMAN (*with a coughing laugh*). Oh, I don't mean any stowed-away embezzlings. Don't worry about that, Ella. (*Stops and points.*) Look, a man, *there!* Who *is* it?

(VILHELM FOLDAL, *in an old, snow-spattered greatcoat, with his hat-brim turned down and a large umbrella in his hand, appears, making his way with difficulty toward the corner of the house. He limps markedly on his left foot.*)

BORKMAN. Vilhelm! What are you doing back here?

FOLDAL (*looks up*). Good Lord—you're out on the steps, John Gabriel? (*Bows.*) And Mrs. Borkman, too, I see.

BORKMAN (*curtly*). This isn't my wife.

FOLDAL. Oh, excuse me. The thing is, I lost my glasses in the snow. But what's brought you, who never go out of doors—?

BORKMAN (*with a careless gaiety*). It's about time I became an outdoorsman again, don't you think? Nearly three years in detention; five years in the cell; eight years in that salon up there—

ELLA (*with concern*). John Gabriel—please—!

FOLDAL. Ah me, yes, yes—

BORKMAN. But what do you want of me?

FOLDAL (*remains standing at the foot of the steps*). I wanted to see you, John Gabriel. I felt I *had* to come up and see you in the salon. Dear me, that salon—!

BORKMAN. Wanted to see me, after I showed you the door?

FOLDAL. Good Lord, that's not important.

BORKMAN. What did you do to your foot? You were limping.

FOLDAL. Yes, you know what—I was run over.

ELLA. Run over!

FOLDAL. Yes, by a sleigh.

BORKMAN. Aha!

FOLDAL. With two horses. They came sweeping down the hill. I couldn't get out of the way fast enough, and so—

ELLA. So they ran over you.

FOLDAL. They bore right down on me, Mrs.—or Miss. Right down on me, so that I rolled in the snow and lost my glasses and got my umbrella broken— (*Rubs his leg.*) —and injured my foot a bit, too.

BORKMAN (*laughs silently*). You know who was in that sleigh, Vilhelm?

FOLDAL. No, how could I see? It was a closed sleigh, and the curtains were drawn. And the coachman didn't slow one iota when I went spinning. But what's the difference, because— (*Impulsively.*) Oh, I'm so wonderfully happy!

BORKMAN. Happy?

FOLDAL. Well, I really don't know what to call it. But the nearest word for it is happy. Because something so extraordinary has happened! And that's why I *couldn't* resist—why I simply *had* to come back and share my joy with you, John Gabriel.

BORKMAN (*gruffly*). Well, let's have my share, then.

ELLA. Invite your friend in with you first, John Gabriel.

BORKMAN (*adamantly*). I told you, I'm not going into that house.

ELLA. But you heard that he's been run over!

BORKMAN. Oh, we all get run over—sometime in life. But then you have to pick yourself up. And pretend it was nothing.

FOLDAL. Those were deep words, John Gabriel. But I can just as well tell you quickly out here.

BORKMAN (*more gently*). Yes, if you'd be so kind, Vilhelm.

FOLDAL. Well, listen to this! When I got home this evening from your place—would you believe it?—I found a letter. Can you guess who it was from?

BORKMAN. From your little Frida perhaps?

FOLDAL. Exactly! To think, you guessed it right off! Yes, it was a long—a fairly long letter from Frida. A servant had brought it. And can you imagine what she wrote?

BORKMAN. Was it possibly a farewell message to her parents?

FOLDAL. Precisely! It's incredible the way you can guess, John Gabriel! Yes, she wrote that Mrs. Wilton had taken such a great liking for her. And now she wants to travel abroad with her. So Frida can study more music, she writes. And Mrs. Wilton's arranged for a highly capable tutor to go along to give Frida private instruction. Because, unfortunately, she's fallen behind a bit in some of her subjects, you see.

BORKMAN (*shaking with silent laughter*). Why, yes, yes, I see the whole thing amazingly well.

FOLDAL (*continues enthusiastically*). And just think, she only found out about the trip this evening. That was at the party that you know—uh, hm! And still she took time to write. And the letter's so warm and so beautiful and so heartfelt; it really is. Not a trace of contempt for her father. And what a thoughtful gesture, her wanting to say good-bye to us in writing—before she went. (*Laughs.*) But we can't have anything like *that*!

BORKMAN (*looks inquiringly at him*). Like what?

FOLDAL. She writes that they're leaving tomorrow, quite early.

BORKMAN. I see, I see—tomorrow. She writes that?

FOLDAL (*laughs and rubs his hands*). Yes, but I'm the sly one, see! I'm on my way right now to Mrs. Wilton's—

BORKMAN. Tonight?

FOLDAL. My goodness, yes. It still isn't so very late. And if the house is dark, I'll ring. Without hesitation. For I will and I must see Frida before she leaves. Good night, good night! (*He starts off.*)

BORKMAN. Vilhelm, listen—you can save yourself that hard piece of road.

FOLDAL. Oh, you mean my foot—

BORKMAN. Yes, and you'll never get in anyway at Mrs. Wilton's.

FOLDAL. Oh, I will definitely. I'll keep on ringing and ringing till somebody comes and opens up. Because I simply have to see Frida.

ELLA. Your daughter's already left, Mr. Foldal.

FOLDAL (*thunderstruck*). Frida's left, already! Are you positive? Who told you that?

BORKMAN. Her future tutor.

FOLDAL. Oh? And who's he?

BORKMAN. A student named Erhart Borkman.

FOLDAL (*radiant with delight*). Your son, John Gabriel! Is *he* going with them?

BORKMAN. That's right. He's the one who'll help Mrs. Wilton with your little Frida's education.

FOLDAL. Well, thank God! Then the child's in the best of hands. But is it really for certain that they've left already with her?

BORKMAN. They drove off in the sleigh that ran you down.

FOLDAL (*clasps his hands*). Imagine, my little Frida in that elegant sleigh!

BORKMAN (*nods*). Oh yes, Vilhelm—your daughter's riding high these days. And son Erhart as well. Did you notice those silver bells?

FOLDAL. Well, now—silver bells, you say. Were they silver bells? Genuine, solid silver?

BORKMAN. You can bet your life they were. Everything was solid. Both outside and—and in.

FOLDAL (*with quiet feeling*). Isn't it curious, the way good fortune can unfold for a person? It's my—my frail talent for poetry that's transformed itself to music in Frida. So really, it hasn't come to nothing that I've been a poet. For now she has her chance to go out in the great, wide world that I once dreamed so hopefully of seeing. Little Frida, riding in a closed sleigh. And with silver bells on the harness—

BORKMAN. And riding down her father—

FOLDAL (*joyously*). Oh, now! What's that to me—as long as the child— Well, so I did come too late, after all. I'd better go home then and comfort her mother, who's sitting in the kitchen, crying.

BORKMAN. She's crying?

FOLDAL. Yes, can you imagine? She was crying as if her heart would break when I left.

BORKMAN. And you laugh, Vilhelm.

FOLDAL. Quite so, I do! But she, poor thing, she doesn't know any better, you see. Well, good-bye. It's lucky I have the streetcar so near. Good-bye, good-bye, John Gabriel! Good-bye, miss! (*He bows and hobbles back the same way he came.*)

BORKMAN (*stands silently a moment, gazing into space*). Good-bye, Vilhelm! It's not the first time in life you've been run over, old friend.

ELLA (*looks at him with suppressed anxiety*). You're so pale, so pale, John—

BORKMAN. That's from the prison air upstairs.

ELLA. I've never seen you like this before.

BORKMAN. Probably because you've never seen an escaped convict before.

ELLA. Oh, please, John, come in with me now!

BORKMAN. You can drop the cajoling voice. I've already told you—

(*The* MAID *appears out on the steps.*)

MAID. Begging your pardon, but Madam has said I should lock up the front door now.

BORKMAN (*in an undertone to* ELLA). Hear that! Now they want to lock me in again.

ELLA (*to the* MAID). The master isn't too well. He'd like a little fresh air first.

MAID. Yes, but Madam said to me herself—

ELLA. I'll lock up the door. Just leave the key in it—

MAID. Oh, all right then; that's what I'll do. (*She goes back into the house.*)

BORKMAN (*stands quietly a moment, listening, then goes hurriedly down onto the open ground*). Now I'm outside the walls, Ella. They'll never get me again!

ELLA (*going down beside him*). But you're a free man in there, too, John. You can come and go as you will.

BORKMAN (*hushed, as if in fright*). Under a roof for the last time! It's so good being out here in the night. If I went up in the salon now, the ceiling and walls would close in and crush me—grind me flat as a fly—

ELLA. But where will you go?

BORKMAN. Just walk and walk and walk. See if I can

win my way through to freedom, and life, and people again. Will you go with me, Ella?

ELLA. I? Now?

BORKMAN. Yes, yes—at once!

ELLA. But how far?

BORKMAN. As far as I can manage.

ELLA. Oh, but what are you thinking! Out in this wet, cold winter night—

BORKMAN (*in a hoarse, rasping voice*). Aha—the lady's worried about her health? Yes, of course—it *is* fragile.

ELLA. It's *your* health I'm worried about.

BORKMAN (*with a laugh*). A dead man's health! I have to laugh at you, Ella! (*He walks farther on.*)

ELLA (*follows him and holds him back*). What did you say you were?

BORKMAN. I said, a dead man. Don't you remember Gunhild telling me to rest quietly where I lay?

ELLA (*decisively, throwing her coat about her*). I'll go with you, John.

BORKMAN. Yes, we two, we really belong together, Ella. (*Proceeds farther.*) Come on!

(*Little by little they enter the low trees to the left, which increasingly conceal them until they disappear from sight. The house and the open land are lost to view. The landscape, with its slopes and ridges, alters slowly and becomes wilder and wilder.*)

ELLA'S VOICE (*heard from within the trees, right*). Where are we going, John? I don't know where this is.

BORKMAN'S VOICE (*higher up*). Keep following my footprints in the snow.

ELLA'S VOICE. But why do we need to climb so high?

BORKMAN'S VOICE (*nearer*). We have to go up the winding path.

ELLA (*still hidden*). Oh, I'm not good for much more.

BORKMAN (*at the edge of the forest, right*). Come on!

We're not far now from the view. There used to be a
bench here once—

ELLA (*becoming visible through the trees*). You remember that?

BORKMAN. You can rest yourself there.

(*They have emerged in a small clearing, high in the
woods. The slope rises sharply behind them. To the left,
far below, is an expansive landscape, with fjords and high,
distant mountain ranges towering one after another. In the
clearing at the left is a dead fir-tree, with a bench beneath
it. The snow lies deep on the ground.* BORKMAN *and, behind him,* ELLA *struggle across from the right through the
snow.*)

BORKMAN (*stops where the clearing falls off at the left*).
Come here, Ella, so you can see.

ELLA (*joining him*). What do you want to show me,
John?

BORKMAN (*pointing out*). You see how the land lies
before us, free and open—all the way out.

ELLA. We often used to sit on that bench—and look
even farther still.

BORKMAN. It was a dreamland we were seeing then.

ELLA. The dreamland of our lives, yes. And now it's a
land of snow. And the old tree is dead.

BORKMAN (*not hearing her*). Can you see the smoke
from the great steamers out on the fjord?

ELLA. No.

BORKMAN. I can. They come and they go. They make
this whole round earth into one community. They spread
light and warmth into human hearts in countless thousands
of homes. *That's* the thing I dreamed of doing.

ELLA (*softly*). And it stayed a dream.

BORKMAN. It stayed a dream, yes. (*Listening.*) Hear
that? Down by the river, the factories whirring! *My* factories! All the ones *I* would have built! Can you hear how
they're going? It's the night shift. Night and day they're
working. Listen, listen! The wheels are spinning, and the

gears are gleaming—around and around! Don't you hear them, Ella?

ELLA. No.

BORKMAN. *I* hear them.

ELLA (*fearfully*). I think you're mistaken, John.

BORKMAN (*more and more exhilarated*). Oh, but all this —it's only a kind of outworks enclosing the kingdom, you know!

ELLA. The kingdom? What kingdom?

BORKMAN. My kingdom, of course! The kingdom I was on the verge of possessing when I—when I died.

ELLA (*quietly shaken*). Oh, John, John!

BORKMAN. And now it lies there—defenseless, leaderless —exposed to the rape and plunder of thieves—! Ella! Do you see those mountain ranges *there*—far off. One after another. They leap skyward. They tower in space. That's my deep, my endless, inexhaustible kingdom!

ELLA. Yes, but John, the wind blows ice-cold from that kingdom!

BORKMAN. That wind works on me like the breath of life. It comes to me like a greeting from captive spirits. I can sense them, the buried millions. I feel the veins of metal, reaching their curving, branching, beckoning arms out to me. I saw them before me like living shadows—the night I stood in the bank vault with a lantern in my hand. You wanted your freedom then—and I tried to set you free. But I lacked the strength for it. Your treasures sank back in the depths. (*His hands outstretched.*) But I'll whisper to you here in the silence of the night. I love you, lying there unconscious in the depths and the darkness! I love you, you riches straining to be born—with all your shining aura of power and glory! I love you, love you, love you!

ELLA (*with constrained but mounting agitation*). Yes, your love is still down there, John. That's where it's always been. But up here in the daylight—here there was a warm, living human heart that beat for you. And this heart you crushed. Oh, more than that! Ten times worse! You *sold* it for—for—

BORKMAN (*a cold tremor seems to go through him*). For the kingdom—and the power—and the glory—you mean?

ELLA. Yes, it's what I mean. I said it once before to you this evening: you've murdered the capacity to love in the woman that loved you. And that you loved in return—as far as you *could* love anyone. (*Her arm upraised.*) And so I prophesy this for you, John Gabriel Borkman—you'll never win the prize you murdered for. You'll never ride in triumph into your cold, dark kingdom!

BORKMAN (*falters over to the bench and sinks down heavily*). I'm almost afraid your prophecy is right, Ella.

ELLA (*over beside him*). It's nothing to be afraid of, John. It would be exactly the best that could ever happen to you.

BORKMAN (*with a cry, clutches his chest*). Ah—! (*Faintly.*) There it let me go.

ELLA (*shaking him*). What was it, John?

BORKMAN (*slumps against the back of the bench*). A hand of ice—that choked my heart.

ELLA. John! Now you feel it, the ice hand!

BORKMAN (*murmurs*). No—no ice hand. It was a hand of metal. (*He slides down upon the bench.*)

ELLA (*tearing her coat off and spreading it over him*). Lie still and rest quietly! I'll go for help. (*She moves several steps to the right, then stops, returns, and feels his pulse and his face for a long moment.*) No. It's best, John Borkman. Best like this for you. (*She tucks the coat more tightly around him and sits down in the snow in front of the bench.*)

(*After a short silence,* MRS. BORKMAN, *wrapped in her overcoat, comes through the snow from the right. The* MAID *goes ahead of her with a lit lantern.*)

MAID (*shining the light on the snow*). Oh, yes, ma'am. It's their footprints here—

MRS. BORKMAN (*peering about*). Yes, there they are! Over there on the bench. (*Calls.*) Ella!

ELLA (*getting up*). Are you searching for us?

MRS. BORKMAN (*acidly*). Yes, I thought I'd better.

ELLA (*pointing*). See, there he lies, Gunhild.

MRS. BORKMAN. Sleeping!

ELLA (*nods*). A deep sleep and a long one, I think.

MRS. BORKMAN (*in an outburst*). Ella! (*Controls herself and asks in a whisper.*) Did it happen—deliberately?

ELLA. No.

MRS. BORKMAN (*relieved*). Not by his own hand, then?

ELLA. No. It was a freezing hand of metal that seized his heart.

MRS. BORKMAN (*to the* MAID). Get some help. Some people from the farm.

MAID. Yes, of course, ma'am. (*Softly.*) In Jesus' name— (*She goes off through the trees to the right.*)

MRS. BORKMAN (*standing behind the bench*). Then the night air killed him—

ELLA. I suppose so.

MRS. BORKMAN. He, that strong man.

ELLA (*moving in front of the bench*). Won't you look at him, Gunhild?

MRS. BORKMAN (*with a gesture of aversion*). No, no, no. (*Lowers her voice.*) He was a miner's son—Borkman, the bank president. He couldn't survive in the fresh air.

ELLA. It was more probably the cold that killed him.

MRS. BORKMAN (*shaking her head*). You say, the cold? The cold—that killed him a long time back.

ELLA (*nodding to her*). And turned the two of us into shadows.

MRS. BORKMAN. You're right about that.

ELLA (*with a painful smile*). A dead man and two shadows—that's what the cold has made.

MRS. BORKMAN. Yes, a coldness in the heart. And so, at last, we two might reach our hands out to each other.

ELLA. Now I think we can.

MRS. BORKMAN. We two twin sisters—over him we both once loved.

ELLA. We two shadows—over the dead man.

(MRS. BORKMAN, *behind the bench, and* ELLA RENTHEIM, *in front of it, reach across and take each other's hands.*)

WHEN WE DEAD AWAKEN

Ibsen's subtitle for his last play, *When We Dead Awaken* (1899), terms it "A Dramatic Epilogue." It was intended to mark the end of a phase and probably a style, but not of a writing career. Three months after its publication, Ibsen wrote his French translator, Count Moritz Prozor, expressing uncertainty about his future plans, but also his expectation of imminent return to the old battlefields, "in new armor, with new weapons." And to C. H. Herford, he remarked that if he could know which play would be his last, he would want to compose it in verse. Those tantalizing hints of future projects were stayed forever when, in 1901, Ibsen suffered the first of several strokes to which his remarkable constitution finally succumbed five years later.

When We Dead Awaken is an epilogue, then, only to the degree that, as Ibsen noted, "it completes the cycle and makes of it an entity." Its action is simple in the extreme. A world-famous sculptor, Arnold Rubek, bored with his young, vivacious, attractive wife Maja, encounters at a seaside health resort, after years of separation, the physical model for, and spiritual collaborator in, his greatest work, a monumental group titled "Resurrection Day." As the setting shifts to the grounds of a mountain sanitarium and finally the treacherous peaks themselves, Rubek sheds his wife for his old attachment, Irene, who embodies madness, guilt, murderous hate, death in life, and an intimation of life in and through death; and concurrently Maja is taken up by a rough-spoken bear hunter and landowner named Ulfhejm, who sees better uses for her animal spirits than sipping champagne and seltzer in a wicker lawn chair.

In what sense can this quadrille of realignments be said to complete the impressively varied segments of the cycle and make them into one entity? A number of possibilities present themselves, of which one is plainly to be avoided. That view interprets Rubek as Ibsen's spokesman, perhaps even costumed and crudely made up in performance as the playwright, venting the stored bitterness and disillusion of a lifetime wasted on art. Rubek may well be, in this regard, an accurate transcript of Ibsen in certain, occasional moods. Nevertheless, our impression from letters, interviews and, in general, the record of Ibsen's life in that period is of something more richly varied than Rubek's repertoire of lamentation. And, even if correspondences exist, as Albert Bermel has warned, "the transmutation of experience into art encompasses distortions we have no way of assessing."

If *When We Dead Awaken* is to yield a stageworthy coherence, it must be as an internally organic, delicately accorded disposition of elements, the lesser characters holding their own importance with the greater—a dramatic poem, in short, in the same respect that Ibsen referred to all his later prose dramas as "poems." It could, as one option, be explored in the light of the psychoanalytic precept that a play is a dream turned inside out (Ibsen was aware of Strindberg's experiments with the dream-play form in *To Damascus I and II*). In this perspective, the last work of the cycle is not summed up in an obsessive message reiterated by a single character; rather, all the characters embody aspects of a dreamer who, since this is an edited and objectified dream, must not facilely be equated with the dramatist.

Thus, Irene and Maja suggest two faces of Eve, of essential woman, that the dreamer must choose between. Irene is woman idealized, whose capacity for inspiration is in direct ratio to her inaccessibility. She is the incitement to creation, the incarnate principle of sublimation, with its terrible, retributive, Blakean corollary: "Pitying I wept to see the woe/ That Love & Beauty undergo/ To be consumed in burning fires/ And in ungratified desires." As Blake's reminder is to "Expect poison from the standing water," Rubek can learn to expect a keenly sharp stiletto in reprisal for exploiting the soul and image, as against embracing the total self, of his inspiration.

Yet only in reconciliation with what Irene represents, in a synthesis of the erotically involved and the aesthetically detached, is there any hope of peace, the very meaning of Irene's name. And for Rubek, as experience, to seek that peace in union with Maja's innocence can only be illusion —the Hindu root of her name—as real and substantial a partner as she may be for Ulfhejm. That voracious huntsman is as integral a component of the dreamer's selfhood as the tormented Rubek, an affirmation of the vitalistic base of existence, an odd anticipation of D. H. Lawrence's Mellors, as previously Allmers and Rita resembled, in physical description, Lawrence himself and his wife Frieda.

The realignment of characters has matched temperaments with symbolic terrain. Rubek and Irene ascend in pursuit of the ideal; and the words that follow them, almost the last of the play, the Nun's "Pax vobiscum," express benediction and forgiveness, the peace of an ending in the ancient language of a once universal Catholic faith. But the last words of the play, indeed of all Ibsen's theater, invoke release and the freedom of beginnings in the language, pure and new-minted, of Maja's song of descent with Ulfhejm to the lowlands, where life is accepted as it is, and perpetually new ideals will generate and new climbers set forth:

> I am free! I am free! I am free!
> No more living in cages for me!
> I am free as a bird! I am free!

THE CHARACTERS

PROFESSOR ARNOLD RUBEK, a sculptor
MAJA RUBEK, his wife
THE MANAGER OF THE SPA
ULFHEJM, owner of an estate
A LADY TRAVELER
A NUN, member of a nursing order
Waiters, guests at the spa, and children

The first act takes place at a health resort by the sea; the second and third acts in the general vicinity of a sanitarium high in the mountains.

⚊⊰ ACT ONE ⊱⚊

Outside the main building of the spa hotel, a portion of which can be glimpsed at the right. An open, parklike place, with a fountain, clumps of shrubbery and groves of fine, old trees. On the left, a table and chairs. In the background, a view over the fjord, extending far out to sea, with promontories and small islands in the distance. It is a still, warm, sun-bright summer morning.

PROFESSOR RUBEK *and his wife* MAJA *are sitting in wicker chairs at a table set for breakfast on the lawn outside the hotel. They have finished eating and now are sipping champagne and seltzer; each is reading a newspaper.* RUBEK *is an older, distinguished-looking man who, apart from a black velvet jacket, is wearing light summer clothes.* MAJA *is in the full bloom of youth, with a vivacious expression and playful, teasing eyes, but with a trace of fatigue about her. She wears an elegant traveling dress. She sits for a moment as if waiting for* RUBEK *to say something, then lowers her newspaper and sighs deeply.*

RUBEK (*looking up from his paper*). Well, Maja? What's the matter?

MAJA. Just listen, how silent it is here.

RUBEK (*smiling indulgently*). Can you hear that?

MAJA. What?

RUBEK. The silence?

MAJA. Yes. Definitely.

RUBEK. Well, *mein Kind*, maybe you're right. Undoubtedly, one can hear silence.

MAJA. Yes, God knows anyone can. When it's as overpowering as it is here—

RUBEK. At the spa, you mean?

MAJA. I mean, everywhere here in this country. Down in the city there was plenty of noise and activity. But nevertheless—I felt that even that noise and activity had something dead about it.

RUBEK (*with a probing look*). You're not happy any more to be home again, Maja?

MAJA (*looking at him*). Are you happy?

RUBEK (*evasively*). I—?

MAJA. Yes. You've been away so very much longer than I have. Are *you* really happy now to be home again?

RUBEK. Truthfully—no—not entirely happy.

MAJA (*animatedly*). There, you see! I knew it!

RUBEK. Maybe I've been away too long. I feel totally detached from all this—this life back home.

MAJA (*eagerly, drawing her chair closer*). There, you see, Rubek! We'd be better off traveling again. Just as soon as we can.

RUBEK (*somewhat impatiently*). Well, that *is* the decision, Maja dear. You know that.

MAJA. But why not right now, today? We could have it so nice and cozy down there in our lovely new house—

RUBEK (*with an indulgent smile*). Or, to put it more exactly: our lovely new *home*.

MAJA (*brusquely*). I prefer *house*. Let's stay with that.

RUBEK (*studying her*). You really are a peculiar little person.

MAJA. Am I so peculiar?

RUBEK. Yes, to my mind.

MAJA. But why? Merely because I have no great desire to go gallivanting around up here—?

RUBEK. Which one of us was just about ready to die if we didn't travel up north this summer?

MAJA. That sounds rather like me.

RUBEK. Well, it certainly wasn't me.

MAJA. But, my Lord—who could have guessed that everything would have changed so drastically up here? And in such a short time! Why, it isn't more than a good four years since I went away—

RUBEK. Got married, you mean.

MAJA. Married? What's *that* got to do with it?

RUBEK (*going on*). And became *Frau Professor* and the mistress of a beautiful home—excuse me—I should say, a most attractive house. And a villa on Lake Taunitz, where only the most fashionable people come. Yes, because I must admit, it's all very choice and inviting, Maja. And spacious, too. We don't always have to be right on top of each other—

MAJA (*casually*). No, no—house room and such, we're not short on that—

RUBEK. So the fact is that, in general, you've been living in a more spacious and elevated style. In a more cultivated society than you were used to at home.

MAJA. Then you think *I'm* the one who's changed?

RUBEK. Yes, I think so, Maja.

MAJA. Only me? Not the people here?

RUBEK. Oh yes, they have, too. A little bit, perhaps. If anything, they've made themselves less endearing, I'll grant you that.

MAJA. Yes, I'm sure you will.

RUBEK (*changing the subject*). You know what kind of feeling comes over me when I see how people live around these parts?

MAJA. No. Tell me.

RUBEK. It takes me back to the night on the train, on our way up here—

MAJA. But you were sound asleep in the compartment.

RUBEK. Not always. I noticed how silent it was at all those little stations we stopped at. I could *hear* the silence —like you, Maja—

MAJA. Hm—like me, yes.

RUBEK. And then I understood that now we'd crossed the border—we really were home now. Because the train was stopping at every tiny station—even though nothing stirred.

MAJA. Why did it stop when there was no reason to?

RUBEK. Don't know. No one got off, and no one got on. And still the train stood there, waiting silently, it seemed like forever. And at every station I could hear two men walking along the platform—one of them with a lantern in his hand—and they talked with each other—low, muffled, meaningless words in the night.

MAJA. Yes, that's true. There are always two men that go by, talking together—

RUBEK. About nothing. (*His tone quickens.*) But now just wait till tomorrow. Then we'll see that great, palatial steamer standing into the harbor. And we'll go on board and sail around the coast—all the way north—right into the Arctic Sea.

MAJA. Yes, but then you'll be seeing nothing of the country—or the people. And that was exactly what you wanted.

RUBEK (*curtly and sullenly*). I've seen more than enough.

MAJA. You think a sea voyage will be better for you?

RUBEK. It's always a change.

MAJA. All right, whatever's the best for *you*—

RUBEK. For me? Best? There's nothing at all wrong with me.

MAJA (*gets up and goes to him*). Yes, there is, Rubek. You must sense that yourself.

RUBEK. But, Maja dearest—what do you mean, specifically?

MAJA (*behind him, bending over the back of his chair*). You tell me. You've begun moving restlessly from place to place. You can't seem to settle anywhere, neither at home nor abroad. And lately you've become so withdrawn, you don't want to see people at all.

RUBEK (*with irony*). No, really—have you noticed *that?*

MAJA. Anyone who knows you could hardly miss it. And then I think it's so distressing that you've lost the urge to work.

RUBEK. *That*, too?

MAJA. You, who once used to work so tirelessly—from dawn on into the night.

RUBEK (*despondently*). Yes, once. Yes—

MAJA. But ever since you finished your masterpiece—

RUBEK (*nodding pensively*). "Resurrection Day."

MAJA. —that's been exhibited all over the world. And that's made you world-famous.

RUBEK. Perhaps that was the great mistake, Maja.

MAJA. But why?

RUBEK. When I'd created this masterpiece of mine— (*With an impassioned sweep of his hand.*) —because "Resurrection Day" *is* a masterpiece! Or *was*, at the start. No, it still is. It must—must be—*must* be a masterpiece!

MAJA (*staring at him, astonished*). Of course, Rubek—the whole world knows it is.

RUBEK (*abruptly, with a deprecating gesture*). The world knows nothing! Understands nothing!

MAJA. It has some degree of awareness, though—

RUBEK. Yes, of things that aren't even there. Things I never had in mind. Oh, but that's what they go into raptures over! (*Muttering to himself.*) It's not worth it to kill yourself, slaving away for the mob—the masses—the "whole world."

MAJA. Do you think it's better—or more worthy of you to go and turn out just a portrait bust now and then?

RUBEK (*with a sly smile*). It's not simply portrait busts that I model, Maja.

MAJA. Yes, that's all you've done, really—in the last two-three years—ever since you got that large group finished and out of your studio—

RUBEK. But they're not portrait busts, pure and simple; that's what I'm saying.

MAJA. Then what are they?

RUBEK. There's something hidden, something sinister behind and within those busts—a secret something that ordinary people can't see—

MAJA. Oh?

RUBEK (*his tone arbitrary*). Only *I* can see it. And it amuses me no end. On the surface is that so-called "striking likeness" that everyone stands and gapes at, transfixed. (*His voice dropping.*) But down at the deepest core are respectable and worthy horse faces and the stubborn muzzles of mules—lop-eared, low-browed dog skulls, and pampered pig snouts—and every so often, the heavy, brutal semblance of a bull—

MAJA (*carelessly*). All our dear, domestic animals.

RUBEK. Only the dear, domestic animals, Maja. All the animals that human beings have distorted in their own image. And that have distorted human beings in return. (*Drains his champagne glass and laughs.*) And these perfidious works of art are what the virtuous rich come and order from me. And pay for in good faith—and through the nose, too. They're almost worth their weight in gold, to coin a phrase.

MAJA (*filling his glass*). Enough, Rubek! Drink up and be happy.

RUBEK (*runs his hand several times over his forehead and leans back in his chair*). I am happy, Maja. Perfectly happy. In one way, at least. (*After a pause.*) For of course there's a certain happiness in feeling totally free and independent—in having plenty of everything one could imagine wishing for. In material terms, anyway. Don't you agree?

MAJA. Oh, indeed yes. It's very nice, in its place. (*Looking at him.*) But can you remember what you promised me that day we resolved our—our difficult situation—

RUBEK (*nods*). Resolved that we two would get married, you mean. You gave yourself a pretty hard time over that, Maja.

MAJA (*continuing unflustered*). —with the proviso that I'd travel abroad with you and live there permanently—and enjoy myself. Can you remember what you promised me then?

RUBEK. No, I really can't. All right, what did I promise?

MAJA. You said you'd take me with you up on top of a high mountain and show me all the glory of the world.

RUBEK (*startled*). I promised you that, too?

MAJA (*looks at him*). Me—too? Who else?

RUBEK (*offhandedly*). No, no, I merely asked if I promised to show you—?

MAJA. All the glory of the world. Yes, you said that. And all that glory would be yours and mine, you said.

RUBEK. That's an old expression I used to use many years ago.

MAJA. Only an expression?

RUBEK. Yes, something from my schooldays. The kind of thing I could coax neighborhood children with, when I wanted them to come out and play with me in the woods or up in the mountains.

MAJA (*looking sharply at him*). Were you only interested in coaxing *me* out to play, too?

RUBEK (*treating it as a joke*). Well, hasn't it been a fairly amusing game?

MAJA (*coolly*). I didn't go off with you just to play games.

RUBEK. No, no, certainly not.

MAJA. And besides, you never took me up on any high mountains to show me—

RUBEK (*irritably*). All the glory of the world? No, I didn't. Because let me tell you something: you're really not made to climb mountains, Maja, my pet.

MAJA (*striving to control herself*). You appeared to think so once.

RUBEK. Some four-five years ago, yes. (*Stretching in his chair.*) Four-five years, that's a long, long time, Maja.

MAJA (*with a barbed look at him*). Has the time seemed so very long to you, Rubek?

RUBEK. It begins to seem a bit long to me now. (*Yawning.*) On occasion, anyway.

MAJA (*returning to her chair*). I won't bore you any more. (*She sits, picks up her paper and starts paging through it. Silence on both sides.*)

RUBEK (*leans forward on his elbows across the table and regards her teasingly*). Is the *Frau Professor* insulted?

MAJA (*icily, without looking up*). No, not at all.

(*Guests at the spa, mostly ladies, begin coming alone or in groups from the right, across the park and out, left. Waiters bring refreshments from the hotel, moving out of view beyond the pavilion. The* MANAGER, *wearing gloves and carrying a walking stick, returns from his rounds of the park and, encountering the guests, greets them deferentially and exchanges a few words with some of them.*)

MANAGER (*proceeds to* PROFESSOR RUBEK'S *table and politely takes off his hat*). A most respectful good morning to you, Mrs. Rubek. Good morning, Professor.

RUBEK. Good morning, sir. Good morning.

MANAGER (*turning to* MAJA). May I presume to inquire if you had a restful night?

MAJA. Yes, thank you; just fine—for *me*, anyway. But then I always sleep like a log.

MANAGER. I'm delighted to hear. The first night in a strange place can often be rather disagreeable— And you, Professor—?

RUBEK. Oh, I make a poor show of sleep. Lately more than ever.

MANAGER (*with a pretense of sympathy*). Oh—I *am* sorry. But a few weeks' stay here at the spa, and that will be straightened out.

RUBEK (*looking up at him*). Tell me—are there any of your patients who use the spa baths at night?

MANAGER (*surprised*). At night? No, that's something I've never heard of.

RUBEK. Never?

MANAGER. No, I don't know anyone here so ill as to call for that.

RUBEK. Well, then is there anyone who goes walking in the park at night?

MANAGER (*smiles and shakes his head*). No, Professor— that would be against the rules.

MAJA (*losing her patience*). Good Lord, Rubek—it's what I told you this morning. You were dreaming.

RUBEK (*drily*). Oh? Was I? Thank you! (*Turns back to the* MANAGER.) You see, I was up during the night, because I couldn't get to sleep. And I thought I'd check on the weather—

MANAGER (*interested*). Yes. So—?

RUBEK. So I looked out the window—and caught a glimpse of a pale figure down there, among the trees.

MAJA (*smiling at the* MANAGER). And Professor Rubek claims that this figure was wearing a bathrobe—

RUBEK. Or something like it, I said. I couldn't make it out too clearly. But I did see something white.

MANAGER. That *is* odd. Was it a man or a woman?

RUBEK. It was my strong impression that it had to be a woman. But following behind, there was another figure. And that was very dark. Like a shadow—

MANAGER (*with a start*). Dark? You mean, all in black?

RUBEK. Yes, to *my* eyes, anyway.

MANAGER (*as if comprehending*). And definitely following the one in white? Close behind her—?

RUBEK. Yes. A short distance—

MANAGER. Aha! Then perhaps I can clear things up for you, Professor.

RUBEK. So what was it then?

MAJA (*simultaneously*). You mean he really wasn't dreaming?

MANAGER (*suddenly whispering as he points toward the background to the right*). Shh! Look over there—and keep your voices down!

(*A slender* LADY, *dressed in fine, cream-white cashmere, followed by a* NUN *in black, with a silver cross on a chain at her breast, comes from behind the corner of the hotel and walks through the park toward the pavilion in the left foreground. Her face is pallid and drawn, like a plaster mask; her eyelids droop and her eyes appear unseeing. Her gown is full-length and clings in long, regular, vertical folds to her body. Over her head, neck, breast, shoulders and arms she has a large, white crepe shawl. Her arms are folded up in a cross over her breast. Her carriage is rigid, her pace stiff and measured. The* NUN's *movements are also measured and convey the role of a servant. Her brown, penetrating eyes are fixed unswervingly on the* LADY. *Waiters with napkins over their arms appear in the hotel doorway and peer curiously after the two strange women, who pay no attention and go, without looking to one side or the other, into the pavilion.*)

RUBEK (*who has risen slowly and involuntarily from his chair to stare at the closed door of the pavilion*). Who was that woman?

MANAGER. She's a lady from abroad, who's rented that little pavilion there.

RUBEK. A foreigner?

MANAGER. Probably. At least, they both arrived here from abroad. Around a week ago. They've never stayed here before.

RUBEK (*firmly, looking at him*). She's the one I saw last night in the park.

MANAGER. She must have been. I thought so immediately.

RUBEK. And the lady's name?

MANAGER. She's on the register as "Madame de Satow and companion." That's all we know.

RUBEK (*mulling it over*). Satow? Satow—?

MAJA (*with a taunting laugh*). Anyone you know, Rubek?

RUBEK (*shaking his head*). Absolutely not. Satow? Sounds Russian. Or Slavic, in any case. (*To the* MANAGER.) What's her native language?

MANAGER. When the two ladies talk together, it's in a language I can't place at all. But otherwise she speaks perfectly good Norwegian.

RUBEK (*exclaims in amazement*). Norwegian! You're not mistaken?

MANAGER. No, I couldn't mistake that.

RUBEK (*avidly, looking at him*). You've heard her yourself!

MANAGER. Yes. I talked with her myself. Several times. No more than a couple of words, though—because she's exceedingly reserved. But—

RUBEK. But it was Norwegian?

MANAGER. Pure Norwegian; the best. With maybe a little trace of a northern accent.

RUBEK (*stares straight ahead, bemused, and whispers*). Even *that*.

MAJA (*faintly disturbed*). Maybe the lady was one of your models once, Rubek? Think back.

RUBEK (*looks witheringly at her*). Models!

MAJA (*with a provocative smile*). Yes, in your younger days, I mean. Because they say you had any number of models—in times past, of course.

RUBEK (*picking up her tone*). Oh no, my little Maja; I've really only had one model. One single model—for everything I've done.

MANAGER (*who has turned and stands looking off to the left*). I'm afraid now that I'd better excuse myself. There's someone coming who's no particular pleasure to meet. Especially around ladies.

RUBEK (*glancing left*). That hunter there? Who's he?

MANAGER. A big landowner, a man named Ulfhejm—

RUBEK. Oh yes, Ulfhejm.

MANAGER. They call him the bear-killer.

RUBEK. I know him.

MANAGER. Yes, who doesn't?

RUBEK. Not at all well, though. Has he come in as a patient—at last?

MANAGER. No, surprisingly—not yet. He just stops by here once a year—when he's on his way up to his hunting grounds. If you'll pardon me— (*He starts off for the hotel.*)

ULFHEJM'S VOICE (*from without*). Wait a second! Wait up! That's a hell of a note! Why do you always run out on me?

MANAGER (*stops*). I am *not* running out, Mr. Ulfhejm.

(ULFHEJM *enters from the left, followed by a servant leading a pair of leashed hounds.* ULFHEJM *is wearing hunting clothes, with high boots and a felt hat with a feather in it. He is a lean, long, sinewy man, with matted hair and beard and a boisterous voice, of an indeterminate age by appearances, but no longer young.*)

ULFHEJM (*closing in on the* MANAGER). Is *that* any way to treat a visitor, uh? Clearing off with your tail between your legs—as if you had the devil at your hindquarters.

MANAGER (*calmly, not answering him*). Did you arrive by the steamer, sir?

ULFHEJM (*growls*). Never had the privilege to see any steamer. (*Arms akimbo.*) Aren't *you* aware that *I* sail by my own cutter? (*To the* SERVANT.) Take good care of your fellow creatures, Lars. But watch you keep 'em on the ravenous side, though. Some fresh marrow bones. But not too much meat on 'em, hear. Bloody and reeking raw, that's the ticket. And get something into your own belly, too. (*Aims a kick after him.*) Ahh, get the hell out of here!

(*The* SERVANT *goes off around the corner of the hotel with the dogs.*)

MANAGER. For the time being, won't the gentleman favor our dining room?

ULFHEJM. In with all those dying flies and half-dead people? No, thanks a million, but not for me.

MANAGER. Oh well, suit your own taste.

ULFHEJM. Just have the maid put up my usual hamper. Lay on the food—and lots of brandy! You can tell her that either Lars or I'll come and raise hell with her if she doesn't—

MANAGER (*breaking in*). We know all that from before. (*Turning.*) Can I have the waiter serve you, Professor? Or anything for Mrs. Rubek?

RUBEK. No, thanks. Nothing for me.

MAJA. Or me, either.

(*The* MANAGER *goes into the hotel.*)

ULFHEJM (*glowers at them a moment, then raises his hat*). Well, strike me dead! What's a country boy doing in this high-toned society?

RUBEK (*glancing up*). And what does *that* mean, Mr. Ulfhejm?

ULFHEJM (*more subdued, minding his manners*). Looks like I've run in with the great sculptor Rubek himself.

RUBEK (*nods*). We met once or twice socially, the autumn of my last visit home.

ULFHEJM. Well, but that was many years ago, and in those days you weren't the famous name that I hear you've become now. Back then even a scruffy bear-hunter could dare approach you.

RUBEK (*smiles*). I don't bite even now.

MAJA (*regarding* ULFHEJM *with interest*). Are you a real, actual bear-hunter?

ULFHEJM (*sitting at the next table, toward the hotel*). Bears by preference, ma'am. But I don't mind taking on anything wild that comes my way. Eagles, wolves, women, elk, reindeer—so long as they're fresh and full-bodied, with plenty of hot blood in their veins— (*He drinks from a pocket flask.*)

MAJA (*studying him intently*). But bears by preference?

ULFHEJM. By preference, yes. Because then, if you're hard put, you can use your knife. (*With a faint smile.*) We both like working with hard material, ma'am—both I and your husband. He likes wrestling with blocks of marble, I imagine—and I wrestle with the hard, straining sinews of bears. And both of us force our material down under control at last. Become lord and master over it. We never give up till we've overcome it, no matter how much it fights back.

RUBEK (*reflectively, to himself*). That's true enough.

ULFHEJM. Yes, because the stone has something to fight for, too, I'm sure. It's dead, and it resists with all its strength being hammered into life. Exactly like a bear when you sneak up and prod it out of its den.

MAJA. Are you going up now in the forests to hunt?

ULFHEJM. I'm heading right up in the high mountains. I don't guess you've ever been up there, ma'am?

MAJA. No, never.

ULFHEJM. Then, by thunder, why don't you come on up there this summer! I'll take you along gladly—both of you.

MAJA. Thanks. But my husband's planning on a sea voyage this summer.

RUBEK. Through the islands, up the coast.

ULFHEJM. Pah—why the devil do you want to be in those damned polluted gutters! Just imagine—lying inshore and paddling around in that soup. Slop is more like it.

MAJA. You heard him, Arnold.

ULFHEJM. No, come up with me instead in the mountains. That's where it's free and clean of people. You don't have any notion what *that* means to me. But such a proper lady—

(*He stops. The* NUN *comes out of the pavilion and goes across into the hotel.* ULFHEJM *follows her with his eyes.*)

ULFHEJM. Look at her there. The big black bird. Who's getting buried?

RUBEK. No one here I know of—

ULFHEJM. Well, someone around here's going to croak. In some corner or other. People who are sickly and weak ought to please see about stashing themselves down under —the sooner, the better.

MAJA. Have you ever been sick, Mr. Ulfhejm?

ULFHEJM. Never. Or I wouldn't be sitting here. But some of my closest friends—*they've* been sick.

MAJA. And what did you do for your closest friends?

ULFHEJM. Shot them, naturally.

RUBEK (*staring at him*). Shot them?

MAJA (*pushing her chair back*). Shot them dead?

ULFHEJM (*nodding*). I never miss, ma'am.

MAJA. But by what right can you shoot a person dead?

ULFHEJM. I'm not talking about people—

MAJA. You said your closest friends—

ULFHEJM. But they're my dogs.

MAJA. Are you closest to your dogs?

ULFHEJM. I've nobody closer. My honest, faithful, true-hearted companions of the hunt. When one of them becomes sick and broken down, then—pow! And with that, my friend is dispatched—over to the other side.

(*The* NUN *comes out of the hotel with a tray of bread and milk, which she sets down on the table outside the pavilion, before going in.*)

ULFHEJM (*laughing scornfully*). That stuff—is that supposed to be feed for humans! Watered-down milk and soft, sticky bread. No, you ought to see my companions eat. Would you like to see that?

MAJA (*gets up, with a smile at* RUBEK). Yes, very much.

ULFHEJM (*also getting up*). I must say, you're a lady of versatile tastes, ma'am. Come along then. Great, huge knucklebones—they swallow them down whole—spew 'em up and choke 'em right down again. Ah, it's pure joy to watch them. Here, come on and I'll show you. And then we'll talk a bit more about that trip in the mountains—

(*He goes out around the corner of the hotel.* MAJA *follows him. Almost simultaneously, the* STRANGE LADY *comes out of the pavilion and seats herself at the table. She raises the glass of milk and is about to drink, then pauses and looks over at Rubek with empty, expressionless eyes.* RUBEK *remains sitting at his table and stares gravely and intently at her. At last he rises, moves some steps toward her and stops.*)

RUBEK (*softly*). I recognize you perfectly, Irene.

IRENE (*tonelessly, setting down her glass*). You've found me out, then, Arnold?

RUBEK (*not answering*). And I see you've recognized me as well.

IRENE. With you, it's quite different.

RUBEK. Why, with me?

IRENE. *You're* still alive.

RUBEK (*baffled*). Alive—?

IRENE (*after a brief pause*). Who was that other one? The woman you had with you—there at the table?

RUBEK (*with some reluctance*). Her? That was my—my wife.

IRENE (*nodding slowly*). I see. That's good, Arnold. Someone who's no concern of mine—

RUBEK (*insecurely*). No, of course not—

IRENE. Someone you got hold of after my lifetime.

RUBEK (*staring fixedly at her*). After your—? What are you saying, Irene?

IRENE (*not answering*). And the child? Our child's done so well. The child's lived after me—in glory and honor.

RUBEK (*smiles as if lost in memories*). Our child? Yes, we did call it that—once.

IRENE. In my lifetime, yes.

RUBEK (*trying to lighten the tone*). Yes, Irene—there's no doubt our child's become world-famous. You must have read about it.

IRENE (*nods*). And about its famous father, too. That was your dream.

RUBEK (*with quiet emotion*). I owe everything, everything, Irene, to you. Thank you.

IRENE (*sits musing for a moment*). If I'd exercised my rights then, Arnold—

RUBEK. What then?

IRENE. I would have killed that child.

RUBEK. Killed it?

IRENE (*in a whisper*). Killed it—before I left you. Smashed it to bits.

RUBEK (*shakes his head reproachfully*). You couldn't have done that, Irene. You wouldn't have had the heart.

IRENE. No, then I didn't have that kind of heart.

RUBEK. But since then? Afterward?

IRENE. Afterward, I killed it innumerable times. In daylight and darkness. Killed it in hate—and revenge—and agony.

RUBEK (*goes up to her table and asks quietly*). Irene— tell me now—after all these years—why did you leave me then? Disappear without a trace—where you couldn't be found—

IRENE (*slowly shakes her head*). Oh Arnold—why should I tell you now—when I've gone to the other side?

RUBEK. Was there someone else you'd come to love?

IRENE. There was someone who didn't need my love—*or* my life anymore.

RUBEK (*evasively*). Hm—let's stop talking about the past—

IRENE. Yes—no more talk of the other world. Because all that is the other world now, for *me*.

RUBEK. Where did you go, Irene? I made inquiries everywhere, and it was as if you'd been erased from this earth.

IRENE. I went into the darkness—while the child stood there, transfigured in the light.

RUBEK. Were you traveling a lot?

IRENE. Yes. Traveling in many lands and countries.

RUBEK (*gazing with compassion at her*). And how did you manage to live?

IRENE (*looks straight at him*). Wait, now, let me see— Yes, now I know. I've stood on revolving platforms in cabarets, as a naked statue in a living tableau. Raked in reams of money that way. That's more than I ever did with you; you never had it. And then I've been with lots of men, the ones I knew how to drive wild. That's also more than I had with you. You held out better.

RUBEK (*letting the matter drop*). And did you get married, as well?

IRENE. Yes, to one of them.

RUBEK. Who is your husband?

IRENE. He was a South American. A high diplomat. (*Staring into space with a stony smile.*) I succeeded in driving him quite mad: insane—incurably, unreachably insane. It was a choice diversion—while it lasted. I could have laughed constantly inside—if I'd *had* anything inside.

RUBEK. And where is he now?

IRENE. In a churchyard somewhere, with an imposing monument raised over him, and a lead bullet rattling around in his skull.

RUBEK. He killed himself?

IRENE. Yes. He was kind enough to anticipate me.

RUBEK. You have no grief for him, Irene?

IRENE (*blankly*). Grief? For whom?

RUBEK. Herr von Satow?

IRENE. That wasn't his name.

RUBEK. No?

IRENE. My second husband is named Satow. He's Russian.

RUBEK. And where is *he?*

IRENE. Far away in the Ural Mountains—with all his gold mines.

RUBEK. He's living there?

IRENE (*shrugs*). Living? Living? Actually, I've killed him—

RUBEK (*with a start*). Killed—?

IRENE. Yes, with a fine, sharp dagger I always have with me in bed.

RUBEK (*explosively*). I don't believe you, Irene!

IRENE (*smiling indulgently*). You can take my word for it, Arnold.

RUBEK (*feelingly*). Did you never have any children?

IRENE. Yes, I've had many.

RUBEK. And where are the children now?

IRENE. I killed them.

RUBEK (*sharply*). Now you're lying to me again!

IRENE. I tell you, I've killed them. Murdered them with a vengeance. Just as soon as they came into the world. No, long, long before that. One after another.

RUBEK (*sadly and somberly*). There's something hidden behind this whole story of yours.

IRENE. I can't help that. Every word I say is being whispered in my ear.

RUBEK. I suppose I'm the only one who can decipher the meaning.

IRENE. You *should* be the only one.

RUBEK (*leans with his hands on the table and looks searchingly at her*). There's a thread inside you—that's snapped.

IRENE (*gently*). That must always happen when a young, full-blooded woman dies.

RUBEK. Oh Irene, give up these wild obsessions—! You're alive! Alive, alive!

IRENE (*rises slowly from her chair and speaks tremulously*). For many years I was dead. They came and bound me. Strapped my arms together behind my back— Then they lowered me down into a tomb, with iron bars for a trapdoor. And the walls were padded—so no one up above on the earth could hear the shrieks from the grave— But now I'm halfway beginning to rise from the dead. (*She sits again.*)

RUBEK (*after a pause*). Do you blame me for all this?

IRENE. Yes.

RUBEK. Blame me—for what you call your death?

IRENE. You're to blame that I had to die. (*Shifts to a neutral tone.*) But why don't you sit down, Arnold?

RUBEK. May I?

IRENE. Yes. Don't be afraid of frostbite. I don't think I've turned quite to ice yet.

RUBEK (*moves a chair and sits at the table*). There now, Irene. We're sitting together again, just like old times.

IRENE. A little apart from each other. Also just like old times.

RUBEK (*moving closer*). It had to be that way then.

IRENE. Had to?

RUBEK (*with finality*). There had to be distance between us—

IRENE. Did there, really, Arnold?

RUBEK (*not acknowledging her*). Do you remember what you answered when I asked if you'd go off with me into the far unknown?

IRENE. I raised three fingers in the air and swore I'd go with you to the world's end and the end of life. And that I'd serve you in all things—

RUBEK. As the model for my art—

IRENE. In full, free nakedness—

RUBEK (*moved*). And you did serve me, Irene—with such buoyancy, and joy, and daring.

IRENE. Yes, with all the throbbing blood of my youth, I served you!

RUBEK (*nodding, with a grateful look*). There's not the least doubt of that.

IRENE. I fell down at your feet then and served you, Arnold! (*Clenching her fists at him.*) But you, you—you—!

RUBEK (*defensively*). I never mistreated you! Never, Irene!

IRENE. Yes, you did! You mistreated the innermost source of my being—

RUBEK (*recoiling*). I—?

IRENE. Yes, *you!* I stripped myself naked for your eyes to explore— (*More quietly.*) And never, not once, did you touch me.

RUBEK. Didn't you realize that there were days on days when your beauty nearly drove me out of my senses?

IRENE (*continues undistracted*). And still—if you'd touched me, I think I'd have killed you on the spot. I always had a sharp needle with me—hidden in my hair. (*Rubs her forehead reflectively.*) Yes, but—still—even so —that you could—

RUBEK (*looking pointedly at her*). I was an artist, Irene.

IRENE (*her voice somber*). Exactly. Exactly.

RUBEK. First and foremost, an artist. And I was sick then—sick with wanting to create the greatest work of my life. (*Lost in memory.*) It would be called "Resurrection Day"—embodied in the form of a young woman who was awakening from the sleep of death—

IRENE. Our child, yes—

RUBEK. As she woke, at that moment, she ought to be the noblest, the purest, the most ideal of women. And then I found *you.* I could use you for everything I needed. And you consented so eagerly and gladly—to leaving your family and home—and going with me.

IRENE. It was the rebirth of my childhood, to go with you.

RUBEK. Just why I could use you best of all. You and no one else. To me you became a sacred creature, to be touched only by worshipful thoughts. I was still so young and innocent then, Irene. And the conviction filled me that, if I touched you, or desired you in sensual terms, then my spirit would be profaned so that I couldn't have created what I was striving for. And I still think there's some truth in that.

IRENE (*nodding, with a hint of scorn*). Art first—and then human life.

RUBEK. Yes, you can condemn it if you want. But I was completely under the spell of my artistic mission in those days. And so happy, so exhilarated by it.

IRENE. And you fulfilled your mission, Arnold.

RUBEK. Thanks and praise be to you—I fulfilled it. I wanted to create woman in all her purity, as I imagined she might awake on Resurrection Day. Not marveling over something new and unknown and inconceivable, but filled with a sacred joy in rediscovering herself unchanged—she, woman, born of earth—in the higher, freer, happier realm —after the long, dreamless sleep of death. (*His voice dropping.*) That's how I created her—in *your* image, Irene.

IRENE (*extends her hands flat on the table and leans back in her chair*). And then you were through with me—

RUBEK (*reproachfully*). Irene!

IRENE. Had no more use for me—

RUBEK. How can you say that!

IRENE. And started looking around for other ideals—

RUBEK. I found none. None after you.

IRENE. No other models, Arnold?

RUBEK. To me you weren't a model. You were the soul of my inspiration.

IRENE (*silent for a moment*). What poetry have you created since? In marble, I mean. Since the day I left you?

RUBEK. No poetry since then. Just putterings in clay.

IRENE. And that woman you're living with now—

RUBEK (*interrupting fiercely*). Let's not discuss her! It's too painful.

IRENE. Where do you plan to go with her?

RUBEK (*weary and dispirited*). On some interminable trip north up the coast, I expect.

IRENE (*looks at him smiling almost imperceptibly, and whispers*). Go instead high up into the mountains. As high as you can go. Higher, higher—always higher, Arnold.

RUBEK (*tensely expectant*). Are *you* going up there?

IRENE. Do you have the courage to meet me one more time?

RUBEK (*struggling inwardly*). If only—oh, if we only could—!

IRENE. And why can't we do what we want? (*Looks at him, her hands folded, and whispers pleadingly*). Come, come, Arnold! Come up to me—!

(MAJA *enters, flushed with pleasure, around the corner of the hotel and hurries to the table where she and* RUBEK *had been sitting.*)

MAJA (*while still at the corner of the hotel, not looking about*). Oh, you can say anything you want, Rubek, but— (*Stops, catching sight of* IRENE.) Oh, I'm sorry—I see you've made a new acquaintance.

RUBEK (*brusquely*). I've renewed an acquaintance. (*Getting up.*) What was it you wanted?

MAJA. Just to tell you—that *you* can do as you please— but *I'm* not going to travel with you on that nauseating steamer.

RUBEK. Why not?

MAJA. Because I want to go up to the mountains and the forests—that's why. (*Cajoling.*) Oh, you have to let me do it, Rubek! I'll be so good, so good to you after!

RUBEK. Who's been putting these ideas in your head?

MAJA. *He* has—that nasty bear-killer. Oh, you can't imagine all the wonders he's been telling me about the mountains—and the life up there! Most of it's ugly, vile, disgusting—a pack of lies. Yes, because I'm practically certain he's lying. But all the same, it's so marvelously attractive. Oh, please, let me go with him? You understand, only to see if it's true, what he's saying. May I, Rubek?

RUBEK. Yes, I don't mind in the least. Go along up to the mountains—just as far and long as you like. Maybe I'll be going the same way myself.

MAJA (*quickly*). No, no, no, really, don't bother! Not for my sake!

RUBEK. But I *want* to go up there. I'm set on it now.

MAJA. Oh, thank you, thank you! May I tell the bear-killer right away, now?

RUBEK. You can tell the bear-killer anything you like.

MAJA. Oh, I do thank you so much! (*Tries to grasp his hand, but he evades her.*) Oh—you're so sweet and kind today, Rubek!

(*She runs into the hotel. At the same moment, the door to the pavilion is gently and soundlessly set ajar. Within the opening the* NUN *stands, surveying the situation. No one sees her.*)

RUBEK (*inwardly resolved, turning to* IRENE.) Then we're meeting up there?

IRENE (*slowly rises.*) Yes, most assuredly we'll meet. I've searched so long for you.

RUBEK. When did you start searching for me, Irene?

IRENE (*with the hint of a wry smile*). From the time I realized that I'd given you something quite irreplaceable. Something one never ought to part with.

RUBEK (*bowing his head*). Yes, that's all too painfully true. You gave me three-four years of your youth.

IRENE. Little prodigal that I was—I gave you far, far more than that.

RUBEK. Yes, you were prodigal, Irene. You gave me all your naked loveliness—

IRENE. To contemplate—

RUBEK. And to glorify—

IRENE. Yes, to glorify yourself. And the child.

RUBEK. And you, too, Irene.

IRENE. But the rarest gift you've forgotten.

RUBEK. Rarest—? What gift was that?

IRENE. I gave you my young, living soul. And that left me empty inside. Soulless. (*Her eyes fixed on him.*) That's why I died, Arnold.

(*The* NUN *opens the door wide, then steps aside for her as she enters the pavilion.*)

RUBEK (*stands staring after her, then whispers*). Irene!

◝ ACT TWO ◜

Near a health resort high in the mountains. The landscape, in the form of an immense treeless plateau, stretches away toward a long mountain lake. On the far side of the water a range of mountain peaks rises, with blue-tinted snow in the crevasses. In the left foreground a stream, split into separate runnels, washes down over a steep wall of rock, then flows quietly across the plateau to the right. Scrub trees, plants and rocks line the banks. In the right foreground, a small rise with a stone bench at the highest point. It is a summer evening, near sunset.

On the far side of the stream, in the distance, a group of singing children play and dance. Some are dressed in ordinary clothes, and others are in peasant costume. Their happy laughter can be heard faintly during the following scene.

PROFESSOR RUBEK *is seated on the bench, with a plaid over his shoulders, watching the children playing below. After a moment* MAJA *appears between some clumps of bushes in the left middle distance and peers about, with her hand shading her eyes. She is wearing a flat tourist cap, a short, gathered-up skirt reaching only halfway down her legs, and high, sturdy, laced boots. In one hand she has a long alpenstock.*

MAJA (*finally catches sight of* RUBEK *and calls*). Hallo! (*She comes across the terrain to the brook, leaps it with the help of her stick and clambers up the rise, arriving out of breath.*) Oh, I've been hunting for you everywhere, Rubek.

RUBEK (*nods indifferently*). Did you come from the hotel?

MAJA. Yes, that flytrap. I just now left it.

RUBEK (*briefly scanning her*). You weren't at lunch, I noticed.

MAJA. No, we had our meal under the open sky.

RUBEK. "We." Who's "we"?

MAJA. I—and that nasty bear-killer, of course.

RUBEK. Oh, him.

MAJA. Yes. And tomorrow, early, we're going out again.

RUBEK. After bears?

MAJA. Yes. Out for big game.

RUBEK. Have you found any tracks?

MAJA (*coolly patronizing*). You don't find bears above the treeline. Anyone knows that.

RUBEK. Where, then?

MAJA. Way down below. On the wooded slopes, where the trees are thickest. Where it's quite inaccessible to ordinary townspeople—

RUBEK. And the two of you are going down there tomorrow?

MAJA (*flinging herself down in the heather*). Yes, that's our plan. Or we might even start out this evening—if you don't have any objection, that is?

RUBEK. I? No, far from it—

MAJA (*quickly*). Lars will be coming, too, of course. With the dogs.

RUBEK. I'm not at all interested in Mr. Lars and his dogs. (*Shifting the subject.*) Wouldn't you rather sit up here properly on the bench?

MAJA (*drowsily*). No, thanks. It's so lovely to lie in the soft heather.

RUBEK. I can see you're tired.

MAJA (*yawning*). I almost think I'm beginning to be.

RUBEK. That usually comes afterward, when the excitement's over—

MAJA (*sleepily*). Yes, I'm going to lie and close my eyes.

(*A brief pause. All at once* MAJA *stirs irritably.*)

MAJA. Ugh, Rubek—how can you bear to sit here and listen to those children screeching! And watch all their capering about!

RUBEK. There's a harmony—almost like music—in their movements, every so often. Right in the middle of all the gawkiness. And it's amusing to sit and watch for those special moments—when they come.

MAJA (*with a faintly scornful laugh*). You're always the artist, aren't you?

RUBEK. I certainly hope so.

MAJA (*rolls over on her side, so her back is turned toward him*). *He* hasn't a trace of the artist in him.

RUBEK (*observantly*). Who hasn't?

MAJA (*her voice drowsy again*). Him. Who else?

RUBEK. You mean the bear-hunter?

MAJA. Yes. No trace of the artist. Not a trace.

RUBEK (*smiling*). No, I think you're absolutely correct in that.

MAJA (*heatedly, without moving*). But he's so ugly! (*Tears a tuft of heather out and throws it aside.*) So ugly! Ugly! Isch!

RUBEK. Is that why you're so eager to push off with him—into the primeval forests?

MAJA (*brusquely*). I don't know. (*Turning toward him.*) You're ugly also, Rubek.

RUBEK. You're just discovering that?

MAJA. No, I saw it long ago.

RUBEK (*shrugs*). People age, Maja. People age.

MAJA. That's not what I mean. No, there's something so weary, so defeated in your eyes—that is, whenever you're gracious enough to look at me—every once in a blue moon.

RUBEK. You think you can see all that?

MAJA (*nods*). Little by little you've taken on this evil look in your eyes. It's almost as if you were dreaming up some insidious plot against me.

RUBEK. Really? (*In an amiable, yet serious tone.*) Come, sit here beside me, Maja. Then we can talk.

MAJA (*raising herself halfway*). Would you let me sit on your knee, then? Like in those first years.

RUBEK. No, you mustn't. People can see us from the hotel. (*Moves a little.*) But you can sit here on the bench—next to me.

MAJA. No, thanks. Then I'd rather go on lying right where I am. I can listen well enough from here. (*Looks inquisitively at him.*) So—what did you want to talk about?

RUBEK (*starting slowly*). What do you think my real purpose was in going along with your idea of this summer trip?

MAJA. Well—among other things, you claimed it would do *me* a great deal of good. But—

RUBEK. But—?

MAJA. But now I don't believe for one second that was why—

RUBEK. And what do you believe now?

MAJA. Now I think it was all because of that pale lady.

RUBEK. Madame von Satow—!

MAJA. Well, look at her, hot on our heels. Last evening she showed up here, too.

RUBEK. But what on earth—?

MAJA. It's obvious you've known her intimately—long before you ever knew *me*.

RUBEK. And I'd also forgotten her again—long before I ever knew you.

MAJA (*sitting up*). Do you find it so easy to forget, Rubek?

RUBEK (*curtly*). Remarkably easy. (*Adds gruffly.*) When I want to.

MAJA. Even a woman who's been your model?

RUBEK (*deprecatingly*). When I have no more use for her—

MAJA. One who's stripped herself naked for you?

RUBEK. Means nothing. Not to an artist. (*Changing his tone.*) And how—might I ask—should I have known that she was here in this country?

MAJA. Oh, you could have read her name in the social notes, in one of our newspapers.

RUBEK. Yes, but she was absolutely unknown to me by her present name. I've never heard tell of any Herr von Satow.

MAJA (*affecting fatigue*). Oh, Lord, Lord—so I suppose you had some other reason for wanting to travel.

RUBEK (*soberly*). Yes, Maja—there *was* another reason. A quite different one. And that's what we need to discuss together.

MAJA (*choking back a fit of laughter*). Ooh, my, you look so solemn!

RUBEK (*studying her suspiciously*). Yes, maybe more solemn than necessary.

MAJA. How so—?

RUBEK. So much the better for both of us.

MAJA. Now you're getting me curious, Rubek.

RUBEK. Only curious? Not just a shade uneasy?

MAJA (*shakes her head*). Not a bit.

RUBEK. Good. Then listen. You said that day down at the spa that you thought I'd become quite nervous lately—

MAJA. Yes, you really have, too.

RUBEK. And what do you think is the cause?

MAJA. How should I know? (*Quickly.*) Maybe you've grown bored with my steady companionship.

RUBEK. Steady—? Incessant is more like it.

MAJA. Daily companionship, then. We've been living down there these four-five years—two solitary people—hardly ever an hour apart from each other. We two, all to ourselves.

RUBEK (*following with interest*). Well? So—?

MAJA (*somewhat depressed*). You're hardly a sociable man, Rubek. You'd rather go your own way and think your own thoughts. And you know I can't talk adequately with you about *your* concerns. About things like art and such. (*With a gesture of frustration.*) And, God knows, *I* care little enough about it!

RUBEK. All too true. Which is why we generally wind up by the fire, prattling about your concerns.

MAJA. Oh Lord—I don't have any concerns to prattle about.

RUBEK. Well, maybe they're not much. But in any case, the time passes for us that way, too, Maja.

MAJA. Yes, you're right there. Time passes. It's passing away from you, Rubek. And it's probably *that* that makes you so nervous—

RUBEK (*nodding emphatically*). And so restless! (*Writhing on the bench.*) No, I can't put up with this shallow life much longer.

MAJA (*gets up and stands a moment, regarding him*). If you want to be rid of me, just say so.

RUBEK. What kind of talk is that? Be rid of you?

MAJA. Yes, if you want to be free of me, then say it straight out—and I'll leave on the spot.

RUBEK (*with a barely perceptible smile*). Do you mean that as a threat, Maja?

MAJA. I can't imagine that's any threat for you.

RUBEK (*rising*). No, I expect you're right. (*After a pause.*) You and I can't possibly go on living like this together—

MAJA. All right. So then—

RUBEK. Doesn't have to be any "so then." (*Measuring his words.*) Because if we can't go on living together in solitude—it doesn't necessarily mean a divorce.

MAJA (*smiles disdainfully*). You mean, just a trial separation?

RUBEK (*shakes his head*). Not that, either.

MAJA. What, then? Explain what you want to do with me.

RUBEK (*hesitantly*). What I now feel so powerfully— even painfully—that I need, is to have someone around me who can reach my innermost self—

MAJA (*interrupting him tensely*). You mean, *I* don't, Rubek?

RUBEK (*hedging*). Not in this particular sense. I need companionship with someone who could fulfill me— complete me—be one with me in everything I'm striving for.

MAJA (*slowly*). Yes, of course in those big things, I could never help you.

RUBEK. No, you have to leave well enough alone.

MAJA (*flaring up*). And, God knows, it's nothing I want, either.

RUBEK. I'm sorely aware of that. And I never had any such role in view for you when we married.

MAJA (*scrutinizing him*). I can see plainly that you're thinking of someone else.

RUBEK. Really? I didn't know you were a mindreader. You can see that?

MAJA. Oh, yes. I know you so well, Rubek.

RUBEK. Then perhaps you can also see who that someone is?

MAJA. Definitely.

RUBEK. Well? If you'd be so kind—?

MAJA. You're thinking of that—that model you once

used for— (*Abruptly switching her train of thought.*) Are you aware that people down at the hotel think she's mad?

RUBEK. Oh? And what do people down at the hotel think about you and the bear-killer?

MAJA. That's beside the point. (*Returns to her former line of thought.*) But it was that pale lady you were thinking about.

RUBEK (*nonchalantly*). About her—absolutely. When I no longer had any use for her—and when she, in turn, walked out on me—vanished—into thin air—

MAJA. Then you took me on as a sort of consolation prize?

RUBEK (*more slightingly*). To be frank, Maja dear, that's about it. For a year, a year and a half, I'd gone on alone and preoccupied, putting the last—the final, finishing touches on my work. "Resurrection Day" went out all over the world and brought me fame—and all the splendors that go with it. (*With greater warmth.*) But I no longer loved my own work. All the bouquets and the incense just about turned my stomach and drove me out in despair to bury myself in the depths of the forest. (*Looks at her.*) You, being a mindreader—can you guess what occurred to me then?

MAJA (*casually*). Yes, it occurred to you to make portrait busts of ladies and gentlemen.

RUBEK (*nodding*). On commission, yes. With animal faces behind the masks. Those were a bonus, thrown into the bargain, you understand. (*Smiles.*) But that's not really what I meant.

MAJA. What, then?

RUBEK (*again serious*). It was the fact that all the talk about the artist's high calling and the artist's mission, and so on, began to strike me as basically empty and hollow and meaningless.

MAJA. What would you put in its place?

RUBEK. Life, Maja.

MAJA. Life?

RUBEK. Yes. Isn't life in sunshine and beauty altogether more worthwhile than to work on till the end of your days in a damp, dripping hole, slaving yourself dead tired over lumps of clay and blocks of stone?

MAJA (*with a faint sigh*). Yes, certainly that's what I've always believed.

RUBEK. And then, at last, I'd become rich enough to live in luxury, in the lazy, shimmering sunlight. To build myself a villa on Lake Taunitz and a palatial town house in the capital, and all the rest of it.

MAJA (*picking up his tone*). And then, to top everything, you had the means to acquire me as well. And you allowed me to play with all your treasures.

RUBEK (*joking to deflect her*). Well, didn't I promise to bring you up on a high mountain and show you all the glories of the world?

MAJA (*with a mild look*). You may have brought me up onto a fairly high mountain, Rubek—but I don't see the glories of the world.

RUBEK (*laughs irritably*). How insatiable you are, Maja! Totally insatiable! (*Explosively.*) But you do know what really drives me to distraction? Can you guess?

MAJA (*quietly defiant*). Yes, probably the fact that you've shackled yourself to me—for life.

RUBEK. I'd prefer a less heartless choice of words.

MAJA. But your meaning would be just as heartless.

RUBEK. You have no conception, really, of the way an artist's mind works.

MAJA (*smiles and shakes her head*). Good heavens. I don't even have any conception of the way my own mind works.

RUBEK (*continues, oblivious to her*). I live at such a high speed, Maja. All artists do. For my part, I've lived through a whole lifetime in these few years we've known each other. I've come to realize that it's absolutely not in me to find happiness by enjoying a life of leisure. For me and my kind, a life like that just doesn't go. I have to stay active—creating work after work—until the day I die.

(*With difficulty.*) That's why I can't go on with you any longer, Maja. Not with you alone.

MAJA (*calmly*). In plain terms, does that mean you've grown tired of me?

RUBEK (*fervently*). Yes, that's what it means! I've grown tired—insufferably tired and bored and worn out by living with you! Now you know. (*Checking himself.*) Those are ugly, brutal things for me to say. I know that all too well. And you're in no way at fault in this; I admit that freely. I'm the one, and no one else, who's undergone another transformation— (*Half to himself.*) —an awakening to what my life really is.

MAJA (*impulsively clasping her hands*). Then why on earth can't we go our separate ways, then?

RUBEK (*looking at her in surprise*). You'd be willing to?

MAJA (*with a shrug*). Yes—if there's nothing else to be done—

RUBEK (*impatiently*). But there *is* something else. Another way out—

MAJA (*raising her forefinger*). Ah, now you're thinking of your pale lady friend again!

RUBEK. Yes. Truthfully, I've been thinking of her all the time. Ever since I met her again. (*Goes a step closer.*) I've something to confess to you, Maja.

MAJA. Well?

RUBEK (*tapping his chest*). In here, you see—here I carry a little, tiny casket with a cunning lock that can never be forced. And in that casket all my visions lie stored away. But when she went off without a trace, the lock on the casket clicked shut. And she had the key—and she took it with her. You, my dear little Maja—you had no key. So everything inside there lies unused. And the years pass! And I can't get at that treasure.

MAJA (*trying to suppress a mischievous smile*). So get her to unlock it again.

RUBEK (*perplexed*). Maja—?

MAJA. Well, she's here, isn't she? And it's probably because of the casket that she's come.

RUBEK. I've never breathed a word of this to her.

MAJA (*with an innocent look*). But, my dear—is it worth making all this fuss and bother over something that's really very simple?

RUBEK. You think this is simple?

MAJA. Why, of course. Just latch on to whomever you need most. (*Nods at him.*) I'll always know how to find a place for myself.

RUBEK. Where do you mean?

MAJA (*coolly evasive*). Well—I could easily move out to the villa, if need be. But there's no necessity. In that great big town house of ours, there surely ought to be—with a little good will—room enough for three.

RUBEK (*doubtfully*). And do you think that could ever work permanently?

MAJA (*lightly*). Good Lord—if it doesn't work, then it doesn't. There's nothing gained by talking about it.

RUBEK. And what will we do, Maja, if it *doesn't* work?

MAJA (*blithely*). Then the two of us would simply get out of each other's way. Split up. I can always find something new for myself somewhere in the world. Where I'll be free! Free! Free! Don't worry on *my* account, Professor Rubek. (*Suddenly points off to the right.*) Look! There she is.

RUBEK (*turning*). Where?

MAJA. On that level stretch. Stalking along—like a marble statue. She's coming this way.

RUBEK (*stands, staring with his hand over his eyes*). Doesn't she look like the living image of Resurrection? (*To himself.*) That I could shift her—consign her to the shadows! Remodel her—what a fool I was!

MAJA. What's *that* all about?

RUBEK (*sidestepping the question.*) Nothing. Not anything you could understand.

(IRENE *approaches from the right across the plateau. The children at play have already spotted her and run to meet her. She is now ringed around by the entire group, some of them exuberant and full of trust, others shy and fearful. She speaks softly to them and indicates that they should go down to the hotel; she herself will rest a bit by the stream. The children run off, left, down the slope in the middle distance.* IRENE *goes over to the wall of rock and lets the divided strands of water run coolly over her hands.*)

MAJA (*in an undertone*). Go down and talk to her alone, Rubek.

RUBEK. And meanwhile, where will *you* go?

MAJA (*gives him a meaningful look*). I'll go my own ways after this.

(*She walks down the rise and leaps the river, again with the help of her alpenstock. She stops by* IRENE.)

MAJA. Professor Rubek's waiting for you up there, madam.

IRENE. What does he want?

MAJA. He needs your help with a casket that's jammed its lock.

IRENE. Can I help him with that?

MAJA. He believes you're the only one who can.

IRENE. Then I'll have to try.

MAJA. Yes, by all means, madam, do try.

(*She goes down the path to the hotel. Shortly after,* RUBEK *descends the slope to* IRENE, *but stops with the stream in between them.*)

IRENE (*after a brief pause*). She—that other one—says you were waiting for me.

RUBEK. I've been waiting for you for years—never knowing it.

IRENE. I couldn't come to you, Arnold. I was lying down there, in a long, deep sleep, full of dreams.

RUBEK. Oh, but now you've awakened, Irene!

IRENE (*shaking her head*). I still have the heavy, deep sleep in my eyes.

RUBEK. You'll see, there'll be the light of a new dawn for both of us.

IRENE. Don't ever believe that.

RUBEK (*ardently*). I do believe it! And I know it! Now that I've found you again—

IRENE. Risen from death.

RUBEK. Transfigured!

IRENE. Only risen, Arnold. Not transfigured.

(*Balancing on steppingstones below the waterfall,* RUBEK *makes his way across the stream to* IRENE.)

RUBEK. Where have you been all day, Irene?

IRENE (*pointing*). Far, far out there in the great dead plains—

RUBEK (*by way of diverting her*). I see you don't have your—your friend with you today.

IRENE (*smiles*). My friend's keeping a sharp eye on me, all the same.

RUBEK. Can she?

IRENE (*glancing furtively about*). You can be sure of that. Wherever I go—I'm never out of her sight— (*Whispers.*) Until, one lovely, sunny morning, I'll kill her.

RUBEK. You would?

IRENE. With pleasure. I'm just waiting my chance.

RUBEK. Why would you do that?

IRENE. Because she's a witch. (*Confiding a secret.*) Can you imagine, Arnold—she's changed herself into my shadow.

RUBEK (*trying to quiet her*). Now, now—we all have shadows. We have to.

IRENE. I'm my own shadow. (*In an outcry.*) Don't you understand that!

RUBEK (*sadly*). Yes, yes, Irene—I understand.

(*He sits on a stone by the stream. She stands behind him, leaning against the wall of rock.*)

IRENE (*after a pause*). Why do you sit with your eyes turned away from me?

RUBEK (*hushed, shaking his head*). I dare not—dare not look at you.

IRENE. Why don't you dare to any more?

RUBEK. You have a shadow that tortures you. And I have the weight of my conscience.

IRENE (*with a joyful cry of relief*). At last!

RUBEK (*jumps to his feet*). Irene—what is it!

IRENE (*waving him back*). Easy now, easy. (*Breathes deeply and speaks as if freed of a burden.*) There. Now they've left me. For a while, anyway. Now we can sit and talk as we used to—in my lifetime.

RUBEK. Oh, if we only could talk as we used to.

IRENE. Sit down there again. I'll sit here beside you.

(*He reoccupies his seat, as she sits on another stone nearby. A brief silence.*)

IRENE. Now I've come back to you, Arnold, from the outermost lands.

RUBEK. Yes, from an interminable journey.

IRENE. Back home to my lord and master—

RUBEK. To our own—to our own domain, Irene.

IRENE. Were you expecting me every day?

RUBEK. What did I dare to expect?

IRENE (*with a sidelong glance*). No, I guess you didn't dare to. Since you understood nothing.

RUBEK. Wasn't it really for someone else's sake that you left me so abruptly?

IRENE. Couldn't it as well have been for *your* sake, Arnold?

RUBEK (*looks at her, disconcerted*). I don't follow you—?

IRENE. After I'd served you with my soul and my body— and the statue stood finished—our child, as you called it— then I laid at your feet the costliest sacrifice of all—by erasing myself from that time on.

RUBEK (*bows his head*). And laying waste to my life.

IRENE (*suddenly flaring up*). But *that* was what I wanted! For you never, never to create anything again—once you'd created our only child.

RUBEK. Was it jealousy in you, then?

IRENE (*coldly*). I think it was closer to hate.

RUBEK. Hate? Hatred for me?

IRENE (*heatedly again*). Yes, for you—for the artist who so casually and unfeelingly took a warm-blooded body, a young human life, and slit the soul out of it—because you could use it to create a work of art.

RUBEK. How can you say that? You who joined in my work with such radiant joy, such a holy passion. That work that we two came together in every morning like a sacrament.

IRENE (*coldly, as before*). I want to tell you something, Arnold.

RUBEK. Well?

IRENE. I never loved your art before I met you. Nor afterward, either.

RUBEK. But the artist, Irene?

IRENE. I detest the artist.

RUBEK. The artist in me, too?

IRENE. Most of all, in you. Whenever I undressed myself and stood there naked for you, I hated you, Arnold—

RUBEK (*intensely*). Irene, you didn't! That isn't true!

IRENE. I hated you because you could stand there so unmoved—

RUBEK (*laughs*). Unmoved? You believe that?

IRENE. So infuriatingly self-controlled, then. And because you were an artist, only an artist. Not a man! (*Her tone changes, becoming warm and intimate.*) But that statue in wet, living clay, *that* I loved—the way a human figure filled with soul emerged out of those raw, shapeless masses. That was *our* creation, *our* child. Mine and yours.

RUBEK (*sadly*). Yes, in spirit and in truth.

IRENE. You see, Arnold—it's for our child's sake that I undertook this long pilgrimage.

RUBEK (*sharply attentive*). For that marble statue—?

IRENE. Call it what you will. It's our child to me.

RUBEK (*troubled*). And now you want to see it, completed? In the marble you always thought was so cold? (*Animatedly.*) Maybe you didn't know that it's been permanently placed in a great museum—far away from here?

IRENE. I heard some story like that.

RUBEK. And museums were always an abomination to you. You called them cemeteries—

IRENE. I want to make a pilgrimage to the spot where my soul and the child of my soul lie buried.

RUBEK (*concerned and anxious*). You mustn't ever see the statue again! You hear that, Irene! I implore you—never, never see it again!

IRENE. Do you think I'd die a second time?

RUBEK (*clenching his fists*). I don't know myself what I think. But then, how could I imagine that you'd focus so obsessively on that statue? You left, after all, before it was finished.

IRENE. It *was* finished. That's why I could leave you, all to yourself.

RUBEK (*sits with elbows on his knees, rocking his head from side to side, hands over his eyes*). But what you remember—later became something else.

IRENE (*silently, with lightning speed, half draws a thin, sharp knife from her bosom, then whispers hoarsely*). Arnold, have you done some harm to our child?

RUBEK (*hedging*). Harm? I can't say for sure what *you'd* call it.

IRENE (*breathlessly*). I must know—what have you done to the child!

RUBEK. I'll tell you if you'll sit and listen quietly to me.

IRENE (*concealing the knife*). I'll sit and listen as quietly as a mother can when she—

RUBEK (*breaking in*). And don't look at me while I talk.

IRENE (*moving over to a stone behind his back*). I'll sit here, behind you. Now tell me.

RUBEK (*drops his hands from his eyes and stares straight ahead*). When I discovered you, I knew right away how I ought to use you for my masterpiece.

IRENE. You called it "Resurrection Day." I call it our child.

RUBEK. I was young then—with no knowledge of life. The Resurrection, I thought, could be most beautifully and most sublimely portrayed as a pure young woman—untouched by worldly experience—awakening to the light and the glory, with nothing ugly or unclean to cast off.

IRENE (*quickly*). Yes—and is that the way I stand now in our work?

RUBEK (*hesitantly*). Not quite that way, Irene.

IRENE (*increasingly tense*). Not quite—? I don't stand there the way I posed for you?

RUBEK (*not answering*). In the following years, Irene, I learned how this world works. My conception of "Resurrection Day" became something larger and more—more complex. The little round pedestal on which your statue stood, erect and isolated—no longer had space for everything I wanted now in the composition—

IRENE (*gropes for the knife, then relinquishes it*). What did you add to it? Tell me!

RUBEK. I enlarged the composition with things I saw through my own eyes in the world around me. I had to. Nothing else would do, Irene. I extended the pedestal—to make it wide and spacious. And on it I set a piece of the curving, bursting earth. And out of the cracks in the earth human beings swarm up now, with disguised animal faces. Women and men—exactly as I knew them from life.

IRENE (*breathless with anticipation*). But the center of all that swarming mass is the young woman, radiant with joy? That's true, Arnold? I'm there?

RUBECK (*evasively*). Not precisely in the center. Unfortunately, I had to move the statue back somewhat. To improve the total composition, you understand. Otherwise, it would have been overly dominant.

IRENE. But my face still shines with that luminous joy, like a revelation?

RUBEK. It still does, Irene. That is, to a degree. A bit toned down, perhaps. To fit in with the change in my outlook.

IRENE (*standing up silently*). That composition expresses life as you now see it, Arnold?

RUBEK. Yes, I suppose it does.

IRENE. And in that composition you've moved me back, a bit faded—a subordinate figure—in a group. (*She draws the knife.*)

RUBEK. Hardly subordinate. At the least, let's call it an intermediate figure—roughly speaking.

IRENE (*in a husky whisper*). Now you've pronounced your own judgment. (*About to stab him.*)

RUBEK (*turns and looks up at her*). Judgment?

IRENE (*quickly hides the knife and speaks as if choked with misery*). My whole soul—you and I—we, we, we and our child were in that one figure alone.

RUBEK (*ardently, pulling off his hat and mopping his forehead*). Yes, but listen now, how I've introduced myself in the composition. In front, by a spring—it could be here —a man sits bowed down by guilt, as if he can't quite detach himself from the earth's crust. I call him remorse for a lapsed life. He sits there and dips his fingers in the flowing water—to rinse them clean—and he's wrung and harrowed by the thought that he'll never, never succeed. In all eternity he'll never be free to experience resurrection. He'll sit there perpetually in his own hell.

IRENE (*cold and harsh*). Poet!

RUBEK. Why poet?

IRENE. Because you're soft and lazy and full of self-forgiveness for every sin of your life, the acts you've done and the thoughts you've had. You killed my soul—and then you model yourself in remorse and penance and contrition— (*Smiles.*) —and you think that settles the score.

RUBEK (*defiantly*). I'm an artist, Irene. And I'm not ashamed of the human frailties I might carry around with me. Because, you see, I was *born* to be an artist. And no matter what, I'll never be anything else.

IRENE (*regards him with a veiled, evil smile and speaks softly and gently*). You're a poet, Arnold. (*Lightly, stroking his hair.*) You're a big, dear, overgrown child, not to see it.

RUBEK (*vexed*). Why do you keep calling me poet?

IRENE (*her eyes full of cunning*). Because, my friend, there's something extenuating in that word. Something self-justifying—that throws a cloak over every sin and human frailty. (*Her tone changing suddenly.*) But *I* was a human being—once! And *I* also had a life to live—and a human destiny to fulfill. See, I let that go—gave it all up to make myself your instrument— Oh, that was suicide. A mortal sin against myself. (*Half whispers.*) And that sin I can never atone for.

(*She settles down near him by the stream, observing him unnoticed, while absently plucking some flowers from the bushes around them. When she speaks, she is seemingly under control.*)

IRENE. I should have brought children into this world. Many children. Real ones, not the kind buried away in mausoleums. That should have been my vocation. That, rather than serving you—poet.

RUBEK (*lost in memories*). Still, those were beautiful days, Irene. Incredibly lovely times—when I think back—

IRENE (*gazing mildly at him*). Can you remember a little word you said—when you were through—through with me and with our child. (*Nods to him.*) Can you recall that little word, Arnold?

RUBEK (*looks quizzically at her*). I said one word then that you still remember?

IRENE. Yes, you did. Have you forgotten that?

RUBEK (*shaking his head*). I really don't remember. Not at the moment, anyway.

IRENE. You took both my hands in yours and pressed them warmly. And I stood there, breathlessly waiting. And then you said, "Thank you from the bottom of my heart, Irene. This," you said, "has been an extraordinary episode for me."

RUBEK (*looking dubious*). I said "episode"? I don't generally use that word.

IRENE. You said "episode."

RUBEK (*passing it off lightly*). Oh well—when you come right down to it, after all, it *was* an episode.

IRENE (*brusquely*). With that word, I left you.

RUBEK. You take everything too much to heart, Irene.

IRENE (*running her hand over her forehead*). Perhaps you're right. Let's throw off all this heavy-heartedness. (*Plucks the petals from a mountain rose and scatters them on the stream.*) See, Arnold. Those are our birds, swimming.

RUBEK. What sort of birds?

IRENE. Flamingoes, of course. Don't you see? They're red as roses.

RUBEK. Flamingoes don't swim. They only wade.

IRENE. Then they aren't flamingoes. They're sea gulls.

RUBEK. Yes, that's possible. Gulls with red beaks. (*Plucks some broad green leaves and tosses them in.*) Now I'm sending my ships out after them.

IRENE. But no hunters on board.

RUBEK. No, there aren't any hunters along. (*Smiling at her.*) Remember the summer we sat like this outside that little peasant cottage on Lake Taunitz.

IRENE (*nods*). On Saturday evenings, yes—when we'd finished our week's work—

RUBEK. And took the train out. And we stayed over Sunday.

IRENE (*a wicked gleam of hate in her eye*). Just an episode, Arnold.

RUBEK (*appearing not to hear*). You had birds swim in that stream, too. They were water lilies that you—

IRENE. They were white swans.

RUBEK. Yes, I meant swans. And I remember that I fastened a broad, downy leaf to one of the swans. A leaf of dock, I suppose—

IRENE. It turned into Lohengrin's boat—with the swan drawing it.

RUBEK. How happy you were with that game, Irene.

IRENE. We played it over and over.

RUBEK. I think, every Saturday. The whole summer long.

IRENE. You said I was the swan that drew your boat.

RUBEK. I said that? Yes, it's possible. (*Engrossed by the game.*) But look how the gulls are swimming down the stream.

IRENE (*laughing*). And all your ships ran aground.

RUBEK (*strewing more leaves in the current*). I have enough ships in reserve. (*Follows the leaves with his eyes, throws in more, then says after a moment.*) Irene—I bought that little peasant cottage on Lake Taunitz.

IRENE. Did you? You said so often you would buy it when you had the means to.

RUBEK. Well, now I have the means. So I bought it.

IRENE (*with a sidelong glance at him*). Are you living out there now—in our old house?

RUBEK. No, I had it torn down a long while ago. Since then, I've built a big, handsome, comfortable villa on the lot—with a park around it. That's where we usually— (*Correcting himself.*) —where I usually spend the summer.

IRENE (*checking herself*). So you and—and that other person stay out there now.

RUBEK (*contentiously*). Yes. When my wife and I aren't traveling—as we are this year.

IRENE (*gazing into the distance*). Lovely, lovely, that life on Lake Taunitz.

RUBEK (*as if delving within himself*). And yet, Irene—

IRENE (*completing his thought*). And yet the two of us let all that loveliness slip by.

RUBEK (*quietly and urgently*). Is it too late now for more than remorse?

IRENE (*sits in silence a moment, not answering, then points across the barren plain*). Look there, Arnold. The sun's just sinking behind those peaks. And look at all those clumps of heather out there, glowing red in that low, slanting light.

RUBEK (*following her eyes*). It's a long time since I've seen a sunset in the mountains.

IRENE. Or a sunrise?

RUBEK. I don't think I've ever seen a sunrise.

IRENE (*smiling as if lost in memory*). I once saw an incredibly beautiful sunrise.

RUBEK. Did you? Where was that?

IRENE. Far, far up on the reeling heights of a mountain top. You inveigled me up there and promised to show me all the glories of the world if I'd only— (*She stops cold.*)

RUBEK. Only—what?

IRENE. Do as you said. Share with you the path to the heights. And right there, I fell on my knees—and worshipped you. And served you. (*Remains silent for a moment, then speaks softly.*) And then I saw the sunrise.

RUBEK (*shifting the subject*). Wouldn't you like to come down and live with us, in the villa on the lake?

IRENE (*looking at him with a disdainful smile*). With you—and that other woman?

RUBEK (*importunately*). With me—just like the days when we created together. You could open up everything that's locked away in me. Couldn't you do that, Irene?

IRENE (*shakes her head*). I don't have the key to you any longer, Arnold.

RUBEK. You have the key! You alone have it! (*Beseeching her.*) Help me—so I can try to live my life over again!

IRENE (*impassively, as before*). Empty dreams. Aimless —dead dreams. *Our* life together can never be resurrected.

RUBEK (*brusquely, dropping the matter*). Then let's just keep playing our game!

IRENE. Yes, playing, playing—only playing!

(*They sit strewing leaves and petals out onto the current and watching them swirl and sail downstream. Coming up over the rock escarpment, in the left background,* ULFHEJM *and* MAJA *appear, dressed in hunting outfits. After them comes the* SERVANT *with the brace of leashed hounds, which he leads out to the right.*)

RUBEK (*catching sight of them*). Look, there goes little Maja with the bear-hunter.

IRENE. Your lady, yes.

RUBEK. Or his.

MAJA (*scanning the terrain as she walks, spotting the two by the stream and calling*). Good night, Professor! Dream of me. I'm off for an adventure!

RUBEK (*calls back*). What are you adventuring after?

MAJA. Life! I'm putting life before everything else.

RUBEK (*mockingly*). Oh, have you thought of that, too, Maja?

MAJA. That's right. And I made up a little song about it—like this:

(*Sings exultantly.*)

I am free! I am free! I am free!
No more living in cages for me!
I am free as a bird! I am free!

MAJA. Yes, because I think I'm awakening now—at last.

RUBEK. It looks that way.

MAJA (*draws a deep breath*). Ahh—I feel light as a feather in paradise, to be awake!

RUBEK. Good night, Maja dear—and good luck—

ULFHEJM (*breaks in with a shout of foreboding*). Shh, quiet! The hell with your good wishes! You'll jinx us. Can't you see, we're out hunting—

RUBEK. What'll you bring home for me, Maja?

MAJA. I'll get you a bird of prey, to model. On a wing shot, all for you.

RUBEK (*with a wry laugh*). Yes, wingshooting—accidentally on purpose—that's an old sport of yours, isn't it?

MAJA (*tossing her head*). Oh, we'll see how it is when I'm on my own feet— (*With a nod and a roguish laugh.*) Bye-bye—and have a nice, quiet summer's night on the moors.

RUBEK (*gaily*). Thanks. And rotten bad luck to you and the hunting!

ULFHEJM (*with a roar of laughter*). Ah, there's a wish after my own heart!

MAJA (*laughing*). Thank you, thank you, Professor!

(*They both have crossed the visible part of the barrens and go off through the bushes, right.*)

RUBEK (*after a brief pause*). A summer's night on the moors. Yes, that would have been life.

IRENE (*suddenly, with a wild expression in her eyes*). You want a summer's night on the moors—with me?

RUBEK (*opening his arms out wide*). Yes, yes—come!

IRENE. You, my beloved lord and master!

RUBEK. Oh, Irene!

IRENE (*hoarsely, smiling and groping at her breast*). It will only be an episode. (*In a rapid whisper.*) Shh, Arnold! Don't look around!

RUBEK (*also whispering*). What is it?

IRENE. A face, staring at me.

RUBEK (*turning despite himself*). Where? (*With a start.*) Ah—!

(*The NUN's head has come halfway in view among the bushes by the path to the left. Her eyes are unswervingly fixed on IRENE.*)

IRENE (*rises and speaks in an undertone*). We have to separate. No, you go on sitting. Listen to me! Don't try to

come with me. (*Bends over him and whispers.*) Till tonight. On the moors.

RUBEK. You'll be there, Irene?

IRENE. Yes, I'll be there, definitely. Wait for me here.

RUBEK (*repeats, as if dreaming*), A summer's night on
the moors. With you. With you. (*His eyes meeting hers.*)
Oh, Irene—that might have been our life—and we lost it,
you and I.

IRENE. We'll see what we've lost only when— (*Breaking
off.*)

RUBEK (*with an inquiring look*). When—?

IRENE. When we dead awaken.

RUBEK (*shakes his head sorrowfully*). Yes, and what,
really, do we see then?

IRENE. We see that we've never lived.

(*She crosses to the rise and descends. The* NUN *makes
room for her, then follows behind.* RUBEK *remains sitting
motionless beside the stream. From higher in the mountains,* MAJA's *song floats jubilantly down.*)

MAJA.   I am free! I am free! I am free!
          No more living in cages for me!
          I am free as a bird! I am free!

⌣ ACT THREE ⌣

A wild mountainside, gashed with fissures. Sheer precipices plunging down in the background. Snow-mantled peaks rise to the right to lose themselves higher up in drifting mist. To the left, on a slope of fallen rock, stands an old, half-tumbled-in hut. It is early morning. Dawn is breaking, but the sun has not yet risen.

MAJA, *flushed and furious, comes clambering down the rocks at the left.* ULFHEJM, *half angry, half laughing, follows her, holding her tightly by the sleeve.*

MAJA (*trying to tear herself loose*). Let me go! Let me go, I say!

ULFHEJM. Easy, easy—are you going to bite me next? You've got the temper of a she-wolf.

MAJA (*beating on his hand*). I said, will you let me go! And act decent—

ULFHEJM. I'll be damned if I will.

MAJA. Good, then I won't go another step with you. Did you hear that—not a single step—!

ULFHEJM. Ho ho—how are you going to lose me here on this rockpile of a mountain?

MAJA. I'll jump right over that cliff there, if I have to—

ULFHEJM. And smash and mash yourself up into dogfood—deliciously bloody—? (*Releases her.*) It's all yours. Go on, jump over the cliff, if you like. It's a sickening drop. Only one narrow path goes down, and it's almost impassable.

MAJA (*smoothes her skirt with her hand and looks at him with blazing eyes.*) Oh, you're really a prize to go out hunting with!

ULFHEJM. Say rather, to do some sporting with.

MAJA. Oh, you call this sport?

ULFHEJM. Yes, I take that esteemed liberty. It's the kind of sport I relish the best.

MAJA (*tosses her head*). Well—I must say! (*After a pause, studying him.*) Why did you let the dogs loose up there?

ULFHEJM (*blinks and grins*). Can't you guess? So they could do a little hunting for a change.

MAJA. That's not true at all! You had no thought of those dogs when you let them go.

ULFHEJM (*still grinning*). All right, why did I do it? You tell me—

MAJA. You let them go to get rid of Lars. You said, he ought to chase after them and bring them back. And meanwhile— Yes, very clever of you!

ULFHEJM. And meanwhile—?

MAJA (*cutting him off*). Never mind about that.

ULFHEJM (*in a confidential tone*). Lars won't find them. You can bet your life on that. He won't bring 'em in before it's time.

MAJA (*looks at him, exasperated*). No, I'm sure he won't.

ULFHEJM (*grasping for her arm*). For Lars—he knows my—hunting methods, he does.

MAJA (*eluding him and gauging him with her eyes*). Do you know what you resemble, Mr. Ulfhejm?

ULFHEJM. I would guess, I most resemble myself.

MAJA. Perfectly correct. Because you're the living image of a satyr.

ULFHEJM. A satyr—?

MAJA. Yes, a satyr, exactly.

ULFHEJM. A satyr—isn't that some kind of monster? Or what you might call a wood demon?

MAJA. Yes, the very thing you are. With a little goatee, and legs like a goat. Yes, and then a satyr has horns, too.

ULFHEJM. Uh-oh—he has horns, too?

MAJA. A pair of disgusting horns, just like you.

ULFHEJM. Can you see those poor horns *I* have?

MAJA. Yes, I think I see them quite distinctly.

ULFHEJM (*takes a dog's leash out of his pocket*). Then it would be best for me to tie you up.

MAJA. Are you utterly mad! Tie me up—?

ULFHEJM. If I'm a demon, then I'll act like one. All right! So you can see the horns?

MAJA (*soothingly*). Now, now, now—behave yourself properly, Mr. Ulfhejm. (*Breaking off.*) But where's that hunting lodge of yours that you've been talking high and low about? It was supposed to lie somewhere around here, according to you.

ULFHEJM (*pointing ostentatiously to the hut*). There it is, right before your eyes.

MAJA. That old pigsty there?

ULFHEJM (*laughs under his breath*). It's put up more than one princess, that one.

MAJA. Is that where the loathsome man you told me about came in to the princess in the shape of a bear?

ULFHEJM. Yes, madam huntress—the very spot. (*With a hospitable gesture.*) If it would so please you to stay within—

MAJA. Isch! I'd never set foot in it—! Isch!

ULFHEJM. Oh, a couple can drowse away a summer

night quite cozily in there. Or a whole summer—if you like.

MAJA. Thanks. But one needs a certain taste for that. (*Impatiently.*) Anyway, I'm bored now, both with you and your hunting trip. I want to go down to the hotel—before everybody wakes up.

ULFHEJM. How do you think you're going to get down?

MAJA. That's your concern. I know there has to be a trail down somewhere.

ULFHEJM (*pointing toward the back*). Why, sure, there's some sort of trail—right across that rock face there—

MAJA. Well, that's better—a little cooperation—

ULFHEJM. But let's see if you have the nerve to try it.

MAJA (*hesitantly*). You don't think so?

ULFHEJM. Not a chance! Unless I help you—

MAJA (*uneasily*). Well then, come and help me! What else are you here for?

ULFHEJM. Would you rather I took you piggyback—

MAJA. Idiot!

ULFHEJM. Or carried you in my arms?

MAJA. Don't start with that drivel again!

ULFHEJM (*with an edge of resentment*). I once did that with a little hussy—picked her up out of the gutter and carried her in my arms. I handled her with kid gloves. I would have carried her that way all through life—so that her slender foot wouldn't be cut by any stone. Because the soles of her shoes were worn pretty thin when I found her.

MAJA. But still you picked her up and carried her like that?

ULFHEJM. Picked her up out of the filth and lifted her as high and as tenderly as I could. (*With a rumbling laugh.*) And you know what thanks I got for that?

MAJA. No. What?

ULFHEJM (*looks at her, smiles and nods*). I got these

horns. The ones you can see so distinctly. Isn't that an amusing story, madam bear-slayer?

MAJA. Oh yes, quite amusing. But I know another story that's even more amusing.

ULFHEJM. What's that?

MAJA. It goes like this. Once upon a time there was a stupid little girl, who had both a father and a mother. But they lived on very little money. Then, one day, a great and celebrated gentleman appeared in the midst of all this poverty. And he took the young maiden up in his arms—just like you—and journeyed far, far away with her.

ULFHEJM. Did she want to be wherever he was?

MAJA. Yes, because she was stupid, you see.

ULFHEJM. And I suppose he was a handsome specimen of manhood?

MAJA. Oh no, he wasn't especially handsome at all. But he fooled her into thinking that she'd go along with him up on top of the highest mountain, where there would always be light and sunshine.

ULFHEJM. So he was a mountain climber, that man?

MAJA. Yes, he was—in his way.

ULFHEJM. So he took the little girl up with him—?

MAJA (*tossing her head*). Oh, I'll say—he took her, but not up! No, he duped her into a cold, dank cage, where there was neither sun nor fresh air—as it seemed to *her*, anyway—but only gilded walls, with great stone phantoms spaced around them.

ULFHEJM. Hang me, but it served her right!

MAJA. Yes; but it makes an even more amusing story, don't you think?

ULFHEJM (*regarding her a moment*). Listen, my fine hunting friend—

MAJA. Well? What now?

ULFHEJM. Shouldn't you and I patch our rags and tatters together?

MAJA. Is milord setting up as a quilt-maker?

ULFHEJM. Yes, I think he is. Couldn't the two of us stitch the pieces together here and there—and make something in the shape of a human life out of them?

MAJA. And when those poor scraps wear out completely —what then?

ULFHEJM (*with a sweeping gesture*). Then we'll stand there, free and easy—exactly as nature made us.

MAJA (*laughing*). You with your goat legs, yes!

ULFHEJM. And you with your—well, enough said.

MAJA. Come on—let's go.

ULFHEJM. Wait! Where to?

MAJA. Down to the hotel, of course.

ULFHEJM. And afterward?

MAJA. Then we'll say respectful goodbyes to each other and "thanks for the conversation."

ULFHEJM. *Can* we separate, you and I? You think we *can?*

MAJA. Well, you never did tie me up, you know.

ULFHEJM. I have a castle to offer you—

MAJA (*pointing to the hut*). A mate to that one?

ULFHEJM. Mine hasn't fallen apart yet.

MAJA. And all the glory of the world, too?

ULFHEJM. One castle, I said—

MAJA. Thanks! I've had my fill of castles.

ULFHEJM. With magnificent hunting grounds stretching for miles around.

MAJA. Are there works of art in your castle?

ULFHEJM (*slowly*). No—actually, there are no works of art, but—

MAJA (*relieved*). Well, that's good news!

ULFHEJM. Will you go with me then—for as far and as long as I want?

MAJA. There's a tame bird of prey keeping watch on me.

ULFHEJM (*wildly*). We'll let him have a bullet in his wing, Maja!

MAJA (*looks at him a moment, then says decisively*). Then carry me down through the depths.

ULFHEJM (*wraps his arm about her waist*). It's high time! The mist is closing in—!

MAJA. Is the trail down awfully dangerous?

ULFHEJM. The mountain mist is worse.

(*She pulls away from him, goes over to the chasm in back, peers down, then recoils with a start.*)

ULFHEJM. Makes your head swim a bit, uh?

MAJA (*weakly*). Yes, that too. But go over and take a look. Those two coming up—

ULFHEJM (*crossing to lean out over the precipice*). It's only your bird of prey and his strange lady.

MAJA. Couldn't we slip by them—without their seeing us?

ULFHEJM. Impossible. The trail's much too narrow. And there's no other way down.

MAJA (*steeling herself*). All right—let's have it out with them here!

ULFHEJM. Spoken like a true bear-killer!

(RUBEK *and* IRENE *emerge into view out of the chasm in the background. He wears his plaid over his shoulders; she has a fur cape thrown loosely over her white dress and a swansdown hood over her head.*)

RUBEK (*still only half visible above the rim of rock*). No—Maja! We meet again?

MAJA (*with feigned poise*). At your service. Do come and join us.

(RUBEK *climbs completely up and extends his hand to* IRENE, *who climbs up as well onto the ledge.*)

RUBEK (*coldly to* MAJA). So you've been all night on the mountain, too—like us?

MAJA. I've been hunting, yes. Remember, you gave me the night off?

ULFHEJM (*pointing toward the chasm*). Did you come up the trail there?

RUBEK. You saw that, I think.

ULFHEJM. And that strange lady, too?

RUBEK. Obviously. (*With a glance at* MAJA.) The strange lady and I plan not to take separate paths in the future.

ULFHEJM. Don't you know it's virtual suicide, the path you took—?

RUBEK. Well, we tried it, anyhow. Because it didn't look too bad at first.

ULFHEJM. No, nothing's too bad at first. But then you come to a tight turning where you can't go forward or back. And then you're stuck, Professor! Rock-trapped, we hunters call it.

RUBEK (*gives him a smiling look*). Are these meant to be wise sayings, Mr. Ulfhejm?

ULFHEJM. I hope to God I never commit a wise saying. (*Urgently, pointing toward the heights.*) But don't you see, there's a storm breaking right over our heads! Don't you hear those wind gusts?

RUBEK (*listening*). Sounds like the overture to the Day of Resurrection.

ULFHEJM. It's a thunder squall from the peaks, man! Just look at how those clouds are churning and rolling down. They'll be on top of us in no time, like a shroud.

IRENE (*shivers*). I know that shroud.

MAJA (*tugging at* ULFHEJM's *arm*). Let's try to get down.

ULFHEJM (*to* RUBEK). I can't help any more than one. Hole yourselves up in the hut for now—till the storm's over. Then I'll send up a party to fetch you down.

IRENE (*in terror*). Fetch us! No! No—!

ULFHEJM (*gruffly*). To take you by force, if necessary.

Because we're talking about life and death now. And don't you forget it. (*To* MAJA.) Come on—you can put yourself safely into my hands.

MAJA (*clinging to him*). Oh, if I come out of this alive, how I'll sing for joy!

ULFHEJM (*begins his descent and shouts to the others*). Wait there in that trail hut till the men come with ropes to fetch you.

(ULFHEJM, *with* MAJA *in his arms, clambers swiftly but carefully down into the chasm.*)

IRENE (*staring a moment at* RUBEK *with terrified eyes*). Hear that, Arnold? There'll be men coming up to take me! Many men, up here—!

RUBEK. Just be calm, Irene!

IRENE (*her fear mounting*). And she—the one in black —she'll come, too. She must have missed me already, for hours. And she'll take hold of me, Arnold! And put me in the straitjacket. Yes, because she has it with her in her trunk. I've seen it myself—

RUBEK. No one will be allowed to lay a hand on you.

IRENE (*with a distracted smile*). No—I've got my own remedy for that.

RUBEK. What remedy?

IRENE (*unsheathing her knife*). This!

RUBEK (*trying to grasp it*). That knife—!

IRENE. Always, always. Day and night. And in bed.

RUBEK. Give me that knife, Irene!

IRENE (*hiding it*). You won't get it. I may very well need it myself.

RUBEK. What would you need it for here?

IRENE (*looks fixedly at him*). It was meant for *you*, Arnold.

RUBEK. For me!

IRENE. As we sat by Lake Taunitz last night.

RUBEK. Lake Taunitz—?

IRENE. Outside the cottage. And played with swans and water lilies—

RUBEK. Yes. Go on.

IRENE. And I heard you say, like an ice-cold voice out of the grave—that I wasn't anything but an episode in your life—

RUBEK. It was you who said that, Irene! Not I.

IRENE (*undeterred*). Then I brought the knife out. Because I wanted to bury it in your back.

RUBEK (*darkly*). And why didn't you?

IRENE. Because it shot through my mind, the horrible thought that you were dead already—from long, long ago.

RUBEK. Dead?

IRENE. Dead. Dead as I was. We sat there by Lake Taunitz, two marble-cold corpses—playing games with each other.

RUBEK. I don't call that dead. But you don't understand me.

IRENE. Then where is that burning desire for me that you struggled and fought against when I stood freely before you as the woman risen from death?

RUBEK. I swear to you, Irene, our love isn't dead.

IRENE. That love that belongs to life on earth—this lovely, miraculous earthly life—this life full of mysteries—*that* love is dead in us both.

RUBEK (*passionately*). Do you realize, it's exactly that love—that scalds and burns in me now more than ever!

IRENE. And what of me? Have you forgotten what I am now?

RUBEK. For me you can be whoever and whatever you want! For me you're the woman I dream of seeing in you.

IRENE. I stood on a turntable—naked—and exposed myself to hundreds of men—after you.

RUBEK. I'm the one who drove you onto that turntable—

blind as I was then! I put the dead clay model above the joys of life—and love.

IRENE (*eyes downcast*). Too late. Too late.

RUBEK. Everything that lies between then and now hasn't lowered you in my eyes by a hairsbreadth.

IRENE (*raising her head high*). Nor in mine, either.

RUBEK. Well, what more, then! At last, we're free! And there's still time for us to live, Irene.

IRENE (*regarding him sadly*). The desire to live has died in me, Arnold. Now I'm risen. And I search for you—and find you. And then I see both you and life lie dead—just as I was lying.

RUBEK. Oh, how totally mistaken you are! Life goes on breeding and spawning in us and around us, as it has forever.

IRENE (*smiles and shakes her head*). Your young woman risen from death can see the whole of life laid out and embalmed.

RUBEK (*throwing his arms around her ardently*). Then let our two dead souls live life to the full for once—before we go down in our graves again!

IRENE (*in an outcry*). Arnold!

RUBEK. But not here, in the half-light! Not here, with that ugly, wet shroud flapping about us—

IRENE (*in an ecstasy of passion*). No, no—up in the light and all its flaming glory. Up to the peak of promise!

RUBEK. Up there we'll celebrate our marriage feast, Irene—my beloved!

IRENE (*proudly*). The sun will look kindly on us, Arnold.

RUBEK. All the powers of light will look kindly on us. And those of darkness, too. (*Seizing her hand.*) Will you go with me, my sacred—my sanctified bride?

IRENE (*as though transfigured*). Freely and joyfully, my lord and master.

RUBEK (*drawing her along with him*). First, up through the mist, Irene, and then—

IRENE. Yes, through all, all the mist—and then up to the topmost peak of the tower that gleams in the sunrise.

(*The mist, billowing down, closes in over the landscape.* RUBEK *and* IRENE, *hand in hand, climb up across the snow-field to the right and soon vanish in the low clouds. Ragged gusts of wind flurry and moan through the air. The* NUN *appears, advancing up the rock slope to the left. She stops and peers about silently. Out of the depths far below,* MAJA *can be heard, singing joyfully.*)

MAJA. I am free! I am free! I am free!
        No more living in cages for me!
        I am free as a bird! I am free!

(*Suddenly, a sound like thunder reverberates high in the snowfield, which gives way and swirls downward in a gathering momentum.* RUBEK *and* IRENE *are indistinctly seen, tumbled in the masses of snow that sweep over and bury them.*)

THE NUN (*with a shriek, reaches her arms out toward them and cries*). Irene! (*For a moment she stands in silence, then forms the sign of the cross in the air before her.*) Pax vobiscum!

(*From farther down the mountain,* MAJA's *song still rises, exultantly rejoicing.*)

APPENDIX

THE PLAYS OF IBSEN

Catiline   (1850)
The Warrior's Barrow   (1850)
Norma   (1851)
St. John's Eve   (1853)
Lady Inger of Østraat   (1885)
The Feast at Solhaug   (1856)
Olaf Liljekrans   (1857)
The Vikings in Helgeland   (1858)
Love's Comedy   (1862)
The Pretenders   (1863)
Brand   (1866)
Peer Gynt   (1867)
The League of Youth   (1869)
Emperor and Galilean   (1873)
Pillars of Society   (1877)
A Doll House   (1879)
Ghosts   (1881)
An Enemy of the People   (1882)
The Wild Duck   (1884)
Rosmersholm   (1886)
The Lady from the Sea   (1888)
Hedda Gabler   (1890)
The Master Builder   (1892)
Little Eyolf   (1894)
John Gabriel Borkman   (1896)
When We Dead Awaken   (1899)

SELECTED BIBLIOGRAPHY

TEXTS OF THE PLAYS

Ibsen, Henrik. *Samlede verker, hundreårsutgave.* Ed. Halvdan Koht, Francis Bull, and Didrik Arup Seip. Oslo: Gyldendal, 1928–1957. 21 vols. (The standard edition in Norwegian.)

Ibsen, Henrik. *The Oxford Ibsen.* Trans. and ed. James W. Mc-Farlane, *et al.* New York: Oxford University Press, 1960–1977. 8 vols. (Drafts, working notes, etc. in translation.)

BIBLIOGRAPHIES

Barranger, M. S. "Ibsen Bibliography 1957–1967." *Scandinavian Studies,* 41, No. 3 (August 1969), 243–58.

Pettersen, Hjalmar. *Henrik Ibsen 1828–1928.* Oslo: Cammermeyer, 1928.

Tedford, Ingrid. *Ibsen Bibliography 1928–1957.* Oslo: Oslo University Press, 1961.

Tiblin, Mariann, Lise-Lone Marker, Harald S. Naess, *et al.* "Ibsen Bibliography: Norwegian Literature; Theatre and Drama." *Scandinavian Studies,* annual supplements.

BIOGRAPHIES AND LETTERS

Ibsen, Bergliot. *The Three Ibsens, Memories of Henrik Ibsen, Suzannah Ibsen and Sigurd Ibsen.* Trans. Gerik Schjelderup. New York: American-Scandinavian Foundation, 1952.

Ibsen, Henrik. *Letters and Speeches.* Ed. Evert Sprinchorn. New York: Hill and Wang, 1964.

Koht, Halvdan. *Life of Ibsen.* New edition. Trans. and ed. Einar Haugen and A. E. Santiello. New York: Benjamin Blom, Inc., 1971.

Meyer, Michael. *Ibsen, A Biography.* Garden City, N.Y.: Doubleday, 1971.

Zucker, Adolf E. *Ibsen the Master Builder.* New York: Octagon Books, 1973 [1929].

BACKGROUND AND INTERPRETATION

Bradbook, M. C. *Ibsen the Norwegian, A Revaluation*. New Edition. London: Chatto and Windus, 1966.

Brandes, Georg. *Henrik Ibsen, A Critical Study*. New York: Benjamin Blom, Inc., 1964 [1899].

Clurman, Harold. *Ibsen* (Makers of Modern Literature Series). New York: The Macmillan Company, 1977.

Downs, Brian W. *Ibsen, The Intellectual Background*. New York: Cambridge University Press, 1948.

————. *Modern Norwegian Literature 1860–1918*. New York: Cambridge University Press, 1966.

Egan, Michael. *Ibsen, The critical heritage*. Boston: Routledge & Kegan Paul, 1972.

Fjelde, Rolf, ed. *Ibsen, A Collection of Critical Essays*. Englewood Cliffs, N.J.: Prentice Hall, 1965.

Flores, Angel. *Ibsen: Four Essays*. New York: Critics Group, 1937 [Engels, Mehring, Plekhanov, Lunacharsky].

Haakonsen, Daniel, *et al.*, eds. *Contemporary Approaches to Ibsen*. Vols. 1, 2, 3. Oslo: Universitetsforlaget, 1966, 1971, 1977.

Hardwick, Elizabeth. *Seduction and Betrayal: Women and Literature*. New York: Random House, 1974. (On Nora Helmer, Hedda Gabler, Rebecca West.)

Holtan, Orley I. *Mythic Patterns in Ibsen's Last Plays*. Minneapolis: University of Minnesota Press, 1970.

Hurt, James. *Catiline's Dream, An Essay on Ibsen's Plays*. Urbana: University of Illinois Press, 1972.

Ibsen Årbok. Skien: O. Rasmussen. 1952–   . ("Ibsen Yearbook"; articles by various hands in English and Norwegian.)

Johnston, Brian. *The Ibsen Cycle, The Design of the Plays from Pillars of Society to When We Dead Awaken*. Boston: Twayne/G. K. Hall & Co., 1975.

Jorgenson, Theodore. *Henrik Ibsen, A Study in Art and Personality*. Northfield, Minn.: St. Olaf College Press, 1945.

Knight, G. Wilson. *Henrik Ibsen*. New York: Grove Press, 1963.

Lucas, F. W. *The Drama of Ibsen and Strindberg*. New York: The Macmillan Company; London: Cassell and Company, 1962.

Lyons, Charles R. *Henrik Ibsen, The Divided Consciousness*. Carbondale: Southern Illinois University Press, 1972.

Marker, Frederick J., and Lise-Lone Marker. *The Scandinavian Theater, A Short History*. Totowa, N.J.: Rowman and Littlefield, 1975.

McFarlane, James W., ed. *Henrik Ibsen, A Critical Anthology*. Harmondsworth, Middlesex: Penguin Books Ltd., 1970.

————. *Ibsen and the Temper of Norwegian Literature*. New York: Oxford University Press, 1960.

Meyer, Hans Georg. *Henrik Ibsen.* Trans. Helen Sebba. New York: Frederick Ungar Publishing Co., 1972.

Northam, John. *Ibsen's Dramatic Method.* London: Faber and Faber Ltd., 1953.

————. *Ibsen, A Critical Study.* New York: Cambridge University Press, 1973.

Robins, Elizabeth. *Ibsen and the Actress.* New York: Haskell House, 1973 [1928].

Shaw, George Bernard. *The Quintessence of Ibsenism.* New York: Hill and Wang, 1957 [1913].

Tennant, P. F. D. *Ibsen's Dramatic Technique.* Cambridge: Bowes and Bowes, 1948.

Valency, Maurice. *The Flower and the Castle, An Introduction to the Modern Drama: Ibsen and Strindberg.* New York: The Macmillan Company, 1963.

Weigand, Hermann. *The Modern Ibsen, A Reconsideration.* New York: E. P. Dutton & Company, 1960 [1925].

IBSEN IN THE AMERICAN THEATER: AN ABBREVIATED STAGE HISTORY OF THE MAJOR PROSE PLAYS

The following compilation covers first professional English-language productions, as well as a representative selection of revivals, of the twelve Ibsen dramas from *Pillars of Society* to *When We Dead Awaken*, as staged in the United States from the single performance of *Thora* (*A Doll House*) on December 7, 1883, in Louisville, Kentucky, by a touring company starring Helena Modjeska and Maurice Barrymore, down to shortly before the playwright's sesquicentennial year of 1978.

Productions have been arranged chronologically by date of opening, under the heading of each play in the sequence of authorship. Where the name of the theater is not followed by the city and state in parentheses, the location is New York City. Production credits (individual or organizational producer, director, settings, costumes, lighting) are fragmentary or nonexistent for many early productions and are supplied as given in contemporary programs and newspaper accounts. Adaptors have been cited in only two instances, where each was a distinguished American playwright. In the cast listings, divergent notations and spellings of roles have been standardized. Where Norwegian names have familiar English equivalents, they have been anglicized, e.g. Hilde to Hilda.

Two caveats are in order. First, the intention has been to provide a tabular summary, limited to the major prose play cycle, of Ibsen in the American theater, not Ibsen on the American stage. The German-language productions of the thriving German theater in lower Manhattan in the 1880s and 1890s, the memorable appearance of Eleanora Duse in *La Donna del Mare* in 1923, a Royal Shakespeare Company *Hedda Gabler* visiting Washington, D.C., may further illuminate Ibsen's contribution to dramatic art, but these stand outside the story of the assimilation of Ibsen into our native theatrical tradition. Recent instances wherein director, designer and leading lady are British and other cast members are American remain borderline cases, but the tendency here has been to include rather than exclude.

Even within the limits set, however, the wealth of material precludes anything approaching a complete summary. At the time of the Ibsen Centennial in 1928, the available data encompassed 173 productions, with an unofficial estimate of considerably over a thousand; fifty years later, the aggregate has soared far beyond those figures. Regretfully, it has been necessary to omit the often highly competent, and occasionally brilliant, mounting of Ibsen productions in college and university, as well as secondary-school, theaters. Likewise, it has been possible to cite the merest fraction of the dedicated work of community theaters throughout the country. The productions listed below reflect essentially the professional theater on Broadway, off-Broadway and off-off-Broadway (showcase and experimental), as well as the regional repertory theater. A few examples of resident theaters attached to universities or conservatories, mixing professionals and students in an auspicious program of master-apprentice relationships, have been included. Indeed, this sampling of the production history of a single modern-classic dramatist traces a revealing profile of the migratory shifts of theatrical activity in America, from the palmy days of Broadway, with two fertile spans of Ibsen interest from 1903 to 1911 and again from 1922 to 1929, succeeded by the rise of off-Broadway in the 1950s and off-off-Broadway in the 1960s. These last have been paralleled over the same period by the burgeoning regional repertory theater movement, which has emulated such pioneers as the Cleveland Play House, whose first Ibsen production, *Rosmersholm*, occurred in 1922.

The second necessary caveat is that this list—although it

aspires toward that end—neither is, nor feasibly can be, a qualitative résumé of the best Ibsen productions over nearly a century. It assuredly includes most of the notable occasions involving Ibsen in the American theater; nevertheless, other productions may qualify for only a single remarkable performance, the inspired solution for one scene, or an innovative concept of staging. Certain of the American premieres themselves, judged by contemporary reviews, which may be unreliable, were ambivalent achievements, or even decorous disasters. Conversely, Ibsen has undoubtedly enjoyed performances of an exceptional level of attainment, which have been inadequately publicized, or recorded, or again, inadvertently overlooked; for any of the latter, the list maker must bear responsibility and offer apologies.

My purpose here has not been to assemble a skeletal essay in greenroom nostalgia, though the vanished and magic names may stir memories for some. Rather, what I hope emerges is a sense of continuity, of linked endeavor; for a great playwright is a mansion with many tenants—actors, directors, designers—all of whom leave something of themselves behind in the rooms their vitality has enlivened. Names, personalities, talents appear, disappear, resurface so regularly in these listings that Ibsen in America has sometimes seemed to belong to a kind of serial stock company, repeatedly drawn to that opportunity which Henry James has observed he affords to actors: "To do the deep and delicate thing—the sort of chance that, in proportion as they are intelligent, they are most on the look out for."

Finally, one hopes that this sense of continuity might become not only a collective but an individual resource as well. It may prove of some worth to, say, an actress who finds herself in the role of Hedvig in *The Wild Duck* to discover, from the record, Bette Davis in 1929 confronting the same complexity of choices, the same challenge to a victorious realization—as did in fact occur—along with others before her, and after. The inestimable contribution of the actor or actress is epitomized in a description by the critic Walter Prichard Eaton of one of the first and finest interpreters of Ibsen's art, Minnie Maddern Fiske, in the hazardous climax of *Pillars of Society*:

> Mrs. Fiske, as Lona, sat quiet, one of the crowd; but gradually, as she saw the man she loved throwing off his yoke of hypocrisy, the light of a great joy radiated from her face, ending in a stifled cry, half sob, half laugh of triumph, of indescribable poignancy. To one beholder, at least, it brought the rush of tears, and made the emotional as well as the intellectual drift of the play suddenly completely clear, completely fused and compelling.

The genius of such acting is less the feeling evoked, which serves the audience, than the clarity of meaning precipitated, which serves the playwright. In Ibsen's scores of roles, his ample gallery of rogues and hypocrites, victims of duty and liberators of truth, there is no lack of opportunity to reinvent the deep and delicate thing and add new luster to what already has been achieved.

PILLARS OF SOCIETY

First published: Gyldendal, Copenhagen, Oct. 11, 1877
First performed: Royal Theater, Copenhagen, Nov. 18, 1877

Lyceum Theater, March 6, 1891

Director, Franklin Sargent (with graduates and students of the American Academy of Dramatic Arts)

Cast: *Bernick*, George Fawcett; *Mrs. Bernick*, Katherine Arnold; *Olaf*, Stella Kenney; *Martha*, Maude Banks; *Johan*, Foster Platt; *Lona*, Alice Fischer; *Hilmar*, R. O. Jenkins; *Rørlund*, W. C. Bellows; *Dina*, Bessie Tyree; *Aune*, Thomas Oberle; *Krap*, P. West

---

Harlem Opera House, March 9, 1891

Producer: Oscar Hammerstein

Cast: *Bernick*, J. B. Studley; *Mrs. Bernick*, Constance Hamblin; *Olaf*, Idella MacDowell; *Martha*, Clara Baker Rust; *Johan*, Robert Hilliard; *Lona*, Henrietta Vaders; *Hilmar*, W. T. Melville; *Rørlund*, Alexis Markham; *Dina*, Ida Van Siclen; *Aune*, J. L. Ottomeyer; *Krap*, Edward Belknap

---

Lyric Theatre, April 15, 1904

Cast: *Bernick*, Wilton Lackaye; *Mrs. Bernick*, Maude Wilson; *Olaf*, Gerald A. Kelley; *Martha*, Margaret Kenman; *Johan*, White Whittlesey; *Lona*, Olive Oliver; *Hilmar*, Kenneth Davenport; *Rørlund*, William O. Hazeltine; *Dina*, Jane Oaker; *Aune*, A. H. Stuart; *Krap*, Edward H. Reardon

---

Lyceum Theater, March 28, 1910

Producer: Harrison Grey Fiske

Cast: *Bernick*, Holbrook Blinn; *Mrs. Bernick*, Virginia Kline; *Olaf*, Gregory Kelly; *Martha*, Alice John; *Johan*, Edward Mackay; *Lona*, Minnie Maddern Fiske; *Hilmar*, Cyril Chadwick; *Rørlund*, Henry Stephenson; *Dina*, Merle Maddern; *Aune*, Sheldon Lewis; *Krap*, R. W. Tucker

---

Copley Theater (Boston, Mass.), April 16, 1917

Producer: The Henry Jewett Players. *Director*, Henry Jewett

Cast: *Bernick*, H. Conway Wingfield; *Mrs. Bernick*, Gwladys Morris; *Olaf*, Ann Remlig; *Martha*, Beatrice Miller; *Johan*, Lionel Glenister; *Lona*, Jessamine Newcombe; *Hilmar*, Nicholas Joy; *Rørlund*, Cameron Matthews; *Dina*, Dorie Sawyer; *Aune*, Leon Gordon; *Krap*, Fred W. Permain

---

Forty-eighth Street Theater, Oct. 14, 1931

Producer: The New York Repertory Co. *Director*, Winifred Lenihan. *Setting*, Rollo Peters

Cast: *Bernick*, Moffat Johnston; *Mrs. Bernick*, Ann Dere; *Olaf*, Richard Jack; *Martha*, Fania Marinoff; *Johan*, Rollo Peters; *Lona*, Armina Marshall; *Hilmar*, Romney Brent; *Rørlund*, Knowles Entrikin; *Dina*, Dorothy Gish; *Aune*, Frank Conlan; *Krap*, Edgar Stehli

Geary Theater (San Francisco, Cal.), Oct. 12, 1974

Producer: The American Conservatory Theatre. *Director*, Allen Fletcher. *Setting*, Ralph Funicello. *Costumes*, Robert Morgan. *Lighting*, F. Mitchell Dana.

Cast: *Bernick*, Earl Boen; *Mrs. Bernick*, Joy Carlin; *Olaf*, David Darling; *Martha*, Anne Lawder; *Johan*, Charles Lanyer; *Lona*, Elizabeth Huddle; *Hilmar*, Sidney Walker; *Rørlund*, James R. Winker; *Dina*, Barbara Dirickson; *Aune*, Joseph Bird; *Krap*, Rick Hamilton

A DOLL HOUSE

First published: Gyldendal, Copenhagen, Dec. 4, 1879
First performed: Royal theater, Copenhagen, Dec. 4, 1879

Macauley's Theater (Louisville, Ky.), Dec. 7, 1883

Cast: *Nora*, Helena Modjeska; *Torvald*, Frank Clements; *Rank*, Ian Robertson; *Krogstad*, Edwin Cleary; *Mrs. Linde*, Mary Shaw; *Anne-Marie*, Mrs. M. A. Pennoyer; *Helene*, Belle Inman

Palmer's Theater, Dec. 21, 1889

Cast: *Nora*, Beatrice Cameron; *Torvald*, Atkins Lawrence; *Rank*, Herbert Druce; *Krogstad*, Mervyn Dallas; *Mrs. Linde*, Helen Gliddon; *Anne-Marie*, Miss Muire; *Helene*, Edith Russell
(First opened at Globe Theater, Boston, Oct. 30, 1889, directed by Miss Cameron's husband, Richard Mansfield, with Ida Jeffreys as Mrs. Linde.)

Empire Theater, Feb. 15, 1894

Cast: *Nora*, Minnie Maddern Fiske; *Torvald*, Courtenay Thorpe; *Rank*, Vincent Sternroyd; *Krogstad*, William H. Thompson; *Mrs. Linde*, Sydney Cowell Holmes; *Anne-Marie*, Alice Leigh; *Helene*, Bijou Fernandez

Garden Theater, March 19, 1896

Director, Henry Greenwall

Cast: *Nora*, Minnie Maddern Fiske; *Torvald*, James Neill; *Rank*, Frank R. Mills; *Krogstad*, Albert Gran; *Mrs. Linde*, Ida Waterman; *Anne-Marie*, Mary Maddern; *Helene*, Helen Macbeth

Manhattan Theater, May 21, 1902

Cast: *Nora*, Minnie Maddern Fiske; *Torvald*, Max Figman; *Rank*, Claus Bogel; *Krogstad*, James Young; *Mrs. Linde*, Eleanor Moretti; *Anne-Marie*, Mary Maddern; *Helene*, Helen Ashley

New Lyceum Theater, May 2, 1905

Producer: Charles Frohman

Cast: *Nora*, Ethel Barrymore; *Torvald*, Bruce McRae; *Rank*, Edgar Selwyn; *Krogstad*, Joseph Brennan; *Mrs. Linde*, Sara Perry; *Anne-Marie*, Eleanor Wilton; *Helene*, Davenport Seymour

Princess Theater, Jan. 14, 1907

Cast: *Nora*, Alla Nazimova; *Torvald*, Dodson Mitchell; *Rank*, Theodore Friebus; *Krogstad*, John Findlay; *Mrs. Linde*, Blanche Stoddard; *Anne-Marie*, Mrs. Jacques Martin; *Helene*, Mabel Findlay

Bijou Theater, Nov. 18, 1907

Cast: *Nora*, Alla Nazimova; *Torvald*, Dodson Mitchell; *Rank*, Walter Hampden; *Krogstad*, Warner Oland; *Mrs. Linde*, Rosalind Ivan; *Anne-Marie*, Mrs. Jacques Martin; *Helene*, Lillian Singleton

Plymouth Theater, April 29, 1918

Producer: Arthur Hopkins. *Director*, Arthur Hopkins. *Settings*, Clifford Pember

Cast: *Nora*, Alla Nazimova; *Torvald*, Lionel Atwill; *Rank*, George Probert; *Krogstad*, Roland Young; *Mrs. Linde*, Katherine Emmet; *Anne-Marie*, Amy Veness; *Helene*, Charity Finney

Morosco Theater, Dec. 27, 1937

Producer: Jed Harris. *Director*, Jed Harris. *Settings and Costumes*, Donald Oenslager. *Adaptor*, Thornton Wilder

Cast: *Nora*, Ruth Gordon; *Torvald*, Dennis King; *Rank*, Paul Lukas; *Krogstad*, Sam Jaffe; *Mrs. Linde*, Margaret Waller; *Anne-Marie*, Grace Mills; *Helene*, Jessica Rogers

Geary Theater (San Francisco, Cal.), Oct. 23, 1944

Producer: James B. Cassidy. *Settings*, Henry Dworkin

Cast: *Nora*, Dale Melbourne; *Torvald*, Francis Lederer; *Rank*, H. B. Warner; *Krogstad*, Lyle Talbot; *Mrs. Linde*, Keven Mc-Clure; *Anne-Marie*, Jane Darwell

---

Greenwich Mews Theater, May 7, 1956

Director, Miriam Goldina. *Setting*, Robert Motley. *Costumes*, Ann Howard. *Lighting*, Adrian Hall. *Music*, Reginald Godden

Cast: *Nora*, Maurine Holbert; *Torvald*, Howard Wierum; *Rank*, James B. McMahon; *Krogstad*, Jack Orrison; *Mrs. Linde*, Miriam Craig; *Anne-Marie*, Charlotte Acheson

---

Theater Four, Feb. 2, 1963

Producer: David Ross. *Director*, David Ross. *Settings and Costumes*, David Ballou

Cast: *Nora*, Astrid Wilsrud; *Torvald*, Paxton Whitehead; *Rank*, Richard Waring; *Krogstad*, Barnard Hughes; *Mrs. Linde*, Louise Troy; *Anne-Marie*, Alice Drummond

---

Actors Theater of Louisville (Louisville, Ky.), Jan. 20, 1966

Director, Richard Block. *Setting*, Brooke Karzen. *Costumes*, Lucile Paris. *Lighting*, Richard Mix

Cast: *Nora*, Patricia Stewart/Jo Deodato; *Torvald*, Grant Sheehan; *Rank*, J. S. Johnson; *Krogstad*, John Seitz; *Mrs. Linde*, Mitzi Friedlander; *Helene*, Judith Wikoff

Center Stage (Baltimore, Md.), April 11, 1969

Producer: Peter W. Culman. *Director*, John Stix. *Scenery and Lighting*, Robert T. William. *Costumes*, Ritchie M. Spencer

Cast: *Nora*, Dorothy Tristan; *Torvald*, Colgate Salsbury; *Krogstad*, Bruce M. Kornbluth; *Rank*, Maury Cooper; *Mrs. Linde*, Laura Esterman; *Anne-Marie*, Hylda Kohn; *Helene*, Barbara Frank

---

Playhouse Theater, Jan. 13, 1971

Producer: Hillard Elkins. *Director*, Patrick Garland. *Setting, Costumes and Lighting*, John Bury

Cast: *Nora*, Claire Bloom; *Torvald*, Donald Madden; *Rank*, Roy Schuman; *Krogstad*, Robert Gerringer; *Mrs. Linde*, Patricia Elliott; *Anne-Marie*, Kate Wilkinson; *Helene*, Eda Reiss Merin

---

Francis E. Drury Theater (Cleveland, Ohio), Oct. 15, 1971

Producer: Cleveland Play House. *Director*, Douglas Seale. *Setting*, Richard Gould. *Costumes*, Joe Dale Lunday. *Lighting*, Jeffrey Dallas

Cast: *Nora*, Carolyn Younger; *Torvald*, John Bergstrom; *Rank*, David O. Frazier; *Krogstad*, Richard Halverson; *Anne-Marie*, Carolyn Prescott; *Helene*, Stephanie Lewis

---

Geary Theater (San Francisco, Cal.), Jan. 9, 1973

Producer: American Conservatory Theater. *Director*, Allen Fletcher. *Setting*, Ralph Funicello. *Costumes*, Robert Blackman. *Lighting*, Fred Kopp

Cast: *Nora*, Marsha Mason; *Torvald*, Peter Donat; *Rank*, Paul Shenar; *Krogstad*, Donald Ewer; *Mrs. Linde*, Barbara Colby; *Anne-Marie*, Anne Lawder; *Helene*, Shirley Slater

---

Goodman Theatre Center (Chicago, Ill.), Nov. 20, 1973

Director, Tormod Skagestad. *Setting*, John Scheffler. *Costumes*, Alicia Finkel. *Lighting*, G. E. Naselius

Cast: *Nora*, Carole Shelley; *Torvald*, Philip Kerr; *Rank*, Anthony Mockus; *Krogstad*, Jeremiah Sullivan; *Mrs. Linde*, Maureen Anderman; *Anne-Marie*, Viola Berwick; *Helene*, Cynthia Baker Johnson

---

Seattle Center Playhouse, Feb. 5, 1975

Producer: Seattle Repertory Theater. *Director*, Eva Le Gallienne. *Setting*, Eldon Elder. *Costumes*, Lewis D. Rampino. *Lighting*, Richard Nelson

Cast: *Nora*, Jeannie Carson; *Torvald*, Curt Dawson; *Rank*, Hurd Hatfield; *Krogstad*, David Hurst; *Mrs. Linde*, Margaret Hilton; *Anne-Marie*, Leah Sluis; *Helene*, Marie Truty

---

Vivian Beaumont Theater, March 5, 1975

Producer: Joseph Papp. *Director*, Tormod Skagestad. *Setting*, Santo Loquasto. *Costumes*, Theoni V. Aldredge. *Lighting*, Martin Aronstein

Cast: *Nora*, Liv Ullmann; *Torvald*, Sam Waterston; *Rank*, Michael Granger; *Krogstad*, Barton Heyman; *Mrs. Linde*, Barbara Colby; *Anne-Marie*, Helen Stenborg; *Helene*, Judith Light

GHOSTS

First published: Gyldendal, Copenhagen, Dec. 13, 1881
First performed: Aurora Turner Hall, Chicago, May 20, 1882

Berkeley Lyceum Theater, Jan. 5, 1894

Director, Charles J. Bell

Cast: *Mrs. Alving*, Ida Jeffreys-Goodfriend; *Osvald*, Courtenay Thorpe; *Manders*, Albert Lawrence; *Engstrand*, G. Herbert Leonard; *Regina*, Eleanor Lane
  (Repeated at the Garden Theater, Jan. 25, 1894, with Olive Oliver as *Regina*, Albert Fisher as *Engstrand*.)

Carnegie Lyceum Theater, May 29, 1899

Director, Emmanuel Reicher

Cast: *Mrs. Alving*, Mary Shaw; *Osvald*, John Blair; *Manders*, William Beach; *Engstrand*, Franz Reicher; *Regina*, Edith Kenward

---

Manhattan Theater, Jan. 26, 1903

Producer: Mr. George Fawcett's Company

Cast: *Mrs. Alving*, Mary Shaw; *Osvald*, Frederick Lewis; *Manders*, Maurice Wilkinson; *Engstrand*, Charles A. Gay; *Regina*, Virginia Kline

Longacre Theater, April 20, 1915

Cast: *Mrs. Alving*, Alberta Gallatin; *Osvald*, Robert Whittier; *Manders*, Dodson Mitchell; *Engstrand*, Harry Neville; *Regina*, Virginia Fox Brooks

Comedy Theater, May 7, 1917

Producer: Washington Square Players. *Director*, Mary Shaw

Cast: *Mrs. Alving*, Mary Shaw: *Osvald*, José Ruben; *Manders*, Arthur E. Hohl; *Engstrand*, T. W. Gibson; *Regina*, Margaret Mower

Longacre Theater, Feb. 7, 1919

Cast: *Mrs. Alving*, Maud Hildyard; *Osvald*, Robert Whittier; *Manders*, Augustin Duncan; *Engstrand*, Wallis Clark; *Regina*, Helen Freeman

Punch and Judy Theater, Feb. 6, 1922

Cast: *Mrs. Alving*, Mary Shaw; *Osvald*, Everett Butterfield; *Manders*, Edward Poland; *Engstrand*, Arthur Shaw; *Regina*, Marion Allen

Comedy Theater, March 16, 1926

Producer: The Actors' Theater. *Director*, Dudley Digges

Cast: *Mrs. Alving*, Lucile Watson; *Osvald*, José Ruben; *Manders*, Edward Fielding; *Engstrand*, J. M. Kerrigan; *Regina*, Hortense Alden

Mansfield Theater, Jan. 10, 1927

Producer: Harrison Grey Fiske. *Directors*, Charles D. Coburn and Patterson McNutt. *Setting and Costumes*, David Gaither

Cast: *Mrs. Alving*, Minnie Maddern Fiske; *Osvald*, Theodore St. John; *Manders*, Walter Ringham; *Engstrand*, William C. Masson; *Regina*, Jarvis Kerr

Sutton Theater, May 23, 1933

Producer: George H. Brennan. *Director*, George H. Brennan

Cast: *Mrs. Alving*, Hilda Englund; *Osvald*, Donald Somers; *Manders*, Stuart Beebe; *Engstrand*, John Ravold; *Regina*, Joan Cordes

Empire Theater, Dec. 12, 1935

Producer: Luther Greene. *Director*, Alla Nazimova. *Setting*, Stewart Chaney. *Lighting*, A. H. Feder

Cast: *Mrs. Alving*, Alla Nazimova; *Osvald*, Harry Ellerbe; *Manders*, McKay Morris; *Engstrand*, Raymond O'Brien; *Regina*, Ona Munson

Cort Theater, Feb. 16, 1947

Producer: Louis J. Singer and the American Repertory Theater. *Director*, Margaret Webster. *Setting*, Watson Barratt

Cast: *Mrs. Alving*, Eva Le Gallienne; *Osvald*, Alfred Ryder; *Manders*, Herbert Berghof; *Engstrand*, Robert Emhardt; *Regina*, Jean Hagen

Fourth Street Theater, Sept. 21, 1961

Producer: David Ross. *Director*, David Ross. *Setting and Lighting*, Charles Bailey. *Costumes*, Theoni V. Aldredge

Cast: *Mrs. Alving*, Leueen MacGrath; *Osvald*, Joseph Marino; *Manders*, Staats Cotsworth; *Engstrand*, John McQuade; *Regina*, Carrie Nye

---

Lydia Mendelsohn Theater (Ann Arbor, Mich.), Oct. 24, 1962

Producer: Association of Producing Artists. *Director*, Eva Le Gallienne. *Settings, Costumes, Lighting,* Geoffrey Brown

Cast: *Mrs. Alving*, Eva Le Gallienne; *Osvald*, Clayton Corzatte; *Manders*, Richard Woods; *Engstrand*, David Hooks; *Regina*, Rosemary Harris

---

Francis E. Drury Theater (Cleveland, Ohio), Jan. 23, 1963

Producer: The Cleveland Play House. *Director and Setting*, David Hager. *Costumes*, Scott Bushnell

Cast: *Mrs. Alving*, Jo Ann Fineli; *Osvald*, Charles Keating; *Manders*, Richard Oberlin; *Engstrand*, Vaughn McBride; *Regina*, Margaret Victor/Linda Ryan

---

Playhouse In The Park (Cincinnati, Ohio), April 7, 1965

Director, Lloyd Richards. *Settings*, Douglas W. Schmidt. *Costumes*, Caley Summers. *Lighting*, Eric Gertner

Cast: *Mrs. Alving*, Mary Sinclair; *Osvald*, Dennis Longwell; *Manders*, Leon Shaw; *Engstrand*, David Hooks; *Regina*, Betty Lou Holland

Long Wharf Theater (New Haven, Conn.), May 2, 1969

Producer: Long Wharf Theater. *Director*, Arvin Brown. *Setting*, Will Steven Armstrong. *Costumes*, Alec Sutherland. *Lighting*, Ronald Wallace

Cast: *Mrs. Alving*, Mildred Dunnock; *Osvald*, Ken Jenkins; *Manders*, William Swetland; *Engstrand*, William Hansen; *Regina*, Joyce Ebert

Roundabout Theater, April 3, 1973

Producer: Roundabout Theater. *Director*, Gene Feist. *Setting*, Holmes Easley. *Costumes*, Sue A. Robbins. *Lighting*, R. S. Winkler

Cast: *Mrs. Alving*, Beatrice Straight; *Osvald*, Victor Garber; *Manders*, Wesley Addy; *Engstrand*, Fred Stuthman; *Regina*, Laura Esterman

Public Theater, April 2, 1975

Producer: Joseph Papp. *Director*, Leonardo Shapiro. *Setting*, Jerry Rojo. *Costumes*, Theodora Skiptares

Cast: *Mrs. Alving*, Mary Zakrzewski; *Osvald*, Chris McCann; *Manders*, Tom Crawley; *Engstrand*, Jerry Mayer; *Regina*, Jane Mandel

Strub Theater (Los Angeles, Cal.), June 1, 1977

Producer: Los Angeles Theatre Co. and ANTA-WEST. *Director*, George Shdanoff. *Setting and Costumes*, Tom Rasmussen. *Lighting*, Gary Raileanu

Cast: *Mrs. Alving*, Patricia Barry; *Osvald*, Robert Hathaway; *Manders*, Philip Lewis-Clarke; *Engstrand*, Michael Mazes; *Regina*, Kathy Paine

AN ENEMY OF THE PEOPLE

First published: Gyldendal, Copenhagen, Nov. 28, 1882
First performed: Christiania Theater, Christiania, Jan. 13, 1883

Chicago Opera House, March 8, 1895

Producer: Messrs. Abbey, Schoeffel & Grau

Cast: *Dr. Stockmann*, Beerbohm Tree; *Mrs. Stockmann*, Frances Ivor; *Petra*, Lily Hanbury; *Mayor Stockmann*, Charles Allen; *Kiil*, Lionel Brough; *Horster*, C. M. Hallard; *Aslaksen*, Alfred Wigley; *Hovstad*, Herbert Ross; *Billing*, Holman Clark
(This first professional performance in English in the United States, by a touring British company, was repeated in New York City at the Abbey's Theater, April 8, 1895.)

Berkeley Lyceum Theater, Jan. 1, 1905

Producer: The Progressive Stage Society

Cast: *Dr. Stockmann*, Charles James; *Mrs. Stockmann*, Astolaine Montgomerie; *Petra*, Eda Bruna; *Mayor Stockmann*, Algernon Eden; *Kiil*, George Low; *Horster*, Joseph Gallow; *Aslaksen*, Owen Craig; *Hovstad*, John de Perria; *Billing*, E. Milton Boyle

Hampden Theater, Oct. 3, 1927

Producer: Walter Hampden. *Director*, Walter Hampden. *Settings*, Claude Bragdon

Cast: *Dr. Stockmann*, Walter Hampden; *Mrs. Stockmann*, Mabel Moore; *Petra*, Marie Adels; *Mayor Stockmann*, C. Norman Hammond; *Kiil*, W. H. Sams; *Horster*, Ernest Rowan; *Aslaksen*, Cecil Yapp; *Hovstad*, Dallas Anderson; *Billing*, Stanley Howlett

---

Pasadena Community Playhouse (Pasadena, Calif.), May 28, 1929

Director, Gilmore Brown

Cast: *Dr. Stockmann*, Gilmore Brown; *Mrs. Stockmann*, Josephine Campbell; *Petra*, Jeane Wood; *Mayor Stockmann*, Joseph Sauers; *Kiil*, Norval Mitchell; *Horster*, Sherwood Walgamott; *Aslaksen*, Robert Young; *Hovstad*, Jerome Coray; *Billing*, Finlay McDermid

---

Hudson Theater, Feb. 15, 1937

Producer: Walter Hampden. *Director*, Walter Hampden. *Settings*, Claude Bragdon

Cast: *Dr. Stockmann*, Walter Hampden; *Mrs. Stockmann*, Mabel Moore; *Petra*, Marjorie Jarecki; *Mayor Stockmann*, C. Norman Hammond; *Kiil*, Dodson Mitchell; *Horster*, Albert Bergh; *Aslaksen*, Hannam Clark; *Hovstad*, Albert Van Dekker; *Billing*, Allen Nourse

---

Broadhurst Theater, Dec. 28, 1950

Producer: Lars Nordenson, with Donald M. Wolin. *Director*, Robert Lewis. *Settings and Costumes*, Aline Bernstein. *Lighting*, Charles Elson. *Adaptor*, Arthur Miller

Cast: *Dr. Stockmann*, Frederic March; *Mrs. Stockmann*, Florence Eldridge; *Petra*, Anna Minot; *Mayor Stockmann*, Morris Carnovsky; *Kiil*, Art Smith; *Horster*, Ralph Dunn; *Aslaksen*, Fred Stewart; *Hovstad*, Martin Brooks; *Billing*, Michael Strong

---

Provincetown Playhouse, Feb. 23, 1958

Director and Settings, Arthur Reel. *Costumes*, E. Blanche Barrett. *Lighting*, Henry Dencygar

Cast: *Dr. Stockmann*, David Moss; *Mrs. Stockmann*, Pat Crawford; *Petra*, Renay Granville; *Mayor Stockmann*, Sherman Lloyd; *Kiil*, James Colby; *Horster*, Lionel Habas; *Aslaksen*, James Alpe; *Hovstad*, Iver Fischman; *Billing*, Jerry Weiss

---

Actors Playhouse, Feb. 4, 1959

Director, Gene Frankel. *Settings*, Richard Bianchi. *Costumes*, Oliver Olsen. *Adaptor*, Arthur Miller

Cast: *Dr. Stockmann*, Ward Costello; *Mrs. Stockmann*, Lois Holmes; *Petra*, Joan De Marrais; *Mayor Stockmann*, Henderson Forsythe; *Kiil*, John Marley; *Horster*, Joseph Warren; *Aslaksen*, Al Sperdito; *Hovstad*, Gerald Hiken; *Billing*, Ronald Nicholas

---

Alley Theater (Houston, Texas), Feb. 22, 1961

Director, Nina Vance. *Settings and Costumes*, Don Bolen. *Lighting*, Jim Jeter. *Adaptor*, Arthur Miller

Cast: *Dr. Stockmann*, James Kenney; *Mrs. Stockmann*, Eleanor Wilson; *Petra*, Ann Williams; *Mayor Stockmann*, Robert Donley; *Kiil*, John Wylie; *Horster*, Hal Burdick; *Aslaksen*, Tom Toner; *Billing*, Robert Quarry; *The Drunk*, Bob Foxworth

Center Stage (Baltimore, Md.), Feb. 16, 1968

Producer: Center Stage. *Director*, Leonardo Cimino. *Settings*, Douglas Seale. *Costumes*, James Edmund Brady. *Lighting*, Lee Dunholter. *Adaptor*, Arthur Miller

Cast: *Dr. Stockmann*, William Newman; *Mrs. Stockmann*, Vivienne Shub; *Petra*, Delores Kenan; *Mayor Stockmann*, William McKereghan; *Kiil*, Bruce M. Kornbluth; *Horster*, Edd K. Gasper; *Aslaksen*, Anthony Brafa; *Hovstad*, David Rohan Sage; *Billing*, Joseph O'Sullivan

---

Repertory Theater (New Orleans, La.), Feb. 28, 1969

Director, David Scanlan. *Settings*, Lloyd Burlingame. *Costumes*, Matthew Ryan. *Lighting*, Fred Allison

Cast: *Dr. Stockmann*, Stuart Vaughan; *Mrs. Stockmann*, Barbara McMahon; *Petra*, Jenneth Webster; *Mayor Stockmann*, Herbert Nelson; *Kiil*, Frank Borgman; *Horster*, Robert Benson; *Aslaksen*, Don Perkins; *Hovstad*, David Byrd; *Billing*, Richard Larson

---

Vivian Beaumont Theater, March 11, 1971

Director, Jules Irving. *Settings*, Douglas W. Schmidt. *Costumes*, Carrie Fishbein Robbins. *Lighting*, John Gleason. *Adaptor*, Arthur Miller

Cast: *Dr. Stockmann*, Stephen Elliott; *Mrs. Stockmann*, Barbara Cason; *Petra*, Tandy Cronyn; *Mayor Stockmann*, Philip Bosco; *Kiil*, Sidney Walker; *Horster*, Don Plumley; *Aslaksen*, Roger De Koven; *Hovstad*, David Birney; *Billing*, James Blendick

---

Syracuse Stage (Syracuse, N.Y.), March 29, 1974

Director, George Sherman. *Settings*, Kenneth E. Lewis. *Costumes*, Lowell Detweiler. *Lighting*, Roger Morgan. *Adaptor*, Arthur Miller

Cast: *Dr. Stockmann*, Robert Lanchester; *Mrs. Stockmann*, Victoria Boothby; *Petra*, Kathy Connell; *Mayor Stockmann*, Tom Brannum; *Kiil*, John Carpenter; *Horster*, Tom Keena; *Aslaksen*, Jack Hollander; *Hovstad*, Vance Jefferis; *Billing*, James Staley

---

Arena Stage (Washington, D.C.), Oct. 29, 1975

Director, Zelda Fichandler. *Settings*, Grady Larkins. *Costumes*, Marjorie Slaiman. *Lighting*, Hugh Lester

Cast: *Dr. Stockmann*, Robert Prosky; *Mrs. Stockmann*, Leslie Kass; *Petra*, Dianne Wiest; *Mayor Stockmann*, Mark Hammer; *Kiil*, Howland Chamberlin; *Horster*, Howard Witt; *Aslaksen*, Terrence Currier; *Hovstad*, David Leary; *Billing*, Gary Bayer

---

Tyrone Guthrie Theater (Minneapolis, Minn.), Sept. 1, 1976

Director, Adrian Hall. *Settings and Costumes*, Sam Kirkpatrick. *Lighting*, Duane Schuler

Cast: *Dr. Stockmann*, Ken Ruta; *Mrs. Stockmann*, Barbara Bryne; *Petra*, Helen Carey; *Mayor Stockmann*, Tony Mockus; *Kiil*, Russell Gold; *Horster*, Oliver Cliff; *Aslaksen*, Wiley Harker; *Hovstad*, Peter Michael Goetz; *Billing*, Tom Hegg

---

Bowne Theater (Madison, N.J.), Aug. 23, 1977

Producer: New Jersey Shakespeare Festival. *Director*, Paul Barry. *Settings*, Don A. Coleman. *Costumes*, Dean H. Reiter. *Lighting*, Gary C. Porto.

Cast: Dr. Stockmann, William Myers; Mrs. Stockmann, Virginia Mattis; Petra, Jody Catlin; Mayor Stockmann, Ronald Steelman; Kiil, Richard Graham; Horster, Nesbitt Blaisdell; Aslaksen, Tom Brennan; Hovstad, Eric Tavaris; Billing, Brian Lynner

THE WILD DUCK

First published: Gyldendal, Copenhagen, Nov. 11, 1884
First performed: Det Norske Theater, Bergen, Jan. 9, 1885

McVicker's Theater (Chicago, Ill.), March 12, 1907

Director, Wright Lorimer

Cast: Werle, William C. Mason; Gregers, Carl Eckstrom; Old Ekdal, Ethelbert Hales; Hjalmar, Wright Lorimer; Gina, Gertrude Berkeley; Hedvig, Marian Ward; Mrs. Sørby, Sylvia Allen; Relling, Mark Price; Molvik, T. F. Tracey

Plymouth Theater, March 11, 1918

Producer: Arthur Hopkins. Director, Arthur Hopkins. Settings, Robert Edmond Jones

Cast: Werle, Dodson Mitchell; Gregers, Harry Mestayer; Old Ekdal, Edward Connelly; Hjalmar, Lionel Atwill; Gina, Amy Veness; Hedvig, Alla Nazimova; Mrs. Sørby, Nora Lamison; Relling, Lyster Chambers; Molvik, St. Clair Bayfield

Forty-eighth Street Theater, Feb. 24, 1925

Producer: The Actors' Theater. *Directors*, Dudley Digges and Clare Eames. *Settings*, Jo Mielziner

Cast: *Werle*, Moffat Johnston; *Gregers*, Tom Powers; *Old Ekdal*, Cecil Yapp; *Hjalmar*, Warburton Gamble; *Gina*, Blanche Yurka; *Hedvig*, Helen Chandler; *Mrs. Sørby*, Pearl Sindelar; *Relling*, Thomas Chalmers; *Molvik*, Philip Leigh (Edgar Henning, Micha Auer)

Goodman Memorial Theater (Chicago, Ill.), Feb. 7, 1928

Director, Whitford Kane. *Settings*, Leslie Marzolf. *Costumes*, Elizabeth Parsons. *Lighting*, Arvid Crandall

Cast: *Werle*, Dennis Martin; *Gregers*, Roman Bohnen; *Old Ekdal*, Art Smith; *Hjalmar*, John Waller; *Gina*, Dorothy Raymond; *Hedvig*, Katherine Krug; *Mrs. Sørby*, Ellen Root; *Relling*, Whitford Kane; *Molvik*, Richard Steele

---

Forty-ninth Street Theater, Nov. 18, 1928

Producer: The Actors' Theater. *Director*, Blanche Yurka

Cast: *Werle*, Reginald Goode; *Gregers*, Ralph Roeder; *Old Ekdal*, John Daly Murphy; *Hjalmar*, Dallas Anderson; *Gina*, Blanche Yurka; *Hedvig*, Linda Watkins; *Mrs. Sørby*, Clare Townshend; *Relling*, Frank Monroe; *Molvik*, Cecil Clovelly

---

Shubert-Belasco Theater, May 6, 1929

Producer: The Actors' Theater. *Director*, Blanche Yurka. *Settings*, Watson Barratt. *Costumes*, Ernest Schrapps

Cast: *Werle*, Edward Fielding; *Gregers*, Cecil Clovelly; *Old Ekdal*, John Daly Murphy; *Hjalmar*, Dallas Anderson; *Gina*,

Blanche Yurka; *Hedvig*, Bette Davis; *Mrs. Sørby*, Clare Townshend; *Relling*, Frank Monroe; *Molvik*, Walter Speakman

---

Francis E. Drury Theater (Cleveland, Ohio), Nov. 6, 1929

Producer: The Cleveland Play House. *Director*, Frederic McConnell. *Settings*, Arch Lauterer. *Costumes*, Helen Forrest. *Lighting*, Sol Cornberg

Cast: *Werle*, Walter Poulter; *Gregers*, Russell Collins; *Old Ekdal*, Elmer Lehr; *Hjalmar*, Noël Leslie; *Gina*, Ruth Feather; *Hedvig*, Katherine Squire; *Mrs. Sørby*, Rowena von Montbé; *Relling*, Emil Klewer; *Molvik*, Thomas B. Gorman

---

Forty-ninth Street Theater, April 16, 1938

Director, Henry Forbes. *Settings*, Harry L. Abbott, Edward Sundquist

Cast: *Werle*, Eric Franson; *Gregers*, William Challee; *Old Ekdal*, Edgar Henning; *Hjalmar*, Emerson Russell; *Gina*, Jane Lyon; *Hedvig*, Arlene Haber; *Mrs. Sørby*, Myrtle Miller; *Relling*, Traver Hutchins; *Molvik*, J. Allen Hamilton

---

City Center Theater, Dec. 26, 1951

Producer: New York City Theater Co. *Director*, Morton DaCosta. *Settings*, Peter Larkin. *Costumes*, Noel Taylor

Cast: *Werle*, Robert Middleton; *Gregers*, Kent Smith; *Old Ekdal*, Philip Loeb; *Hjalmar*, Maurice Evans; *Gina*, Mildred Dunnock; *Hedvig*, Diana Lynn; *Mrs. Sørby*, Nan McFarland; *Relling*, David Lewis; *Molvik*, Leonardo Cimino

---

Lyceum Theater, Jan. 11, 1967

Producer: APA-Phoenix Co. *Director*, Stephen Porter. *Settings*, James Tilton. *Costumes*, Nancy Potts. *Lighting*, Gilbert V. Hemsley, Jr.

Cast: *Werle*, Richard Woods; *Gregers*, Clayton Corzatte; *Old Ekdal*, Sidney Walker; *Hjalmar*, Donald Moffat; *Gina*, Betty Miller; *Hedvig*, Jennifer Harmon; *Mrs. Sørby*, Esther Benson; *Relling*, Joseph Bird; *Molvik*, Nicholas Martin

ROSMERSHOLM

First published: Gyldendal, Copenhagen, Nov. 23, 1886
First performed: Det Norske Theater, Bergen, Jan. 17, 1887

Princess Theater, March 28, 1904

Producer: Sidney Rosenfeld and The Century Players

Cast: *Rosmer*, William Morris; *Rebecca*, Florence Kahn; *Kroll*, Theodore Roberts; *Brendel*, Martin L. Alsop; *Mortensgaard*, Sheridan Tupper; *Mrs. Helseth*, Grace Gayler Clark

---

Lyric Theater, Dec. 30, 1907

Producer: Harrison Grey Fiske. *Directors,* Harrison Grey Fiske and Minnie Maddern Fiske

Cast: *Rosmer*, Bruce McRae; *Rebecca*, Minnie Maddern Fiske; *Kroll*, Fuller Mellish; *Brendel*, George Arliss; *Mortensgaard*, Albert Bruning; *Mrs. Helseth*, Florence Montgomery

Cedar Avenue Theater (Cleveland, Ohio), Feb. 10, 1922

Producer: The Cleveland Play House. *Director*, Frederic Mc-Connell

Cast: *Rosmer*, Frederick S. True; *Rebecca*, Katherine Wick Kelly; *Kroll*, Wallace C. Dunbar; *Brendel*, Ralph Benzies; *Mortensgaard*, Stephen Goby; *Mrs. Helseth*, Helen Haiman Joseph

---

Fifty-second Street Theater, May 5, 1925

Producer: The Stagers. *Director*, Edward Goodman. *Settings*, Cleon Throckmorton. *Costumes*, Fania Mindell

Cast: *Rosmer*, Warren William; *Rebecca*, Margaret Wycherly; *Kroll*, Carl Anthony; *Brendel*, J. M. Kerrigan; *Mortensgaard*, Arthur Hughes; *Mrs. Helseth*, Josephine Hull

---

Shubert Theater, Dec. 2, 1935

Director, Eva Le Gallienne. *Settings and Costumes*, Irene Shareff

Cast: *Rosmer*, Donald Cameron; *Rebecca*, Eva Le Gallienne; *Kroll*, Averell Harris; *Brendel*, Hugh Buckler; *Mortensgaard*, Walter Beck; *Mrs. Helseth*, Leona Roberts

---

Fourth Street Theater, April 11, 1962

Producer: David Ross. *Director*, David Ross. *Setting*, Charles Bailey. *Costumes*, Theoni V. Aldredge

Cast: *Rosmer*, Donald Woods; *Rebecca*, Nancy Wickwire; *Kroll*, Patrick Waddington; *Brendel*, Bramwell Fletcher; *Mortensgaard*, Barnard Hughes; *Mrs. Helseth*, Joan Croydon

Schoenberg Hall Auditorium (Los Angeles, Cal.), Sept. 2, 1964

Producer: The Theater Group. *Director*, Terence Kilburn. *Settings and Lighting*, Myles Harmon. *Costumes*, Niki Minter

Cast: *Rosmer*, Joseph Ruskin; *Rebecca*, Diana Frothingham; *Kroll*, Roger C. Carmel; *Brendel*, E. J. Andre; *Mortensgaard*, Howard Caine; *Mrs. Helseth*, Helen Backlin

---

McCarter Theater (Princeton, N.J.), March 29, 1973

Director, Louis Criss. *Setting*, David Jenkins. *Costumes*, Elizabeth Covey. *Lighting*, John McLain

Cast: *Rosmer*, Mark Lenard; *Rebecca*, Lauri Peters; *Kroll*, I. M. Hobson; *Brendel*, Edward Zang; *Mortensgaard*, Clarence Felder; *Mrs. Helseth*, Anne Sheldon

---

Roundabout Stage Two, Dec. 3, 1974

Producer: Roundabout Theater Co. *Director*, Raphael Kelly. *Setting*, Stuart Wurtzel. *Costumes*, Patrizia Von Brandenstein. *Lighting*, Timmy Harris

Cast: *Rosmer*, Bill Moor; *Rebecca*, Jane White; *Kroll*, Stephen Scott; *Brendel*, Stefan Schnabel; *Mortensgaard*, Steven Gilborn; *Mrs. Helseth*, Virginia Payne

---

Caras Nuevas Theater, May 9, 1977

Producer: Nicholas John Stathis and The Classic Theater. *Director*, Cyril Simon. *Setting*, Tony Giovannetti. *Costumes*, David Samuel Menkes. *Lighting*, Annie Rech. *Music*, David Hollister

Cast: *Rosmer*, Paul Vincent; *Rebecca*, Kathryn Harrold; *Kroll*, Jack Axelrod; *Brendel*, William Myers; *Mortensgaard*, Jeffrey Spolan; *Mrs. Helseth*, Norma Frances

Upstairs Theater (Providence, R.I.), Nov. 22, 1977

Producer: Trinity Square Repertory Company. *Director*, Adrian Hall. *Setting*, Eugene Lee. *Lighting*, Kevin Sean Keating. *Costumes*, Ann Morrell

Cast: *Rosmer*, Richard Kneeland; *Rebecca*, Margo Skinner; *Kroll*, George Martin; *Brendel*, Russell Gold; *Mortensgaard*, Daniel Von Bargen. *Mrs. Helseth*, Barbara Orson

THE LADY FROM THE SEA

First published: Gyldendal, Copenhagen, Nov. 28, 1888
First performed: Christiania Theater, Christiania, Feb. 12, 1889
Hoftheater, Weimar, Feb. 12, 1889

Lyric Theater, Nov. 6, 1911

Producer: The Drama Players. *Director,* Donald Robertson

Cast: *Ellida*, Hedwig Reicher; *Wangel*, Donald Robertson; *Bolette*, Barbara Hall; *Hilda*, Renee Kelly; *Arnholm*, Lionel Belmore; *Lyngstrand*, A. Hylton Allen; *Ballestad*, Edward Emery; *Stranger*, Sheldon Lewis

Bijou Theater, March 18, 1929

Producer: The Actors' Theater. *Director*, Cecil Clovelly

Cast: *Ellida*, Blanche Yurka; *Wangel*, Edward Fielding; *Bolette*, Linda Watkins; *Hilda*, Florida Friebus; *Arnholm*, Dallas Anderson; *Lyngstrand*, Walter Speakman; *Ballestad*, John Daly Murphy; *Stranger*, G. Pat Collins

---

Little Theater, May 1, 1934

Producer: Nathan Zatkin. *Director*, John Houseman. *Settings*, Donald Oenslager

Cast: *Ellida*, Mary Hone; *Wangel*, Moffat Johnston; *Bolette*, Rose Keane; *Hilda*, Margaret English; *Arnholm*, Roman Bohnan; *Lyngstrand*, Richard Whorf; *Stranger*, Clem Wilenchick

---

Fulton Theater, Aug. 7, 1950

Producer: The Festival Theater, *Director*, Sam Wanamaker. *Settings*, May Callas. *Costumes*, Paul du Pont. *Art Director*, Howard Bay

Cast: *Ellida*, Luise Rainer; *Wangel*, Herbert Berghof; *Bolette*, Joan Chandler; *Hilda*, Anne Jackson; *Arnholm*, Theodore Newton; *Lyngstrand*, Steven Hill; *Ballestad*, Eli Wallach; *Stranger*, Jeff Morrow

---

Tempo Playhouse, Dec. 4, 1956

Producers: William Gyimes and A. Woursell. *Director*, William Gyimes. *Settings*, Ben Ardery. *Costumes*, Cliff Capone

Cast: *Ellida*, Christiane Feismann; *Wangel*, Alex Reed; *Bolette*, Helen Quarrier; *Hilda*, Sandy Dennis; *Arnholm*, Lionel Belmore; *Lyngstrand*, Donald Hotten; *Ballestad*, Donald Marye; *Stranger*, Alan Ansara

Mercer-Shaw Arena Theater, Nov. 15, 1971

Producer: C.I.R.C.L.E., Inc. *Director*, Rod Nash. *Settings and Lighting*, Seymour Kleinberg. *Costumes*, Lee Nash

Cast: *Ellida*, Beth Dixon; *Wangel*, Earle Edgerton; *Bolette*, Marina Stefan; *Hilda*, Mareia Lee Merrill; *Arnholm*, Reddy O'Connor; *Lyngstrand*, Ted Henning; *Ballestad*, Joel Bernstein; *Stranger*, Neil Hunt

────────

Gotham Art Theater, Sept. 18, 1973

Producer: New Repertory Co. *Director*, Robert Kalfin. *Settings*, Christopher Thomas. *Costumes*, Elizabeth Covey. *Lighting*, David Sackeroff

Cast: *Ellida*, Marilyn Chris; *Wangel*, Paul Sparer; *Bolette*, Myra Malkin; *Hilda*, Marion McCorry; *Arnholm*, Richard Crook; *Lyngstrand*, Philip Himberg; *Ballestad*, Jerrold Ziman; *Stranger*, Harvey Solin

────────

Circle In The Square Theater, March 18, 1976

Producers: Theodore Mann and Paul Libin. *Director*, Tony Richardson. *Settings and Costumes*, Rouben Ter-Arutunian. *Lighting*, Thomas Skelton. *Music and Sound*, Richard Peaslee

Cast: *Ellida*, Vanessa Redgrave; *Wangel*, Pat Hingle; *Bolette*, Kimberly Farr; *Hilda*, Allison Argo; *Arnholm*, John Heffernan; *Lyngstrand*, Kipp Osborne; *Ballestad*, George Ede; *Stranger*, Richard Lynch

HEDDA GABLER

First published: Gyldendal, Copenhagen, Dec. 16, 1890
First performed: Hoftheater, Munich, Jan. 31, 1891

Fifth Avenue Theater, March 30, 1898

Director, Edwin Knowles

Cast: *Hedda*, Elizabeth Robins; *Tesman*, Leo Ditrichstein; *Brack*, William Courtleigh; *Løvborg*, Ernest Hastings; *Thea*, Maida Craigen; *Aunt Juliana*, Mrs. Griffith; *Berta*, Ellen Cummens

---

Manhattan Theater, Oct. 5, 1903

Cast: *Hedda*, Minnie Maddern Fiske; *Tesman*, William B. Mack; *Brack*, Henry J. Carvill; *Løvborg*, Hobart Bosworth; *Thea*, Carlotta Nillson; *Aunt Juliana*, Mary Maddern; *Berta*, Belle Bohn

---

Broad Street Theater (Philadelphia, Pa.), Feb. 12, 1904

Cast: *Hedda*, Blanche Bates; *Tesman*, Albert Bruning; *Brack*, J. Hany Benrimo; *Løvborg*, Eugene Ormonde; *Thea*, Minnie Dupree; *Aunt Juliana*, Mrs. F. M. Bates; *Berta*, Ada Lewis

Manhattan Theater, Nov. 17, 1904

Cast: *Hedda*, Minnie Maddern Fiske; *Tesman*, William B. Mack; *Brack*, George Arliss; *Løvborg*, John Mason; *Thea*, Laura Mc-Gilvray; *Aunt Juliana*, Mary Maddern; *Berta*, Emily Stevens

Daly's Theater, Nov. 24, 1904

Director, McKee Rankin

Cast: *Hedda*, Nance O'Neill; *Tesman*, Louis Massen; *Brack*, Charles Dalton; *Løvborg*, Charles Millward; *Thea*, Gertrude Binley; *Aunt Juliana*, Clara Thompson; *Berta*, Ricca Allen

Princess Theater, Nov. 13, 1906

Director, Henry Miller

Cast: *Hedda*, Alla Nazimova; *Tesman*, John Finlay; *Brack*, Dodson Mitchell; *Løvborg*, John Blair; *Thea*, Laura Hope Crews; *Aunt Juliana*, Mrs. Thomas Whiffen; *Berta*, Mrs. Jacques Martin

Bijou Theater, March 11, 1907

Cast: *Hedda*, Alla Nazimova; *Tesman*, William B. Mack; *Brack*, Guy Standing; *Løvborg*, John Blair; *Thea*, Florence Kahn; *Aunt Juliana*, Mrs. Jacques Martin; *Berta*, Gertrude Norman

Plymouth Theater, April 8, 1918

Director, Arthur Hopkins. *Setting*, Robert Edmond Jones

Cast: *Hedda*, Alla Nazimova; *Tesman*, Lionel Atwill; *Brack*, Charles Bryant; *Løvborg*, George Probert; *Thea*, Nila Mac; *Aunt Juliana*, Lizzie Hudson Collier; *Berta*, Charity Finney

Forty-eighth Street Theater, May 16, 1924

Cast: *Hedda*, Clare Eames; *Tesman*, Dudley Digges; *Brack*, Roland Young; *Løvborg*, Fritz Leiber; *Thea*, Margalo Gillmore; *Aunt Juliana*, Augusta Haviland; *Berta*, Helen Van Hoose

Comedy Theater, Jan. 26, 1926

Producer: The Actors' Theater. *Director*, Dudley Digges. *Setting*, Woodman Thompson. *Women's Costumes*, Fania Mindell

Cast: *Hedda*, Emily Stevens; *Tesman*, Dudley Digges; *Brack*, Frank Conroy; *Løvborg*, Louis Calhern; *Thea*, Patricia Collinge; *Aunt Juliana*, Hilda Helstrom; *Berta*, Helen Van Hoose

Civic Repertory Theater, March 26, 1928

Producer: Civic Repertory Theater. *Setting and Costumes*, Aline Bernstein

Cast: *Hedda*, Eva Le Gallienne; *Tesman*, Paul Leyssac; *Brack*, Sayre Crawley; *Løvborg*, Donald Cameron; *Thea*, Josephine Hutchison; *Aunt Juliana*, Alma Kruger; *Berta*, Leona Roberts

Forty-ninth Street Theater, Feb. 2, 1929

Producer: The Actors' Theater. *Director*, Blanche Yurka

Cast: *Hedda*, Blanche Yurka; *Tesman*, Dallas Anderson; *Brack*,

Frederic Worlock; *Løvborg*, Ralph Roeder; *Thea*, Linda Watkins; *Aunt Juliana*, Claire Townshend; *Berta*, Genevieve Williams

---

Francis E. Drury Theater (Cleveland, Ohio), May 14, 1930

Producer: The Cleveland Play House. *Director*, Frederic McConnell. *Setting*, Arch Lauterer. *Costumes*, Helen Forrest

Cast: *Hedda*, Katherine Wick Kelly; *Tesman*, K. Elmo Lowe; *Brack*, Walter Poulter; *Løvborg*, Russell Collins, *Thea*, Katherine Squire; *Aunt Juliana*, Irene Tedrow; *Berta*, Katherine Cast

---

Broadhurst Theater, Dec. 8, 1934

Producer: Civic Repertory Company. *Director*, Eva Le Gallienne

Cast: *Hedda*, Eva Le Gallienne; *Tesman*, Paul Leyssac; *Brack*, Hugh Buckler; *Løvborg*, Donald Cameron; *Thea*, Beatrice de Neergaard; *Aunt Juliana*, Marion Evensen; *Berta*, Leona Roberts

---

Longacre Theater, Nov. 16, 1936

Producer: Sam Levey. *Director*, Alla Nazimova. *Setting*, Stewart Chaney. *Lighting*, A. H. Feder

Cast: *Hedda*, Alla Nazimova; *Tesman*, Harry Ellerbe; *Brack*, McKay Morris; *Løvborg*, Edward Trevor; *Thea*, Viola Frayne; *Aunt Juliana*, Leslie Bingham; *Berta*, Grace Mills

Longacre Theater, Jan. 29, 1942

Producer: Luther Greene. *Director*, Luther Greene. *Setting*, Paul Morrison

Cast: *Hedda*, Katina Paxinou; *Tesman*, Ralph Forbes; *Brack*, Cecil Humphreys; *Løvborg*, Henry Daniell; *Thea*, Karen Morley; *Aunt Juliana*, Margaret Wycherly; *Berta*, Octavia Kenmore

---

Cort Theater, Feb. 24, 1948

Producer: Louis J. Singer and The American Repertory Theater. *Directors*, Eva Le Gallienne and Margaret Webster

Cast: *Hedda*, Eva Le Gallienne; *Tesman*, Robert Emhardt; *Brack*, Herbert Berghof; *Løvborg*, Efram Zimbalist, Jr.; *Thea*, Emily McNair; *Aunt Juliana*, Marion Evensen; *Berta*, Merle Maddern

---

Alley Theater (Houston, Texas), Feb. 25, 1956

Director, Nina Vance. *Setting*, Curt Sleight. *Costumes*, Evelyn Norton Anderson and Cecelia West. *Lighting*, Jimmy Jeter

Cast: *Hedda*, Erin O'Brien-Moore; *Tesman*, William Larsen; *Brack*, Jim Hilburn; *Løvborg*, Roy Shuman; *Thea*, Claudine Atkinson; *Aunt Juliana*, Amelia Parker; *Berta*, Betty Williams

---

Fourth Street Theater, Nov. 24, 1960

Producer: David Ross. *Director*, David Ross. *Costumes*, Theoni V. Aldredge

Cast: *Hedda*, Anne Meacham; *Tesman*, Lester Rawlins; *Brack*, Frederick Rolf; *Løvborg*, Mark Lenard; *Thea*, Lori March; *Aunt Juliana*, Lois Holmes; *Berta*, Elizabeth Colquhoun

Goodman Memorial Theater (Chicago, Ill.), Feb. 23, 1962

Director, Melvin Bernhardt. *Setting*, James Maronek. *Costumes*, Francis Morigi. *Lighting*, G. E. Naselius

Cast: *Hedda*, Signe Hasso; *Tesman*, Orest Kinasewich; *Brack*, Dan Bly; *Thea*, Geneva Bugbee; *Løvborg*, Brian Thompson; *Aunt Juliana*, Clementina Luotto; *Berta*, Arlene King

---

Francis E. Drury Theater (Cleveland, Ohio), April 12, 1962

Producer: The Cleveland Play House. *Director and Setting*, David Hager. *Lighting*, Orison Bedell

Cast: *Hedda*, Adale O'Brien; *Tesman*, Richard Oberlin; *Brack*, Michael McGuire; *Løvborg*, Alan Lindgren; *Thea*, Sally Noble; *Aunt Juliana*, Jo Ann Finnelli; *Berta*, Sue Kelly

---

Virginia Museum Theater (Richmond, Va.), Jan. 20, 1965

Director, Kai Jorgensen. *Setting and Lighting*, John H. Döepp. *Costumes*, Anthony Eikenbary

Cast: *Hedda*, Marjorie Arenstein; *Tesman*, Harold Higgens; *Brack*, Lester Woody; *Løvborg*, Frank Brooks; *Thea*, Jane Contessa; *Aunt Juliana*, Molly O'Riordan; *Berta*, Ann Steele

---

Hartford Stage Company (Hartford, Conn.), Jan. 14, 1966

Director, Jacques Cartier. *Setting and Costumes*, Paul Weidner. *Lighting*, Peter Hunt

Cast: *Hedda*, Jane MacLeod; *Tesman*, Charles Kimbrough; *Brack*, David Ford; *Løvborg*, Ken Jenkins; *Thea*, Anne Lynn; *Aunt Juliana*, Ann Driscoll; *Berta*, Elizabeth Lawrence

Playhouse Theater, Feb. 17, 1971

Producer: Hillard Elkins. *Director*, Patrick Garland. *Setting, Costumes and Lighting*, John Bury

Cast: *Hedda*, Claire Bloom; *Tesman*, Roy Schuman; *Brack*, Robert Gerringer; *Løvborg*, Donald Madden; *Thea*, Diana Kagan; *Aunt Juliana*, Kate Wilkinson; *Berta*, Eda Reiss Merin

---

Actors Theater of Louisville (Louisville, Ky.), Feb. 10, 1972

Director, Jon Jory. *Setting*, Grady Larkins. *Costumes*, Paul Owen. *Lighting*, Geoffrey T. Cunningham

Cast: *Hedda*, Peggy Cowles; *Tesman*, Max Wright; *Brack*, Stanley Anderson; *Løvborg*, Patrick Tovatt; *Thea*, Judith Long; *Aunt Juliana*, Dale Carter Cooper; *Berta*, Susan Cardwell Kingsley

---

Stage West (West Springfield, Mass.), Nov. 10, 1972

Producers: Stephen E. Hays and John Ulmer. *Director*, John Ulmer. *Setting and Lighting*, Charles G. Stockton. *Costumes*, Betty Williams

Cast: *Hedda*, Lucy Martin; *Tesman*, Curt Williams; *Brack*, Edward Holmes; *Løvborg*, Anthony McKay; *Thea*, Margery Shaw; *Aunt Juliana*, Virginia Payne; *Berta*, Shirley Jean Measures

---

Cubiculo Theater, Feb. 29, 1974

Director, Philip Meister. *Setting and Costumes*, Andy Milligan. *Lighting*, Eric Tishman

Cast: *Hedda*, Elaine Sulka; *Tesman*, William Shust; *Brack*, Neil Flanagan; *Løvborg*, Toby Tomkins; *Thea*, Darrie Lawrence; *Aunt Juliana*, Patricia Mertens; *Berta*, Pamela Hare

Syracuse Stage (Syracuse, N.Y.), Nov. 22, 1974

Director, John Dillon. *Setting*, David Chapman. *Costumes*, Randy Barcelo. *Lighting*, Arden Fingerhut

Cast: *Hedda*, Sara Croft; *Tesman*, James Secrest; *Brack*, Mervin Goldsmith; *Løvborg*, Paul Collins; *Thea*, Virginia Kiser; *Aunt Juliana*, Sheila Coonan; *Berta*, Anne Ives

---

Abbey Theater, April 8, 1975

Producer: CSC Repertory. *Director and Setting*, Christopher Martin. *Costumes*, Pamela Scofield. *Lighting*, Earl Eidman

Cast: *Hedda*, Karen Sunde; *Tesman*, Tom Donaldson; *Brack*, Christopher Martin; *Løvborg*, Ronald Perlman; *Thea*, Pilar Garcia; *Aunt Juliana*, Linda Lashbrook; *Berta*, Lisa Carling

---

Walnut Street Theater (Philadelphia, Pa.), Feb. 3, 1976

Producer: Philadelphia Drama Guild. *Director*, Douglas Seale. *Setting*, John Kasasda. *Costumes*, Jane Greenwood. *Lighting*, Spenser Mosse

Cast: *Hedda*, Roberta Maxwell; *Tesman*, James Valentine; *Brack*, Robert Gerringer; *Løvborg*, John Glover; *Thea*, Swoosie Kurtz; *Aunt Juliana*, Betty Leighton; *Berta*, Barbara Lester

---

Emelin Theater (Mamaroneck, N.Y.), May 6, 1977

Producer: Westchester-Rockland Regional Theater; *Director*, Nancy Ponder; *Setting*, Karen Sparks Mellon; *Costumes*, Gale Kramer Goldman; *Lighting*, Ruth Roberts

Cast: *Hedda*, Gay Sheldon; *Tesman*, David Washburn; *Brack*, Peter Murphy; *Løvborg*, James Rebhorn; *Thea*, Deborah Arnold; *Aunt Juliana*, Jean Barker; *Berta*, Karen Richter

THE MASTER BUILDER

First published: Gyldendal, Christiania, Dec. 12, 1892
First performed: William Petersens Company, Trondhjem, Jan. 19, 1893
Lessing Theater, Berlin, Jan. 19, 1893

Carnegie Lyceum, Jan. 17, 1900

Cast: *Solness*, W. H. Pascoe; *Aline*, Josephine Wyndham; *Hilda*, Florence Kahn; *Brovik*, Ralph Yoerg; *Ragnar*, Frederick G. Lewis; *Kaja*, Grace Fisher; *Herdal*, John Steppling

---

Murray Hill Theater, April 30, 1905

Producer: Progressive Stage Society. *Director*, Mrs. E. D. Bryan

Cast: *Solness*, J. H. Greene; *Aline*, Nella Holland; *Hilda*, Eda Bruna; *Brovik*, Courtland Hopkins; *Ragnar*, W. D. Howe; *Kaja*, Emerin Campbell; *Herdal*, L. Milton Boyle

---

Madison Square Theater, May 12, 1905

Director, Charles J. Bell

Cast: *Solness*, William Hazeltine; *Aline*, Ida Jeffreys-Goodfriend; *Hilda*, Amy Ricard; *Brovik*, Fred Thompson; *Ragnar*, Douglas J. Wood; *Kaja*, Lottie Alter; *Herdal*, David Elmer

---

Bijou Theater, Sept. 23, 1907

Cast: *Solness*, Walter Hampden; *Aline*, Gertrude Berkeley; *Hilda*, Alla Nazimova; *Brovik*, Cyril Young; *Ragnar*, Warner Oland; *Kaja*, Rosalind Ivan; *Herdal*, H. Reeves-Smith

---

Maxine Elliott's Theater, Nov. 10, 1925

Director, Eva Le Gallienne. *Settings and Costumes*, G. E. Calthrop

Cast: *Solness*, Egon Brecher; *Aline*, Alice John; *Hilda*, Eva Le Gallienne; *Brovik*, Sydney Machet; *Ragnar*, J. Warren Sterling; *Kaja*, Ruth Wilton; *Herdal*, William Raymond

---

Charles S. Brooks Theater (Cleveland, Ohio), April 28, 1936

Producer: The Cleveland Play House. *Director*, K. Elmo Lowe. *Settings*, H. Gunther Gerzso. *Costumes*, Harriet Morley. *Lighting*, Ben Letter

Cast: *Solness*, Howard da Silva; *Aline*, Harriet Borden; *Hilda*, Dorothy Paxton; *Brovik*, John Rowe; *Ragnar*, Newman Burnett; *Kaja*, Elizabeth Flory; *Herdal*, Kirk Willis

---

Cherry Lane Theater, May 25, 1950

Producer: The Repertory Theater, Inc. *Directors*, Audrey Hilliard and Miranda d'Ancona. *Settings*, Eugene Walter

Cast: *Solness*, John Scanlan; *Aline*, Marie Donnet; *Hilda*, Miranda d'Ancona; *Brovik*, Winton Sedgwick; *Ragnar*, Henry Waldon; *Kaja*, Audrey Hilliard; *Herdal*, James Arenton

Phoenix Theater, March 1, 1955

Producers: T. Edward Hambleton, Norris Houghton. *Director*, Oscar Homolka, with Ira Cirker. *Settings*, Boris Aronson. *Costumes*, Alvin Colt. *Lighting*, Lester Polakov

Cast: *Solness*, Oscar Homolka; *Aline*, Margaret Barker; *Hilda*, Joan Tetzel; *Brovik*, Art Smith; *Ragnar*, Gene Saks; *Kaja*, Muriel Berkson; *Herdal*, Joseph Foley

Tyrone Guthrie Theater (Minneapolis, Minn.), June 25, 1968

Producer: Minnesota Theater Company. *Director*, Stephen Porter. *Settings*, Ben Edwards. *Costumes*, Jane Greenwood. *Lighting*, S. Leonard Auerbach. *Music*, Conrad Susa

Cast: *Solness*, Robert Pastene; *Aline*, Helen Harrelson; *Hilda*, Lauri Peters; *Brovik*, Alek Primrose; *Ragnar*, Michael Moriarty; *Kaja*, Helen Carey; *Herdal*, James L. Lawless

Long Wharf Theater (New Haven, Conn.), Oct. 13, 1973

Director, Austin Pendleton. *Settings*, John Conklin. *Costumes*, Whitney Blausen. *Lighting*, Ronald Wallace

Cast: *Solness*, E. G. Marshall; *Aline*, Geraldine Fitzgerald; *Hilda*, Gretchen Corbett; *Brovik*, Emory Battis; *Ragnar*, Fred Cook; *Kaja*, Susanne Lederer; *Herdal*, William Swetland

Berkeley Repertory Theater (Berkeley, Calif.), Nov. 28, 1973

Director, Philip Larson. *Settings and Costumes*, Calvin Tsao. *Lighting*, Richard Reynolds

Cast: *Solness*, Michael Leibert; *Aline*, Holly Barron; *Hilda*, Laurie Walters; *Brovik*, Paul Laramore; *Ragnar*, Dale Elliott; *Kaja*, Karen Ingenthron; *Herdal*, Ron Vernan

---

Eisenhower Theater (Washington, D.C.), June 4, 1977

Director, Edwin Sherin. *Settings*, John Wulp. *Costumes*, Ann Roth. *Lighting*, Roger Morgan

Cast: *Solness*, Richard Kiley; *Aline*, Teresa Wright; *Hilda*, Jane Alexander; *Brovik*, Shepperd Strudwick; *Ragnar*, Joel Stedman; *Kaja*, Mary Catherine Wright; *Herdal*, Thomas Toner

LITTLE EYOLF

First published: Gyldendal, Copenhagen, Dec. 11, 1894
First performed: Deutsches Theater, Berlin, Jan. 12, 1895

Carnegie Lyceum, May 13, 1907

Cast: *Allmers*, Georgio Majeroni; *Rita*, Mme. Oda Neilsen; *Asta*, Schultetus Burolde; *Borghejm*, Munroe Salisbury; *Eyolf*, Gretchen Hartman; *Rat-Wife*, Sarah McVicker

---

Alla Nazimova Theater, April 18, 1910

Producers: the Messrs. Shubert

Cast: *Allmers*, Brandon Tynan; *Rita*, Alla Nazimova; *Asta*, Ida Conquest; *Borghejm*, Robert T. Haines; *Eyolf*, George Tobin; *Rat-Wife*, Gertrude Berkeley

---

Guild Theater, Feb. 2, 1926

Producers: William A. Brady, Jr., and Dwight Deere Wiman. *Settings*, Jo Mielziner. *Costumes*, Jo Mielziner and Robert Edmond Jones

Cast: *Allmers*, Reginald Owen; *Rita*, Clare Eames; *Asta*, Margalo Gillmore; *Borghejm*, John Cromwell; *Eyolf*, William Pearce; *Rat-Wife*, Helen Menken

---

Actors Playhouse, March 16, 1964

Producer: Northwestern Productions. *director*, Marshall W. Mason. *Settings*, Robert Thirkield. *Costumes*, C. M. Nelson. *Lighting*, Dennis Parichy

Cast: *Allmers*, Mark Lenard; *Rita*, Savannah Bentley; *Asta*, Claris Erickson; *Borghejm*, Ronald Willoughby; *Eyolf*, Scott Moore, Jr.; *Rat-Wife*, Dorothy Peterson

---

Manhattan Theater Club, Feb. 4, 1974

Producer: Lynne Meadow. *Director*, Austin Pendleton. *Costumes*, Guus Ligrthart. *Lighting*, Cheryl Thacker

Cast: *Allmers*, David Clennon; *Rita*, Katina Commings; *Asta*, Nancy Donahue; *Borghejm*, Fred Cook; *Eyolf*, Johnny Oakes; *Rat-Wife*, Miriam Lehmann-Haupt

JOHN GABRIEL BORKMAN

First published: Gyldendal, Copenhagen, Dec. 15, 1896
First performed: The Swedish Theater, Helsinki, Jan. 10, 1897
The Finnish Theater, Helsinki, Jan. 10, 1897

Hoyt's Theater, Nov. 18, 1897

Cast: *Borkman*, E. J. Henley; *Gunhild*, Maude Banks; *Ella*, Ann Warrington; *Erhart*, John Blair; *Fanny Wilton*, Carrie Keeler; *Foldal*, Albert Bruning; *Frida*, Dorothy Usner; *Maid*, Miss Parker

---

Forty-eighth Street Theater, April 13, 1915

Producer: The Modern Stage. *Director*, Emanuel Reicher

Cast: *Borkman*, Emanuel Reicher; *Gunhild*, Alice Harrington; *Ella*, Alma Kruger; *Erhart*, Paul Gordon; *Fanny Wilton*, Thais Lawton; *Foldal*, Roland Young; *Frida*, Inez Banghart; *Maid*, Edith Seabury

---

Booth Theater, Jan. 30, 1926

Cast: *Borkman*, Egon Brecher; *Gunhild*, Helen Haye; *Ella*, Eva Le Gallienne; *Erhart*, John Buckler; *Fanny Wilton*, Marian Warring-Manley; *Foldal*, J. Sayre Crawley; *Frida*, Rose Hobert; *Maid*, Beatrice de Neergaard

Civic Repertory Theater, Nov. 9, 1926

Cast: *Borkman*, Egon Brecher; *Gunhild*, Beatrice Terry; *Ella*, Eva Le Gallienne; *Erhart*, Hardie Albright; *Fanny Wilton*, Ellida Pierra; *Foldal*, Sayre Crawley; *Frida*, Ruth Wilton; *Maid*, Beatrice de Neergaard

International Theater, Nov. 12, 1946

Producer: American Repertory Theater. *Director*, Eva Le Gallienne. *Settings and Costumes*, Paul Morrison. *Music*, Lehman Engel

Cast: *Borkman*, Victor Jory; *Gunhild*, Margaret Webster; *Ella*, Eva Le Gallienne; *Erhart*, William Windom; *Fanny Wilton*, Mary Alice Moore; *Foldal*, Ernest Truex; *Frida*, Anne Jackson; *Maid*, Marion Evensen

Stage One Theater, Jan. 19, 1977

Producer: Roundabout Stage Co. *Director*, Gene Feist. *Music*, Philip Campanella

Cast: *Borkman*, Robert Pastene; *Gunhild*, Gale Sondergaard; *Ella*, Jan Ferrand; *Erhart*, Jeffrey David Pomerantz; *Fanny Wilton*, Valerie French; *Foldal*, Truman Gaige; *Frida*, Madelon Thomas; *Maid*, Carolyn Sullivan

WHEN WE DEAD AWAKEN

First published: Gyldendal, Copenhagen, Dec. 19, 1899
First performed: Hoftheater, Stuttgart, Jan. 26, 1900

Knickerbocker Theater, March 7, 1905

Director, Maurice Campbell. *Settings*, L. C. Young and P. J. McDonald

Cast: *Rubek*, Frederick Lewis; *Irene*, Florence Kahn; *Maja*, Dorothy Donnelly; *Ulfhejm*, Frank Lossee; *Manager of the Spa*, James H. Lewis; *Nun*, Evelyn Wood

---

Central Park Theater, May 17, 1926

Producers: Warren & Weir. *Director*, Murray A. Weir. *Settings*, Joseph Physioc

Cast: *Rubek*, Ross Matthews; *Irene*, Eunice Osborne; *Maja*, Sara Floyd; *Ulfhejm*, Murray A. Weir; *Manager of the Spa*, George A. Salem; *Nun*, Ann Morris

---

Goodman Memorial Theater (Chicago, Ill.), Feb. 26, 1929

Director, B. Iden Payne. *Settings*, Leslie Marzolf. *Costumes*, Elizabeth Parsons. *Lighting*, Arvid Crandall. *Music*, Julia Le-Vine

Cast: *Rubek*, B. Iden Payne; *Irene*, Joan Madison; *Maja*, Katherine Krug; *Ulfhejm*, Friendly Leon Ford; *Manager of the Spa*, Donald Willson; *Nun*, Bernard Ostertag

Theater Company of Boston (Boston, Mass.), Feb. 23, 1965

Director, David Wheeler. *Settings*, Alexander Pertzoff. *Costumes*, Mary Lou Matson. *Lighting*, Neville Powers. *Music and Sound*, Ervin Henning

Cast: *Rubek*, Richard Shepard; *Irene*, Bronia Stefan; *Maja*, Janet Lee Parker; *Ulfhejm*, Paul Benedict; *Manager of the Spa*, Jerome Gershman; *Nun*, Louise Sargent

Yale Repertory Theater (New Haven, Conn.), Oct. 14, 1971

Director, Tom Haas. *Settings and Costumes*, Steven Rubin. *Lighting*, Edgar Swift. *Music*, Paul Severtson

Cast: *Rubek*, David Hurst; *Irene*, Nancy Wickwire; *Maja*, Sarah Albertson; *Ulfhejm*, Stephen Mendillo; *Manager of the Spa*, Bill Gearhart; *Nun*, Carmen De Lavallade

Circle Theater Company, April 15, 1973

Director, Marshall Oglesby. *Settings*, Henry Scott III. *Costumes*, Martha Kelly. *Lighting*, Marshall W. Mason

Cast: *Rubek*, Maurice Blanc; *Irene*, Molly Adams; *Maja*, Karen Ludwig; *Ulfhejm*, Ron Seka; *Manager of the Spa*, Chris Romilly; *Nun*, Sharon Madden

Stage West (Springfield, Mass.), Jan. 31, 1977

Director, Rae Allen. *Settings*, Jerry Rojo. *Costumes*, Sigrid Insull. *Lighting*, Ron Wallace

Cast: *Rubek*, Ronald Bishop; *Irene,* Dorrie Kavenaugh; *Maja*, Nancy Sellin; *Ulfhejm*, Brad Sullivan; *Manager of the Spa*, Gwyllum Evans; *Nun*, Timothy Near